Workshop on Intelligent Computing in Engineering (EG-ICE 2021)

Berlin, Germany and Online
30 June – 2 July 2021

Editors:

Jimmy Abualdenien
Andre Borrmann
Lucian Constantin Ungureanu
Timo Hartmann

ISBN: 978-1-7138-5547-7

Printed from e-media with permission by:

Curran Associates, Inc.
57 Morehouse Lane
Red Hook, NY 12571

CURRAN ASSOCIATES INC.
proceedings
.com

Some format issues inherent in the e-media version may also appear in this print version.

European Group for Intelligent Computing in Engineering (eg-ice)
Arcisstrasee 21
D-80290 Munich
Germany

Phone: +49 89 289 25117

https://eg-ice.org/

Additional copies of this publication are available from:

Curran Associates, Inc.
57 Morehouse Lane
Red Hook, NY 12571 USA
Phone: 845-758-0400
Fax: 845-758-2634
Email: curran@proceedings.com
Web: www.proceedings.com

Jimmy Abualdenien | André Borrmann | Lucian-Constantin Ungureanu | Timo Hartmann (eds.)

EG-ICE 2021 Workshop on Intelligent Computing in Engineering

30th June–2nd July 2021, Hybrid
Proceedings

Universitätsverlag der TU Berlin

Technische Universität Berlin

Jimmy Abualdenien, André Borrmann,
Lucian Constantin Ungureanu, Timo Hartmann (eds.)
EG-ICE 2021 Proceedings

EG-ICE 2021 Proceedings:
Workshop on Intelligent Computing in Engineering

30th June–2nd July 2021, Hybrid
Technische Universität Berlin

Editors:
Jimmy Abualdenien
André Bormann
Lucian Constantin Ungureanu
Timo Hartmann

Universitätsverlag der TU Berlin

Bibliographic information published by the Deutsche Nationalbibliothek
The Deutsche Nationalbibliothek lists this publication in the Deutsche Nationalbibliografie; detailed bibliographic data are available in the Internet at http://dnb.dnb.de/

Universitätsverlag der TU Berlin, 2021
http://verlag.tu-berlin.de

Fasanenstr. 88, 10623 Berlin
Tel.: +49 (0)30 314 76131

Print: Schaltungsdienst Lange oHG
Layout/Typesetting: Jimmy Abualdenien | Lucian Constantin Ungureanu

ISBN 978-3-7983-3212-6 (online)

Published online on the institutional repository of the Technische Universität Berlin:
DOI 10.14279/depositonce-12021
http://dx.doi.org/10.14279/depositonce-12021

Preface

Building and infrastructure projects strongly contribute to the gross domestic product (GDP), economic growth, and highly influence the solutions developed for the different social and climate challenges worldwide. The importance of these projects constantly raises the necessity of increasing digitization efforts to improve the quality and outcome of the involved processes. Current advancements in computing and technology provide numerous opportunities for exploring creative solutions capable of substantially supporting projects' success. Realizing such solutions requires an extensive investigation, implementation, and evaluation.

The 28th EG-ICE International Workshop 2021 brings together international experts working at the interface between advanced computing and modern engineering challenges. Many engineering tasks require open-world solutions to support multi-actor collaboration, coping with approximate models, providing effective engineer-computer interaction, search in multi-dimensional solution spaces, accommodating uncertainty, including specialist domain knowledge, performing sensor-data interpretation and dealing with incomplete knowledge. While results from computer science provide much initial support for realizing domain challenges, adaptation is unavoidable, and most importantly, feedback from addressing engineering challenges drives fundamental computer-science research. Competence and knowledge transfer go both ways.

The papers included in this volume were presented at the 28th International Workshop on Intelligent Computing in Engineering of the European Group for Intelligent Computing in Engineering (eg-ice). Due to the CoViD-19 pandemic, the workshop that was originally planned as a face-to-face event, then was quickly transformed into a hybrid one. Attendees were able to join the conference in-person in Berlin as well as online. We thank the authors of the accepted papers for embracing the proposed format and their willingness to disseminate their research results despite the unconventional format forced by the pandemic restrictions.

Moreover, we appreciate the tremendous effort made by reviewers on making the selection of the best papers for the presentation possible. We are grateful for their hard work in providing valuable and constructive feedback to the authors. We believe that the digital transformation, currently disrupting the architecture, engineering, construction, facility management, and operation of the built environment, can gain valuable insight from the scientific work published in this volume.

July, 2021

Jimmy Abualdenien

André Borrmann

Lucian-Constantin Ungureanu

Timo Hartmann

Organization

Organizing Committee

Timo Hartmann (Workshop Chair)	Technische Universität Berlin, Germany
André Borrmann (Scientific Chair)	Technische Universität München, Germany
Jimmy Abualdenien (Scientific Chair)	Technische Universität München, Germany
Lucian-Constantin Ungureanu (Workshop Chair)	Technische Universität Berlin, Germany
Valentina Obradovic (Workshop Secretary)	Technische Universität Berlin, Germany

EG-ICE Committee

Pieter de Wilde (Chair)	University of Plymouth, UK
Philipp Geyer (Vice-chair)	Technische Universität Berlin, Germany
Timo Hartmann (Treasurer)	Technische Universität Berlin, Germany
Christian Koch (International representative)	Bauhaus-Universität Weimar, Germany
HaiJiang Li (Secretary)	Cardiff University, UK
Georg Suter (Auditor)	TU Wien, Austria
Jakob Beetz (Committee Member)	RWTH Aachen University, Germany
Bernd Domer (Committee Member)	University of Applied Sciences, HEPIA, Switzerland
Pieter Pauwels (Committee Member)	Eindhoven University of Technology, Netherlands
André Borrmann (Past Chair)	Technical University Munich, Germany
Ian Smith (EG-ICE Fellow)	Swiss Federal Institute of Technology, EPFL, Switzerland

Scientific Committee

Pieter de Wilde	University of Plymouth
Philipp Geyer	TU Berlin
Timo Hartmann	TU Berlin
Christian Koch	Bauhaus-Universität Weimar
Jakob Beetz	RWTH University of Aachen
Haijiang Li	Cardiff University

Contents

Application of AI methods for the integration of structural engineering knowledge in early planning phases

Univ.-Prof. Dr.-Ing. Martina Schnellenbach-Held, Daniel Steiner, MSc.
University of Duisburg-Essen, Germany
m.schnellenbach-held@uni-due.de

Abstract. The early integration of the structural design expertise in the building design process enables an efficient support of highly complex planning decisions. For this purpose, a knowledge-based system is developed to provide suitable structural engineering experience. Thereby, an intelligent thinking and acting is simulated that is based on the processing of knowledge in the form of transparent structural design rules following the Modus Ponens. Using fuzzy knowledge bases and related inference systems, a human-like decision-making behaviour is achieved. Based on the Fuzzy Logic possibility theory, a rating of structures is included to support design decisions. For appropriate knowledge formalizations, rules are refinable by linguistic hedges. Different methods enable the processing of uncertain design values. Based on structural engineering knowledge, the resulting system provides a structural design assistance through recommendation of design options and structural assessments. An application of the AI methods is demonstrated by an example and related acquirable knowledge.

1. Introduction

In the early phases of the building design process, aesthetic and functional aspects are of high influence on the building design. In contrast, structural decisions are based on only little and uncertain design information, although they are highly relevant for the feasibility, realization effort and costs of a building (Zhang et al., 2018). To meet this challenge, an earliest possible structural design support is highly advisable to achieve an efficient design process (El-Diraby et al., 2017). Common advises in early phases are based on rough calculations and especially on the engineering experience of qualified planners that is acquired during their professional activity. A provision of this structural design expertise initially requires a usable knowledge formalization that sets the phrasing for the knowledge – in the form of "if-then" rules for example – and its applicability in computing. Usually, the knowledge generation for computational uses is based on extensive structural analyses and simulations (Liu et al., 2018). For the utilization of acquired knowledge bases in early design phases, systems are required that are able to process and recommend structural design information based on uncertain parameters (Schnellenbach-Held and Albert, 2003).

The application of knowledge-based systems enables the integration and interpretation of natural-language rules in the computer-aided collaborative design process (Ungureanu and Hartmann, 2017). Involved easily understandable rule bases allow a comprehensible determination of design information (Zhang et al., 2018). At the same time, the exchange, management and communication of knowledge are facilitated (Liu et al., 2019). Applicable experience knowledge is usually associated with different levels of development of the design (Maier et al, 2017) in combination with an uncertainty of the design parameters (Abualdenien et al., 2020). Thus, an appropriate decision support is realizable through the use of knowledge-based systems including development-level dependent fuzzy knowledge bases (Schnellenbach-Held and Steiner 2021).

Using artificial intelligence methods, a knowledge-based system is developed for an efficient provision of structural design knowledge in early design phases. The included knowledge comprises development-level dependent material-specific fuzzy knowledge bases. To access and evaluate this knowledge, intelligent substitution models featuring fuzzy inference systems are incorporated (Schnellenbach-Held and Steiner 2021). Based on structural design experience, the knowledge-based system provides an assessment of bearing structures, the recommendation of design options and the processing of design changes. Thus, an efficient support of design decisions as well as a resulting efficiency increase in the design process are facilitated. In the scope of this paper, fundamentals of the used artificial intelligence methods are presented and the application of the developed system is demonstrated by example.

2. Applied AI methods

Artificial Intelligence (AI) is a subdomain of informatics and covers techniques that allow an intelligent behavior of computer programs. Related methods are often based on the understanding of natural biologic processes. The imitation of such processes or operating principles enables the ability of solving complex problems in computing (Wittpahl, 2019). For an early support of the building design process, the usability of experience knowledge in natural language including a competent assessment of structures as well as an associated decision-making for complex tasks are main advantages of an AI application.

2.1 Knowledge-based systems

Knowledge-based systems (KBS) represent a significant subdomain of AI. They are based on the simulation of intelligent thinking and acting through the integration and processing of knowledge. One of the most proven kinds of KBS are rule-based systems that utilize a knowledge formalization in the form of conditional clauses following the Modus Ponens. The resulting rules are intuitively and easily understandable being phrased as: "If the premise is satisfied, then infer the conclusion". Accordingly, these rules represent relationships between objects or sets in their premises and conclusions. The knowledge base of the KBS is built with respect to these correlations. Knowledge elements are structured and incorporated by the knowledge acquisition component, so that further knowledge is integrated into the knowledge base and thus is acquired for the usage in the KBS. In the process, rule networks can be established by chaining of rules. For instance, the premise of a following rule is specified by the conclusion of the prior one through forward chaining ("data-driven"). For the interpretation of the knowledge, logical operators are used that are included in the inference component of the KBS. Evaluation results are determined through the inference component based on the knowledge and finally added to the data base. Further elements of the KBS are user interfaces that allow an interaction between the system and users like building planners. Most important interfaces are the interrogation component that allows for the request of further information needed by the KBS as well as an explanation component that delivers reasons for the results and thus supports the transparency of the evaluation process (Schnellenbach, 1991, Beierle and Kern-Isberner, 2019).

2.2 Fuzzy Logic

The fuzzy set theory constituted by Prof. Lotfi A. Zadeh in the 1960s is characterized by the usage of fuzzy memberships of members to sets (Zadeh 1965). A main advantage is the simulation of an achieved human-like decision behavior that features the ability of problem solving and decision making even for highly complex tasks. Being based on the classical Boolean set theory with memberships of the conventional 0 "false" or 1 "true", Fuzzy Logic features the extension to continuous membership functions between 0 "totally false" and 1 "totally true". Through these fuzzy memberships, extraordinary generalization abilities as well as a stable and redundant behavior are achievable for rule-based evaluations. The associated rule base commonly consists of knowledge in the form of if-then-rules featuring relationships between fuzzy sets. Based on the classical set theory, generalized logical operators are used for the inference of the rules allowing logical conjunctions of fuzzy sets. On that basis, an approximate reasoning from the fuzzy knowledge base is performed (von Altrock, 1995). Fuzzy Logic is applicable for the logic-based interpretation of knowledge in a KBS that features a fuzzy knowledge base including rules representing relationships between fuzzy sets.

2.3 Functional TSK inference model

For the approximate reasoning through generalized logical operations with fuzzy sets, two functional inference models are commonly used: The MA-model according to Mamdani and Assilian as well as the TSK-model according to Takagi, Sugeno and Kang (Schnellenbach-Held and Albert, 2003). In the following, the TSK-model is addressed, as it generally features a higher numerical precision for approximations and the opportunity of optimizing the quality of evaluation results. To initiate an approximate reasoning using a TSK inference system, the memberships of the input values to the fuzzy sets of the input parameters are determined ("fuzzification"). Subsequently, the memberships of the input values are combined to a resulting acceptance degree for every rule ("aggregation") using generalized logical operators. For instance, fuzzy sets combined through intersection ("and") are aggregated by the application of the minimum operator according to the triangular norm ("T-norm"). The aggregation is followed by the reasoning of the conclusion from the premise for every rule ("implication"). In a TSK inference system, the conclusion is specified through polynomial functions. Using higher order polynomials provides the opportunity of increasing the approximation precision to the basic function within the knowledge. In contrast to the MA-model that involves continuing generalized logical operations, TSK inference systems combine the fusion of the rule conclusions ("accumulation") and the finalizing determination of the inference output ("defuzzification"). For this purpose, the usually crisp output value is calculated through the mean value of the rule conclusions weighted by the rule`s acceptance degrees. Dependencies between parameters are particularly considerable in the inference. For example, such correlations are processible through forward-chaining of TSK inference systems. In doing so, the premise and conclusion of a following system are approximated by the reasoning of a prior one. For instance, the fuzzy set partitioning of the input parameters as well as the polynomials of the conclusions can be determined depending on other parameter values. Thus, the final output is inferred taking into account the dependencies of parameters in the evaluation process.

2.4 Possibility theory

As an alternative to probability theory, the possibility theory was introduced by Prof. Lotfi A. Zadeh as independent uncertainty theory that is based on Fuzzy Logic (Zadeh 1978). It is characterized by the definition of the fuzzy membership as the "possibility" of an element belonging to a set. Thus, possibility distributions π are specified through the membership functions of fuzzy sets. Dual to the possibility, the set function "necessity" is defined as "necessity = 1 – possibility". An application of possibility functions enables the modelling of opinions from qualified planners in the form of "subjective feasibilities". For this purpose, the feasibility can be expressed as possibility function ranging from 0 for "impossible" conditions where other solutions are "totally necessary" to 1 for "totally possible" conditions where other designs are "unnecessary". Thus, information is processible that is included in a specialized planning expertise but doesn't exhibit a stochastic character (Schnellenbach-Held and Steiner 2021).

2.5 Linguistic hedges

A refinement of the linguistic if-then-rules – that form the knowledge base of fuzzy inference systems – is realizable by the application of linguistic hedges. For this purpose, further specifications like "very" or "more or less" can be assigned to fuzzy sets within single rules. Thus, the knowledge used for the inference is specified more precisely. The processing of these hedges is realized through related modifications of the involved membership functions, so that modified membership values are used for fuzzification, for instance. A basic approach for usable membership modifications (see table 1) was suggested by Prof. Lotfi A. Zadeh (Zadeh 1973). An application of linguistic hedges is particularly useful for the expression of qualified opinions, as this kind of knowledge often contains such refining specifications.

Table 1: Linguistic hedges according to Zadeh.

Hedge	Token	Membership modification	Hedge illustration
"very"	CON	$\mu_{CON} = \mu^2$	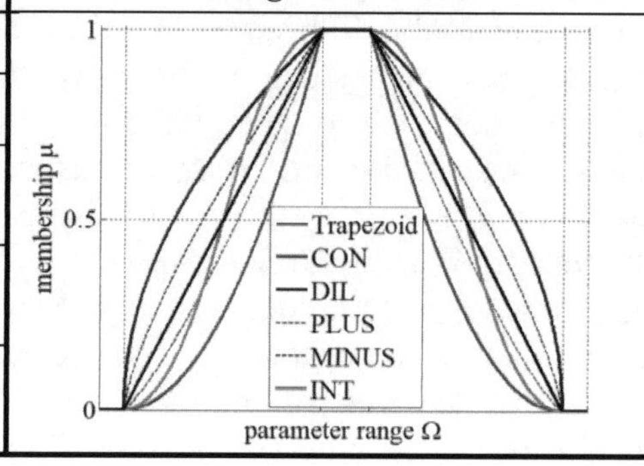
"more or less"	DIL	$\mu_{DIL} = \sqrt{\mu}$	
"plus" (artificial)	PLUS	$\mu_{PLUS} = \mu^{1,25}$	
"minus" (artificial)	MINUS	$\mu_{MINUS} = \mu^{0,75}$	
contrast intensification	INT	$\mu_{INT} = \begin{cases} 1 - 2(1-\mu)^2, if\ \mu > 0,5 \\ 2\mu^2, else \end{cases}$	

3. Application of the AI methods

With the aid of an example, an application of the presented AI methods in the developed knowledge-based system is demonstrated. For this purpose, relevant structural design knowledge as well as the generation of material-specific fuzzy knowledge bases are presented. Intelligent substitution models include the knowledge as well as the related inference systems in dependence on identified adaptive levels of development for structural design. Using the resulting system, the evaluation process and the integration of uncertain design values are exemplified. An overview over the underlying structural design process and considered structures can be found in Schnellenbach-Held and Steiner 2021.

3.1 Example definition and related general structural design knowledge

For demonstrating applicable knowledge and its application, a single-span single-field slab member of reinforced concrete (RC) serves as an example. The identification of this member type in a superstructure of massive construction is based on the following rules according to structural design knowledge in the KBS (see chapter 2.1):

Rule: If slab is supported only on two opposite sides, then single-span field between supports.
Rule: If slab is supported by masonry wall and not continues behind, then support is hinged.

Knowing the member type, the specification of related further knowledge and fuzzy knowledge bases is enabled. Single-span slab members are commonly calculated for the span length L_x in a slab strip of 1 m/m L_y. Suitable life load assumptions are usually in accordance with Eurocode 1. Based on the included knowledge, the load determination is implemented in the KBS through formalization of rules like the following example for residential usage:

Rule: If usage is residential (category A3), then life load is 2 kN/m².

Regarding structural design experience knowledge, an additional dead weight assumption of 1,5 kN/m² is sufficient for early design phases. Further structural design knowledge refers to the valid design standards for the applied structural material type like Eurocode 2 for reinforced concrete (RC) or Eurocode 5 for timber structures. As per experience knowledge for the RC slab member example, the design criteria according to Eurocode 2 are important. Relevant design checks are bending and shear force in ULS, simplified deflection and crack width limitation in SLS, minimum reinforcements for ductility and drain of hydration heat as well as constructive reinforcement elements. Based on the calculation approach according to the design standard, design knowledge is generated and stored in fuzzy knowledge bases, so that a reasoning of design values from the knowledge is rendered possible. A qualification of usable designs is based on the following rule:

Rule: If all design checks are satisfied, then using the member is possible, otherwise not.

3.2 Knowledge acquisition for fuzzy knowledge bases

In structural design practice, the design procedure according to the known standards is applied to a wide range of structural systems. In doing so, the repetition of the design process implies the memorization of relevant information and thus enables an estimation of results in structural engineering. This experience knowledge allows structural assessments relating to feasibility, efficiency and constructive characteristics of structures in early design phases. Thus, it is highly suitable for an effective support of the design process.

Knowledge generation through parametric studies

Simulating the experience-making process, parametric studies are used for the acquisition of fuzzy knowledge bases that include the common structural design procedure. For this purpose, value ranges of the essential parameters are initially specified based on experience (Schnellenbach-Held and Steiner, 2021). Applicable knowledge for value ranges of the slab parameters is:

- Life load q is between 1 kN/m² (minimum) and 10 kN/m² (practice experience),
- Slab height h is between 20 cm (shear minimum) and 70 cm (maximum hollow slab),
- Concrete class minimum is C20/25 (practice experience),
- Span lengths $L = L_x$ are dependent on q, h and concrete class,
- To be calculated: Span length fuzzy set partitioning and reinforcement amount a_s.

Through incremental sampling of the resulting parameter space, the repetition of the design procedure and a related experience-making are simulated. Regarding the RC slab example, this involves the design checks according to Eurocode 2 to determine the length value ranges and the reinforcement amounts for the individual samples. Based on the sampling, design rules are generated that combine the resulting values (see table 2) and are subsequently used to formulate the fuzzy knowledge bases.

Possibility for qualified structural assessments

The inclusion of qualified assessments enables the support of design decisions through providing a rating of structures. Based on the possibility theory (see chapter 2.4), feasibility knowledge is integrated that relates to the acceptance, efficiency and ecology of design parameters. A refinement of associated rules is enabled by using linguistic hedges (see chapter 2.5), as such expressions are often used in the involved subjective criteria. Next to qualified experience knowledge, results of optimizations are also considerable using these possibility criteria. For instance, applied possibility rules for assessments of the slab example (see figure 1) are:

Rule: If usage is residential, then lower concrete classes are good rated.
Rule: If usage is residential, then slab height should be very small.
Rule: If usage is residential, then span length is more or less important.
Rule: If usage is residential, then costs should be very low.

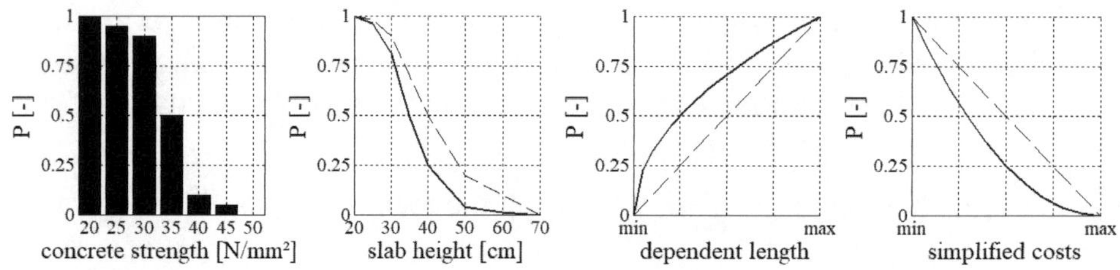

Figure 1: Applied possibility criteria

For the inclusion in the fuzzy knowledge bases, the possibility values P are calculated in the studies and integrated in the rule conclusions (see table 2). In the process, 0,5 indicates the satisfaction of all design checks that is complemented by the criteria P_i aggregated through a generalized compensatory operator:

$$P = 0{,}5 + 0{,}5 \cdot \sqrt[n]{\prod_{i=1}^{n} P_i} \quad with\ P_i \in [0; 1]\ and\ P \triangleq \pi$$

Based on the resulting possibilities, design recommendations are identified through searching for highest possibility values. This enables the complementation of missing design information by suggestions of good rated structural designs. Regarding the slab example, the following rules are identifiable for complementing the structural grid and the slab height:

Rule: If life load is 2 kN/m², then distance between structural axes (span length) is 7,4 m.
Rule: If life load is 2 kN/m² and span length is 7,4 m, then slab height is 30 cm for C30/37.

Table 2: Examples of generated design rules for formalization of fuzzy knowledge bases (extract).

IF premise:	q [kN/m²]	h [m]	L [m]	Concrete	Then conclusion:	a_s [kg/m³]	P [-]
	2,0	0,20	3,0	C20/25		83	0,50
	2,0	0,20	4,4	C20/25		83	1,00
	2,0	0,30	4,6	C30/37		75	0,50
	2,0	0,30	7,4	C30/37		82	0,93

Formalization of fuzzy knowledge bases

For generating the fuzzy knowledge bases from the parametric studies, every value combination of the parameters is used to formulate a design rule. The related fuzzy sets (see figure 2 and chapter 2.2) are integrated through linear connection of adjacent increments. As the concrete class is characterized by integer-like values, it is included through related design options. Due to the dependency of the slab length on other design parameters, a chained TSK inference system (see chapter 2.3) is used. This enables the approximation of the length fuzzy sets based on the influential parameters (see table 3), where the minimum depends on ductility and the maximum on the satisfaction of all design checks. Through the arrangement and density of the increments and the related rules, the resulting approximation quality of the TSK inference system is controllable. Finally, the acquired fuzzy knowledge bases and associated inference systems are integrated in the intelligent substitution models.

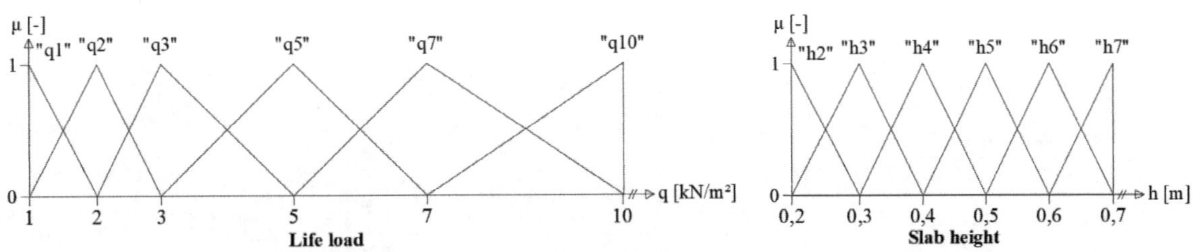

Figure 2: Applicable fuzzy set partitioning

Table 3: Example of a simplified rule for dependent fuzzy set partitioning.

If	q =	h =	C =	
	"q2"	"h3"	C30/37	
Then	ω_{L1}	ω_{L2}	ω_{L3}	ω_{L4}
	4,6 m	6,1 m	7,4 m	7,5 m
And	$a_s(\omega_{L1})$	$a_s(\omega_{L2})$	$a_s(\omega_{L3})$	$a_s(\omega_{L4})$
	75 kg/m³	75 kg/m³	82 kg/m³	83 kg/m³

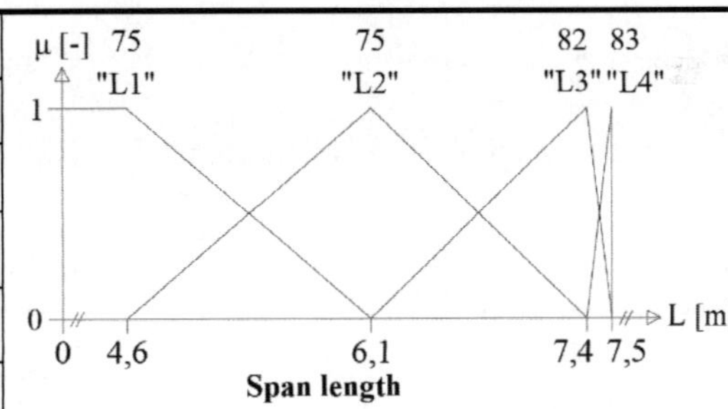

3.3 Design development through inference of fuzzy knowledge bases

To demonstrate the application of the developed system, the inference process is performed for the slab example. For this purpose, residential usage concluding a life load of 2 kN/m² and a span length of 5 m due to the structural grid are considered as predefined. Based on high possibility values, recommended slab heights are ranging from 20 cm for concrete classes over C30/37 up to 23 cm using a C20/25, where 22 cm is considered as an example for further calculations. Through application of a chained TSK inference system, the needed reinforcement amount as well as the achieved possibility are determined (see figure 3) including options for available normal concrete classes (see table 4). In the process, the design values are evaluated by inference of the fuzzy knowledge base that is formulated on the basis of the design-rule samples generated in the parametric studies (see chapter 3.2). As additional reinforcement masses due to constructive reasons – like anchorage and overlapping of reinforcement bars – are not included in the fuzzy knowledge base, subsequent calculations are introduced. Applicable knowledge for related modifications in the KBS is based on structural design experience, concluding an increase of the total steel amount by 15 %, for instance. In the same way, proceeding knowledge is includable, like the determination of grey energy demands (Schneider-Marin et al., 2020).

Additional structural design options are depending on the material type of the member. For instance, a solid GL24 timber construction could be applied for the slab example. Suitable knowledge is available design tables that include relevant design aspects (Lignum, 2012), for instance. To formalize related material-dependent fuzzy knowledge bases, design rules can be extracted, like the following example for recommending the slab height:

Rule: If life load is 2 kN/m² and span length is 5 m, then slab height is 18 cm for GL24.

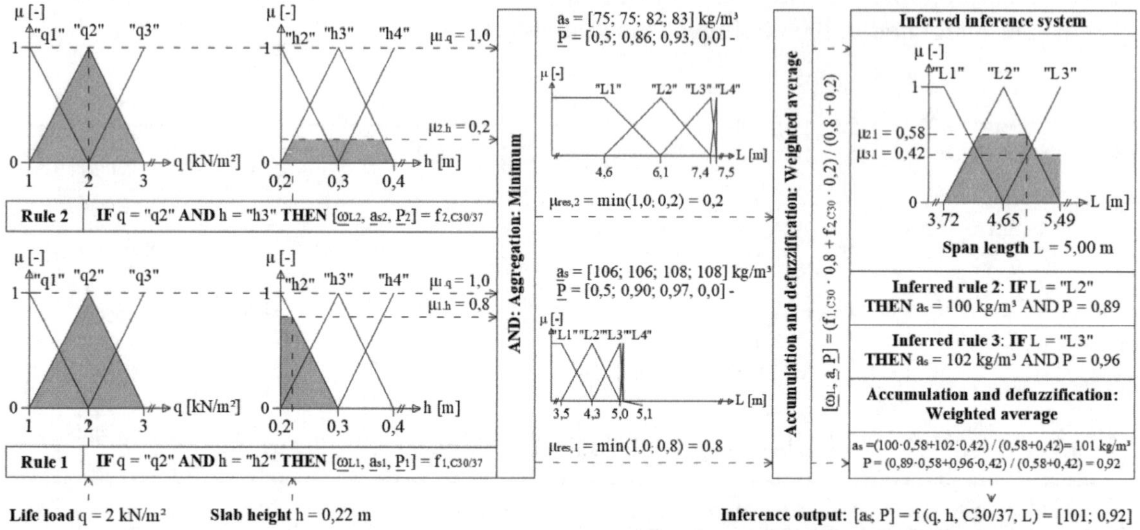

Figure 3: Exemplary Application of fuzzy knowledge bases using a chained TSK inference system

Table 4: Examples of inferred options for normal concrete classes.

Exact material	C20/25	C25/35	C30/37	C35/45	C40/50	C45/55	C50/60
Reinforcement a_s [kg/m³]	-	89	**101**	108	118	127	138
Possibility [-]	0,00	0,96	**0,92**	0,80	0,62	0,57	0,5
Total steel mass [kg/m]	-	113	128	137	149	161	174

3.4 Inclusion of uncertainty

Especially in early phases, the design process of buildings is characterized by uncertain values of design parameters (Abualdenien et al., 2020). Using the presented AI methods, uncertainty is considerable for the support of design decisions. For this purpose, three principal mechanisms are provided. Uncertain input values – expressed as fuzzy sets – are processible during fuzzification in the TSK inference systems. With the input set $A = (X, \mu_{Input})$ and the knowledge set $B_i = (X, \mu_{Rule,i})$ for design value range X, the resulting membership μ_i of rule i is determined and thus the uncertain input is fuzzified using the following generalized logical operator:

$$\mu_i = max\left(min(\mu_A ; \mu_{B_i})\right)$$

In doing so, the most relevant value for both sets at the same time is indirectly used for the aggregation of the rule's premises and their resulting acceptance degrees. As an example, a relatively small variation is considerable for the span length through formalization as input set over an expected value range of [4,75; 5,25] m. For each involved rule, the highest membership within the range is determined for fuzzification (see figure 4a) through the operator and thus the related value is indirectly used for the inference. In contrast, if the value variations of output parameters are to be determined for uncertain input values, multiple evaluations can be conducted with significant crisp values such as the minimum, mean and maximum. For instance, if the span length shows a relatively large value variation between 4 and 6 m, effects on following parameters like the possibility are evaluable (see figure 4b). Multiple evaluations with crisp values following to the variation enable the determination of uncertainty that results from the variation ("uncertainty quantification"). This approach also facilitates the conduction of stochastic analyses for probabilistic parameters (e.g. Monte Carlo simulations) as well as alpha-level optimizations ("membership mapping") for fuzzy parameters. In the case of uncertainty related to the output parameters of the applied knowledge, the relevant value ranges, fuzzy sets or distribution functions can be considered in the rule conclusions. For example, knowledge presenting a needed range of reinforcement is includable through expectable minimum and maximum values (see figure 4c) instead of a single crisp value. By the specification of associated information, the value ranges and variations stated in the knowledge are evaluated by approximation through the inference system.

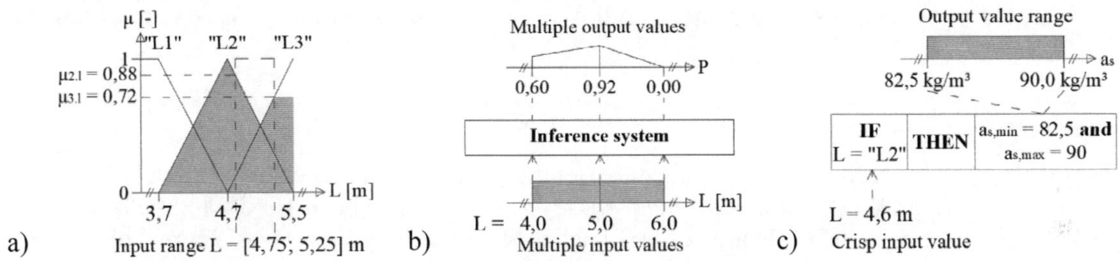

Figure 4: Processing of uncertainty: (a) Fuzzyification of uncertain input values, (b) multiple crisp evaluations for input value variations, (c) reasoning of uncertain output values

4. Summary and outlook

Through the application of AI methods, the support of design decisions is enabled in early phases. The developed knowledge-based system (KBS) performs the provision of structural engineering knowledge. Formalization of the design knowledge is based on Fuzzy Logic methods resulting in fuzzy knowledge bases. A rating of structures is integrated in accordance with the possibility theory, so that design recommendations are included as experience-based assessments of the structural quality. Simulating the human experience-making, the acquisition of fuzzy knowledge bases is realized using parametrical studies to generate rule-based knowledge of structural members. Required boundary conditions and configurations are determined by structural engineering experience knowledge. For the reasoning from the resulting knowledge, functional TSK inference systems are applied. Combining the fuzzy knowledge bases and associated inference systems, intelligent substitution models provide knowledge access and evaluation, thus they relate to the knowledge base and the inference component of the KBS. To consider uncertainty of design parameters, different methods are integrated that allow the processing of value variations. The application of the used AI methods is demonstrated with the aid of an example. The resulting system performs a design support by the early provision of structural design options including a structural engineering rating. Thus, the interdisciplinary and efficient building planning process is facilitated significantly.

Prospectively, complementary components of the KBS are developed regarding the applied artificial intelligence methods. Main aspects are the transferability of the technology to other types of structures and materials, the rule-based consideration of complex interdisciplinary relationships as well as the use of natural linguistic knowledge sources. Additionally, the development of possibility-based models is addressed to enhance the rating of entire superstructures, the transparency of the design process and the interdisciplinary collaboration.

Although the developed system provides a substantial support of the design process, an early inclusion of structural engineers is indispensable. They own the essential experience and design knowledge that qualifies an expertise to supervise designs and structural options and to further develop the knowledge bases as well as systems using them.

Acknowledgements

The outlined work is part of the research unit 2363 "Evaluation of building design variants in early phases on the basis of adaptive detailing strategies" funded by the German Research Foundation (DFG). We are grateful to the DFG for its support of the research unit 2363 and the incorporated partially presented project "Intelligent substitution models for structural design".

References

Abualdenien, J., Schneider-Marin, P., Zahedi, A., Harter, H., Exner, H., Steiner, D., Singh, M.M., Borrmann, A., Lang, W., Petzold, F., König, M., Geyer, P., Schnellenbach-Held, M. (2020). Consistent management and evaluation of building models in early design stages, Journal of Information Technology in Construction 25, pp. 212–232.

Beierle, C., Kern-Isberner, G. (2019). Methoden wissensbasierter Systeme, 6. Auflage, Springer, Berlin.

El-Diraby, T., Krijen, T., Papagelis, M. (2017). BIM-based collaborative design and socio-technical analysis of green buildings, Automation in Construction 82, pp. 59–74.

EN 1991-1-1:2002 + AC:2009. Eurocode 1: Actions on structures – Part 1-1: General actions – Densities, self-weight, imposed loads for buildings [DIN EN 1991-1-1/DE:12-2010].

EN 1992-1-1:2004 + AC:2010. Eurocode 2: Design of concrete structures - Part 1-1: General rules and rules for buildings [DIN EN 1992-1-1/DE:04-2013].

Lignum (2012). Holzbautabellen. HBT1, 4. Auflage, technical documentation.

Liu, H., Ong, Y.S., Cai, J. (2018). A survey of adaptive sampling for global metamodeling in support of simulation-based complex engineering design, Struct. Multidisc. Optim. 57, pp. 393–416.

Liu, F., Anumbra, C., Jallow, A., Carrillo, P. (2019). Integrated change and knowledge management system – development and evaluation, J. Inf. Technol. Constr. 24, pp. 112–128.

Maier, J.F., Eckert, C.M., Clarkson, P.J. (2017). Model granularity in engineering design – concepts and frame-work, Design Science, Volume 3, Cambridge.

Ungureanu, L.-C., Hartmann, T. (2017). Natural language controlled parametric design, Proceedings of the 24th EG-ICE international workshop, Nottingham, UK.

Schneider-Marin, P., Harter, H., Tkachuk, K., Lang, W. (2020). Uncertainty analysis of Embedded Energy and Greenhouse Gas Emissions Using BIM in Early Design Stages, Sustainability 12, 2633.

Schnellenbach, M. (1991). Wissensbasierte Integration und Steuerung computergestützter Entwurfsprozesse im Stahlbetonbau, Technisch-wissenschaftliche Mitteilungen am Institut für konstruktiven Ingenieurbau, Nr. 91-15, doctoral thesis, Ruhr-Universität Bochum.

Schnellenbach-Held, M., Albert, A. (2003). Integrating knowledge based systems with Fuzzy logic to support the early stages of structural design, Bauingenieur 78, pp. 517–524.

Schnellenbach-Held, M., Steiner, D. (2021). AI-methods for the integration of structural design knowledge in early phases of the building design process (in German), Bautechnik, accepted for publication.

Von Altrock, C. (1995). Fuzzy Logic, Oldenbourg Wissenschaftsverlag, München.

Wittpahl, V. (Ed.) (2019). Künstliche Intelligenz: Technologien, Anwendung, Gesellschaft, Springer, Berlin.

Zadeh, L. A. (1965). Fuzzy Sets, Information and Control 8, pp. 338–353.

Zadeh, L. A. (1973). Outline of a New Approach to the Analysis of Complex Systems and Decision Processes, IEEE Transactions on Systems, MAN and Cybernetics, Vol. SMC-3, No. 1, pp. 28–44.

Zadeh, L.A. (1978). Fuzzy Sets as a basis for a Theory of Possibility. Fuzzy Sets and Systems 1, pp. 3–28.

Zhang, J., Li, H., Zhao, Y., Ren, G. (2018). An ontology-based approach supporting holistic structural design with the consideration of safety, environmental impact and cost, Advances in Engineering Software 115, pp. 26–39.

Analysis of the early-design timber models for sound insulation analysis

Camille Châteauvieux-Hellwig [a], Jimmy Abualdenien [b], André Borrmann [b]
[a] TH Rosenheim, Germany, [b] TU Munich, Germany
Camille.Chateauvieux-Hellwig@th-rosenheim.de

Abstract. Timber construction is characterized with its high circularity and sustainability. However, such construction requires a careful evaluation of sound insulation between the different building zones. Currently, acoustic analysis is performed after the design is already detailed, which requires a substantial amount of time and effort to improve the design. Additionally, thus far, performing sound insulation analysis involves manual extraction and processing of building information, which is an error prone task. Hence, this paper proposes a framework for establishing a seamless workflow between building models and acoustic analysis tools across the design phases. In more detail, the junctions between the different elements are extracted and analysed to identify the corresponding acoustic junction types, with the help of topological reasoning and logical rules. The proposed approach was evaluated via a prototypical implementation, where the different possible junction types were extracted successfully.

1. Introduction

The building industry is a major consumer of the world's raw materials and highly contributes to carbon emissions globally (Wong et al. 2013). The circular economy framework aims to separate the economic growth from environmental destruction. In comparison to concrete building structures, timber structures are characterized with high recoverability when disassembled (Finch et al. 2021). Such sustainability of timber construction encourages architects and engineers to choose it for their projects. Using Building Information Modeling (BIM), a model is developed through multiple design phases to satisfy various design and engineering requirements. The decisions made throughout the design stages, especially the early ones, steer a project's success and results (Abualdenien et al. 2019). The impact of the decisions made in the early design stages (conceptual and preliminary stages) is significant, as they form the basis of the following stages.

The planning of sound insulation is very complex, especially in timber construction. The earlier this is included in the planning process, the more likely it is to find a satisfactory solution for the owner. Later modifications due to inadequate planning result in high costs and extensive construction work (Howell 2016). If sound insulation is included in an early planning phase, engineers from different disciplines can find an optimal solution for the individual building use cases (Châteauvieux-Hellwig et al. 2020). However, thus far, there is a lack of seamless integration between BIM-modelers and sounds insulation prognosis. Therefore, this paper proposes a framework for extracting the necessary information from BIM models, then reason about this information to identify the corresponding junction types. This information forms the bases for calculating the sound reduction index and impact sound level. Such calculations use information from databases of component catalogues, collected from standards and domain knowledge to provide a forecast. The result can then be compared with applicable standards and requirements to be optimized if necessary.

The proposed framework in this paper is based on the vendor neutral format industry foundation classes (IFC). IFC is capable of capturing the geometric and semantic building information, including the topological relationships as well as property sets that can include multiple properties. Using IFC makes it possible to establish a seamless workflow between the BIM-modelers and simulation tools. However, as the IFC schema does not have an explicit definition of the junction properties, the proposed framework presents further processing and reasoning to perform the sound insulation analysis.

The aim of this research is to us an IFC data model to find the junctions and define the junction types needed to calculate the prognosis of sound insulation. The process includes the calculation of airborne sound insulation and impact sound insulation. The calculations are performed in building construction according to ISO12354-1 (2017) and are frequency-dependent from 50 to 5000 Hz. The calculation takes into account the joints based on the vibration reduction index, which depends on the direction of the junction, the design of the connection details, and the component types used.

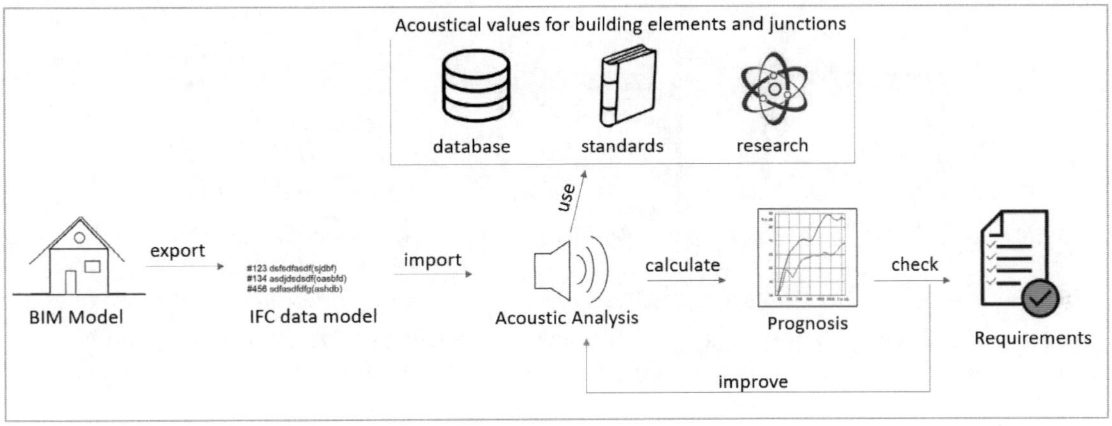

Figure 1: Workflow of an acoustic analysis

2. Sound Transmission in Timber Buildings

The prognosis of sound insulation consists of airborne sound insulation for walls and slabs. Ceilings have an additional impact sound level. The calculations are carried out according to ISO12354-1 (2017). For full information about the element's acoustic properties, the sound insulation needs with frequency depend on values from 50 to 5000 Hz.

$$R_{ij} = \frac{R_i + R_j}{2} + \Delta R + K_{ij} - 10lg\frac{l_{ij}}{\sqrt{a_i \cdot a_j}} + 10lg\frac{S_S}{\sqrt{S_i \cdot S_j}} \quad [\text{dB}] \qquad (1)$$

With

$\overline{D_{v,ij}}$	velocity level difference in dB
R_i, R_j	sound insulation of element *i* and *j* in dB
S_S	surface of separating element in m²
S_i, S_j	surface of element *i* / *j* in m²
ΔR	improvement or deterioration of sound insulation due to wall linings, screeds or suspended ceiling in dB
l_{ij}	junction length between element *i* and *j* in m
a_i, a_j	equivalent absorption length of element *i* / *j* in m
K_{ii}	vibration reduction index in dB

In comparison to the other materials construction methods, such as concrete and steel, timber construction has a low mass. However, existing acoustic prognosis models were designed for concrete constructions. Hence for timber construction, the calculation models are still in development (Rabold et al. 2017, Rabold et al. 2018), and existing models need to be optimized: Due to the lower mass, the flanking transmission's importance is much more important than in usual buildings.

Flanking Transmission

Beneath the direct transmission through an element, it is essential to consider the sound transmission through all flanking elements. When the mass of all elements is low, the flanking paths are more important for the overall result of the sound insulation. Figure 2 shows the sound transmission paths according to the direction and excitation.

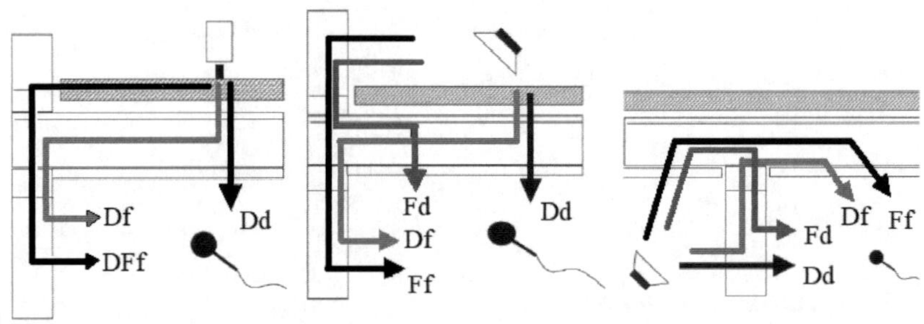

Figure 2: Schematic representation of the transmission paths Ff, Df, Fd and DFf in timber construction: impact sound insulation (left), airborne sound insulation through a slab (middle) or a wall (right)

The vibration reduction index K_{ij} rates the different transmission paths depending on the junction's direction and the design of the connection details, including, the use of elastic layers, the stiffness of the connection devices, separation cuts in flanking elements. The mass ratio between the elements also plays an important role. The excitation and orientation of the junction are necessary to determine the relevant transmission paths. Those are named with *d* for direct element and *f* for flanking element. On the sending room's side, all letters are in capital (*D*, *F*), and on the receiving room's side in small (*d*, *f*). For the general description, all elements on the sending room's side have index *i*, and on the side of the receiving room the index *j*.

Junction Type

The distinction between the junction types is essential to find the correct vibration reduction index. There are 15 different junction types when we consider a junction with one, two or three possible flanking elements. Figure 3 shows all different types and their names depending on their direction.

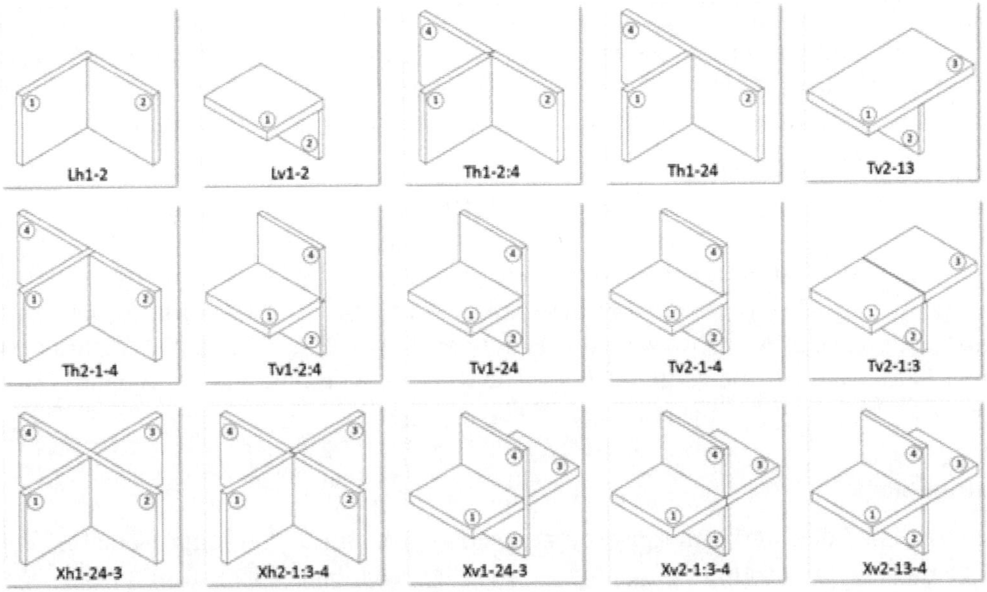

Figure 3: 15 types of junction without consideration of elastic layers for decoupling (Timpte, 2016)

Influence of the vibration reduction index K_{ij}

The joint's influence on the vibration reduction index K_{ij} is very high depending on the construction situation. These values vary from 3 dB to 26 dB depending on the selected joint and transmission path (Timpte 2016). Figure 4 shows the analysis results of a partition wall and four flanking elements. The results show the significant influence of the joint insulation In this example, the same vibration reduction index is used for all three transmission paths (*Df*, *Fd*, *Ff*) of all flanking elements as a simplification. The analysis results vary between 41 and 60 dB. The effect of an additional 10 dBs on the sound level is perceived as approximately doubling the volume (loudness).

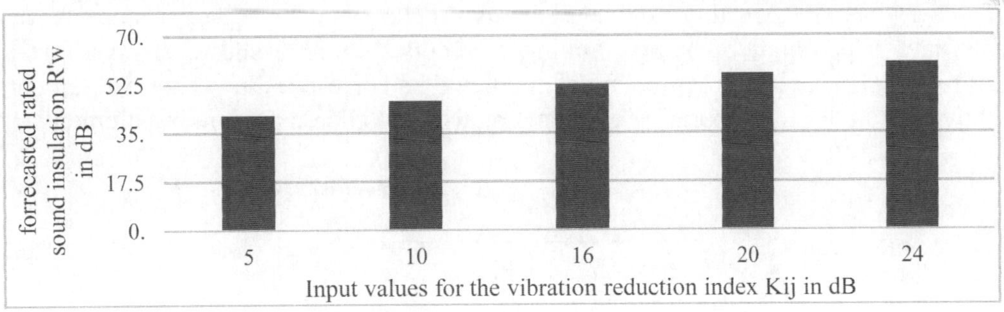

Figure 4: simplified prognosis for the rated sound insulation in which all flanking paths have the same vibration reduction index K_{ij}

3. Junctions in IFC

IFC data models differ in their information value if they are from an early planning phase or for manufacturing. In the early design phase, the models have only rudiment details about the element and connection. Nevertheless, enough information about the used building elements and the overall junction situation should also be provided in this stage.

The IFC standard does not provide an adequate entity to define the junctions for the acoustical analysis. It only allows setting connection relations between elements with *IfcRelConnects*. This class is subdivided into *IfcRelConnectsElements* to connect elements together and *IfcRelContainedInSpatialStructure* to position elements in a space or building storey.

The entity *IfcRelConnectsElements* includes two classes that each attribute to describe where the elements are connected: *AtStart*, *AtEnd* and *AtPath*. The connection geometry is stored in *IfcConnectionGeometry*. Depending on the quality of the model, this information may not be available. That information is not enough to adequately describe the junction from an acoustical perspective, it only allows connection between 2 elements. In this regard, a junction with 4 elements needs 6 relations. Moreover, IFC is not capable of describing a connection between a wall and a slab. Here, attributes like *AtBottom* and *AtTop* would help to define the connection.

4. Methodology

The proposed methodology in this paper is adapted to usual timber buildings. The first approach considers rectangular or almost rectangular building elements. Also all elements are either parallel or in 90 degree angle to each other. This simplification nevertheless makes it possible to represent a large part of the buildings. We assume an IFC data model with a level of detail of 300 to 350 coming from an architect. For this reason we consider the semantic relationships *IfcRelConnects* and *IfcRelSpaceBoundary* in the filter process. But we also do a geometric search for elements in a close range by using *IfcBuildingStorey* because not every BIM software is able to put the correct relationships between elements in the IFC data model. Also not every acoustical relevant space and room is defined by the architect at an early-design phase. So the methodology proposed consists of two main parts: filtering of the relevant components from the IFC data model, and reasoning about the topological relationships between them. In the first part, the separating elements for which the sound insulation has to be calculated are selected. Then we filter the IFC data model to identify possible flanking elements, that has joints with the selected separating elements. Therefore, three aspects are evaluated: Is there an element connection of type *IfcRelConnects*? Is there an *IfcSpace* and other elements adjacent using *IfcRelSpaceBoundary*? Are there other elements on the same or adjacent storey? All those elements have a potential of being flanking elements. Figure 5 shows an example of two adjacent rooms with a wall as separating element and its corresponding flanking elements. The slabs above and under the separating element are also considered as flanking elements.

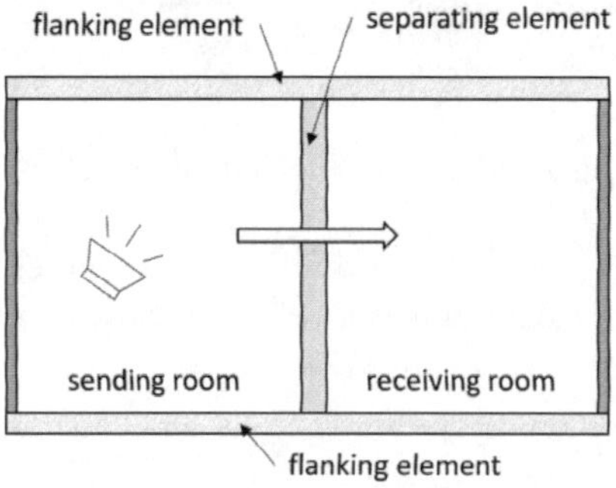

Figure 5: Schematic representation of the separating element and the flanking elements: a standard, rectangular wall has 4 flanking elements: 2 walls and 2 slabs (floor and ceiling)

4.1 Finding Flanking Elements

The first step for finding flanking elements is to filter the IFC data model. This filtering requires the combination of multiple semantic information. When an *IfcRelConnectsElements* exists between the separating element and another element, then, this other element is a flanking element. Additionally those elements may have the same *IfcRelSpaceBoundary*. The last filter option is checking the elements in the building storey around the selecting element. If the separated element is a wall, the filter considers walls and slabs on the same storey and slabs above (as illustrated in Figure 6). For a slab as separating element, walls and slabs of the same storey and walls of the storey below are filtered out. Elements like facades that are described in IFC as *IfcCurtainWall* have the relation *IfcRelReferencedInSpatialStructure* to show in which building storey they are relevant.

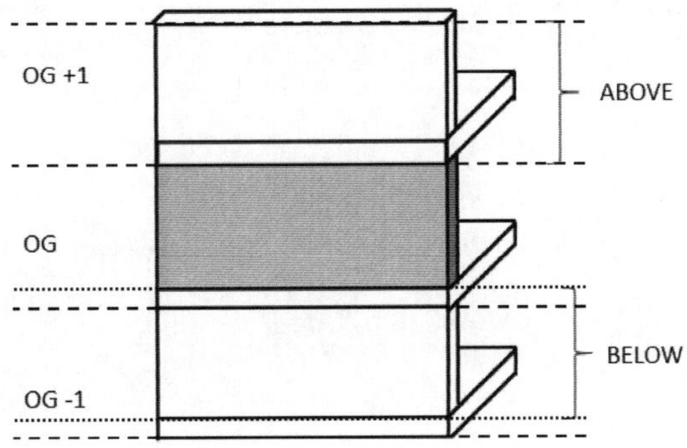

Figure 6: Elements filtered before distance checking: consider all walls and slabs one storey above the separating wall (green), the slabs and walls in the same storey and walls one storey below

In some cases, IFC data models are not rich with enough semantic information (due to issues when exporting to IFC or a modeling error). To overcome such limitation, geometrical operations are used to calculate the distance between the different elements. When the elements are forming a joint, then the distance between (gap) them is evaluated in more detail. Only elements that lay in a range below 0,3 m are still flanking elements. The distance does not need to be zero (as illustrated in Figure 7). Additionally, for flanking elements in a x-junction, another flanking element can lay in between the separating element and the chosen flanking element. For this reason usual collision detection is not suitable to find all flanking elements, because some flanking elements will not touch the separating element. We consider the smallest distance existing between the elements.

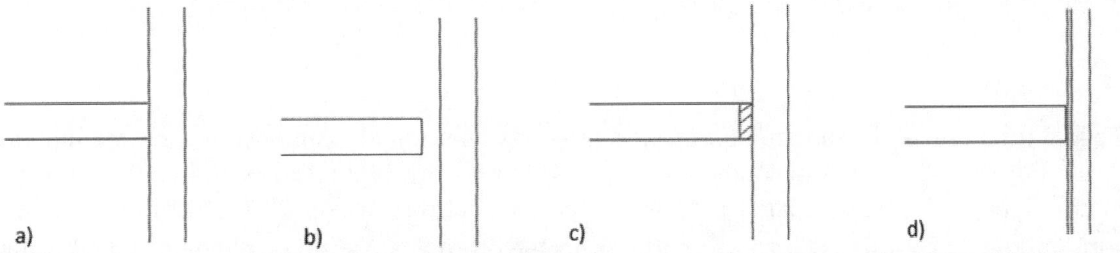

Figure 7: Consideration of junction for an element which is a) touching the separating element (d=0) or adjacent (0 m < d < 0,3 m) to the separated element with b) air in between, c) an elastic layer or d) a facing layer

4.2 Junction-Boxes

To identify the junction type we need different information about its comprising elements. Therefore, we first put every element that will be in the same junction in a separate container. Those containers are called junction boxes. Their position and size are defined by the geometry of the separating element. The vector *n* characterizes the direction of the separating element and the minimum and maximum point of its size and position. With those points, the bounding boxes are created. The following equations show exemplary definition of junction box 1 and junction box 2 for a wall element with n=(1/0/0).

Junction Box 1 for n = (1/0/0)	Junction Box 2 for n = (1/0/0)
JB-Min: X.Min-0,3/Y.Min-0,5/Z.Min	JB-Min: X.Min-0,3/ Y.Min+0,5/ Z.Min
JB-Max: X.Max+0,3/Y.Min+0,5/Z.Max	JB-Max: X.Max+0,3/ Y.Max-0,5/Z.Ma

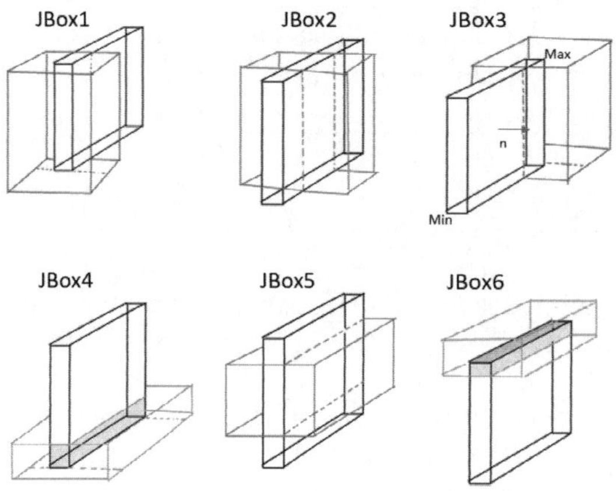

Figure 8: Junction Boxes of a wall element

Every junction box can handle four building elements, one separating element and three flanking elements. The building elements are stored with their entity label from the IFC data model, their element type, their minimum and maximum point, their direction *n*, their distance to the separating element, and the direction in which the distance is calculated. The dimension of each junction box in the y-direction is due to the definition of the junction type. It determines if a junction is an L-junction, or a T-junction, or if opposite elements form a X-junction, or 2 separate T-junctions (see Figure 8).

4.3 Definition of Junction Type

The identification of the junction type takes into consideration all elements in the same junction box. In this regard, each connection needs to be described and represented to identify the exact junction type. For this, this paper proposes three connection zones with respect to its element: short, middle and border. The zone "short" forms the narrow border of an element. The "border" zone is the edge area on the largest element surface, parallel to the element edges. The zone "middle" indicates the remaining area in the middle of the largest area of the element. In addition, the direction of the elements in relation to each other is decisive. For this purpose, the direction "n" is defined starting from a wall element. All wall elements at a 90-degree angle to it are assigned direction "m", while ceiling elements have direction "o". With the element direction and the connection zones, all 15 junction types are identifiable. An excerpt is shown in Figure 10.

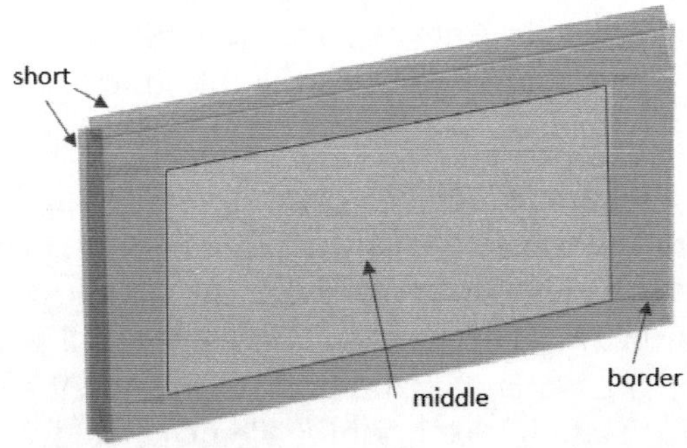

Figure 9: Connection Zones for a wall: short, middle and border

To identify the junction type, the different checks are combined and evaluated in order with if-then-clauses. The following pseudo code shows how this is done for a junction box with 2 elements:

```
For SE.type = wall:
If 2 elements in JunctionBox1 then
         if FE1.n = m AND FE1.dd = n then
                  if FE1.cz(SE) = short then "Lh1-2"
         if FE1.n = m AND FE1.dd = m then
                  if SE.cz(FE1) = border then "Lh1-2"
                  if SE.cz(FE1) = middle then "Th1-24"
End if
```

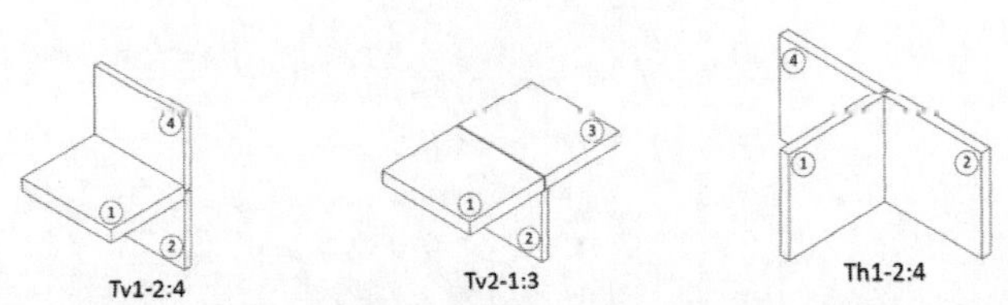

El.Di.	Co.Zo.	
o	short	short
n	border	short
n	border	short

El.Di.	Co.Zo.	
o	border	short
o	border	short
n	short	short

El.Di.	Co.Zo.	
n	short	short
m	border	short
m	border	short

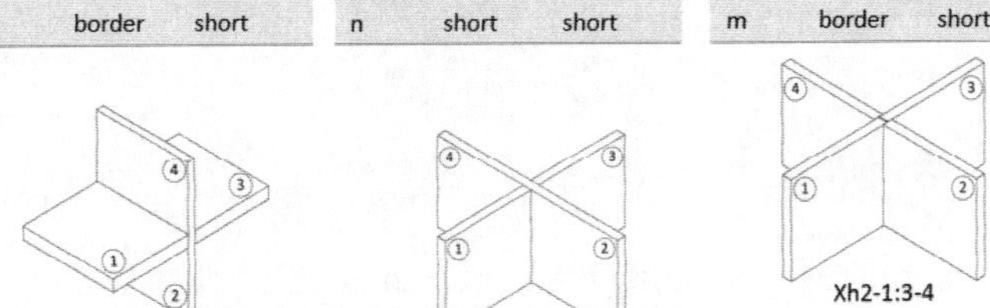

El.Di.	Co.Zo.	
n	middle	middle
o	short	0
o	short	0

El.Di.	Co.Zo.	
n	short	0
m	middle	middle
n	short	0

El.Di.	Co.Zo.		
n	short	short	0
m	border	border	short
m	border	border	short
n	short	short	0

Figure 10: Definition of Junction Type with Element Direction and Connection Zones (excerpt)

5. Use Case

To evaluate the proposed framework, a prototype was implemented as a .Net application, where the xbim Toolkit[1] was used to analyse the IFC data model. Afterwards, a fictions use-case of a model of three storeys was modelled in Autodesk Revit[2], which is then exported into IFC4. The modelling process took into account incorporating the different types of junctions.

Figure 11 shows the result of assigning flanking elements into junction boxes, where the element with number 968 is a separating wall element. As shown in the console, all the flanking elements were correctly detected. The elements were first filtered, then the junction boxes were calculated around the separating element. As a result, the flanking elements were placed into their corresponding junction boxes. The junction boxes 1 and 3 are on the side of the wall element and contain the flanking walls 482 and 623. The element 482 is a façade going from ground floor to the last floor. Junction box 4, for the elements below, includes the slab 206 and the wall 1012, which is located one floor below. The elements above the separating wall are in junction box 6: both slabs 1118 and 1064 and the wall 924. The position of boxes 4 and 6 are also indicated in the illustration. Accordingly, the extracted junction boxes provide the necessary information for identifying the different junction types.

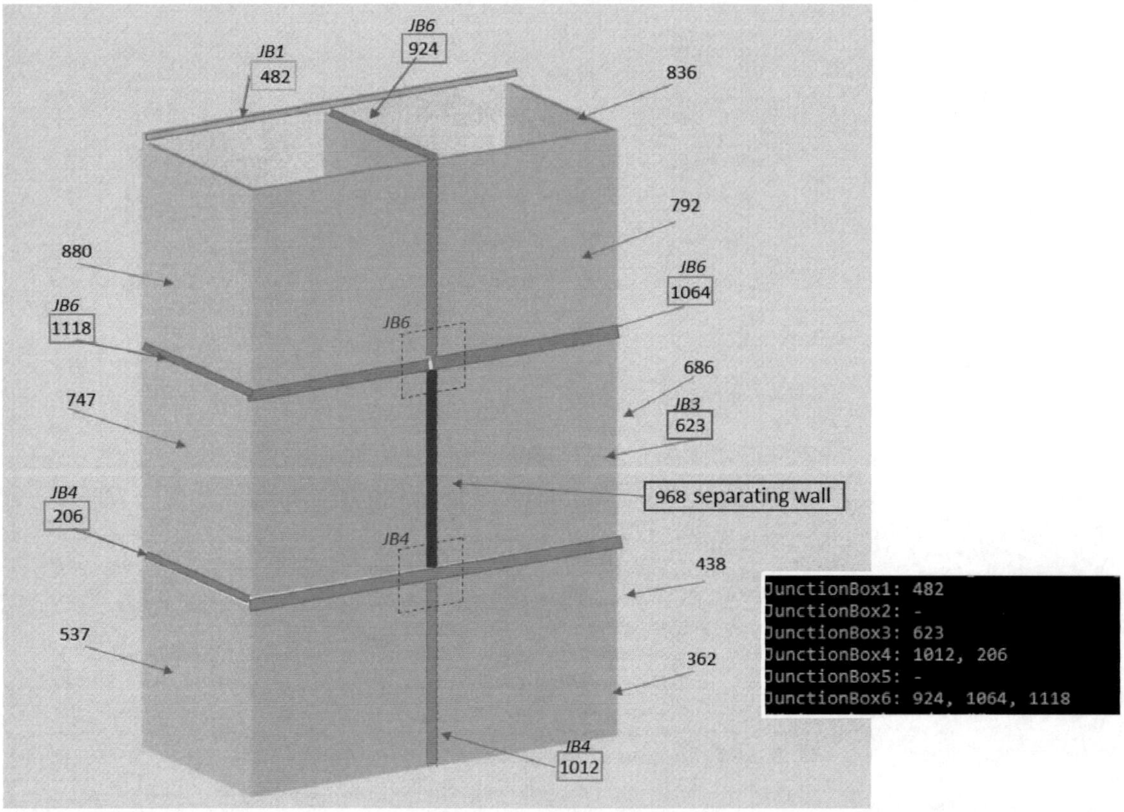

Figure 11: Use Case with *IfcWall* as separating element (red box, number 968) and the result of the assignments of flanking elements into junction boxes. The numbers with a colored frame a flanking elements in the junctions box 1: yellow, box 3: blue, box 4 orange, box 6 green.

[1] https://docs.xbim.net/

[2] https://www.autodesk.eu/

6. Conclusion and Future Work

The planning of sound insulation is a significant challenge while designing timber buildings. The performance forecast is based on calculation models from concrete construction. Moreover, choosing the right input data requires a high level of expertise and a lot of experience in timber construction. Thus far, no software tools can detect and predict the correct junction types from BIM models and interpret them for acoustic analysis. The proposed framework uses geometric analysis to classify zones of elements and distribute them into junction boxes. Based on this information, it is possible to identify the different junction types.

The proposed framework was implemented in a .NET application that automatically extracts the corresponding flanking elements. It is also capable of identifying the geometric placement of flanking elements into junction boxes and deduce the junction type according to that information. The outcome of this research provides a seamless integration with sound insulation prognosis tools, which supports the decision-making process during the design phases.

The current state is that the application does not take into account elements that a not located in the correct building floor. All elements should exist in their corresponding building storey. However, in some cases, some elements geometrically extend to other storeys. Handling this case requires extending the proposed framework to perform special checks. Furthermore, an extensive evaluation for processing complex junctions is necessary, for example, junctions could include double walls. A next step will be to handle building elements with different material layers. This needs detailed filtering of the core layer of the elements, which builds the junction, and the facing layers, which can also get different acoustic characteristics if necessary. To improve the quality of the BIM model, information about the junction type can be included.

References

ISO12354-1 (2017). Building Acoustics – Estimation of acoustic performance of building from the performance of elements- Part 1: Airborne sound insulation between rooms.

Rabold, A., Châteauvieux, C, Schramm, M. (2017). Vibroakustik im Planungsprozess für Holzbauten Modellierung, numerische Simulation, Validierung - Teilprojekt 4: Bauteilprüfung, FEM Modellierung und Validierung. Rosenheim.

Rabold, A., Châteauvieux, C., Mecking, S. (2018). Nachweis von Holzdecken nach DIN 4109 - Möglichkeiten und Grenzen. DAGA, 2018, Munich, Germany.

Timpte, A. (2016). Stoßstellen im Massivholzbau - Konstruktionen, akustische Kenngrößen, Schallschutzprognose. Master Thesis, TH Rosenheim.

Wong, J. K., Li, H., Wang, H.; Huang, T., Luo, E., Li, V. (2013). Toward low-carbon construction processes: the visualisation of predicted emission via virtual prototyping technology. In: Autom. Constr. 33, p. 72–78.

Finch, G. and Marriage, G. and Pelosi, A. and Gjerde, M. (2021). Building envelope systems for the circular economy; Evaluation parameters, current performance and key challenges. In: Sustainable Cities and Society 64.

Abualdenien, J. and Borrmann, A. (2019). A meta-model approach for formal specification and consistent management of multi-LOD building models. In: Advanced Engineering Informatics 40, p.135–153.

Howell, I (2016). The value information has on decision-making. In: New Hampshire Business Review (19), p.19.

Châteauvieux-Hellwig, C., Abualdenien, J., Borrmann, A. (2020). Towards semantic enrichment of early-design timber models for noise and vibration analysis. ECPPM 2020/21. Moscow

Framework proposal for automated generation of production layout scenarios: A parametric design technique to connect production planning and structural industrial building design

Julia Reisinger, Maria Antonia Zahlbruckner, Iva Kovacic, Peter Kán, Xi Wang-Sukalia
TU Wien, Austria
julia.reisinger@tuwien.ac.at

Abstract. To increase the flexibility and expandability of production plants the focus needs to be on a coherent planning of the production layout and building systems. The frequent reconfiguration of production layouts bears challenges on the load-bearing structure of industrial buildings, decreasing the building service life due to rescheduling or demolition. Currently there is no method established to integrate production layout planning into structural building design processes. In this paper, a novel parametric generative design method for automated production layout generation and optimisation (PLGO) is presented, producing layout scenarios to be respected in structural building design. Results of a state-of-the-art analysis and a case study methodology are combined to develop a novel concept of integrated production cubes (IPC). The IPC concept is translated into a parametric PLGO framework, which is tested on a pilot-project of a food-and hygiene production facility and the defined objectives and constraints are validated.

1. Introduction

The economic life cycle of classical building typologies ranges from 50 to 80 years, while industrial buildings are characterised by very short life cycles ranging from 15 to 30 years. The prolongation of industrial buildings service life could increase economic and environmental performance but demands flexible and expandable production layouts, which bears challenges on the structural building design (Gourlis and Kovacic, 2017). Industrial buildings should strive for maximum flexible load-bearing structures, allowing rapid adjustments and simple reconfiguration of production layouts. Thus, the focus needs to be on a coherent planning of the production layout and the building system. An integrated design approach, in which all systems and components work together is one of the most important aspects for well-designed, cost-effective buildings, improving the overall functionality and environmental performance. To have a direct impact on the building performance one need to start early in the design process, such as during the program and schematic design stages, and to develop design alternatives, which must be evaluated, refined, evolved and finally optimised (Butterworth-Heinemann, 2006). Production facilities, referring to a building or area where products are made, and production systems, referring to the methods used in industry to create products from various resources, are generally heavy, fixed, and normally irreversible once construction has been completed (Zhao and Tseng, 2003). By including flexibility early in the design process, the lifetime investment in production facilities that experience change can be reduced (Cardin et al., 2015). However, currently building and production planning processes run sequentially and neglect discipline-specific interactions (Schuh et al., 2011). Integration is complex due to process and interoperability issues and no method is established to integrate production layout planning into structural building design coherently optimising both systems. Current production layout planning methods are mainly conducted manually and are based on assignment activities (Vierschilling et al., 2020). Production layout planning is concerned with the allocation of production segments and functions to meet a set of criteria. One of the most promising methods for automated layout generation is a multi-objective genetic algorithm (MOGA) approach. However, concrete mathematical formalisation of the design space and objectives by which each design scenario can be evaluated is required as basis for optimisation in order to find high performing designs (Nagy et al., 2017). Parametric and performance-based design tools provide design teams an efficient method to explore broad design spaces with quick feedback for well-informed decision-making (Haymaker et al., 2018). Furthermore, parametric modelling offers a sufficient opportunity for integration of multiple design disciplines and generative multi-objective optimisation methods. Various research is conducted on parametric design and optimisation of the building structure (Brown et al., 2020, Pan et al., 2019) but a parametric design method for automated generation and optimisation of production layouts to be integrated into structural building design processes is lacking. The definition of a clear design space scheme to develop a generative parametric design method for production layout generation and optimisation (PLGO), automatically producing production layout scenarios to be integrated into structural design, is the focus of this paper. Therefore, the main research questions investigated in this research are:

1.) What are the design criteria, constraints and objectives for production layout planning in integrated industrial building design (IIBD), respecting flexibility requirements and building criteria, and how can they be mathematically formulated for a MOGA?

2.) What are the requirements and necessary structure of a parametric framework for PLGO, which can be integrated into structural design processes to maximise flexibility and expandability of production plants in long-term?

This paper presents ongoing research conducted within the funded research project BIMFlexi, aiming to develop a holistic digital platform for design and optimisation of industrial buildings towards maximum flexibility by integrating structural design and production processes. In this paper, the design space for PLGO based on a novel concept of integrated production cubes (IPC) is presented, enabling automated generation of production layout scenarios by a MOGA with quantitative objective assessment and layout visualisation for decision-making support. The paper is structured as follows: first, the state of the art on flexibility and automated layout generation in production facility planning through literature review is presented. Second, the applied methodology is described. Based on the results, a novel IPC concept and the PLGO framework is presented. The PLGO framework and the defined objectives and constraints are tested and validated on a pilot-case. Finally, the results and future steps are discussed.

2. Literature Review

The main aim of this research is to create a methodology to optimise the structure of production facilities which allow future adaptations of the production systems without complete rescheduling or demolition. Production systems can be called flexible when they can be easily accommodated to dynamic market requirements (Sahinidis and Grossmann, 1991). A robust production facility must be able to accommodate a range of products; thus moving the facility from a specific product to a more generalized group of products. Thereby, flexibility is not a one-size-fits-all approach; rather it can be cultivated at varying levels by a series of design choices (Madson et al., 2020). Various research define concepts and metrics for the flexibility of residential buildings (De Paris and Lopes, 2018, Cavalliere et al., 2019, Cellucci and Sivo, 2015), the adaptive capacity of buildings (Geraedts, 2016), or the adaptive re-use of office and industrial buildings (Glumac and Islam, 2020). Browne et al. (1984) and Sethi and Sethi (1990) define the 11 most common production flexibility dimensions and Wiendahl et al. (2007) describe five transformation enablers as Universality, Scalability, Modularity, Mobility and Compatibility. Some studies consider the flexible design of a specific facility type, such as food processing facilities (Moline, 2015) and pharmaceutical facilities (Moline, 2017), while Madson et al.

(2020) address the lack of formal design guidance that supports flexibility within architectural and engineering systems of production facilities. No conventional flexibility definition for production layout planning, considering building criteria, has been established. However, Upton (1995) states that the term flexibility is not uniform in production planning. Production managers face a set of flexibility issues: (1) flexibility is not easy to measure; (2) the products that a plant produces do not necessarily reflect its flexibility and (3) it is often unclear which general features of a plant must be changed in order to make its operations flexible.

Research has been conducted on optimisation of product or manufacturing processes (Francalanza et al., 2017, Colledani and Tolio, 2013, Kluczek, 2017, Deif, 2011). On industrial building level, several authors proposed optimisation models that focus on the buildings energy performance (Bleicher et al., 2014, Chinese et al., 2011, Gourlis and Kovacic, 2016). However, integrated optimisation models receive little attention. Indeed, the focus in early industrial building design should be on the optimisation of the load-bearing structure, simultaneously respecting different production layout scenarios. Numerous computational methods have been developed for automation of spatial layout problems, but objectives and scope of these programs vary widely. Automated space allocation algorithms require specific evaluation methods to guide the layout process properly. There are three major solution techniques for automated layout generation: (1) the optimisation of a single criterion function, (2) the graph theoretic approach, (3) and multi-objective optimisation, finding an arrangement that satisfies a diverse set of constraints (position, orientation, adjacency, path, distance) (Liggett, 2000). Despite increasing digitization and extensive computational support in production layout planning, the process of a new design generation including the production logistic aspects still requires manual handling (Vierschilling et al., 2020). Jiang and Nee (2013) and Azadivar and Wang (2000) present automated production layout planning methods based on genetic algorithm and Vierschilling et al. (2020) propose a generative design approach. Furthermore, various research deal with an automated generation of architectural floorplans (Upasani et al., 2020, Dino, 2016, Rodrigues et al., 2013, Lobos and Donath, 2010, Bausys and Pankrašovaite, 2005), mostly utilizing genetic algorithms. To the best of our knowledge, existing research does not provide an algorithm for the automated generation of production layout scenarios, respecting building design criteria during optimisation. Parametric design and performance-based tools offer a great opportunity to integrate discipline-specific systems. Parametric methods have been widely employed by authors in architectural and structural design domain (Brown et al., 2020, Brown and Mueller, 2016, Turrin et al., 2011, Pan et al., 2020). Nourian et al. (2013) develop a design methodology for parametric design of architectural layout plans. Parametric design shows remarkable potential for automated production layout generation and optimisation to integrate into structural building design. A customized PLGO framework on the specificities of IIBD is developed in this paper.

3. Research Methodology

The purpose of the research is the development of the design space (variables, constraints and objectives) and the parametric framework for automated PLGO respecting both, production and building requirements. The methodology is based on an exploratory case study (Yin, 2009), whereby 28 real industrial building projects serve as use-cases, representative for the research objective (Eisenhardt, 1989). Different production types were examined – automotive, food and hygiene, logistic, metal processing and special products – creating a diversity to not exclusively investigate the needs and objectives of a specific production sector. Within the case study, data from production layout planning is collected and the interrelation of architectural, structural and technical building service data is analysed. Results of the state-of-the-art analysis and the case study methodology are combined in a design space for PLGO and a novel integrated production cubes (IPC) concept for parametric production layout planning is developed. The design space representation and the IPC concept is then translated into a parametric framework for PLGO, enabling automated generation of production layout scenarios with quantitative objective assessment and layout visualisation in real-time. The parametric framework is developed in the visual programming tool Grasshopper for Rhino3D (McNeel, 2020). At each research step, care was taken to ensure that the developed PLGO framework follows the same design rules as the parametric structural optimisation script presented in (Reisinger et al., 2021) for successful integration in the next step of the research. The IPC concept and parametric PLGO framework is tested on a pilot-project of a food-and hygiene production and the defined objectives and constraints are validated in a comparative study.

4. Production Layout Generation and Optimisation (PLGO)

This chapter presents the developed IPC concept as basis for parametric production layout planning and the PLGO framework. The description of production requirements is performed manually in the excel-based IPC interface. The IPC concept respects two relation matrices to describe the production flow. Besides the production cube geometry and production-specific information, the IPC concept integrates building related data such as the expected loads from machines and geometry and loads from necessary building service equipment and media supply. This is relevant for the structural building optimisation performed in the next step of the research. A direct link between the IPC interface and the parametric PLGO script is developed, automatically transferring the data to Grasshopper to be respected in the optimisation process. In the PLGO script, the evolutionary algorithm is defined by the IPC concept, constraints and objectives. By appropriate sizing and positioning of the production cubes, the algorithm generates multiple different layout scenarios and ranks them according to their fitness-rating. After the layout scenario generation the design team has to select preferred layout scenarios, which should be further investigated in the structural building design process. The PLGO script collects generated data of the chosen scenarios such as new geometry details and position of production cubes and automatically transfers them into the IPC interface. The chosen production layout scenarios can be integrated into the parametric structural optimisation framework developed by Reisinger et al. (2021). Figure 1 shows the workflow and scope of the paper.

	Scope of this paper – Automated parametric production layout scenario generation and optimisation (PLGO)			Beyond the scope of this paper
Process	**Integrated Production Cubes (IPC) Interface: Input**	**Parametric production layout generation and optimisation**	**IPC Interface: Output**	**Multi-Objective Optimisation of Building Structure**
Data/ Info	1. Input IPC: - Production Cubes: Geometry and data relevant for structural building optimisation - Lean-Factor Matrix - Transport-Intensity Matrix	2. Automated PLGO: - Sizing of production cubes - Positioning of production cubes - Layout scenarios generation - Ranking of layout scenarios 3. Decision-Making: - Selection of layout scenarios to be respected in structural design	4. Automated IPC data output of selected layout scenarios: - Sizing of production cubes - Position of production cubes - Additional production data needed for structural building optimisation (i.e. media supply requirements)	5. Multi-Objective Optimization of Building Structure: - Production layout scenarios (IPC) - Structural system optimisation - Structural layout optimisation - Multi-objective optimisation (life cycle costs, life cycle assessment, flexibility rating)
Tools	*.xls – IPC Interface*	*Rhino/Grasshopper – PLGO script*	*.xls – IPC Interface*	*Rhino/Grasshopper – POD script*

Figure 1: Design process, data and tools of the parametric PLGO framework and scope of the paper

4.1 Integrated production cube (IPC) concept

A novel IPC concept is developed as basis for the parametric production layout generation algorithm. The geometrical description and spatial arrangement of such production cubes is based on the method presented in Reisinger et al. (2021), where one production cube is defined as a rectangular, orthogonal volume described by three variables $C_p\{a_p, b_p, c_p\}$, is allocated to a specific production function (procurement, manufacturing, distribution) and describes a specific sub-process (i.e. storage, milling). Besides the geometrical information of each cube, the IPC concept integrates additional data such as associated loads, media supply, machines or special demands needed for structural optimisation later on. The combination of the production cubes represents the production boundary, the production process and thus the production layout. The production process and material flow, determining the spatial arrangement and the functional sequence of the production cubes and their dependencies, is respected in the optimisation by means of two relation matrices – the *lean-factor matrix* (L) and the *transport-intensity matrix* (T). The lean factor matrix defines the neighbourhood condition of production cubes by *absolutely necessary (AN)*, *important and core (IMPC)*, *unimportant/indifferent (UNIMP)* or *undesirable (UN)*. The number of required dependencies in the cost function is defined by the count of IMPC values in L. While the transport-intensity matrix describes the frequency of needed transports among the production cubes. Figure 2 shows the ICP concept and the geometrical description of production cubes and the integrated data.

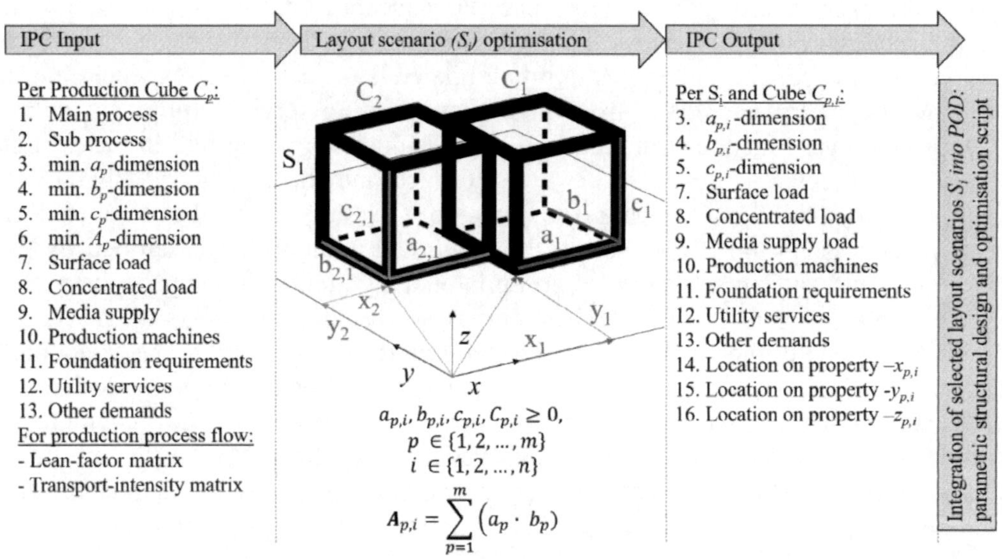

Figure 2: Integrated production cube (IPC) concept: Geometrical formulation and respected data

4.2 PLGO framework development – Constraints and Objectives

To develop the PLGO framework, thus the evolutionary algorithm, five constraints and five objectives were defined based on the IPC concept. We deal with a layout allocation problem that seeks to find non-overlapping geometry and a group of interrelated volumes. We handle this problem with introducing five constraints during optimisation to discover feasible design solutions in the search. The production cubes will be evaluated against their positioning, interrelation and geometry such as (c_1) a cohesively layout, (c_2) layout positioning inside the property, (c_3) lean factor neighbourhood absolutely necessary (c_4) lean factor neighbourhood undesirable and (c_5) adherence of minimum dimensions $(a_{p,min}, b_{p,min})$ of the production cubes. The objectives considered in the PLGO framework rely on a combination of the expert interview results and the flexibility criteria proposed in the literature review. The PLGO objectives defined in the study and respected in the MOGA are: (g_1) maximise the free property area, (g_2) maximise the layout density, (g_3) maximise lean- factor-matrix rating, (g_4) minimise the transport-intensity-matrix length and (g_5) minimise ratio difference of planned and optimised cube dimensions. Table 1 shows the set of constraints and table 2 describes the five PLGO objectives.

Table 1: Set of constraints in the parametric PLGO framework

C	Constraints	Formulation	Description
c_1	*Cohesively layout:* The individual production cube boundaries (R_q, R_r) must not overlap with each other:	$R_q^\circ \cap R_r^\circ = \emptyset$ with $q \neq r$ and $q, r = \{1,2,\ldots,m\}$	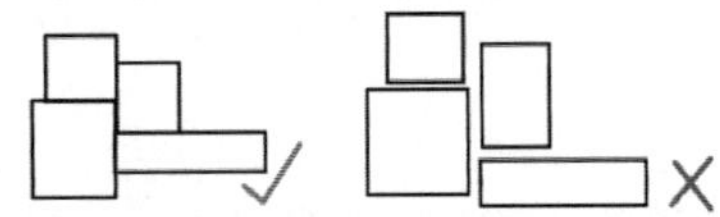
c_2	*Property boundary:* enclosing rectangle of all production cube boundaries R_p must be included into property area boundary R_{Prop}.	$\cup_{(p=1)}^{m} R_p \subseteq R_{Prop}$	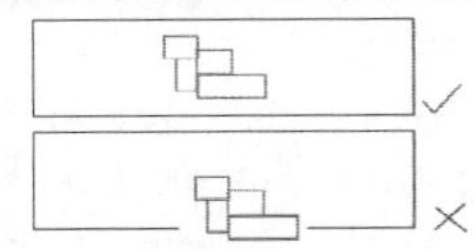
c_3	When *lean factor* neighbourhood is *absolutely necessary*: the edges of the marked production cubes must overlap by at least 1/3.	Min. 1/3 of shorter cube edge must overlap with the other cube edge	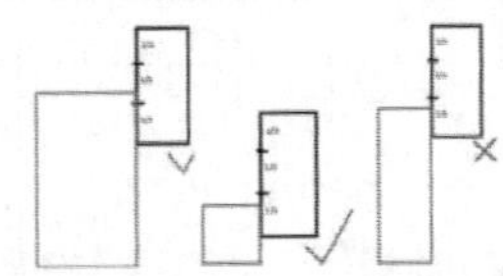
c_4	*Lean Factor* neighbourhood *undesirable:* marked production cubes must not correlate.	Production cubes must not have contact with each other	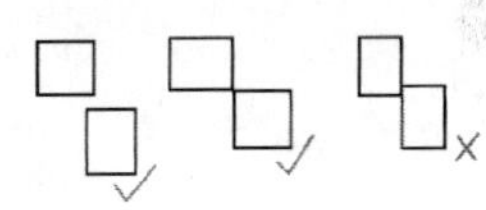
c_5	Adherence of minimum dimension of production cubes	$a_{p,min} \leq a_p$ $b_{p,min} \leq b_p$	

Table 2: Objectives considered in the multi-objective optimisation in the PLGO framework

Nr	Objective	Mathematical objective formulation
g_1	*Maximise the free property area:* for future expansion possibility of the production system	$g_1 = \left(\frac{\sum_{p=1}^{m}(a_p * b_p)}{\sum_{p=1}^{m}(a_{p,min} * b_{p,min})} - 1\right)$
g_2	*Maximise the layout density:* minimise non-usable area between all cubes to avoid unnecessary transport ways	$g_2 = \left(1 - \frac{\sum_{p=1}^{m}(a_p * b_p)}{A_r}\right)$ $A_r \ldots$ area inside the production cube boundary R_p
g_3	*Maximise the rating of the lean-factor-matrix*	$g_3 = 1 - \left(\frac{lfr}{(\sum_{p=1}^{m}\sum_{q=p}^{m} L_{p,q})}\right)$ lfr … lean factor rating (number of fulfilled dependencies)
g_4	*Minimise the length of the transport-intensity-matrix*	$g_4 = \frac{(\sum_{p=1}^{m}\sum_{q=p}^{m}(abs(x_p - x_q) + abs(y_p - y_q)) * T_{p,q})}{(\sum_{p=1}^{m}\sum_{q=p}^{m} T_{p,q}) * (a_{prop} + b_{prop})}$ $a_{prop}, b_{prop} \ldots$ dimension of R_p
g_5	*Minimise the ratio difference* of planned cube dimensions (input) and optimised cube dimensions (output)	$g_5 = \frac{\sum abs\left(\frac{\min(a_{p,min}, b_{p,min})}{\max(a_{p,min}, b_{p,min})} - \frac{\min(a_p, b_p)}{\max(a_p, b_p)}\right)}{m}$

Fitness function for multi-objective optimisation.

The problem we aim to solve is a multi-objective optimisation problem. In this study, the fitness function is minimised and consists of the five presented PLGO objectives. An equal weighting of all objectives is applied in this study to make them test and comparable. The fitness function is mathematically described as follows, whereby f_o is the cost function; g_i describes each objective and w_i is the related weighting ($w_{1-5} = 0.2$):

$$f_o(x) = \sum_{i=1}^{5} g_i * w_i$$

4.3 Implementation of the PLGO framework into parametric design

As described previously, the IPC data is automatically imported into the developed parametric script in Grasshopper for Rhino3D and serves as input for optimisation. The layout generation uses an evolutionary algorithm, implemented in a C# component, and the scalarization method to calculate the fitness to find suitable layouts. Population size, number of generations and the weights for the fitness can be adjusted directly in the script. The layout generation algorithm does not guarantee that layouts do not violate constraints, therefore constraint violation is penalised and inadequate scenarios removed during the generation process. The algorithm ranks the layouts by penalty first and fitness value second.

5. Test Case

This section presents the test case to demonstrate the suitability of the IPC concept, to evaluate the parametric PLGO framework and to validate the defined objectives. The proposed framework is tested on a real use case of a food and hygiene production from the case study, which was chosen because it is particularly representative for flexible production. The production owner has to reconfigure his production machines at regular intervals and constantly expands his production system due to the large growth. The total production layout area is 2 675m² and the property area is 7 125m². The real production layout, its IPC information and the property conditions are used as input for the IPC interface, testing the PLGO framework by comparing the generated production layout scenarios with the real production layout. Figure 3 shows the best-rated layout scenarios using the PLGO framework and the real layout.

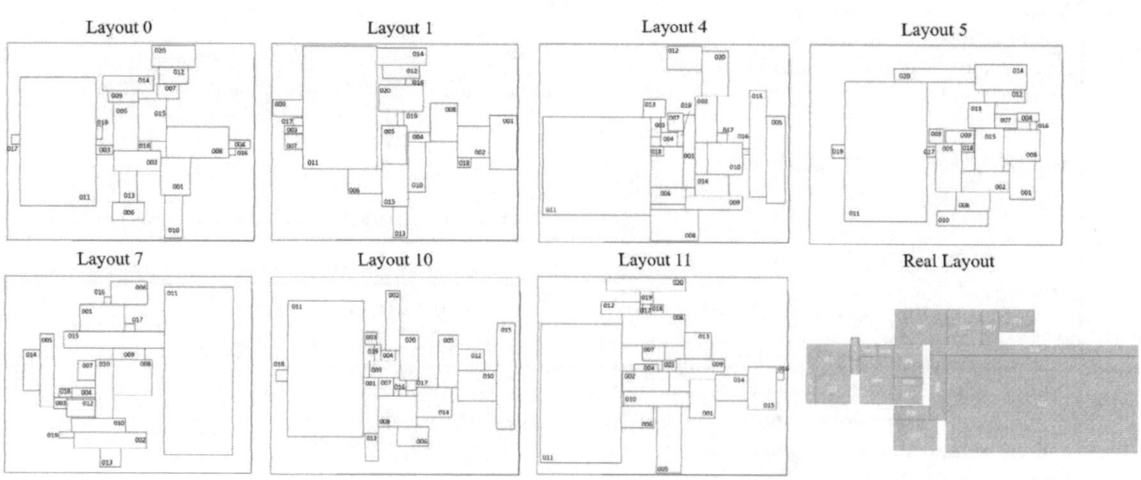

Figure 3: Best-rated layout scenarios generated and real production layout

5.1 Results and discussion

Performing the optimisation, the chosen population size for the test case was 50 with 100 generations. The PLGO algorithm provided 50 different layout s, while the parametric PLGO framework visualised the 21 best-rated layout scenarios. The algorithm penalises constraint violations and removes inadequate scenarios during the generation process. It ranks the found layout solutions according to the constraint violation check first. Then the best-performing layout scenarios within the constraint check are rated according to their fitness. The reason to do the constraint check at first hand is to only find scenarios which best meeting the set of constraints. The ranking results for the constraint violation check are presented in table 3 and the results of the associated fitness-ratings of these layouts are presented in table 4. The conducted test case failed to find layout scenarios which meet all constraints. In future research it is necessary to increase the number of simulations in order to find only non-violating solutions. 14 of the 21 generated scenarios violated constraint 2 by positioning some production cubes outside the property boundary. As these scenarios do not present feasible solutions, they are neglected in the investigation. Constraint 1 requires a cohesive layout but layout 4 is violating this constraint. All investigated scenarios fulfil constraint 2 and 5.

Table 3: Constraint violation check of the best-rated layout scenarios

	Constraint violation check				
Layout ID	**c1**	**c2**	**c3**	**c4**	**c5**
0	✓	✓	1/3 ✓	28/28 ✓	✓
1	✓	✓	1/3 ✓	27/28 ✓	✓
4	×	✓	1/3 ✓	27/28 ✓	✓
5	✓	✓	1/3 ✓	26/28 ✓	✓
7	✓	✓	1/3 ✓	26/28 ✓	✓
10	✓	✓	0/3 ✓	24/28 ✓	✓
11	✓	✓	0/3 ✓	24/28 ✓	✓

Table 4: Results of the single objective evaluation and the final fitness rating of each layout.

	Layout scenario results						
Objective	**0**	**1**	**4**	**5**	**7**	**10**	**11**
g_1	0,036	0,030	0,060	0,050	0,059	0,041	0,064
g_2	0,109	0,111	0,101	0,084	0,097	0,095	0,099
g_3	0,131	0,138	0,131	0,108	0,162	0,138	0,123
g_4	0,041	0,046	0,037	0,045	0,053	0,038	0,039
g_5	0,048	0,054	0,055	0,055	0,053	0,038	0,051
$f(x)$	*0,365*	*0,379*	*0,384*	0,342	*0,424*	*0,350*	*0,376*

5.2 Comparison of best-rated layout scenario with real production layout

Layout 0 represents the best performing scenario as it has the smallest fitness within the least number of constraint violations. Comparing layout 0 with the real production layout of the use-case one can see that the generated layout is not as compact as the real layout. Constraint 1 aims to produce only scenarios with cohesive layouts and the formulation should be refined to reduce large appearing gaps between cubes. The objectives g_1 and g_2 are highly conflicting goals. While the layouts 5 and 10 meet lower fitness-ratings for objective g_2, aiming to maximise the layout density, layout 0 performs better fitness-results at objective g_1, aiming to maximise the free property area for future possible expansion. At this state, it would be up to the decision-maker which layout will be chosen or an objective weighting can be set before running the simulation. The definition and correlation between objective g_1, g_2 and constraint 1 should be further investigated. Constraint 0 is a non-violable constraint, meaning that all minimum dimensions which were adopted from the real layout are also kept in the generated layout scenario. The dimension of the production cubes *001, 003, 004–007, 009–013, 015, 017, 018, 019*, generated in layout 0, are the same dimensions than in the real layout. For the remaining cubes a different ratio of a_p- and b_p-dimensions were chosen by the algorithm in order to come to a feasible solution. The distance of the production cubes 003 and 004 were set to a high transport intensity. However, the algorithm generates a scenario in layout 0, which positions both cubes at a distance of 55 m from each other. Constraint 3 considers the lean-factor matrix and the neighbourhood of *absolutely necessary*. According to the real layout, the neighbourhood of *absolutely necessary* was set for three production cubes. However, constraint 3 is only fulfilled 1 out of 3 times within the conducted test run. The algorithm could not find a solution respecting all adjacency requirements. Thus, the number of simulations should be increased to investigate if the algorithm founds solutions meeting all constraints.

6. Discussion and Conclusion

The applied research method of parametric modelling coupled to a MOGA allows the automated creation of a significant number of layout scenarios according to pre-defined requirements. The results of the test case reveal that the developed PLGO framework is feasible and produces viable layout scenarios to be integrated and investigated in parametric building design processes later on. The PLGO framework serves as an applicable and suitable answer for IIBD, since the optimisation generates feasible production layout scenarios, fulfilling the most important requirements and constraints in production layout planning while also taken into account building aspects. Furthermore, a methodology is created that design teams receive quick quantitative and visual feedback on the layouts for decision-making support. The final choice of which layout scenarios should be further investigated in the building design process is still semi-automated, as the designer must choose the preferred layouts. The circumstance of manual layout selection after the optimisation is explicitly intended in this research as it allows the inclusion of human knowledge and expertise in the design process, not having to rely only on the best-rated scenarios generated by the computational algorithm. In this research, a simple input scheme of minimum width and an aspect ratio range for each production cube has been employed; however, when L-shaped or irregular shaped cubes should be considered, it is challenging to generate a scheme which controls the design of different orthogonal rooms, unless one divides them into rectangles. This current limitation would need to be addressed in future research to generate even more realistic production layouts. In future steps the presented parametric PLGO framework will be coupled to the parametric structural building design framework presented in (Reisinger et al., 2021). The integration of production layout scenarios into the structural design process will allow the evaluation of consequences of changing production layouts on the building structure, enabling integrated multi-objective performance improvement and multidisciplinary decision making support in real-time. The efficiency of the integrated framework, the coupling scheme, the PLC interface and the performance results will be tested within a user-study with experts.

References

Azadivar, F. & Wang, J. 2000. Facility layout optimization using simulation and genetic algorithms. International Journal of Production Research, 38, 4369–4383.

Bausys, R. & Pankrašovaite, I. 2005. Optimization of architectural layout by the improved genetic algorithm. Journal of Civil Engineering and Management - J CIV ENG MANAG, 11, 13–21.

Bleicher, F., Duer, F., Leobner, I., Kovacic, I., Heinzl, B. & Kastner, W. 2014. Co-simulation environment for optimizing energy efficiency in production systems. CIRP Annals, 63, 441–444.

Brown, N. C., Jusiega, V. & Mueller, C. T. 2020. Implementing data-driven parametric building design with a flexible toolbox. Automation in Construction, 118, 103252.

Brown, N. C. & Mueller, C. T. 2016. Design for structural and energy performance of long span buildings using geometric multi-objective optimization. Energy and Buildings, 127, 748–761.

Browne, J., Dubois, D., Rathmill, K., Sethi, S. & Stecke, K. 1984. Classification of Flexible Manufacturing Systems. The FMS Magazine.

Butterworth-Heinemann 2006. 5 - The Design Process—Early Stages. The ASHRAE GreenGuide (Second edition). Burlington: Butterworth-Heinemann.

Cardin, M.-A., Ranjbar-Bourani, M. & De Neufville, R. 2015. Improving the Lifecycle Performance of Engineering Projects with Flexible Strategies: Example of On-Shore LNG Production Design. Systems Engineering, 18.

Cavalliere, C., Dell'osso, G. R., Favia, F. & Lovicario, M. 2019. BIM-based assessment metrics for the functional flexibility of building designs. Automation in Construction, 107, 102925.

Cellucci, C. & Sivo, M. 2015. The Flexible Housing: Criteria and Strategies for Implementation of the Flexibility. Journal of Civil Engineering and Architecture, 9, 845–852.

Chinese, D., Nardin, G. & Saro, O. 2011. Multi-criteria analysis for the selection of space heating systems in an industrial building. Energy, 36, 556–565.

Colledani, M. & Tolio, T. 2013. Integrated process and system modelling for the design of material recycling systems. CIRP Annals, 62, 447–452.

De Paris, S. R. & Lopes, C. N. L. 2018. Housing flexibility problem: Review of recent limitations and solutions. Frontiers of Architectural Research, 7, 80–91.

Deif, A. M. 2011. A system model for green manufacturing. Journal of Cleaner Production, 19, 1553–1559.

Dino, I. G. 2016. An evolutionary approach for 3D architectural space layout design exploration. Automation in Construction, 69, 131–150.

Eisenhardt, K. 1989. Building theories from case study research. The Academy of Management Review, 14, 532–550.

Francalanza, E., Borg, J. & Constantinescu, C. 2017. Development and evaluation of a knowledge-based decision-making approach for designing changeable manufacturing systems. CIRP Journal of Manufacturing Science and Technology, 16, 81–101.

Geraedts, R. 2016. FLEX 4.0, A Practical Instrument to Assess the Adaptive Capacity of Buildings. Energy Procedia, 96, 568–579.

Glumac, B. & Islam, N. 2020. Housing preferences for adaptive re-use of office and industrial buildings: Demand side. Sustainable Cities and Society, 62, 102379.

Gourlis, G. & Kovacic, I. 2016. A study on building performance analysis for energy retrofit of existing industrial facilities. Applied Energy, 184, 1389–1399.

Gourlis, G. & Kovacic, I. 2017. Building Information Modelling for analysis of energy efficient industrial buildings – A case study. Renewable and Sustainable Energy Reviews, 68, 953–963.

Haymaker, J., Bernal, M., Marshall, M. T., Okhoya, V., Szilasi, A., Rezaee, R., Chen, C., Salveson, A., Brechtel, J., Deckinga, L., Hasan, H., Ewing, P. & Welle, B. 2018. Design space construction: A framework to support collaborative, parametric decision making. Journal of Information Technology in Construction (ITcon), 23, 157–178.

Jiang, S. & Nee, A. Y. C. 2013. A novel facility layout planning and optimization methodology. CIRP Annals, 62, 483–486.

Kluczek, A. 2017. An Overall Multi-criteria Approach to Sustainability Assessment of Manufacturing Processes. Procedia Manufacturing, 8, 136–143.

Liggett, R. S. 2000. Automated facilities layout: past, present and future. Automation in Construction, 9, 197–215.

Lobos, D. & Donath, D. 2010. The problem of space layout in architecture: A survey and reflections. Arquitetura Revista, 6, 136–161.

Madson, K. M., Franz, B., Molenaar, K. R. & Okudan Kremer, G. 2020. Strategic development of flexible manufacturing facilities. Engineering, Construction and Architectural Management, 27, 1299-1314.

Mcneel, A. 2020. Grasshopper [Online]. McNeel & Associates. Available: https://www.rhino3d.com/6/new/grasshopper [Accessed 29.01.2020 2020].

Moline, A. 2015. Recipe for change: the flexible food processing plant of the future. DesignFlex2030.

Moline, A. 2017. Rx for change: the flexible biopharma facility of the future. DesignFlex2030.

Nagy, D., Lau, D., Locke, J., Stoddart, J., Villaggi, L., Wang, R., Zhao, D. & Benjamin, D. 2017. Project Discover: An Application of Generative Design for Architectural Space Planning.

Nourian, P., Rezvani, S. & Sariyildiz, S. 2013. Designing with Space Syntax A configurative approach to architectural layout, proposing a computa- tional methodology.

Pan, W., Sun, Y., Turrin, M., Louter, C. & Sariyildiz, S. 2020. Design exploration of quantitative performance and geometry typology for indoor arena based on self-organizing map and multi-layered perceptron neural network. Automation in Construction, 114, 103163.

Pan, W., Turrin, M., Louter, C., Sariyildiz, S. & Sun, Y. 2019. Integrating multi-functional space and long-span structure in the early design stage of indoor sports arenas by using parametric modelling and multi-objective optimization. Journal of Building Engineering, 22, 464–485.

Reisinger, J., Knoll, M. & Kovacic, I. 2021. Design space exploration for flexibility assessment and decision making support in integrated industrial building design. Optimization and Engineering.

Reisinger, J., Kovacic, I., Kaufmann, H., Kan, P. & Podkosova, I. 2020. Framework Proposal for a BIM-Based Digital Platform for Flexible Design and Optimization of Industrial Buildings for Industry 4.0. ICCCBE/W78 Virtual Joint Conference. Sao Paulo, Brazil.

Rodrigues, E., Gaspar, A. R. & Gomes, Á. 2013. An approach to the multi-level space allocation problem in architecture using a hybrid evolutionary technique. Automation in Construction, 35, 482–498.

Sahinidis, N. V. & Grossmann, I. E. 1991. Multiperiod investment model for processing networks with dedicated and flexible plants. Industrial & Engineering Chemistry Research, 30, 1165–1171.

Schuh, G., Kampker, A. & Wesch-Potente, C. 2011. Condition based factory planning. Production Engineering, 5, 89–94.

Sethi, A. K. & Sethi, S. P. 1990. Flexibility in manufacturing: A survey. International Journal of Flexible Manufacturing Systems, 2, 289–328.

Turrin, M., Von Buelow, P. & Stouffs, R. 2011. Design explorations of performance driven geometry in architectural design using parametric modeling and genetic algorithms. Advanced Engineering Informatics, 25, 675.

Upasani, N., Shekhawat, K. & Sachdeva, G. 2020. Automated generation of dimensioned rectangular floorplans. Automation in Construction, 113, 103149.

Upton, D. What Really Makes Factories Flexible. 1995.

Vierschilling, S. P., Dannapfel, M., Losse, S. & Matzke, O. 2020. Generative Design In Factory Layout Planning: An Application Of Evolutionary Computing Within The Creation OfProduction Logistic Concepts.

Wiendahl, H. P., Elmaraghy, H. A., Nyhuis, P., Zäh, M. F., Wiendahl, H. H., Duffie, N. & Brieke, M. 2007. Changeable Manufacturing - Classification, Design and Operation. CIRP Annals, 56, 783–809.

Yin, R. K. 2009. Case study research : design and methods, Los Angeles, Calif. [u.a.], Los Angeles, Calif. [u.a.] : Sage Publ.

Zhao, T. & Tseng, C.-L. 2003. Valuing Flexibility in Infrastructure Expansion. Journal of Infrastructure Systems, 9, 89–97.

Component-based machine learning for predicting representative time-series of energy performance in building design

Xia Chen [a], Manav Mahan Singh [b], Philipp Geyer [a, b]
[a] Technische Universität Berlin, Germany, [b] Katholieke Universiteit Leuven, Belgium
xia.chen@tu-berlin.de

Abstract. The building industry is benefited by building performance simulation (BPS) for design assistance. Machine learning (ML) has been widely used for quick performance prediction; however, it lacks the flexibility to scale for new designs. By spatially and semantically decomposing the building design into components, this article links the ML approach with the system engineering paradigm of BPS to develop component-based machine learning (CBML). While previous use of CMBL focused on point predictions, this study proves that the CBML is able to predict dynamic time-series energy performance for new design cases by deriving a set of reusable model components. We trained and tested the ML model on a dataset of 1000 examples. The objective is to ascertain the ability of the ML model to generalize via different decomposition levels. Hourly energy predictions during the design phase are useful for equipment sizing, controlling peak energy demands, and leveling the load in the networks.

1. Introduction

Digitalization has greatly reshaped the community of architecture (Eastman et al. 2011; Sydora and Stroulia 2020). Simulation for building performance assessment has been applied to the whole life cycle process on a large scale, especially in the design phase (Evins 2013; Østergård et al. 2016; Tian et al. 2018). Regarding the building energy efficiency information such as peak load, cost, etc., performance assessment enables designers, policymakers, and engineers to conduct a wide variety of decision-making and policy implementation toward sustainable energy-efficient buildings (Cao et al. 2016). Among these aspects, one of the important subjects in this domain is building energy prediction at the early stage. Accurately modeling and predicting energy performance provides the foundation for further application (Longo et al. 2019). Accurate predictions of hourly energy consumption will assist in evaluating several design alternatives and operation strategies (Deb et al. 2017a). Especially, the integration of buildings into energy networks exploiting renewable energy and storage capacities requires the prediction of their time-series energy demand.

The development of machine learning (ML) algorithms and cost-efficient computational resources enabled numerous applications for regression, classification, and optimization tasks in an efficient way (Seyedzadeh et al. 2018; Chakraborty and Elzarka 2019). The idea of ML is to feed the data into specific objective functions to capture hidden patterns between input features and outputs by minimizing the error via a recursive training process. The most intuitive approach is training a monolithic model fed with available data from building features and set the target as model output; however, the building features might come from different levels of details. The monolithic approach is incapable of reflecting the internal relationship of variables. In contrast, the component-based machine learning (CBML) approach for energy performance involving the building components relationship into models creates flexibility to integrate domain knowledge (Geyer et al. 2018; Geyer 2009; Geyer and Schlüter 2014; Leblanc et al. 2011). By linking the ML models to general building component structures, the framework offers a possibility to achieve quick support and flexible modeling for energy performance prediction in the early design process. The results show that component-based ML provided a promising accuracy for a variety of design configurations regarding energy demand (Geyer et al. 2018).

In this paper, we intend to take this approach one step further to prove that the component-based ML approach is capable of capturing the energy performance in time-series prediction tasks. A tree-based ensemble machine learning model is implemented as a basic component. The novelty of including time-series prediction instead of point prediction in this framework is as follow:

- By composition in different component structures, the CBML approach contributes to analyzing energy system characteristics in the building design phase learned from time-series training data with certain energy usage patterns and peaks.
- The CBML approach enables an understanding of thermal behavior and its relationship in predicting energy loads for data-driven models.

This paper develops ML models to predict the building energy consumption in time series with validation of model generalization using the CBML approach. To achieve this objective, the remains of the paper is organized as follows: Section 2 introduces the methodology of the CBML framework and the ensemble method; Section 3 describes the database and the setup of the training process; Section 4 discusses the results; Section 5 outlines the limitations and future work, and Section 6 concludes the paper.

2. Methodology

2.1 Component-based machine learning for building energy prediction

Developing a building energy prediction ML model for the early design stage is challenging due to evolving shape and structure of the architectural design. A simpler parametrical representation of building envelope by parameters such as shape coefficient (Catalina et al. 2008) and relative compactness (Cheng and Cao 2014) is insufficient to capture its effect and internal flows on the energy performance. Geyer and Singaravel proposed an approach of component-based machine learning (CBML) to overcome this limitation (Geyer and Singaravel 2018). CBML is based on the decomposition of building into components, each representing its thermal behavior. A building consists of thermal zones connected to walls and windows, ground floors, and roofs. This approach is developed to predict energy demand for new shapes by composing the required ML components to represent any design configuration. A model structure comparison between the monolithic and the CBML approaches for time-series prediction is presented in Figure 1.

We intend to train the monolithic approach as the baseline and compare it to the CBML approach in our use case. The data organization is similar to the previous work (Geyer and Singaravel 2018); we kept the same structure of the data and intermediate value features (heat flow) yet varied each feature's value in a range to represent different building design schemes. The general input building characteristic, output target, and feature engineering used in both approaches are identical. In the CBML approach, we trained building components separately by applying intermediate value as outputs and aggregate for further target output prediction. In the end, the general accuracy of both approaches is compared in average energy performance in time-series format.

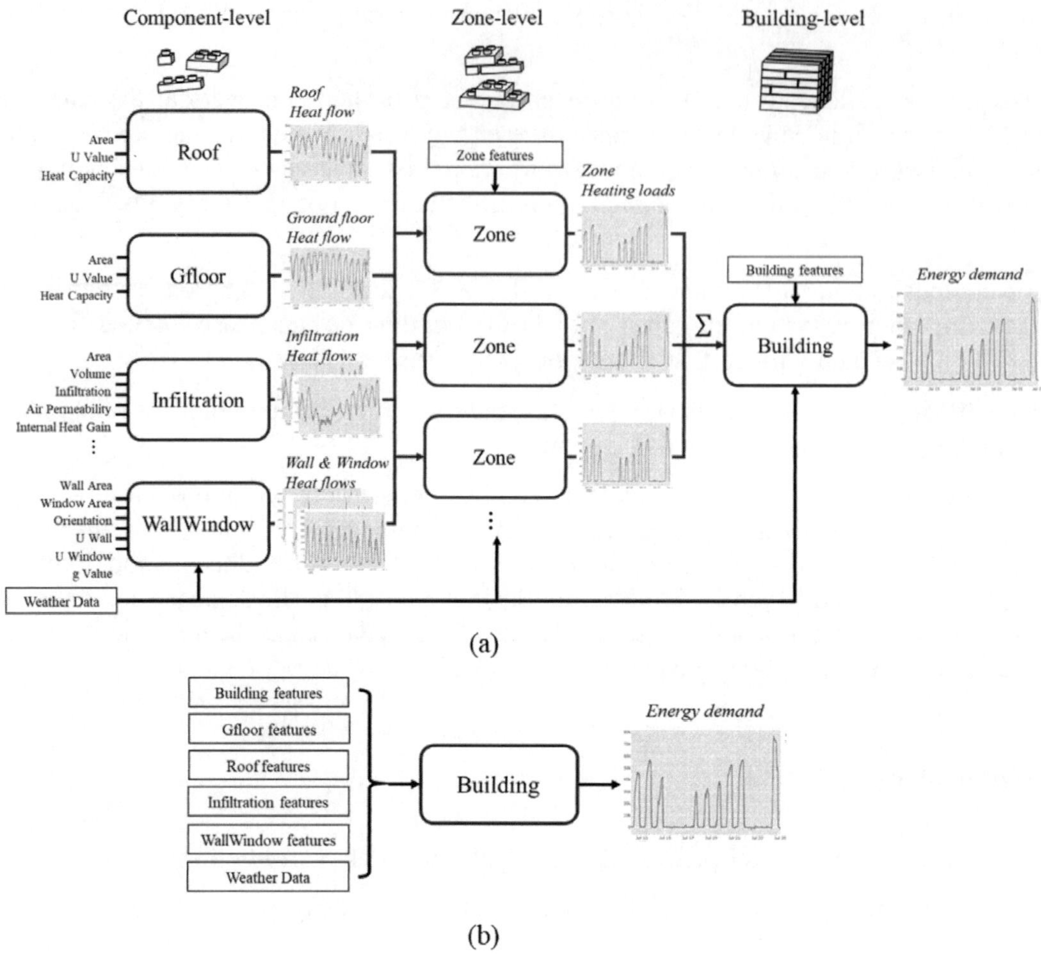

Figure 1: System used for (a) CBML and (b) monolithic ML

2.2 Benchmark: Monolithic ML

In this study, we chose the monolithic ML model approach as a benchmark, which refers to using a single ML model to predict the building's heating and cooling loads. Contrary to the CBML approach, this approach relies on using all relevant design parameters to predict thermal energy loads; hence, compared to CBML, it has less flexibility to be applied for new design cases. Normally, it requires parameters in full detail, making it less practical in the early design phase.

2.3 ML algorithm: LightGBM

A large number of literature reviews (Amasyali and El-Gohary 2018; Machairas et al. 2014; Zhao and Magoulès 2012) indicates that the current mainstream machine learning algorithms in the BPS community are mainly: Artificial Neural Network (ANN), Random Forest (RF), Multiple Linear Regression (MLR), Gaussian Processes (GP), and Support Vector Machine (SVM) (Amasyali and El-Gohary 2018; Deb et al. 2017b; Somu et al. 2020). In addition to the above methods, ensemble methods in both real-world competitions, such as Kaggle[1] and building performance forecasting research (Chakraborty and Elzarka 2019), have been reported

[1] Online survey available: https://www.kaggle.com/kaggle-survey-2020

with an advance in accuracy. In particular, the category of Gradient Boosting Decision Tree (GBDT) (Friedman 2001) has been applied widely and excelled in practice.

In our use case, instead of only using continuous time-series data, building characteristics and discrete features also play an important role in integrating domain knowledge into the prediction. GBDT algorithms are developed under the concept of boosting (Freund et al. 1999), compared with Long short-term memory (LSTM) and Recurrent neural network (RNN), boosting technic in such cases shows benefit in generalization by sequentially random sampling and mixing categorical, numerical feature types with historical observations of the target for training. Hence, in our paper, we use GBDT as the ML method to predict the time-series data. Since the dataset we use contains different shapes of buildings, we expand the sparse discrete building features into the same length as time-based input. In this paper, we chose an efficient algorithm - Light Gradient Boosting Machine (LightGBM) as our ML model. LightGBM implements a highly optimized histogram-based decision tree learning algorithm, which yields great advantages in efficiency and memory consumption. Further insight and an open-source implementation in detail are available in the mentioned reference (Guolin Ke et al.).

3. Case study

3.1 Case study details

This study uses a typical medium-size office building in Munich as a test example. An EnergyPlus model is used to simulate its energy performance. This EnergyPlus model is validated against the yearly energy consumption of the real building. The validation results are available on Mendeley datasets (Singh 2021). The relevant design parameters are modified for creating training and test datasets. The design parameters mentioned in Table 1 are considered in this study to develop datasets. The building shape of training data and test data are shown in Figure 2. The test data has random building shapes to validate that the trained ML components are reusable for new design cases. The random building shapes are generated by arranging squares of varying dimensions. We used the EnergyPlus model to generate time-series energy performance for all the dimension schemes individually. The floor area per floor for random shapes is in the range of 200 to 800 sqm.

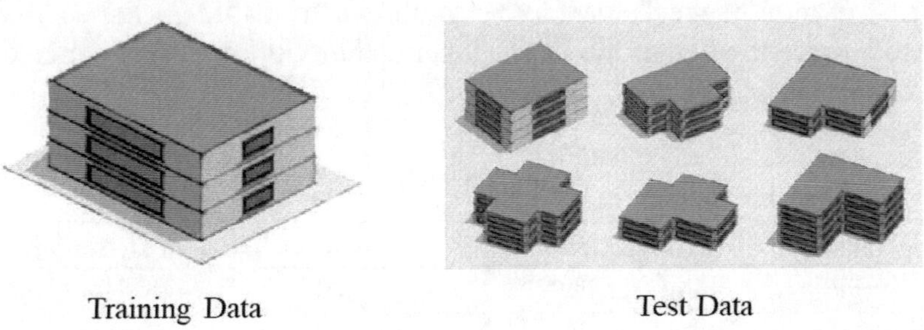

Figure 2: Representation of building shape used for training and test data

Table 1: Design parameters for training and testing

Parameters	Unit	Min	Max	Parameters	Unit	Min	Max
Length	m	12	30	**Heat Capacity (Slab)**	kJ/m^3K	0.8	1.0
Width		12	30	**Window-to-Wall Ratio**	-	0.1	0.5
Floor Height		3.0	4.0	**Internal Mass**	kJ/m^2	60	120
No. of Floors	-	2	4	**Air Permeability**	$m^3/h{\cdot}m^2$	6	9
Orientation	°	0	90	**Operating Hours**	h	10	12
u value (Wall)	W/m^2K	0.15	0.25	**Occupant Load**	m^2/Person	16	24
u value (Ground Floor)		0.15	0.25	**Light Heat Load**	W/m^2	6	10
u value (Roof)		0.15	0.25	**Equipment Heat Load**		10	14
u value (Window)		0.7	1.0	**Heating COP**	-	2.5	4.5
u value (Internal Floor)		0.4	0.6	**Cooling COP**		2.5	4.5
g value	-	0.3	0.6	**Boiler Efficiency**		0.92	0.98

This study makes hourly energy prediction for two typical and two extreme weather conditions to cover a range of representative prediction conditions. Based on the weather information, the days mentioned in Table 2 have been selected to study the proposed approach. These days represent typical weather conditions for calculating the peak energy demand and sizing the energy system.

Table 2: Days selected for hourly energy prediction

Interval	Days	Interval	Days
Winter typical	January 05 – January 17	**Summer typical**	July 12 – July 24
Winter extreme	February 09 – February 21	**Summer extreme**	July 19 – July 31

3.2 Machine learning strategy

Four data categories exist in our dataset: weather, time, building features, and target outputs. As time-series data are required for all categories, we expand the discrete features in Table 1: Design parameters for training and testing to time-series data by repetition. By this transformation, all input features are available in time-series format. As the ensemble tree-based algorithm's split finding mechanism is insensitive to the value range, data scaling is not required (Marsland 2015). In this research, we only decomposed and engineered the cyclical time features such as the month, week, day, etc., as shown in Table 3. Especially, we used the Boolean value to represent whether the day is weekend or workday to enhance the ML model's recognition of energy usage patterns.

Table 3: Decomposition of time features

Name	Definition	Name	Definition
tm_d	Day of month	*tm_wm*	Week of month
tm_w	Week of year	*tm_dw*	Day of week
tm_m	Month	*tm_w_end*	If is weekend

As for hyperparameters' optimization, we kept the default setting of most hyperparameters[2] in LightGBM but fine-tuned the iteration round to prevent model underfitting or overfitting. The cross-validation as hyperparameter tuning technique was used for the best iteration

[2] Default setting of hyperparameters is available on LightGBM 3.2.1.99 documentation (2021): https://lightgbm.readthedocs.io/en/latest/Parameters.html?highlight=default

identification. More specifically, a 3-fold cross-validation method was applied to the training process with 300 early stopping epochs, which means the training dataset is equally split into three subsets, the subsets are repeatedly fed in a model using combinations of two sub-training and one sub-validation set, and the error from each validation was averaged. The averaged error was under supervised during the cross-validation training process until it stops dropping for 300 iterations, then the best iteration rounds are confirmed.

The dataset is split into two independent parts as training and test set. The training set contains a thousand buildings with corresponding components, while in the test set, five hundred buildings of different shapes. We trained all levels of components independently, then used the CBML approach by taking the predicted output of component-level, integrated according to the different composition of zone-levels, further into building-level components to predict the target load, as shown in Figure 1. At the same time, we also trained monolithic ML models for zone-level and building-level as a benchmark. The target periods and outputs are *Heating Load: Winter typical*, *Heating Load: Winter extreme*, *Cooling Load: Summer typical*, and *Cooling Load: Summer extreme*.

4. Results

We took the monolithic ML at the building level as the baseline. The detailed results of components and monolithic MLs in terms of accuracy are available in Table 4. Both accuracy results are concluded by compared with the EnergyPlus model output. To cover all three-level CBML architecture, we also show the results of the monolithic model at zone-level for comparison. Except the *CBML building* is conducted by the CBML approach, the rest rows in Table 4 show results of the monolithic model. In general, both approaches present novel performance in time series prediction in BPS. The accuracy of CBML approaches in all four scenarios degrades only slightly compared to direct prediction, which is impressive by given the fact that: 1. the buildings in the test set are compositionally different from the training set and 2. It requires the variable transfer among the different model components.

Table 4: Accuracy of ML components (R^2 values)

Component	Heating Load		Cooling Load	
	Winter Typical	**Winter Extreme**	**Summer Typical**	**Summer Extreme**
Ground floor	0.9252	0.8941	0.9065	0.8797
Infiltration	0.9743	0.9835	0.9777	0.9826
Roof	0.9462	0.9542	0.9127	0.8967
Wall & Window	0.9726	0.9770	0.9826	0.9823
Zone*	0.9889	0.9877	0.9669	0.9791
Building*	**0.9141**	**0.9731**	**0.9700**	**0.9746**
CBML Building	**0.9274**	**0.9217**	**0.9422**	**0.9597**

* using monolithic ML

If we compare the performance of components closely in Table 4, it is worth noting that components-level performs better at predicting energy demand for infiltration and walls but less accurate for ground floor and roof. The reason might be as follows: In addition to more available features in infiltration and Wall & Window components as inputs, roof and floor normally have a large area; A bigger area brings more uncertainties in heat flow behavior for forecasting; furthermore, due to the horizontal orientation of the roof and floor, they show less sensitiveness to external weather data. Compared to the monolithic model, such a decomposition with a separation reasoning process is only available in the CBML approach, contributing to a better model explainability.

Figure 3 visualizes the performance of energy demand prediction in four different periods. We rendered an extra relative error plot under each prediction to avoid read difficulty due to curves' close overlap. We remove outlier pikes (larger than 1) in the error plot for demonstration purposes when the load is zero. The CBML approach shows a better coverage at peak load in the summer period. Specifically, the visualization shows that inaccurate parts (the absolute value of relative error larger than 0.2) normally appear at the lower part of the load (around 0), contributing the most to accuracy degradation. A common solution for this problem is introducing the intermittent forecasting method to alleviate it in future research. The most important fact is that the CBML approach is capable of capturing the peak load and usage patterns for non-existent buildings, achieve comparable performance as the direct ML approach.

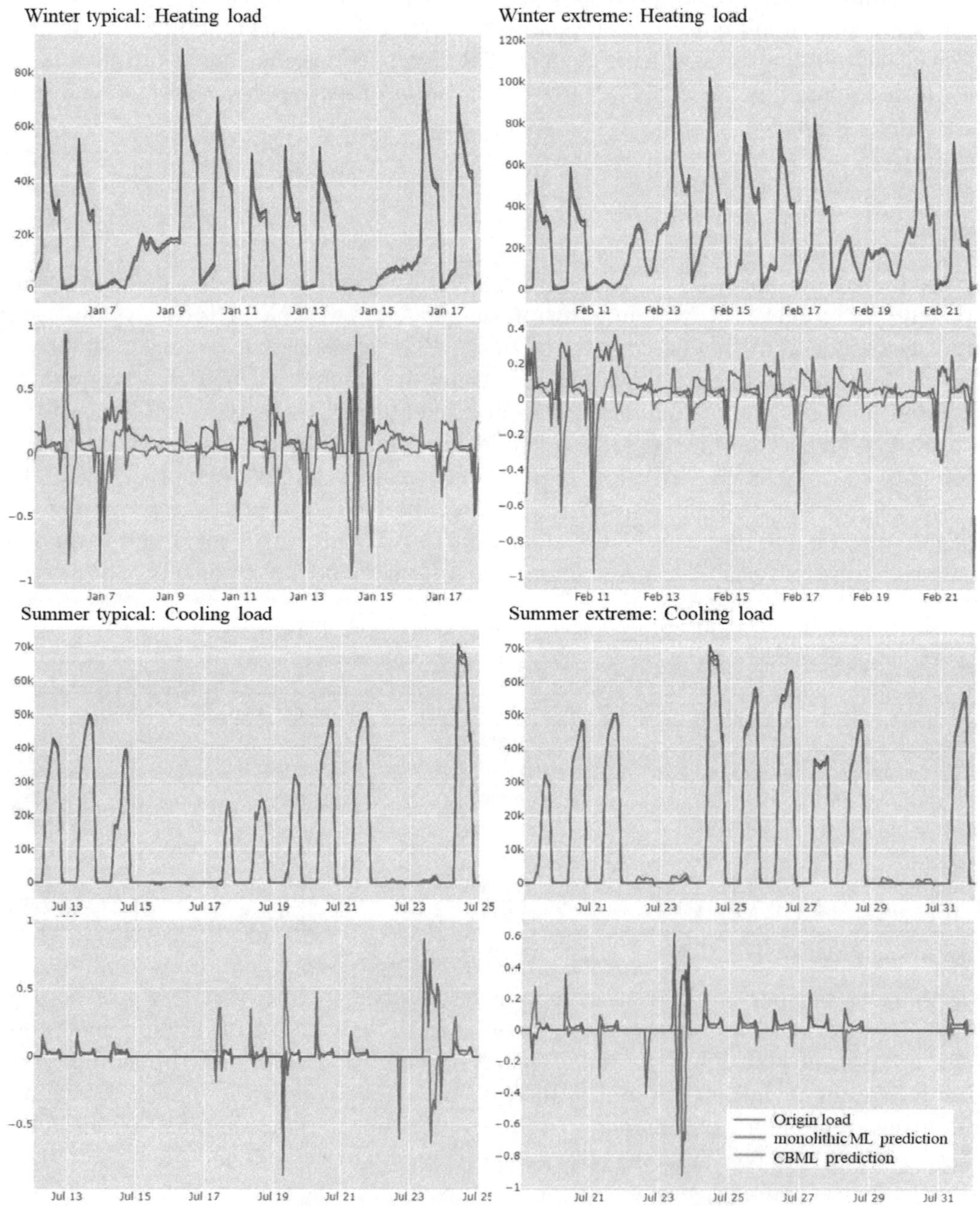

Figure 3: Performance visualization of energy demand prediction with relative error plots

5. Discussion

This paper demonstrated the feasibility of time-series prediction by the CBML approach has been by implementing the tree-based ensemble algorithm for energy demand prediction based on a decomposition scheme for BPS. The hourly CBML prediction has been validated by simulation results against the monolithic ML approach. It is worth pointing out that in Figure 4, the CBML prediction result shows fluctuation at lower load, even negative values. If we consider eliminating the negative value manually, the general performance will be further enhanced. Compared to monolithic ML prediction, it shows the following advantages: (1) CBML covers a range of configurations not included in the training data. The direct ML approach is less likely to build in practice due to the data collection difficulties; Due to the separate component training process, the CBML approach has the flexibility to predict under a certain level of incomplete inputs, which as an essential feature is needed, especially in the early design phase; (2) The CBML approaches provide the possibility to predict the peak load and usage patterns for different shapes of non-exist buildings in the design phase. In practice, they are important indicators for building designers in scheme evaluation, e.g., plant and system dimensioning. (3) Building designers and engineers can access inter-component results to understand why a design performs well or badly. After the deployment, such an extra energy performance time-series data also contributes to model calibration for engineers in simulation; (4) The components integrate seamlessly in digital modeling as performed in BIM, which means fewer efforts are required for the model deployment in real-world scenarios. (5) CBML building components are reusable in different cases once they achieve a certain level of generalization by fed-in enough data. A huge potential to build up a standardized building energy performance library with a limited number of components. Such a library brings the opportunity for fast modelling in the building design assistance.

The accuracy of the model is highly dependent on the data input. As the current model is trained on the synthetic data generated by the energy simulation tool, the study does not address the gap between simulation and actual energy demand. The next step in the component-based ML approach's research is further accuracy validation of error propagation and training under real data, which contains more noise and uncertainty. In addition, a detailed classification of building types due to different energy usage pattern settings needs to be performed, such as for residential buildings, commercial buildings, etc. This may lead to bias in the final prediction results of real cases.

6. Conclusion

To sum up, we incorporated time-series prediction in component-based ML for modeling building performance. The approach provides better generalization than monolithic ML as it allows the use of components assembled in different configurations as required by design. The generalization has been successfully demonstrated because CBML predicts load behavior under representative weather conditions for design configurations not included in the training data. The accuracy of the predictions does not degrade significantly during variables transfer among components. This result demonstrates that the component-based approach owns the transferable flexibility to predict the energy performance of non-exist buildings. This method and its additional information provide vital support in the building early design phase. Especially, the quick and accurate prediction of time-series with peaks and patterns, the integration in digital design and modeling of buildings, and the explainability by inter-component information form important benefits. Such abilities enable machine assistance for building design support with considerable benefit for design process efficiency and solutions.

Acknowledgement

We gratefully acknowledge the support of the German Research Foundation (DFG) for funding the project under grant GE 1652/3-2 in the Researcher Unit FOR 2363.

References

Amasyali, Kadir; El-Gohary, Nora M. (2018): A review of data-driven building energy consumption prediction studies. In *Renewable and Sustainable Energy Reviews* 81, pp. 1192–1205. DOI: 10.1016/j.rser.2017.04.095.

Cao, Xiaodong; Dai, Xilei; Liu, Junjie (2016): Building energy-consumption status worldwide and the state-of-the-art technologies for zero-energy buildings during the past decade. In *Energy and Buildings* 128, pp. 198–213. DOI: 10.1016/j.enbuild.2016.06.089.

Catalina, Tiberiu; Virgone, Joseph; Blanco, Eric (2008): Development and validation of regression models to predict monthly heating demand for residential buildings. In *Energy and Buildings* 40 (10), pp. 1825–1832. DOI: 10.1016/j.enbuild.2008.04.001.

Chakraborty, Debaditya; Elzarka, Hazem (2019): Advanced machine learning techniques for building performance simulation: a comparative analysis. In *Journal of Building Performance Simulation* 12 (2), pp. 193–207.

Deb, Chirag; Zhang, Fan; Yang, Junjing; Lee, Siew Eang; Shah, Kwok Wei (2017a): A review on time series forecasting techniques for building energy consumption. In *Renewable and Sustainable Energy Reviews* 74, pp. 902–924.

Deb, Chirag; Zhang, Fan; Yang, Junjing; Lee, Siew Eang; Shah, Kwok Wei (2017b): A review on time series forecasting techniques for building energy consumption. In *Renewable and Sustainable Energy Reviews* 74, pp. 902–924.

Eastman, Charles M.; Eastman, Chuck; Teicholz, Paul; Sacks, Rafael; Liston, Kathleen (2011): BIM handbook: A guide to building information modeling for owners, managers, designers, engineers and contractors: John Wiley & Sons.

Evins, Ralph (2013): A review of computational optimisation methods applied to sustainable building design. In *Renewable and Sustainable Energy Reviews* 22, pp. 230–245. DOI: 10.1016/j.rser.2013.02.004.

Freund, Yoav; Schapire, Robert; Abe, Naoki (1999): A short introduction to boosting. In *Journal-Japanese Society For Artificial Intelligence* 14 (771–780), p. 1612.

Friedman, Jerome H. (2001): Greedy function approximation: a gradient boosting machine. In *Annals of statistics*, pp. 1189–1232.

Geyer, Philipp (2009): Component-oriented decomposition for multidisciplinary design optimization in building design. In *Advanced Engineering Informatics* 23 (1), pp. 12–31. DOI: 10.1016/j.aei.2008.06.008.

Geyer, Philipp; Schlüter, Arno (2014): Automated metamodel generation for Design Space Exploration and decision-making – A novel method supporting performance-oriented building design and retrofitting. In *Applied Energy* 119, pp. 537–556. DOI: 10.1016/j.apenergy.2013.12.064.

Geyer, Philipp; Singaravel, Sundaravelpandian (2018): Component-based machine learning for performance prediction in building design. In *Applied Energy* 228, pp. 1439–1453. DOI: 10.1016/j.apenergy.2018.07.011.

Geyer, Philipp; Singh, Manav Mahan; Singaravel, Sundaravelpandian (2018): Component-Based Machine Learning for Energy Performance Prediction by MultiLOD Models in the Early Phases of Building Design. In Ian F. C. Smith, Bernd Domer (Eds.): Advanced Computing Strategies for Engineering, vol. 10863. Cham: Springer International Publishing (Lecture Notes in Computer Science), pp. 516–534.

Guolin Ke; Qi Meng; Thomas Finley; Taifeng Wang; Wei Chen; Weidong Ma et al.: LightGBM: A Highly Efficient Gradient Boosting Decision Tree.

Leblanc, Luc; Houle, Jocelyn; Poulin, Pierre (2011): Component-based modeling of complete buildings. In : Graphics Interface, vol. 2011, pp. 87–94.

Longo, Sonia; Montana, Francesco; Riva Sanseverino, Eleonora (2019): A review on optimization and cost-optimal methodologies in low-energy buildings design and environmental considerations. In *Sustainable Cities and Society* 45, pp. 87–104. DOI: 10.1016/j.scs.2018.11.027.

Machairas, Vasileios; Tsangrassoulis, Aris; Axarli, Kleo (2014): Algorithms for optimization of building design: A review. In *Renewable and Sustainable Energy Reviews* 31, pp. 101–112. DOI: 10.1016/j.rser.2013.11.036.

Marsland, Stephen (2015): Machine learning: an algorithmic perspective: CRC Press.

Østergård, Torben; Jensen, Rasmus L.; Maagaard, Steffen E. (2016): Building simulations supporting decision making in early design – A review. In *Renewable and Sustainable Energy Reviews* 61, pp. 187–201. DOI: 10.1016/j.rser.2016.03.045.

Seyedzadeh, Saleh; Rahimian, Farzad Pour; Glesk, Ivan; Roper, Marc (2018): Machine learning for estimation of building energy consumption and performance: a review. In *Vis. in Eng.* 6 (1). DOI: 10.1186/s40327-018-0064-7.

Singh, Manav Mahan (2021): Validation of Early Design Stage EnergyPlus Model for Office Building (one-zone-per-floor model).

Somu, Nivethitha; M R, Gauthama Raman; Ramamritham, Krithi (2020): A hybrid model for building energy consumption forecasting using long short term memory networks. In *Applied Energy* 261, p. 114131. DOI: 10.1016/j.apenergy.2019.114131.

Sydora, Christoph; Stroulia, Eleni (2020): Rule-based compliance checking and generative design for building interiors using BIM. In *Automation in Construction* 120, p. 103368. DOI: 10.1016/j.autcon.2020.103368.

Tian, Zhichao; Zhang, Xinkai; Jin, Xing; Zhou, Xin; Si, Binghui; Shi, Xing (2018): Towards adoption of building energy simulation and optimization for passive building design: A survey and a review. In *Energy and Buildings* 158, pp. 1306–1316. DOI: 10.1016/j.enbuild.2017.11.022.

Zhao, Hai-xiang; Magoulès, Frédéric (2012): A review on the prediction of building energy consumption. In *Renewable and Sustainable Energy Reviews* 16 (6), pp. 3586–3592. DOI: 10.1016/j.rser.2012.02.049.

A hybrid-model time-series forecasting approach for reducing the building energy performance gap

Xia Chen, Tong Guo, Philipp Geyer
Technische Universität Berlin, Germany
xia.chen@tu-berlin.de

Abstract. The performance gap between predicted and actual energy consumption in the building industry remains an unsolved problem in practice. This paper aims to minimize this gap by proposing a hybrid-model using building simulation and machine learning (ML) models inspired by the concept of time-series decomposition: 1. Using first-principles methods in different levels of information to convert the building discrete features and predictable patterns in time-series format. 2. Import the physical model's output into the ML model as input. 3. Training the ML model to align the performance and calibrate the result. The approach is tested in the measured energy load from an office building in Shanghai. Hybrid-model shows higher accuracy in prediction with a better interpretation for gap magnitude investigation in building energy. In summary, the method demonstrates how domain knowledge via building simulation incorporated with data-driven methods, especially ML leads to improved predictions.

1. Introduction

With the global digitalization trend, two major changes have occurred in the building sector: (i) the boom of available data volume, especially operation record (continuous time-series data) and building characteristic data (discrete building features), (ii) the increasing reliance on the building performance simulation (BPS) (Hensen and Lamberts 2011) by constructing prediction models. In this context, a performance gap is reported on the investigation between measured data and predicted output in two major modeling approaches in this domain (Wilde 2014): first-principles models or white-box approaches (simulation tools); and data-driven models or black-box approaches (ML models).

The first-principles model reproduces the physical energy processes of buildings by physical principles. Numerous software tools have been developed to simulate the physical and thermal behavior of buildings, such as TRNSYS (Klein and Beckman 2007), EnergyPlus (Drury B. Crawley et al. 2000), etc.; however, precise modeling and accurate results require detailed building characteristics and a significant amount of modeling effort, making it cost-inefficient in practice with full-scale experiments. Furthermore, compared to detailed building features (u-value, internal mass, etc.), the historical consumption records are easier to obtain yet difficult to utilize for BPS calibration properly.

The difficulties associated with the first-principles modeling process have contributed to the development of alternative approaches based on data-driven models. Especially, machine learning (ML) models that enable computers to adapt energy models without being explicitly programmed have become popular in the recent decade (Seyedzadeh et al. 2018). Since ML approaches are more fit for acquiring unpredictable patterns of data, they have proved to be more efficient and accurate where historical time-series data is available (Chakraborty and Elzarka 2019); however, these black-box models are created directly from data by algorithms without considering the underlying physics of building thermal and energy systems, making ML model training in a relatively inefficient way.

From the discussion above, both the ML and the domain knowledge via simulation are helpful for improving the prediction accuracy. The building simulation domain's current research focuses exclusively on pure ML methods integration, developing new ML approaches for accuracy enhancement or objective functions for discrete and continuous parameters utilization (Banihashemi et al. 2017; Pérez-Lombard et al. 2008). Successful integration of both approaches is reported in the urban energy modeling scale (Nutkiewicz et al. 2018). Following this idea and inspired by the time-series decomposition mindset, the presented approach develops a hybrid model in building energy performance prediction. By integrating predictable information via the output of first-principles models into ML methods, it carries the advantage of capturing both systematic patterns and uncertainties to improve the prediction accuracy further.

To develop the hybrid approach using simulation and ML approaches, Section 2 introduces the methodology of the first-principles model and the ML method used in the approach; Section 3 describes the setup of a case study for validating the approach by data from a commercial building in Shanghai, China; Section 4 discusses the case study results; Section 5 outlines the limitations and future work; and Section 6 concludes the paper.

2. Methodology

2.1 Time-series decomposition: systematic and unsystematic patterns

For building energy demand prediction, the historical data compresses all the information regarding building features, user behavior, operation conditions, as well as unpredicted environmental noise into a compact time-series, which increases the difficulty for the ML model to extract a variety of hidden patterns. In the community of time-series analysis, it is often helpful to split a time-series into several sub-series, each representing an underlying pattern category (Hyndman and Athanasopoulos 2018). The most common and informative decomposition method is Seasonal and Trend decomposition using Loess (STL) (Cleveland et al. 1990) by a purely mathematical process. It defines a series y as an additive or multiplicative combination of trend (T), seasonal or periodicity (P), and random (R) or noise components over time t. Figure 1 visualizes this decomposition, in which the original time-series is illustrated at the first row as observed, accompanied by decomposed series underneath.

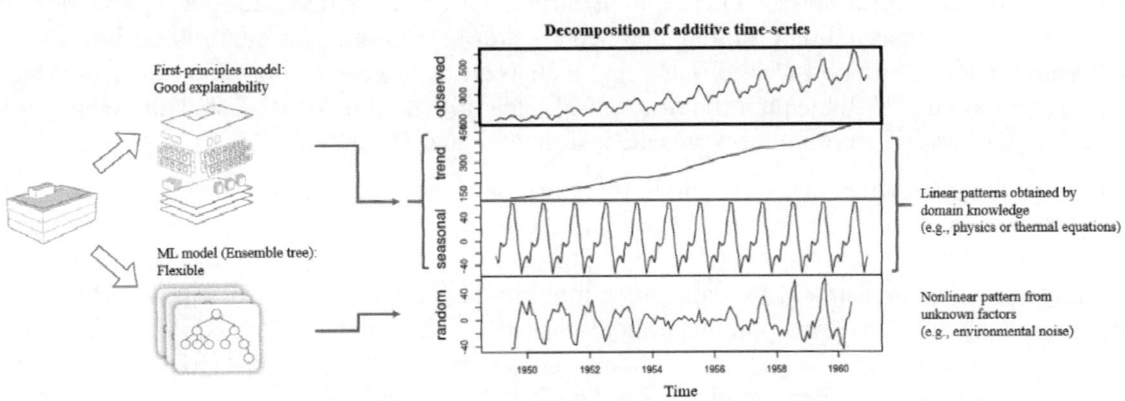

Figure 1: Hybrid concept: analogous of STL decomposition

In general, the STL decomposition includes a useful abstraction mindset to distinguish a time-series into systematic and unsystematic patterns:

- The trend and seasonal component is related to the systematic part, which has consistency or recurrence and can be described and modeled systematically.

- The random component is referred to as the stochastic part, which due to noise or lack of information not to be directly modeled.

Furthermore, this mindset also leverages implicit knowledge of uncertainty decomposition, which refers to two distinct types of uncertainties: aleatory and epistemic (Jeremiah Liu et al.). Although aleatory represents the irreducible randomness from the natural data generation process, it is possible to further decompose epistemic uncertainties into two sub-types: *parametric* and *structural*. The hybrid approach reduces the performance gap by referring both uncertainties to the first-principles approach and ML model:

- The first-principles model is qualified to conduct deterministic processes (trend and seasonal patterns) based on physical laws of thermodynamics. In addition, it offers the domain insight to reduce the epistemic uncertainty due to the ML modeling limit on *structural* (monolithic model).
- The ML model is more efficient to focus on obtaining the stochastic hidden patterns once the decomposition to the residual category is done. This hidden pattern capture ability provides a supplement for the lack of *parametric* specification from simulation (e.g., ignorance of certain building design factors).

Hence, the full available information of a building, including discrete and continuous parameters, is properly allocated into two approaches and integrated under the thought of time-series decomposition, as shown in Figure 1. A process to combine these two approaches is the key in our hybrid approach.

2.2 First-principles model: Modelica

The concept of the first-principles model (or white-box models) in the building simulation domain is thermodynamical modeling of processes, which relies on the mathematical equations describing the physical behavior of thermodynamics and heat transfer. In this paper, we chose Modelica as the simulation platform with two building performance simulation libraries: *AixLib* and *IEA-EBC Annex 60*, which are implemented in the object-oriented modeling language Modelica (Fuchs et al. 2015; Nageler et al. 2019), serve to construct the first-principles model.

As mentioned in Section 1, first-principles models need a full description of the building to be parameterized appropriately. In general, input parameters are classified into four types: exterior information (weather data), building geometry (interior design, zoning information, etc.), buildings physics (wall, constructions, etc.,) as well as boundary conditions (e.g., use conditions and user behavior). With the underlying physical behavior equations, all these parameters with modeling knowledge incorporation provide insight as T and P components.

However, the difficulties on corresponding feature data collection are the major challenge in the first-principles modeling process. More input parameters describe more in detail and lead to better simulation accuracy (Coakley et al. 2011), yet it means also more time consumption and more resource investment for data collection. For this reason, we consider this trade-off in this paper and created corresponding models based on different levels of information. All required input data for the physical model were collected from reliable sources, such as construction plans, equipment brochures, and national weather datasets.

To represent the difference between the level of details intuitively, refinement of geometric and semantic information is described as Levels-of-Information (LOI) - a simplified version of Level-of-Development (LOD) (Hooper 2015) in BIM, which exclusively focuses on available building parameters for the simulation. Three levels of input parameters category are defined in Table 1.

Table 1: Different input parameter levels of detail

Level	Geometry info	Non-geometry info	Integrity
Level 0	Net leased area; Number of floors; u-value;	Construction period; Use of building;	LOI 0 (basic geometry) LOI 1 (coarse representation)
Level 1		Equipment efficiency; Equipment operation time; Temperature setting;	LOI 0, LOI 1, LOI 2 (system settings)
Level 2	Window g-value; Window-to-wall ratio;		LOI 0, LOI 1, LOI 2, LOI 3 (architectural details)

The default level-0 includes the most critical information: basic geometry (LOI 0) and building characteristics (LOI 1), which are required at minimum to build the baseline energy models. The level-1 model requires further information regarding energy system settings (LOI 2). Window-to-wall ratio (WWR) and other architectural details (LOI 3) are offered into final level-2 information. All three data levels for developing physical models are also beneficial for better understanding their importance by integrating them independently with subsequent data models.

2.3 Machine learning model: Ensemble tree-based model

In the building energy sector, a comparative analysis reported that the ensemble learning model produces more accurate results than ANN and ordinary least square regression in a synthetic database from EnergyPlus simulations (Chakraborty and Elzarka 2019). Additionally, based on the split finding mechanism, the ensemble tree-based algorithm is insensitive to the value range. Data scaling is not required (Marsland 2015). In this paper, we chose an efficient algorithm - Light Gradient Boosting Machine (LightGBM) as our ML model. Further insight and an open-source implementation in detail is available in the original paper (Guolin Ke et al.).

The basic idea behind this procedure is to learn sequentially in which the current regression tree is fitted to the residuals (errors) from the previous trees via boosting approach (Marsland 2015), which provides a better blending of different categories of data for learning. A boosting demonstration is presented in the right-bottom corner of Figure 2.

Conducted by the first-principles model, the output time-series is a proper format to carry the domain knowledge, including predictable patterns, building characteristics, and discrete features information (systematic information with T and P). By integrating such information as a reference, it enables the ML model to focus on capturing unsystematic patterns (R) or implicit parametric uncertainties. Hence, the overall hybrid approach contributes to accuracy enhancement and model interpretation, as shown in Figure 2.

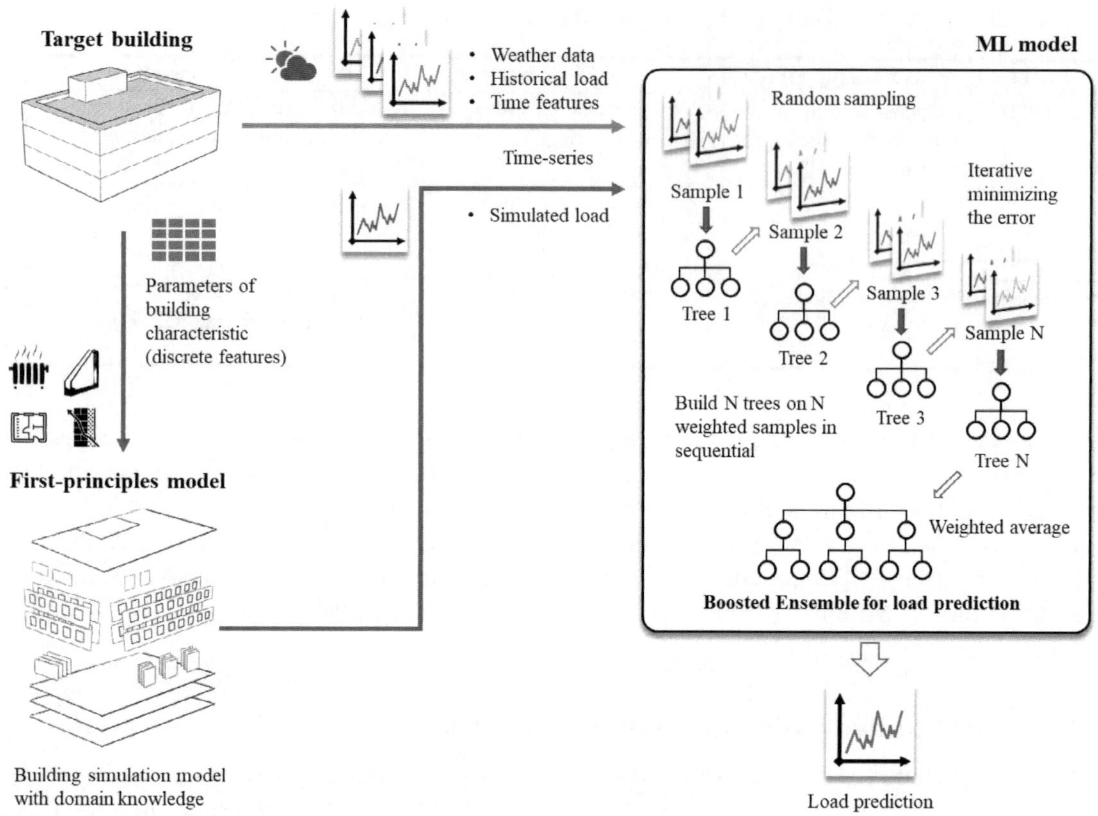

Figure 2: Hybrid framework & boosting algorithm

2.4 Data preparation & Feature engineering

For hourly building performance time-series forecasting, four categories of time-series features are defined for the hybrid approach: weather, time, historical records, and records from the simulation. To strengthen the periodicity information, we processed the time features by:

- decomposing time features such as the month, week, day, etc.
- using sine/cosine transform to turning hour features into 2-dimensions.
- using the Boolean value to represent whether the day is weekend or workday.

More importantly, we used the feature engineering methods from time-series forecasting by adding extra feature columns through all non-time features transformation by:

- Shifting features for 1, 2, and 3 periods
- Rolling average features for 6 and 12 time-windows with shifting 1, 3, 6, 12 periods

We kept the default setting of most hyperparameters[1] in the model but fine-tuned the iteration round to prevent the model under- or over-fitting: A 3-fold cross-validation is used to determine the best iteration.

[1] Default setting of hyperparameters is available on LightGBM 3.2.1.99 documentation (2021): https://lightgbm.readthedocs.io/en/latest/Parameters.html?highlight=default,

3. Case study

In this section, we validate the proposed hybrid approach on a proof of real-world energy prediction case study of a commercial building in Shanghai, China (Xiao et al. 2021). In this database, both the discrete building characteristic and a year of hourly historical load data, as well as the weather data of Shanghai are available.

3.1 Target building data

The scale of data for this case study is represented in Figure 3. We categorized the available data features into different levels based on the classification criteria of LOI from Table 1. As the color darkens from left to right, the higher level of detail results in more accurate simulation performance. However, it also requires more precise building characteristic data. For the unknown data, the system sets default values for level-1 and level-2 to ensure that models of different levels operate normally, represented in Figure 3.

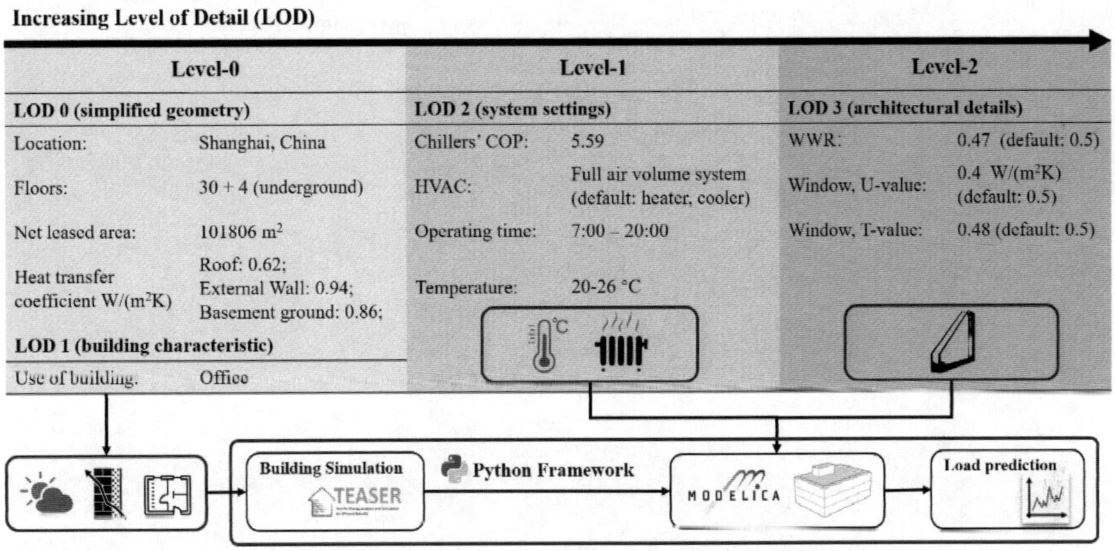

Figure 3: Process of first-principles models with different levels' input

The input difference between the pure ML model and the hybrid model is the extra simulation record input feature (*Simu_Record,* with feature engineering). The detailed information of input features is demonstrated in Table 2.

To prevent data leakage from feature engineering, we split the dataset into two parts, the first eleven months for training and the final month for validation. All approaches are fed-in or applied to the same data, including the pure ML method, three different levels of first-principles models as well as three hybrid framework methods.

Table 2: Input features of hybrid model (shifting and rolling features excluded)

Input feature	description	Input feature	description
*Simu_Record**	The output of the simulation	*tm_h_cos*	Hour of day, cosine transformed
*temp**	Air temperature (°C)	*tm_d*	Day of month
*dew**	Dew point (°C)	*tm_w*	Week of year
*hum**	Relative humidity (%)	*tm_m*	Month

*pres**	Atmospheric pressure (hPa)	*tm_wm*	Week of month
*winds**	Wind speed (m/s)	*tm_dw*	Day of week
tm_h_sin	Hour of day, sine transformed	*tm_w_end*	If is weekend

* also using shifting and rolling feature engineering

4. Results

Figure 4 visualizes the result between the pure ML model, different levels of simulations, and hybrid models. The quantified performances' comparison is shown in Table 3.

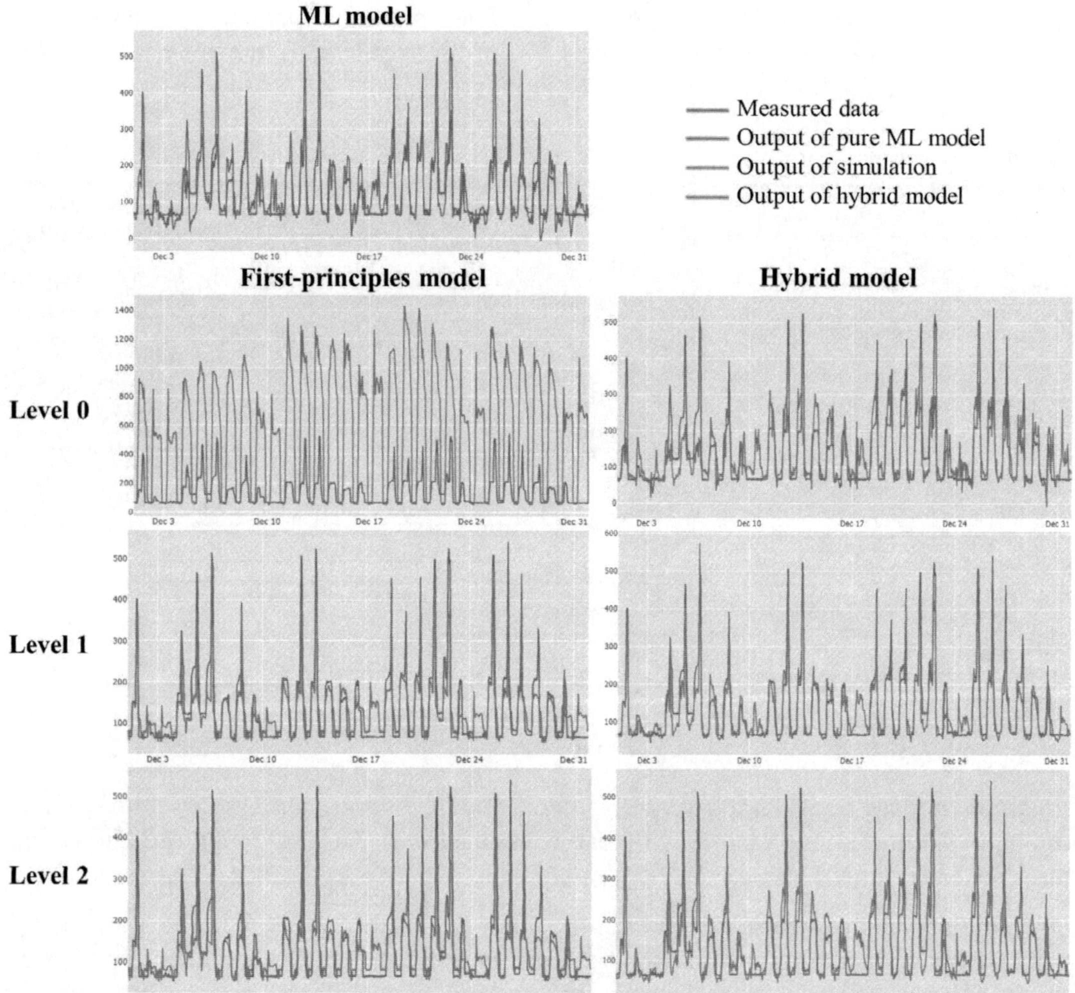

Figure 4: Comparison of results in different levels, one commercial building in Shanghai, China

Table 3: Accuracy of different approaches

	RMSE	**SMAPE**	**R2**
Pure ML model	57.72	29.03	0.62
Simulation – L0	578.53	97.90	-36.18
Simulation – L1	46.20	24.89	0.76
Simulation – L2	49.11	25.85	0.73

Hybrid model – L0	**70.60**	**31.83**	**0.45**
Hybrid model – L1	**39.46**	**20.33**	**0.83**
Hybrid model – L2	**43.16**	**22.16**	**0.79**

Generally, the hybrid framework shows accuracy advantages compared to the same simulation levels and pure ML method. Compared with the result of first-principles models, it enables the ML model to predict the peak load more accurately while performs a reliable output at baseload than the pure ML model.

Several useful pieces of information are summarized therein: (1) It is difficult for pure ML models to overcome the gap of mixed information extraction and energy consumption prediction without domain knowledge. Although it captures a certain degree of periodic variation and average load for the pure ML model result, the output still contains a lot of noise that manifests itself on baseload. Except for Level-0, first-principles models generally perform better than the pure ML model. (2) Systematic information such as trend (T) and periodicity (P) are well extracted through domain knowledge modeling approaches. Contrary to the pure ML method, even Level-0 of the first principles model well captures the periodic change. (3) Non-geometry information such as occupancy behavior, energy system features significantly contribute to the model accuracy enhancement. With additional Level-1 features into the simulation, the prediction performance is greatly optimized from the Level-0 information. (4) A promising path to minimize the gap between predicted and measured load via both approaches integration.

It is worth noting that the accuracy in level-1 is slightly higher than level-2 during the test period (Wintertime) from Table 3. The reason might be that there is shading in the building, such as curtains. Still, the WWR and other window data added in level-2 expand the influence of solar radiation heat, resulting in a slightly higher error than level-1.

5. Discussion

In this paper, we proposed a hybrid approach and demonstrated how domain knowledge via building simulation incorporated with data-driven methods, especially ML leads to improved predictions. Furthermore, compared to physical models, hybrid models reduce the modeling workload and time investment of professional practitioners because they do not require detailed modeling and massive computational resource investment, but simply use the first-principles model to extract sufficient systematic information. Different levels of model detailing have different effects on the output's fineness, sometimes even cause overestimation (e.g., in level-2); We realized that there is a certain trade-off that needs to be further investigated. Furthermore, from measured data, we observed regular patterns of five high peak loads with one or two low peaks, which stand for the working day and weekend load patterns. The hybrid framework obtains the ML model's flexibility to correctly predict the low peak loads (sometimes no load on Sunday, represent for stochastic events in user behavior) than the first-principles model, which is impossible to capture such information by only rely on the law of physic and thermal. Such an accurate and flexible forecasting method provides a solid cornerstone of developing digitalization business models in the future, e.g., dynamic demand-site control, better power market pricing signal, local district prosumer portfolio management, etc.

Of course, the hybrid approach only provides a more effective modeling approach between the limited amount of data and different data forms. In order to increase the acceptance of this data-based method to the industry, further effort should land on the assistance system design based on the hybrid approach, case by case. But still, it does not address the current widespread phenomenon in the building performance simulation community: missing and difficult-to-access situation regarding data collection in the real world.

6. Conclusion

To sum up, we constitute a hybrid framework for predicting building energy consumption by taking physical model results as input variables and feeding them into a machine learning model in the form of a time-series. The hybrid framework provides excellent results that accurately represent the cyclical variation with a certain level of flexibility to capture unpredictable hidden patterns, which also maximizes the use of the building's discrete features and continuous historical load for accurate modeling. Further, the time-series provide a proper form to combines discrete building features with domain knowledge into a machine learning model. This idea of time-series-based decomposition contributes to a further reduction of the uncertainty gap between prediction and measured data.

Acknowledgements

We gratefully acknowledge the German Research Foundation (DFG) support for funding the project under grant GE 1652/3-2 in the Researcher Unit FOR 2363. We would like to thank Prof. Peng Xu and his research group at Tongji University, Shanghai, China, for data resources support.

References

Banihashemi, Saeed; Ding, Grace; Wang, Jack (2017): Developing a Hybrid Model of Prediction and Classification Algorithms for Building Energy Consumption. In Energy Procedia 110, pp. 371–376. DOI: 10.1016/j.egypro.2017.03.155.

Chakraborty, Debaditya; Elzarka, Hazem (2019): Advanced machine learning techniques for building performance simulation: a comparative analysis. In Journal of Building Performance Simulation 12 (2), pp. 193–207.

Cleveland, Robert B.; Cleveland, William S.; McRae, Jean E.; Terpenning, Irma (1990): STL: A seasonal-trend decomposition. In Journal of official statistics 6 (1), pp. 3–73.

Coakley, Daniel; Raftery, Paul; Molloy, Padraig; White, Gearoid (2011): Calibration of a Detailed BES Model to Measured Data Using an Evidence-Based Analytical Optimisation Approach. In.

Fuchs, Marcus; Constantin, Ana; Lauster, Moritz; Remmen, Peter; Streblow, Rita; Müller, Dirk (2015): Structuring the building performance modelica library AixLib for open collaborative development. In : 14th International Conference of the International Building Performance Simulation Association, Hyderabad, India. And see: https://github. com/RWTH-EBC/AixLib.

Guolin Ke; Qi Meng; Thomas Finley; Taifeng Wang; Wei Chen; Weidong Ma et al.: LightGBM: A Highly Efficient Gradient Boosting Decision Tree.

Hensen, Jan; Lamberts, Roberto (2011): Building performance simulation for design and operation. Abingdon, Oxon, New York, NY: Spon Press.

Hooper, Martin (2015): Automated model progression scheduling using level of development. In Construction Innovation 15 (4), pp. 428–448. DOI: 10.1108/CI-09-2014-0048.

Hyndman, Rob J.; Athanasopoulos, George (2018): Forecasting. Principles and practice. Second edition. [Heathmont, Vic.]: OTexts.

Jeremiah Liu; John Paisley; Marianthi-Anna Kioumourtzoglou; Brent Coull: Accurate Uncertainty Estimation and Decomposition in Ensemble Learning.

Klein, S. A.; Beckman, W. A. (2007): TRNSYS 16: A transient system simulation program: mathematical reference. In TRNSYS 5, pp. 389–396.

Marsland, Stephen (2015): Machine learning: an algorithmic perspective: CRC Press.

Nageler, Peter; Mach, Thomas; Heimrath, Richard; Schranzhofer, Hermann; Hochenauer, Christoph (2019): Generation tool for automated thermal city modelling. In : Applied Mechanics and Materials, vol. 887. Trans Tech Publ, pp. 292–299.

Nutkiewicz, Alex; Yang, Zheng; Jain, Rishee K. (2018): Data-driven Urban Energy Simulation (DUE-S): A framework for integrating engineering simulation and machine learning methods in a multi-scale urban energy modeling workflow. In Applied Energy 225, pp. 1176–1189. DOI: 10.1016/j.apenergy.2018.05.023.

Pérez-Lombard, Luis; Ortiz, José; Pout, Christine (2008): A review on buildings energy consumption information. In Energy and Buildings 40 (3), pp. 394–398. DOI: 10.1016/j.enbuild.2007.03.007.

Seyedzadeh, Saleh; Rahimian, Farzad Pour; Glesk, Ivan; Roper, Marc (2018): Machine learning for estimation of building energy consumption and performance: a review. In Vis. in Eng. 6 (1). DOI: 10.1186/s40327-018-0064-7.

Wilde, Pieter de (2014): The gap between predicted and measured energy performance of buildings: A framework for investigation. In Automation in Construction 41, pp. 40–49. DOI: 10.1016/j.autcon.2014.02.009.

Xiao, Tong; Xu, Peng; Sha, Huajing; Chen, Zhe; Gu, Jiefan (2021): XuPengResearchGroup/EnergyDetective2020_dataset.

Deep learning approach for predicting pedestrian dynamics for transportation hubs in early design phases

Jan Clever, Jimmy Abualdenien, André Borrmann
Technical University of Munich, Germany
jan.clever@tum.de

Abstract. A seamless integration of model analysis and simulations into the design process is a key for supporting the different decisions, including deciding upon the position, dimensions, and materiality of building elements. Such design options are explored from the early design phases, where a decision is taken based on their performance. A crucial analysis that is necessary for the different types of buildings, especially transportation hubs, is pedestrian flow dynamics, as it evaluates the occupants' comfort and ability to evacuating the building in case of emergency. Currently, analysing pedestrians' flow is decoupled from the BIM-authoring tools, requires multiple manual steps, and is time consuming. Hence, this paper proposes a framework that leverages the latest advancements of Deep Learning (DL) for replacing pedestrian dynamics simulations by an DL model providing intermediate feedback. In more detail, a representation of the building model, including simulation parameters, is proposed as input and a Convolutional Neural Network (CNN) architecture is developed and trained to predict pedestrians' flow density heatmaps and tracing maps.

1. Introduction

The *Architecture, Engineering and Construction* (AEC) industry is a multidisciplinary sector comprising of various interconnected domain experts. During the design process of a building, each discipline makes multiple design decisions, influencing the resultant design and its performance. Over the last decade, the *Building Information Modeling* (BIM) methodology has gained popularity in fostering collaboration among the project participants and informing the design process from the early phases (Borrmann *et al.*, 2018).

Through the design phases, building models are gradually refined from a rough conceptual design (where many uncertainties are present) to highly complex individual components. In the early design phases (conceptual and preliminary phases), BIM models are subject to multiple changes in the detailed design phases (Knotten *et al.*, 2015). However, changes in the design require a relatively lower cost and efforts (Abualdenien *et al.*, 2019). Typically, architects and engineers explore and evaluate the performance of multiple design options through the comparison of their simulation results. Evaluating a design's performance involves numerous simulations and analysis. Most popularly, analysing the structural system, embodied and operational energy during the life-cycle (Abualdenien *et al.*, 2020), as well as the comfort and evacuation of occupants, a.k.a. pedestrians. Using BIM, the different objects (such as walls, stairs, and zones) can be identified, where each instance has a geometric representation and carries a set of properties (Abualdenien *et al.*, 2019). Such capabilities provide the necessary means for establishing a smooth workflow between BIM-authoring tools and simulators, where customized simulation information can be included in the model. To work independently of a particular software vendor, a variety of the existing authoring tools and simulators support the exchange of models using the open standard *Industry Foundation Classes* (IFC)[1]. Multiple researchers have investigated and proved the capabilities of using IFC BIM models as basis for simulations (Mirahadi *et al.*, 2019).

[1] https://web.archive.org/web/20111024102519/http://buildingsmart-tech.org/implementation/implementations/plominoview.allapplications/?widget=BASIC (visited: 15.03.2021)

In general, integrating simulations into an early design phases can support the decision-making process, which assists in achieving the intended project goals (Abualdenien *et al.*, 2019). Since pedestrians' behavior is essential in normal and panic situations, and highly dependent on the environment (Low, 2000), circulation routes require a special attention during the design process of a building. Therefore, this paper aims for improving the existing workflows for integrated pedestrian simulations into the design process, especially for public buildings, such as train stations.

Typically, the results of pedestrian simulations provide visibility regarding the pedestrians' comfort, circulation, and evacuation in case of emergency. However, the current state of practice involves multiple steps, including exporting building models from the BIM-authoring tool, importing them into the simulator, performing the simulation, and finally, generating a summary of the simulation results. As in addition, agent-based pedestrian simulations require high computational effort and thus long computation times, the entire process is time consuming and error-prone (Andriamamonjy *et al.*, 2018), hindering the interactive exploration of the design space. To overcome this limitation, this paper proposes a framework that leverages *Deep Learning* (DL) methods to facilitate a real-time prediction of pedestrians' comfort and circulation. More specifically, *Machine Learning* (ML) approaches can be used to avoid time-consuming simulations by supporting or even replacing them with predictive tools (Kim *et al.*, 2019). We make use of the rich information provided by BIM models as input for the ML model, thus allowing a direct interaction between creating design options and evaluating them for pedestrian dynamics performance.

This paper is organized into several parts: section 2 introduces background knowledge and related work. In section 3, the concept of our approach is described stepwise, while section 4 presents the outcome. In section 5, a conclusion sums up our results and gives an outlook to future steps.

2. Background and Related Work

2.1 Performance-based Building Design

Designing a building requires many different steps and, hence, considers multiple dependencies on decisions. Therefore, performance-based building design is a crucial method to reduce critical changes to be done in the final phase and maximize a building's performance (Mehrbod *et al.*, 2020). Furthermore, to create reliable results, sufficient data and information must be provided. Especially in early design phases, decisions can influence later performance and cost (Østergård *et al.*, 2016). To improve decisions in the design phase, BIM-based approaches were developed to use the BIM models in the process. In this manner, the authors of Röck *et al.*, 2018 integrate parts of the Life Cycle Assessment (LCA) into BIM by considering the building's materials. In this way, the designer is informed about the chosen materials' potential effects for their embodied energy. Furthermore, Hamidavi *et al.*, 2020 proposes a BIM-based optimization evaluation of a building's structural design. This approach helps to enhance the coordination between architects and structural engineers during the design phase.

2.2 Pedestrian Dynamics Analysis and Simulation Models

The functionality especially of public buildings such as train stations or shopping centres is essential in an emergency evacuation (Løvås, 1994). Moreover, pedestrian dynamics analysis is an essential aspect for efficient crowd routing concerning safety and comfort. That is strongly dependent on the shape of the building (Hanisch *et al.*, 2003). Observations show that individual pedestrians tend to choose polygon-shaped routes, following straight paths to walk on as long as possible in association with visibility. Even though some areas may be crowded, longer travelling times and unknown detours are accepted deliberately or unknowingly (Helbing *et al.*, 2001). Without being externally planned, the crowds' resulting self-organisation is somewhat based on subconscious than communication or expressed strategy, especially with unidirectional pedestrian flows (Helbing *et al.*, 2005). Besides, single persons appear to adjust their walking speed when meeting moving crowd groups within a generally crowded area. Simultaneously, individuals interpret stationary groups as clear obstacles leading to a change in their walking routes (Yi *et al.*, 2015).

Concerning simulation models, three general approaches are distinguished to model pedestrian behaviour, depending on the number of virtual pedestrians (agents). Microscopic methods define the reaction of individual agents, while macroscopic approaches model group behaviour. Furthermore, between these two approaches mesoscopic models provide information about individual agents while staying capable of handling more extensive groups (Ijaz *et al.*, 2015). Because only rule-based approaches appeared to be insufficient (Yang *et al.*, 2020), a more generalized force model was developed in Helbing *et al.*, 2000, known as the *social force* model. In principle, individual agents' repulsive interaction forces take into account other agents and obstacles while moving with a certain velocity.

In contrast to individual behaviour, crowds' demeanour is rather understood as a flow mechanism, ignoring the environment and individual interactions of agents. More specifically, the underlying idea follows the principle of continuum theory proposed by Hughes, 2002. Again, in Yang *et al.*, 2020, other approaches are introduced, like the aggregate dynamics model based on fluid dynamics. Furthermore, to simulate pedestrian crowds' multiple intentions, the potential field model works with navigation- or guidance fields. Due to strict cellular automata structuring, higher pedestrian densities or not completely cell-filling obstacles can lead to a lower representation of reality (Biedermann *et al.*, 2016). To overcome issues like these, hybrid models consider different modelling approaches for particular areas or regions evoking unique behaviour (Biedermann *et al.*, 2021). Another well-known approach is the *optimal steps model* (OSM). Instead of restricting the model to dense crowds or rigid spatial grid only, the authors of Seitz *et al.*, 2012 provide continuous space and free the agents from a strict cell-representation while keeping the stepwise movement in a discretized manner.

2.3 Train Stations and Crowd Dynamics

Concerning waiting areas in train stations, pedestrians tend to uniformly distribute over the respective spaces (Helbing *et al.*, 2001). Furthermore, observations have shown that waiting pedestrians can have a considerable influence on crowd dynamics in train stations. As a result, the walking time of arriving train passengers may increase up to 20%, leaving the platform being influenced by waiting pedestrians as well as by awkwardly positioned attraction points (Davidich *et al.*, 2013). Looking closer at different building elements, Ma *et al.*, 2013 investigated the influence of fences and pillars as separation modules in crowded areas, notably train stations. They point out the increase of pedestrians' flow rate for non-unidirectional movements when using pillars instead of other modules or none at all. Likewise, similar behaviour could be examined by Frank *et al.*, 2011, who showed an improvement in evacuation time for exit areas with pillars placed close to them.

2.4 Deep Learning Methods

In the previous paragraphs, the complexity of pedestrian behaviour and the resulting simulation models could be emphasized. Consequently, pedestrian simulations for complex building structures lead to a considerable increase in computation time. To reduce computation time, AI methods are increasingly considered by the research community. Machine learning (ML) approaches as one specific category of AI methods allow to replace time-consuming simulations by predictive methods. The concept is also known as finding and applying a surrogate function. DL methods became popular to deal with complex problems and different types of data. Various architectures of *Artificial Neural Networks* (ANNs or simply NNs) accomplished different success rates in tackling different kind of tasks, such as detection and segmentation of objects in images or natural language processing.

As a fundamental feedforward NN, commonly, the *Multilayer Perceptron* (MLP) is used for various problems. Here, single values are stored within connected computational nodes organized in (hidden) layers and processed in one direction. The choice of the number of layers is one crucial part of establishing an individual NN suitable for solving a given task. The network's principle is mapping a given input to the desired output, that is to say, a classified label. During the network training, a backpropagation algorithm optimizes the network parameters and, thus, the networks output's accuracy (Nielsen, 2015).

To better deal with images in the form of matrices, *Convolutional Neural Networks* (CNNs) achieved a remarkable success. This kind of feedforward NN consists of several layers, each performing a set of computations. First, a kernel applies a convolution operation to the input matrix that results in a so-called *feature map*. Here, the kernel can be compared to a filter, while different kernels can compute multiple feature maps in parallel within one layer yielding a feature set. Next, a nonlinear activation function like the *rectified linear unit* (ReLU) function is applied to each feature map element. In a final step, the matrix dimensions can be reduced by a pooling operation, known as down-sampling, for instance, maximum pooling. This modification lowers the computational effort of the following layer. Moreover, CNNs can pick out and also detect patterns (features) within a given dataset (Goodfellow *et al.*, 2016).

To train a neural network, a sufficient amount of data is needed. Furthermore, optimization techniques can improve the training process of the network. Providing fewer data can lead to underfitting, while overfitting may occur by using the same training data too often and, thus, the network focuses intensively on these specific examples. Overfitting is why regularization methods like the dropout can enhance the network's computations by simply varying the activated nodes almost randomly. This way, a forced uncertainty is brought into the model, and co-adaptions can be prevented and, thus, overfitting can be reduced (Srivastava *et al.*, 2014). Batch normalization was discovered being useful for strengthening a network's training process (Santurkar *et al.*, 2018). Each layer's inputs are normalized before being passed on to the corresponding activation function in the following computational nodes. Consequently, the downside known as covariate shift is decreased and deep dependencies between multiple layers are relaxed. Besides, the need of regularization methods like dropout in a network may be reduced by integrating batch normalization (Ioffe *et al.*, 2015).

CNNs are a specific ML method particularly tailored for applications in image analysis. For instance, CNNs are able to detect and distinguish cell particles from non-cell particles (Nishida *et al.*, 2018). In Brunton *et al.*, 2020, an ML approach is presented that improves optimization and performance and flow control of calculations in fluid dynamics. Another example is an ML component-based approach supporting estimating a building's heating- and cooling energy (Geyer *et al.*, 2018). Moreover, the authors state an additional benefit of improving the understanding of complex energy calculations for specific parameters.

3. Methodology

The hypothesis of this paper is that deep learning methods can understand the relationship between building information and simulation results, making it possible to replace simulations by real-time predictions. To achieve this, there are two main aspects that need to be identified: (1) how can the geometric and semantic information of the design be represented? (2) What type of simulation results are we trying to predict? The answers of these questions have a high influence on which neural network architecture is suitable, including which operations must be applied on the different layers.

As this paper aims for replacing simulation results, it proposes a framework for an automatic generation of a training dataset as well as predicting the simulation results directly from the BIM representation and simulation parameters. Being part of the workflow shown in Figure 1, a parametric model was developed that is capable of generating a variety of train station models. The train station models include additional parameters that are necessary for performing the pedestrian simulation. Then, each BIM model is exported into IFC, where the geometry and semantics are processed to generate a simulation project file. In this paper, we generate project files that are of the same structure as of the crowd simulator *Crowd:it*[2]. Crowd:it uses the optimal steps model (OSM) (Seitz *et al.*, 2012) for simulating the pedestrian's behaviour. Afterwards, since the simulation parameters are already included in the BIM model, the simulation can run automatically with no manual interaction. Once the simulation is completed, the results are post-processed to produce density heatmaps, path traces, and evacuation times. This process is automatically repeated for design variant that is generated from the parametric model. The generated dataset of BIM models and simulation results is then used to train a neural network.

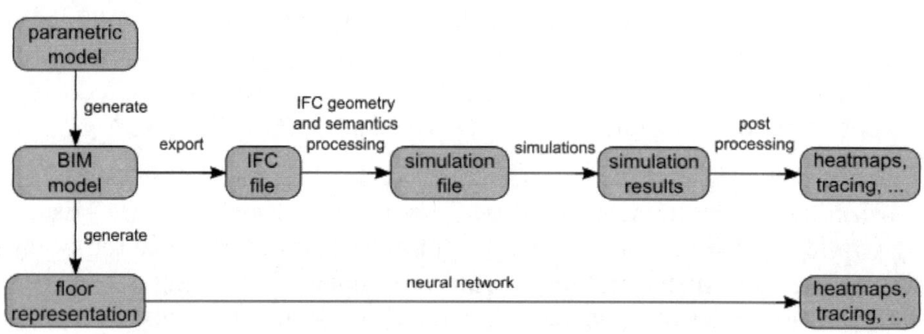

Figure 1: Workflow - conventional way vs. DL approach

3.1 Parametric Models

We developed a parametric model that allows an easy access to different model parameters for variation in the train station models, presented in Figure 2. Now, geometric parameters like the station's length, the platform's width, or the number of escalators can be easily adjusted in the BIM model without tremendous effort. In general, the number of datasets available is crucial for the training of a neural network. In our first attempt, we established in total 432 variations of generic train stations. The corresponding variation parameters are listed in Table 1.

[2] https://www.accu-rate.de/en/software-crowd-it-en/

Table 1: Parameter values for generic train station variation

Abbreviation	Meaning	Variations
F	Number of floors	2
T	Distance between train tracks	15, 25
W	Number of tracks	2, 3, 4, 5
L	Station length	150, 200, 250, 300
H	Floor height	15, 25
E	Number of escalators	1, 2, 3
P	Number of agents (per passenger coach)	5, 20, 50

In addition to the variations, specific semantic information has to be set for the different objects within each train station to ensure an automatic processing of the model by the pedestrian simulation software. In particular, special zones must be marked in the model that, for example, marking agents' spawn areas and destination. Moreover, the number of agents and a mapping of the object types to the simulation object types has to be also specified. Figure 2 shows an example of a parametric platform with four track lines, three escalators at each side, an elevator box in the middle, and two columns in between the track lines. Such building elements are translated into boundaries in the pedestrian simulator.

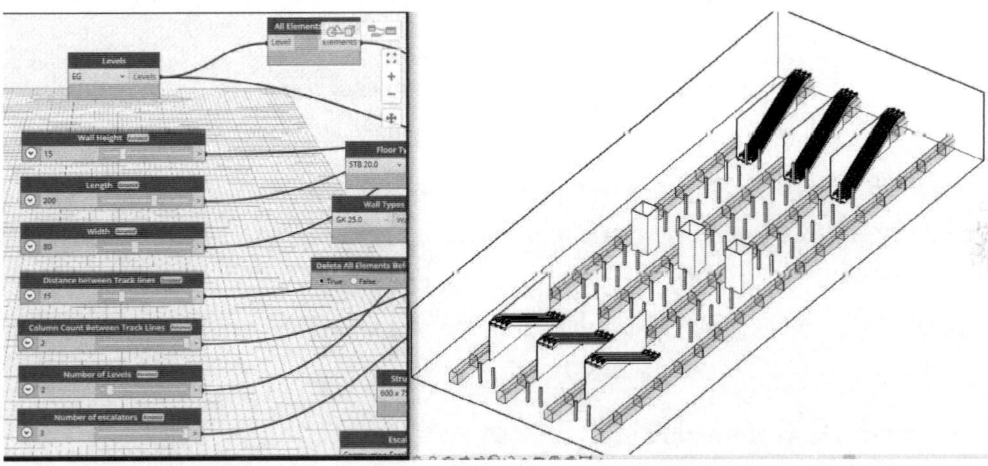

Figure 2: Tool to vary parameters (l.) that create a generic train station (r.)

The toolset used to develop this parametric model are *Autodesk Revit*[3] and *Dynamo*[4]. In this regard, the Deutsche Bahn RIL[5] guidelines were investigated and transformed into logical code that is embedded in the dynamo graph. Such parametric model provides an adaptive train station design, where changing a parameter automatically propagates to the other parameters and regenerates the station design. For the purpose of this paper, as shown in Table 1, all the models were prepared with only two floors. The scenarios we are experimenting with expect that pedestrians will enter the train station via the train coaches and walk to the upper floor. The

[3] https://www.autodesk.com/products/revit/overview?term=1-YEAR
[4] https://www.autodesk.com/products/dynamo-studio/overview
[5] https://www1.deutschebahn.com/sus-infoplattform/start/regelwerk

pedestrians choose the escalators as transition areas to reach the destination zone at the next floor directly after the end of each escalator. In each simulation run, the paths of the pedestrians are chosen according to the simulator's internal logic. Each simulation will end as soon as the last agent has reached the destination zone.

3.2 Floor Representation and Neural Network

To provide an understandable representation of the different object types for training a neural network, we propose the combination of a colour-labelled floorplan and a vector of meta-data (represented by variation parameters in Table 1). For instance, spawning zones are marked in pink while walkable areas are coloured with white, see Figure 3. As the corresponding output, the simulator crowd:it post-processes the simulation results and produces mean density heatmaps (i.e., average of agents per area) and tracing maps according to the selected routes by the agents. Figure 4 depicts an example of generated heat map is illustrated, where mean densities are coloured in blue, the darker the colour, the higher the mean density (brighter zone colour in spawn zones). The agents' traces in orange colour can be seen in Figure 4.

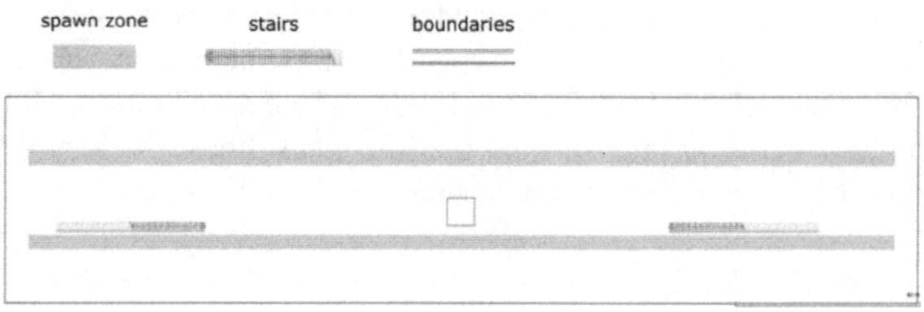

Figure 3: Floorplan representation with colouring

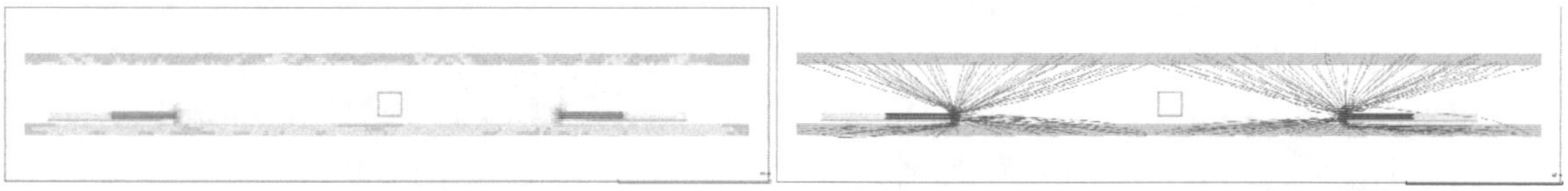

Figure 4: Heat map (l.) and tracing map (r.) examples with 5 agents per passenger coach

4. Neural Network Architecture

Although many different approaches for applying ML in this context are conceivable, in this paper, the focus is on using an image representation as an input and predict an image with densities and traces as output. Hence, we build upon the architecture of *U-Net* (Ronneberger *et al.*, 2015), a fully convolutional network, where pooling operators are replaced with upsampling operators, which improves training performance and the resolution of the output. Additionally, U-Net implements skip connections between the layers and then combines them with a concatenation layer.

Our implementation extends the U-Net architecture by an additional input layer for the meta-data that includes the station dimensions and the pedestrian simulation parameters. In this regard, the placement of the meta-data input layer should be carefully done to avoid encountering the *Vanishing Gradient* problem (Hochreiter, 1998). We optimize our network using minibatch SGD and we apply the Adam solver (Kingma *et al.*, 2014), with a learning rate of 0.002, and momentum parameters $\beta 1 = 0.5$, $\beta 2 = 0.999$, following the recommendations provided by Isola *et al.*, 2017. At inference time, we apply dropout and batch normalization (Ioffe *et al.*, 2015). Figure 5 presents the network architecture. It expects images with a resolution of 1024 * 1024, and produces images with the same size. In between, there is a set of downsampling and upsampling operations are extracting the different features from the image. In the middle, right after flattening the image, the second input of the meta-data is provided and concatenated with the extracted features. The lines between the sampling operations point to the concatenated features passed from each side.

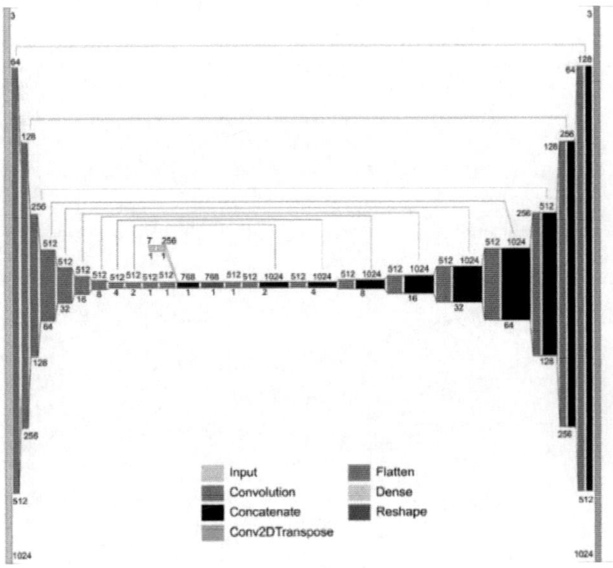

Figure 5: Neural network architecture

5. Neural Network Results & Evaluation

The training process started by splitting the dataset into training and testing. The dataset size is 432 projects with their simulation results, where 20% (87 projects) were used for testing. Before starting the training process, we have applied data augmentation, including resizing, cropping and rotating to double the amount of training data to 690 projects. To the ensure the model performance during training, 20% of the training data was used for validation in every epoch. The training used a batch size of four and ran for 300 epochs. The loss function used to quantify the quality of the predicted heatmaps and traces in comparison to the ground truth during training and validation we used the *mean absolute error* (MAE) per pixel (Asamoah *et al.*, 2018). Figure 6 shows the MAE per pixel of both, training and validation datasets for the training on generating images with heatmaps. In this regard, the error on both sets became less than 0.05 relatively fast (after few epochs). From our observations during training, we noticed that from epoch 20 the predicted images started to generate heatmaps over the right position, however, the density of those heatmaps was low. At epoch 300, the density of the generated heatmaps became fairly comparable to the ground truth by the human eye. Which highlights the need for human's perception in addition to the MAE per pixel to identify the quality of the predictions.

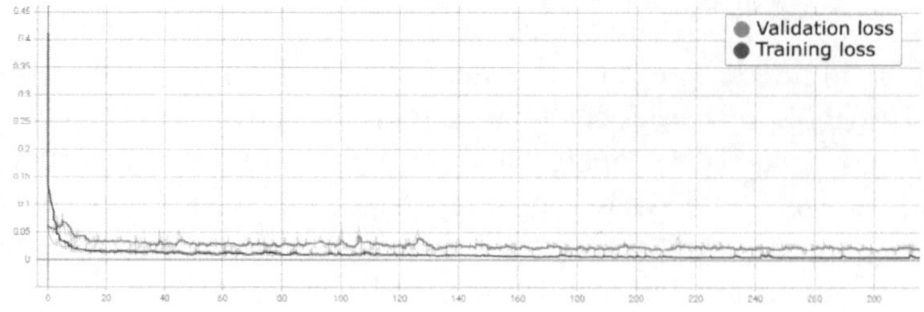

Figure 6: Heatmap – MAE per pixel

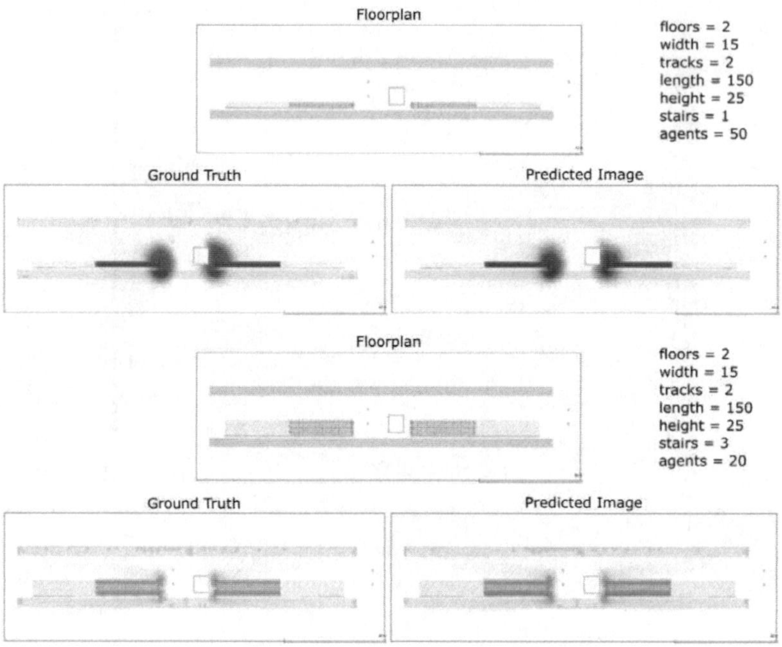

Figure 7: Heatmap – results case 1 (t.) and case 2 (b.)

The prediction of images from the test set are shown in Figure 7, comparing the input floorplan and meta-data, ground truth, and the predicted image. The predicted image in the first case has a similar overall distribution, however, the density at the start of the right stair is less than the ground truth. While in the second case, the predicted image has a slightly denser heatmap than the ground truth. Afterwards, the same process was repeated for training the network on tracing maps, with the same network parameters and loss function. As tracing maps include detailed lines for the different pedestrians, the MAE per pixel is higher than in the case of heatmaps (see Figure 8).

The predicted tracing maps from the test set are shown in Figure 9, comparing the input floorplan and meta-data, ground truth, and the predicted image. In both cases, the network was able to predict reasonable patterns that are close to the ground truth. However, similarly to the heatmaps, the densities deviate.

Overall, the network was able to understand the relation of the input (floorplan + meta-data) to the simulation results (heatmaps and tracing maps). This is shown by predicting different results for different stairs width and number of pedestrians. However, as shown in the training and validation loss figures, increasing the dataset has a high potential for improving the results. Additionally, a different loss function, other than the MAE per pixel, could provide more reasonable assessment for the quality of the predicted images.

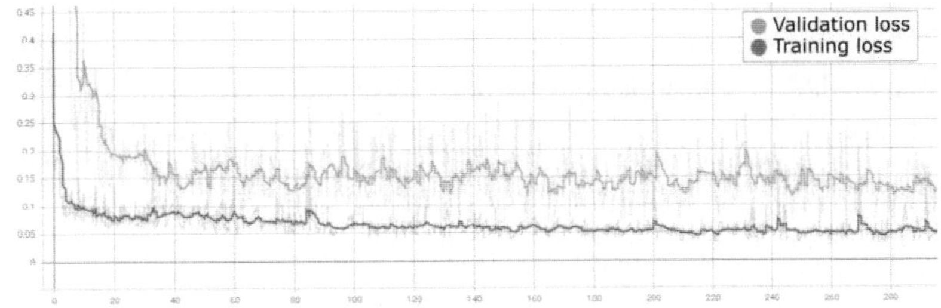

Figure 8: Tracing map – MAE per pixel

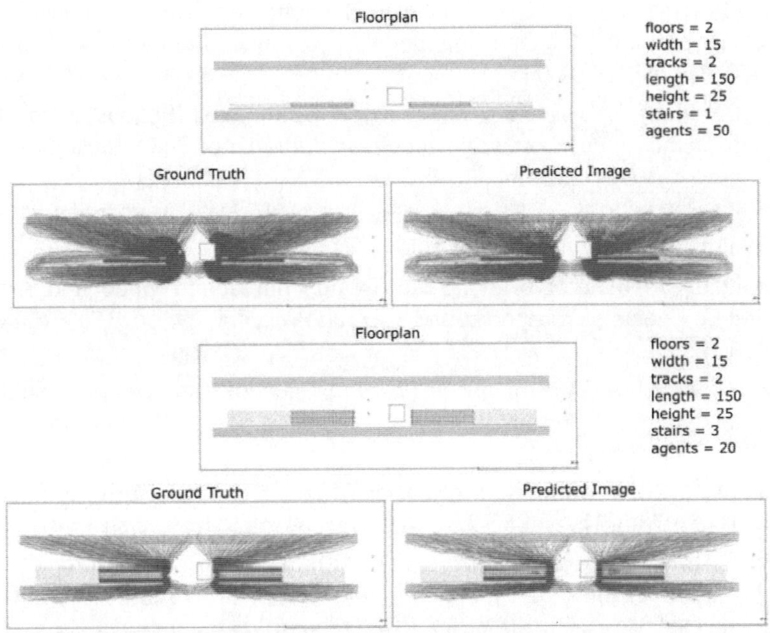

Figure 9: Tracing map – results case 1 (t.) and case 2 (b.)

6. Conclusion & Future Work

In this paper, we presented initial results of providing real-time results for a given train station geometry concerning pedestrian behaviour. Conventional pedestrian simulations can easily become very expensive in computation time. In our approach, training a CNN with image data of the BIM model, we took a first look into practical results for predicting mean densities of pedestrians and their tracing. The approach shows promising results and will be investigated further. In the first place, we clearly see the possibility of using more complex data. That is to say, generic train stations provide similar and rather simple geometric information. As a consequence, remarkable changes in the design may not be considered or understood by the network. Improvements within a predictive tool for pedestrian behavior as presented in this paper can lead to an easy access evaluation of bottlenecks caused by a building environment that is still in design. Thus, an optimal design solution can be developed with less computational effort and remarkable savings in project time.

Acknowledgements

We gratefully acknowledge the support of mFUND – Bundesministerium für Verkehr und digitale Infrastruktur (BMVI) for funding the research project BEYOND.

References

Abualdenien, J. et al. (2020) 'Consistent management and evaluation of building models in the early design stages', Journal of Information Technology in Construction, 25, pp. 212–232. doi: 10.36680/j.itcon.2020.013.

Abualdenien, J. and Borrmann, A. (2019) 'A meta-model approach for formal specification and consistent management of multi-LOD building models', Advanced Engineering Informatics, 40, pp. 135–153. doi: 10.1016/j.aei.2019.04.003.

Andriamamonjy, A., Saelens, D. and Klein, R. (2018) 'An automated IFC-based workflow for building energy performance simulation with Modelica', Automation in Construction, 91, pp. 166–181. doi: 10.1016/j.autcon.2018.03.019.

Asamoah, D. et al. (2018) 'Measuring the Performance of Image Contrast Enhancement Technique', International Journal of Computer Applications, 181(22), pp. 6–13.

Biedermann, D. H. et al. (2016) 'A Hybrid and Multiscale Approach to Model and Simulate Mobility in the Context of Public Events', Transportation Research Procedia, 19, pp. 350–363. doi: 10.1016/j.trpro.2016.12.094.

Biedermann, D. H., Clever, J. and Borrmann, A. (2021) 'A generic and density-sensitive method for multi-scale pedestrian dynamics', Automation in Construction, 122, p. 103489. doi: 10.1016/j.autcon.2020.103489.

Borrmann, A. et al. (eds) (2018) Building Information Modeling. Cham: Springer International Publishing. doi: 10.1007/978-3-319-92862-3.

Brunton, S. L., Noack, B. R. and Koumoutsakos, P. (2020) 'Machine Learning for Fluid Mechanics', Annual Review of Fluid Mechanics, 52(1), pp. 477–508. doi: 10.1146/annurev-fluid-010719-060214.

Davidich, M. et al. (2013) 'Waiting zones for realistic modelling of pedestrian dynamics: A case study using two major German railway stations as examples', Transportation Research Part C: Emerging Technologies, 37, pp. 210–222. doi: 10.1016/j.trc.2013.02.016.

Frank, G. A. and Dorso, C. O. (2011) 'Room evacuation in the presence of an obstacle', Physica A: Statistical Mechanics and its Applications, 390(11), pp. 2135–2145. doi: 10.1016/j.physa.2011.01.015.

Geyer, P. and Singaravel, S. (2018) 'Component-based machine learning for performance prediction in building design', Applied Energy, 228(July), pp. 1439–1453. doi: 10.1016/j.apenergy.2018.07.011.

Goodfellow, I., Bengio, Y. and Courville, A. (2016) Deep Learning. MIT Press.

Hamidavi, T., Abrishami, S. and Hosseini, M. R. (2020) 'Towards intelligent structural design of buildings: A BIM-based solution', Journal of Building Engineering, 32, p. 101685. doi: 10.1016/j.jobe.2020.101685.

Hanisch, A. et al. (2003) 'Online simulation of pedestrian flow in public buildings', in Proceedings of the 2003 International Conference on Machine Learning and Cybernetics (IEEE Cat. No.03EX693). IEEE, pp. 1635–1641. doi: 10.1109/WSC.2003.1261613.

Helbing, D. et al. (2001) 'Self-organizing pedestrian movement', Environment and Planning B: Planning and Design, 28(3), pp. 361–383. doi: 10.1068/b2697.

Helbing, D. et al. (2005) 'Self-organized pedestrian crowd dynamics: Experiments, simulations, and design solutions', Transportation Science, 39(1), pp. 1–24. doi: 10.1287/trsc.1040.0108.

Helbing, D., Farkas, I. and Vicsek, T. (2000) 'Simulating dynamical features of escape panic', Nature, 407(6803), pp. 487–490. doi: 10.1038/35035023.

Hochreiter, S. (1998) 'The vanishing gradient problem during learning recurrent neural nets and problem solutions', International Journal of Uncertainty, Fuzziness and Knowledge-Based Systems, 6(02), pp. 107–116.

Hughes, R. L. (2002) 'A continuum theory for the flow of pedestrians', Transportation Research Part B: Methodological, 36(6), pp. 507–535. doi: 10.1016/S0191-2615(01)00015-7.

Ijaz, K., Sohail, S. and Hashish, S. (2015) 'A Survey of Latest Approaches for Crowd Simulation and Modeling using Hybrid Techniques', 17th UKSIM-AMSS International Conference on Modelling and Simulation, pp. 111–116. doi: 10.1109/UKSim.2015.46.

Ioffe, S. and Szegedy, C. (2015) 'Batch Normalization: Accelerating Deep Network Training by Reducing Internal Covariate Shift'. Available at: http://arxiv.org/abs/1502.03167.

Isola, P. et al. (2017) 'Image-to-image translation with conditional adversarial networks', in Proceedings of the IEEE conference on computer vision and pattern recognition, pp. 1125–1134.

Kim, J. et al. (2019) 'Recurrent inception convolution neural network for multi short-term load forecasting', Energy and Buildings, 194(2019), pp. 328–341. doi: 10.1016/j.enbuild.2019.04.034.

Kingma, D. P. and Ba, J. (2014) 'Adam: A method for stochastic optimization', arXiv preprint arXiv:1412.6980.

Knotten, V. et al. (2015) 'Design management in the building process - a review of current literature', Procedia Economics and Finance, 21, pp. 120–127.

Løvås, G. G. (1994) 'Modeling and simulation of pedestrian traffic flow', Transportation Research Part B: Methodological, 28(6), pp. 429–443. doi: 10.1016/0191-2615(94)90013-2.

Low, D. J. (2000) 'Following the crowd', Nature, 407(6803), pp. 465–466. doi: 10.1038/35035192.

Ma, J. et al. (2013) 'Modeling pedestrian space in complex building for efficient pedestrian traffic simulation', Automation in Construction, 30, pp. 25–36. doi: 10.1016/j.autcon.2012.11.032.

Mehrbod, S., Staub-French, S. and Tory, M. (2020) 'BIM-based building design coordination: processes, bottlenecks, and considerations', Canadian Journal of Civil Engineering, 47(1), pp. 25–36. doi: 10.1139/cjce-2018-0287.

Mirahadi, F., McCabe, B. and Shahi, A. (2019) 'IFC-centric performance-based evaluation of building evacuations using fire dynamics simulation and agent-based modeling', Automation in Construction, 101, pp. 1–16. doi: 10.1016/j.autcon.2019.01.007.

Nielsen, M. A. (2015) Neural networks and deep learning. Determination press San Francisco, CA.

Nishida, K. and Hotta, K. (2018) 'Robust cell particle detection to dense regions and subjective training samples based on prediction of particle center using convolutional neural network', PLOS ONE. Edited by L. Wang, 13(10), p. e0203646. doi: 10.1371/journal.pone.0203646.

Østergård, T., Jensen, R. L. and Maagaard, S. E. (2016) 'Building simulations supporting decision making in early design – A review', Renewable and Sustainable Energy Reviews, 61, pp. 187–201. doi: 10.1016/j.rser.2016.03.045.

Röck, M. et al. (2018) 'LCA and BIM: Visualization of environmental potentials in building construction at early design stages', Building and Environment, 140, pp. 153–161. doi: 10.1016/j.buildenv.2018.05.006.

Ronneberger, O., Fischer, P. and Brox, T. (2015) 'U-Net: Convolutional Networks for Biomedical Image Segmentation'. Available at: http://arxiv.org/abs/1505.04597.

Santurkar, S. et al. (2018) 'How Does Batch Normalization Help Optimization?' Available at: http://arxiv.org/abs/1805.11604.

Seitz, M. J. and Köster, G. (2012) 'Natural discretization of pedestrian movement in continuous space', Physical Review E, 86(4), p. 046108. doi: 10.1103/PhysRevE.86.046108.

Yang, S. et al. (2020) 'A review on crowd simulation and modeling', Graphical Models, 111(October 2019), p. 101081. doi: 10.1016/j.gmod.2020.101081.

Yi, S., Li, H. and Wang, X. (2015) 'Understanding pedestrian behaviors from stationary crowd groups', in 2015 IEEE Conference on Computer Vision and Pattern Recognition (CVPR). IEEE, pp. 3488–3496. doi: 10.1109/CVPR.2015.7298971.

Implementing Information Container for linked Document Delivery (ICDD) as a micro-service

Madhumitha Senthilvel, Jyrki Oraskari, Jakob Beetz
RWTH Aachen University, Germany
senthilvel@dc.rwth-aachen.de

Abstract. Common Data Environments (CDE) are seen as the next steps towards a truly open, accessible and interoperable BIM. Information Containers form the core component based on which CDEs store, manage, exchange and process data between stakeholders in a project. While specifications for Information Containers have gradually evolved with progressive standards, the recently introduced ISO 21597 standard for Information Containers for linked Document Delivery contains specification for linking heterogeneous information. Since this standard is intended for file-based information exchange, in this paper we explore the implementation of ICDD within the context of two web-based CDEs: OpenCDE-API and Linked Data Platform. For this, the functional and operational requirements for using ICDD in both the CDEs are summarized, which are then implemented in a minimalistic prototype for each CDE.

1. Introduction

With the gradual establishment of Building Information Modelling (BIM) for information management across all phases of construction projects, there has been increasing interest in the emphasis on the approach of Common Data Environments (CDEs) (Bucher and Hall, 2020). These environments facilitate data interoperability and exchange between different authoring tools and formats through specifications for standardized information storage, access rights, information management etc. At the core of CDEs lie the concept on Information Containers, which are used to structure meta-information about the data residing within them. In their most rudimentary form, they are virtual enclosures to store relevant data together based on the use case. These data can be uploaded files, files stored in the CDE itself, or even graphs from external Triple Stores.

The notion of containers and CDEs are closely entwined with many existing CDEs containing specifications focusing on container data representation and management. This can be traced back to the fundamental intention of CDEs: to enable collaboration, and centralization of information management. Presently available CDE standards and approaches such as the ISO19650[1], DIN SPEC 91391-2[2], Linked Data Platform (LDP)[3], Open CDE-API[4] have varying levels of specifications for structuring these containers. In addition, a recently introduced standard ISO 21597 Information Containers for linked Document Delivery (ICDD)[5], also focuses on multi-model containers. This approach is particularly relevant in the context of a decentralized open-world BIM, wherein containers and the information inside them also be used for linking disparate, heterogeneous information.

In our previous work, we evaluated how the concepts in ICDD can be leveraged in the existing CDEs introduced earlier (Senthilvel et al., 2020). One of the main issues identified in this

[1] Builds on the previous PAS1192:2003 standard with additional specifications for meta-data for container
[2] German standard defining OpenCDE through requirements for communication interface between CDEs
[3] https://www.w3.org/TR/ldp/
[4] https://github.com/buildingSMART/OpenCDE-API
[5] Formerly "Information Container for Data Drop"

previous work was that ICDD is intended for file-based containers, which store the ontology, payload documents, and the links between these documents in RDF serialization in folders. In this paper, we explore how these container concepts can be implemented in a decentralized web, with all the documents existing as parts of the graph and de-referenceable on the web, accessible by URIs. An implementation for this approach is also briefly presented to demonstrate the concept. In the end, this implementation is envisioned to serve as a micro-service, to be plugged in other CDEs, for extending their container systems.

2. Background

Since the concept of Information Containers has been closely tied with CDEs, there are numerous commercial implementations for it such as BIM 360, Oracle Aconex, Trimble Connect, etc. However, most of these are designed as document management systems, for storing and sharing information as files. While some such as BIM 360 contain added meta-data for version tracking, author information, issue tracking etc., at present there is no mechanism for linking of documents within the containers in these solutions (Gumpert, 2019). As mentioned in the previous section, ICDD provides an approach which uses linked data for creating such linking of information. However, in order to use ICDD in a CDE, the standard does not itself contain specifications such as the use of HTTP requests for information orchestration over the web. Consequently, from the existing standards already introduced in the earlier section, we selected Linked Data Platform (LDP) and OpenCDE-API as candidates for implementing ICDD as a web-based microservice.

For easier comprehension, this section presents a brief introduction to the ICDD standard, OpenCDE-API approach and the Linked Data Platform.

2.1 ISO 21597:2020 - Information Container for linked Document Delivery (ICDD)

The ISO 21597 (from here on referred to as ICDD) is a two-part standard containing specifications for structuring linked documents using the Linked Data approach and the container which contains this information. Its conceptual origins can be traced to the multi-model containers from the Mefisto project and the COINS approach, which introduced preliminary container specifications for managing multiple models (van Nederveen, 2010). Part 1 of this standard defines the container structure and the general linking concepts through the definition of a container-specific ontology, corresponding data types and object properties, along with a linkset ontology with corresponding data types and properties (Technical Committee : ISO/TC 59/SC 13 Organization and digitization of information about buildings and civil engineering works, including building information modelling (BIM), 2020). Part 2 defines additional types of links which form the extended linkset (Technical Committee : ISO/TC 59/SC 13 Organization and digitization of information about buildings and civil engineering works, including building information modelling (BIM), 2020).

Figure 1: Sample ICDD Container

The container has a folder structure with three major components: an Ontology folder containing the schema of the files in the ICDD Zip file format, a linkset folder containing the links, and a payloads folder containing the documents themselves. It also contains an Index file outside of the folders, which contains all the meta-data for the files in the payload folder and the links between these documents. Figure 1 provides a visual representation of a sample ICDD container.

2.2 OpenCDE-API

OpenCDE-API is a buildingSMART initiative, which aims to improve the interoperability within the AEC CDE software ecosystem through closely woven, domain-specific APIs. A project supporting OpenCDE-API would effectively be able to stream information (in containers) between different CDEs with negligible loss in meta-data by providing a common interface standard. The proposed framework contains a host of APIs: Foundations (for authentication, Authorization, Conventions), BCF (for design issues tracking), Documents (for information management), Data Exchange (for proper exchange at component/object level), etc.[6]. Of these APIs, the Documents API and the Data Exchange API are relevant to information management since they handle how information is stored and transmitted. At the time of writing, both of the above APIs are still in early development and not much details are available[6]. Most of the functionalities covered by the above APIs can be traced back to the CDE requirements set by earlier standards such as the ISO 19650, and the DIN SPEC 91391. A more detailed discussion on this topic is presented in Section 3.1.

As introduced in the earlier section, ICDD focuses to specifying container structuring, meta-data management and linking of information inside the container. Consequently, the container concepts from it should be technically feasible to implement in as per OpenCDE-API specifications. Presently, the current API is based on OpenAPI (Swagger) specification which describes a REST interface for the CDEs.

[6] https://github.com/buildingSMART/OpenCDE-API/blob/master/Documentation/20201102.BSI.Summit.Update.pdf

2.3 Linked Data Platform (LDP)

LDP is a specification containing definitions for reading-writing Linked Data architecture. LDP focuses on the use of HTTP to Create, Read, Update, and Delete (CRUD) Linked Data Resources that are part of a collection. To accomplish the above, this W3C recommendation defines guidelines for interacting with both RDF and non-RDF data. These guidelines are focused on what resource, content notations and content serialization formats should be used, how a client can handle changes to resources, container issues including data and meta-data retrieval using GET and updating containers using POST.

In the LDP specification, containers are considered as a very specific web resource, with the capability to respond to HTTP requests relating to the creation and modification operations of resources. Two types of containers are defined, based on how resources are contained, created and deleted: a Basic Container and a Direct/Indirect Container [7].

In the former, links to a `document resource' (as well as a `child container') can be defined by using a predefined predicate. In the Direct and Indirect Container, additional relationships such as domain-specific vocabularies can be used for the link relationships, offering more flexibility for the user to define custom resource relationships, beyond LDP definitions.

It should be noted that in the LDP approach 'anything can be a Container', and these containers can have corresponding RDF-links to their resources in three different ways depending on which container is used. However, this approach is not directly scalable for real building projects, more complex information is usually encoded using specific definitions for links between files/documents, `sub-document level linkages' etc. As LDP is domain agnostic, it provides the flexibility to define link relationships on any domain-specific vocabulary: the links in a Container are left to the discretion of the creator. Currently numerous implementations of LDP exists[8].

3. Implementing ICDD in CDE

With the establishment of the conceptual background of ICDD, OpenCDE-API and LDP in the previous section, the implementation details of ICDD in both these CDEs are elaborated in this section.

In order to publish ICDD container in a CDE platform, two aspects need to be addressed: 1) the requirements in terms of ontologies, vocabularies for meta-information management of data inside the containers and 2) requirements for micro-service architecture of the container. To address the former, we present an assessment on the scope of the vocabularies/scheme defined by the existing standards in conjunction to the ones by ICDD. These include vocabularies for defining meta-information for documents/graphs, specifying base ontologies/schema, version management, file naming conventions, folder structuring and management. A summary of these terms and their corresponding feasibility in both ICDD-Open CDE API and ICDD – LDP is presented in Table 1. The ones with tick mark (✓) are the functionalities implemented in this paper.

[7] https://www.w3.org/TR/ldp/\#ldpc
[8] https://www.w3.org/wiki/LDP_Implementations

Table 1: Consolidated Functionalities as specified by ICDD, OpenCDE-API and LDP

Meta-Classification	Requirement/CDE	ICDD - Open CDE API	ICDD - LDP
Container Structuring	Workflow creation of project templates	×	×
	Information Container Classification System	×	✓
	Nested Containers	×	✓
	Customisable folder structure with highly controlled access	×	✓
Versioning & History	Audit trail and version management	✓	✓
	Status Codes for Information in Container	×	×
	Container history log (status change for username, dates, revisions)	×	×
Container Information Mining	Meta-data based information search (query, filter)	×	×
Access Control	Document Control and Document Actions via workflow engine	×	×
	Access control at Information Container level	×	✓
Meta-Information	Customisable meta-data	✓	×
	Asset tagging	✓	✓
	Definitive meta-data classification based on project context (phases)	×	×
File Naming Conventions	Unique ID for each Information Container	✓	✓
	Definitive document naming rules	×	×
Linking Containers	Document Level	✓	✓
	Sub-Document (model element) level	✓	✓
	Link Type specification for Document Level	✓	✓
	Link Type specification for Sub-Document Level	✓	✓
Container CRUD	CRUD	✓	✓
Container States	Archived	×	×
	Work in Progress	×	×
	Shared	×	×
	Published	×	×
Data Integrity	Data conformance tools	×	×

To achieve the second aspect, as mentioned in section 2, in this section the functionalities of Table 1 are implemented in both OpenCDE-API and LDP. There are three reasons for the selections. First, we base our experiment on the known practices of how to publish linked data using REST-ful architecture, for which we believe that LBD contains the necessarily specifications. Second, we study the Open CDE API since it is an initiative which focuses on the Building Data domain; thus it caters to specific requirements which arises from the AEC industry. It is a good representative of the domain-specific standard for data staring using the micro-service architecture, with its new and developing specification that can be adopted widely in the building data domain. Showing how this can be applied and improved adds knowledge in the field. Third, both specifications are technically detailed, and there are existing implementations. Thus solutions are already established as technically feasible, and it is possible to have a snapshot of the definitions and implement solutions that can be repeated by other groups to validate the results.

Commonly available tools and libraries like React, Node.js, Express etc. are used to add the missing parts of the two technical approaches, do the needed data translations, and orchestrate the experiments. The focus is on the minimal implementation to reveal the differences between the approaches. The implementation decisions are documented. The source code, the used sample data sets are published at our public GitHub source repository.

3.1 Open CDE API

OpenCDE-API for ICDD implements the buildingSMART OpenCDE-API OpenAPI interface specification in the buildingSMART/OpenCDE-API[9] GitHub repository so that the RESTful API can be used to evaluate the ICDD container publication in the server. The code was written in TypeScript for NodeJS and Express and made available in our GitHub repository[10]. The server implements the session creation, file registration, metadata handling, file upload and download, versioning, and version listing. On the other hand, the specification's interactive flow operation has been modified to be tested without user actions to keep the implementation minimalistic.

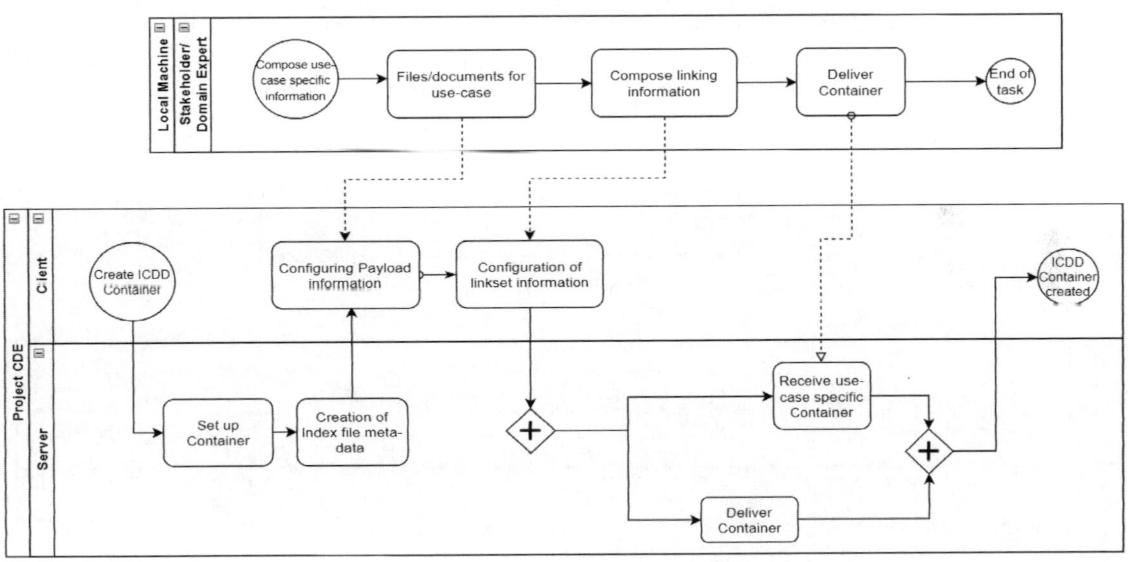

Figure 2: ICDD-OpenCDE-API Interface Usecase

The OpenAPI 3.0 document defines the RESTful API endpoints for an OpenCDE-API server. The accompanying sequence diagrams for the document upload and download flow of actions illustrate the interface's use. In this research, the interface and the associated data types define the Minimum Viable Product (MVP) of the concept (Frank, 2016). The ICDD publication is implemented as an API new interface. The method gets the ICDD input, unzips the content to the document directory of the server, and creates an OpenCDE-API document description for each Internal Document listed in the *index.rdf* in the ICDD container. Furthermore, each

[9] https://github.com/buildingSMART/OpenCDE-API
[10] https://github.com/jyrkioraskari/OpenCDE-API_ICDD

document node's literal property is mapped into a metadata attribute and saved in the application database, and the OpenCDE-API document is created using the metadata.

Since the ICDD publication method fills the OpenCDE-API data structures and file conventions, the files and the metadata can be accessed using the same API calls. Figure 2 shows the sample interface access workflow for the proposed implementation elaborated in this section.

3.2 Linked Data Platform

Existing documentation from W3C defines a list of operations which are must/should/may in order to specify whether a platform conforms to LDP (Speicher and Fernández, 2014). Table 2 documents a sub-set of these operations which are tested for implementing ICDD in conjunction with LDP container specifications. As seen from this table, there are significant differences between the functional operations which are mentioned in the LDP, when compared to the OpenCDE-API. Most notabaly, LDP has a very well-defined classification of operations based on whether they are mandatory and optional. A more extensive list of these operations, though available on the earlier mentioned footnote, is considered as out-of-scope for this paper due to its extensive data.

In the above table, ICDD container can exist in its native form as a Basic Container where the index file directly contains all the meta-data. However, it can also exist as a Direct or Indirect Container, where the links between documents can be present in other containers (such as nested containers). Figure 3 illustrates the workflow of the implemented LDP interface for ICDD using a sample usecase. As seen from the figure, an authentication functionality is added to the workflow for retrieving containers corresponding to each user.

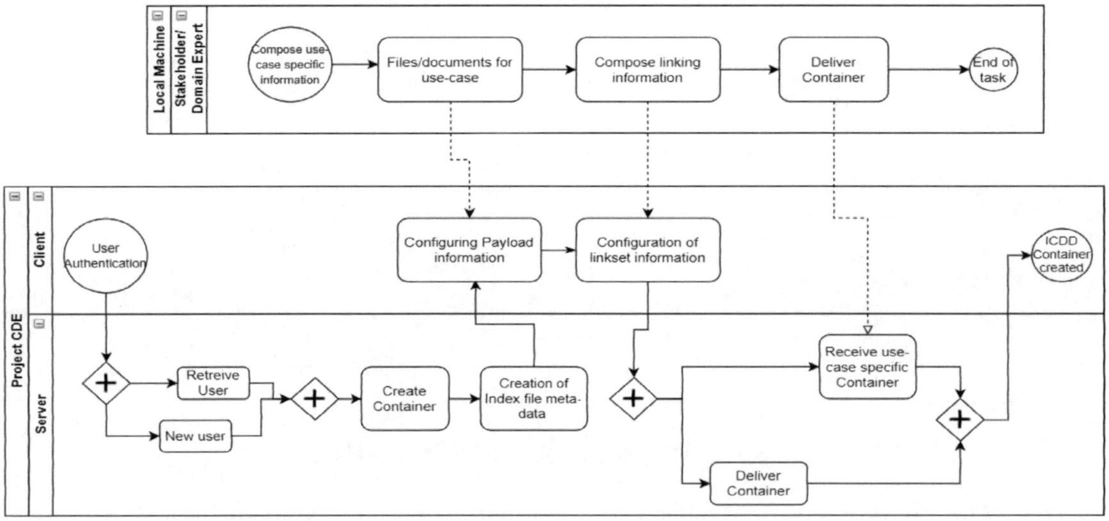

Figure 3: ICDD-LDP integration Interface for a sample Usecase

Table 2: Applicable container operations (as specified by LDP)

S.No	Meta-Classification for Operations	Operation/Container
1	MUST	ConformsBcLdpContainer
2		ContainerSupportsHttpLinkHeader
3		MemberResourceTriple
4		MemberRelationOrIsMemberOfRelationTripleExists
5		RelativeUriResoulutionPost
6		PostResponseStatusAndLocation
7		PostContainer
8		ConformsDcLdpContainer
9		ConformsIcLdpContainer
10		AcceptTurtle
11		GetResource
12		GetResourceAcceptTurtle
13		PostResource
14		ContainerHasInsertedContentRelation
15	SHOULD	ContainsRdfType
16		ReUseVocabularies
17		UseStandardVocabularies
18		4xxErrorHasResponseBody
19		UseMemberPredicate
20		PreferMembershipTriples

As seen from the figure, an authentication functionality is added to the workflow for retrieving containers corresponding to each user. Other parts of the workflow remain the same as the OpenCDE API-ICDD workflow introduced in Figure 2.

4. Discussions and Conclusion

In this paper, we investigated the requirements for the practical aspects of the development of an ICDD container in a CDE based on existing functionalities as specified by the CDEs. We presented two REST-ful implementations, based on LDP and OpenCDE-API, compared quantitatively and qualitatively. We use the data validation use case to evaluate the solutions. At present the approaches implemented in this work focus on uploaded files and future word would include support for data referenceable through triple stores. Additional areas of work would be implementing the features as listed in Table 1 by borrowing specifications from ISO 19650, DIN SPEC 91391 etc.

The benefits of publishing an ICDD container using OpenCDE-API and LDP are 1. The containers and files inside them can be accessed online. They have a Uniform Resource Locator (URL) that can be used for interlinking. 2. The versions of the files may be browsed online. 3. The ICDD metadata can be used to query the container files. They can also be queried between containers. While the level of specifications to conform to varies with each CDE, the overall web architecture of these can still be used for implementing ICDD. As seen in Table 1, OpenCDE-API does not have explicit specifications for container nesting, meta-classification for containers, access control for documents inside containers, thus necessitating use of external ontologies, specifications for implementing them. On the other hand, LDP based approach does not contain specification for operations such as meta-classification for containers, container history and version management etc.

The implementations demonstrate that an ICDD container can be published as OpenCDE-API so that metadata is automatically read from the container files. This can be extended so that, instead of using the OpenCDE API data model, an RDF graph storage is used for the containers' linked data content. The RDF parsing and the memory RDF database for the document query show that this is feasible.

The work presented in this paper is one of the potential ways in which Linked Data supported containers can be represented in CDEs. By combining ICDD's container concepts with the two CDEs, we can leverage ICDD's functionality of accessing linked information at both object and attribute level. This work's main contribution lies in the identification and amalgamation of container concepts from different approaches in order to implement a functional ICDD container in a REST-compliant CDE.

Acknowledgement

This research was funded through the doctoral research grant from the Deutscher Akademischer Austauschdienst (DAAD) and partly through BIM4Ren EU project (Grant No. 820773).

References

Bucher, D., Hall, D., 2020. Common Data Environment within the AEC Ecosystem: moving collaborative platforms beyond the open versus closed dichotomy, in: EG-ICE 2020 Proceedings: Workshop on Intelligent Computing in Engineering. Presented at the 27th International Workshop on IntelligentI Computing in Engineering (EG-ICE 2020) (virtual), Universitätsverlag der TU Berlin, pp. 491–500. https://doi.org/10.3929/ethz-b-000447240

Frank, R., 2016. A proven methodology to maximize return on risk [WWW Document]. URL https://www.syncdev.com/minimum-viable-product/ (accessed 3.15.21).

Gumpert, S., 2019. BIM360 Coordinate – Linking in your BIM360 Design Files for Clashing | Autodesk ANZ Tech Team Blog [WWW Document]. URL https://blogs.autodesk.com/anztechteam/2019/07/22/bim360-coordinate-linking-in-your-bim360-design-files-for-clashing/ (accessed 3.15.21).

Senthilvel, M., Oraskari, J., Beetz, J., 2020. Common Data Environments for the Information Container for linked Document Delivery, in: Proceedings of the 8th Linked Data in Architecture and Construction Workshop. Presented at the 8th Linked Data in Architecture and Construction Workshop, CEUR Workshop Proceedings, Dublin, Ireland (virtually hosted), pp. 132–145. http://ceur-ws.org/Vol-2636/

Speicher, S., Fernández, S., 2014. Linked Data Platform Implementation Conformance Report [WWW Document]. Frédéric GRAND. URL https://dvcs.w3.org/hg/ldpwg/raw-file/default/tests/reports/ldp.html (accessed 3.8.21).

Technical Committee : ISO/TC 59/SC 13 Organization and digitization of information about buildings and civil engineering works, including building information modelling (BIM), 2020a. ISO 21597-1:2020 Information container for linked document delivery Exchange Specification - Part 1: Container.

Technical Committee : ISO/TC 59/SC 13 Organization and digitization of information about buildings and civil engineering works, including building information modelling (BIM), 2020b. ISO 21597-2:2020 Information container for linked document delivery — Exchange specification — Part 2: Link types.

van Nederveen, 2010. Building Information Modelling in the Netherlands: A Status Report, in: 18th CIB World Building Congress. Presented at the CIB W78, CIB, The Lowry, Salford Quays, United Kingdom, p. 13.

An explanatory use case for the implementation of Information Container for linked Document Delivery in Common Data Environments

Janakiram Karlapudi, Prathap Valluru, Karsten Menzel
Technische Universität Dresden, Germany
janakiram.karlapudi@tu-dresden.de

Abstract. The BIM process is highly focused on the enrichment and management of domain data and its interoperability between fields. Many developments were proposed for data integration and sharing in terms of common data environments (CDE), multi-model approach, and open data standards (IFC, IDM), etc. However, often the information in BIM models is still managed in other proprietary formats. In April 2020 ISO 21597 (Information Container for Linked Document Delivery - ICDD) was introduced to enhance the semantic connection of heterogeneous data and document structures in the Architecture, Engineering, Construction and Operation domain (AECO) where the usage of different data formats is still of great diversity. Within this paper, we analyse ICDD capabilities, propose a standardised workflow for ICDD deployment and present a use case demonstrating these abilities of ICDD. Finally, an evaluation of the developed workflow is carried out based on Competency Questions and related SPARQL query profiles.

1. Introduction

The AECO industry is a collaborative environment with the involvement of multiple disciplines throughout the building lifecycle process. This collaboration requires an iterative and cooperated exchange of information, and improves the building design over multiple lifecycle stages (Abualdenien and Borrmann, 2018; Cahill et al., 2012). The management of the project's lifecycle information also ensures the reduction of error-prone operations, data communication problems, and provides significant efficiency benefits, time-saving, etc. (Di Biccari et al., 2018; Karlapudi and Shetty, 2019; Manzoor et al., 2012).

Since the last decade, Building Information Modelling (BIM) is an emerging approach and an enhanced business process in the AECO Industry (Allan and Menzel, 2009; Li et al., 2017). This technical advancement aimed to improve the collaboration and data sharing between the stakeholders involved in construction projects (Keller et al., 2008; Zadeh et al., 2017). Apart from data sharing, it is also a question of managing the continuous growth of the amount of data provided in different formats (Ahmed et al., 2009; Scherer and Katranuschkov, 2019).

IFC (ISO 16739-1, 2018; Karlapudi and Menzel, 2020) and linked data approaches (Karlapudi et al., 2020; Pauwels et al., 2017) support logically consistent data modelling for BIM data sharing. Alternatively, significant developments were introduced for file-based data integration and sharing through so-called level 2 CDE. Such level 2 CDE developments are successfully implemented for the storage and exchange of BIM-documents. However, often BIM and non-BIM data is still managed in proprietary formats (context models). The information heterogeneity between these context models highly affects the project efficiency, co-ordination and causes communication barriers (Beck et al., 2020). A study on industrial reports reveals an average time of 5.5h per week is spent by each professional to extract the related project data from heterogeneous context models (Senthilvel et al., 2020). The appearance of these different context models is usual in different AECO contexts, e.g.: construction management, fire safety, energy-efficient design (Manzoor and Menzel, 2011; Menzel et al., 2008), digital-twins, facility management (Yin et al., 2011), etc.

Thus, research on efficient linking of different data domains (context models) or document structures is carried on for the efficient exchange of context-based information between stakeholders. This research led to the development of three different approaches, the Multi-Model (MM) approach (Scherer and Schapke, 2011), the COINS approach (van Nederveen et al., 2010) and the Linked Building Data (LBD) approach (Beetz et al., 2009; Pauwels et al., 2017). Based on these approaches a new ISO standard – Information Container for Linked Document Delivery (ISO 21597-1, 2020; ISO 21597-2, 2020) was developed by combing the MM approach and LBD approach (Scherer and Katranuschkov, 2019). This new development uses the concept of linked data and ontologies to represent the meta-data of the documents and to produce link-sets between the documents, which further provide information concerning the association of different data structures. The framework developed for the ICDD container is highly enriched with semantic information to better specify heterogeneous data structures in the domain of the AECO sectors. Within this paper, an overview of the development of semantics in the ICDD structure and its usage in CDE platforms is discussed.

2. Related Research and Background

2.1 CDE: Common Data Environment

A CDE is "an agreed source of information for any given project or asset, for collecting, managing and disseminating each information container through a managed process"(ISO 19650-1:2018, 2018). CDE is a solution for structuring, combining, distributing, managing and archiving digital information related to any domain (Preidel et al., 2018). In digital sharing environments (e.g. CDE) it is possible to carry out integrated management of different context models, federated models and documents relating to a project over time (Daniotti et al., 2020). A BIM information repository must not necessarily be kept in one place due to widely dispersed teams. Consequently, CDE workflows can be developed and used across different platforms based on the constraints of collaborative work practice using information containers. These types of workflows are increasingly used in the AECO industries to support collaboration over the whole project life cycle.
As early as in 2013 a distinction between different BIM-Levels was introduced (BSI, 2013). Whereas BIM-Level 2 is defined as "federated file systems" BIM Level 3 is defined as an "integrated, interoperable BIM repository". Numerous commercial collaboration platforms claim to support BIM-Level 3, e.g. BIMCollab, BIMcloud, A360, etc. (Valluru et al., 2021). However, these commercial tools lack of effective integration and interlinking of various data structures or formats. To achieve fully integrated building information models, new workflow specifications should be established concerning AECO-work practice. Such workflows can be strengthened by using the concept of ICDD which specifies the linking of heterogeneous data structures along with its meta-data descriptions.

2.2 ICDD: Information Container

The main objective of the ICDD specifications is to enable the semantic linking of heterogeneous documents and data which contribute significantly to the value of information delivery. It describes file structures and meta-data related to documents. ICDD specifications are defined using RDF, RDFS and OWL semantic web standards and fulfil the linked data principles. Representing the information in widely used semantic web concepts along with ontology descriptions facilitates the interlinking of models and also enables the connection of data with external sources. The defined resource ontologies, Container.rdf, Linkset.rdf and

ExtendedLinkset.rdf in (ISO 21597-1, 2020; ISO 21597-2, 2020) are the core elements to describe the meta-data about the context models and the interrelations between them. The container ontology provides references to linked data sets, including meta-data related to contributors, version management, documents or models, descriptions, etc. Similarly, the Linkset ontology provides the syntax for the link data sets and manages the different links between the documents or with the identifiers inside the document.

Links are defined as a cluster of two or more *ls*[1]*:LinkElements* and can be further explored in the connection process as shown in Figure 1. Links are further categorized into *ls:BinaryLink* which allows only the link between exactly two *ls:LinkElements*. But the class *ls:DirectedLink* can describe the links between many *ls:LinkElements* and the direction of the links is differentiated with the help of *ls:hasFromLinkElement* and *ls:hasToLinkElement* object properties. *ls:Directed1toNLink* is the subclass of *ls:DirectedLink* and which is specialized in restricting the incoming links to only one and as usual outward links are from one to many. Further evolution of both, the *ls:DirectedLink* and *ls:BinaryLink* are the *ls:DirectedBinaryLink* provides exact one and the only link between two *ls:LinkElements*. The *ls:LinkElement* can be related to exactly one *ct:Document* described in the Container ontology using *ls:hasDocuments* object property. Similarly, the *ls:hasIdentifier* object property enables the linkage of the specific entity (string or identifiers) within the document. Basically, for explicit entity identification, these Identifiers are further categorized into various types, in particular, query-based, string-based and URI-based identifiers. In addition to these generic links, ISO 21597-2:2020 describes specializations to these links based on the categories comparative, ordering and dependency. All these specializations of the links and their structure are illustrated comprehensively in Figure 1 with the help of UML.

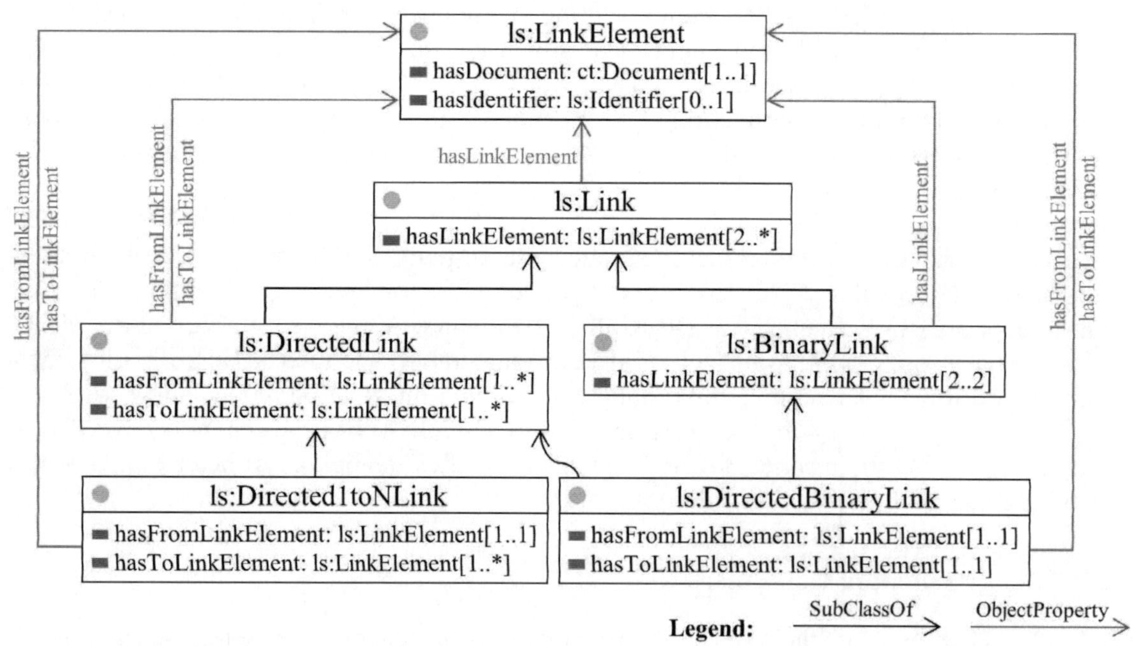

Figure 1: Diagrammatic representations of Link structure (as per ISO 21597-1:2020, 4.2)

[1] https://standards.iso.org/iso/21597/-1/ed-1/en/Linkset.rdf

3. Methodological Workflow

The information generated within a construction project can be categorized into either structured and unstructured data, federated information models, or object-based server models (ISO 19650-1:2018, 2018). To make these information models accessible among project partners, the information models need to be organized, integrated, or linked. The proposed methodology aims to enhance the capabilities of CDE through the implementation of ICDD specifications within CDE workflows. As part of the methodology, an information layer is described in Figure 2 in conjunction with the ICDD concept and CDE workflows. The information layer indicates the information and its source from where the different data structure or formats are generated within a construction project. The generated information can either be a part of a CDE or can be externally located in other data storage systems.

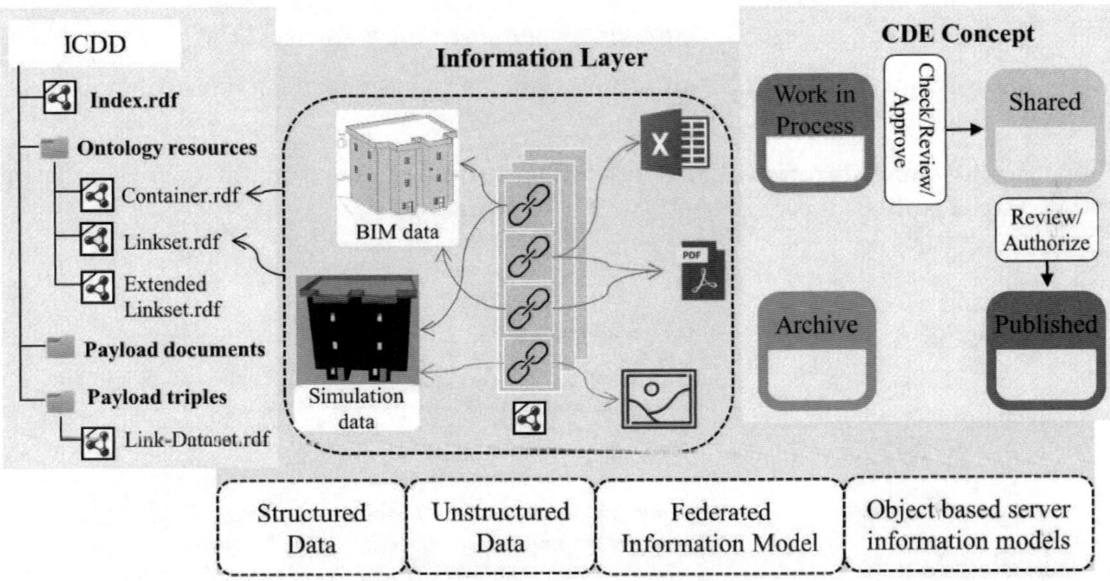

Figure 2: Methodological framework for the Linksets in CDE

To enable this information management and stakeholder collaboration, the ISO standard introduces a common workflow for CDEs (see Figure 10 in (ISO 19650-1:2018, 2018)). This CDE workflow describes the states of each information container (Work in Progress, Shared, Published and Archive) and meta-data assignments to the documents but is in lack of describing the interrelations among the information within the data structures. To enhance these interlinking capabilities, the ICDD container encompasses resource ontologies to specify the meta-data about the data structures and their linking with internal or external data formats. The specifications related to these resource ontologies are adopted to CDE workflows to enhance these link capabilities within the CDE file management systems. These generated link files are incorporated within the CDE environment and provide access to project partners according to their requirements.

As represented in Figure 2, a use case is selected in the domain of building renovation to explain these features additionally adopted to the CDE environment. The set of resource ontologies from ICDD specification is used to generate the relationships between the different data structures categorized in the information layer. A clear demonstration of this process is comprehensively presented in the subsequent section.

4. Demonstration

Based on the comprehensive analysis and understandings of the ICDD framework, this paper progresses with a demonstration exploring the application of ICDD concepts in the process of linking heterogeneous data. For the demonstration, we consider a use-case from the building renovation domain with an emphasis on data management of wall objects in a specific building information model. The use case focuses on the semantic interlinking of data from different sources available both in the CDE environment and outside of the CDE. Data sources considered in this example are:

1. **BuildingMaterial.rdf** is an ontology file that contains the material information and construction details of a specific building.
2. **Building_Model.ifc** is an IFC-based BIM model which represents the geometry and the placement of building objects extracted by surveying services.
3. **Wall10025.jpg** represents the present condition of the wall object (inside and outside).
4. The document **CIB_Plan.pdf** denotes the present renovation plan or retrofitting activities for building objects.
5. **PrecastPanelLibraries.html** is describing the information stored within the company storage profiles. It is represented with a Web link (URL).

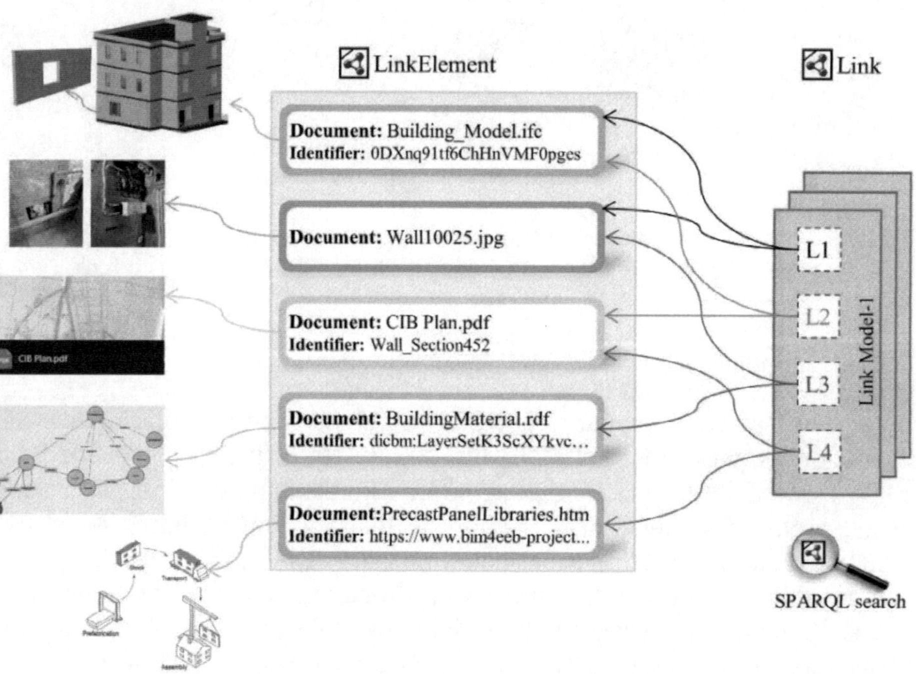

Figure 3: Demonstration example to represent the usage of ICDD ontologies

The different data sources and their linking according to the ICDD framework is represented in Figure 3. The process of documents reading, and link model generation is carried out according to the resource ontologies Container.rdf and Linkset.rdf with the help of a java algorithm. This algorithm can be used to develop minor APIs within a CDE environment to support a user-centric link generation process. Since the paper is restricted to workflow explanations, the present demonstration focuses more on link generation and validation.

Within the example demonstration, several link-scenarios are considered to display or showcase the maximum capabilities of ICDD link specifications. In the linking process, the link elements were considered in such a fashion, some contain a string-based identifier, URI-based identifiers and others with no identifiers, to enable to demonstrate these link-scenarios.

For example, the digital representation of the wall element is considered from an IFC file called "Building_Model.ifc". This originates from "field surveying services" and subsequent "object identification". The GUID of this wall object is a string-based identifier. It is also linked with the image file Wall10025.jpg representing the current condition of the wall. The basic information of these Link elements are represented with the set of data properties such are creator, description, filetype, filename, format, and name, etc. Additionally, this digital wall representation is linked to the specific wall identifier (Wall_section452) used in the renovation plan represented in PDF file format ("CIB Plan.pdf").

Furthermore, current construction and material details of the wall object are saved in an ontology file ("BuildingMaterial.rdf"). The specific details of the layers-system of a wall object are saved as an instance called "dicm[2]:LayerSetK3ScXYk" and is linked to the image file representing the current wall condition. In addition to the representation of the present condition of the wall, a link is generated between the CIB Plan.pdf document and an online Html documentation file PrecastPanelLibraries.html. This documentation provides the relevant information regarding the preparation and installation of the panels to the wall object and as well as the available pre-cast element libraries. Figure 3 illustrates the list of all these link elements (models or documents) and the generated links.

5. Validation

Apart from the link generation, it is also necessary to verify the generated links to specify the efficiency of the interlinking process. It also helps to rectify the mismatches or inconsistencies in linking. The quality and correctness of these generated links are investigated based on appropriate ontology evaluation techniques.

Here, in the validation process, a set of Competency Questions (CQ) are introduced. In general, CQs are natural language questions used to verify the knowledge representation in ontologies. In other terms, these questions assist to specify the information requirements and scope of ontologies. In our case, CQs are developed to identify the different links between the documents or the documents involved in the linking mechanism retrospectively. In a subsequent step, the natural language CQs are translated in SPARQL queries which are further used to extract the knowledge or information from the link ontology.

Table 1: CQ-1: Extracting the basic links between the documents

SPARQL Query	**Query Results**	
SELECT Distinct ?Doc1 ?Doc2 WHERE { ?link ls:hasLinkElement ?l1. ?link ls:hasLinkElement ?l2. filter(?l1!=?l2)	**Doc1**	**Doc2**
	BuildingMaterial.rdf	Wall10025.jpg
	Wall10025.jpg	BuildingMaterial.rdf
	Precast panel Libraries.html	CIB Plan.pdf
	CIB Plan.pdf	Precast panel Libraries.html

[2] https://w3id.org/digitalconstruction/0.5/Materials

?l1 ls:hasDocument [ct:filename ?Doc1]. ?l2 ls:hasDocument [ct:filename ?Doc2]. }	Wall10025.jpg	Building_Model.ifc
	Building_Model.ifc	Wall10025.jpg
	CIB Plan.pdf	Building_Model.ifc
	Building_Model.ifc	CIB Plan.pdf

The SPARQL query described in Table 1 is to identify the list of the documents involved in the linking process along with the representation of their interrelationship. The Query results shown in Table 1 illustrate the eight relationships between Doc1 and Doc2, but in the demonstration, there were only four links between the documents. The table also indicates the duplication of links by interchanging the position of documents between Doc1 and Doc2 columns. This is because of the lack of directional representation of links, i.e. the definition of the link from which element to which element.

Table 2: CQ-2: Extracting the directional relationship between the documents

SPARQL Query	**Query Results**	

`SELECT Distinct ?Doc1 ?Doc2`
`WHERE {`
`?link ls:hasFromLinkElement ?l1.`
`?link ls:hasToLinkElement ?l2.`
`filter(?l1!=?l2)`
`?l1 ls:hasDocument [ct:filename ?Doc1].`
`?l2 ls:hasDocument [ct:filename ?Doc2].}`
	Doc1	**Doc2**

	Building_Model.ifc	Wall10025.jpg
	CIB Plan.pdf	Precast panel Libraries.html
	CIB Plan.pdf	Building_Model.ifc
	BuildingMaterial.rdf	Wall10025.jpg

In the next case, the links were furthermore explicitly defined by using the class ls:DirectedBinaryLink and object properties is:hasFromLinkElement, ls:hasToLinkElement. The CQ-2 and SPARQL query is developed to validate this requirement and the extracted results in Table 2 confirm the achievements by reducing the duplicated links. Apart from the direction specification to links, the typed links can also be generated between the documents according to the ExtendedLinkset ontology defined in (ISO 21597-2, 2020).

Table 3: CQ-3: Extraction of links between the identifiers with in the documents

SPARQL Query

```
SELECT Distinct ?Doc1 ?Identifier1 ?Doc2 ?Identifier2
WHERE {
?link ls:hasFromLinkElement ?l1.
?link ls:hasToLinkElement ?l2.
filter(?l1!=?l2)
?l1 ls:hasDocument [ct:filename ?Doc1].
?l2 ls:hasDocument [ct:filename ?Doc2].
{{?l1 ls:hasIdentifier [ls:identifier ?Identifier1].}
UNION
{?l1 ls:hasIdentifier [ls:url ?Identifier1].}}
{{?l2 ls:hasIdentifier [ls:identifier ?Identifier2].}
UNION
{?l2 ls:hasIdentifier [ls:url ?Identifier2].}}}
```

Query results

Doc1	**Identifier1**	**Doc2**	**Identifier2**
CIB Plan.pdf	Wall_Section452	Building_Model.ifc	0DXnq91tf6ChHnVMF0pges
CIB Plan.pdf	Wall_Section452	Precast panel Libraries.html	https://www.bim4eeb-project.eu/

CQ-3, CQ-4 and the respective SPARQL queries are developed to extract the information related to links between identifiers as well between the identifier and the document. The results in Table 3 from the CQ-3 clearly represent the interrelationship between the identifiers within the documents. The results in Table 4 illustrate the connection of an identifier within a document to other documents. Thus, one can conclude that different link-scenarios can easily be retrieved and shared among users. Retrieved link information can be further used to explore information related to specific objects saved in a CDE environment. This further enhances collaboration and information sharing between project partners.

Table 4: CQ-4: Extraction of links between the identifier in a document to the other document

SPARQL Query

```
SELECT Distinct ?Doc1 ?Identifier1 ?Doc2
WHERE {
       ?link ls:hasFromLinkElement ?l1.
       ?link ls:hasToLinkElement ?l2.
       filter(?l1!=?l2)
       ?l1 ls:hasDocument [ct:filename ?Doc1].
       ?l2 ls:hasDocument [ct:filename ?Doc2].
       {{?l1 ls:hasIdentifier [ls:identifier ?Identifier1].}
       UNION
       {?l1 ls:hasIdentifier [ls:url ?Identifier1].}}
       FILTER (NOT EXISTS
       {{?l2 ls:hasIdentifier [ls:identifier ?Identifier2].}
       UNION
       {?l2 ls:hasIdentifier [ls:url ?Identifier2].}}))}
```

Query results

Doc1	Identifier1	Doc2
Building_Model.ifc	0DXnq91tf6ChHnVMF0pges	Wall10025.jpg
BuildingMaterial.rdf	https://w3id.org/digitalconstruction/BuildingMaterials# LayerSetK3ScXYkvck2p36CZNM	Wall10025.jpg

6. Summary and Future work

The research in this paper presents an analysis of ICDD specifications regarding their semantic representation and interlinking techniques for heterogeneous data structures. Upon the analysis, it demonstrates how these ICDD specifications can enhance the capabilities of CDE platforms concerning efficient management of documents and their interrelation with other data formats. Finally, this paper also validates the enhanced capabilities of CDE workflow using the set of competency questions and SPARQL query profiles. By implementing the ICDD structural framework within a CDE, the abilities of the CDE is enhanced in terms of interlinking the available documents and even enable the links based on sublevels (identifiers) of documents. This implementation also allows the linking of CDE documents with external documents, for example, data on the web. The technical enhancement to CDE progressively increases the efficient structuring of information along with the stakeholder coordination and information access.

The integration of the ICDD concepts into a CDE environment is considered as Future development. The identification of integration requirements and integration process is an ongoing research work in the BIM4EEB Project. Furthermore, the research is extended to the identification of implementation challenges and possible application or API developments.

Acknowledgement

This research is part of the EU project entitled "*BIM4EEB – BIM-based fast toolkit for the Efficient rEnovation in Buildings*" which is supported and funded by European Union's H2020 research and innovation program under grant agreement No 820660. The authors gratefully acknowledge the support and funding from the European Union. The content of this publication reflects the author view only and the Commission is not responsible for any use that may be made of the information it contains.

References

Abualdenien, J. and Borrmann, A. (2018) 'Multi-LOD model for describing uncertainty and checking requirements in different design stages', in Karlshøj, J. and Scherer, R. (eds) eWork and eBusiness in Architecture, Engineering and Construction, CRC Press, pp. 187–195. DOI: https://www.doi.org/10.1201/9780429506215-24.

Ahmed, A., Menzel, K., Ploennigs, J. and Cahill, B. (2009) 'Aspects of multi-dimensional Building Performance Data Management', in Huhnt, W. (ed) Computing in engineering: EG-ICE conference 2009, Aachen, Shaker Verlag, pp. 9–16.

Allan, L. and Menzel, K. (2009) 'Virtual Enterprises for Integrated Energy Service Provision', in Camarinha-Matos, L. M., Afsarmanesh, H. and Paraskakis, I. (eds) Leveraging Knowledge for Innovation in Collaborative Networks: PRO-VE 2009, Thessaloniki, Greece, October 7-9, 2009. [Online], Berlin, Heidelberg, Springer-Verlag Berlin Heidelberg, pp. 659–666. Available at http://site.ebrary.com/lib/alltitles/docDetail.action?docID=10342049.

Beck, F., Borrmann, A. and Kolbe, T. H. (2020) 'The need for a differentiation between heterogeneous information integration approaches in the field of "BIM-GIS Integration": a literature review', ISPRS Annals of Photogrammetry, Remote Sensing and Spatial Information Sciences, VI-4/W1-2020, pp. 21–28. DOI: https://www.doi.org/10.5194/isprs-annals-VI-4-W1-2020-21-2020.

Beetz, J., van Leeuwen, J. and Vries, B. de (2009) 'IfcOWL: A case of transforming EXPRESS schemas into ontologies', Artificial Intelligence for Engineering Design, Analysis and Manufacturing, vol. 23, no. 1, pp. 89–101. DOI: https://www.doi.org/10.1017/S0890060409000122.

BSI (2013) 1192-2:2013: Specification for information management for the capital/delivery phase of construction projects using building information modelling: BSI Standards Limited.

Cahill, B., Menzel, K. and Flynn, D. (2012) 'BIM as a centre piece for Optimised Building Operation', in Gudnason, G. and Scherer, R. (eds) eWork and eBusiness in Architecture, Engineering and Construction: ECPPM 2012, Hoboken, CRC Press, pp. 549–555. DOI: https://www.doi.org/10.1201/b12516-88.

Daniotti, B., Pavan, A., Lupica Spagnolo, S., Caffi, V., Pasini, D. and Mirarchi, C. (2020) BIM-Based Collaborative Building Process Management, Cham, Springer International Publishing. 9783030328894.

Di Biccari, C., Mangialardi, G., Lazoi, M. and Corallo, A. (2018) 'Configuration Views from PLM to Building Lifecycle Management', in Chiabert, P. (ed) Product lifecycle management to support industry 4.0: 15th IFIP WG 5.1 International Conference, PLM 2018, Turin, Italy, July 2-4, 2018, Cham, Springer, pp. 69–79. DOI: https://www.doi.org/10.1007/978-3-030-01614-2_7.

ISO 16739-1 (2018) 16739-1:2018: Industry Foundation Classes (IFC) for data sharing in the construction and facility management industries — Part 1: Data schema, Switzerland: ISO 2020 [Online]. Available at https://www.iso.org/standard/70303.html (Accessed 24 February 2021).

ISO 19650-1:2018 (2018) ISO 19650-1: Organization and digitization of information about buildings and civil engineering works, including building information modelling (BIM) - Information management using building information modelling - Part 1: Concepts and principles: BSI Standards Limited.

ISO 21597-1 (2020) ISO 21597: Information container for linked document delivery — Exchange specification — Part 1: Container, Switzerland: ISO 2020.

ISO 21597-2 (2020) ISO 21597: Information container for linked document delivery — Exchange specification — Part 2: Link types, Switzerland: ISO 2020.

Karlapudi, J. and Menzel, K. (2020) 'Analysis on automatic generation of BEPS models from BIM model', in Monsberger, M., Hopfe, C. J., Krüger, M. and Passer, A. (eds) BauSIM 2020 - 8th IBPSA-Conference (Germany, Austria), 2020th edn, Austria, Verlag der TU Graz, pp. 535–542.

Karlapudi, J., Menzel, K., Törmä, S., Hryshchenko, A. and Valluru, P. (2020) 'Enhancement of BIM Data Representation in Product-Process Modelling for Building Renovation', in Nyffenegger, F., Ríos, J., Rivest, L. and Bouras, A. (eds) Product Lifecycle Management Enabling Smart: 17th ifip wg 5.1, [S.l.], Springer, pp. 738–752. DOI: https://www.doi.org/10.1007/978-3-030-62807-9_58.

Karlapudi, J. and Shetty, S. (2019) 'A methodology to determine and classify data sharing requirements between OpenBIM models and energy simulation models', in Sternal, M., Ungureanu, L.-C., Böger, L. and Bindal-Gutsche, C. (eds) 31. Forum Bauinformatik: 11. bis 13. September 2019 in Berlin : proceedings, Berlin, Universitätsverlag der TU Berlin, pp. 331–338.

Keller, M., O'Donnel, J., Menzel, K. and Keane, M. (2008) 'Integrating the Specification, Acquisition and Processing of Building Performance Information', Tsinghua Science and Technology, vol. 13, no. 1, pp. 1–6.

Li, X., Wu, P., Shen, G. Q., Wang, X. and Teng, Y. (2017) 'Mapping the knowledge domains of Building Information Modeling: A bibliometric approach', Automation in Construction, vol. 84, pp. 195–206. DOI: https://www.doi.org/10.1016/j.autcon.2017.09.011.

Manzoor, F., Linton, D., Loughlin, M. and Menzel, K. (2012) 'RFID based efficient lighting control', International Journal of RF Technologies, vol. 4, no. 1, pp. 1–21 [Online]. DOI: https://www.doi.org/10.3233/RFT-2012-0036.

Manzoor, F. and Menzel, K. (2011) 'Indoor localisation for complex building designs using passive RFID technology', in XXXth URSI general assembly and scientific symposium, 2011: [URSI GASS 2011] ; 13 -20 Aug. 2011, Istanbul, Turkey, Piscataway, NJ, IEEE, pp. 1–4. DOI: https://www.doi.org/10.1109/URSIGASS.2011.6050581.

Menzel, K., Cong, Z. and Allan, L. (2008) 'Potentials for radio frequency identification in AEC/FM', Tsinghua Science and Technology, vol. 13, S1, pp. 329–335. DOI. https://www.doi.org/10.1016/S1007-0214(08)70170-6.

Pauwels, P., Zhang, S. and Lee, Y.-C. (2017) 'Semantic web technologies in AEC industry: A literature overview', Automation in Construction, vol. 73, pp. 145–165. DOI: https://www.doi.org/10.1016/j.autcon.2016.10.003.

Preidel, C., Borrmann, A., Mattern, H., König, M. and Schapke, S.-E. (2018) 'Common Data Environment', in Borrmann, A., König, M., Koch, C. and Beetz, J. (eds) Building Information Modeling -Technologische Grundlagen und Industrielle Praxis: Technology Foundations and Industry Practice, Cham, Springer, pp. 279–291.

Scherer, R. J. and Katranuschkov, P. (2019) 'Context capturing of multi-information resources for the data exchange in collaborative project environments', Proceedings of the 2019 European Conference on Computing in Construction, Jul. 10, 2019, University College Dublin, pp. 359–366. DOI: https://www.doi.org/10.35490/EC3.2019.173.

Scherer, R. J. and Schapke, S.-E. (2011) 'A distributed multi-model-based Management Information System for simulation and decision-making on construction projects', Advanced Engineering Informatics, vol. 25, no. 4, pp. 582–599. DOI: https://www.doi.org/10.1016/j.aei.2011.08.007.

Senthilvel, M., Oraskari, J. and Beetz, J. (2020) 'Common Data Environments for the Information Container for linked Document Delivery', 8th Linked Data in Architecture and Construction Workshop, Dublin (Ireland), 17 Jul 2020 - 19 Jul 2020, pp. 132–145. DOI: https://www.doi.org/10.18154/RWTH-2020-08421.

Valluru, P., Karlapudi, J., Menzel, K., Mätäsniemi, T. and Shemeikka, J. (2021) 'A Semantic Data Model to Represent Building Material Data in AEC Collaborative Workflows', in Camarinha-Matos,

L. M., Afsarmanesh, H. and Ortiz, A. (eds) BOOSTING COLLABORATIVE NETWORKS 4.0, [S.l.], SPRINGER NATURE, pp. 133–142. DOI: https://www.doi.org/10.1007/978-3-030-62412-5_11.

van Nederveen, S., Beheshti, R. and Willems, P. (2010) 'Building Information Modelling in the Netherlands: A Status Report', W078 - Special Track 18th CIB World Building Congress. Salford, United Kingdom, May, CIB Publication 361, pp. 28–40.

Yin, H., Stack, P. and Menzel, K. (2011) 'Decision Support for Building Renovation Strategies', in Zhu, Y. and Issa, R. R. (eds) Computing in civil engineering: Proceedings of the 2011 ASCE International Workshop on Comupting in Civil Engineering, June 19 – 22, 2011, Miami, Florida, Reston, Va., American Society of Civil Engineers, pp. 834–841.
DOI: https://www.doi.org/10.1061/41182(416)103.

Zadeh, P. A., Wang, G., Cavka, H. B., Staub-French, S. and Pottinger, R. (2017) 'Information Quality Assessment for Facility Management', Advanced Engineering Informatics, vol. 33, pp. 181–205 [Online]. DOI: https://www.doi.org/10.1016/j.aei.2017.06.003.

Automatic generation of ISO 19650 compliant templates based on standard construction contracts using a microservices approach

Thomas Bower, Alan Rawdin, Xiaofeng Zhu, Haijiang Li*
Cardiff University, United Kingdom
LiH@cardiff.ac.uk*

Abstract. This study aims to establish a framework for automatically generating evidence for ISO 19650 certification. The study starts with an investigation of the challenges organisations face in compliance with BIM standards ISO 19650, the key areas of interest identified in relation to this are an organisation's ability to understand what their information requirements are. Once requirements have been identified, they are translated into format which is both machine and human readable. Extraction of text from existing project documentation is also investigated, proposing a microservice-based solution which formats and produces documents which meet the standards for information management requirements.

1. Introduction

The concept of Building Information Modelling (BIM) as a process-based information management framework is increasingly being adopted worldwide. There are many standards available defining BIM processes including the recent ISO 19650 series, of which there are currently 4 published parts (ISO, 2018a, 2018b, 2018c, 2020). This standard series is applicable to assets of all sizes and covers the lifecycle management of information from conception to demolition or re-purpose. The concept and principles of information management are designed in terms of BIM maturity, with stage 3 BIM requiring progression towards database and query-based environments.

This study begins with exploration of the concepts and principles of information management, which is divided into specifying, requesting, and delivering information. The collaboration of actors and how they work together is also a key aspect of the standards along with the production of standard methods and procedures.

In line with data-driven BIM stage 3 principles, this work aims to explore the concept of microservices for the purpose of assisting organisations in the AEC industry follow the information management guidance proposed by ISO 19650. This study starts with a requirements analysis of the ISO 19650 series to identify key challenges. This work then explains a framework for document information requirement schemas based on the analysis results, which goes on to inform a proposal for a microservice approach to project data collection and document generation. This study concludes with a summary of the research findings, along with discussions around of limitations of the proposed framework and future steps for improvement.

2. Requirements Analysis - Ethnographic Interviews with Industry

Information requirements and standards of information requirements are a key factor in asset management. BIM is the lifecycle management of asset information relating to not only how the asset is managed during its operational phase but also during the project delivery phase. This involves the process of information management and the data required to deliver and manage it. There are several information requirements during both phases. During interviews held with 23 individuals including asset owners, operators and maintainers along with architects, engineers and building contractors throughout Wales from 2017 – 2020, many issues were raised in relation to building information modelling and how to meet the information requirements. From the asset owner's perspective, there are many challenges in implementing BIM to existing assets (Abdirad and Dossick, 2020) in contrast to implementing BIM in new assets. Facility management systems must be able to capture data that is both relevant and delivered at the correct time to the appropriate actors.

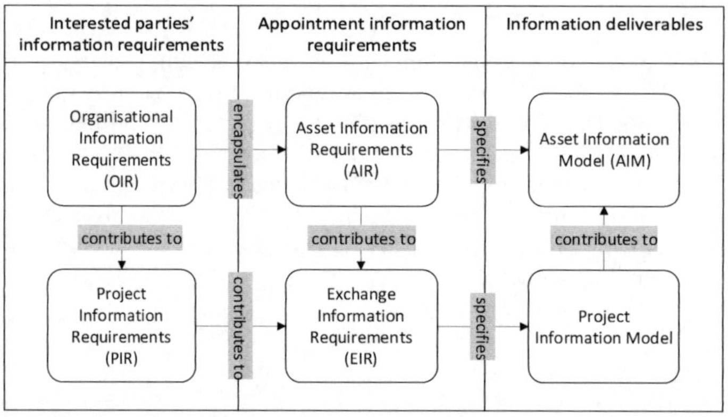

Figure 1: Hierarchy of information requirements as set out in ISO 19650-1 (ISO, 2018a)

Information requirements are specified in ISO 19650 (ISO, 2018a) as relating to one of four areas. The first; Organisation Information Requirements are high-level requirements describing information required for an organisation to run effectively. The second, Project Information Requirements are again a high-level information requirement which allows for a project to request information to answer questions. These questions are usually asked at key decision points of a project which in the UK align with various stages of RIBA scheme of works (Royal Institute of British Architects, 2020). The third requirement, Asset Information Requirements relate to information required about a particular asset during its lifecycle. The final requirement is the Exchange Information Requirements and allows an asset owner to specify how the exchange of information requirements is will occur. This requirement is responded to in the form of an execution plan by one or many of the lead parties termed Lead Appointed Party in the standard. The relationship of these requirements can be seen in Figure *1*.

All the participants stated that whilst they are aware of the requirements within the ISO19650 standard, there are issues related to how the information requirements can be linked together from a practical implementation. During the interviews and case studies, open ended questions were used to prevent biased answers. Closed questions can cause issues when conducting interviews with individuals and study groups leading to bias in the responses (Nuno and St. John, 2014). The results of the interviews were collated and analysed using NVivo (QSR International, 2020). Of note amongst the interviewees and study groups was the responses given to the question "Tell me about your experience with information requirements and exchange and employer information requirements". The responses from the interviewees aligned with each other in their responses. That is, the clients and professionals both had overall negative experiences. The clients' perspectives centred around two key themes: 1) They were unsure how to generate them. 2) They were unsure how they aligned with each other. From the professionals' experiences, the results centred around 1) The quality of information requirements 2) Clients did not understand the role of information requirements surrounding neither PAS1192 nor ISO19650.

From the interviews held with the parties, several key research questions emerged: 1) What are the challenges organisations face in collecting, storing, and reproducing the information requirements? 2) What are the main requirements for ISO19650 compliant documentation? 3) What are the challenges organisations face in collecting, storing and reproducing the information requirements? 4) How can the requirements be addressed? And can generation of some requirements be automated?

3. Information Requirements Schema for ISO 19650 Documentation

Information requirements according to ISO 29481-1 (ISO, 2016) can be formed from defining processes that take place within an organisation. For this research, the key goal is to relate the information requirements together to allow for the flow of information from the Organisation Information Requirements through to the Exchange Information Requirements. All information requirements should be formed, requested, and responded to with a specific purpose. Previous work in this area (Heaton, Parlikad and Schooling, 2019) looked at forming function information requirements as a link between Organisation Information Requirements and Asset Information Requirements. It does not however look at how to link all information requirements between each other. Information requirements can also be formed by following the information schema as defined in ISO 29481-1 (Figure *2*).

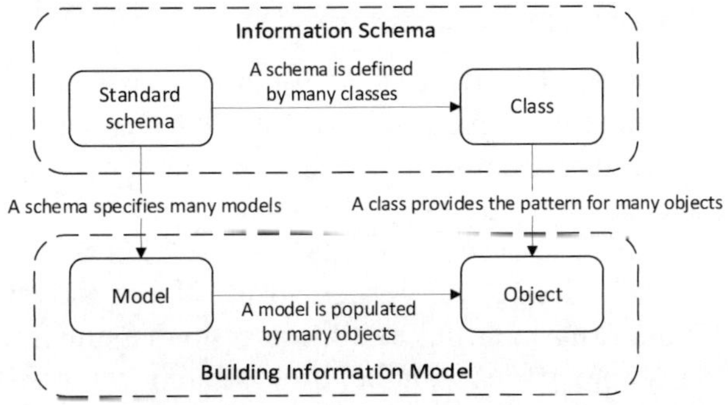

Figure 2: Development of information requirements (ISO, 2016)

For the work undertaken in this research, a simplified schema has been developed which uses activities undertaken at an organisation level to build information requirements that can be linked together using what is defined as information activity reasons. As an example: A local authority has an education department which has many schools. These schools undertake many activities which all require information. At the local authority level, they also undertake activities which require information. These activity-based information requirements have what are called information reasons. These information reasons are used as a link between the remaining information requirements and can be used to connect to questions in project information requirements as well as link them to a specific information delivery point within a defined schema plan of works such as RIBA within the UK or HOAI protocol in Germany.

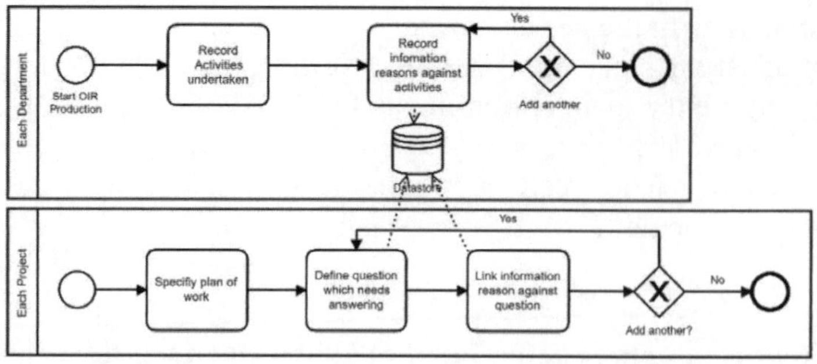

Figure 3: High-level data capture process for activity-based information requirements

The high-level information requirements data schema can be seen in Figure *3*. This shows how each part of the information requirements are linked together along with the data schema for information requirements. From these high-level information requirements, a data schema was constructed for individual models based upon IFC. IFC is designated as an OpenBIM concept for data modelling. Some aspects were not able to be mapped against IFC and for this reason, an extension for the schema has been proposed which includes elements for questions and answers along with information reasons.

4. Container-Based Microservice Architecture

In the context of moving towards UK BIM stage 3 and data-driven environments, there is an increasing need to explore flexible, lightweight, connected web services for management of information. Modularity and interoperability are key considerations to make when designing reusable infrastructure and several authors have made contributions to this idea for BIM applications. Previously studied use-cases for containerised microservice architectures in BIM include linked-data applications (Ferguson, Vardeman and Nabrzyski, 2016), Internet of Things (IoT) infrastructure for supporting building performance management (Kang, Lin and Zhang, 2018). For scalability, multiple nodes can be orchestrated for parallelisation of resource intensive tasks (Fahad and Bus, 2018).

Modularity can be achieved by isolating operations, assigning them suitable endpoints for data access. For example, one processing service can be used by multiple clients. There are several options available for deploying isolated web services such as virtual machines, cloud platforms, Openstack, Kubernetes, and Docker. The latter has been chosen for this work due to its relative simplicity for configuration and installation, and performance advantages over virtual machines which come from the ability for containers to share common resources (Chung *et al.*, 2016). Groups of images can be assembled and linked together using docker-compose files, allowing for simple and consistent installation and configuration of web services.

The broader aim of this project is to create a multi-standards BIM compliance checking environment, and eventually developing 'meta' standards for BIM compliance. The focus of this study is around BS EN ISO 19650, with a particular focus on project certification.

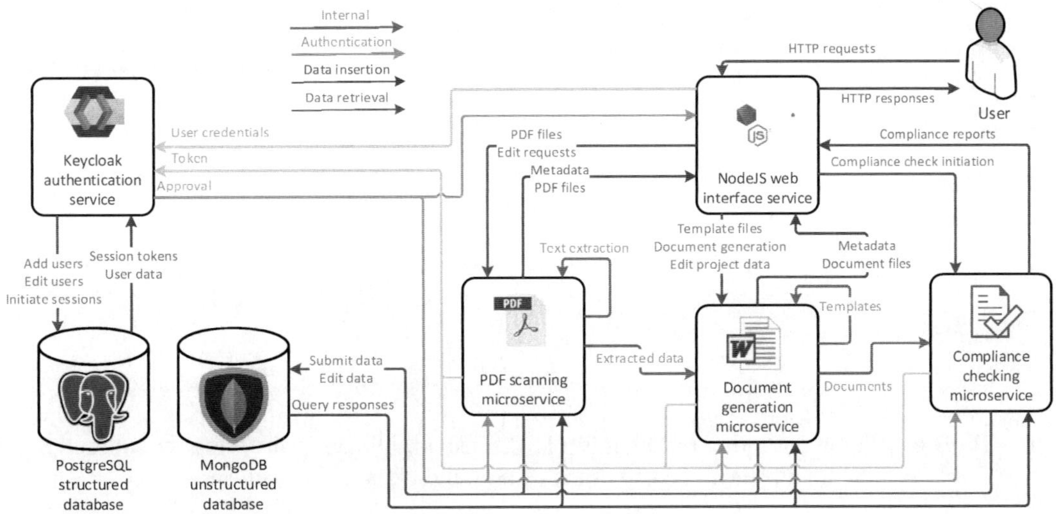

Figure 4: Overall system architecture for container-based infrastructure which incorporates automatic data extraction, document generation and compliance checking. Compliance checking is part of ongoing developments of this project

To address research question 4, this study proposes using microservice architecture with multiple services connected through Application Programming Interfaces (APIs) (Figure *4*). The aim is to start with project documents with standardised structures such as contracts, and automatically produce documentation pursuant to ISO 19650 certification, for the purpose of performing in-house checks on the documents before final submission to a certification body.

4.1 Flask API Microservices

The key processing elements of the system used in this study are undertaken by two Flask microservices. Flask is a web framework for Python which runs as a lightweight web server. The Python library Flask Restplus is used as a wrapper for the Flask microservices. This allows concise definition of RESTful API interfaces, with automatic documentation of the API routes. REST (or Representable State Transfer) is a framework for structuring API endpoints. For a given resource (or URL), there are typically a limited number of requests available on individual items or groups of items, allowing adding, editing, deleting, viewing of resources. Data for the resources is stored in MongoDB collections, with user and project identifiers attached to all data to ensure data isolation between individuals and projects. Data is accessed in the Flask microservices using the Python library PyMongo.

4.2 NodeJS - Express Frontend Microservice

The frontend web service for this project is built using Express; a framework for NodeJS applications. NodeJS allows rendering of dynamic pages to present content from the database on the frontend web interface. Routes are defined for each resource, on the frontend, this typically takes the form of GET routes for rendering pages, or POST requests for submitting form data. For each route, the relevant requests can then be made to microservice API routes.

Specific organisational or project requirements are not necessarily known and cannot be fixed beforehand. Therefore, to embed flexibility into the system, HTML forms have been produced using a dynamic form generation JavaScript library called JSON Form (jsonform, 2020). Figure *5* shows a complex HTML5 form produced from two JSON schemas supplied using this library.

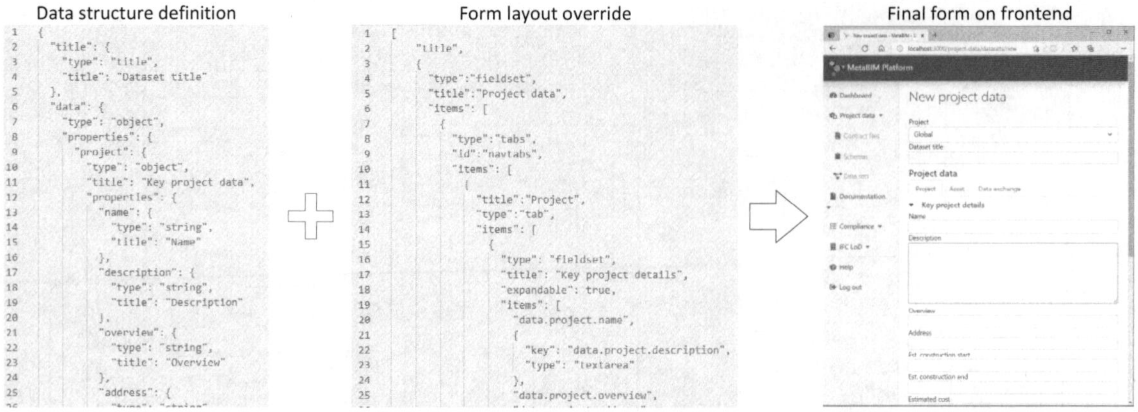

Figure 5: Form schema definition producing HTML5 friendly forms, overriding default options to create advanced layouts such as tabs and expandable fieldsets

Producing forms in this way allows the forms to easily be changed by those with even limited programming experience. Theoretically, this concept could be expanded to have a 'meta' form, generating the required form schemas and overrides. This will be considered in ongoing work.

4.3 Automatic Contract Scanning

The literature surrounding automatic extraction of document data is mature, and there are several approaches available. Generic methods exist for automatically converting semi-structured PDF documents into structured blocks of text (Chao and Fan, 2004). This can be taken a step further to extract and automatically classify blocks of text, for example in extracting known sections from research literature (Ramakrishnan *et al.*, 2012). Extraction from PDF files is less trivial than that of DOCX or HTML data due to its layout-based definition. Consideration needs to be made for size, spacing and alignment of characters and lines (Bast and Korzen, 2017). For example, detection of headings is can be performed through analysis of several thresholds including fonts, size and case (Budhiraja and Mago, 2020).

The contract scanning microservice performs tasks relating to extracting data from PDF files. It is wrapped in a Flask Python environment with a REST API. Within this API there are three main resources: Files, Pages, and Extraction Schemas. Files represent PDF files, and their associated metadata. The File route allows upload and download of files through the API.

The Pages resource represents the page text extracted from the PDF file. A Page resource is created by sending a POST request to the API with the File identifier, to initiate conversion. There are several options available to perform page text extraction, each performing with different accuracies (Bast and Korzen, 2017). In this study, PdfMiner is used, where each page is extracted and stored as a string in a JSON array. It is available as a Python library and performed well in a comparative review by Bast and Korzen (2017) which studied metrics such as missing or additional lines, words, or characters. The primary method for extracting data from contracts in this study is through text markers (Figure *6*), where identifiable phrases in the contract are selected as markers denoting the positions of key values to be extracted.

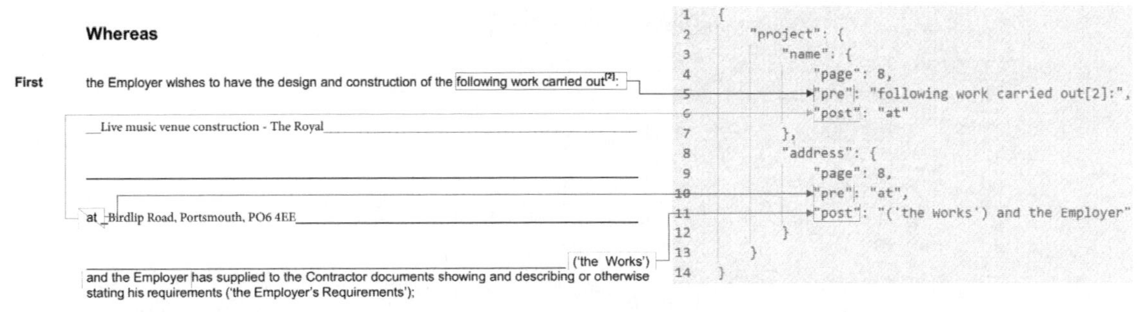

Figure 6: Extraction from JCT Design and Build 2016 contract with content, with mark-up denoting locations of fields

The text is extracted from the page string using REGEX (regular expressions) to search for two strings with a wildcard between. The expression which takes the place of the wildcard character is returned as the field value.

Punctuation which can appear in contract PDF files and can interfere with REGEX searches files has been stripped from both the page text and from the search markers. Alternatively, this REGEX issue could be resolved by converting the strings to escaped characters. To allow working with flexible, and deeply nested structures, a recursive object traversing function is used to navigate objects of any complexity. The function also allows for values to be manually specified, rather than scanned. This is convenient for addressing organisation specific requirements, or contract text which does not change.

4.4 Document generation algorithm

After the completion of contract scanning and extraction of the information related to the project, documents that fulfil the requirements of ISO 19650 can be generated automatically. There are several available approaches for generating documents from templates. The most obvious being Microsoft Word's built-in Mail Merge feature. In its default form, Mail Merge can be used for flat templates only, extracting data from relational or nested objects is not possible without custom modification through writing of macro subroutines.

There are libraries available for Python which allow creation of dynamic documents. Python-docx (Canny, 2013) is one such library, which allows creation of new documents and modification of existing documents. JSON dictionaries containing the project data can be manipulated in Python and written to a document using a template written purely in code. This approach is unlikely to be suitable for BIM project stakeholders, as it requires understanding of Python to implement and customise templates. A second library, python-docx-template (Lapouyade, 2019), builds on python-docx to create templates suitable for use with complex JSON data structures. Tags are written into documents using double braces, and sub-objects can be rendered using dot separators (Figure 7), and repeated data is rendered using loops (Figure 8).

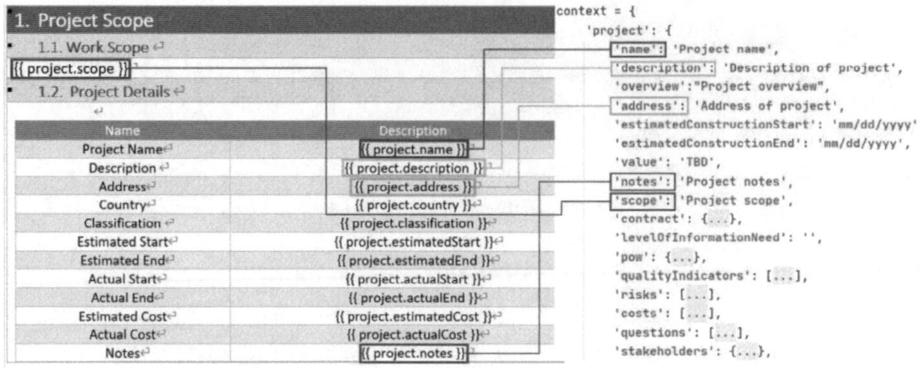

Figure 7: Association between tags in templates and key of the extracted data

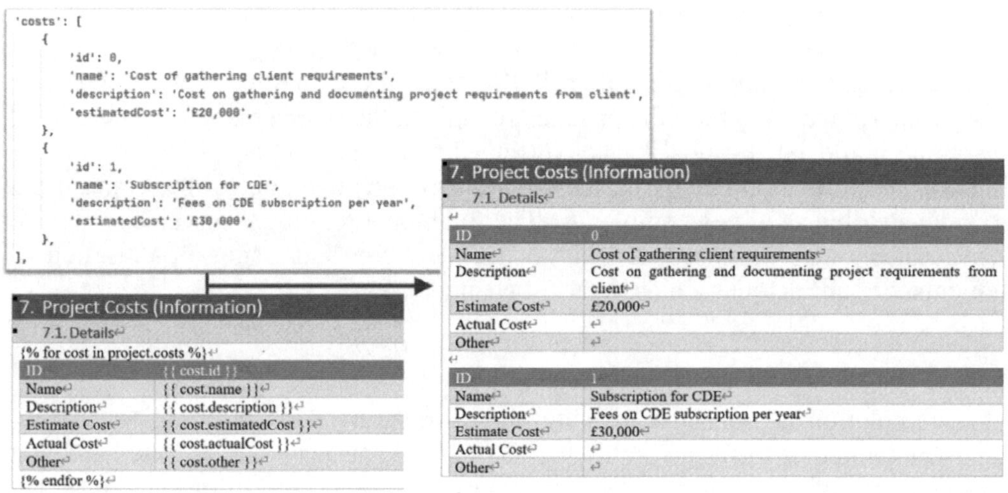

Figure 8: Generating repeated data from JSON list using a for loop in the template

Using a similar approach to the contract scanning microservice, this document generation algorithm is built into a microservice based on Flask and Flask RestPlus. The API allows uploading of templates, and creation of documents.

An important consideration for ISO 19650 compliance is the naming of documents. This is considered in the document generation engine by allowing the user to define naming conventions which extract pieces of information from the JSON schema. The naming convention, as specified in ISO 19650-1 (ISO, 2018a) and the UK National Annex to ISO 19650-2 (ISO, 2018b), is implemented into the document generation API, where the fields, delimiters, field lengths, and blank character are defined using the JSON form JavaScript library, and sent to the document API and stored in the Mongo database. As the document is generated and downloaded by the user, the field names are extracted from the project JSON dictionary and the file name is assembled using the naming convention. Metadata is also added to the document using the python-docx library, allowing metadata fields such as author, status, revision to be specified from the web frontend.

In this study, templates and data structures for project information requirements, asset information requirements, and exchange information requirements were produced. Full templates for these three documents were produced using key project data extracted from the contracts as a basis. Additional project data is entered into the database using flexible web forms.

5. Discussion and Conclusions

The first key objective of this study is to identify the key challenges faced within organisations and how technology could automatically produce the required documentation for ISO 19650 certification. The results of the surveys show that while organisations understand that they require information to comply with the required standard, they are unsure as to the method or suitable formats required to generate them. The organisations interviewed for this research were conducted over a period of 3 years for the Wales region within the UK. Although this may not be a representative picture of the whole of the UK, it shows that although BIM has been around for many years, there remain issues surrounding organisations' understanding of the BIM process and incomplete perception of BIM as a 3D modelling concept.

The development of a data schema which captures these high-level information requirements and transforms them into a machine and human readable format enables organisations to automatically comply with standards. The use of activity-based information requirements also allows generation of information requirements which can be linked together. This prevents organisations having from silos of unrelated information which make it more difficult to construct any required documents that potentially rely on related data.

In this study, a microservice-based architecture is proposed which addresses automated information requirements documentation authoring for ISO 19650 certification. Information extracted from contracts can be enriched with user supplied data using web forms. For JCT contracts, much of the data can be specified directly rather than extracted through markers, as many of the requirements are set out as static content. This approach allows organisations to produce consistent documentation, fulfilling requirements for ISO 19650 certification.

For the contract scanning microservice, the entire PDF is converted to raw text. Depending on the particular use-case there is scope to modify the algorithm to only extract the portions of text which are required on demand. If the required data is very sparsely arranged in the source PDF file, this approach may be more efficient. Use of optical character recognition (OCR) could also potentially improve the framework, allowing for extraction of scanned documents using pure OCR (Bast and Korzen, 2017), probabilistic methods (Hassan and Baumgartner, 2005), or through machine learning approaches (Budhiraja and Mago, 2020), with potential for including handwriting analysis (Baldominos, Saez and Isasi, 2018).

The framework set out for dynamically creating documentation is flexible due to its ability to be nested and recursive and to use filtering and cross referencing. This allows generation of documents from complex data structures. The output from the contract scanning microservice and the web frontend, and the required inputs for the document generation microservice are compatible in structure. These structures can readily be expanded for different use-cases, as the system itself is designed without hard-coding any data structures.

This study also demonstrates the implementation of a containerised microservice-based architecture for BIM complementary services. As the construction industry moves towards stage 3 BIM, web-based services will become more essential. The containerised system used in this study is relatively straight forward to deploy on any operating system, and the system can theoretically be scaled for use in small or large organisations. For large-scale production environments, consideration needs to be made for high levels of traffic. When accessing resources which take time to produce, for example conversion of PDF files to text data, it would be necessary to use message brokering to route all requests through. Systems such as RabbitMQ or Redis can be used to handle queued requests. Cluster orchestration can also be used to scale up the performance and availability of web-based services. Further work in this project will assess in more detail the suitability for utilising container-based systems for use in industry.

References

Abdirad, H. and Dossick, C. S. (2020) 'Rebaselining Asset Data for Existing Facilities and Infrastructure', Journal of Computing in Civil Engineering, 34(1). doi: 10.1061/(ASCE)CP.1943-5487.0000868.

Baldominos, A., Saez, Y. and Isasi, P. (2018) 'Evolutionary convolutional neural networks: An application to handwriting recognition', Neurocomputing, 283, pp. 38–52. doi: 10.1016/j.neucom.2017.12.049.

Bast, H. and Korzen, C. (2017) 'A Benchmark and Evaluation for Text Extraction from PDF', in Proceedings of the ACM/IEEE Joint Conference on Digital Libraries. Institute of Electrical and Electronics Engineers Inc. doi: 10.1109/JCDL.2017.7991564.

Budhiraja, S. S. and Mago, V. (2020) 'A supervised learning approach for heading detection', Expert Systems, 37(4), p. e12520. doi: 10.1111/exsy.12520.

Canny, S. (2013) 'python-docx'. Available at: https://github.com/python-openxml/python-docx (Accessed: 15 March 2021).

Chao, H. and Fan, J. (2004) 'Layout and Content Extraction for PDF Documents', in International Workshop on Document Analysis Systems. Springer, pp. 213–224.

Chung, M. T. et al. (2016) 'Using Docker in high performance computing applications', in 2016 IEEE 6th International Conference on Communications and Electronics, IEEE ICCE 2016. Institute of Electrical and Electronics Engineers Inc., pp. 52–57. doi: 10.1109/CCE.2016.7562612.

Fahad, M. and Bus, N. (2018) 'Conformance Checking of IFC Models via Semantic BIM Reasoner', in Proceedings of the 2018 European Group for Intelligent Computing in Engineering.

Ferguson, H., Vardeman, C. and Nabrzyski, J. (2016) 'Linked data platform for building cloud-based smart applications and connecting API access points with data discovery techniques', in Proceedings - 2016 IEEE International Conference on Big Data, Big Data 2016. Institute of Electrical and Electronics Engineers Inc., pp. 3016–3025. doi: 10.1109/BigData.2016.7840955.

Hassan, T. and Baumgartner, R. (2005) 'Intelligent text extraction from PDF documents', in Proceedings - International Conference on Computational Intelligence for Modelling, Control and Automation, CIMCA 2005 and International Conference on Intelligent Agents, Web Technologies and Internet, pp. 2–6. doi: 10.1109/cimca.2005.1631436.

Heaton, J., Parlikad, A. K. and Schooling, J. (2019) 'A Building Information Modelling approach to the alignment of organisational objectives to Asset Information Requirements', Automation in Construction, 104, pp. 14–26. doi: 10.1016/j.autcon.2019.03.022.

ISO (2016) Building information models — Information delivery manual — Part 1: Methodology and format.

ISO (2018a) ISO 19650-1:2018 - Organization and digitization of information about buildings and civil engineering works, including building information modelling (BIM) — Information management using building information modelling — Part 1: Concepts and principles.

ISO (2018b) ISO 19650-2:2018 - Organization and digitization of information about buildings and civil engineering works, including building information modelling (BIM) — Information management using building information modelling — Part 2: Delivery phase of the asset.

ISO (2018c) ISO 19650-3:2020 - Organization and digitization of information about buildings and civil engineering works , including building information modelling (BIM) — Information management using building information modelling — Part 3: Operational phase of the, Bs En Iso 19650-1:2018.

ISO (2020) ISO 19650-5:2020 Organization and digitization of information about buildings and civil engineering works, including building information modelling (BIM) — Information management using building information modelling — Part 5: Security-minded approach to i.

jsonform (2020) 'JSON Form'. Available at: https://github.com/jsonform/jsonform (Accessed: 17 March 2021).

Kang, K., Lin, J. and Zhang, J. (2018) 'BIM- and IoT-based monitoring framework for building performance management', Journal of Structural Integrity and Maintenance, 3(4), pp. 254–261. doi: 10.1080/24705314.2018.1536318.

Lapouyade, E. (2019) 'python-docx-template'. Available at: https://github.com/elapouya/python-docx-template (Accessed: 15 March 2021).

Nuno, A. and St. John, F. A. V. (2014) 'How to ask sensitive questions in conservation: A review of specialized questioning techniques', Biological Conservation, 189, pp. 5–15. doi: 10.1016/j.biocon.2014.09.047.

QSR International (2020) 'NVivo'.

Ramakrishnan, C. et al. (2012) 'Layout-aware text extraction from full-text PDF of scientific articles', Source Code for Biology and Medicine, 7(1), pp. 1–10. Available at: http://code.google.com/p/lapdftext/. (Accessed: 12 March 2021).

Royal Institute of British Architects (2020) RIBA Plan of Work 2020 Overview. Available at: www.ribaplanofwork.com (Accessed: 15 March 2021).

Graph-based version control for asynchronous BIM level 3 collaboration

Sebastian Esser, Simon Vilgertshofer, André Borrmann
Technical University of Munich, Germany
sebastian.esser@tum.de

Abstract. Collaboration and communication are two essential aspects of Building Information Modeling (BIM). Current standards such as ISO 19650 take this into account by propagating the concept of federated domain models based on file-based information containers (BIM level 2). In consequence, complete models are transmitted every time a new version is shared with the collaborators. As changes in domain models cannot be tracked for individual objects, but for whole files only, high effort for the subsequent coordination across the domains is created. These limitations can be overcome by implementing modern approaches of digital collaboration based on object-level synchronization, as denoted as BIM level 3. To provide a methodological basis, this paper proposes to represent the object-networks of BIM models as formal graphs and describing changes in the model as graph transformations. Consequently, modifications can be transmitted as patches using the graph formalisms, which are to be integrated and interpreted on the receiving side, thus achieving object-level synchronization. The paper discusses in detail the graph-based representation and the implementation of the necessary graph comparison algorithms.

1. Introduction

Collaboration in projects of any size gain increasing importance in the AEC industry. Data exchange across experts of different domains and roles is one of the key aspects of Building Information Modeling (BIM). The degree of support for vendor-neutral data exchange formats by BIM-based software applications has increased during the past years and eases data handover between stakeholders.

Current practice for model-based collaboration, reflected by international standards such as ISO 19650, relies on the concept of federating disciplinary models in a common data environment (CDE) based on so-called information containers. As these information containers are basically a collection of files, the currently implemented mechanisms for model-based collaboration rely on mere file management, where files are the smallest manageable information unit (Preidel *et al.*, 2018).

In consequence, the complete domain model is transferred as monolithic file, each time a new version is made available. While these updates are very frequent during the collaborative design phase, it requires the manual identification of design changes by all other stakeholders. At the same time, the ratio between modified objects and the total number of objects in an updated model is often rather small. Therefore, providing the entire modified model is inefficient if other project participants have already received, understood, and integrated the foreign but outdated model version in their respective software environments.

To overcome the described limitations, improved techniques are required to enable the versioning of BIM models. This versioning includes identifying updates in models and transmitting solely the update information instead of the entire models. The communication between project participants is consequently realized by update patches that represent the update procedure. To this end, a specific focus is put on possible mechanisms to detect changes and integrate update patches in the receiving application.

1.1 Outline

The paper introduces a novel approach that extends file-based collaboration to object-based collaboration using patch-based update mechanisms based on graph formalisms. The entire communication process can be split into three major parts: (i) the update identification, (ii) the patch formulation and distribution, and (iii) the patch integration on the receiver side. The information provided by (disciplinary) BIM models is represented by graph structures, which provide a well-established formalism in data science.

1.2 Preliminary Remarks

The term "model" is broadly used with widely diverging semantics in research and practice and can refer to various structures. The Meta Object Facility (MOF) specifications standardized by the Object Management Group (OMG) distinguish between instance data (M0), data model (M1), meta model (M2) and meta meta model (M3) (Object Management Group, 2019).

By contrast, in the BIM domain the term *model* often refers to the population of instance data. In the context of this paper, we accordingly use the term *BIM model* or *domain model* in the sense of MOF level M0. In addition, the underlying structure, which abstracts the given real-world problem from a certain perspective, is defined as data model or schema specification. The abstraction of a data model in its generic items like datatypes and relationships is defined in a meta model.

2. Background and related work

The increasing growth of digital technologies in the AEC sector has provided industry with opportunities to improve its productivity and operations. A central aspect is the improved communication and collaboration among contractors, coordinators, architects, and engineers. This is accompanied by the need to provide various structures for the transmission of information.

Versioning of structured data representations raises awareness in many industry branches for a long time now. Specifically, in the field of software development, various methods, protocols, and systems exist that enable distributed version control of text files. Prominent examples are Subversion, Mercurial and Git among others. In most approaches, a central database stores the global history of change events, integrates incoming modifications ("commit and push") and allows a user to clone the entire history with all incremental changes to his local machine. Therefore, each user can read and understand the entire history, create, and test modifications locally. If changes are ready to share with others, the user synchronizes his local state with the central database again. The chain of update messages forms the entire history of the project. Incoming updates can be integrated automatically if they do not create any conflicts with existing or concurrent local changes. Only in case of conflicts, the user needs to resolve them and choose the desired content manually (Blischak, Davenport and Wilson, 2016). In the context of this paper, we take inspiration from these version control systems but do not apply their principles on text files, but on graphs.

Existing versioning services use a line-based data comparison and track text lines that have been added, deleted, or modified. Data models used in the AEC-Sector, however, describe complex and highly interconnected information structures that cannot be versioned by a pure text-based approach. For example, the order of entities might be completely different in two versions of a STEP physical file (SPF), regardless that the exact same information content is provided in both versions. Despite these limitations, text-based serialisations of data models are highly used to transfer BIM data in file-based handover scenarios. Looking into current practice in AEC projects, collaboration is mainly realized by means of file-based data exchange (BIM Level 2 according to ISO°19650). Actors from various domains work together using a central database, which is denoted as Common Data Environment (CDE) (DIN, 2019). CDEs help to share and coordinate domain models among involved actors. However, these platforms do not yet offer tools to realize object-level collaboration (BIM level 3).

To overcome the lack of applying object-level versioning in AEC projects, a clear understanding of common principles is necessary, which are used to define data exchange structures. Data models help to describe knowledge of a specific domain and can target various use cases (Turk, 2001). The data model itself is formulated in a schema definition, which defines a skeleton for the piece of information that needs to be exchanged. These skeletons follow mainly the principles of object-oriented programming paradigms. A class defines the frame (i.e., blueprint) on how an information gets stored using attributes and associations. Attributes have a name and a datatype. Associations point to other classes. Furthermore, a class can have one or many relationships to other classes. An instance of a class (an object) fills the given structure with specific values to describe the actual information the user wants to store and exchange. The associations between the instances result in an in-memory graph-like structure, also denoted as object network.

To exchange data stored in such in-memory class instances, an export module serializes the structured information into a file-based representation. These files are often in the ANSI-format and can span several thousands of text lines even for a relatively small scenario. As the term *serialization* implies, a sequential ordering of information is introduced even if the object network does not provide any kind of order. Therefore, text-based versioning systems will fail to correctly identify the modification in the underlying object graph, leading for example to the erroneous detection of massive changes for identical models when the serialization order is changed. Therefore, there is a need to improve the modification detection, which can reflect class instances and their relationships better than in a pure text-based versioning. Principles of graphs and graph transformation appear to be a promising approach to overcome the presented limitations. Graphs are a well-established concept to describe sets of nodes and their relationships among each other.

The application of graph-based systems for information management is not a novel approach in software applications. Many approaches in this field use the term *Graph Data Models* (GDM), which got introduced by Hidders (2001). The essential idea is that each class instance is represented as a node in a graph. Attributes are attached to a node whereas references or associations are represented by edges. Furthermore, graph structures and graph synthesis were successfully applied for information synthesis in other industries (Helms and Shea, 2012).

In the context of model analysis, several publications have investigated the application of graph analysis in recent years. Both, Tauscher, Bargstädt and Smarsly, (2016) and Ismail *et al.*, (2018) have explored graph-based representations of BIM models to navigate and query the object structure. Even though applying graph systems has been applied for various use cases, none of them tackle the problem of versioning model contents in a generic manner. Several established BIM applications expose methods to compare two IFC models (BIM Vision, 2021). These implementations, however, often base on suitable assumptions such as remaining GUIDs through the model versions, but do not capture any possible modification type applied to a model revision.

Shi *et al.* (2018) have proposed an approach that allows detecting differences between two IFC models based on a similarity metric. Their system runs a normalization on all instances stored in the model first and calculates a similarity score afterwards using a recursive depth-first search. A downside, however, is that the resulting similarity rate is presented a mere scalar value. Such score does not expose any kind of understanding of the actual change applied to the model.

3. Proposed framework and approach

The conducted literature has proven the need for versioning systems, explicitly targeting highly structured object-oriented data described according to schema specifications. As largely data models (formats) are currently used for vendor-neutral data exchange in AEC projects, the proposed concept is schema-independent, i.e., it supports diverse schemas if they follow a given set of boundary conditions. Simultaneously, it is not intended to create an entirely new data model that suits any possible use case but rather to keep the structures of existing and well-established standards. This approach acknowledges the development of exchange standards like the Industry Foundation Classes (IFC), RailML, and many others. We address the issue of version control in a generic manner by defining a generic graph meta model. Figure 1 denotes the overall data flow.

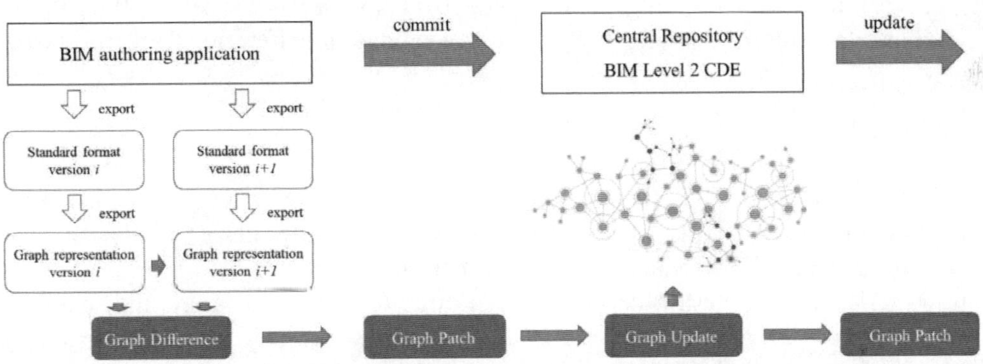

Figure 1: Basic concept of graph-based version control for distributed collaborative BIM development

The use of graph structures appears to be a promising approach. As graph-based representations reflect relationships among objects, we can apply graph theory as profound formalism to analyse a given object network's topological structure. Furthermore, modern graph database systems offer a large range of methods, which help to search, compare, and analyse subsets of the stored information. This is of special interest for the proposed approach as it introduces a large flexibility to handle various data representations and implement generic functionality that can be applied to any kind of versioned data.

3.1 Proposed framework

Due to the wide range of data specifications used in AEC projects, a central aspect of the proposed system is the definition of a meta-structure that is capable of both, reflecting the specific information stored in an instance model and mapping class definitions and relationships onto a generic graph structure. The identification of differences between two versions of a domain model is subsequently based on this graph representation populated with data by the user. The calculation results in a schema independent *DiffResult*, which defines the base for an update patch. The following paragraphs discuss the chosen graph model and present an algorithmic approach to compare two graph-based representations of a domain model.

3.2 Graph characteristics and generation

To ensure applicability for a wide range of schema specifications, a generic graph meta model is introduced. In general, a graph consists of nodes and edges. Nodes and edge can carry additional weights (i.e., attributes in the form of key-value pairs). Furthermore, each node gets one or many labels attached, which help to identify and query a specific set of nodes. Edges can be undirected or directed (Robinson, Webber and Eifrem, 2015). A graph where vertices are associated with attributes is denoted as node attributed graph or property graph. In addition, nodes can be typed leading to a typed attributed graph (Ehrig, Prange and Taentzer, 2004).

The ability to assign attributes as key value pairs to a node matches with the object-oriented paradigm of information modelling (ISO, 1999). Accordingly, we define that each node in the graph represents one class instance. All attributes of a class are attached to the node whereas associations to another class instance are modelled with an edge to represent the relationship among both class instances.

To suit the need of a schema-independent approach, a graph meta model defines a set of rules on how a given object network of an instance model is transferred in the corresponding graph. In the scope of the current paper, we define specific kinds of node labels and formalisms on how aspects of the corresponding schema specification are considered. We use the term *instance graph* to refer to specific type of graph whose specifications are provided in this section.

Node definition

Our graph meta model defines three types of nodes: *primary nodes*, *secondary nodes*, and *connection nodes*. Most schema definitions have an abstract root class that defines a *Globally unique identifier (GUID)* attribute. Due to the inheritance mechanism, all subclasses of such a root class inherit the GUID attribute as well. All other class instances, i.e. instances of classes that does not have a GUID attribute, are represented by secondary nodes in the graph. In the IFC data model for example, classes of the resource layer representing geometry, topology, material etc. do not carry a GUID. They cannot exist independently but can only exist if referenced (directly or indirectly) by one or more entities deriving from IfcRoot. The third type of nodes are denoted as connection nodes. These nodes represent the concept of objectified relationships, which is intensively used by the IFC schema specification. They provide the ability to model one-to-many relationships between class instances and assign attributes to the relationship. Similar to primary nodes, connection nodes carry a unique identifier specified by the schema specification.

Applying these mapping principles exemplary to the IFC schema, ISO 10303 is used to define the mapping of all IFC classes to the node types. ISO 10303-11 defines an entity as "*a class of information defined by common properties*" whereas an entity instance is classified by *"a named unit or data which represents a unit of information within the class defined by an entity"* (ISO, 2004). All IFC classes are either derived from IfcRoot (i.e., have a GUID) or are contained in the resource layer. All classes listed in the resource layer are reflected as secondary nodes. Subtypes of *IfcRelationships* are mapped to connection nodes.

The notion of primary, secondary and connection node will be used to define the equality of two instance graphs and helps to find an efficient implementation of the difference calculation. The detected differences in turn can be interpreted as applied modifications to the object network.

Edge definition

An edge connects two nodes of a graph. Edges can carry an edge weight, which appears as a set of key-value attributes. We use edges to model the associations between objects in an domain model. Each edge has an attribute *relType*, which indicates the association attribute between to class instances.

Graph implementation

Figure 2 depicts a simplified scenario of two classes described in the EXPRESS modelling language (ISO, 2004). The schema definition in the upper left corner defines two entities (i.e. classes without methods). The entity *point* has three attributes with an atomic datatype REAL. The *line* has one atomic attribute "Name" and two complex attributes, which reference the instances of a *Point* entity. A possible instantiation of the given data schema is given in the upper right corner, where one instance of the *Line* entity and two instances of the *Point* entity are filled with individual attribute values.

The mapping into the graph structure follows the rules explained above: Each class instance is represented by an individual node. All attributes are directly attached to the desired node whereas associations between two class instances are modelled as directed graph edges. Each edge carries the attribute name from the parent class, from where the association was initialized. The *Line* instance has a *StartPoint* and an *EndPoint* attribute (in UML/MOF an association to another class), which is reflected by the edges depicted in the graph structure. The class instance of *ShapeElement* is handled as a primary node as it owns a GUID attribute.

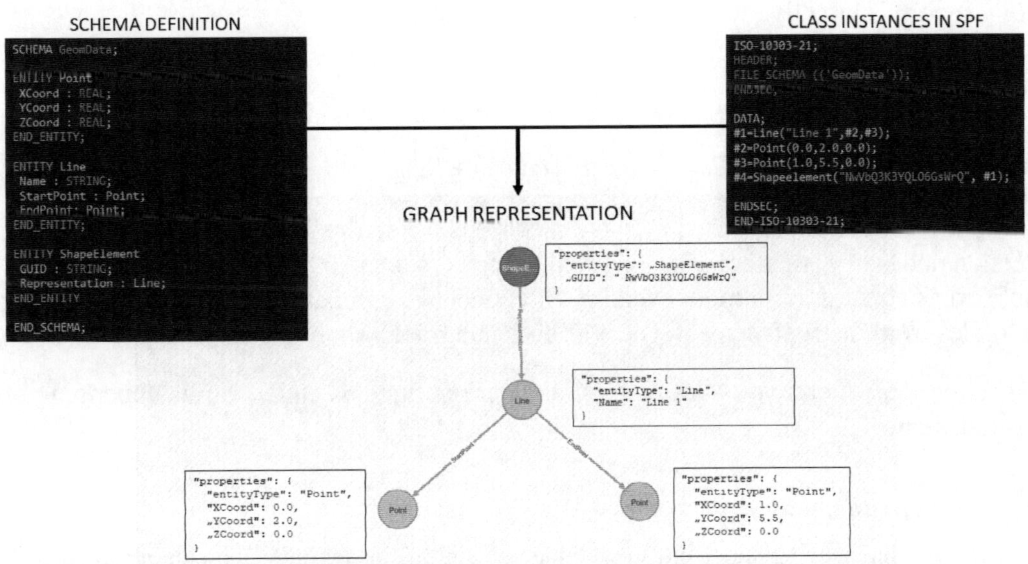

Figure 2: Correlation between schema specification, instance model, and resulting graph structure. The value stated on each edge is the value of the *relType* attribute attached to each edge.

4. Graph-based difference and update calculation

To extract the applied modification between two instance model versions, the generated graph representations of both versions are compared. Possible modifications are adding new class instances, deleting existing instances or changing associations between two instances. Also combinations of add/delete/modify can occur when comparing the object graphs.

From a mathematical point of view, the problem statement for calculating the modifications between two model versions can be defined as the following. The definition of functions follows the notation used by Kriege and Mutzel, (2012).

We denote two graphs $G_{V1} = (N_{V1}, E_{V1})$ and $G_{V2} = (N_{V2}, E_{V2})$ representing two instance model versions 1 and 2. Both are directed, labelled property graphs, where N defines the set of nodes and E the set of edges. Both, nodes, and edges, carry a weight that represents a set of key-value attributes for an individual node or edge, respectively:

$$\mathrm{W(u)}\ \forall\ \mathrm{u} \in \mathrm{N} \tag{1}$$

In addition, we define the node types using labels:

$$l_{type} \in \{\text{primaryNode, secondaryNode, connectionNode}\} \tag{2}$$

Furthermore, an essential feature of property graphs is the flexibility to handle non-distinct node and edge sets. Accordingly, a node with a specific weight (i.e., set of attributes) can occur multiple times in the node set (Robinson, Webber and Eifrem, 2015).

The function L attaches the suitable label to a particular node.

We define a directed edge from node u to r as:

$$(u, r) \in \mathrm{E} \tag{3}$$

The aim of the update computation is to find subgraph isomorphisms between the two graphs G_{V1}, G_{V2} such as a bijective function φ can be defined:

$$\varphi: N_{V1} \rightarrow N_{V2} \tag{4}$$

This bijective function φ preserves adjacencies between two nodes:

$$\forall u, v \in N_{V1}: (u, v) \in E_{V1} \Leftrightarrow \big(\varphi(u), \varphi(v)\big) \in E_{V2} \tag{5}$$

The overall computation is spitted in two major steps. First, the structure of primary nodes and connection nodes of both graphs is compared, which results in a list of primary node tuples that are defined as equal in both model versions. Second, we compare the subgraphs of each node in the tuples from the first step and check if both subgraphs share the same information logic.

The criterion, on which two nodes or subgraphs are defined as equal, varies depending on the calculation step.

4.1 Matching primary node structures

To analyse the base skeleton of both model versions, all nodes labelled as primary nodes are retrieved from the graphs G_{V1} and G_{V2}. This operation results in two nodes sets $N_{V1,primary}$ and $N_{V2,primary}$.

Taking the weight of nodes and thereby their attributes into account, we calculate the relational intersection of both sets and declare the result as $N_{primary,unchanged}$:

$$N_{primary,unchanged} = N_{V1,primary} \cap N_{V2,primary} \tag{6}$$

All nodes in the set $N_{primary,unchanged}$ are present in both, N_{V1} and N_{V2}. Thus, no modification has been applied to the node and their attached attributes.

The relational difference between $N_{primary,unchanged}$ and $N_{V1,primary}$ results in a set of primary nodes, which are included in G_{V1}, but not in G_{V2}. Thus, the result represents a DELETE modification from version 1 to version 2:

$$N_{primary,deleted} = N_{V1,primary} - N_{primary,unchanged} \quad (7)$$

The same principle applies for nodes, which are contained in G_{V2} but not in G_{V1}, which are the result of an ADD modification from version 1 to version 2:

$$N_{primary,added} = N_{V2,primary} - N_{primary,unchanged} \quad (8)$$

Connection nodes are used to implement one-to-many relationships between primary nodes. Each connection node has directed edges, which point to primary nodes. Therefore, the aim is the analysis of the subgraph structure defined by the sets of primary nodes, connection nodes, and all corresponding edges connecting nodes of these two sets.

Therefore, we calculate the adjacency matrices of the node sets $N_{V1,primary}$, $N_{V2,primary}$, $N_{V1,con}$, $N_{V2,con}$. As we want to overcome limitations introduced by a hierarchical ordering in serialization processes, we use either the GUIDs or a calculated hashsum of each node to sort the adjacency matrix. If a relationship in both adjacency matrices is successfully identified, the corresponding *relType* attribute is checked to ensure that the detected relationship between two nodes still represents the same association.

4.2 Matching of component structures

The analysis defined in section 4.1 results in a set of unchanged primary nodes $N_{primary,unchanged}$, which is a subset of both, $N_{V1,primary}$ and $N_{V2,primary}$. As the second step, we need to analyse the subgraph structure, which is introduced by associations between a primary node and a set of secondary nodes. As depicted in Figure 2, a primary node has one or many outgoing edges pointing to secondary nodes to implement associations. Furthermore, a secondary node can have one or many outgoing edges referencing other secondary nodes. Thus, the aim of this step is the calculation of *property* modifications applied to a secondary node (i.e., adding/deleting/modifying node attributes). In addition, the network structure among secondary nodes can be modified as well, which is captured as a *structure* modification.

We define a *component* as a subgraph of the entire graph G:

$$G_{component} \subseteq G \quad (9)$$

Each component subgraph has exactly one primary node u and a set of secondary nodes $q \in N_{secondary}$, which all have a directed path P from u to a particular node q. Thus, the path P is defined by an ordered set of edges:

$$P \subseteq E = \{e_1, \dots, e_n\} \text{ connecting } u \rightarrow q \mid u \in N_{primary}, q \in N_{secondary} \quad (10)$$

To gain knowledge of structure and property modifications, the calculation is divided in several sub-steps.

First, all edges K_{V1}, K_{V2} are queried from G_{V1} and G_{V2}:

$$K_{V1} = \{(u, C(u))\} \mid (u, C(u)) \in E_{V1} \quad (11)$$

$$K_{V2} = \{(v, C(v))\} \mid (v, C(v)) \in E_{V2} \quad (12)$$

We define two edges $k_{V1} \in K_{V1}$ and $k_{V2} \in K_{V2}$ as equivalent if both carry the same value in their *relType* attribute, thus, implementing the same association between two class instances (nodes):

$$b = \begin{cases} true, \ if \ (u, C(u))_{relType} == (v, C(v))_{relType} \\ false, otherwise \end{cases} \quad (13)$$

Next, we take the nodes $q = C(u)$ and $r = C(v)$, which two equivalent edges k_{V1} and k_{V2} point towards (i.e., implement the same association), and compare the node attributes of node u against the node attributes of v. The attribute comparison detects possible property modifications and, thus, finds recently added, deleted, or modified attributes.

If an edge $k_{V1} \in K_{V1}$ exists, which has no counterpart in K_{V2}, we detect a structure modification as k_{V1} got deleted from version 1 to version 2. If an edge k_{V2} is only present in K_{V2}, but no correlation in K_{V1} can be found, we handle a structure modification of type *add* from version 1 to version 2.

To analyse the entire component (i.e., subgraph) structure, we recursively repeat the process denoted in eq. 16 and 17 with the current nodes $C(u)$ and $C(v)$. The recursion limit is reached if a node has no outgoing edges anymore (leaf node).

5. Result and discussion

The presented approach overcomes the limitations of pure file-based versioning systems by introducing a graph-based representation of instance models and their comparison by computing the graph difference. The proposed criteria on which two nodes are defined to be equal enables the user to detect not only structural modifications such as added or deleted nodes but also to find modified attribute values.

The proposed concept was tested with IFC-based instance models from various BIM authoring tools and has shown promising results. Particularly challenging, however, are complex scenarios where the attribute value is composed of nested lists. A critical example is the IFC entity *CartesianPointList3D* (ISO, 2019):

```
ENTITY IfcCartesianPointList3D
 SUBTYPE OF (IfcCartesianPointList);
  CoordList : LIST [1:?] OF LIST [3:3] OF IfcLengthMeasure;
END_ENTITY;
```

Similar discussions have appeared in the scope of ontology representations (Pauwels *et al.*, 2015). Despite these issues, the tested prototype exposes sufficient results, which provide the base for a patch-based collaboration system.

6. Conclusion and outlook

As wide range of software applications already provide export and import interfaces to exchange BIM models on a file basis, improved techniques are required to version models on a component basis. The proposed system overcomes current limitations of a file-based data exchange by abstracting the given information in a domain model into a graph-based representation. By analyzing the topological structure and the attribute data, we can identify the applied modification between two versions by means of graph analysis. On this basis, we will develop a patch-based update system, which is capable to replace the file-based data exchange and overcomes its limitations. As a subsequent step, the formulation of update patches will the next essential development including conflict management concepts. Furthermore, we envision not only an update transfer within a single data specification but also hope to integrate update patches between several schema specifications. Such scenarios must be handled to ensure the consistency of the resulting overall project information.

References

BIM Vision (2021) 'Module: Compare'.

Blischak, J. D., Davenport, E. R. and Wilson, G. (2016) 'A Quick Introduction to Version Control with Git and GitHub', PLoS Computational Biology, 12(1), pp. 1–18. doi: 10.1371/journal.pcbi.1004668.

DIN (2019) DIN SPEC 91391-2: Gemeinsame Datenumgebungen (CDE) für BIM-Projekte – Funktionen und offener Datenaustausch zwischen Plattformen unterschiedlicher Hersteller – Teil 2: Offener Datenaustausch mit Gemeinsamen Datenumgebungen Common. Deutschland.

Ehrig, H., Prange, U. and Taentzer, G. (2004) 'Fundamental theory for typed attributed graph transformation', Lecture Notes in Computer Science (including subseries Lecture Notes in Artificial Intelligence and Lecture Notes in Bioinformatics), 3256(April), pp. 161–177. doi: 10.1007/978-3-540-30203-2_13.

Helms, B. and Shea, K. (2012) 'Computational synthesis of product architectures based on object-oriented graph grammars', Journal of Mechanical Design, Transactions of the ASME, 134(2). doi: 10.1115/1.4005592.

Hidders, J. (2001) A Graph-based Update Language for Object-Oriented Data Models. University Press Facilities, Eindhoven, the Netherlands. doi: 10.6100/IR551259.

Ismail, A., Strug, B. and Ślusarczyk, G. (2018) 'Building Knowledge Extraction from BIM/IFC Data for Analysis in Graph Databases', in Rutkowski, L. et al. (eds) Lecture Notes in Computer Science (including subseries Lecture Notes in Artificial Intelligence and Lecture Notes in Bioinformatics). Cham: Springer International Publishing, pp. 652–664. doi: 10.1007/978-3-319-91262-2_57.

ISO (1999) ISO/IEC 2382-15.

ISO (2004) ISO 10303-11:2004: Industrial automation systems and integration - Product data representation and exchange - Part 21: Implementation methods: Clear text encoding of the exchange structure (ISO 10303-11:1994). Available at: https://www.iso.org/standard/38047.html.

ISO (2019) DIN EN ISO 16739-1: Industry Foundation Classes (IFC) für den Datenaustausch in der Bauwirtschaft und im Anlagenmanagement – Teil 1: Datenschema (ISO 16739-1:2018).

Kriege, N. and Mutzel, P. (2012) 'Subgraph matching kernels for attributed graphs', Proceedings of the 29th International Conference on Machine Learning, ICML 2012, 2, pp. 1015–1022.

Object Management Group (2019) 'OMG Meta Object Facility (MOF) Core Specification', Https://Www.Omg.Org/. Available at: https://www.omg.org/spec/MOF/About-MOF/.

Pauwels, P. et al. (2015) 'Coping with lists in the ifcOWL ontology', EG-ICE 2015 - 22nd Workshop of the European Group of Intelligent Computing in Engineering.

Preidel, C. et al. (2018) 'Common Data Environment', in Building Information Modeling. Cham: Springer International Publishing, pp. 279–291. doi: 10.1007/978-3-319-92862-3_15.

Robinson, I., Webber, J. and Eifrem, E. (2015) Graph Databases, Joe Celko's Complete Guide to NoSQL. Edited by M. Beaugureau. O'Reilly Media, Inc., 1005 Gravenstein Highway North, Sebastopol, CA 95472. doi: 10.1016/b978-0-12-407192-6.00003-0.

Shi, X. et al. (2018) 'IFCdiff: A content-based automatic comparison approach for IFC files', Automation in Construction, 86(June 2016), pp. 53–68. doi: 10.1016/j.autcon.2017.10.013.

Tauscher, E., Bargstädt, H.-J. and Smarsly, K. (2016) 'Generic BIM queries based on the IFC object model using graph theory', in Proceedings of the 16th International Conference on Computing in Civil and Building Engineering. Osaka.

Turk, Ž. (2001) 'Phenomenologial foundations of conceptual product modelling in architecture, engineering and construction', Artificial Intelligence in Engineering, 15(2), pp. 83–92. doi: 10.1016/S0954-1810(01)00008-5.

Image-documentation of existing buildings using a server-based BIM Collaboration Format workflow

Oliver Schulz, Jakob Beetz
RWTH Aachen University, Germany
schulz@dc.rwth-aachen.de

Abstract. This research targets to evaluate the BIM collaboration format's (BCF) applicability in a server-based approach with the BCF API for the use case of existing buildings' image documentation and thus to link this process with the BIM methodology. Although the BCF API already has many functionalities needed for the image documentation of buildings, we have identified that the nested hierarchy of the current version of the API hinders the efficient retrieval of information. This is amplified because all the API filters only refer to one hierarchical level - that of the Topics - which leads to nested queries. We present a possible extension of the API that introduces new routes for Topics, Viewpoints, and Comments, which dissolves the resource hierarchization. Furthermore, we extend the API with the ability to spatialize and link heterogeneous documents and, therefore, apply the BCF principle not only to BIM models but also to 2D plans. Finally, we use the extension and implement it in a prototypical workflow. This consists of an AR application for capturing and spatializing the images, a BCF server for communicating the information, and a viewer used to query and display the collected data. Our research shows that BCF's structure is mostly suitable for documenting existing buildings, but querying this documentation efficiently is still a concern. However, the changes stated in this paper render a possible solution.

1. Introduction

The BIM Collaboration Format (BCF) (*BIM Collaboration Format (BCF)*, no date) is a field-proven method for interchanging issues in a BIM model and is used in the AEC industry. Moreover, the development of a server-based approach with an API (BCF-API) even more strengthens this process's usability.

By contrast, the image documentation of existing buildings is an example of a frequently used process in the AEC industry but is often decoupled from other processes. Images are created and stored on a cloud or the hard drive of a computer. They are often sorted by parameters such as the date of creation. However, sorting can usually only occur according to a single parameter and finding specific images in an extensive collection of data can prove very difficult. A similar finding was reported in (Czerniawski, Ma and Leite, 2020), focusing on facility management. Projects such as Monarch (Stenzer, Woller and Freitag, 2011) show a way to store data, such as images, in the building's context and have also taken the first steps in the direction of BIM. It is focused on historic building sites and requires mainly manual input of data.

This paper focuses on the early phase of documentation of existing buildings, which usually do not have a BIM model. Using the BCF format, we want to show how it can be used even before creating a BIM model to link the process of image documentation with the BIM methodology. This project originated from (Schulz and Beetz, 2019), where a similar attempt was made using a linked data connection. A similarity to the BCF principles of *Topics*, *Viewpoints*, and *Comments* was identified. This research aims to examine the BCF workflow's usability regarding image documentation and describe necessary extensions. It focuses on the possibilities of retrieving information from a BCF-server so that specific images can be quickly retrieved within the building by using different search parameters like author, dates, and the location of an image. By testing the BCF API with the image documentation, it should also be evaluated to what extent this API is suitable for other use cases aside from issue management.

We begin by introducing the process of building documentation and highlighting the core concept of the BCF format in Section 2 and explaining our extensions' necessity. Subsequently, in section 3, we describe how this concept has been applied and tested in a prototype. In section 4, we summarise the results of our work and conclude the research in section 5.

2. Concept

2.1 Building Documentation

The documentation of the current state of and issues inside a building is an integral part of the early work phases when dealing with existing buildings. However, it continues through all phases of a building life cycle. In addition to the traditional methods of building surveys, such as creating deformation-correct building drawings, more approaches exist, such as creating point clouds and models from photogrammetry. Nevertheless, these methods are often costly or time-intensive. A suitable method for documenting buildings and recording issues is still photography (Letellier, 2007). These photos are usually created with a specific intention. After they are sorted into the folder structures of a project, it is not always clear what precisely this intention was or where the photo is located in the building. Therefore, implementing data management for the documentation of the building is an important part (Bruno and Roncella, 2019) since without it, searching and finding specific information is a time-consuming process. By attaching parameters such as labels, dates, authors, and comments, both the accessibility and the transport of the intention of the images and documents can be improved. Usually, when dealing with an existing building, no BIM model is available. However, steps are undertaken, where the documentation is integrated into the BIM methodology, called HBIM, where the buildings are reconstructed using the BIM methodology (Murphy, McGovern and Pavia, 2009), and existing and newly created documents can be linked to the buildings or building elements (Bruno and Roncella, 2019).

2.2 The BIM Collaboration Format

The BIM Collaboration Format (BCF) was developed with the idea of interchanging issues in a BIM model with different project partners, using different software applications. (*BIM Collaboration Format (BCF)*, no date) The *Issues* created can then be assigned to a planner, who can comment or delegate them. The status of an *Issue* in a BCF can be changed so that these *Issues* can be tracked in the BIM workflow. This process is often used in issue management in BIM processes, where the models of the various disciplines are examined for collisions. Any collisions found are then added to *Issues* and assigned to the appropriate discipline. The status and the number of issues can then serve as an indicator for a BIM project's health.

The BCF format exists today in two different variants. On the one hand, there is the BCF XML[1] approach, where the information is written into XML files which are then exported to a ZIP container. Since this variant led to BCF files being sent from one planner to another via email or data storage, the file-based approach evolved into a server-based approach (van Berlo and Krijnen, 2014) the BCF API[2]. It builds on the principle of REpresentational State Transfer (REST) and HTTP Requests. This enables the exchange of BCF information via a server with which the applications can communicate, thus getting rid of the exchange via files.

---

[1] https://github.com/buildingSMART/BCF-XML
[2] https://github.com/buildingSMART/BCF-API

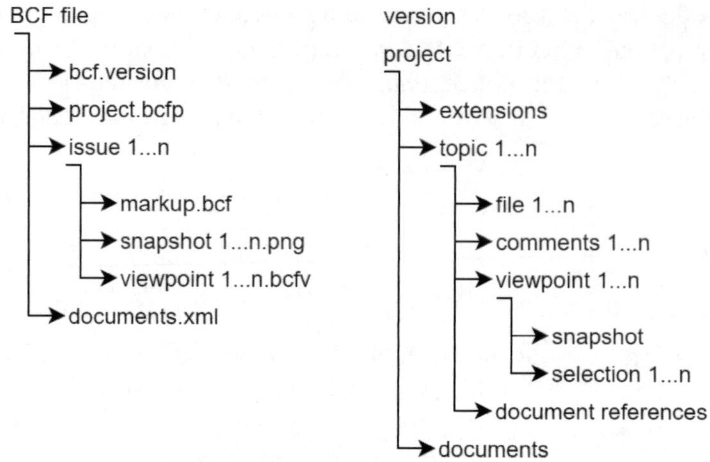

Figure 1: The XML version (left) is based on the concept of markups, which bring together the different resources, whereas the API (right) aggregates the different resources under the *Topics*.

The two formats' structure differs slightly from each other (Figure 1), but compatibility between the two formats is ensured. The essential elements of a BCF can be summarized as follows: An *Issue* consists of a *Topic*, which contains a status, an assignment, a label, and other basic information. Most of the fields must be filled with predefined properties, usually determined at the beginning of a project. Only the title and description are free text fields. A *Topic* occurs only once per *Issue*. The following elements are the *Comments*, which are filled with free text and assigned to an Issue as often as desired. The *Comments* enable a discussion between the project participants. The last main element of an *Issue* is the *Viewpoint*, which stores a position, the selected building elements, the type of camera (orthogonal or perspective), and a link to a screenshot of the *Issue*. The *Viewpoints* are used in conjunction with *Comments* and thus serve as the positioning and transfer of the images. They can also appear any number of times per *Issue*.

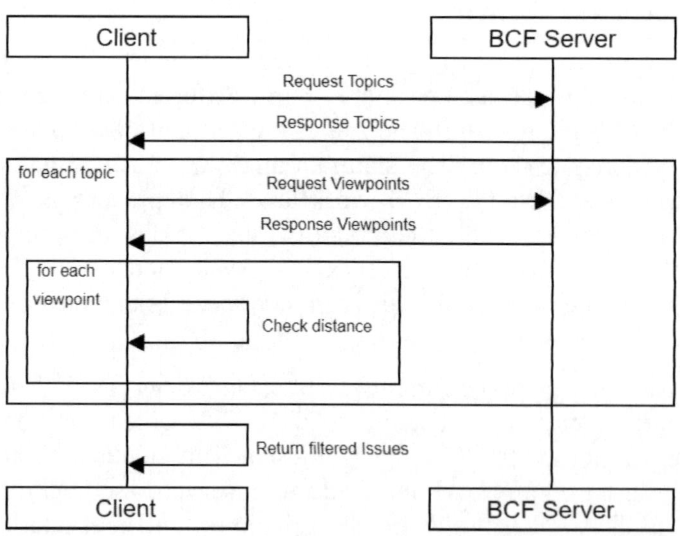

Figure 2: Schematic representation of a request for Viewpoints with a certain distance to a given point. Filtering, for example, for a reference to a building element would require one more request per Topic.

In the BCF XML format are the *Topics* and the *Comments* gathered in the *Markup* file and are referencing the *Viewpoints* and the *Snapshots*. The BCF API assigns the *Issues* to the projects.

First, a request can be made to the server for *Topics* after a certain filtering. For each of these *Topics*, the *Viewpoints*, the *Comments*, and the *Document References* can be requested. The *Viewpoints* are further subdivided and allow, for example, requests to the *Snapshot* and the *Selection*. Furthermore, basic functionality for *Topics* referencing *Documentens* exists in both variants.

The BCF API follows a hierarchical structure, of which *Topics* are identified as the central element. These are assigned to a project and must first be requested to access the data in the *Viewpoints*, *Comments*, and *Document References*. However, this concentration of data around the *Topic* causes an overhead of requests to the server as soon as large numbers of *Issues* are requested. This effect is even intensified if issues are searched for parameters specified in the *Viewpoint* or the *Comment*.

Filtering *Viewpoints* by distance can be used as an example: Frist, all *Topics* must be retrieved from the server. Then, the client requests each *Topic's Viewpoint* to examine if the corresponding *Viewpoint* fulfills the desired distance condition. (Figure 2)

Querying the server, it is unclear how many requests and responses have to be communicated between the server and the client. It should be noted that each request and response between client and server delays the time to process the operation. The event sending an unknown amount of requests is often regarded as the "N + 1 problem" (Ploesser, 2019) and is a known issue when working with REST APIs.

When it comes to the BCF format, the collection of information (a *Topic*, *Viewpoints*, and *Comments*) is often regarded as an *Issue*. Nevertheless, the general structure of the BCF makes it possible to think of other uses than just issue management. BuildingSMART states that the format is intended to exchange information in BIM models (*BIM Collaboration Format (BCF)*, no date). However, the principle can also be applied to non-BIM 3D models, 2D plans, or even actual buildings since it is based on the principle of positioning in a three dimensional cartesian coordinate system.

2.3 Extension of the BCF API

Since BCF already provides many requirements for building documentation and few additions are enough to achieve the objective, we decided to create a BCF server, based on the BCF API, with extended functionalities. The additions are described in the following paragraphs.

Flattening hierarchy of the API: Additional routes have been added for the *Viewpoints*, *Comments*, and *Document References*, which can thus be retrieved from the server independently of the related *Topic* by getting rid of first requesting the *Topic*. (Listing 1) The server then responses with a collection of the respective requested resource.

```
GET /bcf/{version}/projects/{project_id}/viewpoints

GET /bcf/{version}/projects/{project_id}/comments

GET /bcf/{version}/projects/{project_id}/document_references
```

Listing 1: Newly added routes to the BCF API

Furthermore, the *Topic's* Id is added to the *Viewpoints* structure so that the *Viewpoint* always contains a reference to its *Topic*. The assignment is added to the existing JSON schema. Thereby it is possible to reassemble the requested information locally.

Spatial representation of Documents: The existing system for the documents on the BCF server is extended so that the plans can be uploaded to the BCF server and assigned a position, scale, and rotation in the virtual 3D space. This makes it possible to spatially overlay 2D plans with 3D building models and utilize the accumulated information in both building representations. The structure for the extension is exemplified in JSON format in (Listing 2).

```
{
  "documentId": "d5e29473-f414-49df-a255-960d16c8d096",   "alignment": "center",
  "location": {
     "X": 2500,
     "Y": -980,
     "Z": -0.04
  },
  "rotation": {
     "X": 0,
     "Y": 0,
     "Z": 0
  },
  "scale": {
     "X": 0.199637,
     "Y": 0.199637,
     "Z": 0.199637
  }
}
```

Listing 2: Example of a JSON response for the *Spatial Representation* route.

Getting and updating the plans' position is set up under the route presented in (Listing 3).

```
GET /PUT
/bcf/{version}/projects/{project_id}/documents/{document_Id}/spatial_representation
```

Listing 3: A newly added route for the spatial representation of a *Document* in 3D space

The necessity to update the *Spatial Representation* arises from the case that during the process of documenting an existing building, typically, no 3D models are available. However, later on, it is necessary to adjust the plan's positioning to ensure a spatial overlay. The same applies to the *Viewpoints*, which cannot be updated according to the API's current version. Therefore, a corresponding route has been added here as well (Listing 4).

```
PUT /bcf/{version}/projects/{project_id}/viewpoints/{viewpoint_Id}
```

Listing 4: Adding a PUT route for *Viewpoints* for synchronizing the position with a BIM Model

This route allows the *Viewpoints* to be adjusted in their *Spatial Representation* after the 2D plan – on the basis of which the *Snapshots* were created – has been moved. Otherwise, the

Viewpoints would continue to exist at their original position and would no longer be valid for neither the 2D plan nor the 3D model.

By implementing these changes to the BCF API structure, the number of requests and responses is constant at three or four if the document references are requested. This contrasts with the unknown number of requests when trying to achieve the same result with the current version of the BCF API.

3. Implementation and testing of the BCF extension

For this research of documenting an existing building, an extended BCF API was created, and the rooms of the department of Design Computation at the RWTH Aachen are used as an example for testing the functionality. In the following sections, we will describe the required parts of this project and how they are interconnected.

3.1 BCF Server

The BCF Server operates as the central element for this project, handling the communication between the different applications. It builds on buildingSMART's BCF API and is based on Node.js with an Express module and a MongoDB database. Both the BCF server and the documentation of the extended API can be retrieved from the GitHub repository[3].

3.2 Augmented reality application

The mobile phone application is used to capture images and track the user's location in the building. Furthermore, it is possible to attach optional information to each image, such as a status, comments, and descriptions based on the BCF API's standard. The application is built in

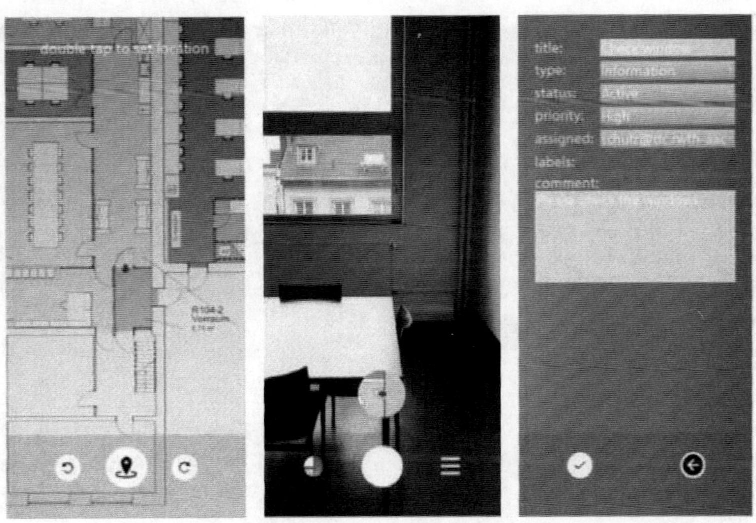

Figure 3: Screenshots of the AR application

the Unreal Engine and can communicate with the BCF Server via HTTP requests. This section describes the general structure of the application and the steps necessary to retrieve the BCF Viewpoints' location from the AR application. To track the user in the building during

[3] https://github.com/Design-Computation-RWTH/bcfServer/tree/extension

documenting, the software development kit ARcore[4] is used, which is built natively into the Unreal Engine. Motion tracking uses the function of simultaneous localization and mapping (SLAM), which can track a movement in real space through internal sensors and the detection of features in the camera feed. The application of AR use-cases in the construction industry is growing. An overview of different use-cases is presented in (Davila Delgado *et al.*, 2020). The entry barrier for using SLAM is low due to the implementation in game engines such as Unity3D or the Unreal Engine and software development environments such as Android Studio or XCode for Apple devices. Although this method can lead to deviations (Kim, Chen and Cho, 2018) over long distances, high precision (Stojanović and Stojanović, 2014) for small distances are still possible. The main focus for this project is set on the interior of buildings.

Other methods for tracking the position of a mobile application are being developed or even currently in use. Such methods are tracking via GPS, which is not feasible for our use-case since the GPS signal is not strong enough inside buildings (Stojanović and Stojanović, 2014). Another common way of tracking the location inside buildings is triangulating the position via a Bluetooth network (Faragher and Harle, 2015). Although this method seems to be less error-prone than SLAM, as it does not require an actively running camera feed, it was decided not to use it. Setting up a new Bluetooth network in an existing building or even on a construction site has not yet been accepted by the industry.

In the application, after an initial setup, the user is tracked based on the plan *(Document)* uploaded to the BCF Server. The created images are saved to a gallery with their position and rotation, and further information can be attached to them. From the gallery, the images can then be uploaded to or updated from the BCF server.

3.3 IFC Viewer

A custom IFC Viewer[5] is used for querying and setting up the documentation. A building's 2D plan is loaded into the 3D space of the Viewer by a ratio of one pixel to one centimeter.

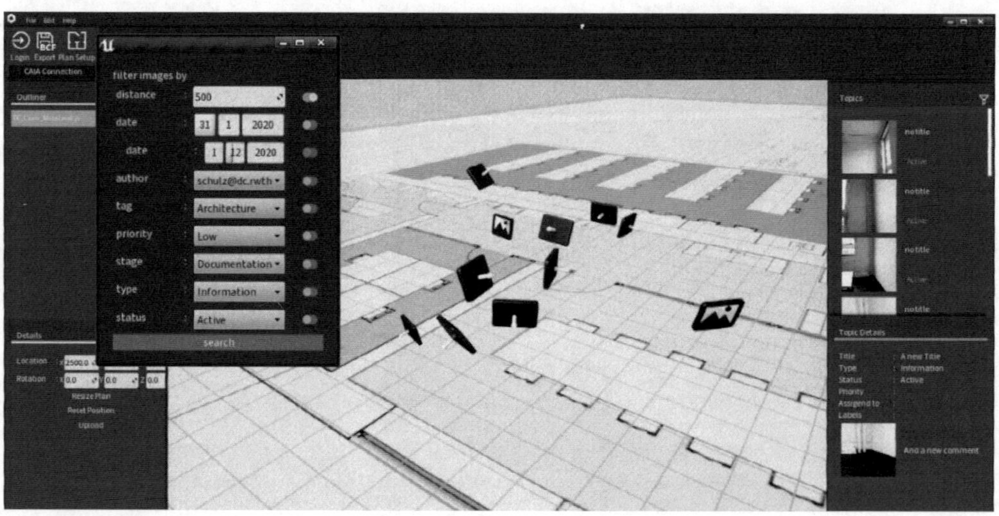

Figure 4: After the filters have been applied, the issues are displayed in 3D space.

However, since this ratio does not correspond to the plan's actual scale, it must be adjusted afterward. Therefore, the user can measure any two points of the plan and enter the actual length. The plan will now be scaled to the correct size. The plan is now uploaded to the BCF

[4] https://developers.google.com/ar

[5] https://github.com/Design-Computation-RWTH/Viewer

server as a *Document* in PNG format. Additionally, the scaling information, the position, and the rotation are uploaded to the new route of the BCF Server for *Spatial Representation* described in section (2.2.). The images created by the mobile application can be downloaded from the BCF Server and reviewed with the Viewer. Therefore, the user first has to select the relating 2D plan, which is requested from the server and placed in the 3D space of the Viewer. The Viewer requests all *Topics*, *Viewpoints*, and *Comments* regarding that plan using the extension to the API (section 3.1).

Now the user can query the BCF data by assigning different filters, such as a filter by date, priority, and distance. The filters are carried out locally at this stage. However, filters already exist in the BCF API for the parameters of the *Topics*. After applying the filter, the *Viewpoints Snapshots* are requested from the server, and the *Issues* are displayed in the 3D viewport. (Figure 4) The final step is to import a BIM model in the IFC format and to align the location of the 2D plan with the model. As soon as the location is adjusted, the spatial information and the *Viewpoints'* location are getting updated on the server. The mobile application functionality is not affected by this process and now uses the adjusted position for 2D plans. This ensures that newly created images are located directly at the correct position in the BIM model.

4. Results

The project's result is an extension of the BCF API, which was tested in a workflow consisting of a mobile application, a BCF server, and an IFC Viewer, collecting images of existing buildings on site and reviewing and filtering them with a viewer. The API's extension became a necessity because early on in this project we recognized, that sticking to the pure BCF API was not appropriate to reach our desired goal because of its nested hierarchy.

To reduce the overhead of requests resulting from the APIs hierarchy, we introduced new routes to the BCF server (section 2.2). Instead of treating *Topics* as the topmost objects, which need to be queried first, before retrieving the additional information, the hierarchy was disbanded by placing *Topics*, *Comments*, and *Viewpoints* on an equivalent level. Furthermore, updating *Viewpoints* and spatialize *Documents* was also added to the BCF API. All these additions are only an extension of the BCF API and do not cause any breaking changes. By introducing a faster search of the server, it was possible to directly download all *Issue* information related to a plan and apply additional filters locally. From the *Issues* filtered in this way, the images were then also downloaded.

As the position on the 2D plan in the mobile application was entered manually, there were slight deviations between the position of the *Issues* in the existing building and the virtual representations of it, which was, however, to be expected. In addition, the result of the tracking by SLAM can also be influenced by external environmental factors such as poor lighting conditions, long tracking distances, and dynamically changing environments (Kim, Chen and Cho, 2018). However, since the user could verify the room's position through the mini-map in the mobile application, it was possible to readjust the position in case of deviations from the plan. Since high precision in the low centimeter range was not a requirement for this documentation project in the existing building, minor deviations were not regarded as a concern.

5. Conclusion

BCF is already a format that is used for documentation. However, for documenting digital and not for existing buildings. Problems occur in the existing building and are recorded there with images as well. The structure of BCF contains many parameters such as the data, the author, comments, and images, which also provide added value for building documentation. Furthermore, BCF is a standard that has found its way into many BIM applications and thus prevents the need to create a new interface explicitly for image documentation. Nevertheless, what is still missing in BCF, especially in the BCF API, is querying this documentation efficiently. The results show this by looking at the limited number of query parameters given by the BCF-API and its hierarchal structure. They all relate to the information in the *Topic* but not in the *Comments* or *Viewpoints*. We removed the nested hierarchy from our BCF server for this experiment, which led to the desired result. This approach could render a possible extension for the BCF API. Further research has to show if these changes are applicable for other use-cases or are just a solution to issues regarding this project's scope.

As described in section 3, the filters of the queries were executed locally in the Viewer. Although this achieved the desired result, it is likely to be a bottleneck as the server's data becomes more extensive. Since the existing search parameters proved insufficient, future work on the API should extend it to include filters that do not refer exclusively to *Topic* information. These include queries for the distance to a given point or the reference to a building element.

Furthermore, updating the *Viewpoints* still proved to be error-prone, as this was handled locally on the computer. The process could potentially not be completed if, for example, the internet connection was interrupted, and thus parts of the *Issues* could be rendered unusable. Proper integration of this function into the BCF server is therefore still pending.

Another solution for tackling the stated problems could be introducing BCF to other query languages, such as GraphQL[6] or SPARQL[7], or a combination of GraphQL and Linked Data, as described in (Werbrouck *et al.*, 2019). GraphQL is increasingly used today as an alternative to REST APIs, addressing issues such as the N+1 problem mentioned above. On the other hand, SPARQL would require graph-based storage of the BCF data, but its expressiveness could allow even more unrestricted data queries. It would also allow BCF to be integrated into the objective of Linked Building Data[8].

The research presented here turned out to be well suited for the example of image documentation. We have shown how the extended BCF API can create a spatial link between heterogeneous representations of buildings. In this case, a 2D plan and a BIM model. Further research will focus on generalizing these spatial links between heterogeneous data and combining semantic linking of data with spatial linking.

Acknowledgment

We thank Epic Games for funding this work with an Epic MegaGrant. Moreover, this project is tested in the H2020 research Project BIM4Ren.

References

van Berlo, L. and Krijnen, T. (2014) 'Using the BIM Collaboration Format in a Server Based Workflow', Procedia Environmental Sciences, 22, pp. 325–332. doi: 10.1016/j.proenv.2014.11.031.

BIM Collaboration Format (BCF) (no date) buildingSMART Technical. Available at: https://technical.buildingsmart.org/standards/bcf/ (Accessed: 7 December 2020).

[6] https://graphql.org/

[7] https://www.w3.org/TR/sparql11-query/

[8] https://www.w3.org/community/lbd/

Bruno, N. and Roncella, R. (2019) 'HBIM for Conservation: A New Proposal for Information Modeling', Remote Sensing, 11, p. 1751. doi: 10.3390/rs11151751.

Czerniawski, T., Ma, J. W. and Leite, F. (2020) 'Metadata-based photo filtering for facility management', EG-ICE 2020 Workshop on Intelligent Computing in Engineering, pp. 333–341.

Davila Delgado, J. M. et al. (2020) 'A research agenda for augmented and virtual reality in architecture, engineering and construction', Advanced Engineering Informatics, 45, p. 101122. doi: 10.1016/j.aei.2020.101122.

Faragher, R. and Harle, R. (2015) 'Location Fingerprinting With Bluetooth Low Energy Beacons', IEEE Journal on Selected Areas in Communications, 33(11), pp. 2418–2428. doi: 10.1109/JSAC.2015.2430281.

Kim, P., Chen, J. and Cho, Y. (2018) 'SLAM-driven robotic mapping and registration of 3D point clouds', Automation in Construction, 89, pp. 38–48. doi: 10.1016/j.autcon.2018.01.009.

Letellier, R. (2007) Recording, Documentation and Information Management for the Conservation of Heritage Places: Guiding Principles. 1st edn. Routledge. doi: 10.4324/9781315793917.

Murphy, M., McGovern, E. and Pavia, S. (2009) 'Historic building information modelling (HBIM)', Structural Survey, 27(4), pp. 311–327. doi: 10.1108/02630800910985108.

Ploesser, K. (2019) 'REST API Design Best Practices for Sub and Nested Resources', REST API Design Best Practices for Sub and Nested Resources | Moesif Blog, 12 March. Available at: https://www.moesif.com/blog/technical/api-design/REST-API-Design-Best-Practices-for-Sub-and-Nested-Resources/ (Accessed: 2 December 2020).

Schulz, O. and Beetz, J. (2019) 'Context-Aware Image Acquisition Approaches for Renovation Building Process Using AR and Linked Data', in eCAADe RIS 2019. Virtually Real. Immersing into the Unbuilt: Proceedings of the 7th eCAADe International Regional Symposium. Virtually Real, Aalborg, Denmark: Aalborg Universitetsforlag, pp. 57–67.

Stenzer, A., Woller, C. and Freitag, B. (2011) 'MonArch: digital archives for cultural heritage', in Proceedings of the 13th International Conference on Information Integration and Web-based Applications and Services. New York, NY, USA: Association for Computing Machinery (iiWAS '11), pp. 144–151. doi: 10.1145/2095536.2095562.

Stojanović, D. and Stojanović, N. (2014) 'INDOOR LOCALIZATION AND TRACKING: METHODS, TECHNOLOGIES AND RESEARCH CHALLENGES', Facta Universitatis, Series: Automatic Control and Robotics; Vol 13, No 1 (2014). Available at: http://casopisi.junis.ni.ac.rs/index.php/FUAutContRob/article/view/208.

Werbrouck, J. et al. (2019) 'Querying heterogeneous linked building datasets with context-expanded GraphQL queries', in Proceedings of the 7th Linked Data in Architecture and Construction Workshop, LDAC 2019. 7th Linked Data in Architecture and Construction Workshop, pp. 21–34. Available at: http://hdl.handle.net/1854/LU-8623179 (Accessed: 17 April 2021).

Unlocking the full potential of Building Information Modelling by applying the principles of Industry 4.0 and Data Governance such as COBIT

Adrian Wildenauer, Prof. Josef Basl
University of Economics and Business, Czech Republic
wila03@vse.cz

Abstract. Construction industry is at crossroads in terms of digital development and empowerment. Lighthouse projects show the practical application of information management based on Building Information Modelling (BIM) in planning and construction. Yet, an overarching international best practice or standard for data governance and maintenance of BIM-based real estate portfolios is lacking. Building owners are often forced to convert or modify received data from construction companies at the time of handover or to enter it manually into their facility or asset management systems. If an overarching data governance approach is not taken, a non-manageable diversification and numerous interfaces in the digital transformation of the construction industry is most likely to occur. This transformation approach has been proven applicable and successful by the manufacturing industry with their Industry 4.0 transformation just a decade ago. The aim of this paper is to examine existing approaches such as the ISACA framework COBIT for IT and data governance for their applicability in the construction industry when ordering BIM based projects from the view of an appointing party.

1. Introduction

Construction industry is not necessarily known as a frontrunner in the digital transformation with a productivity below other industries, frequent project-based massive budget overruns, exceeded deadlines and limited use of digital methods. This has been sufficiently discussed and addressed, among others by Kostka and Anzinger (2016), Barbosa et al. (2017), Bertschek et al. (2019) and Ribeirinho et al. (2020; 2021). A plethora of political initiatives have examined this issue concluding that an overarching regulatory (data) framework is lacking, for example Latham (1994), Egan (1998) and Wolstenholme (2009). The reliable, standardised, automatic and correct end-to-end data transfer and corresponding data governance from a completed construction project based on project information models to an asset management data base of an appointing party based on asset information models and the consequent further use of data is an unsolved problem. Standardisation on international level is starting and must consider a plethora of existing national developments in standardisation. The implementation of information management using Building Information Modelling (cf. Motzel and Möller, 2017) by means of open data and standardised formats such as Industry Foundation Classes IFC (ISO 16739-1, 2018), the buildingSMART International driven BIM Collaboration Format BCF (bsi, 2021) or Construction Operation Building information Exchange COBie (ISO 15686-4, 2014) is possible for planning and construction. McArthur (2015) and Ozturk (2020) confirm this observation that it has become apparent that this applied and current approach needs to move from focusing on the relatively short planning phase to a holistic life-cycle approach. Yet, in projects and portfolios a common, consistent use of data models is still challenging and not or only partially available, as stated in the works of Patacas et al. (2014) and Thabet et al. (2016). There is not an overarching reason for the absence of a consistent structure, but many whys and wherefores. These are, amongst other points, the primary and often single focus on the planning phase (Braun et al., 2013; Barbosa et al., 2017), continuous high fragmentation of the construction sector (Harfmann et al. 2013; Ahmad et al. 2018). This situation affects planners, contractors, and other parties in the value chain, but also clients, so called appointing parties.

Appointing parties frequently lack data competency in ordering and approval of requirements and thus ordered data, but also to test them in conformity with their requirements. This is confirmed in several works, including Eriksson (2010), Bredehorn and Heinz (2016), Interview with Müller (2016), Kuitert et al. (2017), Challender and Whitaker (2019) and Gidez et al. (2020). These inadequacies result in either too little, too much or incorrect data ordered, generated, or made available, which leads to ubiquitous availability of data without purposeful utilisation.

2. Comparison of Industry 4.0 and Construction

The challenges and problems are occurring in an economic sector that has not had to solve these or similar problems for decades – profit margins were low but stable and methods have not changed for centuries. Around 2010, this change took place in an equally large industry in Germany. The manufacturing industry, one of the main pillars of economic growth in Germany (Bauer et al., 2018), was faced with increasing repressive competition within Europe and abroad in the early years of 2010 (European Commission, 2017), leading to a substantial loss of working places (Statista, 2021). The challenges the European manufacturing industry faced at this time were namely (cf. Armstrong et al., 2018):

- the lack of financial resources,
- mismatching skills demands and skill supplies of employers and employees,
- a non-futureproof IT infrastructure,
- a non or low sustainable production and
- the reluctance to change.

These problems are correspondingly observed in the construction industry when considering long-term studies such as Gallaher et al. (2004). These can be allegorised as the typical interdependent crisis components for progress-reluctant or saturated industries, with companies being on a long term successful yet with low but continuous profit without immediate need to change.

Industry 4.0 was coined by the German Ministry of Trade in 2011 (Gneuss, 2014) and considered an initial starting point for the fourth industrial revolution (cf. Pistorius, 2020). Its main goal was to secure the future of the German manufacturing industry (Steven, 2019) with the objectives to make them more robust to foreign competitors by

- preparing the industry's participants to use data-related methods,
- connect production devices with each other,
- enable "smart solutions" (cf. Kagermann et al., 2013) and
- standardise components, processes and appliances (Obermaier, 2019).

Industry 4.0 has had a major impact on the manufacturing industries and is nowadays seen as a business transformation supported by technology rather than the opposite, as stated by Kane et al. (2015). The approach refers in a broader sense to pure process improvements and the raising of efficiencies in manufacturing process such as the production processes described by Amasaka (2002). It is a continuous improvement process of the production lines and production (cf. Johanning, 2019). Tetik et al. (2019) stated that a similar continuous improvement process in the construction industry is yet missing mainly caused by the loose connection to other projects and limited learning from project to project. Already Bresnen and Marshall (2000) pointed to the fact that this lack of continuous learning often undermines attempts to reap the full benefits of collaboration and the transfer of experience across projects, confirmed by the findings of Knecht (2020).

The implementation of Industry 4.0 is based on permanent access to all necessary information for automation of processes, which requires the networking of as many company processes as possible (Pistorius, 2020). Moreover, it is combining cross-company and cross-project processes including the entire supply chain to support and promote alliances in the sense of creating ecosystems not only on product level, but also for research and development and other business areas (Kagermann et al., 2016). Construction is still connected with Taylorism (Wildenauer and Basl, 2021) with high investments needed on monetary, competence-technical and cross-company level to overcome the status quo, corroborated by Zaidin et al. (2014) and Obermaier (2019).

The approaches concerning optimization and automation of processes is about to happen in the construction industry, which has only just begun to develop digitally, verified by Vornholz (2017) and Bertschek et al. (2019). However, digital techniques and methods will only be successful if they can be applied without media discontinuity and across phases, projects, and companies (Rock et al. 2019), not depending on the industry.

2.1 Construction and digital twin versus Industry 4.0 and cyber-physical systems

An increasing number of authors suggest to implement the foundations laid by Industry 4.0 to the construction industry, enabling a "Construction 4.0" with "cyber-physical building management systems" similar to the "cyber-physical production systems" in Industry 4.0, amongst others Aigbavboa and Thwala (2019), Beddiar et al. (2019), Pruskova (2019), Wilde et al. (2019), Lalic et al. (2020), Sawhney et al. (2020) and Spisakova and Kozlovska (2020). However, these authors define Construction 4.0 very differently. According to Oesterreich and Teuteberg (2016), it can be described as the introduction of a popular term to describe the trend for the increasing use of information and automation technologies in the [construction] environment. Yet, it mostly suggested to implement the digital twin approach to the not yet thoroughly digitalised construction industry, too. The comparison is misleading, as two different industries with different pace of digitalisation are benchmarked. Resulting, the basics of the digital twin should be elucidated first. The term "digital twin" was made known to the aerospace industry in 2003 by Grieves (2014). The aim and purpose of the digital twin in spaceflight was to create a "digital doppelganger", physically and digitally, and thus to be able to further develop the product development faster, more reliably and in a more targeted manner. Both systems – physical product and digital twin – shall be in constant data exchange as stated by Grieves (2016). According to the authors, the digital twin concept consists of three parts:

- the physical products in real space,
- the virtual products in virtual space and
- the connections of data and information that ties the virtual and real products together.

The interesting fact is that only the set of virtual information for the creation of a digital image of a project is a "digital twin". However, the term "digital twin" is now widely seen as a general digital image of an asset, so it requires attentiveness due to the widespread misuse of terms and definitions. In the United Kingdom, the Centre for Digital Built Britain started in 2018 stating the first principles for the use of a digital twin in construction, called the "Gemini Principles". Bolton et al. (2018) defined the digital twin generically as "*a realistic digital representation of something physical. What distinguishes a digital twin from any other digital model is its* ***connection*** *to the physical twin.* "

The concept of Grieves (2016) was further refined by Boje et al. (2020) as a cyber-physical integration, comparable to Industry 4.0. The physical part can be considered the asset, while the "cyber-part" is the generated data from daily operation. However, these authors made the exclusion that the *"digital twin is the ultimate, unachievable goal, as no model abstraction can mirror real world things with identical fidelity"*. ISO/TR 24464 (2020) defines the digital twin in the manufacturing industry as *"compound model composed of a physical asset, an avatar and an interface"* respectively a *"digital asset [...] on which services [...] can be performed that provide value to an organization"* stated in ISO/TS 18101-1 (2019). Tao et al. (2019) conducted a large overview of the digital twin in their intensive literature research, showing that the different research fields are diverse in details, having not set a common understanding of a digital twin.

However, there are extraordinarily strong overlaps and similarities between these approaches in the manufacturing and construction industry, but unfortunately named differently, which leads to different definitions of terms, processes, and applications. Exemplarily, Figure 1 contrasts these approaches. Firstly, the models of the construction industry are listed according to international standards, then the models of the manufacturing industry based on the product life cycle models of Sudarsan et al. (2005) respectively Le Duigou and Bernard (2011), the definition of Grösser (2018) concluding with the concept of Grieves (2016).

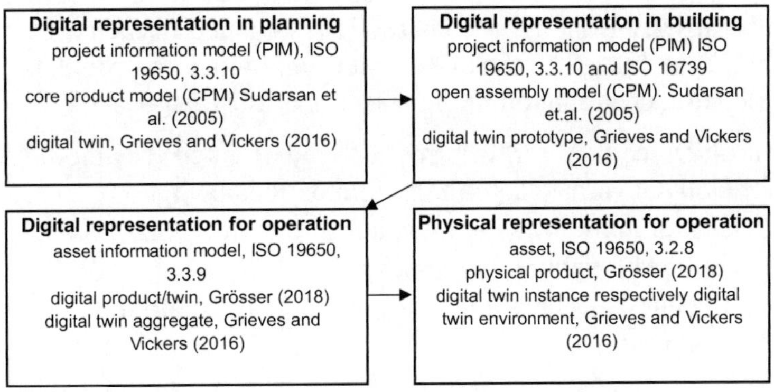

Figure 1: Comparison between manufacturing and construction industry

Interestingly, the approaches are certainly comparable, apart from the different wording of the individual conditions and dependencies. However, it is only partly understandable why there are different terms and state definitions per industry for the same technical aspect (cf. project information model in the construction industry and digital twin in aerospace). The construction industry incorrectly simplifies the term "digital twin" by naming the digital representation for building and operation so. Moreover, the expression "digital twin" is commonly used for representing digital consolidated building models from point clouds surveys for erecting manufacturing facilities (cf. Hiekata, 2019). In summary, construction industry participants use the term "digital twin" incorrectly, inflationary, and inconsistently. This can be attributed to the fact that two different industries have taken up this topic in parallel without clarifying and harmonising necessary terms.

2.2 Data / Information governance and the relation to Building Information Modelling

As with Industry 4.0, Construction 4.0 will not be only about implementing a digital twin environment for planning and realisation with BIM. It is also necessary managing it and understanding this digital twin accordingly as an asset (Errandonea et al. 2020) with the need of an overarching data governance. This was already discussed by Chen and Wang (2011) pointing to a holistic, not temporary project-based approach. The principles of data governance are often interchanged with information governance according to Efe (2016). The aim is to provide stakeholder value with a holistic and tailored approach covering an enterprise end-to-end providing a dynamic framework which is distinct from the daily management (ISACA 2019). However, data management resulting out of BIM processes must be aligned with the business needs in order to be successful and create value (Brunner et al., 2021). This was already stated by Haes et al. (2013) affirming that value creation means realising benefits at an optimal resource cost while optimising risk. The objective of the consequently developed COBIT Framework (ISACA, 2021) is to ensure this balance between value creation and the optimization of risks and resources related to Information **and** Technology. COBIT also defines the information cycle from the alignment between business and IT processes that generate and process data. These data are connected by adding meaning and context to generate information, which in turn becomes knowledge (Liu, 2020). Value can be generated from this knowledge, from which business and IT are driven in a continuous improvement process (ISACA, 2012).

Data Governance principles are common in other industries and have existed for decades (cf the extensive works of Haes et al. (2013), Gelbstein (2016) and Ampe et al. (2020)), but are almost unknown in the construction industry. One reason could be that data is not treated as an asset as raised by Brisson and Savoie (2018) and Grünewald et al. (2020). Though, Data Governance is only partially existing in construction, as stated in the surveys of Rezgui et al. (2013) and Alreshidi et al. (2018), in the event of an economic crisis project- or portfolio-based reinvented or developed, depending on the severeness of the crisis.

COBIT (for "Control Objectives for Information and Related Technology") defines seven generic enablers for Data Governance, with the foundations being

- principles, policies and frameworks and the accompanying enablers being processes
- organizational structures (enabling processes)
- culture, ethics, and behaviour (enabling communication, collaboration, and coordination)
- the information itself (data)
- services, infrastructure, and applications (tools for data generation, exchange, utilisation)
- people, skills, and competencies (personal abilities).

The enablers are designed to be applied in practical situations and must be considered as a surrounding bases for the information model (Figure 1) and can be used for organisational design (Zia-ur-Rehman, 2016). Naturally, these enabler dimensions are interdependent from each other, e.g. stakeholder can change over the life cycle and develop different and differing information needs. However, this goal cascade shall translate the needs of internal and external stakeholders into specific, actionable, and customised enterprise goals. From these, IT-related goals and enabler goals derive. BIM projects can support here by delivering data sets and graphic representations of the asset to the enterprise and are an enabler, too.

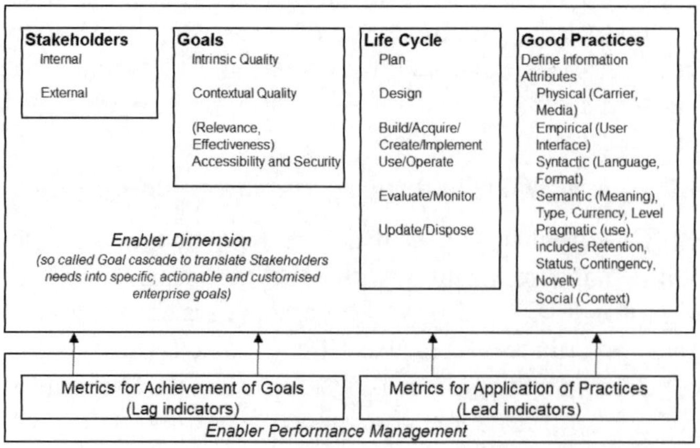

Figure 2: COBIT 5 Information Model (simplified)

2.3 Comparison of ISACA COBIT 5 and ISO 19650 (2018)

Comparing the approaches of COBIT and the information management based on Building Information Modelling BIM according to ISO 19650-1 (2018) (and following numbers used in the construction industry, there are manifold commonalities but also some significant deviations (see Table 1). Both standards supply guidelines for applying information management. However, the ISO 19650 series is mostly focussing on an asset-, project-, respectively portfolio-based approach for information management, where COBIT is focusing on the enterprise including human resources deployments.

Table 1: Comparison between ISACA COBIT 5 and ISO 19650 series

Issue	ISACA COBIT 5	ISO 19650 series	Comparison
Stakeholders internal / external	Information producers (creating the information) Information custodian (storing and maintaining information) Information users (using the information)	Appointing party Appointed party (provider of information) with lead appointed parties possible forming a delivery team Indications that every role is information producer, custodian, and user.	Approach comparable in terms of roles, covering the necessary involved parties and their information requirements
Goals	Information must be fulfilling the following goals. **Intrinsic goals:** Accuracy (correct and reliable) Objectivity (unbiased, unprejudiced, impartial) Believability (true and credible) Reputation (highly regarded in terms of source or content)	ISO 19650, 3.3.16: "level of information need: Framework which defines the extent and granularity of information" in concordance with CEN/TR 17654, ISO 29481-1:2016, EN 17412-1, where geometrical and alphanumerical information as well as documentation is necessary to define the level of information need. ISO 15686-4 supplies guidance on structuring information from existing data sources to enable delivery of their information content in a structure that conforms to international standards for information exchange. In particular, reference is made to ISO 16739-1 Yet, data governance, comparable to COBIT 5 principles are missing in the international standards.	Partly comparable, as the quality criteria of data are not included in the standard but asset-, project or portfolio-based approach. However, the related process management for obtaining, reviewing and accept information is included. Governance on data is not mentioned in ISO 19650 and must therefore be aligned on an asset-, project or portfolio-based approach.
	Contextual goals: Relevancy (applicable and helpful) Completeness (of sufficient depth) Currency (sufficiently for the task) Appropriate Amount (appropriate for the use) Concise Representation (compactly represented) Consistent Representation	The Definition on the "Level of Information Need" (cf. EN 17412-1) states the avoidance of overdelivering information and implicates the necessities for contextual goals as demanded by COBIT. The structuring can be applied in reference to the open IFC Standard as defined in ISO 16739-1	Contextuals goals are implicitly mentioned in ISO 19650 series. Governance on data is not mentioned in ISO 19650 and must therefore be aligned on an asset-, project

	(in the same format) Interpretability (clear definitions) Understandability (easily comprehensible) Ease of Manipulation (applicable to different tasks)		or portfolio-based approach.
	Security/Accessibility goals: Availability (available when required, easily and quickly retrievable) Restricted Access (restricted appropriately to authorised parties)	Security minded approach to information management mentioned in ISO 19650-5	Comparable approaches with a more detailed view in COBIT
Life Cycle (Phases concerned on the product or project)	Plan Design Build/Acquire Use/Operate (Store, Share, Use) Evaluate/Monitor (Monitor, Maintain) Dispose (Archive, Destroy)	ISO 19650 3.2.10: "Life of the asset from the definition of its requirements to the termination of its use, covering its conception, development, operation, maintenance support and disposal" in addition to ISO 22263 (inception, brief, design, production, maintenance, demolition)	Comparable phases of the life cycle
Good Practices	*Define Information Attributes*	*Information attributes are partially defined, the standard deals more with the process*	Not or only partially defined in ISO 19650, providing a very generic framework what to implement, but not as detailed as in COBIT 5. The foreword of the standard ISO 19650 states that best practices based on this standard are not yet available to a sufficient extent. Overarching approach missing in ISO 19650
	Physical: Information Carrier, Media	**Physical**: Paper, models, databases	
	Empirical: Information Access Channel	**Empirical** use for modelling based on realised projects, no European or international accepted standard	
	Syntactic: Code, Language	**Syntactical** Layer IFC according to ISO 16739-1 as well as ISO 23386 and ISO 23387	
	Semantic: Meaning of information, Type, Currency (time horizon), Level	**Semantical** Information Type and Currency (past, present, future), Information Level according EN 17412	
	Pragmatic: Pragmatic use, includes Retention Period, Status, Contingency, Novelty	**Pragmatic**: Novelty in the construction industry and based on done practice or legislation in terms of retention period	
	Social: Context	**Social**: Context of Assets in the Built Environment	
Lag indicators	Metrics for achievement of goals with corresponding Key Performance Indicators and continuous measurements of achievement (strategic and tactical level)	Not included in ISO 19650 but indications to the acceptance criteria and Master Information Delivery Plans	Overarching approach missing in ISO 19 650, asset-, project or portfolio-based approach
Lead indicators	Metrics for application of good practice with corresponding Key	Not included in ISO 19650 but indications to the acceptance	Overarching approach missing in

	Performance Indicators (operational level)	criteria and use of Task Information Delivery Plans	ISO 19 650, asset-, project or portfolio-based approach

Taken this into account, it can be stated that for the metrics an overarching approach is missing and must be incorporated at asset-, project or portfolio-based basis, as well as for the best practice approach. The enterprise must create and implement Data and information security at the organisation level, as these are not exclusively project related. The resulting overall requirements must be then implemented specifically in the project with the directive that the enterprise controls the security requirements of data and information for the portfolio, not the project.

2.4 Recommendation for COBIT extension

The construction industry has not taken part in the development of the COBIT framework. However, there are strong overlaps in manufacturing and construction industry. Figure 3 shows the process framework of COBIT, marked with stars are the recommendations for appointing parties to include in projects planned or erected by the use of information management based on BIM ("BIM projects"). Marked with squares are the COBIT processes which must be aligned and coordinated at enterprise level, all other processes must be included at enterprise level and coordinated/supported/enhanced in BIM projects and consequently portfolios.

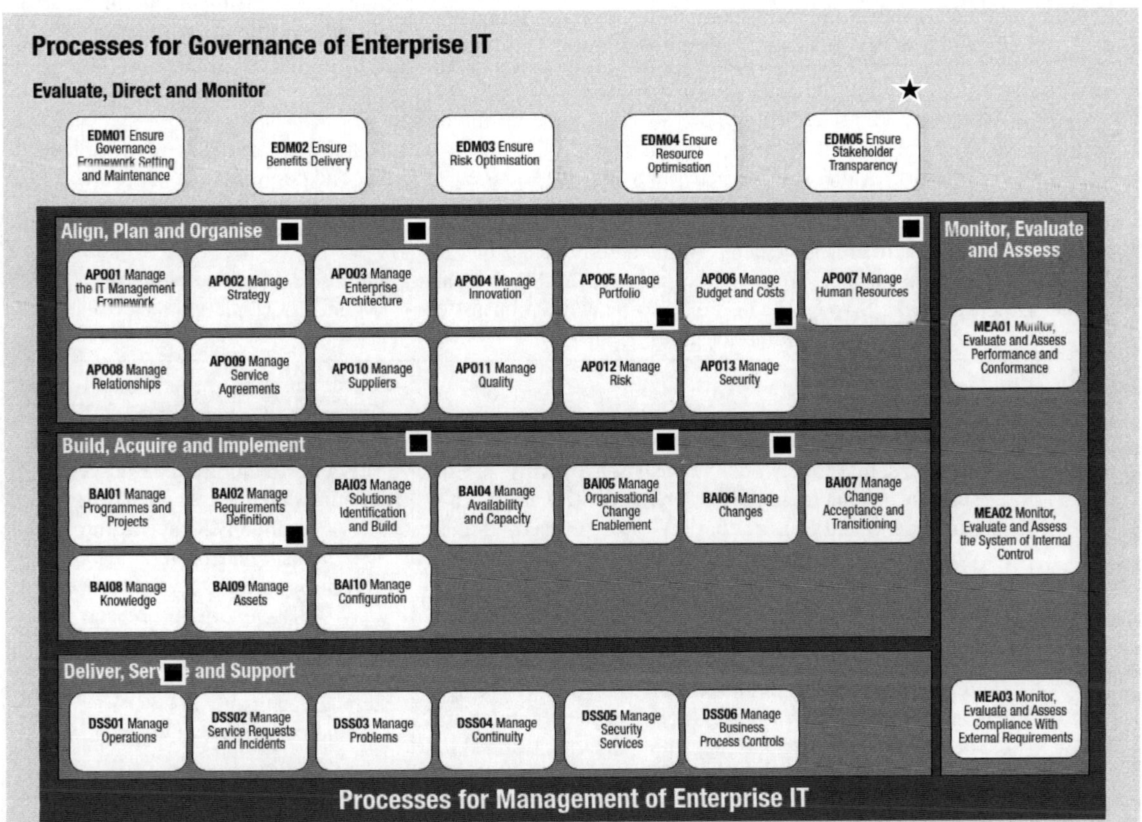

Figure 3: Processes for Governance of Enterprise IT

In table 2, the business-related processes for governance and management of COBIT 5 (cf. ISACA ,2012). are compared to the approach of the ISO 19650 series with the expression "project" conferring to a project executed based on the principles of the ISO Standard. Where the COBIT process description refers to enterprise, the appointing party is understood for the purposes of simplified comparison. However, it is recommended for appointing parties not to resolve general governance issues at the operational (project) level, but at the strategic (enterprise) level. Therefore, the list in table 2 recommends the necessary points to include on an enterprise wide level for appointing parties without questioning the one standard from another.

Table 2: Recommendations for appointing parties using ISO 19650 based on ISACA COBIT 5 Processes for Governance to include in the enterprise strategy

COBIT Process	Description of Process purpose of COBIT 5 / ISACA	Recommendation for appointing parties using ISO 19650
EDM01	Provide a consistent approach integrated and aligned with the enterprise governance approach. To ensure that IT-related decisions are made in line with the enterprise's strategies and objectives, ensure that IT-related processes are overseen effectively and transparently, compliance with legal and regulatory requirements is confirmed, and the governance requirements for board members are met.	Include at enterprise level and coordinate in the project using an Organisational Information Requirement (OIR)
EDM02	Secure optimal value from IT-enabled initiatives, services and assets; cost-efficient delivery of solutions and services; and a reliable and accurate picture of costs and likely benefits so that business needs are supported effectively and efficiently.	Include and ensure at enterprise level and coordinate in the project
EDM03	Ensure that IT-related enterprise risk does not exceed risk appetite and risk tolerance, the impact of IT risk to enterprise value is identified and managed, and the potential for compliance failures is minimised.	Issue and ensure at enterprise level and coordinate in the project
EDM04	Ensure that the resource needs of the enterprise are met in the optimal manner, IT costs are optimised, and there is an increased likelihood of benefit realisation and readiness for future change.	Include and ensure at enterprise level and coordinate in the project
EDM05	Make sure that the communication to stakeholders is effective and timely and the basis for reporting is established to increase performance, identify areas for improvement, and confirm that IT-related objectives and strategies are in line with the enterprise's strategy.	Coordinate in the project mostly with appointments according 3.2.2 (and following numbers) and equivalent information requirements (Organisation OIR, Asset AIR, Project PIR, Exchange EIR) according 3.3.2 by using a Common Data Environment CDE workflow and corresponding processes
APO01	Provide a consistent management approach to enable the enterprise governance requirements to be met, covering management processes, organisational structures, roles and responsibilities, reliable and repeatable activities, and skills and competencies.	Include and ensure at enterprise level and coordinate in the project
APO02	Align strategic IT plans with business objectives. Clearly communicate the objectives and associated accountabilities so they are understood by all, with the IT strategic options identified, structured and integrated with the business plans.	Include and ensure at enterprise level and coordinate in the project by applying a responsibility matrix and the EIR
APO03	Represent the different building blocks that make up the enterprise and their inter-relationships as well as the	Include and ensure at enterprise level and coordinate in the project with the

COBIT Process	Description of Process purpose of COBIT 5 / ISACA	Recommendation for appointing parties using ISO 19650
	principles guiding their design and evolution over time, enabling a standard, responsive and efficient delivery of operational and strategic objectives.	federation strategy and the responsibility matrix
APO04	Achieve competitive advantage, business innovation, and improved operational effectiveness and efficiency by exploiting information technology developments.	Include and ensure at enterprise level, support in the project
APO05	Optimise the performance of the overall portfolio of programmes in response to programme and service performance and changing enterprise priorities and demands.	Include and ensure at enterprise level, support in the project
APO06	Foster partnership between IT and enterprise stakeholders to enable the effective and efficient use of IT-related resources and provide transparency and accountability of the cost and business value of solutions and services. Enable the enterprise to make informed decisions regarding the use of IT solutions and services.	Include and ensure at enterprise level, support in the project
APO07	Optimise human resources capabilities to meet enterprise objectives.	Coordinate and ensure at enterprise level and support in the project with the capacity and capability assessment
APO08	Create improved outcomes, increased confidence, trust in IT and effective use of resources.	Create and ensure at enterprise level, support in the project
APO09	Ensure that IT services and service levels meet current and future enterprise needs.	Ensure at enterprise level, support in the project supplied with OIR/AIR
APO10	Minimise the risk associated with non-performing suppliers and ensure competitive pricing.	Issue and ensure at enterprise level, support in the project with risk register
APO11	Ensure consistent delivery of solutions and services to meet the quality requirements of the enterprise and satisfy stakeholder needs.	Issue and ensure at enterprise level, support in the project supplied with EIR
APO12	Integrate the management of IT-related enterprise risk with overall ERM and balance the costs and benefits of managing IT-related enterprise risk.	Integrate and ensure at enterprise level, observe at project level
APO13	Keep the impact and occurrence of information security incidents within the enterprise's risk appetite levels.	Coordinate at enterprise level and support in the project with the approaches of ISO 19650-5
BAI01	Realise business benefits and reduce the risk of unexpected delays, costs and value erosion by improving communications to and involvement of business and end users, ensuring the value and quality of project deliverables and maximising their contribution to the investment and services portfolio.	Issue and coordinate at enterprise level, observe and support in the project supplied with capacity and capability assessment and the deliverables coordinated with a CDE workflow and solution
BAI02	Create feasible optimal solutions that meet enterprise needs while minimising risk.	Issue and coordinate at enterprise level, support in the project with information management processes
BAI03	Establish timely and cost-effective solutions capable of supporting enterprise strategic and operational objectives.	Establish and coordinate at enterprise level, support in the project
BAI04	Maintain service availability, efficient management of resources, and optimisation of system performance through prediction of future performance and capacity requirements.	Issue and maintain at enterprise level, support in the project with supporting AIR/AIM

COBIT Process	Description of Process purpose of COBIT 5 / ISACA	Recommendation for appointing parties using ISO 19650
BAI05	Prepare and commit stakeholders for business change and reduce the risk of failure.	Issue and ensure at enterprise level
BAI06	Enable fast and reliable delivery of change to the business and mitigation of the risk of negatively impacting the stability or integrity of the changed environment.	Issue and ensure at enterprise level
BAI07	Implement solutions safely and in line with the agreed-on expectations and outcomes.	Implement and ensure at enterprise level, support in the project
BAI08	Provide the knowledge required to support all staff in their work activities and for informed decision making and enhanced productivity.	Coordinated at enterprise level, support in the project by implementing a CDE workflow and solution
BAI09	Account for all IT assets and optimise the value provided by these assets.	Issue and ensure at enterprise level
BAI10	Provide sufficient information about service assets to enable the service to be effectively managed, assess the impact of changes and deal with service incidents.	Issue and ensure at enterprise level, support in the project
DSS01	Deliver IT operational service outcomes as planned.	Issue and ensure at enterprise level
DSS02	Achieve increased productivity and minimise disruptions through quick resolution of user queries and incidents.	Issue and ensure at enterprise level, support in the project with the principles of managing collaborative production of information
DSS03	Increase availability, improve service levels, reduce costs, and improve customer convenience and satisfaction by reducing the number of operational problems.	Issue and ensure at enterprise level, support in the project by the use of information management
DSS04	Continue critical business operations and maintain availability of information at a level acceptable to the enterprise in the event of a significant disruption.	Issue and ensure at enterprise level, support in the project with the principles of managing collaborative production of information
DSS05	Minimise the business impact of operational information security vulnerabilities and incidents.	Issue and ensure at enterprise level, support in the project with the principles of managing collaborative production of information
DSS06	Maintain information integrity and the security of information assets handled within business processes in the enterprise or outsourced.	Issue and ensure at enterprise level, support in the project with the principles of managing collaborative production of information and their security/safety
MEA01	Provide transparency of performance and conformance and drive achievement of goals.	Issue and ensure at enterprise level, support in the project
MEA02	Obtain transparency for key stakeholders on the adequacy of the system of internal controls and thus provide trust in operations, confidence in the achievement of enterprise objectives and an adequate understanding of residual risk.	Issue and ensure at enterprise level, support in the project
MEA03	Ensure that the enterprise is compliant with all applicable external requirements.	Issue and ensure at enterprise level, support in the project with the application of OIR, AIR and their corresponding regulatory framework

3. Conclusion

An overarching data governance approach is missing in the current processes, tools and roles which are suggested with the development of the ISO 19650 series in the information management standard development with the use of Building Information Modelling BIM. However, clear indications are existing but needs refinement. The similarities between these model theories of the digital twin and the existing ecosystems of the manufacturing industry and the digital development of the construction industry and their evolving digital ecosystems are high and consistently overlapping. Due to the advancing digitalisation, the construction industry shall not run the risk of setting up new concepts here that counteract other, already existing models, frameworks, processes, and procedures. It is highly recommended to use well-established and proven information management and data governance models. However, it is not advisable for the construction industry to implement new techniques, methods et cetera before existing ones are used effectively, too. It needs to be a balanced approach in the application of information management by the use of Building Information Modelling in order to create value by realising benefits at an optimal resource cost while optimising risk on an enterprise value.

References

Ahmad, Z., Thaheem, M.J. and Maqsoom, A. (2018). Building information modeling as a risk transformer: An evolutionary insight into the project uncertainty. Automation in Construction 92, pp.103–119. https://doi.org/10.1016/j.autcon.2018.03.032.

Aigbavboa, C. and Thwala, W. (Eds.) (2019). The construction industry in the fourth industrial revolution. Proceedings of 11th Construction Industry Development Board (CIDB) Postgraduate Research Conference. Cham, Springer International Publishing; Springer.

Alreshidi, E., Mourshed, M. and Rezgui, Y. (2018). Requirements for cloud-based BIM governance solutions to facilitate team collaboration in construction projects. Requirements Engineering 23 (1), pp.1–31. https://doi.org/10.1007/s00766-016-0254-6.

Amasaka, K. (2002). "New JIT": A new management technology principle at Toyota. International Journal of Production Economics 80 (2), pp.135–144.https://doi.org/10.1016/S0925-5273(02)00313-4.

Ampe, F., Du Preez, G., Grijp, S., Hardy, G., Peeters, B. and Steuperaert, D. (2020). COBIT 5. Enabling Processes. Rolling Meadows, IL, ISACA.

Armstrong, K., Parmelee, M., Santifort, S., Burley, J. and van Fleet, J.W. (2018). Preparing tomorrow's workforce for the Fourth Industrial Revolution. For business: A framework for action. Globald Business Coalition for Education. Available online at https://gbc-education.org/wp-content/uploads/2018/11/Deloitte_Preparing-tomorrows-workforce-for-4IR-revised-08.11.pdf, accessed November 2020.

Barbosa, F., Woetzel, J., Mischke, J., Ribeirinho, M.J., Sridhar, M., Parsons, M., Bertram, N. and Brown, S., (2017). Executive summary. A route to higher productivity. McKinsey. Available online at https://www.mckinsey.com/industries/capital-projects-and-infrastructure/our-insights/reinventing-construction-through-a-productivity-revolution, accessed January 2019.

Bauer, W., Schlund, S., Hornung, T. and Schuler, S. (2018). Digitalization of Industrial Value Chains. A review and evaluation of exisiting use cases of Industry 4.0 in Germany. Logforum 14 (3), pp.331–340. https://doi.org/10.17270/J.LOG.2018.288.

Beddiar, K., Grellier, C. and Woods, E. (2019). Construction 4.0. Réinventer le bâtiment grâce au numérique : BIM, DfMA, Lean Management. Malakoff, Dunod.

Bertschek, I., Niebel, T. and Ohnemus, J. (2019). Zukunft Bau – Beitrag der Digitalisierung zur Produktivität in der Baubranche. Endbericht. Mannheim,

Boje, C., Guerriero, A., Kubicki, S. and Rezgui, Y. (2020). Towards a semantic Construction Digital Twin: Directions for future research. Automation in Construction. https://doi.org/10.1016/j.autcon.2020.103179.

Bolton, A., Butler, L., Dabson, I., Enzer, M., Evans, M., Fenemore, T., Harradence, F., Keaney, E., Kemp, A., Luck, A., Pawsey, N., Saville, S., Schooling, J., Sharp, M., Smith, T., Tennison, J., Whyte, J., Wilson, A. and Makri, C. (2018). Gemini Principles. https://doi.org/10.17863/CAM.32260.

Braun, H.P., Reents, M., Zahn, P. and Wenzel, P. (2013). Facility Management. Erfolg in der Immobilienbewirtschaftung. Hg. von Hans-Peter Braun. 6th ed. Berlin, Heidelberg, Springer Berlin Heidelberg.

Bredehorn, J. and Heinz, M. (2016). BIM - Einstieg kompakt für Bauherren. Mehrwerte und Potentiale für Bauherren, Investoren und Betreiber. Hg. von Jakob Przybylo. Berlin, Beuth Verlag GmbH.

Bresnen, M. and Marshall, N. (2000). Partnering in construction: a critical review of issues, problems and dilemmas. Construction Management and Economics 18 (2), pp.229–237. https://doi.org/10.1080/014461900370852.

Brisson, M.N. and Savoie, M. (2018). Data Governance: Cybersecurity Oversight and Strategy for Real Estate. Real Estate Issues 42 (10), 1–7. Available online at https://www.cre.org/wp-content/uploads/2018/08/Real-Estate-Issues-Data-Governance-Counselors-of-Real-Estate-1.pdf, accessed May 2021.

Brunner, A., Wildenauer, A.A. and Tatar, A. (2021). Die Verwendung von BIM mittels «Business Use Cases». Anforderungen aus dem Business verstehen, um BIM optimal anzuwenden. Der Eisenbahningenieur 72 (2), pp.14–17.

bsi (2021). BIM Collaboration Format (BCF). Available online at https://technical.buildingsmart.org/standards/bcf/, accessed February 2021.

CEN/TR 17654. Final Draft FprCEN/TR 17654, 2021. CEN. Brussels.

Challender, J. and Whitaker, R. (Eds.) (2019). The Client Role in Successful Construction Projects. Abingdon, Oxon/New York, NY, Routledge is an imprint of the Taylor & Francis Group, an Informa Business, 2019., Routledge.

Chen, X. and Wang, Y. (2011). IT Governance of Construction Information Based on COBIT Model. In: Mark Zhou (Ed.). Education and Management. Berlin, Heidelberg, Springer Berlin Heidelberg, pp.14–20.

Efe, A. (2016). Unearthing and Enhancing Intelligence and Wisdom Within the COBIT 5 Governance of Information model. COBIT Focus. Available online at https://www.researchgate.net/publication/309673974_Unearthing_and_Enhancing_Intelligence_and_Wisdom_Within_the_COBIT_5_Governance_of_Information_Model, accessed March 2021.

Egan (1998). Rethinking Construction. Report of the Construction Task Force. Available online at http://constructingexcellence.org.uk/resources/rethinking-construction-the-egan-report/, accessed October 2019.

EN 17412-1. Building Information Modelling - Level of Information Need, 2020. CEN. Brussels.

Eriksson, P.E. (2010). Understanding the Construction Client. Construction Management and Economics 28 (11), pp.1197–1198. https://doi.org/10.1080/01446191003702450.

Errandonea, I., Beltrán, S. and Arrizabalaga, S. (2020). Digital Twin for maintenance: A literature review. Computers in Industry 123, pp.1–14. https://doi.org/10.1016/j.compind.2020.103316.

European Commission (2017). Germany: Industrie 4.0. Digital Transformation Monitor. European Commission. Available online at https://ec.europa.eu/growth/tools-databases/dem/monitor/sites/default/files/DTM_Industrie%204.0.pdf, accessed September 2020.

Fürstenberg, D. (2021). Information Management in AEC Projects: A Study of Applied Research Approaches. In: Eduardo Toledo Santos/Sergio Scheer (Eds.). Proceedings of the 18th International Conference on Computing in Civil and Building Engineering. Cham, Springer International Publishing, pp.272–284.

Gallaher, M.P., O'Connor, A.C., Dettbarn, Jr., J.L., Gilday, L.T. (2004). Cost Analysis of Inadequate Interoperability in the U.S. Capital Facilities Industry. NIST GCR 04–867. https://doi.org/10.6028/NIST.GCR.04-867.

Gelbstein, E. (2016). The Domains of Data and Information Audits. ISACA Journal (6). Available online at https://www.isaca.org/resources/isaca-journal/issues/2016/volume-6/is-audit-basics-the-domains-of-data-and-information-audits, accessed March 2020.

Gidez, G., Gillchrist, B., Mangin, F., Mollenkopf, J., Konchar, M., Perniconi, M., Kunnath, R., Rawlins, D., Vandezande, J., Loulakis, M.C. and Whitaker, J. (2020). Professional's Guide to Managing the Design Phase of a Design-Build Project. Available online at https://static1.squarespace.com/static/5c73f31eb10f25809eb82de2/t/5f0484760b167351b10049c9/1594131602459/Design-Build-Design-Management-Guide-Edition-2.pdf, accessed July 2020.

Gneuss, M. (2014). Industrie 4.0. Die vierte industrielle Revolution. Available online at https://www.industrie40-info.de/application/files/7814/5752/7317/Industrie40_1403.pdf, accessed November 2020.

Grieves, M., (2014). Digital Twin: Manufacturing Excellence through Virtual Factory Replication. self-published. Available online at https://www.researchgate.net/publication/275211047_Digital_Twin_Manufacturing_Excellence_through_Virtual_Factory_Replication, accessed December 2020.

Grieves, M., (2016). Origins of the Digital Twin Concept. Available online at https://www.researchgate.net/publication/307509727, accessed May 2021.

Grösser, S., (2018). Digitaler Zwilling. Available online at https://wirtschaftslexikon.gabler.de/definition/digitaler-zwilling-54371/version-277410, accessed December 2020.

Grünewald, S., Beijersbergen, M., Overtoom, B. and Geldof, S., (2020). Set up your real estate data foundation as a corporate and start building. Five key areas to focus on to start leveraging Data & Analytics. Available online at https://assets.kpmg/content/dam/kpmg/nl/pdf/2020/services/set-up-your-real-estate-data-foundation.pdf, accessed January 2021.

Haes, S., Betz, C., Douglas, M. and Stachtchenko, P. (2013). COBIT 5: Enabling information. Rolling Meadows, Ill., ISACA.

Harfmann, A.C., Bray, J., Carlo, C., Carl, S., Gentry, T. and Russell, J. (2013). Defragmenting the AEC Industry through a Single, Component-Based Building Information Model. In: Brian J. Leshko/Jonathan McHugh (Eds.). Structures Congress 2013, Structures Congress 2013, Pittsburgh, Pennsylvania, United States, May 2–4, 2013. Reston, VA, American Society of Civil Engineers, pp.938–947.

Hiekata, K. (2019). Transdisciplinary engineering for complex socio-technical systems. Proceedings of the 26th ISTE international conference on transdisciplinary engineering, July 30 – August 1, 2019. Amsterdam/Berlin/Washington, District of Columbia, IOS Press.

ISACA (2012). COBIT 5. A business framework for the governance and management of enterprise IT. Rolling Meadows, IL, ISACA.

ISACA (2019). COBIT 2019 Framework Introduction and Methodology. Rolling Meadows, IL, ISACA.

ISACA (2021). History of ISACA. ISACA. Available online at https://www.isaca.org/why-isaca/about-us, accessed March 2021.

ISO 15686-4. Building Construction — Service Life Planning, 2014. ISO. Geneva. Available online at https://www.iso.org/standard/59150.html, accessed March 2021.

ISO 16739-1. Industry Foundation Classes (IFC) for data sharing in the construction and facility management industries, 2018-11. ISO. Geneva. Available online at https://www.iso.org/standard/70303.html, accessed March 2021.

ISO 19650-1. Organization and digitization of information about buildings and civil engineering works, including building information modelling (BIM), 2018-12. ISO. Geneva. Available online at https://www.iso.org/standard/68078.html, accessed March 2021.

ISO 19650-5. Organization and digitization of information about buildings and civil engineering works, including building information modelling (BIM), 2020. ISO. Geneva. Available online at https://www.iso.org/standard/74206.html, accessed March 2021.

ISO 22263. Organization of information about construction works — Framework for management of project information, 2008. ISO. Geneva. Available online at https://www.iso.org/standard/40835.html, accessed March 2021.

ISO 23386. Building information modelling and other digital processes used in construction, 2020. ISO. Geneva. Available online at https://www.iso.org/standard/75401.html, accessed March 2021.

ISO 23387. Building information modelling (BIM) — Data templates for construction objects used in the life cycle of built assets — Concepts and principles, 2020. ISO. Geneva. Available online at https://www.iso.org/standard/75403.html, accessed March 2021.

ISO 29481-1:2016. Building information models — Information delivery manual, 2016. ISO. Geneva. Available online at https://www.iso.org/standard/60553.html, accessed March 2021.

ISO/TR 24464. Automation systems and integration — Industrial data — Visualization elements of digital twins, 2020. ISO. Geneva. Available online at https://www.iso.org/standard/78836.html, accessed March 2021.

ISO/TS 18101-1. Automation Systems and Integration - Oil and Gas Interoperability, 2019. ISO. Geneva. Available online at https://www.iso.org/standard/68521.html, accessed March 2021.

Johanning, V., (2019). IT-Strategie. Die IT für die digitale Transformation in der Industrie fit machen. 2nd ed. Wiesbaden, Springer Fachmedien Wiesbaden.

Kagermann, H., Anderl, R., Gausemeier, J., Schuh, G. and Wahlster W.,(Eds.) (2016). Industrie 4.0 im globalen Kontext. Strategien der Zusammenarbeit mit internationalen Partnern. München, Herbert Utz Verlag GmbH.

Kagermann, H., Wahlster, W. and Helbig, J. (2013). Recommendations for implementing the strategic initiative INDUSTRIE 4.0. Final report of the Industrie 4.0 Working Group. Federal Ministry of Education and Research. Available online at https://www.din.de/blob/76902/e8cac883f42bf28536e7e8165993f1fd/recommendations-for-implementing-industry-4-0-data.pdf. accessed September 2020.

Kane, G.C., Palmer, D., Phillips, A.N., Kiron, D. and Buckley, N. (2015). Strategy, not Technology drives digital transformation. Becoming a Digitally Mature Enterprise. Available online at https://sloanreview.mit.edu/projects/strategy-drives-digital-transformation/, accessed September 2020.

Knecht, P. (2020). Eine psychologische Analyse über Zusammenarbeit, Informationsaustausch und Wissenstransfer im Bauwesen. Quantitative Expertenbefragung auf Basis von evaluierten Kernaussagen der Publikation «Integrating Project Delivery» über die integrierte Projektabwicklung IPD. Master Thesis. Olten, Fachhochschule Nordwestschweiz.

Kostka, G. and Anzinger, N. (2016). Large Infrastructure Projects in Germany: A Cross-sectoral Analysis. In: Kostka, G. and Fiedler, J. (Eds.). Large Infrastructure Projects in Germany. Cham, Springer International Publishing, pp.15–38.

Kuitert, L., Hermans, M., and van Zoest, S. (2017). Professionalism of construction client organisations. In: 24th Annual European Real Estate Society Conference, 24th Annual European Real Estate Society Conference, Delft, Netherlands. European Real Estate Society.

Lalic, B., Majstorovic, V. and Marjanovic, U. (Eds.) (2020). Advances in Production Management Systems. Towards Smart and Digital Manufacturing. IFIP WG 5.7 International Conference APMS 2020 Novi Sad Serbia August 30 – September 3 2020 Proceedings Part II. Cham, Springer International Publishing; Springer.

Latham, M. (1994). Constructing the Team. Final report of the Government/Industry Review of Procurement and contractual arrangements in the UK construction industry. HMSO (ISBN 0 11 752994 X). Available online at http://constructingexcellence.org.uk/wp-content/uploads/2014/10/Constructing-the-team-The-Latham-Report.pdf, accessed October 2019

Le Duigou, J. and Bernard, A. (2011). Product Lifecycle Management Model for Design Information Management in Mechanical Field. In: 21st CIRP Design Conference. 21st ed. Daejeon, pp.207–213.

Liu, S. (2020). Knowledge management. An interdisciplinary approach for business decisions. London, United Kingdom, Kogan Page Limited.

McArthur, J.J. (2015). A Building Information Management (BIM) Framework and Supporting Case Study for Existing Building Operations, Maintenance and Sustainability. Procedia Engineering 118, pp.1104–1111. https://doi.org/10.1016/j.proeng.2015.08.450.

Motzel, E. and Möller T. (2017). Projektmanagement Lexikon. Referenzwerk zu den aktuellen nationalen und internationalen PM-Standards. 3rd ed. Weinheim, Wiley-VCH Verlag GmbH & Co. KGaA.

Müller, T. (2016). Digitalisierung wird Qualität von Bauten verbessern. Interviewed by Papazoglou of 2016. Available online at https://www.zeitschrift-wohnen.ch/heft/beitrag/interview/digitalisierung-wird-qualitaet-von-bauten-verbessern.html, accessed October 2020.

Obermaier, R. (Ed.) (2019). Handbuch Industrie 4.0 und Digitale Transformation. Betriebswirtschaftliche technische und rechtliche Herausforderungen. Wiesbaden, Springer Gabler.

Oesterreich, T.D. and Teuteberg, F. (2016). Understanding the implications of digitisation and automation in the context of Industry 4.0: A triangulation approach and elements of a research agenda for the construction industry. Computers in Industry 83, pp.121–139. https://doi.org/10.1016/j.compind.2016.09.006.

Ozturk, G.B. (2020). Interoperability in building information modeling for AECO/FM industry. Automation in Construction 113, pp.1–14. https://doi.org/10.1016/j.autcon.2020.103122.

Patacas, J., Dawood, N. and Kassem, M. (2014). Evaluation of IFC and COBIE as data sources for asset register creation and service life planning. In: Proceedings of the 14th International Conference on Construction Applications of Virtual Reality.

Pistorius, J. (2020). Industrie 4.0 – Schlüsseltechnologien für die Produktion. Grundlagen • Potenziale • Anwendungen. Berlin, Heidelberg, Springer Berlin Heidelberg; Springer Vieweg.

Pruskova, K. (2019). Beginning of Real Wide us of BIM Technology in Czech Republic. IOP Conference Series: Materials Science and Engineering 471, pp.1–6. https://doi.org/10.1088/1757-899X/471/10/102010.

Rezgui, Y., Beach, T. and Rana, O. (2013). A Governance Approach for BIM Management across Lifecycle and Supply Chains using mixed-modes of Information Delivery. Journal of Civil Engineering and Management 19 (2), pp.239–258. https://doi.org/10.3846/13923730.2012.760480.

Ribeirinho, M.J., Mischke, J., Strube, G., Sjödin, E., Blanco, J.L., Palter R., Biörck, J., Rockhill, D and Andersson, T. (2020). The next normal in construction. How disruption is reshaping the world's largest ecosystem. Available online at https://www.mckinsey.com/industries/capital-projects-and-infrastructure/our-insights/the-next-normal-in-construction-how-disruption-is-reshaping-the-worlds-largest-ecosystem, accessed June 2020.

Rock, V., Schumacher, C. and Bäumer, H. (Eds.) (2019). Praxishandbuch Immobilienfondsmanagement und -investment. 2nd ed. Wiesbaden, Springer Gabler.

Sawhney, A., Riley, M., Irizarry, J. and Riley, M. (2020). Construction 4.0. Routledge.

Spisakova, M. and Kozlovska, M. (2020). Options of Customization in Industrialized Methods of Construction in Terms of Construction 4.0. In: Blikharskyy, Z., Koszelnik, P. and Mesaros, P. (Eds.). Proceedings of CEE 2019. Cham, Springer International Publishing, pp.444–451.

Statista (Ed.) (2021). Maschinenbau in Deutschland. Hamburg, Statista. Available online at https://de-statista-com.zdroje.vse.cz/statistik/studie/id/6374/dokument/maschinenbau-statista-dossier/, accessed February 2021.

Steven, M. (2019). Industrie 4.0. Grundlagen - Teilbereiche - Perspektiven. Stuttgart, Verlag W. Kohlhammer.

Sudarsan, R., Fenves, S.J., Sriram, R. D. and Wang, F. (2005). A product information modeling framework for product lifecycle management. Computer-Aided Design 37 (13), pp.1399–1411. https://doi.org/10.1016/j.cad.2005.02.010.

Tao, F., Zhang, M. and Nee, A.Y.C. (2019). Digital twin driven smart manufacturing. London, United Kingdom, Academic Press, an imprint of Elsevier.

Tetik, M., Peltokorpi, A., Seppänen, O., and Holmström, J. (2019). Direct digital construction: Technology-based operations management practice for continuous improvement of construction industry performance. Automation in Construction 107, https://doi.org/10.1016/j.autcon.2019.102910.

Thabet, W., Lucas, J. and Johnston, S. (2016). Case Study for Improving BIM-FM Handover for a Large Educational Institution. In: Perdomo-Rivera/Gonzalez-Quevedo/Del Lopez Puerto et al. (Eds.). Construction Research Congress 2016. Old and New Construction Technologies Converge in Historic San Juan. Reston, American Society of Civil Engineers, pp.2177–2186.

Vornholz, G. (2017). Entwicklungen und Megatrends der Immobilienwirtschaft. 3rd ed. Berlin/Boston, De Gruyter Oldenbourg.

Wilde, W.P., Mahdjoubi, L. and Galiano Garrigos, A. (Eds.) (2019). Building Information Modelling (BIM) in Design, Construction and Operations III, BIM 2019, Seville, Spain, 09.10.2019 – 11.10.2019. WIT PressSouthampton UK.

Wildenauer, A.A. and Basl, J. (2021). An Exploration of COVID-19 and Its Consideration as a Black Swan for the Construction Industry in Switzerland. International Journal of Digital Innovation in the Built Environment 10 (1), pp.62–82. https://doi.org/10.4018/IJDIBE.20210101.oa1.

Wolstenholme, A. (2009). Never waste a good crisis. A review of progress since Rethinking Construction and Thoughs of our future. Available online at http://constructingexcellence.org.uk/wp-content/uploads/2014/10/Wolstenholme_Report_Oct_2009.pdf, accessed October 2019.

Zaidin, N.H.M., Diah, M.N.M., Po, H.Y. and Sorooshian, S. (2014). Quality Management in Industry 4.0 Era. Journal of Management and Science 4 (3), pp.82–91. Available online at https://www.researchgate.net/profile/Po_Hui_Yee/publication/328630839_Quality_Management_in_Industry_40_Era/links/5bd970b1299bf1124fafa291/Quality-Management-in-Industry-40-Era.pdf, accessed November 2020.

Zia-ur-Rehman, A. (2016). Using COBIT for IT Organizational Design. Available online at https://www.isaca.org/resources/news-and-trends/industry-news/2016/using-cobit-for-it-organizational-design, accessed November 2020.

Data Quality in Building Productivity Assessment – the Case of Acute Care Environments

Jack Morewood[a,b], Matthew Bacon[a], Pieter de Wilde[b]
[a] TCC-CASEMIX® Ltd, United Kingdom, [b] University of Plymouth, United Kingdom
pieter.dewilde@plymouth.ac.uk

Abstract. Acute care environments are typically cost- and energy-intensive facilities. This paper presents a methodology to map operational processes to predict occupancy. Veracity of occupancy data is assured by an enhanced brief, quality measurement and quality improvement. A major development over existing and more general frameworks applied in this domain, this new approach challenges the basis of engineering. Feedback loops and roles set based on expected competencies instates strong governance. Application to a knowledge intensive case study for a hospital in Gothenburg, Sweden, sees data quality improvements facilitate improved occupancy modelling. Revising energy consumption from 94 to 81 $kWhm^{-2}a^{-1}$, a typical "performance gap" is avoided. Analysis modelled and optimised the space use, informed by knowledge of operational policy, increasing productivity, reducing energy consumption and need for capital-intensive plant.

1. Introduction

Hospital buildings are both energy intensive spaces (CIBSE, 2020) and capital-intensive assets, with operating time attracting great cost (Macario, 2010). Indeed, acute care admissions in the UK cost £27.8 billion in the last period (NHS, 2020b). The financial cost and carbon use attributed to this makes operating theatres a worthy target for building productivity assessment and improvement. However existing approaches to occupancy surveys to facilitate understanding of enhanced productivity, such as direct observation, surveys and field monitoring (Hong *et al.*, 2015b), are impracticable in sterile settings. Yet beyond this, it is important not only to understand occupancy, but *why it is what it is.* Without understanding this causation from operational policy, no control can ever be exercised over building occupancy. In turn, this risks the need to oversize engineering systems to meet the demand of the peaks that arise. Occupancy is related closely with energy use (Ahn *et al.*, 2017). Likewise, the extent of the energy performance gap, where measured performance deviates from design performance, correlates to uncertainties in occupant behaviour (de Wilde, 2014). However, occupancy in healthcare is highly structured and predictable by its congruence with clinical processes and patient pathways. Considered a "new horizon for achieving energy-saving" (Hong *et al.*, 2017), improved understanding of occupancy and space use that quality data facilitates is vital to achieving carbon- and cost-saving targets. This paper will report on the development of a framework to model and predict occupancy in acute care environments. This model gathers and uses this high-quality data to model occupancy patterns in buildings that facilitate highly structured processes such as operating theatres.

This paper critically evaluates the state-of-the-art in building occupancy studies, then builds on the state-of-the-art in data quality to develop a theoretical framework for the gathering of occupancy data and assuring its quality. This is implemented in a commercial tool: the *TCC-Health Activity Model™*. Understanding contextual considerations in acute care environments, this general framework and bespoke software will then be applied to a case study hospital. Implementing the framework, occupant profiles derived from the output data will then be prepared to optimise building services and systems, the use of operating theatres and hence management of patient waiting lists, and ultimately to achieving carbon savings at the building level. The use of the framework to improve hospital productivity will be demonstrated through application to the analysis of a new hospital in Gothenburg, Sweden. This case study demonstrates how this data is used, including in a building energy simulation (BES) tool, IDA-ICE. This allows realistic energy targets to be set in conjunction with operational policy making, optimisation of space use and patient pathway re-engineering to raise building productivity. Appraisal and evaluation of this case study will verify and validate the occupancy model, as well as the data quality framework developed.

2. State-of-the-art in building occupancy studies

Occupancy is strongly correlated with energy use (Mahdavi and Tahmasebi, 2019; Ahn *et al.*, 2017; de Wilde, 2014). The first implication of this is that improving the productivity of processes will reduce energy use. The second is that improved modelling of occupancy is pivotal to improving the reliability of planning. This has already been applied to acute care environments with success under the current status quo in data quality, achieving a 34% reduction in carbon emissions (Bacon, 2014). Poor understanding of occupancy meanwhile leads to deviations from expected performance (de Wilde, 2014). CIBSE *TM54* addresses this "performance gap" with a series of measures to improve design-stage estimations (CIBSE, 2013). Recommending that a structured interview on "occupancy factors" takes place to estimate occupancy input more reliably for use in a dynamic simulation, building performance simulators should question occupant density, density variability (across days, weeks and years), activity, window access (whether occupants can control these) and equipment use (CIBSE, 2013). Despite the known need of this information, typically it is unavailable, because the data simply does not exist, ensuring that assumptions are made and uncertainties in performance remain. Floor area uncertainties are identified as another source of uncertainty in energy use intensity calculations, highlighting trivial causes of performance gaps, to wide and complex occupancy causes, from lighting and servers to operational processes such as catering (*ibid.*).

The International Energy Agency ran two annexes concerning occupant behaviour. *Annex 66* agreed that occupant behaviour had "significant impacts" on both energy use and thermal comfort, evidenced by a series of case studies, concluding that "data collection is fundamental for occupant behaviour" (IEA, 2018a). *Annex 79* further highlighted the potential of "big data" in the sector to implement these in-situ measurements, with techniques such as data mining (D'Oca and Hong, 2015), machine learning (*ibid.*) and sensing technologies used to inform building occupancy modelling, forecasting that "data related to occupants' behaviour" will increase rapidly, therefore offering a large opportunity to building performance analysts (IEA, 2018b). This contrasts with the approach in CIBSE *TM54* where occupancy modelling improvement centred around bettering assumptions, rather than implementing new data to evidence and enhance occupancy prediction.

Existing work is divided into two groups. The first recognises the limitations of current occupancy modelling yet treats this with scepticism of building simulation rather than an evidence-driven solution. The second appreciates role of data in creating accurate occupancy models and therefore improving building simulation, where occupant behaviour is categorised and monitored. This emerging work appreciates that the effects and impact of behaviour are diverse and categorisable. While the state-of-the-art in this domain is found in the latter, even this can set unrealistic data needs or be jeopardised by poor data quality.

3. Theoretical framework development: assuring quality in occupancy data

The framework developed follows significant advancements made in recent times with the rise of information technology, high-performance computing, big data and machine learning. The current state-of-the-art will be aligned to the framework's activities, designed with the objective to improve data quality and better meet the needs of consumers of occupancy data.

In occupancy modelling specifically, new and disparate datasets are now increasingly used in modelling, yet too little is known about their quality. Processes must be effectively captured to successfully model occupant behaviour (CIBSE, 2013) and use data in building information modelling (BIM), where data quality has been identified as one major "pitfall" (Bilal *et al.*, 2016). It is typical to find "null values, misleading values, outliers, non-standardised values", described as "essential traits" that cause misleading and incorrect data, attracting inevitable pessimism (*ibid.*). Structured occupancy schema, such as *obXML*, address poor standardisation and consistency to improve quality (Hong *et al.*, 2015a; Hong *et al.*, 2015b). Evidence points to numerous applications of data quality improvement (DQI) spanning building performance and health engineering. To overcome big data challenges and obtain reliable results, and therefore produce accurate occupancy models, DQI is essential.

3.1 Methodology

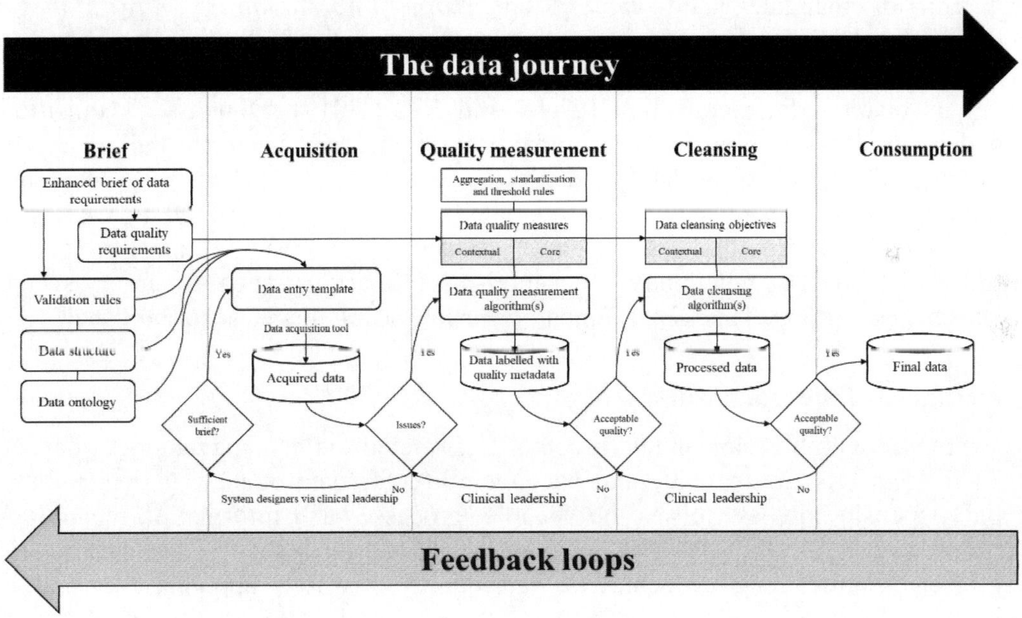

Figure 1: Summary process map of the data quality framework

First, data quality is defined in an enhanced brief. *BS ISO 8000* defines data quality as the "degree to which a set of inherent characteristics of data fulfils requirements" (BSI, 2020). Data quality then must be defined contextually as "requirements" fundamentally differ (*ibid.*). Indeed, building performance literature highlights that definitions of data quality "depends on the use" and benchmarking data quality between different applications is challenging due to deviating quality objectives, especially for different building types (de Wilde, 2018). Establishing "informational requirements" for occupancy models and hence data quality is key (Mahdavi and Tahmasebi, 2019). The developed framework (Figure 1) incorporates these contextual data quality needs through definition at the briefing stage, establishing needs early (both its quality and the structure of data) through a process of elicitation and consultation.

Second, this brief must then be used to select DQI techniques (both at acquisition stage and in post-processing) and data quality measures (DQMs) that are appropriate to data needs. DQMs are essential to monitor the effectiveness of DQI and indeed are fundamentally a subset of performance measures, describing the quality of data numerically (de Wilde, 2018). Use of DQMs is reported widely in literature on data quality assessment (Batini *et al.*, 2009; Berndt *et al.*, 2015; Houston *et al.*, 2018; Kerr, Norris and Stockdale, 2008; Vetrò *et al.*, 2016) and in standards such as *BS ISO 8000* (BSI, 2015). Attributes used in this body of research include completeness, similarity, accuracy, currency, timeliness, volatility (or information stability), record linkage, validation rules and custom business rules. Batini *et al.* (2009) underscore the sheer variability in existing data quality methodologies in a comprehensive review, with some frameworks using as few as four and as many as seventeen DQMs. To reflect this contextuality in defining data quality and application-specific data needs (de Wilde, 2018), the framework provided in this paper divides DQMs developed into core DQMs that apply to all data (such as completeness) and contextual DQMs, specific to occupancy modelling.

This contextuality also applies to DQI itself, the goal of which is to improve the standard of data (Cichy and Rass, 2019), with several strategies existing. DQI can take place during acquisition, for instance in migrating from unstructured to structured data (sometimes through semi-structured data such as extendable mark-up language schemas) to improve data usability (Batini *et al.*, 2009). The design of acquisition tools matters too, including data entry rules to prevent null or mandate valid values. The *Total Information Quality Management* methodology labels "improve information process quality", the first of two key processes in quality improvement. "Information product improvement" meanwhile extracts data and improves its quality after acquisition (Cichy and Rass, 2019). DQI after acquisition can include data processing, preparation, standardisation and cleansing (Wang *et al.*, 2019). Verification and validation of DQI is key to prevent unintended risks to data quality. Spanning acquisition, design and cleansing, the framework applies DQI at each stage to prepare data for consumption in building productivity assessment and the occupancy modelling tool, as well as potentially wider inter-disciplinary use such as surgery scheduling or services benchmarking. This improvement is verified using the DQMs established.

3.2 Governance of the framework

Data governance will "develop and enforce policies related to the management of data" (BSI, 2020). This demands transparency and accountability for data quality, understanding data roles and responsibilities as well as the "people, processes and information technology" in DQI (Houston *et al.*, 2018). Strategies must appreciate that those involved in data acquisition usually receive "no training" in achieving data quality, nor fully appreciate its importance (Nahm, 2012). Existing strategies and frameworks are blind to this reality, often appointing data stewards but failing to align this with typical competency levels or clearly scoping their activities. *BS ISO 8000* for example introduces "technicians", "administrators", "managers" and "stewards" in the process (BSI, 2020), but goes no further in bridging the gap between those who acquire information (likely to have basic or no data science skills) and those who consume, interpret, process and manage information (with specialist skills and data quality training). With big data and passive acquisition, such a bridge is vital as these two groups of actors become increasingly distant. More widely in an age of machine learning and autonomy governance for data quality becomes a moral and ethical consideration (Centre for Data Ethics and Innovation, 2020). For occupancy modelling, proper governance of data will prevent inaccuracies in simulation and ensure effective energy and operational decision-making.

To these limitations emerges a key innovation for this framework: the humanisation of the data quality process (Table 1), centred around expert observers that recognise nuances in the data acquisition context. For example, an occupancy sensor may simply provide data largely abstract from context, whereas informed observers can provide metadata that only becomes apparent during the acquisition process, to understand data quality. The clinical leadership, including analysts at the hospital, work alongside data acquirers who are not only trained in data quality and data science concepts, but are subject experts in the context in which data is being acquired, who are able to discern data quality issues at an early stage. These, alongside system designers who manage the acquisition tool, contribute to a process of continuous data quality improvement aligned to the framework, adding value for occupancy data consumers.

Table 1: Roles of the data quality framework

Role	**Activity** *(When?)*					**Function**	**Competencies**
Who?	Enhanced brief	Acquisition	Measurement	Cleansing	Consumption	*What?*	*How?*
Data consumer	✓				✓	Provide data requirements, cost and resource constraints and consume data.	Contextual
System designers	✓	✓				Creates, improves and manages data acquisition tools and entry templates.	Systems and software engineering
Data acquirers		✓				Collects, modifies and deletes data according to policy.	Software proficiency Subject domain knowledge.
Clinical leadership		✓	✓	✓		Expert observers who identify errors, train data acquirers where necessary and flag bugs to system designers.	Fundamental data science and quality. Subject domain experts.
Data analyst			✓	✓		Processes and cleanses data, assuring and measuring quality and highlighting data deficiencies to clinical leadership.	Advanced data science and quality

3.3 Cost and resource constraints on data quality improvement

A constraint applied to the entire framework is cost and resources, which must be proportionate. Costs and benefits must be defined to do this. Now having a "critical role" in business and government, poor data quality can incur high costs: both "process costs" directly from poor data and "opportunity costs" from missed revenues (Batini *et al.*, 2009). Unsurprisingly, this is highly relevant to acute care organisations where data quality remains a major challenge, particularly for processing big clinical datasets (Wang *et al.*, 2019). In the NHS for example, consistent clinical coding is vital to quality data, yet this has long been poor: relying on this to distribute expenditure, an audit of 8,990 health episodes in 2014 found that clinical coding errors were as high as 45.8% for some trusts, with a gross financial impact of 4.1% (CAPITA, 2014). For occupancy modelling, these opportunity costs can be derived from added value from data quality improvement in occupancy modelling, for example energy or equipment savings. Poor quality process data will jeopardise occupancy data, and hence system optimisation. Total added value must exceed the cost of DQI as a golden rule. This positioning of cost and resources aligns with *AIMQuality*, which established benchmarks for DQMs representing best practice. This helps understand when DQI has been sufficient and where quality is poorest to either prioritise resources for DQI or exclude DQI where it is unfeasible (Cichy and Rass, 2019). This approach relies on setting appropriate benchmarks for desired quality, with gap analysis against this benchmark used to target resources for DQI.

4 Knowledge-intensive case study: patient pathway re-engineering in Gothenburg, Sweden

As an exemplar case study, the framework has been operationalised in the *TCC-Health Activity Model*™ and applied to the Gothenburg hospital in Sweden, with the ambition of re-engineering patient movement pathways to better manage the diversity of occupancy and use this knowledge to optimise building energy performance. The objective is to forecast occupancy diversity of use, typically one of the major assumptions required to make in establishing the basis of engineering design.

The model relies on the ascertainment of two key measurements. The first is dwell time: how long a patient, accompanying person or staff member remains in a space. The rationale is to model occupancy at departmental level of abstraction first because the need is to model occupancy flux based on patient flux out of the department as a representation of the efficiency of process within it. Consequently, the longer the dwell time, the greater the likelihood of patients backing up, upstream in the process. The second is inter-departmental flux: how patients move into, out of and between different treatment departments. This acknowledges that there is a demand and capacity profile for each department based on operational process around patient processing and staffing ratios. For example, 'batch-processing', where patients are requested to arrive no later than 08:00 and wait throughout the morning before they are processed through their patient pathway, leads to substantial peak in occupancy early on, depleting slowly afterwards. Consequently, the peak demand profile on the engineering systems must be sized to accommodate this 'artificial stressing' of the facility.

A data entry template was used with the hospital data analysts to record patient demand and dwell time (Table 3). A year-long monitoring period ensured seasonal variations were captured. Maternity use was derived from 10,000 births per year occurring, with an annual growth factor. The data analyst worked with the hospital's staff and analysts, recording key datasets for different departments. Meta-data was created by analysis of the hospital's clinical information systems. Guidance was provided to hospital teams and a briefing to data analysts. By mapping the operational policy with inter-departmental flux (Table 2), occupancy profiles were correlated with a process logic. This was based on foundational analytics with the hospital's clinical leadership and resulted in a whole facility patient pathway to represent inter-departmental flux (Figure 2). Dwell time (Table 3) and equipment use (Table 4) were calculated according to expected time in use, resource utilisation and the amount of equipment. A standard deviation of 10% of occupancy was derived for equipment.

Finally, this occupancy data was then machine processed and used in the IDA-ICE software, making a significant enhancement over conventional BES which relies on standardised occupancy profile templates based on many assumptions. This stochastic approach appreciates known uncertainties in occupancy while reducing variability through acquiring granular data at the department and space level.

Forecast energy consumption by the client's engineering consultancy for maternity and the attached high dependency unit and intensive care unit was 81 $kWhm^{-2}a^{-1}$. The upper bound of the model's forecast, the preferred probability of the client, was instead 94 $kWhm^{-2}a^{-1}$, which reflects typical prevalence of the energy performance gap. Granulating this into the root causes, previously forecast lighting energy consumption was 20% lower while equipment consumption was 58% lower than where the model was applied as the basis of engineering design. Even further, occupancy can be correlated with individual pieces of equipment, such as an air handling unit or boiler. For instance, buildings were assumed to be unoccupied overnight and therefore heated from a chilled state. When challenged, several spaces were in fact occupied overnight, instead heated from 16°C hence heating demand was far reduced.

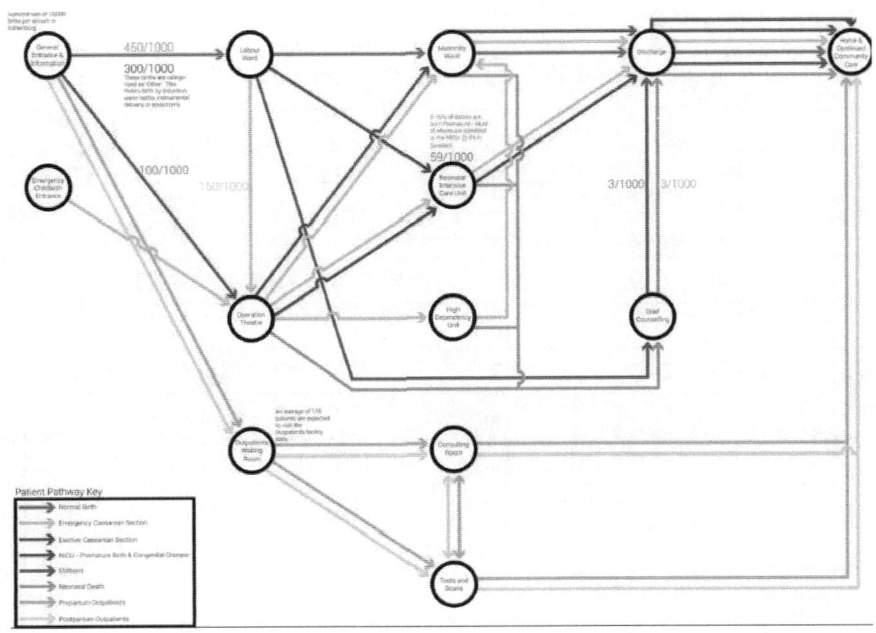

Figure 2: Whole-facility patient pathways – interacting specialties at Gothenburg hospital.

Table 2: Interdepartmental flux analysis from the data entry template for Gothenburg hospital maternity ward

Interdepartmental Traffic			
From Department	To Department	Schedule	Ratio of patients
Reception	Labour Zone	8am - 2pm	30%
		2pm - 6pm	25%
		6pm - 12am	15%
		12am - 8am	30%
Labour Ward	Maternity Zone	8am - 2pm	15%
		2pm - 6pm	25%
		6pm - 12am	25%
		12am - 8am	25%
Maternity Zone	Discharge	8am - 2pm	50%
		2pm - 6pm	50%
Emergency Entrance	Theatre	-	21%
		-	10%
	High Dependency Unit Zone	-	40%

		-	41%
	Neonatal Intensive Care Unit	-	10%
		-	10%
Theatre	Neonatal Intensive Care Unit	-	
	High Dependency Unit	-	
	Maternity Zone	-	10%

Table 3: Dwell time analysis for circulation spaces

Horizontal Spaces					Vertical Spaces		
Name	Stage	Level	Time Spent by Type (sec.)		Name	Design Code	Time Spent (sec.)
			Patient	Staffs & Other			
ME1	1	1	16.0	10.0	BL	Core 1-1-L1A/B/C/D	120
CA11	1	1	22.5	14.1	L11	Core 1-2-L1A/B	120
CC11	1	1	20.0	12.5	L21	Core 1-3-L2A/B	120
CA12	1	2	30.0	18.8	L41	Core 1-9-L1A/B	120
CA13	1	3	16.0	10.0	L1121	L11 or L21	120
CD111	1	11	14.0	8.8	L12	Core 2-2-L1A/B	120
ME2	2	1	8.0	5.0	L12C	Core 2-2-L1C	120

Table 4: Equipment process use for Gothenburg hospital

Department	**Equipment Name**	**No. of Equipment**	**Ratio of patients Using Equipment**		**Slot Length (minutes)**
			OP	IP	
Radiotherapy	Linacs	6	79%		20
	Orthovoltage Machine	1	10%		20
	CT Planning	2	4%		30
Nuclear Medicine	Cardia Gamma	1	32%		15
	PET	1	20%		20
	SPECT CT	2	16%		40
	Gamma Camera	1	16%		30
Imaging Cold	Angio	1	0%	0%	35
	CT	2	12%	0%	15
	Fluoroscopy	3	4%	19%	35
	MRI	4	22%	11%	38
	X-ray	3	41%	51%	10
	Ultrasound	4	21%	19%	25

5 Discussion and conclusion

A novel approach to building productivity assessment was used, aggregating process data to improve the occupancy modelling of an acute care facility. This was underpinned by an improvement in data quality through an applied framework, which ensured rigour in the measurements that underpin predictions of interdepartmental flux, equipment process use and dwell time. The data was derived from clinical information systems data and repurposed for the required analysis using the model and data quality framework. Following this, it was possible to overcome two major causes of the energy performance gap: building occupancy diversity and operational process demand.

The establishment of clear roles for strong data governance in the framework was highly valuable and ensured that the data acquisition system reflected different competencies. This overcame the limitations of data acquisition for big process data, with feedback from subject domain experts successfully overcoming system issues and highlighting quality limitations. The results are clear and enabled rigour in assumptions about design occupancy in energy use. The impact of this analysis was profound. A major operational concern of the client team was there may not be sufficient maternity rooms for post-partum mothers. An analysis of the operational policy found that the length of stay (LoS) assumption for first time mothers was based on 2.6 days. This seemed excessive compared to European standards. For example, in the Netherlands, the equivalent LoS is just one day, but in this situation there is a community care nursing team that supports the new mothers in the early days of motherhood. In contrast the Gothenburg team had assumed that extended care would be provided in the hospital, with the consequential demand on space. Different operational scenarios were created and correlated each to the demand on space. In one of these, the consequence was that only 50% of all rooms would be occupied at peak times, but in another capacity would have been saturated. For each scenario there was a corresponding space and energy impact. The data thus provided the client team with the means to balance competing objectives.

Data quality assurance is highly applicable to both occupancy modelling and care delivery, owing to the close correlation between occupancy and energy use. This is essential to achieve national health policy objectives: for instance in the UK, the NHS seeks to achieve net-zero carbon emissions by 2040 (NHS, 2020a) and demands "short waits" for care in its *Long Term Plan* (NHS, 2019). Such requirements are replicated in international markets. Future work will consume this quality assured process data within a bigger data system, with other subsets used in a prospective theatre management tool. The joining of this data into the enhanced briefing process will see improvements downstream in building management for beneficiaries such as control engineers who currently must make the same poor assumptions to programme building services. The quality improvement process is also applicable in BIM where data quality has been identified as poor, dealing with building use data derived from occupancy and processes; the framework is a significant opportunity to enhance its reliability and quality.

References

Ahn, K.-U., Kim, D.-W., Park, C.-S. and de Wilde, P. (2017). Predictability of occupant presence and performance gap in building energy simulation, Applied Energy, 208, pp. 1639–1652.

Bacon, M. (2014). Occupancy analytics: a new basis for low-energy–low-carbon hospital design and operation in the UK, Architectural Engineering and Design Management, 10(1–2), pp. 146–163.

Batini, C., Cappiello, C., Francalanci, C. and Maurino, A. (2009). Methodologies for data quality assessment and improvement, ACM Computing Surveys, 41(3), pp. 1–52.

Berndt, D. J., McCart, J. A., Finch, D. K. and Luther, S. L. (2015). A Case Study of Data Quality in Text Mining Clinical Progress Notes, ACM Transactions on Management Information Systems, 6(1), pp. 1–21.

Bilal, M., Oyedele, L. O., Qadir, J., Munir, K., Ajayi, S. O., Akinade, O. O., Owolabi, H. A., Alaka, H. A. and Pasha, M. (2016). Big Data in the construction industry: A review of present status, opportunities, and future trends, Advanced Engineering Informatics, 30(3), pp. 500–521.

BSI (2015). BS ISO 8000-8:2015: Data quality: British Standards Institution.

BSI (2020). BS ISO 8000-2:2020: Data quality. London: British Standards Institution.

CAPITA (2014). The quality of clinical coding in the NHS, Alcester.

Centre for Data Ethics and Innovation (2020). Review into bias in algorithmic decision-making, London: Centre for Data Ethics and Innovation.

CIBSE (2013). CIBSE TM54: 2013: Evaluating operational energy performance of buildings at the design stage. London: Chartered Institution of Building Services Engineers.

CIBSE (2020). CIBSE Benchmarking Tool Dashboard. Available at: https://www.cibse.org/Knowledge/Benchmarking (Accessed: 2020-12-04 2020).

Cichy, C. and Rass, S. (2019). An Overview of Data Quality Frameworks, IEEE Access, 7, pp. 24634–24648.

D'Oca, S. and Hong, T. (2015). Occupancy schedules learning process through a data mining framework, Energy and Buildings, 88, pp. 395–408.

de Wilde, P. (2014). The gap between predicted and measured energy performance of buildings: A framework for investigation, Automation in Construction, 41, pp. 40–49.

de Wilde, P. (2018). Building performance analysis. Chichester: John Wiley & Sons, Ltd., pp. 186–7.

Hong, T., D'Oca, S., Turner, W. J. N. and Taylor-Lange, S. C. (2015a). An ontology to represent energy-related occupant behavior in buildings. Part I: Introduction to the DNAs framework, Building and Environment, 92, pp. 764–777.

Hong, T., D'Oca, S., Taylor-Lange, S. C., Turner, W. J. N., Chen, Y. and Corgnati, S. P. (2015b). An ontology to represent energy-related occupant behavior in buildings. Part II: Implementation of the DNAS framework using an XML schema, Building and Environment, 94, pp. 196–205.

Hong, T., Yan, D., D'Oca, S. and Chen, C.-F. (2017). Ten questions concerning occupant behavior in buildings: The big picture, Building and Environment, 114, pp. 518–530.

Houston, M. L., Yu, A. P. P., Martin, D. A. and Probst, D. Y. (2018). Defining and Developing a Generic Framework for Monitoring Data Quality in Clinical Research, AMIA ... Annual Symposium proceedings. AMIA Symposium, 2018, pp. 1300–1309.

International Energy Agency (2018a). Annex 66: Definition and Simulation of Occupant Behavior in Buildings. Berkeley: Energy in Buildings and Communities Programme.

International Energy Agency (2018b) Occupant behaviour centric building design and operation EBC Annex 79. Berkeley: Energy in Buildings and Communities Programme.

Kerr, K. A., Norris, T. and Stockdale, R. (2008). The strategic management of data quality in healthcare, Health Informatics J, 14(4), pp. 259–66.

Macario, A. (2010). What does one minute of operating room time cost? Journal of Clinical Anesthesia, 22(4), pp. 233–236.

Mahdavi, A. and Tahmasebi, F. (2019). People in building performance simulation. In: Jan, L.M.H. and Roberto, L. (eds.) Building Performance Simulation for Design and Operation: CRC Press.

Nahm, M. (2012). Data Quality in Clinical Research: Springer London, pp. 175–201.

NHS (2019). NHS Long Term Plan: London: National Health Service. Available at: http://www.longtermplan.nhs.uk/, accessed February 2021.

NHS (2020a). Delivering a Net Zero National Health Service, London: National Health Service.

NHS (2020b). National Cost Collection 2019, London: National Health Service.

Vetrò, A., Canova, L., Torchiano, M., Minotas, C. O., Iemma, R. and Morando, F. (2016). Open data quality measurement framework: Definition and application to Open Government Data, Government Information Quarterly, 33(2), pp. 325–337.

Wang, X., Williams, C., Liu, Z. H. and Croghan, J. (2019). Big data management challenges in health research-a literature review, Brief Bioinform, 20(1), pp. 156–167.

An Approach for Cross-Data Querying and Spatial Reasoning of Tunnel Alignments

Marcel Stepien, Andre Vonthron, Markus König
Ruhr-Universität Bochum, Germany
marcel.stepien@ruhr-uni-bochum.de

Abstract. In mechanized tunnelling projects, finding a low-risk and cost-effective alignment is an important task. Several alignment variants are usually created and intensively evaluated. Variants often have different advantages and disadvantages and can lead to different constructive designs of the tunnel. To compare variants systematically, ontology databases can be utilized to merge BIM and GIS at data level to create an integrated model of the entire tunnelling project. Relevant information for decision-making can then be inferred. On the one hand, the implementation of queries is a popular and frequently used approach to check for semantic properties. On the other hand, using a query language to derive information from geometric data can be challenging, due to the necessity of processing geometric data prior to and during query execution. For this purpose, information from different sources must be linked and evaluated in a structured way. In particular, spatial relationships are investigated and implemented by adopting GeoSPARQL methods.

1. Introduction

In mechanized tunnelling projects, finding an optimal alignment is a crucial process. An alignment defines the most suitable path for the tunnel by considering cost-efficiency, safety and usability. Typically, variants of alignments are considered and investigated since given constraints and conditions allow the evaluation of alternative approaches. In the end, a preferred alignment is selected by including experts' feedback and investigation results, usually comparing data using a weighted decision matrix (WDM) method. This is a resource intensive and laborious process which requires a holistic analysis and comprehensive knowledge.

Alignments are created based on planning data and must especially consider geometric constraints and conditions, such as a consistent curve continuity and acceptable curvature. Based on the orientation and design of the cross-section a geometric model of the tunnel can be subsequently created using parametric modelling methods (Figure 1.a). In the context of the Building Information Modelling (BIM) method, semantic information is provided by the model structure and object properties, while the geometric representation is declared distinctly. In this case, the Industry Foundation Classes (IFC) are used to enable an interoperable and open data exchange. From version IFC4x1 (buildingSMART, 2018) the IFC support the representation of alignments. Traditionally, the IFC format is used for building construction projects. However, in recent years, the IFC are increasingly gaining attention from the civil engineering community for developing extensions to infrastructure domains, such as bridges, rails, and roads. A currently developing IFC-Tunnel extension focuses on the support of elements and attributes in the tunnel domain (buildingSMART, 2020).

To support decision making for the evaluation and selection of a preferred alignment, this paper investigates the use of query-languages for the validation of constraints and conditions, which are scattered over multiple documents. Particularly, data and documents used in Geographic Information Systems (GIS) contain required information for planning and construction of tunnelling projects, such as cadastral data, city models, surveys, and surface models (Figure 1.b).

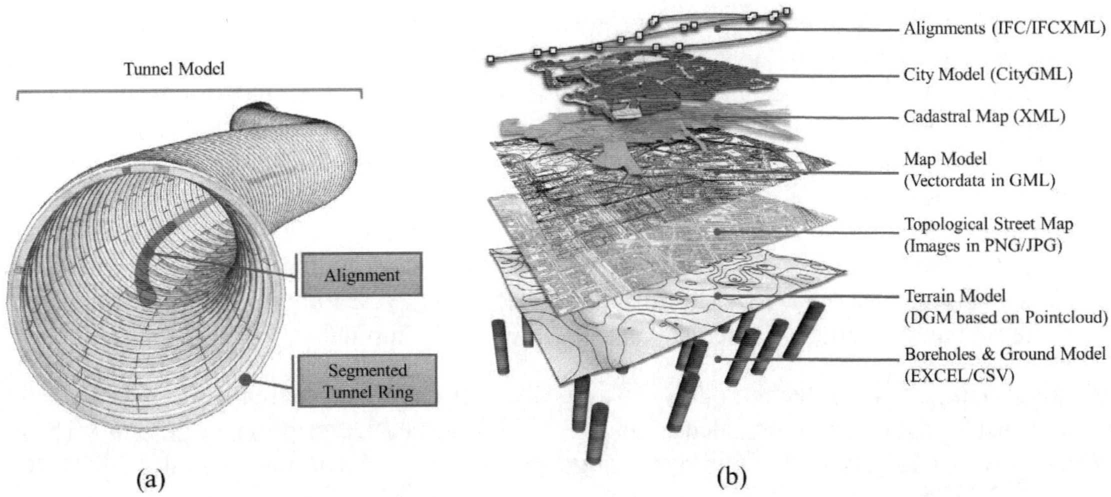

Figure 1: A tunnel model using an alignment (a) and a collection of aggregated planning data (b)

In general, these data cannot be combined without considerable effort, since digital documents differ in format, structure, semantic and geometry. There is often no direct semantic relation in distinct models that can be used to combine the data directly. In some cases, this is caused by the fact that the documents are only delivered in distinct layers. For example, it is not possible that built environment and cadastral maps can be matched based on assigned identifications. Therefore, relations must be created and a method for querying across multiple documents must be developed.

To establish links between the documents, the spatial relationship of geometric properties can be investigated. This is possible for geometric representations that are defined or transferable into the same coordinate reference system (CRS), using the spatial reference for a linked data approach. On the one hand, the implementation of queries is a popular and frequently used method to filter and check for semantic properties. On the other hand, using a query language to derive information from geometric data is challenging, due to the necessity of processing geometric data before and during query execution. This is especially challenging for mechanized tunnelling projects, where multiple documents and models must be compiled. Therefore, in this paper, an approach for querying geometric information across multiple models is described. First, a method for geometric and semantic data transformation is applied, to create a holistic database, which only consists of the required information for the spatial reasoning. This approach will be implemented based on a former developed framework for interactive exploration of alignments (Stepien et al., 2020). By extending this approach, generated tunnel models and planning data can be directly evaluated. As a result, the decision-making process in a collaborative and interactive planning environment for mechanized tunnelling projects can be significantly improved.

2. Related Work

For the development of ontology-based linked data a lot of existing approaches are relevant that deal with spatial information. This includes BIM and GIS integration, methods for processing geometric representation using spatial reasoning, methods to handle geo-localization, and frameworks for inferencing geometrical information. The research and developments in these areas are summarized accordingly.

BIM and GIS data are often integrated because they can benefit from each other, such as in planning phases or the reuse in city models. However, the integration is not trivial due to differences in coordinates systems and level of detail. Herle et al. (2020) found out that the issues in interoperability originate from in differences in the general purpose and perspectives of the modelling context. They also introduced the term Geospatial Information Modelling (GIM), which describes a composition of characteristics and geospatial features defined by location and orientation in Spatial Reference Systems (SRS). To be able to integrate the data from the different systems, they discussed four solutions, including model transformation, linked data approaches, the creation of unified models and the creation of integrated models, of which the first and second approach are already intensively applied.

By using Sematic Web technologies, linked data approaches are realized, which utilize ontology-based data structures, such as using the Resources Description Framework (RDF) (Miller, 1998) and the Web Ontology Language (OWL) (McGuinness et al., 2004). The produced RDF data structure consists of triples, declared by subject, predicate, and object, which form an RDF graph structure that can be used to easily represent facts and relations. To perform queries on these data structures, the SPARQL Protocol and RDF Query Language (SPARQL) presents the de facto standard.

Approaches, to integrate BIM and GIS with these technologies, have been investigated in recent years, but they are primarily focussing on semantics in construction of buildings. A general method has been presented by Hor et al. (2016) and Vilgertshofer et al. (2017). They utilize RDF-graphs to create ontology-based information models and to realize an intergration at the data level. For the integration in the infrastructure domain, Beetz and Borrmann (2018) presented an approachs which links OKSTRA road models and a CityGML built environment to perform queries on a combined context. The applications in the contexts of BIM and GIS use specific SPARQL extensions, such as BimSPARQL (Zhang et al., 2018) and GeoSPARQL (Open Geospatial Consortium, 2012). GeoSPARQL contains methods for spatial reasoning by implementing the Dimensionally Extended 9-Intersection Model (DE-9IM), which has been developed by Egenhofer (1989) and Kurata (2008). The DE-9IM method allows to check the intersections of boundaries, exterior and interior representations between geometries and organizes the results into a matrix. The general pattern of the matrix then enables to draw detailed conclusions about the spatial relation of the geometry, representing operators such as *intersection*, *disjoint*, *touch*, *equals*, *contains* or *covers*. Battle and Kolas (2012) validated this approach of using GeoSPARQL to create semantic links.

However, when performing queries on a combined context, it must be considered, that overlapping contents are specified by the originating schema, such as GML and IFC, and can completely differ in their definition concept. This especially applies to the definition of geometries. In a GIS context, most geometries are defined in a 2D context, originating from applications such as cartography, urban planning, or logistics. Also, it is possible to have 3D contexts, when dealing with CityGML models. Another important fact in the GIS context is, that the geometries are usually provided in different level of detail. In the BIM context, however, when models are exchanged using the IFC, there are lot of ways to represent the geometric information, both in design geometries as well as in tessellated representation forms. For both areas, it has been recognized, that they can produce very complex and cumbersome data structures, when converting them into RDF-graphs. This is due to the fact, that the IFC make intensive use of list representations (Pauwels et al., 2017). This produces a lot of semantic overhead, which not leads to a simple processing and understanding of queries. As a solution, the geometries can be converted to Well Known Text (WKT) representations (Herring, 2011), which provide a compact literals of the underlying geometries (Figure 2). This allows to process geometric comparisions in queries, which support the evaluation on machine level as well as support a human-readable understanding. This procedure has also already been validated by Beetz and Borrmann (2018).

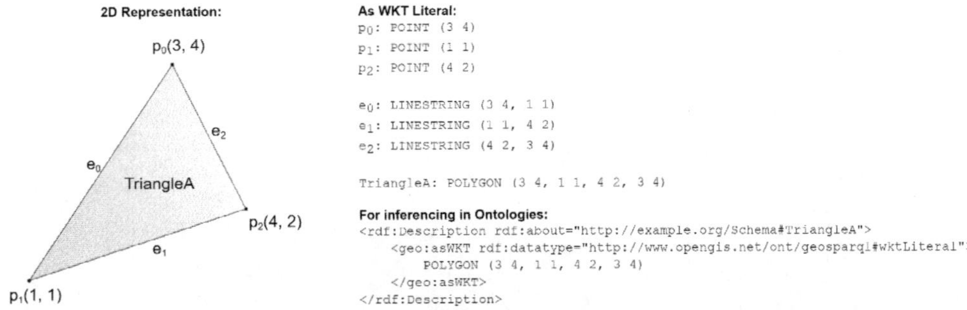

Figure 2: Example of translating geometric data to WKT literals.

When processing queries on a combined BIM and GIS context, another issue must be considered, which relates to the use of different coordinates references systems (CRS). GIS applications are usually covering areas of large dimensions, where distortions must be taken into account. Therefore, geometries are usually provided in absolute coordinates and in combination with a definition to the CRS. However, BIM-Models are created in a local context and therefore define only local coordinates in a cartesian coordinate system. The model then is put into a global context, by defining the related CRS and north direction as a global reference. To be able to process geometric operations in combination, the coordinates of both models must act within the same CRS. Additionally, the coordinates of the BIM model also must be projected into its CRS. GIS data usually operate in a local CRS, such as European Terrestrial Reference System 1989 (ETRS89), while BIM Models are usually referenced using the World Geodetic System WGS84. Using the definitions of European Petroleum Survey Group Geodesy (EPSG), most of these CRS have an equivalent EPSG-Code and transformation definition, which allows to easily transform between different CRS. To allow a direct transformation into WKT literals, the Open Spatial Consortium (2019) developed an WKT-CRS extension to allow a native support.

3. Methodology

The presented approach incorporates methods, which have also been used for approaches from Beetz and Borrmann (2018) and Vilgertshofer et al. (2017). They recommend the use of integrated ontology data structures for Linked Data to provide a semantically rich connection between BIM and GIS. In this approach, a similar method has been developed, which addresses the challenge of working with multiple documents and models that contain disjoint geometric representations in mechanized tunnelling. According to the methods described by Herle et al. (2020), the proposed approach is a combination of model transformation and linked data.

Therefore, semantic information will be queried across multiple documents and models by utilizing spatial relationships and query functions to check for geometric intersections based on the DE-9IM method. These can already be performed on simplified 2D geometries using the GeoSPARQL framework. However, for the application to BIM-based models, a 3D based context must be addressed. This additional geometric dimension presents further challenges since geometric operations in 3D require to take more degrees of freedom into account. To apply the DE-9IM method, in this case, it must be considered that a tunnel is geometrically located beneath the ground level and is typically modelled spatially disjoint in the vertical direction. Therefore, a method for spatial reasoning is developed by projecting complex 3D geometry to geometric 2D profiles (WKT profile) and the inferencing spatial relationships by querying primarily in cardinal directions. The method is divided into three stages (Figure 3).

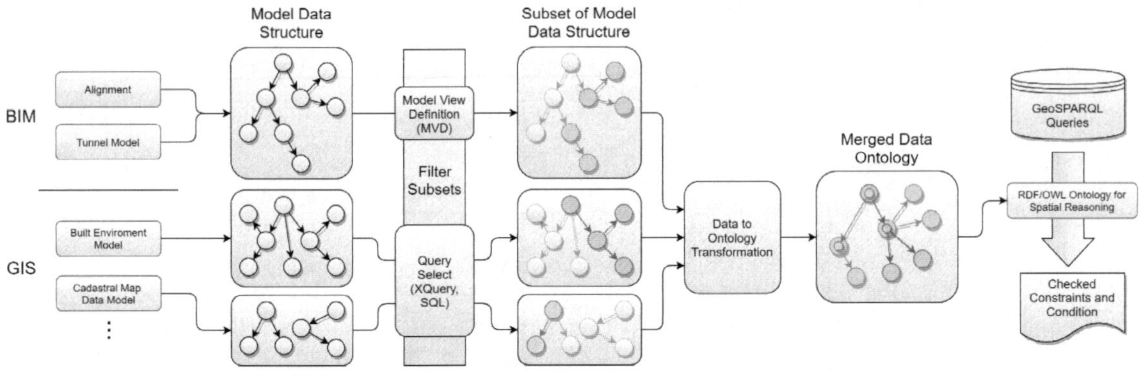

Figure 3: The general method for ontology-based querying across multiple models.

In the first stage, the BIM and GIS model data are filtered to consider only a subset of relevant semantic and geometric information. This procedure serves as data preparation for the implementation of ontology data structures and reduces the size of generated ontologies, as these can turn out into enormous proportions, otherwise. The data is reorganized in this process to enable direct integration into an ontology. Essentially, used data is assumed to be transferable into graph-based structures, which is a prerequisite for the next stage. The creation of the subsets can be achieved by individually transforming documents and models, for example, using Model View Definitions for IFC models and XQuery for XML documents.

The second stage addresses an approach for data to ontology transformation. Each subset of a model or document is thereby transformed from the original format into standalone ontology-based data structures. These data structures will be linked by inferencing their spatial relation. Consequently, an integrated cross-domain ontology is created that contains only geometric information for spatial reasoning. That includes a set of spatial objects that contain a representation and an identification pointing at its originating element (Figure *4*).

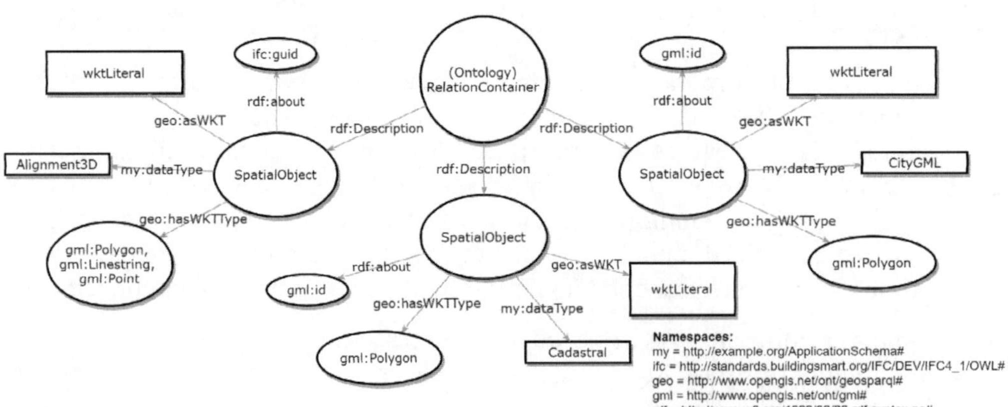

Figure 4: General structure of the ontology for spatial reasoning

Only the profiles of the elements will be substitutionally passed on to the data structure of the spatial ontology, consisting of 2D polygons, lines, or points. These are generated by projecting the original 3D representation on a 2D plane. The generated geometric representations are then translated into WKT literals for further use in the ontologies data structures (see Figure 2).

Finally, in the third stage, the instances of the ontology data structures are combined and queried as a collective. Database technologies can be utilized to enable efficient and comprehensive processing, such as triplestore databases. Incorporating the spatial relations in the querying process enables the establishment of links between documents and models. In this case, the geometric functions of the GeoSPARQL framework are used, since they can directly interpret the geometric profiles stored as WKT representations.

4. Case Studies

A prototypical implementation has been developed, including an RDF/OWL triplestore extension as well as a controlled execution of predefined queries, and which is based on an interactive planning environment for tunnel alignments (Stepien et al., 2020). In this paper, specifically, the Apache Jena framework (Apache Software Foundation, 2021) has been used, since it is already bundled with an implementation of the GeoSPARQL extension. An example project was created for testing query executions and to visualize the results (Figure 5). The project includes a built environment, tunnel alignments and cadastral map documents. The built environment is generated by querying available servers distributed by OpenStreetMap (OSM), using the Overpass-API (OpenStreetMap Wiki, 2020). The alignments are modelled and stored as IFC documents, using the IFC4x1 (alignment extension). Cadastral maps are included as GML documents. In following case-studies, a combination of geographic-geometric requirements and socio-cultural factors were investigated.

For the generation of the 2D WKT profiles, two different approaches where considered. On the on hand, for the BIM models (alignments and tunnel), the parametric definitions of the 3D geometry stored and provided in the model has been utilized, such as radius, length, and positions. This provides a necessary control over the general shape and level of detail of profiles (Figure 5, red profiles). On the other hand, retrieved GIS data contains explicit geometric information as facetted data. These are processed into 2D profiles, including the removal of overlapping geometrical structures (Figure 5, blue profiles). In some cases, such as for cadastral data, the geometric representation can be extracted directly, because they are already defined in a 2D profile structure (Figure 5, green profiles).

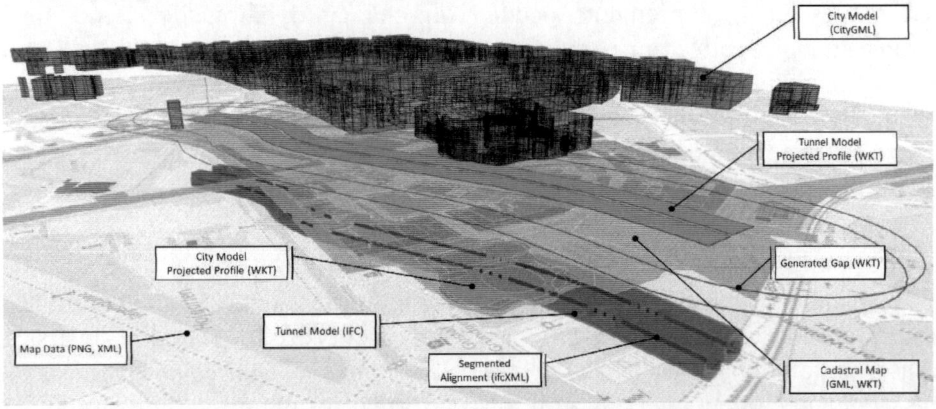

Figure 5: Composition of components used in the example project.

To solve the georeferencing of models from different context, the coordinates from the cartesian BIM models (alignment and tunnel models) are projected into their CRS and then transformed to the corresponding CRS of the GIS context. In this case all coordinates are considered in an WGS84 CRS, which are then easily convertible into WKT-CRS literals, and enable spatial queries among the models.

Case A. Finding all buildings that are located directly above the tunnel.

Finding all buildings that are close to the planned alignment is a relevant prerequisite, which are important for the planning process to investigate buildings and building types that are in the immediate vicinity of the planned alignment. In this case, the 2D profile of the tunnel model is utilized, to filter all buildings that are located directly above the planned tunnel, by inferencing the intersection between WKT profile representations (Figure 6).

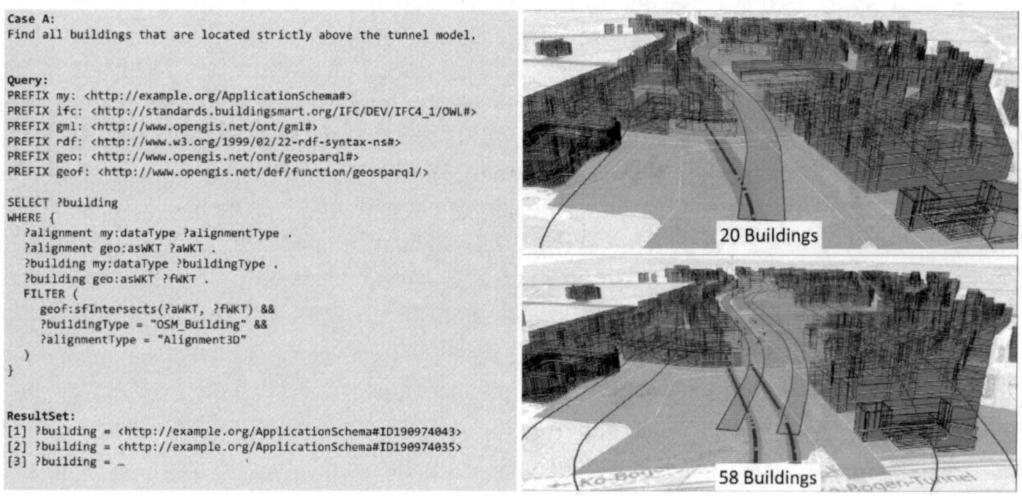

(a) (b)

Figure 6: The query performed in Case A (a) and the results visualized in the project environment (b)

Case B. Querying buildings under historical preservation that are in range of the alignment.

To find buildings that are in a specific range of the alignment, e.g. for the determination of the impact of settlements, a distance check is commonly performed. However, in tunnelling the considered range, where settlements occur, can change dynamically, depending on soil investigations, tunnel depth, tunnel diameter etc. In the process, an irregular shape for the geometric profile along the alignment that is represented as a gap around the tunnel profile is created. Using this gap for inferencing the intersection on WKT profiles is interpreted as a range constraint. To restrict the query also to selected buildings, which are under historic preservation (Figure 7), the attribute *heritage* (for OSM buildings) has been utilized.

Case C. Querying private buildings above the tunnel alignment and built on specific property.

Cadastral maps are commonly subdivided into multiple documents, containing specific interrelated information. In this case, two GML documents are inspected: The first document contains information about the land usage, such as *industrial and commercial* or *residential* areas. The second document contains additional information about building structures, such as

```
Case B:
Find all buildings that are considered cultural heritage in range around
the alignment.

Query: (Prefixes are omitted)

SELECT ?building
WHERE {
  ?area my:DataType "AlignmentGap" .
  ?area geo:asWKT ?aWKT .
  ?building my:DataType ?buildingType .
  ?building geo:asWKT ?bWKT .
  ?building my:heritage ?hValue .
  FILTER (
    geof:sfIntersects(?aWKT, ?bWKT) &&
    ?buildingType = "OSM_Building" &&
    ?hValue = "8"
  )
}

ResultSet:
[1] ?building = <http://example.org/ApplicationSchema#ID143672612>
```

(a)

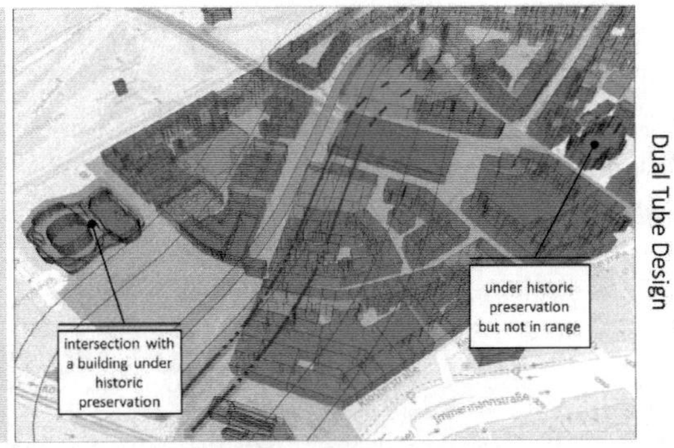

(b)

Figure 7: The query performed in Case B (a) and the results visualized in the project environment (b)

```
Case C:
Querying buildings marked as private above the tunnel alignment that are
built on specific property.

Query: (Prefixes are ommited)

SELECT ?buildingArea ?cadastral
WHERE {
  ?alignment my:DataType ?alignmentType .
  ?alignment geo:asWKT ?aWKT .
  ?cadastral my:DataType ?cadastralType .
  ?cadastral geo:asWKT ?cWKT .
  ?cadastral my:usage ?cadastralUsage .
  ?buildingArea my:DataType ?buildingAreaType .
  ?buildingArea geo:asWKT ?bWKT .
  ?buildingArea my:usage ?buildingUsage .
  FILTER (
    geof:sfIntersects(?aWKT, ?cWKT) &&
    geof:sfIntersects(?cWKT, ?bWKT) &&
    ?cadastralType = "CadastralLand" &&
    ?buildingAreaType = "CadastralBuilding" &&
    ?alignmentType = "Alignment3D" &&
    ?cadastralUsage = "Industrie- und Gewerbefläche" &&
    ?buildingUsage = "1100"
  )
}

ResultSet:
[1]
(?cadastral = <http://example.org/ApplicationSchema#DENW20AL00010QHPTN>)
(?buildingArea = <http://example.org/ApplicationSchema#DENW20AL0000qXbk>)

[2]
(?cadastral = <http://example.org/ApplicationSchema#DENW20AL00010QHPTN>)
(?buildingArea = <http://example.org/ApplicationSchema#DENW20AL0000qXb8>)
…
```

(a)

(b)

Figure 8: The query performed in Case C (a) and the results visualized in the project environment (b)

properties that distinguish between *private*, *civil* or *public* usage. Despite both are considered as cadastral maps, these documents do not have a direct semantic connection. By utilizing their spatial properties, the intended relations across multiple documents can be derived (Figure 8).

5. Conclusion and Discussion

Working with multiple semantically different resources, our approach is using spatial reasoning methods to establish linked data models. For this purpose, information has been merged into ontology data structures and queries has been systematically applied, which makes it possible to check geographic-geometric requirements and socio-cultural factors across documents and models. As noted, checking spatial relations is particularly challenging for projects in mechanized tunnelling, because in 3D geometric representations they are commonly spatially disjoint and defined in different levels of detail and distinct data structures. Therefore, to enable spatial reasoning in cardinal directions, geometric representations were transformed into WKT profiles representations and merged into a holistic spatial ontology. These profiles are not limited to simple projections of geometric representations but can also be utilized to handle constraints and conditions, such as inferencing spatial relations by range. Integrating the presented approach into an interactive and responsive planning environment, the decision-making process for planning tunnel alignments can be improved. Assuming that such an environment could process queries in a reasonable amount of time would be a valuable asset in collaborative approaches for planning in mechanized tunnelling.

However, some challenges remain to be investigated. Producing RDF graph from the input data results into very large datasets, for example, IFC models result into amounts by a factor of ten. Especially for geometric representations, this would require a scalable approach already for performance reasons. Therefore, it is common practice to reduce the considered amount of data to a manageable minimum. However, when it is necessary to reintroduce more data afterwards, it is not trivial to maintain the consistency and integrity of the RDF graph. Another challenge is the general integration and efficient implementation of 3D based operators into the relating query languages. Progress in this direction has already been addressed (Borrmann and Rank, 2008, 2009), but requires further investigation and the integration into the infrastructure domain. For example, retrieving the actual excavation volume between the tunnel and soil in mechanized tunnelling projects.

Acknowledgments

The authors wish to thank the German Research Foundation (DFG) for their financial support of this work within the framework of the subproject D1 of the Collaborative Research Center SFB 837 *Interaction models in mechanized tunnelling*.

References

Apache Software Foundation (2021) Apache Jena (3.16.0) [Computer program]. Available at https://jena.apache.org/ (Accessed 1 March 2021).

Battle, R. and Kolas, D. (2012) 'Enabling the Geospatial Semantic Web with Parliament and GeoSPARQL', Semantic Web Journal, vol. 3, no. 4, pp.355–370.

Beetz, J. and Borrmann, A. (2018) 'Benefits and limitations of linked data approaches for road modeling and data exchange', Workshop of the European Group for Intelligent Computing in Engineering, pp.245–261.

Borrmann, A. and Rank, E. (2008) 'Topological operators in a 3D spatial query language for building information models', Proceedings of the 12th ICCCBE, vol. 2.

Borrmann, A. and Rank, E. (2009) 'Specification and implementation of directional operators in a 3D spatial query language for building information models', Advanced Engineering Informatics, vol. 23, no. 1, pp.32–44.

buildingSMART (2018) Industry Foundation Classes: IFC4.1 [Online]. Available at https://standards.buildingsmart.org/IFC/RELEASE/IFC4_1/FINAL/HTML/ (Accessed March 2021).

buildingSMART (2020) Infrastructure Room: IFC-Tunnel Requirements Analysis Report [Online]. Available at https://www.buildingsmart.org/standards/rooms/infrastructure/ (Accessed 1 March 2021).

Egenhofer, M. J. (1989) 'A formal definition of binary topological relationships', International conference on foundations of data organization and algorithms, pp.457–472.

Herle, S., Becker, R., Wollenberg, R. and Blankenbach, J. (2020) 'GIM and BIM', PFG – Journal of Photogrammetry, Remote Sensing and Geoinformation Science, vol. 88, no. 1, pp.33–42.

Hor, A. H., Jadidi, A. and Sohn, G. (2016) 'BIM-GIS integrated geospatial information model using semantic web and RDF graphs', ISPRS Ann. Photogramm. Remote Sens. Spat. Inf. Sci, vol. 3, no. 4, pp.73–79.

Kurata, Y. (2008) 'The 9+-intersection: A universal framework for modeling topological relations', International Conference on Geographic Information Science, pp.181–198.

McGuinness, D. L., van Harmelen, F. and others (2004) 'OWL web ontology language overview', W3C recommendation, vol. 10, no. 10, p. 2004.

Miller, E. (1998) 'An introduction to the resource description framework', Bulletin of the American Society for Information Science and Technology, vol. 25, no. 1, pp.15–19.

Open Geospatial Consortium (2012) A Geographic Query Language for RDF Data [Online]. Available at https://www.ogc.org/standards/geosparql (Accessed 1 March 2021).

Open Geospatial Consortium (2019) Geographic information - Well-known text representation of coordinate reference systems [Online]. Available at http://www.opengis.net/doc/is/wkt-crs/2.0.6 (Accessed 1 March 2021).

(2011) OpenGIS® Implementation Standard for Geographic information - Simple feature access - Part 1: Common architecture [Corrigendum], Open Geospatial Consortium and Wayland, MA.

OpenStreetMap Wiki (2020) Overpass API - OpenStreetMap Wiki [Online]. Available at https://wiki.openstreetmap.org/w/index.php?title=Overpass_API.

Pauwels, P., Krijnen, T., Terkaj, W. and Beetz, J. (2017) 'Enhancing the ifcOWL ontology with an alternative representation for geometric data', Automation in Construction, vol. 80, pp.77–94.

Stepien, M., Vonthron, A. and König, M. (2020) 'Integrated Platform for Interactive and Collaborative Exploration of Tunnel Alignments', Proceedings of the 18th International Conference on Computing in Civil and Building Engineering: ICCCBE 2020. Cham, 2020. Cham, Springer International Publishing; Imprint: Springer, pp.320–334.

Vilgertshofer, S., Amann, J., Willenborg, B., Borrmann, A. and Kolbe, T. H. (2017) 'Linking BIM and GIS models in infrastructure by example of IFC and CityGML', in Computing in Civil Engineering 2017, pp.133–140.

Zhang, C., Beetz, J. and Vries, B. de (2018) 'BimSPARQL: Domain-specific functional SPARQL extensions for querying RDF building data', Semantic Web, vol. 9, no. 6, pp.829–855.

Ontological reasoning in factory-BIM: An industrial case study for an automotive OEM

Jeremias Merz[a,b], Timo Hartmann[a]
[a] Technische Universität Berlin, Germany, [b] Volkswagen AG, Germany
jeremias.merz@volkswagen.de

Abstract. In the factory planning process of a large German automotive original equipment manufacturer (OEM), the integration of all planning disciplines (e.g. the assembly line equipment) in one federated 3D factory model is state of the art. However, the massive layer-based factory models are limited in their knowledge about the contained assets. The implicit constraints between production and building domain are not formalized explicitly and the process depends on manual checks and interdisciplinary communication. This research proposes the formalization of some exemplary constraints through ontological modelling. The competency questions were derived in a bottom-up manner through an ethnographic approach with focus on interface constraints. An exemplary process integration shows how the ontology can be used in three different use cases addressing the spatial, functional and accessibility claim of an asset in the factory.

1. Introduction

The architecture, engineering and construction (AEC) industry increasingly adopts methods of Building Information Modelling (BIM) which aims at the comprehensive digital representation of buildings (Borrmann et al. 2018). Its counterpart in the manufacturing industry and the respective factory planning process is the Digital Factory, representing the data from a product and production centric view (Wiendahl et al. 2015).

The current state of the art for BIM systems has the maturity level 2 (Bew, Richards 2008), facing interoperability issues due to custom data structures and dependency on proprietary file formats. BIM maturity level 3 (Bew, Richards 2008) is currently being developed by efforts such as the Linked Building Data Community Group (LBD-CG), aiming at interdisciplinary interoperability through open web-based standards (Rasmussen et al. 2020). These developments are highly relevant for the factory building planning because the product life cycle provokes cyclical remodeling activities. For automotive factories the change from fuel-based models to battery electric vehicles causes many large remodeling efforts to existing factories in the years to come. Additionally, building models and their respective data structuring ontologies can form the base for new technologies, such as big data and machine learning, that emerge with the new landscape of Industry 4.0 and Digital Twin applications in the manufacturing industry (Lu 2017).

Factory planning involves even more stakeholders than the planning process of a traditional housing project. Hence, the adoption of BIM technologies to the production domain is a complex matter. Burggräf et al. (2019) found that the interface of these traditionally separated planning fields needs further investigation. The integration of geometric 3D-data for all stakeholders involved in factory planning, including process information in the form of static hull geometries in one model, is state of the art (Wiendahl et al. 2015). However, semantic interoperability in the federated factory environment, which is one of the key objectives for BIM (Eastman et al. 2010), is a goal yet to be achieved.

This research aims at conceptualizing knowledge that can be used to express interface constraints between physical assets of different disciplines in the factory. It is assumed that all the assets have an assigned geometry in the federated model. With an exemplary process integration, this research demonstrates how an ontology can be used to constantly elicit knowledge, and therefore expand the knowledge base to fulfil the practitioner's needs. Its alignment with semantic web technologies ensures the future usability and maintenance of the ontology in practice. However, knowledge formalization is a complex task. This research follows an ethnographic approach proposed by Hartmann and Trappey (2020) to collect relevant interface information. Practitioners were closely monitored and relevant interface information, that has led to cost overruns and schedule delays, was gathered. This knowledge can be used to assure compliance in the federated environment. The interface description of assets is based on the building topology ontology (BOT) developed by the LBD-CG (Rasmussen et al. 2020).

2. Point of Departure

Ontologies formally conceptualize information about physical or abstract objects and their relations. They can represent the knowledge of a specific domain and enable its computational usage and automation (Hartmann and Trappey 2020). More importantly, an ontology is an explicit specification of a shared conceptualization (Gruber 1995). For interfaces several cross-functional experts have to agree on their shared understanding to obtain interoperability. Therefore, ontologies play an important role for interoperability between different computer systems for both the manufacturing industry and the AEC-industry. The standard data format for information exchange in manufacturing is ISO-STEP (Standard for the Exchange of Product model data, ISO 10303), while the AEC-industry aims at semantic operability with IFC (Industry Foundation Classes, ISO 16739), IDM (Information Delivery Manual, ISO 29481) and MVD process (Model View Definition) (Eastman et al. 2010).

This research formalizes knowledge at the interface of manufacturing and building. Within this research field, Beetz et al. (2018) introduced a six step IDM/MVD process for information exchange with IFC. The schema allows companies to map their native data structures into open standards. This enables restructuring existing layer-based legacy data (ISO 13567) as well as decrease one-sided dependencies on software vendors. However, MVDs have to be implemented specifically for every software system. Triggering such IDM/MVD activities for factory planning is a complex undertaking that needs to be justified beforehand. The reference to new technologies, e.g. model-based quantity take-off for procurement or reasoning and model checking mechanisms, are not sufficient in this context.

In the manufacturing domain ontologies have a long history. For factory planning, their main fields of application are systems for modelling of processes, kinematics, ergonomics and logistics (Wiendahl et al. 2015). However, ontological frameworks for manufacturing such as the Virtual Factory Data Model (VFDM, Terkaj et al. 2012) integrate the product, process and resource domain for Product Lifecycle Management (PLM), rather than focusing on the planning aspects of the factory. The framework can be used for simulation to ensure the manufacturing performance in a product and process oriented way. Thus, it exceeds the scope of this research which focusses on modelling relations between physical assets for factory construction planning.

Interoperability efforts generally result in high complexity because they integrate a large number of concepts and views on the data. Accounting for its extensive approach, Eastman et al. (2010) described IFC as complex and redundant. A recent literature review on interoperability in BIM conducted by Sattler et al. (2019) found many research efforts that deal with making data available through integrative approaches.

However, data integration comes with the drawback of the aforementioned complexity. An illustrative example for this is the ifcOWL (OWL, web ontology language) ontology introduced by Pauwels and Terkaj (2016). It maps the semantic web language to the IFC schema and currently consists of 1331 classes and 1599 properties for IFC4_ADD2. Evidently, its size makes ifcOWL complex, difficult to understand and manage as well as inefficient for semantic reasoning (Rasmussen et al. 2020). However, the serialization of IFC data in OWL enables direct querying and inferences through semantic query languages (SPARQL) and rule languages, e.g. semantic web rule language (SWRL) or shapes constraint language (SHACL).

A contrast to this complexity is the building topology ontology developed by the LBD-CG (Rasmussen et al. 2020). BOT is expressed in OWL and focuses on modeling the high-level topology of a building and the respective relations between building elements. The lightweight orientation and the intention for usage with other ontologies offers a good base for the ontology development in this research. In the current version 0.3.1, BOT consists of 7 classes, 14 object properties and one datatype property (Rasmussen et al. 2020). In particular, it builds on three main concepts, namely bot:Zone, bot:Element and bot:Interface. While an element is a tangible object, a zone is a spatial concept in the world that can serve as a frame for several objects. Both can be assigned 3D geometries and be connected by interfaces which can carry additional information to qualify the interface. The geometry specification is the focus of another research project by the LBD-CG. The ontology for managing geometry (OMG) is an upper ontology for representation of geometry and dependencies between geometric and non-geometric properties (Wagner et al. 2019). The concept of dependencies between multiple geometries for the same element is promising. Nevertheless, for the first representation approach of dependencies in this research, a geometric description is considered out of scope.

Both domains manufacturing and building have been introduced. Nonetheless, the research gap described by Burggräf et al. (2019) persists. This research aims at the conceptualization of interface constraints in a federated factory environment through an ontology.

3. Research approach

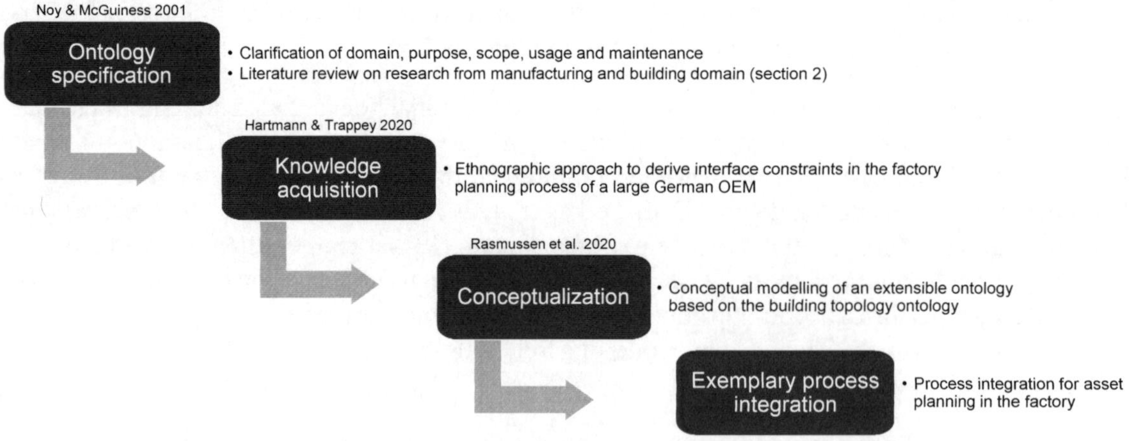

Figure 1: Research approach

This research is based on a hybrid approach that includes several methods from literature depicted in Figure 1. The four main steps are: 1) Firstly, the ontology was specified following the approach from Noy and McGuiness (2001). 2) Secondly, the knowledge to represent in the ontology was retrieved. This was conducted through an ethnographic approach suggested by Hartmann and Trappey (2020). 3) Thirdly, the baseline principles from the collected knowledge were extracted, generalized into core principles and expressed according to BOT (Rasmussen et al. 2020). 4) The last step shows an exemplary process integration addressing the spatial claim of an asset in the factory planning process. It can be expanded the accessibility and functional claims of the asset. The workflow shows how the formalized knowledge can help within the current process and assure the compliance of the federated environment with predefined rules.

The ontology specification follows a set of questions from Noy and McGuiness (2001). Its goal is to clarify the scope of the ontological model and clearly define the research purpose.

Domain – What is the domain that the ontology will cover? The ontology is developed to highlight exemplary constraints between disciplines in the factory planning process of a large German automotive OEM. The focus on interface constraints was derived from the literature review. It was shown that there is a gap, that can be filled by conceptualizing domain specific knowledge.

Purpose 1 – For what will the ontology be used? The ontology will mainly be used to ensure the planning quality and to avoid cost overruns and schedule delays, caused by insufficient project communication. As a side effect, the retrieved and administrated assets can be used to enable BIM-capabilities, such as quantity take-off for procurement or facility management tasks during the operation phase of the factory.

Purpose 2 – For what types of questions should the information in the ontology provide answers? Generally, the ontology will cover interface constraints between different planning disciplines. An exemplary question would be: Is the welding robot connected to a compressed air outlet? It is therefore built in an extensible manner. The competency questions are retrieved through an ethnographic approach.

Usage & Maintenance – Who will use and maintain the ontology? The intended end users of the ontology are factory planners of the automotive OEM analyzed in this paper. They will use the knowledge base to assure quality in the planning process throughout the company's worldwide construction activities. The main usages are the checking of missing data and the support of project communication between internal and external planners through digital representation. The proposed workflow integration helps to create a knowledge base which is maintained and expanded by the planners themselves. It enables to elicit individual knowledge from a single planer and create collective knowledge. This shared conceptualization can be retrieved more easily and standardized.

4. Development of an ontology to highlight interdisciplinary constraints in automotive factory projects

4.1 Knowledge acquisition

Hartmann et al. (2012) found that many software tools do not fulfill the initial expectations on capabilities from engineers. This can be prevented by closely targeting the actual purpose of the engineers. Therefore, the knowledge needs to be extracted directly from the context they work in. Hartmann and Trappey (2020) proposed that this can be achieved by ethnographic exploration through bottom-up knowledge modelling.

This research was conducted in the planning process of a large German automotive OEM closely monitoring planning activities and key stakeholders. Generally, it can be stated that hundreds, even thousands of interface-rules exist in an automotive factory. In the process that was analyzed in this research there was no formalization mechanism for such constraints. Hence, the checking of rule-sets was completely dependent on manual processes and based on implicit expert knowledge. The collected rules and constraints are examples that help to extract the general underlying principles. They were chosen because their non-compliance either has caused large cost overruns in past projects or is the focus of many manual checking activities. The rules are expressed as requirements (first-order logic) and listed in Table 1. In a next research step, they can be implemented through rule languages such as SWRL or SHACL.

Table 1: Exemplary Interface Constraints for Factory Planning.

No	Subject (Discipline*)	Predicate	Object (Discipline*)	Constraint-Type
1	Column (B)	requires	Construction range (B)	Spatial
2	Electric suspension track (CT)	requires	Moving range (CT)	Spatial
3	Material elevator (A / CT)	requires	Moving range (A / CT)	Spatial
4	Logistic route (TL)	requires	Moving range (TL)	Spatial
5	Handling robot (A)	requires	Material Supply Area (A)	Functional
6	Material Supply Area (A)	requires	Logistic route (TL)	Accessibility
7	Welding robot (A)	requires	Exhaust air duct (HVAC)	Functional
8	Electrical duct (EE)	requires	Electric control cabinet (EE)	Functional
9	Electric control cabinet (EE)	requires	Steel-works platform (SW)	Functional
10	Assembly Line (A)	requires	Filling station (A)	Functional
11	Filling Station (A)	requires	Steel-works platform (SW)	Functional
12	Assembly Line (A)	requires	Car under body station (A)	Functional
13	Car Underbody Station (A)	requires	Steel-works platform (SW)	Functional
14	Steel-works platform (SW)	requires	Sprinkler system (FS)	Functional
15	Steel-works platform (SW)	requires	Light-installation (EE)	Functional
*Discipline abbreviations: B = Building, CT = Conveyor Technique, EE = Electrical Equipment, SW = Steel-Works, A = Assembly, TL = Transport Logistics, FS = Fire Safety, HVAC = Heating, Ventilation and Air Conditioning				

Generally, the rules can be classified into three categories namely spatial, accessibility and functional. In the planning phase, an asset's interface requirement to other disciplines can be described as a specific claim in relation to other disciplines. If this claim is met, the asset will work properly during the operation phase of the factory.

The first four rules (1–4) describe code compliance issues. In these cases the object is a static assistance geometry that conceptualizes process information for usability ensuring the spatial claim of an asset in the factory. The following rules (4–6) work together in order to ensure the accessibility claim of an asset, in this case a handling robot. This robot must be approachable by a logistic route which itself requires an assigned geometry to assure its spatial claim.

Additional inherent manufacturing knowledge is modeled through the three rule chains (8–9–14–15, 10–11–14–15 and 12–13–14–15). An assembly line (A) requires a filling station (A) which is built on a steel-works-platform (SW). Moreover, this platform needs sprinklers (FS) and light-installations (EE). These components all have dependencies and are all planned by different disciplines. Hence, extensive communication is required. If the knowledge for these interface constraints is not formalized, some of the components might be forgotten in the model and will cause additional costs on the construction site.

4.2 Conceptualization

The factory model evolves around the assets which will be represented as elements. The point of departure in section 2 introduced the building topology ontology. In this section, a conceptual ontology based on BOT is created (see Figure 2). Generally, the zone-concepts bot:Site, bot:Building, bot:Storey can be matched to FactorySite, FactoryBuilding and Storey. For the application on factory legacy data, the existing zones are not explicitly expressed in the model and can be matched to the respective elements through spatial calculation of their coordinates to the defined zone concepts. As a starting point for the conceptualization of data from different disciplines, this view is introduced to cluster the data. It follows the structure of planning departments that each use their own specialized software tool to carry out their planning task, resulting in diverse custom data structures (Rasmussen et al. 2020). The disciplines carry a data-property through <hasClassification> with the cardinality (1:1) which defines their classification in relation to the other disciplines. This is needed for a semi-automated identification of the discipline's priority in clash evaluation.

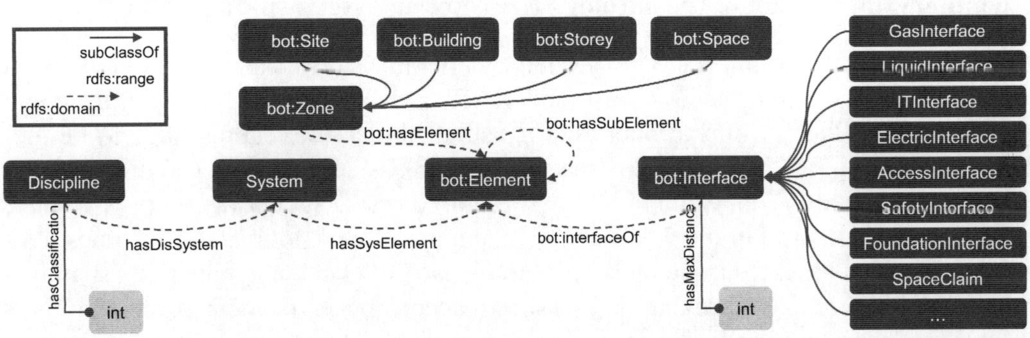

Figure 2: Representation of elements for the ontology

A discipline can have several subsystems. The System-class is connected through the property <hasDisSystem> (1:n). They cluster the elements into groups in order to match a custom layer-structure into this ontology. The need for such a comprehensive class becomes evident for robotic installations that are usually clustered into stations. The Element-class is connected through the property <hasSysElement> (1:n) and can itself be an assembly of several sub-elements in alignment with BOT.

The bot:interface class can qualify a relation between elements or zones (range) through its property <bot:interfaceOf>. Through data-properties the interface can receive quantifiable attributes. For this ontology, this circumstance is used to prepare the relation for a spatial query matching algorithm. The data-property <hasMaxDistance> serves as an input, if the interface partner is not explicitly modeled. The specific interface requirements between elements can be expressed through subclasses of bot:Interface and the reification of <bot:interfaceOf>, creating sub-properties. Exemplary subclasses of bot:Interface for the use case of a factory are

GasInterface, LiquidInterface, ITInterface, ElectricInterface, AccessInterface, SafetyInterface, FoundationInterface and SpaceClaim. Some according sub-properties for <bot:interfaceOf> are depicted in Table 2.

Table 2: Exemplary sub-properties of <bot:interfaceOf> for a factory

Name	Domain	Range
gasInterfaceOf	GasInterface	WeldingRobot, HandlingRobot, Workplace, FreshAirDuctOutlet, ExhaustAirHood, CompressedAirOutlet, AcetlyenOutlet, …
liquidInterfaceOf	LiquidInterface	WeldingRobot, CoolingFluidDuct, ...
accessInterfaceOf	AccessInterface	HandlingRobot, LogisticRoute, …
spaceClaimOf	SpaceClaim	InstallationRange, ConstructionRange, WorkingRange, MaintenanceRange, …
electricInterfaceOf	ElectricInterface	WeldingRobot, HandlingRobot, Workplace, ElectricityDuct, …

Many different interfaces in the factory can be expressed and specified by these sub-properties. In a first step, the creation of such connections can be carried out manually by the practitioner. Later on, for every instance of e.g. a welding robot that has many interfaces, the respective interface elements can be acquired by spatial querying. This can be done as a next research step through a constraint language such as SHACL. Furthermore, the knowledge about the interfaces can be integrated into the workflow of the practitioner.

4.3 Exemplary application of the ontology to assure an asset's spatial claim

An asset can have many interface constraints. Generally, they can be clustered into three different categories: spatial, accessibility and functional (see Table 1). For fully compliant performance in the factory during operation phase all the asset's claims have to be met. An asset works properly if it has sufficient space (no clash), is accessible for maintenance works or material supply and is connected to all other required assets such as a compressed air outlet or a special foundation. Figure 3 shows an exemplary workflow that illustrates how the knowledge about an asset from the ontology can be used to check and ensure its spatial claim. The other claims can be checked and ensured accordingly, if their respective interface constraints are saved within the ontology.

In a factory, an element's spatial claim consists of three ranges namely the installation range, the construction range and the working range. The element's installation range is assumed to be inherent to the model through its geometry. However, the other two ranges have to be assigned to the element explicitly. The ontology can help to identify whether the elements are available or not. An exemplary process for the spatial claim checking of a welding robot is depicted in Figure 3.

The first check reviews the SpaceClaim-Interface of the robot with its working range. If the <spaceClaimOf> property between welding robot and working range is not fulfilled at instance level, the partner needs to be assigned. This spatial query can be implemented in the federated environment with the datatype-property <hasMaxDistance>. It indicates the allowed maximum distance between the interface-elements. Either an interface-partner is available and assigned, or a request for information (RFI) is triggered. This can result in the working range being added to the model or in finding another solution through involvement of other stakeholders in the hierarchy. The next check repeats the aforementioned steps for the property <spaceClaimOf> between welding robot and construction range.

After this process step, the three spatial interface requirements for the respective element's instance have been defined. This part of the workflow evolves around the spatial query that matches the respective elements. The checking of non-geometric constrains ends after this process step (above the dashed line in Figure 3). The geometric constraints such as the spatial claim can then be checked through a clash analysis in a second process step. The type of clash analysis is not scope of this paper. However, the clash analysis is conducted at the lowest element level. The ontology can then be used to group the clashes up to the highest element level (example depicted on the left in Figure 3). Subsequently, the clashes can be classified by the discipline hierarchy defined through the datatype property <hasClassification> (see Figure 2). The outcome of this classification can be used for the resolving of the clash in a next step. The hierarchy of the clash partner defines if the partner must be moved or the respective robot. If the partner is moved, the spatial claim for the robot is validated. If the robot is moved a new clash analysis is required, starting a new iteration of the described second process (below the dashed line in Figure 3).

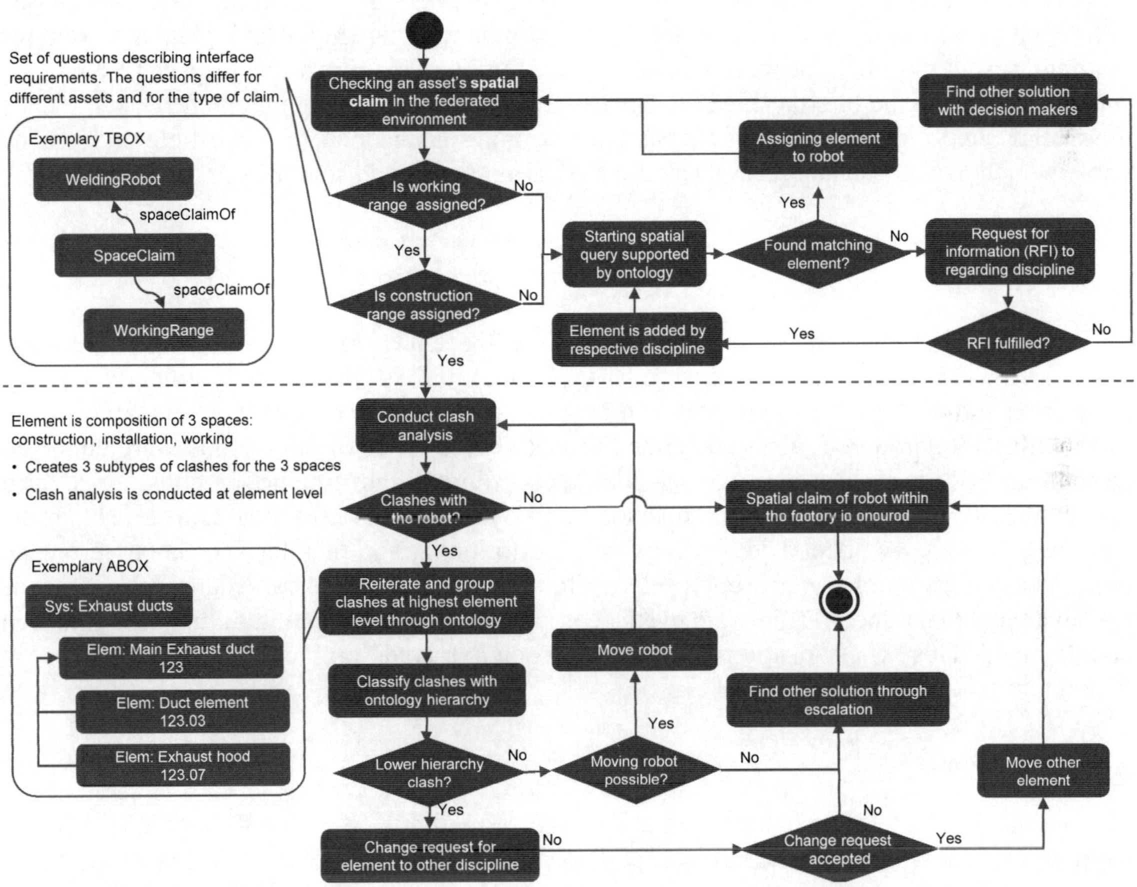

Figure 3: Planning an asset in a federated factory model

5. Discussion

Many research activities evolve around both the ontological modelling of factories and implementing interoperability for building information modelling. Some researchers have addressed the gap that hardly any focus has been set on the combination of the two research fields (Burggräf et al. 2019). One of the proposed solutions is to highlight the production domain, including its interdisciplinary dependencies. The proposed conceptual framework can serve as a base to collect operational knowledge in a larger case study for a specific discipline. It is open to expansion and further refinement. Within the factory planning process, the formalization of interdependencies can avoid human errors that cause cost overruns and schedule delays and beyond that it can enable larger potentials, such as the qualification of more complex interface information. This could prevent the installation of over dimensioned technical equipment based on manual communication, therefore decreasing costs during the operation phase.

In practice, the usage of this ontology depends on its automatic population. Technologies like the ifcOWL ontology (Pauwels and Terkaj 2016) automatically create the data from the model in the required format. Such mapping of object libraries to open standards is a key enabler of this technology. However, it is important that the complexity is minimized for end-users.

Another important aspect of an ontology that captures interface requirements is the seamless process integration. It is essential to validate that the applied rules are up to date. This can be developed into a framework of automated code compliance checking. The logical next step for the ontology is the implementation of the spatial query. This maps the respective elements connected through the interface and checks the federated model. For implementation, the need for spatial querying was highlighted. Spatial reasoning is an open research field and can be implemented using rule languages such as SHACL as suggested by Stolk and McGlinn (2020).

6. Conclusion

This research introduces a framework that enables the elicitation of implicit rules between assets in the factory planning process of a large automotive OEM. The exemplary process integration shows, how the framework can be used in practice to ensure the compliance of an asset with its environment in the federated model. Three types of constraints were collected through an ethnographic approach: spatial, accessibility and functional constraints. The examples show that cost overruns and schedule delays related to assets described through the framework can be avoided. The ontology and the formalization of interfaces is based on the building topology ontology, making it interoperable with other concepts. Additionally, this has the advantage that a specification and even a computational quantification of the interfaces, can be integrated. This benefit distinguishes the approach to manual project communication.

Acknowledgements

This research has been funded through a research cooperation between Volkswagen AG and Civil and Building Systems Department at Technical University Berlin. The results, opinions and conclusions expressed in this article are not necessarily those of Volkswagen AG.

References

Beetz, J.; Borrmann, A.; Weise, M. (2018): Process-Based Definition of Model Content. In A. Borrmann, M. König, C. Koch, J. Beetz (Eds.): Building Information Modeling. Technology Foundations and Industry Practice, pp.127–138.

Bew, M.; Richards, M. (2008): Bim Maturity Model. Construct IT Autumn 2008 Members' Meeting.

Borrmann, A.; König, M.; Koch, C.; Beetz, J. (Eds.) (2018): Building Information Modeling. Technology Foundations and Industry Practice.

Burggräf, P.; Dannapfel, M.; Schneidermann, D.; Ebade Esfahani, M.; Schwamborn, N. (2019): Integrated Factory Modelling: Using BIM to disrupt the interface between manufacturing and construction in factory planning. In W. P. de Wilde, L. Mahdjoubi, A. G. Garrigós (Eds.): BIM 2019. Seville, Spain, 9–11 October 2019: WIT Press Southampton UK (WIT Transactions on The Built Environment), pp.143–155.

Eastman, C. M.; Jeong, Y.-S.; Sacks, R.; Kaner, I. (2010): Exchange Model and Exchange Object Concepts for Implementation of National BIM Standards. In J. Comput. Civ. Eng. 24 (1), pp.25–34. DOI: 10.1061/(ASCE)0887-3801(2010)24:1(25).

Hartmann, T.; Trappey, A. (2020): Advanced Engineering Informatics - Philosophical and methodological foundations with examples from civil and construction engineering. In DIBE 4 (12), p. 100020. DOI: 10.1016/j.dibe.2020.100020.

Hartmann, T.; van Meerveld, H.; Vossebeld, N.; Adriaanse, A. (2012): Aligning building information model tools and construction management methods. In Autom. Constr. 22, pp.605–613. DOI: 10.1016/j.autcon.2011.12.011.

Lu, Y. (2017): Industry 4.0. A survey on technologies, applications and open research issues. In J. Ind. Inf. Integr. 6 (4), pp.1–10. DOI: 10.1016/j.jii.2017.04.005.

Noy, N. F.; McGuiness, D. L. (2001): Ontology Development 101: A Guide to Creating Your First Ontology (Tech. Rep., KSL-01-05). Available online at http://ksl.stanford.edu/people/dlm/papers/ontology-tutorial-noy-mcguinness.pdf.

Pauwels, P.; Terkaj, W. (2016): EXPRESS to OWL for construction industry. Towards a recommendable and usable ifcOWL ontology. In Autom. Constr. 63, pp.100–133. DOI: 10.1016/j.autcon.2015.12.003.

Rasmussen, M. H.; Lefrançois, M.; Schneider, G. F.; Pauwels, P.; Janowicz, K. (2020): BOT. The Building Topology Ontology of the W3C Linked Building Data Group. In SW 12 (1), pp.143–161. DOI: 10.3233/SW-200385.

Sattler, L.; Lamouri, S.; Pellerin, R.; Maigne, T. (2019): Interoperability aims in Building Information Modeling exchanges. A literature review. In IFAC 52 (13), pp.271–276. DOI: 10.1016/j.ifacol.2019.11.180.

Stolk, S.; McGlinn, K. (2020): Validation of ifcOWL datasets using SHACL. In M. Poveda-Villlón, A. Roxin, K. McGlinn, P. Pauwels (Eds.): Proceedings of the 8th Linked Data in Architecture and Construction Workshop. LDAC 2020. Dublin, Ireland, 17-19 June, pp.91–104.

Terkaj, W.; Pedrielli, G.; Sacco, M. (2012): Virtual Factory Data Model. In CEUR Workshop Proceedings 886.

Wagner, A.; Bonduel, M.; Pauwels, P.; Uwe, R. (2019): Relating geometry descriptions to its derivatives on the web. In : European Conference on Computing 2019, pp.304–313.

Wiendahl, H.-P.; Reichardt, J.; Nyhuis, P. (2015): Handbook Factory Planning and Design: Springer Berlin.

IFCNet: A Benchmark Dataset for IFC Entity Classification

Christoph Emunds, Nicolas Pauen, Veronika Richter, Jérôme Frisch, Christoph van Treeck
RWTH Aachen University, Germany
emunds@e3d.rwth-aachen.de

Abstract. Enhancing interoperability and information exchange between domain-specific software products for BIM is an important aspect in the Architecture, Engineering, Construction and Operations industry. Recent research started investigating methods from the areas of machine and deep learning for semantic enrichment of BIM models. However, training and evaluation of these machine learning algorithms requires sufficiently large and comprehensive datasets. This work presents IFCNet, a dataset of single-entity IFC files spanning a broad range of IFC classes containing both geometric and semantic information. Using only the geometric information of objects, the experiments show that three different deep learning models are able to achieve good classification performance.

1. Introduction

Enhancing interoperability between domain-specific information modeling processes and, thus, software products for Building Information Modeling (BIM) is an important aspect to improve the lifecycle support of buildings and to facilitate the collaboration of the different disciplines across Architecture, Engineering, Construction and Operations (AECO). The Industry Foundation Classes (IFC) provide an open data exchange format for sharing information between these stakeholders.

However, since the IFC standard has to cover a broad spectrum of concepts, it contains a large number of entities and is highly complex. Past studies have shown that IFC-based exchanges of models are prone to an information loss due to reduction, simplification or interpretation when sharing data between multiple specialized software products (Bazjanac & Kiviniemi, 2007). One major issue is a potential mismapping between native BIM elements and IFC entities, which can arise through e.g. manual error during model creation or the reliance on default templates (Belsky, et al., 2016). Furthermore, CAD software products interpret specifications differently when processing in- and output data.

When sharing BIM models with other teams, semantic integrity is a prerequisite for a seamless workflow and effective collaboration. Many specialized applications rely on accurate semantic information to perform their tasks, e.g. energy efficiency modelling (Schlueter & Thesseling, 2009; Ham & Golparvar-Fard, 2015) or code compliance checking (Eastman, et al., 2009). Inconsistent object classification has been identified to be a common interoperability issue between different BIM authoring software suites (Belsky et al., 2016; Lai & Deng, 2018).

Researchers have started approaching this issue with methods from the area of machine and deep learning (Bloch & Sacks, 2018). These algorithms typically need labelled datasets to learn from. However, comprehensive and rich datasets in the domain of BIM and IFC are scarce, which makes the development and verification of such models difficult. In this work, the authors introduce a benchmark dataset of single-entity IFC files covering a broad range of IFC classes. This dataset, named *IFCNet*[1], should contribute to the standardization of performance

[1] https://ifcnet.e3d.rwth-aachen.de

evaluations of future work in this domain. To evaluate the usefulness of IFCNet, three deep learning methods are trained to classify the entities and their performance is reviewed.

The key contributions of this research paper can be summarized as follows:

- A benchmark dataset for IFC entity classification, named *IFCNet*, is released.
- The application of recent advances in the area of geometric deep learning to the classification of IFC elements is shown using three different approaches.
- An evaluation of these deep learning methods is conducted to demonstrate the opportunities and challenges posed by IFCNet.

2. Related Work

Existing approaches for the classification of BIM and IFC elements can be categorized into rule-based and machine-learning-based methods. Thomson and Boehm (2015) use RANSAC to identify dominant planes and reconstruct IFC geometry from 3D point clouds, followed by an optional step of geometric reasoning. Others have used region growing (Dimitrov & Golparvar-Fard, 2015) or surface normal approaches (Barnea & Filin, 2013). Sacks et al. (2017) derived rules for object classification using object features and spatial relationships between object pairs. Ma et al. (2017) devise a semantic enrichment process by establishing a knowledge base that associates objects via their geometric and spatial features.

While these methods proof to work well on specific cases, Bloch & Sacks (2018) argue that rule-based workflows are not applicable to all problems. In recent work, researchers started exploring algorithms from the areas of machine and deep learning. Koo et al. (2020) apply PointNet (Qi, et al., 2017) and a Multi-view Convolutional Neural Network (MVCNN) (Su, et al., 2015) to classify elements of road infrastructure. Kim et al. (2019) use images of objects to train a 2D CNN to recognize furniture elements. Leonhardt et al. (2020) also employ PointNet for classification of IFC objects and for semantic segmentation of rooms.

Many of these works assemble their own datasets, but do not release them publicly. On one hand, this is inefficient, since these datasets cannot be used by the research community and thus work is done repeatedly. On the other hand, it makes comparisons between different methods impossible. IFCNet's goal is to serve as a benchmark to be used by other researchers to develop, train, and test their methods and algorithms on and offer a common ground for comparing them.

3. The IFCNet Dataset

Figure 1: Example objects for each of the 20 classes of IFCNetCore.

To assemble IFCNet, around 1000 IFC models were collected from real-world projects, student works and online sources, such as the open IFC model repository of the university of Auckland

(Dimyadi, et al., 2010). The models were created with different authoring software products, most notably Autodesk Revit and ArchiCAD. Afterwards, the models were decomposed into individual entities by extracting all objects into separate files. For the first version of IFCNet, the focus has been put on the subtypes of IfcDistributionElement, IfcBuildingElement and IfcFurnishingElement. Additionally, the attached IfcPropertySets have been extracted as well. The extraction results in roughly 1.2M entities from 82 different IFC classes. The data contain several different representation types, including Brep, AdvancedBrep, MappedRepresentation, SweptSolid, Tesselation and CSG.

The resulting IFC files are deduplicated to eliminate objects with identical geometry. To be able to perform this deduplication in linear time, the vertices of every object are normalized to the unit sphere and used as the key in a hash map. Objects with identical sets of vertices are then mapped onto the same key and can thus be eliminated. This, of course, assumes that the vertices match exactly, meaning that the vertices of two different objects which are in fact duplicates need to be in the same order. However, this was found to be true for the majority of objects, judging by the fact that this naïve way of deduplicating geometries reduces the aforementioned 1.2M to around 290k entities. Since objects are only deduplicated within their respective class, this process can easily be parallelized.

In the next step, the entities are reviewed manually and misclassifications are corrected. To support this process, a web-based tool was developed, which allows users to review an entity's geometric representation and attached metadata before confirming or changing its class and enables quick switching between the different IFC classes and their objects. Furthermore, the tool supports exploring the already labelled data to document the current progress of the dataset. The labelling process has been carried out and supervised by domain experts to ensure the quality of the dataset. A view of this tool is shown in Figure 2, displaying an IfcValve.

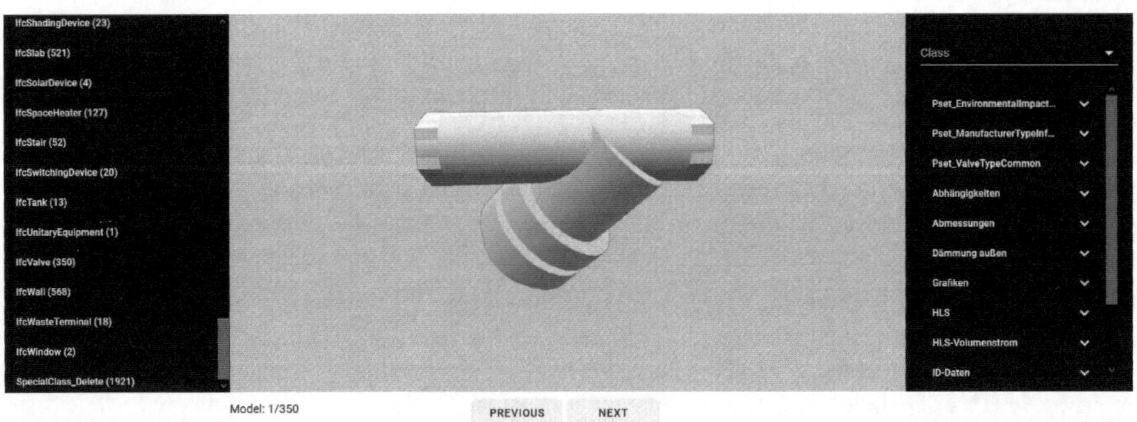

Figure 2: View of the tool used during the labelling process. The menu on the left allows switching between IFC classes. The menu on the right displays the current object's properties. The central canvas shows objects of the selected class in 3D.

The full IFCNet dataset currently consists of 19,613 confirmed objects distributed over 65 classes, most of which are highly imbalanced with respect to the number of objects they contain. Therefore, a subset of 20 classes is selected for the experiments in Section 4. The first version of this sub-dataset, called *IFCNetCore*, contains a total of 7,930 objects (Figure 1). Table 1 shows the number of objects per class before and after deduplication of the full dataset, as well as the training and test split for IFCNetCore.

Some classes, like IfcWall, have little intra-class variance, while others have very large intra-class variance. IfcFurniture for example contains vastly different types of furniture, from chairs and tables to wardrobes. An additional challenge is posed by a small inter-class variance between certain classes like IfcWall and IfcPlate, both of which are rectangular shapes with varying thickness and little to no details with respect to their geometry. To better reflect the reality of people working with IFC, models and elements of different Level of Information Need (LOIN) have been included, which also covers objects that have a placeholder appearance (e.g. generic-looking cubes) and are thus likely to only be classifiable through their metadata.

Most IFC objects have additional metadata in the form of IfcProperties, which are grouped together via IfcPropertySets. The simplest and most frequently used kind of properties are user-defined key-value pairs, which often come in different languages. For instance, German, English, Dutch and French have been observed throughout the labelling process.

Table 1: Number of objects per class in IFCNet and IFCNetCore. A class in IFCNetCore can have more objects than there were after deduplication, since e.g. IfcBuildingElementProxy objects could have moved into that class during the labelling process. Note that not all of the objects listed under *after deduplication* have been reviewed and confirmed, yet.

Class	Before deduplication	After deduplication	Training set	Test set
IfcAirTerminal	6,227	496	333	142
IfcBeam	128,027	17,957	198	84
IfcCableCarrierFitting	2,913	511	361	155
IfcCableCarrierSegment	4,135	2,820	370	159
IfcDoor	11,569	1,833	216	93
IfcDuctFitting	29,409	7,590	455	195
IfcDuctSegment	28,783	22,129	372	159
IfcFurniture	7,943	218	157	67
IfcLamp	0	0	65	27
IfcOutlet	1,559	34	41	18
IfcPipeFitting	117,979	5,510	454	194
IfcPipeSegment	170,308	86,979	454	195
IfcPlate	20,472	3,436	366	157
IfcRailing	3,112	967	295	127
IfcSanitaryTerminal	289	32	316	136
IfcSlab	8,787	4,018	355	152
IfcSpaceHeater	392	51	89	38
IfcStair	807	80	36	16
IfcValve	15,335	362	242	104
IfcWall	21,336	8,348	376	161
Total			5551	2379

4. Experiments

The following experiments apply three neural network approaches to the IFCNetCore dataset. These architectures were chosen because they are among the current state-of-the-art and cover a broad range of intuitive representations for 3D data, i.e. 2D projections, point clouds and triangulated meshes. However, all of these methods only consider the objects' geometric information. Investigating ways to combine geometric and semantic information during training is beyond the scope of this paper. The code for the neural network models is based on the PyTorch implementations of the original publications.

All experiments follow the same training protocol: The IFCNetCore dataset is split into a training and a test set. Afterwards, the data is transformed into the format expected by the different architectures. To determine the best set of hyperparameters, 30% of the training data is split off into a validation set. The models are then trained on the remaining 70% of the training data and evaluated on the validation set after each epoch. The balanced accuracy metric is used to decide for the best performing configuration of hyperparameters. Finally, the models are trained once more on the whole training set with fixed hyperparameters. Evaluation on the test set only occurs once at the end of this procedure. The code used to conduct these experiments will be released along with this work[2].

5. MVCNN

Figure 3: Example of a set of 12 views to be consumed by the MVCNN

The Multi-View Convolutional Neural Network (MVCNN) combines information from multiple views of a 3D shape to learn a shape descriptor (Su, et al., 2015). Since MVCNN uses rendered 2D views of an object from several perspectives, it has two advantages over the other methods presented here. First, neural networks for image classification have received much more attention in Deep Learning research over the last years. Neural network building blocks like 2D convolutions have been specifically designed to work well on image data. Second, MVCNN benefits from the existence of other large-scale image datasets like ImageNet (Deng, et al., 2009). CNN architectures are commonly pre-trained on these massive datasets and can later be fine-tuned on much smaller datasets while still performing well.

To prepare the IFCNetCore dataset to be consumed by MVCNN, 12 views are rendered for each object by a camera rotating around the object's up-axis in 30° increments (Figure 3).

[2] https://github.com/cemunds/ifcnet-models

Similar to Su et al. (2015), the Phong reflection model (Phong, 1975) is used to generate the rendered views. Figure 4 shows the results of the evaluation on the test set.

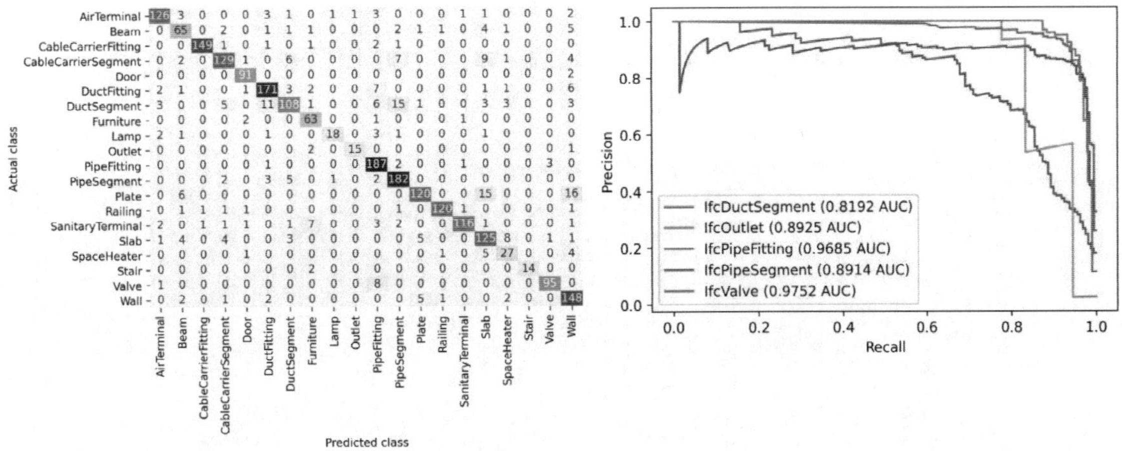

Figure 4: **Left**: Confusion matrix of the MVCNN model. **Right**: Precision-recall curves for selected IFC classes with corresponding values for Area Under the Curve (AUC).

6. DGCNN

The Dynamic Graph Convolutional Neural Network (DGCNN) (Wang, et al., 2019) is inspired by PointNet (Qi, et al., 2017), but operates on neighborhoods of points by using convolution operations. This allows DGCNN to exploit local geometric structures.

During pre-processing, 2048 points are sampled uniformly at random from each object in IFCNetCore. The point clouds are normalized to the unit sphere before they are fed through the model. The results of the evaluation on the test set are shown in Figure 5.

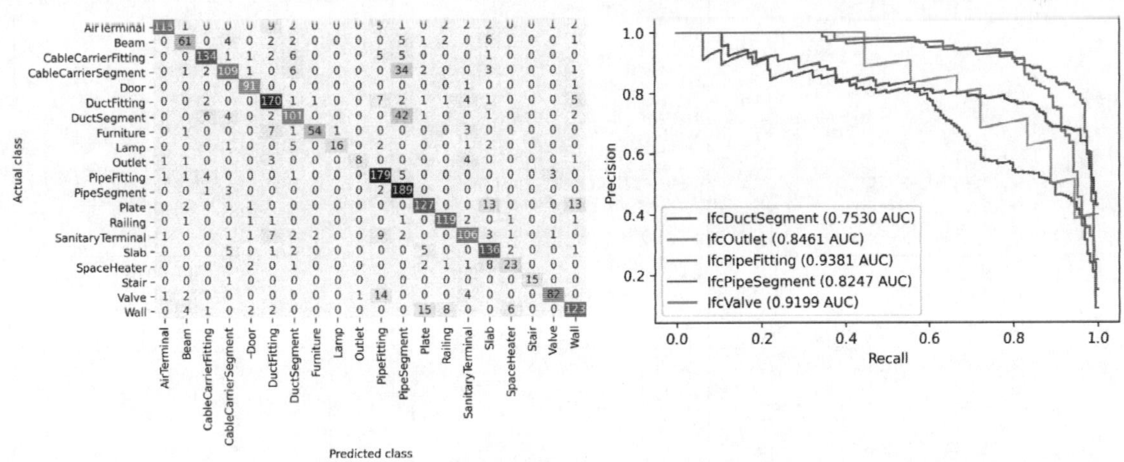

Figure 5: **Left**: Confusion matrix of the DGCNN model. **Right**: Precision-recall curves for selected IFC entities with corresponding values for Area Under the Curve (AUC).

7. MeshNet

In contrast to the previous two methods, MeshNet (Feng, et al., 2018) uses the geometric information of the mesh directly to learn a classifier. It solves the complexity and irregularity problem of mesh data by regarding the faces as the unit and using per-face processes and a symmetry function. Moreover, it splits faces into spatial and structural features by using a spatial and structural descriptor and a mesh convolution block.

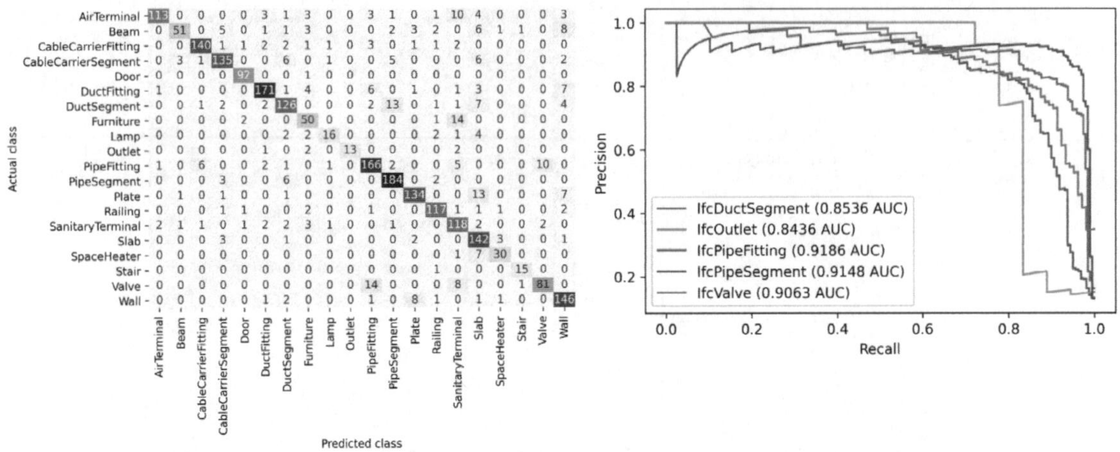

Figure 6: **Left**: Confusion matrix of the MeshNet model. **Right**: Precision-recall curves for selected IFC entities with corresponding values for Area Under the Curve (AUC).

Before training, the meshes are simplified to a maximum of 2048 faces using MeshLab's (Cignoni, et al., 2008) implementation of Quadric Edge Collapse Decimation. Afterwards, the meshes are converted into lists of faces containing information about their center, corners and normal as well as their immediate neighboring faces. The results on the test set are shown in Figure 6.

8. Comparison

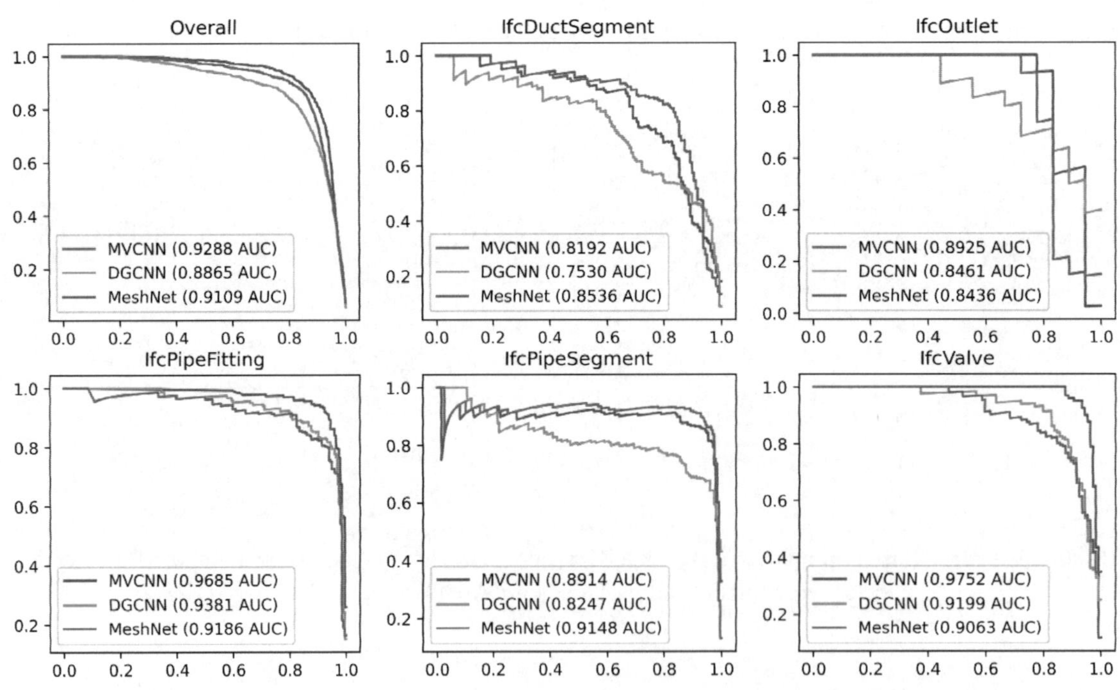

Figure 7: Comparison of precision-recall curves for selected classes. The top-left plot shows the micro-averaged precision-recall curve over all classes.

A comparison of precision-recall curves for selected classes can be seen in Figure 7. Not surprisingly, classes for which there are very few objects like IfcOutlet show a worse performance. However, MVCNN still achieves better results than DGCNN and MeshNet.

Table 2: Results of the evaluation on the test set for the three models.

Model	Balanced Accuracy	F1 score
MVCNN	**85.54%**	**86.93%**
DGCNN	79.11%	82.15%
MeshNet	83.32%	85.72%

Table 2 shows the balanced accuracy and F1 score for the three models. MVCNN achieves the best overall results. The confusion matrices show that each of the three models has its own strengths and weaknesses, but that they also make similar mistakes. For instance, plates, slabs and walls are among the most confused classes. Another example of commonly confused classes are duct segments and pipe segments. However, all three models show a reasonable performance and proof that they are able to learn from the dataset.

9. Limitations

Notably, the absolute sizes of objects are lost due to normalization of the data before training. Incorporating this information into the classification process is likely to improve results for objects that might look similar, but differ greatly in size. Moreover, some objects, especially those with few geometric details, might be very hard to classify when taken out of the context of the full BIM model or without regarding their semantic information. However, most current neural network architectures are trained end-to-end from raw data and were not designed to consume such explicit features.

With such a large quantity of objects, it is difficult to ensure uniqueness. The deduplication process is able to eliminate objects with identical geometry. However, there are many objects that look alike to a human observer, but are not identical on the mesh level. Such cases include permutations of a mesh's vertices or non-uniform scaling along axes. To conduct an exhaustive search and also detect objects that are *almost* identical is not feasible. Further research will have to investigate more efficient methods to eliminate near-duplicate objects.

Many objects use a mix of languages in their metadata. Sometimes the value of a key-value pair might be missing if a field in the authoring software was left unset. Moreover, it is common to encounter abbreviations and acronyms, which require a certain amount of domain knowledge to make use of. In some cases, properties might also be inaccurate or simply wrong. These issues make it difficult to incorporate the semantic properties into the classification process without thorough pre-processing.

10. Conclusion and Future Work

The first version of IFCNetCore offers a common benchmark for model training and evaluation. Expanding IFCNet with more objects, classes, and semantic information is an ongoing effort to create a large-scale dataset for the BIM and IFC domain. Since the labelling process requires specific domain knowledge, creating this dataset is even more resource intensive than other datasets used in machine and deep learning. The goal for IFCNet is to become a useful resource for other researchers working on semantic enrichment of BIM models.

The results of the experiments conducted on IFCNetCore show a good classification performance, despite only using the geometric information of objects. Further research could investigate models that can take the properties and semantic information into account to improve on these results. Moreover, in the domain of 2D images, models used for segmentation or detection are commonly pre-trained on large-scale image datasets. How to effectively use such transfer learning approaches for 3D data is an area of active research. One could imagine that, with sufficient size of IFCNet, it should be possible to use the dataset for similar pre-training purposes.

The classification process presented in this work can be integrated into the BIM workflow similarly to the SEEBIM method of Belsky et al. (2016). Upon import of an IFC file into a BIM tool, the trained network is used to infer the classes of the individual elements of the model. Afterwards, the author is prompted with a screen showing the potential misclassifications and can then decide to accept or reject the propositions of the network.

Acknowledgements

The research within the project EnergyTWIN leading to these results has received funding from the German Ministry for Industry and Energy under grant agreement no. 03EN1026A. The authors would like to thank the Geodetic Institute and Chair for Computing in Civil Engineering & Geo Information Systems at RWTH Aachen, aedifion GmbH, DiConneX GmbH, TEMA Technologie Marketing AG, Internet Marketing Services GmbH and Aachener Grundvermögen Kapitalverwaltungsgesellschaft mbH for their contribution to the project.

References

Barnea, S. & Filin, S., 2013. Segmentation of terrestrial laser scanning data using geometry and image information. ISPRS Journal of Photogrammetry and Remote Sensing Volume 76, pp.33–48.

Bazjanac, V. & Kiviniemi, A., 2007. Reduction, simplification, translation and interpretation in the exchange of model data. Proceedings of the 24th W78 Conference Maribor, pp.163–168.

Belsky, M., Sacks, R. & Brilakis, I., 2016. Semantic Enrichment for Building Information Modeling. Computer-Aided Civil and Infrastructure Engineering.

Bloch, T. & Sacks, R., 2018. Comparing machine learning and rule-based inferencing for semantic enrichment of BIM models. Automation in Construction Volume 91, pp.256–272.

Cignoni, P. et al., 2008. MeshLab: an Open-Source Mesh Processing Tool. In: Eurographics Italian Chapter Conference. s.l.:The Eurographics Association, pp.129–136.

Deng, J. et al., 2009. ImageNet: A large-scale hierarchical image database. IEEE Conference on Computer Vision and Pattern Recognition, pp.248–255.

Dimitrov, A. & Golparvar-Fard, M., 2015. Segmentation of building point cloud models including detailed architectural/structural features and MEP systems. Automation in Construction Volume 51, pp.32–45.

Dimyadi, J., Henderson, S. & Dimalen, D., 2010. Open IFC Model Repository. [Online] Available at: http://openifcmodel.cs.auckland.ac.nz/[Accessed 17th December 2020].

Eastman, C. M., Lee, J.-m., Jeong, Y.-s. & Lee, J.-k., 2009. Automatic rule-based checking of building designs. Automation in Construction, December, pp.1011–1033.

Feng, Y. et al., 2018. MeshNet: Mesh Neural Network for 3D Shape Representation. AAAI 2019.

Ham, Y. & Golparvar-Fard, M., 2015. Three-Dimensional Thermography-Based Method for Cost-Benefit Analysis of Energy Efficiency Building Envelope Retrofits. Journal of Computing in Civil Engineering, July.

Kim, J., Song, J. & Lee, J.-K., 2019. Recognizing and Classifying Unknown Object in BIM Using 2D CNN. Computer-Aided Architectural Design.

Koo, B., Jung, R., Yu, Y. & Kim, I., 2020. A geometric deep learning approach for checking element-to-entity mappings in infrastructure building information models. Journal of Computational Design and Engineering, 11.

Lai, H. & Deng, X., 2018. Interoperability analysis of IFC-based data exchange between heterogeneous BIM software. Journal of Civil Engineering and Management, pp.537–555.

Leonhardt, M. et al., 2020. Implementierung von KI-basierten Referenzprozessen für die computergestützte Objekterkennung im Gebäude. BauSIM, September, pp.599–606.

Ma, L., Sacks, R. & Kattel, U., 2017. Building Model Object Classification for Semantic Enrichment Using Geometric Features and Pairwise Spatial Relationships. Lean and Computing in Construction Congress - Joint Conference on Computing in Construction.

Phong, B. T., 1975. Illumination for Computer Generated Pictures. Communications of the ACM, June, p. 311–317.

Qi, C. R., Su, H., Mo, K. & Guibas, L. J., 2017. PointNet: Deep Learning on Point Sets for 3D Classification and Segmentation. Conference on Computer Vision and Pattern Recognition (CVPR).

Sacks, R. et al., 2017. Semantic Enrichment for Building Information Modeling: Procedure for Compiling Inference Rules and Operators for Complex Geometry. Journal of Computing in Civil Engineering, November.

Schlueter, A. & Thesseling, F., 2009. Building information model based energy/exergy performance assessment in early design stages. Automation in Construction, March, pp.153–163.

Su, H., Maji, S., Kalogerakis, E. & Learned-Miller, E., 2015. Multi-view Convolutional Neural Networks for 3D Shape Recognition. Proceedings of ICCV.

Thomson, C. & Boehm, J., 2015. Automatic Geometry Generation from Point Clouds for BIM. Remote Sensing, pp.11753–11775.

Wang, Y. et al., 2019. Dynamic Graph CNN for Learning on Point Clouds. ACM Transactions on Graphics (TOG).

IFC based Framework for Generating, Modeling and Visualizing Spalling Defect Geometries

Mathias Artus, Mohamed Alabassy, Christian Koch
Bauhaus-Universität Weimar, Germany
mathias.artus@uni-weimar.de

Abstract. Current traditional bridge inspection practices rely on paper-based data acquisition, its digitization, and multiple conversions in between incompatible formats to facilitate data exchange. This practice is time consuming, error prone, cumbersome, and leads to information loss. One aim for future inspection procedures is to have a fully digitized workflow that achieves loss free data exchange, which lowers costs and offers higher efficiency. Up-to-date, image and depth sensors are increasingly utilized by engineers that could be ground-based or drone-fitted to collect visual inspection data, such as videos or photos. For further processing potentials, like structural analyses, the huge amount of collected visuals needs to be interpreted and transformed into meaningful information. This paper proposes and explains a framework, that creates defect geometries from photos and saves them into an object-oriented data model utilizing the standardized IFC format. Potential strengths to this framework include the automated import of a damaged component into a finite analysis software to support further simulation tasks.

1. Introduction

Asset management is a crucial task during the operation phase. One part of this management is the registration of defects. For example, infrastructure and heritage buildings need defect registration. Furthermore, the resulting damage data has to be exchanged between different stakeholders.

Numerous research have shown the applicability of Unmanned Aerial Systems (UAS) for damage data acquisition. For instance, Morgenthal et al. have proposed a framework for the data acquisition starting from the task definition up to photogrammetric reconstruction, anomaly detection, and assessment of bridges (Morgenthal et al., 2019). However, this framework operates on raw point clouds and does not relate defects to a BIM model.

Bruno et al. have shown how to use Building Information Modeling (BIM) for the assessment of heritage buildings (Bruno and Fatiguso, 2018). In general, the concept allows storing photos and textual descriptions of a heritage building. This is the basic requirement for most assessment frameworks. Hüthwohl et al. proposed a Damage Information Model (DIM) with defects and related photos as textures (Hüthwohl et al., 2018). Further extensions provide additional semantic data and geometries (Hamdan and Scherer, 2018). The research mainly focuses on how to support include inspection practices into BIM. This paper shows the potential of a BIM-based DIM in future inspection processes. Rakha et al. reviewed different applications of UAS and concluded "The increased accessibility, efficiency, and safety [of UAS] present a unique opportunity to expedite the improvement and retrofitting of aging and energy inefficient building stock and infrastructure." Furthermore, "Existing software and mathematical concepts present a variety of options for post processing, analysis, and visual representation with reduced manual workflow, as a step closer towards fully automated building performance inspections using drones." (Rakha and Gorodetsky, 2018)

Condition ratings might be calculated based on simulation outputs, such as results from Finite Element Analyses (FEA) or probabilistic durability simulation result, instead of being defined by an engineer based on subjective experience. Currently, this approach is time consuming because all data has to be digitized and manually transferred. A digital DIM leads to faster data transfer between data acquisition and related simulation, for example, the engineer can import the geometry of a damaged component from an IFC file directly into a FEA software and needs only to add the meshing and load scenarios.

Isailović et al. have demonstrated a use case for enriching an IFC-based bridge model with spalling defects geometrically (Isailović et al., 2020). However, two limitations were identified in their proposed approach. The first is mainly related to the reliance on the quality of the as-is point cloud representation for the multi-view classification of damaged elements, as well as the optimal points' size to allow for a meaningful classification of projected cubemap images. Thus, requiring a significant human interference to estimate the correct values with trial and error depending on the quality and density of the point cloud generated. This could be dispensed with as proposed in this paper, if the identification of spalling defects is directly undertaken on photos of the structure under inspection instead of relying on its point cloud representation. The second limitation identified, is the way the spalling meshes were modeled to have an outer surface coinciding to that of the damaged IFC element and scaled up by means of some empirically predetermined scaling factor to circumvent the failure of the CSG boolean difference operation, which consequently changes the actual size of defects in comparison with that of the real structure, making it impossible to compare it to previous and future states of modeled defects.

2. Problem statement

Defects, like cracks and spallings, have geometries. To draw such defects manually is a cumbersome and an error prone work for engineers. Instead, we propose a semi-automatic algorithm, which created the defect geometry based on photos of the related defect. These defect geometries are included in a damage information model for later use. Furthermore, improving the data exchange between different stakeholders, by using digital file formats instead of printed documents, lowers information loss and errors and, hence, lowers the costs for inspection and maintenance. At this point, we present a framework, which derives defect geometries from photos and stores them as entities in an IFC file. Subsequent processes, like visualization or simulations may use this information.

Given the current state of literature on the geometric modelling methods of defects already published, there exists a need for a more efficient and reliable approach to modelling them in a BIM context with a particular focus on seamless compatibility with the IFC format. Although the proposed workflow does solve the limitations identified in currently published methods and opens the door for further processing steps previously not easily achievable, it raises other sorts of challenges and limitations that requires further investigation to solve and mitigate. Among which are a relatively long modelling time taken to implement the complicated workflow in full as proposed, the accumulation of estimation errors for the defects' depth estimation and positioning in the main 3D information model, determining an optimal meshing density for such free-form defect geometries that provides both accurate shapes representation on one hand and maintains a small disk size on the other that doesn't slow down the interaction with a main data model nor hurdle the proper rendering of geometries in IFC viewers when numerus defects are included. Moreover, the sole reliance on images would expectedly pose a limitation in situations where uncontrolled factors like the scene's complexity, the lighting conditions and the quality of inspection images determine the results of segmented damages in photos, which directly impacts the proposed workflow's output.

3. Process pipeline

Figure 1 shows an overview of the entire process pipeline. The data acquisition is done as the first step. As conservation processes rely on visual inspections by engineers, we assume in this paper to receive extensive visual data from Unmanned Aerial Systems (UAS), for example, drones. This means, the input is a huge number of photos of defects.

During the **generation of defect geometry**, the photos are processed. This process generates geometrical and visual information of the defects. The **defect linking** identifies afflicted building components by a nearest neighbor algorithm.

The resulting textures and geometry are saved in a data structure which allows the storage of semantical and geometry data. This data structure is implemented using the IFC 4x1 standard, resulting in a **Damage loaded BIM**. This damage loaded BIM is the input for further processes, such as **structural simulation**, **visualization**, or **condition prediction**.

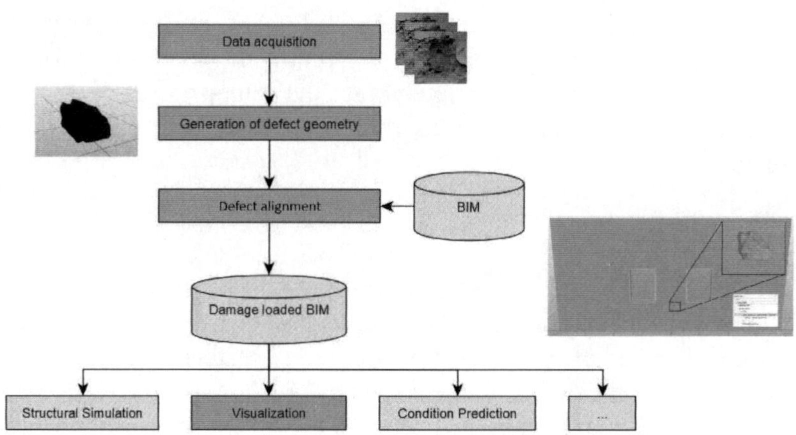

Figure 1: Process pipeline. Orange elements are described in this paper.

4. Geometry Generation

To generate the geometry of spallings, a five-step workflow was devised as described in Figure 2. The first step requires the calibration of the camera(s) used for shooting the images during inspection using a set of calibration photos with a checkerboard pattern to determine the intrinsic parameters needed for the 3D reconstruction through Structure from Motion (SfM), as well as the radial distortion coefficients for undistorting the images and their segmented masks using OpenCV (Bradski and Kaehler, 2008) to be later generated through inference from a retrained TernausNet16 model.

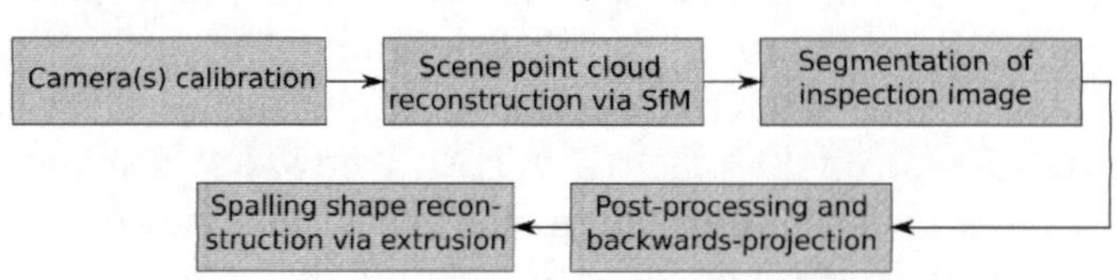

Figure 2: Workflow for the geometry generation of spalling in 5 steps.

Using the images collected from the inspection and the intrinsic parameters estimated from calibration, a dense point cloud of the region of interest is reconstructed in the second step using OpenSfM. This library was chosen in particular for the advantages of providing a superior quality of its resulting point clouds in comparison with other alternatives, the capability to run its commands for 3D reconstruction seamlessly in a background process without the need for manual interaction with a GUI and the flexibility of using its default methods and debug files to retrieve the estimated pose of the camera for each image required for backwards projection.

Based on the well-established performance of convolution neural networks (CNN's) in solving object recognition tasks as demonstrated through the Kaggle challenges and their successful implementation for spallings detection (Yang et al., 2017, 2018, Isailović et al., 2020), a semantic CNN was considered the best approach to identify the spalling regions on pixel level in a user-defined inspection image needed in the third step. To that end, the TernausNet16 based on the UNet with the first 16 layers of VGG encoder architecture (Shvets et al., 2018) was retrained by means of transfer learning on the spalling part of the Concrete Structure Spalling and Crack (CSSC) database used to train the InspectionNet (Yang et al., 2017, 2018). The transfer learning process followed a similar approach to that published for the original TernausNet16, implementing a 5-Fold cross validation with 15 epochs per fold, instead of a classical train-test split due to the limited number of labeled images available for training the model. The evaluation of the fifth fold used for the pixelwise segmentation in the proposed workflow scored Jaccard and validation losses of 0.832 and 0.173 respectively. The inspection image selected for modeling the spalling geometry in the presented use case and the resulting greyscale prediction map of spalling pixels from inference of the retrained model are shown in Figure 3.

In the fourth step, a connected component labeling algorithm was used on the undistorted binary image resulting from thresholding the prediction map obtained in the previous step. In addition to the point cloud of the scene reconstructed through OpenSfM and all the depth information entailed from that process, the regions of interest classified as spallings in the prediction map could be converted from pixel units into 3D world coordinates in metric units up to scale by back-projecting the identified spalling pixels into 3D space.

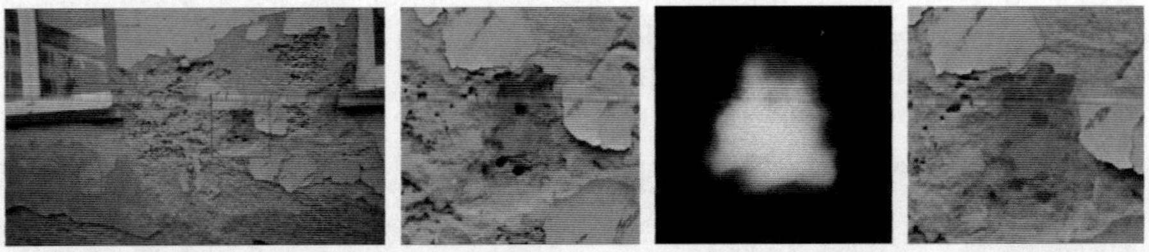

(a) (b) (c) (d)

Figure 3: Segmentation of the use case inspection image containing a spalling defect shown in subfigure (a), a zoom-in crop in (b), the zoom-in crop of the prediction map generated via inference from the retrained TernausNet16 model is shown in (c) and an overlay of the segmented spalling region in red on top of the image in (d).

In the fifth and final step, the actual shape of the spalling is reconstructed using Gmsh library's API for Python (Geuzaine and Remacle, 2009). The geometric modeling approach developed is to estimate the unit vector of an extrusion direction based on the arithmetic mean of all conformed normals of the segmented spalling patch vertices in the point cloud. Extruding the meshed patch of spalling defect along that direction for a distance value thrice that of the depth of the damaged component (i.e., thickness of *IfcWall*) ensures the creation of a defect geometry that its outer surface always protrudes from the surface of the damaged building element to avoid the possibility of failures in the ensuing boolean difference operation to create the voids.

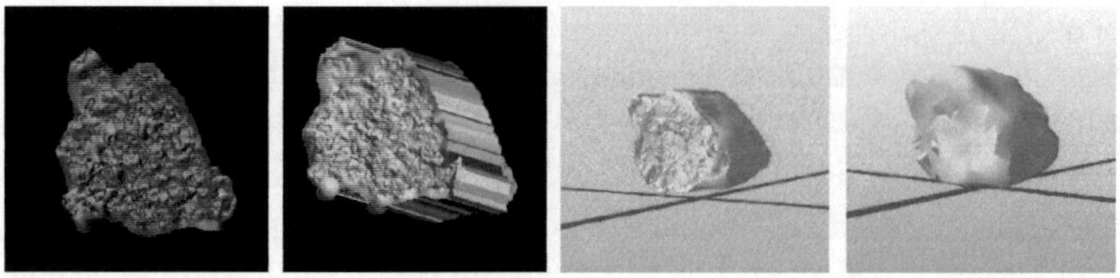

(a) (b) (c) (d)

Figure 4: The construction of the spalling geometry. The mesh of segmented spalling region after backprojection into 3D space is shown in subfigure (a), the extrusion along the average direction of normals of its comprising vertices results in a volumetric geometry shown in (b), the exported *IfcBuildingElementProxy* in the third viewed in XbimXplorer (Lockley et al., 2020) in (c) and a simplified representation of its geometry in (d).

5. Defect Alignment

There exists a misalignment of the reconstructed point cloud representation if segmented spalling defect patches are to be directly added into the model due to the difference of origin in the world coordinate systems of both the point cloud and that of the BIM model. Hence, a globally optimal ICP (GoICP) algorithm (Yang et al. 2013, 2016) was utilized to solve that problem by estimating the rotation and translation required to transform the pose of the point cloud (i.e., source) to align with the coordinate system of the 3D model (i.e., target). For that purpose, the damaged wall presented in the use case was modeled in Autodesk Revit then exported into IFC. The IFC model was then imported into Blender for fine triangulation of its shapes to extract a dense point cloud from the generated meshes' vertices.

The use of GoICP provided for a more reliable alignment independent of an initial guess that is more robust against noise in the source point cloud resulting from registering a 3D reconstructed point cloud of a rough-textured wall in the use case model to a very smooth-surfaced target where the resulting transformation of the global registration of the 3D reconstructed dense point cloud via OpenSfM to the point cloud of the IFC model shown in figure 5.

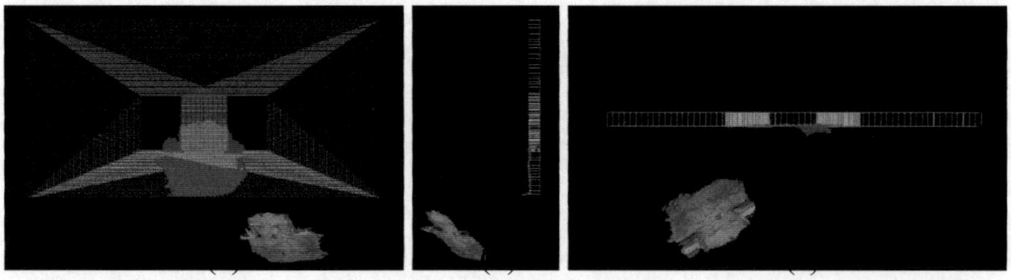

Figure 5: Transformed source point cloud after applying the estimated transformation displayed in red that results from aligning the 3D reconstructed point cloud of the scene with grey-toned real texture colors to the point cloud of the wall in the 3D model displayed in cyan using GoICP shown from elevation in subfigure (a), side view in (b) and plan in (c).

6. Damage Loaded BIM

Artus et al. have shown how to store photos and geometries with relations to a building information model (Artus and Koch, 2020, 2021). This approach has been extended by further typification to enable searches for defects within the extended BIM. Figure 6 shows an overview of the semantic information of the damage model. The defect annotation is an objectified representation of the defect. Furthermore, the *DefectProductRelation* represents the relationship to an existing component of the building. Last, the *DefectType* provides the mentioned typification of the defect. The model is inspired by the IFC standard and, hence, shows similarities. This eases later implementation by using the IFC.

The later visualization of the defect needs geometries and textures. Geometries are incorporated by a special interpretation of the relation between the defect and the afflicted component. An additional parameter shows how to interpret the geometry, for example, cutout would mean that the geometry of the defect has to be subtracted from the geometry of the component as shown in Figure 7 for the UML model of a defect with a geometry.

A photo of the defect may be added to the model by simply referencing the photo or by depicting the photo as texture onto the model. By using the document reference from Figure 6, a picture is stored as external reference. In contrast to the external reference, Figure 8 illustrates storing the photo as texture for a geometry or a part of the geometry. This approach has been published first by Hüthwohl et al. (Hüthwohl et al., 2018).

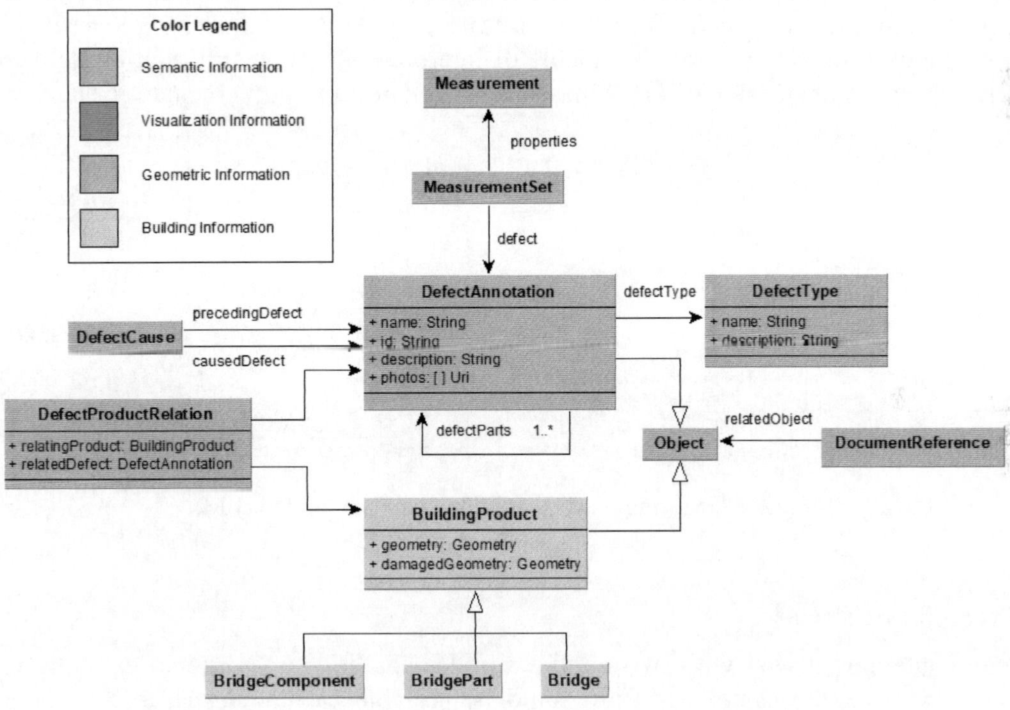

Figure 6: Semantic defect information in the damage loaded BIM.

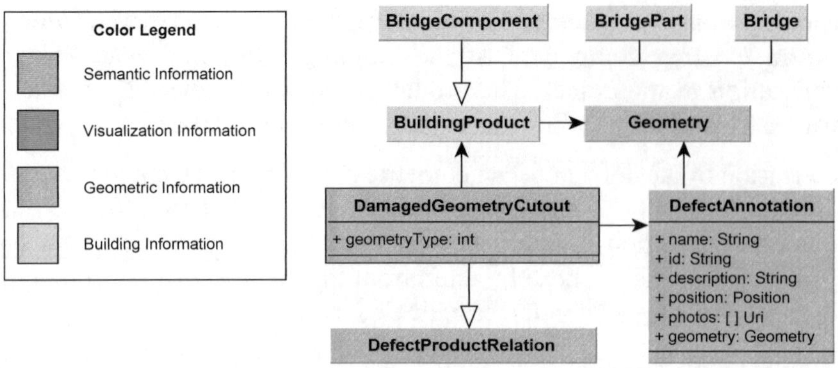

Figure 7: Geometry data within the damage loaded BIM.

The damage loaded BIM is implemented by using the IFC 4 Standard. A defect entity is modeled by using an *IfcVoidingFeature*. This class is designed to store subtractions of other components. *IfcRelVoidsElement*s represent the relation between the defect and the afflicted component. Finally, an *IfcImageTexture* is used to include the texture for the visualization. None of the existing IFC viewers is capable of interpreting texture information delivered by IFC files. Hence, an extension of xBIM has been developed and implemented for later testing.

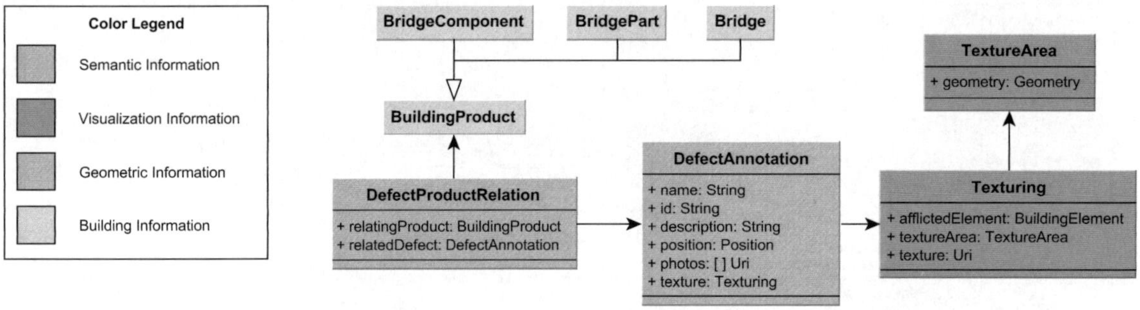

Figure 8: Storing textures within a damage loaded BIM.

7. Exemplary Use Case

A scene containing a wall with two windows and a spalling served as an example for this process. However, the same workflow could be scalable to model spallings in larger 3D information models including those for buildings and bridges. First, numerous photos have been taken from that wall. A sample of these photos is shown in Figure 9 (a). Figure 9 (b) depicts the identified defect area. Finally, Figure 9 (c) shows the resulting defect geometry.

To create the damage loaded BIM model as explained in Figure 7, the spalling geometry was exported into IFC as an *IfcBuildingElementProxy* using BlenderBIM add-on with the help of a script developed in C# utilizing XbimToolkit (Lockley et al., 2017) implementing the approach programmatically for the creation of a voided subtraction via boolean difference. The spalling element (i.e., *IfcBuildingElementProxy*) is to be copied into the IFC project. A new instance of *IfcVoidingFeature* is instantiated and assigned a name 'Void', a GUID and an object type labelled 'voiding feature' and given a type of label 'CUTOUT'. The shape representation of the spalling's proxy could then be assigned to the newly created voiding feature using *IfcProductRepresentation*. The voiding feature location is assigned based on that of the spalling's *IfcProduct* using *IfcObjectPlacement*. A decomposition relationship of type

IfcRelAggregates may be created to relate the new voiding feature to the *IfcWall* in the model selected by the user. The feature element subtraction is generated by creating another decomposition relation linking the related opening element (i.e., the *IfcVoidingFeature*) to the relating building element (i.e., the *IfcWall*) using *IfcRelVoidsElement*. Finally, the *IfcBuildingElementProxy* entity for the spalling blocking the view of the voiding feature is deleted from the project. An excerpt of the generated IFC Model for the use case with the spalling defect geometrically modelled as an *IfcVoidingFeature* is shown in Figure 10.

(a) (b) (c)

Figure 9: (a) photos used for the entire process. (b) defect segmentation. (c) resulting geometry

The final BIM model consists of a wall with the openings for the windows and the spalling. Figure 11 shows a screenshot from the software XbimXplorer. A detailed view of the spalling is shown on the top right of the figure. Furthermore, on the bottom right is a view of the hierarchical view of the defect. This model may be used now for further processing, e.g., in stress or damage propagation analyses.

```
#186=IFCWALL('1MNw2bNCD5BfVJugZB0gHb',#42,
    'Basic Wall:Generic - 200mm:357807',$,'$',#147,
    #180,'357807',.NOTDEFINED.);
#757=IFCSHAPEREPRESENTATION(#758,
    'Body','Tessellation',(#759));
#759=IFCPOLYGONALFACESET(#760,$,
    (#761,...));
#760=IFCCARTESIANPOINTLIST3D((...));
#761=IFCINDEXEDPOLYGONALFACE((33,4,19));
#1600=IFCVOIDINGFEATURE('eNDSdir2ekCSo2AsJtWkiQ',
    #711,'Spalling',$,'Spalling at the wall',
    #727,#1601,$,.CUTOUT.);
#1601=IFCPRODUCTDEFINITIONSHAPE($,$,(#757));
#1602=IFCRELVOIDSELEMENT('22utqtIgr6zRNr7LcfTor3',
    #711,$,$,#186,#1600);
```

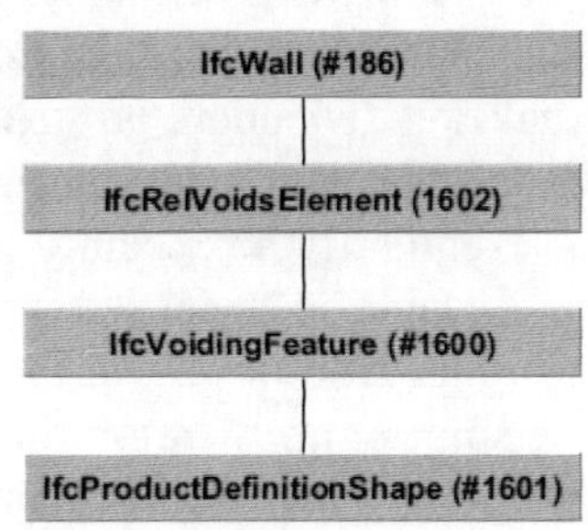

Figure 10: Left: an excerpt showing the result of the modified IFC script with a defect geometry as voiding feature. Right: an UML diagram showing the structure of the IFC file

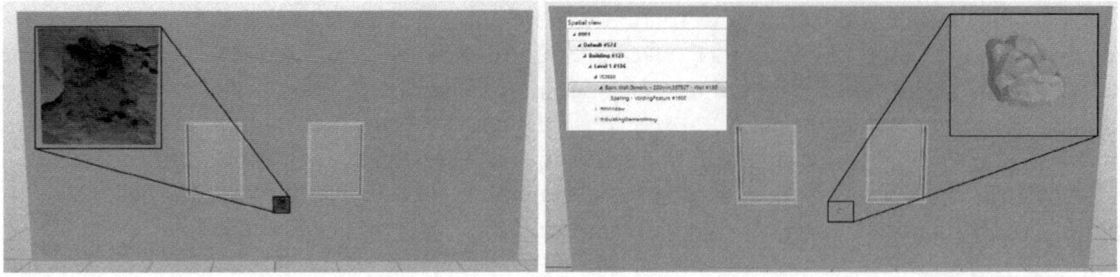

Figure 11: Screenshots from XbimXplorer (Lockley et al., 2020) with the resulting IFC file. On the left is the screenshot with a texture. The right image shows a detailed view of the spalling on the right top. The hierarchy is depicted on the bottom right.

8. Summary and Conclusion

With novel technologies, numerous photos may be taken for bridge inspections. This paper has shown how to generate and position a geometry of a spalling at an existing 3-dimensional building model by automatically processing defect photos. Furthermore, the defect information is modelled and represented with its geometry and texture by using the existent IFC 4 standard. This paper has shown an approach of a semiautomatic workflow starting from defect images up to a damaged Building Information Model with a proper defect geometry. Such an as-is model may be used for inspection reviews, simulations, and reviews. Using fully automated workflows, inspections and assessments become more accurate, faster, and cheaper. The damage information model is inspired by the IFC and assumes a complete model of the structure in the IFC format. This is a problem because few structure and building stocks have digital models. Furthermore, IFC is less established in the civil engineering sector as in the building construction sector.

However, spallings as well as cracks are not the only defects a buildings or structures. Other defects, like chemical defects, are not recognized by the image processing nor included in the data model. Another disadvantage is a missing interface for a user to add information manually. Moreover, the retrained TernausNet16 model for segmenting spalling images is not robust enough to detect spallings in some difficult lighting conditions or complicated scenes even though it did achieve a good Jaccard score. The sole reliance on images in the proposed workflow makes it dependent on several external factors like camera sensor's quality, light and weather conditions. While the use of OpenSfM for reconstructing the scene's point cloud did fulfil the task required, the execution time for generating the point cloud highly depends on the depth maps' resolution specified by the user which could take a significantly long time to generate at higher resolutions and the generated point clouds tend to be very dense that they often require some simplification for practical use. The same disadvantage is faced when using Gmsh for modelling the defect geometry, as the resulting shape tends to be finely meshed to pass the validity checks performed while generating the shape per se that has to be decimated afterwards to achieve a reasonable number of faces and vertices to avoid having rendering errors of the voided geometry when viewed in IFC viewers and a lagging response while interacting with the model.

Splitting the modelling process of all defects simultaneously into minor modelling tasks for individual spalling patches could be a solution to reduce the complexity of the whole process. A mixed use of a very sparse point cloud for the entire model could be first used to determine a general transformation required for estimating an alignment with the 3D model and reserving the use of dense point clouds only at segmented defect patches to produce accurate geometries.

The estimation of a secondary transformation from a single defect patch in any image relative to that of the sparse point cloud applies to every other patch within the same image, saving time and computational resources by eliminating redundant repetitive steps.

References

Artus, M. and Koch, C. (2020), Modeling Geometry and Semantics of Physical Defects using IFC, paper presented at Workshop on Intelligent Computing in Engineering, 1.7.-04.07.2020, Berlin (digital), available at: https://www.researchgate.net/publication/342947221_Modeling_Geometry_and_Semantics_of_Physical_Defects_using_IFC.

Artus, M. and Koch, C. (2021), Modeling Physical Defects Using the Industry Foundation Classes – A Software Evaluation, in Toledo Santos, E. and Scheer, S. (Eds.), Proceedings of the 18th International Conference on Computing in Civil and Building Engineering, Lecture Notes in Civil Engineering, Vol. 98, Springer International Publishing, Cham, pp.507–518.

Bruno, S. and Fatiguso, F. (2018), Building conditions assessment of built heritage in historic building information modeling, International Journal of Sustainable Development and Planning, Vol. 13 No. 01, pp.36–48.

Hamdan, A.-H. and Scherer, J.R. (2018), A Generic Model for the Digitalization of Structural Damage, in Caspeele, R., Taerwe, L. and Frangopol, D.M. (Eds.), Life Cycle Analysis and Assessment in Civil Engineering: Proceedings of the Sixth International Symposium on Life-Cycle Civil Engineering (IALCCE 2018), 28–31 October 2018, Ghent, Belgium, Chapman and Hall/CRC, Milton.

Hüthwohl, P., Brilakis, I., Borrmann, A. and Sacks, R. (2018), Integrating RC Bridge Defect Information into BIM Models, Journal of Computing in Civil Engineering, No. 32, pp.1–14.

Isailović, D., Stojanovic, V., Trapp, M., Richter, R., Hajdin, R. and Döllner, J. (2020), Bridge damage: Detection, IFC-based semantic enrichment and visualization, Automation in Construction, Vol. 112, p. 103088.

Bradski, G.R. and Kaehler, A. (2008), Learning OpenCV: Computer vision with the OpenCV library, O'Reilly, Farnham, Cambridge.

Shvets, A.A., Rakhlin, A., Kalinin, A.A. and Iglovikov, V.I. (2018 - 2018), Automatic Instrument Segmentation in Robot-Assisted Surgery using Deep Learning, in 2018 17th IEEE International Conference on Machine Learning and Applications (ICMLA), Orlando, FL, 17/12/2018 - 20/12/2018, IEEE, pp.624–628.

Yang, L., Li, B., Li, W., Liu, Z., Yang, G. and Xiao, J. (2017 - 2017), A robotic system towards concrete structure spalling and crack database, in 2017 IEEE International Conference on Robotics and Biomimetics (ROBIO), Macau, 05/12/2017 - 08/12/2017, IEEE, pp.1276–1281.

Yang, L., Li, B., Li, W., Liu, Z., Yang, G. and Xiao, J. (Eds.) (2017), Deep Concrete Inspection Using Unmanned Aerial Vehicle Towards CSSC Database, Intelligent Robots and Systems (IROS), 2017 IEEE/RSJ.

Yang, L., Li, B., Li, W., Jiang, B. and Xiao, J. (2018 - 2018), Semantic Metric 3D Reconstruction for Concrete Inspection, in 2018 IEEE/CVF Conference on Computer Vision and Pattern Recognition Workshops (CVPRW), Salt Lake City, UT, USA, 18/06/2018 - 22/06/2018, IEEE, pp.1624–16248.

Yang, J., Li, H. and Jia, Y. (2013 - 2013), Go-ICP: Solving 3D Registration Efficiently and Globally Optimally, in 2013 IEEE International Conference on Computer Vision, Sydney, Australia, 01/12/2013 - 08/12/2013, IEEE, pp.1457–1464.

Yang, J., Li, H., Campbell, D. and Jia, Y. (2016), Go-ICP: A Globally Optimal Solution to 3D ICP Point-Set Registration, IEEE transactions on pattern analysis and machine intelligence, Vol. 38 No. 11, pp.2241–2254.

Geuzaine, C. and Remacle, J.-F. (2009), Gmsh: A 3-D finite element mesh generator with built-in pre- and post-processing facilities, International Journal for Numerical Methods in Engineering, Vol. 79 No. 11, pp.1309–1331.

Lockley, S., Ward, A., Cerny, M. and Artus, M. (2020), xBIM Xplorer, available at: https://github.com/Noranius/XbimWindowsUI.

Lockley, S., Benghi, C. and Černý, M. (2017), Xbim.Essentials: a library for interoperable building information applications, The Journal of Open Source Software, Vol. 2 No. 20, p. 473.

Morgenthal, G., Hallermann, N., Kersten, J., Taraben, J., Debus, P., Helmrich, M. and Rodehorst, V. (2019), Framework for automated UAS-based structural condition assessment of bridges, Automation in Construction, Vol. 97, pp.77–95.

Nagel, L.-M., Pauly, M., Mucha, V., Setzer, J. and Wilhelm, F. (2016), Wettlauf gegen den Verfall, available at: http://www.welt.de/politik/interaktiv/bruecken/deutschlands-bruecken-wettlauf-gegen-den-verfall.html (accessed 27 September 2018).

Rakha, T. and Gorodetsky, A. (2018), Review of Unmanned Aerial System (UAS) applications in the built environment: Towards automated building inspection procedures using drones, Automation in Construction, Vol. 93, pp.252–264.

Schach, R., Otto, J., Häupel, H. and Fritzsche, M. (2006), Lebenszykluskosten von Brücken, Bauingenieur, No. 81, pp.7–14.

Automatic generation of IFC models from point cloud data of transport infrastructure environments

Andrés Justo[a], Mario Soilán[b], Ana Sánchez-Rodríguez[a], Belén Riveiro [a]
[a] Universidade de Vigo, Spain, [b] University of Salamanca, Spain
andres.justo.dominguez@uvigo.es

Abstract. Transport infrastructure is heavily used and subjected to weather condition and other extreme hazards, regardless if they are man-made or natural. Therefore, an adequate monitoring is necessary to ensure that they operate at optimal conditions, enhancing its safety and reducing maintenance cost and time. A digital representation of the asset, such as a BIM (Building Information Model) model, can assist in this task. For this work, data surveyed using LiDAR (Light Detection And Ranging) is processed depending on the desired IFC entity to be parametrized. It is a top-down approach that starts with defining the minimum needed parameters to model an element and then designing a fitting point cloud processing methodology. The objective of this work is to present a modularized methodology for the automatic generation of IFC models of infrastructure elements using point cloud data as input, while also being applicable across the different domains.

1. Introduction

Critical Infrastructure Systems (CIS) are those whose failure would cause direct damage to the economy and society of a nation. These systems are often dependent on one another and grow in size and complexity to accommodate the necessity of the ever-increasing population. Therefore, improving the resilience of these assets is an urgent need, as the collapse of a single element could create a ripple effect to the rest of the network. This would not only help to prevent hazards, accidents, and failures, but also mitigate their effects if they take place. While there are many CISs, such as banking or water supply, the context of this work revolves around the transport infrastructure, which is considered a CIS due to the importance of the transport of goods and people (Boin and McConnell, 2007; Ouyang, 2014). The expansion of the transport network to meet the demands of the population calls for efficient and cost-effective technologies for its construction, monitoring and management (Costin *et al.*, 2018). A digital model, or more specifically, a Building Information Model (BIM) of the asset can fulfil this need. A correct BIM implementation carries several applications, such as integration with other technologies (e.g., Mobile Laser Scanning (MLS)), risk management, and safety control. The BIM approach aids in planning, designing, resource management, construction, maintenance, and monitoring, amongst others. Its benefits could be summarized in reducing cost and time requirements, facilitating decision making and analysis, and boosting integration with other technologies that might provide information of interest. As a result, the overall quality and efficiency of the asset are improved (Azhar, 2011; Costin *et al.*, 2018). Furthermore, its resilience is also enhanced since data that might affect its optimal operation, such as extreme weather data or structural defects, can be analysed alongside the model and set the best course of action. One of the main reasons behind these results is its collaborative nature and multidisciplinary workflow that involves all members of a project. It is based around a Common Data Environment (CDE) that centralizes the relevant data, eliminating the issue with fragmented heterogeneous sources. To do so, it requires an interoperable and standardized data model that guides the different data interactions and exchanges that might occur amongst teams. The Industry Foundation Classes (IFC) is an open international standard (ISO 16739-1:2018) that provides a digital description of the built environment. As with BIM, it was first developed for the building environment, hence the name "Building" information model/modeling.

However, over the last few years, IFC has been evolving towards the infrastructure domain with its IFC4.X releases (*IFC Release Notes - buildingSMART Technical*, no date). The IFC4.1 version introduced the alignment and linear placement as a way to align the infrastructure and place all of its elements relative to it. The newly released IFC4.3 RC2 candidate standard is still very recent, so most of the existing infrastructure modelling efforts based on IFC rely on previous versions. For example, (Kwon *et al.*, 2020) presented an extension to the IFC4.2 version in order to model alignment-based railway tracks. In this context, the creation of an infrastructure BIM model can be broken down into several components that might be tackled independently, or as part of an integrated pipeline. First, the data acquisition is handled by laser technologies that provide high quality point clouds of the as-is state of the asset (Soilán *et al.*, 2019; Lu *et al.*, 2020). That data is then processed for different purposes, such as the detection of the different elements that compose the structure or the identification of possible defects that it might present (Radopoulou and Brilakis, 2017; Brackenbury, Brilakis and Dejong, 2019; Lu, Brilakis and Middleton, 2019). The geometric information can be then used to generate a digital model of the captured data (Hüthwohl *et al.*, 2018; Sánchez-Rodríguez *et al.*, 2020). If left at this point, the model is simply a 3D representation of the asset. However, it can be further enriched to introduce what a BIM model is intended to include besides 3D data, semantics (Belsky, Sacks and Brilakis, 2016). As mentioned, research efforts might deal with several components at once. For instance, (Barazzetti, Previtali and Scaioni, 2020) presented an automatic procedure to detect and classify road assets from LiDAR point clouds using Autodesk Infraworks. In a similar manner, (Sacks *et al.*, 2018) presents an integrated pipeline process for the modelling of bridges which encompasses data acquisition, 3D geometric reconstruction, semantic enrichment, and damage detection and assessment. Furthermore, georeferencing is also a key component in infrastructure modelling since links the model to its real world position, which allows the analysis to account for environmental variables specific for that area (Jaud, Donaubauer and Borrmann, 2019). This paper is focused on the creation of a BIM model that includes both geometry definitions and semantics and that is linked to an alignment definition. To do so, in an analogous manner to previously cited works, the type of information used as source for geometrical data is set as a point cloud obtained by Mobile Laser Scanning (MLS).

MLS has been set as viable technology to elaborate infrastructure inventories or high definition 3D maps. There are various reviews that cover the current state of this topic (Gargoum and El-Basyouny, 2017; Ma *et al.*, 2018; Wang, Peethambaran and Chen, 2018; Soilán *et al.*, 2019). However, most of the efforts lay in automating the point cloud processing, instead of the integration with information models, which is the objective of this methodology. The purpose of this article is to present the modelling possibilities of the IFC schema for infrastructure, and its integration with point cloud data. The key component is the alignment and its linkage with all of the elements of the model, allowing for the abstraction of the infrastructure type. This means that by striping the modelling into its fundamental parts and setting the alignment as the cornerstone, the modelling methodology is applicable to any infrastructure supported by IFC (e.g., road or railway). The authors believe that this type of approach will gain more importance as the existing software tools start supporting the IFC4.3 candidate standard. As a final clarification, the IFC entities and attributes mentioned in the modelling sections will be given in the context of IFC4.1 since it is the schema followed in the programming as by the use of the xBIM toolkit. Additionally, the alignment generation procedure was explained in a previous publication (Soilán *et al.*, 2020) which also used IFC4.1, so it is best to maintain the same naming convention. Nevertheless, the methodology was designed to be as upwards compatible as possible, with minor nomenclature changes. The structure of this work is as follows. Section 2 describes both the cloud processing used to obtain different data inputs and the infrastructure modelling following IFC. Then, Section 3 presents the obtained IFC models guided by figures from the visualization software. Finally, Section 4 offers the conclusions and future lines of research.

2. Methodology

As mentioned, this section is split between the cloud processing and the infrastructure modelling following the IFC schema. The main focus of this work is how to approach the infrastructure modelling at a high level, tackling its fundamentals using traffic signs and guardrails as examples. Furthermore, the alignment generation has been covered in other publications for both the road (Soilán *et al.*, 2020) and the railway domain (Soilán *et al.*, 2021). Also, the generation of IFC models for road infrastructure, including traffic signs, guardrails, and semantics; has also been covered in another publication (Justo *et al.*, 2021). Please refer to the mentioned articles for a more detailed explanation. Figure 1 presents a simple flowchart representing the information flow and the results of each stage. Following this, Section 2.1 presents a brief summary of the methodology used to obtain the data that is to be fed into the modelling program. Section 2.2 is separated following the three key components in infrastructure modelling: positioning, geometric representation, and semantics. Nevertheless, these aspects are often not completely isolated and influence one another, as will be explained at the beginning of Section 2.2.

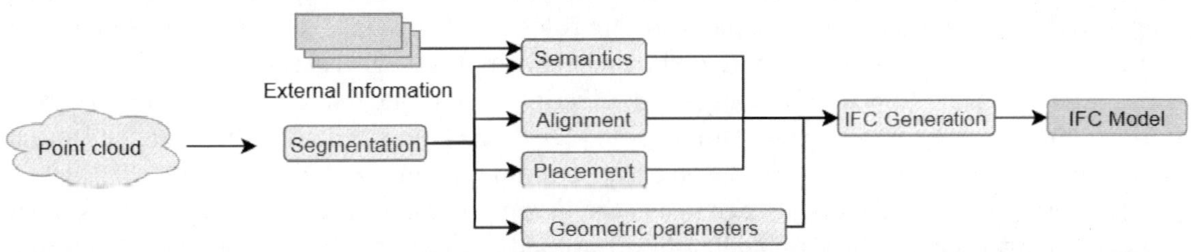

Figure 1: General flowchart

2.1 Point cloud processing

Alignment. 3D point clouds acquired by Mobile Mapping Systems can offer a precise and accurate representation of the geometry of a surveyed infrastructure. These surveys usually include trajectory data as recorded by the navigation system of the vehicle, providing contextual information to the 3D point cloud spatial data. Furthermore, as it was introduced in Section 1, it is possible to implement automated methodologies for the inventory of several infrastructure assets. Under these assumptions, it is clear that obtaining the alignment of the infrastructure from 3D point cloud data is a plausible task. First, the problem statement requires two questions to be answered: (1) How is the alignment defined in the surveyed infrastructure, and (2) which features can be extracted from the point cloud that assist to its computation. Once these questions are answered, the extraction of the alignment is solved by developing an adequate and automated point cloud processing methodology. Previous work in Soilán et al. (2020) shows this workflow, by defining the road alignment as the central axis of the road, and the road markings as main features to define road edges and, subsequently, the geometry of the alignment. Therefore, the point cloud processing step is reduced to a road marking detection problem. By defining the position of the road markings and their spatial context, it is possible to extract not only the road alignment, but also the central axis of each lane of the road, which can be defined as an offset alignment. Analogously, the alignment in the railway environment is defined as the central axis of each rail track, and the features that allow this definition are the rails. Consequently, a rail extraction methodology on the 3D point cloud is a required step for the definition of the alignment.

Asset inventory. While the definition of certain assets from the 3D point cloud is a prerequisite for the computation of the alignment, there are many other assets that can be considered for its inventory. This work focuses on two important assets for road safety: Traffic signs and guardrails. Traffic signs are one of the most distinguishable assets in a 3D point cloud due to its retroreflective properties as well as its standardized geometry. For that reason, the intensity attribute of the point cloud (which is related with the energy reflected by the surface as it returns to the laser scanner receiver) is typically used to segment traffic sign panels, whose points have to be grouped, filtering out those groups of points that do not comply with the standardized geometries of traffic signs. Once the traffic sign panels are isolated, their close environment can be analysed to position its pole and its point of contact with the ground, which are relevant parameters towards its positioning with respect to the alignment. Differently, guardrails cannot be distinguished as straightforwardly as traffic signs. First, the intensity attribute is not a relevant feature for segmentation, and second, they are a linear asset while traffic signs are punctual assets. Having this into account, guardrail inventory is based on two criteria: (1) Spatial context, as they are physical barriers positioned over the edge of the road. (2) Local geometry features, such as the orientation of their surface, height, or dimensionality. Under these assumptions, a set of heuristic rules can be defined to segment the guardrails. Furthermore, if the guardrail geometries are restrained in the case study, or there is enough data from the different types of barriers, the heuristic rules can be embedded in a supervised learning framework training classification models to perform this segmentation task. Finally, it is relevant to note that the position of any point of a 3D point cloud can be expressed with respect to the alignment as a set of three parameters: (1) DistanceAlong, which is the distance from the first point of the alignment to the closest alignment segment of the given point, (2) OffsetLateral, which is the distance between the given point and its closest alignment segment, and (3) OffsetVertical, which is the height difference between the two points used to compute the OffsetLateral parameter.

2.2 IFC model generation

In a modelling level, one element can be characterized by its position, geometrical representation, and semantics. In a civil infrastructure context, the position is guided by the alignment, which allows elements to be placed relative to it. While the geometrical representation simply describes the shape of the element, the semantics encompass any information that further characterizes and differentiates the object. The data source for both position and geometrical representation is the point cloud. However, the semantics usually, but not always, require other external sources. It should be noted that these three components are the result of a simplification, since they can intertwine themselves. For instance, the alignment can be used as the base curve for geometrical representations that follow extrusions. Nevertheless, the abstraction into these groups eases the explanation and follows a modularity that is also exerted in the software.

Linear placement. The placement of the elements can be ruled by different IFC entities. In this work, only the linear and local placement will be mentioned. The local placement is a simple XYZ coordinate system that allows for the relative placement of objects with respect to another placement or the origin. This is the placement used to place the spatial structural elements and the alignment in the project. However, every other entity in the model is placed using a linear placement (*IfcLinearPlacement*) whose basis curve is related to, or is, the main alignment of the infrastructure. To aid in the following explanation, Figure 2a shows an example of linear placement relative to an alignment. The linear placement is characterized by three key attributes that allow to place any element anywhere in space, while keeping it linked to the alignment: (i) Basis curve (*IfcCurve*), (ii) orientation (*IfcOrientationExpression*), and (iii) distance (*IfcDistanceExpression)*. The basis curve is the curve that serves as base for the linear reference system. As mentioned, it should be the alignment or a curve that is defined relative to it. The orientation is formed by the lateral and axial directions (*IfcDirection*) of the element. The distance parameter, however, is also described by other three attributes that serve as relative coordinates in the linear reference system: (a) DistanceAlong, (b) OffsetLateral, and (c) OffsetVertical. The OffsetLateral represents a horizontal offset, perpendicular to the basis curve. The OffsetVertical sets the upwards vertical offset (+Z) relative to the basis curve, regardless of the curve. The DistanceAlong is the distance measured along the basis curve where OffsetLateral and OffsetVertical values are applied.

Alignment. The alignment generation procedure was covered in a previous publication (Soilán *et al.*, 2020) which explained the methodology in detail. The objective is to obtain an alignment hierarchy where a main alignment stands on top of different offset alignments that depend on the main one for their geometric representation. In the road scenario, the main alignment describes the centre of the road, while the offset alignments define the centre of each traffic lane. This hierarchic approach is also valid for a railway scenario, where the main alignment represents the centre of the track, while the offset alignments denote the inner-top part of the rails. In modelling terms, the shape of the alignment can be represented in several ways. The documentation allows for any representation as long as it fits the definitions set by an *IfcCurve*. However, it is advisable to utilize *IfcBoundedCurve* definitions, since they have clear start and end points. The importance of this distinction lies in the DistanceAlong attribute, because it measures a distance from the start of the curve. The chosen representations are *IfcAlignmentCurve* for the main alignment and *IfcOffsetCurveByDistances* for the offset alignments. The *IfcAlignmentCurve* describes a curve by splitting it into vertical and horizontal components (*IfcAlignment2DVertical* and *IfcAlignment2DHorizontal*) formed by a series of segments (*IfcAlignment2DVerticalSegment* and *IfcAlignment2DHorizontalSegment*). Therefore, the core aspect of the alignment generation procedure is to accurately represent the input polyline into the mentioned segments. Horizontal segments describe the behaviour of the alignment in the XY plane, meaning that all of their parameters can be extracted by analysing the X and Y coordinates of the polyline points. The vertical segments, however, describe the slope or gradient of the alignment between two points. These points are described by a start distance measured along the horizontal component (*IfcAlignment2DHorizontal*), and a length measured in the same way. Therefore, to model these segments, the Z coordinate of the polyline points is processed along the horizontal segment lengths. As a result, a dependence is formed, meaning that while it is possible to define a solely horizontal alignment, a uniquely vertical alignment is impossible to model.

Geometric representation. The geometric representation of an element can be defined in several ways. For instance, it is possible to generate a tessellated surface from a mesh that was defined from the point cloud. However, many elements can be defined as an extrusion of simple profiles or combination of primitive shapes. This is the case for the road elements studied in this work, traffic signs and guardrails. The traffic sign and guardrail elements are different in both the positioning and the extrusion operations used to generate their solids. However, they are similar in that they are described as assemblies of simpler elements and that they use a profile definition (*IfcProfileDef*) to characterize their extruded geometries. To emphasize these similitudes and differences, Figure 2b presents a diagram of how the IFC entities of these elements are related to one another. The guardrail can be divided into the railing (*IfcRailing*) and the shoes (*IfcMember*), which are modelled using *IfcSectionedSolidHorizontal* and *IfcExtrudedAreaSolid*, respectively. The key difference between these two representations is that the latter uses a straight line or direction (*IfcDirection*) for its extrusion, while the former employs a curve. As such, the shoes of the guardrail are described by a profile (*IfcProfileDef*), extruded for a certain length, in a certain direction (*IfcDirection*). On the other hand, the railing extrusion, while also using a profile (*IfcProfileDef*), it utilizes a curve (*IfcCurve*) to describe the extrusion. This solid definition allows the use of different profiles, placed in different points relative to the alignment (*IfcDistanceExpression*), which, once connected following the shape of the alignment, forms the desired solid. Nevertheless, the railing profile is expected to be constant throughout the extrusion, meaning that only the start and end positions are required. As for the traffic sign, it can be split into the post (*IfcMember*) and the plate or plates (*IfcPlate*). Both of these elements are modelled in the same manner as the shoes of the guardrail. Their representation is *IfcExtrudedAreaSolid*, meaning that they use a profile definition (*IfcProfileDef*) that is extruded along a direction (*IfcDirection*) for a certain length. Another difference in the modelling of guardrails and traffic signs is the input of their profiles. The parametric values that describe the profiles of the traffic sign components can be extracted directly from the point cloud. Contrary to that, the profiles of the railing and each of the shoes are not easily obtainable. However, they are often standardized and their dimensions can be found in their respective standards. Therefore, the railing profile is characterized as a polyline approximation of the one depicted in the UNE 135121:2012 standard, while the shoes have a predefined rectangular profile. To construct these elements, the linearly extruded components (shoes, plates and posts) are extruded at the origin in the direction of the positive Z axis. Then, using the linear placement, these elements are repositioned and reoriented to fit the alignment direction in the target location. Finally, the elements are assembled under an *IfcElementAssembly* that is used to refer to the combination of elements, instead of the single components. For instance, when placing the guardrail in the spatial structure of the project, the target entity is the *IfcElementAssembly*, not each of the shoes and the railing.

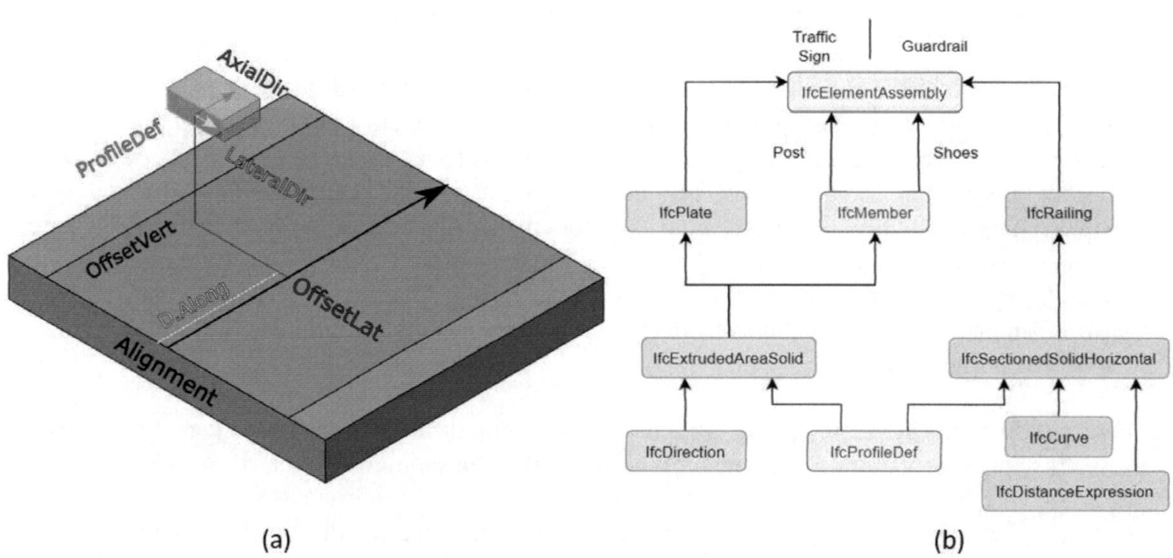

Figure 2: (a) Linear placement example. (b) Guardrail & sign IFC entities

Semantics. The semantic data of an element, entity or object is the information that further enriches it, beyond its 3D representation or position. As such, it encompasses the spatial structure, material definitions, property sets, identification parameters (names, descriptions), amongst others. In the context of this work and the scan-to-BIM methodologies, this information is usually not directly obtainable by processing the point cloud. Therefore, it is introduced in the model by other means. For instance, there is no way to obtain the spatial structure of the project from a point cloud. The spatial structure is a hierarchy of spatial elements (*IfcSpatialStructureElement*) that serve to organize the project in different levels. The top level is occupied by the unique project entity, which branches into sites (zones where the project takes place). These sites can be formed by facilities (roads, railways, etc.). Finally, these facilities contain different facility parts, like road segments. While this can be made more complex, the project > site > facility > facility part hierarchy is enough to give an insight in how a project might be organized. Any other non-spatial element in the model is to be fit in one level of the hierarchy. For example, the spatial structure element that contains the alignment is a site. Therefore, its position is affected by the position of the site since it uses a relative placement. Similarly to the spatial structure, certain property sets cannot be extracted from the point cloud. Once introduced in the model, both the spatial structure and property sets are related to the different elements present in the model by the use of *IfcRelContainedInSpatialStructure* and *IfcRelDefinesByProperties* relationships, respectively.

3. Results

The automatic IFC entity generation explained in Section 3.2 used the data obtained from the point cloud processing methods described in Section 3.1. This IFC model generation methodology is based on the IFC 4.1 version of the schema. Nevertheless, as mentioned in the introduction, the development of this work took into account the online documentations and reports regarding the newly released IFC 4.3 RC2 candidate standard. To promote upwards compatibility, IFC 4.3 RC2 information was prioritized and the chosen IFC entities were the ones that best fit or closes to that version. However, the definitions provided for the alignment and elements, as well as the modularized methodology, which is the main focus of this work, are still valid for newer versions even if they are to be subjected to nomenclature or minor changes when the program is updated. Nevertheless, they could be improved once certain aspects not present in IFC 4.1 become available, such as the lateral profile inclination. To showcase the results, Figure 3 and Figure 4 are shown below. In one hand, Figure 3 illustrates the shape representations and placement of the traffic sign and the guardrails. Both are related to the alignment, which is seen as the blue line in the figure.

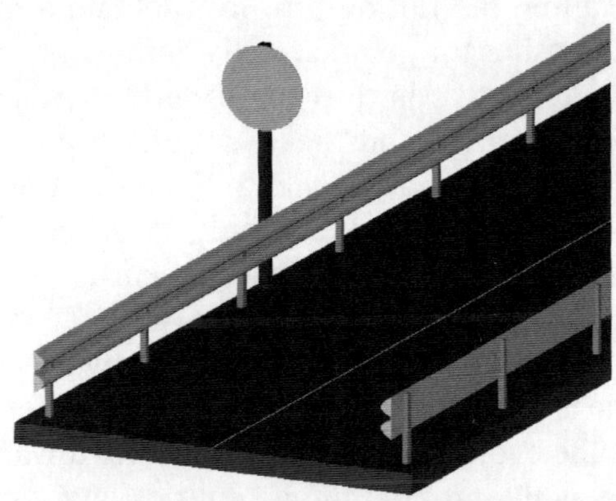

Figure 3: Traffic sign and guardrail model

On the other hand, Figure 4 presents an example of the semantics that might be included in the model. Figure 4a shows a possible spatial hierarchy of the project, where the alignment and road are linked to a site, and where the elements are children of the facility part. In the case of the property sets, Figure 4b presents *Pset_PlateCommon* and *Pset_MemberCommon*, which are associated to the traffic sign assembly.

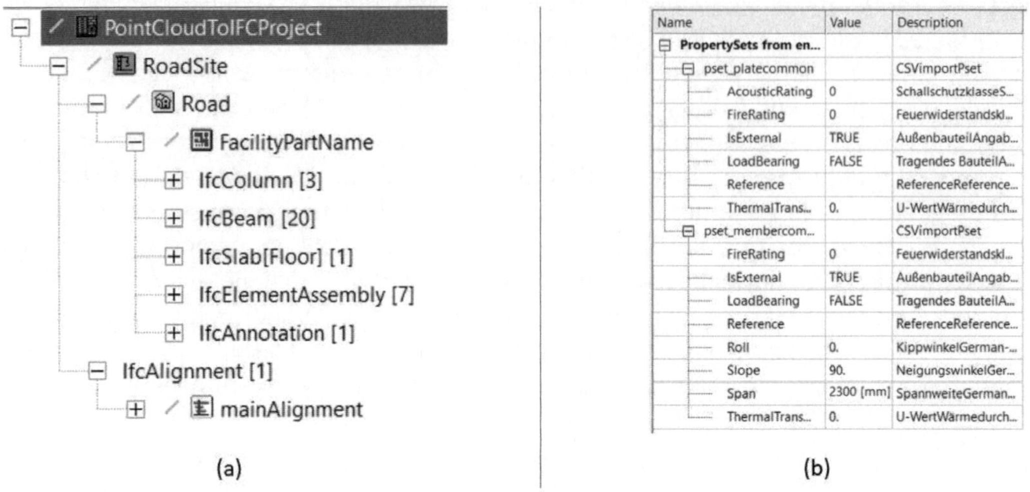

Figure 4: Modelling example. (a) Spatial structure hierarchy. (b) Property sets of the traffic sign model

4. Conclusions

This work showcases the firsts steps towards an automatic alignment-based generation of IFC models for the infrastructure domain. It uses point cloud data as the main source for geometric parameters and positioning, while also semantically enriching the model with additional external sources. The cornerstone of the methodology is the alignment definition that guides the positioning and, in some cases, the geometry of the infrastructure elements. To illustrate the procedure, the modelling of traffic signs and guardrails was described using the different IFC entities involved in their definition. While both types of elements were successfully modelled, including relevant semantics, the methodology is still under development, and therefore, there is room for improvement. Refining changes would imply refining the representation of the elements. For instance, detailing the railing profile to obtain a more accurate representation. Also, the use for simplified meshes for geometrically complex elements (e.g., railway catenary posts) is being studied. The objective is to reach a middle ground between simple and light parametric definitions and detailed and heavy mesh representations. Another type of improvement is the addition of new components to the methodology, such as the inclusion of material definitions, which at the moment has only been tested manually in simple cases. Regardless of the possible changes, the use of the alignment as the cornerstone for infrastructure modelling seems promising. The newly released IFC4.3 RC2 candidate standard introduces several changes to the schema and that implies that some tweaks are to be done to include the new possibilities in alignment definition and implement the different nomenclature changes in IFC entities. Nevertheless, the evolution of the IFC schema towards the infrastructure domain will open new possibilities as the programming libraries and viewers that support it become available.

References

Azhar, S. (2011) 'Building information modeling (BIM): Trends, benefits, risks, and challenges for the AEC industry', Leadership and Management in Engineering, 11(3), pp.241–252. doi: 10.1061/(ASCE)LM.1943-5630.0000127.

Barazzetti, L., Previtali, M. and Scaioni, M. (2020) 'Roads Detection and Parametrization in Integrated BIM-GIS Using LiDAR', Infrastructures. MDPI Multidisciplinary Digital Publishing Institute, 5(7), p. 55. doi: 10.3390/infrastructures5070055.

Belsky, M., Sacks, R. and Brilakis, I. (2016) 'Semantic Enrichment for Building Information Modeling', Computer-Aided Civil and Infrastructure Engineering. Blackwell Publishing Inc., 31(4), pp.261–274. doi: 10.1111/mice.12128.

Boin, A. and McConnell, A. (2007) 'Preparing for critical infrastructure breakdowns: The limits of crisis management and the need for resilience', Journal of Contingencies and Crisis Management. John Wiley & Sons, Ltd, 15(1), pp.50–59. doi: 10.1111/j.1468-5973.2007.00504.x.

Brackenbury, D., Brilakis, I. and Dejong, M. (2019) 'Automated defect detection for masonry arch bridges', in International Conference on Smart Infrastructure and Construction 2019, ICSIC 2019: Driving Data-Informed Decision-Making. ICE Publishing, pp.3–10. doi: 10.1680/icsic.64669.003.

Costin, A. et al. (2018) 'Building Information Modeling (BIM) for transportation infrastructure – Literature review, applications, challenges, and recommendations', Automation in Construction. Elsevier, 94(June), pp.257–281. doi: 10.1016/j.autcon.2018.07.001.

Gargoum, S. and El-Basyouny, K. (2017) 'Automated extraction of road features using LiDAR data: A review of LiDAR applications in transportation', 2017 4th International Conference on Transportation Information and Safety, ICTIS 2017 - Proceedings, pp.563–574. doi: 10.1109/ICTIS.2017.8047822.

Hüthwohl, P. et al. (2018) 'Integrating RC Bridge Defect Information into BIM Models', Journal of Computing in Civil Engineering. American Society of Civil Engineers (ASCE), 32(3), p. 04018013. doi: 10.1061/(asce)cp.1943-5487.0000744.

IFC Release Notes - buildingSMART Technical (no date). Available at: https://technical.buildingsmart.org/standards/ifc/ifc-schema-specifications/ifc-release-notes/ (Accessed: 9 December 2020).

Jaud, Š., Donaubauer, A. and Borrmann, A. (2019) 'Georeferencing within IFC: A Novel Approach for Infrastructure Objects', in Computing in Civil Engineering 2019: Visualization, Information Modeling, and Simulation - Selected Papers from the ASCE International Conference on Computing in Civil Engineering 2019. American Society of Civil Engineers (ASCE), pp.377–384. doi: 10.1061/9780784482421.048.

Justo, A. et al. (2021) 'Scan-to-BIM for the infrastructure domain: Generation of IFC-complaint models of road infrastructure assets and semantics using 3D point cloud data', Automation in Construction. Elsevier, 127, p. 103703. doi: https://doi.org/10.1016/j.autcon.2021.103703.

Kwon, T. H. et al. (2020) 'Design of Railway Track Model with Three-Dimensional Alignment Based on Extended Industry Foundation Classes', Applied Sciences. MDPI AG, 10(10), p. 3649. doi: 10.3390/app10103649.

Lu, R. et al. (2020) 'An Automated Target-Oriented Scanning System for Infrastructure Applications', in Construction Research Congress 2020: Computer Applications - Selected Papers from the Construction Research Congress 2020. American Society of Civil Engineers (ASCE), pp.457–467. doi: 10.1061/9780784482865.049.

Lu, R., Brilakis, I. and Middleton, C. R. (2019) 'Detection of Structural Components in Point Clouds of Existing RC Bridges', Computer-Aided Civil and Infrastructure Engineering. Blackwell Publishing Inc., 34(3), pp.191–212. doi: 10.1111/mice.12407.

Ma, L. et al. (2018) 'Mobile laser scanned point-clouds for road object detection and extraction: A review', Remote Sensing, 10(10), pp.1–33. doi: 10.3390/rs10101531.

Ouyang, M. (2014) 'Review on modeling and simulation of interdependent critical infrastructure systems', Reliability Engineering and System Safety. Elsevier Ltd, pp.43–60. doi: 10.1016/j.ress.2013.06.040.

Radopoulou, S. C. and Brilakis, I. (2017) 'Automated Detection of Multiple Pavement Defects', Journal of Computing in Civil Engineering. American Society of Civil Engineers (ASCE), 31(2), p. 04016057. doi: 10.1061/(asce)cp.1943-5487.0000623.

Sacks, R. et al. (2018) 'SeeBridge as next generation bridge inspection: Overview, Information Delivery Manual and Model View Definition', Automation in Construction. Elsevier B.V., 90, pp.134–145. doi: 10.1016/j.autcon.2018.02.033.

Sánchez-Rodríguez, A. et al. (2020) 'From point cloud to IFC: A masonry arch bridge case study', in EG-ICE 2020 Workshop on Intelligent Computing in Engineering, Proceedings. Universitatsverlag der TU Berlin, pp.422–431.

Soilán, M. et al. (2019) 'Review of Laser Scanning Technologies and Their Applications for Road and Railway Infrastructure Monitoring', Infrastructures, 4(4), p. 58. doi: https://doi.org/10.3390/infrastructures4040058.

Soilán, M. et al. (2020) '3D Point Cloud to BIM: Semi-Automated Framework to Define IFC Alignment Entities from MLS-Acquired LiDAR Data of Highway Roads', Remote Sensing. MDPI AG, 12(14), p. 2301. doi: 10.3390/rs12142301.

Soilán, M. et al. (2021) 'Fully automated methodology for the delineation of railway lanes and the generation of IFC alignment models using 3D point cloud data', Automation in Construction. Elsevier, 126(February), p. 103684. doi: 10.1016/j.autcon.2021.103684.

Wang, R., Peethambaran, J. and Chen, D. (2018) 'LiDAR Point Clouds to 3-D Urban Models : A Review', IEEE Journal of Selected Topics in Applied Earth Observations and Remote Sensing. IEEE, 11(2), pp.606–627. doi: 10.1109/JSTARS.2017.2781132.

A Proposed Ontology for Knowledge Representation in Designing Indoor Inspection Robot Systems

Leyuan Ma, Timo Hartmann
Technische Universität Berlin, Germany
leyuan.ma@campus.tu-berlin.de

Abstract. Robotic technology is now rapidly penetrating the building inspection field and has great potential in improving inspection efficiency and accuracy. However, existing building inspection robot systems are still far from being able to meet the requirements of inspection professionals because of the knowledge gap between robot designers and building inspectors. To facilitate knowledge sharing between the building inspection and robotics domains and improve the robotic design, an ontology is developed in this study to formalize the knowledge that is relevant to the design of an indoor inspection robot system. It contains two main domain ontology models including Building Interior Model and Inspection Robot System Model. After future verification and validation, the proposed ontology is expected to allow for a more effective inquiry of indoor inspection robot design related knowledge and pave the way for the automatic design of robots in the building inspection field.

1. Introduction

Regular inspections for existing residential buildings have drawn increasing attention from both researchers and occupants since building defects can not only impact a building's performance but also threaten users' health and safety if left untreated. However, a thorough building investigation usually involves a substantial amount of time and manpower and highly depends on well-trained inspectors in various disciplines. In recent years, robotic technology is increasingly being used in building inspection and auditing because it reduces the dependency on humans and offers major efficiency and accuracy advantages over traditional approaches. The design of a building inspection robot system is an interdisciplinary work that requires integrated knowledge from robotics and building inspection fields. Currently, significant research has focused on developing new robotic hardware and software applications to help human inspectors conduct tasks such as post-construction quality assessment (Yan et al., 2019) and environmental data collection (Mantha et al., 2018) and to automate auditing processes (Ham and Golparvar-Fard, 2013; López-Fernández et al., 2017). However, existing robotic systems are still often far from being able to perform as expected from building inspectors because it is quite challenging and time-consuming for robot designers to acquire knowledge and requirements from the building inspection field and integrate them into the system design. Thus, it is critical to systematically formalize extracted knowledge from the building inspection domain and make it useful for robotic design.

As formal and explicit specifications of shared conceptualizations, ontologies not only provide enough concepts and relations to articulate models of specific situations in a given domain but also can be used to generate knowledge with inference methods (Ramos et al., 2018). It has been widely used in architecture, engineering, and construction (AEC) industries and the robotics domain. In the building inspection and maintenance domain, dozens of ontologies have been developed around construction quality inspection (Zhong et al., 2012), building facility management (Gouda Mohamed et al., 2020) and building environmental monitoring (Lork et al., 2019). In terms of robotics ontologies, IEEE Ontologies for Robotics and Automation (ORA) Working Group devoted a lot of efforts to developing ontologies to standardize the knowledge representation in the Robotics and Automation field (Balakirsky et al., 2017; Prestes et al., 2013). Besides, several ontologies for robotics subdomains such as service robotics, industrial robotics and autonomous robots have also been proposed to define robots (Schlenoff and Messina, 2005) and to describe the robot environment (Chella et al., 2002), robot actions and robot tasks (Bernardo et al., 2018; Ji et al., 2012). However, to the best of our knowledge, there is still no ontology incorporating fragmented knowledge from both building inspection and robotics fields with the purpose of informing the design of the building inspection robot.

In this study, we propose an ontology that integrates the knowledge related to the design of the robot system from both building inspection and robotic domains. It shows existing concepts and relationships among building information, building defects, and requirements for the robot system, which plays a vital role in facilitating the robot design process and finally improving the performance of the robot system. Though the ontology aims to be general and extensible, to limit the scope of demonstration in this paper, the knowledge required for the design of the indoor inspection robot system in residential buildings was chosen as an area of focus to represent in this ontology. This paper is structured as follows. Section 2 introduces existing efforts on developing ontologies in building inspection and robotics industries. Section 3 presents the methodology we implemented for ontology specification, knowledge acquisition and conceptualization. Section 4 describes the details about the developed ontology. Discussion and conclusion are presented in Section 5 and Section 6, respectively.

2. Related Work

2.1 Ontologies and Knowledge Representation in Building Inspection Domain

Building defects may influence the building in various ways, such as structural performance, energy performance and indoor environmental conditions. It usually requires inspectors from different professional backgrounds using different survey instrumentation to acquire and analyse defect data. Knowledge regarding inspection activities, checklist, defects information and instrument characteristics is often scattered and disconnected. In recent years, the development of ontologies in the building inspection domain has shown great potential for improving knowledge management and workflow. For example, Park et al. (2013) developed a construction defects domain ontology for the user to easily retrieve necessary defect information; Zhong et al. (2012) proposed a regulation constraints ontology allowing for automated construction quality compliance checking; Gouda Mohamed et al. (2020) integrated as-is record ontology converted from as-is BIM into building facilities ontology to facilitate retrieving existing building facilities information; Building management system ontology, benchmarking ontology, and evaluation & control ontology were created by Lork et al. (2019) to help efficiently identify energy-related abnormalities in existing buildings. These ontologies can serve as the base for digital building inspection systems and have paved the way towards automated building inspection. However, existing ontologies mainly focus on formalizing building inspection knowledge, the link between building inspection information and the design of automated building inspection systems is still missing.

2.2 Ontologies and Knowledge Representation for Robotics

The use of ontologies for knowledge representation in the robotics domain is becoming increasingly important because the growing complexity of behaviours that robots are expected to conduct demand increasingly complex knowledge (Prestes et al., 2013). IEEE ORA Working Group has been working with standardizing knowledge representation in Robotics and

Automation field for over ten years. The first output of this group is a Core Ontology for Robotics and Automation (CORA) (Prestes et al., 2013) which describes what a robot is and how it relates to other concepts at a general level. In 2015, IEEE Standard Ontologies for Robotics and Automation (ORA) (IEEE ORA WG, 2015) consisting of CORA and other sub-ontologies was released. It provides a unified way of representing and reasoning knowledge and provides general notions behind Robotics and Automation. In recent 5 years, several IEEE working groups are working on extending the ORA standard for different purposes. For example, the IEEE Task Representation (RTR) Study Group is developing a broad standard that offers a common representation and framework when describing tasks in the industrial robotics domain (Balakirsky et al., 2017; Fiorini et al., 2017). Autonomous Robot (AuR) subgroup is working on defining key concepts needed in the design of autonomous robots operating in the air, ground and underwater (Fiorini et al., 2017).

Apart from the standard ontologies, many ontologies have been developed to support the robot design and operation in robotics subdomains by describing their structural and operation capabilities. Preece et al. (2008) proposed an ontology to formally represent the knowledge about sensors and their requirements for a given mission in the military context. It addressed the decision-making problem when selecting appropriate sensors to be mounted on the robot platform using automated reasoning; The Automatic Design of Robots Ontology (ADROn) developed by Ramos et al. (2018) defines concepts regarding robot actions, structural robot parts, structural requirements and robot types, which allows for inferring structural parts that a robot should have to achieve required actions; In order for the autonomous personal robot to achieve a more flexible operation, Tenorth and Beetz (2013) built a knowledge processing framework (KnowRob) which equips the robot with a comprehensive body of knowledge and dedicated knowledge processing capacities. Robotics have benefited a lot from ontology-based knowledge modelling since it provides an efficient way to capture, share and process knowledge about robots' physical structures, actions and tasks. However, most of them focused on representing generic knowledge in the robotics domain, and there is a lack of study focusing on making use of engineering knowledge in a given domain to inform the robotics design for a specific application. The proposed ontology represents robot design related knowledge extracted from building inspection and robotics domains, aiming to open up new opportunities to promote the interdisciplinary design of indoor inspection robot systems.

3. Research Methodology

3.1 Defining the Purpose and the Scope of the Ontology

According to the METHONTOLOGY proposed by Fernández-López et al. (1997), the development of the ontology starts from identifying its purpose and scope. The purpose of the proposed ontology is to represent the concepts related to the design of the indoor inspection robot system and to support robot designers in choosing optimal components of the system which fulfils the requirements of building inspection professionals. The ontology will include concepts and relations regarding building interior spaces and components in residential buildings, interior defects information, robot system components and requirements for the robot system. The intended end-users of this ontology can be not only robot designers but also building inspectors, and they are supposed to use the ontology for knowledge sharing and effective communication.

3.2 Knowledge Acquisition and Conceptualization

The knowledge that is relevant to the design of the indoor inspection robot system is from two domains: indoor inspection and robotics. Regarding the former, we consider that building interior spaces which offers the robot a working environment and defects on interior components which determines the inspection tasks the robot needs to accomplish are critical to the design of the robot system. Sources for capturing building interior information and defects information include OmniClass (2012), Guide for a Sustainable Energy Audit of Buildings (Dall'O', 2013), State of the Art on Building Pathology Report (CIB, 2013) and several existing studies on developing building inspection systems (Bay et al., 2017; Bortolini and Forcada, 2018; Ferraz et al., 2016). In terms of the robotics domain, knowledge about robot system components and capabilities is acquired from existing literature defining elements of robotics (Ben-Ari and Mondada, 2018) and standards like ISO 8373 (ISO, 2020) and ORA (IEEE ORA WG, 2015). After a thorough reading and analysis of the above documents, we extract the knowledge that is needed in designing the indoor inspection robot system and structure it in a conceptual model. The next section describes the proposed ontology in the conceptual level.

4. Ontology for Designing Indoor Inspection Robot System in Residential Buildings

The Ontology for Designing Indoor Inspection Robot System in Residential Buildings (ODIIRS) defines concepts and their relations that should be considered when selecting appropriate components of robotic systems to perform specific inspection tasks inside residential buildings. As shown in Fig.1, the ontology consists of two main domain ontology models including *Building Interior Model* and *Inspection Robot System Model*. *Building Interior Model* determines the working environment and tasks for the *Inspection Robot System*.

Building Interior Model (Fig.2) contains *InteriorSpaces* that the robot works in, *BuildingComponents* that the robot may have contact with and *Defect*s of *BuildingComponents* that the robot system needs to detect. Different *InteriorSpaces* and *BuildingComponents* are prone to different types of *Defects*. For example, *Cracking*, *SurfaceProblems* and *EnergyRelatedProblems* are the main *Defects* in *Walls* and *Ceilings*, and *MoistureProblems* usually happens on *Walls*, *Ceilings* and *PlumbingSystems* in the *Bathroom*. The *Documentation* of the *BuildingInterior* records details of *InteriorSpaces* and the *Characteristics* of *BuildingComponent*s. Types of *Defects*, *Attributes* of *BuildingComponents* and *Characteristics* of *Material* determine the *Requirements* for the *InspectionRobotSystem*. For instance, *EnergyRelatedProblems* usually require a *ThermalCamera* with a *SpectralResolution* of long wavelength infrared radiation within the electromagnetic spectrum, the *Height* of the *CrawlSpace* determines the *dimension* of the robot, and the *CoefficientOfFriction* of the surface material influences the *MechanicalStructureSpecifications* of the robot.

Inspection Robot System Model (Fig.3) includes *RobotSystemComponents* and *Requirements* for the system. According to the Standard ISO/DIS 8373 Robotics-Vocabulary, the robot system comprises Robot(s), EndEffector(s) and AuxiliaryEquipment. The robot system may have more than one robot because different inspection tasks may require different types of robots. For example, indoor inspection drones or wall-climbing robots are usually used in high spaces which are not accessible to ground-based mobile robots, and specialized crawling robots are needed in crawl spaces. A thorough inspection of the building needs a cooperative fleet of Robots. AuxiliaryEquipment contains Sensors and OtherInspectionInstrument supporting the robot to performing tasks. For instance, thermographic inspection through the use of a ThermalCamera is an important approach to detect EnergyRelatedProblems like ThermalBridges, InsulationProblems and MoistureProblems.

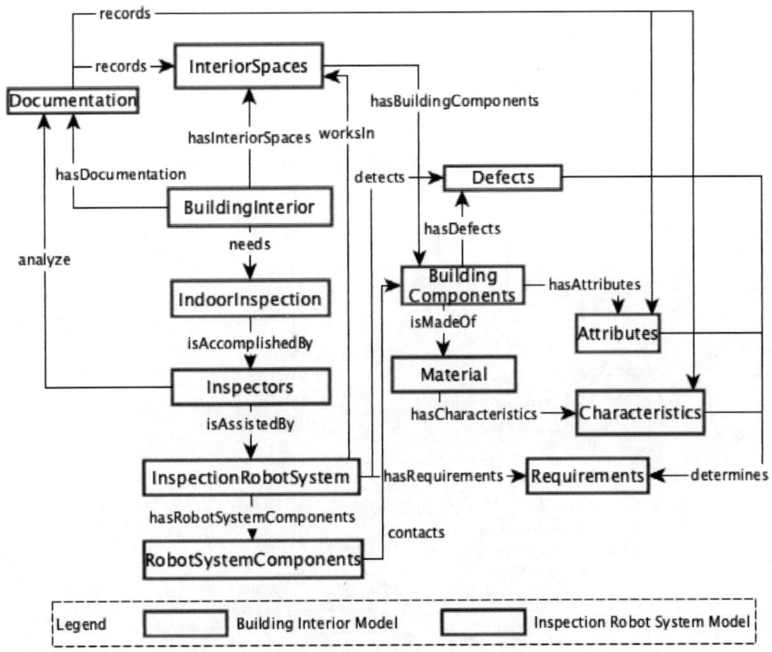

Figure 1: The ODIIRS Ontology

The Requirements class is further represented in Fig.4. It includes three subclasses, namely Specifications, FunctionalRequirements and PerformanceRequirements. Specifications contain GeneralSpecifications and ComponentsSpecifications. GeneralSpecifications relate to the specifications of the whole robot such as Weight, Dimension, BatteryLife and Cost. ComponentsSpecifications specify major parameters that need to be considered when selecting robot components. For instance, *RPM (Revolutions per minute)* of the *DCMotor* is a crucial factor if a high-speed rotation is required. *FunctionalRequirements* define functions that the robot system should possess to accomplish inspection tasks. *DataCollection* is the most important functional requirement for the robot system because collecting data is the most difficult and time-intensive work for human inspectors. Gathering data continuously as robots travelling through the building can significantly improve the work efficiency and accuracy. The robot can operate either semi-autonomously or fully autonomously. Depending on the required degree of autonomy, navigational strategies including navigating indoors, Simultaneous localization and Mapping (SLAM), exploration and target identification solutions need to be considered to achieve the desired *Navigation* function. Besides. To fulfil automatic *DataAnalysis* and offer *DefectsAlarming* in real-time, data processing algorithms should be integrated into the system. *PerformanceRequirements* comprise a set of criteria stipulating how the robot should perform. *SteeringAbility*, for example, indicates the ability of the robot to move omnidirectionally. The requirement of the *SteeringAbility* will consequently influence the design of the *LocomotionMechanisim*.

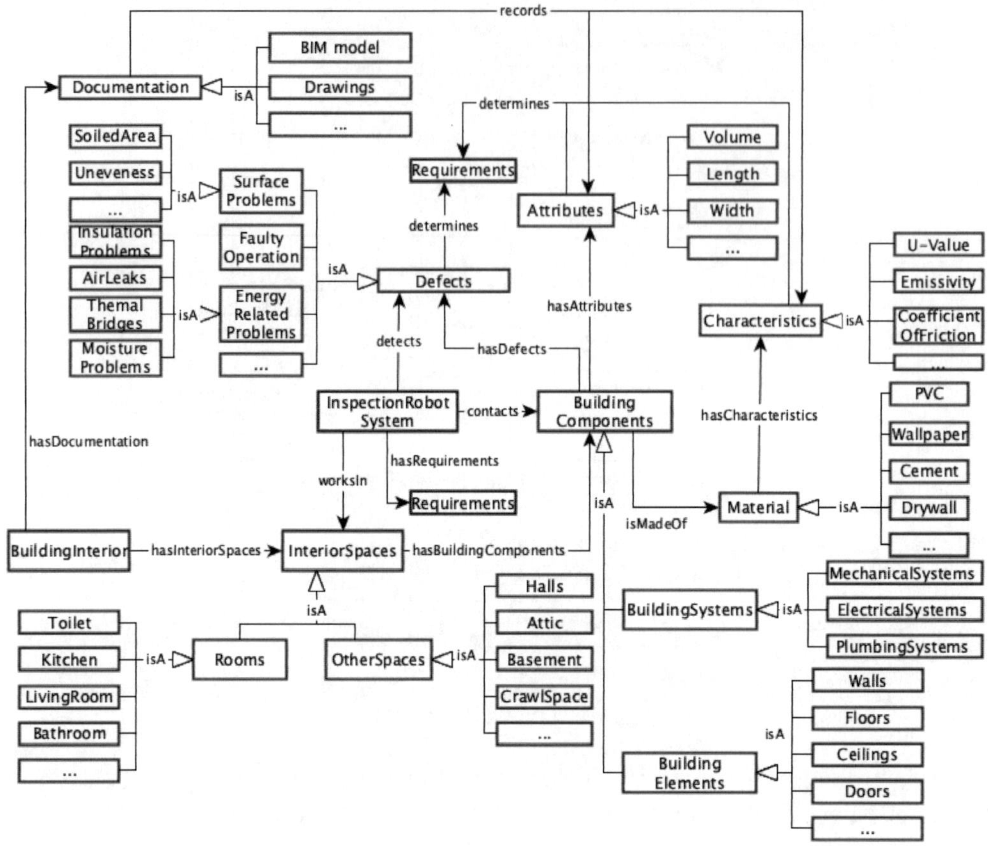

Figure 2: Building Interior Model

5. Discussion

The ODIIRS Ontology systematically formalizes the key concepts and relations that are essential in the design of the indoor inspection robot system. This ontology covers the description of building interior information and interior defects as well as the robot system components with which inspection tasks can be accomplished. It provides a model of the knowledge base for robot designers and building inspectors to query and share knowledge.

However, one of the limitations of this study lies in the knowledge capture process. First, the knowledge sources for identifying relevant concepts are limited to existing standards, guidelines and research work. Since implicit knowledge especially experiences from inspection professionals and robot experts is also important to the robot system design, several workshops, interviews and field practices will be conducted to collect input from trade workers in future research. Second, more information, such as the anomaly behaviour of interior defects which is important for automated defect data analysis, indoor spatial information which is required for better indoor route planning and navigation and rules for the evaluation of the robot performance, needs to be added in this ontology. After incorporating the above supplementary knowledge, the content and the structure of the updated conceptual model will be verified to ensure that the axioms of the ontology reflect the intentions of the author. The ontology will be presented again to building inspectors and robot experts in a workshop to evaluate whether the represented concepts, attributes and taxonomy correspond to the real world. Future work should also involve the implementation of the proposed ontology using OWL/RDF language in Protégé to provide a machine-readable model, where knowledge reasoning can be carried out to evaluate the internal consistency of the ontology and to infer new knowledge that is related to the robot design. A real indoor inspection robot design case will be used to validate the practical value of the ontology. The ontology will be instantiated with the information from the case study, and a set of queries will be executed to get information that needs to be considered in the design process of the robot.

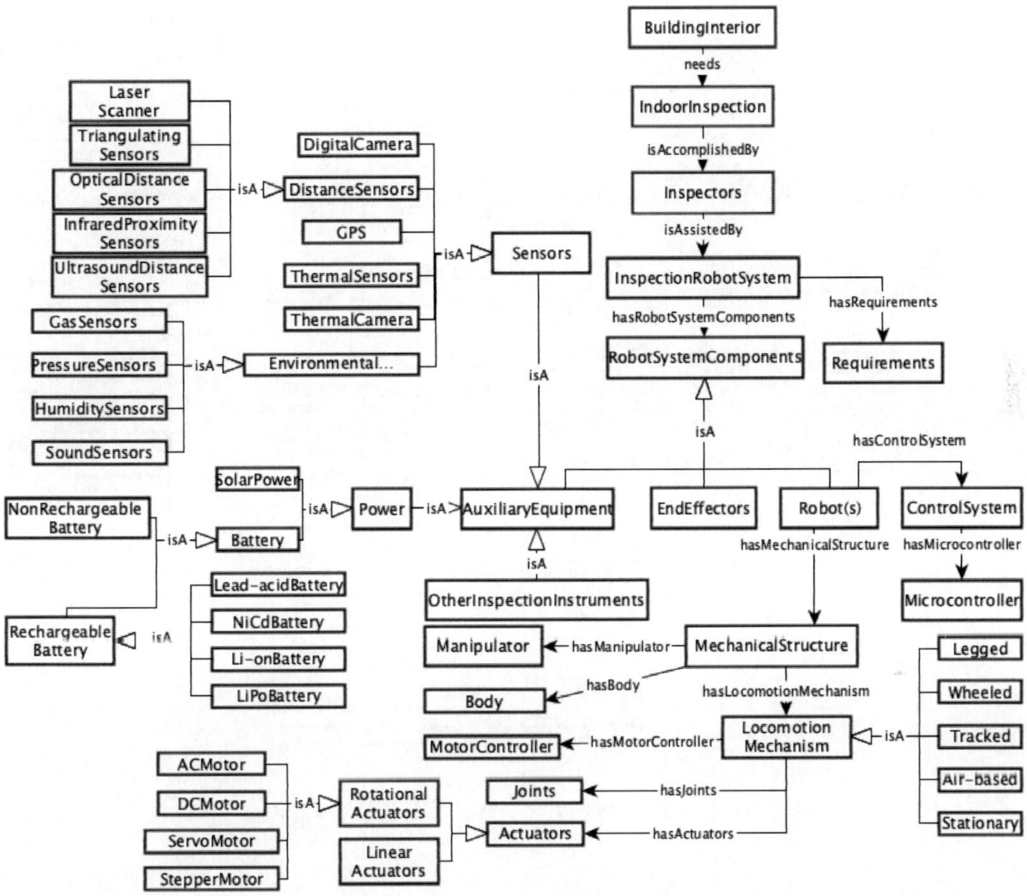

Figure 3: Inspection Robot System Model

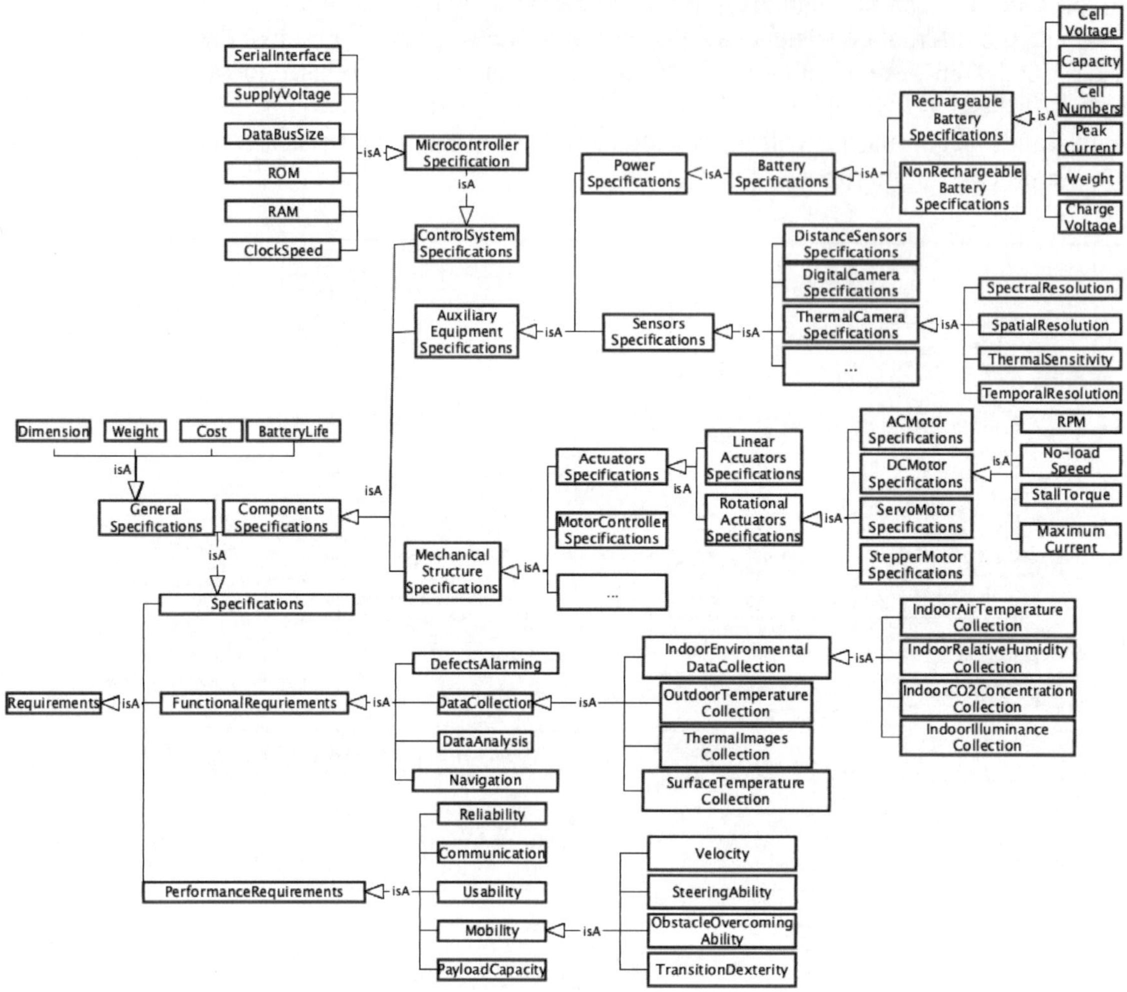

Figure 4: *Requirements* Class in ODIIRS Ontology

6. Conclusion

This paper presents an ontology focusing on the information that is relevant to the design of the indoor inspection robot system. It integrates knowledge from both the indoor inspection domain and robotics domain, which will not only facilitate knowledge sharing between inspection professionals and robot designers but also allow for a more efficient design process and eventually delivering high-quality products. This work is an initial exploratory attempt to carefully leverage formalized engineering knowledge to inform the building inspection robot design. Further goals of future research should be representing the validated design-related knowledge in a machine-friendly format and realizing automatic design of robots in the building inspection field.

References

Balakirsky, S., Schlenoff, C., Rama Fiorini, S., Redfield, S., Barreto, M., Nakawala, H., Carbonera, J.L., Soldatova, L., Bermejo-Alonso, J., Maikore, F., Goncalves, P.J.S., De Momi, E., Sampath Kumar, V.R., Haidegger, T., 2017. Towards a Robot Task Ontology Standard. In: Volume 3:

Manufacturing Equipment and Systems. Presented at the ASME 2017 12th International Manufacturing Science and Engineering Conference collocated with the JSME/ASME 2017 6th International Conference on Materials and Processing, American Society of Mechanical Engineers, Los Angeles, California, USA, p. V003T04A049.

Bay, C.J., Terrill, T.J., Rasmussen, B.P., 2017. Autonomous Robotic Building Energy Audits: Demonstrated Capabilities and Open Challenges. In: Ashrae Transactions 2017, Vol 123, Pt 2. Amer Soc Heating, Refrigerating and Air-Conditioning Engs, Atlanta, pp.3–20.

Ben-Ari, M., Mondada, F., 2018. Elements of Robotics. Springer International Publishing, Cham.

Bernardo, R., Farinha, R., Gonçalves, P.J.S., 2018. Knowledge and Tasks Representation for an Industrial Robotic Application. In: Ollero, A., Sanfeliu, A., Montano, L., Lau, N., Cardeira, C. (Eds.), ROBOT 2017: Third Iberian Robotics Conference, Advances in Intelligent Systems and Computing. Springer International Publishing, Cham, pp.441–451.

Bortolini, R., Forcada, N., 2018. Building Inspection System for Evaluating the Technical Performance of Existing Buildings. J. Perform. Constr. Facil. 32, 04018073.

Chella, A., Cossentino, M., Pirrone, R., Ruisi, A., 2002. Modeling ontologies for robotic environments. In: Proceedings of the 14th International Conference on Software Engineering and Knowledge Engineering, SEKE '02. Association for Computing Machinery, New York, NY, USA, pp.77–80.

CIB, 2013. A state-of-the-art report on building pathology, CIB Rep. Publication 393. CIB Working Commission W86, Delft, Netherlands.

Dall'O', G., 2013. Green Energy Audit of Buildings, Green Energy and Technology. Springer London, London.

Fernández-López, M., Gomez-Perez, A., Juristo, N., 1997. METHONTOLOGY: from ontological art towards ontological engineering. Engineering Workshop on Ontological Engineering (AAAI97).

Ferraz, G.T., de Brito, J., de Freitas, V.P., Silvestre, J.D., 2016. State-of-the-Art Review of Building Inspection Systems. J. Perform. Constr. Facil. 30, 04016018.

Fiorini, S.R., Bermejo-Alonso, J., Goncalves, P., Pignaton de Freitas, E., Olivares Alarcos, A., Olszewska, J.I., Prestes, E., Schlenoff, C., Ragavan, S.V., Redfield, S., Spencer, B., Li, H., 2017. A Suite of Ontologies for Robotics and Automation [Industrial Activities]. IEEE Robot. Automat. Mag. 24, 8–11.

Gouda Mohamed, A., Abdallah, M.R., Marzouk, M., 2020. BIM and semantic web-based maintenance information for existing buildings. Automation in Construction 116, 103209.

Ham, Y., Golparvar-Fard, M., 2013. An automated vision-based method for rapid 3D energy performance modeling of existing buildings using thermal and digital imagery. Advanced Engineering Informatics 27, 395–409.

IEEE ORA WG, 2015. IEEE Standard Ontologies for Robotics and Automation. IEEE Std 1872-2015 1–60.

ISO, 2020. Robots and robotic devices-Vocabulary.

Ji, Z., Qiu, R., Noyvirt, A., Soroka, A., Packianather, M., Setchi, R., Li, D., Xu, S., 2012. Towards automated task planning for service robots using semantic knowledge representation. In: 2012 10th Ieee International Conference on Industrial Informatics (Indin). Ieee, New York, pp.1194–1201.

López-Fernández, L., Lagüela, S., González-Aguilera, D., Lorenzo, H., 2017. Thermographic and mobile indoor mapping for the computation of energy losses in buildings. Indoor and Built Environment 26, 771–784.

Lork, C., Choudhary, V., Hassan, N.U., Tushar, W., Yuen, C., Ng, B.K.K., Wang, X., Liu, X., 2019. An Ontology-Based Framework for Building Energy Management with IoT. Electronics 8, 485.

Mantha, B.R.K., Menassa, C.C., Kamat, V.R., 2018. Robotic data collection and simulation for evaluation of building retrofit performance. Automation in Construction 92, 88–102.

OmniClass, 2012. OmniClass: A strategy for classifying the built environment [WWW Document]. URL https://www.csiresources.org/standards/omniclass (accessed 3.19.21).

Park, C.-S., Lee, D.-Y., Kwon, O.-S., Wang, X., 2013. A framework for proactive construction defect management using BIM, augmented reality and ontology-based data collection template. Automation in Construction 33, 61–71.

Preece, A., Gómez Martínez, M., Mel, G., Vasconcelos, W., Sleeman, D., Colley, S., Pearson, G., Pham, T., Porta, T., 2008. Matching sensors to missions using a knowledge-based approach. Proceedings of SPIE - The International Society for Optical Engineering.

Prestes, E., Carbonera, J.L., Rama Fiorini, S., M. Jorge, V.A., Abel, M., Madhavan, R., Locoro, A., Goncalves, P., E. Barreto, M., Habib, M., Chibani, A., Gérard, S., Amirat, Y., Schlenoff, C., 2013. Towards a core ontology for robotics and automation. Robotics and Autonomous Systems, Ubiquitous Robotics 61, 1193–1204.

Ramos, F., Vázquez, A.S., Fernández, R., Olivares-Alarcos, A., 2018. Ontology based design, control and programming of modular robots. ICA 25, 173–192.

Schlenoff, C., Messina, E., 2005. A Robot Ontology for Urban Search and Rescue.

Tenorth, M., Beetz, M., 2013. KnowRob: A knowledge processing infrastructure for cognition-enabled robots. The International Journal of Robotics Research 32, 566–590.

Yan, R.-J., Kayacan, E., Chen, I.-M., Tiong, L.K., Wu, J., 2019. QuicaBot: Quality Inspection and Assessment Robot. IEEE Trans. Automat. Sci. Eng. 16, 506–517.

Zhong, B.T., Ding, L.Y., Luo, H.B., Zhou, Y., Hu, Y.Z., Hu, H.M., 2012. Ontology-based semantic modeling of regulation constraint for automated construction quality compliance checking. Automation in Construction 28, 58–70.

Bidirectional coupling of Building Information Modeling and Building Simulation using ontologies

Elisabeth Eckstädt
Fraunhofer IIS/EAS Dresden, Germany
elisabeth.eckstaedt@eas.iis.fraunhofer.de

Abstract. Building performance simulation can contribute to necessary energy savings in the buildings sector when applied early in the design phase. A major obstacle to put that into operation is the cumbersome task of model preparation, although significant simplification is anticipated by the adoption of BIM in the design phase. In this paper a workflow is shown for the bidirectional coupling of IFC and Modelica simulation models based on semantic tools (also facilitating the BRICK ontology). Bidirectionality allows for better integration in the building design workflow as it enables iterative approaches. A show case is made for an air handling system.

1. Context

1.1 Motivation

Building performance simulation (BPS) can contribute to necessary energy savings in the buildings sector when applied early in the design phase. Building and system simulation can contribute to greater system efficiency, as it helps to avoid oversizing, find optimal operating points and specify suitable boundary conditions for building automation. It enables transient conditions to be considered and unconventional configurations to be evaluated. In the operating phase, the simulation model serves as a digital twin and enables the rapid detection of operating errors.

A major obstacle to put that into operation is the cumbersome task of model preparation as it is not an integral part of current building design regulations, thus, no additional budget in terms of time and money is available. Fortunately BIM (building information modeling) is used in an increasing amount of design processes, offering the chance to facilitate model generation for BPS.

1.2 Task and Use Case

Although BIM stands for Building Information Modelling, it is often misunderstood as the exchange of 3D geometries. This falls far short of the actual possibilities of the method and hinders workflows such as the one described in this paper. If BIM is used in the true sense of the word, it opens up a wide range of possibilities. In this case, one is no longer limited to the IFC file format, but the integration of other data formats such as BRICK and Modelica becomes possible. If BIM is understood in this extended/genuine sense of the word, it is also possible to transfer planning tasks that were not previously solved with BIM methods into the BIM context and thus to make the results interoperable. This includes the workflow described in chapter 3 for the planning of a ventilation system.

In BIM- and simulation-based design processes there are amongst others two widely adopted file formats: IFC-files in STEP notation (buildingSMART, 2017) and Modelica files (Modelica Association, 2021). Thus, the requirement for a converter between the two arises. As building design processes are usually iterative - especially when simulation methodologies are involved - a bidirectional conversion is desirable.

The focus of the paper will be on the simulation of HVAC equipment rather than on building physics.

As already issued in (Eckstädt, et al., 2020) there is no single *building performance simulation*, instead there are several scenarios for BPS. A scenario is characterised by its assignment to the planning phase and actor, as well as the variable and evaluated quantities. This leads to requirements for the simulation models with regard to

- Which components are to be included in the analysis?
- At which level of detail are these to be represented?
- How close the coupling of the components has to be?

Based on this, six scenarios were defined. In this paper, the workflow is exemplified for the scenario 6 "Plant detailed investigation" using the example of a ventilation system. The quantity to be evaluated is the secondary energy demand of the system, variable are the flow temperatures to the ventilation registers, as well as the supply air temperature to the rooms. Therefore the complete energy conversion chain must be represented in the simulation. The room delivery and the generation must be modelled temperature-dependent; a modelling of the energy flows is not sufficient. As a result of the simulation, it can be decided which supply air temperatures should be set centrally and which decentrally, possibly resulting in the need to add additional decentralised ventilation coils to the IFC model.

1.3 Status Quo concerning IFC-based generation of Modelica Models

Major work concerning the generation of Modelica models from IFC has been accomplished in the Annex 60 project (van Treeck, 2017). Tool chains have been presented mainly by KU Leuven (Andriamamonjy, 2018) (Reynders, 2017) and RWTH Aachen with UdK Berlin (van Treeck, 2017) (Nytsch-Geusen, 2019). Among this, only (van Treeck, 2017) and (Andriamamonjy, 2018) have covered the building equipment to a limited amount, the main focus of most papers has been the translation of the building physics. The plant technology considered in the above-mentioned publications is limited to boilers and heat pumps as generators, hot water storage tanks and radiators as delivery elements, as well as ventilation systems. Cases in which close coupling is necessary, for example component-integrated heating surfaces or CHP units, were not dealt with. The presented tool chains are limited to the IFC → Modelica direction, which is a major drawback.

2. Methodology: ontology-based translation

2.1 Ontology based knowledge representation and its advantages

In contrast to the discussed conversion tools an ontology-based "translation" is proposed in this paper. Ontologies are formal knowledge representations consisting of terms and their relations. This allows for storing not only data but also its meaning (semantics) in a machine readable manner – forming a self-contained data description. Although classic programming approaches also deal with meaning of the handled data, they hold this meaning inside their algorithms and data schemas. The ontology-based approach keeps the semantics separate from the algorithm. Making use of W3C standards for the representation of the semantics enable their availability for other applications. This follows the paradigm of modularization with all its advantages, such as reusability, maintainability, etc.

Once in a semantic representation an alignment between the involved ontologies can be made. In contrast to the aforementioned converter tools the semantic approach allows for the separation of

- the representation of the knowledge about relations between the IFC and Modelica domain (alignment) and
- the algorithm that interprets this knowledge to generate a particular file format from the other

Based on that no further efforts are necessary to allow for a bidirectional translation, if the alignment meet the requirements described in the next chapter.

2.2 Prerequesites

A translation in both directions is basically only possible if there is a unambiguity between the terms in both worlds, which is neither naturally given in human language nor in different modelling domains (as exemplified in Table 1). An essential preliminary work is therefore to establish this unambiguity.

An obvious approach to this is the introduction of a higher-level "language" that contains the necessary subsets of terms from both domains for the selected translation problem and relates them to each other; such an approach has been pursued for example with SimModel (Cao, 2014) and ESIM (Kaiser, 2015). In this translation, the information exchange requirement can then also be defined and missing information modules can be added, if necessary. However, we do not consider this approach to be effective, as it hinders the already hesitant adoption of simulation into planning processes by adding another "hurdle" in the form of a translation tool that is not yet familiar to any of the participants and that will only ever be used for this one application and thus can never become a "common" tool.

In contrast, the approach proposed here consists of an alignment that contains only terms from the domains involved and can thus be created by the participating experts and does not require any (potentially expensive) third party translation experts.

2.3 Software architecture

The overall process consists of three major steps as shown in Figure 1. As a first step the semantics inherent to data standards such as IFC and Modelica have to be "transcribed" to a semantic format[1]. As a second step the semantic "translation" is conducted. The last step will usually be a "transcription" back to the file-based representation. For a transformation from the file-based representation to the semantic representation the term "transcription" will be used, while a transformation between semantic representations will be called "translation". Whilst a transcription is lossless and unambigous by definition this is not the case for translations.

Although it would be possible to translate directly from IFC-RDF to Modelica-RDF with the described workflow, BRICK is also used, as it is focused on the modeling of control and operational relationships, where IFC is less adopted. Modelica, BRICK and IFC files can serve as source and target of translation respectively.

---

[1] A "semantic format" of a model is a serialization with triples according to the RDF framework and its link to the used ontologies.

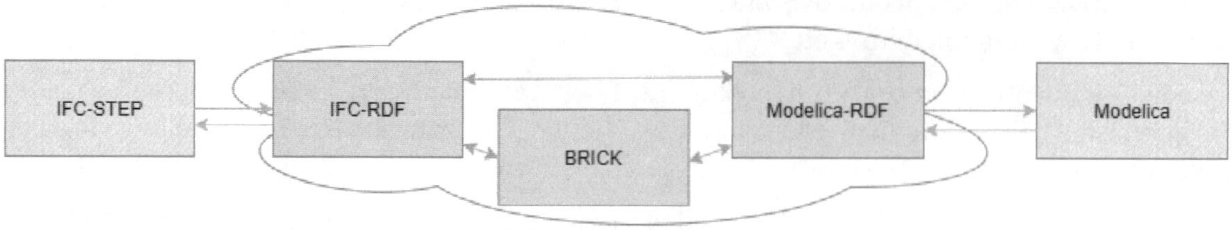

Figure 1: schematics of the coupling, orange arrow: transcription, green arrow: translation, orange box: “file based representation”, green box: “semantic representation”

2.4 Description of the applied ontologies

IFCOWL „ifcOWL provides a Web Ontology Language (OWL) representation of the Industry Foundation Classes (IFC) schema“ (buildingSMART, 2017). It is a thorough and equivalent representation to the EXPRESS schema. It is provided by buildingSMART (Pauwels, 2019) in RDF and TTL formats.

Besides the architectural domain the current official release IFC 4.0.2.1 also covers the domains of HVAC und Building Control. Yet it is not widely adopted in these domains and the features are rarely used, as these domains were underdeveloped in the widespread older IFC version IFC2x3. Up to now, IFC has essentially been used for geometry exchange although IFC enables the mapping of numerous relations through objectified relationships, including topological and compositional relationships.

BRICK is an ontology covering physical, logical and virtual assets in buildings from the HVAC and electrical domain including the building automation domain. It is a native semantic format - designed to represent the technical relationships of these objects - and does not claim to represent geometry, so it does not run the risk of being misused for this purpose. Since Brick might close gaps of the IFC specification and is actively developed by a broad community, we decided to integrate it into the workflow and investigate its capability.

BRICK has been published open source by an consortium of US universities (Balaji, 2018) and has industrial and public supporters. It is still under development.

MoOnt and IBPLib “The Modelica Language is a non-proprietary, object-oriented, equation-based language to conveniently model complex physical systems” containing subcomponents from several domains (Modelica Association, 2021). Since its introduction in 1997 it has been widely adopted. It is maintained by the Modelica Association an can be applied using commercial or non-commercial simulation environments. In addition to the Modelica Standard Library, there are numerous other (open source) libraries. Of particular interest for the building sector are the libraries AixLib, Buildings, IDEAS and BuildingSystems, which were brought together in the context of the Annex60 project. These cover both building physics and building systems engineering and overlap to a large extent.

Semantic representations of Modelica were considered by Pop in 2003 and 2004 - "Modelica users and library developers would benefit from Semantic Web technologies" (Pop, 2004) but no further publications followed. Delgoshaei (Delgoshaei, 2017) explored the use of semantic representations of different simulation models in Dymola and MATLAB for coupling HVAC and control engineering simulations, but confined to storing merely simulation results in semantic format. The SPRINT project proposed the “use of OWL ontologies to represent several modeling tool languages, so that full models maintained in different tools could be represented in RDF" (Shani, 2017). In this context the Wolfram Modelica Ontology was published (Wolfram Research Inc. 2014). It represents the basic language constructs. Further work or applications on this have not been published.

Based on the Wolfram Modelica ontology, an ontology of the basic Modelica components (MoOnt) and the aformentioned IBPSA libraries (IBPLib) was created (Eckstädt, 2021).

2.5 Implementation

IFC and Modelica Transcription There are good open source tools for the transciption. For the transciption from IFC to ttl (Pauwels, 2020) was used, for the return path (Zhang, 2019).

For the transformation of Modelica files into a semantic representation, a parser using ANTLR (Parr, 2021) and the corresponding Modelica grammar (Everett, 2016) was implemented in Java. The return path was also implemented in Java. Both are available as command line applications (Eckstädt, 2021).

Semantic Translation The alignments for IFCOWL, MoOnt, IBPLib and BRICK have been implemented manually using Protégé (Eckstädt, 2021). A prototype for the translator has been implemented using the Apache Jena framework and its OWL reasoner.

As already mentioned, a two-direction translation is only possible if the assignment is unambiguous. Table 1 shows that this is rarely the case by itself - in this example only for the entity space. Ambiguities can in general be resolved by adapting the ontology, but this is not an option for a well established standard such as IFC.

Problem Classes for Semantic Translation The problems with the alignment can be divided into the following classes, for each of which the solution approach is also given:

1. Mapping is ambiguous on class level, but can be resolved with the help of mandatory properties: Since in BRICK as well as in the IFC schema almost all properties or relations are optional, there is no example from this area. On the Modelica side, for example, the mapping of a IBPSA.Fluid.Mover to fan or pump results from the contained medium. (Lines 1, 2 in Table 1)
2. Although there are hardly any mandatory properties in IFC, there are predefined types and property sets. These can be used to create uniqueness. For example the assignment of an IfcFan to Supply or Exhaust fan in BRICK according to the affiliation to a system with the help of the relations IfcRelNests or IfcRelAssignsToGroup. Nevertheless there is no example of this problem class in the ventilation system, as it has been decided to map IfcFan to the brick:fan superclass.
3. Alternatively, it is possible that the assignment is made on the basis of a logical linkage of (several) properties, e.g. whether a coil is a Heating Coil or Cooling Coil results from its temperature level.
4. If predefined types and property sets are not available the coupling must be done via loose properties, e.g. tags in BRICK and annotations in Modelica.
5. As a last option, a naming convention can be used – this would for instance be necessary, to distinguish between the assignment of Modelica PressureDrop to brick:filter or brick:louver. Alternatively, an enhancement of the ontology is also an option here in order to make this more formal and thus less subject to reconciliation.
6. If correspondence is completely missing, only modelling of the partial components is possible (e.g. instead of heat recovery: two heat exchangers with pump and valve).

The solution approaches get less universal in the order of the preceeding list. Conventions in the creation of the model must then be observed. Table 1 contains examples for the ventilation system in chapter 3

Regardless of the aforementioned problem classes, it is common that the mapping is dependent on the issue to be addressed, for example whether an brick:HVAC_Zone is to be assigned to an IfcSpace or IfcZone, or whether a brick:water_pump is to be assigned to a IBPSA.Fluid.Movers.FlowControlled_dp or IBPSA.Fluid.Movers.FlowControlled_m_flow. Typical questions in the planning process were summarized into scenarios in (Eckstädt, 2020). In order to address the problem mentioned, the alignments must be created on a scenario-specific basis. Alignments might also include default values for information that will not be included in the source model according to the dedicated level of detail.

Table 1: IFC-BRICK-Modelica-Mapping (red: non unique items) for the exemplified scenario 6

no	IFC4.2.0.1	*	BRICK 1.1	*	Modelica IBPSA
1	IFCFan	-	Fan	1	Fluid.Movers.FlowControlled_m_flow
2	ifcPump	-	Water_pump	1	Fluid.Movers.FlowControlled_m_flow
3	ifcAirtoAirHeatRecov-ery	4	HeatExchanger	1	Fluid.HeatExchangers.DryCoilEffectivenessNTU
4	IfcCoil	4	HeatExchanger	1	Fluid.HeatExchangers.DryCoilEffectivenessNTU
5	ifcFilter	-	Filter	5	Fluid.FixedResistances.PressureDrop
6	IfcDamper	-	Damper	5	Fluid.FixedResistances.PressureDrop
7	ifcDuctSilencer	4	Louver	5	Fluid.FixedResistances.PressureDrop
8	IfcAirTerminal	4	Louver	5	Fluid.FixedResistances.PressureDrop
9	IfcValve	-	Ventil	1	Fluid.Actuators.Valves.TwoWayLinear
10	IfcAirTerminalBox	-	VAV	1	Fluid.Actuators.Valves.TwoWayLinear
11	ifcSpace	-	HVAC_Zone	-	ThermalZones.ReducedOrder.RC.OneElement

* problem class with respect to the above paragraph

IFC-BRICK-Alignment The mapping between IFC and BRICK can be done for most cases simply with the help of the owl:equivalentClass relation, in the case of Fan and Coil the mapping is done on the level of the "super" classes, not on the basis of the subclasses (e.g. Return Fan or Heating Coil). For the described use case of transfer to a simulation model, this does not involve any loss of information. The mapping of heat recovery and heating/cooling coils can be designed unambiguously with the help of the included medium. The mapping of silencers and air outlets can only be represented in BRICK with the help of tags, the BRICK ontology is not expressive enough at this point. The alignment in ttl format is available online (Eckstädt & Urbanski, 2021), which contains not only the mapping of the classes but also the mapping of the properties, which was not discussed here for brevity.

BRICK-IBPLib-Alignment The mapping of the BRICK to the Modelica model would be unambiguous as a set-up variant, but for the return path there is ambiguity for almost every element. The distinction between fan and pump, as well as the different types of heat exchangers and valves, can be made with the help of the included media, which are mandatory in a Modelica model. The differentiation of the various PressureDrops must first be done with the help of a naming convention. The alignment in ttl format is available online (Eckstädt & Manotas, 2021), it is based on preliminary work by (Manotas, 2021). In addition to the mapping of the classes, it also contains the mapping of the properties, which was not discussed here for brevity.

Dealing with Surplus Information If one compares the different representations of one and the same plant, as exemplified in Figures 2 and 3 (PI diagram, 3D model, simulation model), it is obvious that, in addition to a number of common information, they each contain a lot of specific and unique information. For example, the 3D model contains information on the position and geometry of the components, which is not contained in the simulation model. However, the several models should not be overloaded with information that does not belong to each of them, even if the technical specifications would allow this. Therefore, the multi-model approach described in (eeEmbedded, 2016) is used here, which works with links between the models.

3. Example

The bidirectional coupling between IFC and Modelica is demonstrated using the example of a ventilation system as shown in Figure 2. The system consists of a supply air unit and an exhaust air unit, which are connected via a closed-loop system. The system supplies four rooms of a canteen each with supply and exhaust air. The rooms are characterised by very different thermal loads; in some cases there is a simultaneous demand for heating and cooling. Therefore, the question arises which supply air temperature should be provided centrally and which treatment should take place decentrally. The basic variant that is shown in the PI diagram in Figure 2 only provides for temperature control in the central unit; in the zones, post-heating or post-cooling is carried out with radiators or fan coils. One result of the simulation may be a need to install decentralised ventilation coils, this needs to be reflected in the IFC model. Furthermore the simulation serves to clarify the question of which mass flows must be supplied by the heating and cooling system to each coil and which return temperature is to be expected for the central heating and cooling generation.

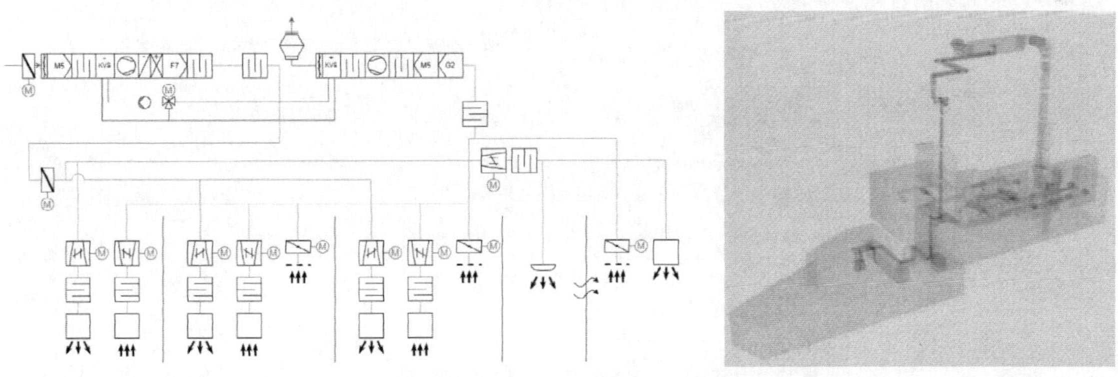

Figure 2: PID diagram and 3D IFC model of the Air Conditioning System comprising of Exhaust and supply air unit, run-around coil and distribution system, as well as the supplied rooms

Table 1 shows the entities contained in BRICK, IFC and Modelica. A 3D rendering of the example is shown in Figure 2 along with an excerpt of the IFC4-File in STEP format (Listing 1). This model also contains topological information encoded by IfcRelConnects objectified relationships, as well as compositional information encoded by IfcRelNests and IfcRelAggregates objectified relationships. The schematics are shown in Figure 2. An excerpt of the BRICK-model in ttl-Notation is given in Listing 2. The Graphic Layer of the Modelica model is shown in Figure 3. The full models in all serializations (IFC-STEP, IFC-RDF, BRICK, Modelica-RDF, Modelica) are available online (Eckstädt, 2021).

```
#2528=IFCFLOWFITTING('2DLin6VGmYy00100420bbx', #102, FF(112)', '?', $, #2533, #2534, $);
#16792=IFCSYSTEM('2AwcmSDGvA6Pv$zMKJI5GP', #102, 'AHU_kitchen_EX', 'AHU_kitchen_EX', $);
#17626=IFCPORT('PORT0033', #102, 'AHU_EX', 'AHU_EX', $, $, $, $, $);
#17632=IFCPORT('PORT0040', #102, 'EX_BEND_1', 'T EX_BEND_1', $, $, $, $, $);
#17654=IFCBUILDINGSTOREY('0wl4…ht', #102, 'Roof_03', '?', $, #17659, $, $, .ELEMENT., 0.);
#18809=IfcUnitaryEquipment('2…a', #102, 'AHU_kitchen', '', ' AIRHANDLER ', #18814, #18815, $);
#19197=IFCRELASSIGNSTOGROUP('3jnK…tTVs', #102, $, $, (#2528, …, #18809), $, #16792);
#19252=IFCRELCONTAINEDINSPATIALSTRUCTURE('3_KQ…MP', #102, $, $, (#106, …, #18809), #17654);
#19291=IFCRELCONNECTSPORTTOELEMENT('ELEMENTCONNECT0033', #102, $, $, #17626, #18809);
#19298=IFCRELCONNECTSPORTTOELEMENT('ELEMENTCONNECT0040', #102, $, $, #17632, #2528);
#19342=IFCRELCONNECTSPORTS('PORTCONNECT028', #102, $, $, #17632, #17626, $);
```

Listing 1: IFC example showing assignment of parts to a system and a room as well as the connection of parts (Eckstädt, 2021)

```
eas:AHU41 a brick: Heating Ventilation Air Conditioning System.
eas:Dining a brick:HVAC_Zone ;
    a brick:Space ;
    brick:isPartOf eas:AHU41;
    brick:feeds eas:Dining_VAV_ETA_Louver ;
    brick:hasInputSubstance eas:Dining_SUP ;
    brick:hasOutputSubstance eas:Dining_ETA .
eas:Dining_VAV_SUP_Louver a brick:Louver ;
    brick:isPartOf eas:AHU41;
    brick:feeds eas:Dining ;
    brick:hasOutputSubstance eas:Dining_SUP ;
    brick:isFedBy eas:Dining_VAV_SUP ;
    brick:hasLocation eas:Dining.
```

Listing 2: BRICK example showing assignment of parts to a system and a room as well as the connection of parts (Eckstädt, 2021)

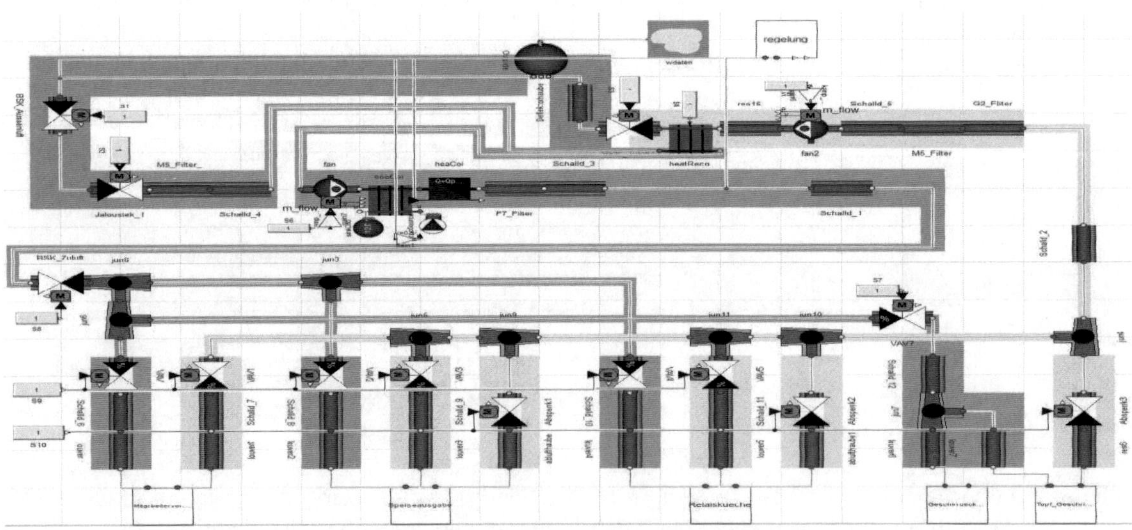

Figure 3: Modelica Model

4. Main Conclusions/Research Findings and Comparison to Classic Converter Tools

A bidirectional coupling of Modelica and IFC has been shown for a real world ventilation system. The data required for the simulation can be transferred in both directions, so it is possible to integrate the simulation into the planning process at different points in time. If a detailed geometric model already exists, as in Figure 2, a simulation model can be derived from it and detailed investigations, such as pressure drops calculations, can be performed. If a geometric model does not exist, the design for the system can also be started in the simulation tool. The configuration that is found to be good can then be output as an IFC and later enriched with geometry.

In contrast to classical converter tools, such as those referenced in chapter 1.3, an additional abstraction layer of the respective native model (Modelica or IFC) was included here in form of the semantic representation. This representation is generated automatically using language parsers, which only require the language grammar as input, which is subject to rare changes. Language constructs that are processed by converter tools change with the further development of file standards, as it is currently happening regularly with IFC. Modelica libraries are subject to even more frequent changes. Newly emerging language elements only have to be included in the alignments with the shown semantic solution approach. The effort required to do this is significantly smaller than incorporating them into the source code of a converter tool, since the translation code and the used dictionary are two separate entities. This corresponds to the modularization paradigm in software development with its associated advantages: better comprehensibility, better handling and better maintainability. The translation is done by reasoning engines. These exist as ready-made software modules for various programming environments and it can be assumed that their software quality is better than dedicated converter tools as they are backed by a broader community.

However, the main advantage of the approach described is the automatically guaranteed translation option in both directions, which would have to be implemented separately for both directions for converter tools. Existing converter tools therefore usually only cover the IFC to Modelica direction and not the reverse direction. This possibility of two-sided translation enables a "simulation first" workflow.

The workflow requires entities that were introduced for the first time in IFC4, so this cannot be implemented with older IFC models. Relevant gaps in the IFC standard were not found for the described use case.

5. Outlook

It turned out that are some shortcomings in the expressivity of BRICK concerning special components of ventilation systems such as duct silencers. An enhancement of the ontology will be considered as well as a direct alignment from IFC to Modelica.

Currently the alignments only cover the air handling domain. They will be enhanced to heating and cooling systems and the respective control equipment. Also more scenarios will be covered, which will mainly affect the Modelica alignment. Formal exchange requirements for the IFC models in the different scenarios will be specified.

The reader might have recognized, that there is a loss of meaning in the models compared to the PID diagram shown in Figure 2. As these diagrams play a significant role in the design processes of building facilities, we will continue to work on their integration.

Acknowledgement

This work has been accomplished within the FMI4BIM project funded by the German Federal Ministry for Economic Affairs and Energy (BMWI) under reference number 03ET1603A. I would like to thank my colleagues and supervisors Hervé Pruvost, Karsten Menzel and Jens

Kaiser for valuable feedback and the student assistants Miguel Manotas and Matthias Urbanski for their support in preparing the example. Special Thanks to all authors of the mentioned open source tools for sharing their work and enabling pursued research.

References

Andriamamonjy, A. (2018). Automated workflows for building design and operation using openBIM and Modelica, PhD thesis, KU Leuven http://dx.doi.org/10.13140/RG.2.2.31108.78729.

Balaji, B. et al. (2018), 'Brick : Metadata schema for portable smart building applications', Applied Energy https://www.sciencedirect.com/science/article/pii/S0306261918302162.

BuildingSMART (2017), 'IFC Specifications Database' https://technical.buildingsmart.org/standards/ifc/ifc-schema-specifications/

Cao, J. et al. (2014), Model transformationfrom SimModel to Modelica for building energy performance simulation, in 'BauSIM2014'. http://hdl.handle.net/10197/11023

Delgoshaei; Austin & Veronica (2017), Semantic Models and Rule-based Reasoning for Fault Detection and Diagnostics: Applications in Heating, Ventilating and Air Conditioning Systems, in 'ICONS 2017 : The Twelfth International Conference on Systems at: Venice, Italy'.

Eckstädt, E. et al. (2020), Simulationsszenarien für Gebäudeenergiesimulation in frühen Planungsphasen, in 'BauSIM 2020 Graz' http://dx.doi.org/10.3217/978-3-85125-786-1.

Eckstädt, E. (2021), 'IBPLib', 'MoOnt', 'Modelica ttl Reader Writer', Translator Example Files'. https://github.com/ElisEck/MO-x-IFC

Eckstädt, E. & Manotas, M. (2021), 'Alignment BRICK-IBPSA'. https://github.com/ElisEck/MO-x-IFC

Eckstädt, E. & Urbanski, M. (2021), 'Alignment IFC-BRICK'. https://github.com/ElisEck/MO-x-IFC

eeEmbedded (2016), 'eeEmbedded – D6.2 Multimodel mapper – Simulation model generator'

EnEff-BIM consortium (2016), 'EnEffBIM_UseCases' https://github.com/EnEff-BIM/EnEffBIM_UseCases.

Everett, T. & Harman, P. (2016), 'Modelica Grammar' https://github.com/antlr/grammars-v4/blob/master/modelica/modelica.g4.

Kaiser, J. & Stenzel, P. (2015), 'eeEmbedded D4.2: Energy System Information Model - ESIM'.

LBNL (2019), 'Modelica Buildings Library' https://simulationresearch.lbl.gov/modelica/

Manotas, M. (2021), 'Untersuchungen zur Simulation Raumlufttechnischer Anlagen zur Unterstützung von Planung und Betrieb von Nichtwohngebäuden', student thesis https://doi.org/10.24406/eas-n-634732

Modelica Association, M. (2021), 'Modelica' https://modelica.org/.

Nytsch-Geusen (2019), BIM2Modelica-An open source toolchain for generating … building models by using structured data from BIM models https://modelica-buildingsystems.de/pub/ModelicaConference2019.pdf.

Parr, T. (2021), 'ANTLR' https://www.antlr.org/.

Pauwels, P. & Terkaj, W. (2019), 'ifcOWL ontology (IFC4_ADD2_TC1)' https://standards.buildingsmart.org/IFC/DEV/IFC4/ADD2_TC1/OWL/index.html.

Pauwels, P. (2020), 'IFCtoRDF' https://github.com/pipauwel/IFCtoRDF.

Pop, A. & Fritzson, P. (2004), 'The Modelica Standard Library as an ontology for modeling and simulation of physical systems' https://www.ida.liu.se/~adrpo33/reports/adrpo-petfr-WS-OSEA.pdf.

Reynders, G.; Andriamamonjy, A.; Klein, R. & Saelens, D. (2017), Towards an IFC-Modelica tool facilitating model complexity selection for building energy simulation https://core.ac.uk/display/251175883.

Shani, U. (2017), 'Can ontologies prevent MBSE models from becoming obsolete?', https://core.ac.uk/download/pdf/144853941.pdf.

van Treeck, C. et al (2017), 'EnEff-BIM: Abschlussbericht', https://doi.org/10.2314/GBV:89124431X.

Wetter, M. & van Treeck, C. (2017), 'New Generation Computational Tools for Building & Community Energy Systems', in IEA EBC Annex 60 http://www.iea-annex60.org/.

Wolfram Research Inc. (2014), 'Wolfram Modelica Ontology' http://www.sprint-iot.eu/Wolfram-Modelica-ontology.zip.

Zhang, B. (2019), 'IfcSTEP-to-IfcOWL_converters' https://github.com/BenzclyZhang/IfcSTEP-to-IfcOWL-converters.

Building Ontology for Preventive Fire Safety

Isabelle Fitkau, Timo Hartmann
Technische Universität Berlin, Germany
i.fitkau@tu-berlin.de

Abstract. The inclusion of preventive fire safety in the planning is always and inevitable necessary. The bases of assessment are complex. In addition to the ubiquitous protection goals, fire protection requirements are asserted and based in the broadest sense on legal texts, which in turn are described in terms of content exclusively by rule-based statements and requirements. The industry currently lacks an ontology that provides the core data for participating in digitalized work processes. In this paper we present the Preventive Fire Safety Ontology (PrevFis). It contains general descriptions, which describe the topology of a building as well as a part of preventive fire safety, in particularly important for other specialized planning, the structural fire safety. We describe how, using the ontology development methodology METHONTOLOGY, a general ontology based on a detailed rule-based data source can be created. Detailed relations are integrated, and we evaluate our approach with the validation of real-world rule-based data implementations. Use cases were collected in close cooperation with fire safety specialists and successfully presented and concluded in PrevFis. These include, for example, the automatic classification of a building according to the possible presence of special construction facts and building classes.

1. Introduction

Many parties involved in the planning process have and take influence on buildings, especially on the building's geometry. Anyone who accesses a building or retrieves information does so with a different background. The information itself and the depth of it can vary greatly. Among other things, the planning derives from fire safety requirements on building materials, components, and escape routes. The work of a fire safety engineer certainly plays a superordinate role within the structural design in case of fire for other specialties (Schjerve, 2017). Fire safety is still strongly underestimated in most used software tools today since it often does not yet have standardized work processes and naming conventions of parameters available for working with the BIM methodology and therefore has not yet received the same support as other departments within the planning process. A current developed fire safety certificate is created as a multi-page paper document. The information in this document has no relationships or connections among each other. If these processes are not revised, there is no possibility for the fire safety engineer to participate in digital work processes demanding several dimensions. Therefore, an attribution of the building regulations must take place. The goal of this ontology is to initiate and lead this process for structural fire safety by creating a suitable building topology for fire safety. A building regulation as a knowledge base for an ontology presents several challenges. First, requirements and concepts within the building regulation are characterized by a high number of if-else statements. The complexity of these statements is difficult to tease apart using simple predicate logic. Second, the immense number of building regulations, ordinances, and codes creates problems. The lack of clarity can be a burden on even experienced fire safety experts in their daily work. This makes a digital, general knowledge representation even more important. The goal of this paper is to develop an ontology that formalizes concepts and relationships between them that allow to define a description of the unambiguous formats of building regulations and related concepts in further guidelines. The PrevFis-ontology is a building topology and will eventually, in expected reuse, enable fundamental processes for fire safety to be initiated and developed, which in turn will strengthen the quality of all parties involved in a construction project. A building model hence a building ontology from the point of view of the fire safety engineer is therefore essential for further implementations regarding e.g. fire safety attributes.

2. Related Work

Ontologies in the field of building modelling. The ontological representation of the Industry Foundation Classes (IFC), called ifcOWL, makes data become available in directed, labeled graphs. The model is intended to allow easy linking of any building data (buildingSMART-Technical, 2020). (Niknam and Karshenas, 2015) propose an ontology which exclusively contains key elements of a building like walls, rooms, elements etc. In terms of an upper ontology, this ontology serves the purpose of being extended with data or entire ontologies depending on the use case. The Building Topology Ontology (BOT) developed by (Rasmussen et al., 2020) is a plain ontology for definition of relationships between components of a building. A few concepts here divide the building into different zones resp. spaces and interfaces. The BOT ontology has been created as a basis for reuse to support other domain-specific ontologies. It has been explicitly omitted a deepening relationship logic between the individual subcomponents as in (Randell et al., 1992). This is also noticeable by the low complexity of the classes and relations.

Ontologies in the field of fire safety. There are only few existing ontologies in the field of fire safety. The work of (Nikulina et al., 2019) largely represents the current state of ontologies in the field of fire safety. The domain ontology of both the Fire ontology (Souza, 2014) as well as the Fire Ontology Network ontology (Garcia-Castro and Corcho, 2008) is intended to be used for fighting wildfires (defensive fire protection). It addresses the use case of managing a wildland fire risk. The Emergency Fire ontology (BITENCOURT et al., 2018), The Building Fire Emergency Response (BFER) (Nunavath et al., 2016) and an ontology by (Wi et al., 2016) propose ontologies for emergency fire situations, especially in buildings. Primarily, these are concepts that describe the emergency protocols necessary in the event of a fire, that depicts firefighting from the perspective of search and rescue operations or aim to identify possible escape routes. The main goal is to enable end users to quickly respond to emergency situations of fires in buildings.

It can be summarized that the majority of current fire safety ontologies either deal with the concept of fire in its vegetative, natural form of being or are used to support rescue operations within buildings. All ontologies share the commonality that a fire must be actively started and, accordingly, processes, protocols, and states are put into action. No ontology currently addresses preventive fire safety with a suitable building topology.

3. Research Approach

To propose an end-to-end validated usage for the ontology for this case and to test competence, several efforts were performed. As a result of studying selected indicators, regulations and, if available, internal fire safety certificates it became clear that compared to existing building topology ontologies, a building in fire safety is viewed topologically different. The goal is to model a building topology that can be used intuitively by a fire safety expert. The ontology should represent the building topology and structural fire safety requirements of a building. Concepts that go extensively beyond this were explored, but no more entire paragraphs of building regulations were reviewed and extracted. In addition, intensive case resp. identifier management was carried out in close cooperation with fire safety experts. The decision making, with the help of the conceptual model (simplified overview see Fig.1), has been conducted in an iterative process during regular interviews. The process stretched over several weeks with one to two consultations a week. Since the current building regulations represent common planning documents and knowledge abstraction of interviews took place, a shared understanding as proposed by (Uschold and Gruninger, 1996) is assumed. There is reason to refrain from reusing existing ontologies if the goal and basis of domain knowledge is fundamentally different from existing but similar ontologies. The effort of considering possible object consolidations (Curry et al., 2013; Hogan et al., 2007) and alignment beforehand must be explicitly compared to the effort of reworking. Since for this proposed ontology the overwhelming goal is that the PrevFis ontology is expected to be reused almost exclusively within the fire safety domain and its service as an upper ontology in this domain, accurate object consolidation to general building ontologies of the AEC industry will not be pursued further at this point in the research. The methodology is strongly based on the well-known METHONTOLOGY (Fernández-López et al., 1997). It divides the development of an ontology into detached parts, which entails an orderly and clear comprehensibility. This is composed of steps such as specification, knowledge acquisition, conceptualization, implementation, and validation.

Specifications. For the purpose of specification we adhere to the proposed questions by (France-Mensah and O'Brien, 2019). The ontology presented in this paper represents a building topology from the perspective of a fire safety engineer. It is also intended to represent the field of structural fire safety, which results in adaptive parametric modelling since the data resource are fire safety requirements for the buildings components itself. The ontologies scope includes knowledge about the building topology based on several legal documents that are needed to certificate a building from a fire safety point of view. The intended end users are fire safety expert planners. Due to the current generality of PrevFis it could be used and extended throughout borders. At the moment, the intended use of the ontology is the ability to infer, through an establishment of detailed relationships, the building class and specific building type of each instantiated building based on its use and components as well as fire safety requirements in terms of structural fire safety.

Knowledge Acquisition & Conceptualization. Fire safety is basically based on national building law. Attributes and relationships of attributes are taken from the law (e.g. the respective state building regulations). For standardized parameter names to be developed and a common planning process to emerge, the written down knowledge of the law must be made digitally and semantically accessible to the fire safety planner and anyone else in the planning process of future buildings. For this specific implementation case, the Berlin building regulation (BauO Bln) (BauO Bln, 2006), the administrative regulation technical building regulation (VV TB Bln) (VV TB Bln, 2020), the DIN 4102-4 (DIN Deutsches Institut für Normung e.V., 2016a), the DIN 277-1 (DIN Deutsches Institut für Normung e.V., 2016b) as well as further model ordinance and sample guidelines (e.g. (MLAR, 2015); (MVKO, 1995)) have been used. Attempts were made to develop superordinate terms grouping several terms in a conceptual model. The most important aspects and concepts detected are (a) all types of fire safety, (b) building components, (c) the categorization of building into building classes and types, (d) the type of certificate and (e) requirements of building components resulting in mandatory attributes. These concepts present general terms needed for the associated preparation of a fire safety certificate. Real buildings including their components, however, represent instances. From these instances, classifications and types can be inferred. OWL, based on the RDF language, is used in order to represent these relationships. RDF is a well-known open standardized language which represents knowledge in a collection of triples. OWL takes advantage of this sort of predicate logic in terms of its more comprehensive description logic. It provides a structural format to present knowledge in a machine-readable format.

Implementation, Verification, Validation. Formalized knowledge of the conceptualization is summarized in a glossary, including concept terms, as well as their relations and attributes. The glossary serves as the fundament of the implementational model since it is representing the class topology of the ontology. For the implementational model to be extensible and reusable it needs to satisfy a set of constraints. The constraints are extracted from the selected regulations. The rule-based data is provided machine-readable by axioms and rules. The alignment of asserted and inferred knowledge is an incremental process. Concepts and instances are determined sequentially through enforcing reasoners and result in verification. To achieve competency and acceptance from experts a validation is important. If information has been successfully defined by the reasoner, validation through determination followed.

4. Preventive Fire Safety-Ontology (PrevFis)

The case was conducted to demonstrate how the proposed ontology deals with real data rule sets from the selected indicators and regulations. The implementation is done in Protégé v5.5.0 (Stanford Center for Biomedical Informatics Research, 2016). The indicator attributes, which have been transferred into a semantic representation by the conceptual model (e.g. building components, requirements for structural fire safety, various types of categorization) are profoundly processed in an implementational model which can then be reasoned for the purpose of verification. The reasoning is done with the Pellet reasoner v2.2.0 (Sirin et al., 2007). The constraints have been manually extracted from the selected documents, as noted before, and formalized into OWL axioms. These Axioms were used in this case to connect the general concepts. However, no effort was made to formulate sophisticated and complex rules using these axioms. Description Logic (DL) rules and Semantic Web Rule Language (SWRL) rules were used for this purpose and are targeting the relationships between instances. Many if-else statements of the selected indicators could be implemented with the non-customized resp. default settings of DL rules. As soon as special Built Ins were needed the syntax of SWRL could be used. Since PrevFis serves as a building topology in its field, important paragraphs in the BauO Bln, which mainly concern building topology and structural fire safety, are implemented: §2 BauO Bln and a large part of the Fourth Section (§26-§32 BauO Bln). To cover resulting unregulated types of buildings other regulations and indicators mentioned under 3. have been used.

4.1 Ontological Model - Overview

The PrevFiS-ontology covers the classification of a building into building classes and building types and assigns structural fire safety requirements for respective components. Building types in the PrevFiS-ontology include *StandardConstruction*, *SpecialConstruction*, and *Garages*. Building facilities are equated to buildings, although not every building facility is a building. However, buildings are the most common structural facility, so this assumption is made.

The *Classification* concept, in which *BuildingClasses* are defined as subclasses, depends essentially on the concepts of *AssessmenBasis* and *GeneralInformation*. The classification is based on defined requirements according to §2 (3) BauO Bln. The categorization of the building into its building type is based on various geometric and numerical concept properties as well as significantly on usage-specific statements. The concept *BuildingInterface* exists so that important components, connections between components, and basic statements about use can be made. It is detached from the concept *BuildingFacility*, to which it is strongly correlated, so an instantiated building can later access all important components of a building (components, information, requirements) from a relatively free position without having to unite the entire structure of a building (the *BuildingInterface*) under itself. The utilization unit and the explicit naming of the user is significant for the classification of the building into *BuildingClasses*. One can imagine the following as intuitive connections: A *BuildingFacility* has (*UtilizationUnit* and *StoreySpace*). A *StoreySpace* has (*UtilizationUnit* and *RoomSpace*). Whereas space-related concepts belong to the concept *SpaceInterface*.

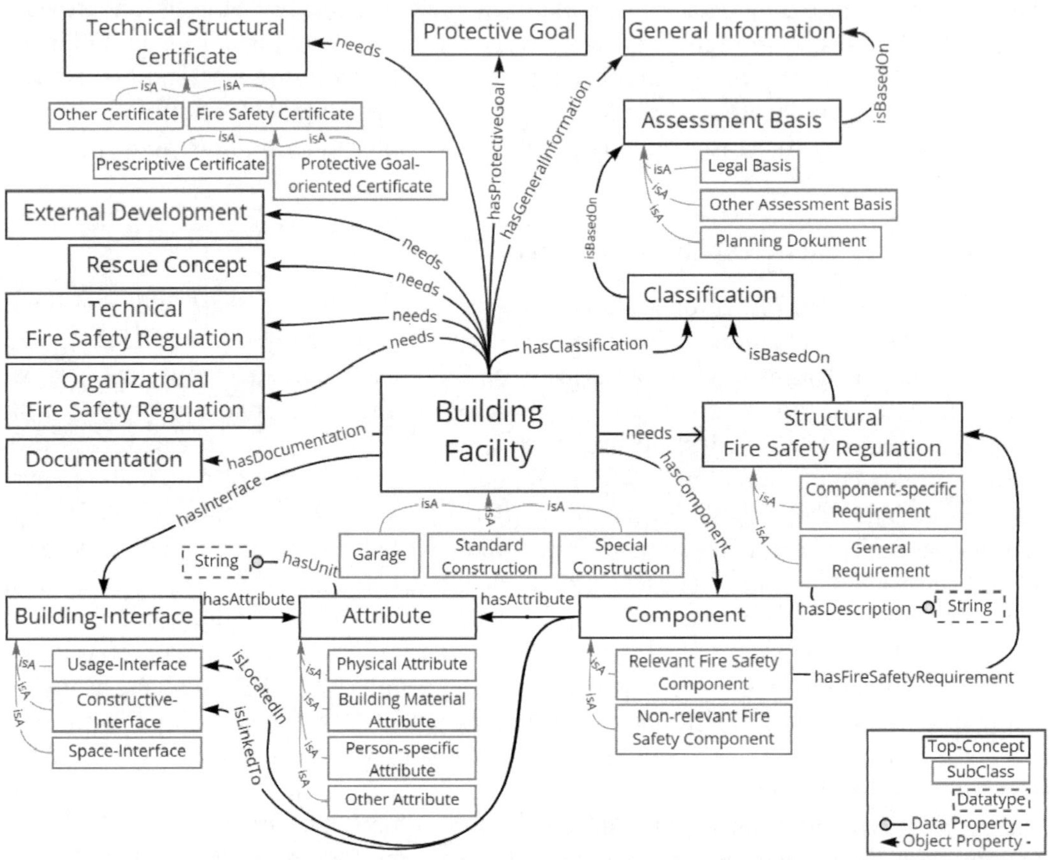

Figure 1: Ontological Overview of Concepts (Concept Map) of PrevFiS-ontology

The usage is determined by the *UsageInterface* within the *BuildingInterface*. For geometrical and numerical requirements, it makes use of the properties in the concept *Attribute*. Mapping attributes in a separate concept arose from the necessity to use the concept map as the basis for conversation that is understandable to ontology laypersons, and that anyone outside the OWL syntax can understand. For example, in §2 (4) 9. BauO Bln it is defined that a nursing home fulfils a special construction fact if the utilization unit meets e.g. the numerical requirements of either a) *individually for more than eight persons* or b) *intended for persons with intensive care need*. In the concept *Attribute* → *PersonSpecificAttribute* resulting concepts for each requirement is defined, e.g. a) the concept *NumberOfPersons* and for b) the concept *NeedForCare*.

The PrevFiS-ontology also contains the types of fire safety certificates. Therefore, a *ProtectiveGoalOrientedCertification* can be assigned to an *UnregulatedSpecialConstruction* with the help of *TechnicalStructuralCertificate* → *FireSafetyCertificate*. The protective goals can then be described in a detached concept called *ProtectiveGoal*.

Building products and types, which are mentioned in the BauO Bln and are subject to fire safety requirements and thus structural fire safety requirements, were combined within the PrevFiS-ontology in the concept *Component*. The concept *Component* was then subdivided into the subclasses *RelevantFireSafetyComponent* and *NonRelevantFireSafetyComponent*. This type of division was chosen so that it is intuitively immediately recognizable to the end user which components must be provided with fire safety requirements by BauO Bln. In the PrevFiS-ontology, elements of a building are first differentiated according to whether they require structural fire safety requirements from the selected regulation. This is in no way related to other building topologies (like IFC (buildingSMART-Technical, 2020) or the BOT-ontology (Rasmussen et al., 2020), in which components incl. building elements are often hierarchically classified in the building structure (e.g. exterior elements and interior elements leads to exterior wall, exterior column and interior wall, interior column). Components also have the strong spatial relationship to the utility of the building (*isLocatedIn*), as well as linking to various geometric relationships (*ConstructiveInterface*) among themselves (*isLinkedTo*). The concept *StructuralFireSafetyRegulation* includes all given requirements described by BauO Bln and is in turn based on the classification of the building and its final *BuildingClass*. The concepts *ExternalDevelopment*, *RescueConcept*, *TechnicalFireSafetyRegulation* and *OrganizationalFireSafetyRegulation* are conceived as superconcepts and for the explicit purpose of future reuse. They are *needed* to allow a full mapping of the BauO Bln. The concept *Documentation* is also used for completeness, as every planning process in construction is recorded and documented.

4.2 Validation

The Validation of the PrevFiS-ontology is accomplished through rule-based data, which have been selected together with fire safety experts, using example implementations. These examples contain complex data (if-else statements) that the PrevFiS-ontology attempts to represent. After the implementation, reasoners are used to check whether the knowledge can be inferred automatically according to the implemented rules. Thus, every check will verify whether the PrevFiS ontology is exhaustively enough for its intended purpose.

It is checked whether an instantiated building can be classified into its building type on the basis of its parameters. This will be done using a sample building *Building01* with the special construction fact of a sales outlet and the gross floor area of its salesrooms. According to §2 (4) 4. BauO Bln applies:

(4) Special buildings are facilities and premises of a special type or use that meet one of the following criteria:
4. sales outlets whose sales rooms and shopping streets have a total gross floor area of more than 800 m2,

The process of formulating a SWRL rule, in order to verify the necessity according to §2 (4) 4. BauO Bln, is presented. The aim is to classify a building if it fulfils the requirements according to §2 (4) 4. BauO Bln, into its type. Possible building types here refer to either regulated special construction or unregulated special construction based on the gross ground floor of the sales rooms or store streets. In the first step, it is to be defined which parameters a building must fulfil in order to constitute a special construction according to §2 (4) 4. BauO Bln and to receive the simultaneous assignment of the special construction fact of sales outlet.

```
BuildingFacility(?ba) ^ StoreySpace(?ge) ^ hasInterface(?ba, ?ge) ^ RoomSpace(?r) ^
isLocatedIn(?r, ?ge) ^ SalesRoom(?vr) ^ hasRoomUsage(?r, ?vr) ^ GrossFloorArea(?bgf)
^ hasValue(?bgf, ?wl) ^ hasAttribute(?r, ?bgf) ^ swrlb:greaterThan(?wl, 800.0) ->
SpecialConstruction(?ba) ^ hasInterface(?ba, SalesOutlet)
```

In the 2nd and 3rd step, a further classification according to regulated and unregulated special construction shall take place. Since the steps are identical except for the comparison of the gross ground floors, they are listed together except for the last step. In addition to the above excerpt from §2 (4) 4. BauO Bln, these steps are based on §1 MVKO as follows:

The provisions of this ordinance apply to any sales outlets whose sales rooms and store streets, including their components, have a total area of more than 2000m².

Figure 2: Results of inferring the abstracted rule-based knowledge from §2 (4) 4. BauO Bln

Accordingly, buildings that meet the facts according to §2 (4) 4. BauO Bln and whose gross ground floors of the sales rooms are in total more than 800m² and less than or equal to 2000m² are unregulated special constructions.

```
SpecialConstruction(?sb) ^ hasInterface(?sb, SalesOutlet) ^ StoreySpace(?ge) ^
isInterfaceOf(?ge, ?sb) ^ RoomSpace(?r) ^ isLocatedIn(?r, ?ge) ^ SalesRoom(?vr) ^
hasRoomUsage(?r, ?vr) ^ GrossFloorArea(?bgf) ^ hasValue(?bgf, ?w1) ^ hasAttribute(?r,
?bgf) ^ …
```

This is where the difference from unregulated to regulated special construction begins. Unregulated special construction:

```
… swrlb:greaterThan(?w1, 800.0) ^ swrlb:lessThanOrEqual(?w1, 2000.0) ->
UnregulatedSpecialConstruction(?sb)
```

Regulated special construction:

```
… swrlb:greaterThan(?w1, 2000.0) -> RegulatedSpecialConstruction(?sb)
```

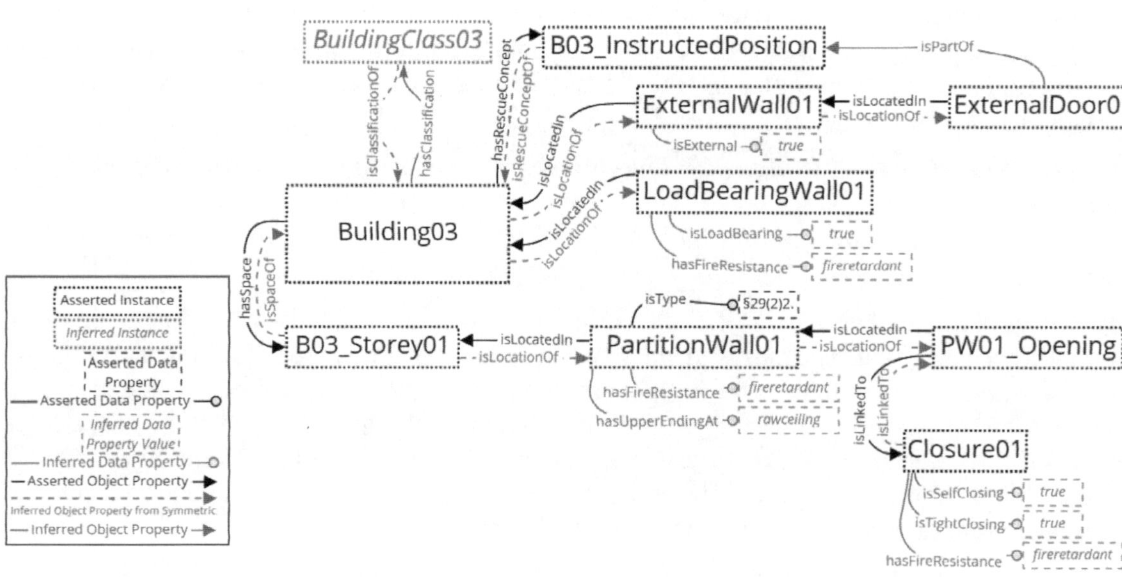

Figure 3: Asserted and inferred knowledge from §29 BauO Bln.

After enforcing the reasoner, it was automatically concluded that the instantiated *Building01* represents an unregulated special construction. (see Fig. 2) With a total gross floor area of $1000m^2$ of the sales rooms, it falls exactly into the unregulated area. The example successfully inferred the rule-based data to the desire. Therefore, a plain, real-world application could thus be illustrated.

In addition to the previous mentioned implementation, parameter values of fire safety requirements for building components, closures and doors were also explicitly examined, which are partly also aimed at the assessment and preparation of rescue concepts during a successful planning process. Fig. 3 shows partial results of the conclusions of the sample building *Building03* of building class 3. These are based entirely on the extracted rule-based data from §29 BauO Bln and were proven to be successful in automatically inferring data that is important for planning. §29 (5) BauO Bln may serve here as a subsample (DL-safe rule):

```
DifferentFrom (?cl, BuildingClass1), hasClassification(?trwba, ?cl), DifferentFrom
(?cl, BuildingClass2), isLocatedIn(?öff, ?trw), isLinkedTo(?öff, ?ab), Opening(?öff),
isLocatedIn(?trw, ?sttrw), PartitionWall(?trw), isZoneOf(?sttrw, ?trwba),
Closure(?ab) -> isTightClosing(?ab, true), hasFireResistance(?ab, "fireretardant"),
isSelfClosing(?ab, true)
```

5. Discussion and Limits

The work processes of a fire safety engineer are based on the data resources and its specific requirements used in this work. Therefore, buildings are categorized and processed differently by a fire safety expert than by other involved departments. Other building topologies are not suitable for reuse since they lack these special points of view. The PrevFis ontology fills the gap by making a building topologically and intuitively useful for the domain of fire safety and its engineers. After further detailed elaboration one could also consider alignment with already existing ontologies. Parallels such as an interface and the division of a building into zones resp. spaces according to the BOT ontology (Rasmussen and Lefrançois, 2018) have also already been attempted to be drawn in PrevFiS using concepts such as *BuildingInterface* and its *SpaceInterface*. Regarding a broader applicability in practice, an alignment to IFC (buildingSMART-Technical, 2020) may be beneficial. However, effort must be weighed up against use in a very needs-oriented manner. After further modifications of the ontology, it will be able to support the work of a fire safety expert in an efficient way as it can resp. serve as the basis referring to query domain knowledge. It could then clarify queries such as "When is a storey defined as a basement?" or "From which length must an extended building be subdivided with fire walls?". This can strongly support the creation of required fire safety concepts. It could also serve as a kind of database. Existing buildings could be instantiated in the ontology. Hence, fire safety requirements including their justifications and deviations could be 'stored' in the PrevFiS ontology. PrevFiS was also formulated as a basis for extensions, such as the technical and organizational fire safety. Thus, the developers of extensions are spared the foundational work of creating a building topology from a fire safety perspective. The exemplary implementation of real-world examples using rules in the present work has been able to show that the implemented PrevFiS ontology behaves positively in end users practice as expected by the developers.

All in all, every selected rule-based data could be successfully implemented and inferred with the help of the advance syntax of DL and SWRL rules. It must be noted that Protégé experienced significant losses in the runtime of the reasoner's work (several seconds) after enforcing a certain number of rules. A transfer towards stronger runtime solutions such as using graph databases should be considered. Also OWLs open-world assumption limits modelling possibilities by forcing the user to make some unintuitively definitions. However, it must be made clear that OWL is a language of inference rather than of constraint (rule) creation, neither is designed for it. A more suitable language (e.g. one that supports closed-world assumptions) may be able to remedy some issues. However, with respect to the assumptions made, a positive conclusion can be drawn from the study of implementations. From a technical perspective, the machine-readable implementational model of PrevFis sets the first step towards a digital fire safety certificate. Resulting from the structure of data from the selected data resources, an inclusion of 3D geometry is clearly not a necessity at this point of research. Considering that attributes extracted from the regulations have fixed values, like design values, which only varies according to the classification that has been made for the building and the fact that this topic did not come up in discussions with experts and that the rule sets were successfully implemented under the chosen assumptions proves this.

6. Conclusion

The present work investigated to what extent a semantic-based approach for the representation of data within the fire safety domain is possible with the help of the representation of an ontology. The goal was to obtain data necessary for a fire safety certification from the data source (mainly BauO Bln, 2006) and to represent it in a machine-readable way. An attempt was made to align some concepts of existing ontologies from the building topology domain during the development of the Preventive Fire Safety (PrevFiS) ontology. In the many interviews with fire safety experts conducted by the authors, a different view of the building as a product emerged. A rule-based data source such as the BauO Bln requires an upper ontology based on its structure before detailed relationships between the components of a building can be created using rules so that more multidimensional relationship strings can be expressed. Thus, it was decided to create a general ontology of the fire safety domain. It primarily represents a building topology as well as the focus of structural fire safety. Its value has also been confirmed by the validation carried out.

Acknowledgement

This research was supported by hhpberlin. We are thankful for all provided insights and shared expertise knowledge during interviews that greatly assisted the research, since we were able to provide an ontology that can serve and support directly our intended end users.

References

BauO Bln, (2006). Bauordnung für Berlin – BauO Bln – vom 29.September 2005.

Bitencourt, K., Durão, F., Mendonça, M., Santana, L., (2018). An Ontological Model for Fire Emergency Situations. In: IEICE Transactions on Information and Systems E101.D, 108–115.

buildingSMART-Technical, (2020). ifcOWL. buildingSMART Technical. https://technical.buildingsmart.org/standards/ifc/ifc-formats/ifcowl/, accessed November 2020.

Curry, E., O Donnel, J., Corry, E., Hasan, S., Keane, M., O'Riain, S., (2013). Linking building data in the cloud: Integrating cross-domain building data using linked data. In: Advanced Engineering Informatics 27, 206–219.

DIN Deutsches Institut für Normung e.V., (2016a). DIN 4102-4, Brandverhalten von Baustoffen und Bauteilen – Teil 4: Zusammenstellung und Anwendung klassifizierter Baustoffe, Bauteile und Sonderbauteile.

DIN Deutsches Institut für Normung e.V., (2016b). DIN 277-1, Grundflächen und Rauminhalte im Bauwesen – Teil 1: Hochbau.

Fernández-López, M., Gomez-Perez, A., Juristo, N., (1997). METHONTOLOGY: from ontological art towards ontological engineering. Engineering Workshop on Ontological Engineering (AAAI97).

France-Mensah, J., O'Brian, W.J., (2019). A shared ontology for integrated highway planning. In: Advanced Engineering Informatics 41, 100929.

Garcia-Castro, R., Corcho, O., (2008). Fire ontology network. http://linkeddata4.dia.fi.upm.es/ssg4env/index.php/ontologies/12-fire-ontology-network/default.htm, accessed November 2020.

Hogan, A., Harth, A., Decker, S., (2007). Performing Object Consolidation on the Semantic Web Data Graph. In: Proceedings of the WWW2007 Workshop I³: Identity, Identifiers, Identification, Entity-Centric Approaches to Information and Knowledge Management on the Web, Banff, Canada, May 8, 2007.

Muster-Richtlinie über brandschutztechnische Anforderungen an Leitungsanlagen (Muster-Leitungsanlagen-Richtlinie MLAR), (2015).

Musterverordnung über den Bau und Betrieb von Verkaufsstätten (Muster-Verkaufsstättenverordnung – MVKO), (1995).

Niknam, M., Karshenas, S., (2015). Integrating distributed sources of information for construction cost estimating using Semantic Web and Semantic Web Service technologies. In: Automation in Construction 57, 222–238.

Nikulina, Y., Shulga, T., Sytnik, A., Frolova, N., Toropova, O., (2019). Ontologies of the Fire Safety Domain. In: Dolinina, O., Brovko, A., Pechenkin, V., Lvov, A., Zhmud, V., Kreinovich, V., (Eds.), Recent Research in Control Engineering and Decision Making, Studies in Systems, Decision and Control. Springer International Publishing, Cham, pp.457–467.

Nunavath, V., Prinz, A., Comes, T., Radianti, J., (2016). Representing Fire Emergency Response Knowledge Through a Domain Modelling Approach. NOKOBIT 24, Bergen, Norway.

Randell, D., Cui, Z., Cohn, A., (1992). A Spatial Logic based on Regions and Connection. In: The Principles of Knowledge Representation and Reasoning: Proceedings of the 1st International Conference, pp.165–176.

Rasmussen, M.H., Lefrançois, M., (2018). Ontology for Property Management (Draft Community Group Report). W3C.

Rasmussen, M.H., Pauwels, P., Lefrançois, M., Schneider, G.F., (2020). Building Topology Ontology (Draft Community Group Report). W3C.

Schjerve, Dipl.Ing. Dr. techn. N., (2017). Brandschutz im BIM – Neues Arbeitswerkzeug. Trockenbau Journal 80.

Sirin, E., Parsia, B., Grau, B.C., Kalyanpur, A., Katz, Y., (2007). Pellet: A practical OWL-DL reasoner. In: Journal of Web Semantics, Software Engineering and the Semantic Web 5, 51–53.

Souza, A., (2014). Fire Ontology - Summary. NCBO BioPortal. https://bioportal.bioontology.org/ontologies/FIRE, accessed November 2020.

Stanford Center for Biomedical Informatics Research, (2016). Protégé. https://protege.stanford.edu/, accessed March 2021.

Uschold, M., Gruninger, M., (1996). Ontologies: principles, methods and applications. In: The Knowledge Engineering Review 11, 93–136.

Verwaltungsvorschrift Technische Baubestimmungen (VV TB Bln), (2020). Berlin, vom 10.Juli 2020.

Wi, N., Botzheim, J., Kubota, N., (2016). Building Ontology for Fire Emergency Planning and Support. In: E-Journal of Advance Maintenance Vol.8-2, 2016, 13–22.

A Framework for Intelligent Building Information Spoken Dialogue System (iBISDS)

Ning Wang, Raja R.A. Issa, Chimay J. Anumba
University of Florida, United States
n.wang@ufl.edu, raymond-issa@ufl.edu, anumba@ufl.edu

Abstract. Existing Building Information Modeling (BIM) information extraction (IE) methods require users to spend more time learning different query languages and database structures, which is difficult for non-BIM experts. Natural language-based IE from building information models is required by both BIM experts and non-experts. Conversational Artificial Intelligence (CAI) technologies improve the generation of speech-based IE from databases. However, existing research on speech-based IE from building information models is limited. Therefore, this research develops a framework for intelligent Building Information Spoken Dialogue System (iBISDS) to achieve speech-based IE from building information models. This study is focused on extracting attribute information of building components. The iBISDS is a speech-based question answering (QA) system that can provide information support for on-site and off-site construction project team members. The iBISDS framework will facilitate the further adoption of CAI technologies in the construction area.

1. Introduction

One of the major characteristics of the current construction industry is that it is information-intensive with a lower level of information integration (Sacks et al., 2018; Wang et al., 2011). Due to its information-intensive nature, Building Information Modeling (BIM) has been proposed to provide information support for architects, engineers, constructors, and facility managers with considerable building information. BIM has been extensively adopted in the Architecture, Engineering, Construction, and Operation (AECO) industry, and BIM has been used in the lifecycle of projects. The size and complexity of BIM/IFC models increase as information is added (Zhang and Issa, 2013). As more data is aggregated in building information models, further use of the building information to support construction activities becomes important. However, building information searching and extraction involve many time-consuming tasks (Sacks et al., 2018). Existing methods for information extraction (IE) from building information models focus on extracting structured building data from the BIM database by keyboard input using a structured query language (SQL) or SPARQL Protocol and RDF Query Language (SPARQL) (Karan et al., 2016). Conventional methods of building data acquisition require BIM users to be agile with BIM software and tools to obtain useful building information from BIM databases. However, it is difficult for non-BIM experts to understand SQL-related language and database structures. With the increase in the data size of BIM models and the complexity of software functions, BIM users will need more time to study BIM software manipulation, and the process of information acquisition will become more difficult (Lin et al., 2016). In comparison to SQL-related language, speech queries and responses are expected to be more acceptable and friendly to BIM users. Speech-based IE from building information models is useful to both BIM experts and non-experts.

In the era of Big Data, automatic speech recognition plays an indispensable contributing role in improving the generation of intelligent virtual assistant systems. An increasing number of organizations and companies are conducting research to develop spoken dialogue systems to support human daily life, such as Apple Siri, Amazon Alexa, Google Assistant, IBM Watson, Microsoft Cortana, and NVIDIA Jarvis. A spoken dialogue system (SDS) is an intelligent human-machine interactive conversation system that provides information support to humans via voice (Park and Kang, 2019). SDS aims to mimic the dialogue capabilities of natural human language. An SDS can be developed into an intelligent virtual agent or chatbot to provide information support for users via spoken interaction. Compared to other industries, the construction industry lags in developing spoken dialogue systems. Existing research on SDS for building information extraction is limited. Although other industries have developed their virtual assistants, most of them are template-based spoken dialogue systems which are unscalable to the construction industry, which means existing spoken dialogue systems cannot be directly implemented to building information extraction. Therefore, it is necessary to develop a customized SDS for building information extraction in the construction industry.

This study aims to develop a framework for intelligent Building Information Spoken Dialogue System (iBISDS) to provide building information support for the AECO industry. The iBISDS requires: 1) recognizing a speech query and transforming it into a textual query; 2) identifying and classifying different keywords within the textual query; 3) extracting corresponding data from building information models; 4) generating a textual natural language answer based on input keywords and extracted building data; 5) and converting the textual answer into speech. To achieve the research goal, this study developed a framework for the iBISDS, which consists of five main modules: Automatic Speech Recognition (ASR), Natural Language Understanding (NLU), Building Information Extraction (BIM), Natural Language Generation (NLG), and Text-to-Speech (TTS). This study used open-source building information models in Industry Foundation Classes (IFC) format as the knowledge base for information extraction use, and the version of the IFC specifications is IFC4 Addendum 2 Technical Corrigendum 1 (IFC4 ADD2 TC1). This study is focused on directly extracting attribute information of building components (i.e., *IfcBuildingElement*) without additional computation and reasoning. A Python-based prototype program was developed based on the iBISDS framework to verify the functionalities and algorithms. The preliminary result indicated that the iBISDS framework satisfies the requirements of iBISDS. The iBISDS enables non-BIM experts to extract useful information via voice. Compared to existing BIM IE methods, the iBISDS can recognize speech queries and generate corresponding speech responses for BIM users who have limited BIM experience. Non-BIM experts can use speech to query building information models, instead of conventional SQL or SPARQL, and the spoken natural language responses are expected to be more acceptable to BIM users. The iBISDS can also provide flexible information extraction, instead of template-based keyword matching.

2. Literature Review

Traditional building information acquisition is through manually searching information from PDF drawings and specifications, which is a low-efficient job for construction project team members. The concept of BIM was first proposed in the 1970s (Eastman et al., 1974). Since then, BIM has been applied by different parties in the AECO industry, and it has become extremely popular in recent years. BIM can be considered as "a verb or an adjective phrase to describe tools, processes and technologies that are facilitated by digital, machine-readable documentation about a building, its performance, its planning, its construction and later its operation" (Sacks et al., 2018). With the adoption of BIM technologies, building information acquisition has become more efficient. However, existing applications for building information retrieval require users to be agile with BIM software and tools to obtain useful data from building information models. Some research proposed SQL-related information retrieval methods to retrieve building information, but it is necessary to transfer building information from an IFC file into another knowledge base, such as Relational Database Management System

(RDBMS), RDF (Resource Description Framework), and OWL (Web Ontology Language) (Karan et al., 2016; Lin et al., 2016; Liu et al., 2016; Wang and Issa, 2020a). That data transfer process is a time-consuming and complicated process with a possibility of data loss and error, and users need to learn SQL-related queries which is difficult for inexperienced BIM users. Flexible and effective information acquisition from BIM is required for both BIM professionals and non-professionals (Lin et al., 2016). Natural language-based information acquisition becomes necessary. A spoken dialogue system (SDS) enables non-BIM experts to extract useful building information by using spoken natural language. SDS can provide flexible information extraction from building information models. However, research on SDS for building information retrieval and extraction is limited. The construction industry lags other industries in developing spoken dialogue systems.

In Industry 4.0, spoken dialogue systems have become more and more popular to support human daily life, and many industries are developing their custom spoken dialogue systems (Ralston et al., 2019). Various names have been used to describe an SDS, such as chatbot, personal assistant, virtual assistant, intelligent virtual assistant, digital assistant, and voice assistant (Kepuska and Bohouta, 2018). SDS is commonly used on smartphones, smart speakers, smart TVs, and intelligent robots (Yamamoto et al., 2019). The basic structure of a general-purpose SDS includes Automatic Speech Recognition (ASR), Natural Language Understanding (NLU), Dialog Manager (DM), Natural Language Generation (NLG), and Text-to-Speech (TTS) (Kepuska and Bohouta, 2018; Park and Kang, 2019). ASR aims to convert speech queries into textual queries using one of many speech recognition technologies, such as Google speech recognition, Microsoft Bing voice recognition, and IBM speech to text. NLU is a sub-field of natural language processing that focuses on getting a machine to interpret natural language. Most existing general-purpose spoken dialogue systems detect exact keywords to recognize the information from voice command (Kobayashi et al., 2019). For example, some keywords like "calendar" are used in general-purpose spoken dialogue systems to fulfill related "calendar" jobs from users. Many general-purpose spoken dialogue systems have been designed by using the exact keyword to complete speech commands. Google Assistant was used by some IoT-based smart home devices for the aforementioned job. When Google Assistant detects the keywords "Turn on" and "TV", the corresponding job will be finished by Google Assistant (Isyanto et al., 2020). If the input keyword is out of domain, a general-purpose SDS will use an online search engine and retrieve relevant information by connecting the SDS with the Internet (Jucks et al., 2018). Most existing general-purpose SDS applications commonly detect exact keywords to recognize the key information from speech commands. For DM and NLG, most existing SDS applications have implemented structured input-output pairs for dialogue databases (Kajinami et al., 2018). General-purpose SDS applications were developed for customer services, and the template-based input-output pairs were manually developed. Also, template-based NLG is commonly utilized in most general-purpose spoken dialogue systems (Wen and Young, 2020). For TTS, many companies have developed Text-to-Speech technologies to convert a textual sentence into speech, e.g., Google, Microsoft, and IBM.

3. IBISDS Architecture

To achieve the research goal, a framework for iBISDS was designed and developed based on the basic architecture of a general-purpose interactive system. The iBISDS is a server-based system to increase the efficiency of information acquisition, which means users can use a web browser on any smart device to get the services from the iBISDS. The iBISDS framework for iBISDS was designed on the server-side, which consists of five major modules: Automatic

Speech Recognition (ASR), Natural Language Understanding (NLU), Building Information Extraction (BIE), Natural Language Generation (NLG), and Text-to-Speech (TTS) (see Figure 1). The ASR module converts the natural language query speech into textual one. The NLU module identifies and classifies different keywords within the textual natural language query. The BIE module was developed to extract corresponding structured data from a building information model, according to the classified keywords from the NLU module. The format of building information models implemented in this study is Industry Foundation Classes (IFC). The NLG module uses structured information including keywords from the NLU module and extracted building data from the BIE module to generate the textual natural language response. The final TTS module enables the conversion from textual natural language into speech.

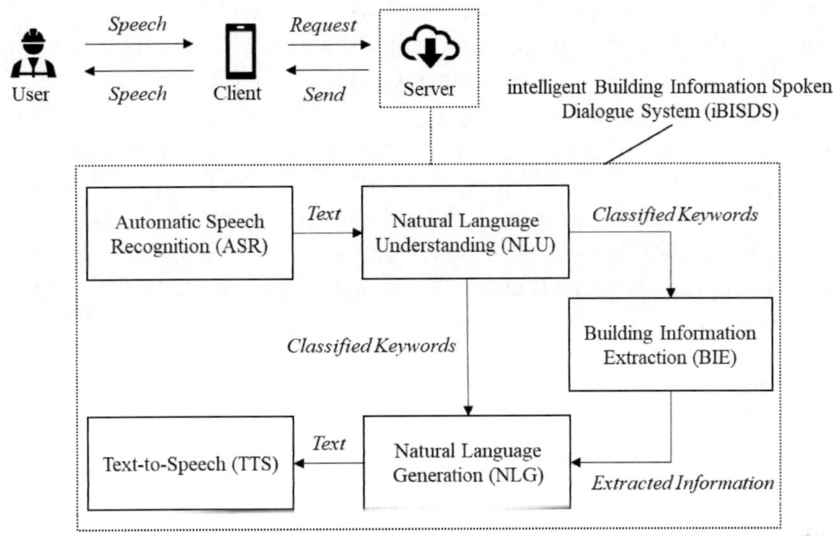

Figure 1: iBISDS Framework

3.1 Automatic Speech Recognition Module

The ASR module aims to convert a spoken natural language query into a textual through existing ASR technologies. Many companies and organizations have developed ASR technologies like Google, IBM, and NVIDIA. The iBISDS framework adopted the Google speech recognition engine to convert the input speech query into a textual one. The transcription accuracy of Google speech recognition has reached 100% with 50 dBA to 78 dBA background noise using natural language speech (Palconit et al., 2019). That means the ASR module of the iBISDS can provide a very accurate transformation from voice into textual natural language query. This study implemented the Google speech recognition Python package to develop the prototype program. To implement the Google speech recognition engine, microphones from PCs and smartphones were utilized to receive speech queries on the client-side in the iBISDS framework.

3.2 Natural Language Understanding Module

The NLU module aims to identify the intent of a user's query. Most existing applications in NLU were developed to detect exact keywords to understand user's intentions. This study utilized semantic and syntactic analysis of natural language processing. Compared to the detection of exact keywords, the NLU allows for more flexible word choices for natural language queries. Some research reported that Deep Neural Networks (DNN) methods can improve the flexibility of natural language understanding (Kepuska and Bohouta, 2018; Packowski and Lakhana, 2017). However, training a deep learning language model for an SDS requires a large amount of dialogue data, and such data is limited in the construction industry. Therefore, this study implemented natural language processing methods for the NLU module. The NLU module was developed to identify content keywords and classify them. This study focused on directly extracting attribute information from "*IfcBuildingElement*", so the speech query is targeting *IfcDoor*, *IfcWindow*, *IfcWall*, etc. For example, consider a non-BIM expert project manager who is reading a PDF drawing, and the manager would like to know the height information for a window with a known tag. The manager used the spoken natural language query "What is the height of the window 356213?" which contains the content keywords "height", "window", and "356213". These content keywords would be identified and classified into *attribute word* (i.e., "height"), *type word* (i.e., "window"), and *name phrase* (i.e., "window 356213") by this module. The developed algorithm uses natural language processing methods, like sentence tokenization and Part-of-Speech tagging, to analyze the semantic contents and syntactic structure of the textual natural language query (see Figure 2). After tokenization and Part-of-Speech tagging, content keywords (i.e., noun, adjective, and cardinal number) are identified. Although the *attribute word* (i.e., "height") and *type word* (i.e., "window") are all nouns, the *type word* is within a prepositional phrase (PP) (i.e., of the window). The *name phrase* (i.e., "window 356213") consists of *type word* with a cardinal number or adjective. The identified keywords are used to locate the target IFC data and generate the corresponding textual natural language response.

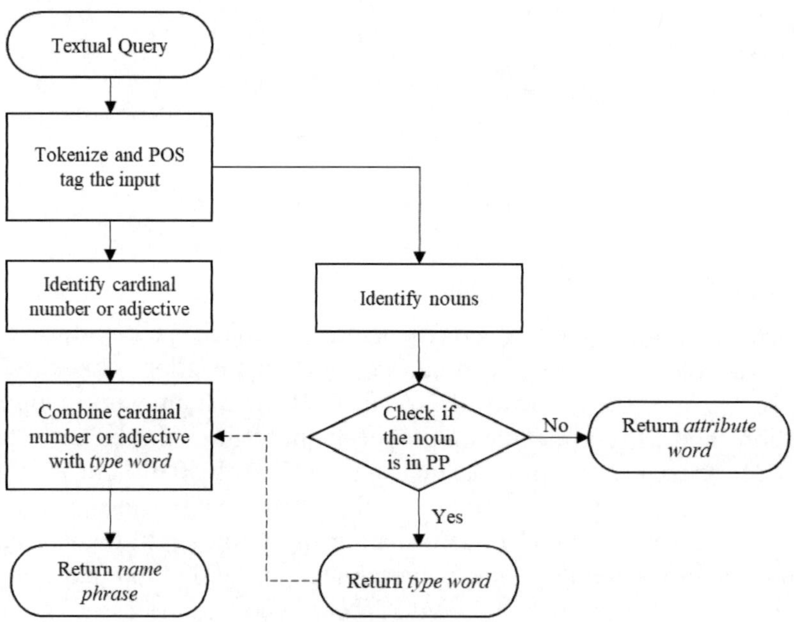

Figure 2: NLU Algorithm for iBISDS Framework

3.3 Building Information Extraction Module

The BIE module extracts the target building information, for example, "the height of window 356213". The building information model in the iBISDS framework is an IFC-STEP file. Although IFC is an open-source specification, the data structure of an IFC-STEP file is complex. To parse an IFC-STEP file and improve the efficiency of information extraction, this study developed an open-source Python package – *IfcReader*, which was published in GitHub (https://github.com/wangningstar/IfcReader). The BIE module was developed based on

IfcReader, which can extract organized IFC data based on the IFC schema. The detailed algorithm for the BIM module is shown in Figure 3. The identified *type word* (i.e., "window") by the NLU is used to find the target IFC entity type (i.e., *IfcWindow*). To locate the target type, all IFC entity types of *IfcBuildingElement* within an IFC-STEP file are extracted into a list. The next step is to check whether the *type word* or its synonym is within the list. This study implemented WordNet to find synonyms of the *type word.* After the target IFC entity type is located, the next step is to locate the target IFC entity. The BIE module checks whether the *name phrase* (i.e., "window 356213") is a substring of one IFC entity. If so, the next step is to extract the queried data from the target IFC entity by checking whether the *attribute word* (i.e., "height") or its synonym is a substring of an attribute name of the target IFC entity. *IfcReader* is utilized to extract all attribute names of the target IFC entity into a list based on the IFC4 ADD2 TC1 schema. For example, the list of attribute names of an *IfcWindow* is "['GlobalId', 'OwnerHistory', 'Name', 'Description', 'ObjectType', 'ObjectPlacement', 'Representation', 'Tag', 'OverallHeight', 'OverallWidth', 'PredefinedType', 'PartitioningType', 'UserDefinedPartitioningType']". The BIE module uses the *attribute word* (i.e., "height") or its synonym to match the target attribute 'OverallHeight' of the target *IfcWindow* and extract the corresponding value. The target value is utilized to generate a natural language response.

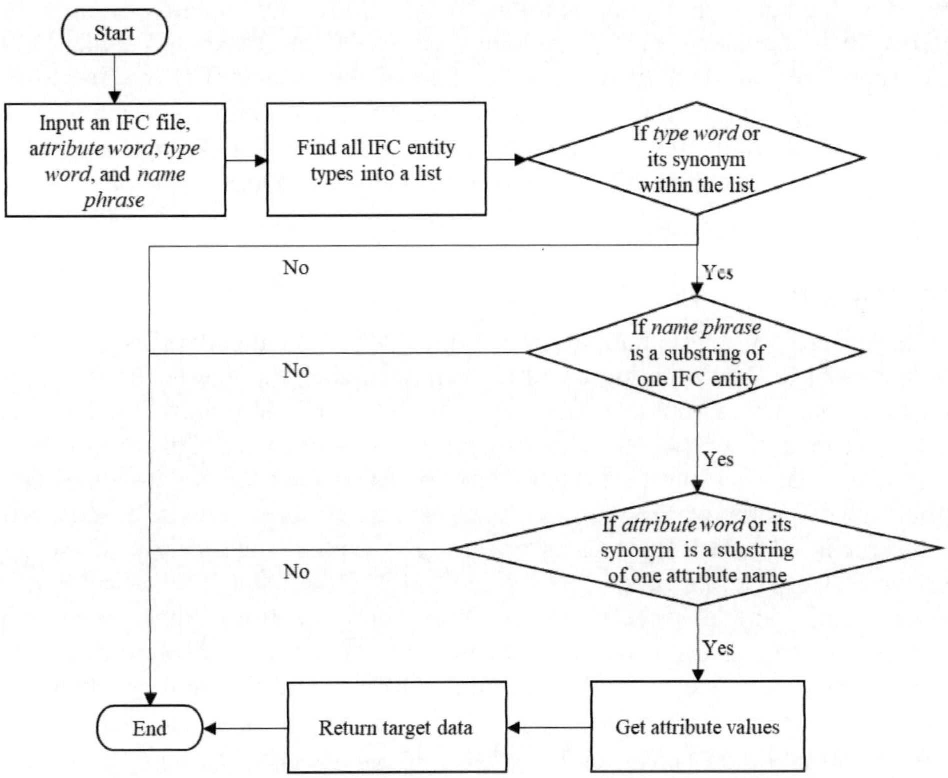

Figure 3: BIE Algorithm for iBISDS Framework

3.4 Natural Language Generation Module

The NLG module aims to generate a natural language sentence based on the structured information from the NLU and BIE modules. The algorithm of this module was developed in previous efforts (Wang and Issa, 2020b). The NLG module used Part-of-Speech to generate a natural language sentence. The generated natural language sentence is a template-based pattern: "The" (determiner) <*attribute word*> "of" (preposition) "the" (determiner) <name phrase> "is" (verb) <extracted IFC data> <unit>. The pattern is following the basic structure of English syntax: noun phrase and verb phrase. "The" (determiner) *<attribute word>* "of" (preposition) "the" (determiner) <name phrase> is a noun phrase, while "is" (verb) <extracted IFC data> <unit> is a verb phrase. Classified keywords from the NLU module and extracted IFC data from the BIE module were utilized as content words to generate the sentence. The <unit> information is extracted from the entity *IfcConversionBasedUnit*. The <unit> can be imperial or metric which is predefined in the IFC file by users. If the <extracted IFC data> is a cardinal number that is not "1", the <unit> will be changed to the plural format. For example, the generated natural language for "the height of window 356213" is "The height of the window 356213 is 4 feet". In addition, the <unit> is unnecessary, if the <extracted IFC data> is not a cardinal number. For example, if a user queried the type information of a window, the generated natural language would be "The type of the window 356255 is fixed:36" x 48".".

3.5 Text-to-Speech Module

The TTS module aims to convert the generated textual natural language into a speech response back to a user. The TTS module is the key to achieve the "spoken" part of an SDS. Many companies and organizations have been developing TTS technologies, e.g., Google, IBM, and Microsoft. With the adoption of deep learning methods, the sound quality and naturalness of synthesized speech of existing TTS technologies have been improved (Joo et al., 2020; Sun et al., 2020). Therefore, the iBISDS framework adopted the Google TTS engine to convert a textual response into a speech one. After the conversion, the generated speech was played by the developed TTS module. The synthesized speech response is a more convenient way for construction practitioners to obtain the queried information response.

4. Verification and Discussion

A Python-based prototype program was developed based on the iBISDS framework. The prototype was used to verify the logic and algorithm of each module in the framework. The integrated development environment (IDE) was the PyCharm community 2020.3 version, and the Python interpreter was Python 3.8.5 distributed by Anaconda. This study developed a preliminary Graphical User Interface (GUI) based on *Tkinter* for the client-side of the iBISDS (see Figure 4). The prototype program is a server-based system. The server-side generates a port, and the client-side can request a service through the port. The server-side was developed based on the iBISDS framework: ASR, NLU, BIE, NLG, and TTS. The ASR module implemented the Google speech recognition service from the Python package *speech_recognition* to convert a speech query into a textual one. A desktop microphone was used to receive the speech query. The NLU module utilized the *nltk* Python package to Part-of-Speech tag the textural natural language query. This module was developed based on syntactic analysis to identify and classify keywords. The developed package *IfcReader* was used to parse an IFC-STEP file and extract organized data in the BIE module. Also, the synonyms function was developed based on the WordNet with the *nltk* version to find all synonyms of *attribute word* and *type word*. The BIE was developed based on a substring matching algorithm to extract the target building information. The NLG module utilized the natural language pattern to generate a textual response. The <unit> information was also extracted by *IfcReader* if the extracted building information is a cardinal number. The TTS module adopted the Google Text-to-Speech package *gTTS* to convert the generated textual response into a speech stored in a .mp3 file and played it for users.

The preliminary results indicated that the iBISDS framework yielded valid results. The ASR module correctly converted a speech query into a textual one. The NLU correctly identified and classified keywords within the textual query. The target IFC data could be extracted by the BIE module. The NLG and TTS modules generated a natural language response and converted it into speech back to users. Compared to the detection of exact keywords, the iBISDS framework enabled a flexible option for speech queries. Construction project team members can use speech to query iBISDS, and the iBISDS will provide a speech response back to them. Also, a smartphone can be the client-side of iBISDS. Users can receive responses to queried building information to support construction activities on the construction site. The iBISDS framework still has some limitations. The NLU module implemented Part-of-Speech and syntactic analysis methods to identify and classify keywords within the textual query, because of the lack of dialogue training data for the construction industry. The NLU uses tags to locate target building elements which restricts the syntactic structure of the speech query. To provide a more flexible NLU, training data should be collected and labeled for deep learning use in the future. This study focused on directly extracting attribute information from *IfcBuildingElement* without computation and reasoning. After the development of a deep learning-based NLU, future research should explore quantity information extraction and ontology-based reasoning. For example, the BIE module with ontology-based reasoning can locate the window in room 101 instead of using tags to locate target building elements. The developed iBISDS is modularized which means each module in iBISDS can be substituted for by future efforts.

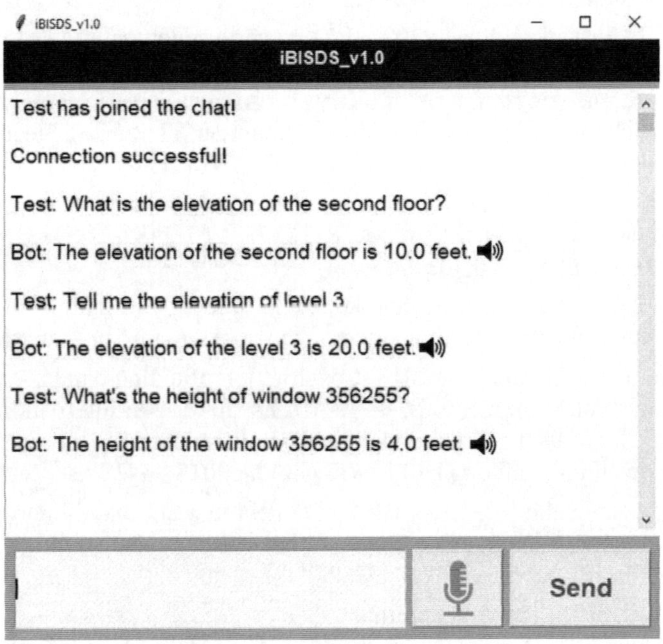

Figure 4: Preliminary Graphical User Interface of iBISDS

5. Summary and Conclusions

Existing building information acquisition methods require BIM users to spend more time studying the BIM database structure and software manipulation. Compared to conventional SQL or SPARQL-based IE methods, the speech-based IE is expected to be more acceptable to BIM users. With the development of conversational AI technologies, SDS has become increasingly more popular in human daily life. Therefore, this research developed an iBISDS framework with a focus on directly extracting attribute information from *IfcBuildingElement*. The basic architecture of the iBISDS consists of five modules: Automatic Speech Recognition, Natural Language Understanding, Building Information Extraction, Natural Language Generation, and Text-to-Speech. Detailed algorithms for each module were developed in this study. A Python-based prototype program was developed to verify the iBISDS framework and algorithms. The preliminary results indicated that the iBISDS framework is valid for recognizing natural language speech queries, extracting the target building information, and generating the corresponding speech responses. The iBISDS enables a machine to use speech natural language to respond to a user's speech query. The framework is just the start of iBISDS, and it currently has some limitations. To provide a more intelligent SDS for BIM, deep learning methods and ontology will be implemented in future research. Also, the iBISDS framework provides a basic architecture for developing an SDS for other research areas, such as construction safety. For example, an SDS for Occupational Safety and Health Administration (OSHA) standards can provide spoken safety instructions for on-site construction laborers via speech queries. It is expected that the iBISDS framework will lead to further adoption of conversational AI technologies in the AECO industry.

References

Eastman, C., Fisher, D., Lafue, G., Lividini, J., Stoker, D., Yessios, C., 1974. An Outline of the Building Description System. Research Report No. 50.

Isyanto, H., Arifin, A.S., Suryanegara, M., 2020. Design and Implementation of IoT-Based Smart Home Voice Commands for disabled people using Google Assistant, in: Proceeding - ICoSTA 2020: 2020 International Conference on Smart Technology and Applications: Empowering Industrial IoT by Implementing Green Technology for Sustainable Development. Institute of Electrical and Electronics Engineers Inc. https://doi.org/10.1109/ICoSTA48221.2020.1570613925

Joo, Y.S., Bae, H., Kim, Y.I., Cho, H.Y., Kang, H.G., 2020. Effective Emotion Transplantation in an End-to-End Text-to-Speech System. IEEE Access 8, 161713–161719. https://doi.org/10.1109/ACCESS.2020.3021758

Jucks, R., Linnemann, G.A., Brummernhenrich, B., 2018. Student Evaluations of a (Rude) Spoken Dialogue System Insights from an Experimental Study. Adv. Human-Computer Interact.

Kajinami, K., Nishimura, R., Kitaoka, N., 2018. Construction of dialog database for development of spoken dialog breakdown detection methods, in: ICAICTA 2018 - 5th International Conference on Advanced Informatics: Concepts Theory and Applications. Institute of Electrical and Electronics Engineers Inc., pp.91–95. https://doi.org/10.1109/ICAICTA.2018.8541273

Karan, E.P., Irizarry, J., Haymaker, J., 2016. BIM and GIS Integration and Interoperability Based on Semantic Web Technology. J. Comput. Civ. Eng. 30, 04015043-1-04015043–11. https://doi.org/10.1061/(asce)cp.1943-5487.0000519

Kepuska, V., Bohouta, G., 2018. Next-generation of virtual personal assistants (Microsoft Cortana, Apple Siri, Amazon Alexa and Google Home), in: 2018 IEEE 8th Annual Computing and Communication Workshop and Conference, CCWC 2018. Institute of Electrical and Electronics Engineers Inc., pp.99–103. https://doi.org/10.1109/CCWC.2018.8301638

Kobayashi, Y., Yoshida, T., Iwata, K., Fujimura, H., Akamine, M., 2019. Out-of-Domain Slot Value Detection for Spoken Dialogue Systems with Context Information, in: 2018 IEEE Spoken Language Technology Workshop, SLT 2018 - Proceedings. Institute of Electrical and Electronics Engineers Inc., pp.854–861. https://doi.org/10.1109/SLT.2018.8639671

Lin, J., Hu, Z., Zhang, J., Yu, F., 2016. A Natural-Language-Based Approach to Intelligent Data Retrieval and Representation for Cloud BIM. Comput. Civ. Infrastruct. Eng. 31, 18–33. https://doi.org/10.1111/mice.12151

Liu, H., Lu, M., Al-Hussein, M., 2016. Ontology-based semantic approach for construction-oriented quantity take-off from BIM models in the light-frame building industry. Adv. Eng. Informatics 30, 190–207. https://doi.org/10.1016/j.aei.2016.03.001

Packowski, S., Lakhana, A., 2017. Using IBM Watson Cloud Services to Build Natural Language Processing Solutions to Leverage Chat Tools, in: Proceedings of the 27th Annual International Conference on Computer Science and Software Engineering, CASCON '17. IBM Corp., USA, pp.211–218.

Palconit, M.G.B., Formentera, A.L., Aying, R.J., Dianon, K.J.A., Tadle, J.B., Dadios, E.P., 2019. Speech Activation for Internet of Things Security System in Public Utility Vehicles and Taxicabs, in: 2019 IEEE 11th International Conference on Humanoid, Nanotechnology, Information Technology, Communication and Control, Environment, and Management, HNICEM 2019. Institute of Electrical and Electronics Engineers Inc. https://doi.org/10.1109/HNICEM48295.2019.9073370

Park, Y., Kang, S., 2019. Natural Language Generation Using Dependency Tree Decoding for Spoken Dialog Systems. IEEE Access 7, 7250–7258. https://doi.org/10.1109/ACCESS.2018.2889556

Ralston, K., Chen, Y., Isah, H., Zulkernine, F., 2019. A voice interactive multilingual student support system using IBM watson, in: Proceedings - 18th IEEE International Conference on Machine Learning and Applications, ICMLA 2019. Institute of Electrical and Electronics Engineers Inc., pp.1924–1929. https://doi.org/10.1109/ICMLA.2019.00309

Sacks, R., Eastman, C.M., Teicholz, P.M., Lee, G., 2018. BIM handbook : a guide to building information modeling for owners, designers, engineers, contractors, and facility managers, Third edit. ed. John Wiley & Sons, Inc., Hoboken, New Jersey.

Sun, G., Zhang, Y., Weiss, R.J., Cao, Y., Zen, H., Rosenberg, A., Ramabhadran, B., Wu, Y., 2020. Generating Diverse and Natural Text-to-Speech Samples Using a Quantized Fine-Grained VAE and Autoregressive Prosody Prior, in: ICASSP, IEEE International Conference on Acoustics, Speech and Signal Processing - Proceedings. Institute of Electrical and Electronics Engineers Inc., pp.6699–6703. https://doi.org/10.1109/ICASSP40776.2020.9053436

Wang, H.-H., Boukamp, F., Elghamrawy, T., 2011. Ontology-Based Approach to Context Representation and Reasoning for Managing Context-Sensitive Construction Information. J. Comput. Civ. Eng. 25, 331–346. https://doi.org/10.1061/(ASCE)CP.1943-5487.0000094

Wang, N., Issa, R.R.A., 2020a. Ontology-Based Integration of BIM and GIS for Indoor Routing, in: Construction Research Congress 2020. Tempe, AZ.

Wang, N., Issa, R.R.A., 2020b. Natural Language Generation from Building Information Models for Intelligent NLP-based Information Extraction, in: Ungureanu, L.C., Hartmann, T. (Eds.), EG-ICE 2020 Workshop on Intelligent Computing in Engineering. Universitätsverlag der TU Berlin, Berlin, pp.275–284. https://doi.org/10.14279/depositonce-9977

Wen, T.H., Young, S., 2020. Recurrent neural network language generation for spoken dialogue systems. Comput. Speech Lang. 63, 101017. https://doi.org/10.1016/j.csl.2019.06.008

Yamamoto, K., Tamagawa, A., Nakagawa, S., 2019. Evaluation of real robot agent interface for spoken dialogue system, in: 2019 IEEE 8th Global Conference on Consumer Electronics, GCCE 2019. Institute of Electrical and Electronics Engineers Inc., pp.694–695. https://doi.org/10.1109/GCCE46687.2019.9015424

Zhang, L., Issa, R.R.A., 2013. Ontology-Based Partial Building Information Model Extraction. J. Comput. Civ. Eng. 27, 576–584. https://doi.org/10.1061/(asce)cp.1943-5487.0000277

A Design Recommender System: A Rule-based Approach to Exploit Natural Language Imprecision using Belief and Fuzzy Theories

Lucian-Constantin Ungureanu
Technische Universität Berlin, Germany
l.ungureanu@tu-berlin.de

Abstract. This paper proposes a framework to handle the natural language imprecision using belief and fuzzy theories. The goal is to provide a stepping-stone towards the creation of more flexible natural language interfaces between humans and computers to support design. The focus is on the natural language, as a result of verbal communication in design collaboration. Language imprecision in such setups is essential to design creativity, and the current design support systems do not accept such imprecise input. The proposed approach drafts a set of rules which are then implemented as a computer program to showcase the achieved behaviour. The achieved behaviour needs to be validated with designers, but it showcases how procedural power of the ambiguous and vague language can be harnessed to generate a population of design alternatives as recommendations.

1. Introduction

We can still argue that nowadays computers cannot compute with words. It is still the imprecise character of the natural language that poses significant computational challenges. Language imprecision is defined as a lack of clarity and precision (Zhang, 1998). On the one hand, it allows listeners to hypothesize about meaning, creating various interpretations. On the other hand, it allows speakers to cope with the lack of information and knowledge for a given situation. In design and engineering, language imprecision is seen as an integral part which enables creativity. Previous studies (Ungureanu & Hartmann, 2021) show that designers' language, when communicating design changes, is imprecise. In design studies, researchers highlighted the benefits of language imprecisions, such as helping creativity (Durrant et al., 2018; Wiegers et al., 2011) and allowing for interpretative flexibility (Glock, 2009). However, at the intersection between humans and computers, human language imprecision hinders the human-computer dynamic. Computers are seen as inflexible, passive and formal (Dossick & Neff, 2011), characteristics which require precise formalization of the input. To break this barrier, flexible human-computer interfaces must allow users to use imprecise language to interact with computers, especially in specialized environments such as design sessions where language imprecision is a key characteristic to a creative process.

Imprecise language expressions encapsulate sufficient information to provide recommendations (Jurafsky & Martin, 2013). To this end, imprecise language such as vague expressions, convey procedural meaning (Jucker et al., 2003). Recent interest on more natural interfaces between computers and humans resurrected the interest of creating systems that make sense of language vagueness when searching for products (Papenmeier et al., 2020), or which provide guidelines on how to interpret approximate numerical expressions (Lefort et al., 2017). Other than acknowledging its presence in design and engineering there is very little done in the direction of allowing the design support systems to harness the power of imprecise and vague language. One remarkable effort (Abualdenien & Borrmann, 2020) in this direction proposes a method to visualize vagueness in design models. While this focuses on information representation, to my knowledge, there is no previous research looking into how to incorporate ambiguous and vague input into a design model.

This paper proposes an approach using belief theory and fuzzy logic to support the creation of a design recommendation system using as input ambiguous and vague language expressions. The research presented in this paper focuses on a very small subset of possible problems related to language ambiguity and vagueness with the purpose of providing a precedent in the direction of handling imprecise input. This paper adopts a listener perspective, which is characterized by the following information flow: Statement ➔ Interpretation ➔ Action ➔ Modified Situation (Sowa, 1999). The research in this paper aims to covers aspects related to interpretation and action and their mathematical formalization. It proposes the creation of a set of rules that serve as possible routes of dealing with the ambiguity related to the attribute naming when communicating a change and vagueness related to the attribute value with the focus on continuous numerical attributes. Moreover, the paper adopts a design science research method with problem-centered initiation. This allowed to create a prototype implementation of the proposed approach, to evaluate it, to identify possible limitations, and propose future research directions based. The behavior achieved after the implementation of the proposed framework is showcased on a small theoretical parametric model of a room. The rest of the paper is structured as follows: next section present some more insight into language imprecision in design and computational approaches to handle it. Next section introduces the proposed approach, followed by the research methodology, implementation, and results. The final two sections of the paper discuss the implementation and the results and present the conclusions of the study.

2. Language imprecision in design and computational approaches

Language imprecision in design can take various forms. It is mainly related on how designers use words to covey their ideas. Some of the previous studies focused on designers' language and their use of metaphors and hedges (Christensen & Schunn, 2007, 2009), polysemy (Georgiev & Taura, 2014), slang and jargon (D'Souza & Dastmalchi, 2017; Kleinsmann & Valkenburg, 2008). In short, language imprecision can take various forms classified as fuzziness, uncertainty, vagueness, possibility, and probability (Raskin & Taylor, 2014). In spoken language, these correspond to various intentional commitments a speaker might make. In the communication between designers, especially when communicating design changes, it has been shown that ambiguity and vagueness are present (Ungureanu & Hartmann, 2021). To this end, a human-computer interface needs to be flexible enough to handle such cases of language ambiguity and vagueness.

Some of the approaches in the field of linguistics propose various strategies to deal with language ambiguity and vagueness. While the humans are wired to make sense of the imprecise input, information systems need precise information to work. When it comes to ambiguity, a common strategy is to identify the meaning of the word in context through disambiguation. Some of the state-of-the-art approaches in this direction are proposed by Pasini & Navigli (2020) and Wang et al. (2020). This solved half of the problem. Once the real meaning of the word is identified how to recommend something to the user? Considering the use of the word size, a disambiguation method might identify to which of the artefact attributes it is connected, such as in the case of a room to length, width, and height. Yet, it might not provide directions regarding which one of these parameters to change to reach the design change impact envisioned by the speaker. Language vagueness can also have multiple facets. In connection with design changes communication, vagueness is linked to communicating the extend of a change (Ungureanu & Hartmann, 2021). Examples of possible linguistic expressions are "a little bit bigger", "a little bit wider", "about" (Khan & Tunçer, 2019; Ungureanu & Hartmann, 2021; Wiegers et al., 2011). To handle language vagueness, Zadeh, (1996) proposed the use of fuzzy logic, terming this as computing with words. While this approach is far from being an automated one, it relies on the knowledge linked to the vague expressions used in the day-to-day conversations and allows computing using this knowledge formalized in the form of rules. It is one of the common approaches used in control systems. For instance, a rule like "*if(cold) then (Increase temperature)*" is a simple example of a rule in a control system using fuzzy logic. The closest to come to deal with language imprecision in design is (Lawson & Loke, 1997) who proposed the use of sliders to allow designers to manually vary attributes' values. In this paper, we proposed the use of belief theory to handle language ambiguity and the use of fuzzy logic to handle language vagueness. The approach we proposed in this paper is presented in the next section.

3. Proposed Approach

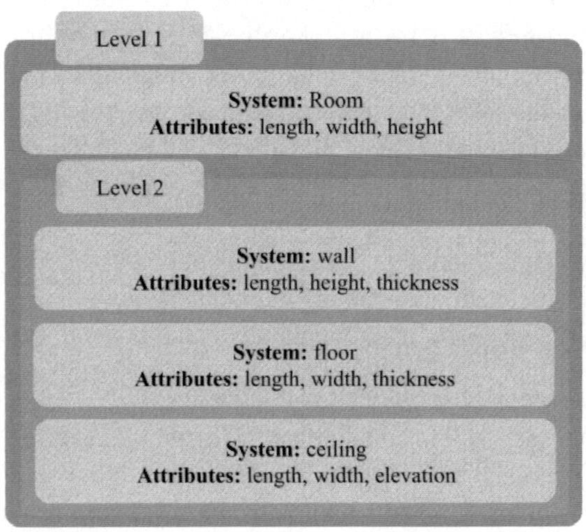

Figure 1: Systems Decomposition – The example of a simple rectangular room

In this paper, the perspective we embrace over the design is following the reasoning laid down by the systems-in-systems theory. Figure 1 showcases a very simple example of a rectangular room. A very first step within this approach is to establish the boundaries of the system. In this case, even if the room is usually part of a higher-level system such as a building, we see the room as the main system. This system can be decomposed further in smaller elements such as the ones shown at Level 2 (e.g., wall, floor, ceiling). At each level, no matter the decomposition granularity, a system has specific attributes driving its design. Another boundary related aspect we consider in this paper, is that our focus is on the numerical attributes associated with a system at a given level. We can represent this mathematically as $D(S) = \{A_i, i = 1 \le i \le n\}$ where D(S) is the design function of the system S, dependent on the set of numerical attributes $\{A_i\}$. Considering the example of our room, this formulation is exemplified as *D(Room) = {A_1: length, A_2: width, A_3: height}*. In the same way, the design function of the wall can be formulated as *D(wall) = {A_1: length, A_2: height, A_3: thickness}*. The design is developed as a succession of states $j = \overline{1, m}$, where j is the current state and j+1 a future possible state. In each state j an attribute A_i has a value v_{ij}. These values have a predefined range called the universe of discourse. The universe of discourse of a given attribute value can be mathematically represented as a bounded interval such as $v_{ij} \in [v_i^{min}, v_i^{max}]$. We can mathematically capture this logic as following:

$$D_j(S) = \{A_i = \{v_{ij} \in [v_i^{min}, v_i^{max}]\}, 1 \le i \le n\}$$

The transition of the design from current state $D_j(S)$ to a next state $D_{j+1}(S)$ is subject of a transformation operator and a goal G to be achieved (Eastman, 1969). If the goal G lacks a precise formulation the transformation is termed by Eastman (1969) as a ill-defined problem. Eastman (1969) did not considered the lack of precise formulation of the transformation operator. In this paper, we consider both aspects. The goal is to formulate an information processing pipeline to handle the cases when the definition of the goal and transformation operator lack precision. As mentioned in the introduction, we focus on the verbal communication of the designers, when communicating changes related to various parts of the design. Designers' communications include the natural language formulation of a specific transformation and the desired goal. In most of the cases, their communication lacks precision – ambiguous and vague linguistic expressions are used instead of precise formulations (Ungureanu & Hartmann, 2021). In this paper, we focus on the ambiguous communication of the ATTRIBUTE subjected to changes and vague communication of VALUE change of the attribute. A precise natural language formulation of a design change implies that a given ATTRIBUTE is named and the extent of the change (i.e., VALUE) are clearly communicated. An example, related to our example in Figure 1 will be "*increase the length of the room with 300mm.*" (E1) In information processing, a such precise formulation can be captured in the form of an IF-THEN rule.

Rule (1): Given the system S: IF (ATTRIBUTE in $\{A_i, i = 1 \le i \le n\}$ AND VALUE is PRECISE) THEN f(ATTRIBUTE, VALUE)

where, f() is a change function dependent on the communicated operation. Given the example, the function f() is an increase function indicated by the action word "*increase*" and the design state *j* function:

$$D_j(Room) = \{A_1: Length = v_{1j},\ A_2: width = v_{2j},\ A_3: height = v_{3j}\}$$

is transformed to the next *j+1* state as following.

$$D_{j+1}(Room) = \{A_1: Length\ is\ ATTRIBUTE = \{v_{1j+1} = v_{1j} + VALUE\},$$
$$A_2: width = \{v_{2j+1} = v_{2j}\},\ A_3: height = \{v_{3j+1} = v_{3j}\}\}$$

Ambiguity and vagueness are two natural language characteristics associated with language imprecision. The expression "*increase the size of the room*" (E2) is a frequent expression used by designers (Ungureanu & Hartmann, 2021). In this case, the ambiguity gives the listener the freedom to hypothesize about a combination of attributes which can be changed to increase the generic attribute *size*. We update Rule (1) to cover the case when the attribute is ambiguous using the belief theory.

Rule (2): Given the system S: IF (ATTRIBUTE not in $\{A_i, i = 1 \le i \le n\}$ AND VALUE is PRECISE) THEN $\binom{n}{k}\{f(Ai,\ VALUE),\ \beta_i\}$, where $\sum_{i-1}^{n} \beta_i \le 1$

β_i called degree of belief, and $\binom{n}{k}$ denote the k-combinations of the n attributes with k taking values from 1 to n. The sum of all the assigned degrees of believe need to be smaller or equal to 1 (Yang et al., 2006). For the room example, the rule (2) can be detailed as following:

Rule (2): Given the system S: IF (**size** not in $\{A_i, i = 1 \le i \le n\ \}$ AND VALUE is PRECISE) THEN

$$\binom{n}{k}\begin{Bmatrix} A1: length\ is\ ATTRIBUTE = \{v1j + 1 = v1j + VALUE\}, \beta_1 = 0.45 \\ A2: width\ is\ ATTRIBUTE = \{v2j + 1 = v2j + VALUE\}, \beta_2 = 0.45 \\ A3: height\ is\ ATTRIBUTE = \{v3j + 1 = v3j + VALUE\}, \beta_3 = 0.1 \end{Bmatrix}$$

Considering the attribute space of the room example, the solution space provided by the rule (2) is $\binom{3}{1} + \binom{3}{2} + \binom{3}{3} = 7$ consisting of solutions taking individually or combinations of each parameter in the attribute space. The assignment $\beta_1 = 0.45$ means that there is *45%* belief that the attribute A_1*:length* is the attribute to be increased. Considering the low degree of belief assigned to $\beta_3 = 0.1$ this can be argued from the perspective of the domain knowledge. Usually, the height of a room is not changed individually; in most of the cases the designer will change the height of the entire floor, and consequently the height of all the rooms on the floor.

We can take further the expression (E2) and, besides ambiguity, we can add the expression "*a little bit*" as a vague indicator of the extent of the change. We get the expression "*increase a little bit the size of the room*" (E3). As shown by the previous research (Khan & Tunçer, 2019;

Ungureanu & Hartmann, 2021; Wiegers et al., 2011) designers use qualitative quantifiers to communicate the extend of a change. To handle this case of linguistic imprecision we propose the use of fuzzy logic. Thus, we consider each attribute A_i as a linguistic variable, rather than a numerical variable. In fuzzy logic, a linguistic variable is defined as:

$$Linguistic\ variable\ =\ \langle x, T(x), U, G, M\rangle$$

where: x is the variable name, T(x) is a set of terms, U is the universe of discourse, G a set of syntactic rules, and M a set of semantic rules. Figure 2 exemplify all the elements of a linguistic variable and provides an example of fuzzification. A linguistic variable such as *Length* can be communicated through linguistic syntax using a set of soft linguistic terms. This set of terms, through semantic rules are represented as fuzzy subsets distributed over the universe of discourse of the linguistic variable using some membership functions. Using the fuzzy subsets, we can represent the crisp number 3 as a fuzzy number [0.66, 0.34, 0.00].

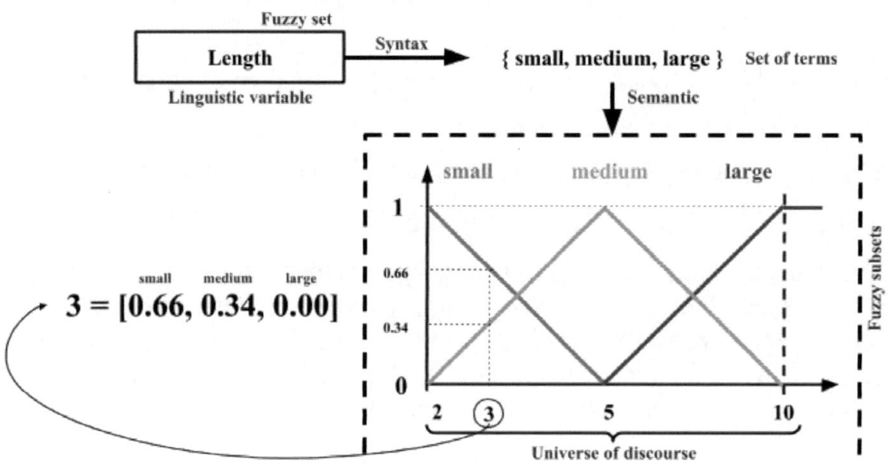

Figure 2: Linguistic variable; example fuzzification length = 3

Table 1: Knowledge base matrix for rules creation

Current value \ Input	Increase			Decrease		
	a little bit bigger	bigger	much bigger	a little bit smaller	smaller	much smaller
Small (S)	ALBB	B	MB	ALBS	S	MS
Medium (M)	ALBB	B	MB	ALBS	S	MS
Large (L)	ALBB	B	MB	ALBS	S	MS

In our case, the universe of discourse for an attribute, usually defined by designers, takes values between [min, max]. Different membership functions can be defined to indicate, based on domain and situational knowledge, the membership of various values to each term from the set. The simplest function which can be defined is the triangular one (Figure 2). We adopt this approach for the fuzzification of the attribute's values. Each attribute will have a universe of discourse between minimum and maximum values assigned by designers with a certain degree of membership to a linguistic term. Table 1 presents a proposed knowledge base to build the set of rules to be used for inference. For example, a rule which can be created based on Table 1 is: IF (Current value is Small) AND (input is "*a little bit bigger*") THEN output is ALBB. The membership functions are assumed as trapezoidal functions following the percentages distributions indicated in Figure 3. Moreover, Figure 3 shows how the inference is done based on this rule. The output is represented by the grey area under the "*a little bigger*" membership function. The final step is to define a strategy for the defuzzification. A common approach is to consider the centre of gravity of the grey area, approach adopted in this paper.

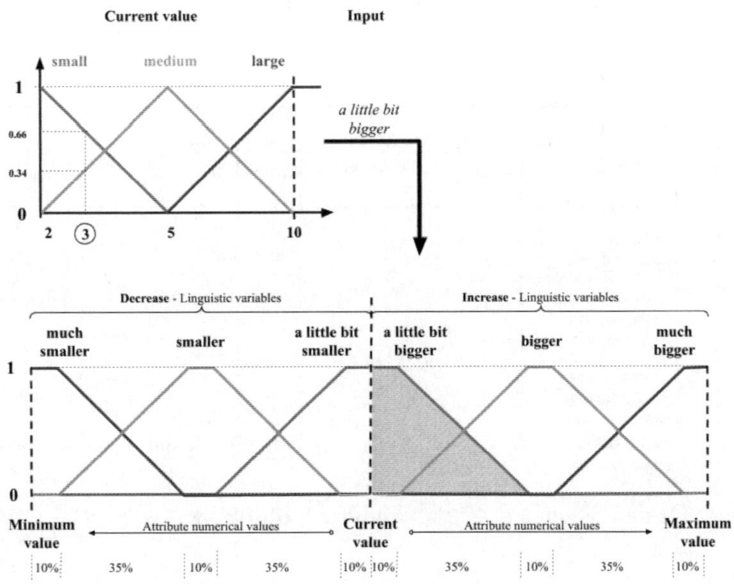

Figure 3: Example inference

To this end, rules (1) and (2) can be updated to reflect the cases when the VALUE is imprecisely communicated by the user.

Rule (3): Given the system S: **IF** (ATTRIBUTE in $\{A_i, 1 \leq i \leq n\}$ **AND** VALUE is not PRECISE) **THEN** f(ATTRIBUTE, g(VALUE))

Rule (4): Given the system S: **IF** (ATTRIBUTE not in $\{A_i, 1 \leq i \leq n\}$ **AND** VALUE is not PRECISE) **THEN** $\binom{n}{k}\{f(Ai, g(VALUE)), \beta_i\}$, where $\sum_{i=1}^{n} \beta_i \leq 1$

where g(VALUE) represents the fuzzy function.

4. Research Methodology

This paper employs a design science research method following the framework proposed by Peffers et al., (2007). Figure 4 presents the problem-centered research method which consists of five main components. The main objective of the current paper is to develop a prototype recommender system that exploits the imprecise input provided by users and provides as output various design alternatives. Figure 5 presents the architecture adopted for the envisioned voice interface. It takes the form of a voice-based command system making use of the state-of-the-art pipeline for automatic speech recognition and natural language processing provided by Amazon Alexa. The output from Alexa represents the content of a set of slots. These slots, together with the intent are predefined for this implementation via Alexa Developer console. The slots represent the semantic elements related to {ATTRIBUTE, VALUE}, where ATTRIBUTE can be any of the attributes of the parametric model presented in Figure 6. As parametric modeling tool, the proposed implementation is using Dynamo BIM, a design automation and parametric modeling tool. The implementation of the proposed approach is made as a view extension for Dynamo, programmed using C# and deployed as a *.dll class library. DynAlexa starts a Http server and based on user query to an Alexa device it receives an Alexa post request input as an intent with its slots. The intent serves to distinguish the conditional cases, and the content of the slots are sent further for processing using the implementation of the proposed approach. The four generic rules of the proposed approach were coded in this implementation using FLS C# library.

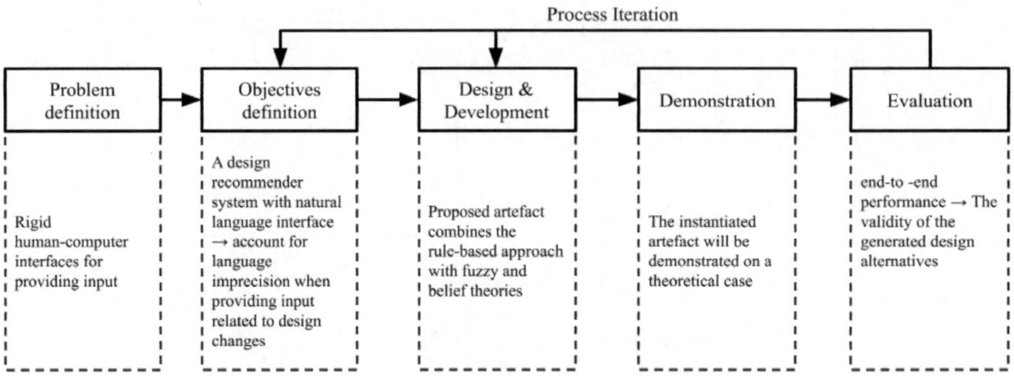

Figure 4: Design Science Research Method with Problem-Centered Initiation

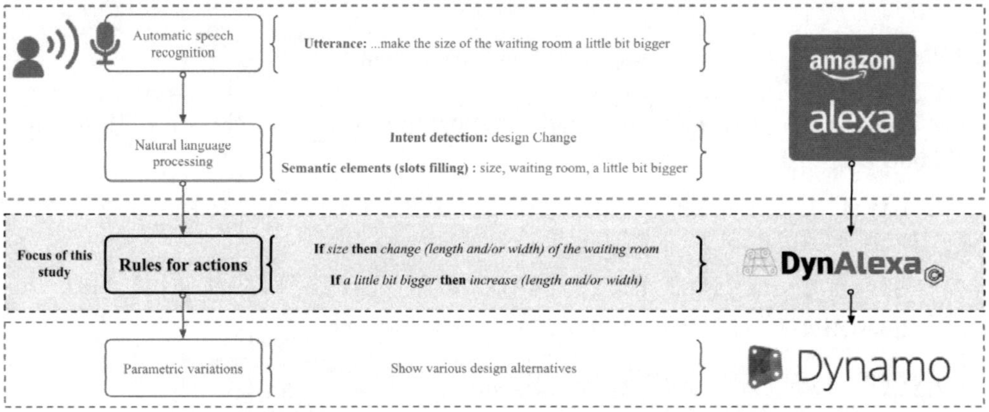

Figure 5: Architecture of the envisioned system

4. Implementation and results

The implementation of the proposed framework led to a first working prototype which allow the user to use imprecise language to input changes in a parametric model. The end-to-end verification highlighted that the created prototype behaves as expected, although the implementation itself helped identify several areas which need further attention from the research community. The implementation made use of a simple parametric model of a room shown in Figure 6. The parametric model has three attributes defined as controlling (input)parameters, namely width, length, and height. The universe of discourse of each parameter is present in Figure 6. The degrees of belief (DoBs) for each input parameter were generically defined in advanced for the cases when the user communicate an ambiguous attribute such as size as shown in the same figure.

For the cases when an ambiguous attribute is named by the user in an utterance such as "*increase the size of the room*", the user received a set of combinations sorted in descending order based on the general degree of belief (gDoB) calculated for each possible combination as the average of the degrees of belief (DoBs) of the parameters part of the combination. The user has the possibility to click on any of the provided combinations and to visualise in real time how the model is changed.

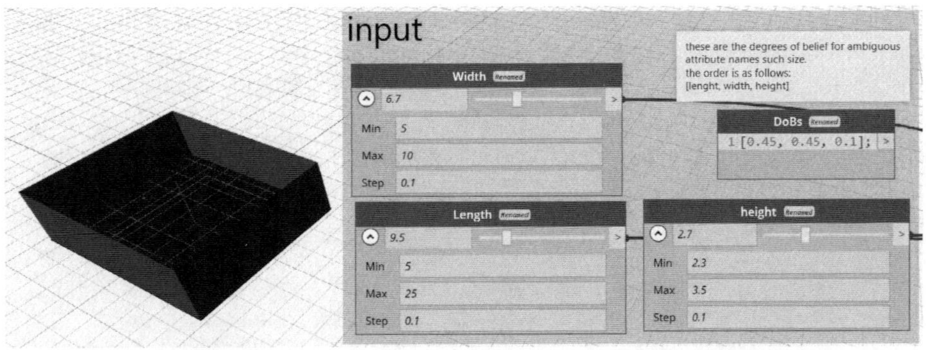

Figure 6: The simple parametric model of a room used for the implementation

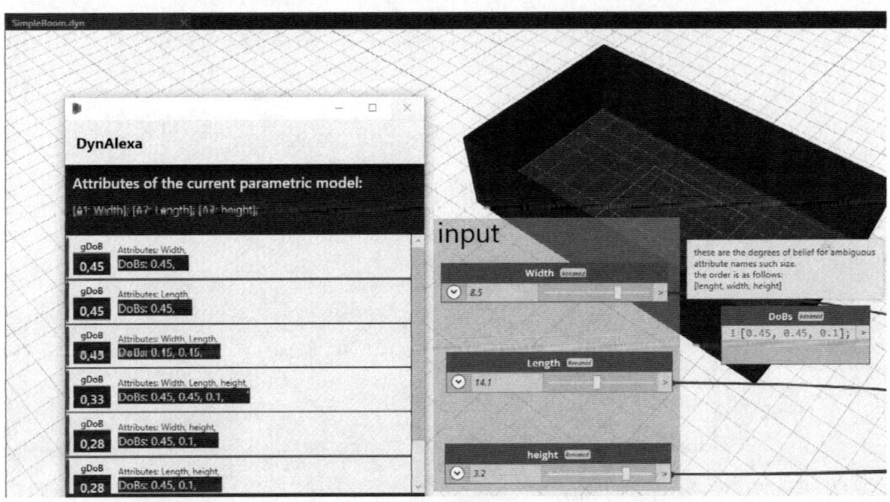

Figure 7: Generated list of design options based on ambiguous attribute naming

Table 2: Results of Fuzzy Logic implementation when the user provides vague qualifiers. The values after each attribute are the [min, max] values. The values after each value assigned to a vague qualifier represent the increase (+) and the decrease (-) relative to the initial value

Attribute	Initial (current) value	Increase			Decrease		
		A little bit bigger	Bigger	Much bigger	A little bit smaller	Smaller	Much smaller
Length [5, 25]	9.5m	11.9 (+2.4)	17.25 (+7.75)	22.6 (+13.1)	8.8 (-0.7)	7.25(-2.25)	5.7 (-3.8)
Width [5,10]	6.7m	7.2 (+0.5)	8.35 (+1.65)	9.5 (+2.8)	6.4 (-0.3)	5.85 (-0.85)	5.2 (-1.5)
Height [2.3, 3.5]	2.7m	2.8 (+0.1)	3.1 (+0.4)	3.4(+0.7)	2.6 (-0.1)	2.5 (-0.2)	2.4 (-0.3)

The results of the fuzzy logic implementation are shown in Table 2. As shown in Figure 3, the fuzzification of the attribute value is made using triangular membership functions, and the defuzzification of the vague qualifiers is made using trapezoidal membership function. Figure 8 shows an example of how the values in the Table 2 were calculated. The trapezoidal functions are defined as ration of the intervals [min, current value] and [current value, max], depending on the operation. If the current value is far away from the min/max values, rate of increase/decrease will be quite significant. If the current value is close to the min/max values, then the rate of increase/decrease will be small. This behaviour is visible in Table 2, and it is because the membership functions are defined using percentages of the remaining intervals from min/max to the current value. This can be seen in the values withing the brackets. Increasing a little bit the length from 9.5m produces an increase of +2.4m. Increasing a little bit the height from 2.7m produces an increase of only +0.1m.

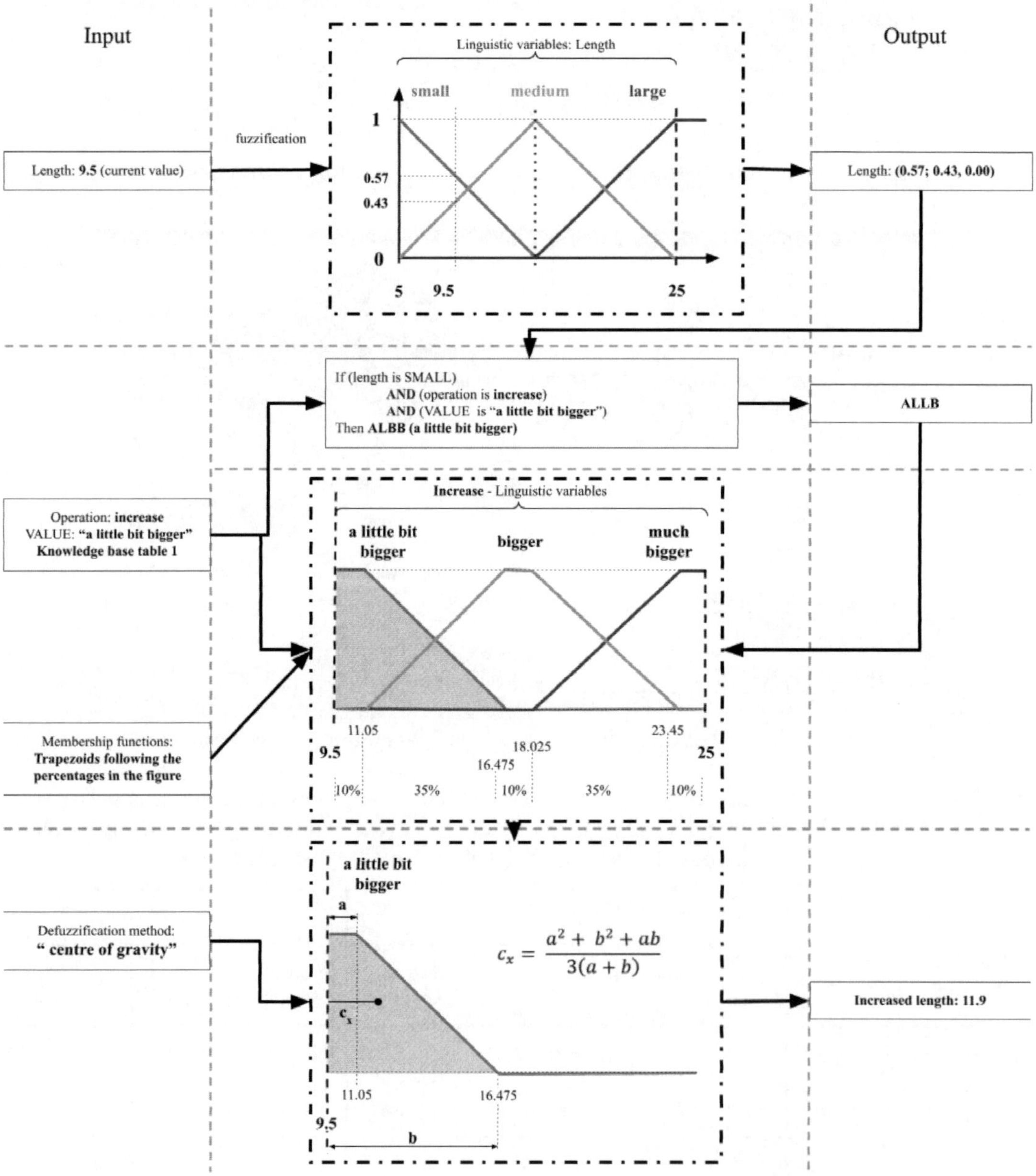

Figure 8: Example showing the steps followed to "***increase***" "***a little bit***" the "***length***" from 9.5m

5. Discussions and Conclusions

Current paper proposes an approach based on belief theory and fuzzy logic to handle the language imprecise input from the user when communicating design changes. The proposed approach can be implemented on any voice-based or text-based user interfaces with the purpose of harnessing imprecise language to provide design recommendations. The implementation showcases a promising direction which allows the user to explore various scenarios when ambiguously communicating the name of an attribute. Moreover, the system allows the users to use vague qualifiers to indicate the extend of a change. The degrees of belief help sort the various scenarios. The fuzzy logic setup allows to convert the vague qualifier into numerical values. The implementation also highlights certain areas for future research.

First and foremost, the entire process needs to be supported by a knowledge base. A parametric model might have various attributes available associated with various parts of the design, named length, width, height. A knowledge base will allow for inferences, so that the system do not confuses for example the length of the bedroom with the length of the living room. Regarding the degrees of belief, future research needs to establish strategies regarding their definition. The approach adopted in this paper to manually define them is tedious and time consuming. When a user refers to the size of a room, to what extend they refer to length, width, or height? Maybe in this direction one might have to think of developing a rule-based system based on domain knowledge. Another option can be a system that learns based on users' preferences. Regarding the fuzzy logic approach, one might need to define the level of granularity of a such system when it comes to the fuzzification and defuzzification in equal measure. In this paper we used a set of three linguistic sets for the input variable, and a set of another three linguistic sets for the defuzzification of the operations. Is this enough or does it require a higher level of granularity? Moreover, when it comes to the defuzzification, is it enough to return a single value based on a method such as centre of gravity or is it better to output a population of values? In addition, the current implementation contains only a small number of rules for a limited number of linguistic variables. Increasing the number of linguistic variables will considerably increase the number of rules needed to be implemented. Smart approaches are needed to identify and handle in a unique manner similar linguistic variable such as *larger* versus *bigger*. The same with ambiguous references to attributes. Our assumption is that computing similarities between various words might serve as an automated approach to assign degrees of belief and to link a generic attribute name to one linked to an artefact. Future research needs to also be done to expand the framework for other types of attributes such as non-numerical ones (e.g. categorical, shape attributes).

While little has been done in this direction, the current paper serves as a steppingstone in the direction of allowing the users to imprecisely provide input to computer. The framework allows for the creation of a design support system that allows designers to get real-time feedback on their design moves. In this direction, research also need to be done to identify whether this approach is beneficial for the design process. To close, the proposed system has the potential to reduce computers inflexibility and allow designers to actively incorporate them in the design process.

References

Abualdenien, J., & Borrmann, A. (2020). Vagueness visualization in building models across different design stages. Advanced Engineering Informatics, 45(April), 101107. https://doi.org/10.1016/j.aei.2020.101107

Christensen, B. T., & Schunn, C. D. (2007). The relationship of analogical distance to analogical function and preinventive structure: The case of engineering design. Memory and Cognition, 35(1), 29–38. https://doi.org/10.3758/BF03195939

Christensen, B. T., & Schunn, C. D. (2009). 'Putting blinkers on a blind man' Providing cognitive support for creative processes with environmental cues. Christensen, B. T. & Schunn, C. D. Tools for Innovation, 48–74.

D'Souza, N., & Dastmalchi, M. (2017). "Comfy" cars for the "awesomely humble": Exploring slang and jargons in a cross-cultural design process. Analysing Design Thinking: Studies of Cross-Cultural Co-Creation, 1993, 311–330. https://doi.org/10.1201/9781315208169

Dossick, C. S., & Neff, G. (2011). Messy talk and clean technology: communication, problem-solving and collaboration using Building Information Modelling. The Engineering Project Organization Journal, 1(2), 83–93.

Durrant, A. C., Kirk, D. S., Moncur, W., Orzech, K. M., Taylor, R., & Pisanty, D. T. (2018). Rich pictures for stakeholder dialogue: A polyphonic picture book. Design Studies, 56, 122–148.

Eastman, C. (1969). Cognitive processes and ill-defined problems: A case study from design. International Joint Conference on Artificial Intelligence: IJCAI, January 1969, 669–690.

Georgiev, G., & Taura, T. (2014). Polysemy in Design Review Conversations. Design Thinking Research Symposium, 2003, 1–19. http://docs.lib.purdue.edu/dtrs/2014/Identity/2

Glock, F. (2009). Aspects of language use in design conversation. CoDesign, 5(1), 5–19.

Jucker, A. H., Smith, S. W., & Lüdge, T. (2003). Interactive aspects of vagueness in conversation. Journal of Pragmatics, 35(12), 1737–1769. https://doi.org/10.1016/S0378-2166(02)00188-1

Jurafsky, D., & Martin, J. H. (2013). Speech and language processing: pearson new international edition. Pearson.

Khan, S., & Tunçer, B. (2019). Speech analysis for conceptual CAD modeling using multi-modal interfaces: An investigation into Architects' and Engineers' speech preferences. AI EDAM, 1–14.

Kleinsmann, M., & Valkenburg, R. (2008). Barriers and enablers for creating shared understanding in co-design projects. Design Studies, 29(4), 369–386.

Lawson, B., & Loke, S. M. (1997). Computers, words and pictures. Design Studies, 18(2), 171–183.

Lefort, S., Zibetti, E., Lesot, M. J., Detyniecki, M., & Tijus, C. (2017). Dimensions for automatic interpretation of approximate numerical expressions: An empirical study. International Conference on Intelligent User Interfaces, Proceedings IUI, 107–117. https://doi.org/10.1145/3025171.3025174

Papenmeier, A., Sliwa, A., Kern, D., Hienert, D., Aker, A., & Fuhr, N. (2020). 'A modern up-to-date laptop' - vagueness in natural language Queries for Product Search. ArXiv, 2077–2089.

Pasini, T., & Navigli, R. (2020). Train-O-Matic: Supervised Word Sense Disambiguation with no (manual) effort. Artificial Intelligence, 279, 103215. https://doi.org/10.1016/j.artint.2019.103215

Peffers, K., Tuunanen, T., Rothenberger, M. A., & Chatterjee, S. (2007). A design science research methodology for information systems research. Journal of Management Information Systems, 24(3), 45–77. https://doi.org/10.2753/MIS0742-1222240302

Raskin, V., & Taylor, J. M. (2014). Fuzziness, Uncertainty, Vagueness, Possibility, and Probability in Natural Language. 2014 IEEE Conference on Norbert Wiener in the 21st Century (21CW), 1–6.

Sowa, J. (1999). Knowledge representation: logical, philosophical and computational foundationsNo Title. Brooks/Cole Publishing Co.

Ungureanu, L., & Hartmann, T. (2021). Analysing frequent natural language expressions from design conversations. Design Studies, 72, 100987. https://doi.org/10.1016/j.destud.2020.100987

Wang, Y., Wang, M., & Fujita, H. (2020). Word Sense Disambiguation: A comprehensive knowledge exploitation framework. Knowledge-Based Systems, 190, 105030. https://doi.org/10.1016/j.knosys.2019.105030

Wiegers, T., Langeveld, L., & Vergeest, J. (2011). Shape language: How people describe shapes and shape operations. Design Studies, 32(4), 333–347.

Yang, J. B., Liu, J., Wang, J., Sii, H. S., & Wang, H. W. (2006). Belief rule-base inference methodology using the evidential reasoning approach - RIMER. IEEE Transactions on Systems, Man, and Cybernetics Part A:Systems and Humans, 36(2), 266–285. https://doi.org/10.1109/TSMCA.2005.851270

Zadeh, L. A. (1996). Fuzzy logic = computing with words. IEEE Transactions on Fuzzy Systems, 4(2), 103–111. https://doi.org/10.1109/91.493904

Zhang, Q. (1998). Fuzziness-vagueness-generality-ambiguity. *Journal of Pragmatics*, *29*(1), 13–31.

Towards the Adoption of Vision Intelligence for Construction Safety: Grounded Theory Methodology based Safety Regulations Analysis

Numan Khan, Muhmmad Khan, Seungwon Cho and Chansik Park*
Chung Ang University, Seoul, South Korea
cpark@cau.ac.kr

Abstract. The construction safety rules play a vital role in mitigating accidents and fatalities at the construction site. Many researchers are currently devoted to monitoring the rule compliance using vision intelligence-based approaches; however, such systems are still not yet mature to be applied in construction job sites. A single autonomous source's job site safety control is a non-trivial task that needs a detailed analysis of safety rules for a compact vision intelligence-based system development. This paper proposes Grounded Theory Methodology (GTM) to systematically classify the safety rules for implementation using vision intelligence technology. The rules are classified into four groups based on the open coding, axial coding, and selective coding approach: (1) Before Work, (2) With Intervals, (3) After Work (4) During Work. The proposed GTM based model linked further with the scene capturing sources such as single scene capturing through smartphones for the rules required: (a) before work and after work, (b) periodic scene capturing using robots, and (c) drones for the rules needed with intervals and (d) CCTVs for the safety rules to continuous monitoring of safety.

1. Introduction

The construction industry is infamous due to the adverse situation of accidents and fatalities happening in the construction job sites. These enormous accidents have made the construction industry one of the most unsafe sectors (Nath, Behzadan and Paal, 2020). The Bureau of Labor Statistics (BLS) in 2017–18 reported 5,250 fatal work injuries, recorded a relative increase of 2 percent concerning the data reported in 2017, (BLS, 2019). The non-fatal injuries also remained at the peak; for instance, the non-fatal accidents recorded during 2017 were 79810, accounting for 9% of the total non-fatal accidents in construction (BLS, 2017). These accidents are expensive and can be prevented by taking excellent safety measures (Park, Lee and Khan, 2020). Numerous safety policy procedures and comprehensive safety regulations have been established worldwide to enhance construction safety and prevent accidents (Fang *et al.*, 2019). The developed safety policies can minimize the alarming statistics mentioned earlier by implementing best safety practices at construction sites.

Construction personnel must understand and access various best practices and safety rules to manage safety and health at the job site (Khan *et al.*, 2019). However, getting knowledge of everything, finding the proper safety rules, and then manually implementing them is tedious and not practical (Park, Lee and Khan, 2020). Thus, construction industry professionals have automatically devoted significant attention to monitoring safety rule compliance using vision intelligence-based approaches. However, the previous efforts to strengthen the safety rules monitoring in the construction job site are limited to specific hazards and not yet mature to apply for life-threatening situations. Also, controlling the entire job site using a single source simultaneously is not practical due to the huge number of participants in a large area and dynamic nature of construction site. Therefore, a GTM based analysis technique is used to develop a structured classification of safety rules for a compact vision intelligence-based system development for construction safety. The Occupational Safety and Health Administration (OSHA) rules are selected as a domain scope of this research. An error and trial-based criteria has been established by authors and experts to extract relevant safety rules from OSHA database. The safety rules are coded using open coding, axial coding and selective codes advised in GTM. The classified into four groups based on the open coding, axial coding, and selective coding approach: (1) Before Work, (2) With Intervals, (3) After Work (4) During Work. This structured classification are then linked with the scene capturing sources such as single scene capturing through smart phones for the rules required before work start and after work finish, periodic scene capturing using robots and drones for the rules required with intervals, and CCTVs for the safety rules required for continuous monitoring. The proposed classification framework is expected to pave the road for the prospect researchers and practitioners adopting vision intelligence-based monitoring systems, promote the bottom-up reporting approach, and enable the relevant safety rules compliance checking at right time.

Computer vision has attracted substantial attention because of the progress made in specific associated parameters with this domain, such as advances in high-definition cameras, convenient accessibility of the internet with excellent speed, developments in augmented storage for databases. As a result, computer vision-based methods have become prevalent for productivity analysis(Roberts and Golparvar-Fard, 2019), project progress monitoring (Golparvar-Fard, Peña-Mora and Savarese, 2015), and safety monitoring (Ding *et al.*, 2018; Fang *et al.*, 2018, 2019; Mneymneh, Abbas and Khoury, 2018; Wang *et al.*, 2019a). Recent research in computer vision-based construction safety monitoring has focused on developing a simple inspection system to detect safety preventive measures. For instance, hard hats detection (Mneymneh, Abbas and Khoury, 2018), safety harness recognition for fall hazards (Fang *et al.*, 2018), proximity detection (Wang *et al.*, 2019b), unsafe behavior detection in traversing structural members such as beams to make shortcuts (Fang *et al.*, 2019). However, the computer vision approach is still rapidly growing due to its cost-effectiveness, ease, and reliability.

2. Applications of Construction Safety Regulations

Construction best practices and regulations provide lessons learned from the previous work (Khan *et al.*, 2019) and have a critical impact in establishing planning, design development, and work execution on job sites (He *et al.*, 2016). The construction task execution requires resources such as workers, materials, tools, and equipment. The interaction of these resources could cause hazards, and the best way might be the application of safety rules to control these hazards at the construction site (Zhang *et al.*, 2013). Even though construction industry professionals and government agencies have made the efforts, the current safety rule compliance still relies on manually auditing and supervising approaches that are inefficient and prone to error (Park, Lee and Khan, 2020). However, the recent trend of design for safety in Building Information Modelling (BIM) (Kasirossafar and Shahbodaghlou, 2013; Zhang *et al.*, 2013; Hongling *et al.*, 2016; Khan *et al.*, 2020), and computer vision-based safety monitoring (Fang *et al.*, 2018, 2019, 2020; Wu and Zhao, 2018) have attracted the interests of many researchers, however, yet in the elementary stages and need more attention for practical application in the construction industry.

3. Need for Construction Safety Rules Classification

There have been tremendous advancements in translating the natural language-based rules to make the machines understand binary languages (Kim *et al.*, 2019). However, due to the enormous number of safety regulations and the inherited complexities with them, finding and implementing the appropriate contents tends to be difficult (Hussain *et al.*, 2017). Previous computer vision-based safety monitoring efforts also revealed that vision-based research is limited to a few specific safety rule compliances. Thus, require comprehensive classification by investigating risk patterns to develop compact vision-based safety monitoring systems (Park, Lee and Khan, 2020). Moreover, controlling the overwhelming number of hazards in a huge job site needs multiple modes and image logistic devices for monitoring and controlling. These challenges require expert understanding and well-structured classification of a safety rule that can be acquired in computer vision-based safety monitoring. Therefore, this study focused on the OSHA regulations to validate the proposed concepts.

4. Methodology and Framework

Establishing safety regulation classification criteria and mechanisms for the real-time provision of rules to safety supervisors is an essential part of safety management.

Table 1: Ground Theory Methodology analysis style

Steps	Tasks
1. Set the review scope	• Research domain definition
2. Research contribution sources selection	• Construction safety rules from OSHA database
3. Keyword selection	• Criterion identification from search term
4. Screening process	• Auto data extraction from OSHA web using parsing technique. • Manually data cleaning and filtering
5. Eligibility	• Using inclusion\exclusion criteria for in-depth analysis
6. Structure and analyze the code	• Axial, open, and selective coding

5. Occupational Safety and Health Administration (OSHA) Rules Analysis

Motivated by the rapid development of industries in the 1970s, OSHA was established to enhance construction health and safety in 1971. Since then, the rate of reported serious workplace injuries (1972-2009) has significantly dropped from 11 out of 100 workers to 3.6 out of 100 workers (OSHA, 2009). OSHA collected and analyzed many accident cases, thereby creating an expert knowledge database. Based on that data, substantial amendments have been made to alleviate the past policies for modern industry compliance. The OSHA regulations for construction are developed under section 107 of the contract work hours and safety standards act, comprise a separate section of 27 subparts (OSHA, 2020).

Table 2: Analysis of OSHA safety Regulations

<table>
<tr><th>Classification</th><th>Type</th><th>Rules</th><th>Percentage</th><th colspan="4"></th></tr>
<tr><td rowspan="5">Application of Image recognition technology</td><td>Procurement</td><td>302</td><td>11.10%</td><td colspan="4"></td></tr>
<tr><td rowspan="4">Construction</td><td rowspan="4">1863</td><td rowspan="4">68.51%</td><td colspan="2">Technology-based classification</td><td colspan="2">Work stage-based classification</td></tr>
<tr><td rowspan="3">Computer vision</td><td rowspan="3">60.54%</td><td>Before work</td><td>32.95%</td></tr>
<tr><td>During work</td><td>41.59%</td></tr>
<tr><td>With intervals</td><td>8.05%</td></tr>
</table>

				Computer vision with sensor integration	12.56%		
						After work	13.09%
				Other	26.9%	Management	4.2%
	Pre-construction	11	0.41%				
	general	543	19.97%				
	Terminologies and definitions	819	30.12%				
Total OSHA safety rules		3535	100%				

The parsing technique has been used to extract the data from the OSHA website automatically. A total of 8970 safety standards has been extracted as raw data. The data was filtered and cleaned using the established criteria in step 4 of Table 1; after the screening process, 5484 safety rules have been finalized for further research. As some sub-parts of OSHA 29-CFR 1926 construction were under amendments such as sub-part Z and sub-part CC, the safety rules analyzed remained 3538. These cited rules were thoroughly reviewed using GTM, such as allocating open codes to each rule. The open codes are then connected using their relationship with each other to form axial codes. After that, the axial codes are further narrowed up to develop the selective code. Based on the selective codes, 15.34% were classified as general rules, 8.5% were categorized under the procurement phase, 0.35% of rules can be adopted in the pre-construction phase, and 52.65% of rules were grouped under the construction phase, as mentioned in Table 2. This 52.65% of the rules were further selected for the analysis of work-stage-based rule classification.

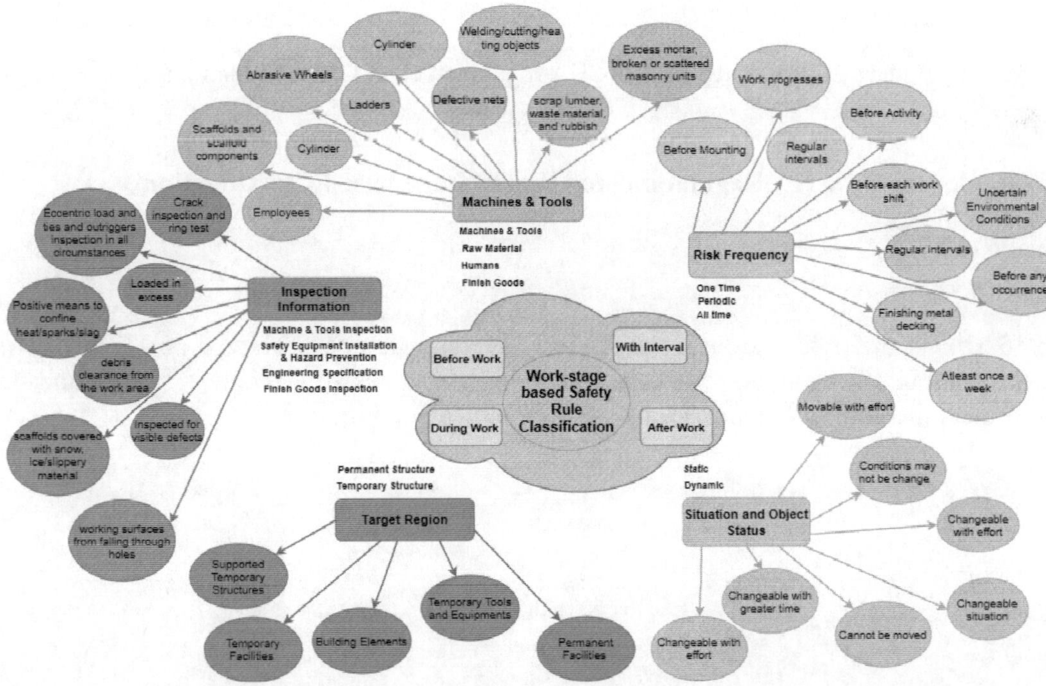

Figure 1: Example of Open coding, axial coding, and selective Coding

In the second stage, the OSHA safety rules that were being grouped under the construction phase were further analysed for computer vision-based safety monitoring using work-stage-based classification. The same approach mentioned in the GTM, such as open codes, axial codes, and selective codes, was formulated for the work-stage-based classification. The selective codes are mentioned in Figure 1. The safety rules are further grouped in four classes for work stage-based classification using the relationship of selective codes such as before work having 32.95% share, 41.59% for during work, 8.05% for with intervals and 13.09% for after work.

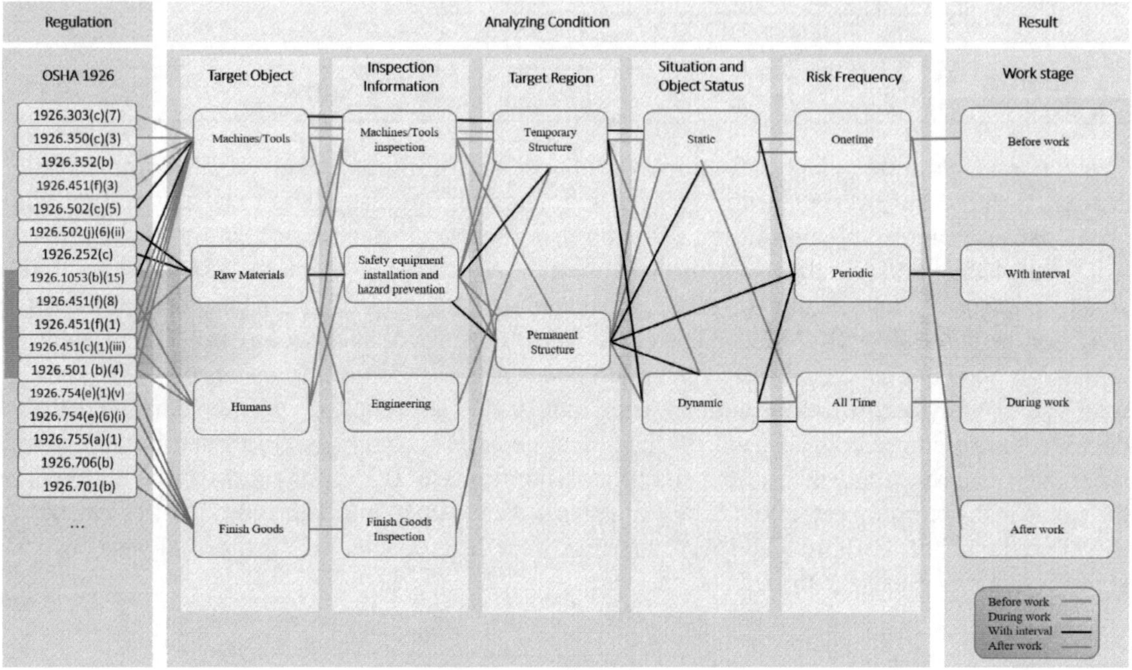

Figure 2: Workstage based OSHA regulation classification conditions

6. Examples from OSHA Regulations for Work-Stage based Classification

Before Work

Case-1

1926.352(b) "If the object to be welded, cut, or heated cannot be moved and if all the fire hazards cannot be removed, positive means shall be taken to confine the heat, sparks, and slag, and to protect the immovable fire hazards from them." (See Figure 2.)

Figure 2: Example of Welding Activity for Safety Equipment Installation Before Work

Case-2

1926.451(f)(3) Scaffolds and scaffold components shall be inspected for visible defects by a competent person before *each work shift*, and after any occurrence which could affect a scaffold's structural integrity. (See Figure 3.)

Figure 3: Example of scaffold components for Tools Inspection Before Work

With Intervals

Case-1

1926.502(j)(6)(ii) "Excess mortar, broken or scattered masonry units, and all other materials and debris shall be kept clear from the work area by removal at *regular intervals*." (See Figure 4.)

Figure 4: Example of Broken or Scattered Masonry for Monitoring with Intervals

Case-2

1926.1053(b)(15) "Ladders shall be inspected by a competent person for visible defects on a *periodic basis* and after any occurrence that could affect their safe use". (See Figure 5.)

Figure 5: Example of Ladder for Monitoring with Intervals

During Work

Case-1

1926.451(c)(1)(iii) "Ties, guys, braces, or outriggers shall be used to prevent the tipping of supported scaffolds (such as mobile scaffold, etc) in all circumstances where an eccentric load, such as a cantilevered work platform, is applied or is transmitted to the scaffold." (See Figure 6.)

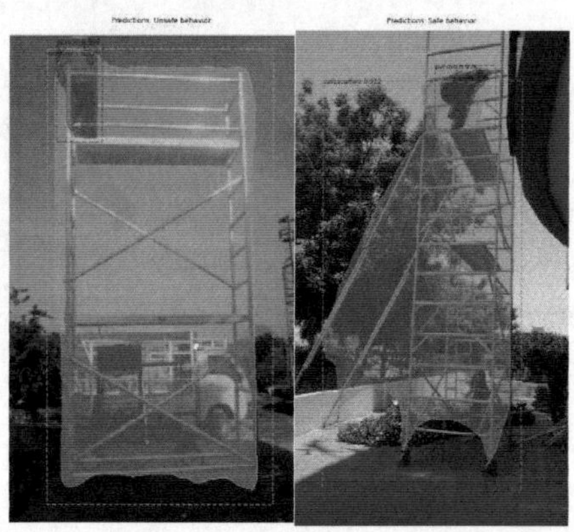

Figure 6: Example of mobile scaffold for Monitoring During the Whole Work

Case-2

1926.451(f)(1) "Scaffolds and scaffold components shall not be loaded in excess of their maximum intended loads or rated capacities, whichever is less." (See Figure 7.)

Figure 7: Example of loaded Scaffolds for Monitoring During the Whole Work

After Work

Case-1

"1926.706(b) All masonry walls over *eight feet in height* shall be adequately braced to prevent overturning and to prevent collapse unless the wall is adequately supported so that it will not overturn or collapse. The bracing shall remain in place until permanent supporting elements of the structure are in place." (See Figure 8.)

Figure 8: Example of masonry walls over eight feet in height for Monitoring after the Work Finish certain Level

Case-2

1926.701(b) Reinforcing steel. All protruding reinforcing steel, onto and into which employees could fall, shall be guarded to eliminate the hazard of impalement." (See Figure 9.)

Figure 9: Example of protruding reinforcing steel for Monitoring Work Finish of Certain Level

7. Conclusion

This paper proposes the classification of OSHA safety rules to develop a compact vision intelligence-based system using ground theory methodology. The rules are classified into two layers. First, the rules are classified in four groups; rules related to (1) procurements phase (8.5%), (2) pre-construction phase (0.35%), (3) construction phase (52.65%), and (4) general rules (15.34%). Second, the construction phase-related rules are further classified for work stage-related rules to adopt computer vision-based safety monitoring. The safety rules are further grouped into four classes such as Before Work, With Intervals, During Work and After Work having 32.95%, 8.05%, 41.59%, and 13.09% of share, respectively. In the extension work, image data capture devices will be compared against the identified classes of work stages.

Acknowledgment

This work is supported by National Research Foundation of Korea (NRF) grant funded by the Korea government (MSIT) (No. NRF-2020R1A4A4078916).

References

BLS (2017) National Census of Fatal Occupational Injuries in 2017, Bureau of Labor Statistics US Department of Labor.

BLS (2019) NATIONAL CENSUS OF FATAL OCCUPATIONAL INJURIES IN 2018. Available at: www.bls.gov/iif (Accessed: 29 January 2020).

Ding, L. et al. (2018) 'A deep hybrid learning model to detect unsafe behavior: Integrating convolution neural networks and long short-term memory', Automation in Construction, 86(March 2017), pp.118–124. doi: 10.1016/j.autcon.2017.11.002.

Fang, W. et al. (2018) 'Falls from heights: A computer vision-based approach for safety harness detection', Automation in Construction, 91(February), pp.53–61. doi: 10.1016/j.autcon.2018.02.018.

Fang, W. et al. (2019) 'A deep learning-based approach for mitigating falls from height with computer vision: Convolutional neural network', Advanced Engineering Informatics, 39(December 2018), pp.170–177. doi: 10.1016/j.aei.2018.12.005.

Fang, W. et al. (2020) 'Computer vision applications in construction safety assurance', Automation in Construction. doi: 10.1016/j.autcon.2019.103013.

Golparvar-Fard, M., Peña-Mora, F. and Savarese, S. (2015) 'Automated Progress Monitoring Using Unordered Daily Construction Photographs and IFC-Based Building Information Models', Journal of Computing in Civil Engineering, 29(1), p. 04014025. doi: 10.1061/(ASCE)CP.1943-5487.0000205.

He, K. et al. (2016) 'Deep residual learning for image recognition', Proceedings of the IEEE Computer Society Conference on Computer Vision and Pattern Recognition, 2016-Decem, pp.770–778. doi: 10.1109/CVPR.2016.90.

Hongling, G. et al. (2016) 'BIM and Safety Rules Based Automated Identification of Unsafe Design Factors in Construction', Procedia Engineering, 164(June), pp.467–472. doi: 10.1016/j.proeng.2016.11.646.

Hussain, R. et al. (2017) 'Safety regulation classification system to support BIM based safety management', ISARC 2017 - Proceedings of the 34th International Symposium on Automation and Robotics in Construction, (Isarc).

Kasirossafar, M. and Shahbodaghlou, F. (2013) 'Building Information Modeling for Construction Safety Planning', Icsdec 2012, pp.1017–1024.

Khan, N. et al. (2019) 'Excavation Safety Modeling Approach Using BIM and VPL', Advances in Civil Engineering, 2019. doi: 10.1155/2019/1515808.

Khan, N. et al. (2020) 'Visual language-aided construction fire safety planning approach in building information modeling', Applied Sciences (Switzerland), 10(5). doi: 10.3390/app10051704.

Kim, H. et al. (2019) 'Visual language approach to representing KBimCode-based Korea building code sentences for automated rule checking', Journal of Computational Design and Engineering, 6(2), pp.143–148. doi: 10.1016/j.jcde.2018.08.002.

Mneymneh, B. E., Abbas, M. and Khoury, H. (2018) 'Vision-Based Framework for Intelligent Monitoring of Hardhat Wearing on Construction Sites'. doi: 10.1061/(ASCE)CP.1943-5487.0000813.

Nath, N. D., Behzadan, A. H. and Paal, S. G. (2020) 'Deep learning for site safety: Real-time detection of personal protective equipment', Automation in Construction, 112. doi: 10.1016/j.autcon.2020.103085.

OSHA (2009) Occupational Safety and Health Administration Timeline. Available at: https://www.osha.gov/osha40/timeline.html (Accessed: 15 March 2021).

OSHA (2020) OSHA 1926 Requirements Graphic Products. Available at: https://www.graphicproducts.com/articles/osha-1926-requirements/ (Accessed: 15 March 2021).

Park, C., Lee, D. and Khan, N. (2020) 'An Analysis on Safety Risk Judgment Patterns Towards Computer Vision Based Construction Safety Management', p. 52. doi: 10.3311/CCC2020-052.

Roberts, D. and Golparvar-Fard, M. (2019) 'End-to-end vision-based detection, tracking and activity analysis of earthmoving equipment filmed at ground level', Automation in Construction, 105, p. 102811. doi: 10.1016/j.autcon.2019.04.006.

Wang, M. et al. (2019a) 'Predicting safety hazards among construction workers and equipment using computer vision and deep learning techniques', Proceedings of the 36th International Symposium on Automation and Robotics in Construction, ISARC 2019, (October), pp.399–406. doi: 10.22260/isarc2019/0054.

Wang, M. et al. (2019b) 'Predicting safety hazards among construction workers and equipment using computer vision and deep learning techniques', in Proceedings of the 36th International Symposium on Automation and Robotics in Construction, ISARC 2019. International Association for Automation and Robotics in Construction I.A.A.R.C), pp.399–406. doi: 10.22260/isarc2019/0054.

Wu, H. and Zhao, J. (2018) 'An intelligent vision-based approach for helmet identification for work safety', Computers in Industry, 100, pp.267–277. doi: 10.1016/j.compind.2018.03.037.

Zhang, S. et al. (2013) 'Building Information Modeling (BIM) and Safety: Automatic Safety Checking of Construction Models and Schedules', Automation in Construction, 29, pp.183–195. doi: 10.1016/j.autcon.2012.05.006.

Concept to support the estimation of static load capacity on construction sites using in-situ AR-based methods

Christian-Dominik Thiele, Tim-Jonathan Huyeng, Pascal Mosler, Uwe Rüppel
TU Darmstadt, Germany
thiele@iib.tu-darmstadt.de

Abstract. Due to the advancing digitization in the AEC industry (Architecture, Engineering and Construction), existing workflows are undergoing a transformation towards modern work patterns. In particular, there is potential for optimization in the area of building in existing structures. For example, the on-site capture of a comprehensive model in the context of Historic Building Information Modeling (HBIM) and especially of building elements can be supported by modern technologies. This paper uses an exemplary use case to demonstrate how such transformation from a traditional to a modern, digitally enhanced workflow is made possible to support an engineer on-site. The use case is the evaluation of a construction state with a temporary local load increase. The traditional workflow consists of multiple manual and partially iterative steps. The proposed workflow uses advanced augmented reality (AR) technology on mobile devices as well as a self-developed Web API for an existing structural analysis software. This enables an on-site estimation of the static load capacity of a structural subsystem.

1. Introduction

Due to the aging real estate stock, especially of the public sector, more and more (infrastructure) buildings reach the end of their planned lifespan (Bigalke et al., 2016). There are no adequate capacities to assess the condition of such buildings and, if necessary, to determine their remaining lifespan. In addition, there is often a desire to maintain and repurpose buildings worthy of preservation rather than demolishing them. In case of protected existing structures and listed buildings, there is no other choice because demolition is out of the question. For the preservation or repurpose of the buildings, BIM models and plans could help in the assessment of the current building state. But these are in the case of historic buildings usually missing or incomplete. In order to apply digital methods such as BIM or HBIM to buildings of this kind and to analyze the current state, a complex stocktaking process is required. This is carried out by means of laser scanning in order to generate a point cloud from which a BIM model can be created. For the scanning, however, it is necessary to remove old pipes, non-load-bearing walls, other shoring and furnishings from the existing building.

For large construction sites in existing structures, there are also concerns about logistics such as material storage. With multiple stages of construction, building materials such as masonry units must be temporarily stored in hallways or rooms. Here, it is often unclear whether the ceiling structures can withstand the point loads. Since the construction progress often is time-sensitive, there is a high interest to make a quick assessment of the static temporary loading capacity. This issue is fundamentally different from BIM-based planning. The structural engineer cannot perform the recalculations on the basis of a model or several plans, as it is usually the case with new buildings, but is dependent on on-site measurements. Due to the lack of a BIM model, the engineer will have to rely on a digital structure model they create for themself in order to perform the necessary calculations.

The aim of this paper is to digitally transform the presented processes, especially in structural planning, with modern in-situ methods like AR and the use of microservices. It is shown that a digital recording of the structure with instant calculation is possible and supports the engineer assessing the situation on-site. This approach has relevance far beyond construction sites and is also applicable, for example, for an immediate assessment of damaged buildings after disasters in order to release operations, e.g., for rescue forces. The focus here is to gain an immediate first impression of the situation, which can be used as a basis for a verifiable structural analysis.

2. Related work

The term HBIM is primarily associated with the preservation of the architectural legacy of historic buildings. In order to generate a HBIM model, the structure is first captured for example by using a laser scanner. This results in a point cloud of the structure. Subsequently, the point cloud can be transformed into 3D component elements. In addition to the captured geometry, information about the material and construction type can be linked to the building elements, adding "intelligence" to the model (Murphy et al., 2013). This whole process is challenging due to the complex structure of historic buildings (Barazzetti and Banfi, 2017).

As described in Barazzetti and Banfi (2017), there is growing interest in developing AR and virtual reality (VR) applications for historic buildings. The authors present several exemplary implementations of HBIM models in smartphone or tablet applications. AR and VR applications are also being developed for specialized engineering applications in an attempt to move the workplace from the office to the construction site. One example mentioned by Barazzetti and Banfi (2017) is Autodesk 360 which highlights the benefits of AR applications. It promises great potential when combined with a BIM model, as relevant information can be obtained on-site from the BIM model, increasing work productivity.

Few professional structural analysis software such as RFEM (Dlubal, 2021) and SOFiSTiK (SOFiSTiK, 2021) have possibilities for interactions that are driven locally by scripts. RFEM, for example, can be accessed with various programming languages using the SDKs published by the manufacturer (Dlubal, 2015). In contrast, SOFiSTiK can be started in headless mode via the command line. Furthermore, the provided interfaces allow the readout and subsequent processing of calculation results. All structure analysis software of this type known to the authors do not have a documented Web Application Programming Interface (API). An exception is SkyCiv, a commercial cloud engineering software (Carigliano, 2020). It offers a (paid) server-side Web API. In addition to the mentioned software, there are freely available packages for various programming languages ("GitHub Finite Element Analysis", 2021).

Kudela et al. (2020) showed the possibilities of a static assessment of historic buildings by means of point clouds. Their approach is based on photogrammetry methods and the finite cell method for determining statically critical areas. The use of augmented reality on construction sites has been studied and discussed by various authors. Shin and Dunston (2009) presented a self-developed "AR prototype system for inspection" to check the placement and alignment of steel columns by distance measurements. Through series of experiments under ideal conditions, they found that the measurement accuracy was inferior to that of a total station but was sufficient for an initial assessment. They concluded that the use on a construction site requires greater robustness and more stable tracking technology.

Zhou et al. (2017) proposed a method for the position control of segments in tunneling. In this approach, marker-based calibration measurements are supposed to be aligned with a deposited BIM model. They found out that the measurements at larger distances are becoming inaccurate. This makes it impossible to reliably detect displacements with millimeter precision. They also pointed out that the use of markers on (tunnel) construction sites is impractical and therefore recommended a system without markers for comparable distance measurements.

Li et al. (2017) proposed a smartphone-based client-server system for finite element analysis at construction sites. The construction models are deposited on a server beforehand and are passed to the user after entering geometric or technical parameters. The smartphone application reads the data and virtually places the model in the environment using image tracking. Li et al. (2017) recommended applying finite element analysis also to dynamic models and to use a more reliable tracking technology.

Park et al. (2013) considered AR in interaction with ontologies for documenting damages in structures using smartphones and tablets ("AR-based Defect Inspection System"). The authors focused on the acquisition and processing of data and used markers for this purpose, as did Zhou et al. (2017).

3. Analysis

The methodology of (H)BIM already enables a detailed description of a building. However, the preparation of the respective model is costly, especially for historical buildings. This is due to the complex structure and shape of irregular building components such as shell and arched structures. In addition, areas that are difficult to access, for example where walls or pipes have been subsequently installed, require time-consuming post-processing of laser scans. Therefore, unless simple structural systems are assumed, it should be estimated which level of detail provides the best value. Numerous researchers such as Barazzetti and Banfi (2017) are using the capabilities of AR and VR to visualize historic buildings in the context of HBIM. Gamification features are used to provide a credible simulation to interested users (storytelling and museum applications). According to Barazzetti and Banfi (2017), AR and VR applications are also increasingly used in specialized applications.

To the best of our knowledge, there is currently no standalone structural analysis software with a Web API available. However, it is possible to implement a Web API as a wrapper on top of the actual, already existing functions. If a structural analysis software is extended by a Web API, on-site calculations are thereby possible. Since using common standalone and established software is used, the on-site recording and the results can be also used for later analysis and can be easily integrated into existing workflows. The integration of the results or input files from non-standard programs into the existing workflow is in contrast much more complex.

The approach presented by Kudela et al. (2020) for the assessment of structures is particularly applicable for exposed and easy-to-reach structures such as bridge structures. However, a quick on-site assessment is not possible due to the complex image processing and subsequent calculation. Furthermore, the focus of the approach is on the detection of weak points of an existing system without considering possible additional loads.

The investigations of Li et al. (2017), Shin and Dunston (2009) and Zhou et al. (2017) have in common that all authors consider AR to be fundamentally suitable for the use on construction sites. In particular, the technical hurdles that were still apparent in the work of Shin and Dunston (2009) such as missing standardized AR-capable hardware and tracking technology were no longer present almost ten years later. The accuracy required for construction sites depends heavily on the use case. Distance measurements using AR currently run up against technical limitations in the millimeter range (Zhou et al., 2017), but are fundamentally faster and less complicated than using a total station. Regarding tracking technology, a trade-off between accuracy and robustness can be observed. Marker-based tracking appears unsuitable for the use on construction sites for logistical reasons (Zhou et al., 2017). Moreover, image tracking technologies such as Vuforia tend to be unreliable (Li et al., 2017). The regarded workflows foresee multiple people involved. Even though immediate results are instantly available after the measurements, like in Li et al. (2017), preliminary work has to be done before the actual use on the construction site. This includes modelling the FEM models and calibrating the tracking technology.

Implications for further procedure

Based on the approaches and findings of the related work, this paper aims to make the handling of the required technology fast and easy. The aim is to avoid any additional personnel and any preparatory work. This seems expedient since distance measurements on vaulted ceilings do not demand an increased accuracy. This will result in time and cost advantages. To further lower the technical hurdles, the use of AR-enabled mobile devices is preferred. VR technologies are not being considered because of the safety risks that would arise when they are used solely on a construction site. Instead, users must always keep an eye on their surrounding, which is only possible using AR. According to Mekni and Lemieux (2014), the three main characteristics of AR are 1) overlaying reality with virtual objects, 2) real-time interaction, and 3) three-dimensional sensing.

In the next chapter, the status quo of the estimation of the static load capacity of a ceiling construction is described. The procedure is illustrated using the example of a common ceiling type in Germany, the Prussian vaulted ceiling.

4. Analysis of the current workflow on the example of a Prussian vaulted ceiling

A slab section constructed as a Prussian vaulted ceiling (as pictured in Figure 1) of a historical building is chosen as an example structure. The choice for this type of construction was made due to the easily visible structure as well as the simple static calculability. However, the discussed workflow is also suitable for other exposed structural systems such as wood beam ceilings. Vaulted ceilings are a historic, widely used construction method consisting of longitudinal beams with intermediate stone vaults. This construction method can be found in numerous old buildings towards the end of the 19th century in Germany (Fischer, 2009). In addition to residential and office buildings, this type of construction is present in some of Berlin's subway stations, such as the Sophie-Charlotte-Platz (Bezirksamt Charlottenburg-Wilmersdorf, 2014).

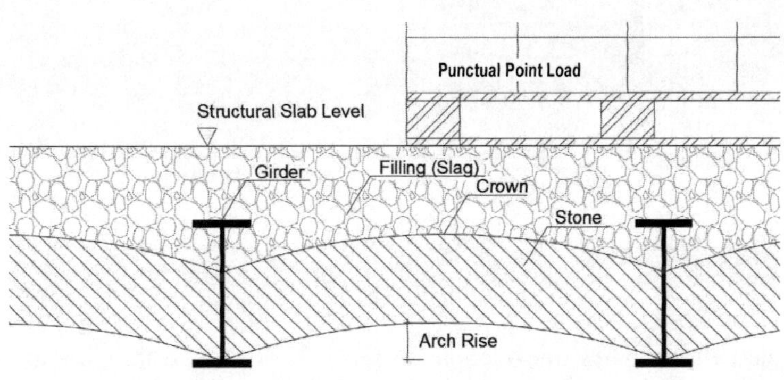

Figure 1: Cross-section of a typical Prussian vaulted ceiling with additional masonry pallet

4.1 Underlying example structural system

In the chosen example (Figure 2), the longitudinal beams rest on the outer wall of the building on one side and are supported by steel girders in the field. This arrangement is typical for buildings with vaulted ceilings. The context is a temporary punctual load increase, e.g., due to a required storage area for building materials on a ceiling, such as masonry blocks. Therefore, the aim is to determine whether the present structural subsystem can handle such loads.

For a significant estimation of the static load capacity of a subsystem, the adjacent technical boundary conditions must always be considered and estimated correctly. Thus, when a partial structure is cut free, the effects from the outside on the subsystem (e.g. supports from floors above that rest on the system) as well as from the modified subsystem on the global system (such as foundations and walls) must be taken into account.

Due to the complexity that quickly arises when calculating an entire system, it can be argued that, for example, the redistribution of loads is not expected to have any effect on the entire system. This would mean that only local subsystems need to be verified. A typical example is a state of construction where temporary load increases are expected in the area of storage areas for construction materials. In this case, single additional loads in the construction state can often be compensated in the global system by omitted live loads from levels above or by missing floor superstructures. Thus, only the considered subsystem has to be examined for the local increased force. The load effect on the underlying walls or foundations mostly remains the same in total and does not have to be verified anew. The responsible engineer must assess whether this is the case. If so, it is possible to consider subsystems isolated in existing buildings and therefore reduce the effort required for the static proof of the structural condition.

For the selected use case, only the steel structure is considered. For an entire structural verification of the subsystem, it is still necessary to verify the static proof of all necessary components of the subsystem as the allowed pressure of the vaulting stones and connected structures. The described example structure of a Prussian vaulted ceiling has been modelled in SOFiSTiK (SOFiSTiK, 2021) to visualize the subsystem (Figure 2).

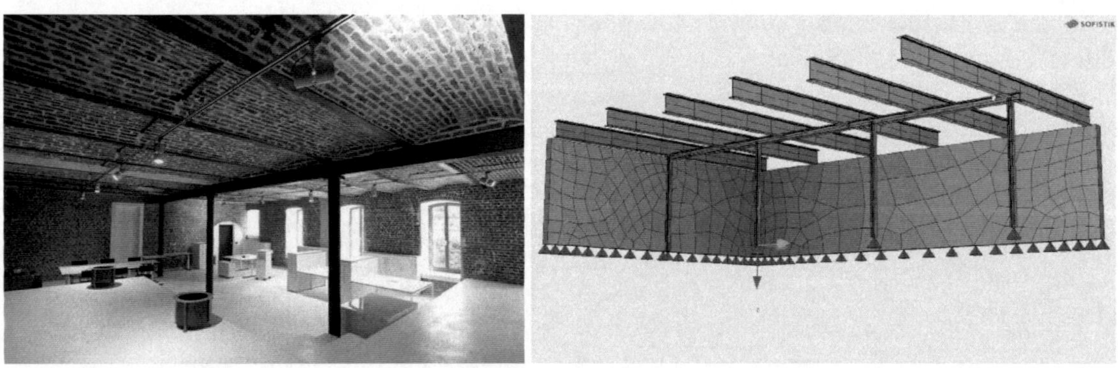

Figure 2: Left: *Alte Brauerei Meerbusch* (source: DEUTSCHE ROCKWOOL), Right: corresponding structural system, modelled in SOFiSTiK

4.2 Current workflow

In order to prove a state of construction, a procedure as it is shown in Figure 3 is common. This process can become time-consuming because it can involve multiple trips to the site. Once the structure and the related subsystem are identified on-site, the recording of the surrounding area can begin. In the presented example of the vaulted ceiling, this would include measuring the length and the cross-section of the longitudinal girders as well as the spacing between two girders. For the purpose of identifying the girder dimensions, the visible flange width can be measured and potentially inferred to technical registers if the year of construction and girder type are known, e.g. from Bargmann (2013). Alternatively, more complex investigations can be necessary in order to get the dimensions of the girder. When columns are present, their length and related girder cross-section must also be measured.

The recording of structural systems on-site is conventionally done by using a folding rule or laser distance meter and handwritten notes and sketches. Depending on the situation on-site, a ladder or scaffolding may be required for recording. Furthermore, the acting loads are estimated. Once the recording is complete, it must be digitally modeled and then calculated using a FEM program, depending on the complexity of the system. When it becomes evident during modeling that values are missing or appear implausible, a new time-consuming recording on the construction site may be necessary. Once the calculation and documentation has been carried out, the intended state of construction can be approved or rejected. The final approval process can vary depending on the local regulations and standards.

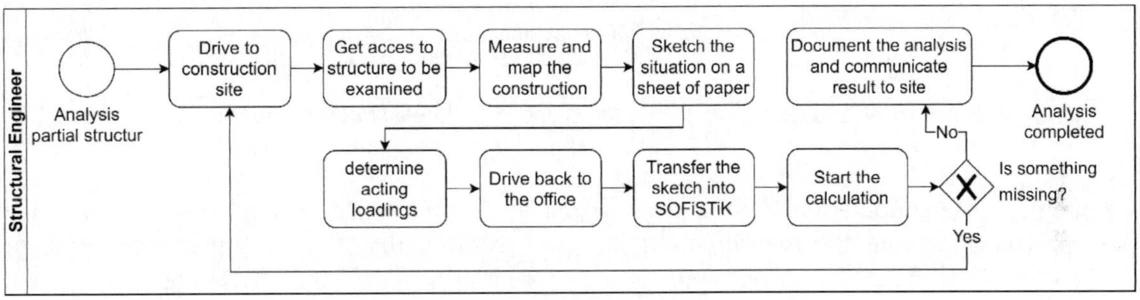

Figure 3: Conventional workflow: recording and calculating a state of construction in terms of structural analysis

Since this process can be time-consuming and can require numerous steps, the authors propose an optimized workflow.

5. Optimization of the traditional workflow

In the following, an approach for an in-situ evaluation of simple static systems by means of AR technologies is proposed. In addition, a Web API is suggested for the connection to an exemplary structural analysis software. Therefore, a Web API has been developed and a mobile application has been designed. For this, the use case described in Chapter 4 has been considered: the structural engineer is called to the construction site and has to assess a structural condition (Chapter 5.1). For this purpose, the engineer uses an AR-based application on their mobile device. The underlying system architecture is described in Chapter 5.2 and the mobile application in Chapter 5.3.

5.1 Proposed workflow

The traditional workflow described in Chapter 4 has been optimized for the vaulted ceiling use case. It is described below and shown in Figure 4.

The developed application enables the digital recording of the subsystem's geometry directly on-site. With the help of AR software development kits (SDKs) for mobile applications, it is possible to perform distance measurements of points and recognize depth information just by using the camera of a mobile device. A vivid example is a tabletop whose surface can be detected using feature points and measuring the dimensions directly in the application. Once the geometry is captured, as described in Chapter 4.2, loads can be applied, cross-sections can be assigned to the line elements and boundary conditions of the system (such as supports) can be defined via the application. The geometric and semantic information will then be sent to the Web API, where the system is automatically calculated by the calculation engine of the structural analysis software SOFiSTiK. Immediately afterwards, the user receives the results of the calculation in the app. Finally, the engineer can check them for plausibility by validating the FEM analysis results directly on-site based on the received plots (like internal forces and bending lines, see Chapter 5.3). This allows the engineer to approve or reject the intended state of construction.

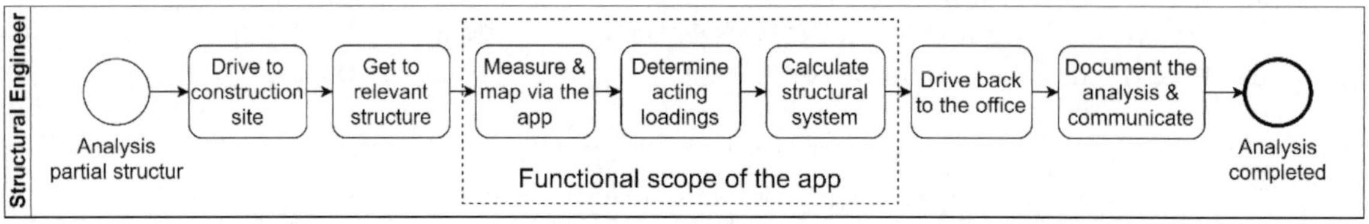

Figure 4: Proposed workflow: efficiently record and calculate a state of construction in terms of structural analysis

To supplement the documentation of the calculation, photos can be taken on-site directly via the application during the measurement process. Additionally, the documentation tools of SOFiSTiK can be used. A later post-processing of the model (e.g. in the office) via the graphical interface of SSD (SOFiSTiK Structural Desktop) is also possible.

5.2 System architecture

Since the chosen structural analysis software SOFiSTiK cannot be installed on mobile devices, the calculation must take place on a stationary computer. Using an established structural analysis software has several advantages over a self-made FEM approach. An expert software is more sophisticated and offers a variety of support, which is essential for the reliability of the calculation. Furthermore, the recorded geometry can be reused in SOFiSTiK's extensive repertoire of calculation options for a later, more comprehensive calculation. It is also possible to use the established integrated tools SOFiSTiK Graphic and SOFiSTiK Report Browser for a concluding documentation. However, since SOFiSTiK is not designed for mobile use, the software does not provide a Web API. Therefore, a separate server application was designed as an interface for the chosen software.

With the help of the web framework FastAPI, a web service was implemented. It can be reached via HTTP(S) requests and represents the web interface to the structural analysis software. The relevant information for SOFiSTiK can be inserted either graphically or in a text-based format. Since the process flow shall be automated, the text-based format (DAT file) was chosen. The DAT file contains all relevant input data on the geometry of the structure. This includes loads, load cases and project information such as the standard on which the calculation is based. The creation of the input file is realized inside the mobile application. As Huyeng et al. (2020) suggested, it is also possible to use an external service for this purpose. SOFiSTiK consists of numerous modules, such as ASE (Advanced Solution Engine), the calculation kernel and the relevant module for the structural analysis itself. ASE can be started directly via the server application by means of a command line call and processes the transferred input file (DAT file). Therefore, no additional action from the user is necessary to perform the calculation.

Once the DAT file is created, it is forwarded to the so-called Sofi-Service which was developed as part of the *SCOPE* (Semantic Construction Project Engineering) research project (Huyeng et al., 2021; "SCOPE" 2018). After computation, the results are stored in a proprietary database (CDBase or CDB). This database can be accessed using program libraries published by SOFiSTiK. The Sofi-Service extracts the relevant parameters and calculation results, such as nodal results and displacements, and sends them back to the mobile application (see Figure 5).

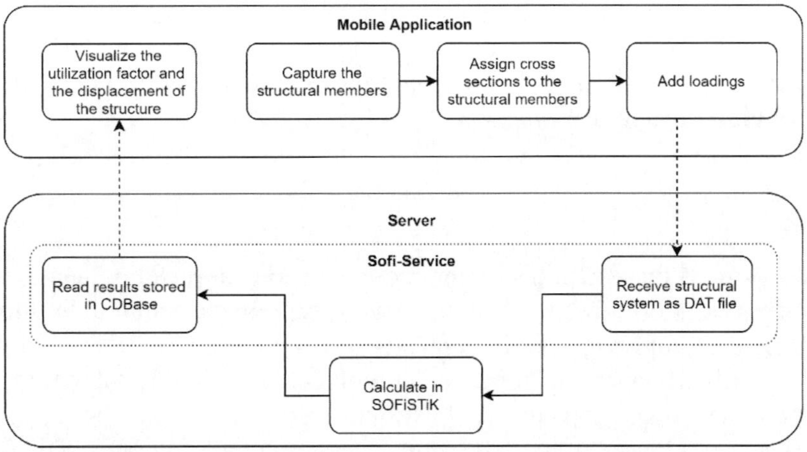

Figure 5: Proposed system architecture and process flow

For documentation and optional later processing, the DAT file can additionally be sent back or stored and made available via a download link. This makes it possible to continue later and post-process the recorded structural system in the graphical user interface of SOFiSTiK (SOFiSTiK Structural Desktop).

5.3 Mobile application

Figure 6: Mock-up of proposed mobile application using the example of *Alte Brauerei Meerbusch* (based on the photo of DEUTSCHE ROCKWOOL)

The proposed application should enable the user to measure the girder dimensions and distances by using built-in functionalities of the AR SDKs as described in Chapter 5.1. To mark the structural elements, the feature of drawing the structural lines onto the captured image of the mobile device camera needs to be provided. Additionally, the material (like HEB steel girders) needs to be assignable. Loads shall be added to the system by clicking on the previous created structural lines. In the same way, hinges and other mechanical parameters can be added to the system, too. Further settings for global parameters like the calculation standard and units can assist the workflow even more. After capturing the geometry and adding loads, the information will be sent to the server where the calculation will be carried out as described in Chapter 5.2. The calculation results can be visualized in different ways. Colored lines or the graphical representation of the deformation of structural elements are conceivable. As described in Chapter 5.1, the responsible engineer is expected to validate the results and to confirm the check for plausibility within the application.

6. Conclusion

In this work, we showed that AR tools integrated in a mobile application can optimize the way structural engineers work on construction sites. This applies in particular to buildings in existing structures. The field of applying mobile application is versatile and offers a high usability. In addition, the described approach supports ecological sustainable planning since analog drawings can be replaced and trips to the construction site can be significantly reduced. Since common AR SDKs are already supported by most common mobile devices, there is no need to purchase special expensive devices. According to Révész (2020), slightly more than a quarter of all smartphones in use are currently AR-enabled. Furthermore, by implementing a Web API, it was possible to connect complex structural analysis software to a mobile application, although it was originally designed as a desktop application. The use of Web APIs implemented as microservices also enables flexibility in the implementation of additional features.

The presented approach demonstrates how the redefined workflow can help to support structural engineers on the basis of already existing equipment (smartphones and tablets) and innovative tools (ARCore). However, it must be made clear that the approach should support engineers rather than replacing their work on-site. In order to prevent the risk of giving up responsibility to the application, the results from the automated calculation workflow always need to be checked for plausibility.

Conceivable further developments could be, as an example, an automated structure recognition, with which bearing elements such as columns and beams can be detected by an image recognition algorithm. In addition to the structural element lines, the whole point cloud of the room could be captured, and an HBIM model can be created and linked to the structural system. This could be realized by using already available techniques of photogrammetry. To increase the user experience and calculation accuracy, the app could be extended by implementing checks for calculability in the background while the user enters the structural model. These checks could consider e.g. the statical determinacy.

References

Barazzetti, L., Banfi, F., 2017. Historic BIM for Mobile VR/AR Applications, in: Ioannides, M., Magnenat-Thalmann, N., Papagiannakis, G. (Eds.), Mixed Reality and Gamification for Cultural Heritage. Springer International Publishing, Cham, pp.271–290.

Bargmann, H., 2013. Historische Bautabellen : Normen und Konstruktionshinweise 1870–1960, 5. Aufl. ed. Köln.

Bezirksamt Charlottenburg-Wilmersdorf, 2014. URL https://www.berlin.de/ba-charlottenburg-wilmersdorf/ueber-den-bezirk/gebaeude-und-anlagen/bahnhoefe/artikel.159800.php (accessed March 2021).

Bigalke, U., Armbruster, A., Lukas, F., Krieger, O., Schuch, C., Kunde, J., 2016. Statistiken und Analysen zur Energieeffizienz im Gebäudebestand, dena-GEBÄUDEREPORT. Deutsche Energie-Agentur GmbH (dena), Berlin.

Carigliano, S., 2020. Strukturanalyse- und Entwurfs-API | SkyCiv. SkyCiv Cloud-Strukturanalyse-Software | Cloud Structural Analysis Software and Calculators. URL https://skyciv.com/structural-analysis-design-api/ (accessed October 2020).

Dlubal, 2021. RFEM [WWW Document]. FEM-Statiksoftware RFEM | Dlubal Software. URL https://www.dlubal.com/de/produkte/fem-statik-software-rfem/was-ist-rfem (accessed March 2021).

Dlubal, 2015. RFEM-/RSTAB-Zusatzmodul RF-COM/RS-COM [WWW Document]. Dlubal. URL https://www.dlubal.com/de/produkte/rfem-und-rstab-zusatzmodule/sonstige/rf-com (accessed February 2021).

Fischer, M., 2009. Steineisendecken im Deutschen Reich 1892–1925. BTU Cottbus - Senftenberg.

GitHub Finite Element Analysis [WWW Document], 2021. Topic: Finite Element Analysis. URL https://github.com/topics/finite-element-analysis (accessed March 2021).

Huyeng, T.-J., Thiele, C.-D., Rüppel, U., Sprenger, W., 2020. An approach to process geometric and semantic information as open graph-based description using a microservice architecture on the example of structural data. Presented at the European Group for Intelligent Computing in Engineering, Berlin.

Huyeng, T.-J., Thiele, C.-D., Wagner, A., Shi, M., Hoffmann, A., Rüppel, U., Sprenger, W., 2021. Interlinking geometric and semantic information for an automated structural analysis of buildings using semantic web. Presented at the European Conference on Product and Process Modelling, Moscow, Russia, p. to appear.

Kudela, L., Kollmannsberger, S., Almac, U., Rank, E., 2020. Direct structural analysis of domains defined by point clouds. Computer Methods in Applied Mechanics and Engineering 358, 112581.

Li, W.K., Nee, A.Y.C., Ong, S.K., 2017. Mobile augmented reality visualization and collaboration techniques for on-site finite element structural analysis. International Journal of Modeling, Simulation, and Scientific Computing 09, 1840001.

Mekni, M., Lemieux, A., 2014. Augmented Reality: Applications, Challenges and Future Trends 10.

Murphy, M., McGovern, E., Pavia, S., 2013. Historic Building Information Modelling – Adding intelligence to laser and image based surveys of European classical architecture. ISPRS Journal of Photogrammetry and Remote Sensing, Terrestrial 3D modelling 76, 89–102.

Park, C.-S., Lee, D.-Y., Kwon, O.-S., Wang, X., 2013. A framework for proactive construction defect management using BIM, augmented reality and ontology-based data collection template. Automation in Construction, Augmented Reality in Architecture, Engineering, and Construction 33, 61–71.

Révész, R., 2020. How many AR enabled phones are in the world? AR-ON Platform. URL https://www.aronplatform.com/mobile-ar-penetration/ (accessed March 2021).

SCOPE – Semantic Construction Project Engineering, 2018. URL https://www.projekt-scope.de/ (accessed February 2021).

Shin, D.H., Dunston, P.S., 2009. Evaluation of Augmented Reality in steel column inspection. Automation in Construction 18, 118–129.

SOFiSTiK, 2021. sofistik.de [WWW Document]. FEM, BIM und CAD Software für Bauingenieure | SOFiSTiK AG. URL https://www.sofistik.de/ (accessed March 2021).

Westfeld, P., Mader, D., Maas, H.-G., 2015. Generation of TIR-attributed 3D Point Clouds from UAV-based Thermal Imagery. Photogrammetrie - Fernerkundung - Geoinformation 2015, 381–393.

Zhou, Y., Luo, H., Yang, Y., 2017. Implementation of augmented reality for segment displacement inspection during tunneling construction. Automation in Construction 82, 112–121.

Using eye-tracking to compare the experienced safety supervisors and novice in identifying job site hazards under a VR environment

Yewei Ouyang, Xiaowei Luo
City University of Hong Kong, Hong Kong
xiaowluo@cityu.edu.hk

Abstract. Hazard-identification experience is a kind of tacit knowledge which is difficult to be extracted from experienced subjects and to be described explicitly in the text. Researchers have applied eye-tracking technology in eliciting the cognitive processes of experienced workers while performing the hazard-identification task. However, the image-based tasks in previous studies are substantially different from how the hazards are perceived on the construction site. To improve the ecological validity of the hazard-identification task, this study develops panoramic VR scenarios of various job sites as the stimulus, and both experienced safety supervisors and students are invited to identify hazards in the virtual sites. Their performances and eye-movement data are compared. The results show the experienced allocate more attention to hazardous areas instead of unimportant things, and they inspect more details which are ignored by the novice. The identified differences may be incorporated into the training courses to educate the hazard-identification of the novice.

1. Introduction

The construction site involves highly dangerous work and harsh work environment, so it is essential to train subjects' hazard-identification ability to avoid them from being hurt. Since hazard-identification is a complex task that requires knowledge of both regulations and experience because of the dynamic nature of construction environments, it might be useful to understand how experts search for and identify hazards and extract their experience to formulate explicit strategies that can be included in training materials. However, the hazard-identification experience is a kind of tacit knowledge which is difficult to be extracted from experienced subjects and to be described explicitly in the text.

Researchers have found the eye-tracking technology which measures eye position and movement, provides eye-tracking information such as fixation location and duration which can indicate one's cognitive strategies and prior knowledge or experience (Hyönä et al., 2002). Hence, researchers tried to utilize eye-tracking in the construction field in eliciting the cognitive processes of experienced workers while performing the hazard-identification task (Dzeng et al., 2016), and they compared the differences among workers with different years of working experiences (Hasanzadeh et al., 2017). Those previous studies used static images as the stimulus, but the image-based tasks are substantially different from how the hazards are perceived on construction site because static images fail to portrait dynamic job sites and the two-dimensional images would lead to information shrinkage and changes in the cognitive process (Sun and Liao, 2019).

To improve the ecological validity of the hazard-identification task, the authors intend to apply virtual job sites created by panoramas of real sites as the stimulus. The panoramic VR creates highly realistic and detailed representations of real construction sites while giving users a sense of immersion(Moore et al., 2019). In such an environment, subjects are allowed to observe their surroundings to identify safety hazards exactly as what they do in real life. The virtual scenes are expected to have more conformities with real-time than the image-based task. Besides, it costs less time and represents details of job sites better than the virtual scenes created by 3D modelling, and compared with the real environment, it allows repeatable experimental conditions, which provides the same conditions for all participants. Besides, due to the simple-to-capture of panoramic pictures, a wide range of job sites covering various construction situations and safety hazards can be captured to acquire a more comprehensive comparison.

This study will integrate panoramic VR technology with eye-tracking technology, where the panoramic VR will be used to develop virtual job sites for subjects to search for hazards, and eye-tracking will be used to indicate subjects' safety experiences. The objective of this study is to find out the differences between the methods employed by experienced safety supervisors and novice of how they identify hazards in the panoramic VR scenes, which can further be incorporated into the training of hazard-identification for the novice.

2. Related Work

Since eye-tracking can provide fixation information to indicate subjects' cognitive strategies and prior knowledge or experience, several studies have successfully applied eye-tracking methodologies to evaluate the difference between the methods used by the experienced and the novice. In the domain of traffic safety, Hosking et al. (2010) evaluated the difference between the visual search patterns that experienced and inexperienced motorcycle riders employ to identify road hazards; Pradhan et al. (2005) compared the scanning behaviour of experienced drivers and novice drivers under risky driving conditions, and they found novice drivers typically look directly ahead and fail to perceive and assess hazard information. These studies from other disciplines facilitate such methods to be applied in the construction industry. Since eye-tracking information can assist in eliciting the cognitive processes of experienced inspectors while performing search tasks (Sadasivan et al., 2005), researchers in the construction field used eye-tracker study the effect of experiences in hazards-identification. Dzeng et al. (2016) invited experienced and novice workers to identify hazards in four screenshots developed by Google SketchUp, which presents both obvious and unobvious hazards of workplaces. They used an eye-tracker to compare the differences in the workers' searching patterns for hazard identification. They reported the experienced workers were found to recognize hazards significantly faster than the novices, and their scanning paths are more consistent. Hasanzadeh et al. (2017) adopted 35 images of job sites as a stimulus to conduct an eye-tracking experiment. They found relative to less-experienced workers (<5 years), more experienced workers (>10 years) need less processing time and deploy more frequent short fixations on hazardous areas to maintain situational awareness of the environment.

However, how subjects perceive hazards on construction sites is substantially different from identifying hazards on images (Sun and Liao, 2019), and some elements of real job sites such as weather and noise are impossible to be expressed (Kushiro et al., 2017). Sun and Liao (2019) proposed to use a civil engineering laboratory on campus as the stimulus for an eye-tracking experiment exploring ability assessment of hazards-identification, they suggest the lab can be a simulated job site because the lab has consistent hazards with job sites and it has stationary site condition. Even though the lab has the same kinds of safety hazards as a job site such as fall-from-height or electric shock, its environment and contained objects are quite different from construction sites. The best choice is to adopt real job sites as the stimulus. Hasanzadeh et al. (2018) used mobile eye-tracking to measure workers' situation awareness towards tripping hazards in a live construction site, but they mentioned the site changes over extended amounts of time so that the research team had a short amount of time to test the subject. However, it is quite hard to invite a large number of participants to conduct such an experiment in job sites as the site condition is changing all the time.

While VR is a sufficiently authentic simulation of a construction site and it also allows repeatable experimental conditions compared with the real environment. Many studies tend to develop virtual scenarios to analyze subjects' behavior in real life, e.g. people's responses during indoor evacuation route-finding (Tian et al., 2019). However, developing VR scenarios using 3d models in game engines such as Unity 3D needs high computational costs, long development times, and has a limited sense of presence and realism (Moore et al., 2019). The panoramic VR would be a better choice. It applies 360-degree panoramas to create true-to-reality simulations of environments and it also gives subjects a high sense of presence when presenting in a VR headset. Hence, this study proposes to use panoramic VR as the stimulus.

3. Research Methodology

Firstly, panoramic VR scenarios representing job sites containing hazards are developed; Secondly, an eye-tracking experiment is conducted where participants are required to search for hazards in the panoramic VR scenarios; Finally, experimental data is analyzed to find out the differences between the experienced and the novice.

3.1 Panoramic VR Development

Firstly, 18 panoramas are shot in job sites of building projects using a panorama camera (THETA Z1, RICOH), with the camera standing on a proper point which ensures the hazards can be seen clearly. Figure *1* shows two of the panoramas. Then the panoramas are added in Tobii Pro Lab as the stimulus, and they are presented to participants using HTC VIVE Pro Headset so that participants can feel immersed in the job sites.

The panoramic VR consists of the 18 job site scenes, covering 8 types of locations (i.e. pile foundation construction, foundation pit construction, construction of the main structure, construction of interior decoration, reinforcement yard, housekeeping area, office area and construction elevator) and 7 types of hazards (i.e. falling-from-height, struck-by objects, collapse, electric shock, improper housekeeping, explosion and improper personal protection). There are 172 hazards in total. Besides, these scenes are of various level of visual clutter. The authors adopt various site conditions aiming at achieving a comprehensive comparison for this study.

a) Indoor scenario b) Outside scenario

Figure 1: Two examples of the Panoramas

3.2 Eye-Tracking Experiment

Participants. 20 undergraduate students in the last year majoring in construction management and 20 safety supervisors with over 3 years of experiences are invited to participate in the study. All participants have uncorrected normal vision or corrected-to-normal vision.

The students have learned all lessons related to construction safety, but they only once visited job sites for a short duration. The students are chosen as participants because they are the same as the novice who just graduate from university and are new to the job site.

The safety supervisors come from various project organizations with a multi-level of positions, including safety managers from the developer, chief safety directors and safety inspectors from both the contractor and sub-contractor and engineers in charge of safety from the supervisor. Their years of experience ranges from 20 to 3, with an average value of 8. Their past working experiences are inquired before the experiment to ensure they have enough experiences to identify the hazards.

Experiment Process. During the experiment, participants wear HTC VIVE Pro Eye (120 HZ), standing inside the playing area (i.e. the square area with the line between the two base stations as a diagonal) and moving around to observe the virtual job sites, as shown in Figure *2*.

Before the formal experiment, participants receive a briefing of the experiment and practice searching hazards in several sample scenes different from the later testing scenes, eliminating the impacts on hazard-identification performances caused by deficient mastery of the experiment requirements and inadaptation to the VR.

Calibration is done first to ensure the accuracy of eye-tracking measurements. Participants are instructed to fixate on five target points at different locations in their VR view. The calibration process establishes a mapping from pupil to gaze coordinates. After successful calibration, a sample scene appears again to ensure the participants can see their front view clearly.

When the testing scene appears, participants move around inside the play area to observe the panoramic job site. They are required to click the mouse in their hand whenever they discover any potential hazard, with their gaze stopping on the hazard. Each scene lasts 90 seconds and participants can switch to the next scene once they finish identification. The 18 scenes are presented randomly among all participants. There is a blank view without time limits designed between two scenes where participants can take a short rest before observing the next scene. The experimenter will direct the participant to the original orientation (participants face the experimenter at the beginning) so that all participants can see the same view when they first see a scene. The experimenter will also direct the participant to the centre of the play area if the participant goes to the edge of the area when observing the previous scene. Participants' mouse-click event and eye movement are recorded during the whole identification.

After the whole identification, the experimenter shows participants the views captured when they click the mouse. Participants are required to explain the hazards they point out. Their identifications will be regarded as correct only when their explanations are correct.

Finally, all participants are required to finish a questionnaire for collecting their personal information and their feedback about this experiment. In terms of personal information, students' major and job site experiences are collected, and supervisors' previous working experiences and their current work positions are collected. In terms of the feedback, both of them are required to describe their dizziness, tiredness and sense of reality towards the panoramic VR, the searching patterns they adopted, and their other feedback. The supervisors are also asked to talk about the use of experiences in hazard-identification.

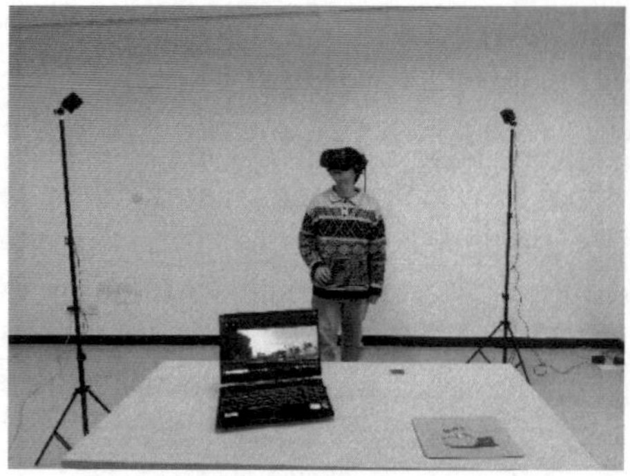

Figure 2: Experimental Set-up

3.3 Data Collection and Analysis

Hypothesis testing for a two-independent sample is used to examine whether there are significant differences in identification performances and eye-movement patterns between the experienced safety supervisors and the students. The identification performances are indicated by identification time and accuracy. The eye-movement patterns are indicated by fixation-related eye-tracking metrics. Fixations are those states when an individual's eyes essentially stop scanning the scene, holding the foveal vision in place so that the visual system can take in detailed information about what is being looked at. Fixation is generally associated with attention, visual processing, and information absorption (Holmqvist et al., 2011). Fixation Counts referring to the number of fixations inside an area and Fixation Duration referring to the time subjects fixated on an area are chosen in this study to indicate participants' attention allocation.

Participants' identification accuracy and final feedback are recorded manually. Participants' identification time and eye-movement are collected by the software Tobii Pro Lab. The identification time of each scene ranges from the stimulus-start to the stimulus-end. To further compare the specific differences of eye-movement patterns, this study defines potential hazardous-areas as AOI (Area of Interest), as shown in Figure *3* (coloured areas are AOIs). In eye-tracking studies, AOI is an area in the display or visual environment that is of interest to the research. There are 6 kinds of AOIs defined, that is "person, scaffold, edge and hole, housekeeping, electric shock and other objects under unsafe status".

Figure 3: An example of AOI definition

4. Results

The results are presented from three levels: the result of the whole scenes (18 scenes), the result of each scene and the result of each AOI. At first, the following two conditions are examined to determine whether the independent-samples T-test can be used: 1) There are no outlier independent variables; 2) The dependent variables in each group obey normal distribution. Otherwise, the non-parametric test method (Mann - Whitney u test) will be used.

Table *1* shows the statistical results of the whole 18 scenes, which shows there are significant differences ($p < 0.05$) in identification time, identification accuracy, fixation counts and percentage of fixations, indicating students spend less time on identification, identify fewer hazards, have fewer fixations and spend less time in fixating.

Table *2* shows the statistical results of identification accuracy on each kind of hazard, that supervisors have significantly higher accuracy ($p < 0.05$) on all kinds of hazards. Students only identify some obvious hazards which can be seen under unsafe status from the appearances, e.g. workers not wearing hardcat, workers being too close to machines, materials stack blocking exits, unlocked electricity box, cables disorderly placed on the ground, holes on the ground without cover. Besides, none hazards caused by unsafe status of scaffold is detected by students.

Table 1: Statistical results of the whole 18 scenes

	Identification time (s)	**Identification accuracy**	**Fixation counts**	**Percentage of fixations**
Mean value of students	1010.10	7	3005	0.480
Mean value of supervisors	1187.01	45	3884	0.559
P-value	0.036	0.000	0.004	0.019
Number of scenes existing significant differences	3	17	11	10

**Percentage of fixations is the ratio between fixation duration and identification time, indicating how much time is spent in fixating.*

Table 2: Statistical results of identification accuracy on various hazard types

	Housekeeping	**Electricity shock**	**Unsafe acts**	**Fall protection**	**Scaffold-related**	**Another unsafe status**
Mean value of students	1.55	0.3	2.35	1.35	0	0.8
Mean value of supervisors	13.35	2.65	6.60	9.8	10.45	5.05
P-value	0.000	0.000	0.000	0.000	0.000	0.000

Table 3: Statistical results of AOI duration and its percentage

AOI_duration (s) / AOI_duration%	**Mean value of students**	**Mean value of supervisors**	**P-value**	**Number of scenes existing significant differences/Number of scenes containing the AOI**
Total AOIs	159.062	249.994	0.000	10/18
	0.315	0.366	0.001	5/18
Housekeeping	27.951	39.926	0.023	8/15
	0.055	0.059	0.461	6/15
Electricity	4.481	9.430	0.001	1/5

	0.009	0.014	0.015	1/5
Person	50.370	34.992	0.052	6/17
	0.103	0.050	0.000	13/17
Edge and hole	13.543	24.123	0.000	6/10
	0.026	0.036	0.001	6/10
Scaffold	30.366	81.727	0.000	13/14
	0.060	0.119	0.000	11/14
Other unsafe status	17.241	28.412	0.001	4/10
	0.034	0.042	0.014	4/10

* *Percentage of AOI duration (AOI_duration%) = fixation time spent on AOI / total fixation time*

Table *3* shows the statistic result of AOI duration and its percentage, where AOI duration refers to the fixation time spent on AOI, indicating how much attention is allocated to a certain AOI; the percentage of AOI duration refers to the ratio between the fixation time spent on AOI and the total fixation time, indicating to what extent attention is allocated to a certain AOI. The differences are significant when calculating the whole AOIs. As for each kind of AOI, the results show supervisors significantly have longer fixation duration on all kinds of AOI except on the person. Similarly, supervisors have a significantly larger percentage of AOI duration on most AOIs except the housekeeping where no significant differences exist and the person where the students have a larger value. The statistical results of each scene are concluded in the last row of Table *1* and the last column of Table *3*, showing the number of scenes where significant differences exist.

Motion sickness occurs on VR players due to the disparity between the users' visual and vestibular stimuli (Clay et al., 2019), nevertheless, the panoramic job sites are static in this study, which greatly reduces participants' dizziness. As a result, none reported dizziness due to VR. One student reported dizziness due to the frequent movement of his body. None reported tiredness during the whole identification.

All students reported they feel going to the job sites personally. Merely one student reported the view resolution is a little lower. All supervisors reported the task is the same as their daily work except they cannot go far in the VR and there is scale distortion in some scenes which bring trouble in exactly determining distance or height.

5. Discussion

5.1 Differences in Identification Time and Accuracy

Table *1* shows supervisors have much higher accuracy ($p = 0.000$), which is not consistent with the study of Dzeng et al. (2016) which reported the experience do not help improve identification accuracy. Such inconformity might come from different experimental stimulus. Their total number (14 in total) and kinds of hazards are quite limited, which might be limited in detecting the differences between the two groups. The simple-to-capture of panoramic pictures allows a large number of safety hazards which helps to acquire a more comprehensive comparison. Besides, the students heavily rely on personal feelings to search for hazards because they lack related knowledge or experience to perceive hazards, so most of their identified hazards are those look obviously.

Even though supervisors spend more time on the whole identification ($p = 0.036$), their unit identification time (identification time / identification accuracy) is significant less than students

($p = 0.000$), indicating they identify faster than students. This is consistent with what Dzeng et al. (2016) found that the experienced identify hazards faster than the novice.

5.2 Differences in Attention Allocation and Search Pattern

Table *1* shows students have significantly fewer fixation counts than supervisors ($p = 0.004$), the authors further examined the Heat Map of fixation counts to analyze the specific differences. The Heat Map uses different colours to illustrate the number of fixations participants made within certain areas of the stimulus. Red indicates the highest number of fixations, and green the least, with varying levels in between. Figure *4* shows a pair of Heat Map. After observing the Heat Map of every scene, the authors found supervisors paid attention to more objects in the scenes, while students ignored some objects. Students' lack of attention to objects might a cause leading to their less identification time and lower accuracy.

When further looking at their attention allocation among the six kinds of AOIs, the specific differences in Table *3* are discussed below:

Person. Students are quite aware of persons in the scenes that they give a larger part of attention on persons than supervisors do ($p = 0.000$), as shown in Figure *4*a, humans are all red in the Heat Map of every scene, while there is no such pattern for supervisors. Nevertheless, students identify less unsafe acts. Supervisors' experiences drive them to inspect more details, that they inspect whether persons tie up their hardcat strap because they know workers not wearing the hardcat well is very common in daily work. Students also fail to identify the hazards requiring professional knowledge even though they notice it, e.g. workers do not place extinguisher when doing hot work.

a) Students' Heat Map b) Supervisors' Heat Map

Figure 4: One scene's Heat Map of fixation counts

Scaffold. Students hardly have awareness to check the safety status of scaffold, while supervisors are quite sensitive ($p = 0.000$). a) Students' Heat Map b) Supervisors' Heat Map

Figure *5* intuitively shows such differences, where students merely go through the scaffold and find no problems, supervisors exactly know the inspection points and they can correctly point out the hazards. In addition, supervisors even carefully inspect the scaffold on the buildings' external surface because they report there are always safety problems in real sites. Students report they once learned related knowledge in class, but they cannot remember and apply it. As a result, students do not identify any hazards caused by unsafe scaffold.

a) Students' Heat Map b) Supervisors' Heat Map

Figure 5: Heat Map of the scene with indoor scaffold

Housekeeping. Students spend less fixation duration in observing housekeeping ($p = 0.023$) even though they put considerable attention on it. The material-stack is less likely to be ignored due to its relatively large volume in the scene, and students are sensitive about its tidiness that they even mistake messy stack as hazards. Even though paying attention to material-stack, students fail to check whether there are extinguishers near flammable materials and to check whether the material-stack is over a safe height.

Edge and Hole. Students aware of the holes' cover on the ground, but they are less sensitive in examining edge protection than supervisors, e.g. they hardly look up at buildings' evaluation surface to ensure whether there are protections alongside the window opening, and they tend to ignore edges with elevation difference less than 2m.

Electricity and Others. Students regard electricity boxes as a source of danger and pay attention to them every time, but their experiences about electric hazards are limited that they fail to detect wherever there is no insulating bush around cables placed on mental objects like scaffold. Likewise, students almost noticed all other objects under unsafe status, but they only pointed out obvious hazards such as a plank is not fixed well on the door frame.

In terms of their differences in each scene. Only three students report they feel harder and need more time for searching when encountering scenes with larger visual clutter (e.g. Figure 6a*)*, while it does not affect supervisors. The authors compare the contained construction locations and level of visual clutter of the scenes existing significant differences and of the other scenes. The significant differences do not exist in certain construction locations or a certain level of visual clutter specifically. Hence, it is inferred that it is the kinds of AOIs and hazards contained in the scenes that might cause the differences.

When it comes to search pattern, 16 of the 20 students report they adopt a constant observation order to totally observe the scene or search hazards more quickly, e.g. one student observed his overhead at first and then the ground and surroundings because he thinks the overhead places are more dangerous. Supervisors reported they do not consciously observe the scenes in a certain order. They just inspect their surroundings exactly as they do in real sites and point out hazards whenever they see. The hazard-identification seems to be a spontaneous behavior for the experienced supervisors.

Dzeng et al. (2016) reported scan paths of the experienced are more consistent than the novice, and Xu et al. (2019) also reported successful participants follow similar searching patterns. The authors observe similar findings in this study by looking at participants' scan paths from their replay. Students seem to find something in a scene following vairous orders and they have more frequent saccades, while supervisors gradually look around the scene along a constant direction and their gaze stop at somewhere to confirm whether there are hazards. This is also consistent with the statistical result in Table *1* that students significantly spend less time in fixations ($p=0.019$), indicating they spend more time in searching instead of identification.

6. Conclusion

Panoramic VR and eye-tracking are integrated to compare the differences in hazard-identification between the experienced and the novice. The panoramic VR provides subjects with an immersive feeling of going to real sites personally, and it allows diverse construction site conditions and a large number of hazards to achieve more comprehensive findings. The eye-tracking provides data which quantificationally reveal the differences of attention allocation and search patterns. The results show the experienced have significantly higher accuracy than the novice. The experiences help supervisors to be more sensitive to hazards. The experienced put more attention on hazardous areas instead of unimportant things, they inspect more details that are ignored by the novice, and they show more solid safety knowledge which enables them to identify correctly hazards once noticing them. It is suggested the training for the novice should educate them to be more aware of hazardous areas, especially those details they tend to ignore and help them enhance safety knowledge at the same time.

There are also some limitations. Participants' limited movement in the scene and the scale distortion reduce participants' sense of reality. The sample is also limited in this study. The future study is suggested to improve the scenario so as to give participants a more authentic feeling and invite more various participants to obtain more findings.

Acknowledgment

This work was jointly supported by Shenzhen Science and Technology Innovation Committee Grant (PJ#JCYJ20180507181647320), National Natural Science Foundation of China (PJ#51778553), and City University of Hong Kong Teaching Development Grant (PJ# 6000687).

References

Clay, v., könig, p. & koenig, s. 2019. Eye tracking in virtual reality. Journal of eye movement research, 12.

Dzeng, r.-j., lin, c.-t. & fang, y.-c. 2016. Using eye-tracker to compare search patterns between experienced and novice workers for site hazard identification. Safety science, 82, 56–67.

Hasanzadeh, s., esmaeili, b. & dodd, m. D. 2017. Measuring the impacts of safety knowledge on construction workers' attentional allocation and hazard detection using remote eye-tracking technology. Journal of management in engineering, 33, 04017024.

Hasanzadeh, s., esmaeili, b. & dodd, m. D. 2018. Examining the relationship between construction workers' visual attention and situation awareness under fall and tripping hazard conditions: using mobile eye tracking. Journal of construction engineering and management, 144, 04018060.

Holmqvist, k., nyström, m., andersson, r., dewhurst, r., jarodzka, h. & van de weijer, j. 2011. Eye tracking: a comprehensive guide to methods and measures, oup oxford.

Hosking, s. G., liu, c. C. & bayly, m. 2010. The visual search patterns and hazard responses of experienced and inexperienced motorcycle riders. Accident analysis & prevention, 42, 196–202.

Hyönä, j., lorch jr, r. F. & kaakinen, j. K. 2002. Individual differences in reading to summarize expository text: evidence from eye fixation patterns. Journal of educational psychology, 94, 44–55.

Kushiro, n., fujita, y. & aoyama, y. 2017. Extracting field oversees' features in risk recognition from data of eyes and utterances. 2017 ieee international conference on data mining workshops (icdmw).

Moore, h. F., eiris, r., gheisari, m. & esmaeili, b. Hazard identification training using 360-degree panorama vs. Virtual reality techniques: a pilot study. Computing in civil engineering 2019: visualization, information modeling, and simulation - selected papers from the asce international conference on computing in civil engineering 2019, 2019. 55–62.

Pradhan, a. K., hammel, k. R., deramus, r., pollatsek, a., noyce, d. A. & fisher, d. L. 2005. Using eye movements to evaluate effects of driver age on risk perception in a driving simulator. Human factors, 47, 840–852.

Sadasivan, s., greenstein, j. S., gramopadhye, a. K. & duchowski, a. T. Use of eye movements as feedforward training for a synthetic aircraft inspection task. Proceedings of the sigchi conference on human factors in computing systems, 2005. 141–149.

Sun, x. & liao, p.-c. 2019. Re-assessing hazard recognition ability in occupational environment with microvascular function in the brain. Safety science, 120, 67–78.

Tian, p., wang, y., lu, y., zhang, y., wang, x. & wang, y. Behavior analysis of indoor escape route-finding based on head-mounted vr and eye tracking. 2019 international conference on internet of things (ithings) and ieee green computing and communications (greencom) and ieee cyber, physical and social computing (cpscom) and ieee smart data (smartdata), 2019. Ieee, 422–427.

Xu, q., chong, h.-y. & liao, p.-c. 2019. Exploring eye-tracking searching strategies for construction hazard recognition in a laboratory scene. Safety science, 120, 824–832.

Virtual Reality Platform for 3D Irregular Packing Problem

Yinghui Zhao[a], JuHyeong Ryu[a], Carl Haas[a], Sriram Narasimhan[b]
[a] University of Waterloo, Canada, [b] University of California, USA
yinghui.zhao@uwaterloo.ca

Abstract. Cutting and packing is an operational research area that supports a wide variety of applications in the chemical industry, robotics, manufacturing engineering, and construction. Construction applications include module packing, 3D printing, volume optimization, and shipping of assemblies. Arguably the most challenging sub-problem in this area is the 3D irregular object packing problem due to its computational complexity. Previous studies on this topic have used heuristics, mathematical modeling, and a hybrid of both these methods. Despite such efforts, limited progress has been achieved for 3D packing of arbitrary objects with multi-objective optimization goals. While not as efficient at computing as computers, humans are naturally superior to a computer in many ways, such as our intuition, strategic thinking, adaptability, and ability to process visual and spatial data quickly and efficiently. Harnessing such capabilities of a human, we propose here a virtual reality (VR) platform which can pack 3D objects into a pre-specified container while optimizing multiple objectives. The platform allows users to virtually pack heavy and potentially hazardous objects (e.g., nuclear waste) while limiting exposure to the hazard and physical fatigue, while also providing an interactive environment which allows users to work with the machine to adjust and improve the overall outcome of packing compared to using either the human or machine alone. Series of preliminary experiments are conducted to explore the feasibility and potential of the VR interactive packing.

1. Introduction

The 3D irregular packing problem consists of arranging irregular-shaped objects into one or a set of containers to optimize one or multiple objectives such as maximizing the packing efficiency or minimizing the container's volume. The primary constraints of 3D irregular packing problems are that the objects must not overlap with each other and are entirely contained inside the containers (Leao *et al.*, 2019). There is a growing interest in the 3D irregular packing problem because of its broad applications and potential impacts in a multitude of industries. The 3D irregular packing problem can generally be applied both to traditional applications such as improving transport efficiency of building parts or pre-fabricated construction assemblies and emerging applications in civil engineering such as 3D printing in construction and facility waste management (Zhao, Rausch and Haas, 2021).

Despite its broad applications and substantial potential, research on 3D irregular cutting and packing problem is still nascent. The primary reason is that the 3D irregular packing problem is known to be NP-hard, i.e., the expected time to find an optimal solution increases exponentially as a function of the number of inputs (Araújo et al., 2019). Researchers have proposed different approaches including constructive heuristics, metaheuristics, mathematical programming, or a hybrid of these. However, none of the existing algorithms for the 3D irregular packing problem can find a globally optimal solution in polynomial time (Cao et al., 2019). Finding a good solution through such autonomous approaches is computationally expensive and time-consuming.

Humans possess intuition are naturally superior to computers in processing visual and spatial data as well as in strategic thinking. Allowing human intervention in the packing process can decrease the time and computation power required, while potentially achieving better outcomes than using machines alone in 3D irregular packing problems. At the same time, virtual reality

(VR) technology can create immersive virtual environments that simulate physical interactions between humans and virtually rendered objects and hence is a powerful tool to establish such an interactive packing environment with humans. This forms the main premise for this paper.

This paper proposes an interactive packing environment supported by VR technology to pack 3D objects into a pre-specified container while optimizing multiple objectives. To the best of the authors' knowledge, this is the first time VR technology is being proposed to tackle the 3D irregular packing problem. A scoring system is developed and integrated into the system to provide users with instant feedback regarding the current configuration and help users to make informed adjustments and decisions. With the help of the proposed platform, users can remotely pack heavy or even hazardous objects without being exposed to potential hazards and physical fatigue.

2. Related Work

2.1 Three-dimensional Irregular Packing Optimization

A variety of optimization techniques have been applied to the 3D irregular packing problem. These approaches include constructive heuristics, metaheuristics, mathematical programming, and hybrids of different techniques. Constructive heuristics refer to low-level heuristics constructed only for a specific class of problems. For instance, the most popular constructive heuristic algorithm for 3D irregular packing problems is the Bottom-left-front (BLF) algorithm, which packs pre-ordered objects one by one at the most bottom left front corner of the container's available space (Wu *et al.*, 2014; Araújo *et al.*, 2019). However, BLF can only explore configurations generated from a fixed packing sequence and fixed object orientations, which reflects a general drawback of construction heuristics. Constrictive heuristics are relatively fast but can only explore limited configurations.

Metaheuristics are high-level heuristics which provide guidelines to develop a process capable of escaping from local optima and finding a good solution. Genetic algorithm, simulated annealing, Tabu-search are some of the metaheuristics applied to the 3D irregular packing (Vanek *et al.*, 2014; Stefan and Paul, 2015; Fakoor, Ghoreishi and Sabaghzadeh, 2016). Metaheuristics explore more potential configurations resulting in significantly more computational time compared to constructive heuristics.

Researchers have also tried to formulate the 3D irregular packing problem using mathematical programming. The most successful approach is based on the phi-function, which provides a tool to mathematically describe non-overlapping constraints, enabling mathematical programming (Romanova *et al.*, 2018; Chugay and Zhuravka, 2021). However, the current state-of-the-art solver cannot directly solve such a problem with a large number of variables and constraints. Heuristics are applied to reduce the problem into a sequence of subproblems with smaller dimensions and fewer constraints that can be solved using a nonlinear programming solver. The drawback of the phi-function-based mathematical programming method is computationally costly and currently futile for non-primary arbitrary shapes.

Despite such efforts, researchers are yet to propose fast, fully autonomous algorithms with adequate packing solution exploration. Alternatively, by harnessing the capabilities of human intuition and visual processing, providing a framework for humans to interact with the machine during the packing process could lead to better packing outcomes in terms of both time and efficiency.

2.2 VR Application in Construction

VR supports the creation of immersive virtual environments, which simulates a physical environment and allows users to interact with virtually rendered objects in real-time (Du *et al.*, 2018; You *et al.*, 2018). In recent years, the architecture, engineering, and construction (AEC) industry have witnessed a growing interest in VR as a potential solution to certain construction problems (Du *et al.*, 2018). VR has been used in training and education, hazard identification, design visualization, and communication. For instance, Muhammad et al. compared the traditional 2D job site layout plan and 3D model in VR for site layout optimization of construction projects (Muhammad *et al.*, 2020). Results indicated that 3D VR-based job site layout planning is more useful to comprehend by users and enhances collision detection. You et al. employ the VR environment to analyze the safety perception in the human-robot collaborative workspace (You *et al.*, 2018). Alizadehsalehi et al. use a 3D model in an extended reality (XR) environment to examine the overall design and evaluate alternative design decisions (Alizadehsalehi, Hadavi and Huang, 2020). Other XR technologies such as augmented reality have been deployed to display packing solutions and guide users in 3D regular packing problems with boxes (Techasarntikul *et al.*, 2020). However, to the best of the authors' knowledge, no previous studies exist which have applied VR to 3D irregular packing problems.

3. Proposed VR platform

Game engines such as Unity3D, with the built-in physics engine mimicking real-world physics (e.g., gravity and collision), are excellent tools to support an intuitive VR interface. The VR packing platform described in this paper is created using the Unity3D game engine. HTC VIVE is used as the VR headset. The matching controllers are developed with functions such as *grab, hold and release* objects and *teleportation* to allow users to navigate the virtual environment. The virtual environment consists of an area with a container at the center and some objects to be packed. Users can load the objects into the container with the aid of the controllers.

A panel showing criteria scores is developed and used to instantaneously evaluate the performance of the ongoing packing configuration, providing critical feedback to workers and guiding better decisions for the following step. Table 1 shows the screenshots of the VR platform under different circumstances. The following criteria are used to evaluate the results of packing experiments:

Packing efficiency. Packing efficiency is calculated by dividing the container volume occupied with packed objects by the total container volume, indicating space utilization inside the container. Higher the packing efficiency, less space in the container is wasted.

Center of gravity (CoG) error. CoG error is the indication of how far the packing CoG is from the optimal CoG. The optimal CoG is defined at the vertical central axis that goes through the geometry center. The more the center of gravity deviates from the central axis, the easier the packed container can be made to destabilize and hence minimizing the deviation between COG of the packed container and optimal COG can lead to more stable configurations.

Weight and radiation criteria. Weight and radiation limitations are imposed on the packed container as in nuclear waste packing and storage problem. By doing so, the VR packing experiment is designed to approximate practical problems with multiple constraints. These two constraints are represented by the percentages of the container's permissible limits reached by the current configuration. For example, if the configuration reaches the container's radiation limit, the radiation limitation criterion is 100%. Warning messages are displayed to the user if weight or radiation limitation is exceeded, informing them of packing configurations which are unacceptable. As long as the weight and radiation limitations are not exceeded, higher values for weight and radiation criteria indicate better container utilization.

Table 1: Screenshots of the VR platform

Initial display	**Display during the packing process**	**Exceeding limitation display**
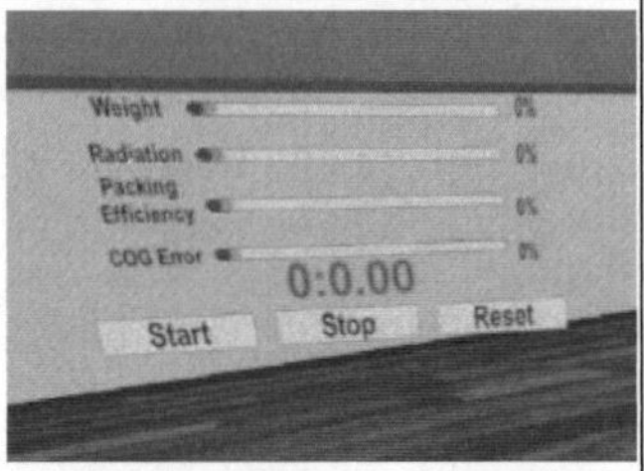	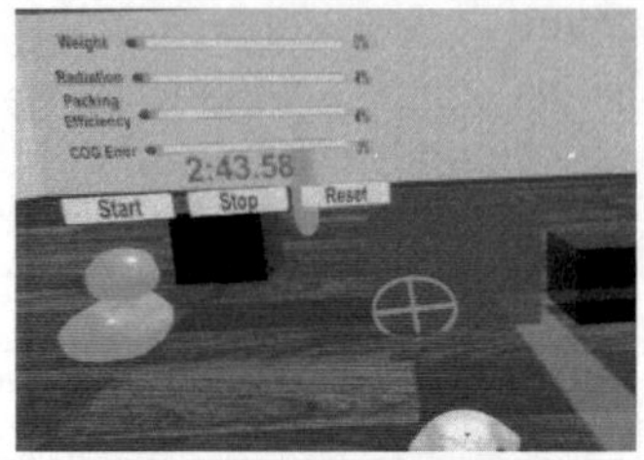	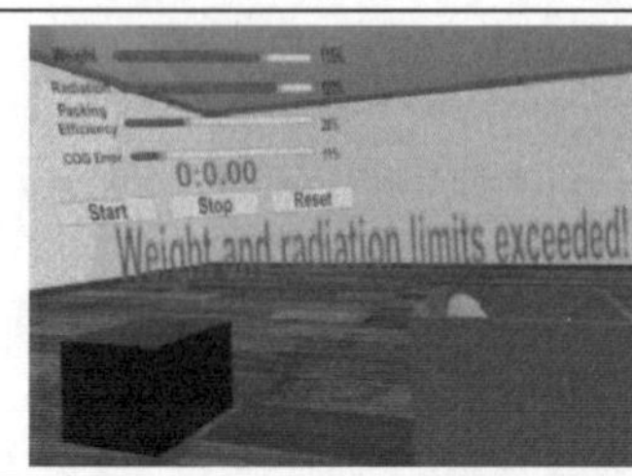

In each packing test, the goal is to achieve preferred packing results (higher packing efficiency and lower CoG error) by arranging objects into the container without exceeding weight and radiation limitation constraints. The VR system shows values of criteria and constraints as feedback in real-time to help the user make informed decisions. A timer is used to record the time a user spends on packing one set of objects into the container.

4. Experiments Design

To test the VR packing platform, experiments were conducted with human participants. The experiment comprised three scenarios of packing different shapes: 1) box-shaped objects, 2) cylinder-shaped objects, and 3) irregular-shaped objects (see Table 2). The variance in objects' shapes is intended to explore the applicability and feasibility of the VR packing platform.

Table 2: Three scenarios of packing different shapes

Packing of box-shaped objects	**Packing of cylinder-shaped objects**	**Packing of irregular-shaped objects**
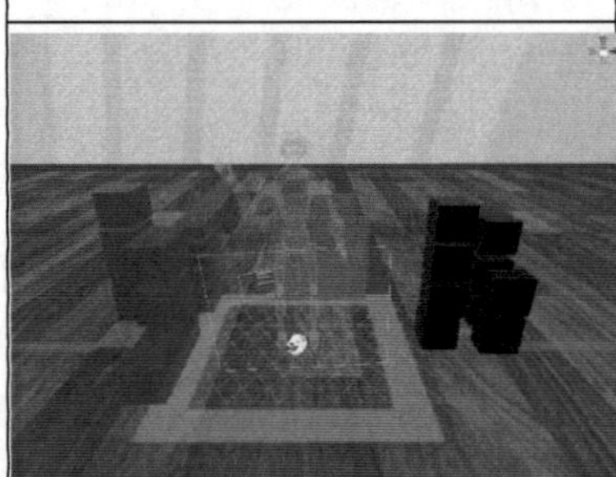		

The experiment involved two volunteer participants due to limitations on in-person interactions during Covid-19. One participant was an experienced user of the developed VR packing platform, whereas the other participant had no previous experience with the platform. Each participant received a written instruction on the VR packing platform and was allowed to practice for five minutes to get familiar with the controls before the actual experiment started.

With the purpose of testing the performance of the VR packing platform, for each scenario, the participants were asked to pack different sets of objects. Each set, consisting of 20 objects, was randomly selected from a pre-established library with 40 different objects. Each object is associated with pre-defined weight and radiation properties. The weight and radiation properties are assumed to be proportional to the object's volume as a first approximation. All objects were assumed to be made from the same material, whereas objects are randomly assigned to two different radiation density levels.

The participants were asked to pack five sets of objects for each scenario and to repeatedly pack the first set of objects (Set1) two times. The Set1's configurations generated from the first and second trials are compared in the next section.

5. Results and discussion

In this section, the experiment results are presented and discussed.

Set1 has been packed two times repeatedly by each participant. Comparisons between the first and second tests for each scenario are presented in Figures 1 to 3. The packing results for Set1 of different shapes are summarized in Table 3.

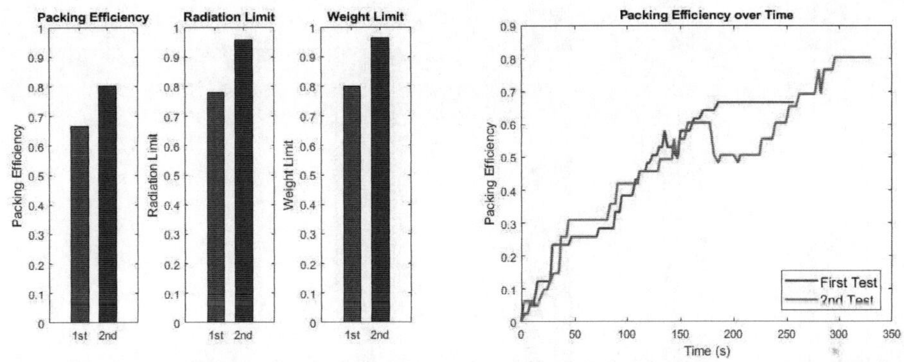

(a)

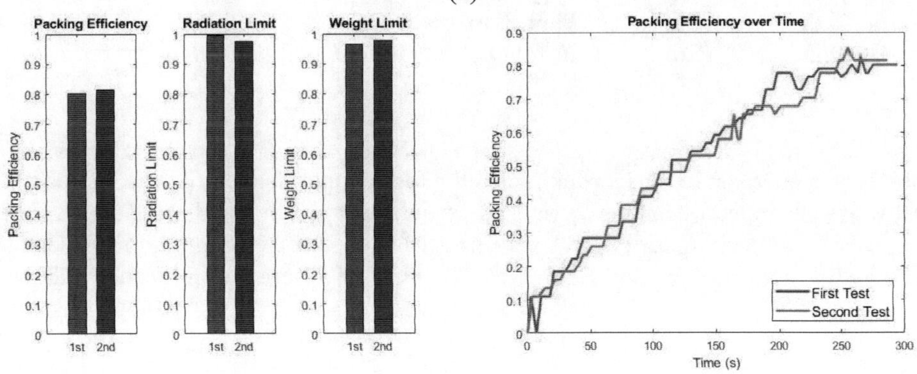

(b)

Figure 1: Comparison of Set1's packing results for box-shaped objects: (a) Comparing configurations generated by the inexperienced participant from first and second tests in terms of different criteria and packing efficiency over time. (b) Comparing configurations generated by the experienced participant from first and second tests in terms of different criteria and packing efficiency over time.

For the inexperienced participant, Table 3 and Figure 1(a) show an approximate 20% ~ 24% improvement in the packing efficiency, achieving the weight and radiation limits in the first test compared to the second trial. There are several reasons which could be attributed to this observed improvement in the packing efficiency in the second test; primarily, after the first test, the user is: 1) better adjusted to the VR platform and controls assigned to the controllers; 2) familiar with the object set. Table 3 and Figure 1(b) show a comparatively very little improvement (1.2%) between the two tests with regards to the packing efficiency for the experienced participant.

It is also worth noting that the inexperienced participant achieved similar configurations in terms of packing efficiency, radiation and weight limits as the experienced participant in the second test.

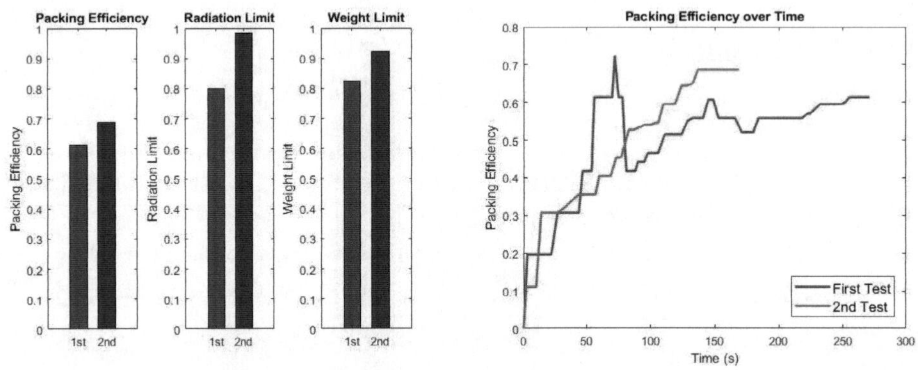

(a)

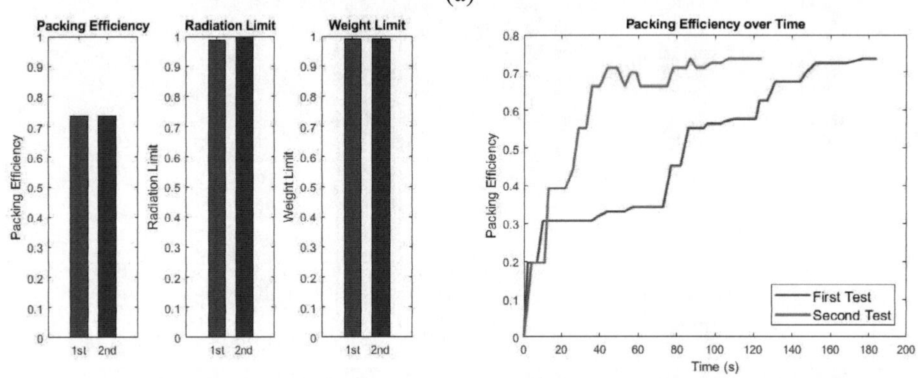

(b)

Figure 2: Comparison of Set1's packing results for cylinder-shaped objects: (a) Comparing configurations generated by the inexperienced participant from first and second tests in terms of different criteria and packing efficiency over time. (b) Comparing configurations generated by the experienced participant from first and second tests in terms of different criteria and packing efficiency over time.

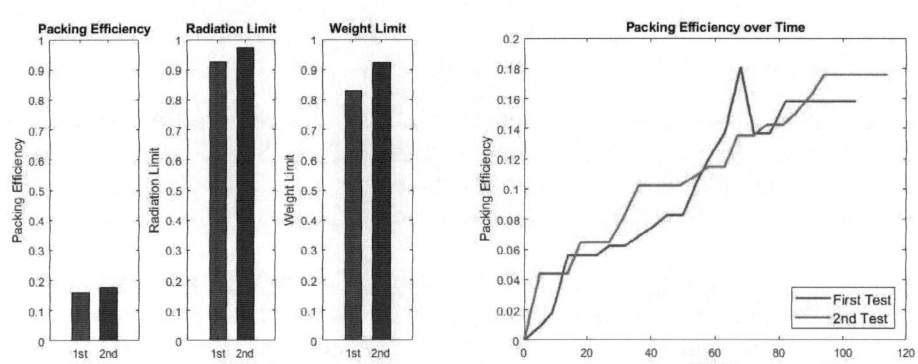

(a)

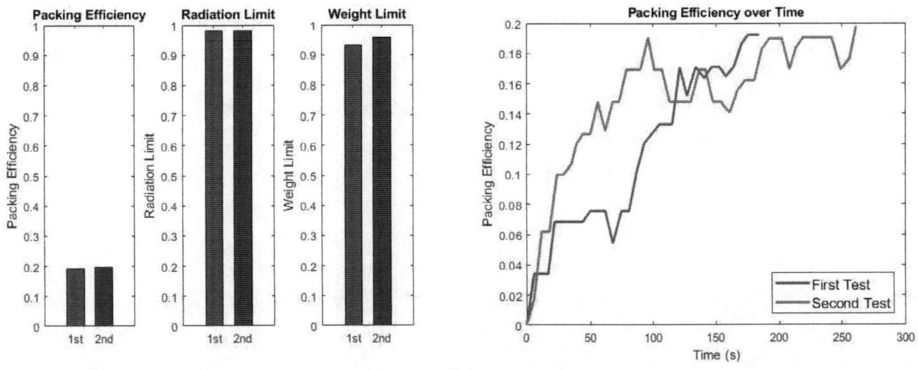

(b)

Figure 3: Comparison of Set1's packing results for irregular-shaped objects: (a) Comparing configurations generated by the inexperienced participant from first and second tests in terms of different criteria and packing efficiency over time. (b) Comparing configurations generated by the experienced participant from first and second tests in terms of different criteria and packing efficiency over time.

Table 3: Comparison of Set1's configurations generated from the first and second tests

		Box		Cylinder		Irregular	
		First test	**Second test**	**First test**	**Second test**	**First test**	**Second test**
Inexperienced	Packing Efficiency	0.667	0.802	0.614	0.687	0.158	0.176
	COG	0.065	0.063	0.056	0.032	0.048	0.057
	Time (s)	208	327	277	167	86	100
	Radiation Limit (%)	77.9%	95.9%	80.1%	98.3%	92.4%	97.2%
	Weight Limit (%)	80.0%	96.3%	82.4%	92.3%	83.0%	92.2%
	No. packed objects	15	18	14	17	12	11
Experienced	Packing Efficiency	0.802	0.815	0.736	0.736	0.192	0.197
	COG	0.064	0.074	0.044	0.036	0.058	0.042
	Time	282	278	198	110	199	260
	Radiation Limit (%)	99.5%	97.7%	98.6%	99.9%	98.0%	98.0%
	Weight Limit (%)	96.3%	97.8%	98.9%	98.9%	93.1%	95.6%
	No. packed objects	17	18	17	8	13	13

In the scenario of packing cylinder-shaped objects, Table 3 and Figure 2(a) still show significant improvement (11.9% in packing efficiency, 22.7% in radiation limitation, and 12.0% in weight limitation) in the second test; while, the two configurations generated by the experienced participant do not exhibit this improvement. When comparing the test results between the inexperienced and experienced participants, though the configuration of the inexperienced participant is still worse than that of the experienced participant, the differences in the configurations' performance are largely reduced in the second test.

In the scenario of packing irregular-shaped objects, a trend, similar to the test results in the other two shapes, can be observed in Table 3 and Figure 3. The packing result generated by the inexperienced participant from the second test shows considerable improvements compared to that from the first test. The experienced participant keeps generating good packing outcomes. It is worth noting that the considerable drop in the packing efficiency in the irregular packing test, compared with the packing test of two other shapes, is because all of the test's irregular objects are non-convex, and most of them are hollow. The concave and hollow parts are hard to fill with other objects, leading to packing efficiency reductions.

To conclude, main observations from the results of the two tests of Set1 are:

(1) For the inexperienced user, the configuration's quality in the second test is better than the configuration in the first test. The potential reasons are a higher degree of familiarity with the VR platform, smoother controls, and a comprehensive understanding of the object set.

(2) Compared to the inexperienced participants, the second test's improvements are negligible for the experienced user. The configurations from the two tests both show good performance.

(3) Although there are significant differences between inexperienced and experienced participants' configurations in the first tests, the packing results' differences are mostly reduced in the second test.

After the two packing tests of Set1, the participants were then asked to pack other randomly selected sets of objects for each shape. The results of the configurations are summarized in Tables 4-6. Since the packing tests of Set1 demonstrated that the differences in the packing results between inexperienced and experienced users could be mostly reduced in the second test, the interesting question is that, from a statistical standpoint, is the inexperienced participant's packing ability and experienced participant's significantly different?

To this end, two-tail t-tests comparing the differences between the means of configurations' packing efficiencies, generated by inexperienced and experienced participants, were completed. Only the packing efficiencies of the packing configurations generated by the two participants are compared. It is the most critical criterion as long as all the other constraints, such as weight and radiation limits, are not exceeded. The null hypothesis (H_0) is that the packing efficiencies of the packing configurations generated by the two participants are not significantly different. For the three different shape types, the t-test results found that the null hypothesis H_0 cannot be rejected, meaning that the packing efficiencies of the packing configurations generated by the two participants are not significantly different at the 5% level of significance. The t-test results show that the inexperienced participant and experienced participant's packing ability may not be significantly different, indicating that the proposed VR platform may be intuitive and easy to use. However, with only five sets of samples from 2 participants at this point, definitive conclusions await further tests.

Table 4: Packing results of 5 sets of box-shaped objects

		Set 1	Set 2	Set 3	Set 4	Set 5
Inexperienced (Participant 1)	Packing Efficiency	0.802	0.753	0.778	0.765	0.790
	COG	0.063	0.053	0.082	0.086	0.075
	Time (s)	327	284	216	205	255
	Radiation Limit (%)	95.9%	96.8%	99.9%	99.5%	99.5%
	Weight Limit (%)	96.3%	90.4%	93.3%	91.9%	94.8%
	No. packed objects	18	15	14	15	16
Experienced ((Participant 2)	Packing Efficiency	0.815	0.790	0.778	0.790	0.802
	COG	0.074	0.062	0.077	0.074	0.071
	Time	278	273	297	205	192
	Radiation Limit (%)	97.7%	99.5%	98.1%	99.9%	98.6%
	Weight Limit (%)	97.8%	94.8%	93.3%	94.8%	96.3%
	No. packed objects	18	15	17	15	17

Table 5: Packing results of 5 sets of cylinder-shaped objects

		Set 1	Set 2	Set 3	Set 4	Set 5
	Packing Efficiency	0.687	0.724	0.699	0.742	0.742
	COG	0.032	0.028	0.046	0.041	0.018
Inexperienced	Time (s)	167	255	118	129	128
(Participant 1)	Radiation Limit (%)	98.3%	93.9%	99.6%	96.8%	98.0%
	Weight Limit (%)	92.3%	97.2%	94.0%	99.7%	99.7%
	No. packed objects	17	15	8	13	14
	Packing Efficiency	0.736	0.736	0.706	0.718	0.742
	COG	0.036	0.037	0.049	0.020	0.018
Experienced	Time	110	85	106	69	161
((Participant 2)	Radiation Limit (%)	99.9%	99.9%	99.3%	99.6%	98.0%
	Weight Limit (%)	98.9%	98.9%	94.8%	96.4%	99.7%
	No. packed objects	8	8	8	10	14

Table 6: Packing results of 5 sets of irregular-shaped objects

		Set 1	Set 2	Set 3	Set 4	Set 5
	Packing Efficiency	0.199	0.203	0.196	0.203	0.204
	COG	0.027	0.024	0.058	0.023	0.025
Inexperienced	Time (s)	92	114	173	198	213
(Participant 1)	Radiation Limit (%)	98.4%	99.9%	97.0%	94.6%	94.1%
	Weight Limit (%)	96.4%	98.5%	95.1%	98.2%	98.8%
	No. packed objects	14	16	15	12	14
	Packing Efficiency	0.203	0.206	0.199	0.204	0.202
	COG	0.049	0.068	0.086	0.013	0.029
Experienced	Time	239	165	299	177	200
((Participant 2)	Radiation Limit (%)	99.4%	94.8%	98.8%	97.4%	96.8%
	Weight Limit (%)	98.5%	99.5%	96.6%	98.7%	98.1%
	No. packed objects	12	13	14	13	13

6. Conclusion

The 3D irregular cutting and packing problem is a challenging problem with emerging applications in construction. Existing approaches demand computationally expensive and time-consuming operations, and even with that are unable to find optimal solutions. This paper presents an interactive VR packing platform to tackle the 3D irregular packing problem with multi-objectives by allowing human intervention. Preliminary experiments demonstrated the framework, technical feasibility and the usefulness of the proposed approach. The VR packing platform is intuitive and user-friendly; experimental results showed that inexperienced users can generate good configurations as experienced users, however more statistical data is necessary prior to reaching definitive conclusions. More potential improvements to the VR packing platform still remain to be explored, such as integrating autonomous packing algorithms with the VR platform and identifying optimal workflows when using the proposed VR packing platform for specific problems. Extended empirical studies will be carried out in the future to compare the VR packing platform's performance with the conventional manual packing and autonomous packing approaches.

References

Alizadehsalehi, S., Hadavi, A. and Huang, J. C. (2020) 'From BIM to extended reality in AEC industry', Automation in Construction. Elsevier, 116(March), p. 103254. doi: 10.1016/j.autcon.2020.103254.

Araújo, L. J. P. et al. (2019) 'An experimental analysis of deepest bottom-left-fill packing methods for additive manufacturing', International Journal of Production Research, 7543. doi: 10.1080/00207543.2019.1686187.

Cao, P. et al. (2019) 'Harnessing multi-objective simulated annealing toward configuration optimization within compact space for additive manufacturing', Robotics and Computer-Integrated Manufacturing. Elsevier Ltd, 57(November 2018), pp.29–45. doi: 10.1016/j.rcim.2018.10.009.

Chugay, A. M. and Zhuravka, A. V. (2021) Packing Optimization Problems and Their Application in 3D Printing, Advances in Intelligent Systems and Computing. Springer International Publishing. doi: 10.1007/978-3-030-55506-1_7.

Du, J. et al. (2018) 'Zero latency: Real-time synchronization of BIM data in virtual reality for collaborative decision-making', Automation in Construction. Elsevier, 85(September 2017), pp.51–64. doi: 10.1016/j.autcon.2017.10.009.

Fakoor, M., Ghoreishi, S. M. N. and Sabaghzadeh, H. (2016) 'Spacecraft Component Adaptive Layout Environment (SCALE): An efficient optimization tool', Advances in Space Research. COSPAR, 58(9), pp.1654–1670. doi: 10.1016/j.asr.2016.07.020.

Leao, A. A. S. et al. (2019) 'Irregular packing problems: A review of mathematical models', European Journal of Operational Research. Elsevier B.V., (xxxx). doi: 10.1016/j.ejor.2019.04.045.

Muhammad, A. A. et al. (2020) 'Adoption of Virtual Reality (VR) for Site Layout Optimization of Construction Projects', Teknik Dergi, pp.9833–9850. doi: 10.18400/tekderg.423448.

Pankratov, A., Romanova, T. and Litvinchev, I. (2020) 'Packing oblique 3D objects', Mathematics, 8(7). doi: 10.3390/math8071130.

Romanova, T. et al. (2018) 'Packing of concave polyhedra with continuous rotations using nonlinear optimisation', European Journal of Operational Research. Elsevier B.V., 268(1), pp.37–53. doi: 10.1016/j.ejor.2018.01.025.

Stefan, E. and Paul, W. (2015) 'Packing Irregular-Shaped Objects for 3D Printing', pp.3–15. doi: 10.1007/978-3-319-24489-1.

Techasarntikul, N. et al. (2020) 'Guidance and visualization of optimized packing solutions', Journal of Information Processing, 28, pp.193–202. doi: 10.2197/ipsjjip.28.193.

Vanek, J. et al. (2014) 'PackMerger: A 3D print volume optimizer', Computer Graphics Forum, 33(6), pp.322–332. doi: 10.1111/cgf.12353.

Wu, S. *et al.* (2014) 'Multi-objective optimization of 3D packing problem in additive manufacturing', in *IIE Annual Conference and Expo 2014*, pp.1485–1494. Available at: https://search.proquest.com/docview/1622299299?pq-origsite=gscholar (Accessed: 3 January 2018).

You, S. *et al.* (2018) 'Enhancing perceived safety in human–robot collaborative construction using immersive virtual environments', *Automation in Construction*. Elsevier, 96(September), pp.161–170. doi: 10.1016/j.autcon.2018.09.008.

Zhao, Y., Rausch, C. and Haas, C. (2021) 'Optimizing 3D Irregular Object Packing from 3D Scans Using Metaheuristics', *Advanced Engineering Informatics*. Elsevier Ltd, 47(December 2020), p. 101234. doi: 10.1016/j.aei.2020.101234.

Reference Architectural Model of Buildings for Virtual City Creator

Agnieszka Mars, Ewa Grabska, Jan Bielański, Paweł Mogiła, Michał Mogiła
Jagiellonian University, Poland
agnieszka.mars@uj.edu.pl

Abstract. This paper presents a new approach to creative building modelling for a virtual city model. The aim of this paper is to propose a simplified generative method that supports the designer in styling city buildings and facilitates interactive control, remaining available to non-expert users. Stylistic preferences are introduced within a reference building model created by the designer through a graphical interface. The main contribution of this paper is an innovative computer tool developed to support the designer in styling architectural objects according to his/her expectations. This tool has been applied to generate buildings of virtual city for computer games. The tool can have other possibilities of applications in the AEC, for example urban design and education in AEC programs. The proposed technology can be also integrated with BIM in future developments.

1. Introduction

This paper proposes a new approach to creative building modelling for a virtual city model. The demand for urban area exists in modern computer games, movies and commercials. Creating this area requires generating buildings. The presented method is used to develop an interactive computer system called Virtual City Creator (VCC) for computer games. The paper describes the stage of VCC development, in which there is a need for generating buildings and recreating their styles. The need to recreate individual building styles is one of the big challenges in the procedural generation of city buildings. It requires a skilled workforce to generate them. Consequently production costs are extremely high (Kelly, McCabe, 2006).

The main objective of this paper is to propose such a simplified generative method that both will support the designer in styling city buildings and will facilitate interactive control, remaining available to non-expert users. In this paper, our attention is focused on the stages of VCC-system in which the following two techniques are used: structural analysis of 3D reference building models and a generative tool enabling stylization of buildings. The remaining phases of VCC system will only be outlined.

Our approach introduces an architectural reference building model that allows the designer to capture his/her style preferences and expectations. The form of such a model is created by the user through a graphical interface. This reference model provides designer's suggested graphical primitives and relationships between them. The reference building is a representative of a class of buildings in his/her style. Other buildings of this class are generated based on structure and attributes of this building model.

The user's aesthetic preferences for building styling are contained within the reference building model he creates using a visual language. In the case of automatic aesthetic evaluation the recreation of the human process of visual perception is needed (Csikzentmihalyi, Robinson, 1990). In this paper the model is based on the Biederman's visual perception model (Biederman, 1987). It is assumed that recognition of an object takes place through the exploration of three-dimensional structural components of the object, together with a description of the way they are connected. The Biederman's structural object has its internal representation in the form of the composition graph (CP-graph) which describes the relations not only between the whole building components but also between fragments of these components at different levels of detail (Mars, Grabska, 2016).

In the VCC-system, evolutionary design will be used as a design aid to stimulate creativity in creating new, unexpected forms of buildings and evaluating their style. The evolutionary approach is a generative approach that has been used for many years to synthesize and evaluate designs during the design process (Marin, et al. 2008). One of the most famous architects in the field of evolutionary design is John Frazer, who has been involved in the use of genetic technology since 1968 (Frazer et al. 2002). He explores the possibilities of expressing designer's actions as generative rules so that their evolution can be evaluated by computer models. The VCC-system will be also used procedural generation describing buildings, in terms of a sequence of generation CP-graph rules, iteratively refining the object by adding more and more details. This type of exploration will be developed with an aesthetic evaluation mechanism encoded in the fitness function. Such an approach to aesthetics was tested in the DARCI system acting as a computational artist of images (Ventura, 2015) and in design characteristics-oriented method (Mars, et al, 2020).

The basis for implementing the VCC-system has been Python as a Blender Addon. Blender is a free and open-source software toolset including 3D modelling, rendering and interactive 3D applications. VCC-system consists of two main modules – the GUI which enables interaction with the user and the graph module that performs operations on the internal representations of the designs.

The main contribution in this paper is an innovative computer tool developed to support the designer in styling architectural objects according to his/her stylistic preferences and aesthetic expectations. This tool has been applied to generate buildings of virtual city for computer games. It is worth noticing that the tool can have other possibilities of applications in the AEC, such as urban design and education in AEC programs. The architect is the decision maker about the future of urban space in which he/she creates buildings with different architectural styles. For that reason, a course in aesthetics in architectural education seems necessary. Currently, the basis of such education is the development of interactive systems that give students a platform for experimentation and artistic freedom in styling architectural objects (Uzunoglu, 2012). The tool proposed in this paper can provide students with the opportunity to create architectural objects depending on their personal aesthetic preferences. It can also be used by architects, for example for redesign of cities.

Our research to date has mainly been related to the conceptual design therefore we have not used BIM technology. Admittedly, there are examples such as the Masdar headquarters, Basrah stadium and Lotte Super Tower that realize the conceptual design potential of BIM technology (Keresmeh, 2012). But while BIM is presented as an integrated tool in the design process, a fully supported workflow has yet to be achieved. For example, conceptual design areas such as methods for generating and evaluating innovative solutions are not supported by BIM. Considering the role of artificial intelligence in the modern world, not only BIM technology should motivate the implementation of innovative solutions, but also new methodologies that result from the creative CAD process should inspire the application and/or development of BIM technology.

2. A Theoretical Framework for VCC-system

This section presents the basic concepts of the VCC-system, such as an architectural reference building that describes the stylistic characteristics of buildings, a composition graph (CP-graph) representing internal design structures, and the CP-graph grammar system used to automatically generate design solutions.

2.1 An Architectural Reference Building

An architectural reference building is the form (appearance) of a building model consisting of both components and relationships between them reflecting the user's preferences and expectations. In VCC-system the designer creates his reference buildings through a graphical interface using the geon-based representation proposed by Irving Biederman. It is the qualitative volumetric solid representation proposed both as a computer model and a model of human vision in which 3D object are reconstructed using three-dimensional generic primitives, called geons. Biederman developed a catalogue of 36 geons which are classified by four qualitative features: edge (straight or curved), types of symmetry, size variation (constant, expanding), axis (straight or curved). However, the lack of quantitative information makes it impossible to distinguish between qualitatively similar but quantitatively different objects. For that reason a boundary representation that describes an object by a finite number of faces represented by their edges and vertices will be also used in our approach.

2.2 A Composition Graph (CP-graph)

In the proposed VCC-system both a reference building and new buildings generated on the base of its design structure are internally represented by means of CP-graphs (Grabska, 1994). The representation of design structures in the form of a CP-graph is especially useful for creative design in engineering. It is used in a composite representation of the design knowledge where the internal structure of the artefact is clearly separated from the description of its geometrical features. This methodology has proven successful in both Civil Engineering and Mechanical Engineering (Grabska, Borkowski, 1996). It has been implemented as a design tool for architectural and graphic designing (Szuba, Borkowski, 2003). This tool, which includes the generator of CP-graphs, the library of primitives and a visualization module, is modified depending on the application. Since 2007, CP-graphs have been used in modeling the parallel direct solver algorithm utilized by the hp finite element method (hp-FEM) (Paszynski, Schaefer, 2010).

The structure of the designed artefact is represented by a CP-graph. Two types of nodes are defined: object nodes and bond nodes. The whole artefact component is represented by the object node, while the bond nodes specify its parts that take part in the relations. In other words, in CP-graphs the relations usually defined between graph nodes can be additionally detailed by means of bond nodes, treated as arguments of the relations. In this paper CP-graphs represent structure of architectural objects, describing the way in which distinct object components are attached together. To each object node a number of bonds is assigned and edges of CP-graph connect pairs of bonds. Object nodes are equipped with two types of bonds: source-bonds and target-bonds and directed edges are drawn from source-bonds to target-bonds. Bonds of CP-graph nodes can be a hierarchical elements. Bonds that are neither source nor target are called free. Formally,

Definition 1. Let Σ be an alphabet of node labels and edge labels. By a *composition graph (CP-graph)* over Σ we mean a tuple $C = (V, E, B, ch, bd, s, t, lb)$, where

- V, E, B are pairwise disjoint sets, whose elements are called object nodes, bond nodes and edges, respectively;
- $ch: B \rightarrow P(B)$ is a function of nesting descendants such that none a bond cannot be nested in two different bonds, and a bond cannot be its own descendant;
- $bd: V \rightarrow B^*$ is a function specifying a sequence of different bond nodes for each object node, such that $\forall b \in B\ \exists v_1 \in V: (b \in bd(v_1) \wedge \forall v_2 \in V: (b \in bd(v_2) => v_2 = v_1))$,

i.e., each bond node is assigned to exactly one object node;

- $s, t\colon E \rightarrow B$ are functions assigning to edges source and target bond nodes, respectively, in such a way, that
  $\forall e \in E\ \exists v_1, v_2\colon s(e) \in bd(v_1) \wedge t(e) \in bd(v_2)$;
- $lb\colon E \cup V \rightarrow \Sigma$ is an edge and object node labelling function.

Fig. 1 shows an architectural object consisting of solids with its CP-graph representation. The set $\{r, b1, b2, b3, b4\} \subset \Sigma$ contains node labels which correspond to components whose icons are also placed in the nodes. For each components the graphic code for any bond is a small circle placed on the border of the node or of the bond (for hierarchical bonds). Bonds are numbered and represent the faces or parts of the faces for hierarchical bonds. Two Biederman's adjacency relations between solids: "end-to-side" and "end-to-end" are represented by edge labels, i.e., the edge label set $\{end\text{-}to\text{-}side, end\text{-}to\text{-}end\} \subset \Sigma$. For simplicity, edges in Fig. 1 are drawn as a solid line for the first label and a dashed line for the second.

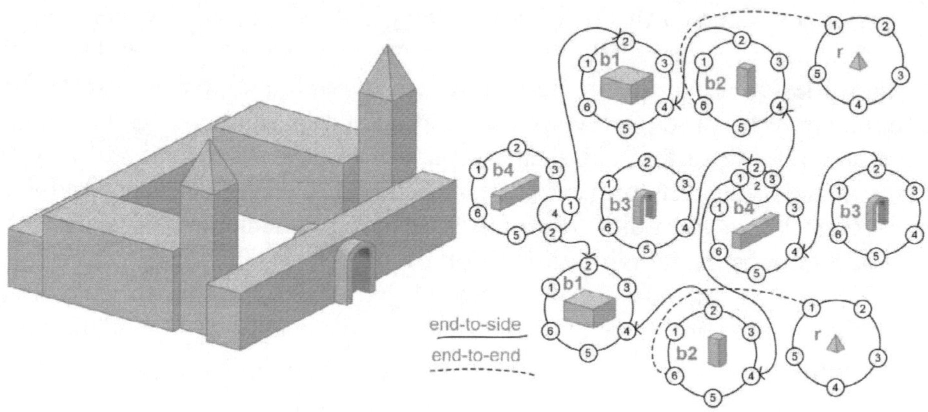

Figure 1: An architectural object and its CP-graphs

In VCC-system attributed CP-graphs are used. Attributes specifying properties of components are assigned to nodes, while attributes for bond nodes define data on the relation between component bonds.

2.3 A CP-graph Grammar

Constructing a CP-graph of the architectural object provides information about its structure. However, if this object is to be the reference model further analysis is needed to define a design space. Buildings compliant with the characteristics of the reference model are elements of this space. The generation system is one of the basic tools for generating a set of such design solutions. In our approach, a CP-graph grammar is used to automatically generate building structures. It is a system for the local transformation of graphs according to formal rules called productions. A production is a pair of CP-graphs in which the first element of the pair is called the left hand-side of production, and the second – its right-hand side. If a production is applied to a given CP-graph, its result is a local transformation of the given graph into a new graph. This new graph is obtained from a given graph by replacing its subgraph, which is a copy of the left production side with the right production side, and connecting the edges of this right production side with the rest of the given graph, according to the so-called embedding rule. An application production to a given graph is called a directly derivation, while the sequence of directly derivations is called a derivation in the CP-grammar. The key property of the procedural generation is that it describes the objects, in terms of a sequence of productions rather than as a static block of data.

In our approach, two CP-graph grammars are defined. The productions of the first grammar describe the addition of individual components of the created object. The second is called a coupled grammar and it allows for additional elements of relations, where source and target bonds are determined by free bonds of the reference model CP-graph. Fig. 2 shows a set of productions of the CP-graph grammar, which describe the architectural object shown in Fig. 1.

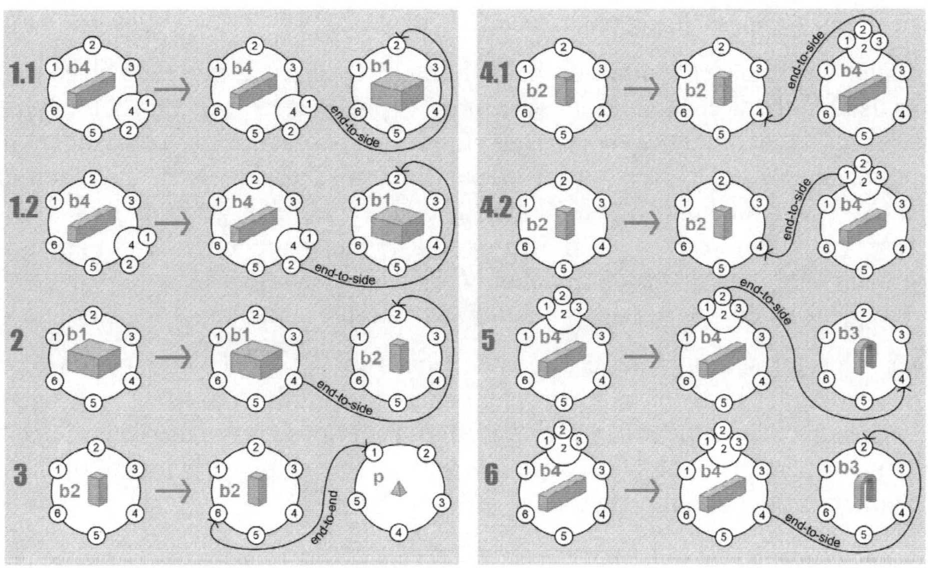

Figure 2: A CP-graph grammar for the architectural object in Fig.1

CP-graph sample productions of the coupled grammar along with their visualization are presented in Fig. 3.

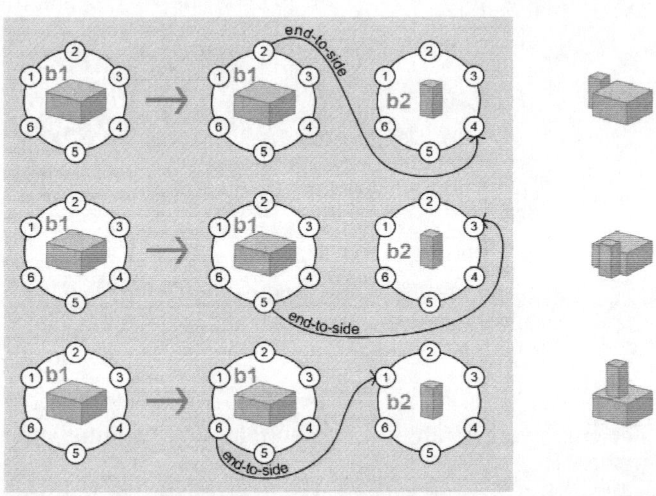

Figure 3: CP-graph sample productions of the coupled grammar

At this point it is worth noting that there is a generative tool called a shape grammar which enables design styles to be recreated (Benrós, Duarte, Hanna, 2012). However, it is a less universal method than the approach proposed in this paper. For a shape grammar, new grammar rules must be created for each style. Experts are needed to generate them. In our approach, rules describing style are generated automatically on the base of the reference building that can be created by non-experts users.

3. Evolutionary Design

In this paper, an evolutionary algorithm serves as a design aid to stimulate creativity in generating forms of buildings and evaluating their style. It is driven by an aesthetic measure. In evolutionary process, objects are represented in two forms: in the encoded of genotypes and in the decoded of phenotypes (Strug, Grabska, Ślusarczyk, 2014).

In the presented approach, a genotype of the building is represented by a sequences of CP-graph productions used to the derivation of its structure. Its phenotypes is a configurations of geons. During the process of evolution, genotypes are modified by mutation and crossover operations. The evolutionary design starts with a population of individuals with required design characteristics. In our method, the population contains buildings generated by the CP-graph grammar describing the reference building as well as by its coupled CP-graph grammar. Since in our approach the evolutionary algorithm works on genotypes represented by CP-graph production sequences, the genetic operators for such a representation must be defined.

A crossover is performed on two selected sequences of CP-graph productions representing genotypes. A crossover operator requires establishing one production from each sequence that would be exchanged during the process of evolution. Fig. 4 presents in the second line the result of the crossover operator at the phenotype level. First line shows arguments of the operator. They are elements of the initial populations.

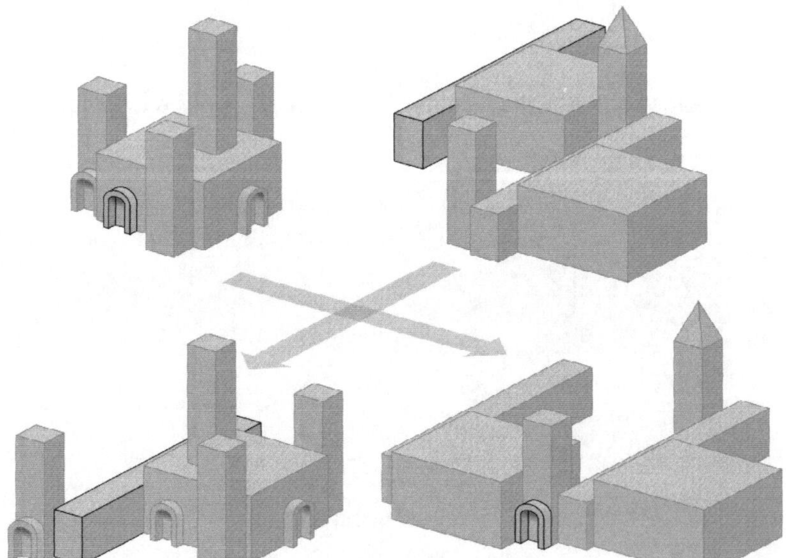

Figure 4: The crossover operator for two buildings of the initial population

The mutation operator is used to introduce new features to the population. In this paper, the mutation operator can modify the structure of the building by removing and adding CP-graph production or changing the value of a single geon attribute.

The fitness function is determined by evaluation of buildings based on aesthetic measure which takes into account the user's aesthetic preferences contained within the reference building he creates. Therefore, one of the most important factor of the automatic aesthetic evaluation is prototyping, i.e. the use of the measure of representativeness of each generated building in the category meeting the user's expectations (Whitfield, Slatter, 1979). In assessment of character similarity between two buildings, the following factors should be considered: a number of component, a number of component types, balance and alignment of component surfaces. The first two of the mentioned factors are provided by the generator, which uses graph grammars with adequate rules. The optimization process needs then to concentrate on verification of balance and alignment levels.The aesthetic measure of buildings is under development and testing.

4. Virtual City Creator

The Virtual City Creator is a computer system which, based on the design structure of a given reference building model, will automatically create building models in a similar style. The derived buildings will be arranged on the generated city map. The goal of the VCC-system is to make it easier for computer game developers to get ready scenery for the game. VCC-system consists of two main modules – the GUI which enables interaction with the user and the graph module that performs operations on the internal representations of the designs. The communication diagram between modules in VCC-system is presented in Fig. 5.

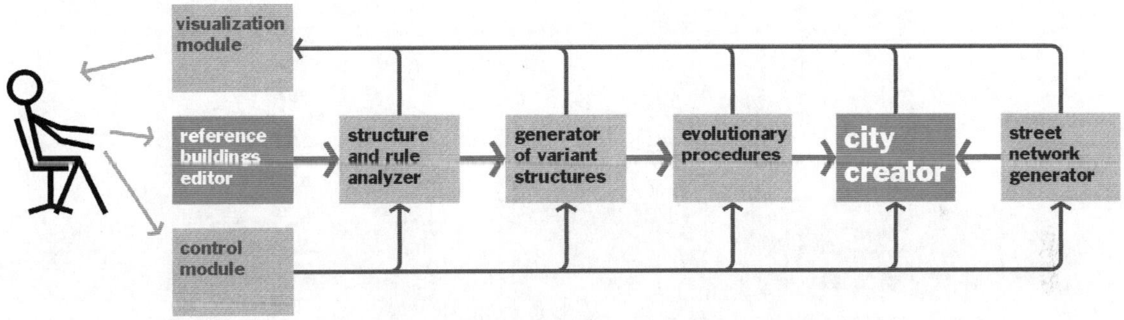

Figure 5: The communication diagram between modules in VCC-system

A reference building is created by the designer through a graphical interface using the Reference Building Editor. Fig. 6 shows a sample reference building generated with the use of Addon written in Python interface integrated with Blender. Addon is integrated with the Structure and Rule Analyzer module which generates a CP-graph representation of the reference building and the set of productions of both the CP-graph grammar describing this building and its coupled grammar.

The Generator of Variant Structures module generates buildings on the base of these productions. A number of these buildings, chosen by the designer, constitute the starting population for the Evolutionary Procedure. Initial population based on the reference building in Fig. 6 is shown in Fig. 7.

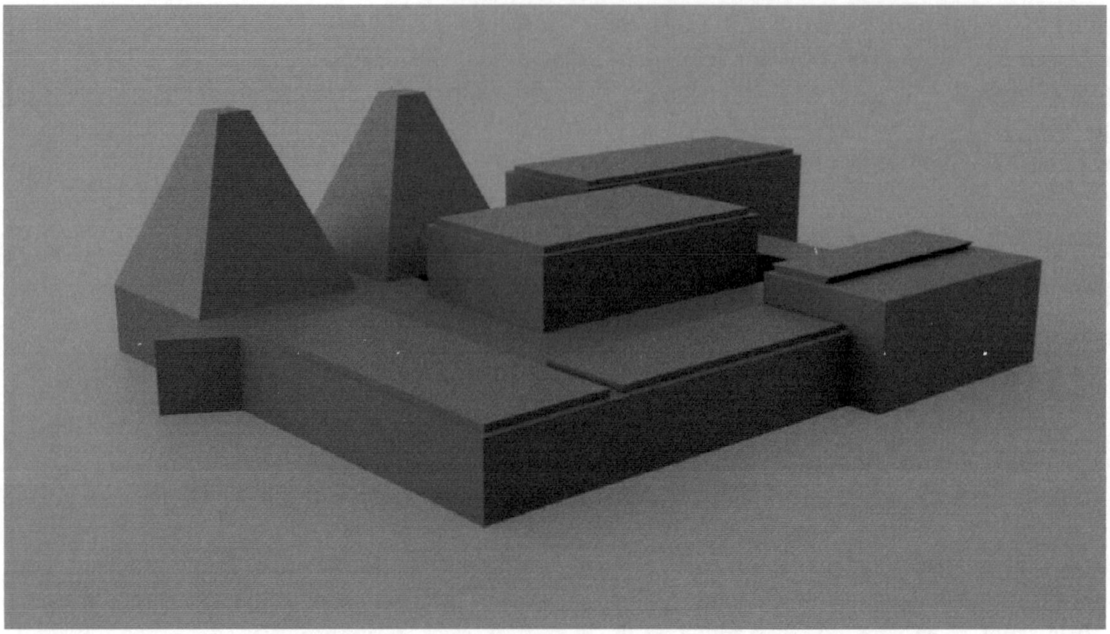

Figure 6: A reference building example

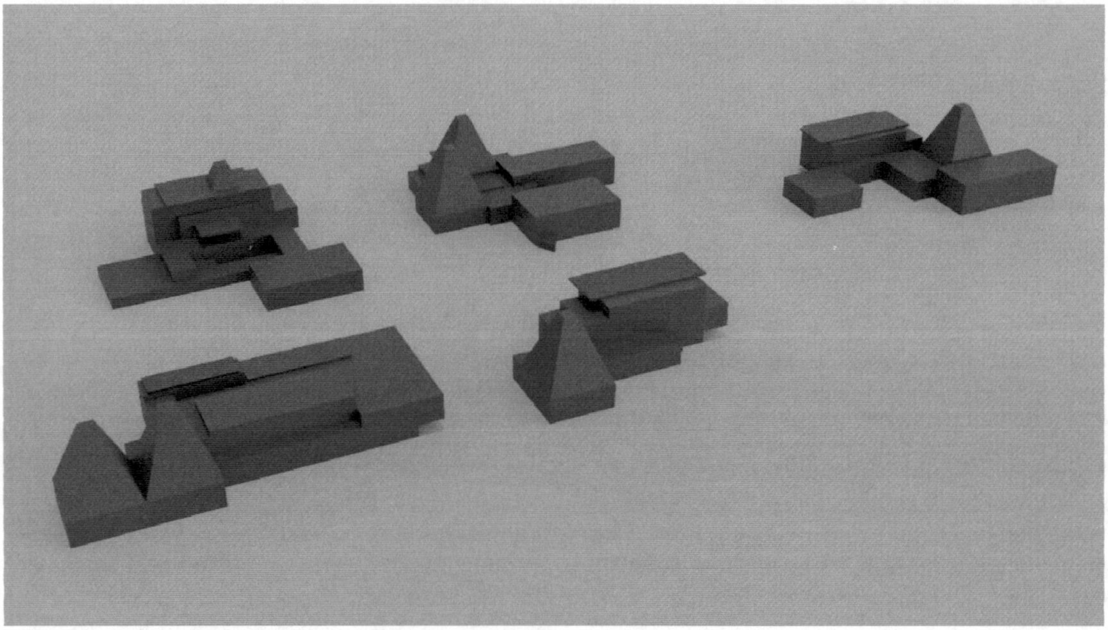

Figure 7: Initial populations based on the reference building in Figure 6

The buildings for virtual city are generated and evaluated in terms of styling with the help of evaluation mechanism. They can be additionally modified by the designer. Currently, a Street Network Generator module is being tested. The street generator is equipped with many parameters matched to configure the style of the virtual city. In the presented method, random distributions with different properties are created by pseudorandom number generators. Some of them are used to generate a network of streets in a given area, others created around a central point determine the basic geometrical properties of buildings - their height and complexity. The user by modifying the properties of random distributions, it can freely create the characteristics of the city. Fig. 8 shows an example of the arrangement of low buildings on the suburbs of the city.

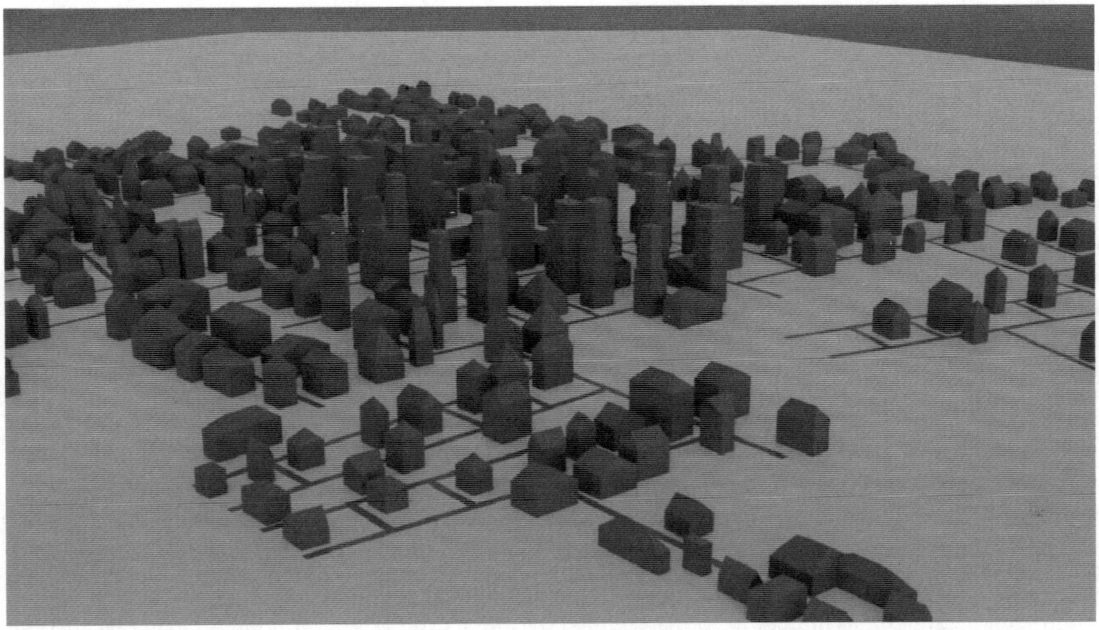

Figure 8: An example of the arrangement of low buildings on the suburbs of the city

In this paper we propose a computer tool that both supports the designer in styling city buildings and allows him/her to interactively control each design level by means of the Control Module.

5. Conclusion

The actions of modern computer games often take place in a large urban area with arranged stylish buildings properly. From the gaming industry's point of view, the complexity of virtual urban areas generates extremely high production costs. The paper has proposed a simplified generative methods implemented in the form of a computer design tool to support the designer in styling city buildings at the conceptual stage. This tool has been applied to generate buildings of virtual city for computer games.

The main contribution is the introduction of aesthetic preferences for building styling within a reference building model created by the designer through a graphical interface. From an evolutionary design point of view, genotypes of buildings represented by sequences of graph productions were an inspiration to define new genetic operators. In future research, we will focus on testing our method in education in AEC programs.

Acknowledgements

The project is funded by a grant from the National Centre for Research and Development (NCBR), POIR.01.01.01-00-0718/18. NCBR's support is gratefully acknowledged. Any opinion, findings, conclusions or recommendations presented in this paper are those of authors and do not necessarily reflect the views of the NCBR.

References

Kelly, G., McCabe, H. (2006). A Survey of Procedural Techniques for City Generation," The ITB Journal: Vol. 7: Is. 2, Article 5.

Csikzentmihalyi, M., Robinson, R.E. (1990). The Art of Seeing. The J Paul Getty Trust Office of Publications.

Biederman, I. (1987). Recognition-by-Components: A Theory of Human Image Understanding. Psychological Review 94, 115–147.

Mars, A., Grabska, E. (2016). Generation of 3D Architectural Objects with the Use of an Aesthetic Oriented Multi-agent System. In: Yuhua Luo (Ed.). Cooperative Design, Visualization, and Engineering, LNCS 992, pp.340–347.

Marin, P., Bignon, J-C., Lequay, H. (2008). A Genetic Algorithm for use in Creative Design Processes. Annual Conference of the Association for Computer Aided Design in Architecture (ACADIA), Minneapolis, United States.

Frazer, J., Frazer, J., Liu, X., Tang, M. Janssen, P. (2002). Generative and evolutionary techniques for building envelope design, Generative 2002.

Ventura, D. (2015). The Computational Creativity Complex. In: Besold, T., Schorlemmer, M., Smaill, A., (Eds). Computational Creativity Research: Towards Creative Machines, Atlantis Press. 2015.

Whitfield, T. W. A., Slatter, P. E. (1979). The effects of categorisation and prototypicality on aesthetic choice in a furniture selection task. British Journal of Psychology, 70, pp.65–75.

Mars, A., Grabska, E., Ślusarczyk, G., Strug, B. (2020). Design characteristics and aesthetics in evolutionary design of architectural forms directed by fuzzy evaluation. Artif. Intell. Eng. Des. Anal. Manuf. 34(2), 2020, pp.147–159.

Uzunoglu, S.S. (2012). Aesthetic and Architectural Education. Procedia-Social and Behavioral Sciences 51, pp.90–98.

Keresmeh, A. (2012). Building Information Modelling in Concept Design Stage. University of Salford, Manchester.

Grabska, E.: (1994) Graph and Designing. In: Schneider, H.J., Ehrig, H. (eds) Graph transformations in Computer Science, LNCS, vol. 776, pp.188–202, Springer, Heidelberg.

Grabska, E., Borkowski, A. (1996). Assisting creativity by composite representation. In: Gero, J.S., Sudweeks, F. (eds). Artificial Intelligence in Design '96, pp.743–759, Kluwer Academic Publisher.

Szuba, J., Borkowski, A. (2003). Graph transformations in architectural design. Computer Assisted Mechanics and Engineering Sciences, vol. 10, pp.93–109, IPPT-PAN, Warsaw.

Paszynski, M., Schaefer, R. (2010). Graph grammar-driven parallel partial differential equation solver. Concurrency and Computation: Practice and Experience, pp.1063–1097, Wiley Online Library

Benrós, D., Duarte, J. P., Hanna, S. (2012). A New Palladian Shape Grammar. International Journal of Architectural Computing 10(4), pp.521–540.

Strug, B., Grabska, E., Ślusarczyk, G. (2014). Supporting the design process with hypergraph genetic operators. Advanced Engineering Informatics, 28 (1), pp.11–27.

Data shortage for urban energy simulations? An empirical survey on data availability and enrichment methods using machine learning?

Gerald Schweiger[a], Johannes Exenberger[a], Avichal Malhotra[b], Thomas Schranz[a], Theresa Boiger[a], Christoph van Treeck[b], James O'Donnell[c]
[a] Graz University of Technology, Austria, [b] RWTH Aachen University, Germany, [c] University College Dublin, Ireland
gerald.schweiger@tugraz.at

Abstract. Building energy simulations at district and urban scales are vital to design and operate sustainable energy systems. In many cases, these simulations rely on enrichment methods as the required detailed data on building characteristics are often unavailable. Approaches using machine learning to address this problem have already been proposed in the literature. However, research on this topic is still at an early stage and the question of whether machine learning can offer substantial solutions has not yet been answered. The goal of this work is twofold; based on an expert survey, we identify the main challenges regarding data availability for urban energy simulations. Furthermore, we identify possibilities of machine learning methods in the field of data enrichment and city information models to offer an initial contribution in defining further research perspectives in this domain.

1. Introduction

The building sector is responsible for around 40% of total final energy consumption in the European Union (European Commission, 2019) and holds enormous potential for saving energy and reducing CO2 emissions in a cost-effective way. In recent years, building energy demand simulations on district or urban scale have become an increasingly relevant topic in academic research and practical applications. Energy performance simulations are crucial for (a) energy management and control, (b) the design of smart systems to reduce overall energy consumption and (c) the design of solutions for efficiently incorporating new sources of renewable energy within the supply system (Schweiger *et al.*, 2020). 3D city models are vital for energy simulations, as they provide information about buildings in a standardized manner. An overview of models and formats can be found in (Hong *et al.*, 2020; Malhotra *et al.*, 2021).

As detailed data about those building characteristics is often not available (especially on district and urban scale) most modelers enrich models with data from other sources (Malhotra *et al.*, 2020). Another way to enrich building-related data is the inference of certain building features from other features using Machine Learning (ML) techniques. In general, data enrichment can be classified into two main categories: a) the enrichment of geometry, and b) the enrichment of semantic data. The first category includes all approaches that use enrichment to create more complex 3D models through data enrichment. ML has for instance been used to identify roof geometries from LiDAR data (Biljecki and Dehbi, 2019). Semantic data enrichment, on the other hand, includes all approaches that identify additional building features that are stored as attributes within the geometrical model. Henn et al. (Henn *et al.*, 2012) for example, use ML for building type classification from a LOD1 city model. Using a different approach, von Platten et al. (Von Platten *et al.*, 2020) combine ML and expert knowledge to identify building types from Google Street View images for estimating energy retrofitting potential.

ML based enrichment methods are a new and emerging field, making it necessary to define potential applications and research paths. As ML cannot be discussed without an assessment of the availability of required data sources, this paper therefore envisions:

- to identify the main challenges researchers are facing regarding data availability for urban energy simulations.
- to identify potential applications for ML in enriching data for district and urban energy simulations.

2. Method

An exploratory expert survey was conducted to explore data availability and enrichment methods using ML for urban energy simulations. Expert surveys are usually conducted in cases where experts have knowledge that is not yet available in the scientific community and the public (Flick *et al.*, 2018). The empirical methodology is similar to the one in (Skov *et al.*, 2021) and (Schweiger, Kuttin and Posch, 2019). We selected academic experts based on (i) their number of publications on city information modeling that are listed in the literature database Scopus and (ii) their active involvement in international projects on city information modeling. Practitioners were chosen according to their actual involvement in projects using city information modeling. 44 experts received the link to an online survey constructed with the survey tool Lime Survey (Limesurvey, 2021),leading to a total number of 28 complete answers. Thus, the response rate was 64%. The questionnaire consists of 18 questions ranging from simple yes/no questions to Likert-scale questions and short-answer questions. To accommodate for additional answers, an extra open field was provided where appropriate. The results of the quantitative questions are presented in a bar chart and, if applicable, evaluated in terms of median and mean, which ensures a transparent presentation of the results.

There are clear limitations associated with the method that was applied in this paper. A well-known problem in interviewing experts is the representativeness of the sample population (Christopoulos, 2011). Exploratory expert surveys gather facts and information to explore new research topics or to establish an initial orientation in a nascent field (Flick *et al.*, 2018). In general, the method implies rather small sample sizes. Since exploratory expert surveys do not aim at generalization, there is no special requirement to have a representative sample or even to interview all relevant experts (Kaiser, 2014). Helfferich, for example, recommends interviewing between 6 and 30 experts (Helfferich, 2011).

3. Results

The first question of the survey concerns the field of applications of city information models for researchers and practitioners working in the domain of urban energy simulation (see Figure 1). The majority of the respondents (70%) have been or are currently using city information models for heating demand prediction of buildings, with an additional 19% of respondents planning to do so within the next year. The second major application for city information models is the visualization of energy demand, which was already done by 65% of the respondents and planned by another 31%. More than half of all respondents have applied digital city models in the context of electric energy (58%) and cooling energy (52%) demand prediction and simulation. Although currently not used as frequent as applications for heating demand prediction, 27% and 30% plan to use city information models for electricity and cooling demand computations respectively. This trend correlates with the increasing importance of cooling systems for overall energy consumption in the future due to rising temperatures, especially in urban areas. Optimal planning and operation of energy production were not considered as applications for city information models by as many respondents. 35% use city models for optimal planning, 38% intend to do so in the coming 12 months. For optimal operation, 38% worked or are working with such models, while 23% are planning to work on this topic in combination with city information models. The data from the survey does not allow statements about the general importance of individual research topics, but the results indicate that the use of city information models is less beneficial for optimal planning and control, at least given the current state of the art methods.

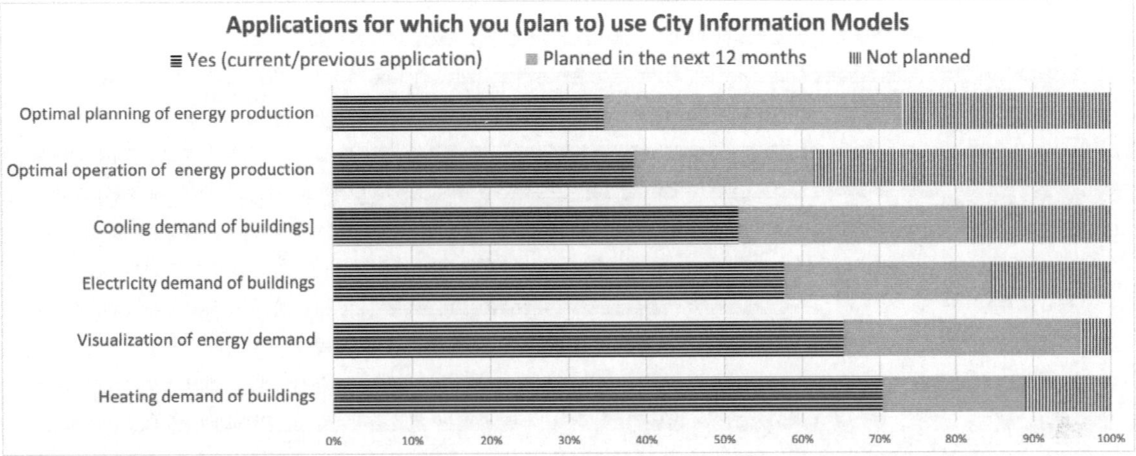

Figure 1: Field of applications for city information models

About one third of the experts mentioned additional applications that were not included in the survey. The applications mentioned can be categorized into the following main objectives: reduction of greenhouse gas emissions; research on urban heat islands; agent-based modeling and traffic modeling; simulation of energy networks; other simulations (noise, pollution, ...); urban planning and smart cities.

In the following question (Figure 2), the respondents are asked how time and effort in a their projects is usually distributed across the following work packages: data acquisition, development of the simulation model, simulation and results analysis. This was done to identify existing bottlenecks in the workflow of projects regarding urban energy simulations, highlighting potential applications for ML. Data acquisition is considered the most time consuming part of the workflow, with an average of 44% (median = 40%) of the whole project time dedicated to data acquisition. Additionally, more than 40% of all respondents spend at least half of their time on data acquisition, indicating that acquiring and pre-processing data is still a major bottleneck regarding research in the domain of urban energy simulations. The development of a simulation model accounts for less time according to the respondents (average = 30%, median = 25 %). Performing the simulation and analyzing the results on average makes up for 27% of the overall time consumption, with a median value of 37%, indicating that across all respondents, variations in time consumption are largest for this work package.

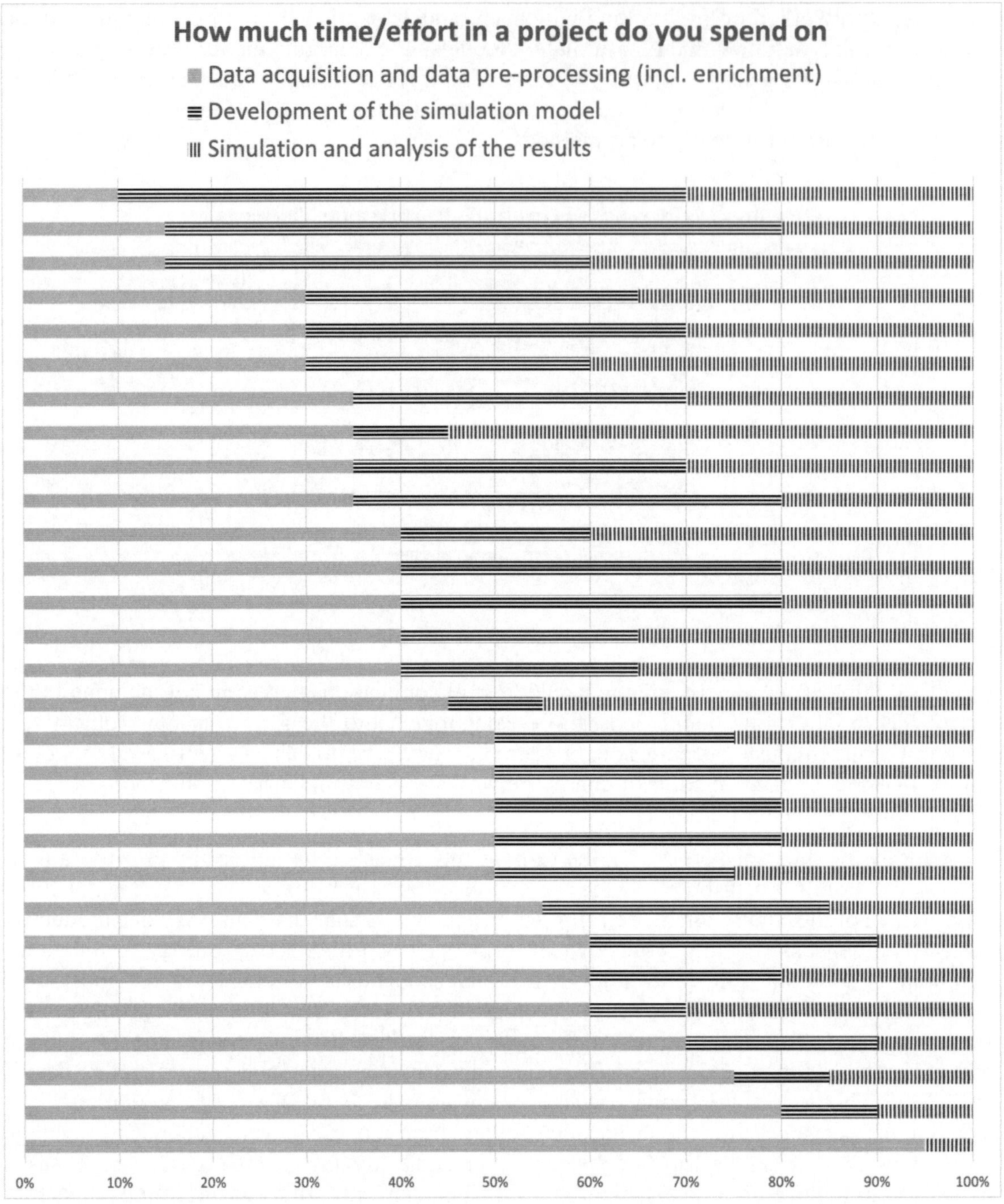

Figure 2: Distribution of workload across different phases of a project

For energy performance applications, efficient use of technology has also proven to be an important milestone in the development of workflows offering sustainable energy management solutions. Methods such as ML or image processing have already been used for building energy assessments. However, these are generally limited to individual buildings and lack implementations on an urban scale. Furthermore, for urban energy simulations, efficient usage of virtual 3D city models along with the previously mentioned methods can be a big step towards energy efficient districts. Virtual data models at a city scale are generally limited in their availability. As the landscape of available data sources is quite complex, with varying restrictions for usage and publication, an approach by Malhotra, et al. (Malhotra *et al.*, 2020) categorizes different availability types of data for energy-related applications. Using these categories, the participants of the present survey were asked to name the types of data they are frequently using (see Figure 3).

All the participants agreed to use open source datasets, whereas, only 18% acknowledged the use of commercial data sets. Commercial data refers to information that is licensed and can be used by paying an agreed fee. Moreover, 89% of the respondents utilize public sector information where a charge may apply for a certain usage. Academic data that is free of charge for scientific research studies is used by 68% of the participants. Industry restricted data that can only be used for specific applications is used by 29%. Furthermore, 68% of the respondents do not acknowledge the usage of private data that is not available to the people outside an institution, university or industry. Conclusively, as a majority of participants rely on open data sets and public sector information, it is quite important for governmental organizations to make urban scale data publicly available for urban energy applications.

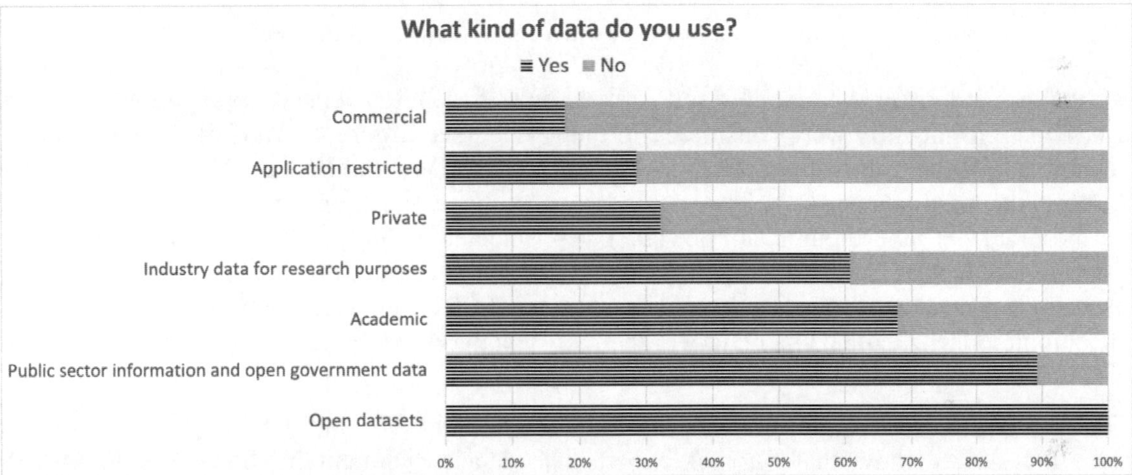

Figure 3: Types of data sources used

Geometrical and energy-specific data is the core requirement for energy related applications. Though many different data models and formats exist, some of them are prominently used in the field of urban building energy modeling (UBEM). City Geographical Markup Language (CityGML) (Gröger *et al.*, 2012), an open XML-based data format, facilitates the representation of semantical and topological information in 3D city models. Although some cities and municipalities offer open LoD1-2 CityGML datasets, there still exists a lack of data models for many different urban areas. Furthermore, CityGML datasets mainly contain geometrical information of the buildings. To include additional information, these models can also be extended using the Application Domain Extension (ADE) mechanism. For energy-relevant information, the CityGML Energy ADE (Agugiaro *et al.*, 2018) is mainly used. Green Building XML (gbXML) (Cheng and Das, 2014), an open data format, also supports information exchange between BIM models and other related analysis tools. Furthermore, the Industry foundation Classes (IFC) (Laakso and Kiviniemi, 2012) can also be used for representing 3D BIM models. The GeoJSON (Dorman, 2020), based on JavaScript Object Notation, defines JSON objects and their relation by which they are combined to represent data about geographic features, their properties and their spatial extents. The ESRI Shapefile format is a geospatial vector data format for geographic information system (GIS) software (ESRI, 1998).

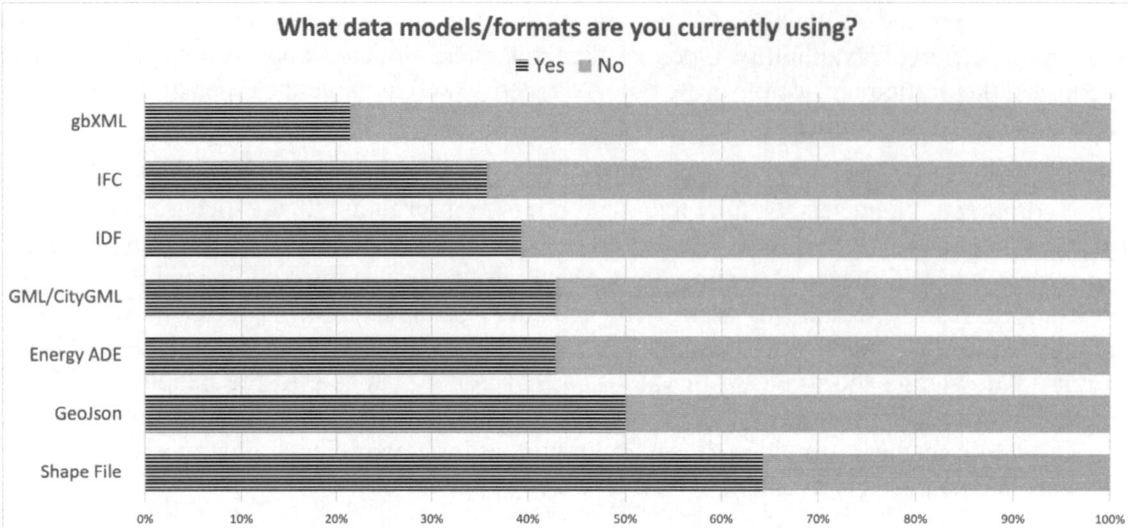

Figure 4: Data models/formats used by the respondents

Although many other data models and formats exist for energy related applications, the ones used most prominently were considered in the survey (see Figure 4). Half of the respondents acknowledged the usage of GeoJSON, whereas the CityGML and Energy ADE are utilized by 43% of the participants. 64% also agreed to use shape files for urban scale applications. Furthermore, IFC and Input Data File (IDF) were selected by 36% and 39% of the respondents respectively. Only 21% considered the usage of gbXML. Furthermore, some experts mentioned the usage of csv, xml, GeoPackage files (gpkg), ESRI File Geodatabase (GDB), Digital elevation models, Geotiff, OpenDRIVE, the UtilityNetwork ADE, 3D pointclouds, 3D meshes, glTF, COLLADA, KML and 3DTiles.

The next section of the questionnaire concerns the topic of ML and data enrichment. Results from the survey show that 82% of experts use data enrichment methods (see Figure 5). Archetype approaches are applied by 75% of the study participants, statistical approaches by 50% and ML methods by 36%. The high percentage of participants using ML methods for data enrichment is surprising, given the relatively low number of publications concerning this topic. Besides these approaches, the participants mentioned other enrichment methods such as engineering models, expert guessing and manual enrichment.

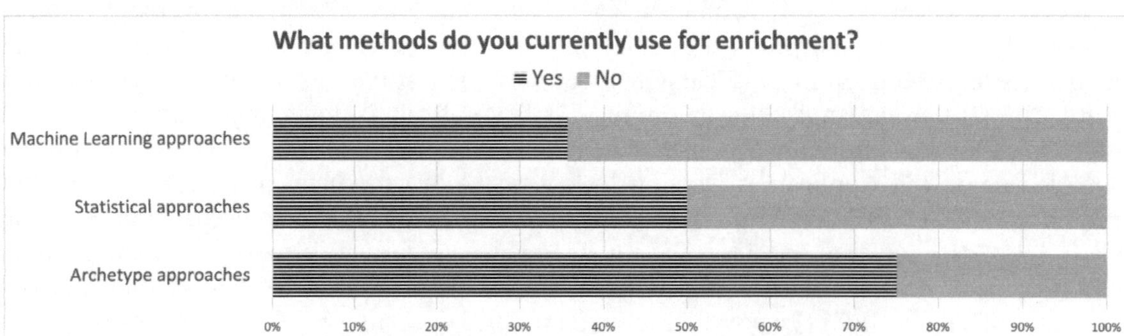

Figure 5: Data enrichment methods used by the participants

68% of experts answered that they have already applied ML techniques in their work. From the remaining 32% percent who have not yet used ML methods, 78% said that they plan to do so in the future. With a share of 86%, Python is the language/framework of choice for most experts. Matlab and R are used by 21% and 25% respectively. Other languages, such as C++ were only mentioned once. ML can be used in a variety of tasks, such as data pre-processing, data analysis or enrichment. 39% of experts use ML methods for pre-processing, 36% use it for input data analysis and data enrichment and 32% use it to analyze simulation results. Other applications mentioned only by one participant each are modeling and LiDAR image processing. Most experts identify a moderate to high potential for ML techniques in all of these areas (see Figure 6). In data enrichment and input data analysis ML is considered to have a high potential by 64% and 61% of the survey participants respectively. Moderate potential in data enrichment is identified by 28% of the experts and 30% consider ML to have moderate potential in input data analysis. 52% of experts see high potential for ML in data pre-processing and within the simulation workflow (e.g. in the form of surrogate modeling). Moderate potential in these two areas is identified by 32% and 29% respectively. In post-processing and in the analysis of the simulation results 42% of the experts see high potential for ML methods and another 42% see moderate potential.

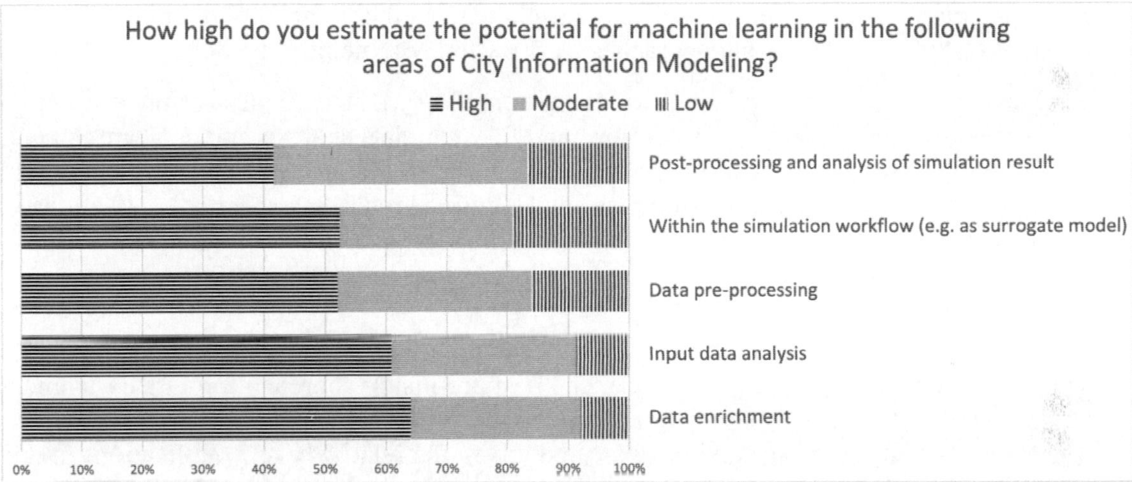

Figure 6: Estimation of potential areas for ML in the domain of city information modeling.

In a following question, the respondents were asked about specific applications in the context of data enrichment they consider promising for the integration of ML. From all the answers, three main topics can be derived: parameter estimation and filling of data gaps, creation of more precise archetypes and image analysis. A majority of experts see the potential of ML in tackling the problems of missing or fragmented data. Closely related is the creation of more accurate building archetypes from data that subsequently can be used to enrich city information models. Image analysis was mentioned several times as well, although exact use cases for image analysis were not specified in most answers. Two experts mentioned image recognition in context of textures for city information models and the detection of building attributes such as windows and PV systems. Data calibration and quality checking was also considered by some respondents. Interestingly, the use of ML for occupancy estimation was only mentioned by one respondent in the survey.

When asked about the potential of ML in the domain of city information models in general, the answers show a less clear opinion across the respondents. While many experts acknowledge the potential of ML for a variety of applications for city information models, many do not settle on definitive use cases, indicating that research in this domain is still in its early stages. Data analysis and processing was also mentioned by several experts. The potential of ML for generative tasks was also considered, proposing the use of ML for 3D model reconstruction from point clouds and meshes and the generation of imaginary 3D data for planning purposes. Using ML in combination with city information models for energy demand prediction was also mentioned by several respondents.

4. Conclusion

District and city energy simulations are vital to design and operate sustainable energy systems. This paper presents an expert assessment on data availability and potentials for ML techniques to enrich data. The main findings from this paper are:

- Data acquisition is considered the most time-consuming part of the workflow, with a median of 40% of the whole project time dedicated to this task.
- All experts who participated in the survey use open-source datasets, whereas only 18% acknowledged the use of commercial data sets.
- More than 80% of experts use data enrichment methods; archetype approaches are applied by 75%, statistical approaches by 50% and ML methods by 36%.
- Most experts identify a medium to high potential of ML techniques for pre- and post-processing, in the simulation workflow, and for input data analysis and data enrichment. Experts expect the highest potential for ML to be in the area of data enrichment and input data analysis. Three main topics can be derived regarding specific applications in the context of data enrichment: parameter estimation and filling of data gaps, creation of more precise archetypes and image analysis.

It can be concluded that many experts consider ML a promising approach for data enrichment in the domain of urban energy simulation. The number of respondents already using ML for this purpose was higher than the authors expected, given the relatively few publications in this field. On the other hand, fragmented data and the complete lack of available sources still persist as a significant limiting factors for researchers. This is also reflected in the survey, with many respondents having to dedicate the biggest share of their time available for a project to data acquisition. This situation puts the use of ML in a different perspective, as data availability is a crucial requirement for the development of functioning ML approaches. While ML thus has potential for many applications in the domain of city information modeling and urban energy simulation, solving the problem of an absence of useful data cannot be addressed merely through ML.

Acknowledgement

This work emerged from the IBPSA Project 1(Wetter *et al.*, 2019), an international project conducted under the umbrella of the International Building Performance Simulation Association (IBPSA). Project 1 will develop and demonstrate a BIM/GIS and Modelica Framework for building and community energy system design and operation. The reported research has been conducted within the project KityVR (879419), which has received funding in the framework of "Stadt der Zukunft".

References

Agugiaro, G. et al. (2018) 'The Energy Application Domain Extension for CityGML: enhancing interoperability for urban energy simulations', Open Geospatial Data, Software and Standards, 5.

Biljecki, F. and Dehbi, Y. (2019) 'Raise the roof: Towards generating LOD2 models without aerial surveys using machine learning', in ISPRS Annals of the Photogrammetry, Remote Sensing and Spatial Information Sciences. doi: 10.5194/isprs-annals-IV-4-W8-27-2019.

Cheng, J. C. P. and Das, M. (2014) 'A bim-based web service framework for green building energy simulation and code checking', Journal of Information Technology in Construction.

Christopoulos, D. C. (2011) 'Towards Representative Expert Surveys: Legitimizing the Collection of Expert Data', SSRN Electronic Journal. doi: 10.2139/ssrn.1353283.

Dorman, M. (2020) 'GeoJSON', in Introduction to Web Mapping. doi: 10.1201/9780429352874-7.

ESRI (1998) 'ESRI Shapefile Technical Description', Computational Statistics. doi: 10.1016/0167-9473(93)90138-J.

European Commission (2019) Energy performance of buildings. Available at: https://ec.europa.eu/energy/en/topics/energy-efficiency/energy-performance-of-buildings.

Flick, U. et al. (2018) 'Generating Qualitative Data with Experts and Elites', in The SAGE Handbook of Qualitative Data Collection. doi: 10.4135/9781526416070.n41.

Gröger, G. et al. (2012) 'OGC City Geography Markup Language (CityGML) En-coding Standard', Ogc.

Helfferich, C. (2011) Die Qualität qualitativer Daten, Die Qualität qualitativer Daten. doi: 10.1007/978-3-531-92076-4.

Henn, A. et al. (2012) 'Automatic classification of building types in 3D city models', GeoInformatica. doi: 10.1007/s10707-011-0131-x.

Hong, T. et al. (2020) 'Ten questions on urban building energy modeling', Building and Environment. doi: 10.1016/j.buildenv.2019.106508.

Kaiser, R. (2014) Qualitative Experten-interviews: Konzeptionelle Grundlagen und praktische Durchf□hrung, Springer.

Laakso, M. and Kiviniemi, A. (2012) 'The IFC standard - A review of history, development, and standardization', Electronic Journal of Information Technology in Construction.

Limesurvey (2021) LimeSurvey: An Open Source survey tool.

Malhotra, A. et al. (2020) 'A review on country specific data availability and acquisition techniques for city quarter information modelling for building energy analysis', in BauSIM 2020.

Malhotra, A. et al. (2021) 'City Quarter Information Modeling for Building Energy - ATaxonomic Review', Under Review.

Von Platten, J. et al. (2020) 'Using machine learning to enrich building databases-methods for tailored energy retrofits', Energies. doi: 10.3390/en13102574.

Schweiger, G. et al. (2020) 'Active consumer participation in smart energy systems', Energy & Buildings.

Schweiger, G., Kuttin, F. and Posch, A. (2019) 'District heating systems: An analysis of strengths, weaknesses, opportunities, and threats of the 4GDH', Energies, 12(24). doi: 10.3390/en12244748.

Skov, I. R. et al. (2021) 'Power-to-X in Denmark: An Analysis of Strengths, Weaknesses, Opportunities and Threats', Energies. Multidisciplinary Digital Publishing Institute, 14(4), p. 913.

Wetter, M. et al. (2019) 'IBPSA Project 1: BIM/GIS and Modelica framework for building and community energy system design and operation - Ongoing developments, lessons learned and challenges', in IOP Conference Series: Earth and Environmental Science. doi: 10.1088/1755-1315/323/1/012114.

End-to-End Framework in support of Virtual Design-Engineering-Manufacturing-Construction Space Exploration

Ebrahim Eldamnhoury[a*], Lewis Healy[b], Renate Fruchter Ph.D.[c]
[a] University of Wisconsin-Madison, USA, [b] The University of Queensland, Australia, [c] Stanford University, USA
Ebrahime@dpr.com

Abstract. To develop a digital strategy towards industrialized construction we consider questions that address: What are current roadblocks? How to involve all stakeholders in the supply chain? How can digitalization and industrialization processes be holistic? How to leverage emergent technologies to develop integrated workflows to explore the solution space, augment informed joint decisions, enhance productivity and agility? This paper presents an End-to-End (E2E) framework that integrates design, engineering, manufacturing, construction, and visualization into interoperable workflows. E2E leverages three technology accelerators - parametric modelling and optimization, AI, and VR. E2E breaks down discipline siloes through interoperability. It enables stakeholders in the supply chain to collaborate and explore the project solution space. E2E integrates discipline-specific workflows that provide real-time assessment and feedback loops. These enabled stakeholders to make joint informed decisions at an early stage of the design process. E2E was implemented and tested by a global project team in 2020.

1. Introduction

Construction is a complex endeavor that encompasses risks and uncertainties. The construction industry is facing challenges including lagging productivity and financial pressure due to its fragmented nature (Chowdhury et al. 2019). Digitalization strategies can transform the construction industry and provide innovative solutions to address these challenges (Woodhead et al. 2018). Industrialized Construction (IC) is the third-ranking top breakthrough to drive improvements in construction productivity. Extant studies focus on benefits of digitalization. However, they address emerging technologies as isolated point solutions with little interoperability to connect IC stages.

The construction industry influences everyone's life by building public infrastructure and contributing a 5%-9% increase in the gross domestic product (GDP) (Bin Ab Halim et al. 2014). In the US, the construction industry contributed approximately $1.49 trillion to the local economy in 2021 (US Census Bureau 2021). An Australian study indicates that a 10% increase in the industry efficiency can improve the overall GDP by 2.5% (Chowdhury et al. 2019), highlighting the significance of technological advancements for the future built environment. To capitalize on these opportunities, the manufacturing sector introduced the concept of Industry 4.0. It is a multifaceted framework encompassing smart manufacturing, AI, and lean production (Oesterreich and Teuteberg 2016). The framework aims to improve productivity, create a digital value chain, and enhance the communication between business partners (Razkenari et al. 2019). Similarly, Construction 4.0 promotes lean principles, automation, digitalization, and manufacturing techniques in IC by using strategies adopted in Industry 4.0 (Qi et al. 2021). Implementation of current frameworks have limited impact due to lack of interoperability between different software platforms (Xue et al. 2018). The fragmented nature of the construction industry leads to isolation between different systems, risking data loss during transfers between applications over the various project stages (Qi et al. 2020). Researchers aim to implement emerging technologies to develop process improvements across IC stages. A recent study explored the state-of-practice of Industry 4.0 emerging technologies in IC. It introduced a conceptual end-to-end digital integration of emerging technologies across the entire value chain (Oesterreich and Teuteberg 2016). Another study introduced a theoretical vertical integration model to improve modular construction supply chain coordination across design and engineering, manufacturing, and construction stages (Eldamnhoury and Hanna 2020). Kedir and Hall (2021) investigated recurring themes for resource efficiency in industrialized housing construction.

This paper presents an End-to-End (E2E) framework that integrates interdisciplinary workflows supported by emerging technologies across different IC stages and demonstrates its application during conceptual development phase. Using intelligent interoperability, the E2E framework integrates design, engineering, manufacturing, construction, and end-of-life stages into a highly streamlined workflow. To achieve this, E2E leverages three technology accelerators - parametric modeling and optimization, Artificial Intelligence (AI), and Virtual Reality (VR) to eliminate discipline-specific siloes between different processes and models across IC stages. The integrated E2E framework: (1) provides real-time assessment and feedback that enables joint informed decisions and (2) allows stakeholders in the value chain to iteratively explore the project solution space in its entirety at early stages of project planning.

2. Points of Departure

IC is the process of producing prefabricated systems in a controlled factory environment and ship them to the construction site for assembly (Razkenari et al. 2019). IC is a holistic term that incorporates a variety of techniques and strategies under its umbrella such as prefabrication, preassembly, and modularization (Eldamnhoury and Hanna 2020). It encompasses a wide range of strategies including standardization, mechanization, cleaner production (Li et al. 2020). IC provides the platform for emerging innovations of resource-efficient construction on both product and process levels (Kedir and Hall 2021). Moreover, IC incorporates input from all supply chain players improving the level of coordination and integration among different project stages.

The adoption of emerging technologies such as AI, VR, parametric modeling and optimization continue to reshape the construction industry (Liu et al. 2020). Over the past two decades construction jobs have gone through major transformations moving from mostly paper-based workflow to a digital workflow which results in an explosion of data sets from diverse sources e.g., digital models, IoT, drones etc. This leads to opportunities for AI and machine learning applications to extract meaningful information from the data sets for agile processes (Patil 2019). VR provides an immersive environment that fosters social and spatial presence, allowing stakeholders to experience the future building, understand design intent, troubleshoot, and receive early client feedback (Liu et al. 2020) and facilitates collaborative design reviews (Chacón et al. 2020). Through parametric design and optimization, designers identify design requirements and explore design variants that best achieve the requirements to improve the building performance.

Currently, these technological advances are often implemented through a discipline specific siloed approach, representing point-solutions rather than contributing to the overall value chain (Veldhuizen et al. 2019). The notion here is that technological advancements can be only one piece to the puzzle to create industry-disrupting business models that stretch beyond technological applications to include process and people (Woodhead et al. 2018). While the software exists to implement such a framework, it must support an approach that optimizes software, interoperability, and platform users. This problem is not foreign to IC due to diversity of tools and platforms across the value chain, resulting in disconnected processes, systems, and poor integration.

2.1 End-to-End (E2E) Integrated Framework Conceptual Model

This paper presents an End-to-End (E2E) framework that integrates design, engineering, manufacturing, transportation, construction, and disassembly IC stages. To implement and demonstrate such an E2E, the authors used a project case study and software integration workflow that eliminate fragmentation among different IC stages. To develop E2E, we: (1) defined workflows for each IC stage, (2) identified specific technologies that support workflow activities, (3) linked the workflows to create feedback loops to support real-time or near real time evidence-based joint decisions. This approach led to early and agile constructability feedback up-stream in the design stage to iteratively improve the design and optimize manufacturing, delivery, and construction. The E2E framework addressed interoperability of information, models, and disciplines. This enabled the project stakeholders to iteratively explore a multi-dimensional solution space by linking: (1) design and engineering; (2) manufacturing; (3) transportation and delivery; (4) on-site assembly and installation; (5) occupancy; and (6) building end of life. Table 1 conceptualizes each stage in the IC lifecycle, description, its significance, and provides a reference to E2E process implementation throughout the paper.

Table 1: Stages of the IC Lifecycle and Impact of E2E Framework

IC Stage	Workflows	Impacts	E2E Implementation (section)
Design	Generate and explore building form and space configuration.	Conduct design iterations to reduce building geometry exploration space.	3.1
Engineering	Explore and determine structural systems, grid layout, member sizes, daylight, energy analysis.	Explore design alternatives and quantify impacts across-disciplines.	3.2, 3.3, 3.4
Manufacturing	Model and explore industrialized-based off-site production of building components.	Optimize production systems, real-time monitoring of production status, and supply chain visibility.	4
Transportation	Deliver - track and transfer - construction components to the final assembly site.	Deliver Just-In-Time (JIT) components to minimize batch size and energy consumption.	4.1
On-site Assembly	On-site operations and logistics to assemble the entire building.	Improve site efficiency, crews utilizations, and on-site assembly.	4.1
Occupancy	Operate and maintain the building.	Minimize lifecycle energy and environmental impacts.	3.4
End of Life	Post-occupancy beyond building initial designed lifetime.	Design joinery and connections for greater reusability opportunities.	4.1, 4.2

2.2 E2E Framework

The E2E integrated framework was developed to (1) enhance team cross-disciplinary business processes, (2) provide real-time integrated workflows of design and engineering, manufacturing, construction utilizing intelligent interoperability of information, models, and disciplines, and (3) formulate feedback loops among different disciplines to explore the solution space efficiently. The framework provides an approach to operationalize Construction 4.0 concepts in the context of IC. E2E framework comprises two main modules: (1) design and modeling – *upstream* module, (2) manufacturing, delivery, on-site assembly and constructions, and end-of-life – *downstream* module. The *upstream* module focused on design for manufacturing assembly and disassembly. This was achieved through generative parametric design optimization and integration of architectural, structural, and mechanical systems focused on conveying the architect's vision, structural, daylight comfort, energy building performance, easy assembly, and disassembly. Rhino, Grasshopper, and Revit software were selected to perform these design, modeling, optimization, integration, and analysis tasks. The *downstream* module addresses manufacturing production optimization, supply chain tracking, constructability factors, just-in-time-delivery (JIT), and end-of-life flexible design solution. To implement the *downstream* module, authors selected MANUFACTON[1] to optimize manufacturing, AnyLogic Simulation[2] to track supply chain and delivery, ALICE[3] to generate and explore scheduling and constructability optimal alternatives, and FUZOR VDC VR[4] to model, simulate, and virtually explore and experience construction site logistics and identify peak workflow bottlenecks. To enhance collaboration among team members, the impacts of design changes across E2E were reviewed by the project team during virtual reality walkthrough and troubleshooting sessions. Prospect (from IrisVR Inc.), MeetinVR (from MeetinVR Inc.), and Enscape (from Enscape Inc.) were selected for virtual review meetings and troubleshooting. The integrated E2E framework implementation is shown in Figure 1.

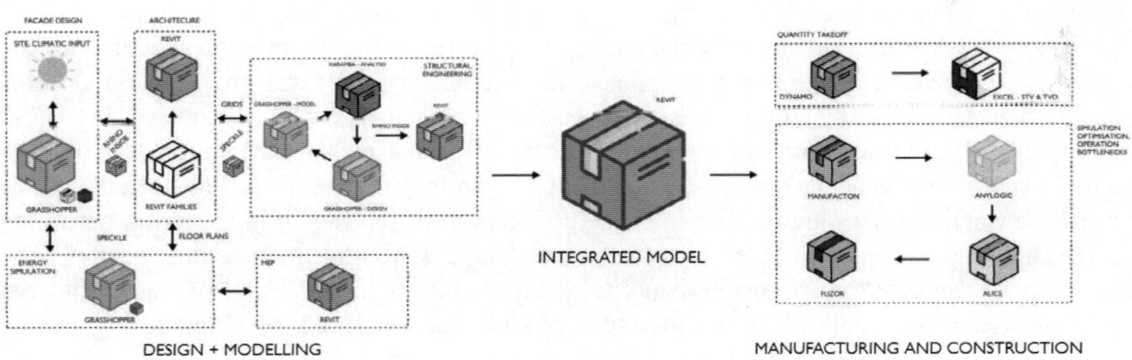

Figure 1: Integrated E2E Framework

The following sections discuss the implementation and testing of the E2E workflows in the context of a global project case study

---

[1] MANUFACTON by MANUFACTON Inc.
[2] AnyLogic Simulation by The AnyLogic Company Inc.
[3] ALICE by ALICE Technologies Inc.
[4] FUZOR by Kalloc Studios Inc.

3. E2E Implementation and Testing in the AEC Global Teamwork

The E2E framework was implemented through a case-based approach and tested by an AEC global project team – Atlantic2020 team – in response to two challenges posed in the 2020 AEC Global Teamwork (Fruchter, 1999): "DPR - Integrating Project Delivery Industrialized Construction" and "BURO HAPPOLD - Intelligent Interoperability Challenge". The Atlantic2020 project is located at the fringe of the University of Wisconsin campus in Madison. The site is constrained by lake Mendota to the north, Muir Woods hill to the south, single site entry, and limited access.

3.1 Design and Modelling

To facilitate a collaborative and holistic method to explore the design solution space, Atlantic2020 team leveraged tools that promoted interoperability between various design and engineering software packages. E2E enabled the team to coordinate all engineering design and modelling efforts into a synchronous process that generated the federated model of the building using Autodesk Revit that acted as the project's single source of truth i.e., the integrated model.

3.2 Architectural Design

The Atlantic2020 team developed a façade that visually expressed the design contributions of each discipline. Since the architectural intent drove many design iterations, it was important for its modelling process to be dynamic and flexible, interoperable and data rich. These factors, along with the building's geometric complexity, made the use of parametric tools desirable in aiding the modelling process. Grasshopper was used for parametric modeling of the building façade, while promoting an interoperable environment for subsequent engineering processes. All disciplines collaborated to determine the key parameters controlling the parametric model. These included (1) the glazing pattern, controlling the transmission of natural light into the building, (2) the vertical member spacing, ensuring adequate support was provided to the floors and (3) the panel size, dictating the ease of assembly and disassembly of the façade. These parameters-imposed constraints on the parametric model and drove the exploration of the design solution space. The façade geometry created from the parametric model was transferred to Revit via Rhino (inside Revit plugin). The interoperable nature of the modelling solution permitted the engineering design processes to occur in real-time with the architectural design. The flexibility of the solution meant the benefits of these simultaneous design processes did not result in redundant work. The architectural model was retrieved by engineering design disciplines in Grasshopper via Speckle (Open-source software), allowing for their respective processes to be executed in a single location.

3.3 Structural Engineering

To further support real-time information flow and interoperability, the structural engineers adopted Karamba 3D for structural analysis, allowing the architectural model to be converted into a complete structural design workflow in a single Grasshopper script. By conducting the analysis and sizing of structural components within Grasshopper, the analysis was driven directly from the architectural model. Using Speckle, the perimeter façade and agreed-upon grids were sent from Revit and retrieved in Grasshopper, with the 2D grid driving the creation of a 3D structural analysis model. The primary inputs in the Grasshopper script included member topology, void locations, a library of permissible sections, and the imposed design criteria. This solution allowed engineering design and member sizing to be completed instantly upon architectural model data being sent from Revit, providing real-time feedback of architectural design implications on structural engineering and vice versa. Further architectural model revisions could then be made with greater confidence and certainty of implications on other design contributors. Finally, 3D models of the structural system could be created directly following the completion of structural analysis and design processes. Element member sizes determined post-analysis were streamed directly into the Revit families and placed in the Revit environment using the Rhino, inside Revit plugin.

3.4 Mechanical, Electrical, Plumbing (MEP)

In the scope of this project, MEP design processes included investigation of building energy efficiency and daylight analysis. In the same Speckle stream containing relevant information for structural engineering, the group's architect provided model data needed to complete MEP design.

- Daylight analysis and simulation. An initial driver of the building form, the daylight analysis and simulation were conducted after generation of the architectural model in Grasshopper, but prior to production of the Revit model. Within the Grasshopper environment, Honeybee and Ladybug were used to complete the simulation directly from the architectural model's driving script. Geometry from this script was transferred to the analysis script via Speckle.
- Energy simulation. After completion of the architectural model, energy analysis was conducted in Grasshopper using the Archsim plugin. From Revit, the interior characteristics of the building could be obtained and used to form a zoning model with different energy characteristics. Subsequent analysis using Archsim would indicate within Grasshopper the requirements of the different zones from an energy perspective. While the following processes of laying out ducts and equipment would be manual, they were driven by real-time analysis results connected to the architecture Revit model.
- Optimizing operational energy efficiency. To control the building lifecycle energy, the team utilized the Sustainable Target Value (STV) (Russell-Smith et. al 2015) tool to track the impact of various design iterations and materials selection on the building's environmental performance. Choosing mass timber and utilizing PV panels allowed to reduce carbon footprint and resource consumption overall.

Figure 2 shows a summary of key design decisions affecting environmental performance and critical building design milestones that led to the final solution presented in May. This upstream design and engineering iterative exploration were continuously impacted by the feedback from the downstream manufacturing and construction workflow optimization discussed in the next sections.

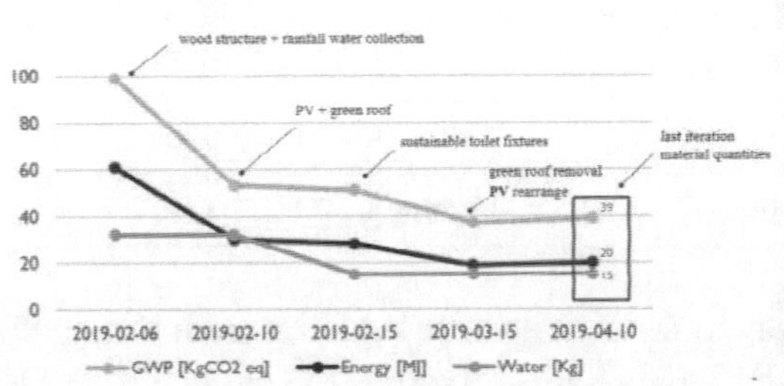

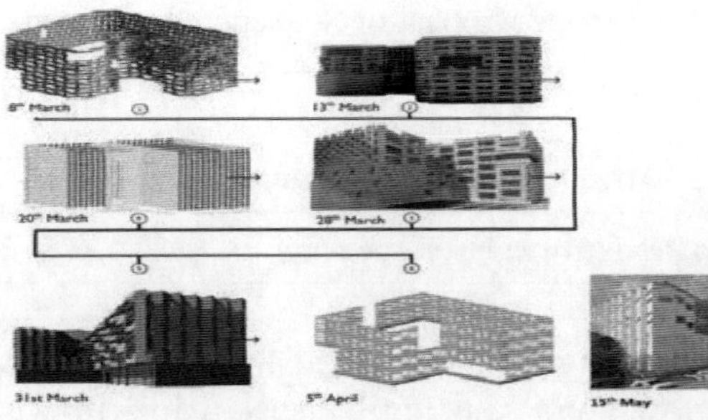

Figure 2: Evolution of Environmental Performance Criteria and Design Exploration

4. Linking Design and Engineering to Manufacturing

To improve the manufacturing stage, real-time assessment of design impacts on industrialized components had to be performed. This requires automated generation of the bill of materials of prefab orders. Moreover, this helps to identifying assembly quantities and cost estimation. In addition, the aim was to track productivity gains in each step in the production that will help mitigate over or underproduction risks. Finally, tracking the prefab orders status across the supply chain helps to connect all stakeholders efficiently. To achieve these goals, Atlantic2020 team used the E2E linked MANUFACTON software, which is an advanced cloud-based software that assists to manage construction materials and off-site production. The façade 3D model from Revit was transferred to MANUFACTON software to perform: (1) automated quantity take-off, (2) prefab orders tracking, and (3) productivity benchmarking.

4.1 Linking Manufacturing to Transportation and On-Site Construction

The second E2E workflow was implemented and tested to simulate and optimize transportation alternatives and on-site construction operations. Different transportation and installing scenarios were analyzed, construction schedules, sequencing, crew numbers were optimized. Peak workflow, site logistics, operations, and safety issues were simulated.

- Transportation and on-site storage analysis. The team compared the process of shipping and installing the façade prefabricated panels for two scenarios. Two scenarios were considered: fully prefabricating the panels, and prefix connections on site. Two KPIs were investigated: (1) total operation time and (2) pre-assembly area required on-site, where total operation time is the summation of time to prefix connections, lift and align panels and fix panels in façade. To achieve the previous analysis, AnyLogic Simulation was utilized. AnyLogic is a simulation modelling software that is used to optimize complex systems and processes. The bill of materials was extracted from MANUFACTON as input to the AnyLogic simulation model. The fully prefabricated alternative yielded better results in all areas, with a total operation time of 31 days compared to 36, and a reduction in on-site storage area of 95%.
- Construction cost and schedule analysis. Atlantic2020 team investigated whether dividing the project in zones would impact cost and time. The comparison showed that no zoning strategy yielded better results. This analysis was carried out using ALICE, a cloud-based platform that leverages AI to generate improved project schedules and optimal resource options. The 3D Revit model was imported into ALICE, a generative scheduling application, to investigate the key drivers for the selected zoning strategy. The results are shown in Table 2. To further optimize cost and schedule, the team ran a second comparison doubling facade crews that worked more shifts vs. having an equal number of crews. The earlier yielded better cost and time results.

Table 2: Impact of Sequencing Alternatives on Construction Time and Cost

	Time (Days)	**Cost (\$)**
Alternative 1: Sequencing in zones	310-400	11,600,000-13,400,000
Alternative 2: No sequencing	150-300	10,250,000-11,500,00

- Site logistics simulations. The following step was to investigate site logistics including peak workflows and site bottlenecks using FUZOR VDC VR software. FUZOR is a VDC software that helps to model, simulate, and virtually experience construction site logistics to better understand the jobsite and identify equipment, material, and crew flow bottlenecks by generating 4D and 5D simulations. The Atlantic2020 team imported the ALICE schedule excel sheet into FUZOR software to build up activities and tasks in the simulation model. Atlantic2020 team simulated the potential of utilizing the water body as an asset due to its proximity to the building. Thus, a barge was simulated to store materials and provide massive preassembly areas if needed. However, pedestrian safety, cost, and material loading were significant drawbacks in this strategy. Peak workflow day was identified using ALICE where complex on-site operations and several crews working within proximity in addition to equipment movement. To avoid space-time congestion, the team investigated shifting the trailers to float over the lake. This helped provide more free space for equipment to move. To check the feasibility of the proposed solution, ALICE schedule was revisited to identify and mitigate rough weather issues.

4.2 Collaboration and Visualization

The last step was to investigate how constructability, safety, and logistical issues can be mitigated early in the design process. After changes were discussed. Integration of clash detection, using BIM360, Prospect VR, Enscape and MeetinVR within the design phase eliminated re-work and increased interdisciplinary rewards. Figure 3 shows images of clash detection analysis and collaborative design review walkthroughs using BIM360 and IrisVR Prospect.

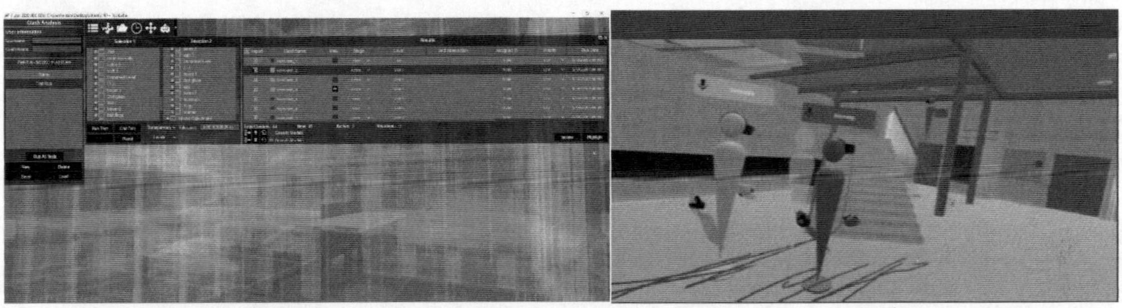

(a) (b)

Figure 3: Interdisciplinary Design Coordination using (a) BIM360 and (b) IrisVR Prospect

5. Discussion and Conclusion

This paper presented an E2E framework implementing a holistic interoperability approach integrating information, models, and disciplines to iteratively explore the design solution space. This was achieved by optimizing and integrating different IC stages and implementing emerging technology accelerators - parametric modelling and optimization, AI, and VR. To this end, the central contribution of this case study is the following:

Holistic E2E mindset. This paper highlights the importance to consider the integration of multiple workflows within the lifecycle of built environment including design-manufacturing-delivery-construction-operation-disassembly-reassambly. The wider and integrated these workflows are, the more informed the joint decision are by all stakeholders engaged in the development of built environment. Technology is constantly evolving. The presented E2E is one instance of an IC holistic mindset that embraces integration across the value chain, instead of emphasizing specific technology with point solution. Determining what are the ends and workflows to be integrated and applied iteratively is an art that vary based on the right mix of people, processes, and tools.

Augmenting human intelligence. Intelligent interoperability supports Construction 4.0 ongoing digital transformation by integrating data, models, disciplines, workflows, and organizations (people) involved in the creation of built environment. It is the convergence of emergent technologies – AI, VR, parametric modeling, and generative design – that foster technology augmented intelligent human exploration, co-creation, and joint decision making demonstrated in this paper through the developed, implemented, and tested E2E framework.

Further validation, refinement, and development of the presented E2E framework is ongoing. In 2021 a new generation of AEC global student teams working on 4 projects adopted the E2E mindset. They expanded E2E framework further, e.g., integrating cashflow liquidity into design-manufacturing-delivery-construction-operation workflows and feedback loops. This highlights the current limitations and opportunities to further consider other key aspects, workflows, and stakeholders that need to be integrated towards a holistic E2E framework, implementation, testing, and deployment. (to view AEC Global Teamwork projects please visit – http://pbl.stanford.edu/AEC%20projects/projpage.htm)

Acknowledgements

The authors thank the Project Based Learning Laboratory at Stanford (PBL Lab) industry partners and their support towards the development of the E2E framework: DPR Construction Inc. and BURO HAPPOLD Inc. who provided insightful challenges, and Facebook Technologies (Oculus) LLC, Kalloc Studios Inc., IrisVR Inc., and MANUFACTON Inc. who provided the VR hardware and cloud-platform technologies. Authors also thank Atlantic2020 team members including Isabella Reynolds (The University of Queensland, Australia); Brandon Byers (Stanford University, United States); Maria Yanez (Denmark Technical University, Denmark) for their effort to implement and test the E2E framework.

References

Bin Ab Halim, M. S., Bin Mat Junoh, M. Z., and Binti Kamil, S. (2014). Financial performance and the management issues of Bumiputera construction firms in the Malaysian construction industry. Advances in Environmental Biology, 8(9 SPEC. ISSUE 4), 654–661.

Chacón, R., Claure, F., and de Coss, O. (2020). Development of VR/AR applications for experimental tests of beams, columns, and frames. Journal of Computing in Civil Engineering, 34(5), 05020003.

Chowdhury, T., Adafin, J., and Wilkinson, S. (2019). Review of digital technologies to improve productivity of New Zealand construction industry. Journal of Information Technology in Construction, 24, 569–587.

Eldamnhoury, E. S., and Hanna, A. S. (2020). Investigating vertical integration strategies in modular construction. Construction Research Congress 2020, American Society of Civil Engineers, Reston, VA, pp.1230–1238.

Fruchter, R. (1999) "Architecture/engineering/construction teamwork: A collaborative design and learning space," Journal of Computing in Civil Engineering, Vol 13 No .4, 261–270.

Global Industry Council. (2018). Five keys to unlocking digital transformation in engineering & construction. Oracle website, https://www.oracle.com/a/ocom/docs/dc/aconex-report-global-industry-council.pdf, accessed March 2021.

Kedir, F., and Hall, D. M. (2021). Resource efficiency in industrialized housing construction – A systematic review of current performance and future opportunities. Journal of Cleaner Production, 286, 125443.

Lessing, J., Hall, D. M., and Pullen, T. (2019). A preliminary overview of emerging trends for industrialized construction in the United States. White Paper. (August). ETH Website: https://www.research-collection.ethz.ch/handle/20.500.11850/331901, accessed March 2021

Li, L., Li, Z., Li, X., Zhang, S., and Luo, X. (2020). A new framework of industrialized construction in China: Towards on-site industrialization. Journal of Cleaner Production, 244.

Liu, Y., Castronovo, F., Messner, J., and Leicht, R. (2020). Evaluating the impact of virtual reality on design review meetings. Journal of Computing in Civil Engineering, 34(1), 04019045.

Oesterreich, T. D., and Teuteberg, F. (2016). Understanding the implications of digitisation and automation in the context of Industry 4.0: A triangulation approach and elements of a research agenda for the construction industry. Computers in Industry, 83, 121–139.

Patil, A. G. (2019). Applications of Artificial Intelligence in construction management. International Journal of Research in Engineering, 32(03), 32–1541.

Qi, B., Razkenari, M., Costin, A., Kibert, C., and Fu, M. (2021). A systematic review of emerging technologies in industrialized construction. 39(February), 102265.

Qi, B., Razkenari, M., Li, J., Costin, A., Kibert, C., and Qian, S. (2020). Investigating U.S. industry practitioners' perspectives towards the adoption of emerging technologies in industrialized construction. Buildings, 10(5), 1–21.

Razkenari, M., Bing, Q., Fenner, A., Hakim, H., Costin, A., and Kibert, C. J. (2019). Industrialized construction: emerging methods and technologies. Computing in Civil Engineering 2019, American Society of Civil Engineers, Reston, VA, 352–359.

Russell-Smith, S., Lepech, M., Fruchter, R., Meyer, Y., (2015). Sustainable Target Value Design: Integrating Life Cycle Assessment and Target Value Design to Improve Building Energy and Environmental Performance. Journal of Cleaner Production, Volume 88, Feb 2015, 43–51.

Veldhuizen, J., Habrakem, I., Sanders, P., and de Jong, R. (2019). Point of view on digital construction - The business case of incorporating digital technologies into the construction industry. Deloitte https://www2.deloitte.com/content/dam/Deloitte/nl/Documents/energy-resources/deloitte-nl-eri-point-of-view-digital-construction.pdf, accessed March 2021.

US Bureau of Labor Statistics. 2021. Current employment statistics highlights. Washington, DC: Dept. of Labor

Wong, P. S. P., Zwar, C., and Gharaie, E. (2017). Examining the drivers and states of organizational change for greater use of prefabrication in construction projects. Journal of Construction Engineering and Management, 143(7), 04017020.

Woodhead, R., Stephenson, P., and Morrey, D. (2018). Digital construction: From point solutions to IoT ecosystem. Automation in Construction 93, 35–46.

Xue, X., Zhang, X., Wang, L., Skitmore, M., and Wang, Q. (2018). Analyzing collaborative relationships among industrialized construction technology innovation organizations: A combined SNA and SEM approach. Journal of Cleaner Production, 173, 265–277.

Accuracy Aspects when Transforming a Boundary Representation of Solids into a Tetrahedral Space Partition

Joanna Zarah Vetter, Wolfgang Huhnt
Technische Universität Berlin, Germany
j.vetter@tu-berlin.de

Abstract. Models, where the geometry of objects is specified by their boundaries (boundary representation), are state of the art in architecture and civil engineering. Nevertheless, an alternative approach is space partition. It covers a description of all solids and the empty space. Advantages of using space partition are obvious: neighboring relations are stored explicitly and navigation becomes simple and efficient. The research presented in this paper is based on the idea of transforming a boundary representation of solids into a tetrahedral space partition. Various existing solutions for this transformation and their problems are discussed. An alternative approach is presented that is based on the idea of accepting round-off errors and using rounded integer coordinates throughout the transformation. This research includes an explanation of why this approach is selected and that the reachable accuracy is sufficient for applications in architecture and civil engineering.

1. Introduction

It is state of the art to model three-dimensional solids in all engineering disciplines. The research presented in this paper is based on the fundamental consideration of modeling the geometry of a set of objects based on space partition. Within this partition, the complete space in which the solids are located is modeled. Topological neighboring relations are stored explicitly. Using space partition for modeling solids is not a new concept (Mäntylä (1988)). The main advantage is the straightforward access to all neighboring relations between the solids and the solids and the empty space.

Fields of possible applications are wide. One possible field of application is the detection of clashes within the model. Additionally to the identification of overlaps, this approach also allows the identification of voids, which are empty spaces in the interior of the model, and touching faces. Because of the complete modeling of both, the empty and non-empty space, another field of application is indoor route planning where neighboring relations play a major role (Wong et al. (2019)).

Even though using space partition for building models has many advantages, it is not state of the art in architecture and civil engineering. Two options exist to introduce space partition in building models: implementing a tool that offers functionalities to construct objects directly based on space partition or transforming the boundary representation of modeled solids into a space partition model. This paper addresses the second option. Resulting data structures store neighboring relations explicitly. Navigation, as well as identification of overlaps and void spaces, are simple without any extensive calculations.

Different solutions for the transformation of boundary representations into a space partition are introduced by Kraft (2016), Huhnt (2018) and Romanschek et al. (2020). Even though Kraft (2016) presented an implementation of his approach for the three-dimensional space it suffers from an uncontrollable refinement of the tetrahedral mesh. Romanschek et al. (2020) presented an implementation of the algorithm introduced by Huhnt (2018) for the two-dimensional space using exact computation. Uncontrollable refinements cannot occur by the nature of this approach. Nevertheless, it is later shown that a transfer of this implementation into the three-dimensional space would be inefficient.

An alternative approach for the three-dimensional space is briefly presented in section 3 which overcomes these problems by accepting round-off errors and using integer coordinates throughout the process of transformation. Because rounded integer coordinates are used, round-off errors occur. Accuracy aspects of this approach are analyzed in section 4 of this paper. Based on the discussed problems of previous approaches it is presented why the new approach is considered to be a reasonable alternative. It is also shown that the occurring round-off errors are acceptable in the architectural and civil engineering field.

2. Related Research

Different research contributes to this field. Theoretical research such as the description of polyhedrons by Nef (1978), the development of location tests and the robust calculation of geometrical predicates (Sunday (2012)) was conducted. In addition, specific data structures play a major role to navigate through solids in an efficient way such as the dual half-edge developed by Boguslawski (2011) and its application in the three-dimensional space.

Kraft (2016) combined existing approaches to accomplish the transformation of given boundary representations of objects into a space partition. His approach is based on the adaptive precision floating-point arithmetic developed by Shewchuk (1997). He achieved the required robustness of his algorithm by using a constraint Delaunay triangulation. He introduces two types of variables to define accuracy in his approach. The first type describes the minimal distance between different points, e.g. points on the boundary of a solid. These variables have a geometrical meaning. They are used to describe whether two objects coincide geometrically. The second type describes the smallest value greater than zero. This value describes the accuracy that can be achieved by floating-point arithmetic. The weakness of the approach of Kraft (2016) is that uncontrollable refinements can occur. So-called Steiner points are necessary to be inserted. There are situations where these points need to be inserted for achieving a robust and valid mesh. Simple examples already show that the number of points increases in an unacceptable way.

Huhnt (2018) introduces an approach based on the idea of using integer values as a starting point to ensure the exact calculation of location tests throughout the process. He showed a general concept and first steps in the process of transforming a boundary representation into a space partition.

Romanschek et al. (2020) introduce a complete implementation of this approach in the two-dimensional space using exact computation with rational numbers for calculated intersection points. Hu et al. (2018) present a similar approach and implementation to Romanschek et al. (2020) but for a single object in the three-dimensional space. They don't analyze the needed memory in theory. Their practical applications show that this approach is very time-consuming in three-dimensional space without analyzing the reasons in detail.

The underlying fundamental problem is that memory in the computer is limited. The resulting problems are well described in the literature, specifically in the context of floating-point operations (Mei et al. (2014)) and the exact computation of geometric predicates such as the location point problem (Shewchuk (1997)). The challenge is to develop a procedure that can handle the inaccuracy so that a robust solution is available that requires an acceptable amount of memory and that has an acceptable runtime behavior.

Because of this consideration, Hu et al. (2020) introduce an approach that uses floating-point numbers for coordinates. This approach has similarities to the approach presented in this paper. However, Hu et al. (2020) consider only a single object. In addition, they cannot guarantee that each triangle of that object can be inserted. The approach presented in this paper considers a set of objects. The insertion of all triangles is guaranteed.

3. Transformation Process

The input for the transformation process is a given model that contains boundary representations of its objects. All objects consist of given triangles that are oriented to the outside and represent the boundary of the object. Coordinates of points of these triangles must be integer values. An example is presented in figure 1.

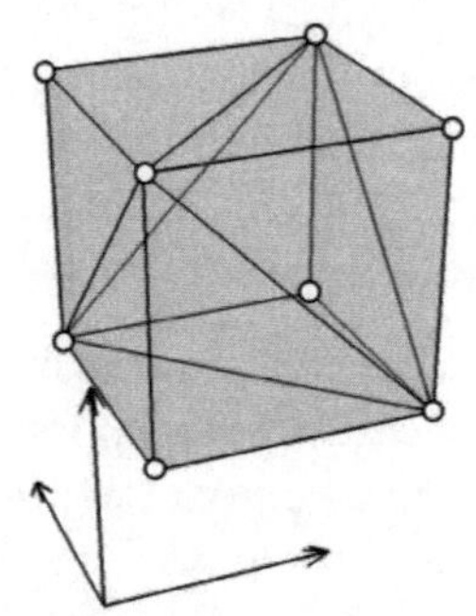

Figure 1: Example of a given object defined by its boundary as a set of triangles

A correct given model has no overlaps of a pair of any two solids and no void spaces in its interior. With all points of the given triangles and additional boundary points, an initial tetrahedral mesh is created. These additional boundary points must lie outside of the convex hull of all objects and are necessary to ensure a sufficient size of the initial mesh. In the example implementation, the initial mesh is created by the tetrahedralization of the area between eight boundary points and the subsequent insertion of all given points by splitting existing tetrahedrons. An example of an initial mesh is shown in figure 2.

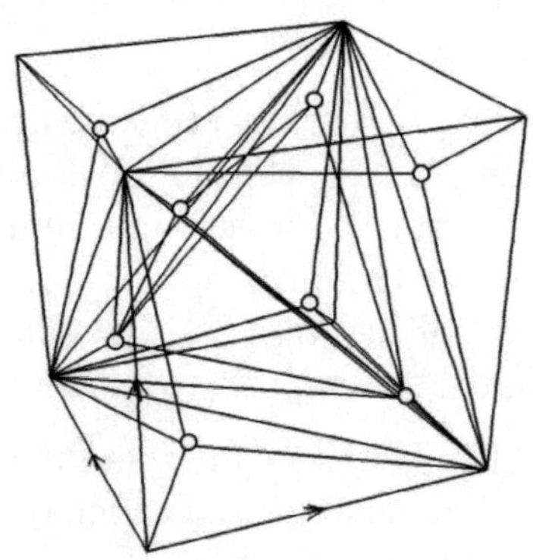

Figure 2: Example of an initial mesh created out of the given model in figure 1

All given points are now vertices of the initial mesh. Additionally, all given points lie in the interior of the initial mesh. This mesh does not preserve the surface of the objects. To achieve this goal, the mesh is now refined step by step for every given triangle of the model. For every triangle, intersection points between the triangle and the tetrahedral mesh are computed and rounded to integer coordinates. Afterward, these rounded intersection points are inserted by splitting existing tetrahedrons. A split always results in a valid tetrahedral mesh. A special treatment guarantees validity. This treatment is not presented here because it does not influence the accuracy which is addressed in this paper.

After refining the tetrahedral mesh, the plane of each given triangle can be represented by a set of mesh triangles. The edges of a triangle are not reconstructed explicitly. But by the stepwise refinement of the tetrahedral mesh, shared edges of given triangles are reconstructed indirectly by processing both triangles one after the other.

The result of the complete refinement procedure is a valid tetrahedral space partition where every given object can be represented by a set of mesh tetrahedrons. The result of the example in figure 1 is shown in figure 3.

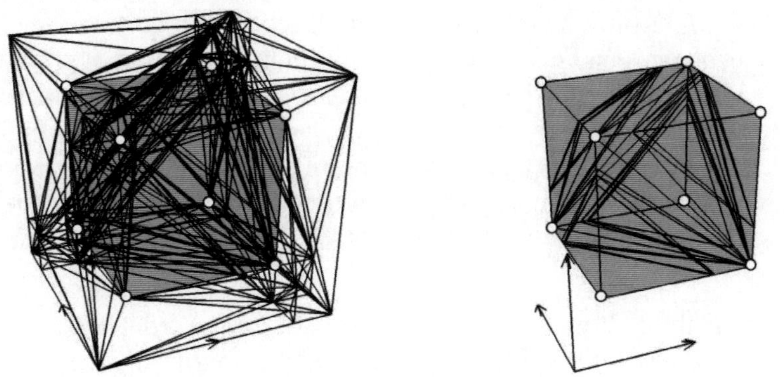

Figure 3: Result of the refinement of the given model in figure 1

Although a great challenge is to ensure topological correctness, it is also necessary to analyze the accuracy of the results in this approach. Round-off errors resulting from rounded integer values may cause issues in practical applications. Therefore, a careful investigation of accuracy aspects is necessary.

4. Accuracy Aspects

To make sure the approach is a reasonable alternative to recent approaches, two questions need to be answered:

- Why is it better to work with rounded integer values instead of exact computation based on rational numbers?
- Is the reachable accuracy sufficient for applications in the civil engineering field?

The first question can be answered by comparing the memory required for coordinates in the two-dimensional and three-dimensional space in the case of using an exact computation based on rational numbers.

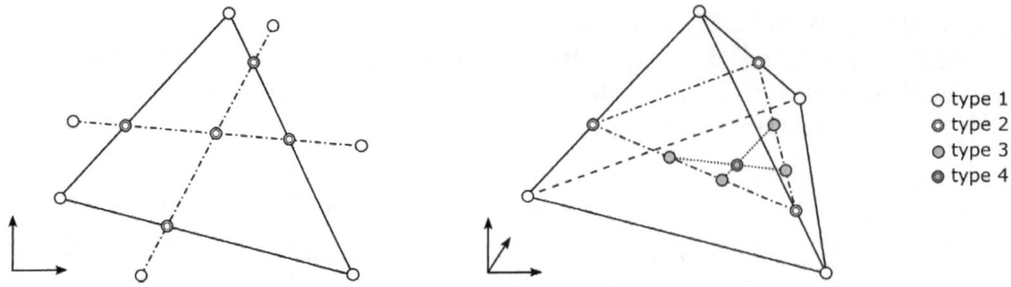

Figure 4: Needed types of points in the two-dimensional and three-dimensional space

Romanschek et al. (2020) implemented the algorithm based on Huhnt (2018) in the two-dimensional space. They used exact computation with rational numbers to represent coordinates of calculated intersection points. All coordinate values of mesh points and given points are positive integer values of 32-bit integer variables. Intersections in the two-dimensional spaces can occur between mesh edges and given edges or two given edges as shown in figure 4. Either way, the calculation of an intersection between two edges in the local coordinate system of each of these edges is based on the original positive integer coordinates. Following the equations described by Romanschek et al. (2020), both, the denominator and the numerator of the fraction need twice as much memory as the input integer coordinates. Therefore no overflow can occur when using a data type for integer values with 64 bits for the denominator and numerator of the fraction.

Intersection points in the three-dimensional space cannot be computed in the same manner since the start and endpoints of two intersecting edges are not necessarily input points as this is true for the two-dimensional space. For the three-dimensional space, different types of intersection points are necessary as shown in figure 4. First, it would be necessary to calculate the intersection points between given triangles and mesh edges. These intersection points are of type 2. Analogous to the two-dimensional space, the exact position of intersection points in the local coordinate system of an edge can be represented by a fraction. This fraction s is calculated as follows:

$$s = \frac{t \cdot (p_{t0} - p_{e0})}{t \cdot (p_{e1} - p_{e0})} \tag{1}$$

We assume that coordinates of all given points p_{t0} and mesh points p_{e0} and p_{e1} are positive values of n-bit integer variables. The normal t of the given triangle is the result of a cross product and can be therefore represented by 2n-bit integer variables. Therefore, 3n-bit integer variables are necessary to store the denominator and the numerator of the fraction for points of type 2. In case two given triangles intersect with each other on the surface of a mesh triangle, intersection points of type 2 are the start and endpoint of intersecting line segments. The intersection point of these line segments is a point of type 3. The calculation of type 3 intersection points is analogous to the calculation of intersections between line segments in the two-dimensional space. Therefore, type 3 intersection points need twice as much memory as type 2 intersection points. Type 4 intersection points occur in case three given triangles intersect in the interior of a mesh tetrahedron. Analogous to the calculation of type 3 intersection points, type 4 intersection points need again twice as much memory as type 3 intersection points. In the end, type 4 intersection points need to be represented by 12n-bit integer variables.

In a conclusion, the necessary bit length of integer values in the two-dimensional and three-dimensional space can be summarized as followed:

Two-dimensional space:

- Type 1: positive values of an n bit variable
- Type 2: 2 times n bits

Three-dimensional space:

- Type 1: positive values of an n bit variable
- Type 2: 3 times n bits
- Type 3: 6 times n bits
- Type 4: 12 times n bits

An implementation of exact computation for all intersection points in the three-dimensional space is possible. However, these considerations show the inefficiency of this approach for computations in the three-dimensional space.

The second question is answered by showing how large the maximum round-off errors of the presented approach can get. As stated in section 3, all calculated intersection points are rounded to integer values. To do so, all coordinates are rounded to the next integer value. In case the calculated coordinate is exactly between two integer values, the bigger integer value is chosen. With this definition, the maximum round-off errors can be 0.5 in every direction. The maximum amount of deviation in a single operation is, therefore, $\sqrt{0.5^2 + 0.5^2} \approx 0.7071$ for the two-dimensional space and $\sqrt{0.5^2 + 0.5^2 + 0.5^2} \approx 0.8660$ for the three-dimensional space.

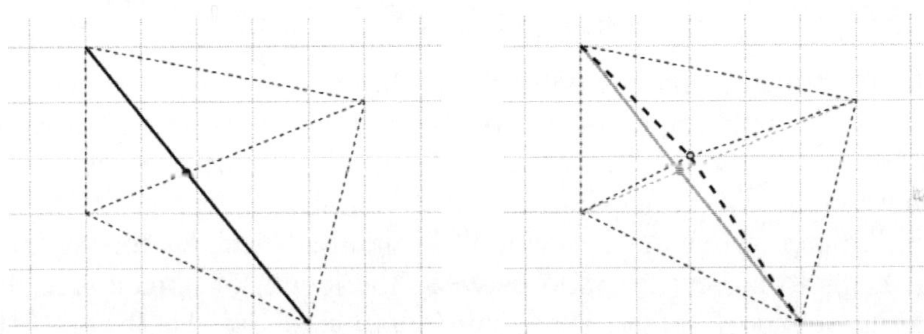

Figure 5: Round-off errors in the two-dimensional space. A given edge (bold) intersect with a mesh edge (dotted) (left). The intersection point is rounded to integer values and inserted into the mesh (bold and dotted edge represents the reconstructed given edge in the mesh) (right).

Figure 5 shows an example of a given edge intersecting with a mesh edge. The computed coordinates of the intersection point are rounded to the next integer values. Both triangles are split into two triangles each. The newly inserted mesh edges form the reconstructed edge in the mesh.

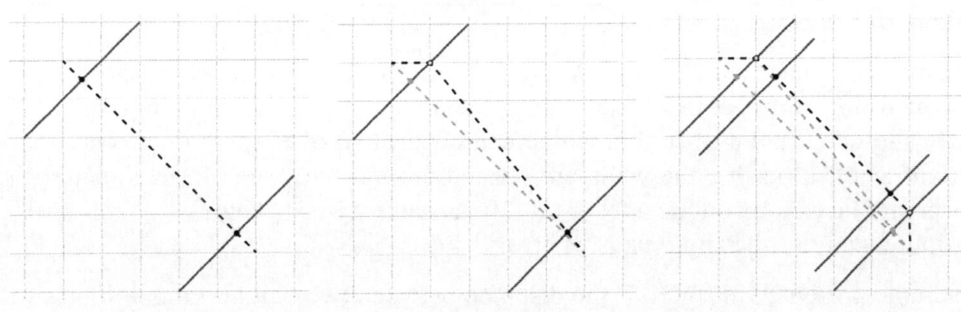

Figure 6: Worst case scenario of round-off errors in the two-dimensional space

There is a theoretical chance of the continuation and increase of round-off errors both, in the two-dimensional space and three-dimensional space. After reconstructing a given edge the mesh does not necessarily consist of given points only anymore. During the reconstruction of a next given edge, the already split mesh edge can be intersected again. This mesh edge is only an approximation of the firstly reconstructed given edge with a maximum distance of 0.7071 to its original. But the computed coordinates of the intersection point between this edge and the second intersecting given edge need also to be rounded to the next integer values. In the worst case, this can double the round-off error compared to the original first given edge. This case is shown in figure 6.

Figure 6 also shows that in the worst case the round-off error can increase with every intersecting given edge. From a geometrical point of view, this increase of the round-off error does not exceed the maximum round-off error of $l/2$ when dealing with a given edge of the length l. This can only occur in case a given edge is intersected by other edges. In this special case, the maximum round-off error of the edge can double with every second intersecting given edge as shown in figure 6.

The presented special case in figure 6 is a theoretical example of what can happen in the worst case. Examples in the civil engineering field do not look like the example in figure 6 and have a very low risk of being affected by the presented problem due to several reasons. The continuation of round-off errors especially occurs due to incorrect input models which include intersecting given triangles or edges in overlapping objects. Although overlapping objects may occur in digital building models, the ratio between the length of an object and the amount of other intersecting objects is rarely as balanced as shown in figure 6.

Additionally, digital building models typically do have limited dimensions. Therefore, it is possible to scale up the input model for the procedure of refinement. This decreases the grid size of the integer values and increases the precision in which the model is calculated. For example, an input model with dimensions of 10000 centimeters can easily be scaled up to be represented in millimeters when dealing with 32-bit integer variables for the input. Scaling up the input model helps to correct the ratio between the length of objects and the intersecting objects to avoid high round-off errors. These considerations show, that the presented theoretical problem shown in figure 6 is not relevant for digital building models.

For correct input models, the maximum round-off error can be determined based on the previous considerations. There are no overlapping objects in a correct input model. Shared edges of given triangles in an object are not reconstructed explicitly but formed by the intersection of two planes. Therefore, the round-off error in a typical building object can be increased by this intersection of the planes as well. All given points of an object are already part of the initial mesh. They must not be formed by the intersection of three reconstructed planes. Due to that fact, the increase of round-off errors is limited to two intersecting planes in typical building objects. This means the maximum round-off error that can occur in correctly modeled building models equals $2 \cdot \sqrt{0.5^2 + 0.5^2 + 0.5^2} \approx 1.7321$.

After showing the maximum possible round-off errors, it is necessary to show how big the average round-off errors get in an example of the architectural and civil engineering field. To effectively show the round-off errors which can occur, two overlapping walls are modeled. It is important to mention that the walls are rotated around the z-axis to make sure, the given triangles do not lie exactly on the integer grid. In case the given triangles would lie perfectly on the grid, there wouldn't be any round-off errors.

In the example presented in figure 7, the distance between two neighboring points is scaled for each coordinate direction as followed: one grid point is one millimeter. The two walls have the following dimensions: 3.2 m x 0.16 m x 2.3 m and 1.6 m x 0.16 m x 2.3 m. This corresponds to 3200 x 160 x 2300 and 1600 x 160 x 2300 grid points.

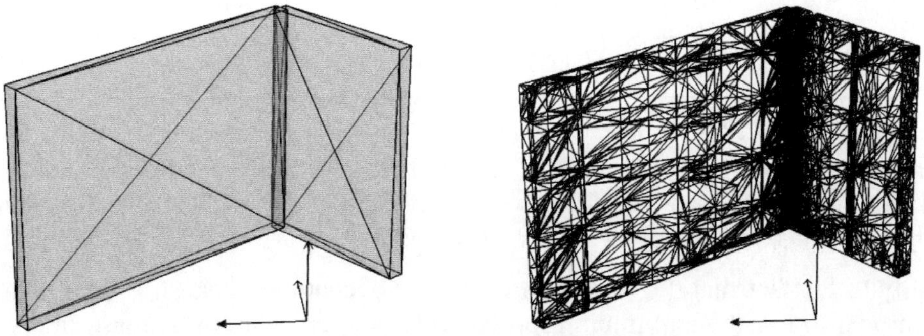

Figure 7: Example of two overlapping walls

The presented example in figure 7 shows two overlapping walls (left) and all mesh tetrahedrons representing the objects after the refinement procedure (right). The resulting surface of the reconstructed objects can be compared to the surface of the input model. There are two different types of round-off errors that can be analyzed. All points on the surface can have a distance due to round-off errors to the original surface of given triangles. Additionally, the mesh points which reconstruct the shared edges of given triangles that are not coplanar can have a distance from the original shared edge. The following table shows the results of the analysis of all round-off errors in this example.

Table 1: Round-off errors of the presented example in figure 7 with an incorrect input model

Type	Average	Standard deviation	Minimum	Maximum
Mesh points to given triangles	0.1127	0.1464	0.0	0.6247
Mesh points to shared edges	0.0796	0.1299	0.0	0.6247

The given model was imported in millimeter precision. This means all deviations are given in millimeters. Although the example is not correctly modeled, the theoretically possible maximum round-off error is not reached at any point. The average round-off error is very low and easily acceptable in the architectural and civil engineering field.

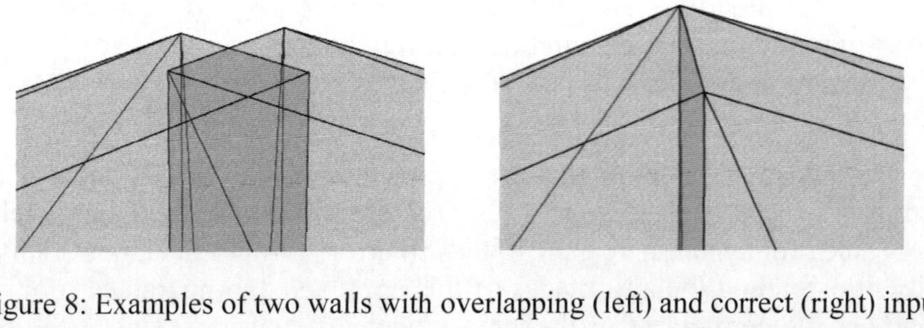

Figure 8: Examples of two walls with overlapping (left) and correct (right) input

The presented example in figure 7 can also be modeled correctly by acceptably connecting the two walls to prevent an overlap of the two walls as shown in figure 8.

Table 2: Round-off errors of the presented example in figure 8 with a correct input model

Type	Average	Standard deviation	Minimum	Maximum
Mesh points to given triangles	0.1182	0.1484	0.0	0.8254
Mesh points to shared edges	0.1021	0.1468	0.0	0.8254

With the comparison of the round-off errors occurring while processing the correctly modeled input and the incorrectly modeled input, it is clear to see that the round-off errors do not differ from each other in a significant way. The average round-off error of the correctly modeled input is even higher than the one from the incorrectly modeled input.

Additionally to the fact that the round-off errors are acceptable, it is still possible to scale up the input model to use the maximum representable integer value to increase the precision in case millimeter precision is not considered to be good enough.

At the beginning of this section, two questions are raised and needed to be answered. With the help of the basic calculation approaches of the reconstruction, it was made clear that the approach of using exact computation for the three-dimensional space is very inefficient. It was also shown that even though round-off errors can occur, the average round-off errors in applications in the civil engineering field are acceptable.

5. Discussion, Conclusion and Outlook

The presented approach of transforming a boundary representation into a space partitioning. The benefit is the explicit storage of neighboring relations. Topological relations between solids and solids and the empty space are easily detected.

The approach is based on integer values and the acceptance of round-off errors. This acceptance influences the possible fields of applications. Some geometrical features may be lost because the resulting representation of the objects suffers from round-off errors, e.g. the parallelism of object surfaces. In fields of application where an exact geometry is necessary the presented approach is not applicable. Nevertheless, the research conducted in this paper shows that the approach is applicable in all other fields where an approximated geometry is sufficient and the exact geometry only plays a subordinate role.

The use of rounded integer values instead of exact computation offers huge potential savings when it comes to both, memory and runtime. Although the presented approach in this paper is implemented with integer values, it would be possible to implement the approach with floating-point numbers if some conditions are met. The exact calculation of geometric predicates is a key condition in this algorithm. Additionally, it is necessary to implement a robust and predictable way of rounding floating numbers that cannot be represented anymore. If those two conditions are met, the use of floating-point numbers is possible.

With showing that the achievable accuracy is sufficient for applications in the architecture and civil engineering industry, it is clear that the approach analyzed in this paper is a reasonable alternative to existing approaches. A next research approach would be the development of a strategy to solve the problem of increasing round-off errors for incorrect input. This would offer the possibility of extending the advantages of this approach and guarantee robust results that are independent of the correctness of the input model. Another next step is the complete and detailed presentation of the briefly mentioned approach. This publication is already in progress. The applicability of the presented approach for real digital building models is another important step in the research that needs to be taken. It is necessary to investigate whether the presented approach is applicable for real building models in terms of memory and runtime.

Acknowledgments

This research is funded by the Deutsche Forschungsgemeinschaft (DFG, German Research Foundation) – Project number: 424641234.

References

Boguslawski, P. (2011). Modelling and analysing 3D building interiors with the dual half-edge data structure, Dissertation, University of Glamorgan, UK.

Hu, Y., Zhou, Q., Gao, X., Jacobson, A., Zorin, D. and Panozzo, D. (2018). Tetrahedral meshing in the wild, ACM Transactions on Graphics, Vol. 37, No. 4.

Hu, Y., Schneider, T., Wang, B., Zorin, D. and Panozzo, D. (2020). Fast tetrahedral meshing in the wild, ACM Transactions on Graphics, Vol. 39, No. 4.

Huhnt, W. (2018). Reconstruction of edges in digital building models, Advanced Engineering Informatics, Vol. 38, pp.474–487.

Kraft, B. (2016). Ein Verfahren der Raumzerlegung als Grundlage zur Prüfung von Geometrie und Topologie digitaler Bauwerksmodelle, Dissertation, Technische Universität Berlin, Germany.

Mäntylä, M. (1988). An Introduction to Solid Modelling, Computer Science Press, pp.72 ff.

Mei, G., Tipper, J. C., and Xu, N. (2014). Numerical Robustness in Geometric Computation: An Expository Summary, Applied Mathematics & Information Sciences, Vol. 8, No. 6, pp.2717–2727.

Nef, W. (1978). Beiträge zur Theorie der Polyeder: mit Anwendungen in der Computergrafik, Beiträge zur Mathematik, Informatik und Nachrichtentechnik, P. Lang.

Romanschek, E., Clemen, C. and Huhnt, W. (2020). From Terrestrial Laser Scans to a Surface Model of a Building; Proof of Concept in 2D, In: 27th International Workshop on Intelligent Computing in Engineering, 2020, Online Workshop.

Shewchuk, J.R. (1997). Adaptive Precision Floating-Point Arithmetic and Fast Robust Geometric Predicates, Dissertation, Carnegie Mellon University, Pittsburgh, USA.

Sunday D. (2012). Geometry Algorithms Home, www.geomalgorithms.com, last visited 11.03.2021.

Wong, M.O. and Lee, S. (2019). A Technical Review on Developing BIM-Oriented Indoor Route Planning, In: ASCE International Conference on Computing in Civil Engineering, 2019, Atlanta, USA.

The influence of topology optimisation's design space—from shell to volume—on the generation of structural systems

Herm Hofmeyer, Diane Schoenmaker, Sjonnie Boonstra, Pieter Pauwels
Eindhoven University of Technology, The Netherlands
h.hofmeyer@tue.nl

Abstract. A part of design (decision) support systems comprises the automatic generation of a structural system for a building spatial design. This generation can be carried out by Topology Optimisation (TO), for which different geometrical design spaces can be selected. Here, three grammars to generate various TO (geometrical) design spaces are studied: (a) the Flat Shell Grammar (FSG), which initiates flat shells for each space surface; (b) a Partial Volume Grammar (PVG), which generates volumes for each surface; and (c) the Volume Grammar (VG) that sees the total volume of the building spatial design as the geometrical design space. By two case studies, it can be concluded that the more freedom a geometrical design space provides, the better the structural performance is. Also, structural systems suggested using PVG, with a large thickness of the volumes, are difficult to interpret. For future research, VG or PVG grammars are advised, including a study for non-rectangular designs and openings.

1. Introduction

Creating a building design is a complex and multi-disciplinary task (Flager et al., 2009). Therefore, design systems exist that (i) optimise building designs for multiple disciplines via evolutionary algorithms; (ii) simulate a design process; and (iii) use these techniques in concert to find alternative and optimised designs (Boonstra et al., 2021). Part of such design systems can be the automatic generation of a structural system for a building spatial design, and this can be carried out by Topology Optimisation (TO). For TO, the spatial design provides the geometrical design space, meshed by finite elements with a variable relative density, and these densities are distributed such that a certain objective is minimised. The result can be interpreted as a structural system. In this paper, the influence of the different TO geometrical design spaces on the suggested structural systems is investigated by using three grammars that help to generate TO geometrical design spaces, see figure 1, and two case studies will be carried out. After this introduction, Section 2 starts with a summary of the background and related work. In Section 3, the used design system is presented. Hereafter, the two case studies are elaborated in Section 4, for which results are discussed in Section 5. Finally, conclusions are given in Section 6.

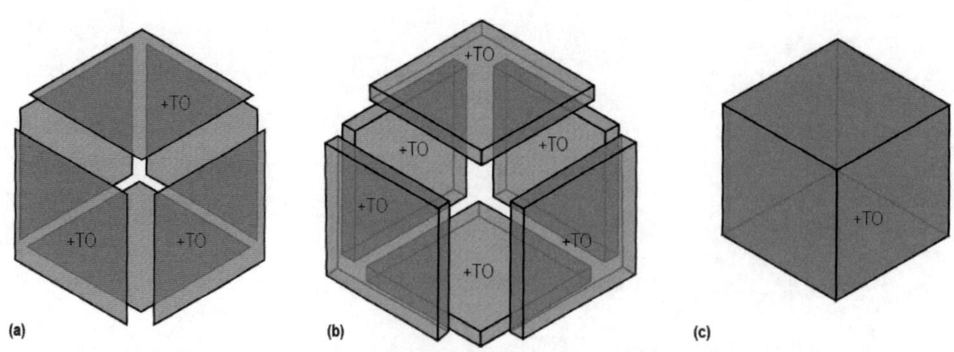

Figure 1: A space of a building design can provide a TO geometrical design space by (a) flat shells; (b) volumes for walls and floors; or (c) by being completely solid, "+TO" stands for "to be optimised by TO"

2. Background and Related Work

TO distributes material (i.e. finite element relative densities) in an optimal fashion to minimise an objective, here strain energy. The resulting distribution can then often be used to suggest (the topology of) a structural system. To solve the topology optimisation problem, common techniques are either gradient- or evolutionary-based. One of the earliest, but still commonly used, gradient-based technique is using Solid Isotropic Material with Penalization (SIMP). Several extensions have been developed to improve SIMP, e.g. projection filters, which are able to create almost Black/White (B/W) solutions (Andreassen et al., 2010), i.e. elements with intermediate material densities are avoided. Combined with techniques to incorporate manufacturing tolerances (Sigmund, 2009), so-called robust TO can be used to show that human-designed hierarchical structures are structurally optimal (Hofmeyer, Schevenels and Boonstra, 2017). As gradient-based techniques may lock into a local optimum, evolutionary based techniques can be used as an alternative, although they are computationally expensive. Examples are Genetic Algorithms (GA) (Wang, Tai and Wang, 2005), and Evolutionary Structural Optimisation (ESO) by Xie & Steven (1993). TO utilises a geometrical design space in which the material is distributed. This geometrical design space is often static but can also be dynamic. For example, in the work of Hofmeyer and Davila Delgado (2015), the building spatial design is optimised in each design loop to match the newly found structural design, and a similar approach can be followed for wind turbine blades (Wang et al., 2020). From a mathematical point of view, the TO geometrical design space influences the outcomes, i.e. the final material distribution. But also for practical building design this holds true: In the work of Steiner et al. (2017), an architectural floorplan is interactively designed, with the future structural layout and performance in mind. Related, in Gan et al. (2019), not only the structural layout for a floorplan is designed and optimised, but also the individual structural elements. And Liang, Xie and Steven (2000) show how the geometrical design space of façades of multi-storey buildings can be used for the generation of bracing systems. Although used for 3D buildings, most TO geometrical design spaces are 2D and pseudo 3D, e.g. Wu et al. (2019). Truly 3D geometrical design spaces can be found only in a few cases, e.g. in the research of Beghini et al. (2014), Christiansen et al. (2015), and Hofmeyer and Davila Delgado (2015).

3. Methodology

The research in this paper uses the open-source Building Spatial design Optimisation (BSO) toolbox (Boonstra & Hofmeyer, 2020). The toolbox starts with the input of a building spatial design, defined as a set of spaces, with each space having an ID, position, and dimensions. Hereafter, the spatial design can be used for the generation of discipline related designs, as explained in the next sections, via the use of a so-called conformal model. This latter model consists of two parts (building and geometry) because domain specific properties may vary within components in the building part, and boundaries between these different properties are handled by being coincident with geometrical boundaries in the geometry part.

3.1 Building Conformal Model

Using the above-mentioned input, the spaces of the building spatial design are used to define their surfaces, in turn realised by edges and points, see figure 2. For this, spaces should not overlap; should be orthogonal; and must all be connected in an orthogonal grid, so "loose" spaces are not allowed. Although not conformal itself (see next section), the intermediate result is already defined as the building conformal model.

3.2 Geometry Conformal Model

A conformal model is defined here as a model in which vertices do not intersect lines, rectangles, or cuboids, which practically means that e.g. a T-joint of two lines should not exist. Such a model is needed to make discipline-related operations possible, like loading external surfaces with wind, or proper finite element meshing. To generate a conformal model, the toolbox uses an automated procedure that associates a so-called geometry conformal model (see figure 2 on the left) to the building conformal model. First to each space an equally shaped cuboid is associated, this cuboid realised by rectangles, in turn realised by lines and vertices. Then, cuboids and their related geometry entities are split iteratively, similar to Hofmeyer, Van Roosmalen and Gelbal (2011), until the geometry entities are conformal. During the split actions, associations between the geometry and building design entities are updated continuously, e.g. a line-to-be-split results in two new lines, which both will be related to the edge that related to the line-to-be-split.

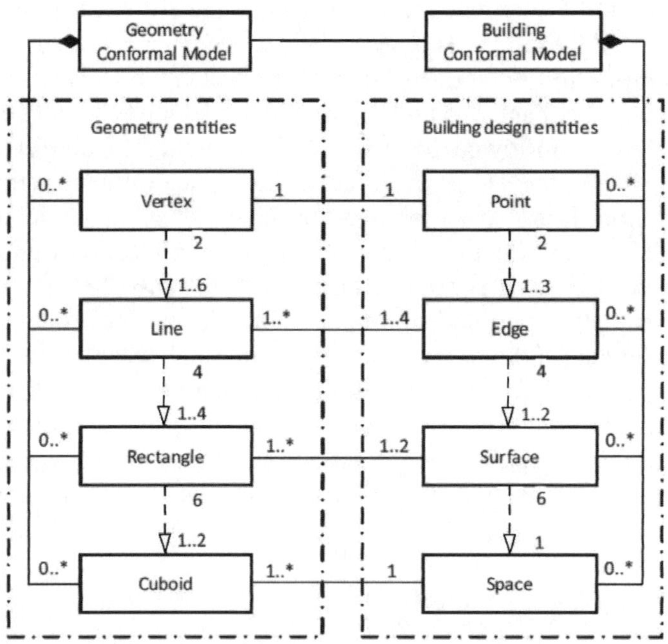

Figure 2: UML diagram of the conformal model, which consists of the geometry and the building conformal models

3.3 Structural Design Model

Based on the conformal model of figure 2, the toolbox can generate a Structural Design (SD) model as shown in figure 3. The SD model is composed of (structural) geometrical components with a type (beam, truss, flat shell, or volume, these types not shown in the figure) with give inheritance to line segments, quadrilaterals, and "quad" (quadrilateral faced) hexahedrons. The components are associated with a general property "Structure", which lists the type, material properties, and dimensions, and may be associated with loads and constraints. To assess a structural design, the toolbox associates the SD model with a finite element model that is composed of (finite) elements, having nodes. Several finite elements are implemented, namely beam, truss, flat shell, and volume (quadrilateral faced hexahedron) elements.

The toolbox offers two fundamentally different approaches to generate a structural system. The first approach applies structural grammars. These generate structural components based on the conformal model. For instance, a grammar can be conceived that adds to each rectangle (in the geometry conformal model) a flat shell component (including material properties and dimensions). A more advanced version of this approach is to use the grammars iteratively, in concert with finite element simulations to assess intermediate design stages, see Boonstra et al. (2020). In both cases, the resulting SD model (a definition within the toolbox) is then regarded as the structural system. The second approach allows for defining structural components mainly to obtain their geometry, and hereafter topology optimisation (as introduced in section 2) finds a material distribution within the geometry outlines (here the TO geometrical design space) that is optimal for the applied load cases. Often, the resulting material distribution suggests a structural system, but the quality of the suggestion varies. Existing and new grammars for this second approach will be presented in the next sections.

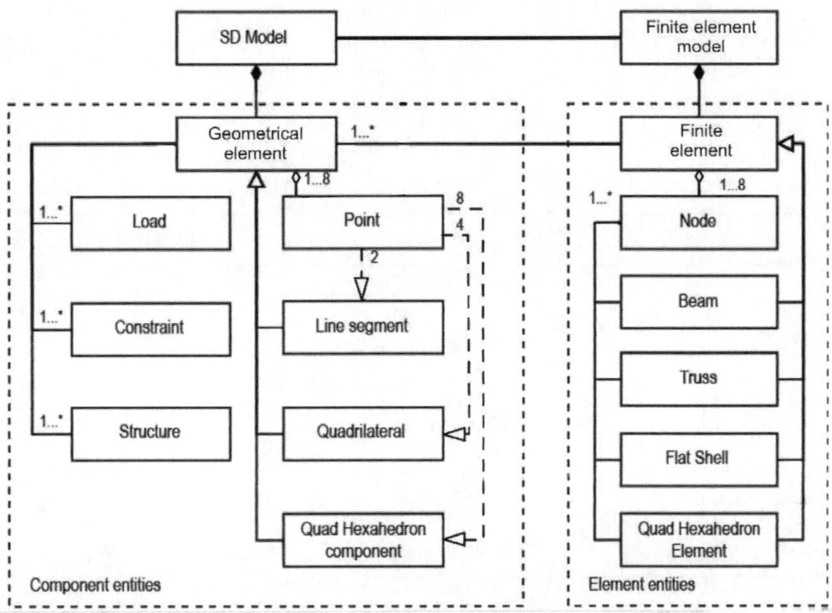

Figure 3: UML diagram of the Structural Design (SD) model and its related finite element model

3.4 Flat Shell Grammar

The existing Flat Shell Grammar (FSG) generates a flat shell structural component with a quadrilateral geometry for each rectangle (see figure 2) that belongs to a (space) surface. Figure 4 shows an example on the bottom left. For this example, it should be noted that there is no structural component in between the two cuboids on the ground level, as there is only a single space there. Loads are first defined on the rectangles, then transferred to the coincident components. Horizontal rectangles coincident with a space surface (a floor) are loaded by a live load equal to 5 kN/m^2, and vertically oriented rectangles are loaded by wind (depending on the orientation: with normal pressure 1.0 kN/m^2, suction 0.8 kN/m^2, or shear 0.4 kN/m^2), but only if they are external (and not internal) with respect to the building spatial design. To model a foundation, lines at the ground are fixed for all degrees of freedom. Hereafter, the flat shell components are meshed with flat shell finite elements, having a certain thickness, and so later topology optimisation will find a material distribution across the shell finite elements. This implies that structural systems are suggested for which the material is localised within the thickness of the flat shell elements, and so at the surfaces of the spaces of the building spatial design.

3.5 Volume Grammar

The existing Volume Grammar (VG) adds a volume structural component (with quadrilateral faced hexahedron geometry) to each cuboid in the conformal model, see figure 4 on the bottom, completely right. Loads, as defined on the rectangles as explained in the previous sections, are assigned to additionally generated quadrilaterals (see figure 3) coincident with the quadrilateral faced hexahedron sides, and during mesh generation this results in the appropriate loads.

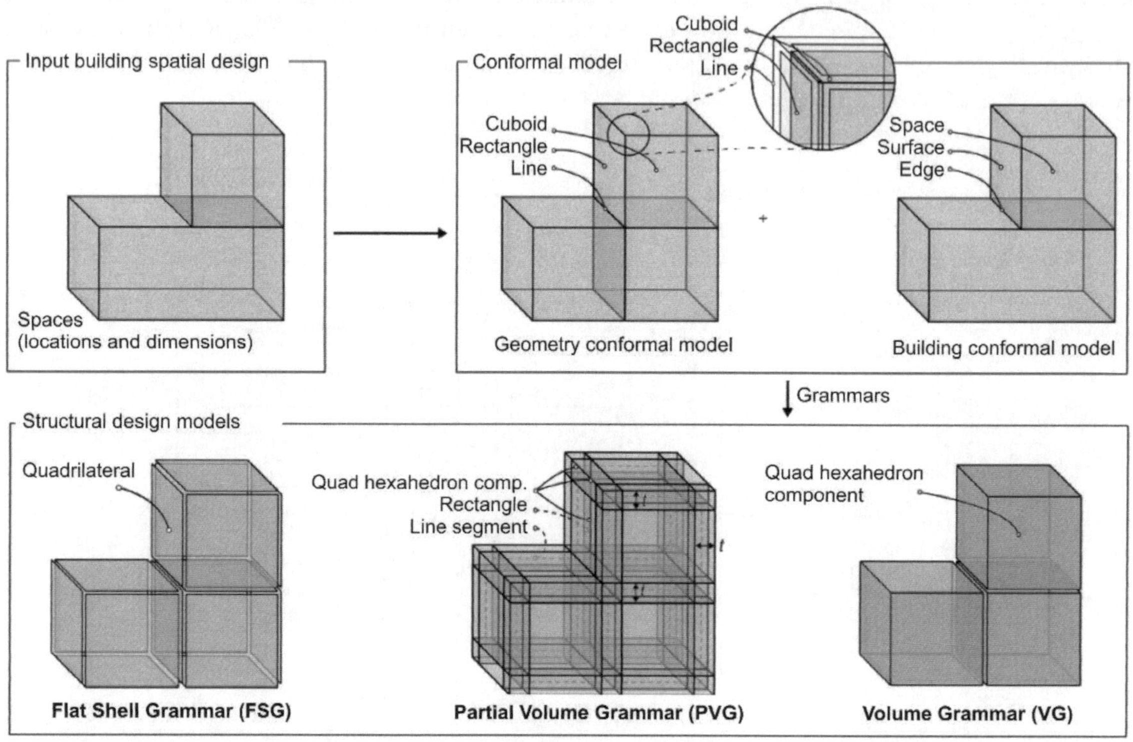

Figure 4: Input is converted into a conformal model, for which FSG, PVG, and VG generate structural components, to be used for topology optimisation to find suggestions for the structural system

3.6 Partial Volume Grammar

As a new grammar, developed for the research in this paper, the Partial Volume Grammar (PVG) aims to create for each rectangle coincident with a space surface (so far similar to the FSG), a volume with a certain thickness in the direction perpendicular to the rectangle. As the volume thickness would lead to intersection of volumes of other nearby rectangles, in practice points, line segments, quadrilaterals, and quadrilateral faced hexahedron components are created as shown in figure 4 at the bottom in the middle. The resulting geometry, with "thick" rectangles and cavities in between, approaches the FSG situation for a very low thickness, and the VG result for a very high thickness. Loads and constraints will still be placed on the rectangles of the conformal model, and so on the middle surfaces of the volumes. More information can be found in Schoenmaker (2020).

4. Case studies

In this section, the three above grammars are applied in two case studies, so the influence can be investigated of the design space on the suggested structural systems.

4.1 Case study 1 - simple building spatial design

As a spatial design, two stacked spaces are used, each 3×3×3 m. For the FSG, the thickness of the flat shell components is 300 mm. The PVG is used three times, respectively with a thickness (in the direction perpendicular to the rectangles) equal to 600, 1200, and 1800 mm. The VG simply uses the complete building volume. Robust TO is carried out, providing clear Black/White (B/W) solutions. As the geometrical design spaces are all different with respect to their volume, the so-called TO volume fraction has been set for each case such that the amount of structural material used will be the same across the grammars. Furthermore, the influence of this amount of structural material is studied too, by carrying out all five grammar cases for different amounts of structural material, namely 17.55, 13.50, 9.45, and 5.4 m^3. Finite elements used are 150×150×150 mm (150×150 mm for the FSG), the material has a Young's modulus equal to $E = 30000$ N/mm^2 and a Poisson's ratio $v = 0.3$, and specific TO settings are $r_{min} = 165$ mm, $p = 3.0$, $\eta = 0.2$, and the tolerance threshold = 0.01, see Hofmeyer, Schevenels and Boonstra (2017) for a further explanation. Results are shown in figure 5.

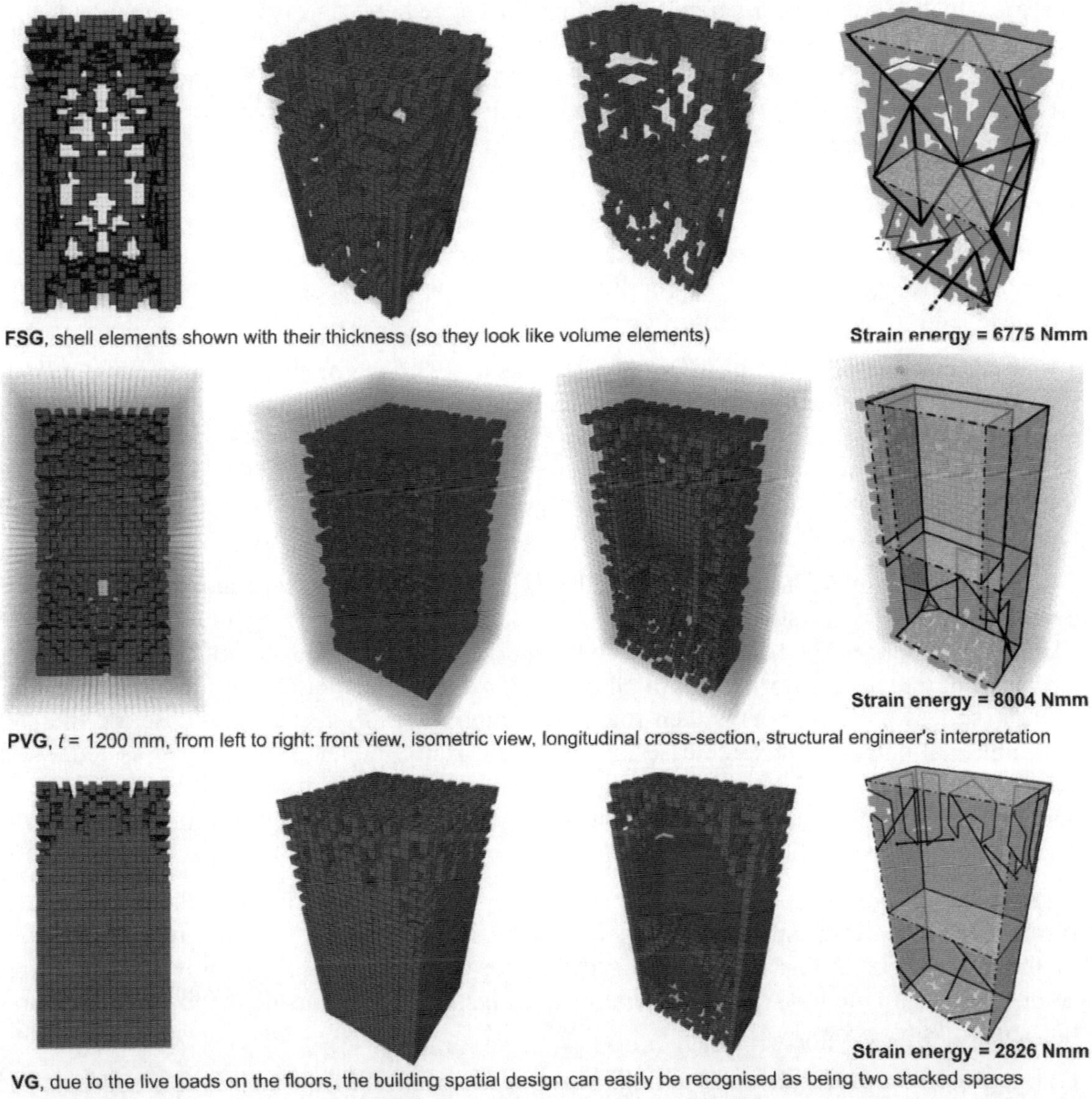

Figure 5: application of robust TO via the FSG, PVG, and VG grammars, structural volume = 13.5 m^3

The material distribution found by the FSG suggest two solid floors, at the top of the upper space (1) and bottom space (2) respectively, connected by a 3D truss, as shown by an interpretation by the authors on the right. Note that during TO for FSG, flat shell elements are used, visualised here with their thickness, as such suggesting volume elements. The cavities of the spaces are naturally conserved, for no TO design space is present there. Interestingly, if the full spatial design is used as a design space, in case of the VG, still these cavities are kept as well (although some use of it is made by bracings in the upper corners at both levels). This is due to the limited amount of structural material available; the loads present at the floors and facades; for this design placing material at the building outside is the better structural choice. The PVG shows results in between the FSG and VG outcomes: it respects the space cavities because there is no design space there, and where material is allowed, a sort of cavity walls are suggested. This is surprising because also the VG can suggest cavity walls, however, shows a single solid wall. Note that for the PVG, where the middle surfaces of the volumes are loaded, the PVG does not suggest material outside the load envelope, visible by the blue ghosting.

The objective of the topology optimisation is the structural compliance (stiffness), i.e. strain energy, which is consequently a measure of performance here. As expected, in general the VG performs the best, followed by a PVG with a large thickness, a PVG with intermediate thickness, and the FSG, which performs the worst, see figure 5 and 6 for indications, and for all data Schoenmaker (2020). If the structural volume to be placed increases, all grammars lead to better performance, and also this is to be expected.

Verification

To verify and interpret the results found in case study 1, studies are carried out that investigate (a) mesh convergence, (b) initial conditions, (c) the PVG design space outside the loading envelope, and (d) an extra convergence criterion.

For mesh convergence, three different mesh sizes are tried for the PVG grammar using a thickness of 600 mm. For all four the amounts of structural volume to be placed, three different element sizes are used: 300×300×300, 150×150×150, and 100×100×100 mm. The two finer mesh sizes yield comparable results, whereas the most coarse mesh shows a little less favourable behaviour, the more so for higher amounts of structural material to be placed. But results are still useful.

By default, topology optimisation starts with all finite element densities equal to the constrained average density. To investigate this initial condition, the simple building above is used with the PVG with a thickness of 1200 mm, but now *starting* with the final solution of the PVG with a thickness of 600 mm. Surprisingly, in all cases (for different material volumes) a higher strain energy (so less performance) is then found, although the design space can describe the PVG 600 mm final outcome. In some cases, also a significantly higher strain energy is found than for the original PVG 1200 mm. This indicates that local minima, and so initial conditions, are an important issue. This is further confirmed by runs of the PVG 1200mm grammar with random density distributions at the start.

As is shown in figure 5, the PVG's so far do not use the design space outside the load envelope. If this part of the design space is removed from the simulations, very similar results are found. In future simulations this may be utilized to save computational time, however for correct comparisons with the FSG (which inevitably does have material outside the loading envelope), this space has been kept.

For an iterative solver, tolerance settings are important, and the most suitable are selected for correct results without a too large burden on computational costs. Instead of controlling the topology optimization with a threshold related to the change of densities, as is normally the case, additionally the change of the compliance can be used. Applying this wisely, the number of iterations can be reduced, so a further reduction of the costs can be achieved. See Schoenmaker (2020) for further details on the verification.

4.2 Case study 2 - portal shaped building

This second case study involves a more realistically sized portal shaped building. The building has four layers, and measures 24×12×24 meters. Due to the realistic size, now an iterative solver is applied (previously a direct solver was used), using multithreading with 4 threads, and the mesh size is set to the coarse 300×300×300 mm, and consequently r_{min} = 330 mm, see Hofmeyer, Schevenels and, Boonstra (2017).

The extra topology optimization threshold is used, and other settings are the same as for the first study. Two amounts of structural volume to be placed are tried, 1037 and 674 m^3, and four grammars are tested: FSG (shell thickness 600 mm), PVG 600 mm, PVG 1800 mm, and the VG. Typical results are shown in figure 6.

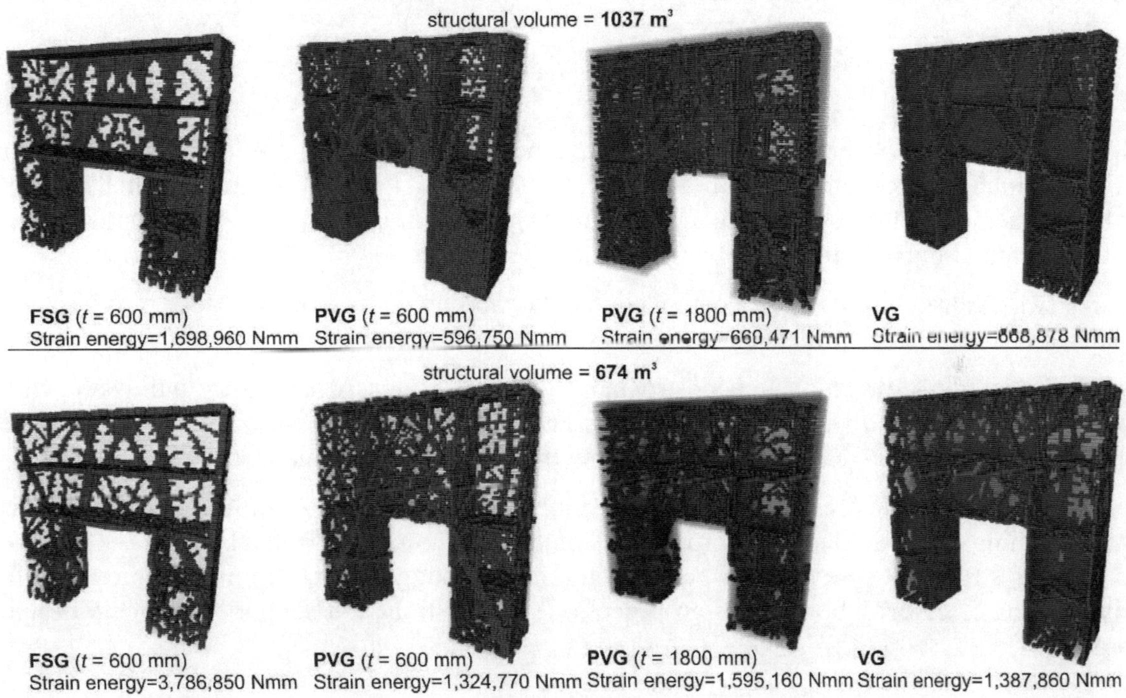

Figure 6: Cross-section of a realistically sized portal shaped building, application of robust topology optimisation on different design spaces, via the use of the FSG, PVG, and VG grammars

With respect to the structural performance (i.e. strain energy) similar outcomes are observed as for the first case study: the more freedom in the design space, the better the performance. However, different from the other grammars, results of PVG 1800 mm are difficult to interpret as a structural system. Thus PVG 600 mm and VG seem to be the most useful. More details can be found in Schoenmaker (2020).

5. Discussion

The different types of TO geometrical design spaces provide suggestions for structural designs, and as such can be used for design suggestions, or can be implemented within simulations of co-evolutionary design processes, which study and support real-world design processes. However, some critical remarks should be made. With respect to the method used, the robust TO approach is a gradient-based optimisation technique, and likely gets locked into local optima, so global optima (i.e. better and probably different looking outcomes) may not be found. Related to the method as well, naturally TO is controlled by the loads. As currently only wind and live loads are considered, the results show relatively flat floors and roofs. Taking self-weight into account, relevant for high-rise and large span structures, could result in other distributions.

With respect to practical applicability, realistic building spatial designs may have non-rectangular spaces, and certainly have openings for lighting and transport. For these more advanced designs, especially the PVG needs significant further developments, and if its computational costs can be accepted, the VG could be a better choice. Secondly, found material distributions are far from realistic and cannot be constructed. Therefore, much interpretation is needed. The question is whether this interpretation is so much of influence on the performance that the initial benefits of TO (an optimal performance) are lost. Additionally, other, faster, and more realistic techniques exist to design structural systems (Boonstra et al., 2020).

6. Conclusions and outlook

Three grammars to generate design spaces have been developed: (a) the Flat Shell Grammar (FSG), which initiates flat shells for each space surface; (b) a Partial Volume Grammar (PVG), which generates volumes for each surface; and (c) the Volume Grammar (VG) that sees the total volume of the building spatial design as the design space.

Using two case studies, it can be concluded that the more freedom a design space provides, the better the structural performance in terms of stiffness (strain energy).

With respect to interpretation and constructability of the designs, outcomes from the PVG with a large thickness are difficult to interpret. As FSG design do not perform well, therefore the designs created by the VG and PVG with a low thickness are recommended.

Future research should focus on the search for global optima; the use of non-rectangular designs with openings; and automatic interpretation of the results (Kazakis et al., 2017). Then the suggested structural systems can be used for design suggestions, or implemented within simulations of co-evolutionary design processes, which study and support real-world design processes.

References

Andreassen, E., Clausen, A., Schevenels, M., Lazarov, B.S., Sigmund, O. (2010). Efficient topology optimization in MATLAB using 88 lines of code. Structural Multidisciplinary Optimisation 43, pp.1–16, https://doi.org/10.1007/s00158-010-0594-7.

Beghini, L.L., Beghini, A., Katz, N., Baker, W.F., Paulino, G.H. (2014) Connecting architecture and engineering through structural topology optimization, Engineering Structures 59, pp.716–726, https://doi.org/10.1016/j.engstruct.2013.10.032.

Boonstra, S., Van der Blom, K., Hofmeyer, H., Emmerich, M.T.M. (2021). Hybridization of Evolutionary Algorithms and Simulations of Co-evolutionary Design Processes for Building Design and Optimization. Automation in Construction 124, 103522, https://doi.org/10.1016/j.autcon.2020.103522.

Boonstra, S., Van der Blom, K., Hofmeyer, H., Emmerich, M.T.M. (2020). Conceptual structural system layouts via design response grammars and evolutionary algorithms, Automation in Construction 116, 103009, https://doi.org/10.1016/j.autcon.2019.103009.

Boonstra, S.; Hofmeyer, H. (2020). TUe-excellent-buildings / BSO-toolbox, version 1.0.0, GitHub, https://doi.org/10.5281/zenodo.3823893.

Christiansen, A.N., Bærentzen, J.A., Nobel-Jørgensen, M., Aage, N., Sigmund, O. (2015). Combined shape and topology optimization of 3D structures, Computers & Graphics 46, pp.25–35, https://doi.org/10.1016/j.cag.2014.09.021.

Flager, F., Welle, B., Bansal, P., Soremekun, G. Haymaker, J. (2009). Multidisciplinary process integration and design optimization of a classroom building, Journal of Information Technology in Construction 14, pp.595–612, http://www.itcon.org/2009/38.

Gan, V.J.L., Wong, C.L., Tse, K.T., Cheng, J.C.P., Lo, I.M.C., Chan, C.M. (2019). Parametric modelling and evolutionary optimization for cost-optimal and low-carbon design of high-rise reinforced concrete buildings, Advanced Engineering Informatics 42, 100962, https://doi.org/10.1016/j.aei.2019.100962.

Hofmeyer, H., Davila Delgado, J.M. (2015). Coevolutionary and Genetic Algorithm Based Building Spatial and Structural Design, AIEDAM 29, pp.351–370, https://doi.org/10.1017/S0890060415000384.

Hofmeyer, H., Schevenels, M., Boonstra, S. (2017). The generation of hierarchic structures via robust 3D topology optimisation, Advanced Engineering Informatics 33, pp.450–455, https://doi.org/10.1016/j.aei.2017.02.002.

Hofmeyer, H., van Roosmalen, M., Gelbal, F. (2011). Pre-processing parallel and orthogonally positioned structural design elements to be used within the finite element method, Advanced Engineering Informatics 25, pp.245–258, https://doi.org/10.1016/j.aei.2010.06.004.

Kazakis, G., Kanellopoulos, I., Sotiropoulos, S., Lagaros, N.D., Topology optimization aided structural design: Interpretation, computational aspects and 3D printing, Heliyon 3, e00431, https://doi.org/10.1016/j.heliyon.2017.e00431

Liang, Q. Q., Xie, Y.M., Steven, G.P. (2000). Optimal Topology Design of Bracing Systems for Multistory Steel Frames, Journal of Structural Engineering 126, pp.823–829, https://doi.org/10.1061.

Schoenmaker, D. (2020). The influence of topology optimisation design space—from shell to volume—on the building structural design, MSc-thesis, Eindhoven University of Technology, https://research.tue.nl/files/165086165/Schoenmaker_0853958_SED.pdf

Sigmund, O. (2009). Manufacturing tolerant topology optimization, Acta Mechanica Sinica 25, pp.227–239, https://doi.org/10.1007/s10409-009-0240-z.

Steiner, B., Mousavian, E., Mehdizadeh Saradj, F., Wimmer, M., Musialski, P. (2017). Integrated Structural-Architectural Design for Interactive Planning. Computer Graphics Forum 36, pp.80–94, https://doi.org/10.1111/cgf.12996.

Wang, S.Y., Tai, K., Wang, M.Y. (2005). An enhanced genetic algorithm for structural topology optimization, International Journal for Numerical Methods in Engineering 65, pp.18–44, https://doi.org/10.1002/nme.1435.

Wang, Z., Suiker, A.S.J., Hofmeyer, H., Van Hooff, T., Blocken, B.J.E. (2020). Coupled aerostructural shape and topology optimization of horizontal-axis wind turbine rotor blades, Energy Conversion and Management 212, 112621, https://doi.org/10.1016/j.enconman.2020.112621.

Wu, Z., Xia, L., Wang, S., & Shi, T. (2019). Topology optimisation of hierarchical lattice structures with substructuring, Computer Methods in Applied Mechanics and Engineering 345, pp.602–617, https://doi.org/10.1016/j.cma.2018.11.003.

Xie, Y.M., Steven, G.P. (1993). A simple evolutionary procedure for structural optimization, Computers & Structures 49, https://doi.org/10.1016/0045-7949(93)90035-C

Qualifying spatial information for underground volumes

Kamel Adouane, Fabian Boujon, Bernd Domer
University of Applied Sciences and Arts Western Switzerland, Switzerland
kamel.adouane@hesge.ch

Abstract. Urbanization and condensation of habitants per m^2 have led to an intense use of subsurface volumes as construction space. Planning and constructing in such spaces is a very challenging task, since knowledge of existing objects is fragmentary and imprecise. An intelligent identification of present objects and thereby detecting available volumes would increase the design quality of projects, since incidents reported during field excavations (Tanoli et al., 2019) are numerous and costly. Combining existing official territorial data with intelligent methods for information completion, compliance checking and data management, is a promising approach as it has been partially demonstrated by the use of ontologies (Caselli et al., 2020; Métral et al., 2020). The minimum level of necessary information for a model-checking framework is identified and formalized by an ontology. The ontology then serves as a basis schema for a triple store database, storing data, completion and compliance rules. The process of data completion allows to qualify the confidence in spatial information delivered.

1. Introduction

Worldwide, the field of construction is influenced by the development of urban underground spaces (Bobylev and Sterling, 2016). However, this increasing utilization should be in phase with functionalities deployed in cities (Admiraal and Cornaro, 2017). The UUS density metric is proposed as an indicator to improve the management of energy demand in urban areas (Bobylev, 2016a). Overall, the Underground Sustainable Project Appraisal Routine (Uspear) provides guidelines structure subsurface projects (Zargarian et al., 2018).

Geneva based experts (SIG, 2020), analyzed ground-penetrating radar (GPR) as a solution to measure missing data of existing utility networks. It has been found, that this solution is costly and not precise enough. Additionally, time consuming post-processes are required to handle measured data-sets. The UK-based project Mapping the Underworld (MTU) proposes ray tracing (Shan et al., 2006) as an alternative.

Shortly after the emergence of the BIM methodology in the AEC industry, it became clear that combining BIM with GIS-type data would increase the quality of territorial and urban planning. Use cases, as checking the occupation of subsurface volumes, explicitly need GIS data to discover free installation space and BIM data to represent, *e.g.*, utility networks.

3D geoinformation embedded in city models can serve as a basis for several use cases, as presented by Biljecki (Biljecki, Stoter, et al., 2015). Examples cited are the energy demand estimation on small scale to assess the return of average building energy retrofits, the visibility analysis using 3D city models in order to determine the sky view factor metric required for thermal comfort analyses or the automatic identification of suitable roof surfaces for the installation of photovoltaic panels. Solar installation potential is especially sensitive to the positioning of the city model (Biljecki, Heuvelink, et al., 2015), as an uncertainty of 50 cm could lead to a variation of 10 % in the estimation of produced energy. It would be advantageous, if such use cases could integrate BIM data. The challenge is that BIM and GIS systems apply different concepts for interoperability, which are difficult to match.

Several proposals have been made to provide convergence for BIM and GIS data structures. Stouffs (Stouffs et al., 2018) uses a triple grammar approach: a solution is developed to map

BIM-IFC type graph towards GIS-CityGML graphs. Adouane (Adouane et al., 2019) presented a specific use case to map a complete building from a BIM-IFC format towards GIS-CityGML. His methodology has been validated on a general architectural model containing complex geometries. Biljecki has developed an ADE (Application Development Extension) to automate the BIM-IFC conversion towards GIS-CityGML format. The conversion strategy has been tested in collaboration with the Building and Construction Authority (BCA) of Singapore (Biljecki et al., 2021).

Interoperability for BIM systems is supported worldwide by buildingSMART international, in particular by their IFC standard. Pauwels (Pauwels et al., 2017) proposes to use Web ontology language (OWL) to specify IFC. An OWL representation facilitates the mapping between data models, like IFC and CityGML.

Xu and Cai (Xu and Cai, 2020) are using ontologies to describe and to manage heterogeneous data sets of underground utilities: they integrate digital conversion tools for spatial relations among objects. Building code compliance is checked through SPARQL queries on triple store databases.

As shown by the examples above, BIM and GIS convergence can be achieved. It should be mentioned, that due to the different objectives of such systems, not all BIM information is transferable into a GIS system and vice versa.

Official GIS databases, like the Geneva "SITG" (SITG, 2020) system, contain precise data for surface objects. When subsurface volumes are considered, existing data is less precise and complete and in most cases not sufficient for a 3D representation. Data completion through in-situ measurements is complicated and costly. This hinders the correct representation of position and geometry of existing subsurface objects.

2. The InnoSubsurface project

The overall objective of the "InnoSubsurface" project is to support subsurface project planning by proposing solutions for a better management of such volumes. As a first step, a taxonomy of subsurface objects and their necessary attributes for 3D representation and planning has been created. This structure is called "minimal data model". The geometric model of the subsurface objects uses only primitives like extruded polygons, cylinders or truncated cones. It accommodates natural elements, like trees, manmade objects, like utility lines and public law restrictions, like contaminated sites. The data model has been transferred into an ontology, which integrates IfcOwl as well as CityGML elements (Caselli et al., 2020; Métral et al., 2020).

The ontology serves as a data schema for a triple store, populated by data from the "SITG" database. As expected, provided information is not sufficient for a 3D representation as defined by the minimal model. Therefore, a completion strategy for positioning and geometrical attributes had to be developed.

Object attributes of the minimal model related to position and geometry are associated to a confidence level. The confidence level might represent measurement precision or the confidence associated to an attribute derived by a completion strategy. Completed objects are stored in the triple store database. Hypotheses used for completion are called "Completion rules". They are derived by construction codes or interviews with practitioners and formulated according to a generic rule model, described in (Caselli et al., 2020). Rules are stored together with subsurface objects.

Although completion rules can be defined for the majority of attributes on a theoretical level, the completed data might give unrealistic results on a practical level. A first proposal for a metric to qualify subsurface volumes is made by Bobylev (Bobylev, 2016b). He relates subsurface volumes to ground surface. His metric does neither provide an indicator on the quality of data used to calculate the volume of subsurface objects nor on the quality of their position.

The paper highlights the following aspects of the "InnoSubsurface" project:

- The integration of confidence levels for positioning and geometric attributes of subsurface objects
- The combination of object confidence on a class level
- The visual representation of the degree of confidence
- A first approach to qualify spatial information for underground volumes with respect to constructability, integrating data completeness, precision as well as the metric proposed by Bobylev.

3. Methodology

3.1 Using probability functions to represent confidence in subsurface object position and geometry attributes.

Positioning and geometrical representation of objects are based on measured and empirical elements (completion rules). In order to represent the precision of such attributes, we propose to use simple probabilistic functions. Their integration vary according to the nature of the imprecision: has the value been measured or derived by a completion rule?

Each object possesses two visual representations:

- The core representation is called "primary object" and specifies the completed object derived by SITG and completion rules.
- The second representation is called "secondary object". The secondary object envelops the primary one and indicates the confidence, that a given object can be found inside its boundaries. The developed stochastic model allows the user to choose the desired confidence level, which affects the size of the secondary object.

3.1.1 Triangle probability function in multiple dimensions

Measured attributes can reach, according to expert interviews, a maximum of 95%. A triangle distribution, with an overall degree of confidence of 95%, is assigned to model the precision of positioning measurements. Based on SITG description, the precision of x and y coordinates of the cantonal database is +/-10 cm. Figure 1 illustrates the model for the x coordinate of a tree root.

The concept of "primary" and "secondary" objects is shown Figure 2. The blue cylinder represents the primary object, the red cylinder the secondary object.

Figure 2 indicates how multiple probabilities for single attributes are modeled. Since horizontal positioning needs x and y coordinates, the confidence interval of the two has to be combined. Depth information is related to a "step" probability function. The uncertainty for the tree root model in Figure 2 is estimated by Equation 1.

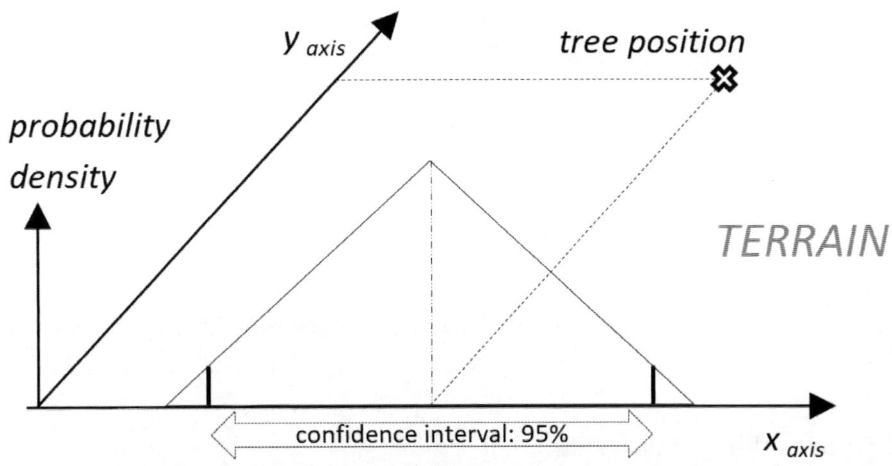

Figure 1: Triangle probability density distribution function for the x coordinate of the tree position

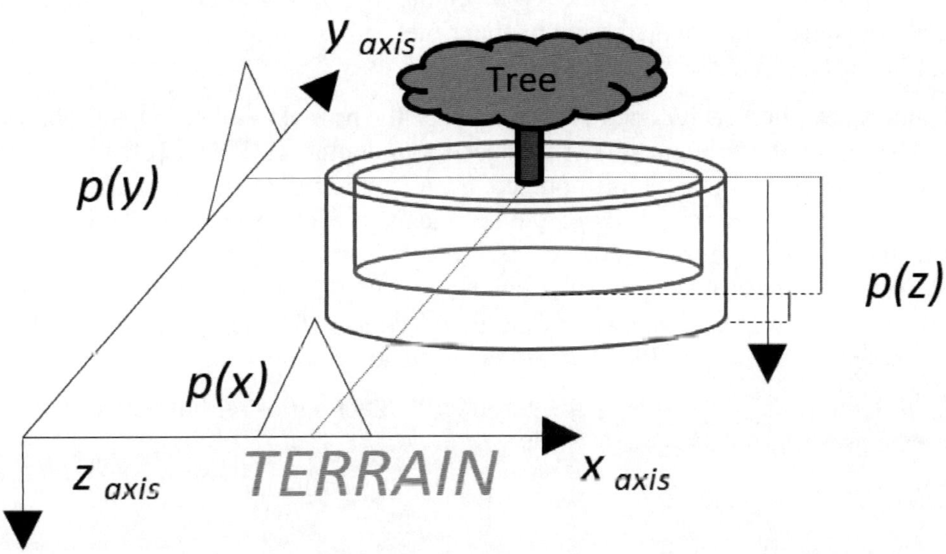

Figure 2: Example for primary (blue cylinder) and secondary objects (red cylinder) of tree roots with primitive probabilistic density functions associated to positioning and depth attributes

Equation 1

$$Object_{uncertainty} = \prod_{dimension} p$$

3.1.2 The Dirac probability density function

The Dirac probability density function represents the confidence used in completion rules for empirical single values. These are, for example, a standard height and quantity for basement floors, a standard diameter for utility pipelines, etc. Figure 3 presents the model of the Dirac primitive for a gas network node.

The maximum level of confidence for such a completion is set to 80 %, based on expert interviews.

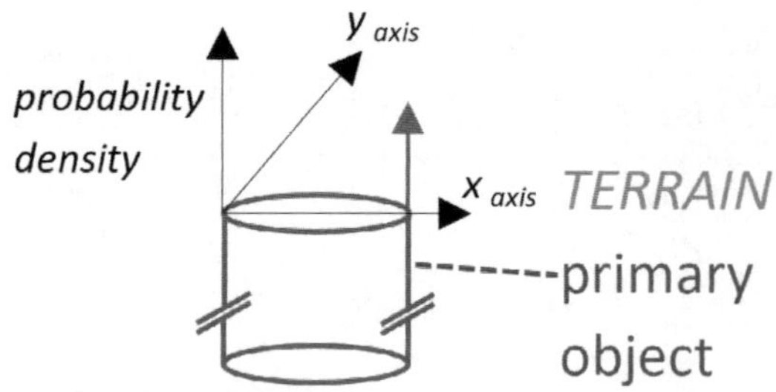

Figure 3: Dirac probability density distribution function (green arrow) applied to the diameter of a gas node

3.1.3 The Pert probability density function

The confidence in the depth of utility networks is modeled by a Pert probability density function. When depth information for a particular network is unknown, a Pert function based on neighboring networks of the same type, containing the desired depth information, is established. The function is characterized by the triplet {a,b,c}, fitted by the least square method to the depth distribution histogram.

Figure 4 shows how the Pert function is used to place the primary and secondary object of a gas network. The top of the primary object is placed at a depth of PERT coeff b, (90 cm in this example). The secondary object is modeled by a bounding rectangle around the pipeline diameter. The maximal lateral limits of the secondary object are obtained using the triangle probability function of Figure 1, since x and y coordinates are known. The upper and lower bounds of the secondary object are calculated by adding a second component, obtained by subtracting the measurement uncertainty from PERT coeff a (for the upper limit) and by adding the measurement uncertainty to PERT coeff c (for the lower limit).

As Figure 4 demonstrates, the size of the secondary object varies with the confidence interval chosen by the user.

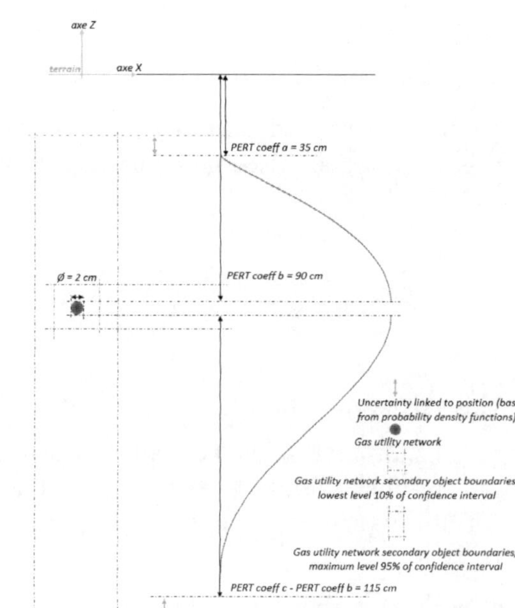

Figure 4: Pert probability density distribution function applied to the positioning of a gas utility network

3.2 Combining attribute confidence for a class of objects

For a given class of objects, like all tree roots, the confidence level can be consolidated according to Equation 2. $Volume_{secondary}$ represents the volume of the secondary volume, $Object_{uncertainty}$ represents the object uncertainty introduced in section 3.1.1.

Equation 2

$$confidence = \frac{\sum(Volume_{secondary} * Object_{uncertainty})}{\sum Volume_{secondary}}$$

3.3 Visual representation of confidence

Each object is visualized by a twofold 3D representation, a primary and a secondary object, as introduced in section 3.1. In general, the secondary object possesses the same geometry as the primary. Figure 5 shows the only exception: for practical reasons, conducts are associated with a cuboid. As the user can choose the confidence level, the right side of the same figure shows the effect on the size of the secondary object.

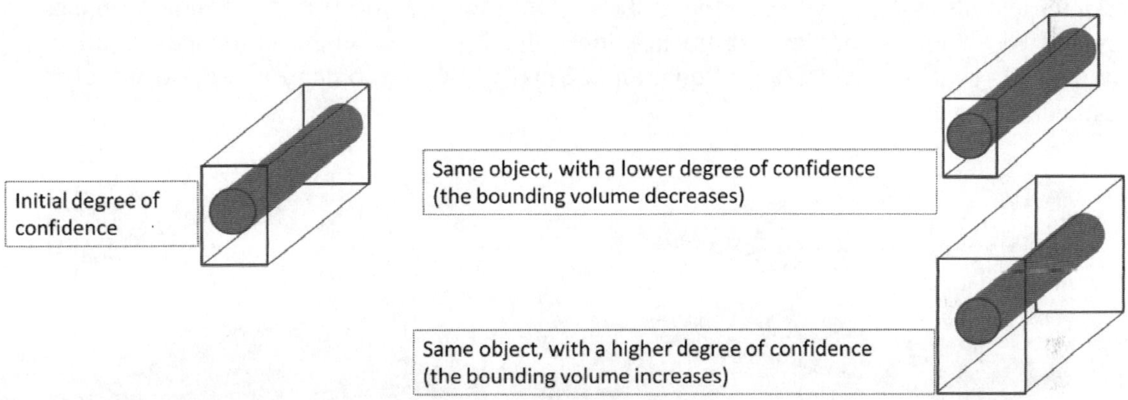

Figure 5: Primary and secondary objects for utility networks. The effect of varying confidence levels is shown on the right.

3.4 A first approach to qualify spatial information for underground volumes

An underground volume contains a finite number of objects with a finite number of geometrical and positioning attributes, which are required to visualize the primary object. Available data is analyzed to identify the number of missing attributes. This number is related to the total number of attributes required.

As the volume of objects is not taken into account, the Completeness Ratio (Equation 3) only describes the information maturity level within the database. Small objects are given the same weight as larger ones.

Equation 3

$$CompletenessRatio = \frac{\sum_{Object_{Class} \in Taxonomy} \sum_{Object \in Object_{Class}} PrimitiveParametersCount_{Existing}(Object)}{\sum_{Object_{Class} \in Taxonomy} \sum_{Object \in Object_{Class}} PrimitiveParametersCount_{Required}(Object)}$$

The Completeness Ratio can be refined (Equation 4) when calculated separately for each object class. An average can then be obtained for all present object classes. This leverages the parasite effects created by objects with a bigger number of attributes or are present in a greater number than others in the evaluated volume.

Equation 4

$$RefinedCompletenessRatio = \frac{\sum_{Object_{Class} \in Taxonomy} \frac{\sum_{Object \in Object_{Class}} PrimitiveParametersCount_{Existing}(Object)}{\sum_{Object \in Object_{Class}} PrimitiveParametersCount_{Required}(Object)}}{Cardinal(Object_{Class} \in Taxonomy)}$$

4. Results/Validation

The methodology has been applied to two subsurface volumes in the center of Geneva: a first one being nearby the main train station (Cornavin, 0.32 km^2) and a second one located around the Arve river (PAV, 0.31 km^2).

4.1 Visual representation of results

Information related to subsurface objects has been extracted from the SITG database for the two zones. The content has been stored in the triple store and missing positioning and geometrical attributes have been found by applying completion rules. Secondary objects are created based on the desired confidence level. In this sector, the confidence for all utility networks is evaluated to 92% by Equation 2. Finally, a GIS-Frontend is used to visualize the results (Figure 6).

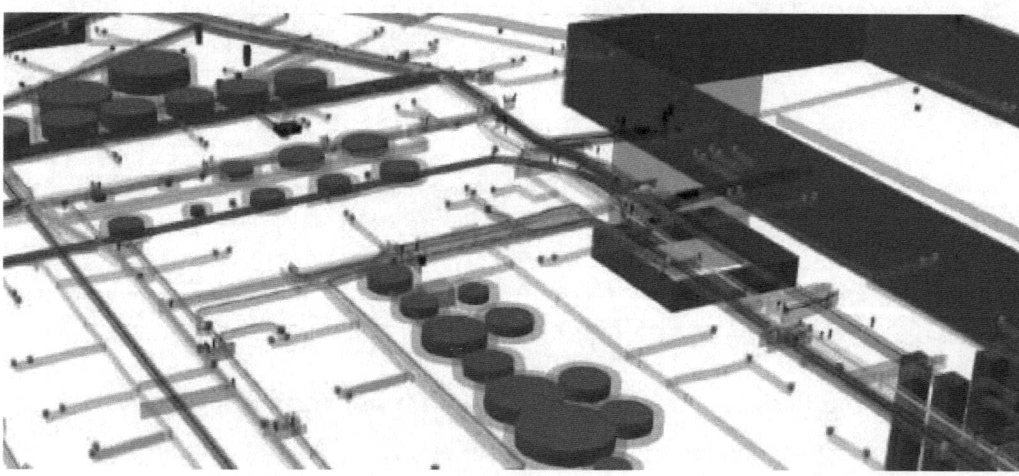

Figure 6: 3D viewing of underground volumes, developed (Topomat, 2021)

Table 1 indicates the colors applied to the different objects, based on Swiss construction codes.

Table 1 : Color codes used in Figure 6

Colour	Object
green	tree root
blue	natural water network
brown	lighting network
red	electricity network
pink	recycling site

grey	geotechnical

4.2 Qualifying existing spatial information for two volumes

The Urban Underground Space metric (UUS) (Bobylev, 2016b) is determined in order to validate the results of our project. For PAV and Cornavin areas, we obtain a density that is comparable to the results of underground volumes in Berlin (Table 2).

Table 2: UUS for PAV and Cornavin zones

metric	PAV sector	Cornavin sector	Berlin (Bobylev, 2016b)
surface, km^2	0.31	0.32	
primary volumes, m^3 (000 000)	0.49	0.42	
UUS m^3/m^2 (in cm)	156.8	133.7	128.0

Table 3 exposes the results of Equation 3 and Equation 4 applied to the two zones (Cornavin and PAV). The completeness ratio is calculated to approximately 80%, the refined metric results in approximately 73%. In addition, the total number of geometric parameters required to represent the volume, is indicated.

Table 3: description of data completeness ratios for PAV and Cornavin zones

Area	Completeness ratio	Refined completeness ratio	Gross geometric parameters
Cornavin	80.22%	72.33%	387'282
PAV	79.36%	73.76%	147'468

5. Conclusion and future work

The AEC industry needs to capture possibilities offered by the digital transition in order to speed up to industry 4.0. Data driven civil and underground engineering are two domains affected by this transition. The wideness and variety of the data available is advantageous but subject to errors. In addition, the data is heterogeneous in precision, completeness, accuracy, level of details and format. Intelligence based processes to automatically correct datasets are therefore required to make those data useful for analysis and design purpose.

Curation and processing of uncertain and incomplete subsurface data prompts research on models to represent uncertainty and to process data with different confidence levels. This paper shows that even imprecise and incomplete data can be applied to provide a coherent representation of subsurface volumes. The proposed concept to associate objects to a confidence level and to inform the user about data quality is unusual but helpful.

Only simple geometric representation and probability functions have been used to facilitate the understanding and control of the workflow. The developed methodology is independent from structure and quality of available subsurface data. Of course, completion strategies and confidence model will have to be checked before being applied to other locations with different database concepts. The overall architecture of the system, based on an ontology and a generic rule model, will nevertheless ease such an adaptation.

A threshold, indicating when data completion strategies will become senseless, is needed. The qualifying metrics employed (UUS, completeness ratio, refined completeness ratio) have to be tested on this question and improved.

The InnoSubsurface project investigated into the application of "Compliance rules", defining spatial constraints on objects, as well. Besides the detection of geometric conflicts, these rules are good candidates to be employed, *e.g.*, in order to automatically disentangle the crossing of multiple utility lines.

Acknowledgements

This research is supported by Innosuisse in the framework of the Innovation project 35265.1 IP-ICT, "Impulse-Subsurface: Efficient data exploitation in subsurface planning". The authors would like to thank, Mr Loïc Neuenschwander and Mr Yohann Schatz (HEPIA)

Ontology creation, conceptualization of the generic rule model and set up of the triple store database: UNIGE (Pr Giovanna Di Marzo Serugendo, Dr Claudine Metral, Pr Gilles Falquet, Dr Vincenzo Daponte, Mr Ashley Caselli)

Industrial partner, GIS-expert, representation and analysis of subsurface volumes in a GIS-Frontend: TOPOMAT (Mr Stéphane Couderq, Mrs Marie-Christine Nicolle, Mr Christophe Suter, Mr Alexandre Gauch)

Provision of data and professional knowledge: State of Geneva (State Direction for Territory Information, Department of Urbanism, Department of Transports, Department of civil engineering, Department of Energy, Department of Water, Industrial Services of Geneva and Geneva Airport)

References

Admiraal, H. and Cornaro, A. (2017) Underground space., Tonbridge, Ice Publishing.

Adouane, K., Stouffs, R., Janssen, P. and Domer, B. (2019) A model-based approach to convert a building BIM-IFC data set model into CityGML, Journal of Spatial Science, pp.1–24 [Online]. DOI: 10.1080/14498596.2019.1658650.

Biljecki, F., Heuvelink, G. B. M., Ledoux, H. and Stoter, J. (2015) Propagation of positional error in 3D GIS: estimation of the solar irradiation of building roofs, International Journal of Geographical Information Science, vol. 29, no. 12, pp.2269–2294 [Online]. DOI: 10.1080/13658816.2015.1073292.

Biljecki, F., Lim, J., Crawford, J., Moraru, D., Tauscher, H., Konde, A., Adouane, K., Lawrence, S., Janssen, P. and Stouffs, R. (2021) Extending CityGML for IFC-sourced 3D city models, Automation in Construction, vol. 121, p. 103440 [Online]. DOI: 10.1016/j.autcon.2020.103440.

Biljecki, F., Stoter, J., Ledoux, H., Zlatanova, S. and Çöltekin, A. (2015) Applications of 3D City Models: State of the Art Review, ISPRS International Journal of Geo-Information, vol. 4, no. 4, pp.2842–2889 [Online]. DOI: 10.3390/ijgi4042842.

Bobylev, N. (2016a) Transitions to a High Density Urban Underground Space, Procedia Engineering, vol. 165, pp.184–192 [Online]. DOI: 10.1016/j.proeng.2016.11.750.

Bobylev, N. (2016b) Underground space as an urban indicator: Measuring use of subsurface, Tunnelling and Underground Space Technology, vol. 55, pp.40–51 [Online]. DOI: 10.1016/j.tust.2015.10.024.

Bobylev, N. and Sterling, R. (2016) Urban underground space: A growing imperative, Tunnelling and Underground Space Technology, vol. 55, pp.1–4 [Online]. DOI: 10.1016/j.tust.2016.02.022.

Caselli, A., Daponte, V., Falquet, G. and Métral, C. (2020) A Rule Language Model for Subsurface Data Refinement,.

Métral, C., Daponte, V., Caselli, A., Di Marzo, G. and Falquet, G. (2020) ONTOLOGY-BASED RULE COMPLIANCE CHECKING FOR SUBSURFACE OBJECTS, London, UK, vol. XLIV-4/W1-2020, 2020 [Online]. DOI: https://doi.org/10.5194/isprs-archives-XLIV-4-W1-2020-91-2020.

Pauwels, P., Zhang, S. and Lee, Y.-C. (2017) Semantic web technologies in AEC industry: A literature overview, Automation in Construction, vol. 73, pp.145–165 [Online]. DOI: 10.1016/j.autcon.2016.10.003.

Shan, Q., Pennock, S. R. and Redfern, M. A. (2006) Investigation of GPR Configurations by Ray-Tracing Methods, 2006 IEEE Conference on Radar, Syracuse, NY, USA, IEEE, pp.335–341 [Online]. DOI: 10.1109/RADAR.2006.1631821 (Accessed 31 March 2021).

SIG, S. I. de G. (2020) [Online]. DOI: https://ww2.sig-ge.ch/.

SITG, L. territoire genevois à la carte, Accessed 26 Feb (2020) [Online]. DOI: https://ge.ch/sitg/.

Stouffs, R., Tauscher, H. and Biljecki, F. (2018) Achieving Complete and Near-Lossless Conversion from IFC to CityGML, ISPRS International Journal of Geo-Information, vol. 7, no. 9, p.355 [Online]. DOI: 10.3390/ijgi7090355.

Tanoli, W. A., Sharafat, A., Park, J. and Seo, J. W. (2019) Damage Prevention for underground utilities using machine guidance, Automation in Construction, vol. 107, p.102893 [Online]. DOI: 10.1016/j.autcon.2019.102893.

Topomat (2021) Switzerland partner for Geographical Information Systems,.

Xu, X. and Cai, H. (2020) Semantic approach to compliance checking of underground utilities, Automation in Construction, vol. 109, p. 103006 [Online]. DOI: 10.1016/j.autcon.2019.103006.

Zargarian, R., Hunt, D. V. L., Braithwaite, P., Bobylev, N. and Rogers, C. D. F. (2018) A new sustainability framework for urban underground space, Proceedings of the Institution of Civil Engineers - Engineering Sustainability, vol. 171, no. 5, pp.238–253 [Online]. DOI: 10.1680/jensu.15.00013.

An algorithmic BIM approach to advance concrete printing

Patricia Peralta Abadia*, Kay Smarsly
Hamburg University of Technology, Germany
patricia.peralta.abadia@tuhh.de

Abstract. Building information modeling (BIM) has the potential to support algorithm-based design and data management, representing a promising methodology to advance concrete printing. In concrete printing, algorithms are used to accomplish critical steps during data modeling, such as slicing and toolpath planning. However, the Industry Foundation Classes (IFC) standard does not support descriptions of algorithms in BIM models, referred to as "algorithmic BIM". Storing algorithm semantics relevant to concrete printing in compliance with the IFC standard advances the replicability of concrete printing. Building upon an IFC-based description of concrete printing, an algorithmic BIM approach, i.e. an IFC-compliant description of algorithm semantics, for concrete printing is proposed in this paper. The algorithmic BIM approach is validated through a case study by describing and integrating a slicing algorithm and a toolpath planning algorithm in an IFC model. The results show that IFC-compliant descriptions of AM algorithms have the potential to enhance data modeling for concrete printing towards standardization.

1. Introduction

Concrete-based additive manufacturing (AM), also referred to as "concrete printing", is a research area that has been gaining traction in the architecture, engineering, and construction (AEC) industry over the last decade. As the implementation of AM in the AEC industry moves forward to automate construction practices, the need to improve quality, repeatability, and reliability of AM processes increases. New data modeling approaches for concrete printing, which encompass the "digital workflow" from 3D models to manufacturing, are developed to improve interoperability between AM software applications as well as repeatability and reliability of the concrete printing technology. As part of the data modeling approaches, sensing-related information as well as algorithm-related information is used to accomplish critical steps along the digital workflow (e.g., slicing, toolpath planning, and motion control). Representing a promising methodology for AM in the AEC industry, building information modeling (BIM) provides semantic and geometric information of buildings and infrastructure and has the potential to support algorithm-based design and data management in concrete printing. The Industry Foundation Classes (IFC), an open standard for BIM, may be extended to support concrete printing in an attempt to advance data management and data exchange between AM software applications employed along the digital workflow, maintaining semantic and geometric information.

To extend the IFC standard towards supporting concrete printing, formal descriptions that define AM semantics, e.g., information generated and exchanged during the digital workflow, is required. In literature, semantic models and ontologies have been developed for conventional AM. Bonnard et al. (2018) have described an AM technology and operation approach based on ISO 14649 for smart AM. To support interoperability, Sanfilippo et al. (2019) have proposed a technology-independent ontology for AM data management, data exchange, and data validation. Specifically for concrete printing, Smarsly et al. (2020) have proposed a semantic modeling approach (i.e., printing information modeling) that takes advantage of BIM concepts and formally represents complex inter-process relationships in concrete printing. While AM formal descriptions usually include sensor-related information, not enough attention has been given to algorithm-related information so far.

Algorithms used in AM processes have a direct impact on designing, planning and manufacturing, affecting the quality of the printed components. Algorithms are executed along the digital workflow for topology optimization, for slicing, as well as for offline and online toolpath planning. However, AM algorithms are not represented semantically in AM formal descriptions, and descriptions of algorithms in general are not fully supported by the IFC standard. Integrating algorithm semantics into BIM models, herein referred to as "algorithmic BIM", will aid in the standardization, interpretation, and data exchange in concrete printing.

The need for standardizing algorithm semantics in the AEC industry has been pointed out in a previous study by Theiler et al. (2018), where an IFC-compliant semantic description of algorithms for structural health monitoring applications has been proposed. Based on the printing information modeling approach proposed by the authors (Smarsly et al., 2020; Peralta et al., 2020), an algorithmic BIM approach for concrete printing is presented in this paper. By analyzing AM algorithms and programming methods in BIM, an IFC-compliant description of AM algorithm semantics is developed and validated through a case study conducted on a direct slicing algorithm and a toolpath planning algorithm that are coupled with an IFC model, underpinning the potential of algorithmic BIM for concrete printing.

The paper is organized as follows. First, background information on AM algorithms and on programming methods in BIM is provided to identify the semantic information required to describe AM algorithms in compliance with the IFC standard. Second, based on the background information, the IFC-compliant description of AM algorithm semantics is developed. Third, the case study, where a direct slicing algorithm and a toolpath planning algorithm are coupled with an IFC model, is used to validate the IFC-compliant description of AM algorithm semantics. The paper concludes with a summary and an outlook on potential future research.

2. Background

Additive manufacturing is a process of building structures on a layer-by-layer basis. The main area of research for AM is the optimization of building processes to improve quality, repeatability, and reliability, as discussed by Leirmo & Martinsen (2019). "Smart AM modeling" may take advantage of semantic information to optimize and adapt manufacturing processes by evaluating components during processing and adapting the build parameters within boundaries defined by semantic specifications (Garanger et al., 2017). Algorithms are used to accomplish critical steps in AM modeling, such as topology optimization (Saadlaoui et al., 2017), build parameters optimization (Rocha et al., 2018), slicing, and toolpath planning (Zhao et al., 2020), all of which influence the quality of the structures to be printed. Relevant to this study are the algorithms for slicing and toolpath planning.

Slicing. Algorithms have been developed for slicing 3D models to improve geometry accuracy while reducing build time through optimizing slicing speed and efficiency. Slicing algorithms may be classified, based on the source of the 3D model, into direct slicing of parametric models, slicing of tessellated models, slicing of models from reverse engineering, and implicit slicing. Slicing algorithms may also be classified according to the shape of sliced layers into planar slicing and non-planar slicing (e.g., curved layers). Commonly, 3D models are sliced into a set of 2D contours with parallel planes, where the main parameters are layer thickness and build direction. The layer thickness may be uniform or variable, while the build direction may be single or multidirectional. The simplest slicing algorithms involve uniform layer thickness and unidirectional build, increasing in complexity for adaptive slicing with variable layer thickness and for multidirectional slicing. A review of slicing processes and algorithms is presented by

Zhao et al. (2020). The main parameters for slicing algorithms are described in Table 1, categorized into attributes, inputs, and outputs.

Table 1: Main parameters for slicing algorithms.

Type	Parameter	Description
Attribute	Name	Name of the algorithm.
	Type	Type of slicing (i.e., uniform/adaptive, unidirectional/multidirectional).
Input	Geometry	Geometry of the 3D models (e.g., parametric models, tessellated models, models from reverse engineering).
	Layer shape	The shape of the layers to be sliced may be planar or non-planar.
	Layer thickness or layer height	Layer thickness or layer height may be uniform or variable. Variable layer thickness or layer height is usually defined based on geometrical features.
	Build direction of cutting planes	Build direction may be unidirectional or multi-directional. Build direction defines the cutting planes using direction vectors.
Output	Contour	Contours of the 3D model per layer.

Toolpath planning. Toolpath planning is the process of defining printhead trajectories in an AM process to fill the boundaries and interior of each sliced layer, influencing surface roughness, dimensional accuracy, and strength of printed components. Toolpaths include outer boundary, inner boundary, filling paths, and paths to build temporary support structures. Toolpath planning may be based on planar slicing (2D), on freeform surfaces (3D), and on topology optimization. For planar slicing, toolpath algorithms may be classified according to path pattern into raster (e.g., unidirectional, multidirectional, and contour), continuous, hybrid-and-continuous, and along-geometry. The most common toolpath planning algorithms use raster patterns, such as unidirectional raster and contour, due to simplicity and robustness (Zhao et al., 2020). Furthermore, toolpath planning may be done offline or online, as discussed by Ibrahim et al. (2018). Online toolpath planning allows adjusting the offline planned toolpath during manufacturing processes to compensate for geometric inaccuracies using sensor data. The main parameters for toolpath algorithms are described in Table 2, categorized into attributes, inputs, and outputs.

AM algorithms are commonly executed by AM software applications. With BIM-based data modeling approaches for AM, software applications that implement BIM concepts can support the execution of algorithms used in AM data modeling. BIM applications and BIM add-ins (e.g., Dynamo and Grasshopper3D) adapt software packages subscribing to the BIM paradigm (e.g., Revit and ArchiCAD) to user-specific needs for managing and processing data based on the IFC exchange format using libraries available for common programming languages. IFC-compliant BIM applications and BIM add-ins can read and write IFC files. The geometry information contained in IFC files is usually interpreted by processing and converting the geometry into triangle networks for visualization and further processing (Amann et al., 2018). An example of developing object-oriented programs to exchange information that can be embedded into the IFC schema has been presented by Amann (2018). Hence, BIM applications and add-ins, as object-oriented programs, may be used to read semantic and geometry information contained in IFC files to be used as inputs, to execute algorithms, and to write IFC files containing algorithm semantics and outputs. In the following section, an IFC-compliant description of algorithms for concrete printing is presented.

Table 2: Main parameters for toolpath algorithms.

Type	Parameter	Description
Attribute	Name	Name of the algorithm.
	Type	Type of toolpath planning (i.e., online/offline, 2D/3D/topology-based).
Input	Contour	Contours of the 3D model per layer.
	Path pattern	The path pattern is part of the printing strategy. For planar slicing (2D), it may be defined as raster (unidirectional, multidirectional, rid, zigzag, contour, spiral, hybrid), continuous (Hilbert, fractal-like, wavy, Fermat spirals), hybrid-and-continuous (zigzag-continuous, zigzag-contour-continuous), and along-geometry (MAT). For freeform surface (3D), it may be defined as directional parallel, contour parallel and space-filling parallel.
	Layer transition	The layer transition is part of the printing strategy. The transition between layers may be defined as upwards, gradually upwards, and interrupted (Bos et al., 2016).
	Filament width or offset distance	Width of the deposited filament or offset distance between infill lines.
	Start point	Start point of the path.
	End point	Endpoint of the path.
Output	Outer boundary	Outer boundary of the contours per layer.
	Inner boundary	Inner boundary of the contours per layer.
	Filling path	Path generated for the infill between the outer and the inner boundary per layer.
	Support path	Path generated for support structures for overhangs and voids per layer.

3. IFC-compliant description of algorithms for concrete printing

Algorithmic BIM, in general, refers to integrating algorithms into BIM models. The algorithms are to be formally defined in compliance with the IFC standard, homogenizing algorithm semantics, aiming to enhance interoperability between AEC software packages and applications. In this regard, an algorithmic BIM approach will aid concrete printing to mature in terms of reliability, thus increasing its acceptance by the AEC industry. Building on an IFC-based description for concrete printing proposed in a previous study (Peralta et al., 2020), an IFC-compliant description of algorithms is developed herein to advance concrete printing. To develop the IFC-compliant description of AM algorithms, the semantic information of slicing and toolpath planning algorithms is represented using technology-independent, semantic models. The semantic models are then mapped into the IFC schema, identifying IFC entities that may be used to store and to link algorithm semantics to BIM elements.

3.1 Semantic models for slicing and toolpath planning algorithms

For AM applications, algorithms are directly related to "products" in the broadest sense, such as printed components and sensor nodes. As illustrated in Figure 1, the abstract class *Product* depends on none or several algorithms (abstract class *Algorithm*) employed in AM processes. Similar to structural health monitoring algorithms (Theiler et al., 2018), AM algorithms take none or several inputs (class *Input*) and one or several algorithm components (abstract class *AlgorithmComponent*), including local variables (class *LocalVariable*), to produce one or several outputs (class *Output*). The algorithm components constitute the workflows or bodies of the algorithms that execute procedures and functions according to rules and constraints. Moreover, algorithms have attributes for identification, such as names, and for classification, such as types.

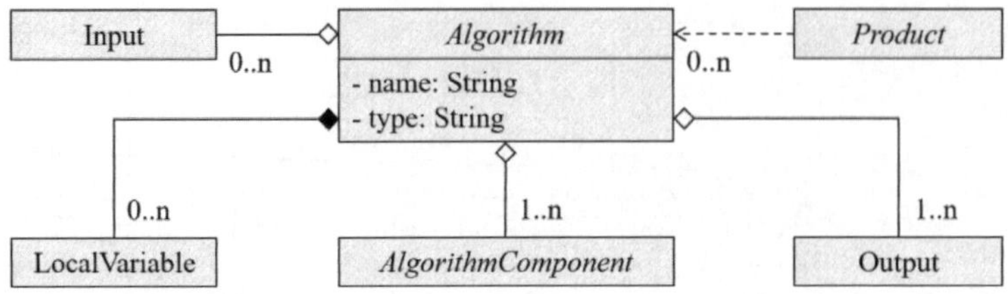

Figure 1: Semantic model for algorithms assigned to products.

Based on the semantic information identified for slicing and toolpath planning algorithms, the main parameters (i.e., inputs and outputs) for the algorithms can be related to products, as shown in Figure 2. Classes specific to slicing and toolpath planning algorithms are highlighted in gray. The geometries of the products are used as input for the slicing algorithms, where the geometries are sliced into contour lines according to layer heights and cutting planes definition (uniform and unidirectional input parameters shown in Figure 2). The toolpath planning algorithms use the outputs of the slicing algorithms as inputs, together with path-pattern and layer-transition strategies, to generate toolpaths for outer and inner boundaries, for fillings, and for support structures.

The printing information model presented in Smarsly et al. (2020) takes into account parameters necessary to execute slicing algorithms and toolpath planning algorithms. The slicing algorithms are executed by the class *ContourLine*, while the toolpath planning algorithms are executed by the class *ToolpathData*. The inputs and outputs of the algorithms form part of the attributes of the classes. In the following subsection, the semantic model for slicing and toolpath algorithms is mapped into the IFC schema for an IFC-compliant description of algorithm semantics for concrete printing.

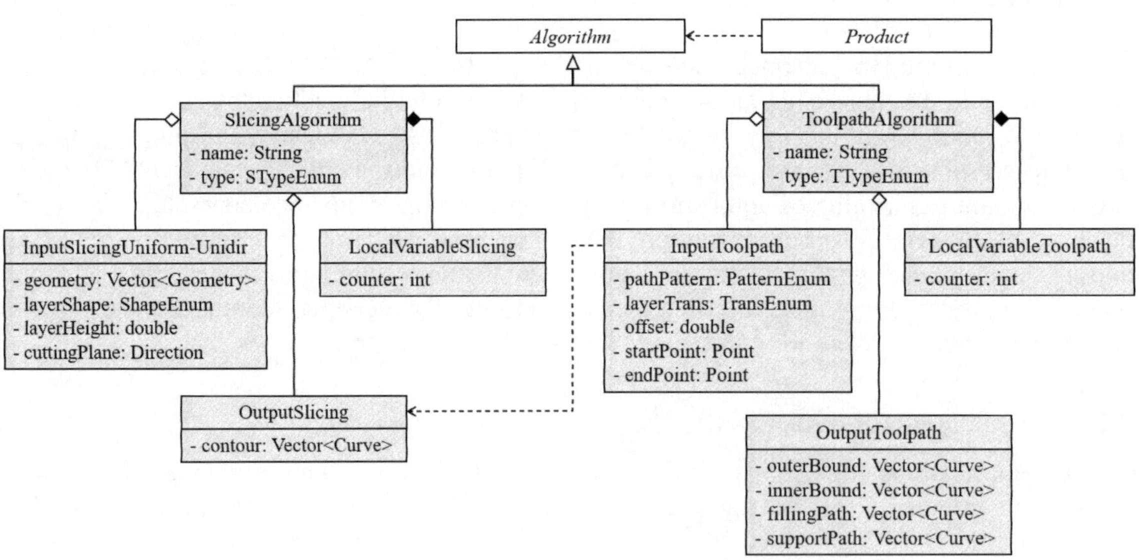

Figure 2: Semantic model for uniform and unidirectional slicing and toolpath algorithms assigned to products. Classes specific to slicing and toolpath planning algorithms are highlighted in gray.

3.2 Mapping AM algorithms onto the IFC schema

The algorithmic BIM approach for concrete printing defines storage preferences for inputs and outputs using IFC entities, providing access to the inputs and visualization of the outputs. It defines details on the connections of algorithms to the AM processes and the AM products represented by BIM models. Moreover, the algorithmic BIM approach defines algorithm semantics, coupled with BIM models, as a step to aid interoperability between AM software applications. The algorithm semantics are mapped onto the current version of the IFC schema "IFC 4 – Addendum 2" (buildingSMART, 2017) to identify IFC entities that may be used and to identify the need to specify new entities. Exemplarily, the mapping of slicing and toolpath planning algorithms onto the IFC schema is presented in the following paragraphs.

Existing IFC entities are reused to describe algorithms in AM processes for concrete printing, and AM processes are represented with *IfcProcess* entities, where algorithms are described using *IfcTask* entities. The AM processes are assigned to *IfcProduct* entities with the entity relationship *IfcRelAssignsToProcess*, when the products are inputs, and with the entity relationship *IfcRelAssignsToProduct*, when the products are outputs. In the case of slicing and toolpath planning algorithms, the algorithms may be described with single tasks (e.g., manufacturing model) that nest subtasks for slicing and subtasks for toolpath planning in sequence.

Similarly, as proposed in the IFC-based printing information model mentioned earlier, contour lines for each layer are represented using the entities *IfcElement* or *IfcElementComponent*, which are aggregated to form an *IfcElement* or an *IfcElementAssembly*. Toolpaths are aligned with the entity *IfcLinearPositioningElement* (to be included in the new version of the IFC schema "IFC4.3 – Release Candidate 2") or represented using the entity *IfcAnnotation* as 3D curves. To access and store the input parameters used by slicing and toolpath planning algorithms, new property sets are required, *Pset_Slice* and *Pset_Toolpath*. The contour lines and the toolpath, represented by the aforementioned existing IFC entities, already store and provide visualization of the output parameters. In Figure 3, the new property sets (highlighted in gray) and the connections of algorithms to the AM processes and the AM products are represented using IFC entities.

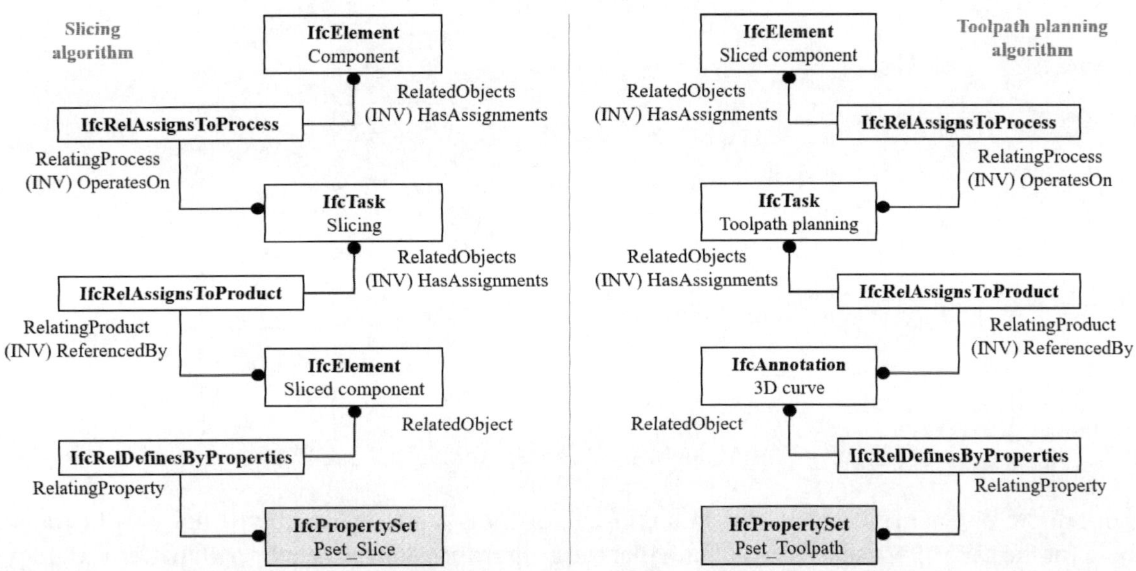

Figure 3: Object typing for slicing algorithms and toolpath algorithms assigned to products. New property sets are highlighted in gray.

During the design and planning of printed components using BIM, information is exchanged between BIM and AM software applications, between finite element analysis and AM software applications, and between AM software applications themselves. The geometry information of the 3D models is usually exchanged as tessellated or parametric models and further processed in AM software applications. With the algorithmic BIM approach for concrete printing, AM semantics are stored in IFC entities together with the main parameters of the AM algorithms used along the digital workflow. To further advance BIM-based concrete printing, Model View Definitions (MVD) or Information Delivery Specifications (IDS) could be defined to specify the IFC entities relevant to data exchange in the digital workflow in AM. However, a detailed analysis of AM software requirements is needed to develop a MVD or an IDS, which is out of the scope of this paper. Before devising a MVD or an IDS, the suitability of mapping the algorithm semantics onto the IFC schema needs to be tested using a case study, which is presented in the following section.

4. Case study

The algorithmic BIM approach for concrete printing is validated via a case study of generating a model of a column taking advantage of BIM concepts, representing steps of the digital workflow for manufacturing ("manufacturing model"). The column, with a hexagonal cross section, is modeled parametrically. The manufacturing model of the column includes the steps of slicing and toolpath planning. The algorithm semantics that generate the manufacturing model are coupled with the IFC model of the column using IFC entities.

Using the concepts of BIM programing, a BIM application is used to generate the parametric BIM model of the column, to execute the slicing algorithm and toolpath planning algorithm, and to store the algorithm semantics using IFC entities, as shown in Figure 4. As proof of concept, the BIM application is devised for direct slicing and for toolpath planning using a contour path pattern strategy and an interrupted layer transition strategy.

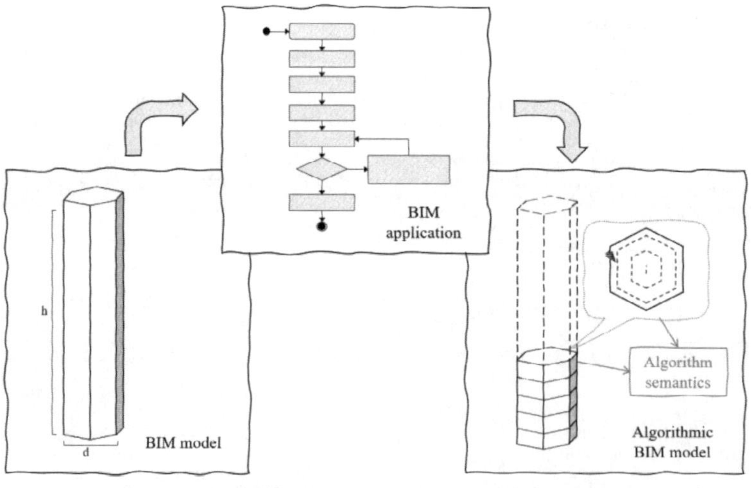

Figure 4: BIM application concept for algorithmic BIM.

For simple parametric models, direct slicing algorithms are trivial and will not be illustrated here for the sake of brevity. The toolpath planning algorithm with a contour path pattern strategy is shown in Figure 5. The contours, which form closed regions, are offset inwards for each layer. The transition between layers is done by temporarily stopping printing once a layer is completed, moving the printhead into position for the subsequent layer, and restarting printing.

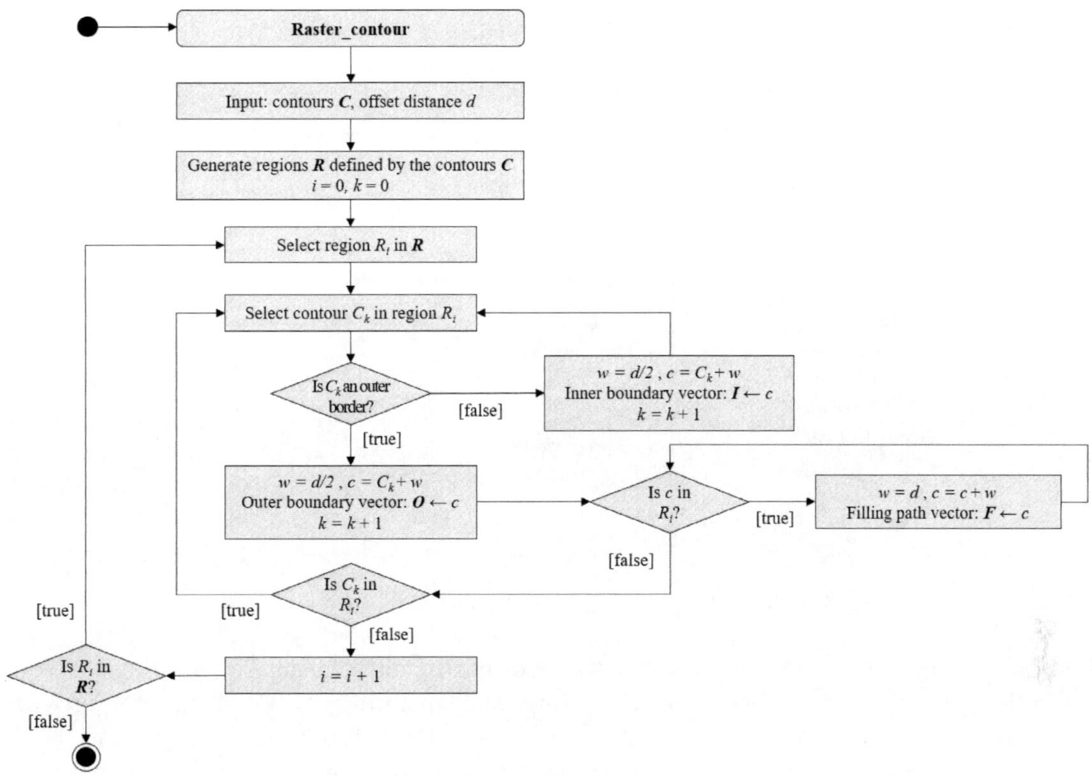

Figure 5: Control flow for a toolpath algorithm with a contour path planning strategy applied to every layer.

The BIM application uses the APSTEX IFC Framework (https://www.apstex.com/) to read, write, create, and modify IFC models. The APSTEX IFC Framework includes the IFC schema extension described by Theiler et al. (2018), which defines two new IFC entities *IfcRelSelection* and *IfcCondition*, and generates Java classes equivalent to the extended IFC schema that are used by the BIM application. The BIM application reads the IFC model of the column, which is described with an *IfcBuildingElementProxy* entity, and generates an equivalent instance using the corresponding Java classes. The raster-contour algorithm is described with an *IfcTask* related to each sliced component. The algorithm is coded in the BIM application and is called by the corresponding *IfcTask*. The inputs are defined by the user, described using *IfcEvent* entities when executing the algorithm. The algorithm components have a nesting relationship with the algorithm, and the statements are described with *IfcProcedure* entities. For sequences, the relation between statements are described with *IfcRelSequence*. For selections and iterations, conditions are described with *IfcCondition* using *IfcRelSelection*. Finally, the outputs of the algorithm are generated, where the toolpath is described using *IfcAnnotiation* entities as 3D curves and the inputs are stored in *Pset_Toolpath* entities.

As a result, an IFC model coupled with algorithm semantics of the manufacturing model is obtained, as shown in Figure 6. The outer boundary and the filling path resulting from the toolpath planning algorithm, as well as the input parameters used to generate the paths, are visualized in the IFC model. By documenting the input parameters and the type of algorithm implemented in this study, the generation of the manufacturing model can be repeated and checked to evaluate the quality of the manufacturing model and of the printed component, thus improving the reliability of concrete printing.

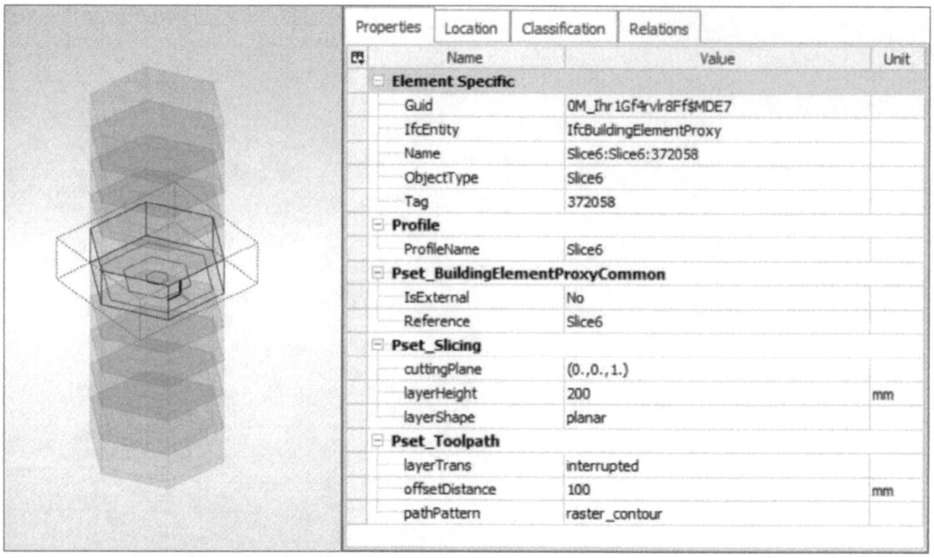

Figure 6: Results of the algorithmic BIM approach for concrete printing.

Therefore, algorithmic BIM approaches for additive manufacturing of buildings have the potential to advance the phases of designing and planning of buildings by providing transparency and repeatability. Moreover, design variants of building components can be analyzed and optimized, without information loss and with minimal misinterpretation of semantics. Additionally, by including algorithm semantics in exchange standards, BIM-compatible platforms that incorporate automatic functions along the design workflow of buildings, such as Hypar (https://hypar.io/), may use the algorithm semantics to train the functions for achieving optimum design variants.

5. Summary and conclusions

Building information modeling has the potential to support algorithm-based design and data management for concrete printing. An algorithmic BIM approach for concrete printing, capable of describing algorithm semantics in compliance with the IFC standard, has been developed and presented in this paper. A case study has been devised to validate the algorithmic BIM approach for a direct slicing algorithm and a toolpath planning algorithm in an IFC model for concrete printing. As has been demonstrated, by storing algorithm semantics in compliance with the IFC standard, the critical additive manufacturing process steps can easily be checked and standardized, improving the communication along the digital workflow and the reliability of concrete printing. In future work, the algorithmic BIM concept can be further explored to be formalized as an IFC extension. Similarly, the IFC-based printing information model can be further explored by defining a model view definition for exchanging information between AM software applications.

Acknowledgments

The authors would like to acknowledge the financial support the German Research Foundation (DFG) through grant SM 281/7-1. Any opinions, findings, conclusions, or recommendations expressed in this paper are those of the authors and do not necessarily reflect the views of DFG.

References

Amann, J. (2018). Eine objektorientierte Sprache zur Einbettung von Interpretationssemantik in digitale Bauwerksmodelle [An object-oriented language for embedding interpretation semantics in digital building models] (Doctoral dissertation, Technical University of Munich). MediaTUM. Retrieved January 28, 2021 at: http://mediatum.ub.tum.de/?id=1453871.

Amann, J., Tauscher, E., & Borrmann, A. (2018). BIM programming. In: A. Borrmann, M. König, C. Koch, & J. Beetz (Eds.), Building Information Modeling: Technology Foundations and Industry Practices. Springer, Cham, Switzerland.

Bonnard, R., Hascoët, J.-Y., Mognol, P., & Stroud, I. (2018). STEP-NC digital thread for additive manufacturing: data model, implementation and validation. International Journal of Computer Integrated Manufacturing, 31(11), pp.1141–1160.

Bos, F. P., Wolfs, R. J. M., Ahmed, Z. Y. & Salet, T. A. M. (2016). Additive manufacturing of concrete in construction: potentials and challenges of 3D concrete printing. Virtual and Physical Prototyping, 11(3), pp.209–225.

buildingSMART (2017). Industry Foundation Classes 4.0.2.1, Version 4.0 – Addendum 2 – Technical Corrigendum 1. Retrieved February 8, 2021 at: https://standards.buildingsmart.org/IFC/RELEASE/ IFC4/ ADD2_TC1/HTML/.

Garanger, K., Feron, E., Garoche, P.-L., Rimoli, J. J., Berrigan, J. D., Grover, M., & Hobbs, K. (2017). Foundations of intelligent additive manufacturing (e-print). ArXiv, abs/1705.00960.

Ibrahim, S., Olbrich, A., Lidermann, H., Gerbers, R., Kloft, H., Dröder, K., & Raatz, A. (2018). Automated additive manufacturing of concrete structures without formwork - Concept for path planning. In: Schüppstuhl, T., Tracht, K., Franke, J. (Eds.), Tagungsband des 3. Kongresses Montage Handhabung Industrieroboter, pp.83–91. Springer Vieweg, Berlin, Germany.

Leirmo, T. S. & Martinsen, K. (2019). Evolutionary algorithms in additive manufacturing systems: Discussion of future prospects. In: Proceedings of the 52nd CIRP Conference on Manufacturing Systems. Ljubljana, Slovenia, June 12, 2019.

Peralta Abadia, P., Heine, S., Ludwig, H.-M., & Smarsly, K. (2020). A BIM-based approach towards additive manufacturing of concrete structure. In: Proceedings of the 27th International Workshop on Intelligent Computing in Engineering (EG-ICE). Berlin, Germany, July 01, 2020.

Rocha, A. M., Pereira, A. I., & Vaz, A. I. (2018). Build orientation optimization problem in additive manufacturing. In: Gervasi, O., et al. (Eds.). Computational Science and Its Applications – ICCSA 2018, pp.669–682. Springer, Cham, Switzerland.

Saadlaoui, Y., Milan, J.-L., Rossi, J.-M., & Chabrand, P. (2017) Topology optimization and additive manufacturing: Comparison of conception methods using industrial codes. Journal of Manufacturing Systems, 43(2017), pp.178–186.

Sanfilippo, E. M., Belkadi, F., & Bernard, A. (2019). Ontology-based knowledge representation for additive manufacturing. Computers in Industry, 109(2019), pp.182–194

Smarsly, K., Peralta, P., Luckey, D., Heine, S., & Ludwig, H.-M. (2020). BIM-based concrete printing. In: Proceedings of the International ICCCBE and CIB W78 Joint Conference on Computing in Civil and Building Engineering 2020. Sao Paolo, Brazil, June 02, 2020

Theiler, M., Dragos, K., & Smarsly, K. (2018). Semantic description of structural health monitoring algorithms using building information modeling. In: Proceedings of the 25th International Workshop on Intelligent Computing in Engineering (EG-ICE). Lausanne, Switzerland, June 10, 2018.

Zhao, D. & Guo, W. (2020). Shape and performance controlled advanced design for additive manufacturing: A review of slicing and path planning. Journal of Manufacturing Science and Engineering, 142 (1), 010801.

A methodological approach to generate robot control algorithms from BIM-Models

Nicolas Mitsch, Karsten Menzel, Adrian Schubert
Technische Universität Dresden, Germany
Nicolas.Mitsch@tu-dresden.de

Abstract. This paper discusses initial achievements in the development of a methodological approach for the development of a framework which aims to support automated generation of robot control algorithms from BIM-models. These control algorithms shall be suitable for modular robot systems, especially dedicated to the deployment in small and medium sized enterprises (SME). Such affordable robot platforms may consist of multiple robot modules which are capable to collaborate with each other during manufacturing. A major step in achieving this goal is the identification of robot modules based on an analysis of construction activities and corresponding control actions.

1. Introduction

The shortage of skilled workers in the construction industry clearly exceeds that of other industries. Low wages, physically demanding work and adverse working conditions make the construction industry less attractive for potential new recruits. While other industrial branches managed to deal with increasing demand by using robots to reduce production time and cost, several factors seem to prevent the use of robotics in the construction industry (Mahbub, 2005).

The biggest problem for the use of robots on construction sites is the uniqueness of each construction project. This requires a very flexible approach to plan and implement the deployment of robots on construction sites. The use of conventional programming methods for robot controllers would require complete reprogramming for each new project. Thus, alternatives are required. Furthermore, the planning process of a construction project is usually ongoing even during the building phase and distributed among several stakeholders (Mahbub, 2005; Martin Keller et al., 2006). This supports the late implementation of quick changes to the desired final product. While these changes usually don't affect the ability of human workers to complete their task, a robot that is programmed for one task specifically couldn't necessarily adapt to the new requirements. Another constraint making it difficult to use robots on construction sites is the unpredictable conditions. Harsh weather conditions, dust, "randomly used" storage spaces and dynamically changing support constructions characterize AEC-workplaces. Furthermore, the AEC-sector allows for comparatively large tolerances for manufacturing and assembly. While compensating for these tolerances is not difficult for humans, a robot must first be programmed to compensate for these tolerances. Additionally, with every wall that has been built, new obstacles 'appear' for the robot. To avoid the above obstacles, robots must be capable to recognize objects seamlessly and instantaneously.

2. Existing and Most Recent Solutions

To deal with the challenges that the use of robots brings to the construction industry there are numerous approaches: (i) Prefabrication of construction elements in easily controllable environments, (ii) controlling the variables on the construction sites, (iii) flexible robot programming using parametric robot control, (iv) increasing the usability of single task robots through autonomy, (v) modularity, and most recently (vi) BIM, embedded intelligence and digital twins.

2.1 Prefabrication of Construction Elements

Since the prefabrication of construction elements such as concrete walls or ceilings transfers the construction process in a controlled environment of a factory building, existing technologies can be adapted quickly (Pan et al., 2018)

Production processes in prefabrication plants are usually highly standardized and thus have a high number of repetitions. Due to the high repeatability, robots can be programmed in a highly specialized manner for individual work steps. For example, robots can be used to lay and tie reinforcement mesh in precast concrete elements, increasing both productivity and quality. While the use of reinforcement mesh laying robots is also possible outside of a factory (ACR, 2019) the possibilities are still very limited due to the reliance on horizontal building elements.

In general, the use of robots in prefabrication plants is not limited to concrete structures. Different branches of the construction industry, such as timber construction is already using robots in prefabrication to a very high degree (Krieg et al., 2015). Stud walls can be constructed fully automated using input from 3D-Models being based on computer-aided design(CAD) and computer-aided manufacturing (CAM) methods. These methods allow a transformation of CAD models into production models for CNC-Milling or even whole production lines (HOMAG, 2020).

While robot-oriented prefabrication of construction elements offers high productivity and quality, it is usually accompanied by high investment costs that small and medium-sized companies in particular cannot usually afford. Therefore, other possibilities of robot uses should be explored to make the advantages of robotic technology accessible to a broader spectrum of AEC-companies.

2.2 Creation of a Controllable Construction Site

In order to create an environment on the construction site that is comparable to a factory, Japanese construction companies and researchers developed the Shimizu Manufacturing System by Advanced Robotics Technology (SMART). The SMART-System consists of an all-weather cover that protects the construction site from environmental influences, an automated crane and mobile robots that perform tasks such as welding, assembly or transport tasks (Maeda, 1994). Within the Smart System, all tasks that occur on a construction site are carried out by a robot alone or in cooperation with other robots (Bock, 2016). In theory, this system makes it possible to build around the clock, if this is not prevented by noise regulations or the like.

Again, this approach requires high upfront investment cost and is therefore suitable to large construction companies. However, in Germany and other European countries the construction sector is dominated by SME. Therefore, different approaches for the introduction of robotic technology are required.

2.3 Flexible Robot Programming

To make the programming of robots more suitable for the fast changing environment of construction sites and building projects in general, new control methods are needed. Parametric robot control makes it possible for the necessary control code to be generated automatically from predefined geometries (Fasih Mohiuddin Syed, 2020). To further increase the flexibility of this methodology, it is possible to control the robot in near real-time (Szulczyński and

Kozłowski, 2015). Production processes for components can thus be quickly adapted to changed conditions.

The foundation for parametric robot control is always a 3D CAD-Model, which contains all information necessary for the generation of the control algorithm (Braumann and Brell-Cokcan, 2011).

In order to obtain robot controls for assembly operations from a 3D model, information regarding geometries and assembly sequence must either already be included in the model or can be derived from it. The derivation of the assembly sequence based on the existing 3D model offers great potential to further advance the automation of production processes in the construction industry. Initial examples from work of our research group are documented in (Khashayar Samiee Moghaddam, 2020).

2.4 New Construction Methods

Robot-Oriented Design: While it is a possible approach to adapt existing solutions from the field of robotics for use in construction, it is equally possible to adapt construction procedures to a robotic approach. Guidelines to be followed for efficient robot use were established as early as in the 1980s (Bock, 1988). Of course, technological developments in the field of robotics have greatly increased the possibilities for use. Nevertheless, basic principles such as standardization are essential for simple and efficient robot use.

Additive Manufacturing: Since the currently used construction methods are one of the main reasons why it is difficult to use robots in construction, it is obvious to adapt them to a robotic use. To achieve this, the existing technology is taken as a basis to explore how buildings can be produced in novel construction methods. Concrete printing has emerged as one of the most popular solutions in this research area, as the shaping possibilities are almost unlimited and the investment costs are manageable.

Another construction method worth mentioning is the so-called mesh-mold technology, which uses reinforcement simultaneously for structural safety and as formwork. This method makes it possible to build concrete walls without the use of heavy formwork elements and at the same time allows shaping comparable to concrete printing.

2.5 Use of Modular Design Approaches

Since the 1920ies so called "industrialized" or "standardized" design and construction methodologies gained increased attraction (Wachsmann and Patzelt, 1989). Major design principles underpinning this approach are – amongst others – modularity (Haller et al., 2015) and Pattern Languages (Alexander, 1980). Modularity characterizes the degree to which systems' can be separated in smaller units aiming to reduce complexity. Abstract description of the parts and precise interface description support the later recombination of those components to larger systems with the benefit of flexibility and variety in use. Fritz Haller is one of the most prominent architects having demonstrated the capabilities of modular design by developing a holistic set of systems, i.e. the "Maxi System", the "Steel Construction System USM Haller Midi 600" and the "USM Furniture System" (Monika Dommann, 2015). Pattern Languages extend the modular design approach by adding flexibility and providing a more comprehensive connectivity across multiple scales (Alexander and Czech, 1995). Late approaches by Haller and his team also propose holistic design approaches considering "core & shell" and building services systems in an integrated way, following a strict "grid based, modular approach" (Hovestadt and Hovestadt, 1999).

2.6 BIM, Embedded Intelligence, and Digital Twins

The technology of Building Information Modelling assumes the availability of product and process data over the whole life-cycle of a building. This includes in many cases the availability of geometrical data (Cahill et al., 2012). However, so far the building elements and the actors modelled in BIM had no or limited capabilities to report their status back "instantaneously".

In the first decade of the 21st century so called "embedded systems" became popular. The broad appearance of RFID- and sensor technology and the increasing usage of wireless data transmission technologies (Menzel et al., 2008) in the AEC-sector supported a more efficient, comprehensive identification and navigation on construction sites and in buildings (Rueppel and Stuebbe, 2008). The usage of localization and identification technologies for intelligent building control (Manzoor et al., 2012; Manzoor and Menzel, 2011) and advanced building operation has been demonstrated for numerous years (Ahmed et al., 2009; Yin et al., 2011). However, these approaches did not consider the dynamic changes of construction sites. Additional technologies, such as laser scanning, were required for advanced progress monitoring on construction sites (Alomari et al., 2016). The necessity for "incremental" surveying activities, irrespectively if executed by surveying personnel or drones, does not fully support the idea of "Digital Twins", since in this case an instantaneous update of the digital model is expected – without time delay. Therefore, autonomy of robots, including the capability to recognize their immediate "work environment" are essential features which must be supported by robotic control software.

3. Proposed Approach

As a possible solution to the problem of robot use in construction we present a concept that uses modularity and flexible robot control for the deployment of robotic technology in construction. Pre-requisites to achieve partial or full automation of construction activities are discussed. We are aware, that especially in the field of on-site manufacturing full automation of the construction site cannot be achieved in the near future. Therefore, it is necessary to analyze which tasks are particularly suitable for the use of robots on construction sites. We present initial results from field studies (Lukas Fuchs, 2020). In order to make an initial robot deployment on the construction site as simple as possible, the following chapters will be limited to construction activities focusing on finishing (e.g. dry-walling, plastering, painting). The deployment of robotics to support core-and-shell construction activities will be excluded from further consideration. Additionally, our framework does not include a discussion of safety aspects, since early discussions with robot developers and manufacturers provide some confidence that appropriate security strategies can be developed and implemented.

3.1 The Framework for the Methodology

From current field studies we have learned that the pure "translation" of features from 3D-models into robot control algorithms or commands will fail. In order to get a more holistic understanding on what activities are suitable for robotic support we developed a three-step approach.

Step 1 – to determine the potential for robotic support: This is the initial step. As a result of a work placement of one of our graduate students in industry an evaluation matrix was developed (Lukas Fuchs, 2020). This matrix serves as an initial tool to determine constraints and evaluate the suitability of activities for robotic support. The result of this process leads to a so called "Suitability Index" and a corresponding "Suitability Evaluation Matrix" (see Table 1 overleaf).

Table 1: Example for an Suitability Evaluation Matrix (as per (Lukas Fuchs, 2020))

Carrying Weight [kg]		Size of required "workplace"		Required tools & materials proc.		Repetition Coefficient		Misc.	Suitability Index	
Weight	points	Size	Points	Number	points	Scope	points		Max 100	
<3	28	Small	24	<3	20	v. high	16		85 <	v. good
4-6	21	Medium	18	4	15	High	12		84-69	Good
7-12	14	Large	12	5	10	Medium	8		68-53	Neutr.
12 <	7	v. large	6	5 <	5	low	4		52-0	poor

Step 2 – to determine the potential for modularization: This step requires an analysis of the sequence of activities to be automated. An important goal of the research is to exploit the modularity of robots so that one robotic-platform can perform different tasks. The purpose of the analysis is, to determine the degree of "coupling" between activities. The more dependencies between activities exist, the higher is the likelihood that activities cannot be decoupled, i.e. modularized. In analogy to software engineering we distinguish between loose coupling and strong coupling.

Step 3 – to determine the concurrency of activities: This step requires the analysis of dependencies between activities. Activities which must be executed in parallel have a high potential to require multiple robotic modules, each supporting a dedicated activity.

The results of step 2 and step 3 are comprehensively documented in a so called "Coupling-and-Concurrency-Matrix" (CCM). An example for a CCM is provided in Table 3.

3.2 Human-Robot or Robot-to-Robot Collaboration

The diversity of tasks in the construction sector places high demands on robotic technologies to be mastered in a timely manner. Therefore, in certain cases it seems to make more sense in the short and medium term to use robots only where they create added value compared to human labor. Processes that are particularly suitable for automation are those that have a high repetition rate and ideally consist of simple but physically demanding activities. Very complex tasks or tasks which are rarely executed can be still performed by humans in the same environment. The prerequisite for this, however, is that the rules of safe human-robot collaboration are examined for their applicability in the construction industry and ultimately also adhered to on the construction site.

In the literature, authors distinguish between four different collaboration scenarios (Matheson et al., 2019), such as:

Coexistence: Robots and humans share a common workspace, but do not interact with each other and each perform their tasks independently.

Synchronised: A work piece is first processed by a human, then passed to the robot for further processing, or vice versa.

Cooperation: Both human and robot both work on the same task and share a workspace. A work piece is processed by only one actor at any given time.

Collaboration: Collaboration is the most complex form of human-robot collaboration, as humans and robots share a workspace and work together on a work piece to complete a task.

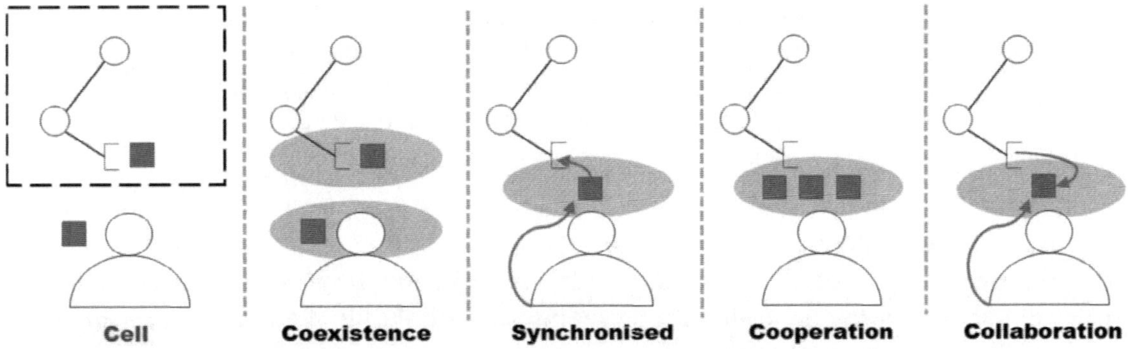

Figure 1: Human-Robot-Collaboration Scenarios in manufacturing (Matheson et al., 2019)

It is obvious that one can develop analogies to robot-to-robot interaction scenarios.

3.3 Classification of Robotic Modules and Related Control Activities

In the previous sections we discussed major constraints. In this section we would like to synthesize our findings. Depending on the activity to be executed, one can distinguish five general types of robotic modules (see rows of Table 2). Each general type of robotic modules shall support selected control activities (see columns of Table 2).

Table 2: Mapping Robotic Modules to Control Actions

Module \ (Control) Action	Visual Sensing	Intelligent Recognition	Localization	Navigation	Position Effector	Actuate Effector	Sense hapitcly	Robot-to-Robot Interaction
Transport	❍	❍	❍	❍				
Drill	❍	❍			❍	❍		
Suspend	❍	❍			❍	❍		
Pick-and-Place	❍	❍	❍		❍	❍	❍	
Assemble	❍	❍	❍	❍	❍	❍	❍	❍

4. Examples for the Deployment of the Framework

In this section we demonstrate the applicability of the developed framework to two major bundled activities, namely Adaptive Robot Control and On-site Manufacturing. Adaptive Robot Control integrates four major control actions (Table 2), such as visual sensing, intelligent recognition, localization and navigation. In comparison On-site Manufacturing integrates effector positioning, effector actuation, haptic sensing and robot-to-robot interaction (Table 2).

4.1 Adaptive Robot Control

Robot actions must be determined in a way that they can be flexibly adapted to changes of design parameters. However, parametric adaptability of building elements not only increases the possibilities to design more complex buildings but also complicates the production process.

Rapidly changing geometries may also lead to the danger that the components to be produced will exceed the physical boundary conditions of the processing robots (Brell-Cokcan and Braumann, 2010). Examples of possible exceedances of the robots' capabilities are unreachable locations due to unfavorably selected component dimensions or large loads.

Regardless of their complex geometries, new problems arise when using solid geometries as a starting point for automated robot control. Solid geometry models must be enriched with information about material, assembly sequence or load-bearing capacity. Alternatively, the robot controller, or the interface between the BIM model and the robot controller, must have sufficient intelligence to derive all the relevant information (Fasih Mohiuddin Syed, 2020).

For the development of initial prove of concept we used a Grasshopper application combined with a plugin for a well-established robot manufacturer (Kuka|Prc). This tool-chain supports parametric programming and related simulation of a robot arm. For demonstration purposes, simple geometries were used to determine the possibilities of the tool in relation to the problem of trajectory specification and picking point determination. This simple "pick-and-place" scenario can be extended to more complex tasks, such as milling, drilling, sawing or screwing. All of these activities can be programmed just by specifying a few reference points.

4.2 On-site Manufacturing

An analysis of construction activities in interior construction (finishing) led to the conclusion that drilling holes is the most common activity (Handwerk Digital, 2019) executed by SME on site. Other relevant tasks executed by SME on construction sites identified were, e.g. suspension (the application of liquids) or simple pick and place activities. Examples for the suspension of liquid materials are painting, plastering, or gluing. Although the consistency of the liquid material to be processed is very diverse, the basic principle how to distribute the liquid material across a surface is comparable. Pick and place applications occur in many on-site activities, such as e.g. the laying of tiles, insulation material, etc.

4.3 Results

As part of Step 1 of our methodology major processes executed by SME were analysed in-depth by students during their work placements. material transport, drilling suspension of liquid materials, pick-and-place of flat elements and assembly activities were classified as having a high potential for execution by robots. Subsequently, we went through steps two and three of our methodology. Based on the initial findings we developed an example for a "Coupling-and-Concurrency-Matrix" (see Table 3).

Table 3: Example for a Coupling-and-Concurrency-Matrix

	Transport	Drill	Suspend	Pick-and-Place	Assemble
Transport	concurrent	concurrent	loose	close	concurrent
Drill	loose	n.a.	none	loose	close
Suspend	loose	none	n.a.	loose	close
Pick-and-Place	close	close	loose	n.a.	close
Assemble	concurrent	close	close	close	concurrent

5. Outlook

Small and medium-sized enterprises (SME) usually execute numerous different tasks in short time intervals. Thus, the availability of modular robot platforms for usage on construction sites becomes indispensable, since highly specialized robots can't be afforded by SME. Ideally, the availability of modular robot platforms will have a positive effect on investment costs and thus makes construction robots more attractive for small and medium-sized companies.

In the medium term, the main focus of research should be on the exploitation of information and knowledge already inherited in BIM models for robot control. Data available in BIM models must be intelligently used to generate control algorithms.

Machine Learning, ontologies and semantic web technologies already provide core technologies to extract further (manufacturing) knowledge through e.g. reasoning (Karlapudi et al., 2020; Valluru et al., 2020). It is also particularly important to determine to what extent the assembly sequence or other boundary conditions critical for manufacturing can be additionally extracted from BIM models.

6. Conclusions

In comparison to many other research approaches the authors of this paper start with an analysis of construction process sequences leading to a so called "robotic suitability index" (ch. 3.1 – Step 1). The authors propose to further progress with the process analysis aiming to identify the possible "degree of coupling" (ch. 3.1 - Step 2). This degree of coupling determines the "modular specification" for a robot-platform. Finally, by determining the capability for concurrent execution of processes the need for multiple robot-modules can be specified.

Simple tools are made available to practitioners, such as the robotic suitability index (Table 1) and the Coupling-and-Concurrency-Matrix (Table 3). In the near future these tools will be used in ongoing research projects.

Acknowledgements

This research was partially funded by the Federal German Ministry for Research and Innovation under the project-acronym "RoPBau".

References

ACR (2019) Construction Robotics | ACR | Pittsburgh, United States [Online]. Available at https://www.acrbots.com/ (Accessed 13 January 2020).

Ahmed, A., Menzel, K., Ploennigs, J. and Cahill, B. (2009) 'Aspects of multi-dimensional Building Performance Data Management', in Huhnt, W. (ed) Computing in engineering: EG-ICE conference 2009 ; [computation in civil engineering, Aachen, Shaker.

Alexander, C. (1980) The timeless way of building, 2nd edn, New York NY u.a., Oxford Univ. Pr.

Alexander, C. and Czech, H. (1995) Eine Muster-Sprache: Städte, Gebäude, Konstruktion, Wien, Löcker.

Alomari, K., Gambatese, J. and Olsen, M. J., eds. (2016) Role of BIM and 3D Laser Scanning on Job sites from the Perspective of Construction Project Management Personnel.

Bock, T. (2016) Construction robotics [Online], 18838049.

Bock, T.-A. (1988) 'Robot-Oriented Design', Proceedings of the 5th International Symposium on Automation and Robotics in Construction (ISARC), pp.135–144.

Braumann, J. and Brell-Cokcan, S. (2011) 'Parametric Robot Control Integrated CAD/CAM for Architectural Design', ACADIA 2011 Proceedings, pp.242–251.

Brell-Cokcan, S. and Braumann, J. (2010) 'A New Parametric Design Tool for Robot Milling', Proceedings of the 30th Annual Conference of the Association for Computer Aided Design in Architecture, pp.357–363.

Cahill, B., Menzel, K. and Flynn, D. (2012) 'BIM as a centre piece for Optimised Building Operation', in Gudnason, G. and Scherer, R. (eds) eWork and eBusiness in Architecture, Engineering and Construction: ECPPM 2012 [Online], Hoboken, CRC Press, pp.549–555. Available at https://www.routledge.com/eWork-and-eBusiness-in-Architecture-Engineering-and-Construction-ECPPM/Gudnason-Scherer/p/book/9780415621281.

Fasih Mohiuddin Syed (2020) Optimization of manufacturing process for sheet metal panels considering shape, tessellation and structural stability (Masterarbeit), Dresden, TU Dresden.

Haller, F., Stalder, L. and Vrachliotis, G., eds. (2015) Fritz Haller: Architekt und Forscher, Zürich, gta Verlag.

Handwerk Digital (2019) Robonet 4.0 | Handwerk-Digital [Online]. Available at https://www.handwerk-digital.org/index.php/robotik-im-handwerk (Accessed 6 January 2020).

Hovestadt, V. and Hovestadt, L. (1999) 'The ARMILLA project', Automation in Construction, vol. 8, no. 3, pp.325–337.

Karlapudi, J., Menzel, K., Törmä, S., Hryshchenko, A. and Valluru, P. (2020) 'Enhancement of BIM Data Representation in Product-Process Modelling for Building Renovation', in Nyffenegger, F., Ríos, J. and Rivest, L. (eds) Product Lifecycle Management Enabling Smart X: 17th IFIP WG 5.1 International Conference, PLM 2020, Rapperswil, Switzerland, July 5–8, 2020, Revised Selected Papers, pp.738–752.

Khashayar Samiee Moghaddam (2020) Analysing trajectories and moments of a one-arm robot to pick up sheet metals and assemble a shell structure (Masterarbeit), Dresden, TU Dresden.

Krieg, O. D., Knippers, J., Li, J., Menges, A., Schmitt, A., Schwieger, V. and Schwinn, T. (2015) 'Roboterfertigung : Entwicklungen und Tendenzen im Holzbau Robotic production : developments and trends in timber construction', pp.1–9.

Lukas Fuchs (2020) Modulare Roboterplattformen im Bauwesen: Potentiale und Einsatzmöglichkeiten (Projektarbeit), Dresden, TU Dresden.

Maeda, J. (1994) 'Development and Application of the SMART System', Automation and Robotics in Construction Xi, pp.457–464.

Mahbub, R. (2005) 'An investigation into the barriers to automation and robotics in construction', Queensland University of Technology Research Week International Conference, QUT Research Week 2005 - Conference Proceedings, June.

Manzoor, F., Linton, D., Loughlin, M. and Menzel, K. (2012) 'RFID based efficient lighting control', International Journal of RF Technologies, vol. 4, no. 1, pp.1–21 [Online]. DOI: 10.3233/RFT-2012-0036.

Manzoor, F. and Menzel, K. (2011) 'Indoor localisation for complex building designs using passive RFID technology', in XXXth URSI general assembly and scientific symposium, 2011: [URSI GASS 2011] ; 13 –20 Aug. 2011, Istanbul, Turkey, Piscataway, NJ, IEEE, pp.1–4.

Martin Keller, Raimar J. Scherer, Karsten Menzel, Thomas Theling, Dominik Vanderhaeghen and Peter Loos (2006) 'Support of collaborative business process networks in AEC', Journal of Information Technology in Construction, vol. 11, Special Issue Process Modelling, Process Management and Collaboration, pp.449–465 [Online]. Available at http://www.itcon.org/2006/34.

Matheson, E., Minto, R., Zampieri, E. G. G., Faccio, M. and Rosati, G. (2019) 'Human–Robot Collaboration in Manufacturing Applications: A Review', Robotics, vol. 8, no. 4 [Online]. DOI: 10.3390/robotics8040100.

Menzel, K., Cong, Z. and Allan, L. (2008) 'Potentials for radio frequency identification in AEC/FM', Tsinghua Science and Technology, vol. 13, S1, pp.329–335.

Monika Dommann (2015) 'Systeme aus dem Mittelland', in Haller, F., Stalder, L. and Vrachliotis, G. (eds) Fritz Haller: Architekt und Forscher, Zürich, gta Verlag, pp.10–35.

Pan, M., Linner, T., Pan, W. and Bock, T. (2018) 'Proceedings of the 21st International Symposium on Advancement of Construction Management and Real Estate', Proceedings of the 21st International Symposium on Advancement of Construction Management and Real Estate, January.

Rueppel, U. and Stuebbe, K. M. (2008) 'BIM-Based Indoor-Emergency-Navigation-System for Complex Buildings', Tsinghua Science and Technology, vol. 13, S1, pp.362–367.

Szulczyński, P. and Kozłowski, K. (2015) 'Parametric programming of industrial robots', Archives of Control Sciences, vol. 25, no. 2, pp.215–225.

Valluru, P., Karlapudi, J., Menzel, K., Mätäsniemi, T. and Shemeika, J. (2020) 'A Semantic Data Model to Represent Building Material Data in AEC Collaborative Workflows', in Camarinha-Matos, L. M., Afsarmanesh, H. and Ortiz, A. (eds) Boosting Collaborative Networks 4.0: 21st ifip wg 5.5 working, Cham, Springer International Publishing.

Wachsmann, K. and Patzelt, O. (1989) Wendepunkt im Bauen, 1959th edn, Dresden, Verl. der Kunst.

Yin, H., Stack, P. and Menzel, K. (2011) 'Decision Support for Building Renovation Strategies', in Zhu, Y. and Issa, R. R. (eds) Computing in civil engineering: Proceedings of the 2011 ASCE International Workshop on Comupting in Civil Engineering, June 19–22, 2011, Miami, Florida, Reston, Va., American Society of Civil Engineers, pp.834–841.

Multi-Level LoD Parametric Design Approach in AEC for Robot-Oriented Construction

Adrian Schubert, Karsten Menzel, Nicolas Mitsch
Technische Universität Dresden, Germany
adrian.schubert@tu-dresden.de

Abstract. This paper aims to discuss early achievements in the development of integrated design and robot-based manufacturing potentially being used in the construction sector. Guided by cross-sectorial research efforts ("Industry 4.0") the emphasis of this paper is on the development of process integration between design and manufacturing. The goal is to demonstrate that the quality of digital building models can be improved using digital design processes in order to use a modelling approach supporting the automatic generation of robot control commands. The applicability of a Multi-Level LoD Parametric Design Approach (ML^2-PDA) is proposed and discussed. The paper illustrates the suitability of Parametric Design for the generation of geometrically highly complex parts. The approach leads to a reduction of subsequent efforts for manufacturing.
In a complementing paper the authors present early developments for modular robot systems, especially dedicated to the deployment in small and medium sized enterprises (SME).

1. Barriers to using robotics in the construction industry

The construction industry faces special challenges when planning its products - the buildings - since almost every building is unique. Well known symptoms characterizing the situation are: (i) architects usually start planning from scratch, (ii) it is expected that changes can be introduced very late (e.g. up to the construction phase, handover and even beyond). On top, the multidisciplinary way of working in the AEC-industry leads to models representing different planning stages for the same building at the same time. The result is a multitude of different models, all of which describe the same building and all of which must be kept up to date as far as possible. This "unstructured" planning approach seems to be a main reason why robotics has not made a significant contribution to efficiency gains in the construction industry in comparison to other industries, which have used robots for efficient production over numerous years (Bock and Linner, 2015).

Although Building Information Modelling is a major and necessary step in the direction of digitization of the building industry, the introduction of this technology seems to present the building industry with completely new challenges. Thus, in the future, specialist planners will need to be trained differently (Menzel and Otreba, 2020; Radisch et al., 2020; Rebolj et al., 2008). It appears that the initial workload of planners might increase. However, it is well known that so called drawing tasks will be replaced by automated generation of drawings from (3D) models (Keller et al., 2006).

Furthermore, the complexity of design tasks is increasing (Cahill et al., 2012). This is mainly due to the complexity and integrated nature of building services and energy technologies used. When it comes to topics such as energy efficiency (Manzoor et al., 2012), integrated, advanced control and operation (Manzoor and Menzel, 2011; Menzel et al., 2008), or life-cycle oriented design (Yin et al., 2011) it becomes obvious that consistent, comprehensive design methods will be required in the future.

Finally, the architectural development of organic structures with the use of free-form surfaces poses additional challenges to engineering (Syed, 2020). One possible consequence is an increasing complexity of construction details and assembly sequences (Moghaddam, 2020).

2. Application of Integrated Digital Design for Prefabricated Building Construction

Modular design and pre-fabrication technologies are well known for more than two centuries. Amongst others, architects like Fritz Haller or Konrad Wachsmann substantially contributed to the development of modular design and construction systems. Well known examples are the USM-system by Haller or the Packaged House by Wachsmann (Wachsmann and Patzelt, 1989). Whereas Haller and Wachsmann worked primarily with steel and wood constructions, later developments in France, Scandinavia or the Eastern European countries focused on the design and manufacturing of modular, pre-fabricated buildings using primarily concrete as the main material (1960ies to 1980ies).

More recently, the shortage of affordable housing in the U.K., Ireland, and the Netherlands has led to another wave of using prefabricated construction methods for residential buildings (Vogler and Eekhout, 2015). Modular, integrated design, off-site prefabrication and on-site assembly complemented by holistic, BIM-based digital design and documentation characterize these recent developments. Architects design different compatible and standardized building modules. Clients can then choose between different options and configure their building.

The above concept has several advantages. On the one hand, prefabrication allows the reduction of construction time on site. On the other hand, it increases the production quality of building elements, since they are manufactured under well-defined conditions. Furthermore, planning costs can be reduced, since not each built artefact has to be designed from scratch.

However, it is argued that the above concept has major disadvantages. It is said that the architectural freedom in the design of built-artefacts is severely limited, as existing building modules are repeatedly used. In their early stages, the production conditions were, due to economic constraints, optimized for mass-manufacturing and led to extreme repetitive usage of a limited number of building modules. In consequence, the scope for architectural development was restricted, less time was spent on the development of new concepts, and instead, existing systems were exhausted until their technical limits were reached.

Most recently the German Science Foundation (DFG) started the funding of four major research initiatives. Table 1 provides a brief characterization of these clusters.

Table 1: A birds eye perspective on relevant, major German research clusters

Innovation	EXC 2021 (Univ. Stuttgart, 2019)	SFB 1244 (Univ. Stuttgart, 2017)	TRR 277 (TU Braunschweig & TU München, 2020)	TRR 280 (TU Dresden & RWTH Aachen, 2020)
Materials & Systems	concrete, fibre-composite (fc)	adaptive systems	concrete, steel, wood	fibre concrete
Design Methods	integrated design	single activities	integrated design for additive manufacturing	invention engineering
Construction Methods	cyber-physical systems	n.a.	integrated BIM and 3D printing	generative construction
Ecology	n.a.	LCA	n.a.	sustainability evaluation
Workforce	new digital literacy	n.a.	n.a.	n.a.

Integrated, digital design and manufacturing processes have the potential to address and overcome the above described limitations. This integration offers possibilities for flexible, parametric design and seamless adaptation of manufacturing systems and the related production processes to a wide spectrum of design shapes and geometries. Thus, a broad variety of modular building components and systems can be realized without significant increase of required resources (e.g. cost, time required). The result is customizable production processes.

However, current research initiatives (see Table 1) are driven by either the development of new materials or systems or/and new design approaches. The integration between design, manufacturing and assembly is less intensively considered in this research.

3. Pre-requisites: Computational Design Methods in AEC

The term Parametric Design refers to an architectural design concept. Rules, constraints, features and associations between various parameters and objects are the basis for defining a model rather than a dedicated geometrical specification. This concept aims to support fast and efficient adaptation of the model by changing input parameters. Thus, the variables of the formulas have a decisive influence on the properties of a model (Aksamija et al., 2011).

In a parametric design process, the designer does not directly specify the geometry. Instead, he describes the shape by using parameters. Thus, different input parameters generate different solutions (Kolarevic, 2005). By setting certain constraints and rules, the entire solution space should correspond to the architect's concept.

The benefit of parametric design is the ability to process design alternatives ad-hoc. Due to the fast adjustment, input parameters can influence the parametric design's output not only according to aesthetic criteria but also to different design criteria. For example, Aksamija et al. describe that shading elements of a building can be easily altered and optimally designed, since the positioning can be executed based on building simulation calculations.

This allows finding the optimum between heat gains in winter, due to solar radiation through transparent components, and energy consumption in summer, caused by air conditioning systems. The integration of building simulation within the design phase of a building can reduce the overall energy consumption over the whole building's life cycle (Aksamija et al., 2011).

3.1 Level of Detail

For the ML²-PDA methodology (as presented in chapter 4) it is desirable to pick up and implement a well-accepted and defined structure for Level of Detail. In general terms, the acronym LoD describes the depth (or accuracy) of modelling. This relates to the geometrical model as well as to the information attached to it. BIMForum differentiates between Level of Detail (LoD) and Level of Development (LOD). The Level of Detail (LoD) describes the amount of detail in the model element. In contrast, the Level of Development (LOD) specifies the degree to which the element geometry and the attached information have been thought through. Thus, according to BIMForum, the LoD is considered the input for the element and the LOD is considered the reliable output (BIMForum, 2018).

Table 1 provides an overview of the different LOD specified by the BIMForum, which correspond to the BIM protocol documents of the American Institute of Architects (AIA). In general, the LOD is classified into the levels LOD 100 up to LOD 500.

Table 2: Description of LOD

LOD	Description
LOD 100	Elements in the model are represented using symbols or other generic representations; Attributes - e.g. costs/m² - can be derived from other elements *Non-geometrical representation, Indicates existence of a component - not the shape, size, position | Information should be considered as an approximation*
LOD 200	Representation of the element in the model as a generic system, object or assembly with approximate quantities, sizes, shape, position and orientation Non-graphical information can be attached to the element *Elements are generic placeholders, information to be considered as approximate*
LOD 300	Representation of the element as a specific system or object in terms of quantity, size, shape, position, orientation | Non-graphical information can be attached. *Quantity, size, shape, position, orientation of the element can be measured directly from the model*
LOD 350	Additionally, to LOD 300: presentation of the interface to other building systems *Modelling of parts necessary for coordination with adjacent or fixed elements* *Quantity, size, shape, position and orientation of the element can be measured directly from the model - without reference to non-modelled information*
LOD 400	Representation of the element in the model as a specific system, object or assembly in terms of quantity, size, shape, position and orientation with detail, manufacturing, assembly and installation information non-graphical information can be attached to the element *Modelling of the represented component with sufficient detail for the production*
LOD 500	field-tested representation in terms of quantity, size, shape, position and orientation non-graphical information can be attached to the element *not defined according to BIMForum*

Source: compare to (American Institute of Architects, 2013) and (BIMForum, 2018).
Italic: Interpretation according to BIMForum

4. Methodology: Multi-Level LoD Parametric Design Approach

An essential step towards overcoming the above problems is to strengthen the interaction between design and production. Model development should encompass the entire life cycle of the building, starting with a rough design model, continuing with the highly detailed production model, and ending with the validated digital twin (Ahmed et al., 2009; Menzel et al., 2009). One evolutionary, dynamic model should be developed for the entire life-cycle covering all modifications in a consistent way.

As addressed above, a central problem with the use of robotics in construction is the uniqueness of the product. In most industries, the economics of robotics are achieved through automation of repetitive tasks, e.g. on assembly lines in the automotive sector (Bock and Linner, 2015a). However, the authors of this paper argue that also highly detailed production models of the construction industry can be generated from digital building models for robot control. In case robot control commands are generated in an automated manner, robots can (pre-)manufacture highly complex components for reasonable cost within affordable time-slots. However, the so called human resources must be trained appropriately to avoid obstacles, such as reduced productivity, increasing error-proneness caused by inexperienced engineering personnel.

Automation of robot control would be conceivable if the consistency (and thus quality) of digital building models can be significantly improved. This means, in the course of digital manufacturing it is necessary being capable to generate digital production models even with high levels of detail. Even the smallest components, such as screw connections, have to be modelled and placed in three-dimensional digital models to enable meaningful documentation. Such precise building models can serve as a foundation for production models and manufacturing control. Therefore, a necessary step for establishing robotics in construction as a key technology is to reduce the modelling effort. Digital and computational design methods, such as Parametric or Generative Design, can contribute to this process. Instead of just proposing a cost shift from the construction phase to the planning phase, the authors argue for the introduction of a "Multi-Level LoD Parametric Design Approach" (ML^2-PDA). It is expected that the ML^2-PDA has the potential to reduce the modelling efforts of geometrical models using a very high LoD by using a so called hierarchically coupled, parametric design approach.

Jia et al. describe in their paper a so-called Product Multi-Level Parametric Design based on skeleton models (Jia et al., 2010). The approach provides for the development of a multi-level parametric design for product models on the basis of three steps.

Top-Down multi-level parameters decomposition and transfer: This is based on a product structure tree. A parameter inheritance structure is set up. A distinction is made between control parameters and inherited parameters.

Product multi-level parametric skeleton modelling: A parametric skeleton model of the product is created. First, models without geometry features are created. Then, the relationship from the multi-level parameter decomposition is taken up and implemented. In a final step, the 3D-geometry features of the skeleton model are created.

Parametric design of the product assembly: Based on the constraints of the skeleton model, the detailed designs of the parts are developed. This step includes setting of parameters of parts, elaboration of the relationships between the part parameters and the inheriting skeleton model, development of the geometry features, and finally the creation of relationships between the feature dimensions and the part parameters.

The authors would like to propose a comparable approach for civil engineering, the Multi-Level LoD Parametric Design Approach (ML^2-PDA). Instead of the described skeleton models, it would be useful for civil engineering to use different levels of detail. This has two advantages. On the one hand, for civil engineering the LoD is comparatively well defined. This ensures that the different development stages of a model are clearly regulated and thus provide for better cooperation between the different parties involved. On the other hand, due to the wide range of application scenarios for digital models in civil engineering, it makes sense to have access to a large number of different LoDs.

An example for ML^2-PDA is cost determination in the construction industry. Usually, one starts with a pre-contractual cost estimation based on the eventual construction volume. The deviation or bandwidth is usually about ± 40 %. In the cost calculation during the tendering process, which should be based on models that are as accurate as possible, the variation is only approx. ± 10 %. Only after procurement, the uncertainty of costs can be lowered further but still entails some uncertainties due to unforeseeable risks.

In the subsequent sections, we illustrate that by using digital and computational design the automatic generation of digital manufacturing models with a high LoD becomes possible. Starting with a low LoD digital BIM model containing building elements as single components enriched with meta-information. Additionally, we discuss how one can build a complementing, suitable data structure in order to use the generated components for robot control and to imply further knowledge from this data structure.

5. Early Verification: High-LoD Model Generation Utilizing Parametric Design

In this chapter, the authors demonstrate the capabilities of a parametric design approach to generate high-LoD models from low LoD inputs. It is shown that this design concept can drastically simplify design processes of high complex constructions.

The generation of high LoD models based on low LoD model inputs is shown in the example of a façade node for a curtain wall façade with a post-beam-system. As shown in Figure 1 (left), a low LoD architecture model was parametrically described. Based on this model, vectors from all intersection points can be extracted, as demonstrated in Figure 1 (right).

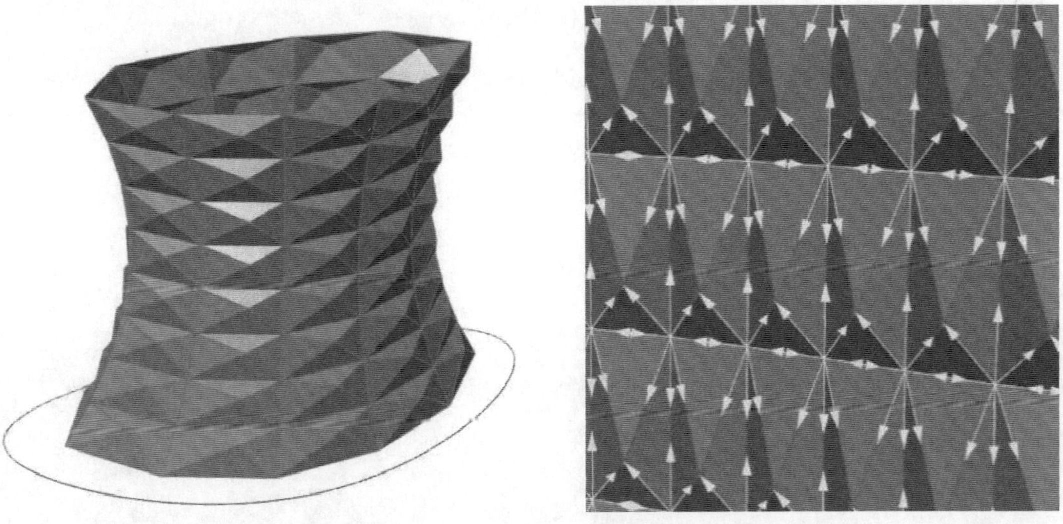

Figure 1: Design model (a) and extraction of vector data (b)

Figure 2 (left) shows the fully parametric façade node that can be controlled by the different input parameters. In Figure 2 (right) we present a control panel which was developed to adjust the parameters of the initial design. The upper five number sliders describe the constellation of the vectors from Figure 1 (right) as angles between those vectors.

In this case, a link between the architecture model and the product model of the parametric façade node was not implemented, but the vectors could be easily translated into those angular inputs.

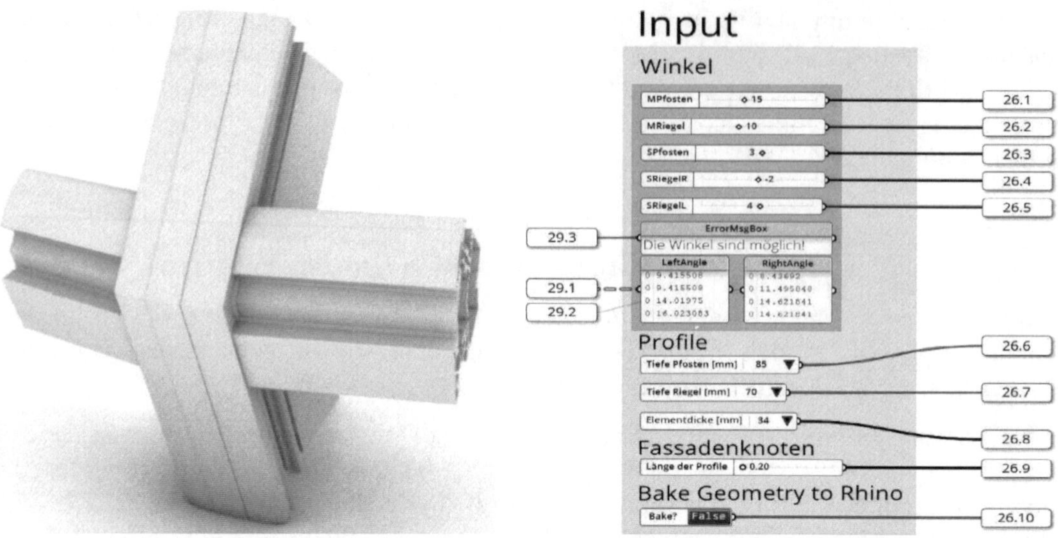

Figure 2: Digital façade node (left) and its input parameters (right)

Figure 3 (left) and (center) show, that the façade node consists of a variety of different elements. In this example, four profiles intersect with each other. Each profile consists out of up to seven different part types. Some parts are used two or four times, so that the total sum of single elements per node can sum up to 54 single elements, screws not included (Schubert, 2019).

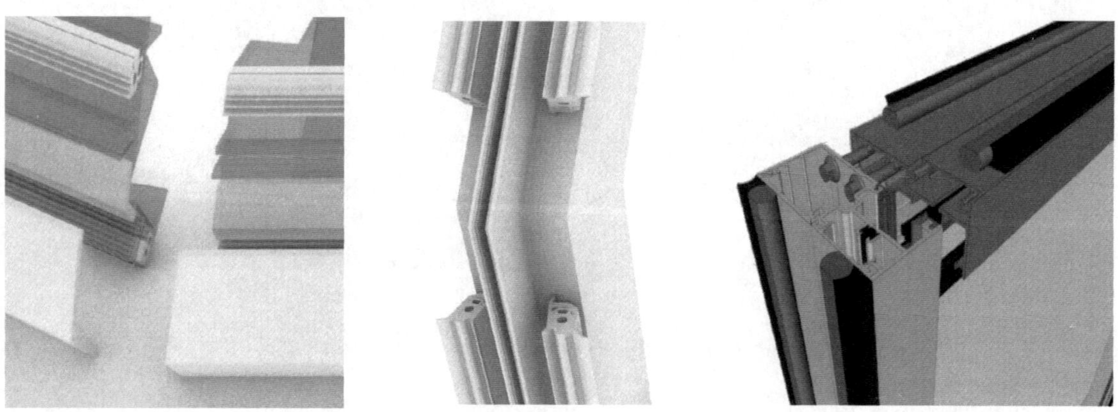

Figure 3: Components of a façade node (left, center), Window in LOD 400 (right) source: BIMForum

From a pure geometrical point of view the model shown can reach LOD 400, except for the missing screws. From an information based view (level of information), the model can reach LOD 300. This is because the current version of the parametric design model does not consider the interface to other building elements (e.g. ifcWall). Since this aspect was not modeled in our own work Figure 3 (right) represents a LOD 400 Model of a window, based on the definition provided in BIMForum (2018, S. 79 ff.).

Due to the very high level of detail, the digital model can be used as a starting point for production. Furthermore, the geometry can be used for additive manufacturing processes, as Strauß (2013) describes it on his Nematox Façade Node (Strauß, 2013). Finally, cutting information can also be obtained from the model. With the help of special profile cutting systems, precise cutting of the individual components would then be possible (Schubert, 2019).

For the entire construction industry, a top-down multi-level parameter decomposition and transfer schema could be developed and introduced, which is based on the definition of the LOD as well as the structure of the Industry Foundation Classes (IFC). Such an approach could facilitate the consistent use of exactly one digital model per building for the construction phase. This model could contain the different LODs and thus meet information requirements of different use case. The end-to-end use of only one model could reduce current problems, such as the recurring loss of data due to the necessity for multiple models. This would also have a positive effect on the increasingly important building documentation, since all development steps would be contained in the model. Finally, the documentation of manufacturing and assembly sequences are valuable information for maintenance, renovation, or deconstruction. It also provides the foundation for more advanced, service-oriented operation of buildings over their whole life-cycle in a circular economy (Allan and Menzel, 2009).

6. Future Work: Robot-Oriented Construction by Utilizing Digital Design Processes

In the course of further research, a fully automated production of functional component modules for a customizable construction method of wood frame constructions will be further investigated. Building elements, for example wall panels, are to be subdivided into components. Such components can be manufactured off-site and assembled on site.

Another promising approach is the intensive exploitation of semantic web and ontology-based modelling approaches (Valluru et al., 2020). The possible enrichment of BIM-models with rules allowing to develop further knowledge (conclusions) from the evaluation of initial design parameters supports the development of more holistic, more comprehensive and finally more consistent building models.

7. Conclusion

This paper presents a new method, the Multi-Level LoD Parametric Design Approach (ML^2-PDA). The method emphasizes on a close integration of parametric design and robotic manufacturing (see ch. 4). It is therefore distinct from other current research approaches (see ch. 2). The verification of the methodology is in its early stages. Initial demonstrations were developed as part of final year projects and Thesis delivered by graduate students (see ch. 5).

References

Ahmed, A., Menzel, K., Ploennigs, J. and Cahill, B. (2009) 'Aspects of multi-dimensional Building Performance Data Management', in Huhnt, W. (ed) Computing in engineering: EG-ICE conference 2009, Aachen, Shaker Verlag, pp.9–16.

Aksamija, A., Guttman, M., Rangarajan, H. P. and Meador, T. (2011) 'Parametric Control of BIM Elements for Sustainable Design in Revit: Linking Design and Analytic Software Applications through Customization', Perkins+Will Research Journal, vol. 03.01, pp.32–45 [Online]. Available at https://www.brikbase.org/sites/default/files/PWRJ_Vol0301.pdf (Accessed 15 March 2021).

Allan, L. and Menzel, K. (2009) 'Virtual Enterprises for Integrated Energy Service Provision', in Camarinha-Matos, L. M., Afsarmanesh, H. and Paraskakis, I. (eds) Leveraging Knowledge for Innovation in Collaborative Networks: 10th IFIP WG 5.5 Working Conference on Virtual Enterprises,

PRO-VE 2009, Thessaloniki, Greece, October 7-9, 2009. Proceedings, Berlin, Heidelberg, Springer-Verlag Berlin Heidelberg, pp.659–666.

American Institute of Architects (2013) G202-2013: Building Information Modeling Protocol Form [Online].

BIMForum (2018) Level of Development (LOD) Specification Part I and Commentary: For Building Information Model and Data [Online].

Bock, T. and Linner, T. (2015) Robot-oriented design: Design and management tools for the deployment of automation and robotics in construction, New York, NY, Cambridge University Press.

Cahill, B., Menzel, K. and Flynn, D. (2012) 'BIM as a centre piece for Optimised Building Operation', in Gudnason, G. and Scherer, R. (eds) eWork and eBusiness in Architecture, Engineering and Construction: ECPPM 2012, Hoboken, CRC Press, pp.549–555.

Jia, H., Wang, A. and Tang, C. ([2010]) 'Product Mutli-level Parametric Design Technology Based on Skeleton Model', in 2010 International Conference on Computer, Mechatronics, Control and Electronic Engineering (CMCE), pp.589–592.

Keller, M., Scherer, R. J., Menzel, K., Theling, T., Vanderhaeghen, D. and Loos, P. (2006) 'Support of collaborative business process networks in AEC', Journal of Information Technology in Construction, vol. 11, Special Issue Process Modelling, Process Management and Collaboration, pp.449–465 [Online]. Available at http://www.itcon.org/2006/34.

Kolarevic, B., ed. (2005) Architecture in the digital age: Design and manufacturing, New York, Taylor & Francis.

Manzoor, F., Linton, D., Loughlin, M. and Menzel, K. (2012) 'RFID based efficient lighting control', International Journal of RF Technologies, vol. 4, no. 1, pp.1–21 [Online]. DOI: 10.3233/RFT-2012-0036.

Manzoor, F. and Menzel, K. (2011) 'Indoor localisation for complex building designs using passive RFID technology', in XXXth URSI general assembly and scientific symposium, 2011: [URSI GASS 2011] ; 13 -20 Aug. 2011, Istanbul, Turkey, Piscataway, NJ, IEEE, pp.1–4.

Menzel, K., Cong, Z. and Allan, L. (2008) 'Potentials for radio frequency identification in AEC/FM', Tsinghua Science and Technology, vol. 13, S1, pp.329–335.

Menzel, K. and Otreba, M. (2020) 'Assessment methods in split-level (PBL)^2 for Building Information Modelling', in Guerra, A., Chen, J., Winther, M. and Kolmos, A. (eds) Educate for the future: PBL, Sustainability and Digitalisation 2020, Aalborg, Aalborg Universitetsforlag, pp.381–394.

Menzel, K., Tobin, E., Brown, K. N. and Burillo, M. (2009) 'Performance Based Maintenance Scheduling for Building Service Components', in Camarinha-Matos, L. M., Afsarmanesh, H. and Paraskakis, I. (eds) Leveraging Knowledge for Innovation in Collaborative Networks: 10th IFIP WG 5.5 Working Conference on Virtual Enterprises, PRO-VE 2009, Thessaloniki, Greece, October 7-9, 2009. Proceedings, Berlin, Heidelberg, Springer-Verlag Berlin Heidelberg, pp.487–494.

Moghaddam, K. S. (2020) Analysing trajectories and moments of a one-arm robot to pick up sheet metals and assemble a shell structure: Master Thesis, Technische Universität Dresden.

Radisch, T., Menzel, K., Schüler, J. F. and Möller, U. (2020) 'Cross disciplinary Project Based Learning', in Guerra, A., Chen, J., Winther, M. and Kolmos, A. (eds) Educate for the future: PBL, Sustainability and Digitalisation 2020, Aalborg, Aalborg Universitetsforlag, pp.369–380.

Rebolj, D., Menzel, K. and Dinevski, D. (2008) 'A virtual classroom for information technology in construction', Computer Applications in Engineering Education, vol. 16, no. 2, pp.105–114.

Schubert, A. (2019) Development of a methodology for the application of digital manufacturing in the construction industry using the example of a parametric façade node: Diplomarbeit, Technische Universität Dresden.

Strauß, H. (2013) AM Envelope: The Potential of Additive Manufacturing for Façade Construction [Online]. Available at https://www.researchgate.net/publication/307823959_AM_Envelope_The_potential_of_Additive_Manufacturing_for_facade_constructions/link/57d37e4208ae6399a38da79f/download (Accessed 15 March 2021).

Syed, F. M. (2020) Optimization of the manufacturing process for sheet metal panels considering shape, tessellation and structural stability.: Masterarbeit, Technische Universität Dresden.

TU Braunschweig & TU München (2020) Additive Manufacturing in Construction (AMC) [Online]. Available at https://www.tu-braunschweig.de/trr277 (Accessed May 2021).

TU Dresden & RWTH Aachen (2020) Konstruktionsstrategien für materialminimierte Carbonbetonstrukturen – Grundlagen für eine neue Art zu bauen [Online]. Available at https://sfbtrr280.de/ (Accessed May 2021).

Univ. Stuttgart (2017) Adaptive Hüllen und Strukturen für die gebaute Umwelt von morgen [Online]. Available at https://www.sfb1244.uni-stuttgart.de/ (Accessed May 2021).

Univ. Stuttgart (2019) EXC 2120 IntCDC: Cluster of Excellence 'Integrative Computational Design and Construction for Architecture [Online]. Available at https://www.intcdc.uni-stuttgart.de/ (Accessed May 2021).

Valluru, P., Karlapudi, J., Menzel, K., Mätäsniemi, T. and Shemeika, J. (2020) 'A Semantic Data Model to Represent Building Material Data in AEC Collaborative Workflows', in Camarinha-Matos, L. M., Afsarmanesh, H. and Ortiz, A. (eds) Boosting Collaborative Networks 4.0: 21st ifip wg 5.5 working, Cham, Springer International Publishing.

Vogler, A. and Eekhout, M. (2015) The house as a product, Amsterdam, IOS Press BV.

Wachsmann, K. and Patzelt, O. (1989) Wendepunkt im Bauen, 1959th edn, Dresden, Verl. der Kunst.

Yin, H., Stack, P. and Menzel, K. (2011) 'Decision Support for Building Renovation Strategies', in Zhu, Y. and Issa, R. R. (eds) Computing in civil engineering: Proceedings of the 2011 ASCE International Workshop on Comupting in Civil Engineering, June 19 - 22, 2011, Miami, Florida, Reston, Va., American Society of Civil Engineers, pp.834–841.

Design and implementation of an optimal sensor system as part of a Digital Twin for a rotary bending machine

D. Haag*, H. Beinersdorf, J. Winge, C. Könke
Bauhaus-Universität Weimar, Germany
daniel.haag@mfpa.de

Abstract. A sensor system is developed for the digital twin of a rotary bending machine. The sensor data is used on the one hand directly for condition monitoring and on the other hand as input variables for calculation and prediction models of the digital twin. A particular focus is the monitoring and prediction of kinematic, thermal and structural mechanical load conditions of critical components that rotate rapidly. The numerical models used to optimize the sensor system are the basis for the design of the (meta-) models of the Digital Twin.

1. Introduction

The concept of Digital Twins (DT) is one of the most significant technological trends of today, according to the market research company Gartner (Gartner, 2019). In the course of digital transformation, the DT is commonly regarded as a key technology, although there is no universally accepted definition of the term. In particular, the distinction between DT, the digital model and digital shadow is not used consistently (Kritzinger, 2018). An indispensable feature of a DT is the interconnection of the physical and the digital representation of an object (Qi, 2018) to a cyber-physical system, which happens with the help of sensors and actuators (Czinchos, 2019).

The paper describes a generalizable concept for the design and implementation of a DT of machines with rotating components focusing on predictive maintenance. An implementation of a suitable sensor system is shown using the example of a rotating bending machine. In order to minimize feedback effects between sensor and machine, contactless measurement technology is primarily used. The presented DT uses prediction models, which allow prognosis about the lifetime and the operating condition of critical components of the machine based on the sensor data.

2. Approach

The developed sensor system is adapted for a DT that describes the condition of a machine and can predict its behaviour in the future. The information and predictions on the machine state are based on the one hand directly on sensor data and on the other hand on model-based calculations. The simplified schematic structure of such a DT is shown in figure 1.

The real asset is supplemented by a sensor system, which provides the data required for the various models of the DT. The sensor data is recorded, filtered and undergoes the necessary conditioning at the location of the physical machine. In order to provide the measurement data independently of the asset, the approach of a cloud-based IoT platform was chosen. The sensor data required for condition monitoring and the following model-based calculations are transferred to the commercial IoT platform Siemens MindSphere© via a data interface. MindSphere is the cloud-based, open 'Internet of Things' (IoT) operating system from Siemens AG that connects products, plants, systems and machines and enables the use of data from the Internet of Things to be combined with extensive analyses.

The chosen implementation in the project (see figure 1) of a Digital Twin enables the provision of sensor data from the physical system and its cloud-based storage. Furthermore, the signal data can be used directly as an input variable in numerical calculation models or in meta models in combination with user input. The results of the model-based calculations can be further processed or visualised by transmitting them to the IoT platform as virtual signal data. The necessary communication generally is realised via the standard TCP/IP interface or, in particular, via REST-based web requests.

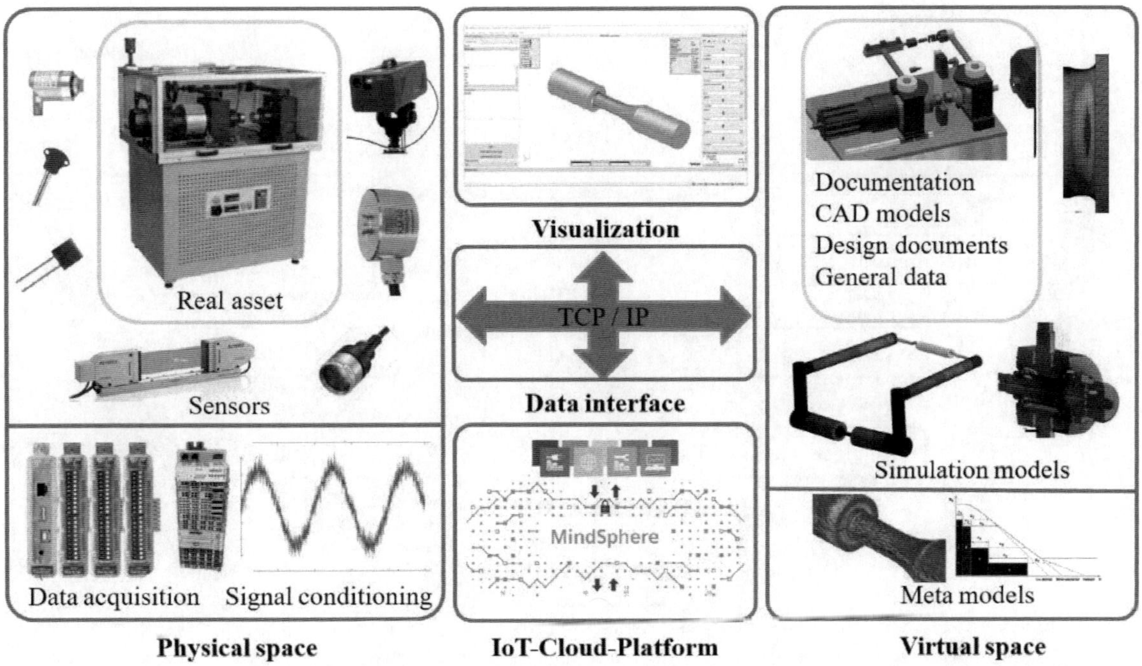

Figure 1: Illustration of the main components of the implemented Digital Twin. The connection of the physical and virtual spaces enables real-time access to sensor and model data at a central access point via IoT cloud platform.

The DT implemented in the project enables the monitoring of machine states (condition monitoring) as well as the calculation of service life estimation (predictive monitoring). The obtained data can show optimisation potentials for further or new developments of the real physical system. The sensor system is a crucial component and must be planned and designed as an integral part of the physical and virtual system (Digital Twin).

VDI Guideline 2206 (VDI 2206) served as orientation for the development and implementation of the Digital Twin. The guideline describes a methodology for the design of mechatronic systems. The schematic of the design and implementation process is shown in Figure 2.

The individual steps of the development phase as well as the implementation phase are usually represented in a V-shape. Starting from a development impulse, the first step is the description of the problem, followed by the development of a list of requirements. This is followed by the system and component development phases. This procedure is carried out for all physical and virtual components of the overall system which have to be developed. This includes the real asset, the sensor technology and the components required for the DT. The designed system is the result of the implementation of partial designs into an overall solution. Implementation is followed by virtual and physical testing of the subsystems, followed by validation and calibration of the individual components. The "V" shape illustrates that all solutions must be evaluated and verified against the original requirements. The procedure is monitored and evaluated by constantly checking all partial results and must be understood as an iterative process. The presented procedure is generally valid for all mechatronic systems and can be used in the same way for the subsequent extension of an existing machine with a Digital Twin (refitting).

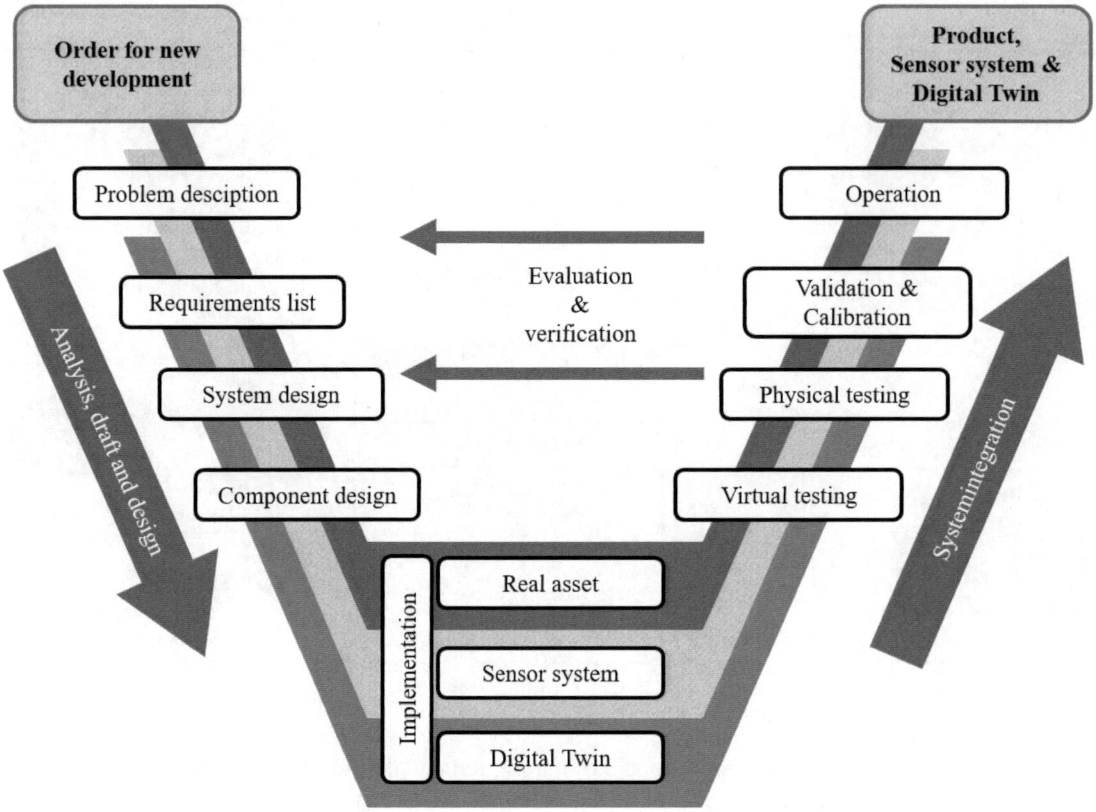

Figure 2: Phases of the development process of a technical product and its Digital Twin. Based on the V-model of VDI 2206.

The sensor system is the link between the real asset and the Digital Twin. Therefore, the requirements for the sensor system from both domains must be coordinated. To determine the requirements, an in-depth system analysis using Failure Mode and Effects Analysis (FMEA, Bertsche 2004) was carried out for the real asset to identify the most likely failure mechanisms of the critical system components. The identified components are to be monitored by sensors in such a way that the expected failure mechanisms can be observed. In the following, the selection, implementation and operation of the sensor system as well as the connection to the Digital Twin of a rotary bending machine are described.

3. Rotary Bending Machine

The research project focuses on machines whose main function is performed by loaded rotating components (generators, machine tools, turbo machines, etc.). A rotating bending testing machine from SincoTec (Power Rotabend 200Nm) was chosen as a demonstrator system for the implementation of a Digital Twin.

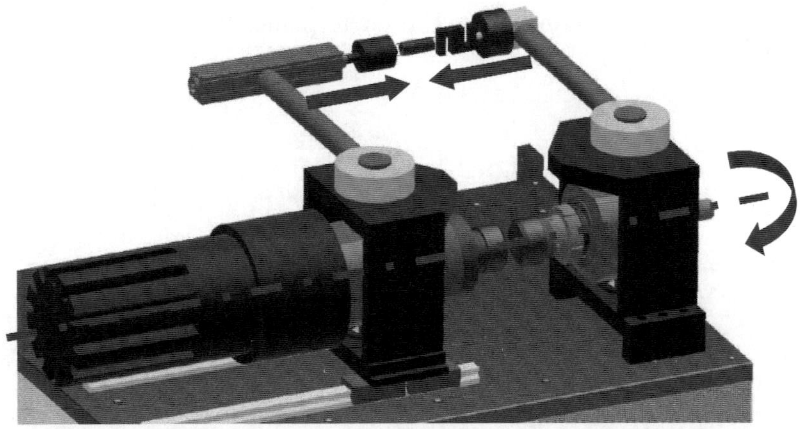

Figure 3: Rotary bending machine used for material testing.

The task of the testing machine is the characterization of materials. Especially for the determination of material properties and material parameters which describe the fatigue strength as well as the operational strength of a component. Figure 3 shows the CAD model of the used rotary bending machine. The two main components of the machine are a drive train with motor and a loading unit. The shaft is loaded by means of two lever arms. The drive unit essentially consists of two bearing units. The right bearing is fixed to the machine table. The left bearing side, on which the motor unit is located, can be moved on rails in axial direction of the shaft. The motor drives a shaft (component sample) that connects the two bearing units. The two lever arms of the load unit are connected by a linear motor and force measuring sensors. By shortening the distances between the lever arms through the linear motor, a force is applied to the lever arms. Mechanically, the shaft experiences a 4-point bending load. The testing machine is controlled by two separate control loops for the bending load and the rotational speed of the shaft.

The FMEA analysis revealed that the machine's shaft and bearings are the most critical components for machine reliability. The underlying damage mechanism of the shaft is component circumferential bending load, which causes material fatigue. Bearing wear represents the second system failure mechanism to be observed. The concentricity of the shaft and the dynamic behaviour of the machine have an influence on the stability of the test, which is critical with regard to the standard-compliant performance of the experiment (see DIN 50113).

4. Damage Model

As an example for the model-based development of a Digital Twin, the damage model of the shaft is described below. The fatigue strength of the component is used as the damage criterion for the shaft. The model development is based on the approaches of the FKM guideline (FKM, 2012). The basis for a service life estimate is the knowledge of load-cycle-dependent damage represented by a material-dependent Wöhler curve. To calculate the service life, the load spectrum of the stress measured over the entire shaft lifetime is required. The combination of a Wöhler curve and a damage accumulation hypothesis is used to calculate the damage of the shaft. In this example, the Wöhler curve was estimated using the "synthetic Wöhler lines (SWL)" method (Bergmann, 1999). For the steel shaft (shaft with undercut) made of 42CrMo4, the main SWL parameters are summarized in Fig. 4. A linear damage accumulation in the form of the "modified Miner rule according to Haibach" (Haibach 2006) was applied as damage accumulation hypothesis.

Wöhler curve exponent:	$k = 4.59$
Number of buckling load cycles:	$N_p = 270$
Number of Corner load cycles:	$N_{Ak} = 515800$
Fatigue strength:	$\sigma_{e,Ak} = 557.2\ MPa$
Wöhler exponent modified	$k^* = 2k - 1 = 8{,}18$

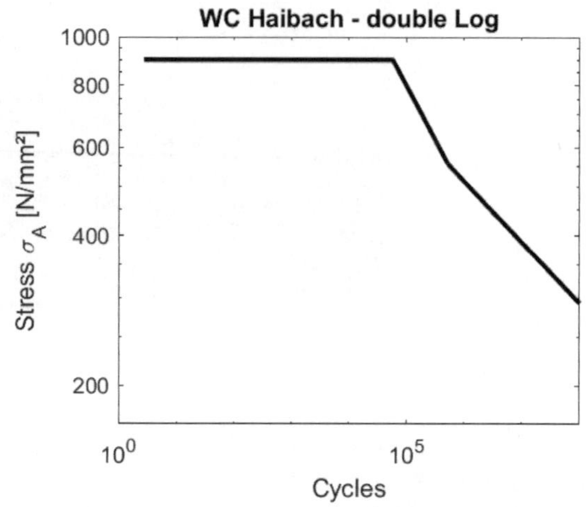

Figure 4: left: SWL results allow the construction of the Wöhler curve for the component, with respect to material, load situation and geometry of the shaft. Right: The diagram shows the Wöhler curve modified according to Haibach in a double logarithmic representation.

The damage D of the component is calculated according to the linear damage accumulation:

$$D = \frac{\sum n_i}{\sum N_i}$$

where N_i is the tolerable number of load cycles from the Wöhler curve, n_i is the occurred load cycles from the load spectrum and the index i indicates the stress class from the Rainflow count.

In the shaft design process, simple load assumptions are usually used for the load spectrum. The Digital Twin allows the load spectrum to be determined based on measured data. The load spectrum is generated from the measured signals using a rainflow counting procedure (FVA, 2010). The method is used to transform a spectrum of variable stress data into a classified equivalent set of damage-relevant hysteresis loops.

To determine the load spectrum, the stress at failure-relevant points on the shaft is required. Direct measurement of the stress is technically challenging due to the rotation of the component and the stress maxima usually located in areas of the shaft surface that are difficult to access (undercuts, bearing seats, thread runouts, keyways). In order to obtain the most accurate information about the condition of the shaft, the notch stress or equivalent strain is not measured directly, but calculated using a model approach. Theoretically, a numerical structural simulation of the stress on the shaft is required for each load combination and shaft geometry that occurs. In order to reduce the time required and to simplify the implementation in the Digital Twin, the simulation is replaced by meta models in the present approach.

The creation of the meta model was carried out by Ansys Dynardo within the research project cooperation with the software packages "Ansys optiSLang" and "Ansys Statistics on Structures". The meta model represents the relationship between the variation of input and resulting output parameters. The underlying parameterized structural mechanical model includes the variation of geometry, material parameters and bending load on the shaft. The stress and strain tensor form the output of the structural mechanics calculation and meta model, respectively. The meta model provides the results for the entire material continuum.

The implementation of the meta model in the Digital Twin is done by a server-client approach. The query of the meta model by the further components of the DT is enabled by web queries. Given knowledge of a (measured) loading condition (e.g. bending moment), the concept allows to derive the stress and strain distribution of the entire component. Accordingly, a load spectrum based on the measured component stresses is available at any point in the shaft's lifetime. The described approach can be adapted for any component, for any simulation model or model approach as well as damage model.

5. Sensor System

Based on the identification of the critical components and the requirements of the selected numerical models, see previous sections, the sensor system was developed and implemented. Additional requirements for the design process of the sensor system result from the construction of the existing testing machine, the safety-related requirements and the installation location. The sensor system has the task of providing measurement data, monitoring the machine condition, providing the manipulated variables for the control system and recording the required information for the Digital Twin. Additional requirements for the design process of the sensor system result from the construction of the existing testing machine, the safety-related requirements and the installation location. The sensor system has the task of providing measurement data, monitoring the machine condition, providing the control variables for the control system as well as collecting the required information for the Digital Twin. The procedure for selecting the right sensors and their implementation is addressed in various guidelines. The VDMA has published a brochure on the selection and implementation of sensors in the context of 'Industrie 4.0' digitalisation initiatives (VDMA, 2018). The sensor technology, available today, enables comprehensive monitoring of machine conditions. The complementary IT and software implementations are provided by the Digital Twin.

Figure 5 shows the sensor technology implemented on the demonstrator. In order to minimise the influence of the sensors on the existing system, non-contact measurement concepts are used. Contactless sensor systems are particularly advantageous on rotating components of the machine. The following section describes the individual sensor systems selected and their implementation.

For the damage model of the shaft described above, the stresses at the critical points and the number of load cycles are required. The necessary maximum stress on the shaft cannot be measured directly. To derive the stress from a model approach, knowledge about the load on the shaft is required. This is recorded with an additional load cell ((8) in Fig. 5). Furthermore, the measured force is one of the control variables for the operation of the machine and is used to keep the load condition constant or to switch off the machine. The actual state of the load is measured for the bending moment controller independently of the force monitoring system. From the measured force magnitude, the boundary conditions for the numerical models are derived and subsequently the true stresses are calculated with a model approach. The applied rotations are recorded with a rotary encoder ((6) in Fig. 5). The encoder enables the assignment of the high-resolution force measurement signals to an exact rotational position and the determination of the number of load cycles. The path of the linear motor, which is responsible for the load, is monitored with a capacitive displacement transducer ((7) in Fig. 5). The controller changes the travel of the linear motor so that the set load value is reached and maintained. The sensor enables statements to be made about changes in machine behaviour before the controller attempts to compensate for them. The applied load causes the shaft to deflect, which is measured without contact using a light strip micrometer ((3) in Fig. 5). The measured deflection can be used to calibrate the models to the load cell signal and monitor changes in shaft stiffness. In addition, unwanted vibrations of the shaft in the plane parallel to the machine table are detected.

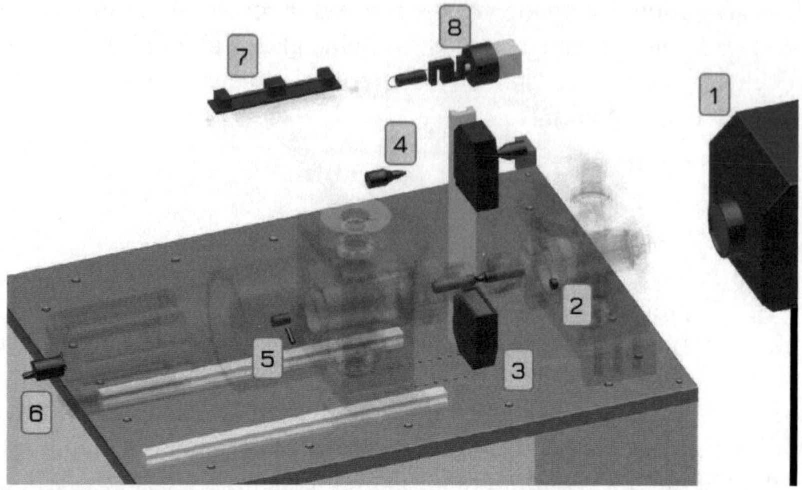

Figure 5: Sensor system for the rotary bending machine. Components: (1) laser Doppler vibrometer, (2) temperature sensor, (3) light strip micrometer, (4) confocal displacement sensor, (5) Engine monitoring (power, electrical key figures), (6) rotary encoder, (7) capacitive displacement sensor, (8) force load cell.

The selection of the measuring method depends to a large extent on the existence of suitable measuring points. In the case described, the measurement technology could be integrated without disturbing the function of the machine or endangering the measurement equipment. This was achieved by integrating the measurement technology into the machine elements (load cell, linear unit), using non-contact measurement technology or the use of models which act as digital sensors. The rigorous integration of (simulation) models into the development process results in additional degrees of freedom for the positioning of the measurement technology and the selection of measurement points.

The service life calculation of rolling bearings in the Digital Twin is based on the ISO 281 standard. Rolling bearing damage and its detection are a difficult subject and require a lot of experience. As source for an overview of damage mechanisms, their frequency and their effect on operating behaviour served a whitepaper from the Schaeffler FAG company (FAG, 2000), which was used to identify the crucial model parameters and operational features. The main input parameters for this model are the rotational speed curve over time, the load curve and the lubricant viscosity, which in turn depends to a large extent on the bearing temperature. The encoder ((6) in Fig. 5) records the time course of the rotational speed. The bearing load is calculated from the measured force ((8) in Fig. 5) via a static mechanical substitution model. The bearing temperature cannot be measured directly. It is obtained by a steady-state thermal simulation model from the temperature measurement on the bearing housing at rest ((2) in Fig. 5). The general procedure is analogous to the service life calculation of the shaft.

Possible wear of the rolling bearings can become noticeable through increased running noise and vibrations of the machine. These can be detected by a high-resolution measurement of the shaft vibration ((3) in Fig. 5) and the longitudinal vibration of the drive train by means of a laser Doppler vibrometer ((1) in Fig. 5). The measurement methods also detect a possible reduction in the operating accuracy of the bearings. This manifests itself primarily in a deterioration of the concentricity characteristics and can lead to alignment errors (radial and/or angular misalignment). Alignment errors can be detected in the frequency spectrum of the Laser

Doppler Vibrometer. Another characteristic of bearing damage is increased friction loss, which is often due to inadequate lubrication. Long-term increased energy consumption by the motor can be detected by monitoring the electrical characteristics of the motor ((5) in Fig. 5).

To ensure the reliability of the test results as well as the availability of the machine, dynamic vibrations during start-up of the machine or in the constant test run must be prevented or minimised. When the speed is ramped up, resonance frequencies are passed through which can cause the load system to oscillate. The detection of this oscillation and its effects are recorded by a confocal displacement measuring system ((4) in Fig. 5) on the lever arms of the rotating bending test machine. The measurement can be used to determine the absolute position of a single arm and the relative movement of the arms to each other. The evaluation of these measurement signals enables the characterisation of the dynamic machine behaviour for different operating conditions and the immediate optimisation of the machine settings as well as the optimisation of future testing machine design.

The coupling of all installed sensors is realized via a data acquisition system. The data acquisition system ensures communication with the widely varying measurement techniques as well as the analog and digital interfaces between the sensor system and the measurement data recording. The topology of the entire sensor system is structured by the data acquisition system (DAQ).For data acquisition, two DAQ systems are used in the demonstrator, which are connected via a bus system. The required sampling rate of the individual sensor signals depends on the observed physical quantity. Structural dynamic effects require a higher digital data resolution than, for example, temperature changes. Thus, temperature data can be recorded synchronously with a recording rate of a few Hz and laser signals with data rates in the GHz range. Signal conditioning is partly performed directly in the integrated sensor systems as well as in the data acquisition system. Signal conditioning includes signal conversion, linearization, signal amplification, filtering, averaging and signal evaluation. Sensor channels are stored directly at the DAQ (on edge) as well as in backup storage systems and directly in the IoT Cloud. For data acquisition, two DAQ systems are used in the demonstrator, which are connected via a bus system. The required sampling rate of the individual sensor signals depends on the observed physical quantity. Structural dynamic effects require a higher digital data resolution than, for example, temperature changes. Thus, temperature data can be recorded synchronously with a recording rate of a few Hz and laser signals with data rates in the GHz range. Signal conditioning is partly performed directly in the integrated sensor systems as well as in the data acquisition system. Signal conditioning includes signal conversion, linearization, signal amplification, filtering, averaging and signal evaluation. The sensor channels are stored directly at the DAQ (edge storage) as well as in backup storage systems and directly in the IoT Cloud. Further conditioning can be performed in the cloud or in the Digital Twin.

6. Digital Twin

At its core, the proposed Digital Twin fulfils three functionalities: It allows access to all relevant information about a real system (including meta-, sensor-, business-, and structural-data), enables simulations based on the available data and allows the visualization of data and simulation results.

These functions are accessed via the Siemens MindSphere IoT Platform, which thus acts as a user interface and are accomplished by means of independent program applications (apps) and data interfaces.

The required data is located on various computers, servers, storage media or a cloud. It is accessed via data interfaces provided by MindSphere. The data can be manipulated or visualized by other apps. Depending on the use of the data, for example the level of detail of a visualization or the update rate of a model, differently resolved data streams were realized. The necessary data reductions (e.g. averaging, collectivization) are performed in parallel to the data recording.

The simulation models employed can be called up by apps in MindSphere. Inputs can be sent to the models and outputs can be retrieved and visualized. The models themselves are hosted on independent servers or computers. As an example, the data flow for the calculation and display of the shaft life is outlined. The conditioned sensor data is stored in a time-series database. An app has access to this database and transfers the data together with the necessary metadata (material parameters, dimensions) to the damage model, which is hosted on a separate web server. The model performs the required calculations and sends the result to another database. There, other apps can access and visualize the data.

The visualization app for the demonstrator is provided by the project partner Orisa Software. The app is capable of visualizing data of different types and sources. The main task is the visualization the condition of the machine (condition monitoring), the provided measurement signals as well as the simulation results from the models of the Digital Twin. The user has access to metadata containing information about the machine, sensors and models. Figure 6 shows the 3D visualization of CAD data within the MindSphere framework.

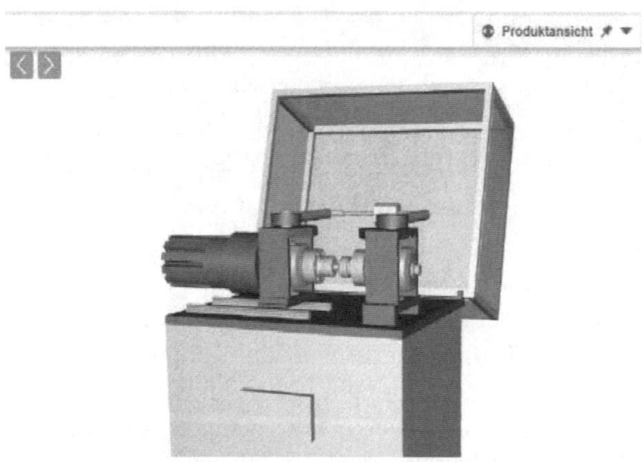

Figure 6: Visualization of CAD data within the DT. Image Source: Orisa Software GmbH.

The DT components presented are suitable for 'condition monitoring' and 'predictive maintenance' of the machine. In the future, the collected measurement data will be used to generate evaluations that can reveal optimization potential of the machine. The DT is designed modular, which allows easy expansion and replacement of components without rendering the DT incapable of working. The models enable physical quantities to be evaluated at locations without an associated sensor. This type of virtual sensors can provide a deeper understanding of the state of the machine.

7. Conclusion

By including the sensor system in the design phase of the DT, an optimal sensor system can be designed based on numerical models. The required models find direct use in the DT and can be used for condition monitoring or prediction of service life. The combination of proven procedures from the field of product development with novel field meta-models for the calculation of damage parameters allows real-time monitoring of the machine with the possibility of making predictions about future behaviour. In this approach, the Digital Twin and all its components (machine, sensor system, models) are considered as a coherent product. This ensures that all components and the overall system are developed and implemented optimally with regard to the requirements. Work is currently underway to standardize all the necessary data interfaces. The aim is to make all the necessary technologies of the Digital Twin widely available, especially for small and medium-sized enterprises, and thus to drive digitization forward.

Acknowledgement

The study, which is base for the present paper, was part of the research project "Wachstumkern VIPO - Digital Twin - product life cycle based on sensor networks and meta-models". The authors acknowledge the financial support by the Federal Ministry of Education and Research of Germany (BMBF) in the framework of VIPO (project number: 03WKDE03B)

In addition, special thanks goes to the project partners Andato GmbH & Co. KG, Orisa Software GmbH and DYNARDO GmbH.

References

Gartner (2019). Gartner study with 599 participants in six countries, Market research company, https://www.gartner.com/smarterwithgartner/prepare-for-the-impact-of-digital-twins/, acc. Dec 2020.

Kritzinger W., Karner, M. Traar, G. Henjes, J. Sihn, W. (2018) 'Digital Twin in manufacturing: A categorical literature review and classification', IFAC PapersOnLine 55-11(2018)1016–1022.

Qi, Q., Tao, F., Zuo, Y., Zhao, D. (2018) 'Digital Twin Service towards Smart Manufacturing', Procedia CIRP 72, 237–242.

Czinchos, H. (2019) ‚Mechatronik – Grundlagen und Anwendungen technischer Systeme', Berlin: Springer Vieweg, pp.333ff.

VDI-Fachbereich Produktentwicklung und Mechatronik (2004), Entwicklungsmethodik für mechatronische Systeme, VDI-Gesellschaft Produkt- und Prozessgestaltung, 29ff.

Bertsche, B., Lechner, G. (2004) ‚Zuverlässigkeit im Fahrzeug- und Maschinenbau', Berlin: Springer Verlag Berlin Heidelberg New York, 106ff.

Hänel, B. (publisher) (2012), ‚Rechnerischer Festigkeitsnachweis für Maschinenbauteile aus Stahl, Eisenguss- und Aluminiumwerkstoffen', FKM-Richtlinie, Frankfurt: VDMA-Verl.

Bergmann, J., Thumser, R. (1999), ‚Synthetische Wöhlerlinien für Eisenwerkstoffe', Forschung für die Praxis P 249, Studiengesellschaft Stahlanwendung e.V.

Haibach, E. (2006): ‚Betriebsfestigkeit: Verfahren und Daten zur Bauteilberechnung', Berlin: Springer-Verlag Berlin Heidelberg New York.

FVA Forschungsvereinigung Antriebstechnik e.V. (Hrsg.) (2010) ‚Zählverfahren zur Bildung von Kollektiven und Matrizen aus Zeitfunktionen, Frankfurt, 19ff.

VDMA & KIT wbk Institut für Produktionstechnik (2018), ‚Leitfaden Sensorik für Industrie 4.0', VDMA Verlag GmbH.

Schaeffler FAG (2000), ‚Wälzlagerschäden', Publication No.: WL 82 102/2 DA, https://www.schaeffler.de/remotemedien/media/_shared_media/08_media_library/01_publications/schaeffler_2/publication/downloads_18/wl_82102_2_de_de.pdf, acc. Nov. 2020, 12f.

The Effects of Fracture Energy on the Interfacial Strength of Self-Healing Concrete

John Hanna
Bauhaus University Weimar, Germany
john.nabil.mikhail.hanna@uni-weimar.de

Abstract. The effects of interfacial fracture energy and strength on fractured microcapsule are investigated computationally. The proposed models based on the combination of eXtended Finite Element Method (XFEM) and cohesive surface techniques to represent the interaction between the microcapsule and the concrete matrix and predict crack propagation under a uniaxial tensile test. Special attention is given to study the effects of interfacial fracture energy and strength on the interaction surface between the microcapsule and the concrete matrix, on the load carrying capacity and fracture probability of the microcapsule. The effect of interfacial strength on microcapsule is found to be significant factor on the load carrying capacity and crack propagation pattern. The interfacial fracture energy has no effect on the load carrying capacity of the specimen, but it effects on the fracture pattern and deboning of the microcapsule.

1. Introduction

The development of self-healing concrete (SHC) has recently attracted a lot of attention due to its inherent ability of automatic crack detection and crack repair with the goal of significantly prolong the service life and reduce the cost of maintenance (Souradeep & Kua, 2016). There are a lot of laboratories studies and experiments were done to study either the fracture interaction between the capsules and the concrete matrix or the healing efficiency and healing performance such as (Snoeck, Malm, Cnudde, Grosse, & Tittelboom, 2018). Recently a lot of computational modeling in SHC is done to study the fracture interaction between the capsules and the concrete matrix with different modeling techniques; using cohesive elements (Mauludin, Zhuang, & Rabczuk, 2018) and using XFEM with cohesive surface which showed high accuracy (Gilabert, Garoz, & Paepegem, 2017). Both techniques focused about studying the effects of the interfacial strength between the capsule and the matrix, capsule radius to thickness ratio, and capsules distribution based on the traction-separation law with regarding to damage evolution of the fracture energy.

Studies on crack healing pattern are more important when incorporated in research on design of self-healing structure because different positioning of healing capsules can lead to different crack healing pattern. In addition there are possibilities where fully bonding is not established in the interfacial zone because surface material properties of the capsules are changed during storing or manufacturing process. In order to model the complicated fracture processes in the multiphase specimen, XFEM technique is used to perform damage analysis for the polymeric microcapsules. The scope of this study is, to understand the effects of the interfacial fracture energy with regarding to the interfacial strength of contact surface between the capsule and the concrete matrix and the reliability of fracture or deboning of the capsule in so-called encapsulation-based self-healing cementitious materials. The efficiency of encapsulation-based self-healing material strongly depends on the leakage of the healing fluid, and this can only be achieved with the breakage of microcapsule. According to the best knowledge of author, it is difficult to find numerical simulation study in the literature discussed about the effects of both main parameters of the interfacial surface between capsule shell and the concrete matrix, these are the bond strength and fracture energy. One of the key novelties from this study is to investigate the effects of interfacial fracture energy on the fracture of microcapsules.

In this study numerical simulations of 2D rectangular plate with single circular microcapsule embedded in a concrete matrix are conducted. Both concrete matrix and the capsule modeled by XFEM elements and combined through cohesive surfaces technique. The specimen is loaded under uniaxial tension. The initial edge-crack length was proposed in order to force the crack to propagate in the capsule zone.

2. XFEM and Cohesive Surface Techniques

The modeling carried out with combination of two computational techniques. The first, the eXtended Finite Element Method (XFEM) to model the crack propagation in the concrete matrix and the capsule shell. The second, the cohesive surface to model the interaction interface surface between the concrete and the capsule. Actually both techniques are governed by a traction-separation law. The eXtended Finite Element Method (XFEM) is used with enrichment terms are added to the normal displacement interpolation, so a crack within an element can be described without the requirement for re-meshing. The enrichment functions, which make the crack independent of the mesh, are expressed as the approximation for a displacement vector function (u), and are written as following (Moës, Dolbow, & Belytschko, 1999):

$$u = \sum_{I \in N} N_1(x) + \left[u_I + H(x)a_I + \sum_{\alpha=1}^{4} F_\alpha(x) b_I^\alpha \right] \qquad (1)$$

$N_I(x)$ is associated with nodal shape functions, u_I is nodal displacement vector, H(x) is associated with discontinuous jump functions to form the crack path, a_I is vector of the nodal enriched degree of freedom, $F_\alpha(x)$ is associated with the crack-tip functions to develop cracks at the tip and b_I^α is the vector of the nodal enriched degree of freedom.

3. Traction-Separation Law

3.1 Damage initiation

For XFEM technique, the damage initiation is defined as part of the material properties, using damage for traction-separation law. There are a lot of damage initiation criterion are available such as Maximum Principal Stress (Maxps) Damage which is used in this paper. With this option, damage will initiate when the maximal principal stress exceeds the critical value. Figure 1 shows the traction-separation response in the normal direction to the crack faces. A crack can appear in the centroid of any element of the mesh when the maximum principal stress calculated in its integration points satisfies the criterion of eq. (2). A more specific description of these techniques can be found in ref. (Dassault Systémes Simulia Corp., Providence, RI, USA., 2016).

$$max\left\{0, \frac{\sigma_{maxps}}{\sigma^*}\right\} \geq 1 \qquad (2)$$

Where σ_{maxps} stands for the calculated maximum principal stress and σ^* stands for the maximum strength of the material.

3.2 Damage evolution

For XFEM technique, the damage evolution law describes the rate at which the cohesive stiffness is degraded once the corresponding initiation criterion is reached. A scalar damage variable, D, represents the averaged overall damage at the intersection between the crack surfaces and the edges of cracked elements. It initially has a value of 0. If damage evolution is modeled, D monotonically evolves from 0 to 1 upon further loading after the initiation of damage. Either the maximal displacement or the fracture energy, which is the area under the curve in a graph of traction versus separation, must be specified (Dassault Systémes Simulia Corp., Providence, RI, USA., 2016).

$$t_n = t_n^* \left(1 - \frac{\delta_n}{\delta_n^*}\right) \tag{3}$$

$$D = 1 - \frac{\delta_n}{\delta_n^u}\left(\frac{\delta_n^* - \delta_n^u}{\delta_n^* - \delta_n}\right) \tag{4}$$

$$\tilde{t}_n = \begin{cases} (1-D)t_n & if\ t_n \geq 0 \\ t_n & if\ t_n < 0\ (compression) \end{cases} \tag{5}$$

Where t_n is the normal traction acting between both crack faces, t_n^* is the maximum allowable stress at fracture initiation, $\tilde{t}_n$ is the unloading value of the normal traction, δ_n is the current normal distance between the crack faces, δ_n^* is the length of the cohesive interaction and δ_n^u indicates the crack opening just before unloading.

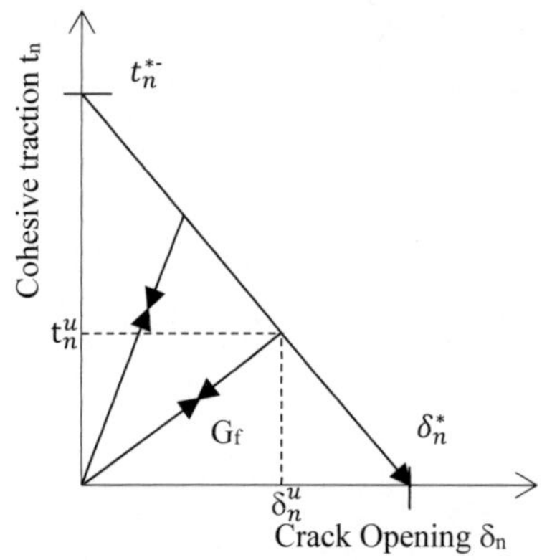

Figure 1: Traction-separation response.

For the cohesive surface technique, is defined as part of interaction and the above mentioned traction-separation law used to model the interaction surface between the concrete and the capsule, which has a zero thickness region that contains only the surface pairs initially in contact. Unlike the treatment for XFEM above mentioned, both the initiation and propagation criteria are integrated in the same formulation. More generally, the initiation criterion is fulfilled when the eq. (6) is satisfied. A more specific description of these techniques can be found in ref. (Dassault Systémes Simulia Corp., Providence, RI, USA., 2016)

$$max\left\{max\left\{0, \frac{t_n}{t_n^*}\right\}, \frac{|t_s|}{t_s^*}, \frac{|t_t|}{t_t^*}\right\} = 1 \tag{6}$$

Where the subscripts n, s, t stand for normal, shear, and tangential components of the interfacial stress. The superscript * represents the maximum strength.

4. Numerical Simulations

Numerical simulations of 2D rectangular plate with single circular microcapsule embedded in a concrete matrix are conducted. The specimen is loaded under uniaxial tension. The dimensions of this plate are 50 mm x 25 mm and the diameter of microcapsule is 2 mm with shell thickness 0.1 mm. The initial edge-crack length was fixed to 4 mm. The schematic of this plate complete with the boundary conditions is shown in Figure 3. Uniform displacements 0.1 mm was applied on the top surface of the specimens. The simulation was done in Abaqus/Static and the samples are meshed with Q4 elements assuming plane stress conditions.

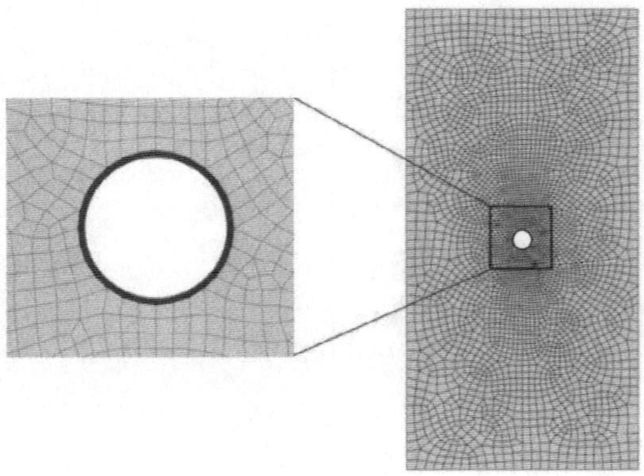

Figure 2: The meshing of the sample.

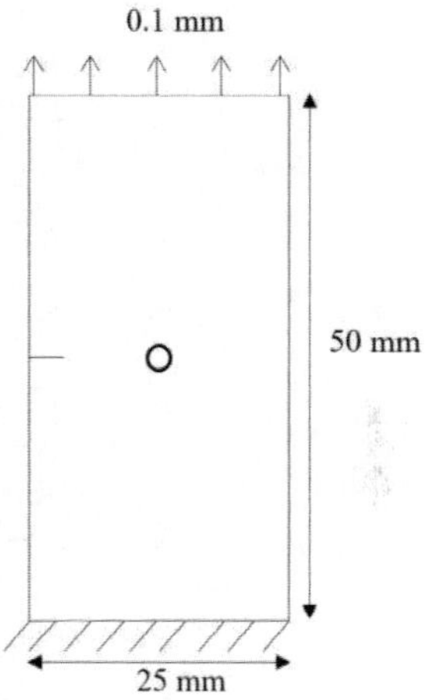

Figure 3: Schematic sketch of rectangular plate model.

In order to establish the degree of mesh refinement required to obtain reliable results, several preliminary calculations using a notched sample without microcapsule have been studied. Overall, all element sizes here tested are well below the value ruled by the critical element size discussed in reference (A. Hillerborg & P.-E., 1976). The outer size mesh of the matrix 1 mm, the single bias seed technique used in order to grantee the smooth mesh transitio n between the outer coarse mesh and the inner fine mesh around the microcapsule opening max. 1 mm and min. 0.2 mm and the circumferential length 0.25 mm around the microcapsule opening. The recommendations for meshing capsules according to (Gilabert, Garoz, & Paepegem, 2017) has been considered and the number of elements through the thickness of the microcapsule was fixed to 4 and the circumferential length 0.05 mm to compromise between accuracy and computational effort as shown in Figure 2. All the material properties used based on (Mauludin, Zhuang, & Rabczuk, 2018; Hilloulin, Tittelboom, Gruyaert, Belie, & Loukili, 2015; Quayum, Zhuang, & Rabczuk, 2015; Wang, 2015) are listed in Table 1. Their parameters are then represented by the Young's modulus (E), Poisson's ratio (ν), maximum tensile strength (σ^*), and fracture energy (G_f).

5. Parametric Studies

In encapsulated-based self-healing system, the breakage of microcapsule is important. The maximum interface tensile strength σ^* which referred to bonding strength and the interfacial fracture toughness which referred to the fracture energy G_f are the most significant components governing the cohesive model. When traction-separation law is used along with linear softening, the failure separations can be directly calculated from the fracture energy G_f.

In order to investigate the effects of interfacial strength and fracture energy of microcapsule shell, parametric studies of six different material inputs for σ^* and G_f were carried out. The default values of material parameters in Table 1 are assigned to cohesive surface between microcapsule shell and concrete matrix (i.e., the interfacial transition zone, itz). Only two parameters, namely, $\sigma^*$and G_f for microcapsule shell and concrete interfaces (itz) were varied relative to the properties of the concrete for each simulation while the other parameters were fixed. Also to study the effects of the interface fracture energy G_f on the interfacial strength, we varied the values of G_f while the interfacial strength remains fixed with other parameters as well.

Table 1: The material properties.

	E (MPa)	**ν**	**σ* (MPa)**	**G_f (N/mm)**
Concrete	25000	0.2	6	0.06
Capsule	3600	0.3	10	0.1
Interface	-	-	6	0.06

6. Results and Discussion

6.1 Effects of fracture properties on the load carrying capacity

Figure 2 shows the effects of variation in fracture properties of the interface (itz) on the load carrying capacity from six samples with different itz values. It is obvious that the specimen strength is highly influenced by interfacial cohesive strength. Figure 2 shows the strength of the interfacial zone (itz) ranging from 0.3 MPa (i.e., 5% of concrete strength) to 6.0 MPa (same as concrete matrix) and Likewise fracture energy of the interfacial zone (itz) ranging from 0.003 N/mm (i.e., 5% of concrete fracture energy) to 0.06 N/mm (same as concrete matrix). It is obvious that the strength of itz is the dominant factor governing the specimen strength. The specimen strength jumps from 104.1 N for itz = 5% to 105.6 N for itz = 100%. It is clear that when the cohesive strength on the interface of microcapsule and the concrete matrix are the same, the specimen strength will reach the higher value. It can be seen from the curves that the higher the itz strength, the larger the load carrying capacity is and vice versa.

Figure 3 shows the force displacement curves with different G_f values with respect to fixed interfacial strength value. For example Figure 3 (a) shows the force displacement curves with different G_f values ranging from 0.06 N/mm (i.e., 100 % of concrete fracture energy) to 0.003 N/mm (i.e., 5% of concrete fracture energy) with respect to interfacial strength σ^* value 6.0 MPa (same as concrete matrix). From Figure 3 (a) can be easily noticed that the curves are coinciding and the peak force is the same 105.6 N regardless the value of G_f. The same principle applied for Figure 3 (b), (c), (d), (e), and (f) except the peak force changes with respect to interfacial strength from 105.59 N for σ^* = 75% to 103.86 N for σ^*= 5%. So, it is obvious that the interfacial fracture energy has no effect on the load carrying capacity of the specimen.

Figure 4 shows the force displacement curves with different σ^* values with respect to fixed interfacial fracture energy. For example Figure 4 (a) shows the force displacement curves for interfacial fracture energy 0.06 N/mm (same as concrete matrix) with different σ* values ranging from 6 MPa (i.e., 100 % of concrete strength) to 0.3 MPa (i.e., 5% of concrete strength). The specimen strength jumps from 104.1 N for σ* = 5% to 105.6 N for σ* = 100%. The same principle applied for Figure 3 (b), (c), (d), (e) and (f). So, it is obvious that the interfacial strength is the dominant factor governing on the load carrying capacity of the specimen.

6.2 Effects of fracture properties on the crack pattern

Figure 5 shows the effects of variation in fracture properties of the interface (itz) on the crack pattern for specimen with ratio itz 100%, 75%, 50%, 25 %, 10 % and 5% of concrete matrix properties respectively. The fracture properties of the interface (itz) is calculated as percentage to the properties of concrete matrix. The samples with itz 100%, 75%, and 50% produced the same crack paths and the approaching crack could break the microcapsule which can be observed from Figure 5 (a), (b), and (c). When the percentage of itz with respect to the strength of the concrete matrix ranging from 0%–25%, an interfacial crack occurs and the microcapsule is deboned from the concrete matrix as illustrated in Figure 5 (d), (e) and (f).

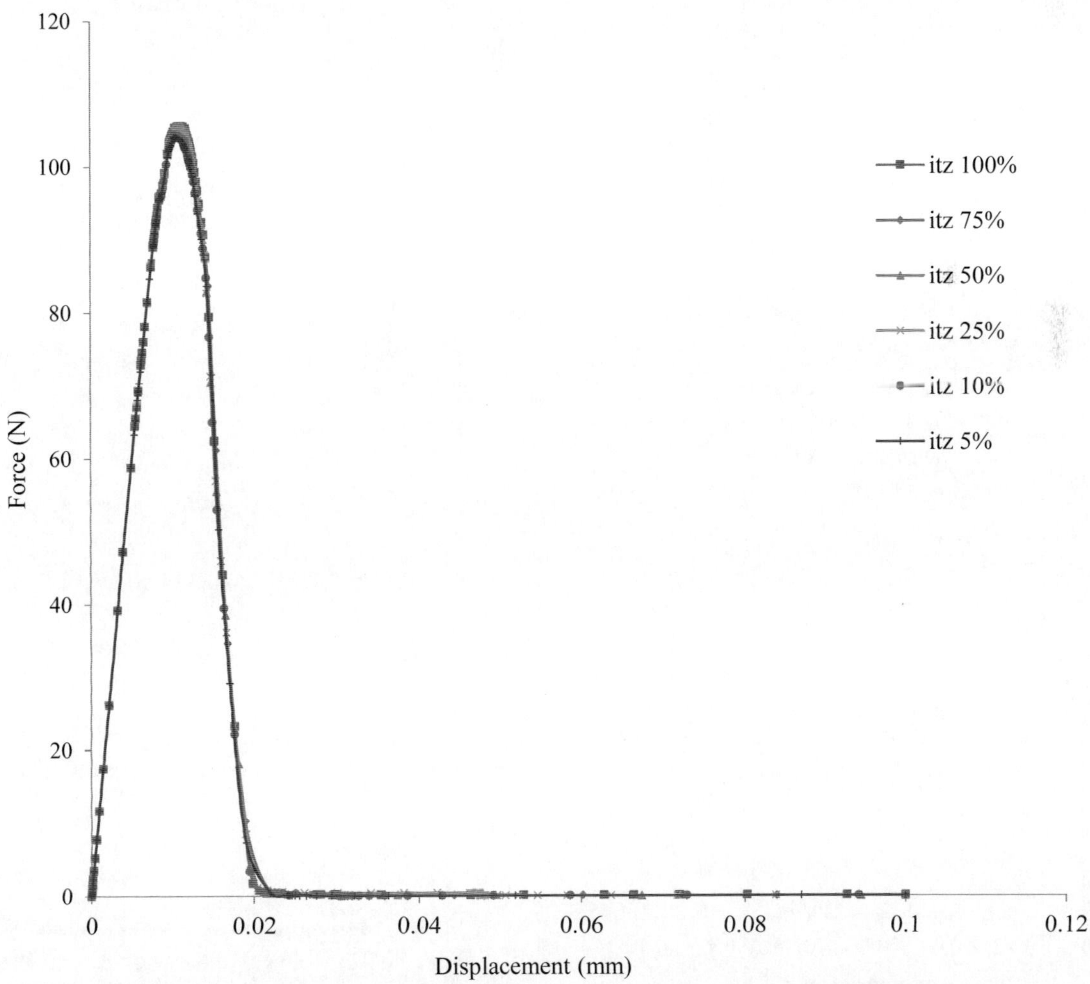

Figure 2: Force displacement curves with different itz values.

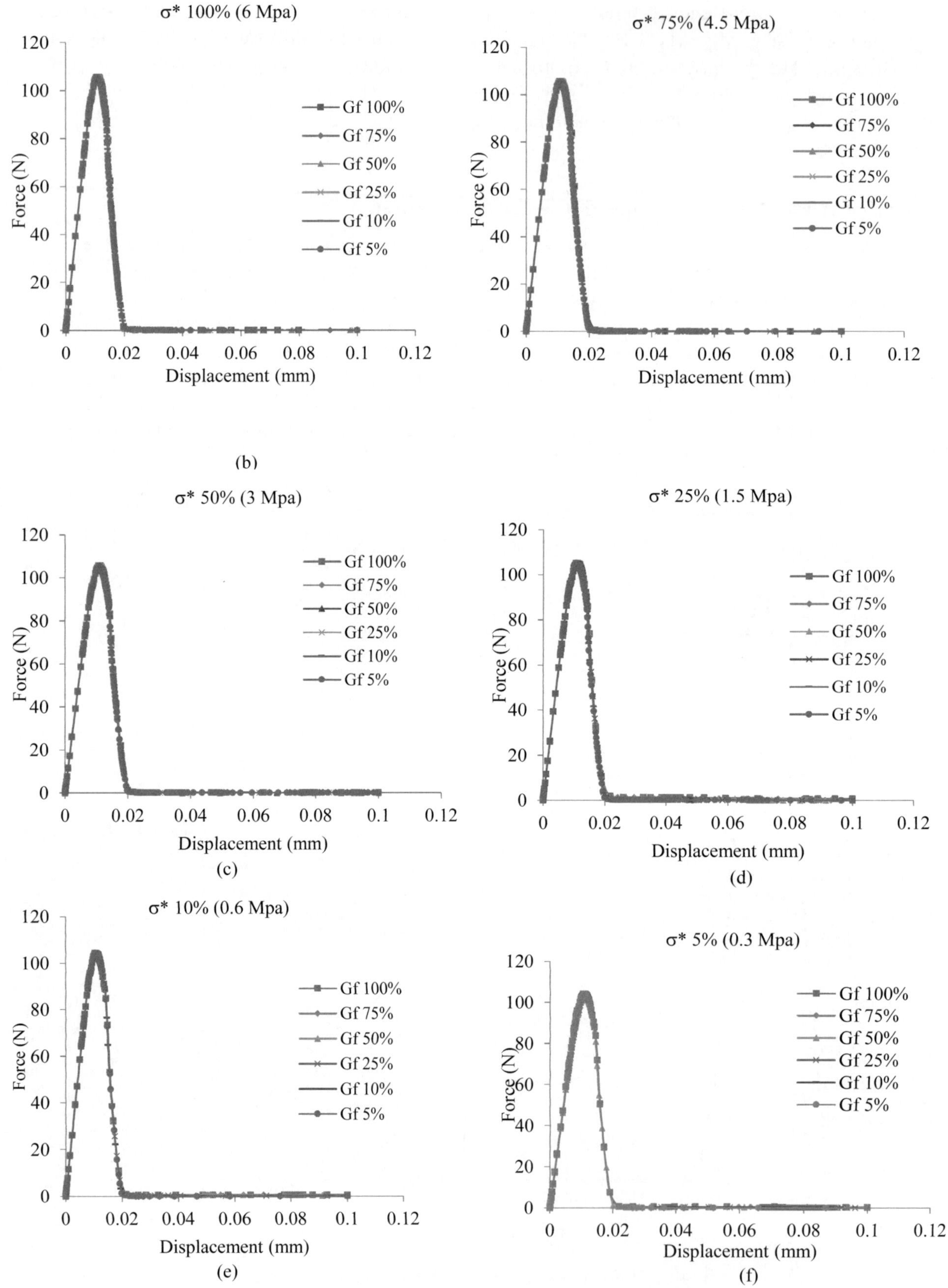

Figure 3: Force displacement curves with different G_f values. (a) σ* 100% (b) σ* 75% (c) σ* 50% (d) σ* 25% (e) σ* 10% (f) σ* 5%

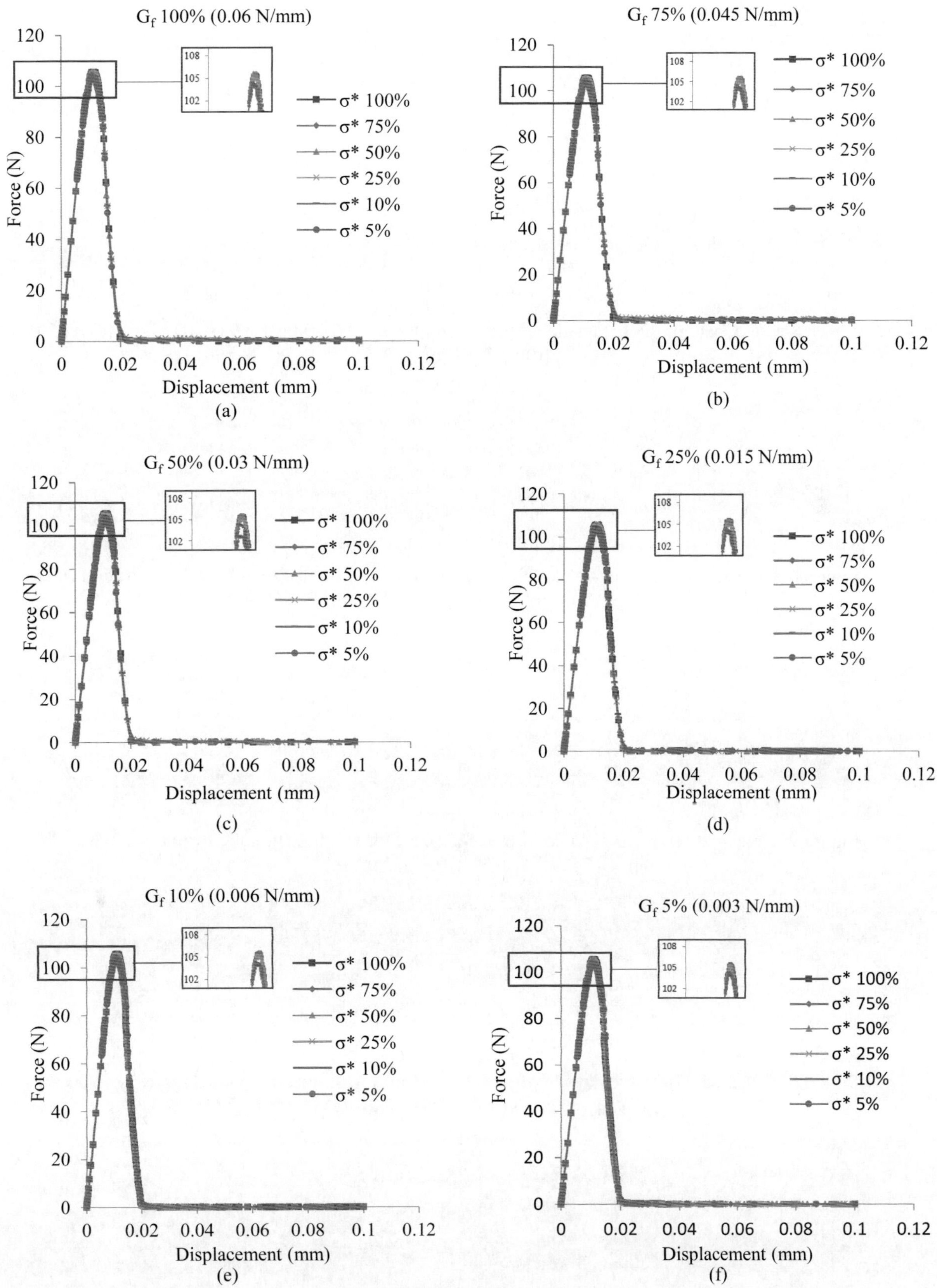

Figure 4: Force displacement curves with different σ* values. (a) G_f 100% (b) G_f 75% (c) G_f 50% (d) G_f 25% (e) G_f 10% (f) G_f 5%

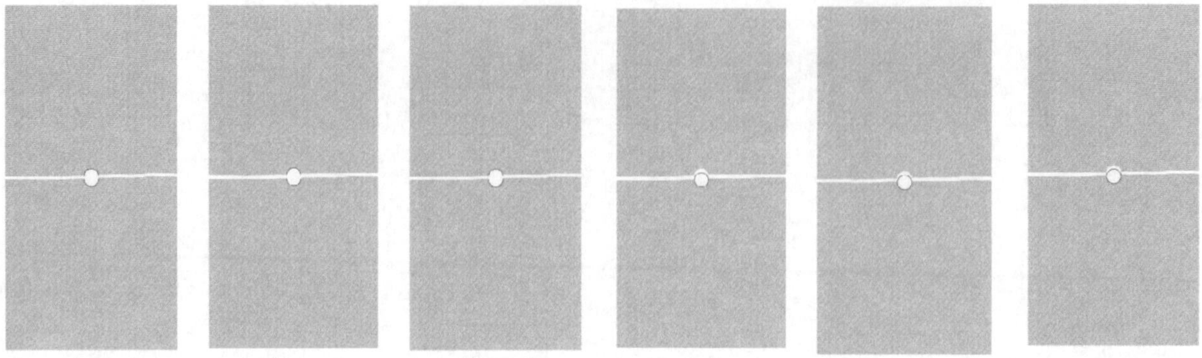

(a) (b) (c) (d) (e) (f)

Figure 5: Crack pattern microcapsule with different itz values. (a) itz 100% (b) itz 75% (c) itz 50% (d) itz 25% (e) itz 10% (f) itz 5%

(a) (b) (c) (d) (e) (f)

Figure 6: Crack pattern microcapsule of σ* 100% (6 Mpa) with different G_f values. (a) G_f 100% (b) G_f 75% (c) G_f 50% (d) G_f 25% (e) G_f 10% (f) G_f 5%

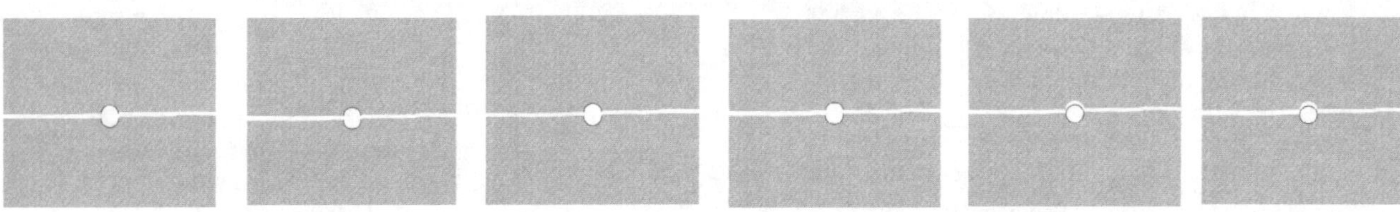

(a) (b) (c) (d) (e) (f)

Figure 7: Crack pattern microcapsule of σ* 75% (4.5 Mpa) with different G_f values. (a) G_f 100% (b) G_f 75% (c) G_f 50% (d) G_f 25% (e) G_f 10% (f) G_f 5%

(a) (b) (c) (d) (e) (f)

Figure 8: Crack pattern microcapsule of σ* 50% (3 Mpa) with different G_f values. (a) G_f 100% (b) G_f 75% (c) G_f 50% (d) G_f 25% (e) G_f 10% (f) G_f 5%

(a) (b) (c) (d) (e) (f)

Figure 9: Crack pattern microcapsule of σ* 25% (1.5 Mpa) with different G_f values. (a) G_f 100% (b) G_f 75% (c) G_f 50% (d) G_f 25% (e) G_f 10% (f) G_f 5%

(a) (b) (c) (d) (e) (f)

Figure 10: Crack pattern microcapsule of σ* 10% (0.6 Mpa) with different G_f values. (a) G_f 100% (b) G_f 75% (c) G_f 50% (d) G_f 25% (e) G_f 10% (f) G_f 5%

(a) (b) (c) (d) (e) (f)

Figure 11: Crack pattern microcapsule of σ* 5% (0.3 Mpa) with different G_f values. (a) G_f 100% (b) G_f 75% (c) G_f 50% (d) G_f 25% (e) G_f 10% (f) G_f 5%

Figure 6 shows the effects of variation in fracture energy of the interfacial G_f on the crack pattern for specimen with ratio G_f 100%, 75%, 50%, 25 %, 10 % and 5% of matrix fracture energy respectively while the interfacial strength is remains fixed 6 MPa (i.e., 100 % of concrete strength). The samples with G_f 100%, 75%, 50%, and 25% produced the same crack paths and the approaching crack could break the microcapsule which can be observed from Figure 6 (a), (b), (c), and (d). When the percentage of interfacial G_f with respect to the fracture energy of the concrete matrix ranging from 0%–10%, an interfacial crack occurs and the microcapsule is deboned from the concrete matrix as illustrated in Figure 6 (e) and (f). An interesting fracture pattern occurred when G_f 10% as the incoming crack that reaches microcapsule shell initially become an interfacial crack and suddenly break the capsule shell from the other side, as illustrated in Figure 6 (e). That means a partial fracture crack developed when the interfacial strength is high value (i.e., 100 % of concrete strength) and fracture energy is low value (i.e., 10 % of concrete fracture energy). Figure 7 and Figure 8 show that interfacial strengths ranging from 75% - 50% of matrix strength have the same crack pattern; the samples with interfacial G_f 100%, 75%, 50%, and 25% of matrix fracture energy produced the same crack paths as the approaching crack could break the microcapsule which can be observed from Figure 7 and Figure 8 (a), (b), (c), and (d). When the percentage of interfacial G_f with respect to the fracture energy of the concrete matrix ranging from 0%–10%, an interfacial crack occurs and the microcapsule is deboned from the concrete matrix as illustrated in Figure 7 and Figure 8 (e) and (f). Figure 9, Figure 10, and Figure 11 show that interfacial strengths ranging from 5% - 25% of matrix strength have the same crack pattern as the microcapsule is deboned from the concrete matrix. An interesting fracture pattern occurred when the interfacial σ* 10% and interfacial G_f 100% of the concrete matrix as the incoming crack could not debone the microcapsule completely, as shown in Figure 9 (a). That means a partial debone crack developed when the interfacial strength is 25 % of concrete strength and fracture energy is high value (same as concrete matrix).

7. Conclusions

Numerical simulations have been carried out to investigate the effects of interfacial strength and fracture energy of microcapsule shell to the fractured microcapsule. A specimen is discretized as three-phase composite composed of concrete, microcapsule shell, and interface between them. To represent the interaction between these components and to predict more realistic crack paths, XFEM technique and cohesive surface in 2D configuration are used. It has been found that the interfacial strength between the microcapsule shell and the concrete matrix has a significant influence on the load carrying capacity and the crack pattern of the sample. The load carrying capacity of self-healing material under tension increases as interfacial properties (itz) between the concrete matrix and the microcapsule shell increases. At fixed value of interfacial strength, the variation interfacial fracture energy of microcapsule has no significant effect on the load carrying capacity of self-healing concrete. But it will effect on the fracture pattern whether fracture or debone of the microcapsule as when the percentage of interface G_f lower than 10% of the concrete fracture energy, an interfacial crack occurs and the microcapsule will deboned from the concrete matrix. It has noticed that the crack path is significantly determined by the fracture properties of the interface of microcapsule shell. Further, having the fracture properties of microcapsule shell interface lower than 25% of concrete matrix, highly favors deboning of the microcapsule. It worth to mention that a partial fracture crack developed when the interfacial strength is high value (same as concrete) and interfacial fracture energy is low value (i.e., 10 % of concrete). In the contrary, a partial debone crack developed when the interfacial strength is 25 % of concrete strength and fracture energy is high value (same as concrete matrix). From all above mentioned conclusions, it is clear that a lot of attention should be considered during the manufacturing of microcapsules surfaces in order to be sure that a sufficient contact interaction surface between the microcapsule and the concrete will be developed to assure the fracture of the microcapsule and then release of the healing agent will happen.

References

A. Hillerborg, M. M., & P.-E., P. (1976). Analysis of crack formation and crack growth in concrete by means of fracture mechanics and finite elements. Cement and Concrete Research, Pages 773–781.

Dassault Systémes Simulia Corp., Providence, RI, USA. (2016). Retrieved from Abaqus user documentation. Tech. Rep.

Gilabert, F., Garoz, D., & Paepegem, W. V. (2017). Macro- and micro-modeling of crack propagation in encapsulation-based self-healing materials: Application of XFEM and cohesive surface techniques. Materials & Design, 130 , 459–478.

Hilloulin, B., Tittelboom, K. V., Gruyaert, E., Belie, N. D., & Loukili, A. (2015). Design of polymeric capsules for self-healing concrete. Cement and Concrete Composites, 55, 298–307.

Mauludin, L. M., Zhuang, X., & Rabczuk, T. (2018). Computational modeling of fracture in encapsulation-based self-healing concrete using cohesive elements. Composite Structures, 196, 63–75.

Moës, N., Dolbow, J., & Belytschko, T. (1999). A finite element method for crack growth without remeshing. 46(1), 131–150.

Quayum, M. S., Zhuang, X., & Rabczuk, T. (2015). Computational model generation and RVE design of self-healing concrete. Frontiers of Structural and Civil Engineering , 9(4), 383–396.

Snoeck, D., Malm, F., Cnudde, V., Grosse, C. U., & Tittelboom, K. V. (2018). Validation of Self-Healing Properties of Construction Materials through Nondestructive and Minimal Invasive Testing. Advanced Materials Interfaces, 5(17), 1800179.

Souradeep, G., & Kua, H. W. (2016). Encapsulation technology and techniques in self-healing concrete. Journal of Materials in Civil Engineering, 28(12), 04016165.

Wang, X. a. (2015). Combined numerical-statistical analyses of damage and failure of 2D and 3D mesoscale heterogeneous concrete. Mathematical Problems in Engineering.

A Performance Metric for the Evaluation of Thermal Anomaly Identification with Ill-Defined Ground Truth

Burak Kakillioglu[a], Yasser El Masri[b], Chenbin Pan[a], Eleanna Panagoulia[b], Norhan Bayomi[c], Kaiwen Chen[b], John E. Fernandez[c], Tarek Rakha[b], and Senem Velipasalar[a]
[a] Syracuse University, USA, [b] Georgia Institute of Technology, USA, [c] Massachusetts Institute of Technology, USA
bkakilli@syr.edu

Abstract. Thermography technology is widely used to inspect thermal anomalies in building façade systems. Computer vision-based techniques provide opportunities to autonomously detect such heat anomalies to significantly improve the efficiency of decision-making for building envelope retrofitting and maintenance. However, traditional performance metrics for evaluation of image segmentation-based anomaly identification methods do not accurately reflect the true performance of the segmentation models. One of the major problems is that labelling suffers from high subjectivity in this task and traditional performance metrics do not account for that. Also, traditional metrics are more skewed towards lower scores due to high sensitivity to overlap ratio. In this work, a novel performance metric, which is robust to the above-mentioned drawbacks, is presented. Experimental results show both qualitatively and quantitatively that the scores that our metric generates better align with the scores provided by building performance experts.

1. Introduction

The residential and commercial building sector accounts for 39% of total U.S. energy consumption and 40% of CO_2 emissions (U.S. Energy Information Administration, 2021). More than half of all U.S. commercial buildings were built before 1970 and have deteriorated severely, which has resulted in general lower efficiency performance (U.S. Department of Energy, 2017). Maintaining the energy efficiency of an increasingly aging built environment is essential in achieving a sustainable living environment. Therefore, to address the inefficiency of deteriorating infrastructure and building stock, energy retrofitting practices should be implemented (U.S. Department of Energy, 2012). The identification, diagnosis, and repair of issues causing additional energy loss in building systems and envelopes are necessary to improve building energy efficiency.

To identify and diagnose energy-related issues in building envelopes, energy auditors typically use professional tools to inspect building envelopes and detect thermal anomaly areas indicating infiltration/exfiltration and thermal bridge issues (Rakha et al., 2018a). Infrared (IR) thermography technology is experiencing a growing trend in building diagnostics, enabling a rapid and accurate detection of thermal anomalies with lower costs and safety risks (Fox et al., 2014). Thermal anomalies (i.e., infiltration/exfiltration and thermal bridges) can be identified from captured infrared images based on their temperature patterns. However, manual scanning and analysis of the captured infrared images is laborious and time consuming. While automation can provide a solution to these issues, there are as well challenges in the processing of infrared images to detect such thermal anomalies through advanced image processing algorithms and computational solutions. These are associated with inconsistent patterns caused by the variation of materials, building components, time of day, and season of year. Emerging deep learning-based segmentation techniques can provide opportunities to autonomously detect, segment and classify such heat anomalies with robustness to handle such inconsistency issues (Rakha et al., 2018b). The output of such automated models can significantly improve the efficiency of

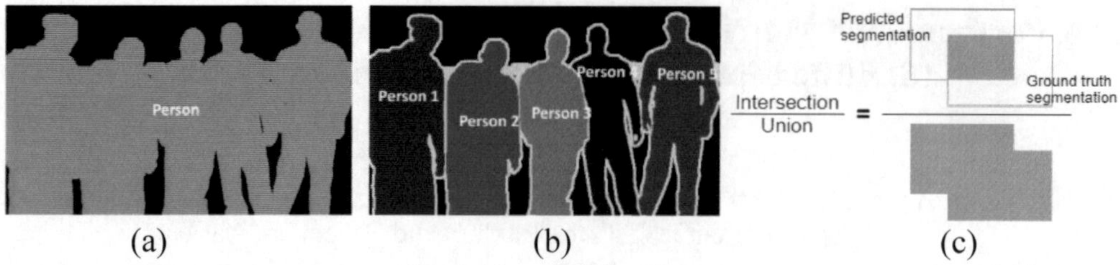

Figure 1: (a) Semantic Segmentation, (b) Instance Segmentation (Sharma, 2019) and (c) Illustration of Intersection-over-Union.

decision-making for building envelope retrofitting and maintenance. There are numerous ways of applying computer vision methodologies to solve the thermal anomaly identification problem. Since anomaly regions can manifest in various random shapes and sizes in IR images, one approach to tackle this problem is *image segmentation*, which is the process of partitioning the image into multiple regions, which correspond to meaningful entities of interest. One type of image segmentation approach that can be used for anomaly detection is *semantic segmentation*, which deals with predicting masks for multiple semantically meaningful entities, as seen in Figure 1-a. Another method is *instance segmentation*, which, different from semantic segmentation, separates/individually segments different instances of the same semantic class, as seen in Figure 1-b. Therefore, instance segmentation provides more information, which makes it a more challenging problem compared to semantic segmentation in computer vision workflows.

The most common metric measuring the overlap performance in segmentation tasks is the Intersection-over-Union (IoU) metric, which is also known as the Jaccard index. IoU is a simple indicator of how well the prediction candidate overlaps with the target ground truth region. As the name suggests, it is calculated by dividing the intersection area with the union area of the candidate prediction and target region, as illustrated in Figure 1-c.

In multi-class semantic segmentation models, IoU is calculated for each different class. The mean IoU (mIoU), which is the average IoU of all classes, is used to represent the performance of the given model on the test data. It does not consider different instances and only measures the ground truth overlap in the entire dataset. On the other hand, when identifying different instances of the same class in an image is also important, then an instance segmentation model is used, for which the average precision (AP) metric is employed for performance evaluation. AP is a measure that combines recall and precision for ranked retrieval results (Zhang and Zhang, 2009). For all "True Positives (TP)", "False Positives (FP)" and "False Negatives (FN)", the precision and recall are defined as $\frac{TP}{TP+FP}$ and $\frac{TP}{TP+FN}$, respectively. A prediction instance must satisfy the IoU threshold to be called as a true positive. If it fails to satisfy the IoU threshold, it becomes a false positive. Similarly, a ground truth (GT) instance is called a false negative (miss) if the IoU of any of the candidate predictions with the GT instance does not satisfy the IoU threshold. In general, the IoU threshold is set as 0.5 to decide whether a prediction is TP or FP (or FN for a GT), although the threshold value can be set to any other value while yielding a precision-recall trade-off.

Generating GT annotations, especially for thermal anomalies on IR images, is usually an expensive, difficult, time-consuming, and oftentimes subjective process. More specifically, for segmentation applications, manually drawing a tight boundary around every target on each image in the dataset is an overly cumbersome process. Yet, the GT in most standard applications is well-defined and less subjective than IR GT (Martin et al., 2001). For instance, when different people are asked to draw the boundary of a dog or a cat, there will not be significant differences between their annotations. However, the annotation of the ground truth for thermal anomaly segmentation suffers from potential subjectivity of thermographers and their interpretations and the difficulty of defining clear cut boundaries for different types of anomalies, making the annotation process ill-defined. Moreover, in some cases one anomaly could be annotated as multiple pieces, or vice versa. Thus, it is important to consider the above identified differences during the performance evaluation methodology of the computer vision workflow. On the other hand, existing metrics perform poorly in indicating the true performance of a model and are more skewed towards smaller scores due to their high sensitivity to overlap (see Figure 4).

Thus, to address the issues and shortcomings mentioned above, a new performance metric, Anomaly Identification Metric (AIM), is presented in this work, for the image segmentation-based thermal anomaly identification problem. Different from traditional segmentation metrics, AIM does not rely on IoU, and can handle the lack of one-to-one correspondences between prediction and ground truth instances. It is shown by rigorous experimental results that the proposed metric is a more suitable and plausible evaluation metric for benchmarking the performance of different computer vision-based segmentation models for thermal anomaly identification on the same data. It represents the true performance of the models more accurately and reliably and is more robust against the aforementioned drawbacks, as compared to traditional evaluation metrics, while being attentive to inspection application needs identified by building experts. In addition to providing many examples for qualitative comparison, we surveyed four building experts to score the performance of an autonomous heat anomaly segmentation algorithm. We first calculated the mean of all the expert scores (μ_E). Then we computed the mean squared error between (i) each expert's scores and μ_E, (ii) mIoU and μ_E, and (iii) proposed metric (AIM) and μ_E for quantitative comparison, showing that our proposed metric does a better job of evaluating the algorithm's performance when compared with the expert scores.

2. Related Work

Since image segmentation is important for many computer vision applications, the evaluation of segmentation algorithms has been covered in the literature, due to the diverse needs of different applications. Martin et al., 2001, present an error metric that objectively quantifies the consistency between segmentations of differing granularities. They empirically show high consistency in human segmentations (ground truth) of the same image, which are generated by different people. This result, however, does not apply to thermal anomaly segmentation, since annotating thermal anomalies is oftentimes subjective, and thermal anomaly shapes are ambiguous, as will be discussed below. Furthermore, it is shown by Polak et al., 2008 that the metric in Martin et al., 2001 can tolerate under-segmentation and over-segmentation, which is not very desirable in many applications. Cardoso et al., 2005 present a generic framework for the evaluation of image segmentation evaluation workflows. Their error measure is based on the partition distance concept, which counts the number of pixels, normalized with respect to the image size, that must be removed from the interpretation, i.e., segmentation of an image until the induced segmentation agrees with the reference image. Unlike the previous work, their method is more sensible to under-segmentation. Polak et al., 2008, proposed a performance metric for image segmentation of multiple objects. Their error measure considers various properties of the objects, such as shape, size, and position, to make object-by-object comparisons. Their measure also penalizes both under-segmentation and over-segmentation. Csurka et al., 2013 surveyed the traditional evaluation metrics and proposed a novel metric based on contours. However, the aforementioned metrics are not readily applicable to the task of thermal anomaly identification due to its highly subjective and ambiguous ground truths.

3. Overview of Anomaly Identification Methods

The purpose of developing the proposed performance metric is to set a standard for benchmarking different thermal anomaly identification methods. These methods can use any algorithm underneath and the performance metric should be agnostic to that. Given the ground truth masks and predictions from each model, the performance metric is used for a commensurate evaluation and comparison. In this section, we summarize three types of models that can be used for thermal anomaly identification.

A simplistic way of identifying thermal anomalies in IR images is classifying thermal pixels based on a pre-defined temperature threshold. Using this method an anomaly analysis being performed outdoors on a cold day, can be carried out by simply marking the pixels of the IR image as anomaly pixels if their value is greater than the pre-set temperature threshold. This threshold value can be set based on the current thermal conditions and expectations, i.e., how cold the outside is, what is the expected indoor temperature etc. Martinez-De Dios et al., 2006 proposed a similar method to identify heat losses through windows. If the thermal properties of the surface are generally uniform, and the anomalies are significant, this simple method could be reliable to some extent. However, these assumptions are too strong and will not always hold. Moreover, there is no one-size-fits-all solution, and to expect a single predefined threshold to work in different scenarios is neither realistic nor practical.

Another approach, which overcomes some of the drawbacks of the fixed threshold-based model, is an adaptive threshold-based model, wherein the temperature threshold is not fixed and adaptively determined per image. By selecting an optimum criteria per image, the robustness of the model greatly increases. Kakillioglu et al., 2018 proposed an adaptive threshold-based thermal heat leakage segmentation method for identification of thermal infiltration/exfiltration on building surfaces. However, this approach also makes some assumptions, which may not always hold, such as all regions with temperature values beyond the adaptive threshold being assumed to be anomaly regions. This assumption might result in false positives, since not all regions with relatively very high or very low temperature values compared to the average thermal signatures in an IR image are necessarily anomaly regions.

Over the last decade, deep learning models have provided the state-of-the-art performance on majority of the computer vision tasks and become the de-facto practice in applying computer vision solutions to many real-world problems. The thermal anomaly identification task is a great candidate to be formulated as an image segmentation problem, which is one of the most common computer vision problems. A data-driven approach is more desirable, especially when annotated data is available, since it removes the need for hand-crafted features or feature engineering, and many assumptions regarding the anomaly identification. Semantic segmentation is a better way to detect heat leakages, since the anomaly can be of any shape, and it is not necessary to differentiate the instances of the same class. In this work, we adopt DeepLabV3+ model (Chen et al., 2019) for semantic segmentation, due to its high performance on various benchmarks, which indicates a great generalization ability on different domains. DeepLabV3+ model applies atrous convolutions to capture multi-scale context. For each location, an atrous convolution filter is applied over the input feature map where the atrous rate corresponds to the stride with which we sample the input signal. By adjusting the rate, we can adaptively modify the field-of-view of the operation. This architecture concatenates feature maps from atrous convolutions with different rates, so it allows us to enlarge the reception field to incorporate larger context and offers an efficient mechanism to control the reception field to find the best trade-off between accurate localization (small field-of-view) and context assimilation (large field-of-view). In other words, we can gather more complete and meaningful information from images using DeepLabV3+. We use the results of DeepLabV3+ model in the evaluation and comparison of our proposed performance metric with the traditional semantic segmentation metric.

There are mainly three modules in DeepLabV3+: (i) backbone neural network model for feature extraction, (ii) atrous spatial pyramid pooling (ASPP) for identification of thermal anomaly regions on the image, and (iii) decoder for mask generation. The input image is firstly sent into the backbone to extract low-level features, and then forwarded to ASPP to extract high-level features with various fields of view. Then, both features are concatenated and fed into the decoder to make predictions for the segmentation mask.

4. Proposed Metric for Segmentation Performance Evaluation

One may ask the following question: "If the employed model is a semantic segmentation model, then why not use the traditional mIoU metric? Why is there a need for a new performance metric?" As will be shown below, both qualitatively and quantitatively, the mIoU-based metric is an inaccurate performance indicator especially when considering how a thermal anomaly segmentation is evaluated by building experts and thermography experts. We observed in our studies with expert analysts that they give more consideration to whether all anomaly instances are identified rather than the overlap ratio. For instance, even if a predicted region does not tightly cover the actual anomaly region, it is, in general, sufficient for identification of that anomaly in thermal inspections. Therefore, it is better to detect and analyze instances, since they are more important than how tightly the GT is covered by a prediction mask. This brings us to the instance segmentation, for which the evaluation metric is the AP. However, there is a drawback when using the traditional AP measure in the thermal anomaly segmentation problem. As opposed to the standard instance segmentation applications, in thermal anomaly identification: 1) anomaly regions are not necessarily associated with single prediction regions; 2) prediction regions are not necessarily associated with single GT regions; and 3) different people may annotate the same anomaly region differently. It is acceptable to have multiple prediction instances covering a GT instance or vice-versa. This is mainly due to the subjectivity of GT instances and ambiguity of thermal anomalies. Therefore, the association requirement must be removed. In this case TP, FP and FN definitions do not hold anymore and AP cannot be determined.

4.1 Separating Instances

Since the semantic segmentation model does not provide instance information and the anomaly instances are of arbitrary shapes, we first apply a preprocessing step to separate instances by the standard connected component analysis. Figure 2 shows a few examples of separating instances via the connected component analysis. Images in the top row, which could be

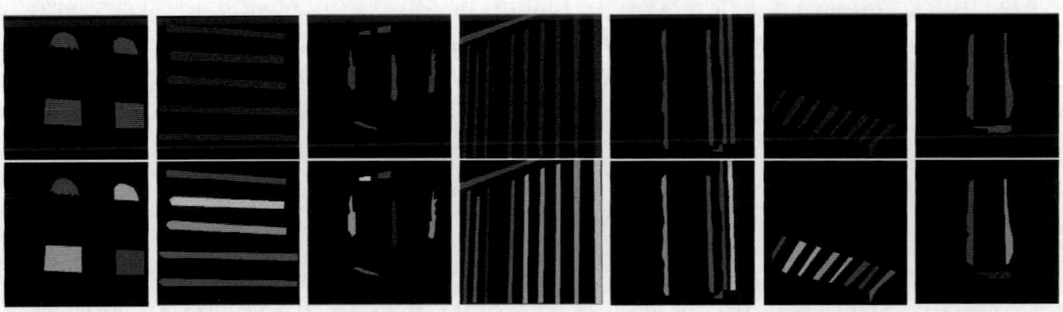

Figure 2: Pre-processing step of separating instances by Connected Component Analysis

annotations or the algorithm output, do not distinguish between different instances, and denote all regions of the same class with the same colour (red or green). Images in the bottom row show the output of the connected component analysis, where each instance is denoted by a different colour.

4.2 Intersection-over-Prediction and Ground Truth Coverage Scores

We define Intersection-over-Prediction (IoP) as a new measure to score each prediction instance, and it is the key component of the entire pipeline. As opposed to the traditional IoU metric, where the total area of the intersection of the prediction and ground truth instance is divided by the total area of their union, in IoP, the intersection area is divided by the area of the prediction instance only (see Figure 3-a). This way, we can break the association requirement, and assign individual scores to each of the prediction instances.

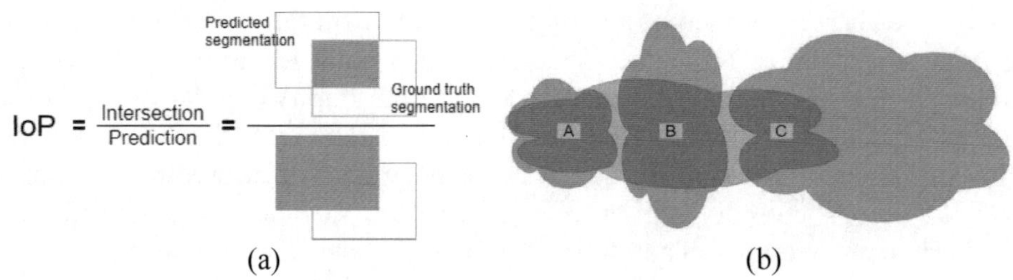

Figure 3: Illustration of the Intersection-over-Prediction

The IoP only assigns scores to the prediction instances. To assign a score to a GT (target) instance, we consider all the prediction instances, which overlap with it, and their IoP score. The score for each GT target is defined as Ground Truth Coverage (GTC), and calculated as follows:

$$GTC = IoP_{P1} * IoT_{P1} + IoP_{P2} * IoT_{P2} + \cdots + IoP_{PN} * IoT_{PN}$$

where IoP_{Pi} is the IoP score of ith prediction instance that overlaps with the target instance and IoT_{Pi} is the Intersection-over-Target Area for i[th] prediction instance.

This formulation ensures that more precise prediction instances, i.e., prediction instances with high IoP value, will have more weight while contributing to a GTC. This effectively prevents imprecise prediction instances from contributing to target identification. For example, in Figure 3-b, although the rightmost prediction instance covers almost 1/3 of the target instance (IoT), its contribution to the GTC of that target instance is greatly reduced due to its very small IoP score (imprecise prediction).

Additionally, our proposed metric does not require one-to-one association between target and predicted instances. One prediction instance can be associated to multiple target instances and vice-versa. This property ensures robustness in cases, where the annotator annotates an anomaly in multiple pieces (see Figure 5-a) or annotates multiple neighboring anomalies as one anomaly (see Figure 5-b).

4.3 Definition of Proposed Anomaly Identification Metric (AIM)

T_{IoP} is defined as the IoP threshold, which is the criteria for an acceptable (precise) prediction score. Similarly, T_{GTC} is defined as the GTC threshold, which is the criteria for an acceptable coverage score for a target instance. We further define the following:

- True Prediction (TP): Number of prediction instances (components) that sufficiently overlap with a ground truth instance. (IoP > T_{IoP})
- False Prediction (FP): Number of prediction instances (components) that do not sufficiently overlap with a ground truth instance. (IoP < T_{IoP})
- Recalled Target (RT): Number of ground truth instances that are sufficiently covered by prediction instances. (GTC > T_{GTC})
- Missed Target (MT): Number of ground truth instances that are not sufficiently covered by prediction instances. (GTC < T_{GTC})

Notice that TP and FP stand for "True Prediction" and "False Prediction" as opposed to the general usage in the literature (True Positive and False Positive). Using TP, FP, RT, and MT we define the precision and recall as $\frac{TP}{TP+FP}$ and $\frac{RT}{RT+MT}$, respectively.

The precision and recall rates indicate how precise the predicted regions are and how much of the ground truth is identified, and they would also be used in the evaluation and benchmarking of multiple models. However, since a single performance score is often desirable, we further define the overall *Anomaly Identification Metric (AIM)* of a given image (or the entire dataset) as follows:

$$AIM = \lambda * precision + (1 - \lambda) * recall$$

In our experiments, λ is set to 0.25, which gives three times more weight to recall compared to precision. The motivation for this is that being able to detect all anomalies is more important than having false predictions by the nature of the thermal anomaly detection problem, and by the expectations of performance analysts. The value of λ is empirically found and can be tuned depending on the needs of the application.

5. Experimental Methodology and Results

For the thermal anomaly identification work, we have collected an extensive amount of IR data (paired with visual RGB images) from various types of buildings in different climate conditions. GT for every single IR image is provided by building performance experts for model training and evaluation. The GT annotation is a cumbersome process, which requires the annotator to draw a tight boundary around every thermal anomaly on every IR image. In GT annotation, two types of anomalies, namely thermal infiltration/exfiltration and thermal bridge were considered. The dataset is split into training and test sets by a 70:30 ratio. A DeepLabV3+ model is trained using the IR images in the training set. After the training is complete, the trained model is used to generate the segmentation masks, which denote the thermal anomalies that are identified by the model on the test set. On the segmentation masks, red colour corresponds to a thermal bridge, while green colour corresponds to infiltration/exfiltration.

The purpose of this work is to define a new metric which will be used to measure how well a model performs on a thermal anomaly dataset. As discussed earlier, a good performance metric should reflect the performance in the most accurate way that is in agreement and alignment with how building or thermography experts would evaluate the anomaly detection performance.

This brings up the following question: "If the assessment of a person is known to be likely subjective, then how can a human assessment be used as the baseline?" To address this issue in our evaluation and comparison experiments, we rely on the evaluations provided by multiple experts, instead of using the assessment of a single expert. We surveyed four building experts to score the performance of an autonomous heat anomaly segmentation algorithm on a

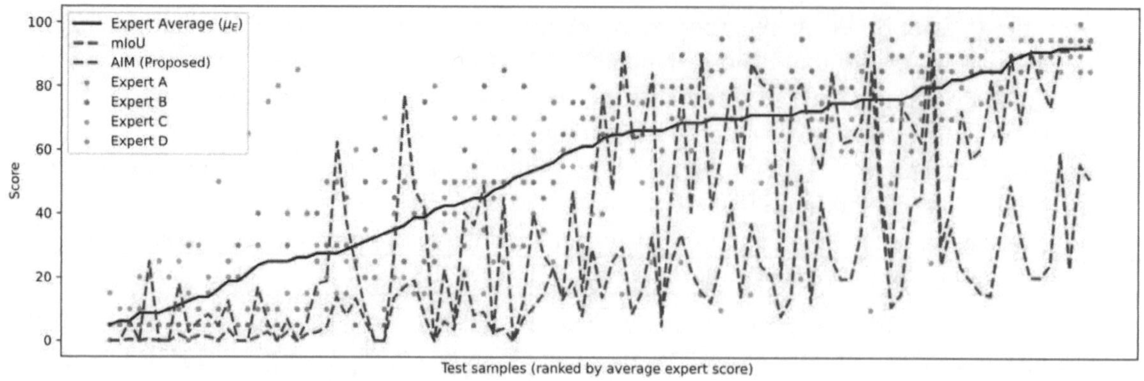

Figure 4: Performances Metrics - Expert Scoring Comparison. The horizontal axis represents the test samples that are sorted in ascending order by the average expert score (blue line).

significant portion of the test data. Given a visible range RGB image, an infrared image and an image showing the segmentation result (prediction) of the algorithm, each expert is asked to provide a performance score for 100 test images. More specifically, the experts were asked to provide a score in the range of 0 to 100, which evaluates "How useful is the algorithm prediction in identifying a thermal anomaly?" for each test sample. It should be emphasized again that the experts assess the prediction by their own judgement, instead of the amount of overlap with the GT data. To avoid any bias, they were not provided with any type of scores, regarding the algorithm performance, and they assessed the performance of each prediction independently.

Figure 4 shows how expert scoring, traditional mIoU metric, and our proposed metric compare to each other. In this figure, all test samples are sorted in ascending order based on the average expert score. Each dot represents a score given by an expert, where different experts' scores are denoted by different colours. The blue line shows the average expert scores per image while red and green dashed lines show the scores of the proposed metric and the traditional mIoU metric, respectively. As can be seen, the proposed metric aligns with the average expert scores much better than the traditional mIoU metric. This result clearly demonstrates that our proposed evaluation metric (i) addresses the issues of annotator subjectivity, lack of clear definition of anomaly boundaries, and not necessarily having one-to-one correspondence between prediction and GT instances; and (ii) robustly and accurately represents the performance of a given thermal anomaly prediction. A similar analysis is provided in Table 1. We first calculated the mean of all the expert scores per image i and denote it by μ_E^i. Then, over 100 sample images, we computed the mean squared error (MSE) between (i) each expert's scores and μ_E, (ii) mIoU and μ_E, and (iii) the proposed metric and μ_E for quantitative comparison. As seen in Table 1, the MSE between each expert's scores and the mean expert score ranges between 0.010 and 0.055. The MSE between our proposed metric and the mean expert score is 0.051, which falls in the above range. This MSE is much lower than the MSE between the traditional segmentation metric and the mean expert score (0.168) showing once again that our proposed metric provides a better way of evaluating the algorithm performance for heat anomaly segmentation by closely matching experts' judgements.

Table 1: Summary of expert scores and compared performance metrics.

Measure Source	Expert A	Expert B	Expert C	Expert D	mIoU	Proposed
MSE	0.015	0.021	0.055	0.010	0.168	0.051

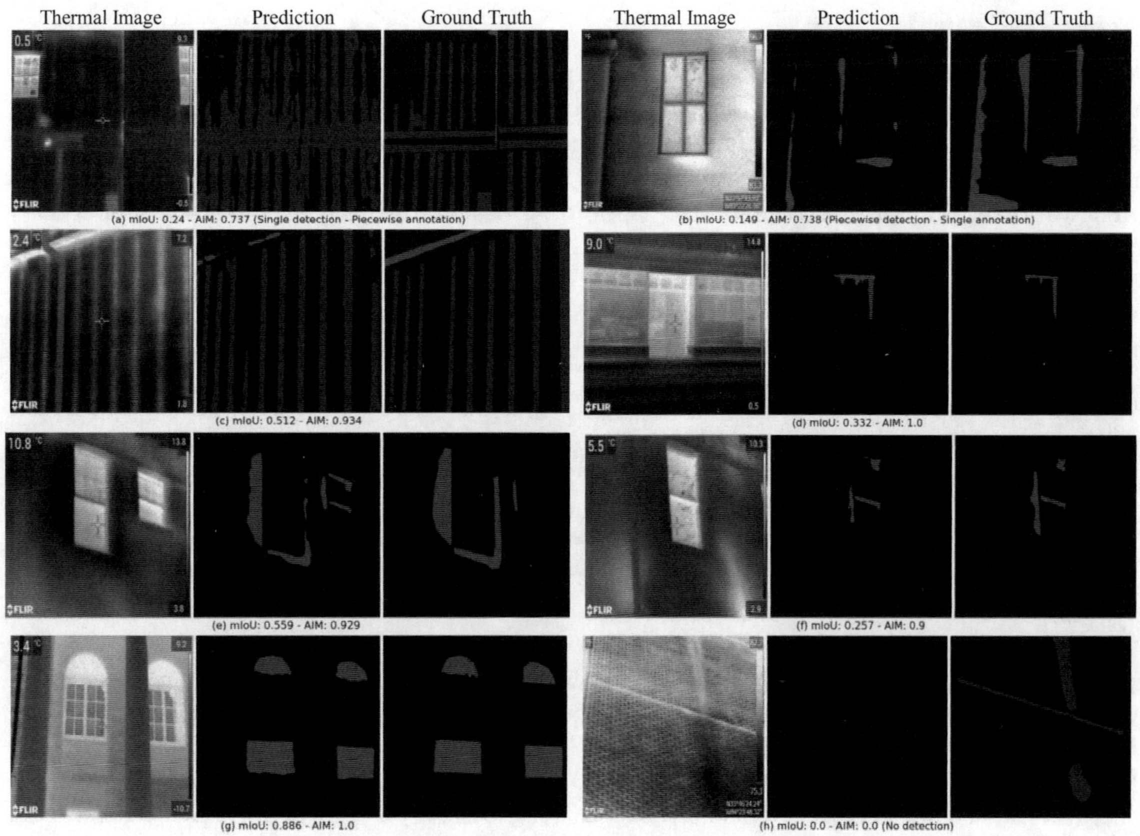

Figure 5: Qualitative Comparison of mIoU and AIM Scores

Figure 5 presents eight qualitative examples showing how our proposed metric better represents the performance in different cases. Each example shows the thermal image (left), algorithm prediction (middle), and ground truth (right), and the scores of both metrics (bottom).

6. Conclusion and Future Work

This paper presented a new metric for performance assessment of thermal anomaly segmentation models. The proposed metric has been developed by computer scientists under the guidance of, and in close collaboration with, building performance experts to provide a better evaluation of thermal anomaly segmentation algorithms and to benchmark different computer vision solutions for the thermal anomaly identification task. We have performed both qualitative and quantitative comparison of the proposed performance metric with the traditional segmentation metric and shown that our proposed performance metric aligns better with expert evaluations.

The performance of various segmentation models will be evaluated by the proposed metric, average precision, and possible other segmentation metrics, and the results will be compared. In addition to the assessment of thermal anomaly identification performance, our proposed metric can also be useful for various other areas, such as civil structure defect detection, machinery fault detection, and oil spill detection based on infrared imagery processing. As future work, the proposed metric can be used as a baseline for an objective function, which can steer the deep learning training for possibly better outcomes compared to the traditional optimization functions.

Acknowledgement

We would like to thank our experts Prof. Les Norford (MIT) and Tyler Pilet (Georgia Tech) for taking their time to provide invaluable contribution to our work by providing performance scoring, and Zachary Lancaster for technical support and data delivery. This material is based upon work supported by the U.S. Department of Energy's Office of Energy Efficiency and Renewable Energy (EERE) under the Buildings Technology Office Award Number DE-EE0008680.

References

U.S. Energy Information Administration, 2021. Total energy monthly data - U.S. Energy Information Administration (EIA). Available at: https://www.eia.gov/totalenergy/data/monthly/index.php [Accessed March 12, 2021].

U.S. Department of Energy, 2012. Thermographic inspections. Available at: https://energy.gov/energysaver/thermographic-inspections [Accessed March 12, 2021].

Rakha, T. and Gorodetsky, A., 2018. Review of Unmanned Aerial System (UAS) applications in the built environment: Towards automated building inspection procedures using drones. Automation in Construction, 93, pp.252–264.

U.S. Energy Information Administration, 2017. How much energy is consumed in U.S. residential and commercial buildings? Available at: https://www.eia.gov/tools/faqs/faq.php?id=86&t=1 [Accessed March 12, 2021].

Fox, M., Coley, D., Goodhew, S. and De Wilde, P., 2014. Thermography methodologies for detecting energy related building defects. Renewable and Sustainable Energy Reviews, 40, pp.296–310.

Rakha, T., Liberty, A., Gorodetsky, A., Kakillioglu, B. and Velipasalar, S., 2018. Heat mapping drones: an autonomous computer-vision-based procedure for building envelope inspection using unmanned aerial systems (UAS). Technology| Architecture+ Design, 2(1), pp.30–44.

Sharma, P., 2019. Image Segmentation: Types Of Image Segmentation. Analytics Vidhya. Available at: https://www.analyticsvidhya.com/blog/2019/04/introduction-image-segmentation-techniques-python/ [Accessed March 12, 2021].

Zhang, E. and Zhang, Y., 2009. Average precision. In: L. LIU and Ö.M. TAMER, eds., Encyclopaedia of Database Systems. [online] Springer US, pp.192–193.

Martin, D., Fowlkes, C., Tal, D. and Malik, J., 2001, July. A database of human segmented natural images and its application to evaluating segmentation algorithms and measuring ecological statistics. In Proceedings Eighth IEEE International Conference on Computer Vision. ICCV 2001 (Vol. 2, pp.416–423). IEEE.

Cardoso, J.S. and Corte-Real, L., 2005. Toward a generic evaluation of image segmentation. IEEE Transactions on Image Processing, 14(11), pp.1773–1782.

Polak, M., Zhang, H. and Pi, M., 2009. An evaluation metric for image segmentation of multiple objects. Image and Vision Computing, 27(8), pp.1223–1227.

Csurka, G., Larlus, D., Perronnin, F. and Meylan, F., 2013, September. What is a good evaluation measure for semantic segmentation?. In BMVC (Vol. 27, No. 2013, pp.10–5244).

Martinez-De Dios, J.R. and Ollero, A., 2006, July. Automatic detection of windows thermal heat losses in buildings using UAVs. In 2006 world automation congress (pp.1–6). IEEE.

Kakillioglu, B., Velipasalar, S. and Rakha, T., 2018, September. Autonomous heat leakage detection from unmanned aerial vehicle-mounted thermal cameras. In Proceedings of the 12th International Conference on Distributed Smart Cameras (pp.1–6).

Chen, L.C., Papandreou, G., Schroff, F. and Adam, H., 2017. Rethinking atrous convolution for semantic image segmentation. arXiv preprint arXiv:1706.05587.

Areas of Interest - Semantic description of component locations for damage assessment

Al-Hakam Hamdan, Raimar J. Scherer
Technische Universität Dresden, Germany
al-hakam.hamdan@tu-dresden.de

Abstract. In the recent years, approaches that utilize Semantic Web Technologies for describing building information enabled the development of semantic representations of constructions and with it the separation of semantic and geometry-based models. Currently developed web ontologies provide functionality for defining a detailed topology, in which direct connections between various components are semantically described. However, a great proportion of tasks that require at least approximate information about the localization of objects in relation to connected components cannot be processed. This is especially a problem in the field of damage inspections, in which this information is mandatory for subsequent damage classification and assessment. To solve this problem, a newly developed ontological approach is presented in this paper, which aims for the semantic description of component areas, called Areas of Interest (AOI). Thereby, a new auxiliary ontology has been conceptualized, which aims for an uncomplicated integration in existing AEC-related ontologies. The paper presents the overall methodology of AOI as well as the corresponding conceptual ontology and the exemplary application for damage assessment utilizing the Damage Topology Ontology (DOT).

1. Introduction

Building Information Modeling (BIM) utilizes digital data models for representing buildings, which not only describe the geometry of a construction, but also additional information such as topological relationships of its consisted components. For instance, aggregations or adjacency relationships between components can be described in a geometry-based BIM-Model by using the Industry Foundation Classes (IFC), which is an open BIM standard defined by ISO 16739-1:2018. Moreover, web ontologies such as the Building Topology Ontology (BOT) (Rasmussen et al., 2017) allow for a geometry-independent way of defining the building topology, which is practical if insufficient or unclear information about the construction geometry is available. Especially for describing the relations between damages and corresponding affected components, a topological model, which is separated from the building geometry, is often preferred, since the detection and modelling of an accurate damage is usually a costly and time-expensive task. In current damage modelling approaches, damage objects are directly assigned topologically to a digital component or construction representation (Artus & Koch, 2019) or to a representation of the material of which the component is made (Cacciotti et al., 2015). However, this results in a loss of semantic data regarding the approximate location of damages in a component, which is often a mandatory information for subsequent classification and assessment. Although, this information can be inferred by evaluating the position data in a geometry-based BIM, it is not explicitly defined in semantic models, which prevents the processing of this information. To solve the problematic of semantically describing the element position relative to a parent component, a newly developed ontological approach is proposed in this paper. Thereby, component areas or volumes are semantically described through specific objects, called Areas of Interest (AOI). By applying AOI, the location of separate objects, such as damages or reinforcing elements, in relation to the affected component or construction is semantically defined and can be used in various Semantic Web processes, e.g., SPARQL queries or logic-based rules. This paper presents the overall methodology of AOI as well as the corresponding conceptual ontology and exemplary applications of the presented approach.

2. Related Work

Although rarely used in modelling practice, approaches already exist that in principle allow a semantic description of the location of objects on a component. In IFC the relative position of an object to another object can be semantically described through subclasses of the objectified relationship class *IfcRelConnects*. Thereby, the class *IfcRelPositions* would be suitable for associating objects to a spatial structure element, instantiated via a subclass of *IfcPositioningElement*, which could represent a certain area of a component, e.g., the upper half or corner of a beam. However, subclasses of *IfcPositioningElement*, such as *IfcGrid* or *IfcLinearPositioningElement* are primarily used for defining geometrical data and not semantic descriptions of the spatial structure. Nonetheless, an annotation through inherited attributes from *IfcRoot*, e.g., *Name* or *Description*, would be possible.

Alternative approaches, which are not geometry-based, are applied for databases of construction management systems. In this regard, the German guideline ASB-ING (Bundesanstalt für Strassenwesen, 2018) dictates how areas of existing bridges and their contained components are semantically defined in a database, which is usually utilized by the bridge management system SIB-Bauwerke[1]. However, these semantic descriptions mainly relate to the overall bridge construction and only to a lesser extent to built-in components. Moreover, component descriptions are limited to bridge- or structural-specific terms, e.g., support sections or areas near a coupling joint.

In the field of Semantic Web for architecture, engineering and construction (AEC), ontologies for building representation, such as ifcOWL (Pauwels & Terkaj, 2016) or BOT (Rasmussen et al., 2017) have been developed. Thereby, ifcOWL functions as an OWL representation of IFC, thus having a similar functionality for describing component areas semantically through subclasses of *IfcRelConnects*. Due to the complexity and monolithical structure of IFC, other more modular approaches such as BOT have been developed, in which the features and objectives of Linked Data are more emphasized. The web ontology BOT provides classes and properties for describing the core topological concepts of a building, such as zones and the contained building elements. In BOT only aggregations and direct connections between zones or elements could be defined, however a semantic description of element localizations is not provided, since this information is not part of the building topology. The same is true for the Building Product Ontology (BPO) (Wagner & Rüppel, 2019), an ontology that is compatible with BOT and which describes the relations between a building product and its subcomponents, but not a semantically formalized location. Furthermore, various approaches exist for representing geometry in an ontology (Wagner et al., 2020), however these solutions provide no method for semantically defining location areas in a component, without the assertion of explicit geometric data.

3. Methodology of Area of Interests (AOI)

The concept of AOI aims for extending current web ontologies that are formalized in the Web Ontology Language (OWL)[2] without significantly changing their proposed modelling concepts. Instead, the AOI ontology[3] provides an additional modelling option, which enhances the extended ontologies with a function to locate objects that are topologically connected. Figure 1 shows the general methodology for assigning an AOI and using it for localization.

---

[1] https://sib-bauwerke.de/

[2] https://www.w3.org/TR/owl2-overview/

[3] https://wisib.de/ontologie/aoi/

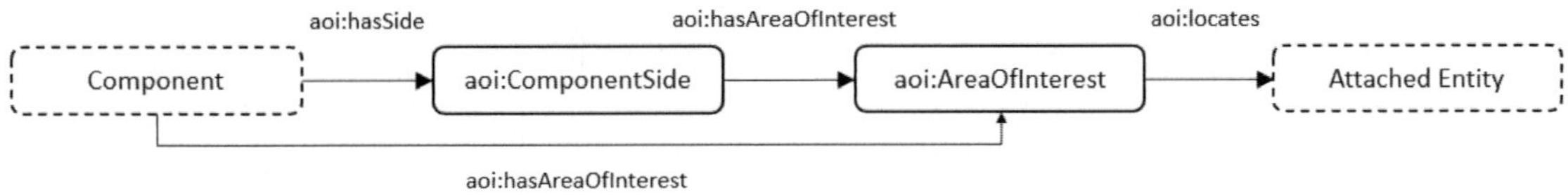

Figure 1: General principle of using an Area of Interest

An AOI is always linked with an individual that represents a physical object, through the Object Property aoi:hasAreaOfInterest. Individuals, which are localized through the AOI, are assigned to it via the Object Property aoi:locates or one corresponding subproperty. The semantic description of the related localization is defined through the AOI itself and additional data properties that could be linked with it.

An AOI is modelled by describing an area on a selected surface of a building component, as it is usually done in damage inspections or when identifying objects on an existing structure (see Fig. 2). Additionally, it is often determined whether the area is located on the surface level of the related component or an internal area. The vertical alignment y of the reference system is determined based on the force direction of the gravity F_g since the structural behaviour and function of each building component is heavily dependent on it. The horizontal axis x of the reference system is orthogonal to the vertical axis and on the components surface (contrary to the axis z for defining the components depth). In this regard, the AOI subclasses for defining horizontal areas are designed in such a way that the direction along the horizontal axis is not relevant, since there is only a distinction between horizontal and peripheral areas.

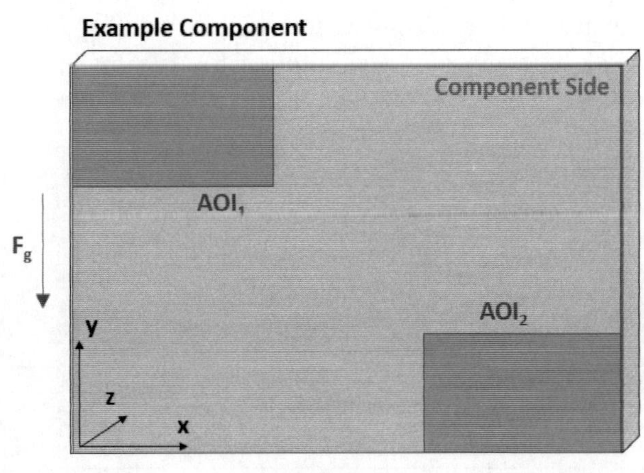

Figure 2: Reference system and structure of a component including a component side and 2 AOIs

Since multiple horizontal areas of a component could be of relevance, it is often necessary to distinguish between them. Therefore, instances of aoi:ComponentSide can be linked with the component representation via aoi:hasSide. Instances of aoi:ComponentSide function as part of the component and similarly can be linked with an AOI. Through a property chain, it is possible to reason the relation between the AOI and the component. Instances of aoi:ComponentSide could be characterized through additional properties e.g., the cardinal direction or whether the side is in an external area of the building for better identification and localization.

To utilize the AOI ontology as extension for an existing ontology, it is recommended to add two components to the provided terminology. This can be accomplished either through modifying the extended ontology, the AOI ontology or by creating an intermediate ontology, which defines the additional axioms. First, a subproperty of aoi:locates should be defined in order to specify, to which class the object belongs that is connected to the component representation. For example, a damage representation classified through the class dot:Damage by the Damage Topology Ontology (DOT)[4] (Hamdan et al., 2019) can be assigned to an AOI via the subproperty aoi:locatesDamage. Second, a property chain axiom should be defined, which is used for inferring the link between a component and the connected object through the intermediate AOI instance. Thereby, an existing assignment property of the extended ontology should be utilized. Following the aforementioned damage example, an instance of bot:Element, is linked with an AOI through aoi:hasAreaOfInterest and an instance of dot:Damage is linked to the same AOI via aoi:locatesDamage. By reasoning a previously defined property chain axiom, it can be inferred that the dot:Damage instance is linked to the bot:Element instance through the Object Property dot:hasDamage (see Figure 3).

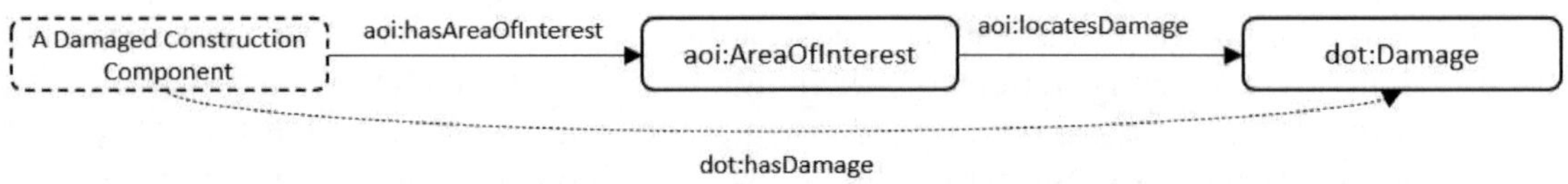

Figure 3: Extension example of AOI for DOT support

The semantic description about the localization area is defined through subclasses of aoi:AreaOfInterest. Thereby, the classification of the areas is performed based on their axial position in three-dimensional space (see Fig. 4). An alternative option considered would have been the definition of the localization area through object properties, however this would have led to overloaded information, since the properties are already used for specifying the object type to which the AOI relates to. Furthermore, changing or adding already defined localization information would usually be a simpler task due to modifying only the classes of an AOI individual compared to linking the AOI object to the same subject through additional object properties.

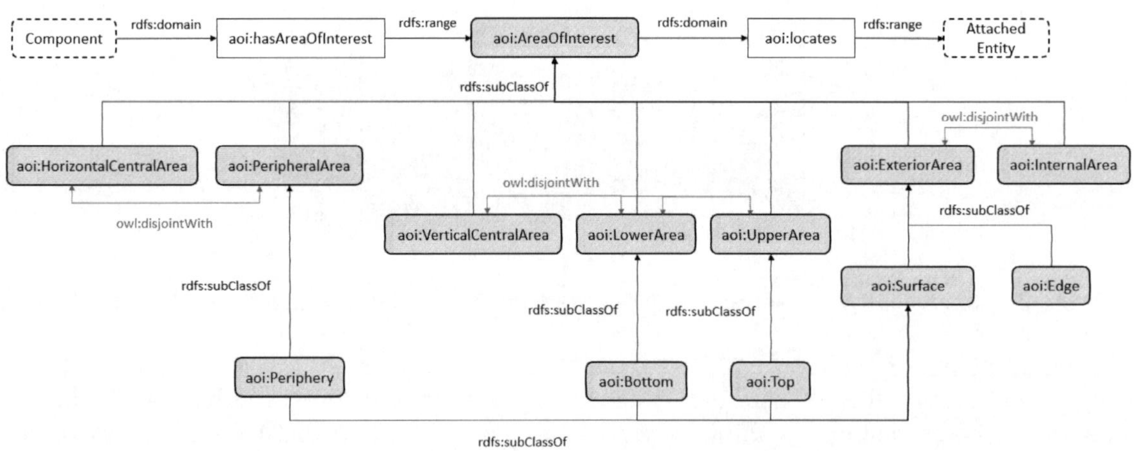

Figure 4: Terminology of the AOI ontology

At the current state of the developed AOI ontology the subclasses, which are used for characterizing an AOI, have been designed towards describing areas in a cubic building component. Since most structural relevant components in a building, such as walls, beams,

[4] https://w3id.org/dot

columns, or slabs, are defined through a cubic geometry, a great amount of the construction can be described via AOI. Consequently, areas in non-cubic objects e.g., some types of support components or shell structures are difficult to represent and localize via AOI. Furthermore, AOI primarily serve for describing an approximate area of a component for semantic localization of topologically linked objects and is not suited for an application in objects that have a complex geometry.

Subclasses, which are related to the same axis, e.g. aoi:HorizontalCentralArea and aoi:PeripheralArea, are disjoint to each other, which is defined through the OWL axiom owl:disjointWith. Consequently, the precise area position in three-dimensional space of an AOI is defined through assigning three classes that are related to different axes. This is to prevent the assignment of classes to instances that would result in inaccurate area descriptions e.g., an AOI that represents the complete side of a component, thus making the purpose of applying AOI for semantic localization obsolete. Therefore, instead of defining one AOI that is classified through multiple classes related to one axis, multiple AOI for each class should be defined.

AOI classes, which are used for representing areas along the horizontal axis of a component, are divided into the two disjoint classes aoi:HorizontalCentralArea and aoi:PeripheralArea, whereby the first one is used for describing the central area of a component along the horizontal axis and the latter one is used for defining areas near the component periphery (see Figure 5). The class aoi:Periphery, an additional subclass of aoi:PeripheralArea, is used for explicitly defining the periphery of the component.

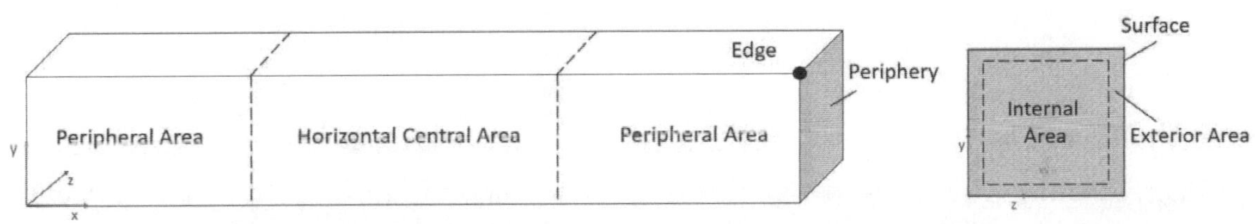

Figure 5: AOI types for representation of areas related to a beams local x- and z axis

The representation of areas that are related to a component's depth is defined through the usage of additional classes that describe external and internal areas along the component's depth. When utilizing an AOI subclass that defines the depth of an area, it is mandatory that the AOI instance is already classified in planar space utilizing a class for either vertical or horizontal localization. Thereby, the class aoi:ExternalArea is used for defining areas near the surface. Its disjointed class aoi:InteriorArea represents the negation area of the exterior area, i.e. the internal area. To explicitly define the surface of a component, aoi:Surface, a subclass of ExteriorArea is used. In addition, aoi:Surface is defined as superclass of aoi:Periphery, so that it could also be implicitly inferred that this subclass is handled as exterior area.

AOI related to the height are represented through one of three classes for defining an area in the upper, lower, or central vertical space of a component (see Figure 6). Additionally, the top and bottom of a component is described through the classes aoi:Top and aoi:Bottom, which are subclasses of either aoi:UpperArea or aoi:Bottom as well as aoi:Surface. In this regard, the top and bottom definition relate to the component boundaries and not the absolute top or bottom, which are specified through geometric coordinates.

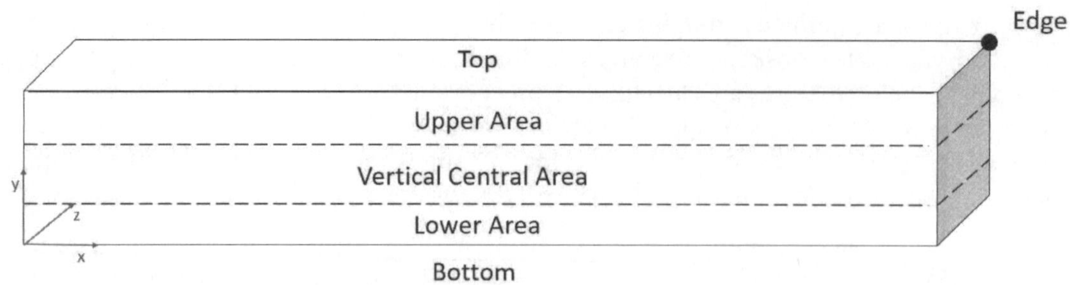

Figure 6: AOI types for representation of areas related to a components local x- and z-axis

A special case is the representation of edges since an edge functions as connection point between multiple AOI. For representing edges, the class aoi:Edge is used.

Although the predefined subclasses of aoi:AreaOfInterest can be used for a superficial semantic description of a location area of connected entities to a component, the overall concept of AOI is not limited to the provided terminology. Therefore, it is also possible to create an instance of aoi:AreaOfInterest without using any of its subclasses and describe it further through properties from other ontologies. The AOI ontology does not provide any terminology for defining geometry data. This is because in corresponding geometric representations of components, their shape and localization are usually not described or segmented through a separate area object, but solely via associated geometric data. When integrating the information of the semantic model in a BIM environment, the AOI information does not need to be linked with geometry data since an implicit connection through its linked instances is defined.

4. Application of AOI

A main benefit of AOI is the description of geometry information without requiring explicit geometry data. Therefore, a primary application would be the recording of existing constructions and corresponding damage since a detailed geometry is often not provided in initial inspections. Additionally, the machine-interpretable information defined via AOI in a model can be utilized for constraint-checking validation processes or automatic evaluations through reasoning of predefined expert knowledge. In this regard, the appropriate AOI information must not be asserted by human experts but can also be processed through geometry analyzing algorithms.

To demonstrate the possibilities of the AOI ontology, two application scenarios are presented in this paper. The first one shows an exemplary application of modelling representations of detected damages in a component via AOI and a corresponding filter example that utilizes the ontology query language SPARQL[5]. In the second application scenario, it is shown how AOI can provide benefits for evaluating damage information through rules that are defined in shapes using the Shape Contraint Language (SHACL)[6]. Both examples are written in RDF using the Turtle notation[7].

4.1 Modeling and filtering damage information

Following the concept of assigning entities to an AOI, which is linked to a component, damage representations modelled via DOT can be assigned to a building element by providing

[5] https://www.w3.org/TR/sparql11-overview/

[6] https://www.w3.org/TR/shacl/

[7] https://www.w3.org/TR/turtle/

additional information about their location. Listing 1 shows an exemplary definition of a damage representation, which extends across multiple affected components. On one component, the damage is located at the upper corner. Thereby, an instance of aoi:ComponentSide has been assigned for better horizontal localization. The damage extends to another connected component and due to its size is located by utilizing two AOI, one for describing an area around the lower corner and another for the central corner of the component.

```
#Damaged components
inst:damagedComponent-1 a bot:Element ;
       aoi:hasSide inst:westSide .
inst:westSide a aoi:ComponentSide ;
       aoi:hasAreaOfInterest inst:AOI-UpperCorner .
inst:damagedComponent-2 a bot:Element ;
       aoi:hasAreaOfInterest inst:AOI-LowerCorner ,
                             inst:AOI-CentralCorner .
#Damage representation
inst:damage-A a dot:DamageElement .
#Damage-A located at upper corner of component-1
inst:AOI-UpperCorner a aoi:PeripheralArea ,
                        aoi:UpperArea ,
                        aoi:Surface ;
       aoi:locatesDamage inst:damage-A .
#Damage-A located at lower corner of component-2
inst:AOI-LowerCorner a aoi:PeripheralArea ,
                        aoi:LowerArea ,
                        aoi:Surface ;
       aoi:locatesDamage inst:damage-A .
#Damage-A located at central corner of component-2
inst:AOI-CentralCorner a aoi:PeripheralArea ,
                        aoi:VerticalCentralArea ,
                        aoi:Surface ;
       aoi:locatesDamage inst:damage-A .
```

Listing 1: Definition of a damaged component and assignment of damages through AOI

Since the AOI ontology has been formalized in RDF, queries utilizing SPARQL could be applied. Listing 2 shows an exemplary query for filtering all entities that are assigned to components, which are part of a specific AOI. Thereby, the example relates to a specific use case, in which all damages located at the surfaces of components are queried.

```
SELECT ?component ?damage ?aoi
WHERE {
       ?component aoi:hasAreaOfInterest ?aoi .
       ?aoi aoi:locatesDamage ?damage .
       ?aoi rdf:type aoi:Surface
}
```

Listing 2: SPARQL query for selecting all damages localized at the component surface

4.2 Reasoning damage information

An important part when inspecting existing constructions is the subsequent evaluation of detected damages and their effect on the structural health. Usually, the damage assessment is done manually by a human expert. For this purpose, expert knowledge is used, which is based on standards and previous research. It is possible to formalize this expert knowledge in digital rules, which then could be reasoned by software applications in an automated process

(Hamdan & Scherer, 2019). An example application of inferring additional information about a detected damage is the classification of a bending crack (see Figure 7). Thereby, a damage object (d_1) that represents a crack, is assigned to an AOI (aoi_1), which is linked to a beam component (be_1) made of reinforced concrete. The AOI is classified as aoi:Surface, aoi:HorizontalCentralArea and aoi:LowerArea.

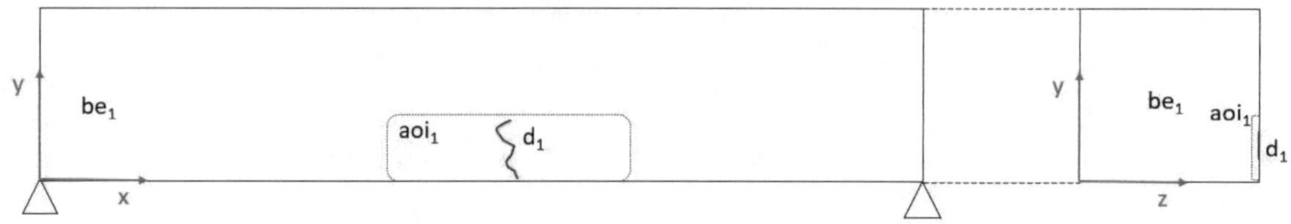

Figure 7: Application of AOI on a concrete beam affected by a bending crack

In general, a logic-based damage evaluation requires not only information about the detected damage properties and affected construction, but also about the component location, in which the damage has occurred. For instance, a damage is usually identified as bending crack in a load-bearing concrete component, if the crack has a vertical alignment and is located at the central lower area of the beam (based on the installed reinforcement). By utilizing the AOI, the crack location is semantically defined, thus allowing the application of rules for inferring bending cracks. The following Equations describe this expert rule. Thereby, the AOI for defining the area where bending cracks appear is defined as A_{bc}. Additionally, vertical cracks are defined as V_c (Hamdan & Scherer, 2019).

$$A_{bc}(aoi) = Surface(aoi) \cap HorizontalCentralArea(aoi) \cap LowerArea(aoi) \tag{1}$$

$$V_c(d) = Crack(d) \cap crackAngle(d, a) \cap (a > 30) \cap (a < 60) \tag{2}$$

$$\forall d \exists be, aoi\ (Beam(be) \cap hasExternalLoads(be, 1) \cap hasAreaOfInterest(be, aoi) \cap A_{bc}(aoi) \cap locatesDamage(aoi, d) \cap V_c(d)) \rightarrow BendingCrack(d) \tag{3}$$

In the example, A_{bc} defines an area *aoi*, which is located on the lower central part of a concrete beam. The depth does not extend above surface level. The damage *d* must be classified as crack and needs to have an angle *a* that must be between 30 and 60 degree to be classified as vertical crack. In this regard, the range for the angle degree has been approximated based on given expert experiences, thus is not covered by any standardized source. Based on these two requirements, the rule in equation 3 defines that each damage that fulfils the constraint V_c and affects a beam *be*, which is affected by external loads e.g., the weight of other components or sources that is not its own dead weight, is a bending crack, if it is located in an area according to A_{bc}.

The rule described in these Equations is digitally formalized through using the advanced features of SHACL (see Listing 3). By utilizing a reasoner that supports the processing of SHACL rules, the shape can be used for automatically classifying bending cracks in a beam, provided that the required information is asserted.

```
cdo:Crack
  a rdfs:Class , sh:NodeShape ;
  sh:rule [
    a sh:SPARQLRule ;
    sh:construct """
      CONSTRUCT {
        $this rdf:type cdo:BendingCrack .}
      WHERE {
        ?component rdf:type product:Beam .
        ?component brstr:hasExternalLoads true .
        ?component aoi:hasAreaOfInterest ?aoi .
        ?aoi rdf:type aoi:Surface .
        ?aoi rdf:type aoi:HorizontalCentralArea .
        ?aoi rdf:type aoi:LowerArea .
        ?aoi aoi:locatesDamage $this .
        $this cdo:crackAngle ?angle .
        FILTER (30 < ?angle && ?angle < 60)}"""].
```

Listing 3: SHACL shape for classifying bending cracks in a beam utilizing a SPARQL rule

5. Conclusion

In this research, a solution is proposed for semantically describing the location of an object in relation to an attached construction component. Therefore, a web ontology for defining Areas of Interest (AOI) has been developed, which functions as an auxiliary ontology for the integration in existing AEC ontologies, such as BOT (Rasmussen et al., 2017). Thereby the conception and development have been aligned towards a suitable implementation in ontologies that represent damaged structures via DOT (Hamdan et al., 2019). AOI define an area or volume in a component that can be annotated with further information. Thereby, the AOI is used as intermediate element between the component and the attached object, which could be another assembled component, a detected damage, etc. In this regard, a localization in a semantic model is possible without relying on previously determined geometry data. Consequently, the utilization of AOI results in new options for querying, validating, and reasoning ontological building representations, of which some examples were presented in this paper.

The examples presented in this paper solely focus on modelling and assessing damage of an existing building. However, AOI could also utilized in other fields since the problem that AOI try to solve is not only limited to damage representations but also affects the semantic modeling of the construction itself. For example, reinforcing elements cannot be accurately described based on their topological properties alone. Besides the aggregation of a reinforcing element in a concrete component, the relative position within the component is of high importance, e.g., whether a reinforcing bar is located at the upper or lower area of a concrete slab, resulting in different loads that affect the bar. Therefore, future developments could focus on other use cases for AOI and lead to a more generic approach of the ontology. Furthermore, the current AOI approach is designed towards the application on components that are defined through a cubic geometry. New updates on the ontology should also support non-cubic geometries such as those of shell constructions. It is also subject of future research, how AOI could be used for BIM models that are not geometry-based, especially digital representations of existing constructions that are created during a BIMification process (Scherer & Katranuschkov, 2018). Moreover, the existing draft version of AOI could be refined based on current standards and practices in AEC in future updates.

Acknowledgments

This research work was enabled by the support of the Federal Ministry of Education and Research of Germany through the funding of the projects BIM-SIS (project number 01-IS18017D).

References

Artus, M., & Koch, C. (2019). State of the Art in Damage Information Modeling for Bridges State of the Art in Damage Information Modeling for Bridges. July, 0–10.

Bundesanstalt für Strassenwesen. (2018). Anweisung Straßeninformationsbank für Ingenieurbauten, Teilsystem Bauwerksdaten (ASB-ING). https://www.bast.de/BASt_2017/DE/Ingenieurbau /Publikationen/Regelwerke/Erhaltung/ASB-ING.html

Cacciotti, R., Blaško, M., & Valach, J. (2015). A diagnostic ontological model for damages to historical constructions. Journal of Cultural Heritage, 16, 40–48. https://doi.org/10.1016/j.culher.2014.02.002

Hamdan, A.-H., Bonduel, M., & Scherer, R. J. (2019). An ontological model for the representation of damage to constructions. 7th Linked Data in Architecture and Construction Workshop.

Hamdan, A.-H., & Scherer, R. J. (2019). A knowledge-based Approach for the Assessment of Damages to Constructions. 36th CIB W78 2019 Conference. https://itc.scix.net/pdfs/w78-2019-paper-055.pdf

International Organization for Standardization. (2018). ISO 16739-1:2018 Preview Industry Foundation Classes (IFC) for data sharing in the construction and facility management industries -- Part 1: Data schema. 2018.

Pauwels, P., & Terkaj, W. (2016). EXPRESS to OWL for construction industry: Towards a recommendable and usable ifcOWL ontology. Automation in Construction, 63, 100–133. https://doi.org/10.1016/J.AUTCON.2015.12.003

Rasmussen, M., Pauwels, P., Lefrançois, M., Schneider, G. F., Hviid, C., & Karlshøj, J. (2017). Recent changes in the Building Topology Ontology. https://hal-emse.ccsd.cnrs.fr/emse-01638305

Scherer, R. J., & Katranuschkov, P. (2018). BIMification: How to create and use BIM for retrofitting. Advanced Engineering Informatics, 38, 54–66. https://doi.org/10.1016/j.aei.2018.05.007

Wagner, A., Bonduel, M., Pauwels, P., & Rüppel, U. (2020). Representing construction-related geometry in a semantic web context: A review of approaches. Automation in Construction, 115(February), 103130. https://doi.org/10.1016/j.autcon.2020.103130

Wagner, A., & Rüppel, U. (2019). BPO: The building product ontology for assembled products. CEUR Workshop Proceedings, 2389, 106–119.

Deep Neural Networks for Visual Bridge Inspections and Defect Visualisation in Civil Engineering

Julia Bush[a]*, Tadeo Corradi[b], Jelena Ninić[a], Georgia Thermou[a], John Bennetts[c]
[a] University of Nottingham, UK, [b] Mind Foundry, UK, [c] WSP, UK
Julia.Bush@nottingham.ac.uk

Abstract. Ageing infrastructure is a global concern, and current structural health monitoring practices are coming under review. With a view to streamline the visual bridge inspection process, we assess the classification performance of two Deep Neural Networks, VGG16 and MobileNet, on a challenging dataset of over 70,000 unprocessed bridge inspection images of three defect categories: corrosion, crack, and spalling. Grad-CAM "heatmap" visualisations on VGG16 predictions provide a coarse localisation of the defect region and some insight into the functioning of the network. Similar performance is attained on MobileNet, for applications where speed or computational cost is a consideration. We conclude that with further optimisation this approach could have an application in automated defect tagging.

1. Introduction

Civil engineering infrastructure asset owners such as Highways England and Network Rail in the UK require asset condition information for several purposes: planning maintenance interventions, assessments of load capacity, exploring trends, leaving audit trails and measuring contracted services (Bennetts et al., 2018). Current practice in bridge inspection produces data with significant uncertainty, and the metrics used in defect description are not optimal for life-cycle analysis of deterioration and cost.

The primary source of bridge condition data are visual bridge inspections (Bennetts et al., 2016). Since these are numerous, costly, and may require disruption to the transport network, it is imperative that the data collected be of high quality and suitable for analysis to obtain the information required. As the value of data is increasingly recognised, data collection and recording processes are coming under review to enable meaningful condition information to be derived and represented, and to then be adequately exchanged between all parties involved.

For the purposes of this paper, only visible defects will be considered, mainly: cracks, corrosion and spalling. The current practice for monitoring defects which have no visible signs (such as chloride migration, carbonation, alkali-silica reaction) is to carry out appropriate intrusive testing. This is planned and managed separately from visual inspections and is beyond the scope of this paper.

2. Background: Computer Vision and Deep Neural Networks for Bridge Inspections

Koch et al. (2015) reviewed Computer Vision based defect detection and condition assessment of concrete and asphalt infrastructure. It was concluded that at the time it was not possible to detect, measure, assess and document defects to provide an integrated and comprehensive approach for inspections. More recently, Azimi et al. (2020) have reviewed deep learning approaches in structural health monitoring more generally. Among the challenges identified in the literature to date, the following two emerge as the most pertinent:

- the lack of standardisation in identifying relevant defect parameters to comprehensively represent defect information, and

- the absence of publicly available large datasets to leverage supervised learning methods for the robust detection and classification of several infrastructure defect types.

This paper is intended to respond to both above issues, with a long-term view towards an automated end-to-end digital bridge inspection process, and eventual digital twinning of infrastructure assets.

Liang (2019) provide a successful precedent for use of VGG16 (Simonyan and Zisserman, 2015) initialised on ImageNet (Russakovsky et al., 2015) for bridge damage classification. Class Activation Mapping (Selvaraju, 2017) has been applied to VGG16 initialised on ImageNet by Perez et al. (2019) to classify and locate building defects. In this paper, we adopt a similar approach to treat images of bridge defects.

3. Methodology

3.1 Image Data

A sample of over 200,000 images of bridge defects was obtained from Highways England for the work presented in this paper. In contrast to many publications to date, the number of images stated here refers to distinct photographs of bridge defects taken on site, which have not been cut up to generate multiple images from a single photograph. Neither have they been cropped to place the object of interest (the defect region in our case) in a prominent position within the image, which would require manual processing of a similar level of labour intensity as bounding box annotations.

The scenes have complex backgrounds and both object position and scale vary (see Figure 2 in Section 5). This, along with other inconsistencies (in lighting and weather conditions, camera, angle, resolution, shadows, background and foreground noise, surface markings, weather-induced surface wetness, irrelevant surface alterations such as small holes or stains) makes this dataset an important step towards developing a benchmark dataset for Computer Vision methods applied to bridge defects.

For any neural network architecture to be usable in real on-site conditions, it must be robust against the noise and variations (as described above) in the images it receives for making predictions. For those who seek to add value to the Civil Engineering industry, therefore, it is imperative to seek methods which move away from the clean laboratory image data and towards accommodating the real complex noisy image data encountered by bridge inspectors on site.

To the best of the authors' knowledge, this is the first time a dataset of this size and complexity has been examined. Inevitably, even an optimally designed methodology will require such a volume of data which is sufficient to overcome the noise. Given the complexity of the features which are sought to be learned, we expect dataset sizes to grow beyond what can be reasonably hand-crafted, even for the simplest case of image-level labels only. To pave the way for handling such datasets, the approach presented in this paper is focused on removing as much human input from data pre-processing as possible.

3.2 Data Set

The dataset consists of 200,852 photographs, tagged with one of a total of 161 possible defect types. Direct classification on the 161 labels is both undesirable and unlikely to succeed, as the classes are heavily imbalanced and, in many cases, represent overlapping concepts. Therefore we decided to create supergroups comprising several classes and selected three of them as a first attempt at an already challenging classification problem (Table 1).

Table 1: 3-class supergroup dataset to train VGG16 and MobileNet classifiers. No data augmentation.

Defect class	Number of images	Data volume, GB
Corrosion	23,474	4.1
Crack	26,775	5.2
Spalling	19,837	3.3
Total	*70 086*	*12.6*

The chosen supergroups represent defect types that ultimately are of highest interest in industry: corrosion, crack and spalling. For the remaining classes (excluding corrosion, crack and spalling), Figure 1 gives an indication of the numbers of images per class, for those classes which contain 1,000 or more images.

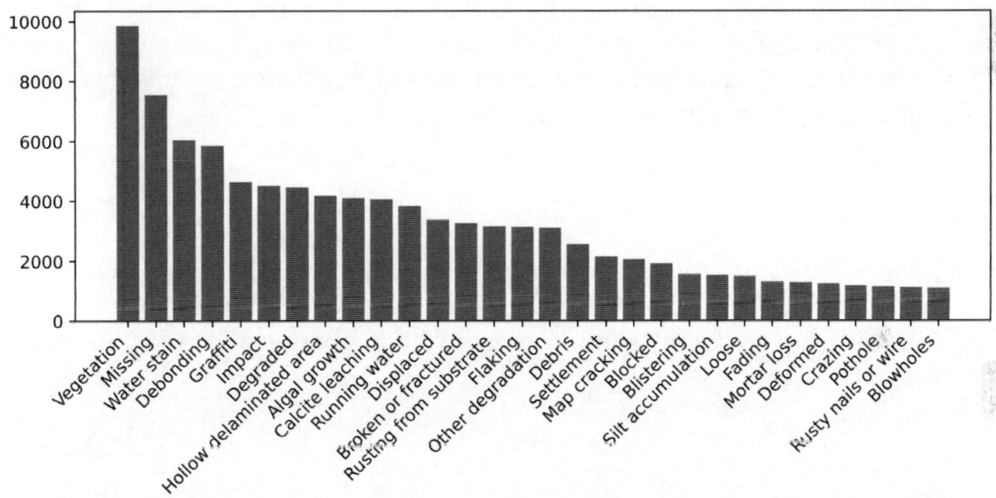

Figure 1: Number of images of other defect types

3.3 Neural Network Architecture

The VGG16 (Simonyan and Zisserman, 2015) was used following the example of previous applications of this architecture to building and bridge defects. In the spirit of searching for the simplest solution which produces predictions of sufficient complexity and accuracy, we also used MobileNet (Howard et al., 2017). The complexity and performance indicators of VGG16 and MobileNet are compared in Table 2, where the top-1 and top-5 accuracy refer to the model's performance on the benchmark ImageNet (Russakovsky, 2015) validation dataset (not on the dataset presented in this paper). Depth refers to the topological depth of the network, and includes activation layers, batch normalisation layers etc.

Table 2: Comparison of complexity and performance of VGG16 and MobileNet.

Architecture	Size, MB	Top-1 Accuracy	Top-5 Accuracy	Parameters	Depth
VGG16	528	0.713	0.901	138,357,544	23
MobileNet	16	0.704	0.895	4,253,864	88

3.4 Localisation

Selvaraju et al. (2017) observe that convolutional layers naturally retain spatial information which is lost in fully-connected layers, so the last convolutional layers are expected to have the best compromise between high-level semantics and detailed spatial information. Their approach, Gradient-weighted Class Activation Mapping (Grad-CAM), uses the gradients of any target concept (say "corrosion" in a bridge defect classifier) flowing into the final convolutional layer to produce a coarse localisation map highlighting the important regions in the image for predicting the concept.

As will be seen in Section 5, this coarse localisation map can provide clues as to the functioning of the trained neural network, allowing us to peek into the model which is traditionally considered "black box". Furthermore, Selvaraju et al. (2017) provide successful examples of Grad-CAM being used as seed for weakly supervised segmentation, an approach which the authors intend to apply to bridge defect images in later work.

4. Implementation

Implementation in Python 3.7 using Keras high-level neural network library, which is in turn built on TensorFlow 2.3.0 machine learning library, using a CUDA[1] 10.1 backend and CUDNN[2] 7. During network training, the dataset was randomly split into 80% training and 20% validation subsets.

4.1 VGG16

The VGG16 was trained using the standard approach of first training the classifier head only, and consequently unfreezing all layers (initialised with ImageNet weights). The classifier head consisted of four layers, namely, flatten, dense, dropout, dense, comprising 3,232,161 trainable parameters.

Firstly, we used the full dataset of 200,852 images belonging to 161 classes as per the original defect type image labels. As expected, this yielded low accuracy (Table 3). Secondly, the dominant classes were grouped into a three-class (corrosion, crack, spalling) dataset, transfer learned for 5 epochs, and fine-tuned for 10 epochs (Figure 2). The latter achieves a considerable validation accuracy of 0.81. Section 5 provides a discussion of possible sources of errors.

---

[1] https://developer.nvidia.com/cuda-toolkit

[2] https://docs.nvidia.com/deeplearning/cudnn/archives/cudnn_765/cudnn-release-notes/index.html

Table 3: VGG16 training and accuracy.

Training mode	Dataset	Epochs	Validation accuracy
Transfer learning	Raw, 161 classes	20	0.23
Fine tuning	Raw, 161 classes	10	0.31
Transfer learning	Selective, 3 classes	5	0.71
Fine tuning	Selective, 3 classes	10	0.81

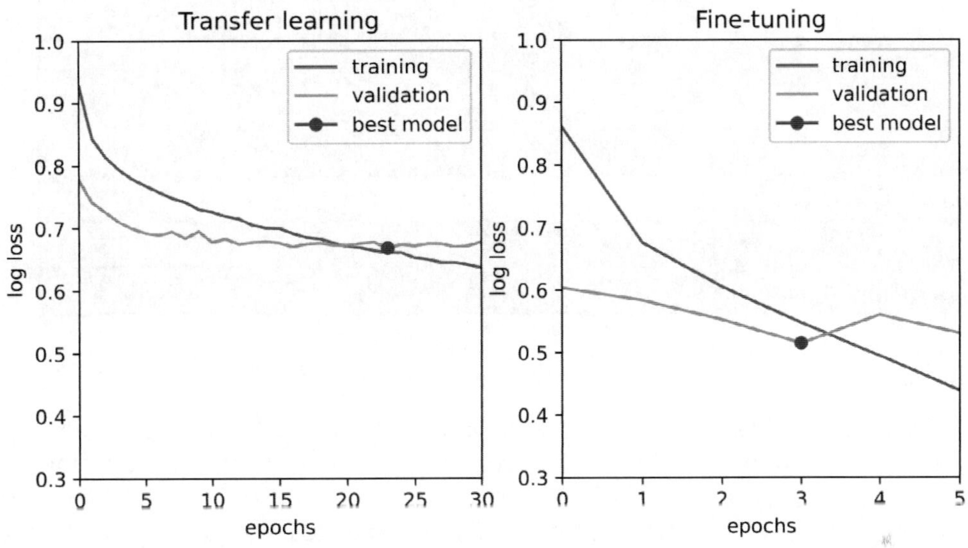

(a) (b)

Figure 2: VGG16 learning curves for the 3-class dataset (train loss in blue and validation loss in orange). (a) transfer learning for 5 epochs; (b) fine-tuning for 10 epochs

In Table 4 True Positives (along the diagonal in blue) indicate the numbers of correct predictions for each of the three classes, corrosion, crack, and spalling. False Positives (upper right in orange) tell us, for example, that 391 images whose true classification is "crack" were predicted to be "corrosion". An example of False Negatives (lower left in pink): 226 whose true classification is "corrosion" and whose predicted classification was "crack".

Table 4: VGG16 confusion matrix.

True class:	***corrosion***	***crack***	***spalling***
Prediction:			
corrosion	4199	391	648
crack	226	4387	787
spalling	269	577	2532

Accuracy (the total number of correct predictions divided by the total number of predictions made) alone can be an overly optimistic indicator of network performance. Table 5 provides a summary of more robust machine learning classification metrics. It is desirable to attain high precision, while low recall is acceptable, in applications where it is not important to identify all positive instances, but it is important that when an instance is identified as positive, this is with high certainty. High recall, on the other hand, corresponds to capturing the maximum number of true positives, and false positives are well tolerated (low precision). Ideally we would like both precision and recall to be high, and the F1 score combines both into a single metric. Weighted average can be very different from macro average if the network is simply guessing by predicting the majority class(es). In our case, all values are similar to the accuracy score, confirming that this is a valid indicator of performance. "Support" is simply the number of images of a given class which were used for validation.

Table 5: VGG16 classification metrics.

	Precision	Recall	F1 score	Support
corrosion	0.80	0.89	0.85	4,694
crack	0.81	0.82	0.82	5,355
spalling	0.75	0.64	0.69	3,967
accuracy			0.79	14,016
macro average	0.79	0.78	0.78	14,016
weighted average	0.79	0.79	0.79	14,016

4.2 MobileNet

MobileNet was designed as an attempt to reduce the intensive computational burden of earlier deep network architectures. It comprises a large number of narrow layers, and can be tuned to achieve a compromise between predictive performance and speed. Its name stems from its intended use on mobile devices, on which it is often important to create a fast prediction without heavy power consumption.

Where VGG16 provides an indication of the ultimate potential of a state-of-the-art neural network for the purpose of bridge defect classification, MobileNet gives a realistic prospect of what could be achievable in an eventual deployed application on a portable mobile device. For the purpose of transfer learning, we remove the top fully-connected layer and replace it with a simple network initialised with random weights (average pooling followed by four dense layers, comprising 164,611 trainable parameters).

Figure 3 shows the train and validation loss at each epoch. Tables 6 and 7 show the performance statistics after 15 epochs (5 for transfer learning). The performance in almost every metric is below that of VGG. However this is attained using considerably less computing power.

Therefore, while we focus primarily on VGG, we consider that smaller architectures such as MobileNet have high potential, particularly for problems in which latency or power consumption are limiting factors.

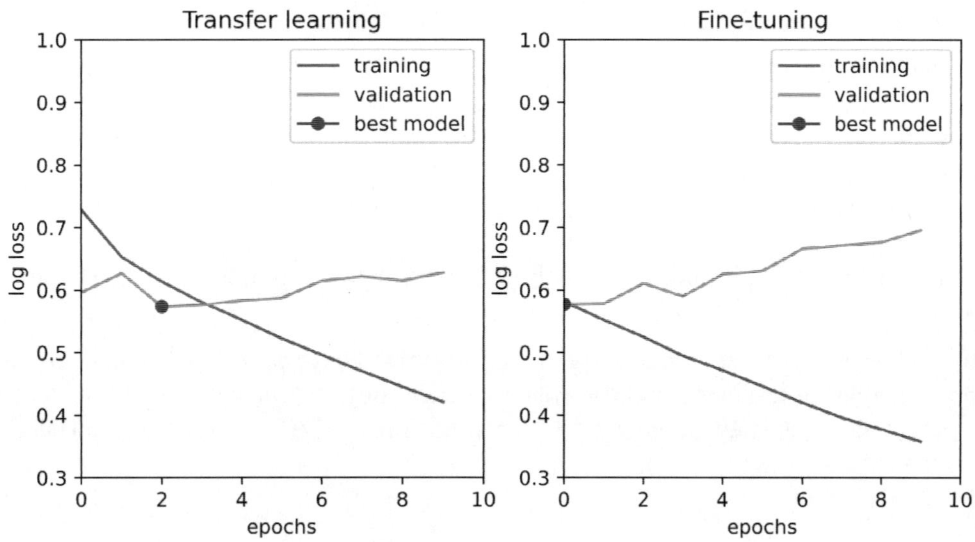

(a) (b)

Figure 3: MobileNet learning curves for the 3-class dataset, during transfer learning (a) and during fine-tuning (b).

Table 6: MobileNet confusion matrix.

True class:	*corrosion*	*crack*	*spalling*
Prediction:			
corrosion	3718	315	411
crack	446	4406	1215
spalling	511	446	2313

Table 7: MobileNet classification metrics.

	Precision	**Recall**	**F1 score**	**Support**
corrosion	0.84	0.80	0.82	4,675
crack	0.73	0.83	0.83	5,315
spalling	0.68	0.59	0.63	3,939
accuracy			0.75	13,929
macro average	0.75	0.74	0.74	13,929
weighted average	0.75	0.75	0.75	13,929

5. Results

While classification accuracy and other metrics stated in Section 4 give some positive indication of the neural network performance, a more informative discussion of results lies in close inspection of classification predictions and their associated Grad-CAM visualisations. All examples given here have been drawn from the validation subset of the VGG16 transfer learned for 5 epochs and fine-tuned for 10 epochs on the 3-class dataset.

Unlike semantic segmentation, which requires a class label for every pixel in every image for training, classification requires only one label for the entire image. By extracting features common to images belonging to the same class, the trained network can not only make class predictions for a given image, but also give some indication of which pixels are more or less pertinent to that prediction. In Figure 4(a) the image is correctly classified as belonging to the "corrosion" class, and the main corroded region is correctly located. This remains true for scenes with complex backgrounds, such as Figure 4(b), where the network largely ignores the irrelevant buildings, trees, fences etc.

Many images in the dataset contain signs of multiple defects, presenting a challenge for prediction accuracy assessment. Grad-CAM visualisations in Figure 5 illustrate that while multiple defect features may be correctly identified, the image has a single "correct" class against which to score the prediction.

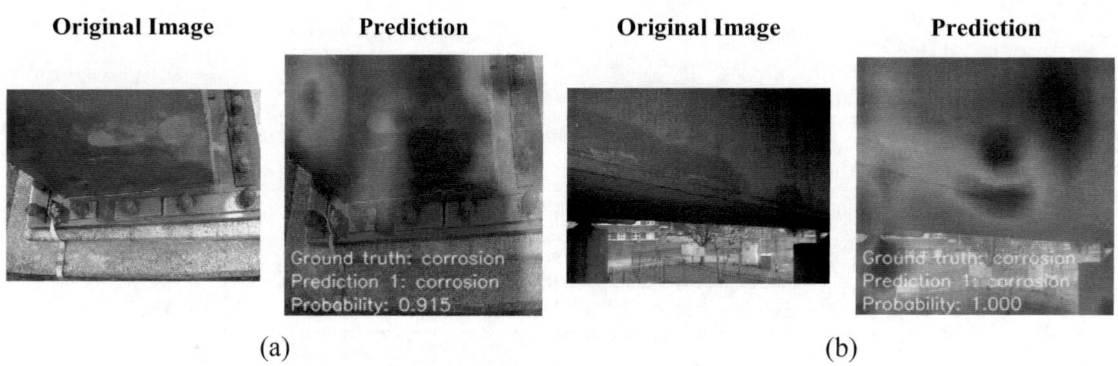

Figure 4: VGG16 trained on corrosion, crack, and spalling classes. Grad-CAM visualisations reveal those regions of the image which have been the most pertinent for the classification process.

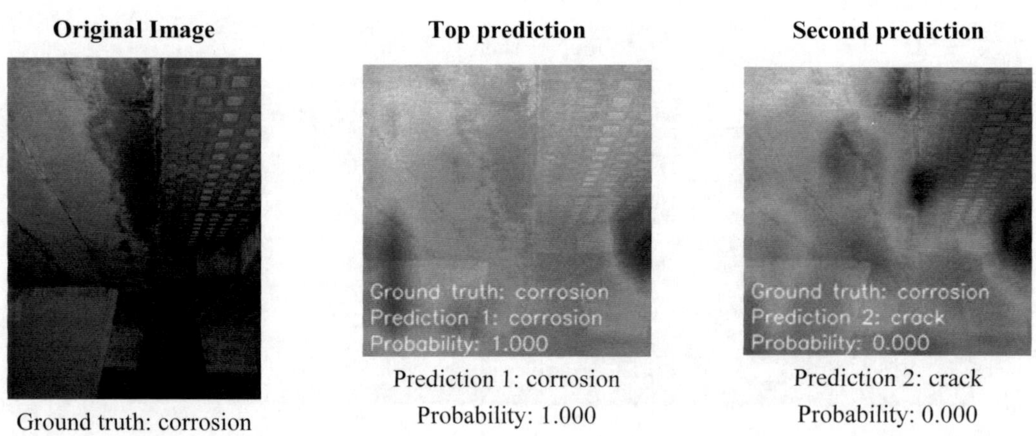

Figure 5: VGG16 trained on corrosion, crack, and spalling classes. Signs of multiple defects on the same image are correctly located.

We gain further insight into the inner workings of the network by observing the examples given in Figure 6. The top row contains examples of correctly predicted image classes, however the heatmaps clearly show that the classifier relied on component features (namely the geometry of the bolt and the steel connection) rather than the defect features (such as the colour and texture typical of corrosion) to make its prediction. This can easily happen where there is positive correlation between a component type and a defect type (for example, if the dataset contains many images of corroded bolts, the network will tend to classify any image containing any bolt as "corrosion" without any signs of corrosion itself). This type of error can be overcome by balancing the dataset (for example, by including images of non-corroded bolts).

Another likely source of errors is poor correspondence between the image scene and the ground truth label. Taking the examples along the bottom row of Figure 5, we see that the network is correctly identifying the crack and spalling features and hence predicting "crack" and "spalling". However this prediction will be scored as erroneous during validation since the ground truth labels are "corrosion" in both cases. This situation may arise when the inspector is not able to gain better access to the defect and has to take the photograph from an unsuitable position, or when the ground truth classification is given according to the underlying causes rather than the visual cues (as per the bottom right example in Figure 6). Moreover, the ground truth classification may sometimes be simply incorrect, for example, due to human error.

Figure 6: VGG16 trained on corrosion, crack, and spalling classes. Top row: images are correctly classified using incorrect features. Bottom row: defect features are correctly identified, however the predictions are scored as "incorrect" due to poor ground truth labels.

6. Conclusions and Future Work

In this paper we presented an application of deep learning to bridge defect image classification using big data acquired from bridge inspections in the UK over the past 20 years. Established machine learning metrics were used for rigorous performance assessment. The achieved accuracy is significant, however further optimisation of network architecture and training methodology remain possible.

Finally, we provide a reference comparison to a smaller neural network (MobileNet), demonstrating that similar performance it attainable, where speed or computational cost is a consideration.

The following improvements are recommended:

- Where a strong positive correlation between a structural component type and defect type exists, include non-defect (normal) component images in the dataset to prevent classification by component features rather than defect features.
- Create partially annotated datasets to guide the feature-learning process.
- Set aside a test dataset of images which the neural network sees neither during training nor during validation to enable complete network performance assessment.
- Guard against overfitting, for example with regularisation, or dropout.

Another meaningful supergroup could be created of other, smaller, defect classes with strong visual cues (for example, graffiti, vegetation, water-related staining). Since these classes contain relatively few images (around 1,000 per class) compared to the dominant classes of corrosion, crack and spalling, isolating them would create a more balanced dataset.

We conclude that this would be a valid approach in the larger framework of automating selected tasks in the visual bridge inspection process, and could be used as a means of automatic defect tagging and coarse localisation in a 2D images, which could in turn be extended to a 3D environment.

Acknowledgements

The authors would like to thank Highways England, UK, for the use of bridge defect images and their associated defect types. This research is part of a project funded by the EPSRC, WSP UK and Highways England, and would not have been possible without their support.

References

Azimi, M., Eslamlou, A.D., Pekcan, G. (2020). Data-driven structural health monitoring and damage detection through deep learning: State-of-the-art review. Sensors (Switzerland) 20. doi:10.3390/s20102778.

Bennetts, J., Vardanega, P.J., Taylor, C.A., Denton, S.R. (2016). Bridge data - What do we collect and how do we use it? in: Transforming the Future of Infrastructure through Smarter Information - Proceedings of the International Conference on Smart Infrastructure and Construction, ICSIC2016, ICE Publishing. pp.531–536. doi:10.1680/tfitsi.61279.531.

Bennetts, J., Webb, G., Denton, S., Vardanega, P.J., Loudon, N. (2018). Quantifying uncertainty in visual inspection data, in: Maintenance, Safety, Risk, Management and Life-Cycle Performance of Bridges - Proceedings of the 9th International Conference on Bridge Maintenance, Safety and Management, IABMAS 2018, CRC Press/Balkema. pp.2252–2259.doi:10.1201/9781315189390-306.

Howard, Andrew & Zhu, Menglong & Chen, Bo & Kalenichenko, Dmitry & Wang, Weijun & Weyand, Tobias & Andreetto, Marco & Adam, Hartwig. (2017). MobileNets: Efficient Convolutional Neural Networks for Mobile Vision Applications.

Koch, C., Georgieva, K., Kasireddy, V., Akinci, B., Fieguth, P. (2015). A review on computer vision based defect detection and condition assessment of concrete and asphalt civil infrastructure. Advanced Engineering Informatics 29, 196–210. doi:10.1016/j.aei.2015.01.008.

Liang X. (2019). Image-based post-disaster inspection of reinforced concrete bridge systems using deep learning with Bayesian optimization. Computer-Aided Civil and Infrastructure Engineering 34:415–430. https://doi.org/10.1111/mice.12425.

Perez, H., Tah, J.H., Mosavi, A. (2019). Deep learning for detecting building defects using convolutional neural networks. Sensors (Switzerland) 19.doi:10.3390/s19163556.

Russakovsky, O., Deng, J., Su, H., Krause, J., Satheesh, S., Ma, S., Huang,Z., Karpathy, A., Khosla, A., Bernstein, M., Berg, A.C., Fei-Fei, L., 2015.ImageNet Large Scale Visual Recognition Challenge. International Journal of Computer Vision 115, 211–252. doi:10.1007/s11263-015-0816-y.

Selvaraju, R.R., Cogswell, M., Das, A., Vedantam, R., Parikh, D., Batra, D. (2017). Grad-CAM: Visual Explanations from Deep Networks via Gradient-Based Localization, in: Proceedings of the IEEE International Conference on Computer Vision, Institute of Electrical and Electronics Engineers Inc..pp.618–626. doi:10.1109/ICCV.2017.74.

Simonyan, K., Zisserman, A. (2015). Very deep convolutional networks for large-scale image recognition, in: 3rd International Conference on Learning Representations, ICLR 2015 - Conference Track Proceedings, International Conference on Learning Representations, ICLR.

Automated decision making in structural health monitoring using explainable artificial intelligence

José Joaquín Peralta Abadía[a], Henrieke Fritz[a], Georgios Dadoulis[b], Kosmas Dragos[a] and Kay Smarsly[a]
[a] Hamburg University of Technology, Germany, [b] Aristotle University of Thessaloniki, Greece
joaquin.peralta@tuhh.de

Abstract. The need for processing large amounts of data from modern structural health monitoring (SHM) systems has been fostering interdisciplinary SHM strategies employing artificial intelligence (AI) algorithms for detecting damage. However, the opacity of several AI algorithms hinders their widespread adoption in SHM practice. To enhance the trust of practitioners in AI algorithms, this paper proposes an explainable artificial intelligence (XAI) approach for SHM. The approach builds upon the capabilities of unsupervised learning algorithms for detecting outliers indicative of structural damage in structural response data. Moreover, features in the data governing outlier detection are "explained" to the user, thus ensuring transparency in decision making. The XAI-SHM approach is validated via simulations of a pedestrian bridge that may or may not include damage. Results show that the XAI-SHM approach is capable of distinguishing between damage and random fluctuations of structural properties, while decisions made by the XAI-SHM approach are clearly explained.

1. Introduction

Structural health monitoring (SHM) strategies usually entail obtaining information extracted from processing structural response data collected by sensor networks. Data processing in SHM builds upon well-established methods drawn from the fields of mechanics and mathematics, usually in a purely data-driven manner, i.e. without considering any physical principles underlying the structural behavior. However, damage may manifest in ways that are too subtle to be captured by data-driven models based on classical mechanics. Moreover, the increasing complexity of civil infrastructure and the heterogeneity of data on which decisions are based have been raising the need for high-complexity models to facilitate decision making. As a result, the SHM community has been actively exploiting the powerful predictive capabilities of artificial intelligence (AI) algorithms for SHM purposes (Smarsly et al., 2007).

Most AI algorithms draw their predictive capabilities from detecting associations and relationships among datapoints (also referred to as "observations") within datasets that are impractical or impossible to approximate with physics-based models or closed-form mathematical expressions. As such, AI algorithms have been gaining increasing popularity across a broad range of scientific and industrial applications (Barr and Feigenbaum, 2014). From an SHM perspective, associations and relationships between datapoints, which are arrays of measurements of structural responses, aim at revealing patterns indicative of structural damage. Particularly in identifying the onset of damage, i.e. the early stages of damage, conventional structural-dynamics-based SHM strategies, such as operational modal analysis, have been proven ineffective due to the low sensitivity to damage (at a localized level) of structural dynamics properties, such as eigenfrequencies (Friswell and Penny, 1997). Evidently, SHM stands to benefit from AI, and its subset machine learning (ML), for damage detection.

Although the vivid interest of the SHM community in AI is relatively recent, early research discussing AI concepts for SHM dates back to the end of the 20th century. The statistical pattern recognition paradigm introduced by Farrar et al. (1999) is one of the earliest attempts to bring concepts of supervised learning and unsupervised learning into discussion over damage detection. The authors have presented damage detection approaches, both "informally", i.e. through manual expert-judgment interpretation of damage-indicative features, and "formally", i.e. using well-established AI algorithms. An elaborate discussion on the statistical pattern recognition paradigm and on machine learning aspects for SHM, in general, can be found in Farrar and Worden (2013). Identifying the onset of damage, which, as previously mentioned, may be a focal point of SHM, has been addressed as "novelty" (outlier) detection by Worden et al. (2000). Further examples of AI-based SHM approaches include using artificial neural networks for damage detection, accounting for uncertainties in data used for training the neural networks (Bakhary et al., 2007) and applying Bayesian regression models for identifying damage in expansion joints of bridges (Ni et al., 2020). Diverging from the objective of damage detection, Smarsly and Law (2014) and Dragos and Smarsly (2016) have demonstrated the applicability of artificial neural networks for sensor diagnostics in SHM systems. Given the increasing interest in adopting AI concepts in SHM, several reviews summarize the state of the art on AI (and ML) in SHM (Worden and Mason, 2006; Salehi and Burgueño, 2018).

Nonetheless, the inner mechanisms of several AI algorithms are opaque ("black-box"), thus raising trust issues with respect to predictions, which eventually hinder the widespread use of AI in SHM practice. This paper presents an approach to overcome the limitations of the black-box nature of AI algorithms used in SHM. Specifically, the emerging paradigm of "explainable artificial intelligence" (XAI) is used as a basis for shedding light into the internal mechanisms of AI algorithms that govern decision making. The proposed XAI-SHM approach is designed around an unsupervised one-class support vector machine (SVM) algorithm. The identification of damage by the one-class SVM algorithm, which after being implemented and trained is referred to as "one-class SVM model", relies on the detection of outliers. As a preprocessing step, continuous wavelet transform (CWT) is applied to the structural response measurements to expose patterns (features) in the data, which are then used as input to the one-class SVM model. With respect to "explaining" the decisions of the SVM model to practitioners, emphasis is placed on the features exposed by the CWT that govern decision making. The proposed XAI-SHM approach is validated through simulations of a pedestrian bridge considering a broad variety of structural behavior scenarios that may or may not include damage. The results show that the XAI-SHM approach is capable of distinguishing structural behaviors attributed to damage from structural behaviors attributed to random fluctuations of the structural properties of the bridge, while the classification of the XAI-SHM outcomes is clearly explained.

In the remainder of the paper, a brief description of the one-class SVM model is given in Section 2, and the details of the XAI-SHM approach are explained in Section 3. The validation tests are presented in Section 4, followed by the summary and conclusions as well as a brief discussion on future research.

2. One-class support vector machine for outlier detection

This section presents a brief description of the one-class SVM unsupervised learning algorithm that is used for outlier detection. Support vector machines have been widely used for classification and regression analysis in ML owing to their robust predictions (Xu et al., 2009). The advantages of SVM algorithms include effectivity in high-dimensional spaces, effectivity in cases where the number of features is greater than the number of datapoints, memory efficiency, and versatility in regard to the number of kernel functions available. Kernel functions are used to "learn" boundaries for separating datapoints into classes within a dataset and include linear kernel, polynomial kernel, radial basis function (RBF) kernel, and sigmoid kernel. SVM for classification problems solves the problem

$$\min \frac{1}{2}\mathbf{w}^T\mathbf{w} + c\sum_{i=1}^{n}\zeta_i : \begin{cases} y_i\left(\mathbf{w}^T\varphi(x_i)\right) + b \geq 1 - \zeta_i \\ \zeta_i \geq 0,\ i = 1 \ldots n \end{cases} \quad (1)$$

Where n is the number of datapoints, ζ_i is the average empirical error, and, given training data $x_i \in \mathbb{R}^p$ (i = 1…n) and target vector $y \in \{1, -1\}^n$, the goal is to find weight $\mathbf{w} \in \mathbb{R}^p$ and bias $b \in \mathbb{R}^p$ such that $y_i(\mathbf{w}^T\varphi(x_i))+b \geq 1-\zeta_i$ for most datapoints. The kernel function applied to x is $\varphi(x_i)$, and p is the number of features characterizing the datapoints in the dataset. The tradeoff between misclassification of training data against the simplicity of the decision boundary is denoted as c. In this study, the one-class SVM algorithm for outlier detection learns a kernel function for outlier detection, where newly collected data is classified as similar or different to training data (Schölkopf et al. 2001).

The one-class SVM algorithm is useful in imbalanced learning problems, where there is abundance of data for a class, e.g. representing normal circumstances of a physical process ("normal scenario"), and insufficient data for a second class that diverges from normal circumstances ("outlier scenario"). The one-class SVM algorithm is trained with normal scenario data, learning the boundaries of the datapoints. For SHM problems, where data is usually in a high-dimensional space, the RBF kernel is usually employed. For training a SVM machine using an RBF kernel, two hyperparameters must be defined, v and γ. The v hyperparameter replaces c in the SVM problem, is bounded between 0 and 1, and represents the expected proportion of outliers in the dataset. The γ hyperparameter represents the influence of a single datapoint on other datapoints. Therefore, the larger the γ parameter is, the closer datapoints must be to each other to be grouped together. Considering two datapoints, x and x', the RBF kernel function is represented mathematically as

$$\varphi(x, x') = e^{-\gamma\|x-x'\|^2}. \quad (2)$$

To better understand how the one-class SVM algorithm works, Figure 1 presents an example of a dataset with datapoints characterized by two features (mapped as horizontal and vertical axes coordinates) and the output of a one-class SVM model trained with the dataset. Both γ and v have been set to 0.1 for the example. Datapoints used for training, new normal datapoints (normal scenario), and new outlier datapoints (outlier scenario) are represented with red circles, light blue circles, and yellow circles, respectively. The boundary learned for the normal scenario data is represented with a red line, enclosing most of the training datapoints. The green contours surrounding the boundary represent the distance of the outlier datapoints from the boundary learned.

From an SHM perspective, the boundary that needs to be learned by the one-class SVM algorithm distinguishes normal structural operation from the presence of anomalies that would indicate structural damage. Specifics on how the one-class SVM algorithm is implemented for the purposes of the XAI-SHM approach presented herein are shown in the next section.

3. Explainable artificial intelligence for SHM using unsupervised learning

In this section, the XAI-SHM approach is illuminated. First, an overview of the XAI-SHM approach is provided, followed by brief descriptions of methods used for data preprocessing and for explanation of one-class SVM outcomes as part of the proposed approach.

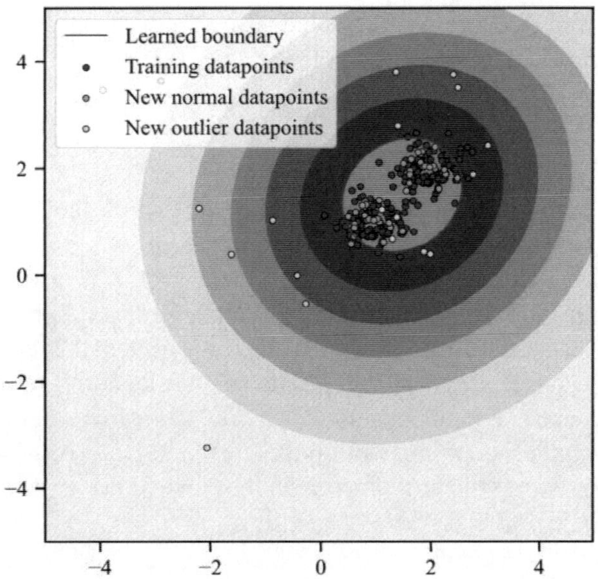

Figure 1: Example dataset as classified by the one-class SVM model.

3.1 Overview of the XAI-SHM approach

Considering a typical SHM strategy, the workflow of the XAI-SHM approach is shown in Figure 2. One of the challenges of the XAI-SHM approach is to distinguish damage from random fluctuations in structural properties and environmental conditions, which are typically part of the "normal" structural condition. These random fluctuations concern, for example, changes in loading conditions (e.g. ice and traffic accumulation) and changes in geometry/stiffness due to temperature variations. Since SHM systems are usually designed on a long-term basis, it is reasonable to assume that the vast majority of structural response measurements collected by SHM systems correspond to normal structural conditions and can be, therefore, used as normal scenario data for training the one-class SVM. Furthermore, since detecting outliers in the structural response data relies on features, raw structural response data is pre-processed using *continuous wavelet transform* to expose features of the normal scenario data prior to being fed to the one-class SVM. Upon completing training, structural response data from an unknown structural condition is collected, pre-processed using CWT, and fed to the one-class SVM, which analyzes the data for the existence of outliers. Finally, the outcome of the one-class SVM algorithm is explained to the user in terms of features contributing to the detection of outliers, using *Shapley values* (Lundberg and Lee, 2017). The main purpose of the explanation is to showcase that the detection of outliers is not random but based on *specific features* existing in the data. In what follows, brief descriptions of the CWT method and of the Shapley values method are provided.

3.2 Continuous wavelet transform

The continuous wavelet transform is a digital signal processing (DSP) technique that enables obtaining information on the frequency content of signals, e.g. datapoints with structural response measurements, at discrete time intervals. While traditional DSP techniques based on the Fourier transform yield the overall frequency content of datapoints over a predefined period of time, the CWT provides a complete picture of which frequency components contribute to structural response measurements coupled with temporal information on the effect of each frequency component, referred to as "coupled time-frequency information". The CWT coefficients L_x of datapoint x over time t are defined as

$$L_x(a,\tau)=\frac{1}{\sqrt{a}}\int_{-\infty}^{+\infty}x(t)\psi\left(\frac{t-\tau}{a}\right)dt, \qquad (3)$$

with a being the "scale" factor of the CWT, and τ being the "shift" factor. The wavelet function, denoted by ψ (also referred to as "mother" wavelet), is a short wave function that is multiplied at every instance in time with datapoint x. The scale factor is used to compute wavelet coefficients across a range of scales, which may be considered as equivalent to the frequency bandwidth of the Fourier transform. The shift factor defines the delay considered when multiplying the mother wavelet with the datapoint, essentially moving the mother wavelet to cover the length of the datapoint. Continuous wavelet transform coefficients are typically depicted in two-dimensional plots (images) with the horizontal axis representing the shift factor and the vertical axis representing the scale factor. In the XAI-SHM approach, CWT coefficients are used as input data to the one-class SVM algorithm.

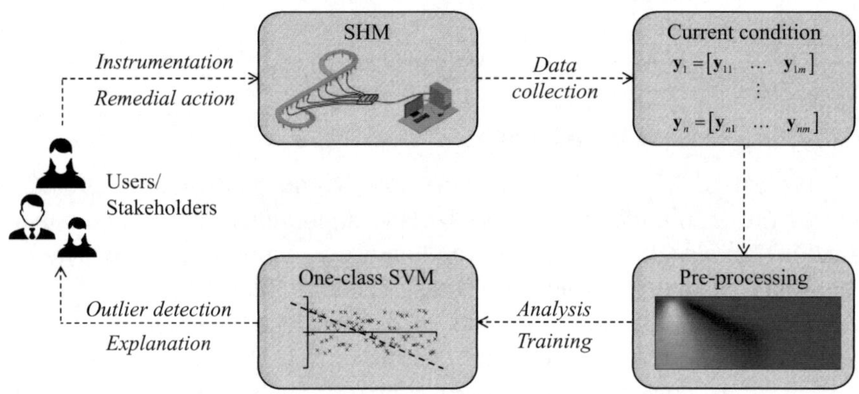

Figure 2: Overview of the XAI-SHM approach.

3.3 Shapley values for explainable AI

Shapley values is a concept based on game theory, where the behavior between several players, whose decisions are interactive, is studied with mathematical methods. From the Shapley values concept, the Shapley additive explanations (SHAP) have been proposed for explaining the output of ML models. SHAP values attribute the change in the prediction of a ML model to changes in the features of a datapoint, thus obtaining the contribution of each feature to the prediction. SHAP values are calculated by retraining ML models on subsets of features $S \subseteq F$, where F is the set of all features, and assigning an importance value λ to each feature i, representing the impact of the feature on the model prediction. The impact is calculated by comparing the predictions of a ML model $f_{S\cup\{i\}}$ trained with the feature present and of the ML model f_s trained with the feature suppressed. The differences are computed for all subsets $S \subseteq F$ for feature i, as the effect of suppressing a feature may depend on the effect of other features of the model. Thus, the SHAP values are calculated as

$$\lambda_i=\sum_{S\subseteq F\setminus i}\frac{|S|!(|F|-|S|-1)!}{|F|!}\left[f_{S\cup\{i\}}\left(x_{S\cup\{i\}}\right)-f_S\left(x_S\right)\right] \qquad (4)$$

Where x_S represents the vales of the input features in subset S.

4. Case study: Simulations of a pedestrian bridge

Validation tests for the proposed XAI-SHM approach are conducted via simulations of a full-scale pedestrian bridge. The simulations involve scenarios that correspond to normal structural condition, i.e. with no damage but with random fluctuations in structural properties, and to damage, i.e. with damage-induced changes in structural conditions. First, the pedestrian bridge is briefly described, and the modeling and simulation of the bridge is illuminated. Finally, the results from applying the XAI-SHM approach are presented and discussed.

4.1 Description of the pedestrian bridge

The pedestrian bridge is a reinforced concrete overpass facilitating pedestrian traffic over a waterfront boulevard in Thessaloniki, Greece. The main span of the bridge deck rests on two piers with variable rectangular cross sections, as shown in Figure 3.

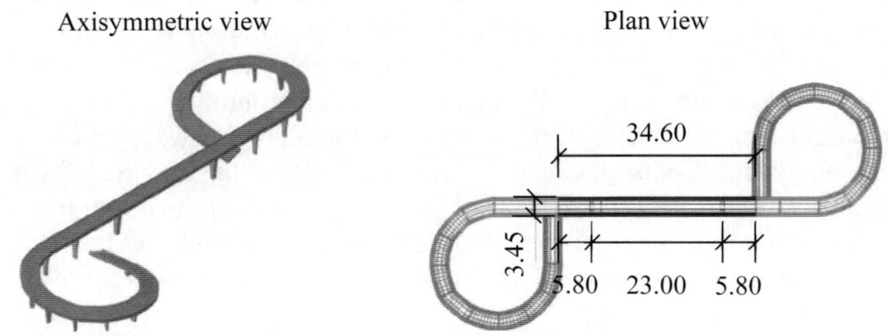

Figure 3: View and geometry of the pedestrian bridge.

The main span has a length of 34.60 m and is connected at its ends to two antisymmetric curved, skewed end-spans (depicted with grey color in the plan view) through expansion joints. As a result, the main span (depicted with black lines in the plan view) essentially behaves as a quasi-autonomous girder with an effective length of 23.00 m between the supports (centroids of piers cross sections), extended by two cantilevers of length 5.80 m, one at each support. Since the main span is located over the boulevard, its importance is higher than the end-spans; therefore, simulations in the validation tests will focus on the main span.

4.2 Modeling and simulation of the pedestrian bridge

The main span of the pedestrian bridge is modeled as a continuous girder ("beam model") using an analytical modeling approach presented in Manolis et al. (2020). The analytical modeling approach builds upon the premise that flexible structures with simple geometries may be considered as "waveguides" undergoing axial, flexural, and torsional vibrations. As such, the following modeling assumptions are made:

- The behavior of the beam model is described by the Bernoulli-Euler differential equation, which is explained below.
- The beam is of constant cross-section and constant mass per unit length.
- Pedestrian traffic is simulated with two point loads, each initially located at one support (pier). The loads move towards the middle of the main span ("moving loads"), i.e. in directions opposite to each other, at constant velocities.
- The presence of pedestrians on the main span would technically increase the structural mass of the main span and would affect its vibration characteristics. However, the mass

of the main span is much larger than the mass of pedestrians, therefore the change in structural mass is neglected and only "gravitational" effects of pedestrian traffic (i.e. the action of the moving loads in the vertical direction) is considered.

- The damping is viscous, i.e. proportional to the velocity response of the beam.
- The main span is simply supported at its connections to the piers.

According to the aforementioned assumptions, the Bernoulli-Euler equation of motion for each moving load is (Fryba, 1999):

$$EI\frac{\partial^4 w(x,t)}{\partial x^4} + \rho A\frac{\partial^2 w(x,t)}{\partial t^2} + C\frac{\partial w(x,t)}{\partial t} = P\cdot\delta(x-ct). \quad (5)$$

In Equation 5, E is the material modulus of elasticity, I is the moment of inertia of the beam cross section in the vertical direction, w is the vertical deflection of the beam, ρ is the material density, and A is the cross section area. The damping coefficient C is equal to $C = 2\rho A\xi\omega$, where ξ is the critical damping ratio and ω is the eigenfrequency of the beam model. For more information on the analytical modeling approach and on the solution of Equation 5, the reader is referred to Manolis et al. (2020). Variable x represents the coordinate (location) in the longitudinal axis of the beam, with $x = 0$ and $x = 23.00$ depicting the position of the left-hand side and of the right-hand side support (as depicted in the plan view), respectively. Variable t represents time, and P and c denote the magnitude and velocity of the moving load, respectively. Finally, δ represents a Dirac function for considering the position of the moving load. Based on information gathered during a previous study using the pedestrian bridge (Manolis et al., 2014), the location for collecting responses is selected at $x = 12.93$ m, and the values for the parameters of Equation 5 are summarized in Table 1.

For training the one-class SVM model, 500 training scenarios with random velocities for the moving loads and random fluctuations of structural parameters, representing normal structural conditions, are simulated. Each scenario comprises measurements collected over a period of 100 seconds with a sampling rate of 100 Hz. For testing the one-class SVM model, an additional 100 testing scenarios are devised, two of which involve damage in the bridge deck (stiffness reduction). The goal of the one-class SVM model is to identify the two damage scenarios as outliers. The results from applying the SVM model are shown in the following subsection.

Table 1: Beam model parameters.

Parameter	**Value**	**Units**
Modulus of elasticity (E)	$27.5\cdot10^6$	kN/m^2
Material density (ρ)	25.00	kN/m^3
Cross section area (A)	1.207	m^2
Cross section moment of inertia (I)	1.178	m^4
Critical damping ratio (ξ)	0.013	-

4.3 Results from outlier detection using the one-class SVM model

Each scenario in the dataset comprises 10000 measurements (with total duration 100 s and sampling rate 100 Hz). To reduce the dimensional space of the dataset and improve the accuracy of the model, while maintaining the information present in the scenario, downsampling to 100 features is performed using the Fourier method. Thereafter, CWT is applied to the dataset, using 40 scales and the *Morlet* function as mother wavelet (Morlet et al, 1982). The one-class SVM model is trained using the RBF kernel, with $\nu = 0.0051$ and $\gamma = 0.02$. Figure 4 presents the confusion matrix of the test predictions obtained from the one-class SVM model. The top-left and bottom-right elements represent correctly predicted scenarios, whereas the top-right and bottom-left elements represent incorrectly predicted scenarios. It can be observed that the one-class SVM model is capable of identifying outliers reliably, with a global accuracy of 92.85% (ratio between correctly predicted scenarios and total observations) and a precision of 95% (ratio between correctly predicted scenarios and total predictions of each scenario).

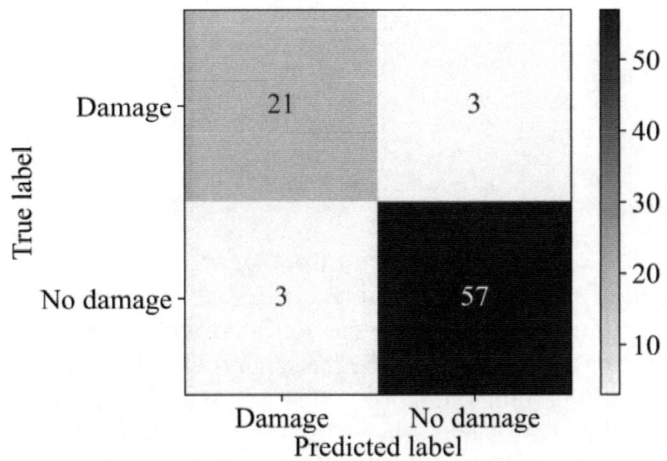

Figure 4: Confusion matrix of the predictions of the one-class SVM model.

4.4 Explanation of outliers detected by the one-class SVM model

After testing the one-class SVM model and obtaining reliable metrics, a SHAP "explainer", i.e. algorithm the computes SHAP values, is trained with the training scenarios. Afterwards, SHAP values are calculated for 20 randomly selected normal scenarios and 1 outlier scenario from the testing scenarios. Each scenario is reevaluated 500 times, representing 500 variations in the features of the scenario. Figure 5 presents exemplarily SHAP explanations for two testing scenarios, (a) a no-damage (normal) scenario and (b) a damage (outlier) scenario. The images on the left are the CWT coefficients for the scenarios and images on the right show the SHAP values overlaid on each CWT image. For each image, the y-axis represents the 40 scale factors of the CWT and the x-axis is the time point of measurement. It may be observed that the no-damage scenario has SHAP values close to zero, represented with almost transparent color, whereas the damage scenario has negative SHAP values, which indicate impact on the prediction. Therefore, it may be inferred that outlier detection is governed by features in the data and are not random. Moreover, the damage scenario has several CWT features marked with SHAP values with varying intensities of blue, revealing the features that have varying degrees of impact on the prediction of outliers.

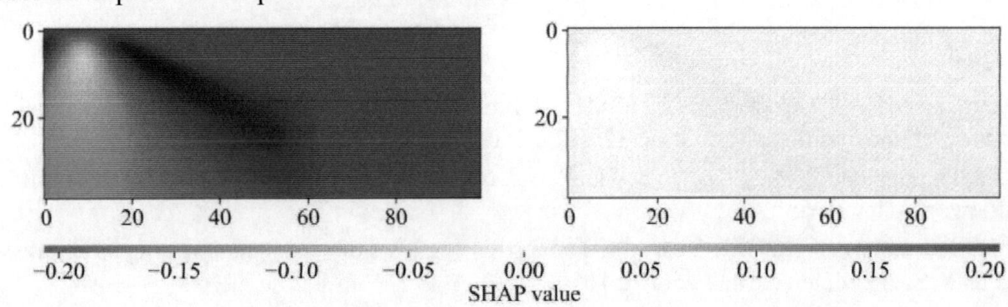

(a)

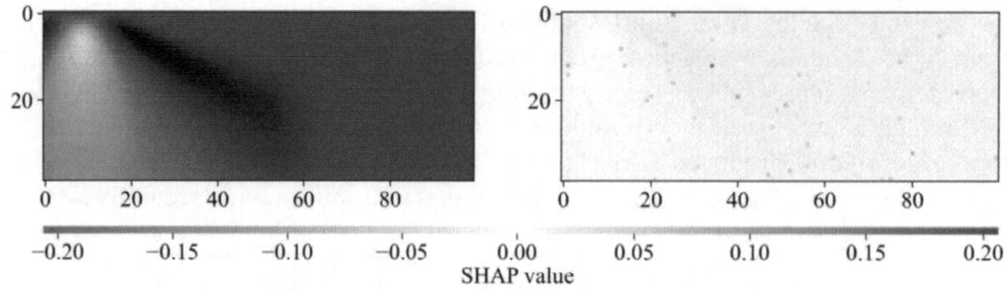

(b)

Figure 5: SHAP explanations for two scenarios, (a) no damage and (b) damage.

5. Summary and conclusions

This paper has presented an explainable artificial intelligence approach for structural health monitoring. The main goal of the proposed approach is to make the decisions of black-box AI models transparent to practitioners and enhance the confidence of the SHM community in AI. The XAI-SHM approach is based on detecting outliers in structural response data that indicate damage using an unsupervised learning one-class support vector machine algorithm. Moreover, the features in the structural response data governing the outcome of the one-class SVM are explained using Shapley values. The XAI-SHM approach has been validated through simulations of a pedestrian bridge including scenarios corresponding to normal structural condition and scenarios corresponding to damage. The results have showcased the ability of the XAI-SHM approach to detect damage scenarios as outliers, while the Shapley values clearly have shown that the detection of outliers is based on specific features existing in the structural response data. Future work will include a more thorough reevaluation of the features for each scenario, also addressing the role of low levels of existing damage at "normal operating conditions", to achieve more reliable and stable estimates of the SHAP values. Moreover, the interpretation of features governing the outcome of the one-class SVM will be investigated. Finally, the convexity of the data will be analyzed to ensure the appropriateness of the chosen SVM kernel.

Acknowledgements

The authors gratefully acknowledge the support offered by the German Research Foundation (DFG) through grants SM 281/12-1, SM 281/14-1, and SM 281/20-1. Any opinions, findings, conclusions or recommendations expressed in this paper are those of the authors and do not necessarily reflect the views of the DFG.

References

Bakhary, N., Hao, H., & Deeks, A.J. (2007). Damage detection using artificial neural network with consideration of uncertainties. Eng. Struct. 29(11), 2806–2815.

Barr, A., & Feigenbaum, E.A. (2014). The Handbook of Artificial Intelligence: Volume 2. Oxford, UK: Butterworth-Heinemann.

Dragos, K., & Smarsly, K. (2016). Distributed adaptive diagnosis of sensor faults using structural response data. Smart Mater. Struct. 25(10), 105019.

Farrar, C.R., Duffey, T.A., Doebling, S.W., & Nix, D.A. (1999). A statistical pattern recognition paradigm for vibration-based structural health monitoring. In: 2nd International Workshop on Structural Health Monitoring, Stanford, CA, USA, 09/08/1999.

Farrar, C.R., & Worden, K. (2013). Structural health monitoring: A machine learning perspective. Chichester, UK: John Wiley & Sons Ltd.

Friswell, M.I., & Penny, J.E.T. (1997). Is damage location using vibration measurements practical? In: International Workshop on Structural Damage Assessment using Advanced Signal Processing Procedures, Sheffield, UK, 06/30/1997.

Fryba, L. (1999). Vibrations of solids and structures under moving loads. London, UK: Thomas Telford, Ltd.

Gardner, P., Fuentes, R., Dervilis, N., Mineo, C., Pierce, S.G., Cross, E.J., & Worden, K. (2020). Machine learning at the interface of structural health monitoring and non-destructive evaluation. Phil. Trans. R. Soc. A. 378, 20190581.

Lundberg, S. M., & Lee, S. 1. (2009). A Unified Approach to Interpreting Model Predictions. In: Conference on Neural Information Processing Systems, Long Beach, CA, USA, 12/04/2017.

Manolis, G.D., Athanatopoulou-Kyriakou, A., Dragos, K., Arabatzis, A., Lavdas, A., & Karakostas, C.Z. (2014). Identification of pedestrian bridge dynamic response through field measurements and numerical modelling: Case Studies. Journal of Theoretical and Applied Mechanics 44(2), pp.03–24.

Manolis, G.D., Dadoulis, G., Pardalopoulos, S.I., & Dragos, K. (2020). Analytical modeling of flexible structures for health monitoring under environmentally induced loads. Acta Mechanica 231(2020), pp.3621–3644.

Morlet, J., Arens, G., Fourgeau, E., & Glard, D. (1982). Wave propagation and sampling theory-Part I: Complex signal and scattering in multilayered media. Geophysics, 47(2), pp.203–221.

Ni, Y.Q., Wang, Y.W., & Zhang, C. (2020). A Bayesian approach for condition assessment and damage alarm of bridge expansion joints using long-term structural health monitoring data. Engineering Structures 212(2020), 110520.

Salehi, H., & Burgueño, R. (2018). Emerging artificial intelligence methods in structural engineering. Engineering Structures 171, pp.170–189.

Schölkopf, B., Platt, J.C., Shawe-Taylor, J., & Smola, A.J., Williamson, R.C. (2001). Estimating the support of a high-dimensional distribution. Neural computation, 13(7), pp.1443–1471.

Smarsly, K., & Hartmann, D. (2007). Artificial intelligence in structural health monitoring. In: 3rd International Conference on Structural Engineering, Cape Town, South Africa, 10/09/2007.

Smarsly, K., & Law, K. H. (2014). Decentralized fault detection and isolation in wireless structural health monitoring systems using analytical redundancy. Advances in Engineering Software 73(2014), pp.1–10.

Worden, K., & Manson, G. (2006). The application of machine learning to structural health monitoring. Phil. Trans. R. Soc. A. 365, pp.515–537.

Worden, K., Manson, G., & Fieller, N.R.J. (2000). Damage detection using outlier analysis. Journal of Sound and Vibration 229(3), pp.647–667.

Xu, H., Caramanis, C., & Mannor, S. (2009). Robustness and regularization of support vector machines. Journal of Machine Learning Research 10(2009), pp.1485–1510.

VOX2BIM – A Fast Method for Automated Point Cloud Segmentation

Jan Martens, Jörg Blankenbach
RWTH Aachen, Germany
jan.martens@gia.rwth-aachen.de, blankenbach@gia.rwth-aachen.de

Abstract. In the past years, 3D reality capturing has consistently evolved to provide ease of use, high accuracy, fast capturing and low costs. Modern image matching algorithms allows even hobbyists to create point clouds from photogrammetric image series, while modern laser scanners are becoming smaller and cheaper, following a trend towards the fast but slightly less accurate mobile laser scanning. Especially laser scanning has become very attractive for reconstructing digital models of buildings and room layouts for facility management. Due to data exchange playing an important role in this field, the segmentation of indoor point clouds into rooms poses a useful step towards breaking large point cloud datasets down into manageable chunks and preparing them for other operations in automated modelling pipelines. Based on this problem, this contribution proposes a fast technique for the segmentation of point clouds into individual rooms based on voxels, 2D representations and morphological operations.

1. Introduction

Throughout the life cycle of buildings, various changes in a building's properties occur during operation or due to reconstructive works. Keeping track of the building's state, Building Information Modeling (BIM) has become an impactful trend in the past years addressing this issue. As thoroughly discussed by Rokooei (2015), the digital characteristics of BIM not only accurately represent the 3D geometry of buildings, they also contain rich semantic information. Consequently, Politi et al. (2018) noted that this makes BIM a useful standard for data exchange between different collaborators and the management of large structures, thus enabling planning, cost estimation, scheduling and Computer Aided Facility Management (CAFM). Despite the benefits of utilizing BIM in existing contexts, the adoption of it is still hindered by the time and effort required for as-is modeling. Becker et al. (2019) describe a rather typical case where either no pre-existing digital model is given or existing floor plans are outdated and do not reflect changes made during reconstruction. This means that the building's as-is or as-built geometry needs to be captured using methods such as laser scanning, with the acquired point cloud forming the foundation for the modeling process. Fortunately, capturing methods such as modern terrestrial laser scanning (TLS) have become more affordable while still providing high-quality data. As an increasingly popular alternative, mobile laser scanning (MLS) features notably higher capturing speed while simultaneously offering sufficient accuracy for modeling purposes.

Other works such as Tang et al. (2010) pointed out that manual modeling and related steps make this a laborious process, hence automated workflows for point cloud processing, modeling and analysis have garnered much attention in recent years. The segmentation of single rooms as non-overlapping, spatial units forms an important step in CAFM for cataloguing them and estimating the room areas and volumes of large facilities.

This work proposes a novel method for subdividing indoor point clouds into rooms for later use by other algorithms. The voxel-based origin of this approach makes it rather fast and robust, making it a useful part in complex processing workflows.

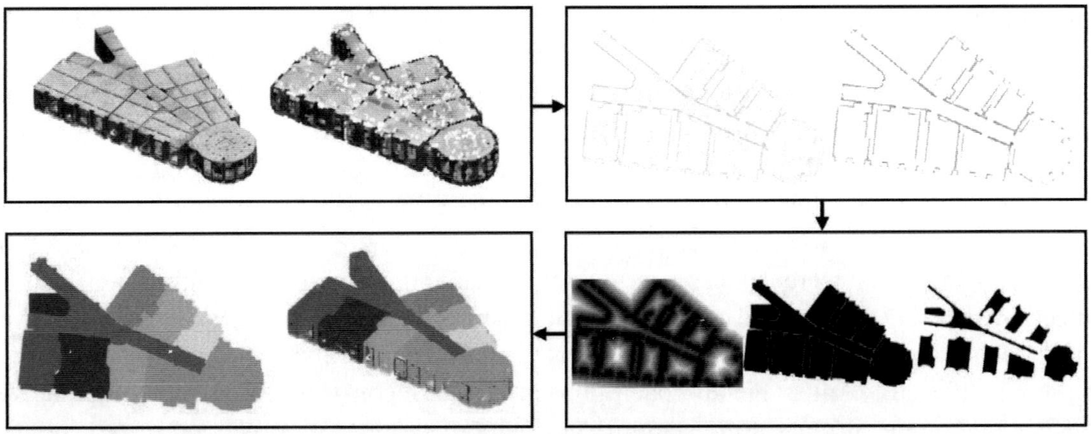

Figure 1: Workflow overview of presented approach. Top left: Load and voxelize point cloud. Top right: Extract vertical voxel densities and wall structures. Bottom right: Compute distance map with respect to walls, building inside area and seed regions for region growing. Bottom left: Estimate rooms by performing region growing, then transfer labels back to input point cloud.

2. Related Work

The fields of robotics and automated indoor reconstruction have resulted in various works concerned with floor plan generation or the detection and subsequent reconstruction of room segments and their geometry from point clouds. Most techniques require scan positions and are either estimating 3D planes in point clouds to reconstruct surfaces, project the data down to a 2D plane or combine 2D and 3D approaches. The creation of room segments is oftentimes either a prerequisite or intermediate step. Taking a closer look at other techniques is therefore worthwhile to pinpoint common and unique aspects among them and understanding the full context of this topic.

In contrast to most other works, Murali et al. (2017) preprocess point clouds by means of regular resampling with a voxel grid to cope with density variations. Subsequent steps deal with the estimation of wall planes where the Manhattan-world assumption plays a central role in re-orienting and rejecting detected planes. In treating planes and their intersections as graphs, cuboids enclosing the rooms are constructed as the final result. In a more generalized approach, the rejection and categorization of segments using the Manhattan-world assumption has been suggested earlier by Sanchez and Zakhor (2012) who labelled points based on their normal vectors, before clustering them into planes oriented along either the global X- or Y-axis of the building coordinate system. Previtali et al. (2014) described an approach which was expanded upon in their follow-up work Previtali et al. (2018). While the focus of both publications is the reconstruction of a room's enclosing planes, assigning points as part of a room was done by exploiting of a voxel-based occupancy map. This occupancy map was used in conjunction with the original scan positions and a ray-casting approach to detect occluding elements such as wall surfaces. Co-authors of the original work picked up on the ray-casting idea for assigning points to individual rooms in Ochmann et al. (2014) and further expanded on it in Ochmann et al. (2016) to create robust, full-fledged building layouts and wall models.

As proven by other works, simplifying the problem from 3D down to a 2D domain has proven to be a useful alternative in many cases. After identifying and removing the floor and ceiling planes from the input point cloud with a histogram-based technique, Oesau et al. (2013)

projected the remaining points to a 2D plane and performed a Hough Transform to extract accurate 2D representations of the wall structures. A graph-based strategy comparable to Murali et al. (2017) was then used to identify cells formed by intersecting lines, thus defining room layouts. Some years before, Okorn et al. (2010) approached the problem with similar ideas, where floor and ceiling planes would be removed through use of a histogram technique and the remaining point data would be projected onto a 2D grid. Determining point densities in vertical direction for each grid cell results in a density map. With high densities indicating their presence, walls were an easy target for extraction through a Hough Transform. A projection to a 2D grid would also be used by Ambrus et al. (2017) for ceiling and wall candidate points. Their combination of energy minimization and flood filling techniques resulted in a decent, multi-stage approach to room layout reconstruction. A rather unique way of using MLS trajectory and time stamp data for room segmentation was presented by Diaz Vilarino et al. (2017). During scanning, differences in the ceiling height profile were detected as they indicate passing through a doorway and therefore entering a new room. As with earlier ray-casting-based approaches, a 2D occlusion map of the point cloud ray-casting would be used to determine if points were visible from a scan position. Keeping track of the scanner's visited rooms and checking point visibilities means that each point can be assigned to the associated room.

3. Methods

As seen in other works, voxelization discretizes point clouds in a fast, robust way and is fairly efficient in highlighting large, connected structures. When dealing with floor and ceiling planes, this advantage becomes particularly apparent. The issue of detecting, filtering and merging wall planes thus becomes irrelevant. With laser scanning point clouds typically being oriented such that the captured floor and ceiling planes are pointing in orthogonal direction to the vector pointing upwards, this means that floor, wall and ceiling planes form continuous structures along at least one of the cardinal directions of the global coordinate system. Reducing voxel grids even further down to 2D images resembling 2D floor plans therefore poses a viable strategy. Inspired by these observations, the following methods illustrated in Figure 1 are proposed for the extraction of room layouts from point clouds.

Figure 2: Steps for wall extraction. From left to right: The input point cloud is voxelized and occupied voxels marked. The sum of occupied voxels in vertical direction forms a 2D density map. Thresholding the density map reveals the location of walls.

The first workflow steps which are focused on extracting wall locations, are illustrated in Figure 2. Initially, the captured point cloud is inserted into a voxel grid. Voxels are subsequently marked as occupied or unoccupied, depending on the number of contained points (see Figure 2, left). Typically, thresholding the number of points p present within a voxel using a user-defined parameter t already suffices for marking it as occupied:

$$Thresh(p) = \begin{cases} \text{occupied if } p \geq t \\ \text{empty if } p < t \end{cases}$$

While for most point clouds the thresholding parameter $t = 1$ which checks if any points are present within a voxel is already enough, but high levels ofnoise and outliers may require higher thresholding values. The distinction into occupied voxels also serves the purpose of ignoring local point density fluctuations and plays a key role for further processing steps. Examining the horizontal slices of the grid indicates that, depending on their height, they either highlight the location of floor/ceiling areas or the room layouts. However, even with normal vectors of each voxel estimated, it is overall hard to differentiate between noise, small vertical objects and actual wall structures. Solving this ambiguity, the number of occupied voxels in each vertical stack is summed up to create a 2D map where each pixel represents the occupancy at given position (see Figure 2, center). As a result, wall structures stick out due to their high densities as compared to other regions which show overall more homogeneous densities. The extraction of wall structures is subsequently done using Otsu's automated thresholding method (Otsu (1979)), resulting in a 2D map describing the location of walls (see Figure 3, right). The advantage of Otsu's method over other strategies is the way it attempts to maximize the in-between class variance for the resulting segments. Because of walls visibly sticking out due to their values, Otsu's method has little problems in identifying and extracting them without any need for parameters or user intervention.

With the location of walls now being known, the layout of the indoor area needs to be estimated next. The corresponding steps are shows in Figure 3, ordered from left to right. To this end, a distance transform (Kimmel et al. (1994)) is performed on the 2D wall map, as it calculates the distance of unoccupied cells to these walls (see Figure 3, left). When considering the voxel grid, it is known that the area outside the building starts at the grid's outer boundaries. Using a region growing method starting at the grid boundaries and following the distance gradient of the distance transform towards the walls fills all voxels of the outside area, allowing for a clean separation between indoor and outdoor area (see Figure 3, center). As a side-effect, this method provides a filling-in effect, where inside areas surrounded by partially visible walls are correctly recognized as such. The slightly jagged edges of the resulting area visible in Figure 3 hardly detract from the overall result.

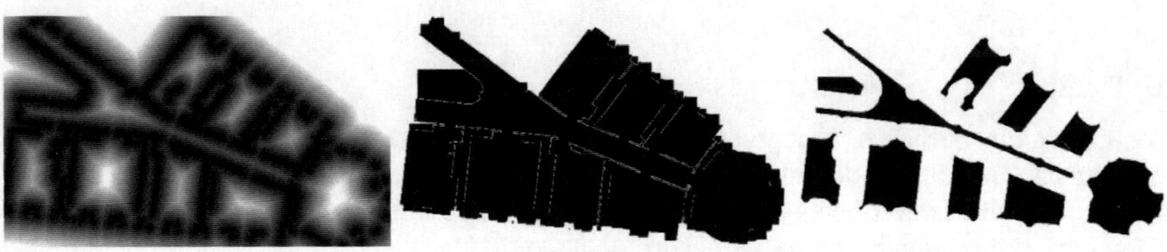

Figure 3: Steps for extraction of inside/outside areas and seed regions. From left to right: Distance transform with respect to the walls. Following the distance gradient from the image borders and marking pixels along the way reveals inside and outside area segments. Thresholding the distance-transformed image creates seed regions for room segmentation.

In the final step both, the detected walls and outside area are subsequently used as the boundaries for a region growing algorithm extracting the areas of each single room. The seed regions for this region growing method are constructed by exploiting the observation that each single room has a characteristic region in its center which maximizes the distances to each wall (as seen in Figure 3, left).

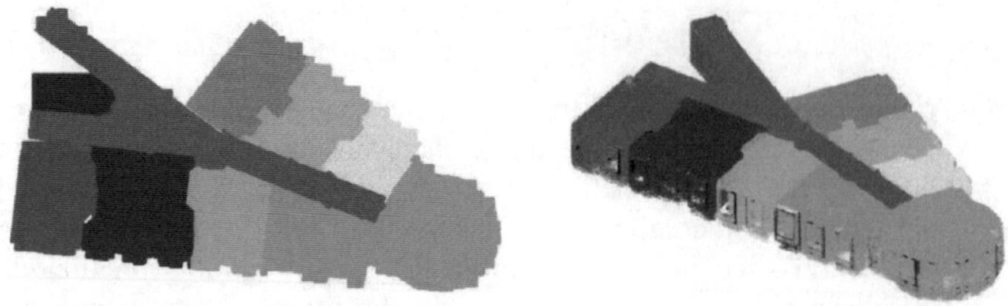

Figure 4: Results of region growing process. From left to right: Growing the seed regions creates the individual room segments. The resulting segments are mapped back to the point cloud.

Taking advantage of this observation, Otsu's automated thresholding is applied to areas of the distance-transformed wall map which have been marked as being inside the building. With Otsu's method choosing a threshold which maximizes the in-between class variance of segmented regions, the resulting individual seed regions are kept separate and still retain a desirable distance towards wall segments. The extracted seed regions (refer to Figure 3, right) are filtered based on their area to remove possible outliers. Afterwards, each seed region is represented as an individual binary image I with a marked region. Iteratively expanding each region is achieved using dilation operations from mathematical morphology as described by Serra (1983). This method leads to a slow growth of the marked regions due to the dilation operator $\oplus$ being defined as the maximum value within a specified (in our case circular) mask B around a reference pixel at position (x, y):

$$I \oplus B(x,y) = \max\{I(x-x', y-y') \mid (x', y') \in B\}$$

Expansions are bounded by the extracted walls, outside area and competing regions, ensuring that regions cannot grow beyond each room's boundaries or claim already marked segments. To improve performance, intermediate steps such as collisions of segments with walls, the outside area and segments can be implemented efficiently by overlaying the binary region images and applying logical "and" and "or" operations. As indicated in Figure 4, once all regions stop expanding, the resulting map denoting the area of each room can be transferred back to the point cloud to form the final result.

4. Results

For evaluation purposes, the given method was used to segment indoor point clouds of varying size and complexity into rooms. As shown in Table 1, execution times are rather swift due to point clouds first being broken down to 3D voxels and afterwards to 2D images. High execution times which normally occur when applying plane-fitting, filtering and post-processing methods to large, dense point clouds are consequently avoided. Interestingly, point cloud volume and area seem to factor into the execution time due to them being a relevant factor after the point cloud has been read and voxelized, but further execution time analysis would be necessary to uncover which steps depend on either point cloud size or point cloud volume and area. Even though full resolution point clouds may be used to accurately estimate the room layouts, subsampled point clouds of sufficient point density could be used as well. A detailed representation of the results is shown in Table 1. On a more relevant note however, choosing the correct voxel grid resolution plays a bigger role in both, performance and accuracy. While finely-resolved voxel grids require more memory and will give sharper results, they are ultimately more sensitive towards noise and poor point cloud resolutions. This may become especially problematic if strong noise is present. Coarse grid resolutions on the other hand strike a good balance between accuracy and robustness, even allowing for the segmentation of mobile laser scanning point clouds. The used voxel size parameter for the experiments is set to 0.025m, and performs generally quite well. In fact, even the segmentation of a photogrammetry point cloud is solid despite severe artefacts as evident in Figure 5. Tests performed on MLS point clouds look consistently convincing as well, proving that the technique can be applied to point clouds captured with a large variety of techniques. Challenging scenarios like staggered ceilings, partially scanned walls and rooms with panorama-like windows pose no problems. The robustness of the wall estimations and the inpainting-like effect of the outside area estimation are quite capable of dealing with these structures.

Figure 5: Segmentation results. In all examples, structures on the edge of the outside area oftentimes remain unmarked. First column: Photogrammetry point cloud. Despite severe artefacts and partially missing ceiling segments, the segmentation even picks up the partially captured room marked in pink. Second column: MLS point cloud. The room layout is rather complex but oversegmentation is mostly avoided.

In terms of drawbacks, it most obvious that unlike methods such as Ochmann (2016) and Previtali (2018) which are based on plane estimations in continuous 3D space, the presented algorithm is only able to operate at the accuracy of the used grid. Corner cases such as large occluded areas or dominant vertical non-wall structures detract from the overall solid quality of the results though, as shown in the right point cloud shown in Figure 6. Closets and shelves represent vertical structures which are notoriously hard to distinguish from actual walls and therefore oftentimes misinterpreted as such. As a result, some room segments will not include their related walls, while other rooms have claimed the seemingly empty area between shelves and walls of their neighbors. Other cases where room segments appear to be slightly inaccurate can occasionally be seen (as evident in Figure 5, right) and result from inaccurate wall estimates. Another issue is the fact that points outside the estimated room boundaries remain unmarked, as seen in Figures 5 and 6. Windows in particular will occasionally suffer from this problem. Oversegmentation is another issue which can occur in elongated corridors. The seed regions used for region growing are hard to estimate, occasionally leading to the formation of multiple seed regions within a single corridor. As described in Section 3, such small disconnected seed regions can be discarded before the region growing process based on their area though. More interestingly, axis-oriented point clouds suffer from this problem to notably lesser degree. This observation appears to be related to the fact that grid structures are used during each step and it is rather obvious that geometries following that Manhattan-world assumption therefore lead to sharper estimations for walls and seed regions.

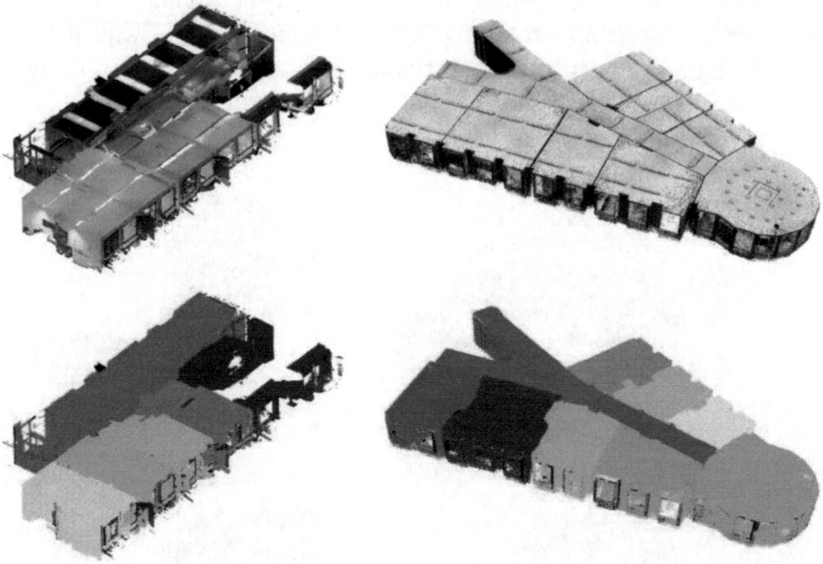

Figure 6: Segmentation results. First column: Downsampled TLS point cloud. Aside from the other rooms, a large, incomplete room section was correctly recognized and marked in dark blue. The staggered ceilings do not detract from the overall results. Second column: MLS point cloud. Despite the non-manhattan layout and geometries of the office rooms and rotunda, segmentation is successful. Shelves are however incorrectly recognized as walls, leading to inaccurate segments.

Table 1: Results for point clouds from varying sources. Execution times are averaged over 10 runs and include the time required for loading the point cloud data and writing the results. Note how execution times are impacted by both, the number of points and voxel grid volume.

Source	**# Points**	**Area [m²]**	**Execution Time [s]**
MLS	5.793.587	15509.25	32.1602
TLS	1.629.143	13901.7	7.6759
TLS	17.527.772	3539.775	22.0541
TLS	1.309.846	9167.0	21.8616
MLS	104.264.098	14751.225	173.4989
MLS	71.120.467	12226.15	91.7616
Photogrammetry	4.567.344	8044.05	10.9378

5. Conclusion and Outlook

As seen, the presented approach exploits multiple concepts also seen in multiple other 2D-based approaches such as Ambrus et al. (2017) and Okorn et al. (2010) and is capable of subdividing point clouds into room segments in a fast, automated way. With the algorithm's focus on and the test scenarios dealing with indoor office point clouds, clutter objects are being dealt with appropriately. Due to lack of data, no tests for special architectures such as slanted ceilings were carried out thus far and with no ground truth being given in the underlying examples, an analysis using error metrics was not possible yet and should be done in future works. An additional deeper execution time analysis and direct comparison with other methods in terms of speed and accuracy should be subject to further analysis. General shortcomings of the presented methods are inaccurate results for corner cases or specific, challenging scenarios like long corridors or entire wall sections removed from the point cloud. Like other methods such as the one proposed by Ambrus et al. (2017), the presented one easily misidentifies large vertical furniture pieces such as shelves as wall segments. On the flipside, Manhattan-like room layouts and point clouds previously oriented along the global axes using either manual or automated methods such as suggested by Martens and Blankenbach (2020) benefit the segmentation and leading to better results during the construction of seed regions with less small, disconnected seeds. In consequence, oversegmentation becomes less of a problem, with results being overall more robust. Combining the presented method with algorithms working without grid structures may additionally help clean up inaccurately segmented regions. In the simplest case, a post-processing step which takes the extracted region boundaries into consideration and deals with un- or mislabeled points would be a possible extension.

As seen in the results, the extracted segments describe the room layouts and the areas captured in the point clouds rather well. In consequence, they can be used for area estimations in the context of CAFM, as the foundation for the construction of spatial units in IFC models or for further processing and segmentation of individual rooms. The current limitations prevent the method from delivering exact results, further improvements are necessary to bring out its full potential. From a holistic perspective, embedding the presented approach into a full Scan-to-BIM workflow where individual building floors are segmented beforehand and parametric wall, floor and ceiling models are constructed is highly attractive. After all, wall locations are already estimated in one of the intermediate steps and used as boundaries for the region growing process. The extracted 2D wall information can therefore be used for full volumetric wall reconstructions by tracing and extruding the given form of the walls. Improvements of the algorithms addressing these ideas are already progress and aim to segment and reconstruct room layouts and parametric wall models of multistory buildings. The resulting BIM models and complementary information will be well-suited for scenarios as described by Politi et al. (2018) and Becker et al. (2019).

References

Rokooei, S. (2015). Building Information Modeling in Project Management: Necessities, Challenges and Outcomes. Procedia - Social and Behavioral Sciences. 210. 87–95. 10.1016/j.sbspro.2015.11.332.

Politi, Ruti and Aktaş, Engin and İlal, Emre. (2018). Project Planning and Management Using Building Information Modeling (BIM).

Becker, R., Lublasser, E., Martens, J., Wollenberg, R., Zhang, H., Brell-Cokcan, S., Blankenbach, J. (2019). Enabling BIM for Property Management of Existing Buildings Based on Automated As-is Capturing. 10.22260/ISARC2019/0028.

Tang, P. and Huber, D. and Akinci, B. and Lipman, R. and Lytle, A. (2010). Automatic reconstruction of as-built building information models from laser-scanned point clouds: A review of related techniques, Automation in Construction, Volume 19, Issue 7, Pages 829–843, ISSN 0926–5805.

Murali, S. and Speciale P., and Oswald, M.R. and Pollefeys, M. (2017). Indoor Scan2BIM: Building information models of house interiors, 2017 IEEE/RSJ International Conference on Intelligent Robots and Systems (IROS), Vancouver, BC, 2017, pp.6126–6133, doi: 10.1109/IROS.2017.8206513.

Zakhor, E. T. and A. (2016). Floor Plan Generation and Room Labeling of Indoor Environments from Laser. Journal of Wound, Ostomy and Continence Nursing, 43(6), 636–640.

Previtali, M., Díaz-Vilariño, L., Scaioni, M., Ochmann, S., Vock, R., Wessel, R., Bringmann, O. (2014). Automatic Generation of Structural Building Descriptions from 3D Point Cloud Scans. Computers and Graphics (Pergamon), 2(September), 8–15.

Previtali, M. and Díaz Vilariño, Lucia and Scaioni, Marco. (2018). Towards Automatic Reconstruction of Indoor Scenes from Incomplete Point Clouds: Door and Window Detection and Regularization. ISPRS - International Archives of the Photogrammetry, Remote Sensing and Spatial Information Sciences. XLII-4. 507–514. 10.5194/isprs-archives-XLII-4-507-2018.

Ochmann, S. and Vock, R. and Wessel, R. and Tamke, M. and Klein, R. (2014). Automatic generation of structural building descriptions from 3D point cloud scans. GRAPP 2014 - Proceedings of the 9th International Conference on Computer Graphics Theory and Applications. 120–127.

Ochmann, S. and Vock, R. and Wessel, R. and Klein, R. (2016) Automatic reconstruction of parametric building models from indoor point clouds, Computers & Graphics, Volume 54, 2016, Pages 94–103, ISSN 0097–8493

Oesau, S. and Lafarge, F. and Alliez, P. (2013). Indoor Scene Reconstruction using Primitive-driven Space Partitioning and Graph-cut.

Okorn B., Xiong, X., Akinci, B., Huber, D. (2010). Toward Automated Modeling of Floor Plans. Visualization and Transmissions (3DPVT).

R. Ambruş, S. Claici and A. Wendt. (2017). Automatic Room Segmentation From Unstructured 3-D Data of Indoor Environments, in IEEE Robotics and Automation Letters, vol. 2, no. 2, pp.749–756, April 2017, doi: 10.1109/LRA.2017.2651939.

V. Sanchez and A. Zakhor (2012). Planar 3D modeling of building interiors from point cloud data, 19th IEEE International Conference on Image Processing, Orlando, FL, 2012, pp.1777–1780, doi: 10.1109/ICIP.2012.6467225.

Díaz Vilariño, L. and Verbree, E. and Zlatanova, S. and Diakité, A. (2017). Indoor Modelling from SLAM-based Laser Scanner: Door Detection to Envelope Reconstruction. ISPRS - International Archives of the Photogrammetry, Remote Sensing and Spatial Information Sciences. XLII-2/W7. 345–352. 10.5194/isprs-archives-XLII-2-W7-345-2017.

Otsu, N. (1979). A Threshold Selection Method from Gray-Level Histograms, in IEEE Transactions on Systems, Man, and Cybernetics, vol. 9, no. 1, pp.62-66, Jan. 1979, doi: 10.1109/TSMC.1979.4310076.

Kimmel, R. and Kiryati, N. and Bruckstein, A.M. (1994). Sub-pixel Distance Maps and Weighted Distance Transforms. Journal of Mathematical Imaging and Vision, vol. 6, pp.223–233.

Serra, J. (1983). Image Analysis and Mathematical Morphology. Academic Press, ISBN: 978-0-12-637240-3, doi: 10.2307/2531038

Martens, J. and Blankenbach, J. (2020). An evaluation of pose-normalization algorithms for point clouds introducing a novel histogram-based approach. Advanced Engineering Informatics, vol. 46, ISSN 1474–0346

Automated Generation of Railway Track Geometric Digital Twins (RailGDT) from Airborne LiDAR Data

M.R. Mahendrini Fernando Ariyachandra, Ioannis Brilakis
University of Cambridge, United Kingdom
mfa47@cam.ac.uk

Abstract. Automated generation of railway track geometric digital twins (RailGDT) from airborne LiDAR data is an unresolved problem. Currently, this onerous manual procedure counteracts the expected benefits of the resulting RailGDT. State-of-the-art methods provided promising results, but are unable to generate RailGDTs over kilometres with complex railway geometries without forfeiting precision and manual cost. The challenge that this paper address is how to efficiently minimise manual cost for generating RailGDTs such that the benefits provide even greater compared to the initial investment in RailGDTs. We tackle this challenge by leveraging the highly standardised nature of railways. The method restricts the search region and segments track elements given their locations relative to masts, using an extended RANSAC algorithm. Next, it converges segmented point clusters with various pre-assembled track element profiles to obtain RailGDTs. Experiments on 18 km datasets yield 95% and 98% average F1 scores for rail and trackbed point cluster segmentation. The RailGDT accuracy is 3.4 cm and 2.7 cm RMSEs for rails and trackbeds.

1. Introduction

A Digital Twin (DT) is a digital copy of a real-world asset (i.e. building, railway, bridge) that is based on massive, cumulative, real-time, real-world data measurements in multiple dimensions (Buckley and Logan, 2017). We use the term 'geometric DT' (GDT) to define the fundamental 3D geometry, without which many DT applications do not exist. A GDT is generated using raw spatial data, [i.e. Point Cloud Datasets (PCD)s] collected with laser scanners. This is beneficial for rail inspection maintenance and practices, which usually require substantial costs and timescales. The method given in this paper is a part of a much larger framework for twinning railways which contains three phases. The 1st phase is the automated removal of noise points and mast segmentation (Ariyachandra and Brilakis, 2020a). The 2nd phase is the generation of Overhead Line Equipment (OLE) GDTs (Ariyachandra and Brilakis, 2020b) and the 3rd phase is the generation of railway track geometric digital twins (RailGDT), which is the scope of this paper. Railway track refers to rails and trackbed, which represent the most critical elements in railway track structure (Dvořák *et al.*, 2017).

Railways are complicated, safety-critical systems (Wilson *et al.*, 2007) that occasionally face catastrophic risks such as derailments and collisions (European Railway Agency, 2020). While these incidents are considered to be rare, the total costs of railway accidents are estimated at £3.4 billion in 2018 (European Railway Agency, 2020). Maintenance, safety management and retrofitting are therefore vital operations in the life-cycle of existing rail infrastructure. Yet, European and UK rail industries are partly built on antiquated legacy systems that are becoming more difficult to maintain. The railway system in the UK is the oldest in the world (Lee, 1945) and comprised of a patchwork of overlapping designs built at different times (RailEngineer, 2020). Current maintenance processes can no longer cope with the increasing complexity of modern complex socio-technical systems (Zio, 2018) due to the absence of Information and Communication Technology (ICT) sector-level data management. This explains why there is a huge market demand for less labour-intensive railway maintenance techniques that can efficiently boost railway operations and productivity. Industry experts believe that the wider adoption of DTs will unlock 15-25% savings to the global infrastructure market by 2025

(Gerbert *et al.*, 2016). The use of a DT is greatest during the design stage, while little use is made in the closeout stage, and almost absent in the maintenance stage (Buckley and Logan, 2017). Our DT focus is on the latter, except as otherwise noted. The adoption of RailGDTs is very limited. Soni (2016) reported that the total time to reconstruct the GDT of 0.5 m length track section using PCDs was between 20-40 minutes. Every DT generation hour saved can prevent critical failures or accidents so that continuous operations of railways can be achieved without impeding the national economy (Rail Delivery Group, 2014).

This paper only focuses on generating 3D models that correspond to LODs which can be achieved through laser scanning technology. Thus, the proposed method in this paper generates RailGDTs in LOD 300, that are in line with the End-User Requirements (EUR)s namely; (1) EUR 1: component-level digital representation which includes the main structural component types of a sensed asset with a component-level resolution (Sacks et al., 2017), (2) EUR 2: component's explicit geometry representation and property sets (Borrmann and Berkhahn, 2018), (3) EUR 3: component's taxonomy by labelling their element types (Koch and Konig, 2018) and (4) EUR 4: all above-listed EURs in a platform-neutral data format, such as Industry Foundation Classes (IFC) (Koch and Konig, 2018).

Leading software vendors such as Autodesk, Bentley, Trimble, AVEVA and ClearEdge3D provide advanced commercial twinning solutions. Yet the automation provided by these software packages is tailored only to generic or pre-defined geometries; it is still far from being fully automatic (Agapaki and Brilakis, 2018). For instance, OpenRail Designer has a certain degree of automation by combining survey, design rules, and operational requirements to generate optimal geometry of the track on a 2D plane (Bentley Systems, 2018). However, it's shape-creation method focuses only on continuous structures belonging to the alignment. The lack of interoperability between the existing software makes the modelling process challenging (Kenley et al., 2016). Other commercial applications cannot fully automate any one of the EURs. We investigated the current railway twinning process using existing software packages for the whole framework mentioned at the beginning of this paper (Ariyachandra and Brilakis, 2019). Our results illustrate that the 'bottlenecks' of digital twinning using current software applications are (1) existing software can semi-automatically extract generic shapes in PCDs. Yet, their ability to extract non-generic shapes is limited and is laborious. Vegetation overlap adds extensive labour hours, (2) the occlusions, data gaps and varying point density slows down the workflow and add hours of adjustments, (3) EURs 1, 3, & 4 can only be manually achieved, (4) there is no single software that can offer a one-stop GDT generation solution.

2. Research Background

We review the existing research methods by dividing them into two parts namely, (1) object segmentation in PCDs and (2) 3D model fitting to segmented point clusters. The point cluster segmentation step delivers labelled point clusters corresponding to track elements (i.e. rail #1, trackbed #2). Model fitting elaborates the methods for representing the 3D geometry of the segmented point clusters in an object-oriented data format (i.e. IFC).

Jwa and Sonh (2015) used Kalman filter-based railway tracking, which approximated the orientation of the rail track trajectory and then segmented track region and railhead points using a Bayesian decision process and a region growing approach. However, the threshold parameters are appropriate only for relatively simple datasets without any switches, bridges, and train stations. Gézero and Antunes (2019), used the scan angle value of the Mobile Laser Scanned (MLS) data to segment rail points. This method was sensitive to the colour information and the scan angle value of the PCD, hence, does not work for mono-colour PCDs. Moreover, it is valid only for straight rail tracks without any slopes and not a fully automated solution for the segmentation of rails. Yang and Fang (2014) employed a moving window filtering operator to analyse elevation patterns in points along MLS scanning lines to segment track structure element points. However, the method was less accurate in extracting forking junctions due to the complexity of track geometry. Lou et al. (2018) addressed some of the above limitations using MLS profile information such as position, velocity, and altitude. Their method is sensitive to the density of their input PCD, hence, do not work well for different input PCDs. Niina et al. (2018) proposed a method that initially clipped the PCD of the rail track and projected those points on the section perpendicular to the rail track position using the trajectory of the MLS scanner. Next, the method localised the position of the gauge corner, by matching the shape of the ideal railhead to the projected points. The method proposed by Sánchez-Rodríguez et al. (2018), used the MLS scanner profile information and a saliency map to classify ground points. They localised rails, curbs and other ground elements with a peak detection algorithm. All the aforesaid methods are highly dependent on MLS scanner profile information. The ALS are unorganised as they do not contain any scanner profile information such as the trajectory of the scanner or scan angle values. Thus, the above methods are ineffective for ALS PCD. The existing methods can segment rail track points without using scanner profile information as proposed by Oude Elberink et al. (2013). The method initially analysed the height distribution of the points using a digital terrain model (DTM). They analysed all points within 0.5 m above DTM height for rail segmentation using the RANSAC algorithm, assuming that the majority of the roughly segmented rail points within a grid cell fit one line within a certain buffer (0.05 m). However, this method was highly dependent on the determination of DTM height, which was sensitive to the density of their PCD. The method is proven to be effective only for small lengths (typically 300 m) and relatively simple datasets without any switches, bridges, and train stations. The method proposed by Jeon and Kim (2019), used contact cable positions (Jeon and Choi, 2013) as references to segment rail tracks, following the same approach developed by Oude Elberink et al. (2013). However, they assumed that rails are straight lines hence this method cannot be used for curved rail tracks. Both of these methods highly rely upon the segmentation of cables. The sparseness of data on foreground elements in railways is expected due to the small size of the cables in relation to the size of the rail track, and likely to occur despite the scanning technology. It creates obstacles that hinder the robustness of cable segmentation as explained before (Ariyachandra and Brilakis, 2020b). These factors reduce the potential performance of the methods discussed in Jeon and Kim (2019) and Oude Elberink et al. (2013) for lengthier datasets. Cheng et al. (2019) proposed a method that segmented track elements with an elevation and 3D local spherical neighbourhood analysis. The method was sensitive to PCD densities and numbers of points in a particular interval; hence it is dubious that this method is suitable for varying densities of input PCD. Some of the parameters were sensitive to the scan angular resolution of the terrestrial laser scanner (TLS). Thus, this method is incompatible with ALS data, as they do not contain any profile information.

Arastounia and Oude Elberink (2016) proposed an approach to segment trackbed points based on the statistical method of the global map. The height difference of the trackbed was small in their input PCD. Therefore, the method calculated the standard deviation in the fixed neighbourhood to obtain a threshold to distinguish the trackbed from other targets. Their input PCD did not contain any large slopes hence, they assumed that the height difference between points remained constant. A similar approach in Pastucha (2016) used MLS trajectory to limit the search area of the trackbed. This method could effectively reduce the amount of the search calculations but it could not provide a uniform threshold for railway corridors in different scenarios. Both aforementioned methods assume that trackbeds are relatively flat. Subsequently, the geometry and elevation features of the track beds made it easy to recognise. Also, these methods require large-scale neighbourhood computation and hence do not work well with real-world scenarios. The real-world railway corridors typically contain vertical elevations span over kilometres hence the above methods are not fit for purpose. Yang and Fang (2014) extracted track beds by analysing spatial patterns on MLS scanning lines. Methods proposed in Lou et al. (2018) and Gézero and Antunes (2019) used scan angle value of MLS data to segment trackbed. In Gézero and Antunes (2019), their method only indicated the mere existence of the trackbed boundaries by extracting top and bottom track bed lines and did not segment point clusters of trackbeds. However, in real-world railways, the trackbed width changes due to the varying horizontal elevation and consequently, the scan angle of the PCD points representing the top and bottom ballast break-lines, will also change. Also, the above-mentioned methods are highly dependent on the geometric patterns and the reflectance characteristics of MLS railway PCD.

The choice of the fitting technique mainly depends on the nature of the object, the modelling approach, and the application scenario where the object needed to be modelled. Implicit representation represents the 3D shape of the objects using mathematical (implicit) functions. Common implicit functions can use to define point segments as planes (Limberger and Oliveira, 2015), spheres, and toruses (Schnabel *et al.*, 2007), among others. These functions can describe few primitives only; therefore, have a very limited usage when describing non-primitives of railway elements such as trackbeds. A model can be described using Boundary Representation (B-rep) by exploiting the information about vertices, edges, loops, and the way of assembling them to form the object. The primitive shapes in construction sites, indoor planer objects, and synthetic building PCDs have been represented using B-rep methods (Oesau *et al.*, 2014; Valero and Cerrada, 2012) yet these methods could hardly smooth the point regions in railway elements when occlusions and data gaps are present. Constructive Solid Geometry (CSG) methods contain information about how an object was constructed and simultaneously functioned as a shape representation method (Deng *et al.*, 2016). CSG methods reconstructed the 3D shape of piping systems (Patil *et al.*, 2017), kitchen objects (Rusu *et al.*, 2008), and indoor environments (Xiao and Furukawa, 2012). Well-designed and complex CSG modelling strategies are needed to model non-primitives of track elements. Another most commonly used method is Swept Solid Representation (SSR), which exploits the 2D cross-sectional profile of the element to represent the volumetric characteristics of the 3D shape, by sweeping it along a defined path in the 3rd dimension. The use of this technique can be found in state-of-the-art methods in indoor environments for building elements (Budroni and Boehm, 2010), steel beams (Laefer and Truong-hong, 2017) and bridge components (Lu and Brilakis, 2020). Its implementation for railway masts and railway OLE elements can be found in our previous work (Ariyachandra and Brilakis, 2020b, 2021). This paper will investigate its implementation for track elements.

The review provided in the previous section demonstrates that the problem of generating RailGDTs automatically from railway ALS data has yet to be solved. The limitations in each method reduce their robustness thus unable to provide the expected automation over kilometres on the ground. We propose a method for automated RailGDT generation, aiming to meet objective 1: automatically segment track structure elements as labelled point clusters and objective 2: automatically reconstruct the 3D geometry of segmented track element point clusters in IFC format. We answer the research questions RQ1: How to automatically segment railway track structure elements in the form of labelled point clusters from real-world railway PCDs with varying horizontal and vertical elevations and complex railway geometries; without using any additional prior information such as neighbourhood structures, scanning geometry and intensity of input data; and where occlusions, data gaps and varying point density exist?; RQ2: How to automatically separate rails from other linear elements adjacent to the railway corridor without relying on prior knowledge and manual inputs?; and RQ3: How to automatically reconstruct labelled point clusters into 3D IFC objects for the railway domain?.

3. Proposed Solution

We hypothesize that the use of railway topology has the theoretical potential to perform better when segmenting and modelling the geometry of railway elements in PCDs with varying geometric patterns. We have tested this hypothesis with three approximately 6 km (total 18 km) long PCDs (Dataset A, B, and C) obtained from the track located between 's-Hertogenbosch and Nijmegen in the Netherlands. Railways are a linear asset type; their geometric relations remain roughly unchanged, often over very long distances. Close inspection of railway PCDs validates this effect, with repeating geometrical features such as, (1) the geometric relationships among railway elements (i.e. masts, cables, and rails) remaining fairly unchanged along the railway corridor (Network Rail, 2018), (2) the connections between masts and cables are placed in regular intervals (60 m intervals on average), (3) the main axis of the railway masts (Z-axis) is roughly perpendicular to the rail track direction (X-axis) [error tolerance is 11° (Network Rail, 2018)] and (4) masts are always positioned as pairs throughout the rail track. We use these four geometric features as assumptions for the proposed method. The method is designed to twin only the typical double-track railways because they make up 70% of the existing and under-construction railway network in the UK and Europe (Eurostat 2019). The method given in this paper is a part of a railway twinning framework as described in the introduction. Hence, inputs of the method in this paper are (1) railway corridor PCD, (2) ground truth mast position coordinates (RM_{Cor}). The ground truth is used, to evaluate the method on its own without adding the error of the segmented mast predictions of the 1st phase (Ariyachandra and Brilakis, 2020a). The outputs of this paper are (1) labelled point clusters of track elements and (2) RailGDTs in .ifc format. Figure 1 illustrates the workflow of the proposed methodology.

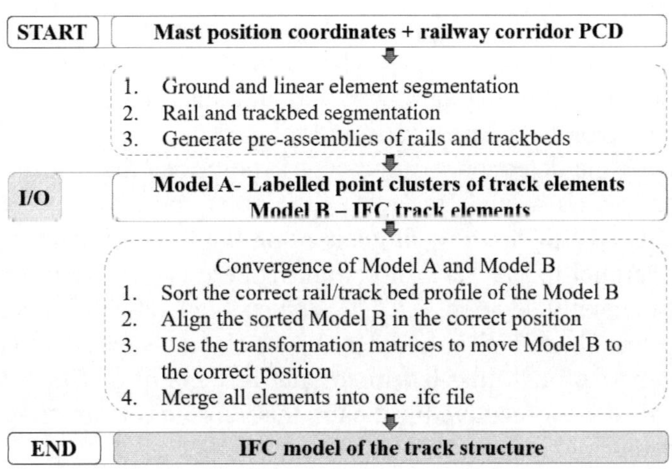

Figure 1: Workflow of the proposed method

The first step is to separate the ground points including horizontal and quasi-horizontal planes from the ALS data. This is an essential and advantageous step because; (1) it permits segmenting points associated with rails and track beds from the railway PCD, (2) it allows one to easily exploit the linearity of rails against the ground using linear feature extraction algorithms, (3) it minimises the effect of false positives that may arise due to other linear elements such as OLE cables in the railway ALS data, and finally (4) it significantly reduces the number of points required for the rail and trackbed segmentation method, leading to faster computational performance. Initially, we use the RANSAC plane detection algorithm to segment point clusters of the horizontal and quasi-horizontal ground planes. A pre-processing step is used before the RANSAC algorithm that divides the PCD into sub boxes, using a crop box filter (CBF). The selected crop box [Crop Box 1 (CB_1)] ensures that only two consecutive pairs of masts fall in each CB_1 (60 m on average). This CBF automatically extracts all the data within a given box, and hence simplifies the cloud by increasing the speed of RANSAC due to the small number of points considered each time. This further removes any noise data that contain vegetation and other rail infrastructure built adjacent to the track. The method computes the minimum and the maximum points of CB_1 using the $RM_{Cor}$of two consecutive pairs of masts. Next, we apply the RANSAC plane detection algorithm for each CB_1. RANSAC algorithm iteratively and randomly sample points to estimate the hypothesis plane and then tests the plane against the remainder of the PCD. We set the parameters of RANSAC plane detection to extract planes that satisfy the steepest incline that exists in the UK railways (*Gradients of the British Main Line Railways*, 2016). A closer observation of the resulting data demonstrates that these horizontal and quasi-horizontal planes contain points associated with rails and trackbeds as well as a few unrelated points. This is because the position and the orientation of a raw railway PCD are not always properly aligned or paralleled to the global axes. In Ariyachandra and Brilakis (2020a), we used PCA to align a railway such that the global X-axis and the horizontal alignment of the input PCD in this study are now roughly paralleled to the global axes. Yet, the alignment is not perfect mainly because PCA provides only a rough estimate and the railway corridor itself contains a certain degree of curvature and slope. As a result, CB_1s are rotated in different directions around the Z-axis. Hence, we calculate the tangent between the resulting and optimum CB_1s to compute the rotation [arctangent (atan2)] around Z-axis and thereby align each CB_1 along the track direction ((1);

$$atan2(Y, X) = \left\{ \arctan \frac{Y_{max} - Y_{min}}{X_{max} - X_{min}} \right\} \tag{1}$$

Where, X_{max}, Y_{max}, X_{min} and Y_{min} represent the maximum and minimum XY coordinates, respectively, sorted from one pair of masts. The method automatically applies this rotation to each CB_1, and then uses CBF to extract horizontal and quasi-horizontal planes inside a given CB_1. We then use a method to segment rails and track beds from the resulting CB_1s based on an extended RANSAC line detection method. We hypothesise that the only linear element on CB_1 PCD now represents rails, while the rest of the points on CB_1 represent track bed points. The previously calculated CB_1 are now aligned along the track direction; yet, it is difficult to segment rail tracks parallel to the track direction, if there is a curvature occurred within any CB_1. Thus, we automatically segment each CB_1 such that the resulting pieces [Crop Box 2 (CB_2)] are relatively straight enough to segment linear elements parallel to track direction. This step also reduces computational time by processing a segment of CB_2 at a time. It creates 8 CB_2s between a set of two consecutive mast pairs that represent near straight pieces of railway PCD and repeats for the next pairs of masts throughout the track (Figure 2).

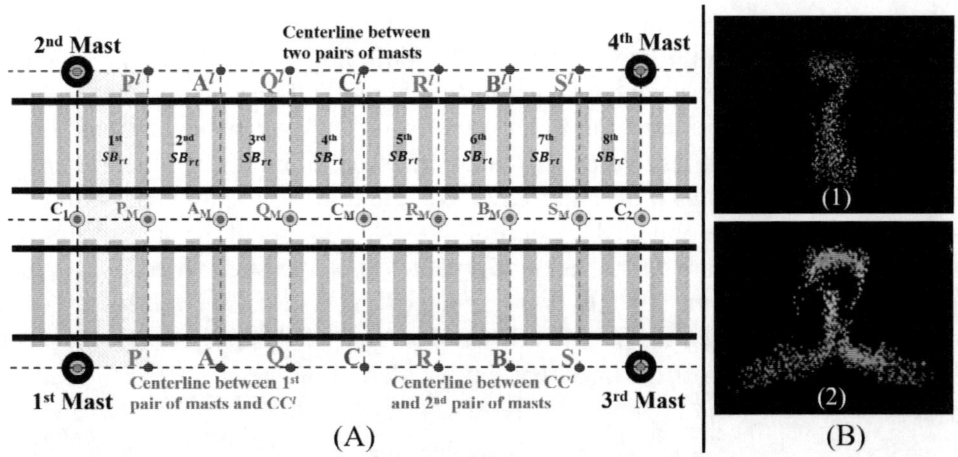

Figure 2: (A) Segmentation step, (B1) Segmented rail, (B2) Segmented rail improved with radius neighbour search

We use a pre-processing step that allows projecting slopes on the rail tracks on to the ground, such that the RANSAC can segment those rails as lines parallel to rail track direction despite their vertical elevations/inclines. Using RANSAC, four lines, which represents four rails in a double-track railway, with maximum inliers are then iteratively generated by determining the most probable hypothesis line for each CB_2. We observed that the resulting four lines do not contain all the points of the rail point cluster (Figure 2B1). Hence, we use a radius neighbour search to include any missing points during RANSAC detection. For a given segmented line of P points (Eq.2);

$$P = \{p_1, \ldots, p_N\}, p_i \in \mathbb{R}^3 \tag{2}$$

We find all the neighbour points of the segmented lines N such that (Eq.3);

$$N(q, r) = \{p \in P\}| \; \|p - q\| < r\} \tag{3}$$

inside a radius $r \in \mathbb{R}^3$ of a query point $r \in \mathbb{R}^3$. We set radius (r) to 0.1 m and this parameter is fine-tuned with experimental results to ensure that only rail points fall in each neighbourhood. (Graphs representing calculations for the parameters are not illustrated due to limited space). We used a regular space portioning; the octree to accelerate the neighbour search in the PCD. The resulting segmented points now consist of rail point clusters including the missing points in the previous stage (Figure 2B). We use the performance matrices to measure the performance of step 2 as expressed below (Eq. 4, Eq. 5, 6). We observe that the segmented linear elements at this stage represent both rails and other linear elements along the rail track direction in railway PCDs. As a result, the segmentation performance reached a precision of 91.7%, a recall of 94.4%, and an F1 score of 93.1% (Table 1). False positives in these numbers include other linear elements such as walls, fences adjacent to the track, lines segmented on the trackbed and ground, among others.

$$Precision = \frac{Correctly\ segmented\ rail\ tracks\ (TP)}{Total\ segmented\ linear\ elements\ (TP + FP)} \tag{4}$$

$$Recall = \frac{Correctly\ segmented\ rail\ tracks\ (TP)}{Total\ number\ of\ rail\ tracks\ (TP + FN)} \qquad F1\ Score = 2\ x\ \frac{Precision\ x\ Recall}{Precision + Recall} \tag{5,6}$$

A closer observation of the railway PCD shows that (1) the number of points per other linear elements such as walls, fences are considerably higher than those of the rails; (2) the number of points per other linear elements such as lines on the trackbed and ground are considerably lower than those of the rails. These observations are expected despite the density of the input

PCD, which likely to occur regardless of the scanning technology used. Therefore, we hypothesis that the number of points per each rail should not drastically vary as the geometric properties of the rails are consistent throughout the whole PCD. Hence, we use a point-based calculation method to differentiate point clusters of rails from other linear elements. Initially, we experimentally define a threshold D_1, by calculating the ratio between the number of points per other liner elements such as walls and fences over the number of points per rail point cluster along the track direction. We obtained the optimum D_1 as 2.12 for all the datasets by computing precision, recall, and F1 score for different D_1 values. For the segmented point clusters, we compute the number of points of the 1st segmented line and repeat the same for the next optimum subset of points, i.e., the 2nd line, that is chosen by RANSAC. Next, we calculate D_1 of these two lines and true positive lines that represented by $\widehat{K}$; where, D_k is the ratio between the point counts of the 1st and 2nd lines.

$$\widehat{K} = \begin{cases} 1 & D_k \leq D_1;\ true\ positive \\ 0 & otherwise;\ false\ positive \end{cases} \quad (7)$$

We filter the lines using Eq. 7. We replicate this procedure until there are 4 lines per CB_2 (as there are 4 rails in a double-track railway) and repeat for next CB_2 s throughout the track. This step increased the precision, recall, and F1 score up to 93.2%, 95.4%, and 94.3%, respectively (Table 1). Yet, the segmented linear elements still represent both rails and other linear elements along the rail track direction such as lines on trackbed and ground that contain a smaller number of points per element compared to the rails. Next, we experimentally define a threshold D_2 to filter false positives of lines on the trackbed and ground. This threshold is obtained by calculating the ratio between the number of points per rail point cluster over the number of points per other liner elements such as lines on the trackbed and ground along the track direction. We obtain the optimum D_2 = 1.7 by computing precision, recall and F1 score for different D_2 values. We compute D_2 of these two lines and true positive lines that represented by $\widehat{M}$; where, D_m is the ratio between the point count of the previous line over the point count of the current line. We filter lines using Eq. 2. This procedure only loops over the first 4 lines chosen by RANSAC. The linear elements with higher points counts are already discarded at the 1st step. Hence, we only need to remove linear elements with lower point counts compared to rails to minimise the false positives at this stage.

$$\widehat{M} = \begin{cases} 1 & D_m \leq D_2;\ true\ positive \\ 0 & otherwise;\ false\ positive \end{cases} \quad (8)$$

The 2nd step increased the precision, recall, and F1 score up to 95.6%, 94.2%, and 94.9%, respectively (Table 1). We initially hypothesised that the points on CB_1 PCD represent rails and track beds only. Hence, once we removed the segmented rail point clusters from CB_1 PCD, the rest of the points in CB_1 PCD is the trackbed point cluster. Thus, our proposed method removes the extracted rail point clusters and overwrites the CB_1 PCD, once all the lines are segmented during the RANSAC line segmentation. The resulting CB_1 PCD represents the trackbed point cluster. Our proposed method has a precision of 100.0%, recall of 96.3%, and F1 score of 98.1% for trackbed segmentation (Table 1). Different colours are assigned to each labelled point cluster (i.e. rail #1, trackbed #2) and are hereinafter denoted as 'Model A's (Figure 3). Next, we design pre-assemblies of track structure elements; hereafter known as 'Model B' using standard railway guidelines (Network Rail, 2018) to represent the geometry of the real track structure elements. These models preserve the geometric properties of the elements, such as different web thicknesses, head widths in rail profiles. We have created 10 different rail and 5 different track bed profiles, compatible with EU and UK railway standards (European Commission, 2017; Network Rail, 2018). We define each of the track elements using extruded area solid definition in IFC format. We use the standard cross-sectional dimensions (European Commission, 2017; Network Rail, 2018) to define the 2D area profile for each element. The method takes the extruded distance by computing the length of each segmented point cluster. The method then uses the Iterative closest point (ICP) algorithm to automatically converge Model B to Model A. We set Model A as the reference cloud (R_C); is kept fixed while different profiles of Model B are source clouds (S_C). The method first converts Model B into .pcd files and then these S_C are transformed to find the best match with the R_C by minimising the distance ($RMSD$) between the two (Eq. 3), where T – transformation, for a set of pairs of points $C = (s_i, r_j)$, $s_i \in S_C, r_j \in R_C$.

$$RMSD\ (T\ (S_C), \mu\ (R_C)) = \frac{\sum_C dist\ (r_j, T(s_i))^2}{|C|}, s_i, r_j \in \mathrm{C} \tag{9}$$

Hence, by using ICP we first sort the correct rail profile or trackbed profile as the correct profile ideally has the minimum sum of squared differences between the coordinates of the target and reference clouds. Once we sorted the correct profile, our method then converges the sorted model to the correct position and finally gives a transformation matrix which provides the corresponding translation vector and rotation matrix of Model B (model) relative to Model A (point cluster). Finally, the method moves the .ifc format of Model B to the correct position using the resulting transformation matrices and finally merges all units (including rail and trackbed sections) into one file to get the final IFC model of the track structure (Figure 3).

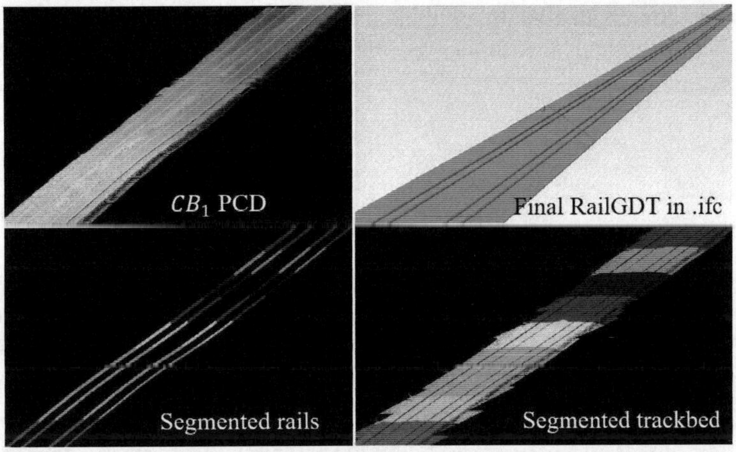

Figure 3: Results of the RailGDT generation

4. Experiments and Evaluation

We manually generated two sets of Ground Truth (GT) datasets consist of three sub-datasets each per one railway PCD; (1) GT A: Manually extracted point clusters of track elements from raw railway PCD. They are used to compare against the automatically detected point clusters of track elements, and (2) GT B: Manually created RailGDTs and used to compare against automated RailGDTs. We implemented the solution with the point cloud library (PCL) version 1.8.0 using C++ on Visual Studio 2017, on a laptop (Intel Core i7-8550U 1.8GHz CPU, 16 GB RAM, Samsung 256GB SSD). We gauged the average segmentation accuracies as explained in section 3 (Table 1).

Table 1: Performance matrices for three datasets

Sequence of steps	Dataset	Precision	Recall	F1 score
Segmentation of rails and other linear elements	A	88.1%	96.5%	92.1%
	B	93.7%	93.0%	93.4%
	C	93.8%	93.6%	93.7%
	Average	91.7%	94.4%	93.1%
Segmentation of rails with 1st refinement	A	91.6%	98.8%	95.0%
	B	93.0%	92.4%	92.7%
	C	95.0%	94.8%	94.9%
	Average	93.2%	95.4%	94.3%
Segmentation of rails with 2nd refinement	A	96.9%	97.8%	97.3%
	B	93.6%	91.6%	92.6%
	C	96.1%	93.1%	94.6%
	Average	95.6%	94.2%	94.9%
Segmentation of the trackbed	A	100.0%	95.8%	97.9%
	B	100.0%	97.8%	98.9%
	C	100.0%	95.6%	97.8%
	Average	100.0%	96.3%	98.1%

We use cloud-to-cloud distance evaluation to detect changes between GT B and the automated ones. Initially, we converted the GT B and the automated GDTs into .pcd files. The evaluation method computed the Root Mean Square Error (RMSE) between each unit of automated GDT of track elements and the corresponding GT B model. The average model distance between the two for all 18 km 3.4 cm RMSE for rails and 2.7 cm RMSE for track beds. The proposed method reduces manual twinning time by 82%. This implies the proposed method outperforms the manual operation.

5. Conclusions

We presented a novel automated method that exploits the highly regulated and standardised railway topology to generate RailGDTs for existing railways from PCD and tested it on an 18 km railway PCDs. Our method does not request any human intervention even though the railway PCDs are highly occluded, sparse, and with varying horizontal and vertical elevations. Based on the high performance delivers, our method; (1) can deal with real-world railway PCD consists of varying track geometries and yet outperforms the existing methods by achieving remarkably high performance; (2) is effective in handling challenges inherited in PCDs such as occlusions, extreme vegetation around the track, and local variable densities of points; (3) provided high-performance matrices despite the different track arrangements such as crossings, turnouts, overbridges and passing loops; (4) offers significant computational cost reductions by automatically cropping a lengthy railway PCD into relatively straight segments. This enables a considerably improved large-scale object detection generally required over kilometres without forfeiting precision and manual cost; and (5) is the first to automatically and robustly solve the RailGDT generation by exploiting reiterating railway geometric patterns which lengths over kilometres of spans.

Acknowledgements

We express our gratitude to Fugro NL Land B.V. who provided data for evaluation. This research is funded by Cambridge Commonwealth, European & International Trust and Bentley Systems UK Plc. We gratefully acknowledge their support. Any opinions, findings and conclusions expressed in this paper are those of the authors and do not necessarily reflect the views of the institutes mentioned above.

References

Agapaki, E. and Brilakis, I. (2018), "State-of-practice on As-Is Modelling of Industrial Facilities", in Smith, I. and Domer, B. (Eds.), Advanced Computing Strategies for Engineering. EG-ICE 2018. Lecture Notes in Computer Science, Springer, Lausanne, Switzerland, available at:https://doi.org/10.1007/978-3-319-91635-4_6.

Arastounia, M. and Elberink, S.O. (2016), "Application of template matching for improving classification of urban railroad point clouds", Sensors (Switzerland), Vol. 16 No. 12, available at:https://doi.org/10.3390/s16122112.

Ariyachandra, M.R.M.F. and Brilakis, I. (2019), "Understanding the challenge of digitally twinning the geometry of existing rail infrastructure", 12th FARU International Research Conference (Faculty of Architecture Research Unit), Faculty of Architecture Research Unit, Univeristy of Moratuwa, Colombo, Sri Lanka, pp.25–32.

Ariyachandra, M.R.M.F. and Brilakis, I. (2020a), "Detection of Railway Masts in Air-Borne LiDAR Data", Journal of Construction Engineering and Management, Vol. 146 No. 9, available at:https://doi.org/10.1061/(ASCE)CO.1943-7862.0001894.

Ariyachandra, M.R.M.F. and Brilakis, I. (2020b), "Digital Twinning of Railway Overhead Line Equipment from Airborne LiDAR Data", Proceedings of the 37th International Symposium on Automation and Robotics in Construction (ISARC), pp.1270–1277.

Ariyachandra, M.R.M.F. and Brilakis, I. (2021), "Application of Railway Topology for the Automated Generation of Geometric Digital Twins of Railway Masts", Proceedings of the 13th European Conference on Product & Process Modelling, European Association of Product and Process Modelling (EAPPM), Moscow, Russia, available at:https://doi.org/10.17863/CAM.62196.

Bentley Systems. (2018), Bentley Systems ' New OpenRail Is First to Advance BIM for the Full Rail and Transit Lifecycle.

Borrmann, A. and Berkhahn, V. (2018), Principles of Geometric Modeling, edited by Borrmann A., König M., Koch C., B.J., Springer International Publishing AG, available at:https://doi.org/https://doi.org/10.1007/978-3-319-92862-3_2.

Buckley, B. and Logan, K. (2017), SmartMarket Report The Business Value of BIM for Infrastructure.

Budroni, A. and Boehm, J. (2010), "Automated 3D Reconstruction of Interiors from Point Clouds", International Journal of Architectural Computing, Vol. 8 No. 1, pp.55–73.

Cheng, Y.J., Qiu, W.G. and Duan, D.Y. (2019), "Automatic creation of as-is building information model from single-track railway tunnel point clouds", Automation in Construction, Elsevier, Vol. 106 No. August, available at:https://doi.org/10.1016/j.autcon.2019.102911.

Deng, Y., Cheng, J.C.P. and Anumba, C. (2016), "Mapping between BIM and 3D GIS in different levels of detail using schema mediation and instance comparison", Automation in Construction, Vol. 67 No. July, pp.1–21.

Dvořák, Z., Sventeková, E., Řehák, D. and Čekerevac, Z. (2017), "Assessment of Critical Infrastructure Elements in Transport", Procedia Engineering, Vol. 187 No. June, pp.548–555.

European Commission. (2017), Technical Specifications for Interoperability Relating to the "infrastructure" Subsystem of the Rail System in the European Union, Vol. 10, pp.1–21.

European Railway Agency. (2020), Report on Railway Safety and Interoperability in the EU, available at:https://doi.org/10.2821/30980.

Gerbert, P., Castagnino, S., Rothballer, C., Renz, A. and Filitz, R. (2016), Digital in Engineering and Construction: The Transformative Power of Building Information Modeling, available at: http://futureofconstruction.org/content/uploads/2016/09/BCG-Digital-in-Engineering-and-Construction-Mar-2016.pdf.

Gézero, L. and Antunes, C. (2019), "Automated three-dimensional linear elements extraction from mobile lidar point clouds in railway environments", Infrastructures, Vol. 4 No. 3, available at:https://doi.org/10.3390/infrastructures4030046.

Gradients of the British Main Line Railways. (2016), Ian Allan Publishing.

Jeon, W.G. and Choi, B.G. (2013), "A study on the automatic detection of railroad power lines using LiDAR data and RANSAC algorithm", Journal of the Korean Society of Surveying Geodesy Photogrammetry and Cartography, Vol. 31 No. 4, pp.331–339.

Jeon, W.G. and Kim, E.M. (2019), "Automated reconstruction of railroad rail using helicopter-borne light detection and ranging in a train station", Sensors and Materials, Vol. 31 No. 10, pp.3289–3302.

Jwa, Y. and Sonh, G. (2015), "Kalman filter based railway tracking from mobile lidar data", ISPRS Annals of the Photogrammetry, Remote Sensing and Spatial Information Sciences, Vol. 2 No. 3W5, pp.159–164.

Kenley, R., Harfield, T. and Behnam, A. (2016), "BIM Interoperability Limitations: Australian and Malaysian Rail Projects", MATEC Web of Conferences, Vol. 66, p. 00102.

Koch, C. and Konig, M. (2018), "Data Modeling", Building Information Modeling, Springer International Publishing AG, part of Springer Nature 2018, pp.43–62.

Laefer, D.F. and Truong-hong, L. (2017), "Toward automatic generation of 3D steel structures for building information modelling", Automation in Construction, No. November, available at:https://doi.org/10.1016/j.autcon.2016.11.011.

Lee, C.E. (1945), "The World's Oldest Railway", Transactions of the Newcomen Society, Vol. 25 No. 1, pp.141–162.

Limberger, F.A. and Oliveira, M.M. (2015), "Real-time detection of planar regions in unorganized point clouds", Pattern Recognition, Elsevier, Vol. 48 No. 6, pp.2043–2053.

Lou, Y., Zhang, T., Tang, J., Song, W., Zhang, Y. and Chen, L. (2018), "A fast algorithm for rail extraction using mobile laser scanning data", Remote Sensing, Vol. 10 No. 12, available at:https://doi.org/10.3390/rs10121998.

Lu, R. and Brilakis, I. (2020), "A benchmarked framework for geometric digital twinning of slab and beam-and-slab bridges", Vol. 172 No. 2019, pp.3–18.

Network Rail. (2018), "Catalogue of Network Rail Standards", available at: https://www.networkrail.co.uk/wp-content/uploads/2018/04/Network-Rail-Standards-Catalogue.pdf (accessed 5 January 2019).

Niina, Y., Honma, R., Honma, Y., Kondo, K., Tsuji, K., Hiramatsu, T. and Oketani, E. (2018), "Automatic rail extraction and celarance check with a point cloud captured by MLS in a Railway", International Archives of the Photogrammetry, Remote Sensing and Spatial Information Sciences - ISPRS Archives, Vol. 42 No. 2, pp.767–771.

Oesau, S., Lafarge, F. and Alliez, P. (2014), "Indoor scene reconstruction using feature sensitive primitive extraction and graph-cut", ISPRS Journal of Photogrammetry and Remote Sensing, International Society for Photogrammetry and Remote Sensing, Inc. (ISPRS), Vol. 90, pp.68–82.

Oude Elberink, S., Khoshelham, K., Arastounia, M. and Diaz Benito, D. (2013), "Rail Track Detection and Modelling in Mobile Laser Scanner Data", ISPRS Annals of Photogrammetry, Remote Sensing and Spatial Information Sciences, Vol. II-5/W2 No. November, pp.223–228.

Pastucha, E. (2016), "Catenary system detection, localization and classification using mobile scanning data", Remote Sensing, Vol. 8 No. 10, available at:https://doi.org/10.3390/rs8100801.

Patil, A.K., Holi, P., Lee, S.K. and Chai, Y.H. (2017), "An adaptive approach for the reconstruction and modeling of as-built 3D pipelines from point clouds Automation in Construction An adaptive approach for the reconstruction and modeling of as-built 3D pipelines from point clouds", Automation in Construction, Elsevier B.V., Vol. 75 No. November 2018, pp.65–78.

Rail Delivery Group. (2014), What Is the Contribution of Rail to the UK Economy?, available at: https://www.oxera.com/wp-content/uploads/2018/07/Contribution-of-rail-to-the-UK-economy-140714.pdf.pdf.

RailEngineer. (2020), Why Rail Electrification Is Key?

Rusu, R.B., Marton, Z.C., Blodow, N., Dolha, M. and Beetz, M. (2008), "Towards 3D Point cloud based object maps for household environments", Robotics and Autonomous Systems, Elsevier B.V., Vol. 56 No. 11, pp.927–941.

Sacks, R., Ma, L., Yosef, R., Borrmann, A., Daum, S. and Kattel, U. (2017), "Semantic Enrichment for Building Information Modeling: Procedure for Compiling Inference Rules and Operators for Complex Geometry", Journal of Computing in Civil Engineering, Vol. 31 No. 6, p. 04017062.

Sánchez-Rodríguez, A., Riveiro, B., Soilán, M. and González-deSantos, L.M. (2018), "Automated detection and decomposition of railway tunnels from Mobile Laser Scanning Datasets", Automation in Construction, Elsevier, Vol. 96 No. April, pp.171–179.

Schnabel, R., Wahl, R. and Klein, R. (2007), "Efficient RANSAC for Point-Cloud Shape Detection", Computer Graphics Forum, Vol. 26 No. 2, pp.214–226.

Soni, A. (2016), Non-Contact Monitoring of Railway Infrastructure with Terrestrial Laser Scanning and Photogrammetry at Network Rail, available at: https://discovery.ucl.ac.uk/id/eprint/1477352/.

Valero, E. and Cerrada, C. (2012), "Automatic Method for Building Indoor Boundary Models from Dense Point Clouds Collected by Laser Scanners", Sensors, Vol. 12, pp.16099–16115.

Wilson, J.R., Farrington-Darby, T., Cox, G., Bye, R. and Hockey, G.R.J. (2007), "The railway as a socio-technical system: Human factors at the heart of successful rail engineering", Proceedings of the Institution of Mechanical Engineers, Part F: Journal of Rail and Rapid Transit, Vol. 221 No. 1, pp.101–115.

Xiao, J. and Furukawa, Y. (2012), "Reconstructing the World ' s Museums", International Journal of Computer Vision, Vol. 110 No. 3, pp.668–681.

Yang, B. and Fang, L. (2014), "Automated Extraction of 3-D Railway Tracks from Mobile Laser Scanning Point Clouds", IEEE Journal of Selected Topics in Applied Earth Observations and Remote Sensing, Vol. 7 No. 12, pp.1–12.

Zio, E. (2018), "The future of risk assessment", Reliability Engineering and System Safety, Elsevier Ltd, Vol. 177 No. June 2017, pp.176–190.

Deriving Digital Twin Models of Existing Bridges from Point Cloud Data Using Parametric Models and Metaheuristic Algorithms

M. Saeed Mafipour, Simon Vilgertshofer, André Borrmann
Technical University of Munich, Germany
m.saeed.mafipour@tum.de

Abstract. In building information modeling (BIM), a digital twin (DT) is a model that represents the current status of an existing structure; thus, facilitating the operation and management process. Due to higher measurement speed and accuracy, laser scanning and photogrammetry are generally employed, resulting in point cloud data (PCD). Today, the required volumetric models are created in a laborious and costly manual process from PCD. This paper aims to automate this process by applying metaheuristic optimization algorithms to fit highly parametric BIM models of bridges into given point clouds. For this purpose, parametric base models of elements are created and instantiated by adjusting their parameters' value using metaheuristic algorithms. This optimization process leads to extracting the parameters for a model from PCD and creating 3-D volumetric shapes. The paper's results show that metaheuristic algorithms can be successfully used for parametric modeling even in point clouds with occlusion and clutter.

1. Introduction

Building information modeling (BIM) is an efficient tool for supporting the design and construction of buildings and infrastructure facilities. BIM can also assist in the operation and maintenance process. *As-is* BIM models represent the digital replica of an existing facility, such as a bridge, and provide an appropriate basis for inspection, condition assessment, and repair planning (Sacks et al., 2018). They also provide an integrated and single unit in which all the gathered information from the construction site can be imported. The main advantages of a digital as-is model are the possibility of accessing and querying structured data and the visualization of information.

Most recently, the concept of as-is BIM has been extended to digital twin (DT) (Pan et al., 2019; Lu et al., 2020). A DT is updated frequently, thus keeping the digital replica consistent with the physical reality. However, the frequency of these updates depends on the product type, its dynamics, and the model's purpose. While the DT of a jet engine is updated in minute intervals, it is suitable to update the DT yearly in bridge maintenance management. However, a significant challenge is that the vast majority of existing bridges were constructed decades ago, which means DT models must be created from the existing asset as well.

Laser scanning and photogrammetry are two of the best-known methods to capture the geometry of an existing facility (Bosché et al., 2015; Laing et al., 2015; Technion, 2015; Adán et al., 2018; Rocha et al., 2020). The output of these techniques is point cloud data (PCD). Compared with a visual inspection, PCD is provided in a lower time and has higher measurement accuracy (Zhu et al. 2010). However, DT modeling based on PCD is laborious and error-prone. In current practice, these models are created manually, which in turn, increases the duration and costs. Hence, infrastructure authorities mostly do not undertake high costs and potential risks of DT models and still prefer the old rating system to manage structures (Zhu et al. 2011). To utilize the benefits of DT models and reduce the modeling costs, the digital twinning process needs to be automated. Recently, several attempts have been made towards this goal (Sacks et al., 2016; Sacks et al., 2018), which mostly follow a bottom-up approach, which has limitations, especially in point clouds with occlusion and clutter.

In this paper, we propose a method based on metaheuristic algorithms to automate the creation of parametric BIM models. We use a top-down approach for parametric modeling of bridges from PCD and combine it with a bottom-up approach by instantiating parametric profiles of bridge elements. These profiles are created based on pre-knowledge about the existing elements in a typical bridge. Hence, the profiles comprise all the human-definable features such as parallelism, symmetricity, and orthogonality. Since the scope of the paper is on parametric modeling, we use element-wisely segmented point clouds. Also, it is assumed that elements can be defined by an extrude function. To extract the parameters' value, the required cross-section or face for the extrude function is recognized and then be used as an input for updating the parameters' value of the corresponding profile. Since closed-form formulations cannot describe these profiles, metaheuristic algorithms are applied. Finally, all the extracted parameters are used to create the parametric model of the elements. The workflow of the proposed approach can be seen in Figure 1.

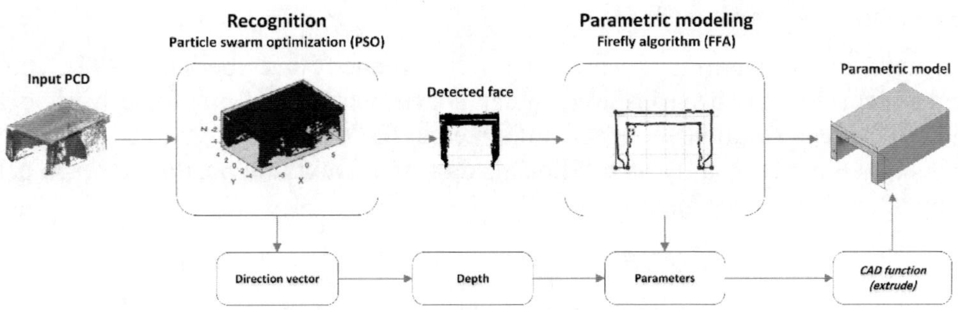

Figure 1: The proposed pipeline of parametric modeling

2. Related research

Bottom-up and top-down are the major approaches for detecting structural elements and modeling based on PCD. The bottom-up methods start from the low-level features to generate a complex system at successively higher levels. Walsh et al. (2013) extracted sharp features of points and used a region-growing algorithm to segment planar faces of bridge elements. Next, surfaces were fitted by the least square algorithm. Zhang et al. (2015) determined the local features of points and clustered them based on the existing linear relationships and finally extracted the planar faces of elements in bridges by singular value decomposition (SVD). Yan et al. (2017) used principal component analysis (PCA) to recognize the endpoints of elements and then applied a voxelization process to modify the real boundaries of bridges to generate a mesh. The bottom-up approach provides an efficient tool for modeling elements. However, created models are vulnerable to occlusion and do not mostly provide a meaningful parametric model in the end.

In contrast to the bottom-up, the top-down methods start from an abstract model and decompose a complex system to the subordinate models. Lu et al. (2019) used a top-down approach for detecting elements in the point cloud of RC bridges and represented the geometry of the bridge by the alpha-concave hull. Qin et al. (2021) also considered a top-down approach for detecting elements in bridges based on the density of points and employed a bottom-up method for parametric modeling of cylindrical and cuboid shapes. Kwon et al. (2004) introduced a fast and accurate local spatial modeling algorithm to fit planes, cuboids, and cylinders to sparse PCD, assuming that the construction site can be modeled by these primitives. Song and Jüttler (2009) improved the performance of implicit modeling by adding sharp features to the models. Cao and Wang (2019) used cuboids and graph-cut energy minimization algorithms for model fitting to unstructured PCD. The top-down methods can provide a completely human-understandable model; however, they have been mostly limited to primitives as they can be mathematically defined in closed-form formulations.

2.1 Overview of metaheuristic algorithms

Metaheuristic algorithms are a sub-branch of optimization algorithms and artificial intelligence. These algorithms have been inspired mainly by natural, biological, and social systems of animals and humans. In contrast to most optimization algorithms, metaheuristic algorithms do not need the closed-form formulation of the loss function. Hence, they can be adequately used for expressing a parametric instance with no closed-form formulation.

Particle swarm optimization (PSO)

PSO, as a metaheuristic algorithm, was proposed by (Kennedy and Eberhart, 1997). This swarm intelligence algorithm has been inspired by the social behavior of birds and herds of fish. A population of random solutions is firstly initialized in PSO, called a swarm of particles. Based on a fitness function, the quality of solutions is assessed. Next, the position of each particle is updated by the following formulas:

$$V_i^{k+1} = w V_i^k + c_1.r_1.(P_{best,i}^k - p_i^k)/\Delta t + c_2.r_2.(G_{best}^k - p_i^k)/\Delta t \quad (1)$$

$$p_i^{k+1} = p_i^k + V_i^{k+1}.\Delta t \quad (2)$$

where p_i is the position of the ith particle, V_i is the velocity vector of the ith particle, $p^k{}_{best,\, i}$ is the best position of the ith particle over its history up to iteration k, $G^k{}_{best}$ is the position of the best particle in the swarm by up to iteration k, c_1 is the cognitive parameter, c_2 is a social parameter, r_1 and r_2 are independent random numbers uniformly distributed between 0 and 1, w is the inertial weight, and Δt is the time interval which is considered equal to 1.

Firefly algorithm (FFA)

FFA is another metaheuristic algorithm that was proposed by (Yang, 2008). This algorithm has been inspired by fireflies' flashing patterns to attract their partners, communicate, and show risk warnings. Every firefly is assumed unisexual in FFA whose attractiveness is proportional to its brightness. This algorithm is based on three parameters, including attractiveness, randomization, and absorption. The position of every firefly is formulated as below:

$$x_i^{t+1} = x_i^t + \beta_0 e_i^{-\gamma r_{ij}^2}(x_j^t - x_i^t) + \alpha_t \varepsilon_i^t \quad (3)$$

where x_i is the position of a firefly at the iteration t, $\beta_0 > 0$ is the attractiveness at the distance zero ($r_{ij} = 0$), γ is the absorption coefficient that controls the visibility of fireflies, ε_i is a vector with random numbers, and α_t is the mutation coefficient.

3. Method for model-to-cloud fitting

To extract the parameters' value of an element from its corresponding point cloud, the cross-section or face of interest should be recognized first. In this paper, the required face for the *extrude* function is only detected since most of the elements in bridges, including piers, wing walls, and direct decks, can be defined by this function. To this end, we evaluate all the faces of the element by a bounding box. Figure 2(a) illustrates the axis-aligned bounding box (AABB) of a point cloud that is not aligned coordinate axes. As can be seen, the lack of alignment in the point cloud has resulted in an AABB that is not the minimal bounding box (MBB) simultaneously (Figure 2(b)). Based on this observation, if the AABB of a point cloud is its MBB at the same time, the point cloud is thus aligned coordinate axes. We denote this resulting bounding box as Minimal Axis Aligned Bounding Box (MAABB) that aligns point cloud in the direction of coordinate axes (see Figure 2(c)). A MAABB is computed the same as an AABB, however, after applying a transformation to the point cloud.

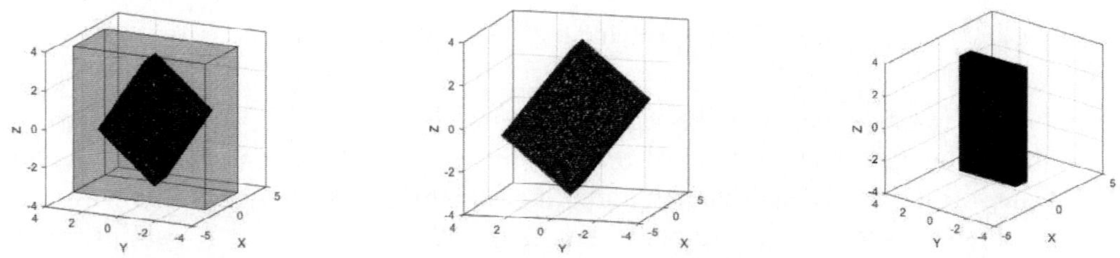

(a) (b) (c)

Figure 2: Different types of bounding box: (a) AABB; (b) MBB; (c) MAABB

To determine this transformation, an optimization problem is defined. As the first step, the point cloud is translated to the origin of the coordinate system. Next, it is transformed using the general form of the rotation matrix in 3-D space. This rotation matrix can be computed by the multiplication of rotation matrices around x, y, and z axes with the angles α, β, and γ, respectively. For every value of α, β, and γ, a new rotation matrix can be obtained, and a volume for the AABB can thus be calculated. Hence, the fitness function of the optimization problem can be defined as below:

$$\textit{To Minimize: } V(\alpha,\beta,\gamma) = l \times w \times h \qquad \textit{Subjected to: } -\pi \le \alpha,\beta,\gamma \le \pi \tag{4}$$

where V is the AABB volume after transformation, l, w, and h are also the dimensions of the bounding box.

All the available real (continuous) metaheuristic algorithms can solve this optimization problem. In this paper, PSO is used as it is simple in coding and results in faster convergence.

3.1 Extrude function

Two parameters are required to extrude a 2D sketch: the direction vector and thickness (depth). Using MAABB, these parameters are simply determined. Figure 3 shows an element created by the extrude operation. As can be seen, the shape's projection (shadow) is a rectangle in all the side views, except for the face of interest (the extrusion base plane). This feature is seen in any shape created by extrusion. Therefore, the face with the lowest similarity to a rectangle is selected as the basis of the extrusion. Subsequently, the vector perpendicular to this face is the direction vector, and the dimension along this vector is the thickness.

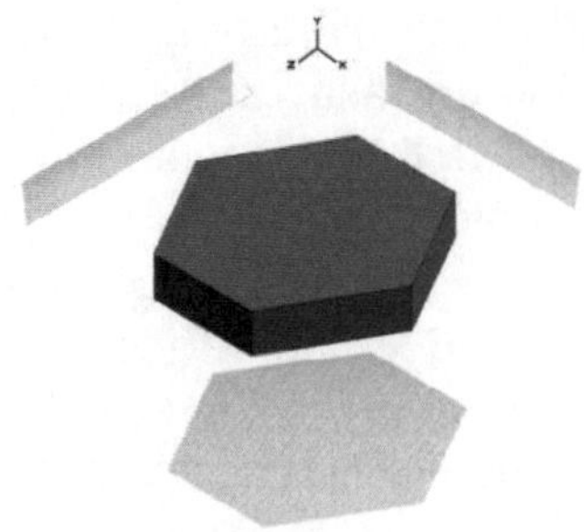

Figure 3: An arbitrary element created by extrude function

To determine the similarity between the faces of a point cloud and a rectangle, the factor of area ratio is defined. This factor is the ratio of the covered area by points and the faces area of the MAABB. The former can be estimated by creating the alpha complex of points with a critical value of alpha that leads to a single region, i.e., a_{xy}, a_{xz}, and a_{yz}, and the latter is simply computed using the dimensions of the MAABB as follows:

$$A_{xy} = L_x L_y \,, \quad A_{xz} = L_x L_z \,, \quad A_{yz} = L_y L_z \tag{5}$$

Considering the calculated values of the area, one area ratio for each direction (x, y, z) can be obtained as below:

$$r_x = a_{yz} / A_{yz} \,, \quad r_y = a_{yz} / A_{yz} \,, \quad r_z = a_{xy} / A_{xy} \tag{6}$$

The minimum area ratio shows the direction of extrusion in MAABB.

3.2 Parametric modeling

The methodology described in the previous section can detect the cross-section of any element that can be modeled by the *extrude* function. This element can be a wing wall, a straight deck, or an abutment in a typical bridge. To extract the parameters' value of elements, the corresponding profiles of the elements can be created based on pre-knowledge, as shown in Figure 4. Although these profiles cannot be expressed by closed-form formulations, they all can be defined by an origin (x_0, y_0) and a set of parameters $\{p_1, p_2, \ldots, p_k\}$.

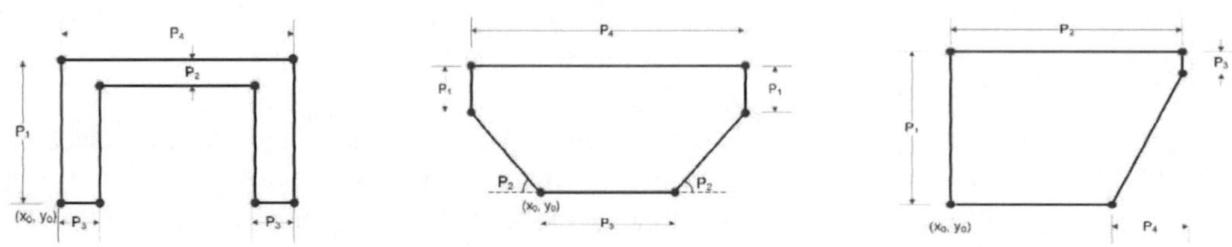

(a) (b) (c)

Figure 4: Parametric profiles: (a) Wing walls; (b) Deck; (c) Abutment

Adjusting the origin and value of the parameters leads to new geometries. Hence, if these profiles are optimized and become closer to the existing points, the obtained parameters at the end of the optimization process will be the actual parameters of the profile. For this purpose, we use metaheuristic algorithms and encode every solution as shown in Figure 5.

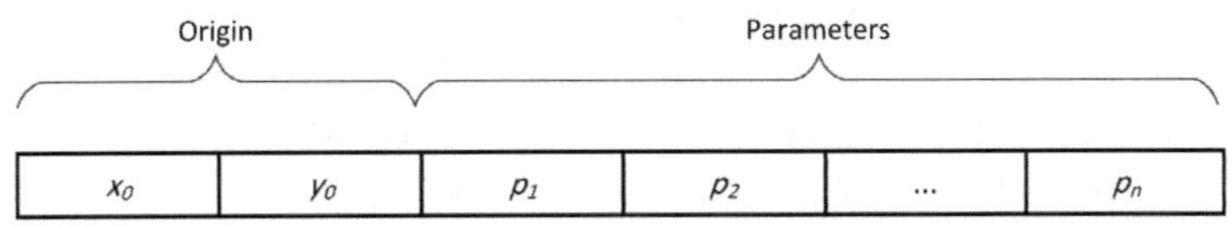

Figure 5: Encoding a profile as a solution in a metaheuristic algorithm

Given a set of points $B = \{b_i = (x_i, y_i), i = 1, 2, \ldots, N\}$ and the profile $F(v_j, e_j)$ with vertices v, edges e, and parameters set $P = \{x_0, y_0, p_1, p_2, \ldots, p_k\}$, the fitness function of the optimization problem can be defined as the root min squared error (*RMSE*) of the minimum distance between the profile and points as below:

$$\text{To minimize: } D(P) = \sqrt{\frac{\sum_{i=1}^{N} \min(d_{ij}(b_i, F(v_j, e_j)))^2}{N}} \quad j = 1, 2, \ldots, M \quad \& \tag{7}$$
$$(v_j, e_j) = f(x_0, y_0, p_1, p_2, \ldots, p_k)$$

where $d_{ij}(b_i, F(v_j, e_j))$ is the distance of the ith point to the jth vertex v or edge e. N is the number of points, M is the number of vertices or edges, and k is the number of parameters.

The range of parameters needs to be defined as well to solve this optimization problem. These ranges can be estimated based on engineering knowledge or can be provided by external resources. Note that the exact ranges are not required, and they should be defined such that the profile can keep its form during the optimization process. However, to make the profiles adaptive, a simple method for estimating these ranges is proposed. For this purpose, all the points are normalized in the range of [-1, 1] using the following formula:

$$(x_i, y_i) = \frac{(x_{io}, y_{io}) - (x_{min}, y_{min})}{(x_{max}, y_{max}) - (x_{min}, y_{min})} \times 2 - 1 \tag{8}$$

where (x_i, y_i) and (x_{io}, y_{io}) are the coordinates of points after and before normalization, respectively. (x_{min}, y_{min}) and (x_{max}, y_{max}) are also the minimum and maximum of points.

After this process, all the points will be mapped in a square bounding box with a length of 2. The range of parameters can then be approximated using this bounding box. To clarify, an example has been shown in Figure 6.

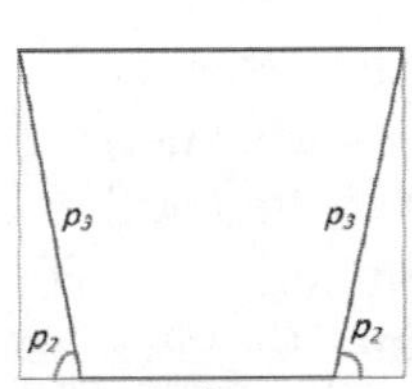

lb:	-1	-1	0	$tan^{-1}(2)$	2
sol:	x_o	y_o	p_1	p_2	p_3
ub:	1	1	2	$\pi/2$	≈ 2.5

lb: lower bound; *ub*: upper bound; *sol*: solution

Figure 6: An example of defining the range of parameters

As the last step, three degrees of freedom for considering the rotation and reflection of the profiles are added to the solution, as shown in Figure 7. These modes create eight regions that are helpful in the parametric modeling of asymmetric profiles. The range of these variables is defined between [-1, 1] so that for values more than 0, the transformations are applied to the profile, and for values lower than 0, no transformation is exerted. The defined optimization problem in this section can be solved by real metaheuristic algorithms. In this paper, FFA is used as it showed more promising performance, especially after adding transformations to the solution.

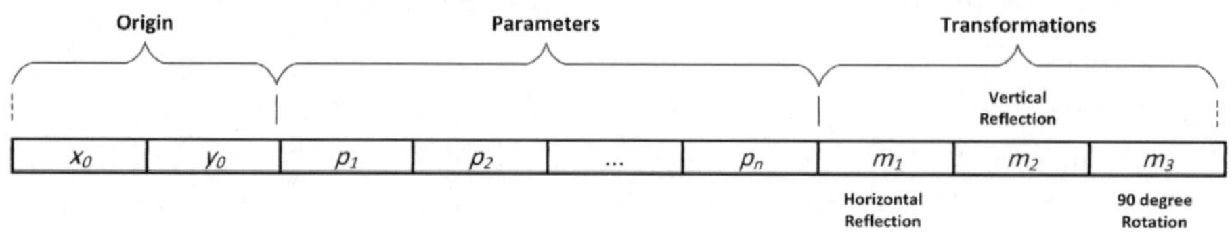

Figure 7: General form of a solution in a metaheuristic algorithm

4. Real-world applications

Two cases are studied to evaluate the performance of the developed methodology on the point cloud of structural elements. The first case is the concrete abutment of a bridge, and the second case is an overpass with two connected wing walls. To validate and compare results, the models are also created manually. The minimum distance of points to the 3-D objects, obtained from our approach and manual modeling, is calculated and finally, a value of *RMSE* is reported in each case.

4.1 Case study 1: Abutment

In this case, an asymmetric point cloud of an abutment has been studied. The point cloud included 56,767 points after down-sampling. Due to occlusion, 2 faces out of 7 faces of the element were not present (the bottom and left face). Also, occlusion and clutter could be seen on the remaining faces, especially the back face of the element. To determine the MAABB (see Section 3), PSO was used. It was seen that considering a swarm with 35 particles and 100 iterations is sufficient for solving the problem. c_1, c_2 coefficients were also set 2, and a damping factor of 0.99 was applied. To calculate the area covered by points, an alpha complex with a critical value of alpha for meshing a single region was employed. The area ratios of r_x, r_y, and r_z were computed 0.8833, 0.7531, and 0.8358, respectively. Hence, the y-direction was detected correctly as the extrusion direction. The cross-section of the point cloud was obtained from the alpha hull with the same value of alpha (0.3839). To extract the parameters of the cross-section, FFA with a parametric model of an abutment profile was used. All the points were normalized, and optimization was conducted in this space. The number of 15 fireflies with 30 iterations was initialized. FFA coefficients including β_0, γ, and α were considered 2, 1, and 0.2, respectively. Figure 8 shows the steps of parametric modeling and Figure 9 demonstrates the final output. Comparing the results of our approach and manual modeling illustrates that the proposed approach not only reduce the modelilng time significantly but also might improve the quality of modeling, i.e. lower value of *RMSE*. This can be due to visual errors and rounding numbers that happens in the manual modeling process.

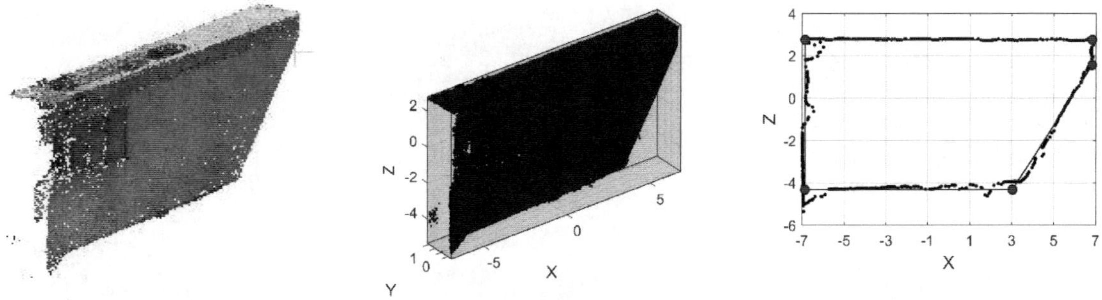

(a) (b) (c)

Figure 8: Parametric modeling process: (a) input PCD; (b) MAABB; (c) Optimized profile

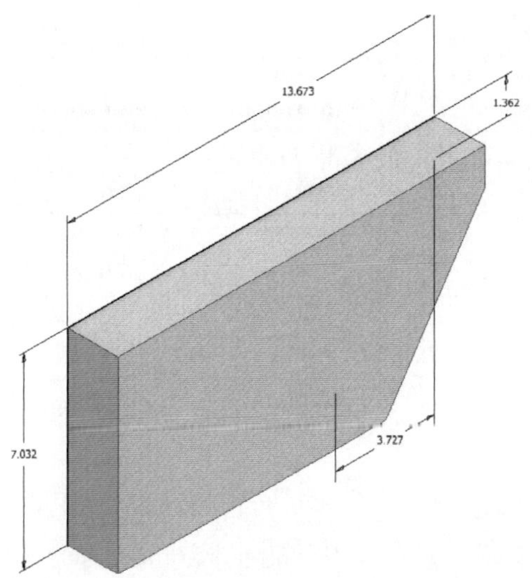

Results	Our approach	Manual modeling
p_1	7.03 m	7.00 m
p_2	13.67 m	13.50 m
p_3	1.36 m	1.40 m
p_4	3.73 m	3.50 m
p_5	1.89 m	1.90 m
RMSE	**0.11 m**	0.25 m
Time	**23.43 sec**	≈ 1200.00 sec

Figure 9: Resulting model of the abutment and its parameters

4.2 Case study 2: Overpass with wing walls

In this case, the point cloud of wing walls connected by an overpass has been studied. In contrast to the previous case, this point cloud has an axis of symmetry. Hence, this feature should also be considered in parametric modeling. The point cloud after down-sampling contained 129,028 points. Two faces of each wing wall were not present, and the other faces had clutter and occlusion. All the parameters of the metaheuristic algorithms were considered the same as the first case study. The area ratios of r_x, r_y, and r_z were computed 0.3543, 0.8015, and 0.9569, respectively. Hence, the x-direction was recognized as the direction vector. The total time necessary for modeling this structure was 43.67 sec. Figure 10 demonstrates all the steps for automatic parametric modeling based on PCD. Figure 11 also shows the final model and a comparison between the proposed method and manual modeling. As can be seen, the obtained parameters in both cases are very close to each other. However, the accuracy of the model derived from our approach is higher, i.e., lower *RMSE*.

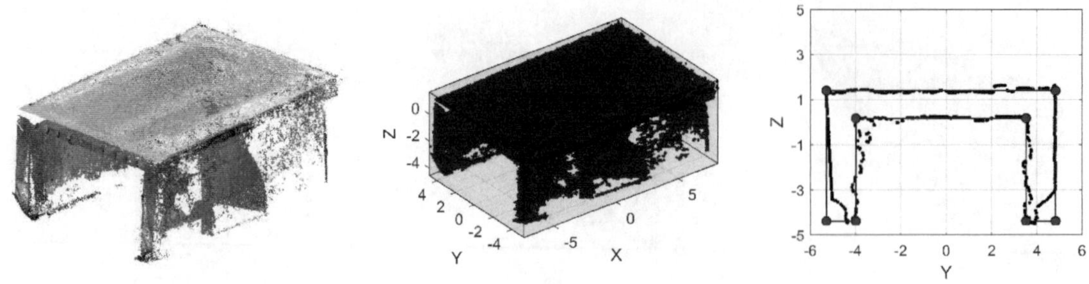

(a) (b) (c)

Figure 10: Parametric modeling process: (a) input PCD; (b) MAABB; (c) Optimized profile

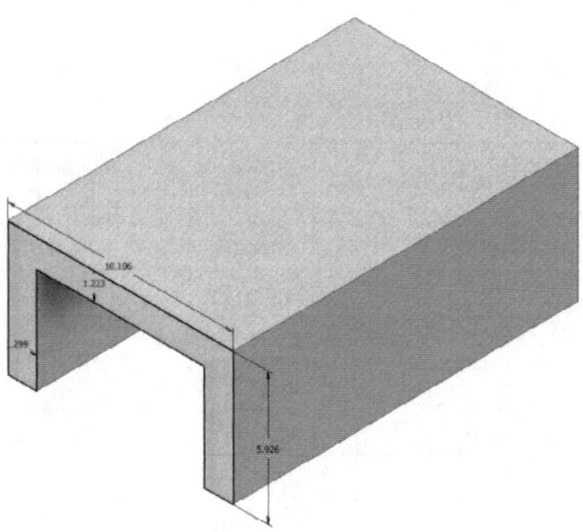

Results	Our approach	Manual modeling
p_1	10.11 m	10.00 m
p_2	5.93 m	6.00 m
p_3	1.22 m	1.30 m
p_4	1.30 m	1.30 m
p_5	15.63 m	15.50 m
RMSE	**0.17 m**	0.38 m
Time	**43.67 sec**	≈ 1200.00 sec

Figure 11: Resulting model of the overpass with wing walls and its parameters

5. Conclusion

In this paper, a method is presented that enables fitting a parametrized bridge model into a given point cloud resulting from a capturing campaign. To this end, metaheuristic algorithms are applied to derive the value of parameters from point cloud data of structural elements. It is shown that these algorithms could extend the conventional *model-based* approach from primitives to more general shapes that are common in infrastructure assets. The presented method consists of three steps: (1) identifying orientation, (2) fitting parametrized cross-section, and (3) applying extrusion operation. In all steps, meta-heuristic optimization approaches were successfully applied. Except for the optimization algorithms' parameters that exist in any problem, no additional parameter or threshold was set. The accuracy of the proposed method was tested on actual point clouds of structural elements that had a significant amount of occlusion and clutter. The results of the paper show that metaheuristic algorithms can be successfully employed for extracting parameters and deriving the volumetric model of the point cloud. The main advantage of the presented method over existing ones is that a high-quality as-is BIM model is generated with a level of abstraction that fulfills the needs of bridge management systems. In this paper, only components with comparatively simple geometries have been investigated. However, the positive results of the presented feasibility analysis provide grounds for further extending the presented approach to represent the most common bridge types in Germany by highly parameterized models for rapid and automated DT generation from point clouds.

Acknowledgment

The research presented has been performed in the profile of the TwinGen project funded by the German Ministry of Transport and Digital Infrastructure (BMVI).

References

Adán, A., B. Quintana, et al. (2018). "Scan-to-BIM for 'secondary'building components." Advanced Engineering Informatics 37: 119–138.

Bosché, F., M. Ahmed, et al. (2015). "The value of integrating Scan-to-BIM and Scan-vs-BIM techniques for construction monitoring using laser scanning and BIM: The case of cylindrical MEP components." Automation in Construction 49: 201–213.

Cao, C. and G. Wang (2019). Fitting Cuboids from the Unstructured 3D Point Cloud. International Conference on Image and Graphics, Springer DOI: http://dx.doi.org/10.1007/978-3-030-34110-7_16.

Kennedy, J. and R. C. Eberhart (1997). A discrete binary version of the particle swarm algorithm. 1997 IEEE International conference on systems, man, and cybernetics. Computational cybernetics and simulation, IEEE.

Kwon, S.-W., F. Bosche, et al. (2004). "Fitting range data to primitives for rapid local 3D modeling using sparse range point clouds." Automation in construction 13(1): 67–81 DOI: http://dx.doi.org/10.1016/j.autcon.2003.08.007.

Laing, R., M. Leon, et al. (2015). "Scan to BIM: the development of a clear workflow for the incorporation of point clouds within a BIM environment." WIT Transactions on The Built Environment 149: 279–289.

Lu, Q., L. Chen, et al. (2020). "Semi-automatic geometric digital twinning for existing buildings based on images and CAD drawings." Automation in Construction 115: 103183.

Lu, R., I. Brilakis, et al. (2019). "Detection of structural components in point clouds of existing RC bridges." Computer-Aided Civil and Infrastructure Engineering 34(3): 191–212 DOI: http://dx.doi.org/10.1111/mice.12407.

Pan, Y., A. Borrmann, et al. (2019). Built Environment Digital Twinning. Report of the International Workshop on Built Environment Digital Twinning presented by TUM Institute for Advanced Study and Siemens AG. Technical University of Munich, Germany.

Qin, G., Y. Zhou, et al. (2021). "Automated Reconstruction of Parametric BIM for Bridge Based on Terrestrial Laser Scanning Data." Advances in Civil Engineering 2021 DOI: https://doi.org/10.1155/2021/8899323.

Rocha, G., L. Mateus, et al. (2020). "A scan-to-BIM methodology applied to heritage buildings." Heritage 3(1): 47–67.

Sacks, R., A. Kedar, et al. (2016). SeeBridge information delivery manual (IDM) for next generation bridge inspection, ISARC.

Sacks, R., A. Kedar, et al. (2018). "SeeBridge as next generation bridge inspection: overview, information delivery manual and model view definition." Automation in Construction 90: 134–145 DOI: 10.1016/j.autcon.2018.02.033.

Song, X. and B. Jüttler (2009). "Modeling and 3D object reconstruction by implicitly defined surfaces with sharp features." Computers & Graphics 33(3): 321–330 DOI: http://dx.doi.org/10.1016/j.cag.2009.03.021.

Technion (2015). SeeBridge—Semantic enrichment engine for bridges, Technion: 77.

Walsh, S. B., D. J. Borello, et al. (2013). "Data processing of point clouds for object detection for structural engineering applications." Computer-Aided Civil and Infrastructure Engineering 28(7): 495–508.

Yan, Y., B. Guldur, et al. (2017). Automated structural modelling of bridges from laser scanning. Structures Congress 2017.

Yang, X.-S. (2008). "Firefly algorithm." Nature-inspired metaheuristic algorithms 20(2008): 79–90.

Zhang, G., P. A. Vela, et al. (2015). "A sparsity-inducing optimization-based algorithm for planar patches extraction from noisy point-cloud data." Computer-Aided Civil and Infrastructure Engineering 30(2): 85–102.

Zhu, Z., S. German, et al. (2010). "Detection of large-scale concrete columns for automated bridge inspection." Automation in construction 19(8): 1047–1055 DOI: http://dx.doi.org/10.1016/j.autcon.2010.07.016.

Zhu, Z., S. German, et al. (2011). "Visual retrieval of concrete crack properties for automated post-earthquake structural safety evaluation." Automation in Construction 20(7): 874–883 DOI: http://dx.doi.org/10.1016/j.autcon.2011.03.004.

Building a balanced and well-rounded dataset for railway asset detection

Felix Eickeler, André Borrmann
Technical University of Munich, Germany
felix.eickeler@tum.de

Abstract. The entire railway network in Europe has a total length of close to 200 thousand kilometres and is one of the main components of European infrastructure (Eurostat Database 2021). Modernising and maintenance is a sizable effort, and due to the long lifespan of railway links, documentation is discontinued, incomplete, or lost. Using survey methods and recreating accurate as-is documentation improve the efficiency and effectivity of maintaining the rail network. In this paper, we present one major building block in creating such a recognition model. While focusing on images and semantic segmentation, the paper describes how a well-rounded dataset for training ML models can be constructed efficiently. Such a dataset is the missing part in adapting modern image recognition systems to railways and providing semantic information for a fully usable building information model (BIM).

1. Introduction

Due to the introduction of digital methods in the construction industry, 2D planning in railway construction is gradually being replaced with BIM-based planning using semantic-geometric models. An essential basis for model-supported planning and maintenance in railway construction is the existence of high-quality geometric-semantic models. Today, existing plans are painstakingly digitised by hand, and the survey data generated by various acquisition methods are manually processed into 3D models. This is a major opportunity for cost and time savings as reconstructed digital models help to better organise and plan changes to rails and roads (Elberink and Khoshelham 2015; Bressi et al. 2020).

Balancing between flexibility, objects count, extent of properties, and precision is one of the challenges in transferring the captured real world to a rich model. Most classic, explicit approaches process an input point cloud to a geometric semantic model focusing on geometric accuracy and sacrificing completeness and flexibility. Especially true in Europe, regulatory influences, differences in survey equipment, and a healthy mix of railway equipment used by different organisations restrict the use of deterministic state-of-the-art approaches. While technologically very similar, an approach created and verified for Spanish tunnels will not work on the complex tunnels of Switzerland, while another built for processing airborne data in Benelux will provide suboptimal results on German turnout areas.

One way to address this diversity is to incorporate implicit techniques in model creation. Implicit and adaptive methods may be extended by additional rules, local models, or datasets of the region, enhancing the correlation of the transferred and the real world. For recognition tasks, statistical models have become an increasingly popular choice. Still, these systems are based on observed or inferred facts, which must be selected, formulated, and prepared before forming a building block in railways model creation. In the railway context, this could be provided by explicit rules provided by the authorities, which have been selected and prepared in a machine-readable form, expert systems that condense best-practices, or training data for deep learning applications. Computer scientists have developed effective and efficient techniques for image recognition, 3D reconstruction, and model generation. These techniques make use of deep learning and are trending in the field of engineering.

Nevertheless, for railway model recognition, these systems are still missing the second key component, the data and facts used to generate a prediction. This component is inevitably bound to the sensors used in the railway survey, which is usually a measurement train. These railcars can cover long tracks quickly and provide multiple sensors for further processing. Following sensors are available: *(i)* multiple mobile laser scanners, *(ii)* inertial measurement units, *(iii)* track radar, *(iv)* global position systems and cameras.

While laser scanners are considered the primary source of automatic railway modelling, this paper develops concepts for processing images, which the authors consider a superior source for semantic information. It focusses on the second component and the challenges that occur during data collection. It provides a solution to these challenges and contours a start-to-end description to acquire this second component, the training data. The data is configured to fit a convolutional neural network (CNN) which can be considered state-of-the-art in machine vision, but the approach can be viewed as generalised. The paper is separated into three main chapters: Background and related work, a description of the task and its complexity, our solution to generate a complete training set, and finally, discussion and outlook.

2. Related Work

Railways are one of the oldest, still existing way of transportation and standards, rules, and best practices have developed over the last 250 years. Relative to this, the use of computers in design, operation and maintenance is a recent development and is thereby heavily influenced by legacy processes. The current trend is to incorporate and expand elements of classical planning into a digital workflow. The most prominent components of this process are the horizontal and vertical alignment, which form the bases of any railway model (Jaud, et al. 2021). Objects and railways are often designed around this alignment using it as a relative curved coordinate system. As the alignment is the basis of the railway model, many approaches have been made to extract it or the closely related centreline of the tracks.

2.1 Railways models from point clouds

Investigations on the extraction of centrelines in point clouds primarily target the explicit geometry of the scan, deriving the local direction of the track for small elements, segmenting the ground and vegetation and matching the gauge (Diaz-Benito 2012; Oude Elberink et al. 2013; Soni et al. 2014; Yang and Fang 2014; Elberink and Khoshelham 2015). These concepts were recently extended by incorporating more information such as GNSS or scan angles (Chen et al. 2020; Wilk et al. 2020; Shankar et al. 2020).

Besides the pure track geometry, railway equipment such as masts, cables, boxes, and signals were extracted from point clouds. The higher the resolution of the model, the more influence has the origin of the point cloud. Work to recognise rails and masts in aerial point from airborne laser scanners was presented in Neubert et al. (2008), Zhu (2014), Arastounia (2015) and Ariyachandra and Brilakis (2020a; 2020b). Simpler capturing technologies such as railcar bound mobile laser scanners where the focus of Sánchez Rodríguez et al. (2018; 2019) and Suárez-González (2020). These already published concepts address the challenge of model creation by imitating the manual process of segmentation. As these results are often close to human interaction, they are easier to incorporate in semi-automatic and existing workflows. Adding to these mostly deterministic algorithms, implicit concepts using machine learning models (e.g. point net) have started to be used to assess railway equipment (Corongiu et al. 2020; Soilán et al. 2020). Nevertheless, these papers are often based on the same data points and datasets as previously investigated concepts leading to similar results.

2.2 Information from images

Many crucial details cannot be detected in point clouds alone, and other sources provided additional insight. Contrary to the laser scans that provide a basic design model, the current major application for image-based detection in railways is fault detection and maintenance tasks. The everyday use cases are inspections of a specialised task by cameras sectionally mounted to observe irregularities, such as damaged or missing parts.

Besides algorithms that analyse the frequency and image space looking for explicit features (E. Resendiz et al. 2013), the currently most influential and general approach is the appliance of supervised neural networks. In the last few years, this approach has matured and, if applied carefully, leads to impressive results. A generalised overview of inspection tasks, especially fasteners, is given in Gibert et al. (2017). Detecting faults in power supply infrastructure was described by Huaxi et al. (2018) using a bilinear network optimised to detect fine-grained visuals. The paper approach predicts if parts belonging to the same category were damaged or still acceptable. The damage detection was later improved to a more generalised approach and extended using a generative adversarial network (GAN) or specialised, including welds (Yao et al. 2020).

Without a prebuilt expectation of the detection, Vilgertshofer et al. (2019) published a concept for detecting the location of railway assets without prior knowledge of the track from video footage. The presented software evaluates hours long capture campaigns resulting in a simple maintenance model. The location along the axis is linked to the track's location, providing some locality to the detection. By combining classical object tracking between frames, the researchers provided over 110 000 bounding boxes for detection in 9 different classes (see Figure 1b).

2.3 Image detection

The problem for most supervised CNNs is the collection of an appropriate dataset. As shown by Vilgertshofer et al. (2019), the amount of training data needed to provide good results is high but can be reduced with an intelligent selection of frames. However, the amount and quality of recognition are heavily dependent on the deep learning model selected. A list of tasks can be seen in Table 1.

Table 1: Computer Vision Tasks

Task	**Image**	**Output**	**Description**
Image Classification	single object	class of the object	
Object Localization	multiple objects	bounding boxes	
Object Detection	multiple objects	bounding boxes and classes	
Object Segmentation	multiple objects	classified pixels	*Can also be provided by boundary descriptions*
Instance Segmentation	multiple objects	classified pixels with instance	*Can also be provided by boundary descriptions*
Keypoint Detection	Multiple objects	Classified pixels with instances and key points	*Can also be provided by boundary descriptions*

Generally, the more specific the results should be, the more data must be provided. Figure 1 shows classification, detection, object segmentation, and instance segmentation applied on a rail dataset.

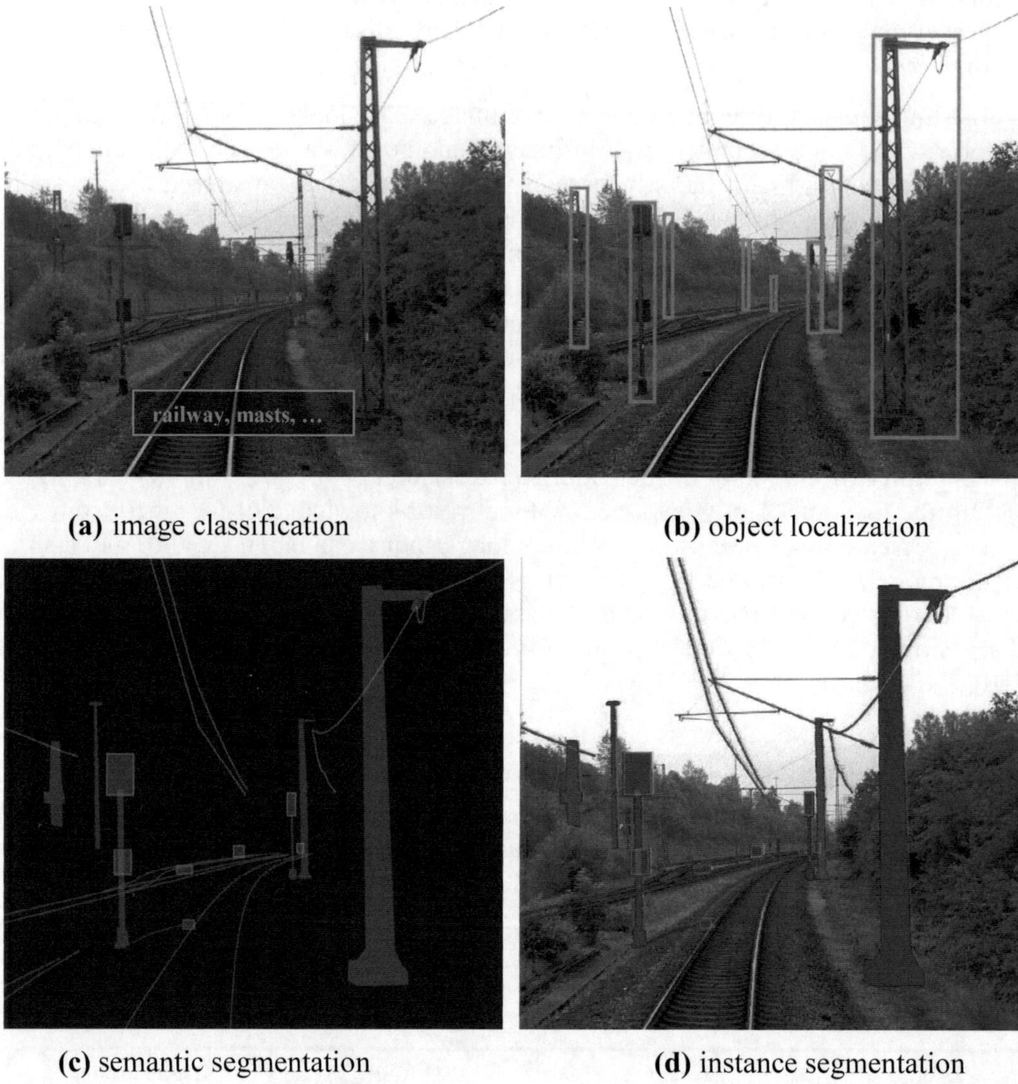

Figure 1: Examples of recognition tasks on the example of rail images. **(a)** shows a classic image classification, **(b)** the object bounding boxes localisation, **(c)** the pixel-based segmentation. The first stage of this works results in **(d)**, an instance segmentation task. Adapted from *Lin et al. (2014).*

For engineers, the application dictates the correct recognition task, the disciplines, and the test data configuration. There is no public railway focused dataset existent to the authors' best knowledge, and only general test data for everyday objects are publicly available. This data can be used to preconfigure the CNN and apply transfer learning to achieve better object detection accuracy (Talukdar et al. 2018).

The creation of the Common Objects in Context (COCO) Panoptic dataset (2017) is well documented. In 123,287 images, 886,284 objects are instance segmented and distributed among 80 classes. While the dataset is large, it is partially unbalanced, only having 225 instances of toasters but close to 66,808 for persons. All labels were created by hand and sourced in multiple steps and quality controls using a self-programmed annotation tool and

Amazon Mechanical Turk (Lin et al. 2014). In the earlier days of machine learning, generating labelled data for neural networks was focused on manual labour. COCO describes the process as extremely time-consuming and states 22 working hours per 1000 segmentations – 1.3 minutes for each segmented entity. This process is the gold standard and highly effective, but the fully manual approach's downside is the immense cost and time needed. This motivation leads to more efficient processes, such as automatic image annotation (Cheng et al. 2018).

3. Requirements & challenges

By assessing the requirements from an engineering perspective, a list of 79 object types should be identified in a captured building information model to fully support the planning process (Bade et al. 2020). The object catalogue presented is created with German railway planning in mind, but most of the objects are relevant for general European railways. These classes do not indicate any general properties such as materials, resulting in farther subcategories inside the catalogue. Starting with the worst case and estimating the same required number of elements as the COCO dataset, this would take around 24 person-months to complete. This process does not include spotting elements, cropping them with a bounding box, sourcing the images from a railcar or any quality control.

Figure 2: Example of a clearance point during recording. The recording was created with 60 frames per second and an approximate speed of 80 km/h. The entity is visible in the next 2 seconds. Clearance point taken from *(jha 2007).*

Additionally, balancing the dataset is not in the nature of a generalised railway dataset. Looking at previous work with bounding boxes, only rail assets present on modern European standardised tracks were selected. This equipment is often sourced from the same manufacturer and has high optical similarity. The similarity explains the excellent results with object tracking during the semi-automatic dataset creation. The complete object catalogue includes objects of varying forms like cables or soundproofing as well as varying content like signal markers. Some of the elements are rare and not as common as others. For example, a clearance point ("Weichengrenzzeichen") will only be present close to a switch (see Figure 2). Switches are generally not present between stations, which can be considered the bulk of the track.

Even if enough clearance points can be found in the datasets, spotting and cropping them will add significant time to the labelling process. As measuring railcars travel with the speed of 16-

22 m/s, the time frame for registering such a small element is tiny. If the shutter needs to be activated in a range of 10 m to a clearance point for visibility, the camera needs to record at least one frame per second to avoid accidentally skipping the element. Revisiting each frame of multiple hours of a measurement run is not feasible.

Before the segmentation, objects need to be cropped to make segmentation possible. This process follows all steps of routine object detection labelling. The speciality arises when the required object catalogue is inspected closely. Some object, such as soundproofing, bridges, station platforms, present themselves in long or wide objects. If these objects are not aligned with the image's axis, the nonaligned bounding box typically spans most of the image. For railcar recording setups with a centralised camera mount, this condition is given in most images as the optical distortion (vanishing point) misalign the objects. The misaligned bounding boxes introduced inefficiencies in the cropping process that precedes the instance segmentation labelling step.

4. Methodology

Facing these challenges in dataset generation, we engineered a three-stage concept that minimised the manual work needed to create a well-rounded, balanced dataset. This process is shown in Figure 3. This concept's design expands on known concepts like assisted labelling and includes the domain-specific knowledge to skip parts of the classification process.

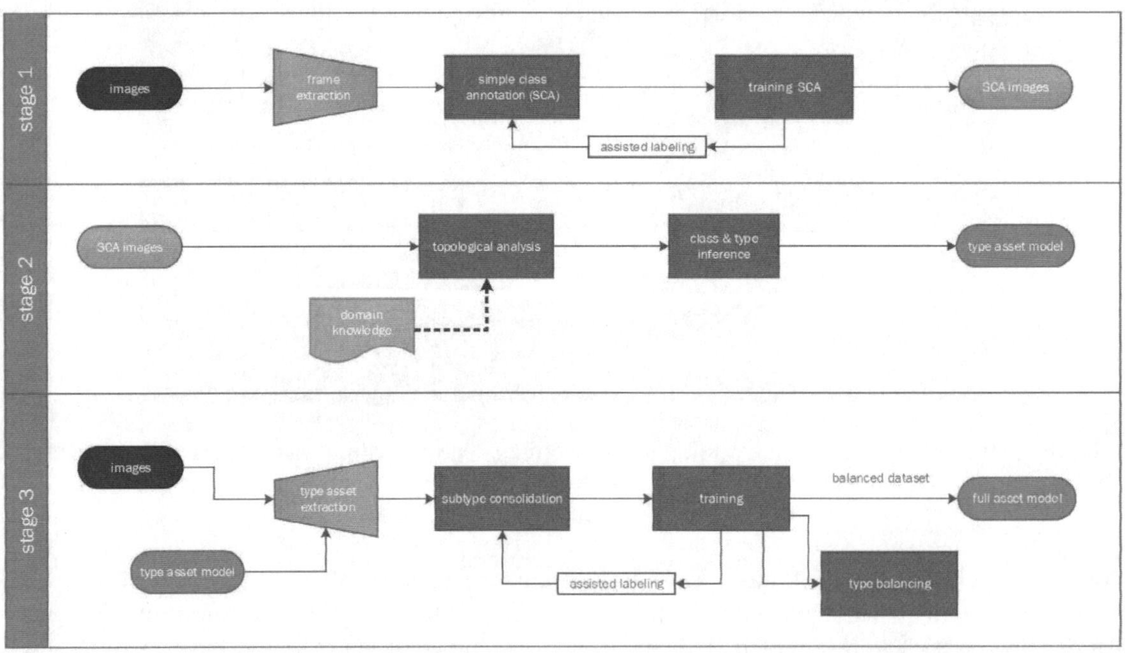

Figure 3: Process of creating a well-rounded and balanced dataset for the detection of infrastructure assets. The approach features three stages: simple class annotation, non-supervised type asset detection, balancing, and type consolidation.

4.1 Stage 1 – Simple Class Annotation (SCA)

The first stage starts by extracting images from multiple continuous sets or videos recorded by a train mounted camera. Instead of using all frames, this stage reduces the processed images down to 0.05 – 0.1 frames per second (fps). The large time steps ensure that the content of the image changes drastically and reduces the load of a 1 h recording to 180 – 360 images. The extracted images are then manually labelled, and a reduced set of the 79 required classes is applied. The reduced set is generated by imposing an artificial hierarchy forming a set of super-classes. The super-classes are generated with two things in mind: label the most occurring elements that have no or a very specialised sub-class and categorise the rest by recording planes. The latter are named point of interest (poi). The recording planes are visualised in Figure 4, the resulting labels in Table 2.

Table 2: Object share in stage 1

Class	Share
powerline	54 %
rail	17 %
pole	10 %
poi_above	7 %
poi_ground	7 %
poi_ground_cable	3 %
poi_generic	2 %

Figure 4: Recording planes used as basis for building a recording hierarchy. Blue to green represents ground, above green is above.

The labelling scheme of stage 1 uses line-based (polylines) labelling, which speeds up the rails, powerlines, and other cables annotation. While this is superior in labelling speed, it adds a layer of complexity since a line does not have a thickness. Therefore, an essential part is the pre-processing, converting, and improving of the line-based labels. The process of extracting rails, cables and powerlines starts by segmenting space around the line. This expanded line, masks the image, which is processed with a Canny edge detection algorithm, exposing the true contour. These contours are then closed by a variable kernel applied in a mix of morphological transformations operations (open/close operations). The kernels are generated by extracting the line direction and only applying them to that segment of the polyline. Additional steps are conducted for each element to fill, filter, and extract the segmentation. The process for powerlines is shown in Figure 5.

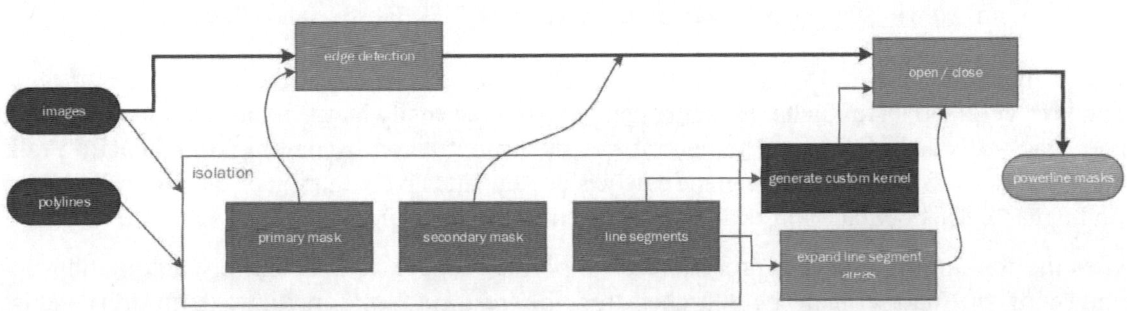

Figure 5: Pre-processing of the manual labels. Cables, powerlines, and rails are provided as polylines that are then converted to the object's actual pixels. The directional vector of the polyline is used to generate a custom kernel.

The final step in this stage is assisted labelling, where training is done early, and the results are manual quality controlled, and only results that diverge from the wanted output are corrected. After a sufficient adaptation of the CNN by stage 1, this model can now be used to filter all datasets' images to extract bounding boxes and parts of interests. By this, we can ensure that all objects in our dataset are selected for further processing.

4.2 Stage 2 – Classification by domain knowledge

In this part, the original subclasses of the entire catalogue are partially inferred by stage 1 and classic image-based analysis results. The analysis uses two dimensions: The temporal one, where information can be inferred from multiple time steps and a connection between different objects, can be implied. This could be the clearance point mentioned above that must be in the temporal vicinity of a switch. The second dimension is the image-space, where an object has a distinct profile with properties such as the recording plane, the format of the bounding box, pixels density, and the locality of the object in the image.

For this stage, a database provides the properties of the object. An instance of the image-space properties is shown in Figure 6. For categorising the objects, three objects are considered: the shape of the bounding box, locality of the centre of the object, the extracted information from the SCA filter. For example, an ETCS Balise is categorised as between rails (*Central*), the bounding box shape is between an aspect ratio of 1:3 to 1:1 and, therefore, categorised as *Box* and was classified as *poi_ground* by the SCA filter. This step reduces the number of possible categories down to a few elements, sometimes resulting in a single category.

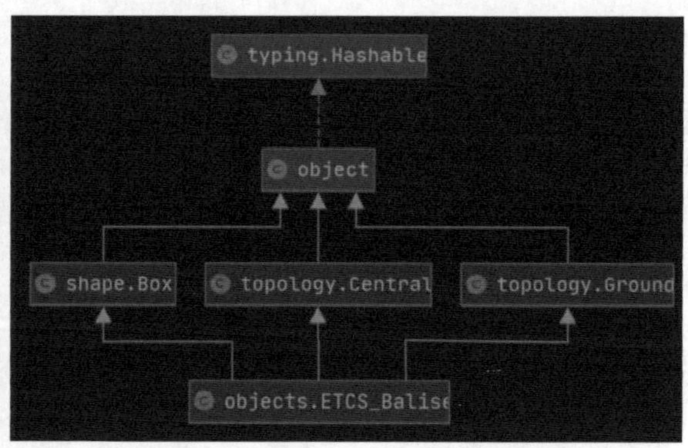

Figure 6 & 7: Example of an ETCS Balise and the topological classification. The colours indicate left, centre, right. The properties of the object are determined and queried in a database, narrowing the possible classification results. ETCS Balise (Halász 2008).

One of the challenges in this step is the horizontal categorisation of the element. While the train is travelling on a rail, where a centre can be extracted easily by the relatively fixed camera, other tracks occur in images. The central spaces are extracted by naming and selecting rail pairs. Due to the SCA results, the plane can be selected, and an estimation of the ground contact can be made. This contact point can then be used to describe the result relative to the rail.

After the initial labelling, the procedure of applying stage 1 & 2 is entirely automatic. All images of the dataset can be searched for the resulting intermediate definitions. This combination creates a balanced and well-rounded dataset for multi-class detection and segmentation that takes rarer elements properly into account.

4.3 Stage 3 – Full Asset Model

This stage reassembles the optimisation steps of the COCO panoptic dataset creation. To create the full asset model, two main tasks remain:

- Additional classification of still ambiguous objects from stage 2. As the preceding stage selected the hierarchical super-category, only the possible sub-classes need to be considered, and cropped images are used. The annotation takes approximately 30 seconds per image that needs further classification (Lin et al. 2014).
- The second task is to complete the panoptic segmentation for objects that need instance segmentation. This is only true for point of interest elements labelled for object detection in the SCA stage.

Both steps are again processed using model-assisted labelling to reduce the manual load. By design, the authors propose using two separate networks, as the time needed to adapt depends on the complexity of the network used. The selection of pre-trained classification networks such as the state-of-the-art *Inception-ResNet-v2* helps to reduce the labels needed.

Simultaneous to the labelling process, the balance of the objects is verified further. If a subclass is now overrepresented, more images from that super-category are pulled to compensate for the lack of images. This will introduce overhead in the "faster" classification tasks but reduce the load on the time-intensive instance segmentation.

5. Conclusion & Outlook

Challenged with recognising various infrastructure assets from different locations and surveys, this paper focused on building a railway dataset by integrating domain knowledge. It describes the first building block in creating a complete deep learning model and incorporating images as sources of information. The use of images has been neglected in full model creation and was, until now, only used for maintenance. While the proposed concept has a higher complexity than standard approaches, it is adaptive and independent of the prediction method (e.g., CNN). Early and intermediate results seem to verify the applicability of our approach.

The following steps for further developing automated modelling from image sources are mainly incorporating localisation of the information extracted from the images. As some of the elements identified in images can be referenced globally (control points), the main tasks are the local projection of the semantic information to the geometric entities. Few techniques have been presented that can be leveraged for this task, including an inertial measurement unit, 3D edge detection or photogrammetry.

Another step is the quality enhancement of the resulting dataset. As research shows, the number of maintenance tasks offered by evaluating images alone is substantial. While this is not part of this investigation, the condition and existence of certain elements can be evaluated. Expanding these to the object catalogue by adding, for example, a fourth stage to fill in properties of essential objects, this approach can be the platform to unify and benchmark existing recognition techniques in maintenance.

References

Arastounia, M. (2015). Automated Recognition of Railroad Infrastructure in Rural Areas from LIDAR Data. Remote Sensing 7, 14916–14938. https://doi.org/10.3390/rs71114916.

Ariyachandra, M.,Brilakis, I. (2020a). Detection of Railway Masts in Airborne LiDAR Data. Journal of Construction Engineering and Management 146. https://doi.org/10.1061/(ASCE)CO.1943-7862.0001894.

Ariyachandra, M.,Brilakis, I. (2020b). Digital Twinning of Railway Overhead Line Equipment from Airborne LiDAR Data. Proceedings of the 37th International Symposium on Automation and Robotics in Construction (ISARC). https://doi.org/10.22260/ISARC2020/0174.

Bade, M. M. Sc.,Schneider, P. M. Sc.,Rampf, F. M.Sc.,Frei, M. Dipl.-Math.,Eickeler, F. Dipl.-Ing. (TUM),Borrmann, A. Prof. Dr.-Ing. (2020). RailTwin Zwischenbericht 2020.

Bressi, S.,Santos, J.,Losa, M. (2020). Optimization of maintenance strategies for railway track-bed considering probabilistic degradation models and different reliability levels. Reliability Engineering & System Safety.

Chen, C.,Zhang, T.,Kan, Y.,Li, S.,Jin, G. (2020). A rail extraction algorithm based on the generalized neighborhood height difference from mobile laser scanning data. SPIE Future Sensing Technologies. https://doi.org/10.1117/12.2580371.

Cheng, Q.,Zhang, Q.,Fu, P.,Tu, C.,Li, S. (2018). A survey and analysis on automatic image annotation. Pattern Recognition 79, 242–259. https://doi.org/10.1016/j.patcog.2018.02.017.

Corongiu, M.,Masiero, A.,Tucci, G. (2020). Classification of Railway Assets in Mobile Mapping Point Clouds. ISPRS - International Archives of the Photogrammetry, Remote Sensing and Spatial Information Sciences, 219–225. https://doi.org/10.5194/isprs-archives-XLIII-B1-2020-219-2020.

Diaz-Benito, D. (2012). Automatic 3D modelling of train rails in a LiDAR point cloud. Master Thesis. University of Twente Faculty of Geo-Information and Earth Observation (ITC).

E. Resendiz,Hart, J. M.,Ahuja, N. (2013). Automated Visual Inspection of Railroad Tracks. IEEE Transactions on Intelligent Transportation Systems (2), 751–760. https://doi.org/10.1109/TITS.2012.2236555.

Elberink, S.,Khoshelham, K. (2015). Automatic Extraction of Railroad Centerlines from Mobile Laser Scanning Data. Remote Sensing 7 (5), 5565–5583. https://doi.org/10.3390/rs70505565.

Gibert, X.,Patel, V. M.,Chellappa, R. (2017). Deep Multitask Learning for Railway Track Inspection. IEEE Transactions on Intelligent Transportation Systems 18 (1), 153–164. https://doi.org/10.1109/TITS.2016.2568758.

Halász, I. (2008). European Train Control System. Available online at https://commons.wikimedia.org/wiki/File:Balizok_az_%C5%90rs%C3%A9gi_vas%C3%BAton2.jpg.

Huaxi, H.,Xu, J.,Zhang, J.,Wu, Q.,Kirsch, C. (2018). Railway Infrastructure Defects Recognition using Fine-grained Deep Convolutional Neural Networks. 2018 Digital Image Computing: Techniques and Applications (DICTA), 1–8. https://doi.org/10.1109/DICTA.2018.8615868.

Jaud,, Š.,Esser, S.,Wikström, L.,Muhič, S.,Borrmann, A. (2021). A critical analysis of linear placement in IFC models.

jha (2007). Deutsches Signal Ra 12/So 12, Grenzzeichen. Available online at https://commons.wikimedia.org/w/index.php?curid=13761614 (accessed 3/21/2021).

Lin, T.-Y.,Maire, M.,Belongie, S.,Bourdev, L.,Girshick, R.,Hays, J.,Perona, P.,Ramanan, D.,Zitnick, C. L.,Dollár, P. (2014). Microsoft COCO: Common Objects in Context. Available online at https://arxiv.org/pdf/1405.0312.

Neubert, M.,Hecht, R.,Gedrange, C.,Trommler, M.,Herold, H.,Krüger, T.,Brimmer, F. (2008). Extraction Of Railroad Objects From Very High Resolution Helicopter-Borne Lidar And Orthoimage Data.

Oude Elberink, S.,Khoshelham, K.,Arastounia, M.,Diaz Benito, D. (2013). Rail Track Detection and Modelling in Mobile Laser Scanner Data. ISPRS Annals of the Photogrammetry, Remote Sensing and Spatial Information Sciences II-5/W2, 223–228. https://doi.org/10.5194/isprsannals-II-5-W2-223-2013.

Sánchez Rodríguez, A.,Riveiro, B.,Soilán, M.,González-deSantos, L. (2018). Automated detection and decomposition of railway tunnels from Mobile Laser Scanning Datasets. Automation in Construction 96, 171–179. https://doi.org/10.1016/j.autcon.2018.09.014.

Sánchez Rodríguez, A.,Soilán, M.,Cabaleiro, M.,Arias, P. (2019). Automated Inspection of Railway Tunnels' Power Line Using LiDAR Point Clouds. Remote Sensing 11, 2567. https://doi.org/10.3390/rs11212567.

Shankar, S.,Roth, M.,Schubert, L. A.,Verstegen, J. A. (2020). Automatic Mapping of Center Line of Railway Tracks using Global Navigation Satellite System, Inertial Measurement Unit and Laser Scanner. Remote Sensing 12 (3), 411. https://doi.org/10.3390/rs12030411.

Soilán, M.,Nóvoa, A.,Sánchez Rodríguez, A.,Riveiro, B.,Arias, P. (2020). Semantic Segmentation Of Point Clouds With Pointnet And Kpconv Architectures Applied To Railway Tunnels. ISPRS Annals of Photogrammetry, Remote Sensing and Spatial Information Sciences V-2-2020, 281–288. https://doi.org/10.5194/isprs-annals-V-2-2020-281-2020.

Soni, A.,Robson, S.,Gleeson, B. (2014). Extracting Rail Track Geometry from Static Terrestrial Laser Scans for Monitoring Purposes. ISPRS - International Archives of the Photogrammetry, Remote Sensing and Spatial Information Sciences XL-5, 553–557. https://doi.org/10.5194/isprsarchives-XL-5-553-2014.

Suárez-González, A. (2020). Automatic Extraction of Power Cables Location in Railways Using Surface LiDAR Systems. Sensors 20, 6222. https://doi.org/10.3390/s20216222.

Talukdar, J.,Gupta, S.,Rajpura, P.,Hegde, R. (2018). Transfer Learning for Object Detection using State-of-the-Art Deep Neural Networks. 2018 5th International Conference on Signal Processing and Integrated Networks (SPIN), 78–83. https://doi.org/10.1109/SPIN.2018.8474198.

Vilgertshofer, S.,Stoitchkov, D.,Borrmann, A.,Menter, A.,Genc, C. (2019). Recognising railway infrastructure elements in videos and drawings using neural networks. Institution of Civil Engineers - Smart Infrastructure and Construction 172 (1). https://doi.org/10.1680/jsmic.19.00017.

Wilk, A.,Koc, W.,Specht, C.,Judek, S.,Karwowski, K.,Chrostowski, P.,Czaplewski, K.,Dąbrowski, P.,Grulkowski, S.,Licow, R.,Skibicki, J.,Specht, M.,Szmagliński, J. (2020). Digital Filtering of Railway Track Coordinates in Mobile Multi–Receiver GNSS Measurements. Sensors 20, 5018. https://doi.org/10.3390/s20185018.

Yang, B.,Fang, L. (2014). Automated Extraction of 3-D Railway Tracks from Mobile Laser Scanning Point Clouds. Selected Topics in Applied Earth Observations and Remote Sensing, IEEE Journal of 7, 4750–4761. https://doi.org/10.1109/JSTARS.2014.2312378.

Yao, N.,Jia, Y.,Tao, K. (2020). Rail Weld Defect Prediction and Related Condition-Based Maintenance. IEEE Access PP. https://doi.org/10.1109/ACCESS.2020.2999385.

Zhu, L. (2014). The Use of Airborne and Mobile Laser Scanning for Modeling Railway Environments in 3D. Remote Sensing 6, 3075–3100. https://doi.org/10.3390/rs6043075.

Panorama-to-digital twin registration using semantic features

Yujie Wei, Burcu Akinci
Carnegie Mellon University, USA
yujiew,bakinci@cmu.edu

Abstract. In recent years, capturing panoramas has become an effective way for documenting the as-is condition of a building in addition to conventional monocular images. Even though having a bigger field of view helps in locating where the image was taken, registering the image to a digital twin model is still challenging due to possible inconsistent visual appearances, such as model vs. image visual differences, lighting condition changes, and different levels of details. In this paper, we present a novel method that registers panoramic images to a digital twin by image retrieval using high-level semantics such as object categories and semantic segmentation. We evaluated the proposed method on a synthetic dataset using images generated from the building information model of an academic building and showed that the proposed method can localize a panorama in less than a second with an average error of 2.3m.

1. Introduction

1.1 Overview

Imagery, as an efficient approach to collect as-built information, has been widely used in many AEC applications, such as progress monitoring, quality inspection, collaboration, and proactive maintenance, in recent years (Kim, Hwang, Chi, & Seo, 2020; Luo et al., 2019; C. Zhang & Huang, 2019). In current industry practices, engineers manually locate images within as-designed models to compare whether what is built matches what is specified. This is often error-prone and time-consuming (Lu & Lee, 2017; Wei, Kasireddy, & Akinci, 2018). With the development of image stitching algorithms and camera rigs, capturing panoramic images instead of monocular images is gaining wider usage since a bigger field-of-view (FoV) is the key to addressing the common repetitive and texture-less structures presented in indoor environments (Z. Zhang, Rebecq, Forster, & Scaramuzza, 2016). However, registering panoramas to a digital twin is still challenging due to the missing 3D information and the cross-domain visual differences between real-world images (Figure 1a) and computer graphic (CG) models (Figure 1b). With the recent development of deep learning-based object recognition techniques, it is possible to obtain semantic segmentation for any query image using a convolutional neural network (CNN) and use it as a consistent cross-domain feature (Figure 1c) for comparing with the as-designed semantics and supporting registration (Figure 1d). In this paper, we proposed a novel method to leverage the predicted semantic segmentation and the existing as-designed semantics in a BIM to perform panorama-to-digital twin registration. Specifically, we generate semantic segmentation for different camera views using a BIM and encode them into a compact vector representation using product quantization (PQ) for fast querying. After the top-K similar images are retrieved, we spawn camera particles around the retrieved images to further minimize the reprojected semantic errors to obtain the predicted camera pose.

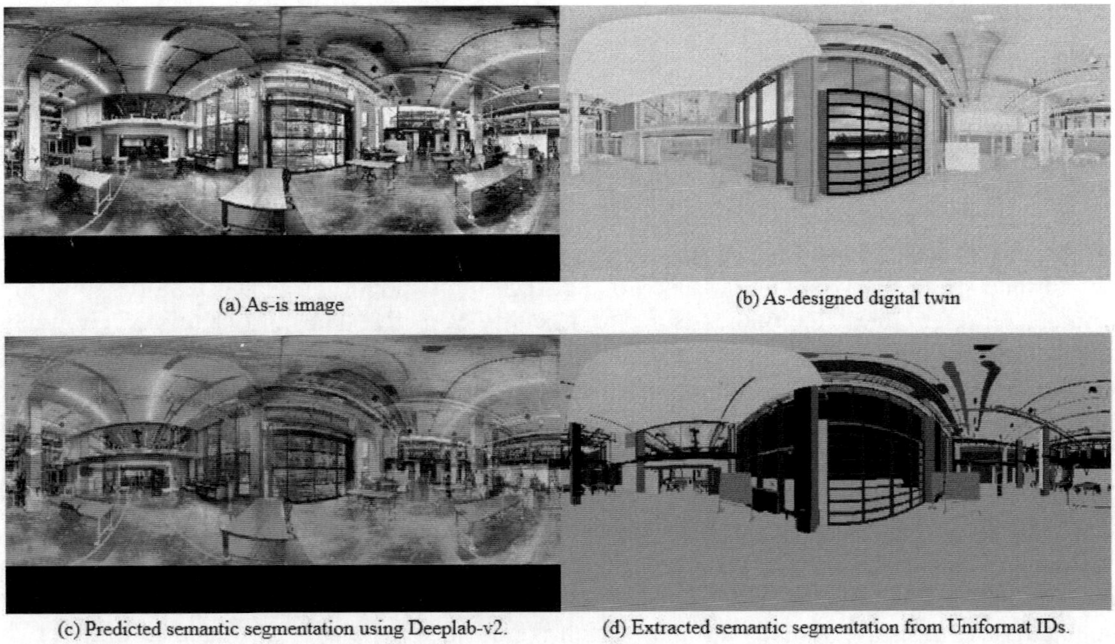

Figure 1: Registering real-world panoramas to a digital twin without available 3D information is challenging due to the visual differences between real-world images (a) and computer graphic models (b). The proposed method leverages semantic segmentation predicted using CNN (c) and extracted from prior information (d) as a cross-domain feature for registration.

1.2 Existing research

Existing image-to-digital twin registration approaches can be broadly categorized into three groups: 1) 3D reconstruction (3D-3D registration), 2) Direct mapping (2D-3D registration), and 3) Image retrieval (2D-2D registration). Below provides a literature review on all three groups of research and discuss their limitations when they are used for AEC applications.

3D-3D registration. 3D-3D registration methods, such as structure from motion (SfM) and simultaneous localization and mapping (SLAM), aim at recovering camera poses and landmark locations from overlapping images and registering the reconstructed 3D model to a digital twin (Engel, Koltun, & Cremers, 2018; Engel, Schöps, & Cremers, 2014; Mur-Artal, Montiel, & Tardos, 2015; Schonberger & Frahm, 2016). In order to estimate the camera pose of a particular image, 3D-3D registration methods rely on capturing depth information or overlapping images to guarantee the geometric accuracy of the reconstructed 3D model, which often requires a dedicated data collection and cannot be used for registering unstructured photos.

2D-3D registration. Instead of reconstructing a 3D model from the captured data first, 2D-3D registration approaches infer camera poses by associating 2D information shown on images to a prior 3D map. One common way to establish such 2D-3D matching is to store local feature descriptors such as SIFT and ORB into a 3D map, and the camera pose of a query image can be estimated using Perspective-n-Points (PnP) methods (Lepetit, Moreno-Noguer, & Fua, 2009). However, due to the visual differences between real images and CG models, it is difficult to establish such 2D-3D matching using handcrafted feature points. Many recent studies use learned features on images to regress a camera pose directly (Acharya, Khoshelham, & Winter, 2019; Kendall, Grimes, & Cipolla, 2015; Wei & Akinci, 2019). However, such 2D-3D mapping models require ground truth camera poses for training and need to be fine-tuned when they are used in a new building, which makes them costly to use and difficult to generalize to new environments.

2D-2D registration. 2D-2D registration methods formulate the localization process as an image retrieval problem. In other words, 2D-2D registration approaches estimate the pose of a query image by fetching the most similar geo-tagged images from a pre-built database. The key to a successful retrieval is to find a compact representation of the original query image and images in the database and make sure two similar images remain close to each other in the transformed space. Early studies focused on aggregating handcrafted visual features to form a compact representation for images, such as Locality-Sensitive Hashing (Kulis & Grauman, 2009), Bag-of-Words (Sivic & Zisserman, 2009), and VLAD (Arandjelovic & Zisserman, 2013). Such methods relying on handcrafted visual features are often used for fetching the most similar real-world image from a database given another real-world image and perform poorly on cross-domain registration. Recent studies started to look into the usage of learned visual features for localizing an image, such as middle-layer activations from a CNN (Baek, Ha, & Kim, 2019) or learned descriptors (Arandjelovic, Gronat, Torii, Pajdla, & Sivic, 2016; Dusmanu et al., 2019; Revaud, Weinzaepfel, de Souza, & Humenberger, 2019; Sarlin, Detone, Malisiewicz, & Rabinovich, 2020). However, these methods assume that the query image and the database images are visually similar, which is not true in the case of image-to-digital twin registration.

Considering the limitations of existing approaches, we introduce a novel panorama-to-digital twin registration approach using semantic features with the following contributions: 1) the proposed method can utilize a bigger FoV provided by panoramas compared to monocular images to address texture-less and repetitive scenes; 2) by leveraging semantic features instead of visual features, the proposed method builds a cross-domain similarity measure between a digital twin model and real-world images; 3) the employment of semantic features allows for the integration of domain knowledge to help localization, such as filtering out moving objects when performing image retrieval. In the rest of the paper, we first formulate the registration process as an image-retrieval problem and introduce the details of the proposed method in Section 2. The experiment setup and the discussion on results will be covered in Section 3 and Section 4 respectively.

2. The proposed method

As mentioned above, the panorama-to-digital twin registration process can be viewed as an image retrieval problem. Figure 2 shows an overview of the proposed workflow that contains two stages: offline database preparation and online localization. During the offline stage, we sample possible camera poses from a digital twin and render semantic panoramas to be encoded into semantic descriptors using Product Quantization (Jégou, Douze, & Schmid, 2011). Since the images in the database are rendered from an existing digital twin, it is easy to obtain their camera poses to create a geo-tagged PQ descriptor database. During the online stage, for any given query panorama, we first compute its semantic segmentation using CNN and encode it into a PQ descriptor to be compared with the ones stored in the database. After retrieving several candidate images with top semantic similarity, the camera pose can be further refined through particle sampling by minimizing the reprojected semantic errors. Below we will give a detailed introduction to each module.

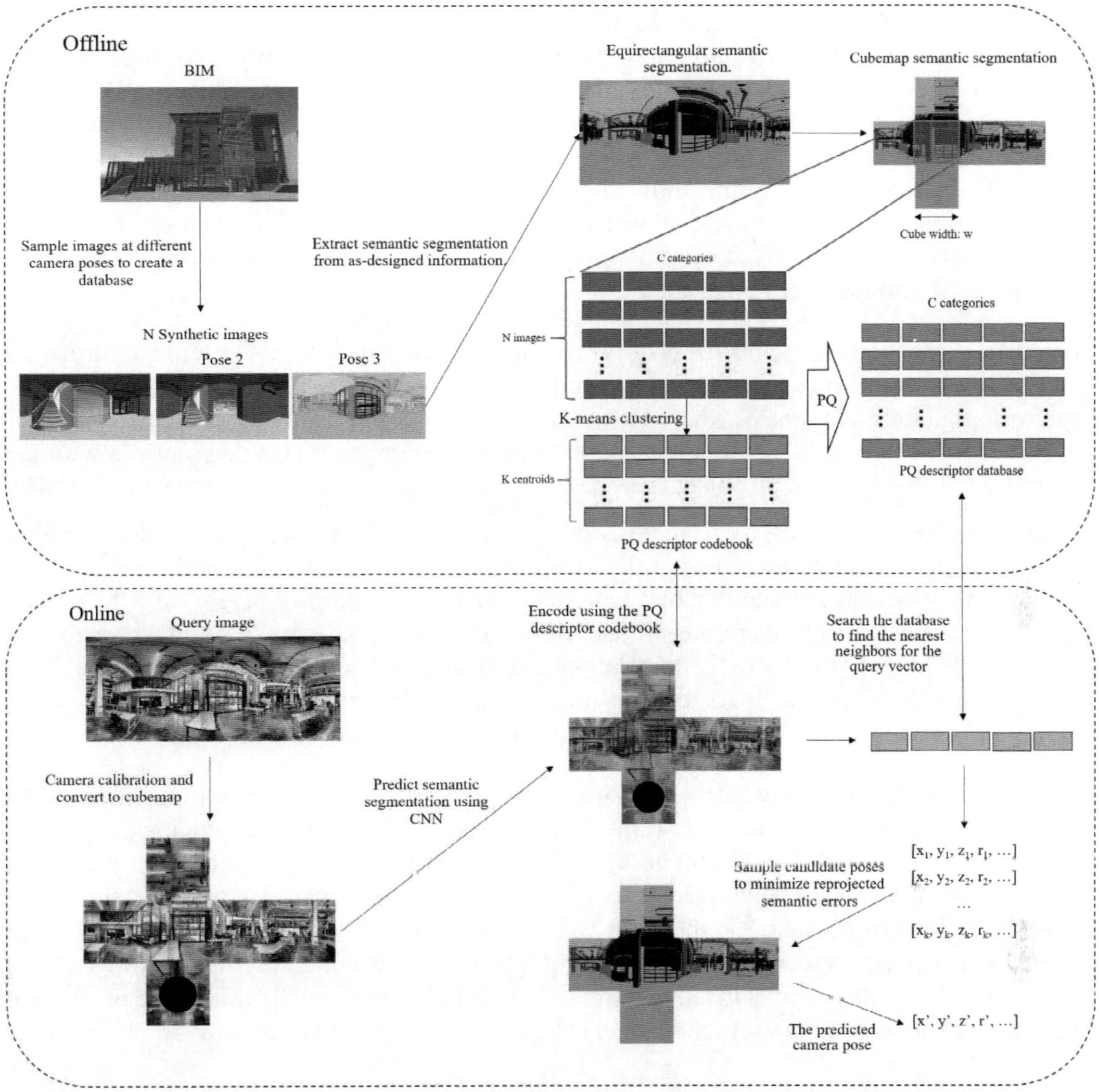

Figure 2: Overview of the panorama-to-digital twin registration workflow

2.1 Offline database preparation

During the offline stage, the proposed workflow needs to build a database that contains compact semantic representations for possible panoramic views in a digital twin. The database creation can be divided into three steps: 1) Define the semantic classification scheme used for registration; 2) Sample semantic images in a BIM given different camera poses; 3) Compute compact representations for semantic images and record their corresponding camera poses to build a geo-tagged descriptor database. We will introduce each step in detail below.

Classification scheme definition. In order to compare the semantics predicted from CNN with the semantics extracted from BIM, we must define a uniform object classification scheme to be used in both real images and model images. In other words, it is not possible to match two classification schemes when one taxonomy contains [cats, dogs, human] but the other one contains [columns, beams, walls]. Instead of using existing object classification taxonomies from the computer vision communities such as ImageNet or COCO, we employed the

Uniformat 2010 standard (CSC CSI, 2010) as the classification scheme since it covers major components common to most buildings and can be generalized to various types of building projects[1]. Besides, it is convenient to extract the Uniformat ID from any existing BIM, since such information is available in a digital twin. This can save the time spent on manually assigning category labels to each component in an as-designed BIM. Notice that a building might only contain a subset of the Uniformat-defined components. For example, an academic building might have institutional equipment (E1040) but not residential equipment (E1060). This problem can be easily fixed by removing irrelevant categories when building the semantic codebook as discussed later in this chapter.

Semantic segmentation generation. Given a digital twin, such as a building information model (BIM), we can place a virtual camera C with a camera pose [**R**, **t**] into the model to capture a semantic panorama S, where **R** stands for a 3x3 rotation matrix and **t** stands for a 3x1 translation vector $[x, y, z]^T$. Notice that on the semantic segmentation image, pixels with the same value belong to the same object class based on the as-designed information stored in BIM.

A key question that needs to be addressed is the sampling space. Due to the curse of dimensionality, it is important to limit the sampling space to a tractable size. In our case, we assume that panoramas are captured by a calibrated camera at the known height from the ground and the camera is leveled. Therefore, we can limit the sampling space to a 4-d pose vector p = $[x, y, z, yaw]^T$ where [x,y,z] are the translation coordinates and yaw is the rotation angle along vertical axis. The sampling space can be further reduced by enabling collision check when moving the virtual camera. We will cover the details in the implementation section.

Creating a descriptor database for querying. In this paper, we employed Product Quantization (PQ) to compute a descriptor for each semantic segmentation image (Furuta, Inoue, & Yamasaki, 2019; Jégou et al., 2011). Specifically, for a panoramic semantic segmentation S, we can first convert it to a cubemap representation that contains six $w \times w$ faces (front, back, left, right, top, bottom) with C categories of objects (w is the width of the cube). Let $i = 1, \cdots, N$ denote the i-th semantic panorama generated from a BIM. Let $j = 1, \cdots, 6 \times w^2$ denote the pixel location. Notice that we now can unroll a semantic segmentation image into a vector and represent the object category using a one-hot vector as shown below:

$$\boldsymbol{s}^i = [\boldsymbol{s}_1^i, \boldsymbol{s}_2^i, \cdots, \boldsymbol{s}_c^i]^T$$

Notice that the semantic segmentation image is now a vector with $6Cw^2$ dimensions. The vector can be naturally divided into C subvectors based on their categories as shown below.

$$\boldsymbol{s}_c^i(j) \in [0,1]^{w^2 \times 6},$$
$$s.t. \quad \forall i, j, \ \ \sum_{c=1}^{C} \boldsymbol{s}_c^i(j) = 1$$

where the constraint means each pixel can only belong to one category. Given N images, we have N semantic segmentation vectors and they form C matrices where each of them has a size of $N \times 6w^2$. Following the PQ technique (Jégou et al., 2011), we can use K-means for each matrix to find K centroids and quantize each image into a PQ vector by representing its subvector using the nearest centroids. For categories that should not be considered when performing localization, we can simply remove the subvector corresponding to that category when building the database. Notice that as the number of categories increases, the one-hot vector representation of a semantic segmentation could become highly sparse and might result in training error during PQ quantization under some random initializations. To avoid such

[1] The complete Uniformat 2010-based classification scheme can be found at https://github.com/yugitw/Construction-Scene-Parsing/blob/master/csp.txt.

computational issues, when the number of object category is large and the number of training images is small, performing PQ on the label-encoding vector rather than one hot-encoding vector is a feasible alternative.

2.2 Online localization

Given a prebuilt database and a query panorama, the online localization module predicts the location of the input panorama in a digital twin model. The online localization contains two steps: rough localization and fine localization. In the first step, we use a fully connected neural network to predict the dense semantic segmentation of a query image. After obtaining the semantic segmentation, the PQ vector will be computed and compared with the ones stored in the database using the asymmetric distance computation (Jégou et al., 2011) to find several candidate camera poses that have the most similar PQ representations as the query image. In the second step, we compute the reprojected semantic errors for each candidate camera pose as shown below:

$$E(\boldsymbol{s}^i, s') = \left\| \boldsymbol{s}^i - \boldsymbol{s}' \right\|_2$$

where s' is the detected semantic segmentation on real-world images and $\boldsymbol{s}^i$ is the rendered semantic segmentation from a BIM. We will use the camera pose with the smallest camera reprojected error as the predicted camera pose.

3. Implementations and results

3.1 Dataset

To verify the proposed workflow, we used a 5-floor academic building in Pittsburgh as our testbed. The testbed contains a building information model that includes architectural, structural, MEP, and furnishing components. For evaluations, we migrated a BIM created in Revit to Unreal Engine 4 and generated a database that contains 72,000 synthetic views for database creation and 150 synthetic views for query. Below we will discuss the detailed implementation of dataset creation.

Figure 3: The building information model (left) and the image (right) of the academic building used as a testbed

BIM-to-Unreal Engine Migration. Since there are many limitations when rendering synthetic views using the Revit APIs, we first convert a BIM from Revit to Unreal Engine 4 (UE4) using Datasmith. As mentioned in the previous section, the proposed method utilizes the built-in Uniformat 2010 in a BIM for component classification. In order to migrate the Uniformat ID information to Unreal Engine as well, we explicitly assigned the Uniformat ID as an entry in the metadata of each component. Therefore, after the model is converted to the fbx format using Datasmith, we can still obtain the Uniformat ID from the metadata conveniently.

Semantic Rendering. In order to render panoramic RGB and semantic segmentation images, we utilized the AirSim (Shah, Dey, Lovett, & Kapoor, 2017) together with UE4 (Epic Games, 2020) as our render engine. It is worth noticing that UE4 does not support spherical panorama rendering intrinsically. Therefore, we created a camera rig inside AirSim with six cameras (front, back, left, right, top, bottom). Each camera has a FoV of 90 degrees and a focal length of exactly half of the image width (256x256 for each cube face). With such a virtual camera rig, we can capture cubemaps without any overlapping, which can then be converted to equirectangular or spherical panorama representations easily.

Automatic data creation. In order to reduce the sampling space, we leveraged the physics engine in UE4 to enable collision check as well. Once a model is imported to UE4, we manually adjust the attribute of each floor into walkable regions and created a 3D occupancy map for collision detection. When enabling collision detection, the sampled camera poses will not be placed at unreachable locations, such as inside a column or a wall.

3.2 Experiments

For evaluation purposes, we randomly placed virtual cameras into the scene to generate 2000 query images and try to localize the query images. For the number of centroids (K) used for training the PQ codebook, we used K = [32, 64, 128, 256] and obtain top-5 candidates from the database. The PQ model was trained on a Pittsburgh Super Computing (PSC) node with two AMD EPYC-7742 CPU (64 cores each) and 512GB of RAM (Towns et al., 2014). The localization accuracy will be measured in terms of the L2 norm of translation error Δt (meters) and the L2 norm of rotation error Δr (L2 norm of Rodrigues difference). Specifically, we measured the localization error at the rough registration stage by using the mean of top-5 candidate poses as our predicted camera pose. The localization error at the fine registration stage will be measured by the final predicted camera pose. Figure 4 shows the intermediate result right after rough localization through image retrieval and the result after fine localization by minimizing the reprojected semantic error. Table 1 reports the localization accuracy on the synthetic testbed and the time spent for registration using a Desktop with an Intel i7-8700k CPU and an Nvidia GTX 1080Ti GPU.

Table 1: Localization accuracy on the synthetic dataset.

		Translation error (m)	**Rotation error ($\|\Delta r\|$)**	**Time spent (s)**
Rough registration	K=32	6.84	0.31	0.032
	K=64	6.22	0.29	0.091
	K=128	6.09	0.26	0.247
	K=256	5.21	0.27	0.534
Fine registration (K=256)		2.31	0.24	0.82

3.3 Discussions

The registration results showed that the proposed method can effectively search for the most similar images using semantic features. Despite that we only verified the proposed method on a synthetic dataset, the method can be extended to real-world images easily when a semantic segmentation CNN is available. From Table 1 we can tell as the number of words (K) increases, the compact descriptors become more discriminative. However, the time spent on localizing each image also increases. Therefore, there is a tradeoff between localization accuracy and computation/storage cost. From Figure 4, we can tell that the top-3 images have similar semantic distributions as the query image. In the third example, we can tell that the best matching was not the top-1 result fetched from the PQ database, which indicates that the semantic reprojection check is necessary for eliminating some confusing cases.

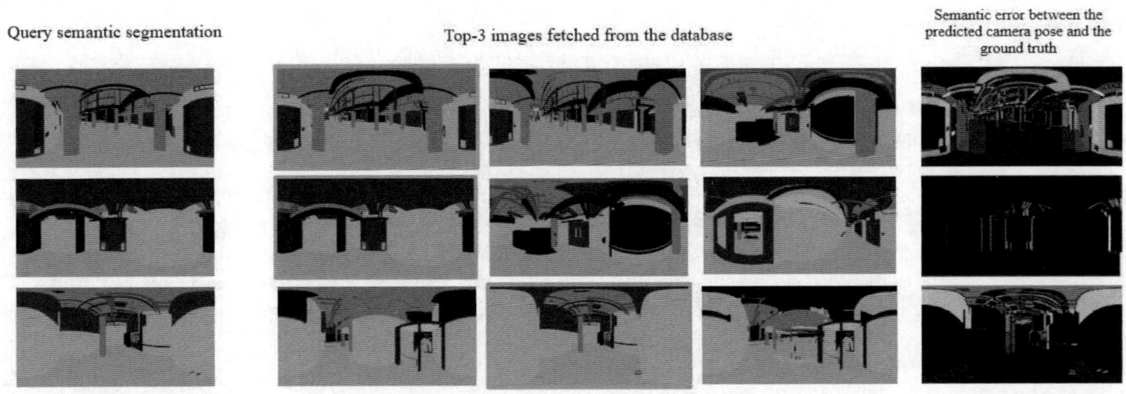

Figure 4: Example queries and registration results. (The ones with an orange bounding box were the results after fine registration)

The computation cost of the proposed method can be decomposed into two parts: database creation and online localization. During the database creation stage, we need to sample possible camera poses and generate their corresponding semantic segmentation. The time needed for building a database depends on the size of the sampling space. In our experiments, sampling 72,000 images from the building takes about two and a half hours on a desktop with an Intel i7-8700k CPU, 32GB RAM, and an Nvidia GTX-1080Ti GPU. Such a sampling space can guarantee that there is a sample for every 0.5 meters and every 20 degrees. The second part of the computation cost comes from the online localization stage. The query image needs to go through a neural network to obtain its semantic segmentation. The predicted semantic segmentation will then be used for comparing with the PQ vectors stored in the database and find the top nearest neighbors. Since we employed a compact representation for image retrieval, this step can often be done in less than one second, showing that the proposed algorithm can be potentially used for visual localization in large buildings.

4. Conclusion

In summary, this paper proposed a method that can register panorama images to a digital twin model with the help of semantic features. The proposed method contains two stages. During the offline database creation stage, we first sample semantic segmentation views with different camera poses and use product quantization to compress semantic features into a set of compact descriptors. During the online localization stage, images with the most similar PQ vectors as the query semantic segmentation will be retrieved from the dataset, and the indoor position is then estimated by finding the candidate pose with the least reprojected semantic error. Preliminary experiment results have shown that the PQ compression and semantic reprojection check allow for efficient and effective visual localization through image retrieval.

It is worth noticing that there are still many engineering challenges that need to be addressed before putting the proposed method into practice. First, the rough image retrieval accuracy will heavily depend on the semantic segmentation accuracy, which has not been validated using real-world images. Second, a digital twin might not reflect the as-is conditions perfectly, which could result in mismatching of the semantics when performing the registration. We will focus on addressing these problems in our future research and improve the proposed registration method so that it be used as a cornerstone for various image-based AEC applications.

Acknowledgments

The project is funded by a grant from the National Science Foundation (NSF), 1534114. NSF's support is gratefully acknowledged. Any opinions, findings, conclusions, or recommendations presented in this paper are those of authors and do not necessarily reflect the views of the NSF.

This work also used the Extreme Science and Engineering Discovery Environment (XSEDE), which is supported by National Science Foundation grant number ACI-1548562. Specifically, it used the Bridges system, which is supported by NSF award number ACI-1445606, at the Pittsburgh Supercomputing Center (PSC).

References

Acharya, D., Khoshelham, K., & Winter, S. (2019). BIM-PoseNet: Indoor camera localisation using a 3D indoor model and deep learning from synthetic images. ISPRS Journal of Photogrammetry and Remote Sensing, 150, 245–258. https://doi.org/10.1016/j.isprsjprs.2019.02.020

Arandjelovic, R., Gronat, P., Torii, A., Pajdla, T., & Sivic, J. (2016). NetVLAD: CNN Architecture for Weakly Supervised Place Recognition. In 2016 IEEE Conference on Computer Vision and Pattern Recognition (CVPR) (pp.5297–5307). IEEE. https://doi.org/10.1109/CVPR.2016.572

Arandjelovic, R., & Zisserman, A. (2013). All About VLAD. In 2013 IEEE Conference on Computer Vision and Pattern Recognition (pp.1578–1585). IEEE. https://doi.org/10.1109/CVPR.2013.207

Baek, F., Ha, I., & Kim, H. (2019). Augmented reality system for facility management using image-based indoor localization. Automation in Construction, 99, 18–26. https://doi.org/10.1016/j.autcon.2018.11.034

CSC CSI. UniFormat, A Uniform Classification of Construction Systems and Assemblies (2010).

Dusmanu, M., Rocco, I., Pajdla, T., Pollefeys, M., Sivic, J., Torii, A., & Sattler, T. (2019). D2-Net: A Trainable CNN for Joint Description and Detection of Local Features. In 2019 IEEE/CVF Conference on Computer Vision and Pattern Recognition (CVPR) (pp.8084–8093). IEEE. https://doi.org/10.1109/CVPR.2019.00828

Engel, J., Koltun, V., & Cremers, D. (2018). Direct Sparse Odometry. IEEE Transactions on Pattern Analysis and Machine Intelligence, 40(3), 611–625. https://doi.org/10.1109/TPAMI.2017.2658577

Engel, J., Schöps, T., & Cremers, D. (2014). LSD-SLAM: Large-Scale Direct monocular SLAM. In Lecture Notes in Computer Science (including subseries Lecture Notes in Artificial Intelligence and Lecture Notes in Bioinformatics) (Vol. 8690 LNCS, pp.834–849). Springer, Cham. https://doi.org/10.1007/978-3-319-10605-2_54

Epic Games. (2020). Unreal Engine. Retrieved December 20, 2020, from https://www.unrealengine.com

Furuta, R., Inoue, N., & Yamasaki, T. (2019). Efficient and interactive spatial-semantic image retrieval. Multimedia Tools and Applications, 78(13), 18713–18733. https://doi.org/10.1007/s11042-018-7148-1

Jégou, H., Douze, M., & Schmid, C. (2011). Product quantization for nearest neighbor search. IEEE Transactions on Pattern Analysis and Machine Intelligence, 33(1), 117–128. https://doi.org/10.1109/TPAMI.2010.57

Kendall, A., Grimes, M., & Cipolla, R. (2015). PoseNet: A convolutional network for real-time 6-dof camera relocalization. In Proceedings of the IEEE International Conference on Computer Vision (Vol. 2015 Inter, pp.2938–2946). https://doi.org/10.1109/ICCV.2015.336

Kim, J., Hwang, J., Chi, S., & Seo, J. O. (2020). Towards database-free vision-based monitoring on construction sites: A deep active learning approach. Automation in Construction, 120, 103376. https://doi.org/10.1016/j.autcon.2020.103376

Kulis, B., & Grauman, K. (2009). Kernelized locality-sensitive hashing for scalable image search. In Proceedings of the IEEE International Conference on Computer Vision (pp.2130–2137). https://doi.org/10.1109/ICCV.2009.5459466

Lepetit, V., Moreno-Noguer, F., & Fua, P. (2009). EPnP: An accurate O(n) solution to the PnP problem. International Journal of Computer Vision, 81(2), 155–166. https://doi.org/10.1007/s11263-008-0152-6

Lu, Q., & Lee, S. (2017). Image-Based Technologies for Constructing As-Is Building Information Models for Existing Buildings. Journal of Chemical Information and Modeling, 31(4). https://doi.org/10.1061/(ASCE)CP.1943-5487.0000652.

Luo, X., Li, H., Wang, H., Wu, Z., Dai, F., & Cao, D. (2019). Vision-based detection and visualization of dynamic workspaces. Automation in Construction, 104, 1–13. https://doi.org/10.1016/j.autcon.2019.04.001

Mur-Artal, R., Montiel, J. M. M. M., & Tardos, J. D. (2015). Orb-slam: a versatile and accurate monocular slam system. IEEE Transactions On, 31(5), 1147–1163. https://doi.org/10.1109/TRO.2015.2463671

Revaud, J., Weinzaepfel, P., de Souza, C., & Humenberger, M. (2019). R2D2: Repeatable and reliable detector and descriptor. In Advances in Neural Information Processing Systems (Vol. 32). Retrieved from https://github.com/naver/r2d2.

Sarlin, P. E., Detone, D., Malisiewicz, T., & Rabinovich, A. (2020). SuperGlue: Learning Feature Matching with Graph Neural Networks. In Proceedings of the IEEE Computer Society Conference on Computer Vision and Pattern Recognition (pp.4937–4946). IEEE Computer Society. https://doi.org/10.1109/CVPR42600.2020.00499

Schonberger, J. L., & Frahm, J.-M. (2016). Structure-from-Motion Revisited. In 2016 IEEE Conference on Computer Vision and Pattern Recognition (CVPR) (pp.4104–4113). IEEE. https://doi.org/10.1109/CVPR.2016.445

Shah, S., Dey, D., Lovett, C., & Kapoor, A. (2017, May 15). AirSim: High-Fidelity Visual and physical simulation for autonomous vehicles. ArXiv. arXiv. https://doi.org/10.1007/978-3-319-67361-5_40

Sivic, J., & Zisserman, A. (2009). Efficient visual search of videos cast as text retrieval. IEEE Transactions on Pattern Analysis and Machine Intelligence, 31(4), 591–606. https://doi.org/10.1109/TPAMI.2008.111

Towns, J., Cockerill, T., Dahan, M., Foster, I., Gaither, K., Grimshaw, A., … Wilkens-Diehr, N. (2014). XSEDE: Accelerating scientific discovery. Computing in Science and Engineering, 16(5), 62–74. https://doi.org/10.1109/MCSE.2014.80

Wei, Y., & Akinci, B. (2019). A vision and learning-based indoor localization and semantic mapping framework for facility operations and management. Automation in Construction, 107, 102915. https://doi.org/10.1016/j.autcon.2019.102915

Wei, Y., Kasireddy, V., & Akinci, B. (2018). 3D imaging in construction and infrastructure management: Technological assessment and future research directions. In Lecture Notes in Computer Science (including subseries Lecture Notes in Artificial Intelligence and Lecture Notes in Bioinformatics) (Vol. 10863 LNCS, pp.37–60). https://doi.org/10.1007/978-3-319-91635-4_3

Zhang, C., & Huang, H. (2019). As-Built BIM Updating Based on Image Processing and Artificial Intelligence. In Computing in Civil Engineering 2019: Visualization, Information Modeling, and Simulation - Selected Papers from the ASCE International Conference on Computing in Civil Engineering 2019 (pp.9–16). https://doi.org/10.1061/9780784482421.002

Zhang, Z., Rebecq, H., Forster, C., & Scaramuzza, D. (2016). Benefit of large field-of-view cameras for visual odometry. In Proceedings - IEEE International Conference on Robotics and Automation (Vol. 2016-June, pp.801–808). Institute of Electrical and Electronics Engineers Inc. https://doi.org/10.1109/ICRA.2016.7487210

AI-based thermal bridge detection of building rooftops on district scale using aerial images

Zoe Mayer M.Sc.[a]*, Yu Hou M.Sc[b], Dr. James Kahn[c], Dr. Rebekka Volk[a],
Prof. Dr. Frank Schultmann[a]
[a] Karlsruhe Institute of Technology, Germany, [b] University of Southern California, USA, [c] Helmholtz AI, Karlsruhe Institute of Technology, Germany
zoe.mayer@partner.kit.edu

Abstract. Thermal bridges are weak areas of building envelopes that conduct more heat to the outside than surrounding envelope areas. They lead to increased energy consumption and the formation of mold. With a neural network approach, we demonstrate a method of automatically detecting thermal bridges on building rooftops from panorama drone images of whole city districts. To train the neural network, we created a dataset including 917 images and 6895 annotations. The images in the dataset contain thermal information for detecting thermal bridges and a height map for rooftop recognition in addition to regular RGB information. Due to the small dataset, our approach currently only has an average recall of 9.4% @IoU:0.5-0.95 (14.4% for large objects). Nevertheless, our approach reliably detects structures only on rooftops and not on other parts of buildings, without any additional segmentation effort of building parts.

1. Introduction

In 2017, building constructions and operations accounted for 36% of global final energy use worldwide and about 40% of energy-related carbon dioxide emissions (GlobalABC, 2018). Thermal energy is a particularly relevant component of this: more than a half of current global household energy use is for space and water heating (IEA, 2014). In addition to high energy standards for new buildings, the energy retrofit of old buildings plays an important role. While new construction adds annually 1% or less to the existing building stock, the other 99% of buildings already existed in the year prior (Power, 2008).

To develop energy-saving approaches for existing buildings in cities, strategies on different aggregation levels can be considered: at the single building scale, the district scale, and the full-city scale. The district scale, the intermediate level between the city and the building scale, is coming increasingly into the focus of building science and urban transition planning. The main strengths of the district scale for the building energy retrofit are summarized by Riechel (2016): Compared to measures for single buildings, measures for whole districts provide the possibility of cost digressions and other economies of scale for energy improvements. For example, the planning and implementation of retrofit measures such as the purchase of retrofit material can be cheaper for a large demand in a small area at the same time. Compared to the city scale, the closeness between habitants and building owners contributes to neighborhood-dynamics in districts. Informal communication among neighbors ("neighborhood gossip") or the copying of a building retrofit in the neighborhood by other owners can have benefits for implementing energy improvement measures. (Riechel, 2016)

There are approaches to systematically use the advantages of the district scale to push urban transition and the retrofit of buildings. One of the most frequently practical and standardized approaches in this field is from Germany called “energetisches Quartierskonzept” (EQ). It describes a policy plan that intends to improve the energy quality of private and public buildings and the energy infrastructure of a whole city district. So far, more than 1,000 EQs have been financially supported by the German government (BES, 2020).

To identify districts with a high need for energy retrofits and to develop effective measures for substantially improving the energy quality of a district, an initial thermal quality analysis of existing buildings is necessary. Currently, such analyses on district scale are expensive and time consuming (Riechel et al., 2016; Neußer, 2017). Therefore, approaches that allow for automatic and simplified analyses are crucial for a higher efficiency of EQs and other retrofit planning approaches.

With the help of unmanned aerial vehicles (UAV, drones), it is possible to collect thermal panorama images of many buildings from different angles with relatively little effort and cost but with a high resolution. A distinction is made between quantitative and qualitative thermography. In quantitative thermography, absolute temperatures are measured as precisely as possible. The process is highly dependent on environmental parameters, the infrared camera used, and the qualifications of the thermography staff. Qualitative thermography, on the other hand, is simpler. It focuses on temperature distributions and differences. Thermal bridges in particular can be easily identified in qualitative images. (Volland et al., 2016)

A thermal bridge is an area of the building envelope that conducts heat easily, thus transporting heat from the warmer inside to the colder outside faster than it does through the adjacent areas. This is caused by different thermal conductivities of used materials or the geometry of constructions. Air leaks can also be subsumed under the term thermal bridge (Schmidt and Windhausen, 2018). Thermal bridges cause high energy losses which can make up to one third of the transmission heat loss of an entire building. Additionally, they lead to the collection of moisture, which in the long term degrades the building fabric or causes mould. A thermal bridge can be seen on a thermographic image as an area with an increased thermal radiation relative to adjacent areas. (Schild, 2018).

2. Research approach

In this study, we analyse how drone-based thermal images can be used for a simple analysis of the thermal quality of building envelopes on district scale. To do so, we investigate the quality of thermal panorama images obtained by drones and analyse how artificial intelligence can help to automatically detect thermal bridges. We focus on thermal bridges on rooftops as they are difficult to access with conventional thermography from terrestrial images.

To motivate our research, we first provide an overview about which publications and studies are known to us in the field of automated computer vision approaches to detect thermal bridges of buildings. We focus on studies that work with imagery data obtained by non-stationary recording approaches - especially with drones - suitable for recording images on district scale.

In the main part of our work, we demonstrate a method to automatically detect thermal bridges on building rooftops in thermal aerial images using a neural network. We employ existing solutions from the domain of object detection to learn to identify the size and location of thermal bridges within each image. For this, we create a dataset of drone images with annotations of thermal bridges on building rooftops. Each image of the dataset consists of a combination of a thermal image, an RGB[1] image recorded from the same angle and converted to the same format, and height information for each pixel (Hou et al., 2021 - a). We select a training dataset for the neural network composed of a subset of the images, and validate our results on the remainder of the dataset.

---

[1] Red, Green, Blue

3. Related work

Non-stationary thermography with the help of cars and drones for the analysis of buildings is becoming increasingly important in thermography studies. The advantage of drones compared to terrestrial methods is that the entire envelope of buildings (including rooftops) can be thermographically assessed. In addition, the influence of facade covering (e.g. by trees or pedestrians walking past) is less prevalent from the bird's eye view.

Publications in the field of automated thermal bridge detection from thermal images obtained with non-stationary cameras are from Garrido et al. (2018), Macher et al. (2020), Martinez-de Dios and Ollero (2006), and Rakha et al. (2018). To automatically detect thermal bridges these publications work with different threshold approaches for temperature differences in the images. They record close-up images of single buildings from different angles, but do not work with panorama images that cover multiple buidlings. Moreover, they use small datasets to validate their approaches and do not focus on entire districts. Garrido et al. (2018) place an infrared camera on the roof of a vehicle to record images at an angle of 45°. The proportion of unrecognized or incorrectly declared thermal bridges is 32% for a test set of three images. Macher et al. (2020) also install their infrared camera on a vehicle and conclude being able to reliably detect thermal bridges between floors and under balconies. No quantitative information is given on the precision of the used algorithm. Martinez-de Dios and Ollero (2006) use a thermal camera placed on a drone helicopter. According to the authors this approach is suitable for detecting thermal bridges on windows. The study lacks precise quality information for evaluating the results. Rakha et al. (2018) also use a drone with a thermal camera to record close-up images of buildings from the air. They state the overall precision of their algorithm of about 75%.

As thermal panorama images contain many different buildings from changing angles and infrastructure in between (e.g. trees, trams, cars, streets, street lights) classic threshold approaches appear unsuitable for the automatic detection of thermal bridges. This is because thermal bridges change in shape from different angles and high temperature differences often occur on objects in the image which are not buildings. For successful thermal bridge detection on panorama images deep learning approaches are very promising, as complex objects such as buildings, certain building parts on that thermal bridges occur (e.g. rooftops), and various thermal bridge types with different shapes can be recognized.

A recent study by Kim et al. (2021) works with a deep learning approach to detect thermal bridges from terrestrial thermographic images. The study uses a method including thermal anomaly area clustering, feature extraction, and an artificial-neural-network-based thermal bridge detection. The average precision of the detection of thermal bridges is for eight test images 89%. However, the images used are close-ups of buildings and cannot be compared to panorama images. To the best of our knowledge there is no study that aims to detect thermal bridges in an entire district on thermal panorama images using deep learning approaches.

4. Dataset

Our dataset of Thermal Bridges on Building Rooftops (TBBR dataset) consists of combined RGB and thermal panorama drone images with a height map (Figure 1). The raw images for our dataset were recorded with a normal (RGB) and a FLIR-XT2 (thermal) camera on a DJI M600 drone. We converted all images to a uniform format of 2400x3200 pixels. They contain RGB, thermal, and GPS information as well as flight altitudes (between 60-80m above ground). The GPS and flight altitude information were used to reconstruct a 3D model out of the 2D images to create the height map. We hypothesize that this will significantly simplify the task of learning to ignore street-level sections of the images and focus instead on rooftops.

The drone images show parts of the Karlsruhe city centre, east of the market square. The recorded area can be divided into six large city blocks of around 20 buildings per block. Because of a high overlap rate of the images, the same buildings are on average about 20 times on different images, recorded from different angles. The dataset contains a total of 5698 images before preselection. During preselection, all images containing no thermal bridges were filtered out, as well as images that are blurred due to rapid turns or other fast movements of the drone. A total of 917 images remain after preselection.

All images were recorded during a drone flight on March 19, 2019 from 7 a.m. to 8 a.m. At this time, temperatures were between 3.78 ° C and 4.97 ° C, humidity between 80% and 98%. There was no rain on the day of the flight, but there was 2.3mm/m^2 48 hours beforehand.[2] For recording the thermographic images an emissivity of 1.0 was set. The global radiation during this period was between 38.59 W / m^2 and 120.86 W / m^2, hence the solar radiation was high enough to visually classify the geometric and structural conditions on the RGB images, but not so high that the surface temperatures of thermal bridges and surrounding components change significantly, thus making it difficult to identify thermal bridges. No direct sunlight can be seen visually in any of the recordings.

Figure 1: Drone images of the city centre of Karlsruhe used for the TBBR dataset A) thermal image B) RGB image C) image with height information (height map)

The annotated images of the TBBR dataset contain a total of 6895 annotations. The annotations only include thermal bridges that are easily identifiable, and thus also include thermal bridges that are not annotated. Because of the image overlap each thermal bridge is annotated on average about 20 times from different angles. An example image with annotations is shown in Figure 2. We have published the dataset with further information in Mayer et al. (2021).

[2] The total absence of moisture can therefore not be fully guaranteed. Moisture falsifies the recording of thermographic images. We recognized puddles on some flat rooftops and removed corresponding images from the dataset during the preselection process; otherwise we could not detect any significant moisture visually on the RGB images.

Figure 2: Example of thermal bridge annotations in the TBBR dataset for the example shown in Figure 1. Colours are only for clarity and do not have any other meaning.[3]

5. Experimental procedure

5.1 Data pre-processing

To prepare the datasets, we align thermal images and height images onto RGB images via a process called image registration (Hou et al., 2021 - a). Since on the collected images, fisheye effects occur (called radial distortion) and the lens is not aligned parallel to the imaging plane (called tangential distortion), we must resolve these two distortions before image registration. Distortions can be solved by $x_{corr,rad} = x(1 + k_1 r^2 + k_2 r^4 + k_3 r^6)$ -$y_{corr,tang} = y + [p_1(r^2 + 2y^2) + 2p_2 xy]$). In these equations, (x, y) represents a point before correction, and (x_{corr}, y_{corr}) represents a point coordinate after correction. Many collected pairs of coordinates of (x, y) and (x_{corr}, y_{corr}) from a collection of calibration images enable the calculation of the distortion coefficients $(k_1, k_2, k_3, p_1, p_2)$. The coefficients (k_1, k_2, k_3) are radial distortion coefficients and (p_1, p_2) are tangential distortion coefficients.

$$x_{corr,rad} = x(1 + k_1 r^2 + k_2 r^4 + k_3 r^6) \quad (1)$$

$$y_{corr,rad} = y(1 + k_1 r^2 + k_2 r^4 + k_3 r^6) \quad (2)$$

$$x_{corr,tang} = x + [2p_1 xy + p_2(r^2 + 2x^2)] \quad (3)$$

$$y_{corr,tang} = y + [p_1(r^2 + 2y^2) + 2p_2 xy] \quad (4)$$

After undistorting all images, we aligned thermal and height images onto the RGB images using $[x_{thermal}, y_{thermal}] = T_{RGB \rightarrow thermal} * [x_{RGB}, y_{RGB}]$ - $[x_{thermal}, y_{thermal}] =$

[3] The borders of the thermal bridge annotations show a slight distortion. The reason for this lies in the data pre-processing and is explained and discussed in more detail in Section 7.

$T_{height \rightarrow thermal} * [x_{height}, y_{height}]$. In these equations, $T_{RGB \rightarrow thermal}$ and $T_{height \rightarrow thermal}$ represent transformation matrices that transform pixels from RGB images to thermal images and pixels from height images to thermal images.

$$[x_{thermal}, y_{thermal}] = T_{RGB \rightarrow thermal} * [x_{RGB}, y_{RGB}] \tag{5}$$

$$[x_{thermal}, y_{thermal}] = T_{height \rightarrow thermal} * [x_{height}, y_{height}] \tag{6}$$

Lastly, we connected the registered thermal and height images to the RGB images to produce single 5-channel images (RGB + thermal + height).

5.2 Neural network details

To identify thermal bridges, we employed a neural network to perform object detection and segmentation. Formally, the task is defined as follows: given a set X containing input images $x_i \in R^{N*H*W*C}$, with image height H, width W, and channels C; and a corresponding annotation set Y containing bounding boxes $y_{i,box} \in R^{N*4}$, where 4 represents the coordinates of the box's four corners, class labels $y_{i,cls} \in R^N$, and masks $y_{i,mask} \in R^{N*H*W}$, where N is the number of annotated object in the given image; learn the mapping $F: X \rightarrow Y$, where F denotes a neural network.

In this work the neural network is the Mask R-CNN framework (He et al., 2017) with a ResNet-18 (He et al., 2016) backbone implemented in the Detectron2 software package (Wu et al., 2019). We select this architecture for two key reasons: firstly, the ResNet architecture has consistently proven to perform at state-of-the-art (SOTA) levels (e.g. as in Bello et al. (2021)); and secondly, self-supervised training methods offer a means of achieving SOTA performance with limited labelled samples. The latter point is discussed further in section 7 and motivates the use of a neural network over classical approaches.

Figure 3 shows the basic structure of Mask R-CNN. It consists of two stages: the first uses a Region Proposal Network (RPN) to propose candidate regions of interest (ROI); the second uses a (convolutional) backbone to extract features which are then used to perform object classification and bounding box regression, as well as prediction of a binary segmentation mask. The former is performed via fully connected layers on the extracted features, while the latter uses further convolutional layers. In practice, learned features are shared by both stages to speed up processing.

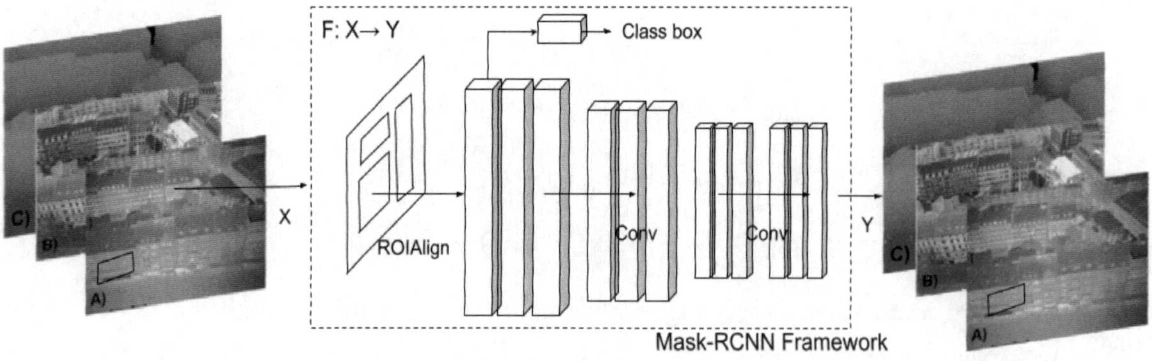

Figure 3: The Mask R-CNN framework

Mask R-CNN uses a multi-task loss on every proposed region of interest: $L = L_{cls} + L_{box} + L_{mask}$. L_{cls} is the categorical cross-entropy loss across $K + 1$ output predictions for K component classes, plus an additional catch-all class for proposed regions containing only background. L_{box} is the bounding box regression (mean squared error) over the predict box corners. L_{mask} is the average binary cross entropy across all pixels in the mask. These are described in further detail in He et al. (2017). Note that for the experiments reported in this work we use a single annotation class (i.e. K=1).

The dataset images were split into 717 training images and 200 test images corresponding to five and one of the city blocks described in the section above, respectively. Training was performed for 30,000 iterations at a batch size of eight, with random weight initialisation (i.e. no pre-training). The remaining hyper-parameter configurations were set to the Detectron2 defaults for the "mask_rcnn_R_50_FPN_3x_gn" model from the Detectron2 model zoo templates, with only changes the number of ResNet layers (18) and the pixel value means (130, 135, 135, 118, 118) and standard deviations (44, 40, 40, 30, 21) for (B, G, R, thermal, height) used by Detectron2 to normalise the inputs. These values were calculated from the full set of training images.

6. Results

To evaluate the performance of our training, we use the Average Recall (AR) metric, defined as:

$$AR = \frac{TP}{TP+FN} \tag{7}$$

where TP and FN refer to the number of true positive and false negative object predictions, respectively. The AR measures the probability of objects in an image being detected. Since not every thermal bridge in the dataset is annotated, we do not report any metrics that work with false positives (such as Average Precision). These metrics are guaranteed to underperform as even correctly predicted thermal bridges will be reported as false positives if the corresponding annotation does not exist.

To determine which predicted bounding boxes correspond to correct predictions, the Intersection-over-Union (IoU) is measured between the predicted and ground truth boxes as:

$$IoU = \frac{area(predicted \cap true)}{area(predicted \cup true)} \tag{8}$$

For a given IoU threshold, predicted bounding boxes that have an IoU with an annotated thermal bridge's bounding box above the threshold are considered true positives. Any annotated thermal bridges without a prediction satisfying this are considered false negatives. Table 1 shows the metric scores for various common variants of the AR metric. An IoU range (i.e. IoU=0.5:0.95) indicates the AR is averaged over the given interval. An area of medium or large corresponds to objects of area between 32^2 and 96^2, and greater than 96^2 pixels, respectively. Max. detections indicates the score given the N highest confidence predictions[4].

We note immediately the comparatively low scores, which we attribute to the low number of annotated examples relative to the large image sizes and sparsity/small size of thermal bridges. Notably, the network performs better at larger scales, which is likely due to larger

[4]Although often reported in object detection tasks, we do not report small (less than 32^2 pixels) thermal bridges as the smallest present in our dataset is 55^2 pixels.

thermal bridges being less ambiguous with regards to non-thermal bridge heat spots in an image.

An interesting result, however, is the location of predicted thermal bridges, regardless of their accuracy. All predictions are on or overlapping with rooftops, indicating the network has an awareness of sensible locations for thermal bridges. We find that this result is consistent across all test images. We posit that this is due to the inclusion of the height map as a signal to the neural network of where to look for thermal bridges. We plan to perform further ablation studies to confirm this.

Given the dataset was produced by a single fly over of six city blocks, some portions of the test dataset images are also present in the training images from different angles. In these instances we note that the neural network has overfitted those thermal bridges and predicts them with at or near 100% confidence. Nonetheless, the network is able to identify thermal bridges unique to the test dataset, albeit with lower confidence and IoU. We expect this to improve with the training techniques discussed in the next section.

Table 1: Bounding box regression metrics on the test images dataset

Metric	Area	Max. detections	Score
AR @ IoU=0.50:0.95	All	1	0.052
AR @ IoU=0.50:0.95	All	10	0.142
AR @ IoU=0.50:0.95	All	100	0.142
AR @ IoU=0.50:0.95	Medium	100	0.114
AR @ IoU=0.50:0.95	Large	100	0.196

7. Discussion

The Average Recall achieved is not currently suitable for thermal bridge detection; however it does provide a baseline score for prediction with a modern computer vision approach directly on the TBBR dataset. This represents a departure from previous approaches which relied on complex multi-stage solutions (as in Rakha et al. (2018)) or fine-tuning of clustering and feature extraction preprocessing steps (as in Kim et al. (2021)).

A key limitation in this work is the comparatively small number of images available for training. This is due to the time required to manually annotate each image. While we used a total of 917 images, common benchmarks often contain hundreds of thousands (e.g. COCO) or even tens of millions (e.g. Imagenet) of images.

We therefore plan to implement a self-supervised pretext task to maximise the use of collected images. Specifically, we intend to utilise the work from Hou et al. (2021 - b) to first train a neural network to predict thermal images from RGB and use these predicted images, along with the real thermal and the height information, as input to the Mask R-CNN network. This approach is similar to that of the Split-Brain Autoencoder described by Zhang et al. (2017). We hypothesise that the predicted thermal images will be nearly identical to the real thermal images, with only the thermal bridges missing[5], thus simplifying the network's task significantly to learn to locate the appropriate differences between the two. If successful, this

[5] The assumption here is that thermal bridges are only visible from the thermal image, which is of course the original motivation for including thermal images in this project in the first place.

would allow full use of all (non-blurry) drone images captured, not only those on which the laborious task of annotation has been performed.

In order to increase the size of the dataset, it is also possible to use panorama images collected from other sources. Since our approach is based on qualitative thermography, the weather conditions and temperatures when recording new images do not have to be identical to the existing dataset (Volland et al., 2016). However, the temperature contrast of new annotated thermal bridges should be high enough to detect, which is the case when there is a difference of more than 10°C between indoor and outdoor temperatures. The distances of the drone to the buildings can also vary, however thermal images with more than 20m distance to the measurement object should be checked in all individual cases for appropriate quality (Fouad and Richter, 2012).

8. Conclusion

We have reported an overall average recall of 14.2% at IoU:0.5-0.95, and 19.6% at IoU:0.5-0.95 for large thermal bridges. We demonstrated the ability of the neural network to propose predictions in reasonable locations (i.e. rooftops only) which we posited is due to the addition of height information to the input images. While this work has shown a promising first result in identifying individual thermal bridges from drone images, we believe there is still significant potential for improvement to be made using a self-supervised pretext task to maximise the information obtain from the entire set of collected images.

This work focuses on a cost-effective and scalable approach to assess thermal bridges using thermographic images from drones. In future, we intend to use financial and environmental criteria to estimate which buildings in a district the retrofit of thermal bridges is recommended and when buildings should be retrofitted more extensively.

Acknowledgements

This project was performed during a PhD project that is financed with a scholarship according to Landesgraduiertenförderungsgesetz (LGFG), the State Graduate Promotion Act, of the Karlsruhe Institute of Technology (KIT). This work is supported by the Helmholtz Association Initiative and Networking Fund, the Helmholtz AI platform grant, and the HAICORE@KIT partition. Furthermore, we thank Marinus Vogl and the Air Bavarian GmbH for their support with equipment and service for the recording of images and Tobias Beiersdörfer who supported us with the development of the TBBR dataset.

References

Begleitforschung Energetische Stadtsanierung (BES) (2020): 3. Fachkonferenz der Begleitforschung zum KfW-Förderprogramm Energetische Stadtsanierung Energiewende im Quartier (English: 3rd specialist conference of the accompanying research to the KfW funding program ‘Energy transition in districts‘). Berlin.

Bello, I. et al. (2021). Revisiting resnets: Improved training and scaling strategies. arXiv preprint arXiv:2103.07579.

Garrido et al. (2018). Thermal-based analysis for the automatic detection and characterization of thermal bridges in buildings. Energy and Buildings, 158, 1358–1367. Doi: https://doi.org/10.1016/j.enbuild.2017.11.031

Global Alliance for Buildings and Construction (GlobalABC) (2018). 2018 Global Status Report Towards a zero-emission, efficient and resilient buildings and construction sector. ISBN No: 978-92-807-3729-5.

He, K. et al. (2017). Mask r-cnn. In Proceedings of the IEEE international conference on computer vision (pp.2961–2969).

He, K. et al. (2016). Deep residual learning for image recognition. In Proceedings of the IEEE conference on computer vision and pattern recognition (pp.770–778).

Hou, Y. et al. (2021 - a). Automation in Construction Fusing tie points - RGB and thermal information for mapping large areas based on aerial images: A study of fusion performance under different flight configurations and experimental conditions', Automation in Construction. Elsevier B.V., 124. Doi: 10.1016/j.autcon.2021.103554.

Hou, Y. et al. (2021 - b). A Novel Building Temperature Simulation Approach Driven by Expanding Semantic Segmentation Training Datasets with Synthetic Aerial Thermal Images. Energies, 14(2). Doi: https://doi.org/10.3390/en14020353

International Energy Agency (IEA) (2014). Energy technology perspectives 2014: Harnessing electricity's potential. OECD/IEA.

Kim, C. et al. (2021). Automatic Detection of Linear Thermal Bridges from Infrared Thermal Images Using Neural Network. Applied Sciences, 11(3), 931. Doi: https://doi.org/10.3390/app11030931

Macher, H. et al. (2020). Automation of Thermal Point Clouds Analysis for the Extraction of Windows and Thermal Bridges of Building Facades. The International Archives of Photogrammetry, Remote Sensing and Spatial Information Sciences, 43, 287–292. Doi: https://doi.org/10.5194/isprs-archives-XLIII-B2-2020-287-2020

Martinez-De Dios, J. R., and Ollero, A. (2006, July). Automatic detection of windows thermal heat losses in buildings using UAVs. In 2006 world automation congress (pp.1–6). IEEE. Doi: 10.1109/WAC.2006.375998

Mayer, Zoe, Hou, Yu, Kahn, James, Beiersdörfer, Tobias, & Volk, Rebekka. (2021). Thermal Bridges on Building Rooftops - Hyperspectral (RGB + Thermal + Height) drone images of Karlsruhe, Germany, with thermal bridge annotations (Version 0.1.0) [Dataset]. Zenodo. http://doi.org/10.5281/zenodo.4767772

Neußer, W. (2017). Energetische Quartierssanierung - Ausblick und externe Rahmenbedingungen. (English: District energy improvement - outlook and external conditions.) Information zur Raumentwicklung, 4/2017. BBSR.

Power, A. (2008). Does demolition or refurbishment of old and inefficient homes help to increase our environmental, social and economic viability. Energy Policy 2008;36: 4487–4501. Doi: https://doi.org/10.1016/j.enpol.2008.09.022

Rakha, T. et al. (2018). Heat mapping drones: an autonomous computer-vision-based procedure for building envelope inspection using unmanned aerial systems (UAS). Technology| Architecture+ Design, 2(1), 30–44. Doi: https://doi.org/10.1080/24751448.2018.1420963

Ren, S. et al. (2016). Faster R-CNN: towards real-time object detection with region proposal networks. IEEE transactions on pattern analysis and machine intelligence, 39(6), 1137–1149. arXiv:1506.01497

Riechel, R. (2016). Zwischen Gebäude und Gesamtstadt: das Quartier als Handlungsraum in der lokalen Wärmewende. (English: Between the building and the city as a whole: the district as field for action in the local heat transition.) Vierteljahrshefte zur Wirtschaftsforschung, 85(4), 89–101.

Schild, K. (2018). Wärmebrücken: Berechnung und Mindestwärmeschutz. (English: Thermal bridges: Calculations and minimum requirements) Springer-Verlag. Doi: 10.1007/978-3-658-20709-0

Schmidt P. and Windhausen S. (2018) Bauphysik-Lehrbuch. (English: Building physics) Bundesanzeiger Verlag, Köln. Doi: https://doi.org/10.1007/978-3-658-21749-5_3-1

Volland J. et al. (2016). Wärmebrücken: erkennen-optimieren-berechnen-vermeiden. (English: Thermal bridges: recognize-optimize-calculate-avoid) 1. Auflage 420 Seiten Verlagsgesellschaft Rudolf Müller GmbH & Co. KG, 978-3-481-03365-1 (ISBN).

Wu Y. et al. (2019). Detectron2.

Zhang, R., Isola, P., & Efros, A. A. (2017). Split-brain autoencoders: Unsupervised learning by cross-channel prediction. In Proceedings of the IEEE Conference on Computer Vision and Pattern Recognition (pp.1058–1067).

Image Captioning in Chinese for Construction Activity Scene Understanding Using a Pre-trained Cross-modal Language Model

Yuexiong Ding, Xiaowei Luo*
City University of Hong Kong, Hong Kong, China
xiaowluo@cityu.edu.hk

Abstract. With the popularity of surveillance cameras, many vision-based artificial intelligence (AI) agents have been applied to construction projects, significantly improving management efficiency and workers' productivity. However, only a few works study scene understanding because it is one of the most challenging topics of intelligent monitoring. Besides, as a big construction country, China lacks corresponding AI research based on Chinese in the construction field, which seriously hinders the further development of China's construction industry. Therefore, this paper proposes a Vision-based BERT (V-BERT) model for construction activity scene understanding. A Chinese caption dataset named Images of Jobsite Daily Activity and Chinese Captions (IJDACC) is created to verify V-BERT's performance. Some data augmentation operations are then used to enlarge the training set further. Two evaluation systems are established to evaluate V-BERT's comprehensive performance. The experimental results show the V-BERT achieves state-of-the-art performance in the construction area with an average performance improvement of 171.20%.

1. Introduction

With the popularity of surveillance cameras in construction sites, a large number of vision-based Artificial Intelligence (AI) agents have been applied to construction projects. The captured visual information can be used to evaluate workers' safety status (Kim et al., 2016) and recognize workers' activities and working conditions (Luo et al., 2018), significantly improving management efficiency the workers' productivity. However, most existing vision-based researches focus only on the part of the image content. Thus, scene understanding, a comprehensive understanding of the captured image content, is worth more exploration. On the other hand, it is well-known that China is a big construction country. As the "Global Construction 2030" report goes, China will become one of the leading countries driving the development of the global construction market by 2030 (Robinson, 2015). However, there are fewer AI-related studies based on Chinese in the construction area, hindering the further intelligence of China's construction industry.

Therefore, in view of the urgent development needs of China's construction industry, a cross-modal language model named the vision-based BERT model (V-BERT) is proposed for scene understanding. To verify the proposed model's effectiveness, this study creates a new Chinese image caption dataset containing everyday construction activity scenes and regulated description sentences. Some data augmentation techniques are then utilized to enlarge the training set for building a better model. Finally, some experiments are conducted, following results showing the state-of-the-art performance in the area of construction. The following article is structured as follows: Section 2 introduces the related work of the existing vision-based techniques in the construction domain. Section 3 describes the proposed methods. Section 4 conducts the experiments and presents the results. Section 5 and Section 6 provide discussion and conclusions.

2. Literature review

In general, the existing vision-based AI models in the construction field can be divided into *object recognition*, *pose estimation*, *activity identification*, and *scene understanding* according to different uses.

Object recognition commonly involving object detection and object tracking. For example, Q. Fang et al. (2018) utilized the Faster R-CNN model to detect whether the workers wore helmets. Roberts and Golparvar-Fard (2019) applied a Tubelets Convolutional Neural Network (CNN) to track the trajectory of the earthmoving equipment such as excavators and dump trucks. However, these object recognition models only identify some of the targets in the activity scene content.

Pose estimation mainly involves the posture recognition of workers and equipment. For example, Zhang et al. (2018) utilize the ergonomic posture recognition (EPR) technique based on three-dimensional skeleton motion captured by the ordinary camera to recognize workers' postures, while Luo et al. (2020) proposed an ensemble model (HG-CPN) for full-body poses estimation of on-site equipment to avoid potential hazards or casualties. However, pose estimation only focuses on describing the detected objects' current state, ignoring their relationship.

Activity identification aims to detect and tag the relationship between the detected objects based on recognizing objects' postures. For example, Luo et al. (2018) proposed a two-streams (spatial and temporal) CNN model to identify workers' activities with an accuracy of 80.5%. Considering the importance of workers' safety, Ding et al. (2018) developed a deep hybrid learning model integrating CNN and long short-term memory (LSTM) to recognize workers' unsafe behaviors automatically. Though activity identification successfully finds out the relationship between the detected objects, it is still limited for describing the whole scene since the activity is just one of the essential scene elements.

Scene understanding requires recognizing objects in the images and identifying various detailed information such as the attributes and states of the objects, the relative positions, and relationships between the objects. According to this functional definition, object, pose, and behavior recognition are only part of scene understanding, indicating it is more challenging than the tasks above. With the development of image caption technologies, an efficient way for scene understanding has gradually been explored. For example, Liu et al. (2020) proposed a CNN-LSTM-based English image captioning model to manifest construction activity scenes. Nevertheless, it cannot be used for non-English contexts. Besides, based on traditional deep neural networks, Liu's model has several limitations, such as large data demand.

Developed from the Transformer(Vaswani et al., 2017), the BERT (Bidirectional Encoder Representations from Transformers) takes the place of RNN in NLP tasks and has achieved the best performance in many NLP tasks (Devlin et al., 2018). BERT is a pre-training model trained on a large corpus, which allows training a better model with fewer data. In addition, BERT utilizes self-attention and position encoding methods to capture the temporal features, which utterly free from the effects of long-term dependence. Therefore, BERT has great potential in image caption task, being worth exploring.

3. Methodology

Figure 1 shows the structure of the V-BERT model. Cross-modal means the model can not only capture visual information from the images but also learn the expression logic from the existing Chinese captions. Specifically, the proposed V-BERT model utilizes a deep CNN to extract visual features and initializes the language model with a pre-trained Chinese BERT model to generate the image captions. The visual components are involved in computing at each Vision-based Conditional Layer Normalization (VCLN) of BERT. After fine-tuning on a small Chinese captions dataset related to the construction activity scenes, the proposed model can generate a fluent and logical Chinese sentence according to the visual information and expression ability the model has captured and learned.

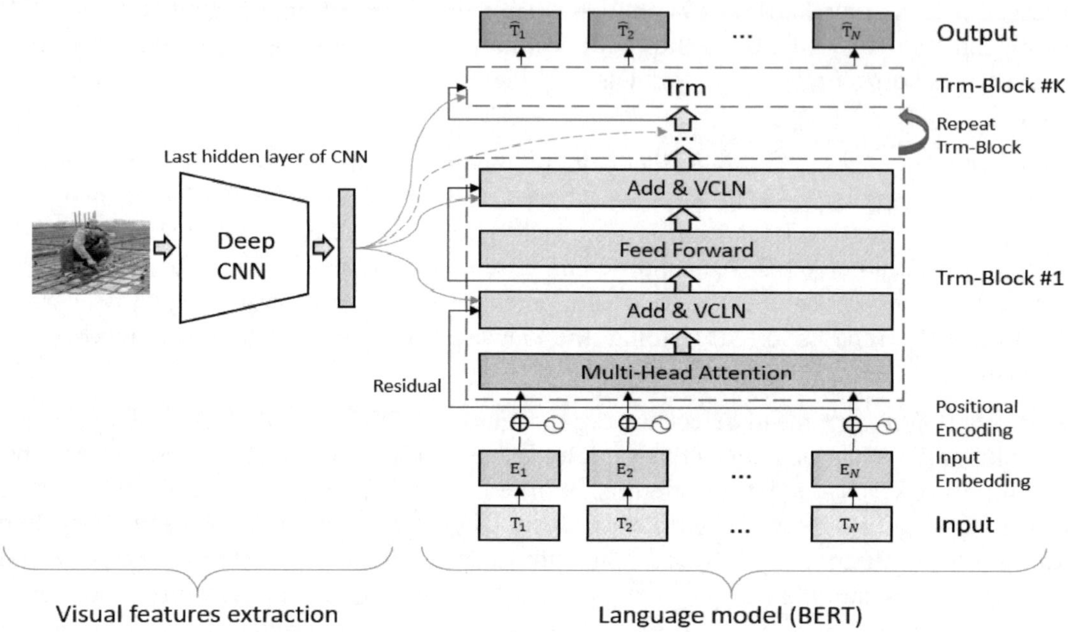

Figure 1: The structure of V-BERT. N is the max length of the input sequence

3.1 Vision-based conditional layer normalization (VCLN)

Intuitively, BERT is created to solve the NLP tasks, which means it can not easily handle the visual information. How to make the BERT can deal with the visual features becomes a crucial problem in this research. To address this problem, therefore, a Vision-based Conditional Layer Normalization (VCLN) technique is adopted.

Layer normalization (LN) used in the original BERT model was proposed by (Ba et al., 2016) mainly to solve the batch size problem of batch normalization (BN). Similar to BN, the LN can be formalized by equations (1), (2), (3). Where $\mathbf{a}^l$ is the activation output of lth layer, μ^l and σ^l denote the mean and variance of the lth layer, N^l denotes the number of hidden units in l^{th} layer, and $\mathbf{h}^l$ represents the output of lth LN. $\mathbf{g}^l$ and $\mathbf{b}^l$ are defined as the trainable gain and bias parameters of the same dimension as $\mathbf{h}^l$. ϵ is a very tiny value avoiding dividing by zero and $\odot$ is the element-wise product.

$$\mu^l = \frac{1}{N^l}\sum_{i=1}^{N^l} a_i^l \tag{1}$$

$$\sigma^l = \sqrt{\frac{1}{N^l}\sum_{=1}^{N^l}\left(a_i^l - \mu^l\right)^2} \tag{2}$$

$$\mathbf{h}^l = \frac{\mathbf{a}^l - \mu^l}{\sqrt{(\sigma^l)^2 + \epsilon}} \odot \mathbf{g}^l + \mathbf{b}^l \tag{3}$$

To make the BERT model be able to process the visual information, the vision-related components are involved in the calculation of LN, which is inspired by conditional batch normalization (CBN) that implements the combination of language features in the process of image feature extraction. The VCLN can be represented by equations (4), (5), (6). Where MLP is the multi-layer perceptron neural network, and f_{img} represents the visual features. Since $\mathbf{g}^l$ and $\mathbf{b}^l$ were the trainable parameters in the pre-trained BERT model, it can not be directly replaced by $\Delta\mathbf{g}^l$ and $\Delta\mathbf{b}^l$ or the knowledge contained in $\mathbf{g}^l$ and $\mathbf{b}^l$ that the BERT model has learned in the pre-training phase would be lost. Therefore, $\Delta\mathbf{g}^l$ and $\Delta\mathbf{b}^l$ are respectively added to $\mathbf{g}^l$ and $\mathbf{b}^l$ as a small increment, which makes the original BERT model able to process and generate language under the constraints of the visual information.

$$\begin{cases} \Delta\mathbf{g}^l = \mathrm{MLP}_{\mathbf{g}}^l(f_{img}) \\ \Delta\mathbf{b}^l = \mathrm{MLP}_{\mathbf{b}}^l(f_{img}) \end{cases} \tag{4}$$

$$\begin{cases} \mathbf{g}_{new}^l = \mathbf{g}^l + \Delta\mathbf{g}^l \\ \mathbf{b}_{new}^l = \mathbf{b}^l + \Delta\mathbf{b}^l \end{cases} \tag{5}$$

$$\mathbf{h}_{new}^l = \frac{\mathbf{a}^l - \mu^l}{\sqrt{(\sigma^l)^2 + \epsilon}} \odot \mathbf{g}_{new}^l + \mathbf{b}_{new}^l \tag{6}$$

3.2 Model training and prediction

The first step of model training is to generate the training samples. As shown in the upper part of Figure 2, a sentence is first mapped word by word to an integer token sequence through the vocabulary dictionary. The Start ID and End ID are then inserted into the head and the tail of the token series, respectively. To make sure the model be able to handle all the samples, the mapped token sequences finally need to be padded with zero to the fixed-length N.

After obtaining an output token sequence, the loss is calculated using the token series $\mathrm{T}[2{:}N]$ and $\hat{\mathrm{T}}[1{:}N-1]$ of input and output, as shown in the bottom part of Figure 2. This is not only because the first token of the input sequence is a meaningless beginning flag but also can make sure the model be able to forecast the first meaningful token when the input sequence only has the start token. Note that the output series has no start token but has the end token, and the padding tokens are excluded when computing the loss.

Figure 3 demonstrates how to predict a sentence according to a given image. At the beginning of the prediction, the model needs to infer the first meaningful token according to the learned knowledge and the input visual features when the input sequence has only the start token and then continues to predict the next single token in turn based on the previous predictions. The Beam Search is used in this stage as the inference method to generate the best sub-sentence according to the predicted token at each step. In practice, the output values of the Softmax layer are commonly used as the score for tokens in each step, and the cumulative sum of each token score is the final score of the sub-sentence. Stop inferring when the End ID appears in a sub-sentence with the best-score or the length of all sub-sentences reaching the max length.

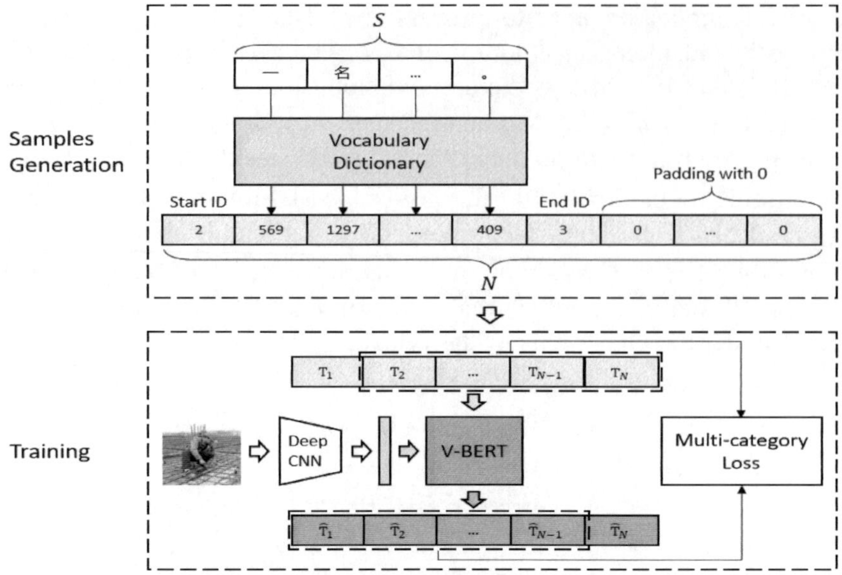

Figure 2: Sample generation and model training.

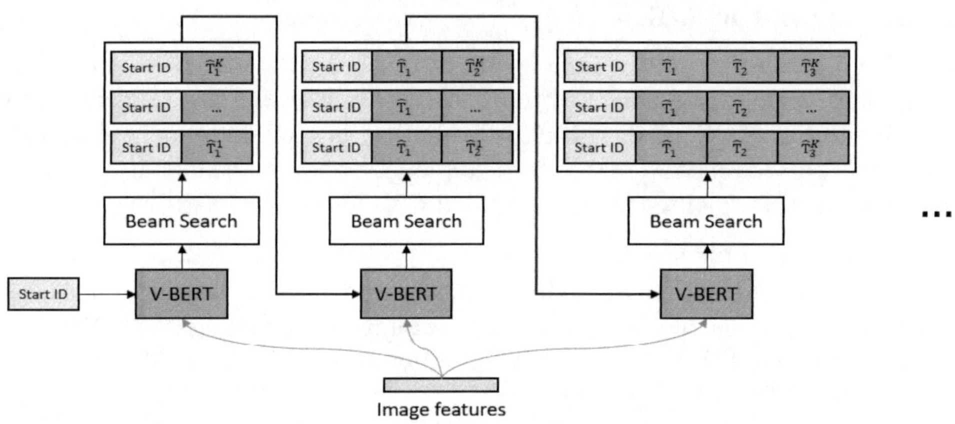

Figure 3: Beam search prediction using V-BERT. Though token $\hat{T}_{t-1}$ in step t may be different, to simplify the drawing, the superscript of token $\hat{T}_{t-1}$ is not shown in the figure after step 1

4. Experiments

4.1 Data collection and preprocessing

To carry out the experiments and validate the proposed model, the authors have created a private dataset named Images of Jobsite Daily Activity and Chinese Captions (IJDACC). In detail, we have collected about 1227 job site daily activity images. The source of the images was diverse. Some were collected directly from the jobsite, some were obtained from the internet, and some were from Liu's research (Liu et al., 2020). Thanks to Liu's generous sharing. Similar to the MS COCO caption dataset (Chen et al., 2015), each image has at least five Chinese descriptive sentences. All the sentences were given by different people through Internet crowd-sourcing to obtain diversified image captions. The annotators were required to read the description rule document carefully to ensure they were trained to give the appropriate Chinese sentences.

The content of the image description includes the type and count of the worker and the related activities, worker-related or construction-related objects (such as helmet, reflective vest, gloves, safety belt, trolley, etc.) and the corresponding color and count. Table 1 shows some examples of the image descriptions for the major types of activities, including *Bricking*, *Rebar Work*, *Transporting*, *Plastering*, *Scaffolding*, *Concreting*, and *Other* activities without workers or can not be clearly identified. To save space, here, we only show a sample picture of the main types of work and some descriptive sentences. Different types of keywords in a sentence are masked with different colors for a more intuitive demonstration, and the color legend is at the bottom of Table 1.

Table 1: Some examples of image captions in IJDACC

Activity	Image Example	Chinese Image Description	English Translation
Bricking （砌筑）		• 一个穿着白色衣服戴着白色手套和橙红色安全帽的砌筑工在室外用红色小砖块砌墙。 • 一名砌筑工人穿着白色短袖戴着白色手套和橙色安全帽正在室外用红色小砖头砌砖墙。	• A bricklayer, dressed in white clothes, white gloves and an orange-red safety helmet, was building walls with small red bricks outside.
Rebar Work （绑钢筋）		• 一个戴着黄色安全帽和红白色手套穿着橙色反光衣的钢筋工人在绑柱子的钢筋。 • 一个穿着橙色反光背心戴红白色手套和黄色安全帽的钢筋工在绑钢筋。	• A steelworker in a yellow helmet, red and white gloves and an orange reflective vest tied the steel bars of the post.
Transporting （搬运）		• 一个穿着绿色反光背心的搬运工人在推着一辆装满混凝土的独轮小推车。 • 一名穿着绿色荧光安全马甲的搬运工人正用一辆独轮手推车运输渣土。	• A porter wearing a green reflective vest is pushing a wheelbarrow full of concrete.
Plastering （抹灰）		• 一个戴着橙红色安全帽穿着白色衣服的抹灰工在给墙抹水泥砂浆。 • 一名戴红色安全帽的抹灰工人正在给墙上水泥砂浆。	• A plasterer in an orange-red safety helmet and white clothes is plastering the wall with cement mortar.
Scaffolding （搭建架子）		• 两名系着安全带戴着黄色安全帽穿红色工作服的架子工人正在高处架设铁架。 • 两个穿着安全背带和红色制服戴着黄色安全帽和手套的架子工在搭建脚手架。 •	• Two scaffolders in seatbelts, red uniforms, yellow helmets and gloves are building scaffolding.
Concreting （混凝土浇筑）		• 一群戴着手套和黄色安全帽的混凝土工在楼层顶部浇筑混凝土。 • 多名戴着黄色安全帽和手套的混凝土工人正在钢筋网上浇筑混凝土。	A group of concrete workers in gloves and yellow helmets poured concrete at the top of the floor.
Others		• 一台黄色的挖掘机正在开挖地面。 • 一台黄色挖掘机正在开挖土方。	A yellow excavator is digging the ground

Type of worker | Valuable object | Activity | Color | Count

Table 2: Data summary before and after data augmentation

Activity	Original						Augmented	
	Image				Sentence		Image	Sentence
	Total	Train	Val	Test	Total	Train	Train	Train
Bricking	382	261	61	60	1910	1305	2088	10440
Rebar Work	350	239	55	56	1750	1195	1912	9560
Transporting	168	119	25	24	840	595	952	4760
Plastering	58	41	9	8	290	205	984	4920
Scaffolding	57	38	10	9	285	190	912	4560
Concreting	42	28	7	7	210	140	896	4480
Others	170	125	23	22	850	625	1000	5000
Sum	1227	851	190	186	6135	4255	8744	43720

After collecting the dataset, we checked all the sentences manually to correct the text errors like omissions, repetitions, and typos, then divided the images and their corresponding descriptions into the training set, validation set, and testing set by 70%, 15%, 15%, respectively. The stratified random sampling method was used when splitting the dataset to ensure that different categories of images are distributed proportionally in the training, verification, and testing set.

To build a better model, some data augmentation operations were adopted to enlarge the training set. Unlike image classification, image captioning in this study needs to see the whole area of the image. Hence, any operation that impairs image quality and integrity did not use during augmenting. In practice, we adopted different combinations of flip (original, vertical and horizontal) and rotating (0°, 90°, 180°, and 270°) and obtained seven new different images finally by removing the repeated ones. The descriptive sentences of the augmented images were directly copied from the original images. After this operation, the number of images and sentences was eight times than before. A simple copy operation was then used to enlarge the image of *Plastering*, *Scaffolding*, and *Concreting* to the nearly same quantity level of the *Transporting*'s, which can not only balance the training set to a great extent but also avoid a significant offset of the predicted distribution. Note that data augmentation only applied to the training set. After enlargement, the total number of training images increased from 851 to 8744, and the sentences rose from 4255 to 43720, as shown in

Table 2.

4.2 Evaluation metrics

In order to comprehensively evaluate the performance of the proposed V-BERT model, two evaluation systems were utilized to reflect the accuracy of the generated text and the generated key elements, respectively.

Evaluation system for text generation. The first one is the text generation evaluation system, which aims to evaluate the accuracy, fluency, and naturalness of the generated text. Some famous metrics in this system are BLEU, ROUGE-L, METEOR, CIDEr-D, and SPICE. The first step in text generation evaluation is to cut the predicted and reference sentences into meta-units. There are two segmentation methods for Chinese sentences, as shown in Figure 4. The traditional way is the single Chinese character segmentation(SCCS) that considers every single Chinese character as a meta-unit. Another method is Chinese word segmentation (CWS). The meta-unit in CWS is a meaningful Chinese word that includes multi-Chinese characters. For CWS, there are many excellent tools, such as Jieba (https://github.com/fxsjy/jieba) and Pkuseg (https://github.com/lancopku/PKUSeg-python), which were also adopted in this paper.

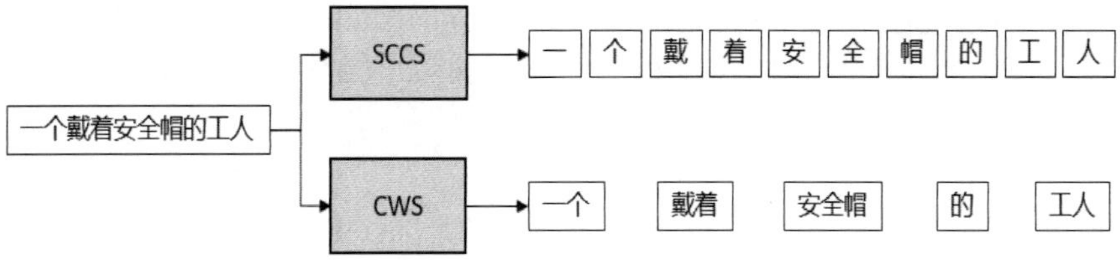

Figure 4: Different segmentation methods

Evaluation system for key-elements generation. Another one is the evaluation system for generated components, which designs to evaluate the key elements' accuracy in the generated sentences. The standard metrics in this system are Precision, Recall, and F-Score. The formulas of these three metrics are shown in Figure 5 (a). When $\beta = 1$, F-Score becomes the F1 score, which was adopted in this paper. Figure 5 (b) shows an example of calculating TP, FN, FP, and TN when the key element is "rebar worker".

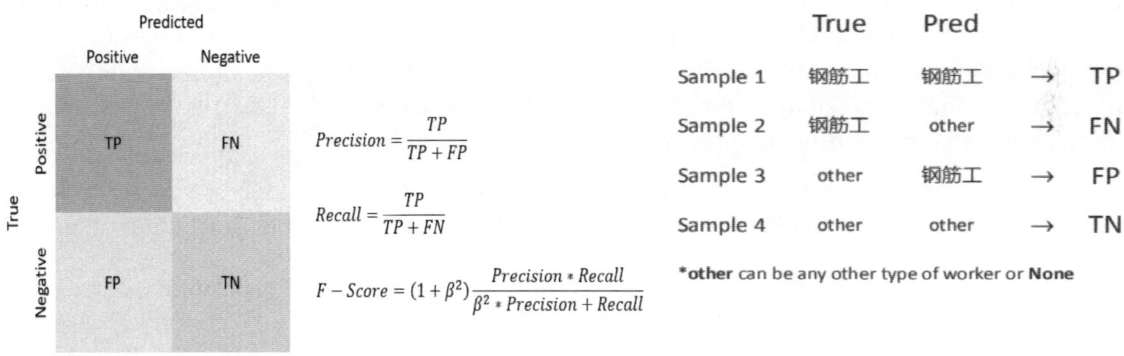

(a) (b)

Figure 5: (a) Calculation of Precision, Recall, and F-score. (b) Calculation of TP, FN, FP, and TN of rebar worker

4.3 V-BERT modeling

We utilized the deep CNN model *Resnet152* (He et al., 2016) trained on *ImageNet* to extract the image features and initial the language model with a pre-trained Chinese BERT model *Chinese_wwm_ext_L-12_H-768_A-12* (https://github.com/ymcui/Chinese-BERT-wwm), which was an advanced edition of Google's Chinese BERT model. The Adam algorithm was chosen to be the optimizer, and the learning rate was set to 1.0E-5. The batch size was equal to 32, and the early stopping strategy was also adopted to prevent over-fitting.

As shown in Table 3, four different types of segmentation methods: SCCS, Jieba_HMM, jieba_noHMM, and Pkuseg, were utilized to divide the meta-units. HMM indicates whether to use Hidden Markov Model. According to the results, all the metric values of method SCCS except **M** were obviously higher than the values of three other methods. However, the metrics values of the three other methods were relatively stable. It might reveal that the performance would be overestimated when only using the SCCS method. Thus, the authors adopted the ***Avg*** value as the final performance in Chinese text generation, which may be more prudent than using any other single method.

We also evaluated the performance in key element generation. According to the results shown in Table 4, the average F1 score of all categories was higher than 0.5, and the average F1 score of the Workers, Activities, and Objects was greater than 0.7.

4.4 Comparison experiments

To make a direct comparison, the authors trained a new V-BERT model based on the dataset used in model E#3 developed by (Liu et al., 2020). Since the dataset was based on English, Google's pre-trained English BERT (*Uncased_l-12_h-768_a-12*) was adopted to initialize the V-BERT model, which was named V-BERT_EN in Table 5. The evaluation results showed that all the metric values of the V-BERT_EN model were obviously higher than E#3's, indicating that the text generation performance of the V-BERT_EN model was significantly better than the E#3 model.

The trained V-BERT_EN model was then used to repeated Liu's another experiment to test key elements generation performance. The results are shown in Table 6. The performance improvement percentage of each category was calculated to show the enhancement. Except *Object I*, the V-BERT_EN's performance in key elements generation of other categories were considerably better than Liu's model, especially in *Object II* and *Relationships*, which got the great improvement percentage of 432.2% and 380.83%, respectively; and finally achieved an incredible mean improvement percentage of 171.20%.

To sum up, after analyzing two comparative experiments, it is reasonable to conclude that the proposed V-BERT model achieves state-of-the-art performance in the field of construction.

Table 3: Text generation performance of the V-BERT model in different segmentation methods with Beam Size = 5

Segment Type	B_1	B_2	B_3	B_4	M	R_L	Cr-D	S
SCCS	0.8105	0.7460	0.6913	0.6422	0.4168	0.7294	1.8197	0.6394
Jieba_HMM	0.7494	0.6472	0.5651	0.4949	0.4168	0.6517	1.3749	0.4859
Jieba_noHMM	0.7794	0.6820	0.6033	0.5352	0.4168	0.6836	1.5107	0.5363
Pkuseg	0.7741	0.6738	0.5953	0.5266	0.4168	0.6700	1.3167	0.5169
Avg	0.7783	0.6873	0.6137	0.5497	0.4168	0.6837	1.5055	0.5447

***B**, **M**, **R_L**, **Cr-D**, **S**, and **T** denote BLEU, METEOR, ROUGE_L, CIDEr-D, SPICE, and forecasting time (the same below).

Table 4: Key elements generation performance of the V-BERT model

Categories	Components	TP	TP+FP	TP+FN	P	R	F1	F1_Avg
Workers	Bricklayer	59	72	60	0.8194	0.9833	0.8939	0.7858
	Rebar worker	43	52	56	0.8269	0.7679	0.7963	
	Mover	18	20	24	0.9000	0.7500	0.8182	
	Plasterer	9	11	9	0.8182	1.0000	0.9000	
	Scaffolder	8	16	9	0.5000	0.8889	0.6400	
	Concreter	5	8	7	0.6250	0.7143	0.6667	
Activities	Bricking	59	72	60	0.8194	0.9833	0.8939	0.7742
	Rebar work	40	49	53	0.8163	0.7547	0.7843	
	Transporting	18	20	24	0.9000	0.7500	0.8182	
	Plastering	8	10	9	0.8000	0.8889	0.8421	
	Scaffolding	8	16	9	0.5000	0.8889	0.6400	
	Concreting	5	8	7	0.6250	0.7143	0.6667	
Objects	Helmet	158	170	162	0.9294	0.9753	0.9518	0.7242
	Reflective vest	40	48	63	0.8333	0.6349	0.7207	
	Gloves	72	97	99	0.7423	0.7273	0.7347	
	Safety belt	2	3	8	0.6667	0.2500	0.3636	
	Trolley	17	19	21	0.8947	0.8095	0.8500	

Colors	H-Red	11	16	32	0.6875	0.3438	0.4583	0.5359
	H-Yellow	85	111	106	0.7658	0.8019	0.7834	
	H-Orange	5	19	11	0.2632	0.4545	0.3333	
	H-White	8	13	13	0.6154	0.6154	0.6154	
	RV-Green	5	6	24	0.8333	0.2083	0.3333	
	RV-Orange	28	42	39	0.6667	0.7179	0.6914	
Counts	W-One	96	112	123	0.8571	0.7805	0.8170	0.6148
	W-Two	16	36	44	0.4444	0.3636	0.4000	
	W-Multi	16	32	19	0.5000	0.8421	0.6275	

*H-Red, RV-Green, W-One, W-Multi denote red helmet, green reflective vest, one worker, more than four workers.

Table 5: Performance comparison in text generation

Model	B_1	B_4	M	R_L	Cr-D	S
E#3	0.680	0.491	/	0.616	1.605	0.354
V-BERT_EN	0.8312	0.7387	0.5083	0.8281	4.0314	0.4894

Table 6: Key elements generation performance comparison

	Object	TP	TP+FP	TP+FN	F1	F1_Avg	F1 of E#3	Improvement (%)
Object I	Worker/man	79	79	80	0.9937	0.9937	0.9937	0.0000
Object II	Cart(s)	15	15	15	1.0000	0.9899	0.1860	432.2038
	Brick(s)	32	34	32	0.9697			
	Bar(s)	31	31	31	1.0000			
Object III	Helmet	51	52	68	0.8500	0.8472	0.7070	19.8334
	Reflctive vest(s)	19	19	26	0.8444			
Relationships	Lay(ing)/ Build(ing)	26	27	27	0.9630	0.9136	0.1900	380.8317
	Tie(Tying)	30	30	30	1.0000			
	Pull(ing)/ Push(ing)	7	7	11	0.7778			
Attributes	H-Yellow	24	26	39	0.7385	0.8471	0.6880	23.1260
	W-One	54	55	58	0.9558			
Mean	/	/	/	/	/	/	/	171.1990

5. Discussion

By understanding the image content, the proposed V-BERT model can be applied to several aspects to facilitate the development of Intelligent Jobsite.

First of all, the V-BERT model can be used to assess worker's safety status by analyzing the presence or absence of specific keywords in the generated image captions such as helmet, reflective vest, gloves, safety belt, etc. As shown in Figure 6 (a), After matching the keywords, the condition of the worker can be got (he is bricking outdoor, wearing a helmet and gloves). Then the corresponding pre-defined rules under this condition are used to evaluate worker's safety status and finally output the assessment result. Similarly, by matching the keywords related to work activities, it is easy to identify ongoing activities in the image. Therefore, the V-BERT model can be used for automatic progress monitoring or construction process monitoring.

Moreover, with the development of smart construction sites, a large number of images would be produced every day by many visual sensors. It would be another challenge to store and retrieve such a large-scale image dataset efficiently. Fortunately, the image captions output from the V-BERT model can also be used to generate tags as images index, as shown in Figure 6 (b), which can significantly reduce the stress of image storage and retrieval.

Last but not least, since Google has publicly released a multilingual BERT model, it is also significant that this study provides some inspiration (such as the V-BERT framework) for those countries that do not speak English to quickly develop the text generation models based on their national language using a small dataset.

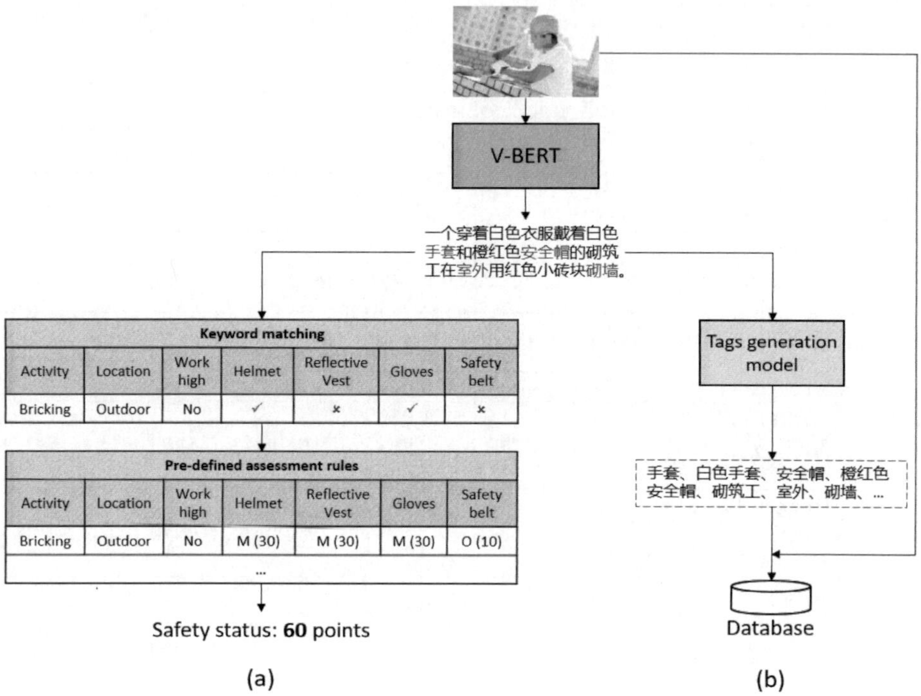

Figure 6: Examples of possible application prospects of the V-BERT model. M and O denote mandatory and optional, respectively.

6. Conclusion

This study proposed a V-BERT model for job site scene understanding. An IJDACC dataset was created, and some data augmentation operations were adopted to enlarge the training set. The experimental results show that the proposed V-BERT model achieves state-of-the-art performance in the construction area with an average performance improvement of 171.20%.

The limitation of this study mainly lies in the amount of data, the diversity of sentences, and the accuracy of some critical elements like *Colors* and *Counts*. In the future, continue to enlarge the IJDACC dataset is one of the crucial steps. Besides, developing some augmentation methods for descriptive sentences is also a desirable research direction. Finally, it is also worth exploring some different methods of extracting visual features or combining visual features with the BERT model.

Acknowledgment

This work was jointly supported by Shenzhen Science and Technology Innovation Committee Grant (PJ#JCYJ20180507181647320), National Natural Science Foundation of

China (PJ#51778553), and City University of Hong Kong Strategic Research Grant (PJ# 7005240).

References

Ba, J.L., Kiros, J.R., Hinton, G.E., 2016. Layer normalization. ArXiv Prepr. ArXiv160706450.

Chen, X., Fang, H., Lin, T.-Y., Vedantam, R., Gupta, S., Dollár, P., Zitnick, C.L., 2015. Microsoft COCO Captions: Data Collection and Evaluation Server. CoRR abs/1504.00325.

Devlin, J., Chang, M.-W., Lee, K., Toutanova, K., 2018. BERT: Pre-training of Deep Bidirectional Transformers for Language Understanding. CoRR abs/1810.04805.

Ding, L., Fang, W., Luo, H., Love, P.E.D., Zhong, B., Ouyang, X., 2018. A deep hybrid learning model to detect unsafe behavior: Integrating convolution neural networks and long short-term memory. Autom. Constr. 86, 118–124. https://doi.org/10.1016/j.autcon.2017.11.002

Fang, Q., Li, H., Luo, X., Ding, L., Luo, H., Rose, T.M., An, W., 2018. Detecting non-hardhat-use by a deep learning method from far-field surveillance videos. Autom. Constr. 85, 1–9. https://doi.org/10.1016/j.autcon.2017.09.018

He, K., Zhang, X., Ren, S., Sun, J., 2016. Deep residual learning for image recognition, in: Proceedings of the IEEE Conference on Computer Vision and Pattern Recognition. pp.770–778.

Kim, Hongjo, Kim, K., Kim, Hyoungkwan, 2016. Vision-Based Object-Centric Safety Assessment Using Fuzzy Inference: Monitoring Struck-By Accidents with Moving Objects. J. Comput. Civ. Eng. 30, 04015075. https://doi.org/10.1061/(ASCE)CP.1943-5487.0000562

Liu, H., Wang, G., Huang, T., He, P., Skitmore, M., Luo, X., 2020. Manifesting construction activity scenes via image captioning. Autom. Constr. 119, 103334. https://doi.org/10.1016/j.autcon.2020.103334

Luo, H., Wang, M., Wong, P.K.-Y., Cheng, J.C.P., 2020. Full body pose estimation of construction equipment using computer vision and deep learning techniques. Autom. Constr. 110, 103016. https://doi.org/10.1016/j.autcon.2019.103016

Luo, X., Li, H., Cao, D., Yu, Y., Yang, X., Huang, T., 2018. Towards efficient and objective work sampling: Recognizing workers' activities in site surveillance videos with two-stream convolutional networks. Autom. Constr. 94, 360–370. https://doi.org/10.1016/j.autcon.2018.07.011

Roberts, D., Golparvar-Fard, M., 2019. End-to-end vision-based detection, tracking and activity analysis of earthmoving equipment filmed at ground level. Autom. Constr. 105, 102811. https://doi.org/10.1016/j.autcon.2019.04.006

Robinson, G., 2015. Global construction market to grow $8 trillion by 2030: driven by China, US and India. Global Construction.

Vaswani, A., Shazeer, N., Parmar, N., Uszkoreit, J., Jones, L., Gomez, A.N., Kaiser, \Lukasz, Polosukhin, I., 2017. Attention is all you need, in: Advances in Neural Information Processing Systems. pp.5998–6008.

Zhang, H., Yan, X., Li, H., 2018. Ergonomic posture recognition using 3D view-invariant features from single ordinary camera. Autom. Constr. 94, 1–10. https://doi.org/10.1016/j.autcon.2018.05.033

Process Pattern-based Hybrid Simulation for Emission Estimation of the Construction Processes

Danh Toan Nguyen[a] and Walter Sharmak[b]
[a] University of Kassel, Germany, [b] TH Lübeck-University of Applied Sciences, Germany
dtnguyen@student.uni-kassel.de

Abstract. Simulation-based calculation methods are increasingly being used in construction emissions assessments. However, to properly simulate a construction process, modellers face a number of challenges in obtaining input data and taking into account uncertainties and dynamics. This paper proposes a hybrid simulation method to combine multi-agent systems (MAS) and dynamics systems (SD) based on process patterns for estimating emissions during the construction phase. The agents in the model, which are generated based on the predefined process patterns, represent the products, tasks, and resources of the building process. The modellers will be able analyse the emissions of different construction operation strategies through the agents' interaction under the influence of uncertainties and dynamic factors in both specific and holistic perspectives.

1. Introduction

The execution of building projects is intrinsically harmful to the environment because of material consumption, energy consumption, and emissions. The construction phase occurs in the short term and emits fewer emissions than the operation and maintenance phases. (Wu *et al.*, 2012). However, some researchers recognized that strong short-term emissions in overcrowded areas could harm the environment and the community than to a mild level in the long term, so the construction phase's emission must be adequately assessed and mitigated (Tam, Deng, and Zeng, 2002).

The life-cycle assessment (LCA) has been widely applied to environmental impact assessments in the construction field. Fundamentally, there are three principal approaches in LCA research, including a process-based, an economic input/output-based, and hybrid approach (Combination of process-based and economic Input/Output-based)(Abd Rashid and Yusoff, 2015). The process-based LCA method analyses each process associated with the assessed product and then sums the total impacts. The pLCA is considered to be the most accurate method, so most LCA studies in the construction sector are applying process-based methods (Ding, 2004). However, preparing the input data for the pLCA in the construction field can become time-consuming as the necessary data collection required is mostly performed manually, which includes construction tasks, constraints, their respective resource consumption, and the related environmental data. Moreover, construction processes are relatively difficult to analyse because they are affected by numerous uncertainties and dynamic factors such as altered on-site conditions, traffic situation, and machine breakdown, working under high schedule pressure, the skill level of the workforce, and error generation. These factors can lead to waste generation, deadlines slips, rework, and thus indirectly increasing the environmental impact. To overcome these challenges, some researchers integrated simulation methods such as discrete event simulation (DES), system dynamics (SD), and agent-based simulation (ABS) into the pLCA method (Ozcan-Deniz, Zhu and Ceron, 2012; Feng, 2020; Nguyen and Sharmak, 2020a). Utilizing the simulation methods can assess the duration and resource consumption of different construction operation strategies and capture the variability of events in complex systems, thereby increasing the reliability of the estimation. Each simulation approach has an outstanding advantage, such as DES and ABS can analyse construction processes at a micro level while SD can evaluate problems from a macro and holistic-thinking perspective. Currently, existing environmental impact assessment studies are often conducted independently without incorporating the advantages of these simulation methods. However, these approaches have a great potential to be more effective if they are used together.

This research aims to improve the pLCA approach by proposing an innovative method to combine a multi-agent system and system dynamics (MAS-SD) based on process patterns. Construction logic knowledge is generalized as reusable process patterns and task packages for similar projects. Task packages describe atomic tasks in process patterns with the most necessary data, especially the related data to the environmental impact indicators. The agents in the multi-agent system represent products, tasks, and resources of construction processes. Through the interaction between agents, the modeller can analyse the construction processes under different operating mechanisms. Besides, the causal-effect loops of the system dynamics approach are integrated into the agents in the MAS model to consider the influence of the macro factors on the environmental performance of construction processes. To test the applicability of the proposed method, a case study of a reinforced concrete high-building shell is implemented.

2. Hybrid simulation model

2.1 Process patterns and task packages

Typically, the construction of a high-building consists of several similar components, such as the foundation, columns, beams, slabs of the building shell structure. Accordingly, the construction workers execute the same processes repetitively to construct these components of the building shell. The needed construction processes for a building components are formalized as predefined process patterns(Wu *et al.*, 2010; Sigalov and König, 2017; Nguyen and Sharmak, 2020b) . A process pattern describes the process logic of how construction tasks are organized and performed. This description can be a hierarchical one, which consists of subprocesses and atomic tasks. Previous research, which applied process patterns for the construction processes, usually defines an atomic task as a specialized technical task such as to reinforce, to set up the formwork, to concrete, to cure concrete, and to strip formwork in a cast-in-place reinforced concrete process (level 2 in Figure *1*). However, these tasks should be disaggregated into more detailed tasks to align with the pLCA approach. For example, the reinforcement should be divided into rebar transport (off-site and on-site), processing (straightening, cutting, bending), and erection (level 3 in Figure 1).

The tasks in Figure 1 play an essential role since the pLCA approach can only estimate the environmental impact by analyzing the task on the atomic level. Therefore, they need to store more specific data related to environmental impact assessment. To minimize the possibility of making errors and omissions in the task description, a task package patterns concept was applied. A task package describes an atomic construction task with all corresponding data such as constraints, required resources, and environmental impact indicators. For example, a task package named rebar installation of a slab by the cast-in-place method is described in Figure *2*. The needed resources of the task are explicitly illustrated. The environmental impact indicators of resources can be referred from the available LCA dataset of each country, such as Ökobau.dat in Germany. The performance factor shows how this task consumes the resources, which can be referred from the construction company's oriented construction norms. Besides, some other important information, which is needed for the simulation process, such as the malfunction rate of the equipment, wasted material consumption rate, and the error rate of crew, are added. It is not easy to get exactly the value of these indicators, but they can be collected from the available historical records of the construction company in similar previous projects or through experienced staff.

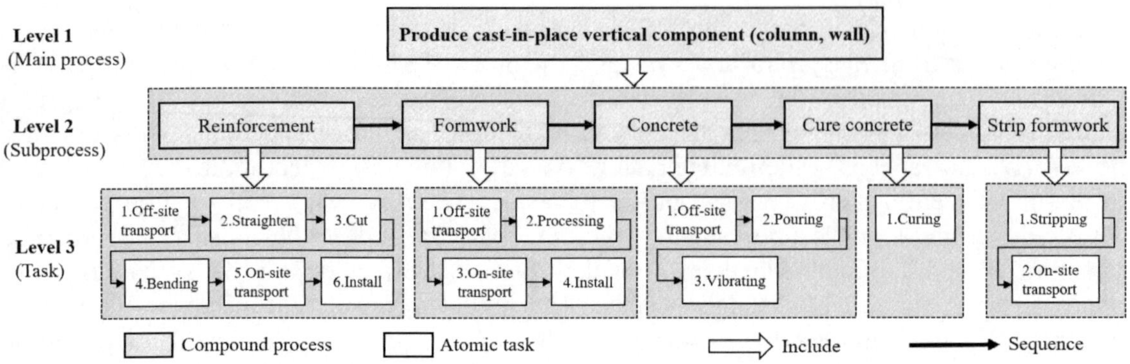

Figure 1: Process pattern for cast-in-place reinforced concrete method

Process patterns and task packages significantly expedite the preparation time of the pLCA method, since the modeller only selects the appropriate process, after which the rest parts are generated almost automatically. However, breaking down construction activities into many atomic tasks challenges the pLCA method of evaluating the processes in a complex constraint environment. To cope with this complexity, A multi-agent system was developed to support pLCA method for construction processes.

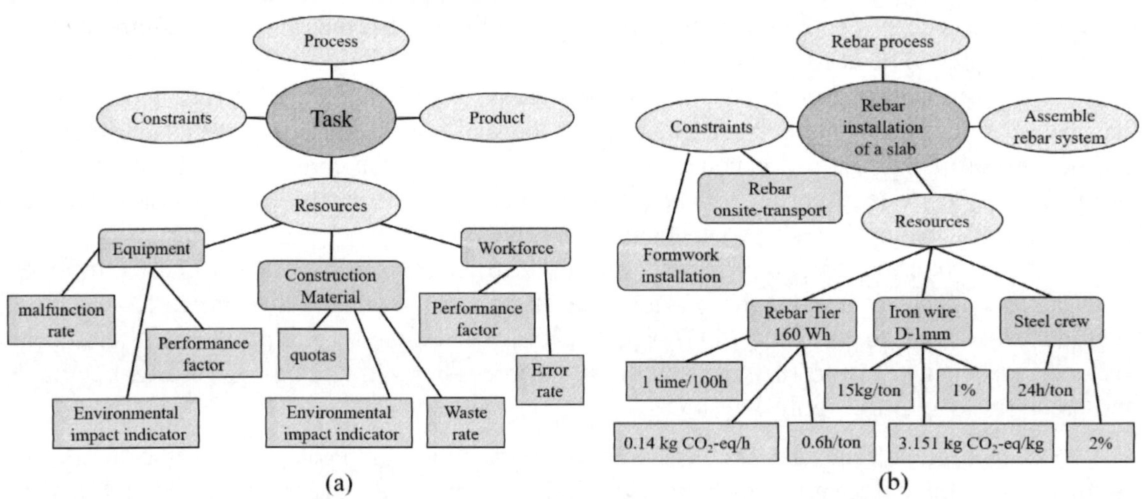

Figure 2: Task package pattern: content (a) and an instance (b)

2.2 Multi-agent system development

Multi-agent system. MAS models are based on the bottom-up methodology that suits properly modeling complex systems. In which, the modeler assumes that it is impossible to understand the whole considering situation but can perceive, on a micro-level, and tries to recognize their behaviors. These agents interact and communicate with each other, and they form a coherent whole on a macro-level, often emerging and unpredictable behaviors. MAS is defined as a group of intelligent autonomic agents representing real-world parties without global control and unified objective (Ren and Anumba, 2004). The adoption of MAS increases modeling realism because individual agents can represent not only physical entities such as machines, vehicles, workforce, products but also abstract objects like the proposals, orders, processes. The MAS model in this study uses agent technology for products, tasks, and resources in the construction process of a high-building shell. To model the construction phase, the modeller needs both product and process data of the building shell. The process patterns and task package mentioned above can provide the process data of a typical high-building shell. The product data can be extracted from the BIM model of the high-building. Both data types can support the MAS model in the initialization agents and their attributes. A database is suggested in this paper to store process, product, and resource data to support the development of the MAS model (Figure 3).

Figure 3: The schema of the suggested relational database

Product agent. This agent type represents construction components such as columns, beams, slabs. The product agent's attribute, including related workload, location, sequence index, is extracted from the BIM model. The BIM model is created as a construction-oriented model to fit the modeller's intentions. For instance, in a 4D-BIM model, the construction zones and their sequence constraints should be defined to present the construction order. One story can be divided into several zones, which are assigned parameters indicating the planned construction method, zone identification, sequence indicator, and the quantity take-off of construction components.

Process agent. Based on the predefined construction method of construction components, the product agents initialize their process agents by querying the process pattern database. After that, the new process agents continue to initialize their sub-processes agents. This cycle is repeated until the atomic tasks are initialized, called the task agents.

Task agent. Task agents automatically infer their predecessors and successors based on the relationships among process agents and product agents. Each agent processes this information, calculates task duration, priority index, manipulates its state, and operates accordingly. The priority index is calculated based on the longest path following, which stands for the accumulated maximum duration of all successors (Horenburg, Wimmer and Günthner, 2012). For this purpose, a recursive function was implemented, which determines the longest path through the network by self-referencing. Consequently, tasks close to the critical path tend to have a higher priority index.

Resource agent. The resource agents represent vehicles, machines, building materials, or workers. Each resource agent contains essential information related to the applicable construction norms, environmental impact indicators, resources description, which were mentioned in the task package (Figure 2).

Agent interation. In the operating phase of the MAS, a control system updates all resource agents' proposals and receives task agents' resource orders (Figure 4). A task agent can only send the orders to the control system if their prerequisites are satisfied. The control system can allocate the resource for the task agent by some different mechanisms following the defined patterns. For example, the tasks with a high priority index and have no constraints will be allocated first. The tasks with no constraints but have a low priority cannot be immediately allocated unless they can use and release resources before the specified time of other tasks, which also use the same resource but their predecessors are unfinished. Thereby, this process will be repeated until all the tasks have been completed. Based on the time implementation of equipment, the material consumption, the emission of the process will be calculated parallel to the running of the model.

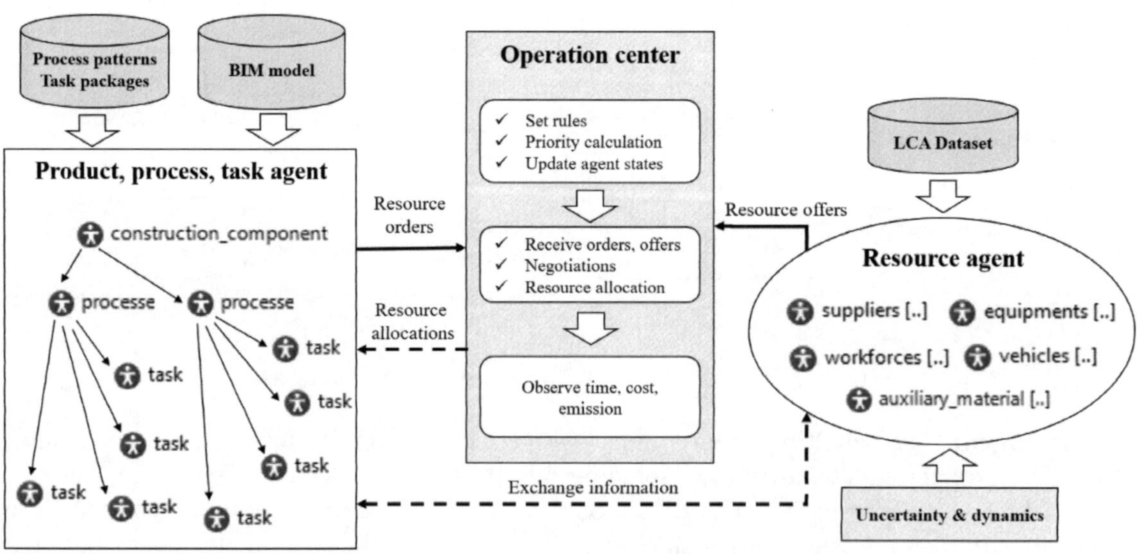

Figure 4: The control center of MAS model

2.3 Integration System Dynamics into the Multi-agent System

The control system in the MAS model can set the rules to drive the construction operation process. However, as assessed by the MAS approach, the environmental impact does not change much if the process is performed with the same construction method and the same resource type, although the operating mechanism has changed. In fact, some important factors such as high schedule pressure, skill level, overtime, and error generation can influence the construction productivity, thus indirectly increasing the environmental impact. The reason for omitting indirect effects is that the MAS ignores the interactions between agents and macro factors in the holistic perspective.

System Dynamics. SD is a top-down approach based on the information feedback method. The SD model aims to analyze a complex system behavior from a macro and holistic perspective within a predefined boundary (Ding *et al.*, 2018). Analyzing the construction process by the SD method can quantify the effect of many macro factors that are difficult to solve by MAS. For example, a high schedule pressure had caused a requirement for increase construction production beyond normal limits. When the actual productivity of a project falls behind the perceived required productivity, the anticipated completion date becomes invisible. Consequently, the management must adopt specific solutions to reduce the harmful effects of the productivity loss. These policies can be overtime, hiring new workers, extending the project completion duration to improve productivity, etc., in order to attempt to finish the project on time. In construction, it is usual that not all completed work meets quality requirements. Therefore, a rework cycle during the construction phase is mostly unavoidable, and the correction work may cause as well secondary errors. As a result, these described negative effects indirectly increase the environmental impact.

Hybrid Simulation Model. To integrate the SD approach into the MAS model, two causal-effect loops were developed to describe the cognitive behavior of task agents in the interaction with macroscopic factors (Figure 5). These loops are rigorously studied and quoted in literature by many researchers (Alzraiee, Zayed and Moselhi, 2015).

*Schedule pressure loop***.** Schedule pressure is defined as schedule discrepancy, which is the difference between planned and actual progress. When the schedule pressure is too low, participants realize that they have more time to complete their tasks than planned, so their productivity may be reduced. However, excessive schedule pressure can deteriorate productivity considerably. To decrease the schedule pressure, one simple solution is adopting overtime, which might cause fatigue, result in lower quality and lead to generate more error.

Rework feedback loop. The rework cycle consumes more materials, time, and labor than expected, so the impact on the environment also increases significantly. Rework can itself be flawed, requiring additional rework in a recursive cycle that can extend project duration and workload beyond what is originally conceived. The rework cycle is affected by the skill level of the workforce and their productivity, the quality of the performed work, and the time of error discovery. The traditional environmental impact assessment methods treat the project as being composed of a set of individual, static, and discrete tasks. They tend not to account for the flaws in work and the need to rework.

The task agents in the MAS model are analyzed under the effect of two causal-effect loops (Figure 5). In which the planned productivity and the initial error rate is calculated based on the capacity of the resource. The deadline is set based on the task's late finish or milestone of the construction process. The proposed SD model included workflow and rework. The workflow module illustrates the workflow from execution to completion. A rework cycle module is added to account for work that does not pass the quality standards and needs to be reworked. The schedule pressure resulting from low productivity and increasing rework is captured as well. If the schedule pressure reaches a high level, an overtime solution will be considered for the current crews. The SD model structure was developed to capture the effects of schedule pressure, fatigue, overtime, and rework cycle on quality of work and project completion duration. Consequently, the additional emission of processes was indirectly quantified.

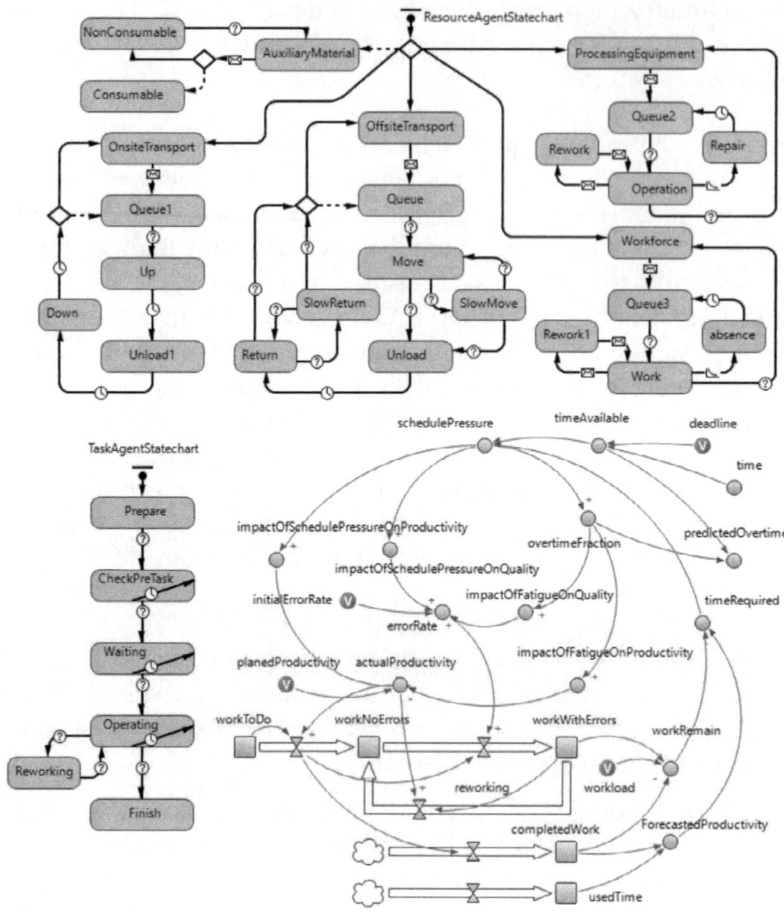

Figure 5: The statechart of agents and effect-causal loops of the hybrid model

3. Model Test

3.1 Example Description

A BIM model, which is an example in the Revit library, was used to test the proposed method (Figure 6). The building has a reinforced concrete shell with three storys based on the pile foundation system. The construction operations cause environmental impacts by equipment and auxiliary materials usage alongside the offsite materials supply chains and onsite construction. These impact sources are within contractors' area of decision-making, while other major building materials are determined by the upstream design stage. Therefore, the scope of the simulation in this case study includes upstream auxiliary materials extraction, processing, and production; offsite materials transportation (major and auxiliary materials); and the onsite construction operation process, using the cast-in-place reinforced concrete method. One floor of the building was divided into three zones, matching the production capacity of assumed construction resources. Each zone has two parts are vertical components (columns, walls) and horizontal components (beams, slabs). The workload of each component was extracted from the BIM model (Figure 6). The information of the construction phase, such as material supplier, vehicle, equipment, workforce, was assumed at a certain detail level to suit the simulation model (Nguyen, 2019). All of the data was stored in a database (Figure 3) that is the input of the simulation tool (Anylogic 8.7 Personal Learning Edition). To consider the emissions of different construction operation alternatives, three scenarios were tested.

Scenario 1: The process is operated using the critical path method (CPM). Construction tasks try to own their required resources to start at the earliest possible date so as not to delay their successors. The project control aims at adhering to the initial schedule, so the simulation model sets the late finish as the deadline of the process.

Scenario 2: The operation mechanism is the same as scenario 1, but the target end dates of activities were adjusted. The task's due date was set later 25% compared to the task's late finish.

Scenario 3: in contrast to scenario 1, after the activity prerequisites are complete, instead of calling the resource immediately, the task waits until it receives a pull signal from its successors. The operating mechanism applies the pull technique of the lean principle. Furthermore, each task only holds resources if all the required resources are available at the same time. Before this point, they do not keep any resources in their queue. This scenario also sets the deadline 25% later than the late finish.

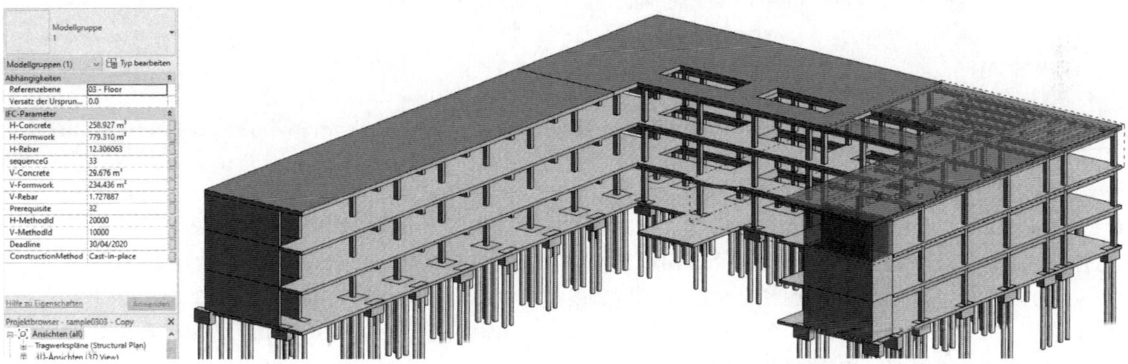

Figure 6: BIM model of the building in the case study

3.2 Result and Discussion

This example selected the global warming potential index (GWP), expressed as CO_{2eq}, for analysis. In which, the CO_{2eq} emission of the construction processes of the 3rd floor of the building is assessed in two ways: using MAS model, and using the hybrid model MAS-SD. In both cases, auxiliary material consumption contributed to the highest CO_{2eq} (63%-65%) among all impact resources during the construction phase (Figure 7). This result is consistent with results from previous studies, in which auxiliary materials are found to contribute about 60%-80% of the CO_{2eq} ratio depending on the type of construction (Feng, 2020). The proportion of CO_{2eq} emissions due to material consumption increased slightly compared to other resource groups when using a hybrid model for assessment. The reason is that in the hybrid model, the rework of the unsatisfactory works leads to the use of more materials.

The process duration in scenario 1 is the highest (243 hours) (Table 1). The main reason is that while some tasks cannot possess the resources needed to get started at their early start time, they still try to keep their required resources, which were available, in their queue. Therefore, these resources have no chance to combine with other tasks, have the same priority as the task under consideration, but have submitted the resource order late. Thus, the overall schedule affected leads to higher progress pressures that negatively affected productivity and generate errors. As a result, the emissions of the process increased significantly by 16.67% compared with the predicted emissions using only MAS model, regardless of schedule pressure. Scenario 2 can control the increase in schedule pressure by setting the deadline 25% later than the end of scenario 1. However, it maintains the same method of resource allocation; thus, the duration is still 10% longer than scenario 3, adopting the pull-driven process management. In scenario 3, resources are allocated selectively, since the task of processing them is started only when all of its needed resources are available at the same time. Besides, the tasks are drawn according to the needs of their successors, following the pull mechanism of the lean principle. As such, avoid multiple tasks trying to get access to resources to get started as soon as possible.

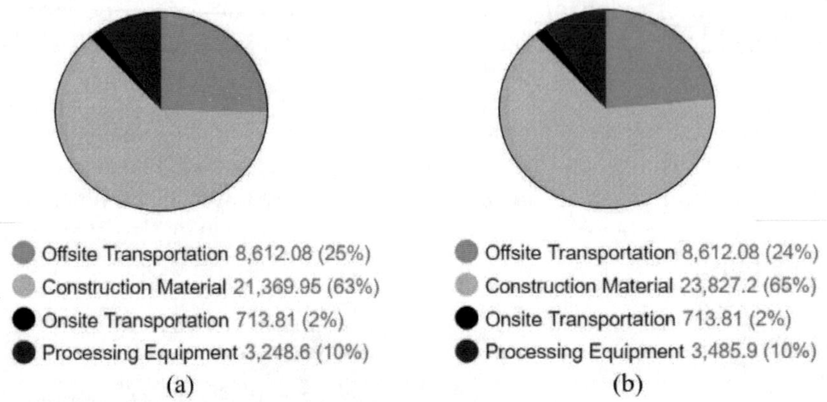

Figure 7: Emission propotion of resource groups assessing by MAS (a), and MAS-SD (b) in scenario 3.

Through the case study, even though the proposed hybrid model provided an emission assessment that considered process uncertainties and dynamic environments, some limitations need to be solved in the future. The probability distributions of uncertainty, the error rate of crews and equipment, the traffic situation, the input data for lookup function in deducing the effect of schedule pressure on the productivity, quality of work in this study are based on experience, literature, and assumptions.

Table 1: Comparison of emission estimation between MAS model and MAS-SD model.

Scenarios	CO2eq-ton (MAS)	CO2eq-ton (MAS-SD)	Deviation (%)	Duration (hours)
Scenario 1	34.61	40.38	16.67	243
Scenario 2	34.14	38.03	11.39	201
Scenario 3	33.94	36.73	8.22	183

4. Conclusion

In this paper a hybrid simulation model is proposed to integrate system dynamics into a multi-agent system to simulate construction processes while assessing emissions. Process patterns were used to support the MAS in an agent initialization and determine the agent constraints. Tasks and resources during the construction phase were modeled as autonomous agents following their own objectives. Modeller can analyse different construction operation strategies through the agents' interaction under the influence of uncertainties and dynamic factors in both specific and holistic perspectives. By analyzing some scenarios in the case study, a significant increase in the emission estimation was detected as the result of taking into account the influence of schedule pressure, error generation rate on the construction process. Furthermore, adopting pull techniques can improve resource allocation to reduce schedule pressures, thereby indirectly reducing emissions during construction. In the future, it is necessary to reinforce the proposed method to explore the impact of lean theory on the environment during the construction phase in a more comprehensive way.

References

Abd Rashid, A. F. and Yusoff, S. (2015) 'A review of life cycle assessment method for building industry', Renewable and Sustainable Energy Reviews. Elsevier Ltd, 45, pp.244–248. doi: 10.1016/j.rser.2015.01.043.

Alzraiee, H., Zayed, T. and Moselhi, O. (2015) 'Dynamic planning of construction activities using hybrid simulation', Automation in Construction. Elsevier B.V., 49, pp.176–192. doi: 10.1016/j.autcon.2014.08.011.

Ding, G. K. C. (2004) The development of a multi-criteria approach for the measurement of sustainable performance for built projects and facilities. PhD Thesis. University of Technology, Sydney.

Ding, Z. et al. (2018) 'System dynamics versus agent-based modeling: A review of complexity simulation in construction waste management', Sustainability (Switzerland), 10(7). doi: 10.3390/su10072484.

Feng, K. (2020) Environmentally friendly construction processes under uncertainty: Assessment, Optimisaton and Robus Decision-Making. PhD Thesis. Lulea University of Technology.

Horenburg, T., Wimmer, J. and Günthner, W. a (2012) 'Resource Allocation in Construction Scheduling based on Multi-Agent Negotiation', in Proceedings of the 14th International Conference on Computing in Civil and Building Engineering. Moscow, Russia.

Nguyen, D. T. (2019) 'A knowledge-based value stream mapping simulation framework for predicting the environmental impact of the construction process', in Forum Bauinformatik 2019. Berlin, Germany: Technische Universität Berlin, p. 25.

Nguyen, D. T. and Sharmak, W. (2020a) 'Agent-based simulation for gas and dust emissions assessment during construction: A case study in Vietnam', IOP Conference Series: Materials Science and Engineering, 869(4). doi: 10.1088/1757-899X/869/4/042015.

Nguyen, D. T. and Sharmak, W. (2020b) 'BIM-based Ontology for sustainabilty-oriented building construction', in Construction Digitalisation for Sustainable Development 2020. Hanoi, Vietnam.

Ozcan-Deniz, G., Zhu, Y. and Ceron, V. (2012) 'Time, Cost, and Environmental Impact Analysis on Construction Operation Optimization Using Genetic Algorithms', Journal of Management in Engineering, 28(3), pp.265–272. doi: 10.1061/(asce)me.1943-5479.0000098.

Ren, Z. and Anumba, C. J. (2004) 'Multi-agent systems in construction-state of the art and prospects', Automation in Construction, 13(3), pp.421–434. doi: 10.1016/j.autcon.2003.12.002.

Sigalov, K. and König, M. (2017) 'Recognition of process patterns for BIM-based construction schedules', Advanced Engineering Informatics. Elsevier Ltd, 33, pp.456–472. doi: 10.1016/j.aei.2016.12.003.

Tam, C. M., Deng, Z. M. and Zeng, S. X. (2002) 'Evaluation of construction methods and performance for high rise public housing construction in Hong Kong', Building and Environment. Elsevier, 37(10), pp.983–991.

Wu, H. J. et al. (2012) 'Life cycle energy consumption and CO2 emission of an office building in China', International Journal of Life Cycle Assessment, 17(2), pp.105–118. doi: 10.1007/s11367-011-0342-2.

Wu, I. C. et al. (2010) 'Bridge construction schedule generation with pattern-based construction methods and constraint-based simulation', Advanced Engineering Informatics. Elsevier Ltd, 24(4), pp.379–388. doi: 10.1016/j.aei.2010.07.002.

Automatic image analysis of mineral construction and demolition waste (CDW) using machine learning methods and deep learning

M. Sc. Jurij Walz, Dr. -Ing. Elske Linß, Prof. Dr. -Ing. habil. Carsten Könke
Materialforschungs- und -prüfanstalt Weimar, Coudraystr. 4, 99423 Weimar, Germany
jurij.walz@mfpa.de

Abstract. In science and technology, artificial intelligence and machine learning are becoming more and more important. For example, they are used for object recognition in image processing. This investigation aims to improve the rate of reuse for different types of CDW, reduce processing costs and improve processing performance by using machine learning methods and revolutionary deep learning approaches. To achieve this, classifiers with various features have been used. They are support vector machines, multilayer perceptron, k-nearest-neighbor, and pre-trained neural network by MVTec HALCON. Comparisons were made using the recognition rates achieved with actual data sets. The results showed that both classical classifiers, and convolutional neural networks, generate excellent results. They vary little from that of deep learning algorithms. The task is to find feature combinations that optimally characterize the classes.

1. Introduction

The cover of raw materials is a prerequisite for economic value chains and is therefore of great importance for the efficiency of the economy. The demand for raw materials for the building sector in Germany is covered by the extraction from domestic deposits, the use of secondary raw materials from the recycling of construction waste and other industrial processes, as well as from imports. For more than 20 years, the Building Materials Industry, the Construction Sector, and the Waste Management Industry have been working intensively to promote closed material cycles in the construction sector. The focus is on mineral construction and demolition waste (CDW). This is the largest material flow in the national waste balance (KrWB, 2018). According to the report (KrWB, 2018) in Germany, the proportion of CDW incurred yearly is about 58.8 million tons 45.5 million tons (or 77.7 %) were recycled. Most of them are used in road pavements and fillings. The fraction of the material that flows back in the production of new concrete is with 1-5 % very little. The possibilities for the recycling of recycled aggregates produced from CDW depend on their material and environmental properties as well as on their material composition. Thus, the recovery of secondary material makes a significant contribution to the substitution of primary raw materials. With both, better quality control of recycled aggregates in the construction industry and the further advancement of sensor-supported technologies, the loop of the building materials can be better closed. Quality-monitored goods are better positioned in the market and thus results in an improvement in the reputation of the recycling industry and better utilization of resources. This fact is contributing to an increased interest in machine learning processes. The significant increase in interest is mainly due to the development of new algorithms and increasingly powerful computer technology. These technologies are primarily used for object recognition in image processing. In the field of quality management, monitoring, and recognition of recycling aggregates in the construction industry, recycled aggregates have to be characterized concerning their material composition. Nowadays the recognition analysis during the quality monitoring and reporting are performed manually according to the standards DIN EN 12620 and DIN EN 933-11 (DIN EN 12620, 2008; DIN EN 933-11, 2011). On one hand, this is very time-consuming and highly subjective, on the other hand, it is not possible to analyze bigger amounts of CDW by hand. The given sample quantities are limited and do not represent a significant amount if small contents of foreign materials are to prove. This requires innovative methods for the analysis of the recycled aggregates that deliver precise, fast, and above all, representative results. It is a contribution to increasing the recycling rate of the different materials in building waste (Anding, et al., 2011).

In this research work, modern methods for quality control and identification of mineral recycled aggregates based on optical pattern recognition methods have been explored and compared between each other. Analysis of the material composition can be automated by using sensor-based image recognition in combination with artificial intelligence and machine learning methods. The aim is to develop an automatic optical analysis for better quality assurance of recycled aggregates. The challenge is the high amount of classes and the high heterogeneity of the investigated different classes. The super-classes contain different sub-classes which makes it difficult to a high precision identification. In the future, the sensor-based recognition and future sorting of materials will be the bases of classification methods, which can separate the classes by specific features.

2. Materials and Methods

2.1 Experimental material

Table 1 gives an overview of all super- and sub-classes and shows the exact composition and a few examples of the data set used.

Table 1: Examples and number of particles in the super classes of the data set

Classes	**Ra**	**Rb**	**Rc**	**Ru**	**X**	**Y**	**Z**
Number	1,760	4,136	1,902	2,207	8,233	2,445	870
Example images							

A data set consisting of typically recycled aggregate materials has been created for this paper. The super-classes are graded according to the construction waste classes based on DIN EN 12620: Ra (asphalt, tarpaper, and roofing felt), Rb (brick, masonry porous and dense, sand-lime brick and not floating aerated concrete), Rc (concrete, concrete products, concrete masonry blocks, and mortar), Ru (natural stone, not bounded aggregates, and hydraulic bounded aggregates, lightweight concrete), X (clay and soil, not iron metal slag, gypsum, rubber, plastic, metal, not floating wood, organic materials, paper, glass, and others), Y (floating aerated concrete, floating wood and styrofoam / polysterol) and Z (composite particles). The class "Z" is not included in the DIN EN 12620. It was added by us to examine the recognition of composite materials. The subclass "glass" was added to the main class "X". In total, the collected data consists of more than 20,000 images of individual particles. The variability in size of the classes, together with the fact that the individual classes are themselves not homogeneous, represent the challenge of this study. The results of own investigations by using image processing techniques (Anding, et al., 2011) and (Kuritcyn, et al., 2019) shoved, that by using larger datasets and new modern classification algorithms (deep learning), it is possible to improve the accuracy of analysis.

2.2 Experimental equipment

The images were taken by using a static image acquisition system called QualiLeo. It is possible with this system to illuminate objects under observation in different ways, such as top light, ring light, and transmitted light. The transmitted light is used to segment objects from the background. The built-in 12 MP CMOS camera allows the generation of high-resolution images of objects. This setup was used to analyze various lighting scenarios: Lighting number 1 with complete ring light on (L1). Here, all samples are illuminated equally. With lighting number 2, in which just one half of the ring light is turned on (L2), simulating side lighting. The last set of lighting number 3 uses direct light from above, top light (L3). By implementing these three different lighting scenarios on the samples, the importance of the illumination should be investigated. Thus, three data sets with different lighting have been created and analyzed. Table 2 gives an example of the used types of lighting options before the segmentation of objects.

Table 2: Different lighting scenarios on the example of brick particles

Lighting 1 (ring light)	Lighting 2 (half of a ring light)	Lighting 3 (top light)
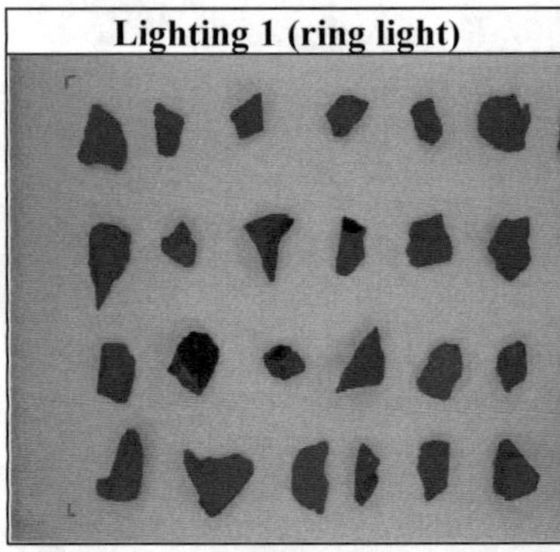	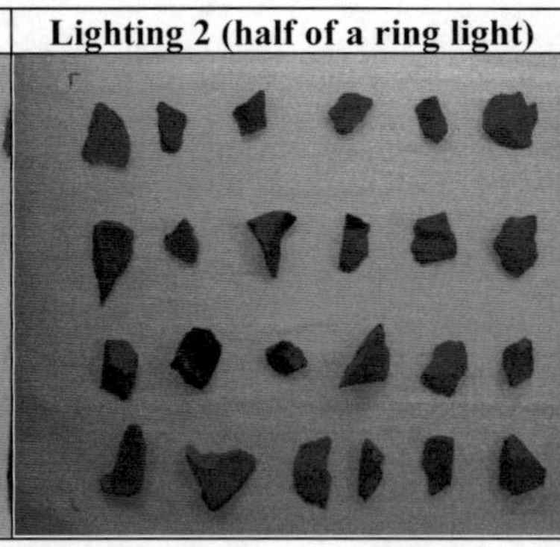	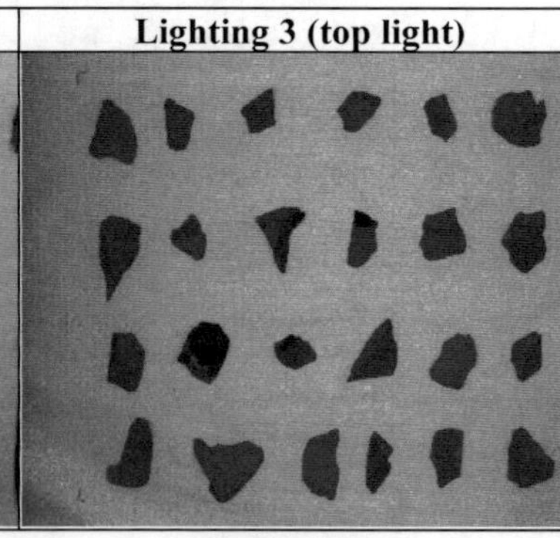

2.3 Data processing

The full processing of the data was carried out following the image processing chain based on VDI 2632 (Haar, 2019). This process is shown in figure 1. The main points are explained below.

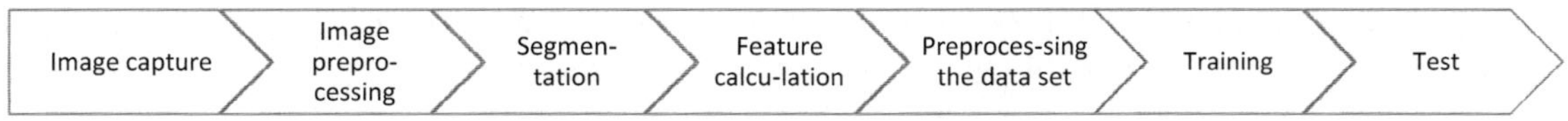

Figure 1: Image processing chain (Haar, 2019)

The procedure starts with the capture of the images. The images should contain all relevant characteristics of the test objects. The main focus is on optical features such as texture, color, and shape. As part of the next step – preprocessing of the images, different measures are taken to adapt the image, which should simplify the implementation of further steps and the evaluation. This is important for the reduction of systematic and random disturbances. During the segmentation, the foreground is separated from the background and therefore the relevant regions of the image are detected. The aim is to find coherent and significant regions within the image scene and to pass them on to further processing steps. The feature vector is extracted from the images for each identified object. It represents the actual input of the classifier and contains all the important differences and the relevant information. The current data set is preprocessed to achieve good recognition results. This includes the removal of outliers and reduction of the feature vector, because at the beginning the feature vector also contains a lot of noise. During the training phase, the classifier is selected and the model is created. The results are evaluated in the last step and the recognition rate as well as the standard deviation are determined.

2.4 Classification method

Classical supervised machine learning methods were compared with modern deep learning (DL) methods in this study. Classifiers with various characteristics and complexity are chosen to make the investigations as detailed as possible. These are presented below.

2.4.1 Classical classification

The first algorithm is the *k*-nearest-neighbor (*k*-NN). Existing training data is stored in the memory and the distances between the data and the new object are determined. The *k*-objects, which have the smallest distance to the data point, are determined and classified in the future space. Assuming that these nearest *k*-neighbors are most similar to the unknown object, the new object it is assigned to the class to which most of the examples under consideration belong (Runkler, 2010).

As a further machine learning method support vector machine (SVM) was chosen. The basic idea of the support vector machine is based on the linear separation of classes. If this is given, a dividing line can be drawn in a two-dimensional feature space or a linear hyperplane in a multi-dimensional feature space, which defines classes and enables the classification of unknown objects (Cleve & Lämmel, 2014). Such linear separability is not always provided. In such cases, the SVM uses the so-called kernel trick. Data is transferred to higher-dimensional feature spaces with the help of a kernel function until linear separation is possible. Then the dividing plane is determined and the data is transferred back to the original feature space. Now the dividing plane is no longer linear and can separate classes from each other (Cortes & Vapnik, 1995).

The third option was a simple neural network called perceptron. This was presented by Rosenblatt and contains a direct graph in which the individual nodes have been modeled as neurons (Rosenblatt, 1958). After running, the input feature vector is converted into the output vector. The weights of the individual neurons are changed, which are used more often and become stronger (from the weighting). The complex task can be solved with hidden layers, hence the name multilayer perceptron (MLP). This also increases the complexity of the structure and the time needed for computing (Runkler, 2010).

With all classical classifiers, the determination of the features is the most important step in the calculation process. As explained above, the features are calculated from the object images and describe the physical characteristics of the recorded objects, such as texture, color, and shape. A feature vector consists of several hundred features per object to be considered. The feature vectors created in this way must be further optimized, as they still contain noise. For this purpose, feature selection methods are used in which the most relevant features of the feature vector are reduced without compromising the recognition rate. In contrast, the deep learning (DL) approach has the advantage of calculating the features of the neural network, which takes place automatically within the algorithm, so that the user does not have to worry about the correct calculation of the features (Sesselmann, et al., 2019). One of the disadvantages of using DL compared to classical algorithms is the need for a large data set and a modern graphics processing unit (GPU) (Witten, et al., 2017).

2.4.2 Deep learning classification

An artificial neural network is a representation of a biological network of nerve cells (Ertel, 2016). Such a network can be created from individual artificial computing units, the neurons (McCulloch & Pitts, 1990). Each neural network consists of three main layers, the input layer, the hidden layer, and the output layers. The important role here is the hidden layer, which can consist of several connected layers. The structure of the hidden layers also differs depending on the type of application of the neural network and thus it forms different topology types (Biethahn, et al., 1998). The more hidden layers available, the more complex systems the network can map. As a result, a large number of layers ensure a "deep" neural network (Witten, et al., 2017). At the same time, a large number of hidden layers lead to computationally intensive tasks when implementing DL systems. Complex problems also make the implementation of the network difficult. Large training data is required for such tasks, leading to an increase in training time (Marcus, 2018). The number of object examples can increase to millions. Transfer learning with the so-called pre-trained network is used to speed up the learning process and reducing the computing effort (MVTec Software GmbH, 2020). DL structures are used in a variety of areas. Pattern recognition in all aspects is one of the most important cases. In the present study, a convolutional neural network (CNN) was used. It has been specially developed for image processing (LeCun, et al., 1998). The images are processed in a matrix (width x height x color channels). Because the calculation does not take place based on the manually created features, the training step takes place directly on the images or the image sections (Sesselmann, et al., 2019). The most important distinguishing feature of other architectures lies in the structure of hidden layers. They consist of three subgroups, which include alternated convolutional layers and pooling layers, being followed by fully connected layers. At first, CNN recognizes location independent basic structures such as lines, edges, and colored pixels, later the combination of these structures and complex parts, which are combined into an object and viewed as a whole, are learned (Quoc V. Le; Google Brain; Google Inc, 2015). A pre-trained CNN from MVTec HALCON 18.11 was used for this study's task. HALCON is a program library for industrial image processing with the graphical user interface HDevelop of MVTec Software GmbH (MVTec Software GmbH, 2018). This means that it is not necessary to create and train a network independently from the ground up. The classifier provided and pre-trained by HALCON is specially prepared for solving industrial image classification tasks. It is only required to retrain this CNN network with an own limited data set. Another aspect that matters is that neural networks are black boxes and the user cannot understand the final decision-making process. In addition, many parameters need to be optimized for each task. These include activation function, learning rate, and batch size. It is also difficult to predict how such a change will affect the results. To examine the exact differences in the recognition efficiency, classical machine learning approaches are compared with innovative deep neural networks.

3. Results and discussion

The methods are evaluated using the presented data set with different properties and the achieved average recognition rate (RR). All results are compared with each other based on the achieved recognition rates and standard deviation (Stdev). The investigations have been implemented in the programming environment of HALCON.

3.1 Settings of the classifiers

3.1.1 Classical machine learning methods

The classifiers used in the investigations have different setting parameters. The *k*-NN classifier is distance-based and the value of the nearest *k*-neighbors has been set to 5. While using SVM, the rbf-kernel was used and the γ parameter was set to 0.02. Classification mode has been used as one-versus-all. This implies that a multi-class problem is reduced to a binary decision. With the chosen implementation, a classifier is generated for each class, which is then compared to all the remaining classes (MVTec Software GmbH, 2020). MLP creates a neural network in the form of a multilayer perceptron. Softmax is used as an activation function, as it is particularly suited for classification tasks with several independent classification outputs. The number of hidden units in the hidden layer is set to 15. The data set is divided into two parts in these analyses: 80 % and 20 %. The higher percentage of the data set is used to train the classifier, while the smaller part is used to test the classifier.

3.1.2 Deep Learning method

As mentioned above, a pre-trained CNN from HALCON was used as a DL method. It just needs to be complemented with our own data set. This avoids the problem of too little data for the training phase of a new neural network. According to the HALCON reference book, depending on the problem, only hundreds to thousands of image objects per class are needed (MVTec Software GmbH, 2020). For this purpose, the training phase can only be run with a modern GPU. HALCON has three pre-trained networks. In this study, the "pretrained_dl_classifier_enhanced.hdl" (CNN_enhanced) and "pretrained_dl_classifier_resnet50.hdl" (CNN_resnet50) were used. The CNN_enhanced neural network has many hidden layers and is, therefore, better suited to more complex classification tasks (MVTec Software GmbH, 2020). Other parameters were determined as follows: batch size with 64 and the number of epochs with 16. Like the neural network CNN_enhanced, the CNN_resnet50 classifier is suitable for more complex tasks. However, due to the different structures, this classifier has the advantage of making the training more stable and internally more robust (MVTec Software GmbH, 2020). Here, the batch size parameter was set to a value of 21 due to limited hardware. Other parameters remained the same like in CNN_enhanced. An adaptive learning rate is used for both deep neural networks. It starts with a value of 0.001 and is reduced by 1/10 by each epoch. No further settings can be changed and MVTec provides no information on the exact structure of the networks. Here for using neuronal networks, the data set is divided into three parts. The majority of the data (70 %) is used for training, 15 % for validation, and the remaining 15 % is used for testing.

3.2 Experimental results

Classical classifiers (*k*-NN, SVM, and MLP) were analyzed at the beginning. The best feature groups have been searched for each one of three data sets (lighting L1, L2, and L3). These results are summarized in table 3.

Table 3: Comparison of the recognition performance of classical classification methods with different feature groups

Features	**Classical classifier (RR in %)**								
	***k*-NN**			**SVM**			**MLP**		
	L1	**L2**	**L3**	**L1**	**L2**	**L3**	**L1**	**L2**	**L3**
Color	84.94	74.27	88.31	77.54	66.43	84.64	83.51	81.88	89.63
Region	31.65	32.18	33.50	32.13	35.08	32.52	49.62	49.30	49.86
Texture	53.16	50.26	56.17	86.54	81.48	86.38	81.11	78.12	81.11
Gray	31.21	31.62	30.70	81.53	78.12	83.53	81.55	76.80	81.25
All	39.88	38.42	43.04	83.97	83.39	87.94	88.66	87.03	89.74

The experiments have shown that the features of the region contribute little to the classification and thus they have achieved the lowest RR. For example, on one hand, the best performance for MLP was in the L3 data set with 49.86 %. On the other hand, the classification has mainly achieved the best results with color or texture features. From all the remaining classifiers in the L3 data set, MLP achieved the best performance in this feature category with 89.63 %. However, regarding texture features, SVM achieved the highest result at 86.54 % in the L1 data set. The combination of all the features led to different performance results for all three classifiers. With MLP, the best result remained relatively the same as the best performance with color features in the L3 data set. RR has changed from 89.63 % with only color features to 89.74 % with all features. SVM improved by about 2 %, from 86.38 % with texture features to 87.94 % with all features at the L3 data set. There was a decrease of the results with the *k*-NN classifier, from 88.31 % with color features to 43.04 % with all features also at the L3 data set. It is an unacceptable performance, being the reason for this, that the *k*-NN classifier is more susceptible to redundant features than the more robust classifiers (such as SVM or MLP). This investigation revealed that using the most possible number of features does not always lead to a better result, or the improvement is minor because many of the features are redundant. Furthermore, the training time of the classifier increased with a large number of features. A feature selection must be carried out to find the optimal and only the most relevant features for the current classification problem. HALCON employs an approach in which the most promising feature at the time is added to the selection. The goal of this method is to improve recognition results. It can be said, that good results with *k*-NN can be achieved with mainly color features. According to the classification results, the L2 data set usually showed lower performance than the L1 and L3 data sets. This data set has been excluded from the following investigations.

Finally, the performance of classical classification methods was compared with the performance of DL methods. Classical methods have been applied to the optimization of feature vectors, such as the feature selection method. With this algorithm, an optimal subset for a particular classification problem is selected from a list of features. The current most successful feature is added to the feature vector (MVTec Software GmbH, 2020). Thus, a different feature vector was created for each classical classifier. These results can be seen in table 4.

Table 4: Comparison of the recognition performance of classical classification methods with DL

RR and Stdev (%)	Data sets			
	L1		L3	
Classifier	**RR**	**Stdev**	**RR**	**Stdev**
***k*-NN**	90.63	0.25	93.13	0.26
SVM	95.61	0.31	96.97	0.24
MLP	90.34	0.23	92.56	0.41
CNN_enhanced	93.96	0.36	94.76	0.23
CNN_resnet50	97.20	0.17	97.30	0.14

At first sight, table 4 shows good results for both data sets with all classifiers methods. The average RR is over 90 % for all classifiers and both data sets L1 and L3. Therefore, the different light settings had only a low effect on the result of the optimized classifier. Performance for both data sets L1 and L3 are very similar, but the data set of L3 always shows a slightly higher RR than the data set of L1. The standard deviation is low, indicating a stable classification process. Above all, the simple *k*-NN classifier shows an improvement of 5 %. An RR of 93.13 % and a Stdev of 0.26 % were achieved with an optimized feature vector. In this study, MLP achieved 92.56 % the lowest performance of all classifiers. To counteract this, the parameter values could be adapted for further investigations. SVM achieved the best result with an RR of 96.97 % among the classical methods. That is a 9 % improvement. This exceeds the performance of the DL method CNN_enhanced with RR of 94.76 %. Although CNN_resnet50 achieved the highest RR (97.3 %) for this data set. However, it is important to note that the classical classifier (SVM) led to a result, as good as the one obtained with the deep neural networks for this complex data set.

The recognition within the classes in the L3 data set for the best-achieved result is shown in the following figure 2. The class asphalt and tarpaper can be determined with 99 % accuracy using SVM. Except for the composite particles, the RR of other classes is at least 95 %. The performance of the last class is only 89 %. SVM outperforms the other classical classifiers in the present task in terms of class recognition. The class asphalt and tarpaper is the best-recognized class for both MLP and *k*-NN classifiers, with over 95 % RR. Except for the classes concrete, mortar, and composite particles, all other classes have at least 90 % RR. The problem class composite particles have the lowest RR, with only 70 % for MLP and 80 % for *k*-NN. A similar pattern result can be seen in the deep neural networks. Except for the composite particles class, CNN_resnet50 has a detection rate of over 95 % across all classes. The RR for the problem class is at 92 %. In comparison, the CNN_enhanced performs worse, with an RR of 82 % in the problem class. The poor results of the problem class composite particles are because it is the smallest class in the data set, with only 870 image objects. Thus, it does not have enough images to complete this complex recognition task. It can be summarized, that the optimized SVM and CNN_resnet50 are the best classifiers for this data set.

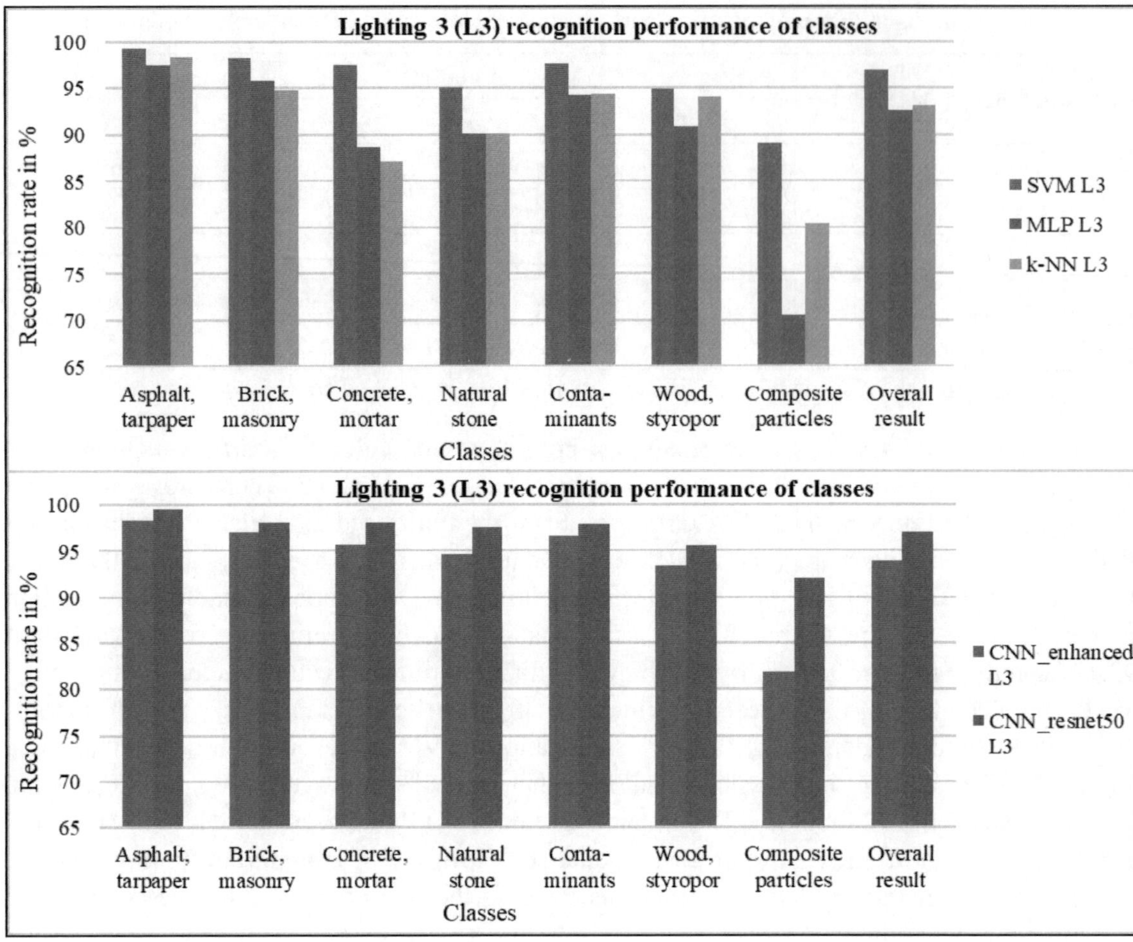

Figure 2: Recognition performance according to individual classes and classifiers

4. Conclusion

The progressive development of neural networks and, above all, the pre-trained CNNs show very good results in the use of complex recognition tasks. The omission of some pre-processing steps in the image processing chain, such as the calculation of features or the selection of features, makes the application of deep networks easier compared to the classical classifiers because these steps are carried out automatically in the network. Compared to classical methods, the disadvantage of deep neural networks is that a large amount of training data is needed also for pre-trained networks. An expensive computer with a modern GPU is needed to run a DL algorithm. Calculation time is also significantly higher than with classical methods. As the number of data increases, so does the time of calculation.

The aim of the present study was, on the one hand, to use DL for recognition purposes and, on the other hand, to compare recognition rates with classical classification methods. The investigation of the performance of pre-trained deep neural networks by HALCON shows very good results of the achieved RR with the given data set of recycled aggregates. However, with optimized classical methods, almost the same performance is possible. The result of the recognition task of SVM with 96.97 % is not significantly lower than that of CNN_resnet50 with 97.3 %. This shows that high performance can be achieved also with classical classifiers with a well-executed feature selection algorithm. Nevertheless, this kind of application is also not always trivial. Even though a pre-trained deep neural network gives positive results, it should be kept in mind that e.g. CNN_resnet50 requires significantly more time and needs a modern GPU for training than the SVM method. However, again, the use of pre-trained CNN is very simple since no segmentation or feature calculation is required.

References

Anding, K., Linß, E., Träger, H., Rückwardt, M., Göpfert, A., 2011. Optical Identification of construction and demolition waste by using image processing and machine learning methods, Jena, Germany: International IMEKO TC1+ TC7+ TC13 Symposium.

Biethahn, J. et al., 1998. Betriebswirtschaftliche Anwendungen des Soft Computing. s.l.:Vieweg+Teubner Verlag.

Cleve, J. & Lämmel, U., 2014. Data Mining. München: De Gruyter Oldenbourg.

Cortes, C. & Vapnik, V., 1995. Support-vector networks. In: Machine Learning. s.l.:s.n., pp.273–297.

DIN EN 12620, 2008. Gesteinskörnungen für Beton, s.l.: Beuth.

DIN EN 933-11, 2011. Gesteinskörnungen - Teil 11: Einteilung der Bestandteile in grober recyclierter Gesteinskörnung, s.l.: Beuth.

Ertel, W., 2016. Grundkurs Künstliche Intelligenz: eine praxisorientierte Einführung. Wiesbaden: Vieweg + Teubner.

Haar, L., 2019. Möglichkeiten des unterstützenden Einsatzes unüberwachter maschineller Lernverfahren entlang der Bildverarbeitungskette, Ilmenau: Dissertation.

KrWB, 2018. Kreislaufwirtschaft Bau: Mineralische Bauabfälle Monitoring 2016: Bericht zum Aufkommen und zum Verbleib, Berlin: Bundesverband Baustoffe - Steine und Erden e.V.

Kuritcyn, P., Anding, K., Linß, E. & Notni, G., 2019. Using hybrid information of colour image analysis and SWIR-spectrum for high-precision analysis of construction and demolition waste, Karlsruhe, Germany: Optical Characterization of Materials (OCM).

LeCun, Y., B. L., Bengio, Y. & Haffner, P., 1998. Gradient-based learning applied to document recognition. Proceedings of the IEEE, pp.2278–2324.

Marcus, G., 2018. Deep Learning: A Critical Appraisal, s.l.: s.n.

McCulloch, W. S. & Pitts, W., 1990. A logical calculus of the ideas immanent in nervous activity. Bulletin of Mathematical Biology, Issue 52, pp.99–115.

MVTec Software GmbH, 2018. HALCON: Quick Guide, s.l.: s.n.

MVTec Software GmbH, 2020. HALCON/HDevelop. Operator-Referenz (de), s.l.: s.n.

Quoc V. Le; Google Brain; Google Inc, 2015. A Tutorial on Deep Learning Part 2: Autoencoders, Convolutional Neural Networks and Recurrent Neural Networks, Mountain View, CA: s.n.

Rosenblatt, F., 1958. The perceptron: A probabilistic model for information storage and organization in the brain. In: Psychological Review, 65(6). s.l.:s.n., pp.386–408.

Runkler, T. A., 2010. Data Mining: Methoden und Algorithmen intelligenter Datenanalyse. s.l.:Vieweg+Teubner Verlag.

Sesselmann, M., Stricker, R. & Eisenbach, M., 2019. Einsatz von Deep Learning zur automatischen Detektion und Klassifikation von Fahrbahnschäden aus mobilen LiDAR-Daten. AGIT - Journal für Angewandte Geoinformatik, Issue 5, pp.100–114.

Witten, I. H., Frank, E., Hall, M. A. & Pal, C. J., 2017. Data Mining: Practical Machine Learning Tools and Techniques. Cambridge: Morgan Kaufmann.

Fast Crack Detection Using Convolutional Neural Network

Jiesheng Yang[a], Fangzheng Lin[a], Yusheng Xiang[b], Peter Katranuschkov[a], Raimar J. Scherer[a]
[a]Technische Universität Dresden, Germany, [b]Karlsruhe Institute of Technology, Germany
jiesheng.yang@tu-dresden.de

Abstract. To improve the efficiency and reduce the labour cost of the renovation process, this study presents a lightweight Convolutional Neural Network (CNN)-based architecture to extract crack-like features, such as cracks and joints. Moreover, Transfer Learning (TF) method was used to save training time while offering comparable prediction results. For three different objectives: 1) Detection of the concrete cracks; 2) Detection of natural stone cracks; 3) Differentiation between joints and cracks in natural stone; We built a natural stone dataset with joints and cracks information as complementary for the concrete benchmark dataset. As the results shown, our model is demonstrated as an effective tool for the industry use.

1. Introduction

In the field of non-destructive stone defect testing, different methods, e.g., Visual inspection Test (VT) Magnetic particle Testing (MT) and Ultrasonic Testing (UT), have been used to test surface defects. In practical use, every method has obvious imperfections: the MT equipment costs 904,48 € (UV Magnetic Yoke Flaw Detector - AJE-220 | Katex Ltd, 2021), and UT equipment costs 17.253,69 € (Olympus Panametrics Omniscan MX 32:128 Ultraschall Phased Feld Pa Flaw | eBay, 2021). Issues from high expense on MT equipment and UT equipment have not been adequately addressed. Moreover, disadvantages of VT can also not be overlooked. The test result of VT strongly depends on the tester's experience and thus subjective.

Hence, empowering VT with increasing computing power to improving efficiency and productivity and avoid the high cost of special equipment in renovation works is the starting point of this research. Abdel-Qader (2003) proved a Fast Haar Transform edge detection method in bridge crack identification. Based on that, Yeum and Dyke (2015) proposed a sliding windows technique in image processing techniques to detect cracks on steel. However, the results of edge detection are mainly affected by the noises. Thus, deep learning is employed in later application: Cha (2017) trained models to recognize concrete cracks with 97.95% accuracy on his test dataset. Similarly, Satyen (2019) achieved 85% accuracy with his test dataset in the crack recognition task. Unfortunately, those models are trained in labs with expensive powerful machines, for example, Cha performed all task on a workstation with two GPUs (CPU: Intel Xeon E5-2650 v3 @2.3GHz, RAM:64GB and GPU: Nvidia GeForce Titan X × 2ea), which limit the promotion of their approach.

As a consensus, stone crack images are more difficult to obtain compared with brick crack ones. At the same time, the TF can apply the weights of an already trained deep learning model to a different but related problem, and it shall be used if the old task has more data than the new task (Yosinski, 2015). Instead of starting the training process from scratch, this method starts with features that have been learned from a previous task, where a lot of labelled training data are available. As evidence, many studies in construction domain have mentioned that they have followed this idea and benefited from it (Xiang, 2020a; Xiang, 2020b). Hence the TF method is used to address this problem.

Given the above-mentioned facts, the scope of this research is focused on: Building a lightweight convolutional neural network (CNN) architecture to make training on laptops possible and improving training efficiency with the TF method. During the study, a total of three datasets are built and three models are trained for different objectives, namely:

- Detection of the concrete cracks;
- Detection of natural stone cracks;
- Differentiation between joints and cracks in natural stone.

This paper is organized as follows: in the next section, the design of proposed network architecture is presented; in Section 3, three datasets for each objective are build; section 4 demonstrates how the models are trained and how they benefit from the TF; section 5 shows the results of the study; section 6 makes conclusions of this article.

2. Methodology and Implementation

2.1 Network Architectures for Crack-like Features Detection

Each layer of the network has its own role in a deep learning network. The term convolution refers to an orderly mathematical procedure, in which two sources of information are intertwined and a new information is produced. The role of the convolution layer is a feature identifier (see Figure 1(a)). If features of input generally matched with filter, summation of multiplication will result in a large value in output (Fukushima, 1980). The Pooling (see Figure 1 (b)) layer can reduce the feature map size as the layers get deeper while at the same time keep the significant information. It helps to reduce the number of parameters and memory consumption in the network (Fukushima, 1980). The Rectified Linear Unit (ReLU) activation function (Glorot, 2011) is most commonly used in CNN based neural networks currently. With equation $R(x) = \max(0, x)$, the range of ReLU is $[0, \infty)$, which means that only a non-negative x-value yields and outputs. The uncomplicated and efficient mathematical form gives ReLU activation function layer a big advantage: It makes randomly initialized network very light, because of the characteristic of ReLU, approximately half of the neurons have 0 as output. This can cause several neurons to die and reduce parameters during training process. Fully Connected (FC) layer connects with high level features that extracted from convolutional layer with particular weights, and outputs the probabilities of different classes. As can be seen from Figure 2.14, in a FC layer, every neuron is connected with all the neurons in the previous layer. FC layers in CNN are identical to a fully connected multilayer perception structure. With suitable weight parameters, FC layers could create a stochastic likelihood representation.

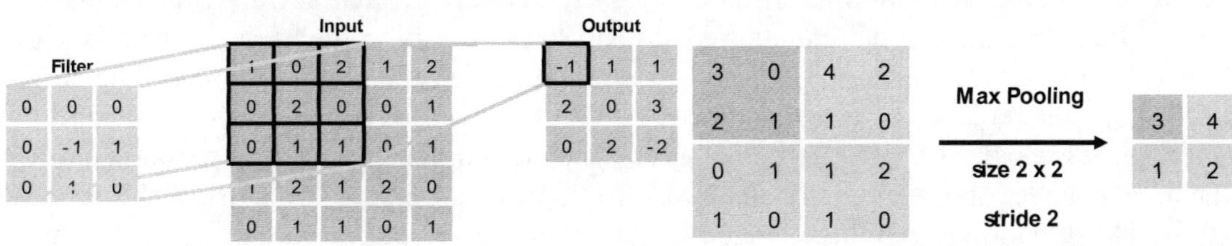

(a) Convoluting (b) Max pooling

Figure 1: Convoluting and pooling (Glorot, 2011)

All popular network architectures are composed of above-mentioned basic layers. A comparison between most used architectures in Table 1 shows performance, depth and parameter number of those networks: On the one hand, the accuracy for image classification have been dramatically increased from 1998 to 2015. On the other hand, the architecture of network become deeper and more complex. In other words, the computer needs to process more than 60 million parameters to train a model.

Table 1: Comparing between different CNN architecture (Russakovsky et al., 2015)

Name	LeNet-5	AlexNet	VGG	GoogLeNet	ResNet
Year	1998	2021	2014	2014	2015
Top-5-Error	-	15.30%	7.30%	6.67%	3.57%
Data Augmentation	-	+	+	+	+
Number of Convolutional Layers	3	5	16	21	151
Layer Number	7	8	19	22	152
Parameter Number	6.E+04	6.E+07	1.E+08	7.E+06	6.E+07

After the comparison, LeNet-5 is chosen to be basic architecture in this study for following reasons: First and most important, it meets the need of computational cost. Second, it has an acceptable accuracy. LeNet-5 is a classic CNN architecture proposed by Yann LeCun (1998). It was applied in banking to recognize handwritten numbers on checks. Because of the limited computing power at that time, grayscale images in 32 ×32 pixel is considered as inputs. LeNet-5 has 7 layers, 3 of them are convolutional layers. (see Figure 2).

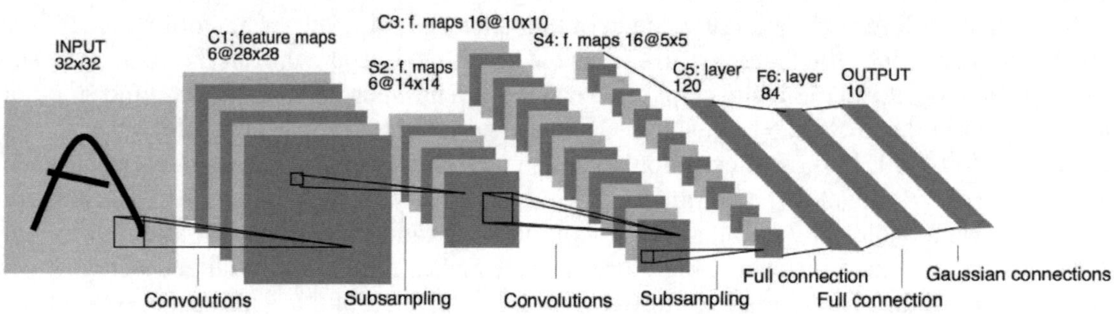

Figure 2: LeNet-5 architecture (Lecun, Bottou, Bengio and Haffner, 1998)

A number of modifications based on LeNet-5 need to be done to fit this architecture to the research goal: 1) Instead of one channel (black and white) images of original LeNet-5, the modified architecture takes three channels colour images as input. All inputs are re-sized into 228×228 pixels to avoid calculation errors, which caused by different image sizes in the dataset. 2) Instead of Sigmoid activation function of original network, which suffers from vanishing gradient problem, the modified architecture uses ReLU as activation function. 3) Max-Pooling and Local Response Normalization is used to keep features on the feature map. 4) The single 5x5 CONV layer is replaced by a stack of two 3x3 CONV layer to reduce parameters. A multi-FC layer set composed of FC1 and FC2 gives the network a stronger expression ability nonlinear to connect those extracted features from previous layers. 6) During the CNOV operation, SAME padding technique is used, which uses zeros to pad around the image to make sure the size of output and input are same. 7) On the end of the network architecture is a SoftMax layer to calculate the probabilities for each class. The modified network architecture is shown in Figure 3. Size and Parameters of each layer are shown in Table 2.

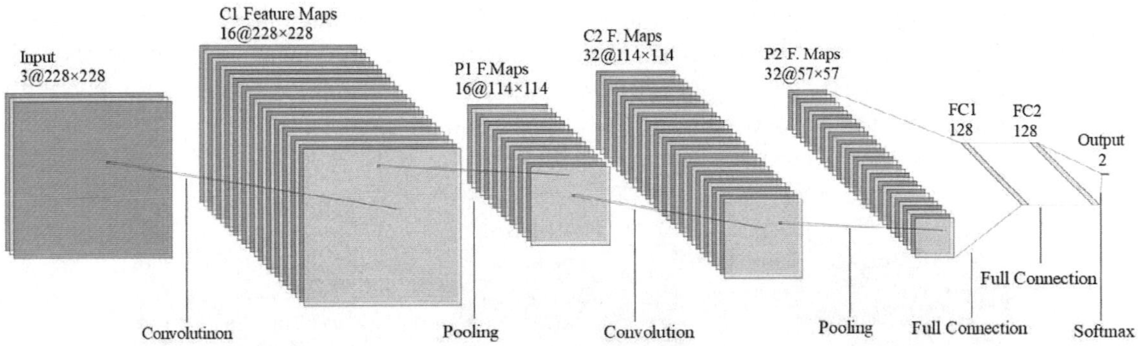

Figure 3: Network architecture for crack-like feature detection

Table 2: Size and parameters of network architecture for crack-like feature detection

Layer	Input Volume			Filter Size			Stride		Output Volume			Parameters
	D_i	H_i	W_i	K	F_x	F_y	S_x	S_y	D_o	H_o	W_o	
Input	3	228	228	-	-	-	-	-	3	228	228	0
C1	3	228	228	16	3	3	1	1	16	228	228	448
P1	16	228	228		3	3	2	2	16	114	114	0
C2	16	114	114	32	3	3	1	1	32	114	114	4640
P2	32	114	114		3	3	2	2	32	57	57	0
FC1	32	57	57	1	-	128	-	-	1	128	-	13308032
FC2	1	128	-	1	-	128	-	-	1	2		258

With the parameters trained after the transfer learning process for the target task, the size of SoftMax layer should also be changed (see Table 3). For example, to make the model able to different joints and crack in natural stone, the size of SoftMax layer is set to be 3 for different prediction results, namely cracks, joints and no defects.

Table 3: Changes of SoftMax layer for different training goals

Training goals	Size of SoftMax layer
Detection of the concrete cracks	2
Detection of natural stone cracks	2
Differentiation between joints and cracks in natural stone	3

2.2 Datasets

The concrete cracks dataset (see Figure 4 (a)) contain a total of 40,000 images with 227×227 pixel resolutions (Zhang, 2016). The whole dataset is evenly divided into two groups as positive crack and negative crack images for classification. Data augmentation like random rotation or flipping is not used in this dataset. This dataset is divided into a training set with 39600 images and a test set with 2400 images.

The natural stone cracks dataset (see Figure 4 (b)) contain 150 small images with different Resolutions. The whole dataset is divided into a test set of 10 images and a train set of 140 images. In the training set, 70 images are labelled with crack and other 70 images are labelled with negative. Different types of cracks are contained in the dataset, such as hair crack and splitting.

The cracks and joints of natural stones dataset (see Figure 4 (c)) is made of natural stone contains 150 images with different pixel resolutions. All images related to natural stone cracks are cut from RGB images with a resolution of 2560×1920. The whole dataset is divided into a test set of 10 images and a train set of 140 images. The training set consists of 70 pictures with natural stone crack and 70 pictures with joints. In the test sets, 5 images are natural stone with cracks and others images are about joints.

(a) Concrete crack (b) Natural stone crack (c) Joints of nature stones

Figure 4: Examples of cracks and joints in datasets

2.3 Training Process and Results

An overview of training process can be seen from Figure 5: Step 1: Feed the images and labels into the network. Step 2: Iterate over each example in the training dataset within one step by grabbing its features and label. Step 3: Compare the prediction of inputs with the real label. Measure the SoftMax value of the prediction and use that to calculate the model's loss and gradients. Step 4: Update the model's variables with Adam optimizer. Step 5: Repeat for each epoch. The loss value ls calculated with $Loss = logS_j$. The SoftMax function can be described with $S_j = e^{a_j}/\sigma_{k=1}^{T} e^{a_k}$, where S_j is the SoftMax value of element j, a_j is the original value of the element, and T is the number of elements in the vector.

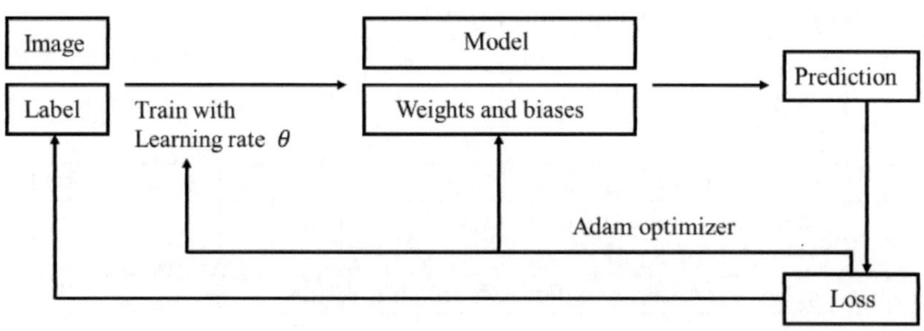

Figure 5: Training process overview

The Training process of the **concrete cracks detection model** took 3038 seconds. Figure 6 summarizes the loss and accuracy changes during training process of this model. As can be seen from Figure 6 (a), those lines in purple and orange show the fluctuation of training loss and testing loss separately. They both show sharp fluctuation before 10,800 training steps and trend to become steady after 11,100 training steps. Until 15,000 training steps, the accuracy of testing gets stable around 100%. Taking the model with 14,199 training steps for example, when the test loss is near to 0, the test accuracy is near to 1. We hence keep the model with 14,199 training steps for validation and the TF.

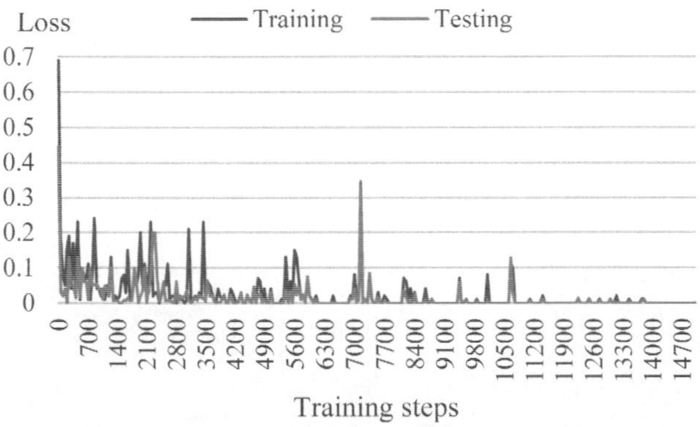

(a) Loss

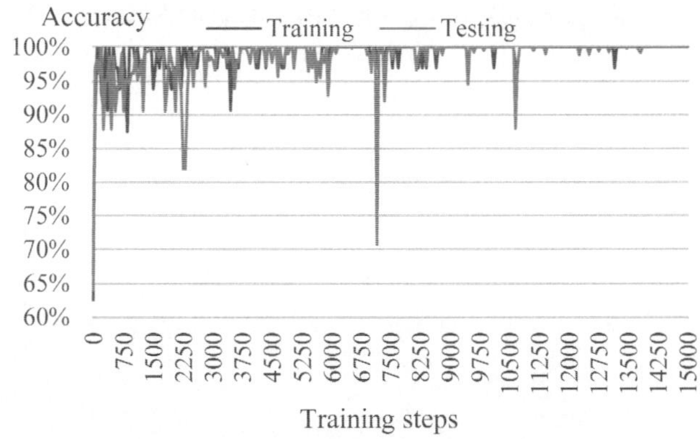

(b) Accuracy

Figure 6: Loss and accuracy changes of concrete crack detection model

As can be seen in Figure 7(a) for natural stone cracks detection model, the red line stands for the accuracy using the TF, and the light purple line stands for the accuracy without using the TF. After first 50 training steps, training accuracy of the TF is 87.5%, which is higher than the one without (53.12%). Additionally, it took 36 seconds for training with TF to get a training accuracy over 97%, while it took 62 seconds for the training without TF. Similarly for Cracks and joints detection model, Figure 7(b) shows that TF needs less time (28 seconds) compared to normal training (44 seconds) to get an accuracy over 97%.

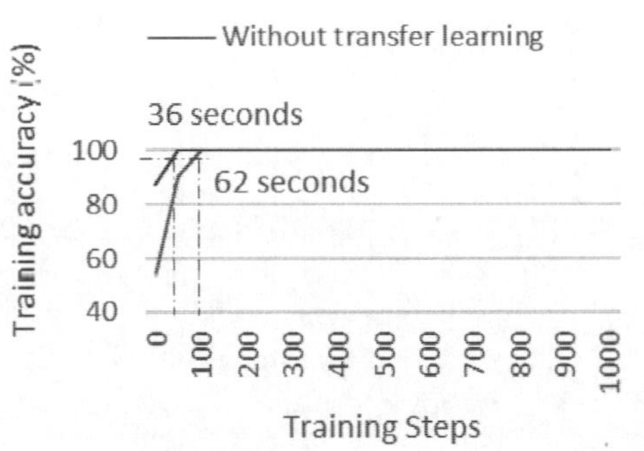

(a) Natural stone cracks detection model

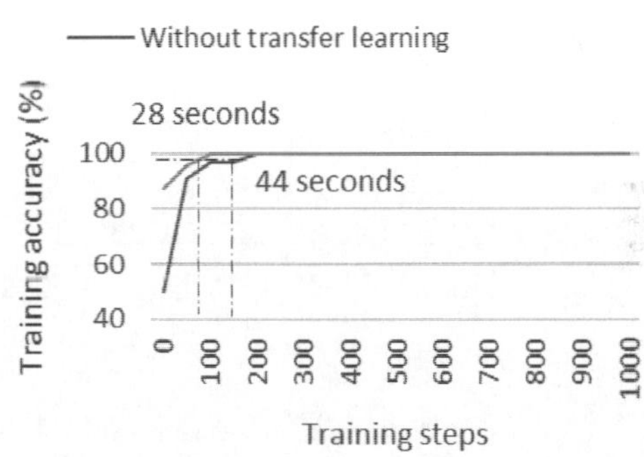

(b) Cracks and joints detection model

Figure 7: Comparison between training with and without the TF

The training process of **the natural stone cracks detection model** took 367 seconds. Figure 8 provides data regarding loss and accuracy changes while the model was training. Both training accuracies and testing accuracies keep steady after 150 train steps, where training accuracy is around 100 % and testing accuracy is around 90 %.

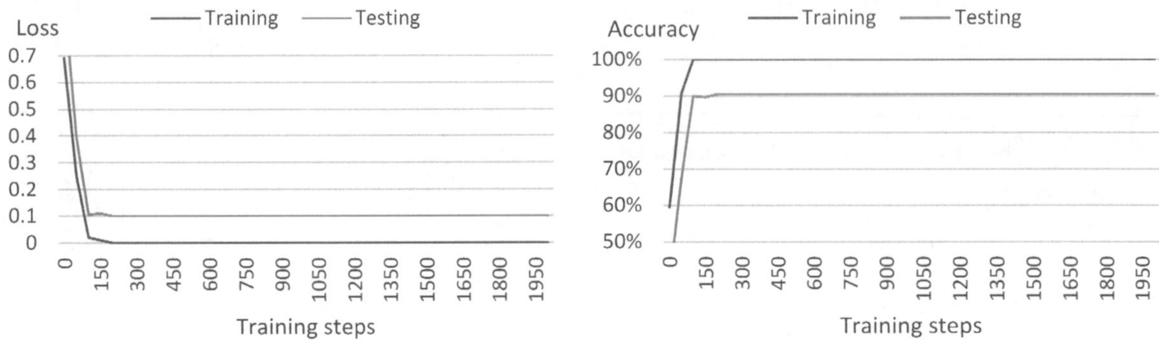

(a) Loss (b) Accuracy

Figure 8: Loss and accuracy changes of natural stone crack detection model

The training process of the **cracks and joints of natural stones detection model** took 84 seconds. As can be seen in Figure 9, training accuracy and testing accuracy increase to around 100 % and around 82 separately after 400 steps.

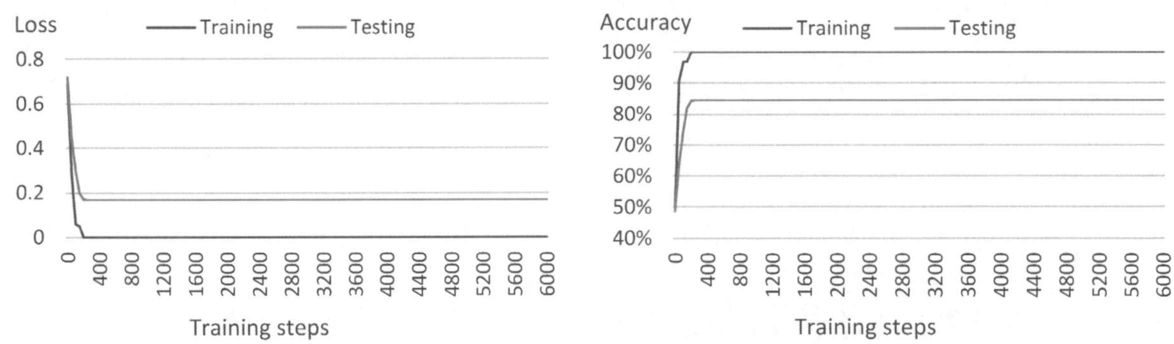

(a) Loss (b) Accuracy

Figure 9: Loss and accuracy changes of cracks and joints detection model

3. Results

After loading the **concrete cracks detection model** with 141999 training steps, Figure 10(a) and 10 (b) shows the prediction results of a concrete with 0.506732 probability of having no crack and with 1.000000 probability of having a crack separately. After loading the **natural stone cracks detection model** with 1999 training steps, Figure 10(c) and 10 (d) shows the prediction results of a natural stone with 0.999998 and 0.951548 probability to have a crack separately.

It should be pointed out that the probability value indicates the confidence degree of the computer on the prediction result. It is calculated with $probability = e^{-Loss}$.

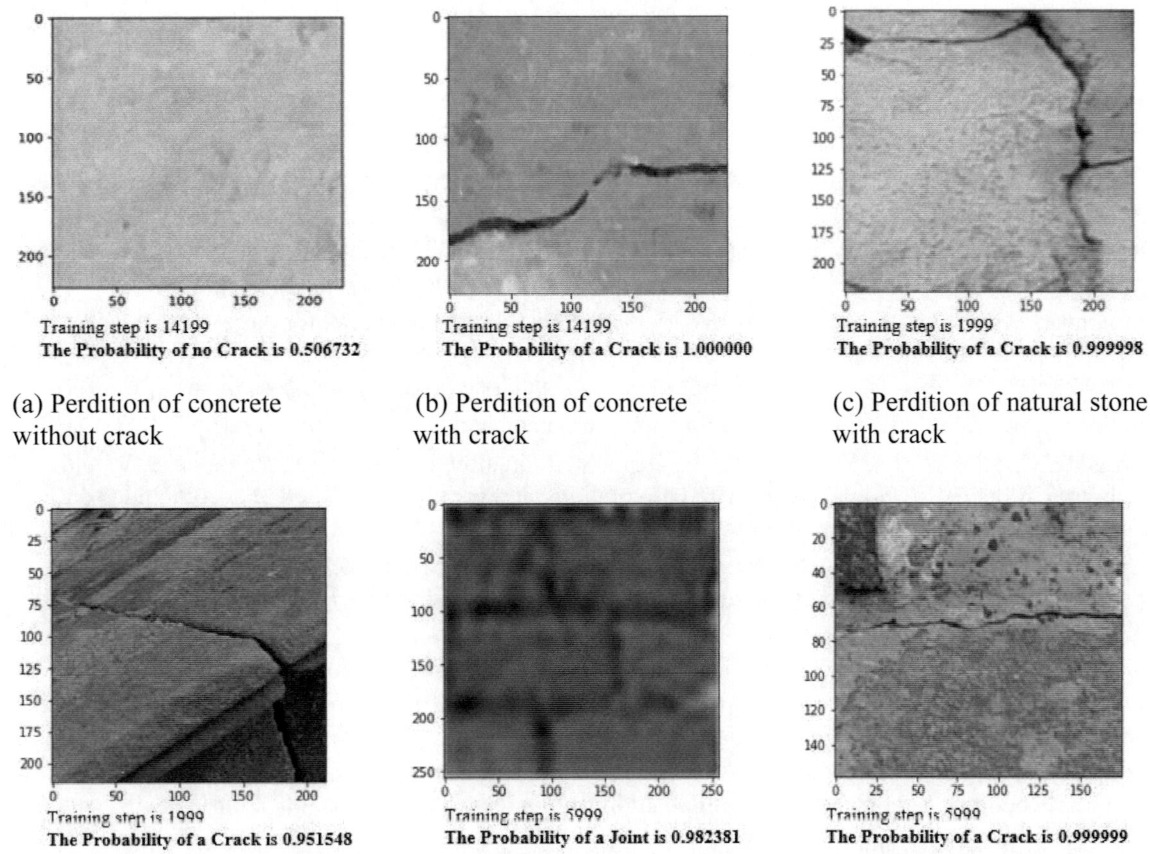

(a) Perdition of concrete without crack

(b) Perdition of concrete with crack

(c) Perdition of natural stone with crack

(d) Perdition of natural stone wit crack

(e) Perdition of natural stone with joint

(f) Perdition of natural stone with crack

Figure 10: Utilization of the models

4. Conclusion and Discussion

The whole study consists mainly of four parts. A lightweight CNN architecture is built. A CNN model is then trained so that it can detect whether there are concrete cracks in images. After that, the TF method is used in the training process to train a natural stone detection model with few training data. Consequently, the training steps and training time to get the comparable result are significantly reduced. Since there are not only cracks in a natural stone façade, a further advanced CNN, to promote the usage scenarios of this CNN in renovation works, is trained, so that the computer is able to distinguish, if there are cracks, joints, or nothing special in the input image.

From the comparative studies, which also used CNN to detect concrete cracks, this proposed light weighted CNN architecture shows a possibility to training models on laptops compared to the Cha (2017). Training time of all three models in this work are within one hour. Also, our results suggest that the main advantages of transfer learning are the potential of saving training time as well as solve the problem of insufficient training data (see Figure 7). As shown in results, our work is demonstrated as an effective tool for the industry use.

Although there are discoveries revealed by this study, there are also limitations. The size of data set with cracks is quite small, which makes the trained model not robust enough because not all the features from diverse cracks are including in the dataset. Thanks to the relative lightweight architecture of our model, we encourage future research to implement our model on mobile applications, such as smart phone, to make the renovation process more efficient and smoother.

References

LeCun, Y., Bottou, L., Bengio, Y. and Haffner, P., 1998. Gradient-based learning applied to document recognition. Proceedings of the IEEE, 86(11), pp.2278–2324.

Krizhevsky, A., Sutskever, I. and Hinton, G.E., 2012. Imagenet classification with deep convolutional neural networks. Advances in neural information processing systems, 25, pp.1097–1105.

Simonyan, K. and Zisserman, A., 2014. Very deep convolutional networks for large-scale image recognition. arXiv preprint arXiv:1409.1556.

He, K., Zhang, X., Ren, S. and Sun, J., 2016. Deep residual learning for image recognition. In Proceedings of the IEEE conference on computer vision and pattern recognition (pp.770–778).

Szegedy, C., Liu, W., Jia, Y., Sermanet, P., Reed, S., Anguelov, D., Erhan, D., Vanhoucke, V. and Rabinovich, A., 2015. Going deeper with convolutions. In Proceedings of the IEEE conference on computer vision and pattern recognition (pp.1–9).

Cha, Y.J., Choi, W. and Büyüköztürk, O., 2017. Deep learning-based crack damage detection using convolutional neural networks. Computer-Aided Civil and Infrastructure Engineering, 32(5), pp.361–378.

Kang, D. and Cha, Y., 2018. Autonomous UAVs for Structural Health Monitoring Using Deep Learning and an Ultrasonic Beacon System with Geo-Tagging. Computer-Aided Civil and Infrastructure Engineering, 33(10), pp.885–902.

Fukushima, K., 1980. Neocognitron: A self-organizing neural network model for a mechanism of pattern recognition unaffected by shift in position. Biological Cybernetics, 36(4), pp.193–202.

Glorot, X., Bordes, A. and Bengio, Y., 2011, June. Deep sparse rectifier neural networks. In Proceedings of the fourteenth international conference on artificial intelligence and statistics (pp.315–323). JMLR Workshop and Conference Proceedings.Russakovsky, O., Deng, J., Su, H., Krause, J., Satheesh, S., Ma, S., Huang, Z., Karpathy, A., Khosla, A., Bernstein, M., Berg, A. and Fei-Fei, L., 2015. ImageNet Large Scale Visual Recognition Challenge. International Journal of Computer Vision, 115(3), pp.211–252.

Zhang, L., Yang, F., Zhang, Y.D. and Zhu, Y.J., 2016, September. Road crack detection using deep convolutional neural network. In 2016 IEEE international conference on image processing (ICIP) (pp.3708–3712). IEEE.

Yosinski, J., Clune, J., Bengio, Y. and Lipson, H., 2014. How transferable are features in deep neural networks?. arXiv preprint arXiv:1411.1792.

Xiang, Y., Tang, T., Su, T., Brach, C., Liu, L., Mao, S. and Geimer, M., 2020. Fast crdnn: Towards on site training of mobile construction machines. arXiv preprint arXiv:2006.03169.

Xiang, Y., Wang, H., Su, T., Li, R., Brach, C., Mao, S.S. and Geimer, M., 2020. Kit moma: A mobile machines dataset. arXiv preprint arXiv:2007.04198.

ASHRAE, (2005). Handbook of Fundamentals. Atlanta: American Society of Heating, Refrigerating and Air Conditioning Engineers.

AbdelQader, I., Abudayyeh, O. and Kelly, M.E., 2003. Analysis of edge-detection techniques for crack identification in bridges. Journal of Computing in Civil Engineering, 17(4), pp.255–263.

Yeum, C.M. and Dyke, S.J., 2015. Vision-based automated crack detection for bridge inspection. Computer-Aided Civil and Infrastructure Engineering, 30(10), pp.759–770.

Zhou, B., Khosla, A., Lapedriza, A., Oliva, A. and Torralba, A., 2014. Object detectors emerge in deep scene cnns. arXiv preprint arXiv:1412.6856.

Szegedy, C., Vanhoucke, V., Ioffe, S., Shlens, J. and Wojna, Z., 2016. Rethinking the inception architecture for computer vision. In Proceedings of the IEEE conference on computer vision and pattern recognition (pp.2818–2826).

Smith, L.N., 2017, March. Cyclical learning rates for training neural networks. In 2017 IEEE winter conference on applications of computer vision (WACV) (pp.464–472). IEEE.

Khan, S., Rahmani, H., Shah, S.A.A. and Bennamoun, M., 2018. A guide to convolutional neural networks for computer vision. Synthesis Lectures on Computer Vision, 8(1), pp.1–207.

Kang, D. and Cha, Y.J., 2018. Autonomous UAVs for structural health monitoring using deep learning and an ultrasonic beacon system with geo-tagging. Computer-Aided Civil and Infrastructure Engineering, 33(10), pp.885–902.

Neto, N. and De Brito, J., 2011. Inspection and defect diagnosis system for natural stone cladding. Journal of Materials in Civil Engineering, 23(10), pp.1433–1443.

Cs.toronto.edu. 2021. CSC321 Winter 2018.

Satyen, R., 2019. [online] Available at: <https://github.com/satyenrajpal/Concrete-Crack-Detection> [Accessed 17 May 2020].

Katex NDT Equipment. 2021. UV Magnetic Yoke Flaw Detector - AJE-220 | Katex Ltd. [online] Available at: <https://www.katex.co.uk/product/aje-220-ac-uv-magnetic-yoke-flaw-detector/> [Accessed 19 May 2021].

eBay. 2021. Olympus Panametrics Omniscan MX 32 : 128 Ultraschall Phased Feld Pa Flaw | eBay. [online] Available at: <https://www.ebay.de/itm/393249231234?mkevt=1&mkcid=1&mkrid=707-53477-19255-0&campid=5338805019&toolid=20006&customid=1250078041622-g_Cj0KCQjw7pKFBhDUARIsAFUoMDZU_S37KnAtbmEdSh96x15OBk9A7oD-IPHHHrAL7bSiE2EOZeD-ycAaArPOEALw_wcB> [Accessed 19 May 2021].

An Integrated Computational GIS Platform for UAV-based Building Façade Inspection

Kaiwen Chen, Xin Xu, Georg Reichard, Abiola Akanmu
Georgia Institute of Technology, U.S.
kaiwen.chen@design.gatech.edu

Abstract. Nowadays periodic inspections of building façades are required to maintain a safe and well-performed built environment. An Unmanned Aerial Vehicle (UAV) equipped with a high-definition or infrared camera can help capture numerous multi-spectral images or videos for close-up inspection of building façades. However, there is a lack of management and application for UAV-captured imagery data, which brings difficulties in the localization, assessment, and documentation of detected anomalies. This paper thus proposes an integrated, computational GIS platform for UAV-based building façade inspections, embedded with two computational methods: 1) computer vision-based registration of UAV-images into a GIS model, and 2) deep learning-based façade anomaly detection. The proposed GIS platform for UAV-based façade inspection shows its advances in the management of multi-type data, contributing to the automated retrieval and analysis of UAV-images, and therefore allowing for the assessment and documentation of anomalies to support the decision-making of maintenance throughout a building's service lifecycle.

1. Introduction

Over 15,000 buildings in the U.S. are required by local municipal laws to take periodic inspections of their facades, mostly for safety reasons (Moghtadernejad 2013). However, the detection and assessment of building façade anomalies or defects (e.g., cracks, detachment, corrosion) is also valuable for monitoring the façade performance (e.g., thermal bridging, heat losses from failing insulation materials, moisture damage, or structural durability). In recent years, there has been a trend in employing professional imagery sensors in building facade inspections, such as High Definition (HD) cameras, infrared thermography (IRT) cameras, laser scanners (LS). Equipped on an Unmanned Aerial Vehicle (UAV) system, large amounts of facade photos with spectral and locational data can be collected and analyzed using computational imagery analysis techniques.

Previous studies have focused on the application of different imagery sensors (Remondino et al. 2011; Eschmann et al. 2012), the methods of during-flight data collection (Lagüela et al. 2015), the post-flight processing of the collected images (Yahyanejad and Rinner 2015; Bemis et al. 2014; Eltner et al. 2016), and imagery analytics for the defect detection (Mohan and Poobal 2017; Costa et al. 2014). However, the processing of UAV-images to reconstruct a 3D building model through photogrammetry techniques generates redundant model information and causes heavy loss of image data, which impedes the inspection purposes especially for the detection of micro-level façade anomalies such as cracks and corrosion (Chen et al. 2021). Additionally, for an in-depth image analysis, a reconstructed 3D building point cloud or mesh model generally lacks access to professional image analytical solutions. Therefore, it is important to manage these massive imagery data with a flexible computing environment to get access to the developed and abundant resources of professional image analytics methodologies.

This paper proposes a Geographic Information System (GIS)-based modeling solution for the management and analytics of multi-sourced and multi-type building façade inspection data, including imagery data, geographical and geometric data, and temporal data. GIS applications typically specialize in the storage management and analytical functions for spatial and raster data. It can provide a working platform for archiving and analyzing the massive imagery data, building model information, and other inspection information to support the inspection of building façade anomalies. In the following sections, this paper reviews UAV-based image processing studies in the building and geoscience fields to emphasize the motivation of applying GIS for UAV-based façade inspection management. This paper then develops an integrated and computational GIS platform with technical solutions and workflow for image transformation and advanced processing analytics. In the end, a real-world case is studied to demonstrate and validate the proposed GIS platform's advantages in management, analytics, and documentation of the multi-sourced data and inspection information to support the UAV-based façade inspection practices.

2. Integrated Computational GIS Platform for UAV-Based Façade Inspection

This paper proposed an integrated, computational GIS platform to integrate UAV-captured imagery data and spatial information of building model, empowered with a series of automation functions including computer vision-based image registration, machine learning-based image processing to support a computer-aided management and analysis platform for UAV-based building façade inspections. The GIS platform aims at serving for the detection, localization, assessment, and documentation of visible façade anomalies based on the UAV-captured closeup façade inspection images.

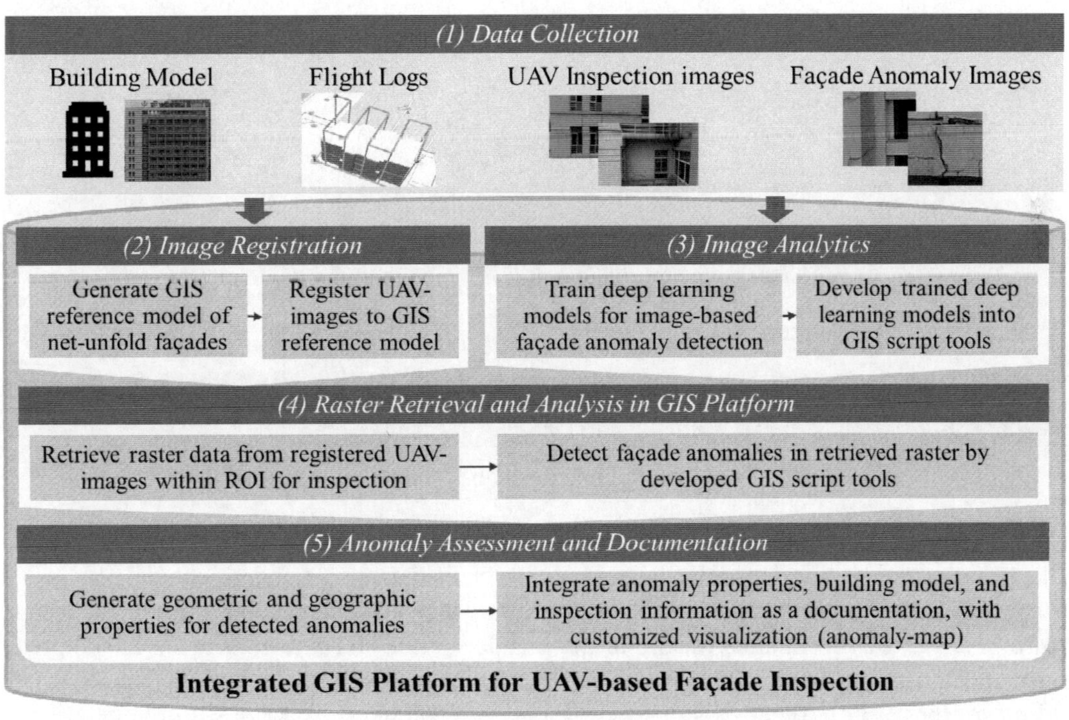

Figure 1: Workflow of UAV-based façade inspection in proposed GIS platform

Figure 1 presents an overview of the workflow of UAV-based façade inspection based on the proposed GIS platform. In the first step, images for façade inspection and building modeling are respectively collected by flying UAVs in different flight patterns. Then, the UAV-collected images are registered to a GIS spatial model where facades are net-unfolded along the building footprint. Meanwhile, in the third step, deep learning models are designed and trained with the preparation of training dataset for predicting façade anomalies. The trained models are further integrated into GIS script tools to provide a user-friendly interface for raster analytics. In the fourth step, the registered UAV-images from Step 2 are retrieved by selecting a region of interest (ROI) and are then processed by GIS scripting tools for façade anomaly detection. Lastly, the detected anomalies are assessed by measuring their geometric properties and extracting their geographic information. As such, an integrated documentation of building façade inspection information in a GIS system is achieved, which can provide a visualization of anomaly-maps to help the decision-making in the buildings' periodical and preventive maintenance work. One experimental case study was conducted to illustrate the overall process, detailed as follows.

3. Experimental Case Study

3.1 Data Collection

A real-world case is studied to present and validate the proposed workflow. The case study was performed at a 13-story classroom building in Jiangsu Vocational College, Yangzhou, China. This 13-story building was built in 2005. It is 56 m high above the ground with an area of 1154.5 m2. Figure 2 (a) presents the 2D building footprint in open map; Figure 2 (b) shows the 3D wireframe building model.

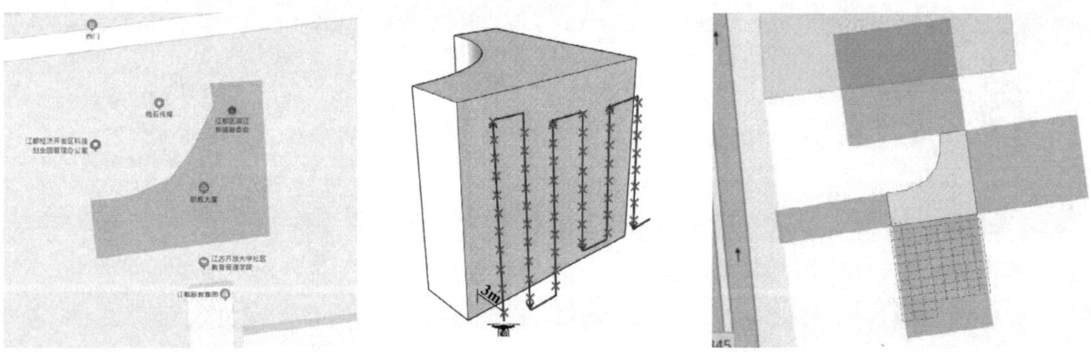

(a) building footprint **(b) drone flight path** **(c) image capturing grid in NU facades**

Figure 2: Overview of building model and flight information

A DJI Inspire drone was deployed to collect images for close-up visual inspection of the southern façade. Table 1 presents the technical specifications of the selected UAV system. Flying in a vertical strip path as shown in Figure 2 0(b), the camera-equipped UAV system capture 63 5472×3078p images for the target façade within 10 minutes. Figure 2 0(c) presents the image capturing grid for the target façade which were net-unfolded along the edge of 2D building footprint. The lower two or three floors were blocked by fences and vegetation, and thus were omitted during this inspection activity.

Table 1: Technical specifications of DJI Inspire

	Take-off weight	3060g
	GPS hovering accuracy	Vertical: ±0.5m
		Horizontal: ±1.5m
	Camera model	FC6510
	Camera sensor	1/2.3" CMOS
	35mm focal length	24mm f/4.5
	Image size	5472×3078p
	Video recording	Frame size: 3840×2160p
		Frame rate: 29.97 frames/second

3.2 Registration of UAV-images to GIS-based Façade Model

This section presents the registration of the UAV-collected image data into a GIS building footprint with façade surfaces net-unfolded along this footprint. The readers are referred to the authors' previous work for the detailed registration process (Chen et al. 2021). For illustration purpose, Figure 3 summarizes the image registration process into the following four steps:

1) Create GIS polygons that represent the building façade's geometric shapes and net-unfold them along the building's roofline projecting the roof area to its footprint, which in turn becomes the flatted base façade model.
2) Geo-reference the whole view façade images to the GIS polygons to serve as references or base maps for the geo-registration of UAV-collected images.
3) Detect imagery feature keypoint matches between UAV-images and corresponding reference images through CV-based feature detectors (i.e., SIFT) and matching algorithms (i.e., KNN, RANSAC). Note that the reference images are obtained through narrowing the scope of the whole view façade images to the camera view of each UAV-image based on camera positions.
4) Geo-register each UAV-image to the corresponding reference image via projection transformation computed from the keypoint matches and their geo coordinate information.

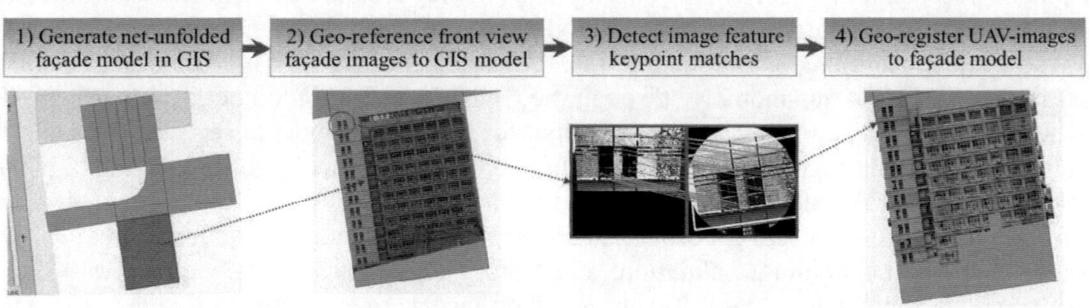

Figure 3: Process of automated registration of UAV-images to GIS façade model

Following this process, the 63 UAV-collected high-resolution images were registered to the 2D net-unfolded façade model in GIS. Through this workflow, pixels in the UAV-captured images were assigned with geocoordinates within the net-unfolded façade model, and therefore can be stored as multi-spectral raster data embedded with spatial information.

3.3 Image-Based Façade Anomaly Detection

1) Deep Learning Model for Façade Crack Detection

To proceed with a detailed analysis of the UAV-captured images that were previously registered in the GIS model, this paper explored deep learning solutions to develop robust and reusable image analytics tools for façade anomaly segmentation. Specifically, the authors previously studied two-step neural networks (Figure 4) to segment façade cracks among complicated background noises. The two-step method has the robustness to handle diverse façade background noises (e.g., windows, columns, seamlines, joints, pipes, mechanical devices). Attributed to this merit, this paper also designed a two-step method, which is combined with a patch-level classification model (CNN) and pixel-level segmentation model (UNet) for façade crack detection. The training, validation, and testing details of the CNN and UNet models are presented as follows.

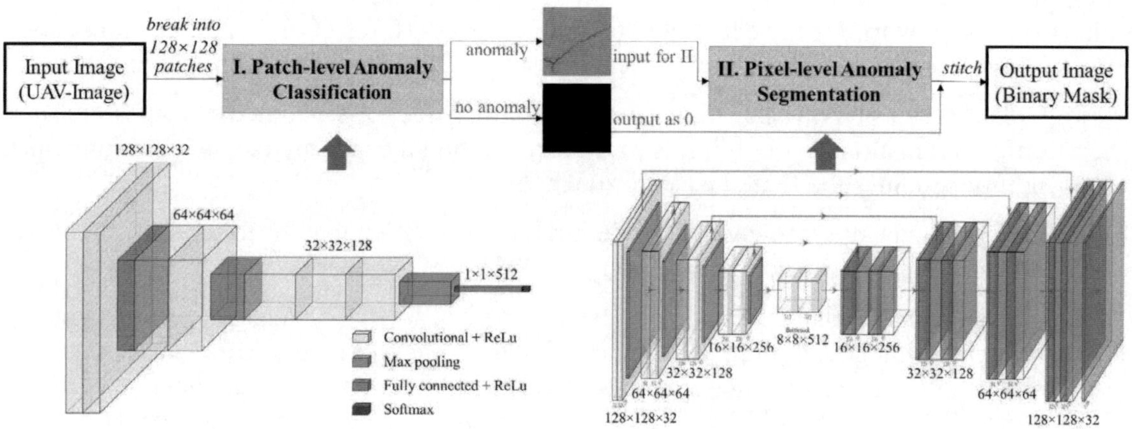

Figure 4: Two-step neural networks for image-based façade anomaly predictions

During the prediction process, an input raster from the previously registered UAV-image is firstly divided into patches in a fixed size of 128×128 pixels to match the size of input data for the trained deep learning models. Then, the divided patches need to be transformed into encoded data following the data processing used in model training, such as normalization and standard deviation adjustment transformation. The transformed patches are then predicted as a specified class of "anomaly" or "no anomaly" through the CNN classification model. Among them, the patches predicted as "anomaly" become the input for the U-Net model to segment the anomaly pixels. In the end, the segmentation of anomaly pixels for each patch are stitched into a binary mask as the output of prediction results. The researchers have collected large amounts of façade inspection images and prepare classification and segmentation labels for crack anomalies. The split of data for the training, validation, and testing of the two neural network models is summarized as Table 2 and sample images and their labels are presented in Figure 5.

Table 2: Statistics for CNN and UNet model training/validation/test datasets

	Datasets	Crack	Non-Crack	Total	Image Size
Patch-level CNN Classification Model	Train	4,310	21,867	26,177	128×128
	Validation	461	2,448	2,909	128×128
	Test	547	2,685	3,232	128×128
Pixel-level UNet Segmentation Model	Train	2,045,605	44,976,475	47,022,080	128×128
	Validation	583,009	12,851,871	13,434,880	128×128
	Test	188,062	4,039,010	4,227,072	128×128

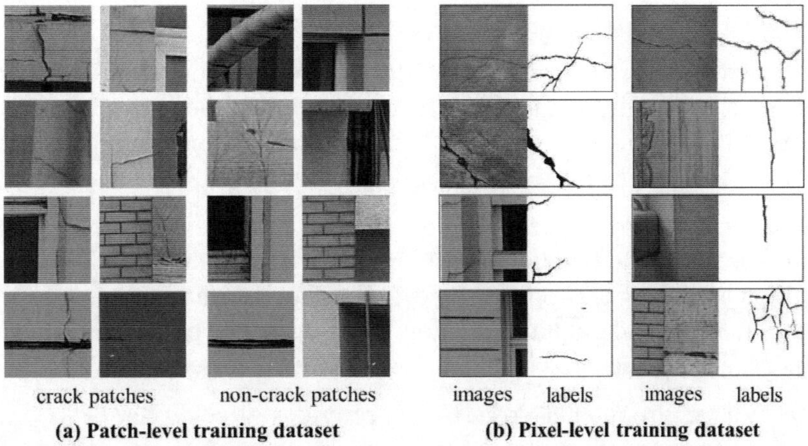

Figure 5: Sample images for patch-level classification and pixel-level segmentation training data

Three metrics were used to evaluate the training and validation process: loss, IoU, and accuracy. The loss value of the neural networks is measured by the commonly used cross-entropy loss function; the accuracy is the ratio of correct predictions. IoU (Intersection over Union), also known as the Jaccard index, is a common and effective evaluation metric used for image semantic segmentation tasks. The IoU is the ratio of the intersection area of the predicted crack pixels and ground truth crack pixels to their union area. The IoU metric can effectively measure the performance of the segmentation of the crack pixels, given that the crack pixels only account for around 3~5% of an entire image. Figure 6 shows the change of loss, IoU, and accuracy values throughout the training and evaluation process, which indicates a good convergence of both neural networks. In the end, the trained CNN model reached an accuracy of 94% and the U-Net model reached an IoU of about 0.65 for both the training and validation dataset.

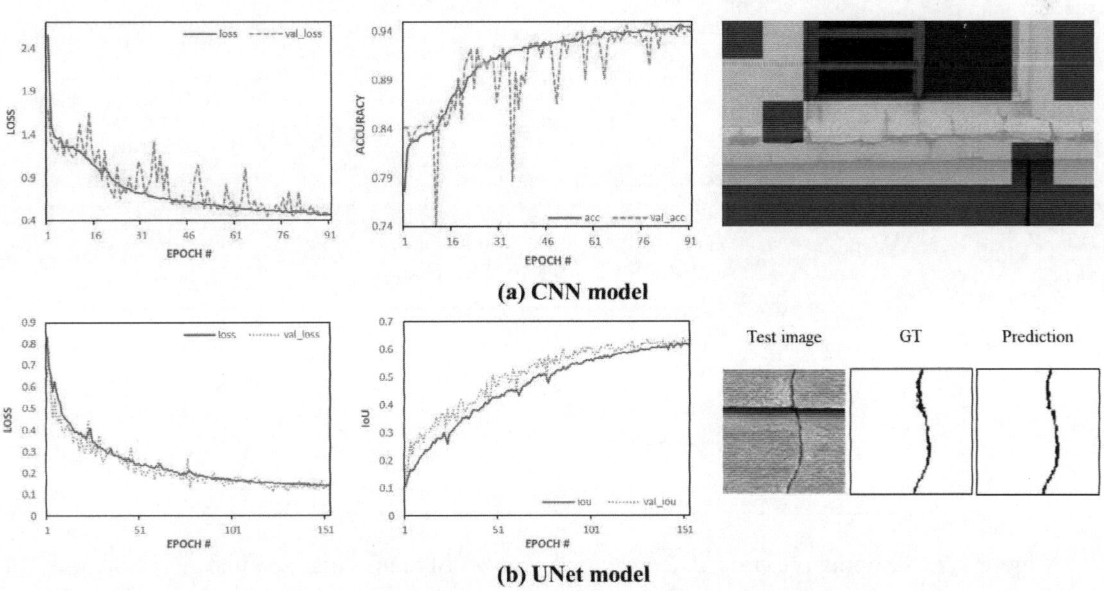

Figure 6: Loss and accuracy/IoU of the train and validation set, with test data prediction examples

2) *GIS Scripting Tools for Façade Crack Segmentation*

The trained models were then developed into GIS tools via python scripts in GIS. The input of the processing tool is geo-registered imagery raster data, while the output is a GIS raster, where each cell represents the prediction value of 1 ("crack") or 0 ("non-crack"). The cells predicted as "crack" class can then be visualized and highlighted in the GIS model.

This paper selected ArcGIS Pro as the working platform to develop user-friendly geoprocessing tools. ArcGIS Pro provides the functionality of creating scripting tools in a custom toolbox and running the python script as a geoprocessing tool. The interface of the geoprocessing tool requests the input imagery and output prediction raster data. The python script using the trained models to segment façade crack pixels is embedded within the geoprocessing tool.

To work with python environments, ArcGIS Pro provides direct accesses to Conda, an open-source package management system and environmental system (Kadiyala and Kumar 2017). Specifically, the execution of a python script for deep learning-based predictions requires the installation and utilization of python packages such as OpenCV, TensorFlow, and ArcPy. Among them, OpenCV is an open source library for the computer vision-based analytics and processing of image data or video data (Culjak et al. 2012); TensorFlow is used for the operation and implementation of machine learning algorithms (Abadi et al. 2016); ArcPy provides functions to call and run ArcGIS tools in python scripts (Tateosian and Tateosian 2015). The integration of these packages in the GIS compiling environment allows for the generation of a user-friendly GIS geoprocessing tool to execute image-based façade inspections via the previously trained deep learning models of anomaly detection.

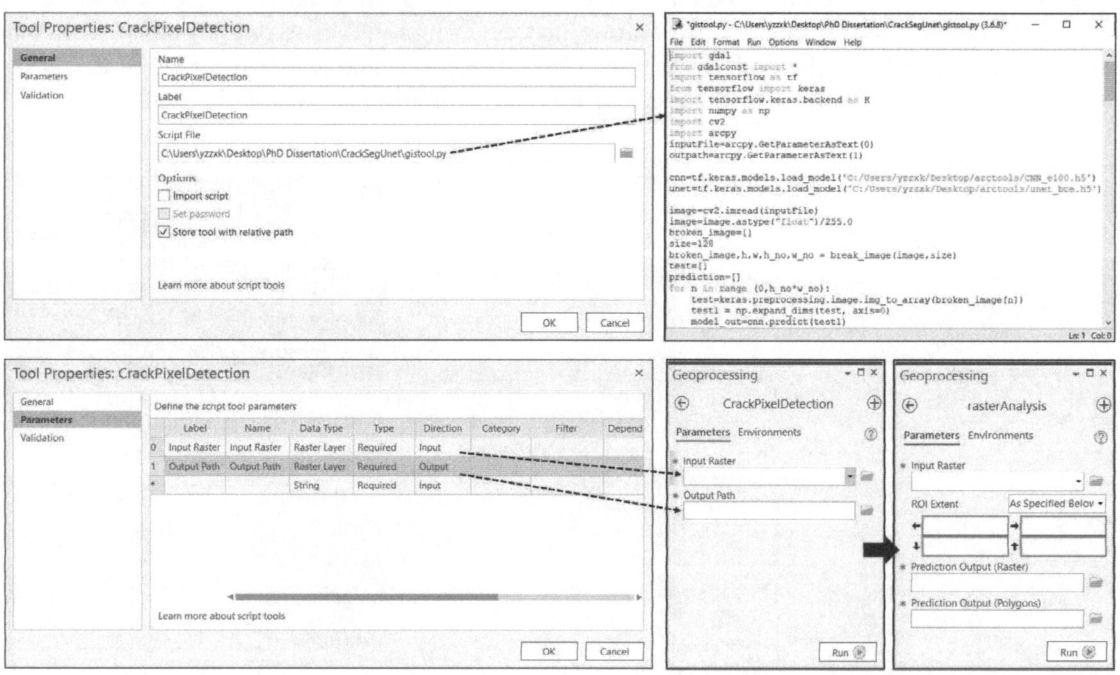

Figure 7: Developing pre-trained deep learning model of crack detection into ArcGIS tools

As shown in Figure 7, the upper-right python script, which used the pre-trained CNN and U-Net deep learning models to detect crack pixels within a raster image, was imported as the script file for the customized geoprocessing tool named "CrackPixelDetection". Then, the paths for input file and output file were set as interactive parameters that would require users' operations.

Furthermore, the "CrackPixelDetection" geoprocessing tool could be integrated into a comprehensive workflow to generate a geoprocessing tool called "rasterAnalysis", enabling the crop of imagery raster within an area of interest for deep learning-based imagery analysis. As shown in the two dialog boxes in the bottom-right corner of Figure 7, the "CrackPixelDetection" tool requires users to select an interested raster for processing as well as define a path to save the predicted output; while the "rasterAnalysis" tool also requires specifying the ROI extent and defining the paths to save the prediction results in raster and polygon format. The developed "rasterAnalysis" geoprocessing tool brings many benefits including: automating the retrieval and analysis of the specified imagery data of interest; providing a user-friendly interface that allows effective human operation and control of machine without the necessity for understanding long and complicated source codes; displaying customized visualization of the prediction results; and the generation of prediction raster dataset to support the documentation in the following steps.

3.4 Imagery Raster Data Retrieval for Façade Anomaly Detection

With the integration of the previously developed GIS tools for façade crack segmentation, the UAV-imagery data registered in GIS façade model could be automatically retrieved and analyzed for anomaly detection. Following the workflow in Figure 5, the ROI of target imagery raster data were firstly specified simply by zooming and moving the current display to the appropriate extent. The input raster was then clipped into the ROI extent for analysis using the trained deep learning models. The prediction results through deep learning were then exported as raster and polygon outputs, which were respectively stored in the specified saving paths.

Figure 8: Execution of developed GIS tools for the detection of crack pixels using trained models

As an example shown in Figure 8, the raster "mosaic_all.tif" became the input raster file for the developed GIS script tool of "rasterAnalysis"; the ROI extent were defined by zooming to the interested region and selecting "Current Display Extent"; the output paths were defined by users to save the prediction results respectively in raster and polygon data format. The predicted cracks pixels were represented by raster cells valued as 1 ("crack") and were visualized and highlighted as red color. It can be observed that most cracks were successfully detected and segmented through the developed geoprocessing tools, which reflects the superior reusability and robustness of the developed deep learning tool.

3.5 Assessment and Documentation of Detected Façade Cracks

The properties of cracks (e.g., areas, lengths, widths) can be computed by calculating geometry attributes for vectors. Through the developed "rasterAnalysis" geoprocessing tool, the predicted crack pixels were converted into polygons in the final step. The geometry attributes of each crack polygon such as areas and perimeters were calculated by GIS tools; the length of each crack were measured by generating centerlines for each polygon; and their average width of each crack can be estimated based on calculated area and perimeter as Equation 1.

Table 3 presents the areas, length, mean width of each crack within the previously retrieved raster with ROI extent. Their geolocational information is represented by the longitude and latitude of the centroid of each polygon. It can be summarized that the crack lengths fluctuate between 0.09m to 1.71m; their mean widths range between 4mm to 8mm; and their coverage area are in the range between 6cm² to 40cm². Inspectors could rank these detected cracks based on their lengths, widths, and coverage areas, which helps them make decisions including if a further inspection or repair action should be executed timely.

$$Mean\ Width = (Perimeter - Sqrt(Perimeter^2 - 16 \times Area))/4 \quad (1)$$

Table 3: Attribute table for predicted cracks using developed GIS deep learning tools

FID	Anomaly Type	Length (m)	Perimeter (m)	Area (m^2)	Mean_Width (m)	Centroid_Lon	Centroid_Lat
1	crack	0.53	1.057549	0.00404	0.007748	13312929.98	3814289.758
2	crack	1.71	3.427110	0.01080	0.006325	13312928.87	3814289.655
3	crack	0.52	1.041498	0.00281	0.005455	13312927.58	3814289.515
4	crack	0.49	0.977577	0.00213	0.004391	13312928.07	3814289.558
5	crack	0.18	0.364745	0.00094	0.005323	13312931.14	3814289.27
6	crack	0.09	0.187699	0.00062	0.007184	13312928.83	3814289.224
7	crack	1.33	2.659434	0.00738	0.005572	13312928.69	3814288.99

4. Conclusion

This paper put forward an innovative GIS-based management system to support UAV-based building façade inspections. The proposed GIS working platform improves the management and documentation of the multi-sourced large amounts of data collected by UAVs, with the integration of the spatial information of building and façades. Moreover, GIS can provide user-friendly tools and interfaces for developing python scripts, which allows access to open-source processing tools and developed algorithms for image analysis. In this paper, we integrated trained deep learning models (i.e., CNN and UNet) into GIS scripting tools to support image-based façade crack segmentation, which demonstrated potentials of developing professional GIS image processing tools for the detection of various façade defects through diverse deep learning models. The newly developed GIS tools, together with fundamental GIS geoprocessing tools, can facilitate the automated detection of façade anomalies and comprehensive analysis of their properties based on UAV-captured images. Additionally, the implementation of a geodatabase proves its ability to store and manage various types of datasets including building facades, imagery sets, and tabular files. The interrelated and integrated datasets in the geodatabase can provide sorting and retrieval functions to search interested textual, spectral, spatial, and time-series data to achieve a thorough analysis and track of façade anomalies.

The practical application of the proposed GIS-based management system can revolutionize and automate the process of UAV-based façade inspection. It demonstrates a reduction of information loss and improves the integration of multi-sourced data. With the storage, analysis, and display capabilities and specialties of GIS systems, the multi-types of façade inspection data become more accessible, processible, and can be readily visualized. It supports the effective identification and quantification of façade anomalies for better understanding of overall façade conditions. Moreover, for UAV-based periodic façade inspections during a building's service lifecycle, the GIS-based management system enables the documentation of temporal information, which allows spatiotemporal queries and analyses of UAV-images to track or estimate trends of façade anomalies. It also provides opportunities of prioritizing inspection and maintenance programs for specific building groups with the consideration of regional weather effects.

Future work will study how to manage the commonly captured infrared images and integrate them with high-resolution images to support the detection of moisture issues and the evaluation of building façade performance. Also, more UAV-images for larger building groups throughout multiple inspection cycles could be collected and managed in the GIS-based management system to support the decision-making of early-interventions and maintenance prioritization. Furthermore, additional algorithms and GIS tools will need to be developed for the image-based detection of various other types of façade anomalies as well as time-sequence trend analysis of the detected anomalies, to further improve and support an overall risk evaluation and maintenance decision-making for building façades.

References

Abadi, M., Agarwal, A., Barham, P., Brevdo, E., Chen, Z., Citro, C., Corrado, G. S., Davis, A., Dean, J., Devin, M., Ghemawat, S., Goodfellow, I., Harp, A., Irving, G., Isard, M., Jia, Y., Jozefowicz, R., Kaiser, L., Kudlur, M., Levenberg, J., Mane, D., Monga, R., Moore, S., Murray, D., Olah, C., Schuster, M., Shlens, J., Steiner, B., Sutskever, I., Talwar, K., Tucker, P., Vanhoucke, V., Vasudevan, V., Viegas, F., Vinyals, O., Warden, P., Wattenberg, M., Wicke, M., Yu, Y., and Zheng, X. (2016). "TensorFlow: Large-Scale Machine Learning on Heterogeneous Distributed Systems." https://arxiv.org/abs/1603.04467, accessed May 2021.

Bemis, S. P., Micklethwaite, S., Turner, D., James, M. R., Akciz, S., Thiele, S. T., and Bangash, H. A. (2014). "Ground-based and UAV-Based photogrammetry: A multi-scale, high-resolution mapping tool for structural geology and paleoseismology." Journal of Structural Geology, 69, 163–178.

Chen, K., Reichard, G., Akanmu, A., and Xu, X. (2021). "Geo-registering UAV-captured close-range images to GIS-based spatial model for building façade inspections." Automation in Construction, 122, 103503.

Culjak, I., Abram, D., Pribanic, T., Dzapo, H., and Cifrek, M. (2012). "A brief introduction to OpenCV." MIPRO 2012 - 35th International Convention on Information and Communication Technology, Electronics and Microelectronics - Proceedings, 2012 Proceedings of the 35th International Convention MIPRO, IEEE, 1725–1730.

Eltner, A., Kaiser, A., Castillo, C., Rock, G., Neugirg, F., and Abellán, A. (2016). "Image-based surface reconstruction in geomorphometry - merits, limits and developments." Earth Surface Dynamics, 4(2), 359–389.

Kadiyala, A., and Kumar, A. (2017). "Applications of Python to evaluate environmental data science problems." Environmental Progress and Sustainable Energy, John Wiley and Sons Inc.

Lagüela, S., Díaz−Vilariño, L., Roca, D., and Lorenzo, H. (2015). "Aerial thermography from low-cost UAV for the generation of thermographic digital terrain models." Opto-Electronics Review, 23(1), 78–84.

Moghtadernejad, S. (2013). "Design, inspection, maintenance, life cycle performance and integrity of building facades." McGill University, Montreal, Quebec, Canada.

Mohan, A., and Poobal, S. (2017). "Crack detection using image processing: A critical review and analysis." Alexandria Engineering Journal.

Remondino, F., Barazzetti, L., Nex, F., Scaioni, M., and Sarazzi, D. (2011). "UAV photogrammetry for mapping and 3d modeling–current status and future perspectives." International Archives of the Photogrammetry, Remote Sensing and Spatial Information Sciences, 38(1), C22.

Tateosian, L., and Tateosian, L. (2015). "Calling Tools with Arcpy." Python For ArcGIS, Springer International Publishing, 95–117.

Yahyanejad, S., and Rinner, B. (2015). "A fast and mobile system for registration of low-altitude visual and thermal aerial images using multiple small-scale UAVs." ISPRS Journal of Photogrammetry and Remote Sensing, 104, 189–202.

A Computer Vision Approach for Building Facade Component Segmentation on 3D Point Cloud Models Reconstructed by Aerial Images

Yu Hou M.Sc.[a*], Zoe Mayer M.Sc.[b], Zhaoyang Li[a], Dr. Rebekka Volk[b], Dr. Lucio Soibelman[a]
[a] University of Southern California, USA, [b] Karlsruhe Institute of Technology, Germany
yuhou@usc.edu

Abstract. Segmenting windows and doors on 3D point cloud models allows for heat loss audits around these areas. Researchers have collected aerial images to reconstruct 3D models for large districts, but easily accessible training datasets with data acquired on ground level cannot be directly used for segmentation on 3D models reconstructed by aerial images. Additionally, building a new dataset is a time-consuming and labour-intensive process. Therefore, we propose a segmentation approach that uses open source training datasets to segment windows and doors on façade images rendered from 3D point clouds. The results show that our approach can make full use of open source datasets to segment windows and doors, and that such trained segmentation models performs differently for different building styles. In addition, different algorithms result in various degrees of accuracy and segmentation on windows performs better than on doors.

1. Introduction

Thermography, a non-destructive inspection technology, is used for heat loss energy audits. However, the most common current data collection approaches only allow individual building energy audit by deploying handheld infrared thermography cameras to collect thermal information from building facades. The biggest downside of current data collection approaches is efficiency. Such approaches also do not consider groups of buildings in large district areas in which interconnected buildings impact each other's thermal behaviors, especially, those connected within the same district heating network. More precisely speaking, if one building that is located in the middle of a heating network has unfixed heat loss issues, it will force buildings located downstream in the network to draw more heat to keep warm, resulting in more energy wasted through the middle-network buildings. Thus, there is a need to investigate novel methods and frameworks for building heat energy audits for large districts. Driven by the need of efficient and thorough energy audits for large districts, researchers have been deploying unmanned aircraft systems (UASs) to improve the data collection process (Hou *et al.*, 2019).

The benefits of using UASs to collect both thermal (infrared spectrum) and RGB (red-green-blue visible light) images include the higher data collection speed and availability of a bird's eye view, which can improve collection efficiency and comprehensively explore high areas of building façades that handheld thermal cameras cannot reach. Thermal and RGB imagery data collected from UASs allow the reconstruction of 3D point cloud models using photogrammetry technology. In order to obtain the 3D point cloud models that can integrate both thermal and RGB information, researchers have deployed different data fusion approaches (Hou *et al.*, 2021; Shahandashti *et al.*, 2010).

Distinguishing windows and other heat loss related building façade elements is an important step for energy audits. Semantic segmentation using 3D point cloud building models fused with thermal information allows researchers to detect heat loss from window and door edges and to monitor thermal bridges and areas of moisture on walls. The first step is to distinguish these façade components. However, in available open source image databases, facade images with their labeled components (the ground truth information) that were taken from the ground cannot be directly used to train a model to segment façade elements either in drone-based aerial images or in point cloud models reconstructed by these aerial images. To manually label newly captured aerial images and then build a new dataset is a potential option. However, conducting ground truth coding on these aerial images is both time-consuming and labor-intensive. Therefore, studies on the use of open source databases obtained from the ground to train artificial neural network (ANN) models for façade components segmentation using aerial images can provide an alternative that does not require the building of a new database.

To reduce labeling time and maintain the benefits of using UAS-based data collection, we propose a framework to train segmentation models using open source terrestrial image datasets taken from the ground to predict semantic information on building façades. In this paper, we introduce the results of our approach that was tested on two different datasets from Karlsruhe, Germany, one from a university campus, and the other from a central business district (Mayer *et al.*, 2021). The research introduced in this paper was designed to answer the following questions: (1) How does the proposed approach perform on different testing datasets with different building styles? and (2) How does the segmentation accuracy vary for different building components? This paper is organized as follows. We introduce and detail our approach in Section 2. Experiment results are described in Section 3, followed by evaluation and discussion in Section 4. Finally, we present our conclusions in Section 5.

2. Methodology

The proposed approach consists of the following four steps: (1) reconstructing a 3D point cloud model with aerial imagery data, (2) rendering 2D images from the 3D model, (3) training a semantic segmentation ANN model with open source datasets, and (4) predicting segmentation results on the rendered 2D images. We also designed the evaluation and validation metrics for the proposed approach.

Note that with the exception of the 3D models that were reconstructed by ContextCapture, a commercial photogrammetry software kit (Shi and Ergan, 2020; Chen *et al.*, 2020), most of the algorithms used in this study (e.g. Thermal-RGB data fusion, ANN model training, image rendering) were implemented using Python. The involved implementing libraries include Open3D (Zhou et al., 2018), OpenCV (Bradski, 2000), scikit-learn (Pedregosa *et al.*, 2019), and PyRender (Matl, Mahler and Goldberg, 2017).

2.1 Photogrammetry and 3D Point Cloud Model Reconstruction

There are many approaches to detecting defects in building envelops, such as fan pressurization (blower door test), ultrasound (tone test), and thermography. Thermography, as a non-destructive technique, is considered the most useful method because it can detect thermal values in envelops allowing for heat loss and moisture detection. However, current thermography methods mostly focus on handheld data collection (Dino *et al.*, 2020; Yang, Su and Lin, 2018), which is not recommended for an energy audit for a group of buildings in a large district. As such, researchers have mounted thermal and RGB cameras on UASs for more efficient large district data collection.

As shown in Figure 1, the data acquisition system used in this study included the drone (DJI M600), camera (FLIR Duo Pro R), control modules, and other equipment. The DJI M600 is a state-of-the-art aerial platform designed for industrial data collection. The FLIR Duo Pro R camera has both photographic and thermal lenses integrated into a single package that enables simultaneous RGB and thermal image data collection. Additionally, the control system allows to remotely operate the drones and the FLIR camera to collect data with the desired flight altitude and camera angles.

(1) Gimbal - Connection to DJI M600; (2) Gimbal - Frame for Camera; (3) FLIR DUO Pro R – Visible Lens Barrel; (4) FLIR DUO Pro R – IR Lens Barrel; (5) FLIR DUO Pro R – Electric Wires; (6) FLIR DUO Pro R – Integration Cable; (7) FLIR DUO Pro R – GPS Antenna Cable; (8) FLIR DUO Pro R – USB Cable.

Figure 1: Cameras Setup for the Unmanned Aircraft System

After both RGB and thermal images with designed image overlapping rates were collected with the drone, images were used to reconstruct 3D point cloud models over the survey areas using the photogrammetry technique. We collected over 10,000 images for both campus and city areas. There were over 12 buildings included for these two areas. Photogrammetry is the technology for 3D modeling of physical objects such as buildings, infrastructures, and their environment through the process of measuring and interpreting overlapped images. There are many well-established photogrammetry commercial software tools. We chose to use ContextCapture since this software provides an application programming interface (API) that support further extended developments, such as extracting parameters of image-orientation estimations to indicate the relative relationships between images and reconstructed 3D models (Fischer, Dosovitskiy and Brox, 2015; Verykokou *et al.*, 2018).

Photogrammetric modeling reconstructed by aerial images can support the investigation of groups of buildings in large districts. As shown in Figure 2 (a), a 3D point cloud model of some residential buildings was reconstructed by a series of aerial RGB images. To audit the heat-related defects of these residential buildings, researchers can also reconstruct a 3D thermal model. Many current approaches directly use thermal images to build thermal-mapping models. We choose to use high-resolution RGB images to reconstruct a 3D RGB model and then project corresponding thermal information onto the RGB model to create a thermal point cloud model (Hou *et al.*, 2021), as the FLIR camera can simultaneously take thermal and RGB images from the same angle and at the same altitude. Additionally, image-orientation estimations provided by ContextCapture support the data fusion process. Figure 2 (b) represents a 3D thermal model of a group of residential buildings created based on the RGB model in Figure 2 (a). In Figure 2 (b), the dark purple color represents a lower thermal value and a lighter yellow color represents a higher value. Another example is a group of 3D models on a campus shown in Figure 2 (c) and (d).

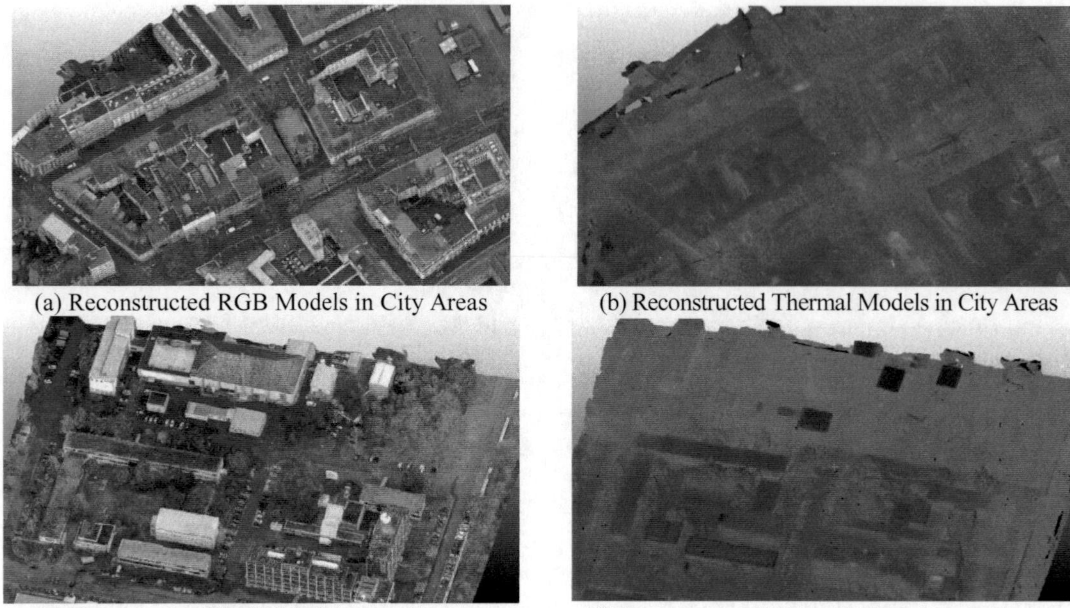

(a) Reconstructed RGB Models in City Areas
(b) Reconstructed Thermal Models in City Areas
(c) Reconstructed RGB Models on a Campus
(d) Reconstructed Thermal Models on a Campus

Figure 2: 3D point clouds reconstructed by overlapped images

2.2 Rendering 2D Images from a Reconstructed 3D model

After the development of the 3D point cloud model as described in Section 2.1, the next step focus on how to use the model to audit heat loss. At this step it is important to recognize/classify door and windows elements in the model because those are the most relevant elements when auditing building façade heat loss. Therefore, in this step, we developed a process to render 2D images from the reconstructed 3D models.

We created a virtual camera in the 3D model, which was essential for rendering images that we needed to investigate. In our study, we used the perspective projection, and the default camera position was at the origin and facing the negative Z-axis. To move the camera from its origin position to a position from which the façade image can be rendered, we defined a 4x4 matrix that contains rotation and transformation information, as shown in Eq. (1).

$$\begin{bmatrix} Right_x & Right_y & Right_z & 0 \\ Up_x & Up_y & Up_z & 0 \\ Forward_x & Forward_y & Forward_z & 0 \\ T_x & T_y & T_z & 1 \end{bmatrix} \qquad \text{Eq. (1)}$$

First, we defined the $Forward$ vector. To set a camera position, the computer must know an initial point, which we refer to as the $From$ point. To know the camera's orientation, the computer must also know the point at which the camera looks. We refer to as the To point. As shown in Figure 3 (a), as an example, the $From$ point is (-5.0, 5.0, 5.0), and the To point is (0.0, 0.0, 0.0), and thus we define the $Forward$ vector as $Forward = normalize\ (From - To)$. Next, we define the $Temporary$ vector, which does not have to be precise. The typical value is (0, 0, 1). Thus, the $Right$ vector is perpendicular to the space that $Forward$ and $Temporary$ create. Finally, Cartesian coordinates are defined by three mutually perpendicular vectors, and thus we can calculate the Up vector based on the $Forward$ and $Right$ vectors. Note that $Forward, Right,$ and Up vectors are mutually perpendicular, and they are all normalized unit vectors. Therefore, a rendered image by our current camera settings can be shown in Figure 3 (b). Additionally, we need to define the transformation vector T, which is

$T = From - Origin$. Since the $Origin$ is (0, 0, 0), vector T is the coordinate of the $From$ point.

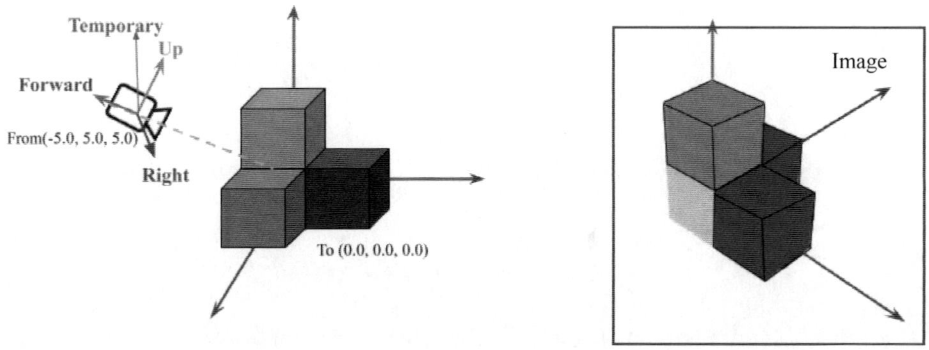

(a) The Camera Aiming at a Point (b) The Image Can Be Rendered by Such Settings

Figure 3: The Local Coordinate System of the Camera Aiming at a Point

As we have defined the 4x4 rotation and transformation matrix, we can render façade images by the given pairs of $From$ and To points. After we selected the $From$ points on streets and the To points inside of buildings, the façade images can be then rendered.

2.3 Training a Semantic Segmentation ANN Model

In this step, we used an open source database to train a segmentation ANN model based on different algorithms. This open source dataset is annotated into eight classes (e.g. Loft, Top, Wall, window, Shop, Door, and Balcony), which is available from the studies of Mathias, *et al.*, 2016 and Simon *et al.*, 2011 and can be freely downloaded from the webpage of *Ecole Centrale Paris Facades Database* (Teboul, 2008). The data contains 400 images for training and 100 images for testing. The images of facades are taken from different cities including Paris, Barcelona, and San Francisco, among others.

Many state-of-the-art ANN algorithms exist to train the segmentation models, including DeepLab, MaskRCNN, and Generative Adversarial Networks (GAN) (Goodfellow *et al.*, 2014). Among these algorithms, GAN can learn density distributions of imagery datasets and explore their internal representations (Hou, *et al.*, 2021). Additionally, as the detailed architecture of a GAN shows in Figure 4, the main difference between the GAN and other ANNs is that the GAN has two separated networks including a generator network and discriminator network; therefore, the GAN architecture is more flexible than other neural network approaches. The function of the discriminator network is to decide if the generated samples are similar to the ground truth samples, and the differences are calculated by the loss function. Further, the backpropagation improves the parameters in generator and discriminator networks based on the loss function. After several epochs, the samples generated by the generator network evolve from random noise to predicted results, and then the model is trained for use in testing datasets. As previously discussed, the GAN architecture is flexible. Thus, it is easy for us to replace the network architecture. We choose to use two different network architectures to build the generator network including "Resnet+9 blocks" and "Unet256".

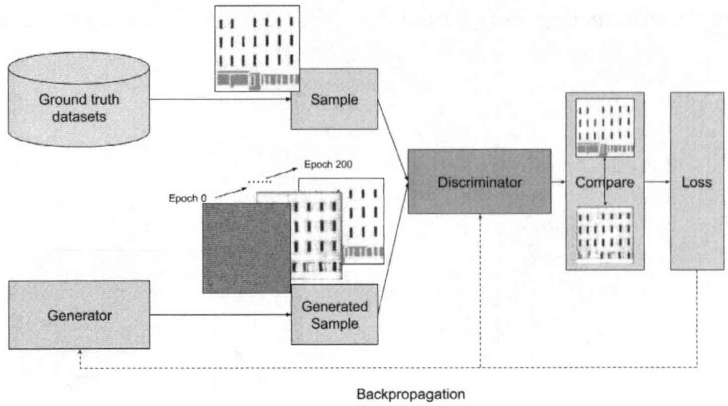

Figure 4: The Detailed Architecture of a GAN

2.4 Segmentation Results and Evaluation of the Proposed Approach

As rendering the façade images and building the semantic segmentation ANN model, we were able to use the trained model to evaluate the segmentation results of the rendered images. We applied trained ANN models (both "Resnet+9 blocks" and "Unet256" versions) on two datasets, including the campus and city areas as shown in Figure 2. As for the evaluation metrics, we chose two evaluation criteria to analyze the performance of the proposed method: (1) an accuracy analysis of the segmentation performance on the open source datasets, and (2) a performance analysis on the rendered images.

We applied four methods to evaluate the segmentation performance on images, including (1) precision, (2) recall, (3) Jaccard/intersection-over-union (IOU), and (4) the dice coefficient /F1-score, as shown in Eqs. (2-5). In these equations, TP (true positive) represents the area of overlap between the predicted segmentation and the ground truth in the images. FP (false positive) represents the areas that belong to the correct class but that the algorithms cannot recognize, and FN (false negative) represents the areas that do not belong to the correct class, but that the algorithms incorrectly recognize them do. Using TP, FP and FN, we can calculate the evaluation metrics. Precision, also known as positive predictive value, is the fraction of the correctly classified area among the actual result area in the ground truth images. Recall, also called sensitivity, is the fraction of the correctly classified pixel area among the predicted result area in the predicted images. Next, IOU, is the fraction of the correctly classified pixel area among the union areas of the actual result areas and predicted result areas. Last, F1 is a harmonic mean that combines precision and recall score.

$$Precision = \frac{TP}{TP+FP} \qquad \text{Eq. (2)}$$

$$Recall = \frac{TP}{TP+FN} \qquad \text{Eq. (3)}$$

$$IOU = \frac{TP}{TP+FP+FN} \qquad \text{Eq. (4)}$$

$$F1 = \frac{2TP}{2TP+FP+FN} \qquad \text{Eq. (5)}$$

3. Experiment

Thermography inspection needs a special experimental condition in which the temperature difference between the indoors and outdoors should be at least 10 °C (18 °F) (FLIR Systems, 2011). To meet this requirement, inspections need to be conducted in a hot summer or a cold winter. However, the sun radiation can cause an inaccurate façade temperature measurement and further impact the cooling energy loss audits. Therefore, thermography inspection on hot days is usually conducted in early morning or late afternoon to avoid sun radiation. However, it is still difficult to guarantee the needed temperature differences during such inspection times in the summer. Considering these facts, we conducted a heat loss inspection on a college campus and in a city area during a cold winter in Karlsruhe, Germany. In collecting data for our experiments, room temperatures were higher (the average temperature was 17 °C (63 °F) for indoor spaces when the research was conducted), and the outside ambient temperatures were lower (the outdoor temperature was -5 °C (23°F) in the early morning).

The open source dataset in which the cameras were set on the ground is annotated into 8 classes. However, we only focused on two categories (doors and windows) related to the heat loss audits for this study. As shown in Figure 5, Figure 5 (a) and (e) are two examples in the open source datasets, (b) and (f) are ground truths for these two examples, (c) and (g) are segmentation results for these two examples, and (d) and (h) are segmentation results using another algorithm.

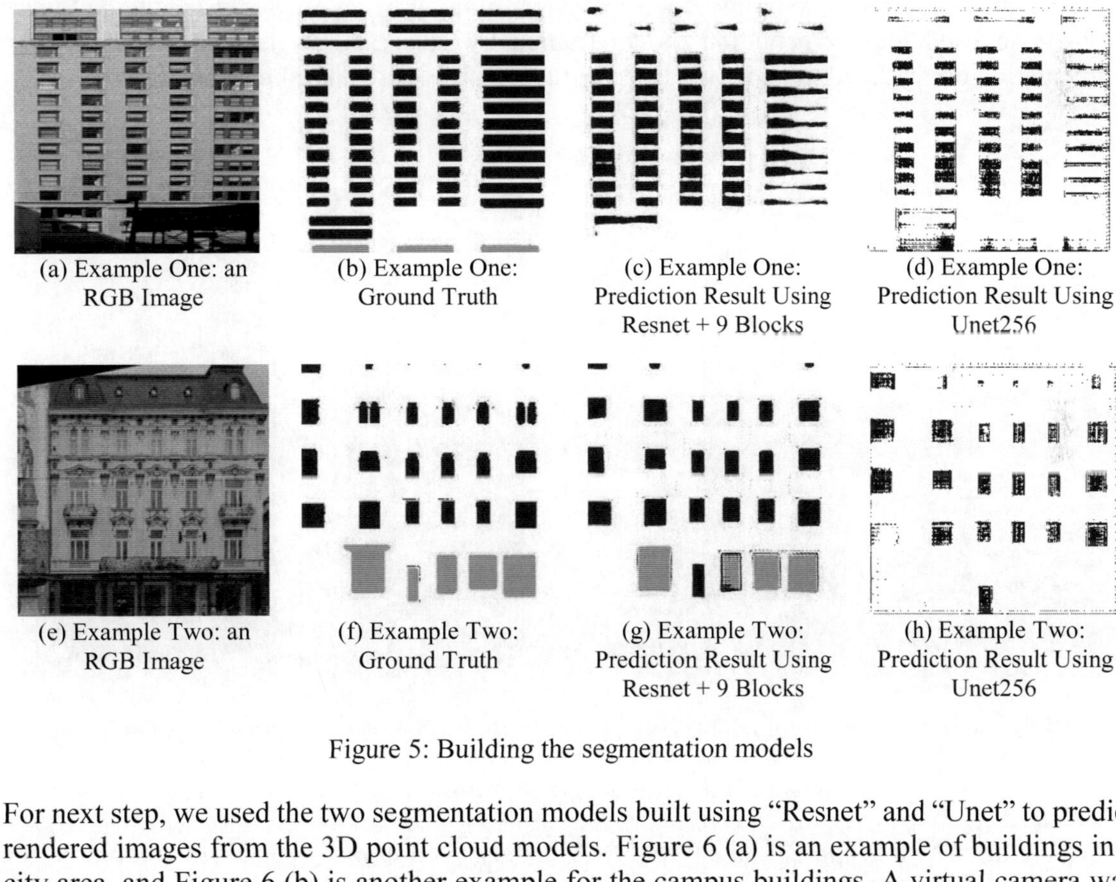

(a) Example One: an RGB Image

(b) Example One: Ground Truth

(c) Example One: Prediction Result Using Resnet + 9 Blocks

(d) Example One: Prediction Result Using Unet256

(e) Example Two: an RGB Image

(f) Example Two: Ground Truth

(g) Example Two: Prediction Result Using Resnet + 9 Blocks

(h) Example Two: Prediction Result Using Unet256

Figure 5: Building the segmentation models

For next step, we used the two segmentation models built using "Resnet" and "Unet" to predict rendered images from the 3D point cloud models. Figure 6 (a) is an example of buildings in a city area, and Figure 6 (b) is another example for the campus buildings. A virtual camera was set in the 3D model, and a façade image with its ground truth were rendered.

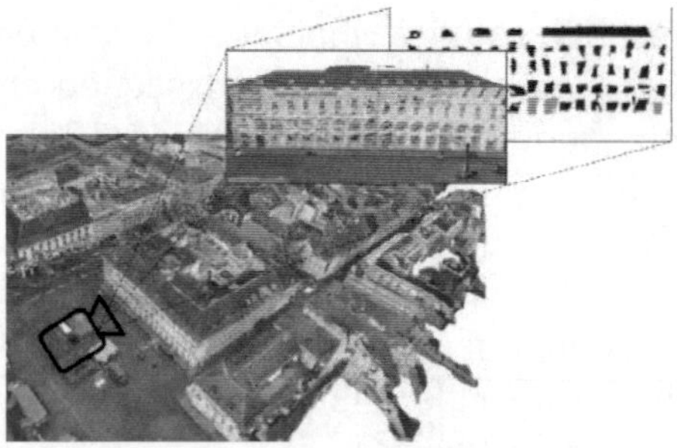

(a) Example One: an RGB Image

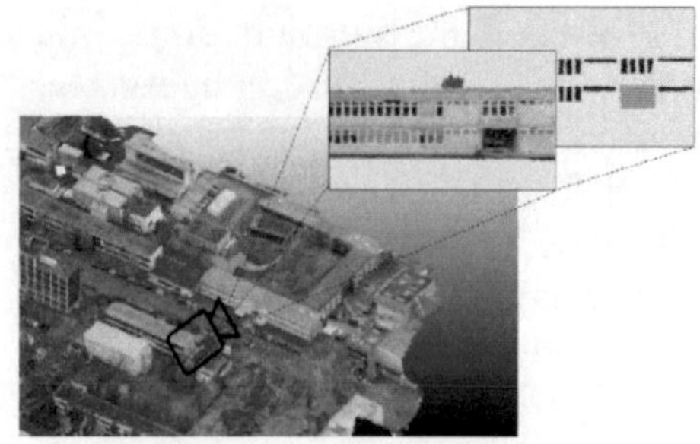

(b) Example Two: Ground Truth

Figure 6: Segmentation on Rendered Images

4. Results and Discussion

Based on the Eqs. (2-5), we conducted accuracy analysis of the segmentation performance for the open source datasets and performance analysis for the rendered images, as shown in Figure 7. We also used the segmentation model trained by open source datasets to predict the segmentation on rendered images, and the accuracy analyses are also shown in Figure 7.

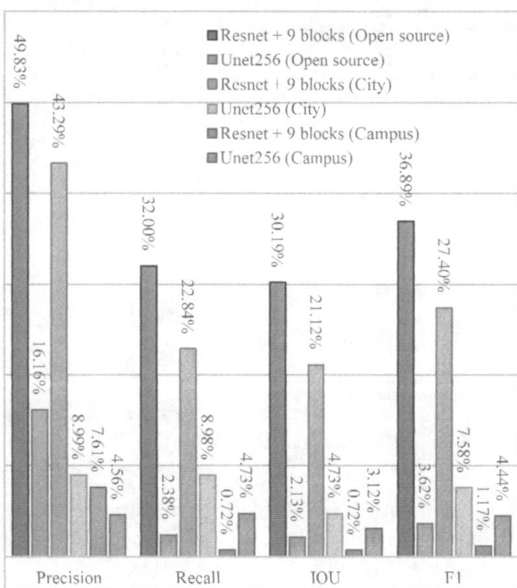

(a) Performance Analysis for Door Class

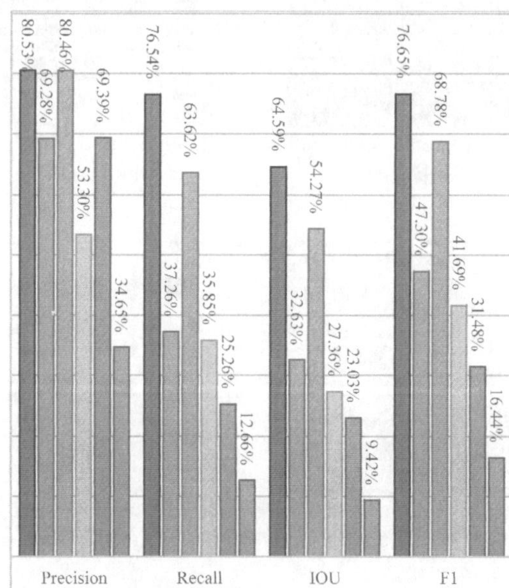

(b) Performance Analysis for Window Class

Figure 7: Segmentation Performance Analysis

We also plotted a Precision-Recall curve (PRC) as shown in Figure 8. The blue color represents "Resnet+9blocks" GAN algorithm, and red represents "Unet256" GAN algorithm. As the yellow lines shown in figure (a), the ideal test should have a PRC that passes through the upper right corner representing the 100% precision and 100% recall. In general, the closer the blue or red area is to the yellow lines, the better the performance.

There were some important findings from the results. First, as the results in Figure 7 show, "Resnet+9blocks" outperformed "Unet256" in all cases except predicting door class in rendered images from the campus datasets. Second, in general, predicting window class was more accurate than predicting door class. The blue areas are always on top of the red areas in Figure 8. This is potentially because of the unbalanced datasets. In every image in the datasets, there were more pixels belonging to window class than pixels belonging to door class. A solution needs to be found for this unbalanced dataset issue in future studies. Third, in general, our proposed approach performed better in city datasets than in campus datasets, potentially because the building styles in the open source are closer to the styles in city datasets.

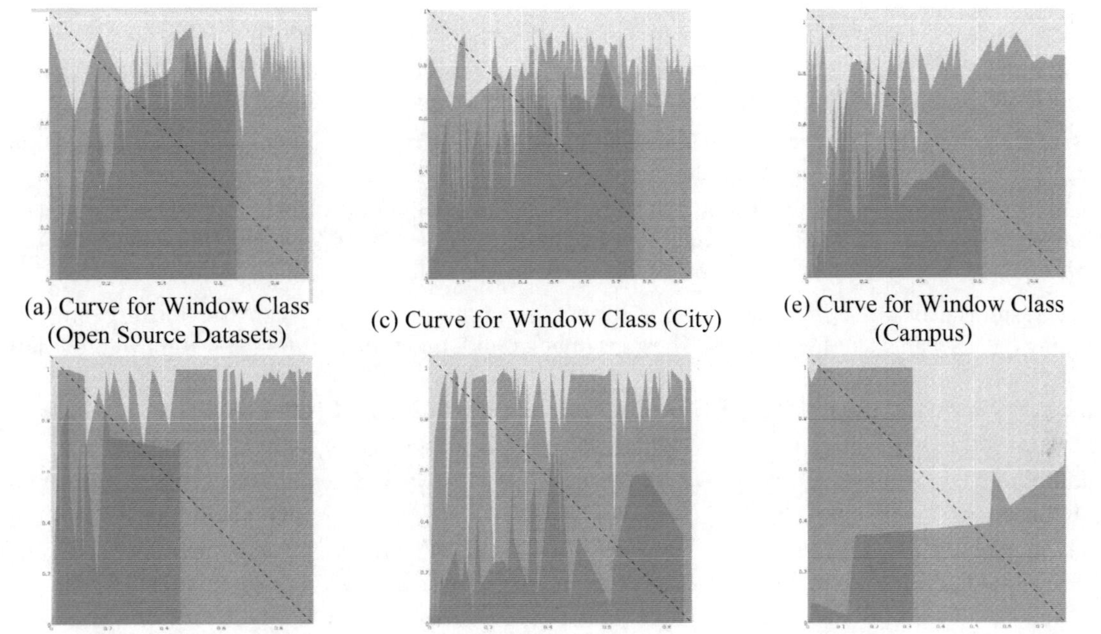

(a) Curve for Window Class (Open Source Datasets)

(c) Curve for Window Class (City)

(e) Curve for Window Class (Campus)

(b) Curve for Door Class (Open Source Datasets)

(d) Curve for Door Class (City)

(f) Curve for Door Class (Campus)

Figure 8: Precision-Recall Curve

5. Conclusion and Outlook

Our results show that a 3D point cloud model can be created using aerial images and that rendered façade images for segmentation can be successfully generated by a virtual camera in the model. As the results show, the segmentation accuracy decreases from the evaluation of the segmentation performance on the open source datasets to the evaluation of the rendered images. Particularly, the performance decreases more when using the "Unet256" algorithm. Second, the accuracy of segmenting windows is higher than segmenting doors. Finally, the results show that the accuracy of semantic segmentation is higher when the approach is conducted on buildings in a city than in a university campus. In the future, there is a need to consider the unbalanced dataset issue related to the higher incidence of windows objects when compared to door objects on existing databases. Additionally, there are two options for improving the segmentation performances; one is by improving the quality of the rendered images, and the other one is by improving the segmentation algorithms.

Acknowledgement

The authors thank the CSC (China Scholarship Council), the KIT International Department, and DAAD (Deutscher Akademischer Austauschdienst, German Academic Exchange Service) for their support. Furthermore, the authors thank Marinus Vogl and Air Bavarian GmbH, his drone company, for their support with equipment and service. Last, the authors thank Leslie Ramos, Wenyun Lu, and Tianyou Dong for their time and effort in ground truth coding.

References

Bradski, G. (2000) 'The OpenCV Library', Dr. Dobb's Journal of Software Tools.

Chen, M. et al. (2020) 'Semantic Segmentation and Data Fusion of Microsoft Bing 3D Cities and Small UAV-based Photogrammetric Data', (20220), pp.1–12. doi: arXiv:2008.09648v1.

Dino, I. G. et al. (2020) 'Image-based construction of building energy models using computer vision', Automation in Construction, 116(1). doi: 10.1016/j.autcon.2020.103231.

Fischer, P., Dosovitskiy, A. and Brox, T. (2015) 'Image orientation estimation with convolutional networks', German Conference on Pattern Recognition, pp.368–378. doi: 10.1007/978-3-319-24947-6_30.

FLIR Systems (2011) An informative guide for the use of thermal imaging cameras for inspecting buildings, solar panels and windmills. Thermal Image Guidebook for Building and Renewable Energy Applications Content. Available at: http://www.flirmedia.com/MMC/THG/Brochures/T820325/T820325_EN.pdf (Accessed: 13 June 2020).

Goodfellow, I. et al. (2014) 'Generative Adversarial Nets', Advances in neural information processing systems, pp.2672–2680. doi: 10.1109/ICCVW.2019.00369.

Hou, Y. et al. (2019) 'Factors affecting the performance of 3D thermal mapping for energy audits in a district by using infrared thermography (IRT) mounted on unmanned aircraft systems (UAS)', in Proceedings of the 36th International Symposium on Automation and Robotics in Construction, ISARC 2019, pp.266–273. doi: https://doi.org/10.22260/ISARC2019/0036.

Hou, Y. et al. (2021) 'Automation in Construction Fusing tie points' RGB and thermal information for mapping large areas based on aerial images : A study of fusion performance under different flight configurations and experimental conditions', Automation in Construction. Elsevier B.V., 124. doi: 10.1016/j.autcon.2021.103554.

Hou, Y., Volk, R. and Soibelman, L. (2021) 'A Novel Building Temperature Simulation Approach Driven by Expanding Semantic Segmentation Training Datasets with Synthetic Aerial Thermal Images', Energies, 14(2). doi: https://doi.org/10.3390/en14020353.

Mathias, M., Martinović, A. and Van Gool, L. (2016) 'ATLAS: A Three-Layered Approach to Facade Parsing', International Journal of Computer Vision, 118(1), pp.22–48. doi: 10.1007/s11263-015-0868-z.

Matl, M., Mahler, J. and Goldberg, K. (2017) 'An algorithm for transferring parallel-jaw grasps between 3D mesh subsegments', IEEE International Conference on Automation Science and Engineering, 2017-Augus, pp.756–763. doi: 10.1109/COASE.2017.8256195.

Mayer, Z. et al. (2021) 'Thermal Bridges on Building Rooftops - Hyperspectral (RGB + Thermal + Height) drone images of Karlsruhe, Germany, with thermal bridge annotations (Version 0.1.0)', in Zenodo. Zenodo. doi: http://doi.org/10.5281/zenodo.4767772.

Pedregosa, F. et al. (2019) 'Generating the blood exposome database using a comprehensive text mining and database fusion approach', Environmental Health Perspectives, 127(9), pp.2825–2830. doi: 10.1289/EHP4713.

Shahandashti, S. M. et al. (2010) 'Data-Fusion Approaches and Applications for Construction Engineering', Journal of Construction Engineering and Management, 137(10), pp.863–869. doi: 10.1061/(ASCE)CO.1943-7862.0000287.

Shi, Z. and Ergan, S. (2020) 'Towards Point Cloud and Model-Based Urban Façade Inspection: Challenges in the Urban Façade Inspection Process', Construction Research Congress 2020, p. 385. doi: https://doi.org/10.1061/9780784482872.042.

Simon, L. et al. (2011) 'Random Exploration of the Procedural Space for Single-View', International Journal of Computer Vision, 93(2), pp.253–271. doi: https://doi.org/10.1007/s11263-010-0370-6.

Teboul, O. (2008) Ecole Centrale Paris Facades Database. doi: http://vision.mas.ecp.fr/Personnel/teboul/data.php.

Verykokou, S. et al. (2018) 'A Photogrammetry-Based Structure From Motion Algorithm Using Robust Iterative Boundle Adjustment Techniques', ISPRS Annals of Photogrammetry, Remote Sensing & Spatial Information Sciences, IV(October), pp.1–2. doi: https://doi.org/10.5194/isprs-annals-IV-4-W6-73-2018.

Yang, M. Der, Su, T. C. and Lin, H. Y. (2018) 'Fusion of infrared thermal image and visible image for 3D thermal model reconstruction using smartphone sensors', Sensors (Switzerland), 18(7). doi: 10.3390/s18072003.

Feasibility Study of Urban Flood Mapping Using Traffic Signs for Route Optimization

Bahareh Alizadeh, Diya Li, Zhe Zhang, Amir H. Behzadan
Texas A&M University, USA
abehzadan@tamu.edu

Abstract. Water events are the most frequent and costliest climate disasters around the world. In the U.S., an estimated 127 million people who live in coastal areas are at risk of substantial home damage from hurricanes or flooding. In flood emergency management, timely and effective spatial decision-making and intelligent routing depend on flood depth information at a fine spatiotemporal scale. In this paper, crowdsourcing is utilized to collect photos of submerged stop signs, and pair each photo with a pre-flood photo taken at the same location. Each photo pair is then analyzed using deep neural network and image processing to estimate the depth of floodwater in the location of the photo. Generated point-by-point depth data is converted to a flood inundation map and used by an A* search algorithm to determine an optimal flood-free path connecting points of interest. Results provide crucial information to rescue teams and evacuees by enabling effective wayfinding during flooding events.

1. Introduction

In recent decades, rapid land development, mass migrations, and deforestation in many parts of the world have overloaded critical infrastructure including road networks and drainage systems especially in at-risk communities and coastal population centers (Sahin & Hall, 1996; Bjorvatn, 2000). This problem is exacerbated by excessive stormwater runoff on impermeable surfaces (e.g., roads, parking lots, driveways, roofs, sidewalks), putting additional strain on the deteriorating drainage systems. The socioeconomic and environmental costs of urban floods can be significant spanning chronic health problems (Du et al., 2010; Paterson et al., 2018), overwhelming insurance claims (Michel-Kerjan, 2010), decreased property values (Bin & Polasky, 2004), lost business income (Browne & Hoyt, 2000), eroded streams and riverbeds (Galay, 1983), and degraded quality of drinking water (Masciopinto et al., 2019).

In the immediate aftermath of a flood event, emergency managers and first responders are tasked with surveying inundated dwellings and neighborhoods, and rescuing those trapped in floodwaters. A key barrier to successful search and rescue (SAR) operation is the limited scope and high variability of field data describing the extent of flood damage and road network vulnerability that could potentially disrupt or prevent timely resource deployment (Keech et al., 2019; Helderop and Grubesic, 2019; Abdullah et al., 2020). Moving floodwater and changing water levels over time necessitates access to (near-) real time floodwater depth information to help people and first responders avoid flooded areas and passages (Liu et al., 2006). In Hurricane Katrina in 2017, for example, emergency responders were frequently querying information about the extent of flood depth to deploy the right type of vehicles for SAR missions and determine the best route for accessing victims (Brecht, 2008). In the absence of such data, people tend to estimate the floodwater depth and level of destruction in their neighbourhoods using social media posts or news stories which can contain outdated data or misinformation (Brecht, 2008; Fan et al., 2020).

In this paper, we conduct a feasibility study with the goal of developing an intelligent spatial decision support system that integrates street-level flood inundation mapping and data-driven routing system using geographic information system (GIS), computer vision, and crowdsourcing. The project aims to support risk-informed spatial decision-making for first responders and communities by providing flood-prone regions with reliable, scalable, and (near-) real time estimation of floodwater depth in the surrounding areas.

2. Literature Review

Conventional methods of floodwater depth calculation use sparse data from contact water level gauges, water depth sensors, flood gauges, and water wells (Nair and Rao, 2016; Water Systems Council, 2014; Chetpattananondh et al., 2014; Töyrä et al., 2002; Odli et al., 2016). However, these devices may fail or be washed away in heavy rain (Nair and Rao, 2016). Moreover, water gauges have limited coverage areas (primarily in and around riverine or coastal lands), and need major effort for installation, calibration, and maintenance in flood susceptible locations. Researchers have also used hydrodynamic modeling to estimate flood water depth (Patel et al., 2017; Salimi et al., 2008). However, surface variability and inconsistency (particularly in urban areas) along with the difficulty in differentiating saturated surface soil from standing water in aerial images makes it difficult for these models to yield accurate results. Besides the high cost of sensor installation and operation, a key challenge in floodwater depth analysis in urban places is the low granularity of flood information relative to road and neighborhood data, which makes it extremely difficult to properly overlay road network maps with flood data (Bales and Wagner, 2009; Merwade et al., 2008; Cohen et al., 2018).

In our previous work, we utilized crowdsourcing for large-scale collection of highly granular flood data (Alizadeh Kharazi and Behzadan, 2021). In particular, standardized traffic signs were employed as ubiquitous markers to measure the depth of floodwater in user-contributed photos using artificial intelligence (AI)-based image processing techniques. The motivation behind this approach is the significantly large number of traffic signs that are vastly distributed on the road network in and around residential areas. In the U.S., for example, there are more than 500 types of federally approved traffic signs which have unique shapes and colors, as described in the Manual on Uniform Traffic Control Devices (MUTCD) (FHA, 2004). These signs contain symbols that are recognizable by both humans and computers, e.g., autonomous vehicles use pre-trained models to detect traffic signs on roads (Kurnianggoro et al., 2014). Many such traffic signs are also adopted to a greater degree internationally, thus providing an opportunity for creating a scalable methodological framework for using traffic signs for large-area flood inundation mapping. In this paper, we built upon our past work by generating practical movement plans for evacuees and first responders based on the crowdsourced data through implementing a routing optimization model on a street-level flood inundation map.

The routing problem is one of the most studied combinatorial optimization problems, first mentioned in 1959 as *truck dispatching problem* to determine an optimal route for a fleet of gasoline delivery trucks between a terminal and a number of service stations (Dantzig and Ramser, 1959). One classic variant of this problem is routing in the presence of obstacles (Golden et al., 2008), which is directly applicable to scenarios where people, rescue teams, or other resources need to evacuate disaster-affected areas while avoiding hazardous encounters (e.g., debris fields, flooded areas, blocked roads). In computational geometry, the *watchman route problem* (Chin and Ntafos, 1986) attempts to solve this scenario by computing the shortest route that a watchman should take to guard a particular area with obstacles. Previous research has used polynomial time algorithms to find the shortest route given an area on a map with preset conditions (Carlsson et al., 1999; Tan 2001; Chin and Ntafos, 1986). In graph theory, the same can be modeled as an optimization problem where the goal is to find the shortest path between a subset of nodes. Dijkstra's algorithm is one of the widely recognized solutions to this optimization problem. For example, Li and Klette (2006) used a rubber-band algorithm to find the shortest path between two points in a graph with $O(n \ log \ n)$ time complexity. Other researchers have investigated routing problems in real world cases such as flood events and proposed various algorithms (Wang and Zlatanova, 2013; Kapoor et al., 2007; Golden et al., 2008; Lu et al., 2003). For instance, Lu et al. (2003) designed a capacity-constrained routing algorithm with heuristic methods that incorporated evacuation time to perform route planning with avoidance. More recently, several commercial applications and open-source solutions have been developed to provide convenient routing services. Among others, examples include Nedkov and Zlatanova (2011) who used Google Directions API to extend web direction for routing with avoidance, as well as Engelmann et al. (2020) who used GraphHopper (Karich and Schröder, 2014) to create a route planning method that minimizes the emission of harmful gases from vehicles. However, existing decision support systems for emergency management lack the ability to integrate street-level flood information, risk-informed routing system, and spatial decision-making capabilities, which could weaken the efficiency of the SAR operations. As described in this paper, we incorporate floodwater depth information as an additional constraint into the routing problem to produce practical movement plans for evacuees and first responders.

3. Methodology

Line detection for pole length calculation. We use stop signs as standardized measurement benchmarks and estimate the depth of the flood by comparing the length of the visible portion of the pole (on which the stop sign is mounted) in pre- and post-flood photos taken from the same location. As shown in Figure 1, Mask Regional Convolutional Neural Network (in short, Mask R-CNN), an object detection and instance segmentation model (He et al., 2017), is used to detect stop signs in paired stop sign photos of the same location prior and after the flood event. After the stop sign is detected, two image processing techniques, namely Canny edge detector (Ogawa et al., 2010; Rong et al., 2014) and probabilistic Hough transform (Zhu and Brilakis, 2009), are used to detect the sign pole in each photo and estimate their lengths. Using this technique, first, all possible edges in each photo are explored. Selected edge candidates are then merged to reconstruct and measure the length of the straight line that is likely to represent the sign pole. The depth of floodwater is subsequently calculated as the difference in pole lengths in paired pre- and post-flood photos. A detailed description of this step is beyond the scope of this paper and can be found in Alizadeh Kharazi and Behzadan (2021).

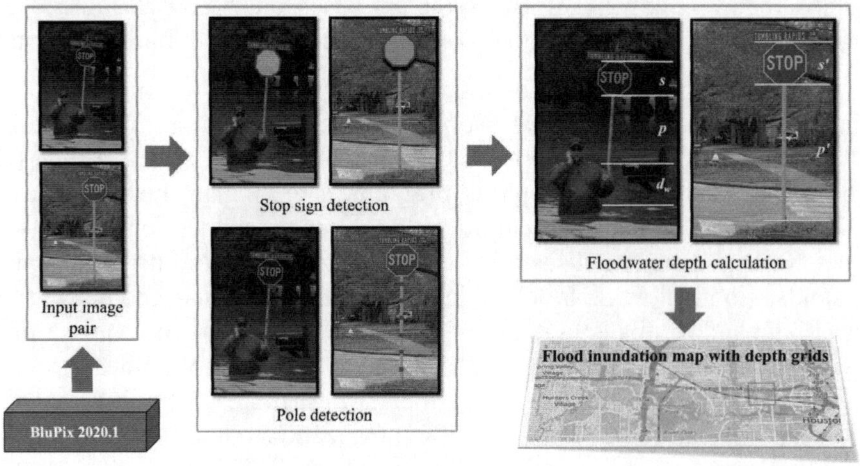

Figure 1: Framework for Estimation of Floodwater Depth by Visual Analysis of Paired Stop Sign Flood Photos. (base post-flood photo: courtesy of Erich Schlegel/Getty Images)

Simulate flooded areas using GIS and Stop Sign detection results. Volunteered Geographic Information (VGI) has been utilized in flood studies (Goodchild 2007; Huang et al., 2018). Huang et al. (2018) used an inverse distance weighted height filter to build a probability index distribution (PID) layer from the high-resolution digital elevation model data. Inspired by that work, we use a distance-decay function along with isohypse information to transform point-by-point floodwater depth data into area-wide flood inundation maps. Several forms of this function are widely used to describe systematic spatial variations where spatial information has the tendency to vanish with distance (Haining, 2001). In this research, we create a flooding confidence area around detected floodwater depth points to simulate flooded regions. In the future, this approach can be compared and validated using hydrological-based modeling (Liu et al., 2006) to improve the accuracy of flood inundation mapping. Suppose an estimated flooded area A that is defined by a discrete point grid $\{X_1, X_2, \ldots, X_i, \ldots, X_j\}$. The Gaussian buffering function shown in Equation 1 is applied to approximate the depth of floodwater at point X_j in area A. In this Equation, X_0 is the detected floodwater depth at the center point of area A, I_0 is the elevation at the center point of area A, I_j is the elevation in point j, d_j is the geographic distance between the center point of area A and X_j, and b is a fixed bandwidth for the Gaussian function. As the distance d_j varies around area A, the estimated floodwater depth also changes with distance-decay and isohypse information. This approach is commonly used in GIS research such as social-media flood mapping (Huang et al., 2018) and distance-decay weight regression model (Gutiérrez et al., 2011).

$$X_j = X_0 \, exp\,[-1/2(d_j/b)^2] + (I_0 - I_j) \tag{1}$$

Description of the routing problem. Given the flood inundation information, the routing problem from an origin to a destination point can be modeled as a multi-stage decision process, where each decision stage includes the location of the current decision point as well as the time needed to complete the remainder of the process. The designed optimization-based algorithm proposes a routing solution that avoids flood inundated areas and supports SAR operations during a flood event. The routing problem is further modified by including several decision objectives, and transforming the otherwise single-objective optimization into a multi objective decision process. From the taxonomy of navigation for emergency response (Wang and Zlatanova, 2013), this problem can be defined using $X = < X_1, X_2, X_3, X_4, \ldots >$, where X_i denotes an environment factor, and contains the quantity (one or many), and the type (e.g., destination, responder object, obstacle) of that factor. For example, for a person whose goal is to go back home while avoiding flooded roads, the navigation route can be defined as $< \{one\ moving\ object\}, \{one\ static\ destination\}, \{one\ static\ obstacles\} >$. Since the traditional Dijkstra algorithms may not work well for X that contains obstacle factors, we propose to use the A* search algorithm (Russell and Norvig, 2002; Lerner et al., 2009). For this purpose, the following concepts are adopted before we formalize each iteration of the A* search algorithm:

1. Search area: Given a prepared base map that contains spatial entities, each entity is represented as a graph node in the search area.
2. Open vs. closed list: All nearest nodes waiting to be searched are stored in an open list; and those already searched are stored in a closed list.
3. Path sorting: To define the direction of the next movement, we use a path sorting function expressed by Equation 2.

$$F(n) = G + H \tag{2}$$

In this Equation, H denotes a heuristic function, and G is the moving cost from the initial location to the next node in the open list. The heuristic function takes the Manhattan distance to calculate the cost of moving from each of the candidate next nodes in the open list to the final destination node. Figure 2 presents the pseudo algorithm for the A* search. A demonstration of how this algorithm is used in a flooded area (routing with obstacles) is shown in Figure 3. In this Figure, different shades of blue represent different floodwater depth values, diamonds stand for start and destination points, and orange pixels mark the simulated routing path. The cost value is displayed in each searched pixel. This information is used as threshold conditions to check whether a vehicle can pass through a particular area.

```
Initialize open_list and close_list, start with initial point;
Add start node s to open_list;  F(s) = 0 (smallest);
If open_list is not Null, select node n with smallest F(n):
  If n is destination node:
    Find parent node from destination node to start node then return;
  If n is not destination node:
    Move n from open_list to close_list;
    Traverse eight nearest nodes of n:
      If nearest node m in close_list: continue;
      If nearest node not in open_list:
        Set parent node n for m; Update cost function; add m to open_list
Connect parent node from initial node and generate path;
```

Figure 2: Pseudo Algorithm for A* Search.

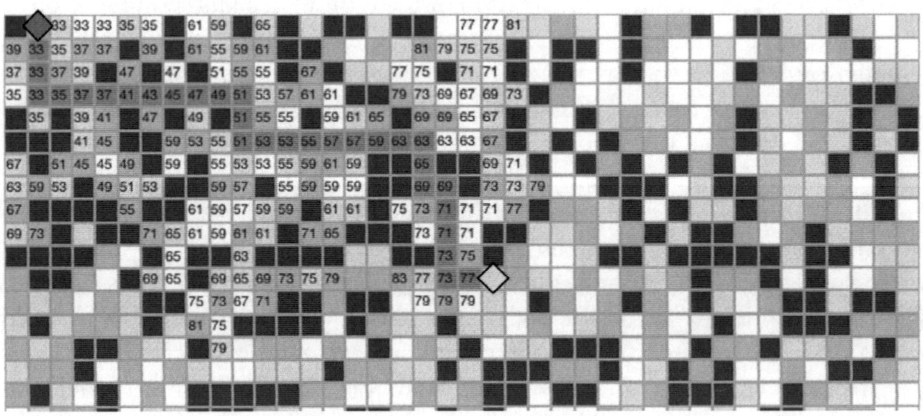

Figure 3: Sample Output of A* Search Algorithm with Obstacles.

4. Proof-of-Concept Experiment

As shown in Figure 4, for the flood scenario presented in this paper, six paired photos from the 2017 Hurricane Harvey in Houston, Texas, taken approximately on the same date in the month of September, are selected from BluPix v.2020.1, a crowdsourcing platform developed in this research to collect user-contributed photos of flooded stop signs.

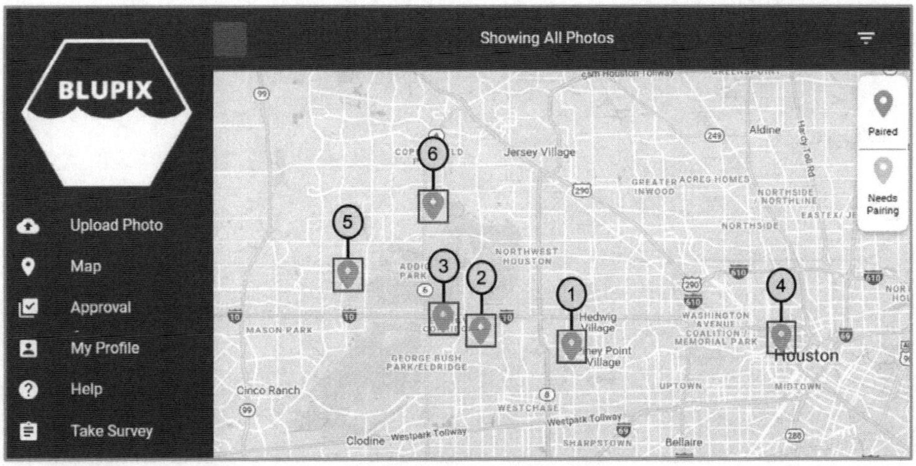

Figure 4: Locations of Selected Paired Flood Photos in Houston, TX after Hurricane Harvey (2017).

Table 1 shows a summary of floodwater depth calculations applied to pre- and post-flood photos. As shown in this Table, the root mean square error (RMSE) of the flood depth estimation model on the six pairs of pre- and post-flood photos is 4.69 inches, and the average processing time for floodwater depth calculation is 11.6 seconds.

Table 1: Performance of floodwater depth estimation on paired pre- and post-flood photos.

Calculation	Metric	Pre-flood photos ($n = 6$)	Post-flood photos ($n = 6$)
Stop sign detection	Intersection over union (IOU) %	96.73	95.24
	Precision %	100	100
	Recall %	100	100
	Average precision (AP) %	100	100
	Average processing time (s)	1.08	1.26
Pole detection	RMSE (in.)	2.64	5.80
	Average processing time (s)	0.13	0.10
Flood depth estimation	Average total processing time (s)	2.57	
	RMSE (in.)	4.69	

Floodwater depth estimates are subsequently used to generate a flood inundation map with depth grids. Figure 5 demonstrates the application of A* search algorithm to calculate the shortest flood-free route. In this example, each of the previously selected six paired points is taken as the central point of a flooded area. To implement the distance-decay function (Equation 1), elevation data is queried from Google Elevation API. The Graphhopper library (Karich and Schröder, 2014) is used for route search, and Openrouteservice is utilized to overlay the base map with generated flooded areas. The basic spatial information for building the base map is taken from OpenStreetMap (Planet OpenStreetMap, 2021).

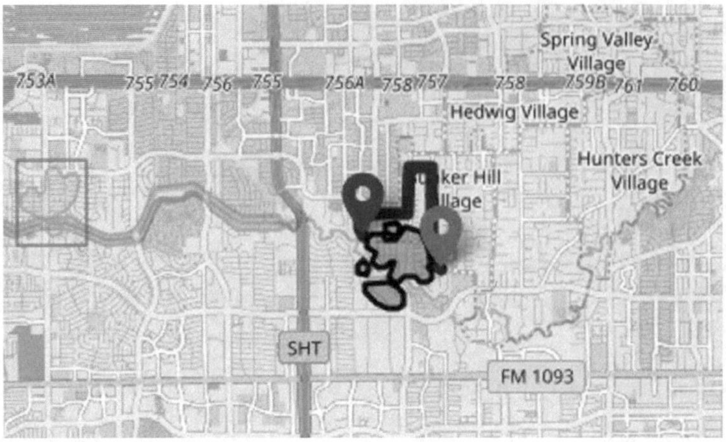

Figure 5: Illustration of the routing algorithm using buffered points that represent estimate floodwater depths collected from inundated areas.

5. Summary and Conclusion

Flood is the most common type of climate disaster in the U.S. and around the world. An impediment to timely SAR and routing of resources during flood events is the lack of street-level floodwater depth information. Since water levels change over time, it is necessary to have access to (near-) real time floodwater depth information to help people and first responders avoid flooded areas and passages. This paper proposed the use of standardized traffic signs as ubiquitous markers for measuring the depth of floodwater in user-contributed street photos. We used Mask R-CNN, a deep neural network, to detect stop signs in photos, and applied two image processing techniques (Canny edge detector and probabilistic Hough transform) to determine the length of the sign pole in pre- and post-flood photos. Floodwater depth was then estimated as the difference between pole lengths of the same stop sign in paired pre- and post-flood photos. We achieved an RMSE of 4.69 inches in estimating the floodwater depth for a set of six paired flood photos taken in Houston, TX after the 2017 Hurricane Harvey.

Next, distance-decay function was implemented to transform point-by-point floodwater depth data into area-wide flood inundation maps. The generated map was used to develop a risk-informed routing system based upon the A* search algorithm to calculate the shortest flood-free route between points of interest (i.e., intelligent wayfinding). In the current implementation of the route optimization algorithm, all flooded areas are avoided. However, one can set a threshold value and customize their search based on the vehicle type used to navigate in a flooded area. Clearly, increased public awareness and improved user experience can help gather a large number of floodwater depth points and improve the reliability of the algorithm. In the meantime, when only limited data points are available for flood mapping, additional flood depth data can be generated using advanced hydrological models. The minimum number of flood depth data needed for flood mapping may also depend on the type, topography, and other characteristics of the flooded surface. In a flat area, for example, fewer data points are generally sufficient to generate accurate flood maps. In contrast, more points may be needed in rugged areas or where surface characteristics and shape change abruptly. In this paper, using a Gaussian distance-decay function with each pole independently allowed us to relax the minimum number requirement when generating flood maps with sparse data.

The developed methods in this paper are sought to interface with other sources of spatial information (e.g., high-resolution point cloud terrain), leading to further improvement of flood mapping and wayfinding. Moreover, paired photos are stored with time and location information, allowing a host of spatiotemporal analyses of past flood events. All in all, the designed route optimization will provide crucial information to rescue teams and evacuees and enable effective wayfinding during flooding events. In the long term, the generalizability and robustness of the designed platform will be rigorously evaluated as more user-contributed photos are collected and paired on the BluPix crowdsourcing application.

Acknowledgments

This study is funded by award #NA18OAR4170088 from the National Oceanic and Atmospheric Administration (NOAA), U.S. Department of Commerce. We are thankful to Dr. Courtney Thompson and Dr. Michelle Meyer (project collaborators at Texas A&M University) for their supporting role in this project. Additionally, we would like to thank Mr. Nathan Young (undergraduate student at Texas A&M University) for his assistance in data collection. Any opinions, findings, conclusions, and recommendations expressed in this paper are those of the authors and do not necessarily represent the views of the NOAA, Department of Commerce, or the individuals named above.

References

Abdullah, M., Suliman, M.S., Daud, M.S.M., Hamid, Z.J.M.H., Noor, M.R.M. Ngadiman, N.I. (2019). Humanitarian logistic relief team challenges during flood. In: International Research Conference and Innovation Exhibition, 2019, Johor Bahru, Malaysia.

Alizadeh Kharazi, B., & Behzadan, A. H. (2021). Flood depth mapping in street photos with image processing and deep neural networks. Computers, Environment and Urban Systems, 88, pp.101628.

Bales, J.D., Wagner, C.R. (2009). Sources of uncertainty in flood inundation maps, J. Flood Risk Management, 2(2), pp.139–147.

Bin, O., Polasky, S. (2004). Effects of flood hazards on property values: evidence before and after Hurricane Floyd, J. Land Economics, 80(4), pp.490–500.

Djorvatn, K. (2000). Urban infrastructure and industrialization, J. Urban Economics, 48(2), pp.205–218.

Brecht, H. (2008). The application of geo-technologies after Hurricane Katrina. In: Nayak, S., Zlatanova, S. (Eds.). Remote Sensing and GIS Technologies for Monitoring and Prediction of Disasters, Berlin: Springer-Verlag, pp.281–304.

Browne, M.J., Hoyt, R.E. (2000). The demand for flood insurance: empirical evidence, J. Risk and Uncertainty, 20(3), 291–306.

Carlsson, S., Jonsson, H., Nilsson, B.J. (1999). Finding the shortest watchman route in a simple polygon, J. Discrete and Computational Geometry, 22(3), pp.377–402.

Chetpattananondh, K., Tapoanoi, T., Phukpattaranont, P., Jindapetch, N. (2014). A self-calibration water level measurement using an interdigital capacitive sensor, J. Sensors and Actuators A: Physical, 209, pp.175–182.

Chin, W.P., Ntafos, S. (1986). Optimum watchman routes. In: Second Annual Symposium on Computational Geometry, 1986, New York, NY.

Cohen, S., Brakenridge, G.R., Kettner, A., Bates, B., Nelson, J., McDonald, R., Huang, Y.F., Munasinghe, D., Zhang, J. (2018), Estimating floodwater depths from flood inundation maps and topography, JAWRA J. of the American Water Resources Association, 54(4), pp.847–858.

Dantzig, G.B., Ramser, J.H. (1959). The truck dispatching problem, J. Management Science, 6(1), pp.80–91.

Du, W., Fitzgerald, G.J., Clark, M., Hou, X.Y. (2010). Health impacts of floods, J. Prehospital and Disaster Medicine, 25(3), pp.265–272.

Engelmann, M., Schulze, P., Wittmann, J. (2020). Emission-based routing using the GraphHopper API and OpenStreetMap. In: Schaldach, R., Simon, K.H., Weismüller, J., Wohlgemuth, V. (Eds.). Advances and New Trends in Environmental Informatics, Progress in IS. Springer, Cham, pp.91–104.

Fan, C., Esparza, M., Dargin, J., Wu, F., Oztekin, B., Mostafavi, A. (2020). Spatial biases in crowdsourced data: Social media content attention concentrates on populous areas in disasters. J. Computers, Environment and Urban Systems, 83, 101514.

FHA, (2004). Manual of Uniform Traffic Control Devices (MUTCD): Standard Highway Signs. Washington: Federal Highway Administration.

Galay, V.J. (1983). Causes of riverbed degradation, J. Water Resources Research, 19(5), pp.1057–1090.

Golden, B.L., Raghavan, S., Wasil, E.A. (2008). The Vehicle Routing Problem: Latest Advances and New Challenges (Vol. 43). Berlin: Springer-Verlag.

Goodchild, M. F. (2007). Citizens as sensors: The world of volunteered geography, GeoJournal, 69(4), 211–221.

Gutiérrez, J., Cardozo, O.D., García-Palomares, J.C. (2011). Transit ridership forecasting at station level: An approach based on distance-decay weighted regression, J. Transport Geography, 19(6), pp.1081–1092.

Haining, R.P. (2001). Spatial Sampling. In: Smelser, N.J., Baltes, P.B. (Eds.). International Encyclopedia of the Social and Behavioral Sciences. Oxford: Pergamon.

He, K., Gkioxari, G., Dollár, P., Girshick, R. (2017). Mask R-CNN. In: IEEE International Conference on Computer Vision (ICCV), 2017, Venice, Italy.

Helderop, E., Grubesic, T.H. (2019). Streets, storm surge, and the frailty of urban transport systems: A grid-based approach for identifying informal street network connections to facilitate mobility. Transportation Research Part D: Transport and Environment, 77, 337–351.

Huang, X., Wang, C., Li, Z. (2018). A near real-time flood-mapping approach by integrating social media and post-event satellite imagery, Annals of GIS, 24(2), 113–123.

Kapoor, S., Maheshwari, S.N., Mitchell, J.S. (1997). An efficient algorithm for Euclidean shortest paths among polygonal obstacles in the plane, J. Discrete and Computational Geometry, 18(4), pp.377–383.

Karich, P., Schröder, S. (2014). Graphhopper, http://www.graphhopper.com, accessed March 2021.

Keech, J.J., Smith, S.R., Peden, A.E., Hagger, M.S. Hamilton, K. (2019). The lived experience of rescuing people who have driven into floodwater: Understanding challenges and identifying areas for providing support, Health Promotion J. of Australia, 30(2), pp.252–257.

Kurnianggoro, L., Hariyono, J., Jo, K.H. (2014). Traffic sign recognition system for autonomous vehicle using cascade SVM classifier. In: 40th Annual Conference of the IEEE Industrial Electronics Society, 2014, Dallas, TX.

Lerner, J., Wagner, D., Zweig, K. (2009). Algorithmics of Large and Complex Networks: Design, Analysis, and Simulation (Vol. 5515). Berlin: Springer-Verlag.

Li, F., Klette, R. (2006). Finding the shortest path between two points in a simple polygon by applying a rubberband algorithm. In: Pacific-Rim Symposium on Image and Video Technology, 2006, Hsinchu, Taiwan.

Liu, Y., Hatayama, M., Okada, N. (2006). Development of an adaptive evacuation route algorithm under flood disaster. Annuals of Disaster Prevention Research Institute, Kyoto University, 49, 189–195.

Lu, Q., Huang, Y., Shekhar, S. (2003). Evacuation planning: a capacity constrained routing approach. In: International Conference on Intelligence and Security Informatics, 2003, Tucson, AZ.

Masciopinto, C., De Giglio, O., Scrascia, M., Fortunato, F., La Rosa, G., Suffredini, E., Pazzani, C., Prato, R., Montagna, M.T. (2019). Human health risk assessment for the occurrence of enteric viruses in drinking water from wells: Role of flood runoff injections, J. Science of the Total Environment, 666, pp.559–571.

Merwade, V., Olivera, F., Arabi, M., Edleman, S. (2008). Uncertainty in flood inundation mapping: current issues and future directions, J. Hydrologic Engineering, 13(7), 608–620.

Michel-Kerjan, E.O. (2010). Catastrophe economics: the national flood insurance program, J. Economic Perspectives, 24(4), pp.165–186.

Nair, B.B., Rao, S. (2016). Flood water depth estimation: A survey. In: IEEE International Conference on Computational Intelligence and Computing Research (ICCIC), 2016, Tamil Nadu, India.

Nedkov, S., Zlatanova, S. (2011). Enabling obstacle avoidance for Google maps' navigation service. In: GeoInformation for Disaster Management, 2011, Antalya, Turkey.

Odli, Z.S.M., Izhar, T.N.T., Razak, A.R.A., Yusuf, S.Y., Zakarya, I.A., Saad, F.N.M., Nor, M.Z.M. (2016). Development of portable water level sensor for flood management system, J. Engineering and Applied Sciences, 11(8), pp.5352–5357.

Ogawa, K., Ito, Y., Nakano, K. (2010). Efficient Canny edge detection using a GPU. In: IEEE First International Conference on Networking and Computing, 2010, Higashi, Japan.

Planet OpenStreetMap. (2021). Planet dump [Data file from June 4th. 2017 dumps], https://planet.openstreetmap.org, accessed May 2021.

Patel, D.P., Ramirez, J.A., Srivastava, P.K., Bray, M., Han, D. (2017). Assessment of flood inundation mapping of Surat city by coupled 1D/2D hydrodynamic modeling: A case application of the new HEC-RAS 5, J. Natural Hazards, 89(1), pp.93–130.

Paterson, D.L., Wright, H., Harris, P.N. (2018). Health risks of flood disasters, J. Clinical Infectious Diseases, 67(9), pp.1450–1454.

Rong, W., Li, Z., Zhang, W., Sun, L. (2014). An improved Canny edge detection algorithm. In: IEEE International Conference on Mechatronics and Automation, 2014, Tianjin, China.

Russell, S., Norvig, P. (2002). Artificial Intelligence: A Modern Approach. Upper Saddle River: Prentice Hall.

Sahin, V., Hall, M.J. (1996). The effects of afforestation and deforestation on water yields, J. Hydrology, 178(1–4), pp.293–309.

Salimi, S., Ghanbarpour, M.R., Solaimani, K., Ahmadi, M.Z. (2008). Floodplain mapping using hydraulic simulation model in GIS, J. Applied Sciences, 8, pp.660–665.

Tan, X. (2001). Fast computation of shortest watchman routes in simple polygons, Information Processing Letters, 77(1), pp.27–33.

Töyrä, J., Pietroniro, A., Martz, L.W., Prowse, T.D. (2002). A multi-sensor approach to wetland flood monitoring, J. Hydrological Processes, 16(8), pp.1569–1581.

Wang, Z., Zlatanova, S. (2013). Taxonomy of navigation for first responders. In: Krisp, J.M. (Ed.). Progress in Location-Based Services, Berlin: Springer-Verlag, pp.297–315.

Water Systems Council (2020). Well Owner's Manual, https://www.watersystemscouncil.org/download/3430/, accessed February 2021.

Zhu, Z., Brilakis, I. (2009). Comparison of optical sensor-based spatial data collection techniques for civil infrastructure modelling, J. Computing in Civil Engineering, 23(3), 170–177.

Developing indicators for measuring the effectiveness of visualizations applied in construction safety management using eye-tracking

Yewei Ouyang, Xiaowei Luo
City University of Hong Kong, Hong Kong
xiaowluo@cityu.edu.hk

Abstract. Visualizations can help construction safety personnel understand the abstract, dynamic and massive construction information due to its ability in supporting human cognition. However, the effectiveness of cognition support is influenced by the design of visualization and individual differences in cognition ability. To help select appropriate visualizations, this study aims to develop indicators for measuring visualizations' effectiveness in supporting human cognition. Firstly, human's cognitive process of processing visualizations is analysed to obtain the requirements on indicators, then three eye-tracking metrics potential for the measurement are extracted from previous studies, namely, Time to first fixation, Fixation counts and Fixation duration. Finally, an eye-tracking experiment using the indicators to compare visualizations commonly used in construction safety management is conducted for demonstration. The results show using the developed indicators to compare visualizations can help us to understand the effect of visualization design on human cognition. The developed indicators could be used to select more appropriate visualizations and guide the visualization design.

1. Introduction

The construction industry has caused a high incident rate worldwide due to it involves highly dangerous work and harsh work environment. Visualization technologies such as BIM (Building Information Modelling), VR (Virtual Reality) and AR (Augmented Reality) have been extensively explored in the construction field to aid construction safety management because the use of visualization conveys information through images, diagrams or animations, which might help construction personnel understand the abstract, dynamic and massive construction information(Guo et al., 2017).

Psychologists found that visualization leads to more effective information communication and presentation because it can amplify human cognition (Spence, 2001), but such function is influenced by the design of visualization (Simkin and Hastie, 1987, Heer and Stone, 2012) and individual differences in cognition ability (Galotti, 2017). If inappropriate visualizations are adopted, it would overwhelm the viewer and undo the benefits of cognitive support (Huang et al., 2009). Therefore, it becomes critical to select an appropriate visualization to be presented to the decision-maker for optimally supporting their cognitions. However, previous studies applying visualization technology in aiding construction safety focused on dealing with technical difficulties to create visualizations, without validating the effectiveness of the visualizations in supporting human cognition (Guo et al., 2017).

To fill this gap, the authors propose this study to help select appropriate visualizations by providing indicators for measuring the effectiveness of visualizations. Effectiveness here refers to the ability to support human cognition.

2. Methods for Measuring Visualization Effectiveness

Previous studies have proposed several measurement methods, namely, task-centred method, user-centred method, heuristic evaluation, and cognition measurement(Zhu, 2007). The task-centred method looks at the time people spend on tasks and their accuracy rate, e.g. Cleveland and McGill (1984) measured task efficiency of visualization, but it ignores the feelings of users (e.g. how much efforts they have to put, user convenience). In hence, some studies stand at the place of users to assess visualization effectiveness, that they conducted user studies to collect feedback of the participants, e.g. Nowell et al. (2002) record the subjects' judgments of the quantitative information on graphs. Nevertheless, the user-centred method depends on the subjective responses of users that might not be reliable and easy to quantify. Heuristic evaluation invites experts to evaluate the visualization designs based on certain rules and principles (Tory and Moller, 2005). However, the rules and principles for effectiveness measurement are not empirically validated, and there have not been standard procedures for conducting.

To objectively understand people's feeling towards a visualization, cognition measurement has been utilized to evaluate visualization effectiveness(Riche, 2010, Anderson, 2012). Psychological devices such as electroencephalography (EEG) and eye-tracking are utilized to measure cognitive load in visualization perception (Huang et al., 2009, Anderson et al., 2011, Zagermann et al., 2016, Anderson, 2012). The cognitive load is an important indicator of visualization effectiveness due to that it indicates users' mental efforts put in processing a visualization. Even though EEG is a direct measurement for cognitive load, it is quite intrusive to the user and requires a time-consuming setup and its analysis is often complex. Instead, eye-tracking is non-intrusive and easy-to-setup. It is possible to use eye-tracking to measure users' cognitive processes during system usage to allow the system to adapt to users current cognitive load (Zagermann et al., 2016).

Except for measuring cognitive load, eye-tracking also provides a set of eye movement metrics measuring human attention and visual search, which can be used to indicate the cognitive process in processing visualizations. Furthermore, previous studies also proposed that compared to the traditional measurement for assessment such as accuracy and performance time which are typically collected after the conclusion of an assigned task, the eye-tracking adds a new added dimension to the assessment by allowing access to the gaze activity of human subjects and providing objective quantitative data, e.g. Atik and Arslan (2019) explored using eye-tracking to evaluate electronic navigation competency in maritime training, and their findings show that eye tracking provides the assessor data such as the focus of attention to enable evaluation of the cognitive process and competency, while this kind of data is impossible to be obtained by traditional observation methods used in simulation training. Therefore, eye-tracking is selected to be the cognition measurement method for measuring visualization effectiveness.

3. Research Methodology

Eye-tracking metrics which are potential to be the measuring indicators are extracted from previous studies at first, based on the analysis of the cognitive process of processing visualizations. Then, an eye-tracking experiment is conducted to demonstrate how to use the extracted indicators to compare various visualizations.

3.1 Extracting Eye-Tracking Metrics for Measurement from Previous Studies

Figure 1 shows a general Human Information Processing model proposed by Wickens (Wickens et al., 2015). This model describes the cognitive processes when people interact with the outside environment. The authors apply this model to reflect people' cognitive process in visualization processing. The whole processing is concluded as two key stages, as shown by the two dashed boxes in Figure 1. In the first stage, people use their eyes to look through visualizations for searching their wanted information, which can be regarded as a searching stage. Next, people perceive the wanted information and make decisions based on the perception results, which can be regarded as an encoding stage. In the searching stage, the cognition support is indicated by how difficult it is for people to find out their wanted information, it is indicated by how many efforts are required to perceive the information in the encoding stage.

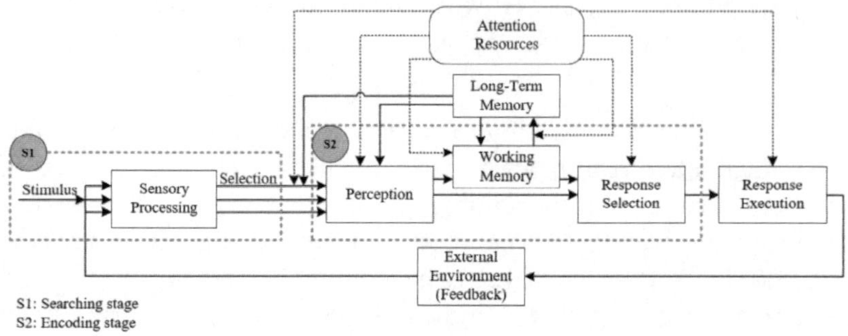

Figure 1: The cognition model of visualization processing

The authors extract a set of eye-tracking metrics which are used to indicate the difficulty level of visual searching and mental effort for perception from previous studies, as shown in Table *1*. These metrics are expected to indicate cognition support.

Table 1: Eye-tracking metrics extracted from previous studies for indicating cognition support of visualization

Cognition stage	**Eye-tracking metrics**	**Descriptions**	**Indication of cognition support**
Searching stage	Time to first fixation	Time spent from stimuli onset to the first fixation arrival	How fast people can find an area containing useful information
	Total fixation counts	Number of fixations within a stimulus	Searching efficiency
Encoding stage	Total fixation duration	Time spent on fixations within a stimulus	Cognitive load

In terms of eye-tracking metrics, fixation means times when our eyes essentially stop scanning about the scene, holding the central foveal vision in place so that the visual system can take in detailed information about what is being looked at. It is generally associated with attention, visual processing, and information absorption(Holmqvist et al., 2011).

Time to first fixation refers to the time from a stimuli onset to the first fixation arrival, e.g. (Sørensen et al., 2012) used it to measure which element in the food package firstly attracts consumers' attention. If we calculate the time people spent from a stimuli onset to firstly fixating on a key area (i.e. an area containing useful information), we can know how fast a visualization can attract people's attention to key areas.

Fixation count refers to the number of fixations. A larger number of fixations indicates the complex situation that decreased efficiency in searching for the desired targets(Ehmke and

Wilson, 2007). If we calculate the total number of fixations within a stimulus, we can know the efficiency in finding wanted information within a visualization.

Tao et al. (2019) reviewed the blink rate, pupil diameter, and fixation duration were the most frequently used to measure cognitive load. However, blink rate, pupil diameter and blink duration are less applicable than fixation duration for the current situation. On one hand, they are influenced by the environmental brightness, e.g. variations in the brightness of the environment produce changes in the pupil size. It is crucial to control environmental brightness and display luminance when pupil dilation is investigated in experiments, which reduces the applicability. On the other hand, they also indicate other aspects so that it is hard to extract influences from the mental workload. Blink is also an indicator of fatigue, and pupil diameter is also associated with the degree of interest(Rosenbaum, 2009). Fixation duration refers to the time spent on fixation, and it is an indication of task difficulty and complexity (Pan et al., 2004). When perceiving a visualization, the longer duration means the participant needs to put more efforts for perception. If we calculate the total fixation duration people spend within a stimulus, we can use it to measure people's mental efforts in processing a visualization, and the mental effort is positively related to cognitive load (Paas and Van Merriënboer, 1994).

3.2 Eye-Tracking Experiment for Demonstration

Participants. 36 participants from job sites who are responsible for job site safety management are invited to join this study. As shown in Figure 2, they are of different ages (25-year-old to 55-year-old), work positions (project manager, safety manager, safety inspector), years of working (3years to 25 years) and construction parties (owner, supervisor, contractor). All participants had normal or corrected-to-normal vision.

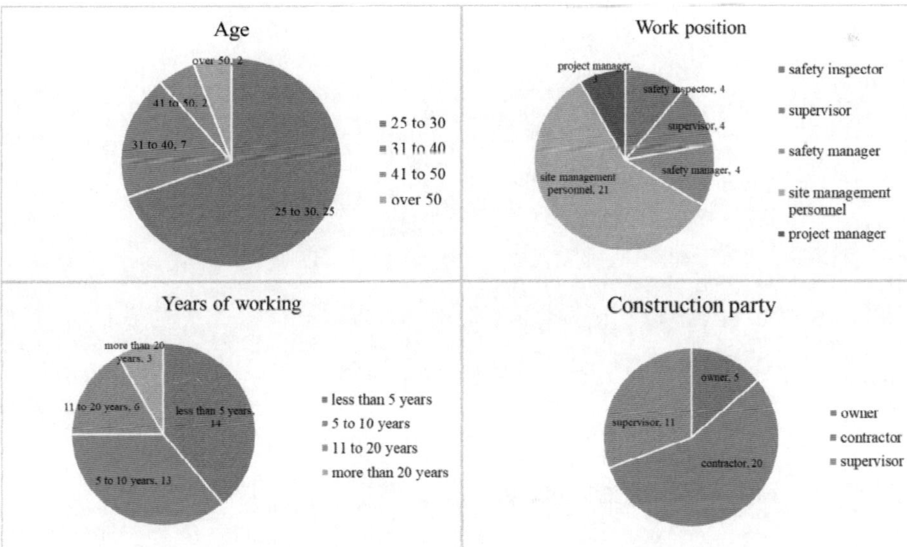

Figure 2: Backgrounds of eye-tracking experimental participants

Apparatus. As shown in Figure 3, the stimulus is presented on a laptop (15.6 in., 1920*1080) and the experimenter monitor the participants' real-time screen through an external screen connected to the laptop. The eye-tracker is Tobii Pro Nano, with a sampling rate of 60 Hz. The eye-tracker is attached to the bottom edge of the laptop screen to track and record the participants' eye movements. Participants sit approximately 30 cm to 60 cm from the laptop screen.

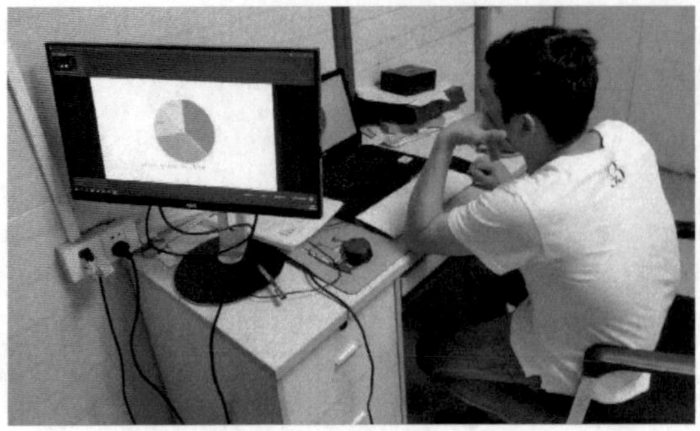

Figure 3: Experimental Set-up

Table 2: Descriptions of the stimulus

Group	Type I	Type II	Task
Group1: Statistics of the causes of safety accidents	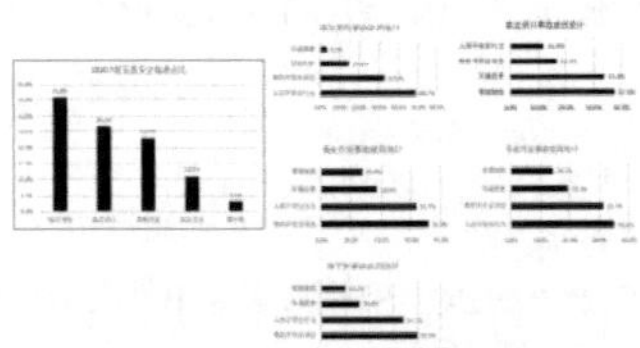 Five separate bar graphs. Five types of accidents and four causes contained.	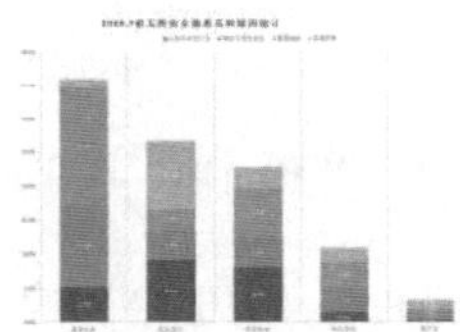 One bar graph. Five types of accidents and four causes contained.	Find out the most serious accident type and its main cause
Group 2: The procedure of safety management	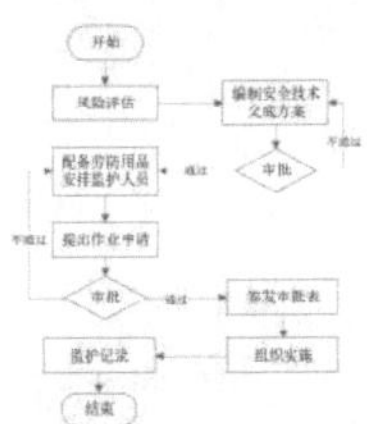 A flow chart showing the procedure of managing risky work.	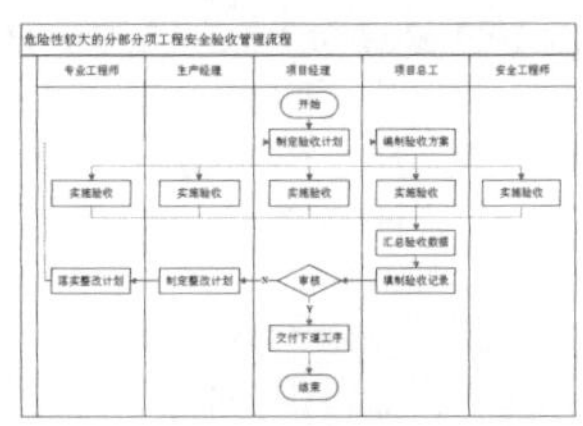 A cross-functional flow chart showing the procedure of inspecting highly risky sub-projects.	Find out what to do next in a given situation.
Group 3: Cause analysis of safety accidents	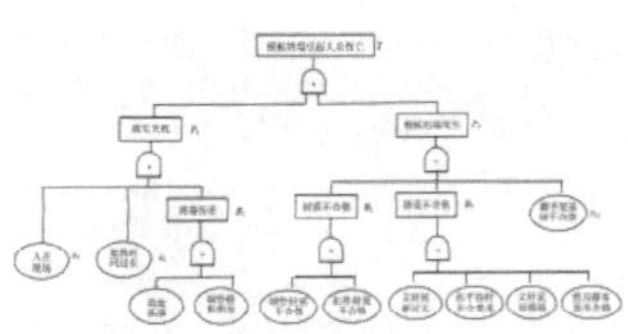 A tree diagram showing the causes of formwork collapse.	 A fishbone chart showing the causes of foundation pit collapse.	Infer what the safety status will be under a given condition.
Group4: Construction schedule	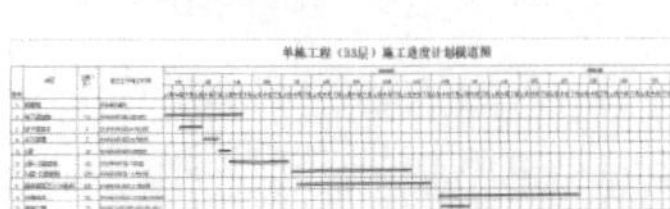 A Gantt chart showing the schedule of a high-rise building.	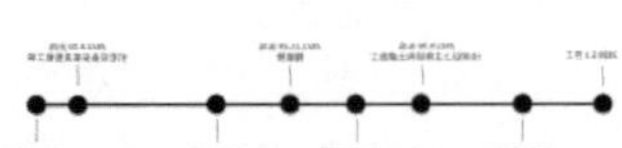 A timeline showing the schedule of a project.	Identify what kind of hazard will be the most serious in a given duration.

Stimulus. Details of the stimulus are shown in Table 2. There are four groups of images, and each group contains two images of various types. In each group, the two types of images present the same kind of safety information or safety knowledge without differences in difficulty.

Participants are required to complete the same task after observing the two images. The eight images are presented in random order. All stimulus is presented in Chinese. The authors select these types of visualizations because they are commonly used in safety management. Task-related areas are defined as AOI (Area of Interest) in each stimulus. In eye-tracking studies, AOI is an area in the display or visual environment that is of interest to the research.

Procedure. Before the formal experiment, participants receive a briefing of the experiments and practise an experimental demo to ensure they have understood their tasks. Calibration was done first to ensure the accuracy of eye-tracking measurements. Participants were instructed to fixate on five target points at different locations on the screen during the calibration.

In the formal experiment, participants were asked to follow the procedure as shown in Figure 4. There are three steps for each stimulus. Firstly, the instruction showing the name of the stimulus to be presented and the question to be answered. Participants are asked to read it through and press any key to continue after they finish reading. Then, the stimulus appears and participants can observe it without time limits. The stimulus ends its presentation when participants press any key to switch to the question page which examines participants' information perception towards the stimulus. Finally, participants answer the single choice question and press any key to continue the next stimulus. At the end of the test, participants state which kind of visualization they prefer in each group and their feedback towards this experiment.

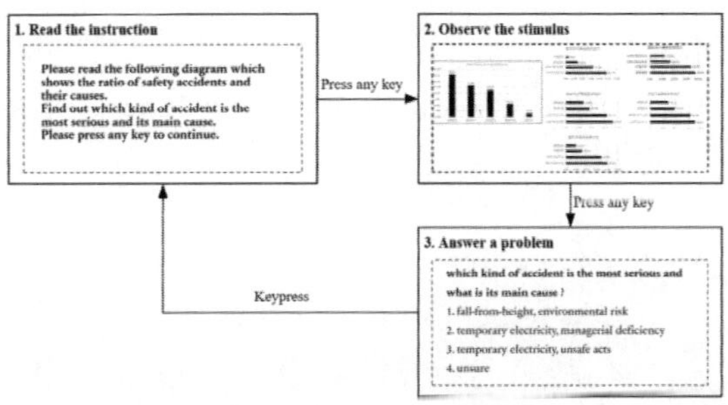

Figure 4: Procedure of participants' task

3.3 Data Collection and Analysis

Participants' keypress and eye-movements are recorded throughout the experiment. Task accuracy and completion time are extracted from the keypress information. The eye-tracking metrics are extracted from the collected eye-movements.

Hypothesis testing is done on the indicators to see whether there are significant differences between the two types of visualization within a group. Task accuracy is a type variable (true or false), so McNemar-test is used. The other variables are all constant, so the normality test is executed first, if the variables are normally distributed, Paired Sample T-Test will be used, otherwise, Wilcoxon's Sign Rank Test will be used.

4. Results

Table *3* shows the results of hypothesis testing. In group 1, there are significant differences between Task completion time, Time to first fixation and Total fixation counts. Participants finish the task more quickly, fixate on the key areas faster and have fewer fixation counts in the second diagram.

In group 2, significant differences exist in all indicators. Participants spend more time and have higher accuracy on the cross-functional flow chart. When observing the flow chart, participants can find out the key areas faster, and they have fewer fixation counts and shorter fixation durations.

As for group 3, significant differences only exist in the eye-tracking metrics. Participants fixated on the task-related area faster in the fishbone chart. Also, even though participants have more fixation counts on the fishbone chart, they have shorter durations in total.

For group 4, Time to first fixation and Total fixation counts are significantly different. Participants search for their wanted information faster and have fewer fixation counts in the timeline.

Table 3: Results of hypothesis testing

	Group 1		**Group 2**		**Group 3**		**Group 4**	
Task completion time(s)	Mean	P-value	Mean	P-value	Mean	P-value	Mean	P-value
Type 1	33.33	0.012	19.44	0.001	26.10	0.649	30.44	0.083
Type 2	27.50		26.35		24.67		24.64	
Task accuracy (%)	Mean	P-value	Mean	P-value	Mean	P-value	Mean	P-value
Type 1	80.56	0.405	91.67	0.001	77.78	0.293	72.22	0.586
Type 2	72.22		55.56		66.67		77.78	
Time to first fixation (ms)	Mean	P value	Mean	P value	Mean	P value	Mean	P value
Type 1	2.00	0.002	1.30	0.000	3.93	0.000	1.81	0.002
Type 2	0.95		7.00		0.93		0.24	
Total fixation counts	Mean	P-value	Mean	P-value	Mean	P-value	Mean	P-value
Type 1	99.50	0.047	59.39	0.000	62.89	0.039	85.14	0.018
Type 2	82.23		80.93		77.98		69.50	
Fixation duration (ms)	Mean	P-value	Mean	P-value	Mean	P-value	Mean	P-value
Type1	26.35	0.730	14.93	0.003	20.56	0.006	23.54	0.090
Type2	20.76		20.50		20.02		18.34	

5. Discussion

The above results show the three indicators can indicate the significant differences in various visualizations, which helps analyze the influences of the design of the visualization on supporting human cognition. Specific causes of the significant differences between the indicators of each group are discussed below.

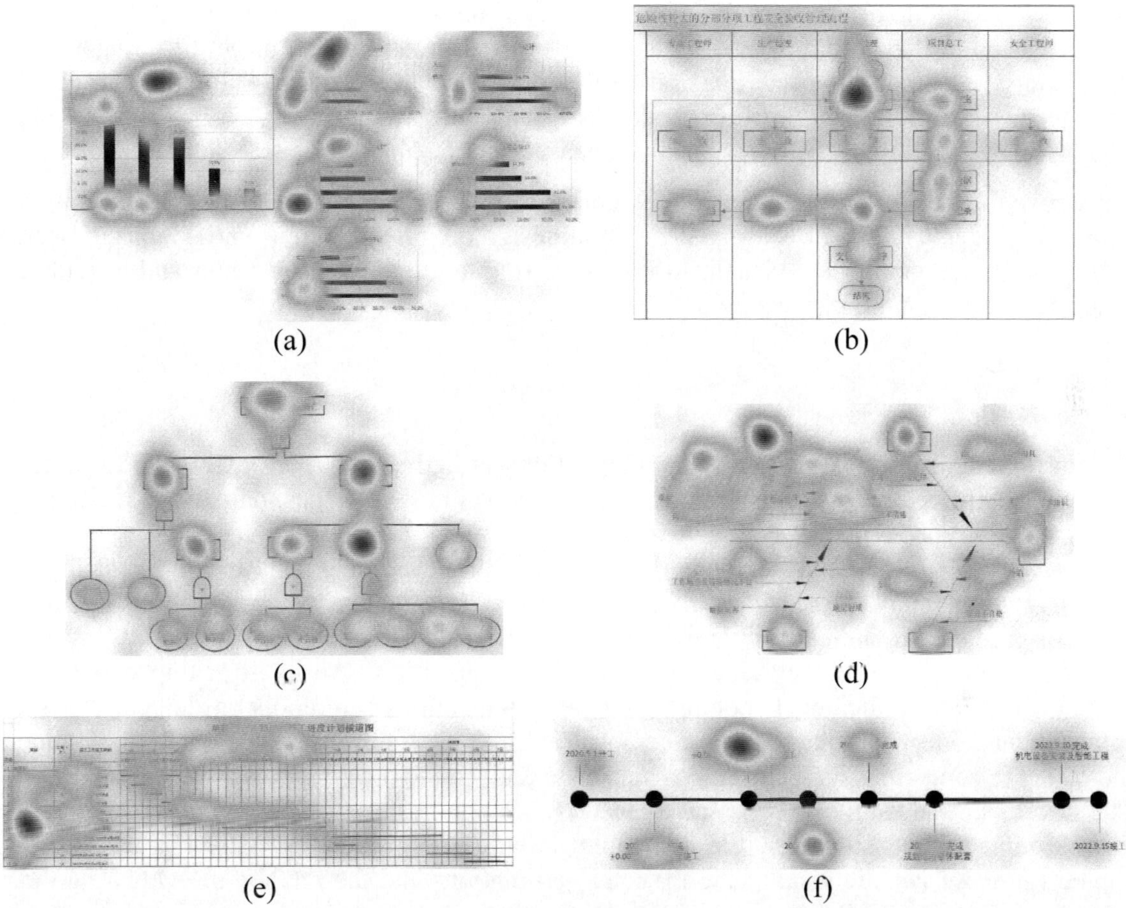

Figure 5: Heat Map

**The Heat Map uses different colours to illustrate the number or the duration of fixations participants made within certain areas of the stimulus. Red indicates the highest number or the longest duration of fixations, and green the least, with varying levels in between.*

In group 1, the second stimuli gather all information in a diagram, so participants are less likely to be distracted by other unimportant information, as shown in the Heat Map (Figure 5a), participants also allocate some attention to other irrelevant diagrams. The intensive information might facilitate participants to quickly fixate on the key areas and search within them more efficiently.

In group 2, the cross-functional flow chart has an additional information dimension (i.e. the functional information), which might impede participants quickly fixating on the task-related area, attract participants' some attention and subjects might need to put more efforts to understand it. The Heat Map (Figure 5b) also reflects the differences that participants did allocate attention to the functional information.

In group 3, the fishbone chart places the same kind of accident causes together and it looks more compact, which might help participants search their wanted information faster. It shows from the Heat Map (Figure 5c and Figure 5d) that participants can concentrate on the task-related area when processing the fishbone chart, while they have focused on several areas in the tree diagram to determine the answer.

In group 4, the schedule and the planned task are put together as a block and all the blocks are apart from each other in the timeline; while in the Gantt chart, the schedule and the planned task are listed in two columns, and there is also a row of time scale. It might be easier to find out the targeted time in the timeline and fixated on the key areas quickly. In contrast, people need to observe more areas to fully understand the Gantt chart, as shown in the Heat Map (Figure 5e and Figure 5f), participants also look through the upper time scale in the Gantt chart.

The above discussion shows that using the developed indicators to compare visualizations can help us to understand the effect of visualization design on human cognition, which can further help us to select appropriate visualizations supporting human cognition better and provide us with suggestions on the visualization design.

6. Conclusion

To develop indicators for measuring visualizations effectiveness, firstly, this study divides human's cognitive process of processing visualizations into two stages, namely, the searching stage and the encoding stage, and it analyses indicators' requirements for the two stages respectively. Then this study extracts three eye-tracking metrics which are potential for the measurement, namely, Time to first fixation, Fixation counts and Fixation duration. The three indicators are used to indicate how fast subjects can find an area containing useful information, subjects' searching efficiency and cognitive load respectively. An eye-tracking experiment using the extracted indicators to compare several visualizations commonly used in construction safety management is conducted for demonstration. The results show using the developed indicators to compare visualizations can help us to understand the effect of visualization design. The developed indicators can be used to select more appropriate visualizations and guide the visualization design. However, the compared stimulus only contains statistic images. How subjects process statistic visualizations such as animations and the method of evaluating their effectiveness might be different, which need to be further studied in the future.

Acknowledgment

This work was jointly supported by Hong Kong Research Grant Council (PJ# 11214518), National Natural Science Foundation of China (PJ#51778553), and City University of Hong Kong Strategic Research Grant (PJ# 7005240).

References

Anderson, e. W. Evaluating visualization using cognitive measures. Proceedings of the 2012 beliv workshop: beyond time and errors-novel evaluation methods for visualization, 2012. 1–4.

Anderson, e. W., potter, k. C., matzen, l. E., shepherd, j. F., preston, g. A. & silva, c. T. 2011. A user study of visualization effectiveness using eeg and cognitive load. Computer graphics forum, 30, 791–800.

Cleveland, w. S. & mcgill, r. 1984. Graphical perception: theory, experimentation, and application to the development of graphical methods. Journal of the american statistical association, 79, 531–554.

Ehmke, c. & wilson, s. 2007. Identifying web usability problems from eyetracking data.

Galotti, k. M. 2017. Cognitive psychology in and out of the laboratory, sage publications.

Guo, h., yu, y. & skitmore, m. 2017. Visualization technology-based construction safety management: a review. Automation in construction, 73, 135–144.

Heer, j. & stone, m. Color naming models for color selection, image editing and palette design. Proceedings of the sigchi conference on human factors in computing systems, 2012. 1007–1016.

Holmqvist, k., nyström, m., andersson, r., dewhurst, r., jarodzka, h. & van de weijer, j. 2011. Eye tracking: a comprehensive guide to methods and measures, oup oxford.

Huang, w., eades, p. & hong, s.-h. 2009. Measuring effectiveness of graph visualizations: a cognitive load perspective. Information visualization, 8, 139–152.

Nowell, l., schulman, r. & hix, d. Graphical encoding for information visualization: an empirical study. Ieee symposium on information visualization, 2002. Infovis 2002., 2002. Ieee, 43–50.

Paas, f. G. & van merriënboer, j. J. 1994. Instructional control of cognitive load in the training of complex cognitive tasks. Educational psychology review, 6, 351–371.

Pan, b., hembrooke, h. A., gay, g. K., granka, l. A., feusner, m. K. & newman, j. K. The determinants of web page viewing behavior: an eye-tracking study. Proceedings of the 2004 symposium on eye tracking research & applications, 2004. 147–154.

Riche, n. Beyond system logging: human logging for evaluating information visualization. Position paper presented orally at the beliv 2010 conference, 2010. Citeseer.

Rosenbaum, d. A. 2009. Human motor control, academic press.

Simkin, d. & hastie, r. 1987. An information-processing analysis of graph perception. Journal of the american statistical association, 82, 454–465.

Sørensen, h. S., clement, j. & gabrielsen, g. 2012. Food labels–an exploratory study into label information and what consumers see and understand. The international review of retail, distribution and consumer research, 22, 101–114.

Spence, r. 2001. Information visualization, springer.

Tao, d., tan, h., wang, h., zhang, x., qu, x. & zhang, t. 2019. A systematic review of physiological measures of mental workload. Int j environ res public health, 16.

Tory, m. & moller, t. 2005. Evaluating visualizations: do expert reviews work? Ieee computer graphics and applications, 25, 8–11.

Wickens, c. D., hollands, j. G., banbury, s. & parasuraman, r. 2015. Engineering psychology and human performance, psychology press.

Zagermann, j., pfeil, u. & reiterer, h. 2016. Measuring cognitive load using eye tracking technology in visual computing. Proceedings of the beyond time and errors on novel evaluation methods for visualization - beliv '16.

Zhu, y. Measuring effective data visualization. International symposium on visual computing, 2007. Springer, 652–661.

Real-time LiDAR for Monitoring Construction Worker Presence Near Hazards and in Work Areas in a Virtual Reality Environment

Emil L. Jacobsen, Jochen Teizer
Aarhus University, Denmark
elj@cae.au.dk, teizer@cae.au.dk

Abstract. In this paper, a novel sensor system is used to detect worker presence near hazards and in key locations tied to productivity through geo-fencing. The systems' main component is real-time monitoring via LiDAR, which allows for more precise detection of the workers' position relative to the locations. The method involves LiDAR change and use-time event detections. The system is tested in a virtual environment resembling a real construction site, allowing for a safe evaluation while initial results are produced. Preliminary findings demonstrate the usability and the potential of this type of monitoring system, because of the precise detection of workers in geo-fenced locations in general. It could potentially be incorporated into live construction work environments.

1. Introduction

The labor productivity in the construction industry has not met the average growth of the world economy for decades (Barbosa, 2017; Neve, 2020). This compared with the safety records of the very same industry has been declining as well (Bureau of Labor Statistics, 2019) – with an increase in fatalities, now being the largest amount since 2007. This combination shows an industry in need of optimization. To do this, several actions have been previously taken throughout the literature, for example, hazard identification, mitigation, and training (Teizer et al., 2013) and tracking of heavy machinery for productivity improvements (Chen et al., 2020). Because of the often confined spaces of a construction site, most literature regarding detection does not focus on the workers, but rather the hazards.

By focusing on hazardous spaces and monitor these through sensor fusion and geo-fencing, it is possible to monitor hazardous events in near real-time. Some hazards can be relatively small, which is why a LiDAR system is implemented, as this gives precision not possible by RGB cameras or RTLS equipment and also works in rough conditions, such as in low lightning or with bright lights shining. The system is tested through a Virtual Reality (VR) scene, to ensure the safety of all participants. The test is conducted to showcase the system without introducing people to real hazards. This paper (1) gives a brief introduction to hazard detection and monitoring, (2) shows a novel sensor system and its capabilities in 3D monitoring, (3) introduces a virtual environment, which allows for initial experiments without real hazards, (4) shows the early implementation and preliminary results, and (5) discusses the remaining challenges and gives an outlook.

2. Background

For a construction project to be successful, it needs to meet the requirements of duration, quality, and cost while ensuring the construction workers' health and safety. As construction projects can become very large with many confined spaces it is a necessity to be able to monitor workers to ensure their well-being. Several monitoring solutions have previously been presented throughout the literature.

2.1 Hazard Detection and Reporting Systems

Hazard detection is being used in several applications, as a way to ensure safety on construction sites. Hazard detection is used to analyze models of the projects, i.e. model checking for evaluating safety compliance of BIM models (Schultz et al., 2020; Zhang et al., 2013) and analyzing point clouds to check for compliance issues with scaffolding (Wang, 2019). This type of research is utilizing various forms of project models and can work as a foundation for additional research as it discovers hazards within the project. Others attempt to detect hazards during the construction phase, for example, Kim et al. (2016) detect hazards by comparing actual routes to optimal routes using a real-time location system and the building information model. This system can define hazardous areas, but not in a definitive way, as the system uses predictions. Some of these hazards are not possible to mitigate, and therefore monitoring is needed. As the hazards vary in type, multiple solutions can be used.

2.2 Use-time Monitoring

Several papers use vision-based algorithms for their detection (Gong and Caldas, 2011; Kim and Chi, 2020; Kim et al., 2020). The vision-based algorithms often use regular RGB footage as the data input, which has shortcomings as this method does not record depth. They create a limitation in terms of accuracy. These types of systems also have a limitation in terms of reach, as the cameras will have a limited view only allowing the monitoring to happen in the vicinity of the camera. A majority of the vision-based studies are being used for heavy machinery instead of workers (Chen et al., 2020; Kim et al., 2018; Kim et al., 2020), as these are easier to track because of the lesser likelihood of some of the key areas of the machine being obscured by itself.

To work around these limitations, research has used several non-vision-based methods. Here several directions have previously been explored. Location-tracking has been widely researched as a base for safety monitoring systems (Li et al., 2018; Cheng and Teizer, 2013). This method has limitations in terms of reach, as location tracking throughout the literature has shown the limitation of not working indoors, due to the signal being blocked by construction elements. Several papers have investigated close call events and created systems to detect and report these (Marks and Teizer, 2013; Golovina et al., 2019a; Teizer et al., 2010). These approaches use sensors to determine the relative position of the worker in relation to the hazard. This approach has been applied to both stationary hazards and moving hazards in a virtual test environment, if combined with a warning system, this would allow the worker to know that they were close to a hazard and thereby allowing them to safely traverse the construction site.

2.3 Monitoring via Real-time LiDAR Detection

Active monitoring of human body motions in relation to hazards embedded in a workstation with external devices relies critically on extrospection sensors to determine the range to the objects. This provides the ground truth information on how safely the human participant navigates around obstacles and maps its work environment at the same time, hence facilitates detailed scene and workflow understanding. However, there is a requirement for a large-field range imaging system that can determine the distances to any object in a camera lens's field of view (FOV) accurately and in run-time. Since 2004, forward-looking research includes grand challenges on sensor systems for autonomously driving vehicles (Hooper, 2004). An example of a more recent construction safety-related application includes pro-active safety workspace mapping for planning mobile crane lifting operations (Fang et al., 2016).

The literature classifies the terminology and working principle into passive and active optical range imaging systems (Teizer and Kahlmann, 2007). While passive approaches like video cameras often require post-processing of the raw image data to obtain range values to objects and scene, depth sensors transmit some form of energy, such as ultrasonic waves or infrared beams, into the scene to receive a return signal that determines range values in run-time. However, developments in the processing of images using methods such as deep learning and dense models have allowed for computing depth and camera motion from images (Ummenhofer et al., 2016; Newcombe et al., 2011; Facil et al., 2019). Examples of such active depth sensing sensors are Light Detection and Ranging (LiDAR) and 3D range imaging. Latter includes RGB cameras, infrared projectors, and detectors that map depth through either structured light or time of flight (TOF) calculations (Ray and Teizer, 2012a).

Based on the current development status, the unique advantage of using 3D range imaging is to track the position of moving objects in 3D at high range frame update rates approximately close to human vision. The cameras acquire a high range point density that allows imaging multiple objects and scenes in run-time. While depth sensors over time have become steadily more popular in commercial gaming application to track body motions since 2005, early research in construction around the same time has explored applicability in safety applications (Teizer, 2008), including but not limited to head pose estimation (Ray and Teizer, 2012b) and object manipulation and identification (Arif et al., 2014). However, interest in this technology was lost in the construction industry due to an increase in research on physiological status monitoring (PSM) of construction workers (Cheng et al., 2013). These applications eventually seek millimeter precision at run-time acquisition rates. While commercial 3D range imaging cameras were not envisioned for such research purpose, recent research has been using more intrusive electronic devices like Inertial Measurement Units (IMU) (Ryu et al., 2016; Ryu et al., 2020) that lack monitoring the surrounding work environment.

2.4 Data Collection for VR Environments

The run time data collection has in the research been done in the virtual environment itself. This restricts the level of information, as most of these experiences use virtual reality headsets with controllers, only allowing for tracking of these three elements (head and hands). Solberg et al. (2020) also apply tracking of feet, via an HTC Vive tracker attached to each foot, allowing for two additional data streams. Even with this tracking setup, it still only allows for potential tracking of the body's extremities. It is, however, possible to approximate other body positions based on this data, which could allow for approximated data points for the whole (Chryssolouris et al., 2000).

Positional data of the player is used in several papers, as it allows to analyze the performance of the participant. This can be done for safety measures (Golovina et al., 2019b) and productivity (Michalos et al., 2018). Positional data has also been recorded for other objects in the virtual environment, such as bucket movements of an excavator, allowing for further analysis related to both productivity and safety by having data from not only the worker but also the hazard (Morosi et al., 2019).

As part of the preliminary research scope limitation, data collection in VR was not conducted. For further analysis, this will be collected for benchmarking purposes.

3. Method

To benchmark, the performance of the system, a virtual environment with the same dimensions as the physical space has been used. In the environment, several hazardous areas have been created. These are then located in the physical environment and it is here the zones are created.

The process of the experiment is shown in Figure 1. Here the dotted line represents the division between processes regarding reality and processes regarding the virtual environment. If a task is in the middle of the line, this means that the task is done in both environments.

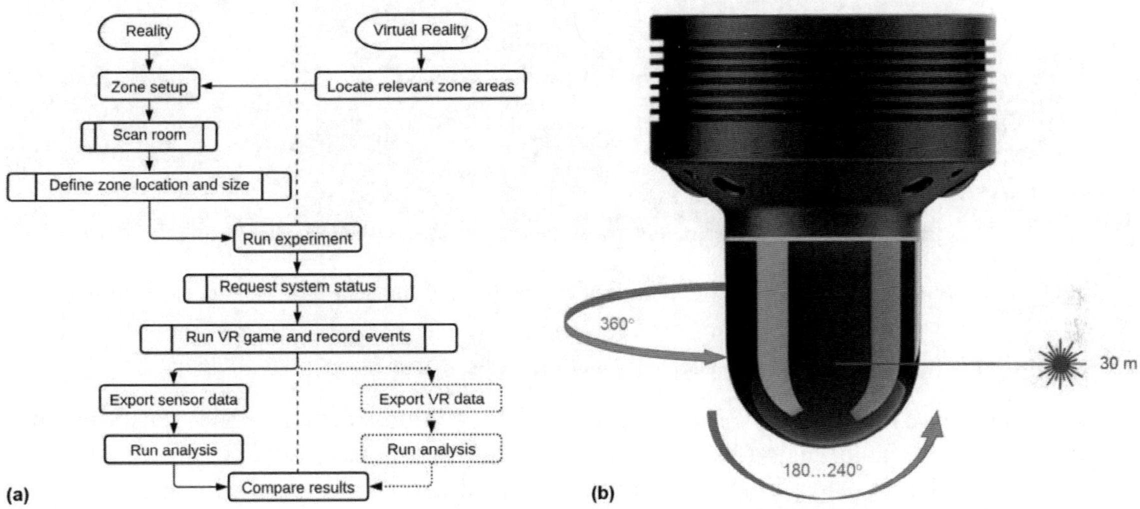

Figure 1: (a) Flowchart of the process (dotted lines show future work) and (b) sensor system

3.1 Experimental Setup

Four zones are defined in total. These have been defined by walking the scene and defining areas that are of interest. Figure 2 shows an overview of the zones' placements via the graphical user interface of the sensor system.

Zone 1 has been defined around a hole in the ground as this is seen as a potential hazard with a risk of people having their foot caught in the hole leading to possible injuries. Zone 2 has been defined around a leading-edge without guard rails, as there is a risk that people will fall off the building, as the participants are not wearing anything to protect against this. Both hazards can be rectified, as the area contains a cover for the hole and a guard rail for the leading edge. Zone 3 and 4 are created around the areas where the worker interacts with the bricks. The last two zones are placed to be able to monitor the productivity of the worker, as these two areas are necessary areas to be in for the worker to be productive. To calculate the productivity, the number of times they are within each zone is needed as well as the total time of the work.

The virtual environment from Solberg et al. (2020) is used to simulate a real construction site in virtuality, which allows for a more immersive experiment, allowing the participant to see hazards where the zones have been placed, and hereby interact with the environment as they normally would. The VR scene can be seen in Figure 2b. The task is to move 6 bricks between two stations, with two hazards being present in the near vicinity.

The sensor system is placed at a height of 2 m, which allows it to monitor the whole experimental setup. A mat is placed on the floor resembling the size of the virtual setup but is not used by the sensor. This is only for the worker to know if they are close to any physical objects, to ensure their safety, not only in virtual reality but also in reality.

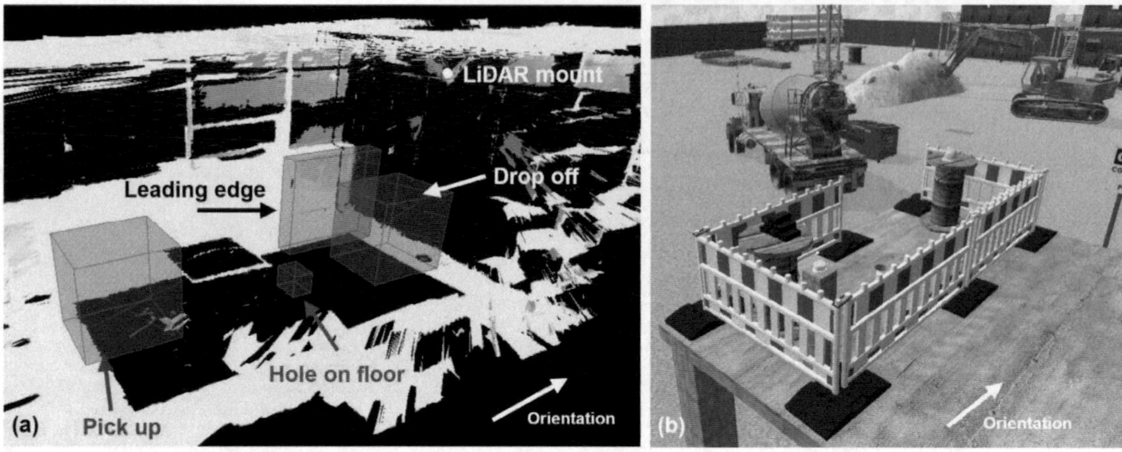

Figure 2: Placements of zones: (a) in the LiDAR scan and (b) the scene in the VR environment.

3.2 Sensing Technology for the Physical Environment

This research uses a novel smart sensor system. Its main component is a LiDAR sensor that has the advantage over regular vision-based cameras as it is independent from external light sources and able to function in bright light and darkness. LiDAR can also directly measure the size of objects that are in its FOV. The LiDAR sensor has a maximum scan rate of 200.000 points/second and a 3D point accuracy of ±3mm at 10m distance (according to vendor specification). The wavelength of the LiDAR is 830 nm. The LiDAR uses Wave Form Digitizer (WFD), which allows for long-range, high measurement accuracy and a fast measuring time (Maar and Zogg, 2014). It has a maximum range of 30m and a FOV of 360x270°. In addition, the system has two RGB cameras of which both have fisheye lenses and a 12 megapixels resolution. The individual images can be stitched to a 360x180° field of view (FOV) and can be streamed at 1080p. The system supports from 10 to 30 frames per second.

The sensor system uses data fusion that is based on the available data types. Its software detects movements and changes in the observable environment. It can differentiate between bounding box sizes of persons or other sized objects in movement. This allows for the detection of entry into predefined zones, e.g. those that are restricted according to safety protocols. For this research, the system is used to detect the true size and distance of the objects when they enter these zones. This is done using geo-fencing in a 3D environment created by the LiDAR sensor. The system also examines the LiDAR scan for changes that would resemble a bounding box within the given size parameters. Finally, all changes in the LiDAR scan that are found are examined but only bounding boxes that fulfill the size requirements are returned.

3.3 Run-time Data Collection

The data collection is a two-flow process, with data being collected both in the VR scene, but also through the sensor system. As data is recorded in both VR and through the sensor system, it is necessary for two processing streams. One using JSON, as this is the output of the sensor system, and one using CSV, as this is the output from the VR environment. For the physical environment, the system's API is used to make requests. There are several requests supported by the API, but throughout this research, only four calls are examined (Table 1).

Table 1: API requests and their applications.

Requests	Description
Status	Allowing to connect to the device and check the system status, i.e. on/off.
LiDAR toggling	Toggling the LiDAR on and off and enables the point cloud streaming
Events	Requests that allow to receive all events in a timespan in JSON format.
Live events	The requests allow the user to listen for events and will receive JSON formatted information when an event happens.

In this research, the status request is used to ensure the system is operational before an experiment is started. Currently, the workflow is then running the experiment and afterward use the events API call, to get all events in JSON format, which allows for analysis of the data. This could be further developed by using the live events API request, which would enable a live stream of event data and therefore also a real-time analysis of the events.

An event is automatically created by the sensor system, which analyses the LiDAR scan and examines this scan for differences from the static scene, which has to be created before zones can be made. Having the static scene allows the system to detect changes in the scene, and locate whether or not they are in the zone. When the system detects changes within the zone, an event is created with the defined attachments. For all objects, IDs for media attachments can also be included, which makes it possible to retrieve pictures or videos from the event for further analysis as well. The extent of these attachments is defined when the zone is made, as it is here possible to define what attachments are needed for this specific zone.

3.4 Data Analysis

From the physical system, several JSON objects are outputted. The events are outputted as individual JSON objects, which for the analysis needs to be combined into one JSON file consisting of all the events from the experiment. This file is then imported to the analysis tool developed in Python as a python dictionary for further analysis. Not all data from the JSON is used in this research. The data in Table 2 is what is taken from the JSON file. With this information, the analysis tool determines how many times a person has been within the defined zones, which will allow for monitoring spaces that have been deemed as potentially hazardous areas.

Table 2: Data points used from the JSON file.

Data points	Description
Timestamp	Timestamp of event.
Zone name	The name of the zone in which the event has happened.
Bounding box	X,Y,Z coordinates of the bounding box centroid that caused the event.
Box size	The size of the bounding box.
Box rotation	The rotation of the bounding box.

4. Results

The preliminary work focused on three play rounds with three different participants. The participants were necessary to get an understanding of the system, as the hazardous areas could be recognized by the participants, which means that they would avoid these zones and thereby ending up with zero encounters. The four defined zones (Table 3) were made to showcase multiple use-cases. Zones 1 and 2 were used to determine whether or not a worker was close to a hazard. Zones 3 and 4 were used to track the workers' productivity.

The three participants were within the scene for 68.9s, 88.1s, and 296.2s. This explains the big deviation of the durations between participant 3 and the two others. For all participants combined, the sensor system detected 16 encounters with the hole in the ground (Figure 3). The total duration was measured automatically to 82 seconds. All of them also had encounters with the leading edge, which could have been secured by placing a guardrail. These 8 events had a total duration of 55 seconds according to the sensor system.

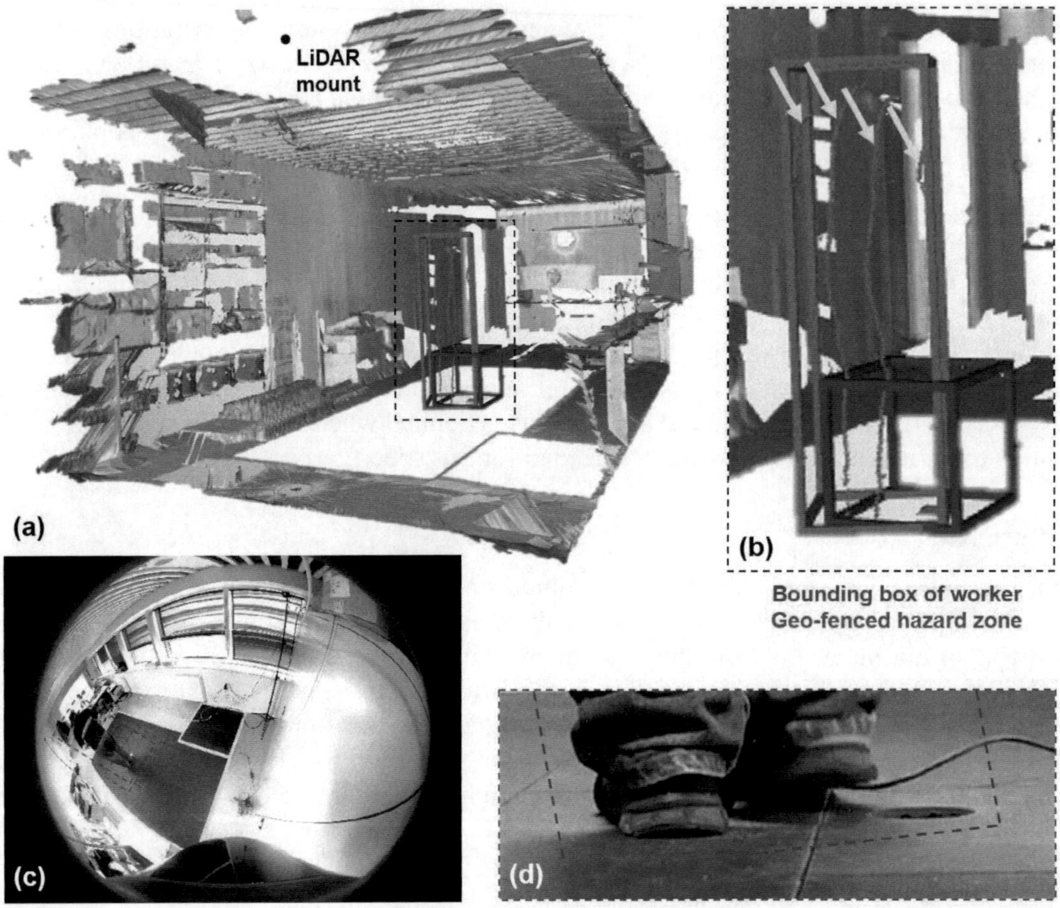

Figure 3: Encounter of the worker with a geo-fenced hazard zone: (a) LiDAR point cloud: detection of a worker (red bounding box) colliding with the geo-fenced hazard zone "hole on floor" (blue bounding box); (b) a detail view shows 4 slices (yellow arrows) of LiDAR data giving the vertical profile of the worker at the time of the encounter; (c) RGB image of LiDAR system; and (d) detailed view (from external video camera positioned on ground) of the event in the physical environment.

Table 3: Presence of the three participating workers, respectively, in the zones.

Zones		Count [No.]	Duration [s]
	Participant ID	1 / 2 / 3	1 / 2 / 3
Hole on floor		5 / 5 / 6	18 / 18 / 46
Leading edge		2 / 2 / 4	6 / 3 / 46
Pick-up		0 / 1 / 3	0 / 1 / 34
Drop-off		4 / 4 / 5	6 / 11 / 12

The productivity measures can only be seen as an estimate, as the objects that are being moved are virtual and thereby not visible to the sensor. This means that the sensor can only detect when the participant is in a zone where the objects are located, assuming that the participant will pick one of the objects up. The results show that the participants were at the pick-up zone 4 times with a total duration of 35 seconds and at the drop-off zone 13 times with a total duration of 29 seconds. Several missed zone encounters were observed while running the experiment, due to occlusion of the zone. This would be possible to mitigate with better sensor placement, potentially at a greater height or by using multiple sensors running simultaneously. Another limitation is the scanning frequency, which is at 2Hz. This means that the participants theoretically could quickly enter a zone and leave it again without being scanned.

5. Next Steps

The next step will be to incorporate the sensor system as a support measuring tool for a VR scene. As the preliminary results only show data capturing done by the sensor system, a comparison to the VR data collection will be done. The VR scenes allow immersive testing of the sensor system, and the sensor system could benefit the VR scenes as an additional data recording and analysis tool. In this next step, data collection will happen in both the virtual and physical environments. For the virtual data collection sensors on feet, hands, and head are used to detect collisions with predefined objects in VR. This will ultimately mean that the experiment has data from both the virtual scene and the scene in reality, which can now be compared to see how the sensor fusion method performs compared to the virtual scene, in which the hazards are located.

6. Conclusion

Monitoring of construction projects has several challenges, from occlusion to weak signals from detection and tracking devices. Having multiple solutions allows for a greater ability to monitor projects by potentially utilizing several different methods of monitoring. This research provides a novel method for monitoring workers on construction sites, with the potential of developing workflows that also monitors machines on-site, allowing for greater monitoring around hazards. The proposed method allows for more precise data than the prior monitoring methods as it is based on LiDAR instead of RGB footage or IMU sensors, which excels not only in precision, but also allows working in conditions such as poorly lighted areas, or very bright areas. The paper shows preliminary findings of an experiment, based in a virtual setting. The virtual setting is used as a testing facility where the hazards are defined in the game, which allows for safe testing of the novel sensor system. To further develop the method, it will be incorporated as an additional data capturing and analysis tool in more elaborate virtual reality testing. This will be done to examine the potential use of the system in a safe environment before it will be tested on physical cases. Furthermore, alarms should be incorporated to let the worker know that the area contains hazards, this can be done with speakers attached to the sensor system. The system also allows for trajectory collection, which would allow for more elaborate analysis and analyzing how close the workers get to hazards and their pathing around them.

References

Arif, O., Ray, S. J., Vela, P. A., Teizer, J. (2014). "Potential of Time-of-Flight Range Imaging for Object Identification and Manipulation in Construction", *Journal of Computing in Civil Engineering*, 28(6), pp. 06014005, https://doi.org/10.1061/(ASCE)CP.1943-5487.0000304.

Barbosa, F. W., Jonathan; Mischke, Jan; Riberirinho, Maria J.; Sridhar, Mukund; Parsons, Matthew; Bertram, Nick; Brown, Stephanie (2017). "Reinventing Construction: A Route To Higher Productivity", McKinsey Global Institute, https://www.mckinsey.com/business-functions/operations/our-insights/reinventing-construction-through-a-productivity-revolution (accessed online March 1, 2021).

Bureau of Labor Statistics, B. (2019). National Census of Fatal Occupational Injuries in 2019. Available at: https://www.bls.gov/news.release/pdf/cfoi.pdf. (accessed online March 1, 2021).

Chen, C., Zhu, Z. and Hammad, A. (2020). "Automated excavators activity recognition and productivity analysis from construction site surveillance videos", *Automation in Construction*, 110, pp.103045, https://doi.org/10.1016/j.autcon.2019.103045.

Cheng, T., Migliaccio, G. C., Teizer, J. and Gatti, U. C. (2013.). "Data Fusion of Real-Time Location Sensing and Physiological Status Monitoring for Ergonomics Analysis of Construction Workers", *Journal of Computing in Civil Engineering*, 27(3), pp.320–335, https://doi.org/10.1061/(ASCE)CP.1943-5487.0000222.

Cheng, T., Teizer, J. (2013). "Real-time resource location data collection and visualization technology for construction safety and activity monitoring applications", Automation in Construction, 34, pp.3–15, https://doi.org/10.1016/j.autcon.2012.10.017.

Chryssolouris, G., Mavrikios, D., Fragos, D. and Karabatsou, V. (2000). "A virtual reality-based experimentation environment for the verification of human-related factors in assembly processes", *Robotics and Computer-Integrated Manufacturing*, 16(4), pp.267–276, https://doi.org/10.1016/s0736-5845(00)00013-2

Facil, J. M., Ummenhofer, B., Zhou, H., Montesano, L., Brox, T., and Civera, J. (2019). "CAM-Convs: Camera-Aware Multi-Scale Convolutions for Single-View Depth", *IEEE Conference on Computer Vision and Pattern Recognition (CVPR)*, https://arxiv.org/abs/1904.02028

Fang, Y., Cho, K, Chen, J. (2016). "A framework for real-time pro-active safety assistance for mobile crane lifting operations", *Automation in Construction*, 72(3), 367–379, https://doi.org/10.1016/j.autcon.2016.08.025.

Golovina, O., Perschewski, M., Teizer, J. and König, M. (2019a). "Algorithm for quantitative analysis of close call events and personalized feedback in construction safety", *Automation in Construction*, 99, pp.206–222, https://doi.org/10.1016/j.autcon.2018.11.014.

Golovina, O., Kazanci, C., Teizer, J., König, M. (2019b). "Using Serious Games in Virtual Reality for Automated Close Call and Contact Collision Analysis in Construction Safety." *36th International Symposium on Automation and Robotics in Construction*, Banff, Canada, https://doi.org/10.22260/ISARC2019/0129.

Gong, J. and Caldas, C. H. (2011). "An object recognition, tracking, and contextual reasoning-based video interpretation method for rapid productivity analysis of construction operations", *Automation in Construction*, 20(8), pp.1211–1226, https://doi.org/10.1016/j.autcon.2011.05.005.

Hooper, J. (2004). "From Darpa Grand Challenge 2004: DARPA's Debacle in the Desert", *Popular Science*, https://www.popsci.com/scitech/article/2004-06/darpa-grand-challenge-2004darpas-debacle-desert/ (last accessed, March 15, 2021).

Kim, H., Bang, S., Jeong, H., Ham, Y. and Kim, H. (2018). "Analyzing context and productivity of tunnel earthmoving processes using imaging and simulation", *Automation in Construction*, 92, pp.188–198, https://doi.org/10.1016/j.autcon.2018.04.002.

Kim, H., Lee, H.-S., Park, M., Chung, B. and Hwang, S. (2016). "Automated hazardous area identification using laborers' actual and optimal routes", *Automation in Construction*, 65, pp.21–32, https://doi.org/10.1016/j.autcon.2016.01.006.

Kim, J. and Chi, S. (2020). “Multi-camera vision-based productivity monitoring of earthmoving operations”, *Automation in Construction*, 112, pp.103121, https://doi.org/10.1016/j.autcon.2020.103121.

Kim, J., Hwang, J., Chi, S. and Seo, J. (2020). “Towards database-free vision-based monitoring on construction sites: A deep active learning approach”, *Automation in Construction*, 120, pp.103376, https://doi.org/10.1016/j.autcon.2020.103376.

Li, Y., Hu, Y., Xia, B., Skitmore, M. and Li, H. (2018). “Proactive behavior-based system for controlling safety risks in urban highway construction megaprojects”, *Automation in Construction*, 95, pp.118–128, https://doi.org/10.1016/j.autcon.2018.07.021

Marks, E. D. and Teizer, J. (2013). “Method for testing proximity detection and alert technology for safe construction equipment operation”, *Construction Management and Economics*, 31(6), pp.636–646, https://doi.org/10.1080/01446193.2013.783705

Michalos, G., Karvouniari, A., Dimitropoulos, N., Togias, T. and Makris, S. (2018). “Workplace analysis and design using virtual reality techniques”, *CIRP Annals*, 67(1), pp.141–144, https://doi.org/10.1016/j.cirp.2018.04.120

Morosi, F., Rossoni, M. and Caruso, G. (2019). “Coordinated control paradigm for hydraulic excavator with haptic device”, *Automation in Construction*, 105, pp.102848, https://doi.org/10.1016/j.autcon.2019.102848

Maar, H. and Zogg, H.-M. (2014). Optimized Measuring Meets Individual Demands – the WFD Technology: Leica Geosystems AG.

Neve, H. H., Wandahl, S., Lindhard, S., and Teizer, J. (2020). “Determining the Relationship between Direct Work and Construction Labor Productivity in North America: Four Decades of Insights”, *Journal of Construction Engineering and Management*, 146(9), https://doi.org/10.1061/(ASCE)CO.1943-7862.0001887

Newcombe, R. A., Lovegrove, S. J., and Davison, A. J. (2011). “DTAM: Dense tracking and mapping in real-time”, *2011 Int. Conf. on Computer Vision*, pp.2320–2327, https://doi.org/10.1109/ICCV.2011.6126513

Ray, S.J. and Teizer J. (2012a). “Real-Time Construction Worker Posture Analysis for Ergonomics Training.” *Advanced Engineering Informatics*, 26, pp.439–455, http://dx.doi.org/10.1016/j.aei.2012.02.011

Ray, S. J. and Teizer, J. (2012b). “Coarse head pose estimation of construction equipment operators to formulate dynamic blind spots”, *Advanced Engineering Informatics*, 26(1), pp.117–130, https://doi.org/10.1016/j.aei.2011.09.005

Ryu, J., McFarland, T., Haas, C. and Rahman, A. (2020). “Automatic Clustering of Proper Working Posture”, *EG-ICE 2020 Workshop on Intelligent Computing in Engineering*, Berlin: Universitätsverlag der TU Berlin, pp.106–114, http://dx.doi.org/10.14279/depositonce-9977.

Ryu, J., Seo, J., Liu, M., Lee, S. and Haas, C. T. (2016). “Action Recognition Using a Wristband-Type Activity Tracker: Case Study of Masonry Work”, *Construction Research Congress*, pp.790–799.

Schultz, C. P. L., Li, B. and Teizer, J. (2020). 'Towards a Unifying Domain Model of Construction Safety: SafeConDM', *EG-ICE 2020 Workshop on Intelligent Computing in Engineering*, Berlin: Universitätsverlag der TU Berlin, pp.363–372, http://dx.doi.org/10.14279/depositonce-9977.

Solberg, A., Hognestad, J., Golovina, O. and Teizer, J. (2020). “Active Personalized Training of Construction Safety Using Run Time Data Collection in Virtual Reality”, *20th International Conference on Construction Application of Virtual Reality*, Middlesbrough, UK: Teesside University Press, pp.19–30.

Teizer, J. (2008). “3D range imaging camera sensing for active safety in construction”, *Journal of Information Technology in Construction*, 13(Sensors in Construction and Infrastructure Management), pp.103-117, https://www.itcon.org/2008/8.

Teizer, J., Allread, B. S., Fullerton, C. E. and Hinze, J. (2010). “Autonomous pro-active real-time construction worker and equipment operator proximity safety alert system”, *Automation in Construction*, 19(5), pp.630–640, https://doi.org/10.1016/j.autcon.2010.02.009.

Teizer, J., Cheng, T. and Fang, Y. (2013). "Location tracking and data visualization technology to advance construction ironworkers' education and training in safety and productivity", *Automation in Construction*, 35, pp.53–68, https://doi.org/10.1016/j.autcon.2013.03.004.

Teizer, J. and Kahlmann, T. (2007) "Range Imaging as Emerging Optical Three-Dimension Measurement Technology", *Transportation Research Record: Journal of the Transportation Research Board*, 2040(1), pp.19–29, https://doi.org/10.3141/2040-03.

Ummenhofer, B., Zhou, H., Uhrig, J., Mayer, N., Ilg, E., Dosovitskiy, A. and Brox, T. (2016). "DeMoN: Depth and Motion Network for Learning Monocular Stereo", *CVPR 2017*, https://doi.org/10.1109/CVPR.2017.596.

Wang, Q. (2019) "Automatic checks from 3D point cloud data for safety regulation compliance for scaffold work platforms", *Automation in Construction*, 104, pp.38–51, https://doi.org/10.1016/j.autcon.2019.04.008.

Zhang, S., Teizer, J., Lee, J.-K., Eastman, C. M. and Venugopal, M. (2013). "Building Information Modeling (BIM) and Safety: Automatic Safety Checking of Construction Models and Schedules", *Automation in Construction*, 29, pp.183–195, https://doi.org/10.1016/j.autcon.2012.05.006.

Universitätsverlag der TU Berlin

eg-ice

European Group for Intelligent Computing in Engineering

EG-ICE 2021 Workshop on Intelligent Computing in Engineering

30th June–2nd July 2021, Hybrid, Proceedings

The 28th EG-ICE International Workshop 2021 brings together international experts working at the interface between advanced computing and modern engineering challenges. Many engineering tasks require open-world resolutions to support multi-actor collaboration, coping with approximate models, providing effective engineer-computer interaction, search in multi-dimensional solution spaces, accommodating uncertainty, including specialist domain knowledge, performing sensor-data interpretation and dealing with incomplete knowledge. While results from computer science provide much initial support for resolution, adaptation is unavoidable and most importantly, feedback from addressing engineering challenges drives fundamental computer-science research. Competence and knowledge transfer goes both ways.

European Group for Intelligent Computing in Engineering (eg-ice)
Arcisstrasee 21
D-80290 Munich
Germany

ISBN 978-1-7138-5547-7

CURRAN ASSOCIATES INC.
proceedings.com